FINAL WHISTLE

Andy Johnson on his way to 21 Premiership goals

FOREWORD

by talkSPORT presenter Patrick Kinghorn

Welcome to Final Whistle, your complete review of the 2004-05 Premiership season.

This year talkSPORT, the UK's number one commercial radio station, has teamed up with Sidan Press to bring you a book that's packed with in-depth stats and expert commentary.

It was another exciting year in the Premiership, with José Mourinho guiding Chelsea to a Premiership and Carling Cup double in his first season in English football. The FA Cup went to Arsenal, as Arsène Wenger's men beat Manchester United 5-4 on penalties at the Millennium Stadium.

Sir Alex Ferguson's charges finished behind their two London rivals in the league, with Everton unexpectedly securing the final Champions League place. The UEFA Cup spots went to Bolton and Middlesbrough.

The relegation battle went right to the wire, with four sides battling for top-flight survival on the final day. As Norwich, Southampton and Crystal Palace all slipped up, Bryan Robson's West Brom leapt off the bottom of the table to safety.

Seven clubs changed their manager over the course of the season, with Sir Bobby Robson among the high-profile casualties. Tottenham's Jacques Santini lasted just a few months in the English game, departing White Hart Lane for personal reasons.

Newcastle was the place for drama, as new boss Graeme Souness had plenty of difficult issues to deal with. Craig Bellamy was loaned to Celtic after branding his manager a "liar", while Lee Bowyer and Kieron Dyer took to fighting each other in a match against Aston Villa.

Chelsea striker Adrian Mutu was sacked by the club after failing a random drugs test. The Romania international was handed a seven-month ban by the FA, keeping him out of action until May.

On the international front, England made good progress in their bid to reach the 2006 World Cup. A 2-2 draw in Austria was followed by five straight wins, leaving Sven-Goran Eriksson's men well-placed to qualify.

Chelsea unsurprisingly dominated the end-of-season awards. Captain John Terry was named PFA Player of the Year, while Frank Lampard took the Football Writers' prize. The two players were joined in the PFA Team of the Season by colleagues Arjen Robben and Petr Cech.

Finally, a big thank you to the guys at Sidan for their help in putting this publication together... we couldn't have done it without you.

Enjoy!

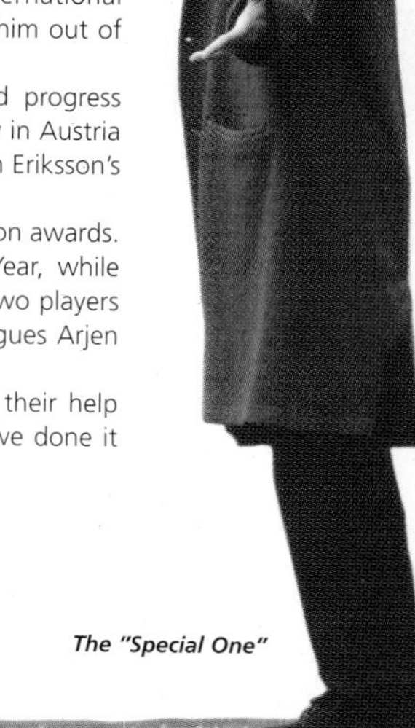

The "Special One"

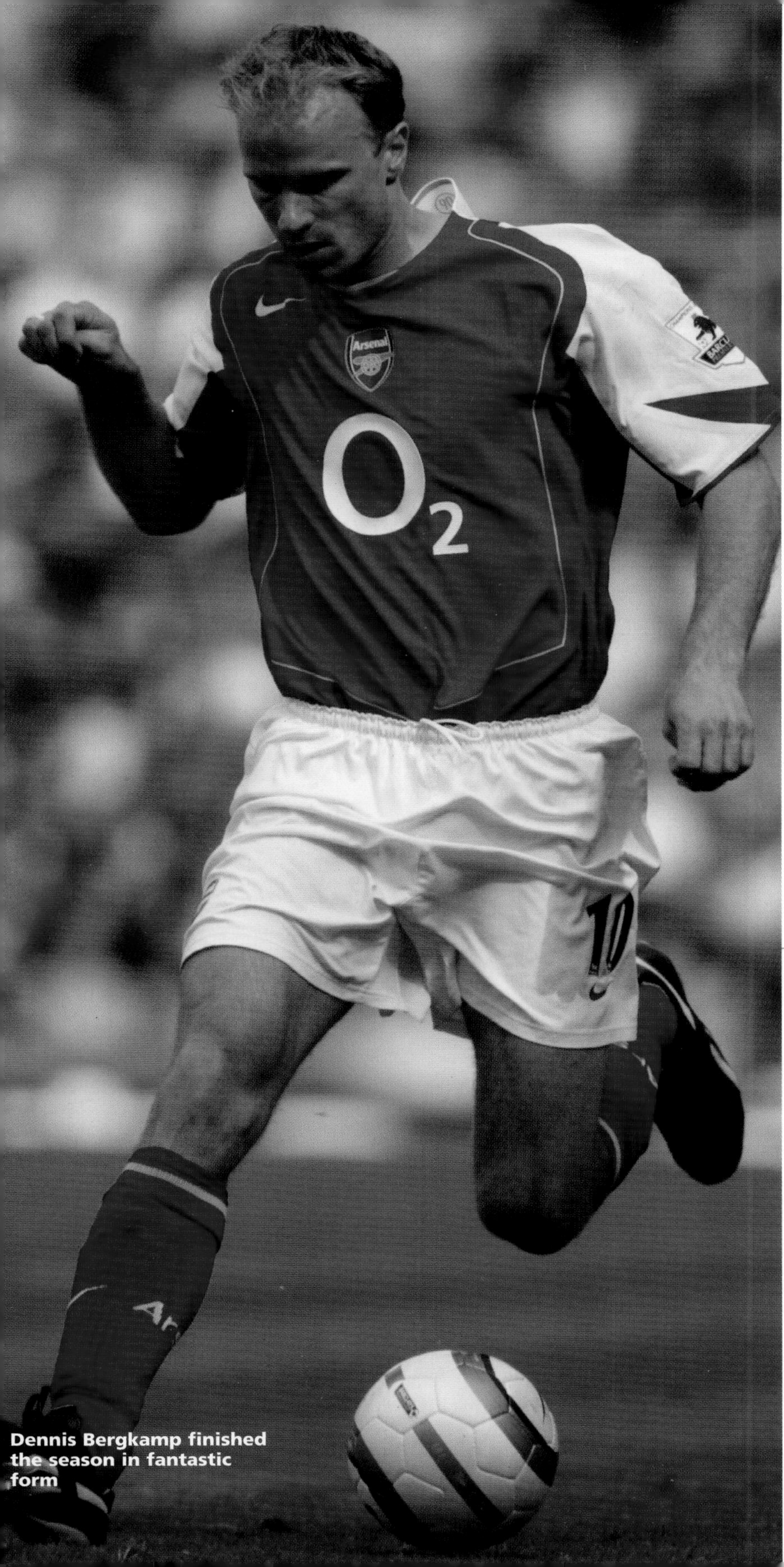

Dennis Bergkamp finished the season in fantastic form

CONTENTS

Publisher Simon Rosen
Editor Mark Peters
Contributing Editors Marc Fiszman, Janet Callcott, Julian Hillwood, Trevor Scimes, John Fitzroy, James Avenue, Jenny Middlemarch, Joan Colville-Scott.
Statisticians Karim Biria, Sean Cronin, Zoe Westbourne, Charles Grove, Ronen Dorfan, Lim Wai-lee, Tim Ryman, Emma Turner, Anders Rasmussen. Adam Regent
Designers Fetherstonhaugh, Nick Thornton, Daniel Anim-Kwapong

Sidan Press Ltd
63-64 Margaret St, London W1W 8SW
tel +44 (0)20 7580 0200
sidanpress.com

PREMIERSHIP FIXTURE HISTORY

Pl: **13** Draws: **4**	Wins	⚽	▢	■
Aston Villa	**6**	**15**	**9**	**1**
Southampton	**3**	**8**	**15**	**1**

STARTING LINE-UPS

Sorensen

Delaney, Mellberg (c), Laursen, Samuel

Hendrie, McCann, Hitzlsperger, Barry

Cole, Vassell

Phillips, Ormerod

Nilsson, Folly, Prutton, Fernandes

Le Saux, Higginbotham, Lundekvam, Dodd (c)

Niemi

Whittingham, Postma, L.Moore, De la Cruz, Berson

Delap, A.Svensson, Crouch, Smith, Kenton

EVENT LINE

12 ⚽ **Vassell (Open Play)**

22 **Hendrie (Off) Whittingham (On)**

34 ⚽ **Cole (Open Play)**

HALF TIME 2 - 0

46 Folly (Off) Delap (On)

46 Nilsson (Off) Svensson A (On)

68 Ormerod (Off) Crouch (On)

75 **Whittingham (Off) De la Cruz (On)**

85 **Vassell (Off) Moore L (On)**

FULL TIME 2 - 0

STATISTICS

Season	Fixture		Fixture	Season
5	**5**	Shots On Target	**2**	**2**
9	**9**	Shots Off Target	**4**	**4**
0	**0**	Hit Woodwork	**0**	**0**
0	**0**	Caught Offside	**2**	**2**
12	**12**	Corners	**6**	**6**
14	**14**	Fouls	**9**	**9**
56%	**56%**	Possession	**44%**	**44%**

LEAGUE STANDINGS

Position (pos before)		W	D	L	F	A	Pts
2 (-)	**Aston Villa**	**1**	**0**	**0**	**2**	**0**	**3**
15 (-)	**Southampton**	**0**	**0**	**1**	**0**	**2**	**0**

Saturday 14th August 2004 | Venue: **Villa Park** | Attendance: **36,690** | Referee: **U.D.Rennie**

ASTON VILLA 2 SOUTHAMPTON 0

Darius Vassell bounced back from his Euro 2004 heartache to help fire Aston Villa to an impressive opening day victory against Southampton at Villa Park.

Vassell, whose penalty miss against Portugal ultimately cost England their place in the European Championships, put his side ahead after just 12 minutes.

He then turned provider for his new strike partner, Carlton Cole, who marked his debut on a season-long loan move from Chelsea with a smartly taken 34th-minute strike.

Southampton were never really in contention and were not helped by the fact that their England international striker James Beattie, who was the target of an unsuccessful £6m bid from Villa, was missing with a thigh strain.

The opening goal did not take long to arrive. A neat move saw Gareth Barry's cross fired goalwards by Lee Hendrie, with Vassell quickest to react as the ball ricocheted around a packed six-yard box.

Other opportunities came and went for the home side, most notably for Peter Whittingham, before the Saints almost levelled matters in the 28th minute.

Danish goalkeeper Thomas Sorensen could only help Brett Ormerod's cross into the path of Southampton's £500,000 summer signing from Halmstad, Mikael Nilsson, but recovered brilliantly to somehow block the Swede's effort on the line, before Mark Delaney completed the clearance.

It was to prove a vital moment in the match, as David O'Leary's side extended their lead just six minutes later.

Vassell fed Cole, who surged towards goal before rifling home a drive from 16 yards that left Niemi rooted to the spot.

That was a blow from which the visitors never fully recovered, but they did at least step up a gear in the second half following the introduction of Rory Delap and Anders Svensson.

Fabrice Fernandes fired narrowly wide just 60 seconds after the restart, before Kevin Phillips tested Sorensen with a low 20-yard drive that was turned away for a corner.

Villa remained on cruise control throughout the second period and spurned several half-chances. For Southampton, defeat meant that they extended their dismal record on the opening day of the season to just one win since the formation of the Premier League.

Carlton Cole fends off Rory Delap

"I thought that we were excellent in the first half and that was when the game was won."

David O'Leary

PREMIERSHIP MILESTONE

Carlton Cole made his Premiership debut for Aston Villa, and scored his first goal for the club

"I am very hopeful he will stay. I want him to be my main striker this season and we missed him today."

Paul Sturrock on James Beattie

PREMIERSHIP MILESTONE

Premiership debuts were made by Martin Laursen and Mikael Nilsson

PREMIERSHIP MILESTONE

Peter Crouch made his Premiership debut for Southampton

PREMIERSHIP FIXTURE HISTORY

Pl: 2 Draws: 2	Wins	⚽	▢	■
Blackburn Rovers	0	2	3	0
West Bromwich Albion	0	2	1	0

STARTING LINE-UPS

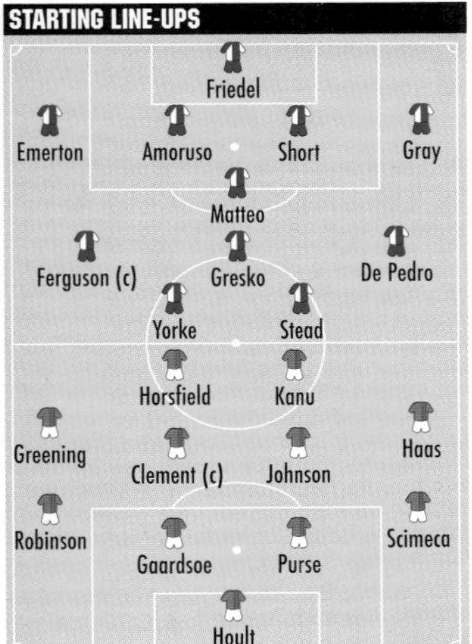

Tugay, Dickov, Gallagher, Enckelman, Johansson

Moore, Dobie, Gera, Kuszczak, O'Connor

EVENT LINE

33 ⚽ Clement (Direct Free Kick)

HALF TIME 0 - 1

46 **De Pedro (Off) Tugay (On)**

46 **Gresko (Off) Dickov (On)**

65 ▢ **Matteo (Foul)**

70 ⚽ **Short (Open Play)**

75 Clement (Off) Moore (On)

76 Horsfield (Off) Dobie (On)

84 **Emerton (Off) Gallagher (On)**

87 Johnson (Off) Gera (On)

FULL TIME 1 - 1

STATISTICS

Season	Fixture (Blackburn)		Fixture (West Brom)	Season
4	4	Shots On Target	2	2
8	8	Shots Off Target	2	2
0	0	Hit Woodwork	0	0
3	3	Caught Offside	4	4
4	4	Corners	5	5
15	15	Fouls	17	17
52%	52%	Possession	48%	48%

LEAGUE STANDINGS

Position (pos before)		W	D	L	F	A	Pts
6 (-)	Blackburn R	0	1	0	1	1	1
14 (-)	West Brom	0	1	0	1	1	1

Saturday 14th August 2004 | Venue: **Ewood Park** | Attendance: **23,475** | Referee: **C.J.Foy**

BLACKBURN ROVERS 1 WEST BROM 1

Bernt Haas takes on Michael Gray

"It was a difficult afternoon for us. It was a typical first day of the season, with people feeling edgy."

Graeme Souness

PREMIERSHIP MILESTONE

Paul Dickov and Dominic Matteo made their first Premiership appearances for Blackburn

"We did ever so well throughout the game. This is a good point for us."

Gary Megson

PREMIERSHIP MILESTONE

Javier De Pedro and Zoltan Gera made their Premiership debuts

PREMIERSHIP MILESTONE

Eight players – Scimeca, Purse, Robinson, Greening, Horsfield, Kanu, Gaardsoe, and Haas - made their first Premiership appearances in a West Brom shirt

Newly-promoted West Bromwich Albion began their top-flight campaign determined to improve on their one previous Premiership experience of 2002-03, when they never really looked like avoiding relegation.

A lack of goals was a major reason why the Baggies had struggled two seasons ago, though their 33rd-minute strike in this game suggested a change in fortune. Neil Clement's fiercely-struck free-kick crashed off Barry Ferguson in the wall and flew beyond a helpless Brad Friedel.

Blackburn were devoid of inspiration and ideas in the first half, with the deployment of Dominic Matteo in front of his back four leaving a gaping hole down the right-hand side of midfield. If he had been positioned there to lessen the threat from Nwankwo Kanu, then the tactic didn't work. The Nigerian was always involved in the action and his languid style constantly posed problems for the Rovers defence.

It was not until Graeme Souness changed things around at half-time, throwing on Tugay and striker Paul Dickov, that the home team began to pose a genuine threat.

Even so, Friedel's alertness rescued his side in the 50th minute after Lorenzo Amoruso's short back-pass had let Kanu in, the American goalkeeper racing out of his area and managing to dispossess the former Arsenal man.

After a Dickov penalty appeal was turned down, Blackburn got the equaliser they had been striving for in the 70th minute. Patient build-up play was rewarded when ageing centre-back Craig Short arrived in the penalty area to meet Jon Stead's inswinging cross from the left with an angled header that seemed to brush Paul Robinson on its way in.

Both sides went close to stealing victory in the closing stages, with Brett Emerton for Blackburn and Robinson for Albion both squandering presentable opportunities. It was a whipped cross from Barry Ferguson that nearly decided the outcome, however, curling inches wide of the far-post.

In the end, a draw was probably a fair result, though better performances will be needed from both sides if they are to steer clear of the relegation battle.

PREMIERSHIP FIXTURE HISTORY

Pl: 4 Draws: 2	Wins	Goals	Yellow	Red
Bolton Wanderers	1	5	7	0
Charlton Athletic	1	3	6	0

STARTING LINE-UPS

Jaaskelainen
Hunt, N'Gotty, Cesar, Gardner
Okocha (c), Campo, Speed
Nolan, Pedersen
Davies

Bartlett
Konchesky, Euell, Murphy, Holland (c), Lisbie
Hreidarsson, Fish, Fortune, Young
Kiely

Giannakopoulos, Ferdinand, Ben Haim, Poole, Barness

Hughes, Rommedahl, Jeffers, Andersen, El Karkouri

EVENT LINE

11 **Okocha (Direct Free Kick)**
12 Holland (Off) Hughes (On)
30 **Pedersen (Open Play)**
HALF TIME 2 - 0
59 **Okocha (Open Play)**
63 Young (Dissent)
67 Lisbie (Corner)
70 Konchesky (Off) Rommedahl (On)
70 Murphy (Off) Jeffers (On)
72 **Pedersen (Open Play)**
75 **Speed (Foul)**
77 **Davies (Off) Ferdinand (On)**
77 **Nolan (Off) Giannakopoulos (On)**
85 **Hunt (Off) Ben Haim (On)**
FULL TIME 4 - 1

STATISTICS

Season	Fixture		Fixture	Season
11	11	Shots On Target	5	5
10	10	Shots Off Target	4	4
0	0	Hit Woodwork	0	0
0	0	Caught Offside	1	1
9	9	Corners	5	5
10	10	Fouls	12	12
62%	62%	Possession	38%	38%

LEAGUE STANDINGS

Position (pos before)		W	D	L	F	A	Pts
1 (-)	Bolton W	1	0	0	4	1	3
16 (-)	Charlton Ath	0	0	1	1	4	0

Saturday 14th August 2004 | Venue: **Reebok Stadium** | Attendance: **24,100** | Referee: **P.Dowd**

BOLTON WANDERERS 4 CHARLTON ATHLETIC 1

Bolton captain Jay-Jay Okocha ended last season without a Premiership goal to his name, yet the birthday boy quickly made amends this time around with a spectacular opening day brace in the 4-1 demolition of disappointing Charlton.

The Nigerian international also laid on another for Henrik Pedersen, the first of a double for the Dane, while he could have celebrated turning 31 with a hat-trick, but for Shaun Bartlett heading another goalbound effort off the line.

Charlton's only consolation was a 67th-minute Kevin Lisbie goal, though their cause had not been helped when captain Matt Holland was forced off with a knee injury in the early stages.

Both managers had been busy over the summer, but only Gary Speed and Julio Cesar for Bolton and Danny Murphy for Charlton were afforded starting places. In fact, the entire visiting bench was made up of new arrivals.

The campaign was just 11 minutes old when one of the stars of last season lit up the Reebok Stadium. An innocuous handball on the left edge of the area provided Jay-Jay Okocha with the chance to fire a stunning free-kick into the far top corner of Dean Kiely's net.

Okocha was then instrumental in Wanderers' second goal on the half-hour, splitting the Charlton defence with a measured pass from which Pedersen coolly converted.

Half-time failed to stop Bolton momentum, as Okocha fired home a low 20-yard effort just before the hour mark.

Two minutes later Okocha could have completed a treble, but this time South African striker Shaun Bartlett was stationed by the post to head away another thunderous free-kick.

Charlton's attempts had been pretty much limited to a Murphy header, but they finally gained some sort of a foothold when Lisbie headed home from a corner.

New-boys Dennis Rommedahl and Francis Jeffers were thrown into the action, but it was Bolton's Henrik Pedersen who completed the scoring in the 72nd minute. Gary Speed's long pass picked out the Dane, who saw his 20-yard shot deflected in off Mark Fish.

Ricardo Gardner narrowly failed to add a fifth, in what was a five-star performance from Sam Allardyce's team.

Henrik Pedersen celebrates a goal

"If we had a problem last season it was turning opportunities into goals. We've gone some way to putting that right already."
Sam Allardyce

PREMIERSHIP MILESTONE
Gary Speed and Les Ferdinand made their first Premiership appearances for Bolton

"This was a shadow of any Charlton team I have ever put out."
Alan Curbishley

PREMIERSHIP MILESTONE
Julio Cesar, Tal Ben Haim and Dennis Rommedahl made their Premiership debuts

PREMIERSHIP MILESTONE
Danny Murphy, Francis Jeffers and Bryan Hughes made their first Premiership appearances for Charlton

PREMIERSHIP FIXTURE HISTORY

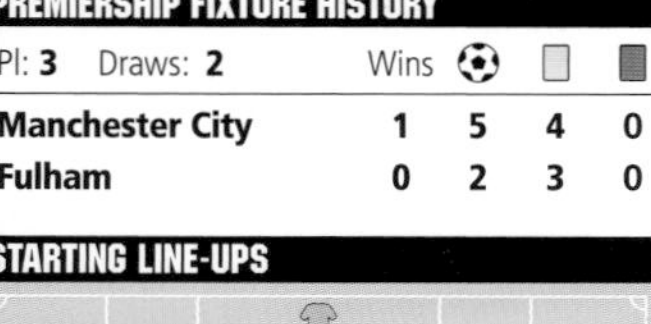

Pl: 3 Draws: 2	Wins	⚽	Yellow	Red
Manchester City	1	5	4	0
Fulham	0	2	3	0

STARTING LINE-UPS

Barton, McManaman, Jihai, Macken, Stuhr-Ellegaard

McBride, Pembridge, Crossley, Goma, Rehman

EVENT LINE

28 ⚽ **Fowler (Open Play)**
40 Cole (Foul)
HALF TIME 1 - 0
56 ⚽ John (Open Play)
63 John (Off) McBride (On)
66 Volz (Foul)
77 **Fowler (Off) Macken (On)**
78 **Bosvelt (Off) Barton (On)**
79 Radzinski (Off) Pembridge (On)
FULL TIME 1 - 1

STATISTICS

Season	Fixture		Fixture	Season
5	5	Shots On Target	2	2
7	7	Shots Off Target	2	2
0	0	Hit Woodwork	0	0
1	1	Caught Offside	7	7
9	9	Corners	4	4
14	14	Fouls	12	12
44%	44%	Possession	56%	56%

LEAGUE STANDINGS

Position (pos before)		W	D	L	F	A	Pts
10 (-)	**Man City**	0	1	0	1	1	1
8 (-)	**Fulham**	0	1	0	1	1	1

Saturday 14th August 2004 | Venue: **City of Manchester Stadium** | Attendance: **44,026** | Referee: **M.D.Messias**

MANCHESTER CITY 1 FULHAM 1

Manchester City's struggles at home continued, as visitors Fulham battled back to earn a 1-1 draw on the opening day of the new Premiership season.

It was the same old story for City, who failed to capitalise on total first half domination and the electrifying forward surges of 22-year-old right winger, Shaun Wright-Phillips. The youngster was in inspirational form, and further enhanced growing claims that he should be included in England coach Sven-Goran Eriksson's immediate plans.

The home side's 28th-minute goal, however, owed more to England past than future. A long throw from summer signing Danny Mills was flicked on at the near-post by Antoine Sibierski, and Robbie Fowler expertly hooked a right-foot shot over his shoulder and into the corner of the net from around the penalty spot.

Having kept Edwin van der Sar busy prior to their goal, City refused to let up after it. Nicolas Anelka made progress down the right, before teeing up Wright-Phillips for a shot that the Dutchman could only parry. Sniffing a second goal, Fowler went in for the loose ball, but a desperate clearance by Zat Knight saved the day for the visitors.

That escape was to prove vital for Fulham, as they regrouped at half-time and levelled the scores 11 minutes after the interval. Claus Jensen, a new £2.5m signing from Charlton, clipped over a ball from the right, and hesitancy in the home defence allowed Collins John to swivel and beat David James with the aid of a deflection from 15 yards out.

The goal jolted Kevin Keegan's men back to life, and Claudio Reyna saw a fierce 20-yard drive superbly turned away by van der Sar.

The visiting custodian produced another breathtaking save soon after, when he tipped behind Sibierski's point-blank near-post header from Reyna's free-kick.

Things almost got worse for City nine minutes from time when Andy Cole produced a neat lay-off to send Jensen clear. However, David James kept his head to snuff out the Dane's weak low finish.

That save ensured that the home team earned a point, which could so easily have been either three or none at all.

"We were outstanding in the first half. We had good shape and created many chances."

Kevin Keegan

PREMIERSHIP MILESTONE

Ben Thatcher and Danny Mills made their first Premiership appearances for Man City

"If we want to equal or do better than we did last season, we cannot afford to play like we did in the first half."

Chris Coleman

PREMIERSHIP MILESTONE

Andy Cole, Claus Jensen and Tomasz Radzinski made their first Premiership appearances for Fulham

PREMIERSHIP MILESTONE

Pape Bouba Diop made his Premiership debut

Carlos Bocanegra attempts to dispossess Jonathan Macken

Manchester City >> 18 | Fulham >> 17

PREMIERSHIP FIXTURE HISTORY

Pl: 9 Draws: 3	Wins			
Middlesbrough	1	10	13	1
Newcastle United	5	17	12	0

STARTING LINE-UPS

Schwarzer
Ehiogu (c) Riggott
Reiziger Parnaby
Parlour Boateng
Mendieta Zenden
Hasselbaink Job

Shearer (c) Bellamy
Robert Milner
Butt Jenas
Bernard Carr
Elliott Hughes
Given

Nemeth, Downing, Nash, Cooper, Doriva

Dyer, Ameobi, Kluivert, Harper, Ramage

EVENT LINE

11 **Parlour (Foul)**
14 Bellamy (Open Play)
29 **Boateng (Foul)**
HALF TIME 0 - 1
46 **Job (Off) Nemeth (On)**
48 **Ehiogu (Foul)**
52 Carr (Dissent)
65 **Parnaby (Off) Downing (On)**
68 Milner (Off) Dyer (On)
73 **Downing (Open Play)**
76 Robert (Off) Ameobi (On)
83 Shearer (Penalty)
87 Shearer (Off) Kluivert (On)
90 **Hasselbaink (Open Play)**
FULL TIME 2 - 2

STATISTICS

Season	Fixture		Fixture	Season
8	8	Shots On Target	5	5
7	7	Shots Off Target	7	7
0	0	Hit Woodwork	0	0
7	7	Caught Offside	5	5
6	6	Corners	7	7
16	16	Fouls	13	13
51%	51%	Possession	49%	49%

LEAGUE STANDINGS

Position (pos before)		W	D	L	F	A	Pts
3 (-)	Middlesbrough	0	1	0	2	2	1
4 (-)	Newcastle Utd	0	1	0	2	2	1

Saturday 14th August 2004 | Venue: **Riverside Stadium** | Attendance: **34,268** | Referee: **S.G.Bennett**

MIDDLESBROUGH 2 NEWCASTLE UNITED 2

Ugo Ehiogu shields the ball from Craig Bellamy

"Obviously, I am pleased with the point after we were twice behind."
Steve McClaren

PREMIERSHIP MILESTONE
Michael Reiziger and Patrick Kluivert made their Premiership debuts

PREMIERSHIP MILESTONE
Stewart Downing scored his first Premiership goal

PREMIERSHIP MILESTONE
Jimmy Floyd Hasselbaink and Ray Parlour both made their first Premiership appearances for Middlesbrough, with Hasselbaink also netting his first goal for the club

"Hasselbaink clearly handled the ball. Sometimes you get decisions, sometimes you don't."
Sir Bobby Robson on Middlesbrough's late equaliser

PREMIERSHIP MILESTONE
Nicky Butt, Stephen Carr and James Milner all made their first Premiership appearances for Newcastle

Newcastle United were unlucky not to take all three points from this Tyne-Tees derby at the Riverside Stadium.

The home side were rescued by a dubious last-gasp goal from Jimmy Floyd Hasselbaink, one of several high-profile new faces on the Middlesbrough teamsheet.

Several Newcastle players had gone down with conjunctivitis earlier in the week, and manager Sir Bobby Robson had described the match preparation as the most testing of his long and distinguished career.

Kieron Dyer's exclusion from the starting XI, amid rumours that he had refused to play on the right-hand side of midfield, did not seem to have an adverse effect on his team-mates, as Craig Bellamy capitalised on a slip by Chris Riggott to round Mark Schwarzer and give his side a 14th-minute lead.

Former rivals in the battle for the Premiership crown, Ray Parlour and Nicky Butt were 100% committed to their respective new colours.

High pre-match expectations seemed to be weighing down on Steve McClaren's revamped charges, and there was a lack of penetration until the introduction of local lad Stewart Downing midway through the second half.

Having already gone close, the England Under-21 international levelled the scores after 73 minutes, steadying himself before dispatching Hasselbaink's low cross under Shay Given from seven-yards out.

Newcastle responded by sending on substitute Shola Ameobi, and in the 83rd minute he was sent crashing to the ground by makeshift left-back Boudewijn Zenden, to earn his side a penalty.

Alan Shearer duly hammered home from the spot, before giving way to debutant Patrick Kluivert three minutes from time.

Jermaine Jenas missed a gilt-edged chance to put the issue beyond doubt in the closing minutes, when he shot wide from close range. The young midfielder was to regret this, as Hasselbaink popped up to salvage a point for his new employers with a 90th minute debut goal.

Boudewijn Zenden delivered a vicious cross from the left, and his fellow Dutchman stooped to turn the ball home at the far post. Television replays later confirmed Newcastle suspicions that Hasselbaink had converted the chance with his hand.

Saturday 14th August 2004	Venue: **Carrow Road**	Attendance: **23,717**	Referee: **P.Walton**

PREMIERSHIP FIXTURE HISTORY

Pl: **3** Draws: **2**	Wins	⚽	▢	■
Norwich City	1	5	2	0
Crystal Palace	0	3	2	0

STARTING LINE-UPS

McVeigh, Edworthy, McKenzie, Ward, Jarvis

Derry, Riihilahti, Freedman, Kiraly, Black

EVENT LINE

16 ⚽ **Huckerby (Open Play)**

HALF TIME 1 - 0

58 ▢ Granville (Foul)

64 **Jonson (Off) McVeigh (On)**

71 **Bentley (Off) Edworthy (On)**

73 ⚽ Johnson (Open Play)

78 Hall (Off) Riihilahti (On)

78 Kolkka (Off) Derry (On)

82 **Svensson (Off) McKenzie (On)**

89 Hughes (Off) Freedman (On)

FULL TIME 1 - 1

STATISTICS

Season	Fixture		Fixture	Season
10	**10**	Shots On Target	**8**	**8**
4	**4**	Shots Off Target	**6**	**6**
0	**0**	Hit Woodwork	**0**	**0**
8	**8**	Caught Offside	**4**	**4**
6	**6**	Corners	**11**	**11**
12	**12**	Fouls	**16**	**16**
46%	**46%**	Possession	**54%**	**54%**

LEAGUE STANDINGS

Position (pos before)		W	D	L	F	A	Pts
11 (-)	**Norwich C**	**0**	**1**	**0**	**1**	**1**	**1**
7 (-)	**Crystal Palace**	**0**	**1**	**0**	**1**	**1**	**1**

Adam Drury keeps a close eye on Sandor Torghelle

"Darren Huckerby showed today that he can do it in the Premiership."

Nigel Worthington

PREMIERSHIP MILESTONE

The attendance of 23,717 was a Premiership record at Carrow Road

PREMIERSHIP MILESTONE

Darren Huckerby netted his first Premiership goal for Norwich

"He makes bright runs and if you keep making those runs you will get goals."

Iain Dowie on Andy Johnson

PREMIERSHIP MILESTONE

Andy Johnson scored his first Premiership goal

PREMIERSHIP MILESTONE

Crystal Palace handed Premiership debuts to 10 players – Johnson, Boyce, Kolkka, Hudson, Popovic, Routledge, Speroni, Torghelle, Derry and Riihilahti

PREMIERSHIP MILESTONE

Danny Granville, Michael Hughes and Fitz Hall made their first Premiership appearances for Crystal Palace

NORWICH CITY 1 CRYSTAL PALACE 1

When Darren Huckerby hit his first Premiership goal for newly-promoted Norwich City, the home side looked odds on to collect all three points.

However, a spirited second half Crystal Palace fightback brought an equaliser from Andrew Johnson, and in the end a draw was probably a fair result.

The visitors began brightly, with Emmerson Boyce and Wayne Routledge combining well down the right, but the home side were soon into their running, forcing three corners in quick succession.

The opening goal took just 16 minutes to arrive as Huckerby nudged Mark Hudson off the ball to collect Matthias Svensson's pass, before advancing and beating Julian Speroni with a blistering shot across goal from an inside right position.

In the 25th minute, Huckerby began his run just too soon and was flagged offside with only the keeper to beat.

This situation was repeated three or four times throughout the game.

Debutant David Bentley, on a season-long loan from Arsenal, was playing a starring role for the Canaries. Having created first half openings for both Huckerby and Simon Charlton, the youngster took less than a minute of the second period to provide Svensson with a headed chance from which he should have done better.

Robert Green then denied Hungarian Sandor Torghelle with a spectacular facial block, after the striker had got clear of the home defence.

At that point the Eagles were playing as well as they had at any stage in the match, forcing Norwich into some desperate defending.

Huckerby was denied a second goal by Speroni's fingertips with half-an-hour left to play, but no home player was alert to the rebound.

With 73 minutes on the clock, Johnson continued where he had left off last season, netting a smartly taken equaliser. The striker was picked out by the impressive Routledge, having run in behind the Norwich defence, and was able to beat Green with a quickly dispatched low effort.

Both sides pushed for a winner, with Speroni clutching an 18-yard Huckerby volley and Green somewhat fortuitously keeping out a Johnson strike at the second attempt.

PREMIERSHIP FIXTURE HISTORY				
Pl: 2 Draws: 1	Wins	Goals	Yellow	Red
Portsmouth	1	4	3	0
Birmingham City	0	2	6	1

STARTING LINE-UPS

Portsmouth: Hislop; Primus, De Zeeuw (c), Stefanovic, Unsworth; Stone, Quashie, Hughes, Berger; Lua Lua, Yakubu

Birmingham City: Heskey, Forssell; Johnson, Izzet, Savage, Gronkjaer; Lazaridis, Upson (c), Martin Taylor, Melchiot; Maik Taylor

Substitutes (Portsmouth): Taylor, Griffin, Ashdown, O'Neil, Berkovic

Substitutes (Birmingham City): Gray, Morrison, Bennett, Clapham, John

EVENT LINE

10 Goal Savage (Direct Free Kick)
16 Goal **Unsworth (Penalty)**
18 Yellow **Hughes (Foul)**
18 Yellow Savage (Ung.Conduct)
25 Yellow Taylor Martin (Foul)

HALF TIME 1 - 1

50 Yellow **Unsworth (Foul)**
67 Sub Gronkjaer (Off) Gray (On)
70 Yellow Izzet (Foul)
80 Yellow Lazaridis (Ung.Conduct)
81 Sub **Berger (Off) Taylor (On)**
85 Sub **Stone (Off) Griffin (On)**
90 Sub Forssell (Off) Morrison (On)

FULL TIME 1 - 1

STATISTICS

Season	Fixture (Portsmouth)		Fixture (Birmingham City)	Season
9	9	Shots On Target	11	11
6	6	Shots Off Target	5	5
0	0	Hit Woodwork	0	0
5	5	Caught Offside	1	1
8	8	Corners	4	4
13	13	Fouls	16	16
51%	51%	Possession	49%	49%

LEAGUE STANDINGS

Position (pos before)		W	D	L	F	A	Pts
12 (-)	Portsmouth	0	1	0	1	1	1
5 (-)	Birmingham C	0	1	0	1	1	1

Saturday 14th August 2004 | Venue: **Fratton Park** | Attendance: **20,021** | Referee: **H.M.Webb**

Lomana Tresor Lua Lua gets away from Mario Melchiot

"It was hard, but my players worked tirelessly all over the pitch and it was good to get a point."

Harry Redknapp

PREMIERSHIP MILESTONE

David Unsworth scored his first Premiership goal for Portsmouth

PREMIERSHIP MILESTONE

Andy Griffin and David Unsworth made their first Premiership appearances for Portsmouth

"I was delighted with the performance of Emile Heskey and you can all see what a good player Muzzy Izzet is."

Steve Bruce

PREMIERSHIP MILESTONE

Five players – Heskey, Izzet, Melchiot, Gronkjaer and Gray – made their first Premiership appearances for Birmingham

PORTSMOUTH 1 BIRMINGHAM CITY 1

Defender David Unsworth capped an impressive debut by firing home an unstoppable penalty, to give Portsmouth a deserved draw in the Fratton Park sunshine against Birmingham City.

Visiting boss Steve Bruce had considerably strengthened his squad over the summer and gave starting places to four high-profile new arrivals, as he aimed to celebrate the signing of a new five-year contract with an opening day victory.

The early signs were good as Robbie Savage curled his side in front from a 10th-minute direct free-kick. Damien Johnson was hauled down on the edge of the area and the Welsh international stepped up to find the top right-hand corner of Shaka Hislop's goal.

The joy was short-lived, however, as within six minutes Portsmouth had equalised. Referee Howard Webb, no stranger to awarding penalties for innocuous offences, spotted a push on Steve Stone and new-boy Unsworth beat Maik Taylor from 12-yards.

Birmingham defender Martin Taylor was lucky not to be sent off in the 25th minute, when he escaped with a yellow card after tripping up Yakubu as he bore down on goal.

The visitors should have regained their advantage four minutes later through Emile Heskey. Jesper Gronkjaer delivered an inviting centre from the left, but the striker headed too close to Hislop, who made a fumbling save, and Izzet blazed the loose ball over the bar.

Yakubu wasted a golden opportunity to open his account on the half-hour mark, when a delightful pass from Patrik Berger left him with just the goalkeeper to beat, but Maik Taylor stood his ground before saving well to his left.

Portsmouth's African strikeforce posed problems all afternoon, but it was Birmingham who had the two best opportunities to net the three points after the interval.

Australian Stan Lazaridis, playing in an unfamiliar left-back role, abandoned his defensive duties and advanced towards goal, eventually unleashing a right-foot shot which fizzed past the far upright.

Then, 90th-minute substitute Clinton Morrison received the ball with his back to goal inside the penalty area in injury time. He managed to turn and get away a shot that was destined for the top left-hand corner, but Hislop flung himself to his right to ensure that the spoils were shared.

PREMIERSHIP FIXTURE HISTORY

Pl: 13 Draws: 4	Wins	Goals	Yellow	Red
Tottenham Hotspur	6	20	18	0
Liverpool	3	18	21	0

STARTING LINE-UPS

Doherty, Atouba, Brown, Keller, Silva

Sinama-Pongolle, Warnock, Biscan, Kirkland, Henchoz

EVENT LINE

6 **Kanoute (Foul)**

24 **Redknapp (Foul)**

38 Cisse (Corner)

HALF TIME 0 - 1

64 Cisse (Off) Sinama-Pongolle (On)

70 **Jackson (Off) Atouba (On)**

70 **Naybet (Off) Doherty (On)**

70 Sinama-Pongolle (Foul)

71 **Defoe (Ung.Conduct)**

71 **Defoe (Open Play)**

79 Baros (Off) Warnock (On)

82 **Redknapp (Off) Brown (On)**

83 Hamann (Off) Biscan (On)

FULL TIME 1 - 1

STATISTICS

Season	Fixture		Fixture	Season
7	7	Shots On Target	8	8
7	7	Shots Off Target	8	8
0	0	Hit Woodwork	0	0
5	5	Caught Offside	1	1
3	3	Corners	8	8
17	17	Fouls	11	11
47%	47%	Possession	53%	53%

LEAGUE STANDINGS

Position (pos before)		W	D	L	F	A	Pts
13 (-)	Tottenham H	0	1	0	1	1	1
9 (-)	Liverpool	0	1	0	1	1	1

Saturday 14th August 2004 | Venue: **White Hart Lane** | Attendance: **35,105** | Referee: **D.J.Gallagher**

TOTTENHAM HOTSPUR 1 LIVERPOOL 1

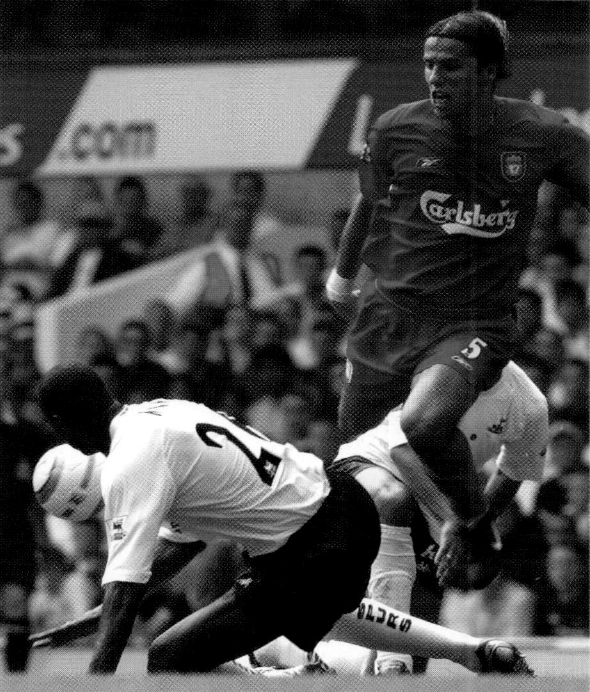

Ledley King wins the ball from Milan Baros

"It's always nice to get a goal with the England manager watching."
Jermain Defoe

PREMIERSHIP MILESTONE

Tottenham handed Premiership debuts to five players – Naybet, Edman, Mendes, Ifil and Atouba

PREMIERSHIP MILESTONE

Paul Robinson and Sean Davis made their first Premiership appearances for Tottenham

"We eased off a bit in the second half, having dominated the first. The manager will be disappointed, but I thought a draw was a fair result."
Steven Gerrard

PREMIERSHIP MILESTONE

Liverpool handed Premiership debuts to Djibril Cisse, Josemi and Stephen Warnock

PREMIERSHIP MILESTONE

Djibril Cisse scored his first Premiership goal

Djibril Cisse proved there is life without Michael Owen, but the French striker's goal was not enough to win the battle of the new managers at White Hart Lane.

On the day England striker Owen was officially unveiled at the Bernabeu, Gerard Houllier's final capture as Liverpool manager began to justify his £14m price tag.

Cisse, who netted 26 times in the French League last term, opened the scoring with a 38th-minute goal former Anfield hero Owen would have been proud of, reacting quickest in the box to sweep home after Spurs failed to clear a corner.

The goal had been coming, as a Tottenham team featuring six debutants struggled to cope with a visiting side that had won just four days earlier in a Champions League Qualifier in Austria.

Milan Baros had gone close with a deflected effort, while Steven Gerrard should have had a penalty when he had his shirt tugged by young defender Philip Ifil.

Rafael Benitez's men nearly went in at the break two goals to the good, but skipper Gerrard's dipping 30-yard volley flew just over the bar.

Jacques Santini must have wondered what he had let himself in for, but would have been delighted by the way in which his players responded to what was said in the dressing room at half-time.

Spurs offered a lot more up front at the start of the second half, with England striker Jermain Defoe shining like a beacon. The confident young forward went on a mazy dribble on 55 minutes, but saw his shot fly wide of Jerzy Dudek's goal.

However, Liverpool were not so lucky on 71 minutes. Defoe latched onto Frederic Kanoute's flick-on, before drilling home at the near post from an acute angle with his unfavoured left foot. It was the ex-West Ham player's eighth goal in 16 Tottenham appearances, and was reward for a spirited performance.

The fact that Defoe's goal did earn a point was down in no small part to new White Hart Lane shot-stopper Paul Robinson. The £1.5m capture from Leeds proved his worth by acrobatically tipping over Jamie Carragher's late bullet header.

PREMIERSHIP FIXTURE HISTORY

Pl: 13 Draws: 5	Wins	Goals	Yellow	Red
Chelsea	4	16	23	1
Manchester United	4	16	19	1

STARTING LINE-UPS

Chelsea: Cech; Ferreira, Gallas, Terry (c), Bridge; Makelele; Geremi, Lampard, Smertin; Gudjohnsen, Drogba

Manchester United: Howard; G.Neville, Keane (c), Silvestre, Fortune; Miller, Djemba-Djemba, O'Shea, Giggs; Smith, Scholes

Chelsea substitutes: Kezman, Parker, Carvalho, Cudicini, Mutu

Manchester United substitutes: Forlan, Richardson, Bellion, Ricardo, P.Neville

EVENT LINE

15	**Gudjohnsen (Open Play)**
	HALF TIME 1 - 0
70	**Drogba (Off) Kezman (On)**
73	Djemba-Djemba (Off) Forlan (On)
82	**Gudjohnsen (Off) Parker (On)**
84	Fortune (Off) Bellion (On)
84	Miller (Off) Richardson (On)
89	**Geremi (Off) Carvalho (On)**
	FULL TIME 1 - 0

STATISTICS

Season	Fixture (Chelsea)		Fixture (Man Utd)	Season
4	4	Shots On Target	2	2
6	6	Shots Off Target	5	5
0	0	Hit Woodwork	0	0
4	4	Caught Offside	2	2
2	2	Corners	3	3
11	11	Fouls	8	8
56%	56%	Possession	44%	44%

LEAGUE STANDINGS

Position (pos before)		W	D	L	F	A	Pts
4 (-)	Chelsea	1	0	0	1	0	3
17 (-)	Man Utd	0	0	1	0	1	0

Sunday 15th August 2004 | Venue: **Stamford Bridge** | Attendance: **41,813** | Referee: **G.Poll**

CHELSEA 1 MANCHESTER UNITED 0

Chelsea kicked off life under Jose Mourinho with a disciplined victory against fellow title pretenders Manchester United.

Eidur Gudjohnsen's 15th-minute bundled finish, after he had latched on to new boy Didier Drogba's cushioned header, proved to be the decisive moment in the match, though the visitors did carve out a couple of good chances to equalise.

Starting debuts were handed to Petr Cech, Paulo Ferreira, Drogba and Alexei Smertin, back from a loan spell at Portsmouth, by Mourinho, while Sir Alex Ferguson introduced Liam Miller and Alan Smith. In the continued absence of Rio Ferdinand, Roy Keane lined up at centre-back.

Chelsea initially seemed to struggle to adapt to a new shape in midfield, as both John O'Shea and Smith missed the target from very presentable heading opportunities. All was forgotten soon after though, as Gudjohnsen illustrated why he had been preferred to £5m signing Mateja Kezman by putting the Londoners in front.

United almost hit back within a minute, when a Paul Scholes piledriver flew inches wide of the right post. Then, on the half-hour mark, a sustained period of away possession nearly resulted in a goal. Firstly, Cech smothered a dangerous cross, before Scholes hit a snap-shot wide.

A Frank Lampard free-kick almost doubled the home side's advantage, arrowing narrowly wide, as the first half drew to a close.

The visitors started the second period in determined fashion, and within a minute John Terry was called upon to make an important block.

A flicked header from Smith, who was a constant menace, drifted wide after 58 minutes, before play switched to the other end as Tim Howard alertly denied Gudjohnsen.

Substitute Diego Forlan spurned two half-chances as United increased the pressure late on. Eventually, with eight minutes remaining, Smith carved out the gilt-edged opening his side had been searching for. Unfortunately, Ryan Giggs somehow managed to direct a free header wide of the target from just ten yards out.

Chelsea comfortably saw out the remainder of the game to repeat their 1-0 success of last season in this fixture.

"I told Sir Alex Ferguson that his side did not deserve to lose."
Jose Mourinho

PREMIERSHIP MILESTONE
Chelsea handed Premiership debuts to five players – Ferreira, Drogba, Cech, Carvalho and Kezman

PREMIERSHIP MILESTONE
Alexei Smertin made his first Premiership appearance in a Chelsea shirt

"I do not need Mourinho telling me we did not deserve to lose."
Sir Alex Ferguson

PREMIERSHIP MILESTONE
Liam Miller made his Premiership debut

PREMIERSHIP MILESTONE
Alan Smith made his first Premiership appearance for Man Utd

Eidur Gudjohnsen turns home the winner

PREMIERSHIP FIXTURE HISTORY

Pl: 13 Draws: 5	Wins	Goals	Yellow cards	Red cards
Everton	2	10	19	1
Arsenal	6	18	22	1

STARTING LINE-UPS

Everton subs: Hibbert, Bent, Ferguson, Wright, Watson

Arsenal subs: Pennant, Pires, Flamini, Almunia, Hoyte

EVENT LINE

23	Goal: Bergkamp (Open Play)
37	Yellow card: **Carsley (Ung.Conduct)**
39	Goal: Reyes (Open Play)
43	Yellow card: **Osman (Ung.Conduct)**
	HALF TIME 0 - 2
46	Sub: **McFadden (Off) Bent (On)**
46	Sub: **Stubbs (Off) Hibbert (On)**
53	Yellow card: Cole (Ung.Conduct)
54	Goal: Ljungberg (Open Play)
64	Goal: **Carsley (Open Play)**
64	Sub: Ljungberg (Off) Pennant (On)
65	Sub: Reyes (Off) Pires (On)
69	Sub: Gilberto (Off) Flamini (On)
71	Sub: **Osman (Off) Ferguson (On)**
83	Goal: Pires (Open Play)
	FULL TIME 1 - 4

STATISTICS

Season	Fixture	Everton / Arsenal	Fixture	Season
5	**5**	Shots On Target	**13**	**13**
4	**4**	Shots Off Target	**4**	**4**
0	**0**	Hit Woodwork	**1**	**1**
10	**10**	Caught Offside	**0**	**0**
0	**0**	Corners	**6**	**6**
16	**16**	Fouls	**15**	**15**
40%	**40%**	Possession	**60%**	**60%**

LEAGUE STANDINGS

Position (pos before)		W	D	L	F	A	Pts
19 (-)	**Everton**	**0**	**0**	**1**	**1**	**4**	**0**
1 (-)	**Arsenal**	**1**	**0**	**0**	**4**	**1**	**3**

Sunday 15th August 2004 | Venue: **Goodison Park** | Attendance: **35,521** | Referee: **M.A.Riley**

EVERTON 1 ARSENAL 4

Arsenal continued from where they had left off last season, brushing Everton aside with a display of free-flowing football.

The champions, buoyed by the news that Patrick Vieira would not be leaving for Real Madrid, began brightly. Young Spaniard Cesc Fabregas slotted seamlessly into the Frenchman's shoes, delivering an assured midfield performance that belied his 17 years.

Freddie Ljungberg was denied twice inside the opening ten minutes by Nigel Martyn, while James McFadden almost punished Pascal Cygan for a mistake at the other end.

The Gunners' first goal of the season arrived courtesy of Dennis Bergkamp in the 23rd minute. A characteristic break from an Everton throw was ended in clinical fashion, as Bergkamp controlled Thierry Henry's neat pass before beating Martyn with a low drive.

A spirited response saw Thomas Gravesen threaten from several free-kicks, while Kevin Kilbane flashed a header narrowly over the bar. However, Arsenal extended their lead after 39 minutes.

Jose Antonio Reyes stole across the front of his marker to angle home an eight-yard header, after Ljungberg had retrieved possession on the left. The goal effectively killed the game as a contest and Ljungberg netted himself nine minutes after the break.

Loose play by Joseph Yobo enabled Bergkamp to pick out Henry on the right. Within seconds the ball was in the back of the net, as the Frenchman sped forward before providing his Swedish colleague with a simple tap-in.

Lee Carsley pulled one back for Everton in the 64th minute, as the Arsenal defence was undone by a sublime looping pass from Gravesen. The Irish midfielder pulled the ball down from the sky, before rounding Jens Lehmann and slotting home.

The goal made little difference to the pattern of play, and substitute Robert Pires grabbed an 83rd-minute fourth. Having parried a shot from Henry, Martyn could only watch as Ashley Cole hit the bar from eight yards before Pires tucked away the rebound.

An injury to Gilberto was the only black spot on a glorious afternoon for the Gunners, while Evertonians had to comfort themselves with the thought that they only had to face Arsenal once more.

Dennis Bergkamp celebrates his goal

"I have the toughest job in the Premiership at the moment, but I still enjoy it."
David Moyes

PREMIERSHIP MILESTONE

Marcus Bent made his first Premiership appearance in the colours of Everton

"Today was a sunny day and everything went well for us."
Arsene Wenger

PREMIERSHIP MILESTONE

Arsene Wenger gave Premiership debuts to Cesc Fabregas and Mathieu Flamini

PREMIERSHIP FIXTURE HISTORY

Pl: **3** Draws: **1**

	Wins	Goals	Yellow cards	Red cards
Birmingham City	0	1	3	0
Chelsea	2	4	8	0

STARTING LINE-UPS

John, Bennett, Tebily, Carter, Clemence

Tiago, Kezman, J.Cole, Cudicini, Gallas

EVENT LINE

HALF TIME 0 - 0

46 Gudjohnsen (Off) Kezman (On)

46 Smertin (Off) Tiago (On)

63 Geremi (Off) Cole J (On)

68 Cole J (Open Play)

76 **Gronkjaer (Off) John (On)**

FULL TIME 0 - 1

STATISTICS

Season	Fixture		Fixture	Season
13	2	Shots On Target	3	7
11	6	Shots Off Target	4	10
1	1	Hit Woodwork	0	0
2	1	Caught Offside	3	7
12	8	Corners	2	4
26	10	Fouls	16	27
46%	44%	Possession	56%	56%

LEAGUE STANDINGS

Position (pos before)		W	D	L	F	A	Pts
19 (7)	Birmingham C	0	1	1	1	2	1
1 (4)	Chelsea	2	0	0	2	0	6

Saturday 21st August 2004 | Venue: **St Andrew's** | Attendance: **28,559** | Referee: **B.Knight**

BIRMINGHAM CITY 0 CHELSEA 1

Joe Cole came off the bench to devastating effect, silencing St Andrew's with a deflected 68th-minute matchwinner.

The ex-West Ham youngster had only been on the field five minutes when his willingness to be positive brought reward. Maik Taylor may well have saved his low drive from the inside left channel, but it took a cruel nick off namesake Martin to leave the Northern Ireland international goalkeeper completely helpless.

The defeat was rough on Birmingham, who had dominated for long spells. With Emile Heskey playing as a lone striker the Blues flooded the midfield, a tactic which the visitors struggled to come to terms with.

Robbie Savage was everywhere as the home side set about knocking the expensively assembled West Londoners out of their stride.

As early as the third minute Chelsea had a lucky escape, Julian Gray firing wide from close range after Damien Johnson had seen his shot blocked. Yet, despite spending most of the opening period on the defensive, the best chance of the half fell to Jose Mourinho's team.

An error of judgement by former player Mario Melchiot handed Didier Drogba a golden 13th-minute opportunity. However, despite reacting quickly, the Ivorian somehow managed to steer the ball beyond the left-hand upright.

Chances continued to come and go for Steve Bruce's side, before they finally beat Petr Cech as half-time approached. Much to the disappointment of the locals the post this time came to Chelsea's rescue, as Gray struck the woodwork from close range before spurning the rebound.

Mateja Kezman and Tiago were introduced by the visitors' at the break, with the former later ending up in a crumpled heap on the floor after a clash with the omnipresent Savage.

The changes brought little relief though, as the home side remained in control and on the front foot. Dutchman Melchiot came closest, flashing a 48th-minute header narrowly over the bar.

Yet, never had the old adage 'goals win games' wrung truer than when Cole stepped off the bench to steal the points. It is also said that the best teams can win when not playing well.

Joe Cole celebrates his deflected winner

"He is committed, wholehearted and can be a pest, but the one thing he wouldn't do is maliciously or deliberately elbow somebody."

Steve Bruce on Robbie Savage

"I was really surprised when this blond player struck Kezman. I hope the disciplinary committee will look at the video."

Jose Mourinho on Robbie Savage

PREMIERSHIP MILESTONE

Tiago made his Premiership debut

PREMIERSHIP FIXTURE HISTORY

Pl: 2 Draws: 1	Wins	Goals	Yellow	Red
Charlton Athletic	1	3	1	0
Portsmouth	0	2	2	0

STARTING LINE-UPS

Jeffers, Konchesky, El Karkouri, Andersen, Hughes

Taylor, Curtis, O'Neil, Ashdown, Schemmel

EVENT LINE

23 **Euell (Open Play)**

HALF TIME 1 - 0

46 Primus (Off) Taylor (On)

53 Berger (Indirect Free Kick)

69 Unsworth (Foul)

70 Griffin (Off) Curtis (On)

75 Berkovic (Off) O'Neil (On)

77 **Bartlett (Off) Jeffers (On)**

83 **Murphy (Off) Konchesky (On)**

87 **Unsworth (Own Goal)**

89 **Rommedahl (Off) El Karkouri (On)**

FULL TIME 2 - 1

STATISTICS

Season	Fixture		Fixture	Season
18	13	Shots On Target	6	15
7	3	Shots Off Target	4	10
1	1	Hit Woodwork	0	0
7	6	Caught Offside	1	6
10	5	Corners	6	14
21	9	Fouls	10	23
44%	51%	Possession	49%	50%

LEAGUE STANDINGS

Position (pos before)	W	D	L	F	A	Pts
11 (19) Charlton Ath	1	0	1	3	5	3
17 (14) Portsmouth	0	1	1	2	3	1

Saturday 21st August 2004 | Venue: **The Valley** | Attendance: **25,204** | Referee: **A.G.Wiley**

CHARLTON ATHLETIC 2 PORTSMOUTH 1

Jonathan Fortune and Radostin Kishishev celebrate a victory

"It didn't matter to me how we won that game, just as long as we did."

Alan Curbishley

PREMIERSHIP MILESTONE

Talal El Karkouri made his first Premiership appearance for Charlton

PREMIERSHIP MILESTONE

150 Luke Young made his 150th Premiership appearance

"I looked upfield to see where Shaka was going to clear it to, so I couldn't tell you exactly what happened, whether it sneaked under him or whatever."

Harry Redknapp on Charlton's winning goal

PREMIERSHIP MILESTONE

100 Dejan Stefanovic made his 100th Premiership appearance

PREMIERSHIP MILESTONE

50 John Curtis made his 50th Premiership appearance

Having started their centenary season in depressing fashion at Bolton, Charlton turned in a thoroughly professional performance to see off visitors Portsmouth at The Valley, thanks in no small part to a goalkeeping howler by Shaka Hislop.

It was Jason Euell who deservedly put Alan Curbishley's men ahead midway through the first half, expertly prodding home a loose ball from eight yards out following a cross from the right.

Four minutes earlier, fellow Jamaican frontman Kevin Lisbie had thumped a header off the Portsmouth crossbar.

Despite struggling defensively, the South Coast side always looked dangerous going forward. Lomana Tresor Lua Lua was a bag of tricks, setting up David Unsworth for a powerful drive and then almost squeezing a close-range effort under Dean Kiely.

Whilst an away goal was always on the cards, nobody could have foreseen its spectacular nature. Collecting a 53rd-minute free-kick with his back to goal some 30 yards out, Patrik Berger swivelled and dispatched a dipping shot in one fluid movement. The ground briefly fell silent in disbelief, before the away fans erupted with joy.

It was a goal worthy of winning any game, yet it turned out not even to be good enough for a point. Furthermore, the Addicks' winner was as ridiculous as Berger's strike was sublime.

With just three minutes left on the clock Jonathan Fortune launched a deep, hopeful free-kick into the Portsmouth area. Though no Charlton player came close to a touch, Unsworth was unsighted by the leap of teammate Arjan De Zeeuw in front of him and inadvertently headed back towards his own goal.

Nonetheless, goalkeeper Hislop appeared set to make a comfortable diving save, only for the ball to somehow wriggle underneath him and into the corner of the net.

There was little time for Harry Redknapp's side to respond as Curbishley quickly introduced debutant Talal El Karkouri in a bid to stiffen up his midfield.

As the final whistle sounded, Portsmouth were left to reflect on the cruel nature of the sport. For Charlton, their centenary season was off and running, albeit a week later than they would have liked.

PREMIERSHIP FIXTURE HISTORY

Pl: 4 Draws: 0	Wins	⚽	□	■
Crystal Palace	1	3	5	0
Everton	3	8	4	1

STARTING LINE-UPS

Crystal Palace: Speroni; Boyce, Hudson, Popovic (c), Granville; Routledge, Hall, Riihilahti, Kolkka; Freedman, Johnson

Everton: Campbell, Bent; Kilbane, Carsley, Gravesen, Osman; Naysmith, Stubbs (c), Yobo, Hibbert; Martyn

Crystal Palace subs: Derry, Kaviedes, Kiraly, Borrowdale, Hughes

Everton subs: Ferguson, Pistone, Watson, Wright, McFadden

EVENT LINE

9 ⚽ **Hudson (Open Play)**
19 ⚽ Gravesen (Penalty)
37 □ **Boyce (Foul)**
HALF TIME 1 - 1
54 Campbell (Off) Ferguson (On)
62 ⚽ Gravesen (Open Play)
71 ■ Naysmith (2nd Bookable Offence)
73 **Riihilahti (Off) Derry (On)**
75 Osman (Off) Pistone (On)
77 **Boyce (Off) Kaviedes (On)**
82 ⚽ Bent (Open Play)
85 Bent (Off) Watson (On)
FULL TIME 1 - 3

STATISTICS

Season	Fixture (Crystal Palace)		Fixture (Everton)	Season
13	5	Shots On Target	5	10
11	5	Shots Off Target	7	11
0	0	Hit Woodwork	0	0
5	1	Caught Offside	0	10
17	6	Corners	6	6
27	11	Fouls	11	27
50%	47%	Possession	53%	46%

LEAGUE STANDINGS

Position (pos before)	W	D	L	F	A	Pts
20 (9) Crystal Palace	0	1	1	2	4	1
9 (20) Everton	1	0	1	4	5	3

Saturday 21st August 2004 | Venue: **Selhurst Park** | Attendance: **23,666** | Referee: **M.Clattenburg**

CRYSTAL PALACE 1 EVERTON 3

Crystal Palace were given a taste of the difficulties that lay in front of them, suffering a comprehensive defeat against a club that had struggled last season.

Things had begun brilliantly for the Londoners with defender Mark Hudson heading them in front inside ten minutes. However, a blunder by goalkeeper Julian Speroni allowed Thomas Gravesen to level the scores from the penalty spot, before Gravesen and then Marcus Bent netted further second half goals.

A lively opening by the Premiership newcomers was rewarded after nine minutes. Andy Johnson's blocked effort found its way to Wayne Routledge, and the young winger slipped past Gary Naysmith down the right before sending over an inviting cross that Hudson powered home with his head from six yards.

The Toffees were having real problems coping with Johnson and strike partner Dougie Freedman at this stage of the game, but were gifted the chance to grab an undeserved equaliser after 19 minutes.

Not content with putting his captain Tony Popovic under pressure from a poor throw, Speroni attempted to skip around the onrushing Kevin Campbell from the Australian's return pass. All he succeeded in doing was upending the former Arsenal striker, enabling Thomas Gravesen to score from the resultant penalty.

That goal took the wind out of Palace's sails and they were a spent force after the break. Lee Carsley and Gravesen became increasingly instrumental in midfield and it came as no surprise when the Dane curled Everton in front from 20 yards in the 62nd minute.

However, Iain Dowie's men were offered a way back into the match after 71 minutes when Naysmith was dismissed for a second bookable offence. Having been cautioned for a first half foul, the Scot could have no complaints after cynically cutting short a breakaway from an Everton corner.

The home team certainly gave it their all, but it was old boy Marcus Bent who netted a decisive third goal, and his first, for the Merseysiders. This time Gravesen was the provider, with Bent racing clear of the defence before finishing coolly.

"We have got to be more ruthless and more clinical."
Iain Dowie

PREMIERSHIP MILESTONE
Mark Hudson netted his first Premiership goal

PREMIERSHIP MILESTONE
Ivan Kaviedes made his Premiership debut

"It was important we got a win away from home and the lads were well aware of that today."
David Moyes

PREMIERSHIP MILESTONE
Marcus Bent scored his first Premiership goal for Everton

Marcus Bent nets on his return to Selhurst Park

PREMIERSHIP FIXTURE HISTORY

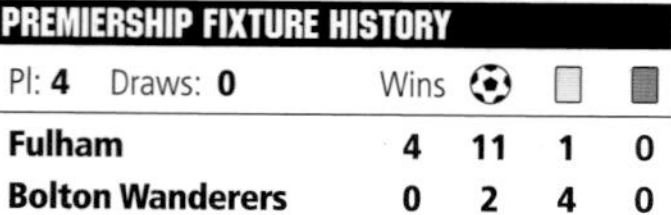

Pl: 4 Draws: 0	Wins	Goals	Yellow	Red
Fulham	4	11	1	0
Bolton Wanderers	0	2	4	0

STARTING LINE-UPS

Fulham subs: Boa Morte, McBride, Pembridge, Crossley, Pearce

Bolton subs: Giannakopoulos, Barness, Hierro, Poole, Ben Haim

EVENT LINE

5 ⚽ **Cole (Corner)**

HALF TIME 1 - 0

51 Pedersen (Off) Giannakopoulos (On)

55 Campo (Off) Barness (On)

65 **John (Off) Boa Morte (On)**

69 **Radzinski (Off) McBride (On)**

75 Gardner (Off) Hierro (On)

82 ⚽ **Cole (Open Play)**

85 **Jensen (Off) Pembridge (On)**

FULL TIME 2 - 0

STATISTICS

Season	Fixture (Fulham)		Fixture (Bolton)	Season
12	10	Shots On Target	4	15
13	11	Shots Off Target	6	16
2	2	Hit Woodwork	0	0
10	3	Caught Offside	2	2
12	8	Corners	4	13
23	11	Fouls	13	23
56%	56%	Possession	44%	53%

LEAGUE STANDINGS

Position (pos before)		W	D	L	F	A	Pts
2 (10)	Fulham	1	1	0	3	1	4
7 (2)	Bolton W	1	0	1	4	3	3

Saturday 21st August 2004 | Venue: **Craven Cottage** | Attendance: **17,541** | Referee: **R.Styles**

FULHAM 2 BOLTON WANDERERS 0

Andy Cole netted both goals as Fulham swept aside Bolton on their return to Craven Cottage.

The first came after just five minutes as the summer signing from Blackburn turned home a low Zat Knight drive from close range. The visitors had failed to fully clear a corner, giving the striker the chance to demonstrate his predatory instincts.

A further 77 minutes elapsed before Cole netted his second, and his 200th league goal, drilling home through the legs of Jussi Jaaskelainen after running onto a Claus Jensen pass in the inside right channel.

In between times, Chris Coleman's side missed a host of opportunities to put the game out of reach. Chance after chance went begging as Cole, Moritz Volz, Sylvain Legwinski and sub Luis Boa Morte all went close to extending the lead.

For their part, Bolton offered little by way of attacking invention. Jay-Jay Okocha was the only bright spark in a midfield bereft of ideas, and signalled his intentions with a first minute shot that was well saved by Edwin van der Sar.

The Dutch goalkeeper had little else to do all afternoon, with most of the play taking place inside the visitors' half.

The outstanding Pape Bouba Diop, scorer of the opening goal in the '2002 World Cup', almost netted with a powerful header from a corner. Fellow home debutant Tomasz Radzinski then cut in from the left to fire a right-foot effort narrowly wide.

Before half-time, the Cottagers came even closer. Having latched on to a weak Ivan Campo backpass, Cole rounded Jaaskelainen before rolling the ball against the foot of the left-hand upright from an acute angle.

Despite introducing Stylianos Giannakopoulos and Anthony Barness in the early stages of the second half, Sam Allardyce's side remained unable to get a foothold in the game.

Home substitute Luis Boa Morte twice went close, before Cole relieved any nervous tension with his crisp 82nd-minute finish.

The final whistle saw Craven Cottage bathed in sunlight by the River Thames. After two years in exile at Loftus Road, Fulham's emotional homecoming had gone swimmingly.

Pape Bouba Diop leads the Fulham celebrations

"Andy Cole was excellent. He missed a couple of chances, but he's got that arrogance to believe he's going to score in the end."

Chris Coleman

PREMIERSHIP MILESTONE

Andy Cole scored his first Premiership goals for Fulham

"Fulham seemed to have all the enthusiasm and that was disappointing. I wasn't at all happy with the performance."

Sam Allardyce

PREMIERSHIP MILESTONE

Fernando Hierro made his Premiership debut

PREMIERSHIP FIXTURE HISTORY

Pl: 8 Draws: 1	Wins	⚽	□	■
Liverpool	6	19	9	0
Manchester City	1	8	16	1

STARTING LINE-UPS

Diao, Warnock, Biscan, Harrison, Sinama-Pongolle

Barton, Sinclair, Stuhr-Ellegaard, Jihai, Macken

EVENT LINE

27	□	Thatcher (Foul)
45	⚽	Anelka (Open Play)
		HALF TIME 0 - 1
48	⚽	**Baros (Open Play)**
61	⇄	**Josemi (Off) Diao (On)**
74	□	Bosvelt (Foul)
75	⚽	**Gerrard (Open Play)**
77	⇄	**Finnan (Off) Warnock (On)**
82	⇄	Bosvelt (Off) Sinclair (On)
82	⇄	Sibierski (Off) Barton (On)
85	■	Dunne (2nd Bookable Offence)
87	□	**Hamann (Foul)**
90	⇄	**Kewell (Off) Biscan (On)**
		FULL TIME 2 - 1

STATISTICS

Season	Fixture (Liverpool)		Fixture (Man City)	Season
18	**10**	Shots On Target	**4**	**9**
13	**5**	Shots Off Target	**3**	**10**
0	**0**	Hit Woodwork	**0**	**0**
4	**3**	Caught Offside	**2**	**3**
16	**8**	Corners	**3**	**12**
20	**9**	Fouls	**17**	**31**
58%	**64%**	Possession	**36%**	**40%**

LEAGUE STANDINGS

Position (pos before)	W	D	L	F	A	Pts
3 (11) Liverpool	**1**	**1**	**0**	**3**	**2**	**4**
15 (12) Man City	**0**	**1**	**1**	**2**	**3**	**1**

Saturday 21st August 2004 | Venue: **Anfield** | Attendance: **42,831** | Referee: **G.Poll**

LIVERPOOL 2 MANCHESTER CITY 1

Paul Bosvelt challenges Steve Finnan

"I said to the players at half-time that we could do it, and in the second half we played well and took our opportunities. We showed a lot of character coming from 1-0 down."

Rafael Benitez

"In the second half they had 'The Kop' behind them. That spurred them on and possibly forced us into our own half more often than we would have liked."

Kevin Keegan

Rafael Benitez's Liverpool began their Anfield Premiership campaign in unconvincing fashion, but still managed to pick up all three points against an equally disappointing Manchester City side.

Second half strikes from Milan Baros and Steven Gerrard overturned a half-time deficit, brought about by former Red Nicolas Anelka's 45th-minute goal.

The result was a fair one on the balance of play, but the Merseysiders showed little sign of a Spanish revolution in some of their uninspiring football.

With Claudio Reyna and Paul Bosvelt in the heart of midfield, City had a solid look about them. Though enjoying plenty of possession, the home side failed to carve out any decent openings and it looked as though the first half would end in stalemate.

However, on the stroke of half-time it was Kevin Keegan's side who took the lead. Sean Wright-Phillips evaded a sequence of challenges before clipping over a speculative ball from the right. An off balance Jamie Carragher could only manage a back header which Jerzy Dudek fumbled, and Anelka was on hand to gobble up the chance.

The second period saw City pinned inside their own half for long spells. Liverpool were clearly playing higher up the pitch, and got an early reward in the 48th minute.

Captain Gerrard was the driving force, darting towards goal before slipping in Baros for an accomplished finish. From then on there was only going to be one winner, and the decisive goal arrived in the 75th minute.

This time the roles were reversed as Baros teed up Gerrard for a goal that sent The Kop wild. Though the Anfield side had not been at their best collectively, Gerrard once again turned in a complete midfield performance.

There was still time for ex-Evertonian Richard Dunne to receive his marching orders. The Irish international was shown a second yellow card for bringing down Baros five minutes from time, having been booked for a crunching challenge on the same player in the first period.

With the new regime still in its infancy, Liverpool supporters could head home disappointed with the performance, but delighted with both the result and the spirit shown by the players.

PREMIERSHIP FIXTURE HISTORY

Pl: **4** Draws: **1**	Wins	Goals	Yellow	Red
Manchester United	**3**	**6**	**1**	**0**
Norwich City	**0**	**3**	**2**	**0**

STARTING LINE-UPS

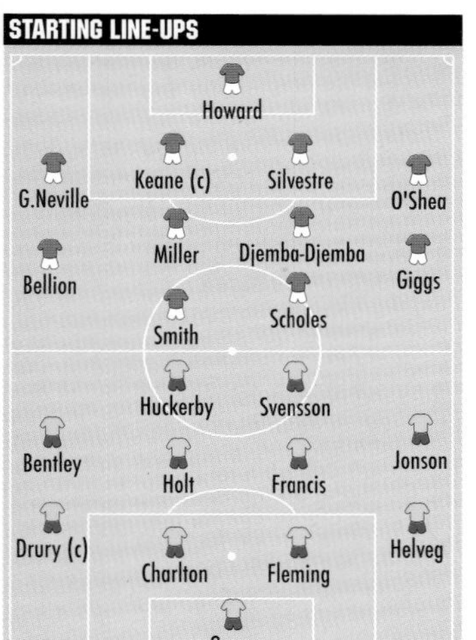

P.Neville, Richardson, Ronaldo, Carroll, Eagles

McVeigh, Doherty, McKenzie, Ward, Edworthy

EVENT LINE

32	**Bellion (Open Play)**
	HALF TIME 1 - 0
46	Jonson (Off) McVeigh (On)
49	Helveg (Foul)
50	**Smith (Open Play)**
69	Svensson (Off) Doherty (On)
73	**Neville G (Off) Neville P (On)**
74	**Bellion (Off) Richardson (On)**
75	McVeigh (Open Play)
76	Bentley (Off) McKenzie (On)
85	**Miller (Off) Ronaldo (On)**
	FULL TIME 2 - 1

STATISTICS

Season	Fixture		Fixture	Season
9	**7**	Shots On Target	**1**	**11**
15	**10**	Shots Off Target	**5**	**9**
0	**0**	Hit Woodwork	**1**	**1**
4	**2**	Caught Offside	**4**	**12**
14	**11**	Corners	**5**	**11**
16	**8**	Fouls	**23**	**35**
50%	**57%**	Possession	**43%**	**44%**

LEAGUE STANDINGS

Position (pos before)	W	D	L	F	A	Pts
8 (17) Man Utd	**1**	**0**	**1**	**2**	**2**	**3**
16 (13) Norwich C	**0**	**1**	**1**	**2**	**3**	**1**

Saturday 21st August 2004 | Venue: **Old Trafford** | Attendance: **67,812** | Referee: **N.S.Barry**

MANCHESTER UNITED 2 NORWICH CITY 1

Manchester United picked up their first points of the season with a less than convincing victory against spirited Premiership newcomers Norwich City at Old Trafford.

French winger David Bellion registered his side's first goal of the campaign in the opening period, before summer signing Alan Smith looked to have secured the victory with a stunning second shortly after the interval. However, the Canaries hit back 15 minutes from time through substitute Paul McVeigh, as Sir Alex Ferguson's side stuttered past the winning post.

With several star names missing from the teamsheet, United began in fairly cautious fashion. Patience seemed to be the watchword, with half-chances for Smith, John O'Shea and Ryan Giggs representing the home team's best efforts.

In fact, it was the visitors who came closest in the opening half-hour, David Bentley almost breaking the crossbar with a 30-yard drive. That let-off seemed to galvanise the Old Trafford side, as they broke upfield to take the lead.

A Giggs cross from the left was flicked on by Smith for Bellion to turn home a 32nd-minute close-range opener. The Frenchman was denied a second four minutes later, when his crisp low shot from the right corner of the penalty area was turned behind by goalkeeper Robert Green.

If Bellion's goal was well worked, Smith's first Premiership strike for United five minutes into the second half was brilliantly executed.

Gary Neville's deep cross from the right was met by a cushioned header from Giggs. Having controlled the ball on his chest with his back to goal, Smith swivelled before dispatching a 12-yard volley over his right shoulder and in off the far post.

Far from using the goal as a springboard to push on, Ferguson's side retreated and invited Norwich back into the game. They duly obliged when McVeigh capitalised on hesitancy in the home defence to cut in from the right and beat Tim Howard with a low left-foot shot.

In truth, the visitors rarely looked likely to snatch a point. However, despite losing, it was probably they that could take away more positives from the game.

David Bellion evades David Bentley

"Alan Smith's goal was absolutely superb. He's similar to Mark Hughes in the way he leads the line."

Sir Alex Ferguson

PREMIERSHIP MILESTONE

Alan Smith netted his first Premiership goal for Man Utd, while Paul McVeigh did likewise for Norwich

"We are disappointed we got nothing from the game. For 35 minutes in the second half, Old Trafford was quiet."

Nigel Worthington

PREMIERSHIP MILESTONE

Gary Doherty made his first Premiership appearance for Norwich

PREMIERSHIP MILESTONE

The attendance of 67,812 was a Premiership record

PREMIERSHIP FIXTURE HISTORY

Pl: 12 Draws: 3	Wins	Goals	Yellow	Red
Newcastle United	6	23	11	1
Tottenham Hotspur	3	12	19	1

STARTING LINE-UPS

Newcastle United: Given; Carr, O'Brien, Hughes, Bernard; Milner, Butt, Jenas, Robert; Bellamy, Shearer (c)

Tottenham Hotspur: Defoe, Kanoute; Atouba, Mendes, Davis, Redknapp (c); Edman, King, Naybet, Ifil; Robinson

Newcastle substitutes: Dyer, Kluivert, Ameobi, Harper, Elliott

Tottenham substitutes: Brown, Gardner, Jackson, Keller, Silva

EVENT LINE

HALF TIME 0 - 0

51 Goal Atouba (Open Play)

68 Yellow Redknapp (Foul)

68 Yellow **Robert (Ung.Conduct)**

69 Sub Redknapp (Off) Brown (On)

77 Sub **Jenas (Off) Dyer (On)**

77 Sub **Milner (Off) Kluivert (On)**

77 Sub **Robert (Off) Ameobi (On)**

80 Sub Kanoute (Off) Gardner (On)

88 Yellow Brown (Ung.Conduct)

90 Sub Atouba (Off) Jackson (On)

FULL TIME 0 - 1

STATISTICS

Season	Fixture (Newcastle)		Fixture (Tottenham)	Season
11	6	Shots On Target	8	15
14	7	Shots Off Target	7	14
0	0	Hit Woodwork	0	0
9	4	Caught Offside	6	11
20	13	Corners	3	6
23	10	Fouls	12	29
48%	48%	Possession	52%	49%

LEAGUE STANDINGS

Position (pos before)		W	D	L	F	A	Pts
18 (6)	Newcastle Utd	0	1	1	2	3	1
4 (15)	Tottenham H	1	1	0	2	1	4

Saturday 21st August 2004 | Venue: St James' Park | Attendance: 52,185 | Referee: M.L.Dean

NEWCASTLE UNITED 0 TOTTENHAM HOTSPUR 1

Thimothee Atouba is the hero at St James' Park

"We lost a match we should have won by half-time, and they mugged us."
Sir Bobby Robson

PREMIERSHIP MILESTONE
100 Laurent Robert made his 100th Premiership appearance

PREMIERSHIP MILESTONE
50 James Milner made his 50th Premiership appearance

"It was a difficult game against a good Newcastle side, and I'm very happy for my young team."
Jacques Santini

PREMIERSHIP MILESTONE
Thimothee Atouba netted his first Premiership goal

PREMIERSHIP MILESTONE
The attendance of 52,185 was a Premiership record at St James' Park

Newcastle continued a recent unwanted tradition of making a poor start to the season, going down to a fine curling effort from Thimothee Atouba.

The goal arrived six minutes into the second half as the Cameroonian international was afforded time and space to advance into the penalty area, before bending a sublime effort beyond the outstretched left arm of Shay Given. Ex-Spurs full-back Stephen Carr could have been forgiven for asking why he had been so badly isolated during the attack.

Sir Bobby Robson's charges had performed well prior to that point, with Craig Bellamy looking particularly lively. The revamped Tottenham defence initially struggled to cope with the Welshman's direct running, highlighted in the second minute when he latched on to an Olivier Bernard ball down the left before testing Paul Robinson at his near post.

The visitors had chances too, Jermain Defoe neatly turning Andy O'Brien in the box before scuffing his effort and Jamie Redknapp firing straight at Given from 25 yards.

However, it was the home side who came closest to leading at the interval as Jermaine Jenas went perilously close.

A flowing move saw the Nottingham-born youngster break clear of the defence and beat the onrushing Robinson to the ball, only to see his effort go under the body of his England colleague and squirt beyond the far post.

James Milner was the next to try his luck, this time meeting Alan Shearer's nod down with a left-foot volley that his former Leeds teammate tipped over the bar.

Having got their noses in front early in the second period, Spurs never really looked like relinquishing the lead. In fact, it was Jacques Santini's side that came closest to a goal in the remainder of the contest, Defoe being denied by the legs of Given and Ledley King seeing a header cleared off the line.

The Magpies finished the match with four strikers on the pitch, yet none of them seemed to have the beating of a defence expertly marshalled by Moroccan international Noureddine Naybet. On this evidence, Newcastle have little hope of claiming a Champions League place come May.

PREMIERSHIP FIXTURE HISTORY

Pl: **11** Draws: **4**	Wins	Goals	Yellow	Red
Southampton	6	21	8	0
Blackburn Rovers	1	11	17	3

STARTING LINE-UPS

Southampton: Niemi; Telfer, Lundekvam, Higginbotham, Le Saux; Fernandes, Prutton, Delap, A.Svensson; Beattie (c), Phillips

Blackburn Rovers: Friedel; Gray, Johansson, Short, Emerton; Matteo, Tugay, Ferguson (c), Flitcroft; Stead, Yorke

Southampton substitutes: Van Damme, Smith, Cranie, Crouch, Best

Blackburn Rovers substitutes: Neill, Dickov, Gresko, Enckelman, De Pedro

EVENT LINE

32	**Phillips (Open Play)**
	HALF TIME 1 - 0
46	Flitcroft (Off) Neill (On)
46	Yorke (Off) Dickov (On)
50	Ferguson (Open Play)
68	Dickov (Open Play)
74	**Svensson A (Open Play)**
78	Dickov (Ung.Conduct)
82	Ferguson (Foul)
85	Johansson (Foul)
89	Gray (Off) Gresko (On)
90	Ferguson (Dissent)
90	**Beattie (Penalty)**
	FULL TIME 3 - 2

STATISTICS

Season	Fixture	Southampton / Blackburn	Fixture	Season
10	8	Shots On Target	6	10
10	6	Shots Off Target	4	12
0	0	Hit Woodwork	0	0
3	1	Caught Offside	3	6
9	3	Corners	6	10
21	12	Fouls	18	33
49%	55%	Possession	45%	48%

LEAGUE STANDINGS

Position (pos before)	W	D	L	F	A	Pts
10 (18) Southampton	1	0	1	3	4	3
14 (8) Blackburn R	0	1	1	3	4	1

Saturday 21st August 2004 | Venue: **Friends Provident St Mary's Stadium** | Attendance: **27,492** | Referee: **A.P.D'Urso**

SOUTHAMPTON 3 BLACKBURN ROVERS 2

A game that began amid rumours surrounding the future of Saints boss Paul Sturrock, ended with all the attention switching to referee Andy D'Urso.

With the scores tied at 2-2, the official awarded a controversial injury-time penalty that was tucked away by Southampton's James Beattie. Furthermore, Barry Ferguson was shown his second yellow card of the match for disputing the decision, yet somehow remained on the pitch.

The first half had given little indication of the excitement to follow, a drab and uninspiring period punctuated only by a 32nd-minute Kevin Phillips goal.

The ex-Sunderland striker showed that he had not lost his eye for goal, ghosting in unmarked at the far post to poke home Fabrice Fernandes' inswinging cross from the right.

The goal lightened what was an uneasy atmosphere inside St Mary's, with most pundits believing that a win was vital if Sturrock was to remain in the managerial hotseat any longer. Unfortunately for the Scot, defensive frailties were exposed as Blackburn came from behind to lead midway through the second half.

Firstly, the home defence parted like the Red Sea as Rovers captain Ferguson was allowed to exchange passes with substitute Paul Dickov and waltz through for a neatly taken 50th-minute goal.

Then, Dickov himself was afforded the freedom of the area as he controlled Brett Emerton's 68th-minute ball in from the right, before hammering home past Antti Niemi from seven yards.

Graeme Souness must have felt confident of victory at this point, but a stunning 74th-minute Anders Svensson strike swerved its way into the top right-hand corner of Brad Friedel's net, to set up a grandstand finish.

With 90 minutes showing on the stadium clock, Paul Telfer launched a hopeful ball into the Blackburn box. James Beattie fell following the slightest of contact from Craig Short, and D'Urso pointed to the spot. Even the Southampton players and fans seemed amazed by the decision.

The three points were duly sealed from the spot by Beattie, but not before Ferguson had evaded a red card when collecting his second yellow of the game for kicking the ball away in disgust at the penalty award.

Anders Svensson is congratulated after making it 2-2

"I didn't think it was going to be our day, but I thought we deserved the win."

Paul Sturrock

"I think the majority of referees wouldn't have given it."

Graeme Souness on the late penalty awarded against his team

PREMIERSHIP MILESTONE

Paul Dickov scored his first Premiership goal for Blackburn

PREMIERSHIP FIXTURE HISTORY

Pl: 10 Draws: 3	Wins	Goals	Yellow	Red
Arsenal	6	23	14	1
Middlesbrough	1	12	22	1

STARTING LINE-UPS

Arsenal: Lehmann; Lauren, Toure, Cygan, Cole; Ljungberg, Gilberto, Fabregas, Reyes; Bergkamp (c), Henry

Middlesbrough: Schwarzer; Queudrue, Cooper (c), Riggott, Reiziger; Zenden, Boateng, Parlour, Mendieta; Job, Hasselbaink

Arsenal subs: Pires, Flamini, Almunia, Hoyte, van Persie

Middlesbrough subs: Parnaby, Nemeth, Nash, Doriva, Maccarone

EVENT LINE

25 **Henry (Open Play)**

43 Job (Open Play)

HALF TIME 1 - 1

50 Hasselbaink (Open Play)

53 Queudrue (Open Play)

54 **Bergkamp (Open Play)**

58 Zenden (Foul)

59 **Bergkamp (Foul)**

61 **Ljungberg (Off) Pires (On)**

65 **Pires (Open Play)**

65 **Reyes (Open Play)**

74 Reiziger (Off) Parnaby (On)

78 **Reyes (Off) Flamini (On)**

78 Zenden (Off) Nemeth (On)

90 **Henry (Open Play)**

FULL TIME 5 - 3

STATISTICS

Season	Fixture (Arsenal)		Fixture (Middlesbrough)	Season
22	9	Shots On Target	5	13
9	5	Shots Off Target	4	11
3	2	Hit Woodwork	0	0
2	2	Caught Offside	5	12
13	7	Corners	5	11
23	8	Fouls	14	30
57%	55%	Possession	45%	48%

LEAGUE STANDINGS

Position (pos before)		W	D	L	F	A	Pts
1 (5)	Arsenal	2	0	0	9	4	6
19 (12)	Middlesbrough	0	1	1	5	7	1

Sunday 22nd August 2004 | Venue: **Highbury** | Attendance: **37,415** | Referee: **S.W.Dunn**

ARSENAL 5 MIDDLESBROUGH 3

Arsenal equalled Nottingham Forest's 42-match unbeaten league run with a thrilling 5-3 victory over Middlesbrough, though the achievement looked improbable when the Gunners found themselves 3-1 down early in the second half.

Despite dominating the opening period, Arsene Wenger's side only had Thierry Henry's 25th-minute goal to show for their efforts as the interval approached. The Frenchman had brilliantly lobbed home over the onrushing Mark Schwarzer following Jose Antonio Reyes' sublime 50 yard diagonal pass from the left.

Then, in the 43rd minute, Joseph-Desire Job levelled things up with a bolt from the blue. The Cameroonian beat Jens Lehmann at his near post with a fiercely struck shot from the inside left channel. Having also hit the post through Reyes and the bar through Henry, Arsenal had even more reason to feel aggrieved at the half-time score.

Worse was to follow early in the second period as Middlesbrough added two more goals. Five minutes in Lehmann was again beaten at his near post, this time by a rasping drive from Jimmy Floyd Hasselbaink. Three minutes later and the German's nightmare was complete, Franck Queudrue catching him out with a shot from distance as the keeper anticipated a cross.

Fortunately for the home team, they did not have long to dwell on the uphill task in front of them. Within a minute of conceding the third, Dennis Bergkamp advanced unchallenged before firing home low to Schwarzer's right from 20 yards.

The game then turned back in Arsenal's favour in a storybook 65th minute. Firstly, Robert Pires tapped home a close range equaliser following Henry's scuffed shot across the face of goal from the left. Then, straight from the restart, Reyes ran on to Bergkamp's pass before stepping inside Michael Reiziger and firing an unstoppable effort high to Schwarzer's left.

Though Middlesbrough kept plugging away, their chance of victory had gone. It came as no surprise when Henry added a coat of gloss to the scoreline by netting an injury time fifth.

Wonderful interplay between Bergkamp and Pires down the left ended when the latter pulled the ball back from the byline for his international colleague to angle home a near-post effort from eight yards out, thus completing an historic day.

Boudewijn Zenden admires Dennis Bergkamp's footwear

"At 3-1 down, it was backs-to-the-wall time. We showed our mental reserves, kept our nerve and kept playing our football."

Arsene Wenger

"There were a lot of things there that bode well for the rest of the season. But we need to be much better at holding a lead, especially away from home."

Steve McClaren

PREMIERSHIP FIXTURE HISTORY

Pl: 2 Draws: 2	Wins	⚽	▢	■
West Bromwich Albion	0	1	5	0
Aston Villa	0	1	5	0

STARTING LINE-UPS

Gera, Dobie, Kuszczak, Moore, Albrechtsen

Angel, De la Cruz, Whittingham, Postma, L.Moore

EVENT LINE

4 ⚽ Mellberg (Indirect Free Kick)
6 ▢ **Horsfield (Foul)**
38 ⚽ **Clement (Indirect Free Kick)**
HALF TIME 1 - 1
52 ▢ Laursen (Foul)
63 ⇄ **Haas (Off) Gera (On)**
70 ▢ Mellberg (Foul)
70 ⇄ Vassell (Off) Angel (On)
74 ⇄ **Horsfield (Off) Dobie (On)**
75 ▢ **Johnson (Ung.Conduct)**
80 ⇄ Solano (Off) De la Cruz (On)
81 ⇄ Barry (Off) Whittingham (On)
FULL TIME 1 - 1

STATISTICS

Season	Fixture		Fixture	Season
7	**5**	Shots On Target	**4**	**9**
12	**10**	Shots Off Target	**5**	**14**
0	**0**	Hit Woodwork	**0**	**0**
7	**3**	Caught Offside	**1**	**1**
17	**12**	Corners	**4**	**16**
29	**12**	Fouls	**20**	**34**
49%	**50%**	Possession	**50%**	**53%**

LEAGUE STANDINGS

Position (pos before)	W	D	L	F	A	Pts
12 (13) West Brom	**0**	**2**	**0**	**2**	**2**	**2**
3 (6) Aston Villa	**1**	**1**	**0**	**3**	**1**	**4**

Sunday 22nd August 2004 | Venue: **The Hawthorns** | Attendance: **26,601** | Referee: **M.R.Halsey**

WEST BROM 1 ASTON VILLA 1

The spoils were shared in this highly competitive West Midlands derby as both sides netted through first half headers.

Aston Villa were first to draw blood as skipper Olof Mellberg rose to meet Thomas Hitzlsperger's inswinging free-kick from the right with a glancing near-post finish in the fourth minute.

Albion responded in the 38th minute through Neil Clement. The versatile midfielder rose unopposed 12 yards out to plant home a firm header from Jonathan Greening's free-kick from the right. It was the ex-Chelsea man's second goal of the season, following on from his deflected opening day strike at Blackburn.

David O'Leary's side, who had opened the season with a comfortable 2-0 win against Southampton, were given a severe examination by their neighbours. Thomas Sorensen had to make several fine saves, particularly in the second period, as Gary Megson's team paid little respect to reputations.

The visitors' best spell of the match came, unsurprisingly, after they had taken the lead. Carlton Cole shot just wide in the eighth minute, while Russell Hoult had to be alert to deny Gareth Barry soon afterwards.

The Baggies then had a major escape after 20 minutes. Nolberto Solano's corner was met by Mellberg, parried by Hoult and then hooked off the line by Paul Robinson. Aston Villa players were justifiably convinced that the ball had crossed the line, but referee Mark Halsey was unmoved.

West Brom responded to this let-off in positive fashion, Geoff Horsfield missing following good work from Nwankwo Kanu. The equaliser soon followed, and Clement then went close to repeating the trick from a corner.

The second half began with Albion in the ascendancy. A whipped free-kick from that man Clement forced a smart save from Sorensen in the 53rd minute, before Darren Purse twice went close with his head.

Tireless running then almost brought a 69th-minute reward for Horsfield, but he pushed his shot wide of the post when put through with just the keeper to beat.

The home side also had strong penalty appeals turned down late on when Gavin McCann appeared to handle the ball, though ultimately they had to settle for a point.

"The players are disappointed that we didn't win the game. We have to make sure that we pick up three points when we play well."

Gary Megson

"I don't think that we defended well enough or passed the ball well enough."

David O'Leary

PREMIERSHIP MILESTONE

50 Ulises De la Cruz made his 50th Premiership appearance

Geoff Horsfield wins a free-kick that leads to a goal

PREMIERSHIP FIXTURE HISTORY

Pl: 3 Draws: 0	Wins	⚽	Yellow	Red
Birmingham City	2	3	5	0
Manchester City	1	3	4	0

STARTING LINE-UPS

John, Clemence, Tebily, Bennett, Martin Taylor

Sinclair, Barton, Macken, Bischoff, Stuhr-Ellegaard

EVENT LINE

8 ⚽ **Heskey (Open Play)**
31 Mills (Foul)
HALF TIME 1 - 0
54 **Heskey (Off) John (On)**
57 Sibierski (Off) Sinclair (On)
59 **Lazaridis (Off) Clemence (On)**
69 **Izzet (Foul)**
79 **Forssell (Off) Tebily (On)**
79 Bosvelt (Off) Barton (On)
79 Fowler (Off) Macken (On)
FULL TIME 1 - 0

STATISTICS

Season	Fixture		Fixture	Season
15	2	Shots On Target	1	10
15	4	Shots Off Target	3	13
1	0	Hit Woodwork	0	0
2	0	Caught Offside	4	7
14	2	Corners	5	17
46	20	Fouls	14	45
49%	55%	Possession	45%	41%

LEAGUE STANDINGS

Position (pos before)	W	D	L	F	A	Pts
7 (18) Birmingham C	1	1	1	2	2	4
19 (14) Man City	0	1	2	2	4	1

Tuesday 24th August 2004 | Venue: **St Andrew's** | Attendance: **28,551** | Referee: **P.Dowd**

BIRMINGHAM CITY 1 MANCHESTER CITY 0

Emile Heskey began to repay the faith shown in him by manager Steve Bruce, netting the only goal of the game with a towering eighth minute header.

Ironically, it was the striker's first goal since scoring at St Andrew's for Liverpool the previous May, and owed much to an excellent ball in from the left by makeshift full-back Stan Lazaridis.

By the time of the goal, however, Manchester City should already have been in front. Great work from Sean Wright-Phillips saw Nicolas Anelka presented with a gilt-edged chance, but the former French international completely missed his kick, before Maik Taylor easily saved the follow-up effort from Robbie Fowler.

Having dominated proceedings without scoring in their previous game against Chelsea, Heskey's goal made the Birmingham players visibly relax. Though chances were at a premium for the home side, they were virtually non-existent for Kevin Keegan's visitors.

The one chance that they mustered before half-time fell to a clearly out-of-sorts Fowler. The ex-Liverpool forward was expertly picked out at the far post by a right-wing cross from Sun Jihai, but could only flash his free header from six yards back across the face of goal.

A combination of poor finishing and fine goalkeeping from England custodian David James prevented the West Midlands side from adding to their one-goal advantage. Mikael Forssell directed a 48th-minute header over the bar, before James then denied substitute Stern John with a marvellous one-handed save.

John had replaced Heskey after 54 minutes, the England striker limping off with a leg injury.

Only once in the second period did Steve Bruce's team have genuine cause for concern. Danny Mills, jeered all night following a run-in with Robbie Savage last season, met a cross from Trevor Sinclair with a close-range header 16 minutes from time. The ball appeared goalbound, but was deflected away from danger by the recovering Damien Johnson.

While Birmingham were able to celebrate their first three points of the season, Heskey's strike sentenced Manchester City to a second successive away defeat following their 2-1 loss at Liverpool at the weekend.

"For me, Emile is the best type of old-style English centre-forward in the country."
Steve Bruce

PREMIERSHIP MILESTONE
Emile Heskey scored his first Premiership goal for Birmingham

"I don't think that Birmingham deserved to win. I feel we had the best of the game, but they got the goal."
Kevin Keegan

Emile Heskey celebrates his goal with Stan Lazaridis

PREMIERSHIP FIXTURE HISTORY

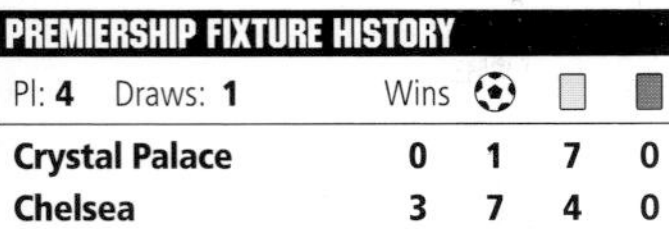

Pl: 4 Draws: 1	Wins			
Crystal Palace	0	1	7	0
Chelsea	3	7	4	0

STARTING LINE-UPS

Hughes, Kiraly, Borrowdale, Derry, Freedman

Mutu, Gudjohnsen, Geremi, Cudicini, Carvalho

EVENT LINE

28 Drogba (Open Play)

HALF TIME 0 - 1

62 Babayaro (Foul)

67 **Kaviedes (Off) Hughes (On)**

70 Kezman (Off) Mutu (On)

72 Tiago (Open Play)

74 **Hudson (Foul)**

75 Drogba (Off) Gudjohnsen (On)

76 Cole J (Off) Geremi (On)

FULL TIME 0 - 2

STATISTICS

Season	Fixture		Fixture	Season
13	0	Shots On Target	5	12
17	6	Shots Off Target	10	20
0	0	Hit Woodwork	0	0
5	0	Caught Offside	2	9
18	1	Corners	6	10
36	9	Fouls	12	39
47%	40%	Possession	60%	57%

LEAGUE STANDINGS

Position (pos before)	W	D	L	F	A	Pts
20 (20) Crystal Palace	0	1	2	2	6	1
1 (2) Chelsea	3	0	0	4	0	9

Tuesday 24th August 2004 | Venue: **Selhurst Park** | Attendance: **24,953** | Referee: **C.J.Foy**

CRYSTAL PALACE 0 CHELSEA 2

Jose Mourinho's Chelsea made it three wins out of three, with expensive summer imports Didier Drogba and Tiago getting the goals that saw off Crystal Palace at Selhurst Park.

The star-studded West Londoners endured a tough opening, as Iain Dowie's determined outfit contested every ball. Indeed, the home side had the first chance after 10 minutes, when Danny Granville failed to make proper contact from a Wayne Routledge corner.

However, the visitors' dominance of possession soon began to tell. Joe Cole forced a flying stop from Julian Speroni, before Didier Drogba opened his account in the 28th minute.

Celestine Babayaro reached the byline down the left and sent over a cross that Drogba powerfully headed home from around the penalty spot.

The goal further strengthened Chelsea's grip on the game, with Joe Cole becoming increasingly influential in his role at the tip of a midfield diamond. The young England international again forced a save from Speroni as the half drew to a close.

Palace regrouped at the interval and again tested their visitors with an early flourish. A long ball out of defence caused problems for John Terry and the livewire Andy Johnson fired wide from the edge of the box.

That was as good as it got for Iain Dowie's team though, as a combination of crisp passing and fluid movement off the ball saw Mourinho's side take complete control.

Again Cole was prominent, a jinking run taking him into the area, though his finish did not match the approach play. The same could not be said of Portuguese teammate Tiago in the 72nd minute. Having collected possession outside the area, the former Benfica midfielder jinked past Granville before drilling a 15-yard effort into the bottom left-hand corner of the net.

The goal meant that Chelsea had scored more than once for the first time under Mourinho. Coupled with their third clean sheet in three league outings, this meant that the Stamford Bridge outfit moved temporarily to the top of the table. Not everything was positive, however, Drogba having limped off following a strong challenge from Mark Hudson.

Didier Drogba savours his first goal in English football

"I cannot fault the effort of the lads. The epitome of our side's commitment was Aki Riihilahti, whose energy levels were colossal."

Iain Dowie

"We have put ice on Didier's ankle and hopefully it is only just bad bruising."

Chelsea Assistant Manager
Steve Clarke

PREMIERSHIP MILESTONE

Both Didier Drogba and Tiago netted their first Premiership goals

PREMIERSHIP FIXTURE HISTORY

Pl: 11 Draws: 4	Wins	Goals	Yellow	Red
Arsenal	4	12	25	1
Blackburn Rovers	3	10	30	3

STARTING LINE-UPS

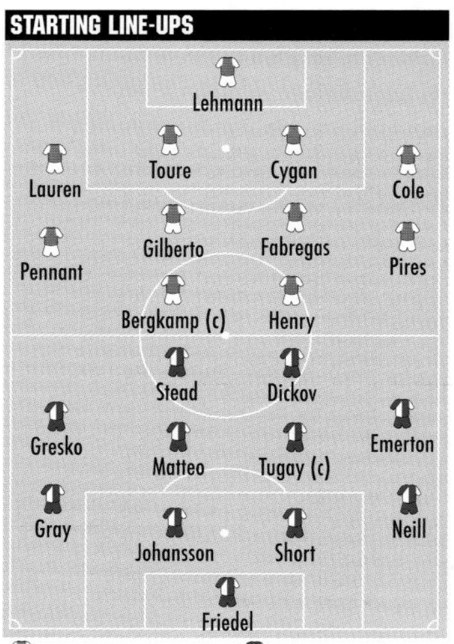

Ljungberg, Reyes, Flamini, Almunia, Hoyte

Yorke, De Pedro, Enckelman, Amoruso, Flitcroft

EVENT LINE

16 Henry (Foul)
21 Emerton (Foul)
27 Neill (Foul)

HALF TIME 0 - 0

50 Henry (Open Play)
58 Fabregas (Corner)
63 Stead (Off) Yorke (On)
72 Fabregas (Foul)
75 Short (Ung.Conduct)
77 Bergkamp (Off) Reyes (On)
77 Pennant (Off) Ljungberg (On)
77 Tugay (Off) De Pedro (On)
79 Reyes (Open Play)
86 Fabregas (Off) Flamini (On)
87 Matteo (Foul)

FULL TIME 3 - 0

STATISTICS

Season	Fixture (Arsenal)		Fixture (Blackburn)	Season
31	9	Shots On Target	0	10
15	6	Shots Off Target	3	15
3	0	Hit Woodwork	0	0
6	4	Caught Offside	8	14
19	6	Corners	5	15
34	11	Fouls	18	51
59%	64%	Possession	36%	44%

LEAGUE STANDINGS

Position (pos before)	W	D	L	F	A	Pts
1 (2) Arsenal	3	0	0	12	4	9
19 (14) Blackburn R	0	1	2	3	7	1

Wednesday 25th August 2004 | Venue: **Highbury** | Attendance: **37,496** | Referee: **N.S.Barry**

Thierry Henry takes on Lucas Neill

"It feels good to beat Forest's record, but the important thing was that we got the three points."
Thierry Henry

PREMIERSHIP MILESTONE

150 Freddie Ljungberg made his 150th Premiership appearance

PREMIERSHIP MILESTONE

Cesc Fabregas scored his first Premiership goal

"Everyone enjoys watching Arsenal play - they're exciting and spectacular. As a manager, you'd want your team to play like them."
Graeme Souness

ARSENAL 3 BLACKBURN ROVERS 0

Champions Arsenal overcame gutsy Blackburn with three second half goals, breaking Nottingham Forest's record of 42 consecutive league games unbeaten in the process.

The record stretched back to December 1978, when defeat at Anfield ended a sequence of 21 wins and 21 draws for Brian Clough's side. The Gunners' figures during the run compare favourably, with 31 victories and just 12 draws.

Perhaps of more importance to the pragmatic Arsene Wenger was that the three points took his side back above Chelsea to the Premiership summit.

A nervous first half display was understandable given the historic nature of the match, with Rovers going very close through ex-Gunner Paul Dickov during a fraught goalmouth scramble.

Brad Friedel was called upon to keep out Thierry Henry on three separate occasions during the first half. Comfortable saves from a curling effort and a dipping free-kick were followed by a fine diving stop to keep out a powerful low drive from the Frenchman.

The second period began with Jermaine Pennant, a surprise inclusion in Wenger's starting XI, warming the palms of the goalkeeper. Then, in the 50th minute, Dennis Bergkamp delivered an inviting low cross from the right that Henry steered high into the net from seven yards out at the back post.

The sense of relief was tangible as Highbury exploded into life.

Teenage midfielder Cesc Fabregas was outstanding, and got his reward with the second goal after 58 minutes.

Blackburn failed to heed an earlier warning as Gilberto again rose unchallenged to power a header goalwards from a left-wing corner. It appeared at first as though the Brazilian had scored, but replays clearly showed the ball striking Fabregas on its way into the net.

Jose Antonio Reyes netted Arsenal's third in the 79th minute, shortly after coming off the bench. The Londoners' team ethos was demonstrated perfectly as, having been denied by a sprawling Friedel, Henry declined a potentially makeable finish to tee up the fast-arriving Spaniard for a simple strike.

This was a fitting way to break the record, emphasising perfectly that football is, above all else, a team game.

PREMIERSHIP FIXTURE HISTORY

Pl: 6 Draws: 1	Wins	Goals	Yellow cards	Red cards
Charlton Athletic	2	11	11	0
Aston Villa	3	8	10	0

STARTING LINE-UPS

Konchesky, El Karkouri, Hughes, Andersen, Johansson

Postma, Angel, De la Cruz, L.Moore, Whittingham

EVENT LINE

29 Jeffers (Open Play)

34 Jeffers (Open Play)

HALF TIME 2 - 0

46 Sorensen (Off) Postma (On)

58 Young (Open Play)

67 Samuel (Ung.Conduct)

72 Cole (Off) Angel (On)

75 Jeffers (Off) Konchesky (On)

78 Kishishev (Off) El Karkouri (On)

82 Rommedahl (Off) Hughes (On)

FULL TIME 3 - 0

STATISTICS

Season	Fixture (Charlton)		Fixture (Villa)	Season
23	5	Shots On Target	5	14
9	2	Shots Off Target	5	19
2	1	Hit Woodwork	1	1
12	5	Caught Offside	3	4
14	4	Corners	12	28
34	13	Fouls	14	48
48%	55%	Possession	45%	50%

LEAGUE STANDINGS

Position (pos before)		W	D	L	F	A	Pts
4 (12)	Charlton Ath	2	0	1	6	5	6
10 (3)	Aston Villa	1	1	1	3	4	4

Wednesday 25th August 2004 | Venue: The Valley | Attendance: 26,190 | Referee: H.M.Webb

CHARLTON ATHLETIC 3 ASTON VILLA 0

Following a fortuitous win against Portsmouth at the weekend, the Addicks really turned on the style in this emphatic 3-0 demolition of Aston Villa.

The visitors, however, made the more encouraging start. Just six minutes had elapsed when Darius Vassell, presented with the most glaring of chances by Nolberto Solano's cut-back, somehow conspired to send the ball thudding against the crossbar from just eight yards out.

The onslaught continued as Thomas Hitzlsperger thundered a drive narrowly over the top, before Dean Kiely had to be on his toes to keep out former Charlton loanee Carlton Cole.

The inability of David O'Leary's side to net the goal their performance deserved came back to haunt them just before the half-hour mark.

Francis Jeffers, making his first start since arriving from Arsenal, rose majestically in the middle to head home Hermann Hreidarsson's cross from the left. Just five minutes later and Jeffers was in dreamland.

Radostin Kishishev's long ball out of defence caused a communication problem between Olof Mellberg and Thomas Sorensen, with the former Everton striker latching on to the Swede's weak header and volleying home across the stranded goalkeeper.

An opportunistic effort by Kevin Lisbie then clipped the crossbar as Villa seemed unable to respond to the enormous pressure they were suddenly under. The striker was then denied by Sorensen on the stroke of half-time, a challenge which resulted in a change of custodian for the visitors at the interval.

His replacement, Stefan Postma, fared little better in the second half, beaten by the unlikely figure of Luke Young in the 58th minute. The former Tottenham defender combined well with Kishishev, before marking his 100th appearance for the club by sliding the ball under the Dutch substitute from the inside right channel.

Any prospect of a second half fightback from O'Leary's men had been quashed, and his side seemed to focus on not conceding a fourth in the remaining half-hour.

There were few noteworthy chances as the game petered to a conclusion, though the home fans went away more than happy with what they had seen earlier on.

Nolberto Solano fails to halt Hermann Hreidarsson

"Bolton was a shocker, saturday was better, but that was back to what we're capable of."

Alan Curbishley

PREMIERSHIP MILESTONE

50 Bryan Hughes made his 50th Premiership appearance

PREMIERSHIP MILESTONE

Francis Jeffers netted his first Premiership goals for Charlton

PREMIERSHIP MILESTONE

Luke Young scored his first Premiership goal

"We gifted goals to Charlton. I thought we were their best player tonight."

David O'Leary

PREMIERSHIP FIXTURE HISTORY

Pl: **4** Draws: **0**	Wins	Goals	Yellow cards	Red cards
Fulham	3	6	2	0
Middlesbrough	1	5	5	0

STARTING LINE-UPS

Fulham subs: McBride, Boa Morte, Crossley, Bonnissel, Pembridge

Middlesbrough subs: Job, Nemeth, Doriva, Nash, Cooper

EVENT LINE

HALF TIME 0 - 0

54 Goal: Viduka (Open Play)

62 Substitution: **John (Off) McBride (On)**

71 Substitution: Viduka (Off) Job (On)

71 Yellow card: Zenden (Ung.Conduct)

74 Substitution: **Diop (Off) Boa Morte (On)**

77 Substitution: Mendieta (Off) Nemeth (On)

79 Goal: Nemeth (Open Play)

89 Substitution: Boateng (Off) Doriva (On)

FULL TIME 0 - 2

STATISTICS

Season	Fixture (Fulham)		Fixture (Middlesbrough)	Season
14	2	Shots On Target	3	16
17	4	Shots Off Target	5	16
2	0	Hit Woodwork	0	0
12	2	Caught Offside	9	21
13	1	Corners	6	17
33	10	Fouls	8	38
52%	46%	Possession	54%	50%

LEAGUE STANDINGS

Position (pos before)		W	D	L	F	A	Pts
8 (4)	Fulham	1	1	1	3	3	4
7 (18)	Middlesbrough	1	1	1	7	7	4

Wednesday 25th August 2004 | Venue: **Craven Cottage** | Attendance: **17,759** | Referee: **D.J.Gallagher**

FULHAM 0 MIDDLESBROUGH 2

After collecting just one point from a tough start against Newcastle and Arsenal, Middlesbrough finally recorded their first victory of the season in an evenly contested clash at Craven Cottage.

Second half goals from debutant Mark Viduka and substitute Szilard Nemeth saw off the challenge of Fulham, as Steve McClaren's side continued their free-scoring start to the season.

The first period offered little to remember it by, with Edwin van der Sar's smart parry from Viduka and counterpart Mark Schwarzer's save from a Collins John header proving the only moments of note. Boudewijn Zenden posed a constant threat down the left, but all too often failed to deliver a telling final ball.

The same could not be said of fellow Dutchman Jimmy Floyd Hasselbaink in the 54th minute though. Having escaped down the right, the ex-Chelsea man looked up before driving in a low cross that his new strike-partner Viduka steered home from close range. Many people had wondered how this temperamental pairing would get on, with this goal proving a very encouraging sign for Middlesbrough fans.

The Cottagers tried in vain to get back in the game. Tomasz Radzinski was inches away from connecting with a cross from Carlos Bocanegra, as Brian McBride and Luis Boa Morte were introduced to supplement the attack.

However, it was a Middlesbrough substitute who ultimately sealed the contest. Having been on the field just two minutes, Slovakian Nemeth bundled home Franck Queudrue's 79th-minute cross at the back post.

That strike served to emphasise just how many options in attack McClaren now has at his disposal. Coupled with a traditionally strong defensive unit, which kept its first clean sheet of the season in this game, the Teesside club look well-set for a productive campaign.

It is difficult to say the same for Chris Coleman's side. Danish international Claus Jensen looked to be the only player capable of unlocking a Premiership defence, while both Radzinski and John looked uncomfortable playing in wide areas.

Mark Viduka demonstrates his ball skills

"We were poor. Middlesbrough were stronger and more determined."
Chris Coleman

"There was evidence there that Jimmy and Mark can work well together in attack."
Steve McClaren

PREMIERSHIP MILESTONE

Mark Viduka celebrated his first Premiership appearance for Middlesbrough with his first goal for the club

PREMIERSHIP FIXTURE HISTORY

Pl: 3 Draws: 1	Wins	⚽	▢	■
Newcastle United	2	8	2	0
Norwich City	0	2	1	0

STARTING LINE-UPS

Ameobi, Bowyer, Harper, Elliott, Kluivert

Jonson, McKenzie, Ward, Helveg, Svensson

EVENT LINE

40 ⚽ **Bellamy (Open Play)**

HALF TIME 1 - 0

50 ⚽ **Hughes (Corner)**

52 ⚽ Bentley (Open Play)

53 ▢ Fleming (Foul)

67 McVeigh (Off) Jonson (On)

71 Bentley (Off) McKenzie (On)

74 ⚽ Doherty (Open Play)

75 **Milner (Off) Ameobi (On)**

84 **Dyer (Off) Bowyer (On)**

FULL TIME 2 - 2

STATISTICS

Season	Fixture		Fixture	Season
26	15	Shots On Target	5	16
22	8	Shots Off Target	8	17
0	0	Hit Woodwork	0	1
9	0	Caught Offside	5	17
32	12	Corners	6	17
40	17	Fouls	10	45
50%	55%	Possession	45%	44%

LEAGUE STANDINGS

Position (pos before)	W	D	L	F	A	Pts
16 (15) Newcastle Utd	0	2	1	4	5	2
15 (16) Norwich C	0	2	1	4	5	2

Wednesday 25th August 2004 | Venue: **St James' Park** | Attendance: **51,574** | Referee: **M.R.Halsey**

NEWCASTLE UNITED 2 NORWICH CITY 2

Newcastle's miserable start to the campaign continued as they squandered a two-goal lead at home to newly-promoted Norwich City.

The Magpies did not win a Premiership match until October last season, a sequence that ultimately cost them a Champions League place.

Goals either side of half-time from ex-Canary Craig Bellamy and defender Aaron Hughes looked to have sealed the three points in this encounter, but strikes from David Bentley and Gary Doherty saw Nigel Worthington's side pick up a valuable away draw.

Sir Bobby Robson's men had started brightly enough, Laurent Robert seeing a header harshly ruled out and James Milner fully stretching Robert Green in the visitors' goal.

At the other end, Darren Huckerby was a coat of paint away from opening the scoring after seeing off the challenge of Olivier Bernard.

It was Newcastle who broke the deadlock through a 40th-minute Bellamy goal. The Welsh international steered home a deflected 12 yard effort after Alan Shearer had knocked down a cross from the right.

Five minutes after the interval, Hughes doubled the home side's advantage from a corner. The versatile defender stooped to head home Robert's inswinging flag-kick from six yards out.

Perhaps the men in black and white were guilty of believing the game was won, as Norwich caught them cold with an almost instant response. Two minutes after Hughes' goal, Bentley was left unchallenged to fire home a low 25-yard swerving effort that Shay Given would have been disappointed to have conceded.

Good chances continued to go begging at both ends, before the Canaries drew level in the 74th minute. Gary Doherty, making his first start since arriving from Tottenham, reacted quickest to turn the ball home from close range after Given had denied Craig Fleming.

Far from sparking the Magpies back into life, the equaliser gave encouragement to the visitors. A spectacular long-range shot from Huckerby almost found the top corner, while a poor first touch was all that prevented substitute Leon McKenzie from netting the winner.

For the second successive home match the jeers that greeted the final whistle left no doubt as to what the Geordie public thought of what they had witnessed.

"The boy Bentley skipped in between two players far too easily."

Sir Bobby Robson on Norwich's opening goal

"We showed people what we could do at Old Trafford for 30 minutes, and today we have done it for the 90 minutes."

Nigel Worthington

PREMIERSHIP MILESTONE

David Bentley scored his first Premiership goal

PREMIERSHIP MILESTONE

Gary Doherty netted his first Premiership goal for Norwich

David Bentley revels in his moment of glory

Wednesday 25th August 2004 | Venue: **Friends Provident St Mary's Stadium** | Attendance: **30,713** | Referee: **S.W.Dunn**

PREMIERSHIP FIXTURE HISTORY

Pl: **6** Draws: **2**	Wins	⚽	☐	■
Southampton	**1**	**3**	**10**	**1**
Bolton Wanderers	**3**	**5**	**13**	**0**

STARTING LINE-UPS

Crouch, Smith, Van Damme, Folly, Ormerod

Nolan, Hierro, Ferdinand, Poole, Ben Haim

EVENT LINE

7 ⚽ Pedersen (Open Play)

27 ⚽ Okocha (Penalty)

30 ☐ **Delap (Foul)**

HALF TIME 0 - 2

52 ☐ Campo (Foul)

69 ⇄ **Delap (Off) Crouch (On)**

80 ⇄ Giannakopoulos (Off) Nolan (On)

85 ⚽ **Crouch (Corner)**

90 ⇄ Davies (Off) Ferdinand (On)

90 ⇄ Pedersen (Off) Hierro (On)

FULL TIME 1 - 2

STATISTICS

Season	Fixture		Fixture	Season
16	**6**	Shots On Target	**6**	**21**
14	**4**	Shots Off Target	**4**	**20**
0	**0**	Hit Woodwork	**0**	**0**
3	**0**	Caught Offside	**7**	**9**
18	**9**	Corners	**6**	**19**
30	**9**	Fouls	**8**	**31**
49%	**48%**	Possession	**52%**	**52%**

LEAGUE STANDINGS

Position (pos before)	W	D	L	F	A	Pts
14 (11) Southampton	**1**	**0**	**2**	**4**	**6**	**3**
3 (8) Bolton W	**2**	**0**	**1**	**6**	**4**	**6**

Jay-Jay Okocha scores from the spot

"The fans gave the team excellent support and we were not worthy of it."

Steve Wigley

PREMIERSHIP MILESTONE

100 Anders Svensson made his 100th Premiership appearance, while Paul Telfer made his 100th Premiership appearance for Southampton

PREMIERSHIP MILESTONE

Peter Crouch scored his first Premiership goal for Southampton

"I thought we controlled and dominated most of the game, and we were only troubled in the last few minutes after Southampton had pulled a goal back."

Sam Allardyce

PREMIERSHIP MILESTONE

Sam Allardyce gave Radhi Jaidi his Premiership debut

SOUTHAMPTON 1 BOLTON WANDERERS 2

Steve Wigley made a losing start in his role as 'Head Coach' at troubled Southampton, as Bolton withstood a spell of late pressure to record their first away win of the season.

The Trotters were two goals to the good inside half-an-hour, capitalising on disorganised, and then clumsy, defending.

Henrik Pedersen was the first beneficiary, taking advantage of a woeful attempt at an offside trap to coolly dispatch a low seventh-minute drive beyond the left hand of Antti Niemi.

Midfielders Gary Speed and Jay-Jay Okocha both tried their luck from distance, before Danny Higginbotham handed the Nigerian a 27th-minute opportunity to net his third goal of the season.

Having been lucky not to concede a penalty just seconds earlier, Stylianos Giannakopoulos was sent sprawling in the box by a rash challenge from the ex-Derby County defender. The spot-kick was confidently stroked home by Okocha and Bolton were cruising.

Home fans directed their anger towards Chairman Rupert Lowe, unsurprising given that he had sacked former boss Paul Sturrock after just 13 games in charge.

Visiting goalkeeper Jussi Jaaskelainen was not called upon to make a meaningful save until the 31st minute. Even then, he was comfortably able to turn away Fabrice Fernandes' long-range effort.

Given the scoreline, it was no surprise that Southampton came out for the second period the more fired up of the two sides. An improved performance was evident, but it was Bolton's Radhi Jaidi who came closest to finding the net with a header from a corner.

A change of philosophy was needed, and Wigley threw on the giant Peter Crouch in the 69th minute. Although the impact was not immediate, the gangly striker did net an 85th-minute goal, his first for the club, to briefly raise hopes of a late comeback.

Paul Telfer's ball in from the right following a corner was not dealt with by Jaaskelainen, allowing Crouch to bundle home an effort at the far post.

An injury-time Claus Lundekvam header drifted agonisingly wide of the right-hand upright, as Sam Allardyce's team almost paid the price for dropping deeper and deeper during the second period.

PREMIERSHIP FIXTURE HISTORY

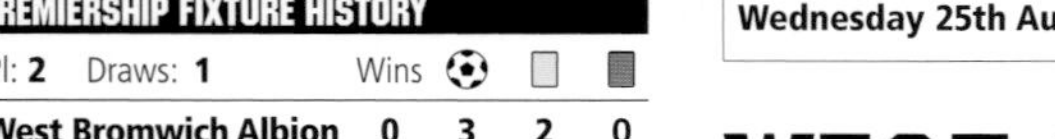

Pl: 2	Draws: 1	Wins ⚽	☐	■
West Bromwich Albion	0	3	2	0
Tottenham Hotspur	1	4	2	0

STARTING LINE-UPS

Dyer, Dobie, Moore, Kuszczak, Albrechtsen

Keane, Brown, Jackson, Keller, Gardner

EVENT LINE

3 ⚽ **Gera (Open Play)**

34 ⚽ Defoe (Open Play)

HALF TIME 1 - 1

54 **Johnson (Off) Dyer (On)**

61 **Horsfield (Off) Dobie (On)**

67 Defoe (Off) Keane (On)

78 Redknapp (Off) Brown (On)

81 **Gera (Off) Moore (On)**

88 Atouba (Off) Jackson (On)

FULL TIME 1 - 1

STATISTICS

Season	Fixture (West Brom)		Fixture (Tottenham)	Season
9	2	Shots On Target	6	21
14	2	Shots Off Target	6	20
0	0	Hit Woodwork	1	1
15	8	Caught Offside	0	11
21	4	Corners	5	11
42	13	Fouls	10	39
49%	50%	Possession	50%	49%

LEAGUE STANDINGS

Position (pos before)	W	D	L	F	A	Pts
11 (13) West Brom	0	3	0	3	3	3
5 (6) Tottenham H	1	2	0	3	2	5

Wednesday 25th August 2004 | Venue: **The Hawthorns** | Attendance: **27,191** | Referee: **B.Knight**

WEST BROM 1 TOTTENHAM HOTSPUR 1

Neil Clement notices that Sean Davis is wearing the same boots

"We made a great start, but we just did not play well enough after we took the lead."

Gary Megson

PREMIERSHIP MILESTONE

Lloyd Dyer and Noe Pamarot both made their Premiership debuts

PREMIERSHIP MILESTONE

Zoltan Gera scored his first Premiership goal

"I am sure that for both sets of fans it was a good game to watch."

Jacques Santini

An early goal from Hungarian international Zoltan Gera was cancelled out by a long-range Jermain Defoe strike, as the points were shared at The Hawthorns.

It took just three minutes for Gera to mark his first start for West Brom with a goal. The £1.5m summer signing from Ferencvaros caught the visitors napping when he raced on to a long ball from Riccardo Scimeca to shrug off the attentions of Noureddine Naybet, before angling a low drive into the bottom left-hand corner of Paul Robinson's net.

The remainder of the half saw Tottenham in the ascendancy. Jacques Santini's side lay siege to the home side's goal, with Defoe seeing a shot deflected narrowly wide and then going close again after Russell Hoult had spilled a drive from distance.

It therefore came as no surprise when Spurs grabbed a 34th-minute equaliser. The move was started and finished by Defoe, who exchanged passes with his strike-partner Frederic Kanoute before driving home from 20 yards with his unfavoured left foot.

Gary Megson's side responded positively. Nwankwo Kanu thought he had restored Albion's advantage, only to see his acrobatic overhead kick ruled out for offside. It was a rare moment of worry for the Londoners, who could easily have put the game out of reach in the opening three minutes of the second half.

The livewire Defoe hit the foot of the post from 15 yards after a pass from Sean Davis, before the supplier of that chance was then denied in spectacular fashion as his rising drive was expertly turned over the bar.

The summer revolution at White Hart Lane had clearly had a positive influence on the team. No less than seven recent acquisitions had started for Tottenham in this game, yet there were few signs of unfamiliarity as they pressed for a winner.

Ultimately, a decisive goal was not forthcoming, as West Brom registered their third 1-1 draw of the season. In the battle for survival home points are vital, though the quality of Spurs' performance suggested that the West Midlands side should look upon this result as a positive one.

PREMIERSHIP FIXTURE HISTORY

Pl: **12** Draws: **5**

	Wins	⚽	☐	■
Aston Villa	2	10	16	0
Newcastle United	5	14	12	1

STARTING LINE-UPS

Aston Villa: Sorensen; De la Cruz, Delaney, Mellberg (c), Samuel; Solano, McCann, Hitzlsperger, Barry; Vassell, Cole

Newcastle United: Given; Bernard, Hughes, O'Brien, Carr (c); Robert, Butt, Jenas, Bowyer; Kluivert, Bellamy

Hendrie, Angel, L.Moore, Postma, Whittingham

Elliott, Shearer, Ameobi, Harper, Milner

EVENT LINE

4 ⚽ **Mellberg (Corner)**
28 ⚽ Kluivert (Open Play)
36 ⚽ O'Brien (Corner)

HALF TIME 1 - 2

52 ☐ **Samuel (Foul)**
53 ⚽ **Cole (Open Play)**
56 ☐ **Sorensen (Handball)**
60 ⇄ **Hitzlsperger (Off) Hendrie (On)**
70 ⇄ **Cole (Off) Angel (On)**
71 ⚽ **Barry (Open Play)**
73 ⇄ Bernard (Off) Elliott (On)
77 ⇄ Bowyer (Off) Ameobi (On)
77 ⇄ Kluivert (Off) Shearer (On)
82 ⚽ **Angel (Open Play)**
86 ⇄ **Vassell (Off) Moore L (On)**
90 ☐ **Hendrie (Ung.Conduct)**
90 ☐ Given (Ung.Conduct)

FULL TIME 4 - 2

STATISTICS

Season	Fixture (Aston Villa)		Fixture (Newcastle)	Season
27	13	Shots On Target	10	36
22	3	Shots Off Target	2	24
2	1	Hit Woodwork	0	0
10	6	Caught Offside	1	10
37	9	Corners	4	36
71	23	Fouls	11	51
49%	48%	Possession	52%	51%

LEAGUE STANDINGS

Position (pos before)	W	D	L	F	A	Pts
5 (10) Aston Villa	2	1	1	7	6	7
16 (15) Newcastle Utd	0	2	2	6	9	2

Saturday 28th August 2004 | Venue: **Villa Park** | Attendance: **36,305** | Referee: **M.A.Riley**

ASTON VILLA 4 NEWCASTLE UNITED 2

Sir Bobby Robson's position as manager of Newcastle United started to look increasingly vulnerable after this 4-2 reverse at Villa Park.

The former England boss had sent shockwaves around the football world by dropping Alan Shearer, an act that had cost Ruud Gullit the same job several years earlier. The striker's replacement, Patrick Kluivert, justified his inclusion with a goal, though Robson will ultimately be judged on results.

Things began disastrously for the Magpies as Villa skipper Olof Mellberg nodded home his second goal in a week. The Swede got on the end of former Newcastle wideman Nolberto Solano's corner after just four minutes.

Carlton Cole headed wide two minutes later as David O'Leary's men threatened to run riot. All that changed, however, when Kluivert netted his first goal for his new employers in the 28th minute.

Neat build-up play was rewarded when the Dutch striker showed all his experience to turn his marker in the box and beat Thomas Sorensen with a quickly taken shot.

Within eight minutes of equalising, the Tyneside club were in front. Defender Andy O'Brien, harshly sent off in this fixture last season, met Craig Bellamy's ball in from the right following a half-cleared corner with a superbly angled header.

There was still time for Solano to hit the bar when it had seemed easier to score as a pulsating 45 minutes drew to a close.

The second period proved far less enjoyable for the Geordie fans as Cole, Gareth Barry and substitute Juan Pablo Angel all netted without reply.

Excellent work by Barry down the left led to an onrushing Cole chesting the ball home from close range in the 53rd minute. The ex-England international midfielder then netted himself with a 71st-minute back-post header from a Solano cross, before Angel sealed the victory with a hopeful 82nd-minute shot that looped cruelly up off O'Brien and over the head of a stranded Shay Given.

The 77th-minute introduction of Shearer, in place of Kluivert, had come too late to change the game. As disheartened Newcastle fans left Villa Park, many were asking whether a first win of the season would come too late to save Robson's job.

Villa's young guns celebrate a goal

"I felt that we were unlucky to be trailing at half-time. But we really went out and took the game to them in the second half."

David O'Leary

"Alan played 90 minutes last weekend and 90 minutes on Wednesday. I thought he looked tired on Wednesday and I chose to rest him."

Sir Bobby Robson

PREMIERSHIP MILESTONE

100 Andy O'Brien made his 100th Premiership appearance for Newcastle

PREMIERSHIP MILESTONE

Patrick Kluivert scored his first Premiership goal

PREMIERSHIP FIXTURE HISTORY

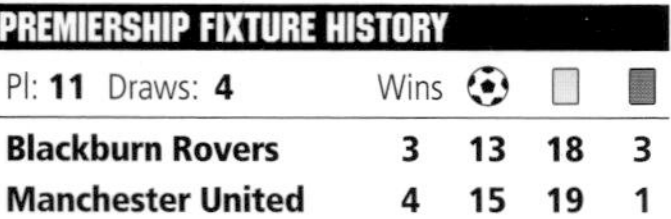

Pl: 11 Draws: 4	Wins	⚽	Yellow	Red
Blackburn Rovers	3	13	18	3
Manchester United	4	15	19	1

STARTING LINE-UPS

Emerton, Johansson, Yorke, De Pedro, Enckelman

Saha, Miller, Bellion, Carroll, P.Neville

EVENT LINE

13 Yellow **Stead (Foul)**
17 Sub **Thompson (Off) Emerton (On)**
17 Goal **Dickov (Open Play)**
35 Yellow Kleberson (Foul)

HALF TIME 1 - 0

46 Sub Kleberson (Off) Saha (On)
64 Sub **Stead (Off) Yorke (On)**
71 Sub **Dickov (Off) Johansson (On)**
71 Red **Amoruso (2nd Bookable Offence)**
75 Sub Spector (Off) Miller (On)
80 Sub Djemba-Djemba (Off) Bellion (On)
90 Goal Smith (Open Play)
90 Yellow **Tugay (Dissent)**

FULL TIME 1 - 1

STATISTICS

Season	Fixture (Blackburn)		Fixture (Man Utd)	Season
14	4	Shots On Target	15	24
19	4	Shots Off Target	9	24
0	0	Hit Woodwork	0	0
17	3	Caught Offside	4	8
19	4	Corners	14	28
77	26	Fouls	18	34
44%	46%	Possession	54%	51%

LEAGUE STANDINGS

Position (pos before)	W	D	L	F	A	Pts
18 (19) Blackburn R	0	2	2	4	8	2
12 (12) Man Utd	1	1	1	3	3	4

Saturday 28th August 2004 | Venue: **Ewood Park** | Attendance: **26,155** | Referee: **A.G.Wiley**

BLACKBURN ROVERS 1 MANCHESTER UNITED 1

An inspirational performance from Brad Friedel looked to have helped secure a famous victory for Blackburn Rovers, until he was finally beaten by Alan Smith's dubious goal in the fourth minute of stoppage time.

The home side seemed set for a remarkable third successive 1-0 win in this fixture, as they clung on to Paul Dickov's 17th-minute strike. The former Leicester forward had opened the scoring with a wonderfully taken near-post finish, withstanding the attentions of Mikael Silvestre to crash home following a long throw.

That followed a bright start from the visitors, with Cristiano Ronaldo causing all sorts of problems down the right. The Portuguese starlet was a constant menace and won numerous free-kicks in dangerous areas for his side.

United responded well to falling behind, Friedel providing a taste of things to come when he blocked Smith's effort with his legs. Brazilian Kleberson, playing in his favoured central midfield position, then struck a fierce shot from distance inches past the post, before Lorenzo Amoruso did likewise at the other end from a free-kick.

The same two players were involved again after 40 minutes, as the Italian defender was cautioned for a cynical foul on the World Cup winner.

The second half brought more one-way traffic, as Friedel demonstrated why he was named in the PFA team of the season in 2002-03.

Half-time substitute Louis Saha was denied in the 55th minute, before Paul Scholes saw his fierce close-range header clawed to safety.

Rovers came under even more pressure after the 71st-minute dismissal of Amoruso. The defender collected his second yellow card for a clumsy bodycheck on Saha.

If Friedel had been special up to that point, he was sensational after it. The American smothered a Scholes effort, turned over a Saha drive with his legs and then produced a wonder-save to deny Smith.

However, just when most teams would have given up hope, United scored. There was a huge element of fortune about the goal as Smith lashed the ball home after it had broken to him off the hand of Saha. The visitors deserved their luck though, having dominated proceedings.

Ryan Giggs embarks upon a trademark run

"We showed great spirit and hung in there against a great team. I am very pleased with the performance."

Graeme Souness

PREMIERSHIP MILESTONE

100 Lucas Neill made his 100th Premiership appearance

PREMIERSHIP MILESTONE

Morten Gamst Pedersen and Jonathan Spector made their Premiership debuts

"You have to give full credit to Brad Friedel, but we kept plugging away and I'm just grateful to get a point."

Sir Alex Ferguson

PREMIERSHIP FIXTURE HISTORY

Pl: 13 Draws: 3	Wins	Goals	Yellow cards	Red cards
Chelsea	8	22	10	1
Southampton	2	11	26	0

STARTING LINE-UPS

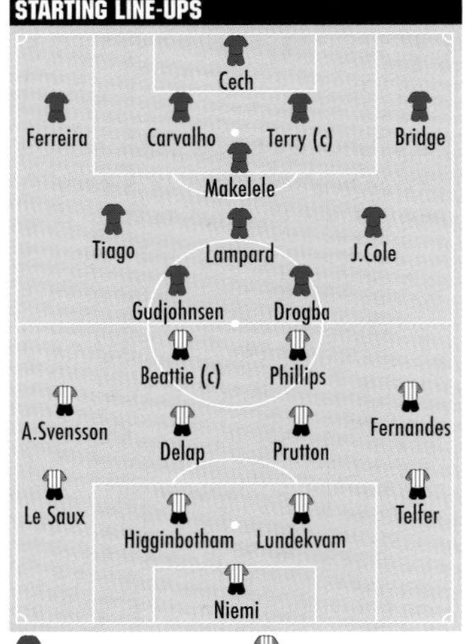

Chelsea subs: Duff, Kezman, Geremi, Pidgeley, Gallas

Southampton subs: Folly, Crouch, Van Damme, Smith, Cranie

EVENT LINE

1 Beattie (Open Play)

23 Fernandes (Off) Folly (On)

34 **Beattie (Own Goal)**

40 Delap (Dissent)

40 Phillips (Dissent)

41 **Lampard (Penalty)**

HALF TIME 2 - 1

57 **Cole J (Off) Duff (On)**

60 **Gudjohnsen (Off) Kezman (On)**

63 Prutton (Ung.Conduct)

70 Folly (Off) Crouch (On)

81 Le Saux (Ung.Conduct)

83 Svensson A (Off) Van Damme (On)

90 **Makelele (Off) Geremi (On)**

FULL TIME 2 - 1

STATISTICS

Season	Fixture (Chelsea)		Fixture (Southampton)	Season
20	8	Shots On Target	2	18
29	9	Shots Off Target	4	18
0	0	Hit Woodwork	0	0
12	3	Caught Offside	0	3
19	9	Corners	0	18
50	11	Fouls	12	42
57%	57%	Possession	43%	47%

LEAGUE STANDINGS

Position (pos before)		W	D	L	F	A	Pts
2 (2)	Chelsea	4	0	0	6	1	12
15 (14)	Southampton	1	0	3	5	8	3

Saturday 28th August 2004 | Venue: **Stamford Bridge** | Attendance: **40,864** | Referee: **S.G.Bennett**

CHELSEA 2 SOUTHAMPTON 1

Chelsea maintained their perfect start to the season, though James Beattie became the first player to breach the West Londoners' water-tight defence.

Jose Mourinho's side got off to the worst possible start, conceding a goal within 14 seconds of the kick-off. A loose pass in midfield by Joe Cole was seized upon by Beattie, who displayed some of the skill that had seen him involved for England in recent seasons by beating Petr Cech with a dipping 25-yard effort into the top left-hand corner of the net.

Eidur Gudjohnsen had an immediate chance to equalise, but could only head Frank Lampard's left-wing cross wide of the target from 12 yards. Antti Niemi then saved well from Didier Drogba on five minutes, as the game continued apace.

Chelsea's Ivorian international frontman couldn't seem to get on the end of anything, failing to latch onto a Cole throughball, narrowly missing out on connecting with a Lampard free-kick, and then being beaten to a Paulo Ferreira cross by Claus Lundekvam.

Indeed, it was a Southampton striker who got the Blues back in the match. Like so many before him, Beattie completed the feat of scoring for both teams in a game when he inadvertently turned Gudjohnsen's flick from a Lampard corner past Niemi in the 34th minute.

Shortly afterwards, Anders Svensson had to clear a Tiago header from another Lampard corner off the line. Then, after 41 minutes, another flag-kick led to the award of a penalty.

Claus Lundekvam was adjudged to have handled the ball by referee Steve Bennett, allowing Lampard the chance to score from the spot. The midfielder duly obliged, though closer inspection showed that he had inadvertently struck the ball twice.

The second period had little of the excitement of the first. The Saints rarely troubled the home defence, while Chelsea seemed content to adopt the continental tactic of sitting on their lead.

Substitutes Damien Duff and Mateja Kezman invigorated proceedings, both forcing Niemi into smart saves, as Mourinho's men ably demonstrated that you don't have to annihilate teams in order to pick up points.

"We want to win the league. If we lose three or four games and win the league, then we will be happy."

Frank Lampard

"Only Michael Owen and Alan Shearer have better strike rates as Englishmen in the Premiership."

Steve Wigley on James Beattie

PREMIERSHIP MILESTONE

200 James Beattie made his 200th Premiership appearance

PREMIERSHIP MILESTONE

Jelle Van Damme made his Premiership debut

Joe Cole skips away from David Prutton

PREMIERSHIP FIXTURE HISTORY

Pl: 2 Draws: 0	Wins	Goals	Yellow cards	Red cards
Everton	2	3	2	0
West Bromwich Albion	0	1	3	0

STARTING LINE-UPS

Everton substitutes: Ferguson, Wright, Weir, Watson, McFadden

West Brom substitutes: Albrechtsen, Haas, Moore, Kuszczak, O'Connor

EVENT LINE

2 Goal **Osman (Open Play)**

7 Goal Dobie (Corner)

23 Substitution Gaardsoe (Off) Albrechtsen (On)

HALF TIME 1 - 1

54 Substitution Gera (Off) Haas (On)

62 Substitution **Campbell (Off) Ferguson (On)**

62 Yellow card Scimeca (Foul)

64 Substitution Robinson (Off) Moore (On)

70 Goal **Osman (Indirect Free Kick)**

FULL TIME 2 - 1

STATISTICS

Season	Fixture	Everton	West Brom	Fixture	Season
20	10	Shots On Target		8	17
17	6	Shots Off Target		4	18
0	0	Hit Woodwork		0	0
13	3	Caught Offside		2	17
13	7	Corners		6	27
38	11	Fouls		16	58
48%	53%	Possession		47%	48%

LEAGUE STANDINGS

Position (pos before)	W	D	L	F	A	Pts
7 (13) Everton	2	0	1	6	6	6
14 (11) West Brom	0	3	1	4	5	3

Saturday 28th August 2004 | Venue: **Goodison Park** | Attendance: **34,510** | Referee: **P.Walton**

EVERTON 2 WEST BROM 1

Leon Osman aptly emphasised that Wayne Rooney is not the only product of an acclaimed Everton youth system, netting both goals in an important 2-1 victory.

Both teams found the net in an opening 10 minutes that set the tone for an entertaining and combative match.

The home side were first to strike as Osman ghosted in unmarked at the back post to head home Kevin Kilbane's flick from a throw on the left in just the second minute. West Brom responded in similar fashion, as Scott Dobie rose on the six-yard line in the seventh minute to score with a header that owed more to luck than judgement from Jonathan Greening's right-wing corner.

Aerial bombardment continued to represent the best route to goal for both sides in this see-saw contest. Joseph Yobo tested Russell Hoult with a header from a set-piece, while Marcus Bent failed to convert a glorious cross from Thomas Gravesen.

Having lost Thomas Gaardsoe to a leg injury midway through the first half, the last thing the Baggies wanted to see was the introduction of giant Scot Duncan Ferguson in the 62nd minute.

The former Newcastle striker's presence in the box for a 70th-minute free-kick clearly distracted the visiting defenders, leaving Osman free to glance home Lee Carsley's whipped delivery from a central position just six yards out.

The remaining 20 minutes didn't see Nigel Martyn troubled unduly, though Nwankwo Kanu did have a half-chance. Unfortunately for Gary Megson's side, the Nigerian was unable to get the necessary purchase on his effort.

The final whistle brought much relief to the Goodison Park terraces. With Rooney almost certainly heading for the 'exit' door, David Moyes' spirited troops had shown their supporters that they could still be a competitive Premiership side in the boy wonder's absence.

For West Brom, this result served to indicate that there are no easy games at this level. The West Midlanders would have seen this as a good time to play Everton, given all their off-field problems, but were ultimately outfought by a side that seemed a little bit hungrier on the day.

Duncan Ferguson takes style tips from Thierry Henry

"He is as good a footballer as we have here at Everton. He can play in a number of positions and is very skilful."

David Moyes on Leon Osman

"There is no use bringing in a striker if we continue to concede goals at set-pieces."

Gary Megson

PREMIERSHIP MILESTONE

Martin Albrechtsen made his Premiership debut

PREMIERSHIP FIXTURE HISTORY

Pl: 4 Draws: 1	Wins	⚽	▢	■
Manchester City	1	6	1	0
Charlton Athletic	2	6	7	0

STARTING LINE-UPS

Macken, Waterreus, Jihai, Bosvelt, McManaman

Johansson, Hughes, Andersen, Konchesky, El Karkouri

EVENT LINE

13 ⚽ **Anelka (Open Play)**

34 ⚽ **Sinclair (Open Play)**

HALF TIME 2 - 0

58 ▢ Murphy (Foul)

60 ⚽ **Anelka (Open Play)**

65 Fortune (Off) El Karkouri (On)

65 Kishishev (Off) Konchesky (On)

65 Rommedahl (Off) Johansson (On)

76 **Barton (Off) McManaman (On)**

78 ⚽ **Wright-Phillips S (Open Play)**

80 **Sinclair (Off) Macken (On)**

FULL TIME 4 - 0

STATISTICS

Season	Fixture		Fixture	Season
20	10	Shots On Target	3	26
19	6	Shots Off Target	3	12
0	0	Hit Woodwork	0	2
9	2	Caught Offside	0	12
23	6	Corners	4	18
56	11	Fouls	8	42
45%	57%	Possession	43%	46%

LEAGUE STANDINGS

Position (pos before)		W	D	L	F	A	Pts
9 (18)	Man City	1	1	2	6	4	4
8 (4)	Charlton Ath	2	0	2	6	9	6

Saturday 28th August 2004 | Venue: **City of Manchester Stadium** | Attendance: **43,593** | Referee: **M.R.Halsey**

MANCHESTER CITY 4 CHARLTON ATHLETIC 0

Charlton's away day blues continued as they shipped four goals in the North-West for the second time this season.

Having suffered a humiliating drubbing at Bolton on the opening day, the South Londoners fared no better at the City of Manchester Stadium. Nicolas Anelka, twice, Trevor Sinclair and Sean Wright-Phillips were on target, and this time the Addicks couldn't even manage a consolation.

Alan Curbishley's teams had always been solid on their travels prior to this campaign, but his current outfit looked lightweight in midfield and sluggish at the back.

The opening goal took 13 minutes to arrive. A clever step-over by Robbie Fowler on the edge of the Charlton area afforded Anelka the time and space he needed to drill Danny Mills' clipped pass just inside Dean Kiely's left-hand upright.

Had Danny Murphy not impatiently fired a gilt-edged chance high over the bar just six minutes later, things might have been different. As it was, Sinclair extended the lead with a comical goal in the 34th minute.

Wright-Phillips' ball in from the right caused a mix up between Kiely and Luke Young, with the defender's desperate attempt at a clearance cannoning into the net off the onrushing Sinclair at close range.

City keeper David James was called upon to make a fine save at the start of the second half, when he dived full-length across goal to turn behind Francis Jeffers' header from a Murphy cross. The chance represented a momentary break in the dominance of Kevin Keegan's side, and they made it 3-0 on the hour.

Anelka showed the fleet of foot that strikes fear into the heart of defences to latch onto Wright-Phillips' pass out of defence, before angling a low 15-yard drive across Kiely and into the bottom left-hand corner of the net.

Having produced a dazzling performance, it was fitting that Wright-Phillips should net a memorable fourth. There was no obvious danger when the recently-capped England international collected possession some 25 yards out in the 78th minute. However, one quick swing of his right boot later and the ball had arrowed home high to the left of Kiely.

Joey Barton wins the award for 'least follicly-challenged Man City player'

"Nicolas Anelka is very important for us. Even on a day when he is only 50% he is incredible. When he is 100% he is unplayable and he was close to that today."

Kevin Keegan

"Over the last few years in the Premiership our away performances have been good, while we have sometimes struggled at home. This season the roles have been reversed and we will have to look at the situation."

Alan Curbishley

PREMIERSHIP MILESTONE

100 Radostin Kishishev made his 100th Premiership appearance

PREMIERSHIP FIXTURE HISTORY

Pl: **2** Draws: **0**

	Wins	Goals	Yellow cards	Red cards
Middlesbrough	1	2	1	0
Crystal Palace	1	2	3	0

STARTING LINE-UPS

Middlesbrough substitutes: Nemeth, Downing, Nash, Ehiogu, Job

Crystal Palace substitutes: Derry, Kaviedes, Kiraly, Borrowdale, Soares

EVENT LINE

23 Yellow card: Hughes (Foul)

HALF TIME 0 - 0

51 Yellow card: **Riggott (Foul)**

52 Goal: Johnson (Penalty)

55 Substitution: **Mendieta (Off) Nemeth (On)**

56 Substitution: **Zenden (Off) Downing (On)**

61 Goal: **Popovic (Own Goal)**

78 Goal: **Hasselbaink (Direct Free Kick)**

80 Substitution: Riihilahti (Off) Derry (On)

84 Substitution: Routledge (Off) Kaviedes (On)

88 Yellow card: Popovic (Dissent)

FULL TIME 2 - 1

STATISTICS

Season	Fixture (Middlesbrough)		Fixture (Crystal Palace)	Season
31	**15**	Shots On Target	**3**	**16**
25	**9**	Shots Off Target	**4**	**21**
0	**0**	Hit Woodwork	**0**	**0**
23	**2**	Caught Offside	**0**	**5**
21	**4**	Corners	**2**	**20**
54	**16**	Fouls	**16**	**52**
52%	**61%**	Possession	**39%**	**45%**

LEAGUE STANDINGS

Position (pos before)		W	D	L	F	A	Pts
4 (7)	**Middlesbrough**	**2**	**1**	**1**	**9**	**8**	**7**
20 (20)	**Crystal Palace**	**0**	**1**	**3**	**3**	**8**	**1**

Saturday 28th August 2004 | Venue: **Riverside Stadium** | Attendance: **31,560** | Referee: **M.L.Dean**

MIDDLESBROUGH 2 CRYSTAL PALACE 1

Middlesbrough climbed to fourth in the table, as they recovered from conceding an early second half penalty to see off the spirited challenge of Crystal Palace.

Former Chelsea striker Jimmy Floyd Hasselbaink was the matchwinner, curling home a 30 yard free-kick 12 minutes from time after a Tony Popovic own goal had cancelled out Andy Johnson's spot-kick.

It was the Dutchman's third goal in four games for his new club and, in view of Juninho's departure to Celtic, he seemed to already have taken on the mantle of fans' favourite at the Riverside.

The first half proved a fairly turgid affair. Iain Dowie opted for a solid look with five men strung across midfield, and the home side struggled to carve out many clear-cut openings. Julian Speroni was his usual erratic self in the Palace goal, but did manage to keep the ball out when called upon.

The former Dundee goalkeeper got something in the way of a powerful Hasselbaink drive, but was fortunate that the rebound fell to Chris Riggott. The defender made poor contact with what was a golden chance and Speroni was able to make a smothering save.

At the other end, Michael Hughes missed a great chance for the visitors, firing Joonas Kolkka's left-wing pass agonisingly beyond the far post.

Seven minutes into the second half, Palace did go in front. A clumsy challenge on Johnson by Riggott left referee Mike Dean with no option, and the striker picked himself up to stroke his side in front from the spot.

The Premiership is a tough enough environment for newly-promoted clubs without helping the opposition. Unfortunately for the South Londoners, captain Tony Popovic did just that when he diverted substitute Stewart Downing's inswinging 61st-minute free-kick into his own net.

Middlesbrough piled on the pressure and were rewarded when Hasselbaink whipped a free-kick over the wall and beyond the despairing right hand of Speroni.

The result was harsh on the Eagles, and boss Iain Dowie had plenty of positives to reflect on. His side have come a long way in eight months, though he must be realising fast that hard work and commitment can only take you so far.

"We would not have won that game last year. We did not have the firepower to win games."
Steve McClaren

"The lads gave me everything they had, but we cannot keep saying that we were a little hard done by."
Iain Dowie

PREMIERSHIP MILESTONE

50 Danny Granville made his 50th Premiership appearance

Emmerson Boyce is closed down by Mark Viduka

PREMIERSHIP FIXTURE HISTORY

Pl: 4 Draws: 3	Wins	⚽	□	■
Norwich City	0	3	6	0
Arsenal	1	6	5	0

STARTING LINE-UPS

Safri, McKenzie, Svensson, Ward, Helveg

Edu, Bergkamp, Clichy, Almunia

EVENT LINE

22 ⚽ Reyes (Open Play)
30 □ Lauren (Foul)
36 ⚽ Henry (Open Play)
40 ⚽ Pires (Open Play)

HALF TIME 0 - 3

46 **Jonson (Off) Safri (On)**
50 ⚽ **Huckerby (Penalty)**
63 **McVeigh (Off) McKenzie (On)**
73 Fabregas (Off) Edu (On)
73 Reyes (Off) Bergkamp (On)
82 **Doherty (Off) Svensson (On)**
83 □ **Safri (Foul)**
84 Pires (Off) Clichy (On)
90 ⚽ Bergkamp (Open Play)

FULL TIME 1 - 4

STATISTICS

Season	Fixture (Norwich)		Fixture (Arsenal)	Season
22	6	Shots On Target	15	46
17	0	Shots Off Target	3	18
1	0	Hit Woodwork	0	3
19	2	Caught Offside	1	7
21	4	Corners	10	29
60	15	Fouls	5	39
43%	38%	Possession	62%	60%

LEAGUE STANDINGS

Position (pos before)	W	D	L	F	A	Pts
17 (16) Norwich C	0	2	2	5	9	2
1 (1) Arsenal	4	0	0	16	5	12

Saturday 28th August 2004 | Venue: **Carrow Road** | Attendance: **23,944** | Referee: **G.Poll**

NORWICH CITY 1 ARSENAL 4

Arsenal continued their mesmeric start to the season, handing out a footballing lesson to the men from East Anglia.

Norwich didn't play badly, but were ripped apart at will by a side with confidence levels in the clouds. Youngster Justin Hoyte slotted in seamlessly alongside Kolo Toure at centre-back, following an injury picked up by Pascal Cygan in the warm-up, as the Gunners demonstrated their growing strength in depth.

The game began with a flurry of corners at both ends, then settled into a rhythm of swift attacks from the visitors. Jose Antonio Reyes and Thierry Henry both tested Robert Green, before the two combined for the opening goal.

Henry used his pace and trickery down the left to lay on a simple close-range tap-in for the Spaniard in the 22nd minute.

Referee Graham Poll then angered the home fans on the half-hour, failing to dismiss Lauren for what appeared to be a blatant professional foul on Darren Huckerby. Home frustrations intensified just six minutes later, when Henry doubled his side's advantage.

Unusually for the French striker, he netted with a bullet header from Freddie Ljungberg's clipped cross from the right.

By the 40th minute it was three. Slack play in his own box from Norwich skipper Adam Drury saw him pick-pocketed by Ljungberg, with Robert Pires clinically sweeping home the loose ball from 12 yards out.

Credit must go to Nigel Worthington and his team, who never gave up and pulled a goal back in the 50th minute. It was Huckerby, the catalyst for so much of their best attacking work, who tempted Hoyte into a challenge that resulted in the award of a penalty. The former Coventry frontman duly stepped up to send Jens Lehmann the wrong way from the spot.

The Canaries were flying, as Huckerby and midfielder Gary Holt both forced fine saves from Arsenal's German goalkeeper, but had their wings clipped in injury time.

Substitute Dennis Bergkamp finished off a pacy break with a rapier-like right-foot finish from 15 yards that swerved beyond the left hand of Green.

Dennis Bergkamp thanks Thierry Henry for his assist

"Although it is always disappointing to lose, Arsenal are a different class, even from Manchester United and Newcastle."

Nigel Worthington

PREMIERSHIP MILESTONE

Youssef Safri made his Premiership debut

"I think Norwich can stay up. They have a good mixture of playing short and long."

Arsene Wenger

PREMIERSHIP FIXTURE HISTORY

Pl: 3	Draws: 0	Wins	⚽	Yellow	Red
Tottenham Hotspur		3	7	5	0
Birmingham City		0	2	2	0

STARTING LINE-UPS

Kanoute, Redknapp, Gardner, Keller, Ifil

Morrison, John, Bennett, Tebily, Martin Taylor,

EVENT LINE

30 Brown (Foul)

35 ⚽ Defoe (Open Play)

38 Defoe (Ung.Conduct)

HALF TIME 1 - 0

64 Keane (Off) Kanoute (On)

69 Jackson (Foul)

72 Forssell (Off) Morrison (On)

79 Clemence (Off) John (On)

85 Heskey (Ung.Conduct)

86 Defoe (Off) Redknapp (On)

90 Mendes (Ung.Conduct)

90 Jackson (Off) Gardner (On)

FULL TIME 1 - 0

STATISTICS

Season	Fixture (Tottenham)		Fixture (Birmingham)	Season
24	3	Shots On Target	2	17
23	3	Shots Off Target	8	23
1	0	Hit Woodwork	0	1
14	3	Caught Offside	7	9
13	2	Corners	8	22
54	15	Fouls	5	51
47%	42%	Possession	58%	51%

LEAGUE STANDINGS

Position (pos before)		W	D	L	F	A	Pts
3 (5)	Tottenham H	2	2	0	4	2	8
13 (9)	Birmingham C	1	1	2	2	3	4

Saturday 28th August 2004 | Venue: **White Hart Lane** | Attendance: **35,290** | Referee: **M.Clattenburg**

TOTTENHAM HOTSPUR 1 BIRMINGHAM CITY 0

Jermain Defoe continued to impress in Tottenham's fine start to the season, netting the only goal of the game to see off Steve Bruce's Birmingham City.

The decisive moment of the match came in the 35th minute as the young striker, showing no signs of the fatigue that his manager feared he was suffering from, advanced from halfway and evaded a couple of challenges, before firing home a powerful 25-yard effort. The ball took a slight nick off the right boot of Matthew Upson, but the deflection did not make a difference to the outcome.

In truth, the goal lit up what had been a dire first period. Any efforts of note tended to be from distance, while neither side found it easy to maintain possession.

Robbie Keane had been passed fit to start for the first time this season, though he was understandably off the pace. The same could not be said of his strike-partner, though Defoe did blot his copybook with a 38th-minute caution for diving in the box.

If Tottenham were sluggish, then Birmingham were asleep. The West Midlanders had not won on the road since December 2003, with a blocked Mikael Forssell effort representing their only real chance of the first 45 minutes.

Things improved marginally after the interval as Steve Bruce's side set about registering a shot on target. After Forssell had wasted a good chance to do just that, Emile Heskey rose to powerfully head a corner goalwards. Fortunately for Spurs, Michael Brown was stationed on the line and made a clearance.

Anxiety on the pitch began to spread to the stands as Jacques Santini's side desperately defended their lead. Julian Gray and Heskey both fired presentable opportunities over the bar, before the latter was, like Defoe, booked for diving in the box.

The burly frontman was incandescent with rage, and almost took out his frustrations on Tottenham with a last-gasp header that drifted narrowly over the crossbar.

The final whistle was greeted with huge sighs of relief around White Hart Lane. The home side had won without producing their best, a well-known attribute of any good team.

"It was a very special goal by Jermain Defoe. He is a good striker for us."

Jacques Santini

"I thought the referee was excellent and I have no complaints about the bookings for Emile and Jermain Defoe. He deemed they went over too easily and I take my hat off to him."

Steve Bruce

Jesper Gronkjaer is unimpressed by Johnnie Jackson's run

PREMIERSHIP FIXTURE HISTORY

Pl: 6 Draws: 2

	Wins	Goals	Yellow cards	Red cards
Bolton Wanderers	2	8	11	0
Liverpool	2	8	9	1

STARTING LINE-UPS

Bolton substitutes: Ferdinand, Nolan, Hierro, Poole, Cesar

Liverpool substitutes: Traore, Cisse, Harrison, Biscan, Diao

EVENT LINE

14 Hyypia (Off) Traore (On)

38 **Davies (Open Play)**

HALF TIME 1 - 0

46 Warnock (Off) Cisse (On)

72 **Davies (Off) Ferdinand (On)**

75 **Giannakopoulos (Off) Nolan (On)**

85 **Okocha (Off) Hierro (On)**

90 **Hierro (Foul)**

90 **Nolan (Foul)**

FULL TIME 1 - 0

STATISTICS

Season	Fixture (Bolton)		Fixture (Liverpool)	Season
29	8	Shots On Target	2	20
22	2	Shots Off Target	5	18
0	0	Hit Woodwork	0	0
10	1	Caught Offside	2	6
24	5	Corners	2	18
46	15	Fouls	14	34
49%	41%	Possession	59%	58%

LEAGUE STANDINGS

Position (pos before)		W	D	L	F	A	Pts
3 (6)	Bolton W	3	0	1	7	4	9
10 (10)	Liverpool	1	1	1	3	3	4

Sunday 29th August 2004 | Venue: **Reebok Stadium** | Attendance: **27,880** | Referee: **U.D.Rennie**

BOLTON WANDERERS 1 LIVERPOOL 0

Bolton emphasised how far they had come under Sam Allardyce, with a victory over Liverpool that would have shocked few people.

The Merseyside club are clearly in a period of transition, and new boss Rafael Benitez handed debuts to recent Spanish recruits Luis Garcia and Xabi Alonso in midfield. The pair had cost £16.5m between them, with big things expected at Anfield.

Things began badly for the visitors when key defender Sami Hyypia was injured in a first-minute aerial clash with Kevin Davies. The Finnish international battled on bravely, but had to be replaced by Djimi Traore in the 14th minute.

Liverpool were playing five men in midfield, and the policy seemed to work early on as they enjoyed the bulk of possession. Milan Baros, operating as a lone striker, fired wide when well-placed, and Dietmar Hamann was unable to round off an intricate passing move when he also missed the target.

For Bolton, ex-Evertonian Gary Speed had a shot deflected over, while Jay-Jay Okocha went through a complete repertoire of tricks down the left in order to set up an aerial chance that Stylianos Giannakopoulos should really have put away.

However, that miss did not prove costly as Kevin Davies poked his side in front after 38 minutes. Henrik Pedersen did the hard work down the left, driving low across the six-yard box where Davies finished with some aplomb.

The Anfield side reverted to a 4-4-2 formation in the second half following the introduction of Djibril Cisse. The visitors initially struggled to adapt to the change, as Wanderers threatened to put the game out of reach.

Jerzy Dudek made saves from Davies, Okocha and Tunisian Radhi Jaidi, before Garcia took centre stage at the other end.

Having missed a far-post sitter from Steven Gerrard's inswinging ball, the Spaniard's composed finish appeared to have levelled things in the 81st minute. Unfortunately for Liverpool, the goal was incorrectly ruled out for offside.

The Merseysiders threw everything at their hosts, Cisse firing over in the dying embers of the game, but were unable to penetrate a resolute Bolton rearguard.

Nicky Hunt and Stephen Warnock compete for possession

"Our players gave 110% against a side which has had an awful lot of money spent on it."

Sam Allardyce

"Our Spanish players played well but they can play better. They need to know that referees allow more contact in England than they do in Spain."

Rafael Benitez

PREMIERSHIP MILESTONE

Xabi Alonso and Luis Garcia both made their Premiership debuts

PREMIERSHIP FIXTURE HISTORY

Pl: 13 Draws: 2	Wins	Goals	Yellow cards	Red cards
Manchester United	10	28	8	0
Everton	1	10	24	1

STARTING LINE-UPS

Djemba-Djemba, Giggs, Bellion, Carroll, P.Neville

Ferguson, Naysmith, Wright, McFadden, Campbell

EVENT LINE

40 Osman (Foul)

HALF TIME 0 - 0

52 Cahill (Foul)

54 Bent (Off) Ferguson (On)

64 **Fletcher (Off) Giggs (On)**

64 **Kleberson (Off) Djemba-Djemba (On)**

70 Cahill (Off) Naysmith (On)

81 **Ronaldo (Off) Bellion (On)**

FULL TIME 0 - 0

STATISTICS

Season	Fixture		Fixture	Season
28	4	Shots On Target	2	22
32	8	Shots Off Target	5	22
2	2	Hit Woodwork	0	0
10	2	Caught Offside	0	13
36	8	Corners	2	15
42	8	Fouls	13	51
52%	56%	Possession	44%	47%

LEAGUE STANDINGS

Position (pos before)		W	D	L	F	A	Pts
9 (12)	Man Utd	1	2	1	3	3	5
7 (7)	Everton	2	1	1	6	6	7

Monday 30th August 2004 | Venue: **Old Trafford** | Attendance: **67,803** | Referee: **D.J.Gallagher**

MANCHESTER UNITED 0 EVERTON 0

With the proposed transfer of Wayne Rooney taking centre stage, this encounter did little to divert attention towards matters on the pitch.

Everton came with a game plan, stringing five men across midfield in a bid to stifle a United team that had begun the season slowly. The tactic worked, as Sir Alex Ferguson's side aptly demonstrated why they are in such need of a player with Rooney's ability to unlock a defence.

The Old Trafford side weren't without chances, striking the woodwork twice, though failed to show the necessary composure in front of goal.

Missing stars such as Roy Keane, Rio Ferdinand and Ruud van Nistelrooy, the men in red relied heavily on youth. Cristiano Ronaldo seemed to be playing in a free role off the front two, a tactic that resulted in the visitors dominating midfield.

Kevin Kilbane raced clear in the sixth minute, only to be denied by a combination of Tim Howard, Kleberson and young defender Jonathan Spector. The American custodian then did well to keep out a point-blank effort from Tim Cahill, before United awoke from their slumber.

Nigel Martyn was tested by a vicious inswinging free-kick from Ronaldo and, after Louis Saha had headed wide, Kleberson then stung the goalkeeper's hands from 25 yards.

The woodwork came to Everton's rescue early in the second period as Ronaldo cut in from the right and unleashed a low 20-yard drive. There followed a lucky escape at the other end, referee Dermot Gallagher turning down strong penalty appeals after Mikael Silvestre appeared to handle from a David Weir header.

A great save from Martyn then kept out the hard-working Saha, before Alan Smith's shot from distance again crashed against his former Leeds teammate's post.

In an exciting finale, the visiting goalkeeper had to tip over a header from his own captain Alan Stubbs, and then proceeded to somehow keep out a low shot from Paul Scholes.

The result left United seven points adrift of title-rivals Arsenal and Chelsea at the top of the Premiership. Even with just four games played, that gap is already starting to look insurmountable.

Alan Stubbs and Louis Saha do their best to avoid heading the ball

"It was really frustrating. They played 4-5-1, and we just couldn't break them down."

Darren Fletcher

"We have done well to make such a decent start to the season and now we are hoping to maintain it."

David Moyes

PREMIERSHIP MILESTONE

100 Steve Watson made his 100th Premiership appearance for Everton

PREMIERSHIP MILESTONE

Tim Cahill made his Premiership debut

Monday 30th August 2004 | Venue: **Fratton Park** | Attendance: **19,728** | Referee: **B.Knight**

PREMIERSHIP FIXTURE HISTORY

Pl: **2** Draws: **1**

	Wins	Goals	Yellow	Red
Portsmouth	1	5	1	0
Fulham	0	4	6	0

STARTING LINE-UPS

Hislop
Primus, De Zeeuw (c), Stefanovic, Unsworth
Stone, Quashie, Berger
Berkovic
Fuller, Yakubu

Cole
Boa Morte, Diop, Jensen, Legwinski (c), Radzinski
Bocanegra, Goma, Knight, Volz
van der Sar

Portsmouth subs: Lua Lua, Taylor, Ashdown, Griffin, O'Neil

Fulham subs: John, McBride, Crossley, McKinlay, Pembridge

EVENT LINE

19 **Berkovic (Open Play)**
22 **Yakubu (Penalty)**
28 **Yakubu (Open Play)**
39 Cole (Open Play)
41 Boa Morte (Open Play)

HALF TIME 3 - 2

68 Legwinski (Ung.Conduct)
68 Radzinski (Off) John (On)
72 **Yakubu (Open Play)**
75 Bocanegra (Indirect Free Kick)
77 Knight (Foul)
79 **Berkovic (Off) Lua Lua (On)**
86 Legwinski (Off) McBride (On)
88 **Yakubu (Off) Taylor (On)**

FULL TIME 4 - 3

STATISTICS

Season	Fixture	Portsmouth	Fixture	Season
24	9	Shots On Target	10	24
14	4	Shots Off Target	4	21
0	0	Hit Woodwork	0	2
8	2	Caught Offside	1	13
19	5	Corners	8	21
36	13	Fouls	13	46
48%	44%	Possession	56%	53%

LEAGUE STANDINGS

Position (pos before)	W	D	L	F	A	Pts
11 (19) Portsmouth	1	1	1	6	6	4
13 (10) Fulham	1	1	2	6	7	4

Yakubu enjoys his evening

"You don't come to football to see a boring 0-0 draw, and that was great entertainment for the fans and for the television cameras."

Harry Redknapp

PREMIERSHIP MILESTONE

50 Eyal Berkovic scored Portsmouth's 50th Premiership goal

PREMIERSHIP MILESTONE

50 Nigel Quashie made his 50th Premiership appearance

"On the ball we could not be much better than that, but every time they went forward they looked like they were going to score."

Chris Coleman

PREMIERSHIP MILESTONE

Ricardo Fuller made his Premiership debut

PREMIERSHIP MILESTONE

Carlos Bocanegra scored his first Premiership goal

PORTSMOUTH 4 FULHAM 3

Portsmouth edged out Fulham in a pulsating seven-goal thriller at Fratton Park, with Nigerian striker Aiyegbeni Yakubu helping himself to a hat-trick.

After a patchy opening, the game appeared dead as a contest when the home side netted three times in nine minutes midway through the first half.

Israeli Eyal Berkovic got the ball rolling in the 19th minute, giving Edwin van der Sar no chance with a swerving 20-yard volley after Yakubu's initial effort had been blocked.

Debutant Ricardo Fuller embarked on a determined mazy run to earn a penalty three minutes later. The former Preston striker was tripped by Luis Boa Morte and Yakubu slammed the resulting spot-kick high into the net.

The Nigerian grabbed his second after 28 minutes, firing a stunning left-footed drive low across van der Sar from the inside left channel, having latched onto a Fuller flick-on. At 3-0, even the most pessimistic of Portsmouth supporters must have felt the game was won, but Fulham had other ideas.

Andy Cole nodded home his third goal of the campaign from Boa Morte's 39th-minute centre from the left, before the pair reversed roles two minutes later as the Portuguese winger beat Shaka Hislop with a low finish from the inside left channel after collecting the striker's return pass.

The second half continued in harum-scarum fashion, with countless chances at both ends. A miraculous one-handed save from Hislop denied Cole what looked a certain equaliser, and within 60 seconds Harry Redknapp's team had scored a fourth.

Slack defending from a 72nd-minute goal-kick allowed Berkovic to find Yakubu in the area, and the Nigerian tucked the ball home with a minimum of fuss.

That was not the end of the scoring though, as the Cottagers hit back just three minutes later. Carlos Bocanegra lost his marker to nod home Boa Morte's deep free-kick from the left from within the six-yard box.

Despite late chances, there were no further goals. The second period was also notable for an incident in which Fulham full-back Moritz Volz fell into the crowd. Luckily, neither the player or anyone in the crowd was badly injured.

Jose Antonio Reyes in action for Arsenal

AUGUST 2004

Champions Arsenal began the new campaign in blistering form, their record of four wins from four games matched only by London rivals Chelsea. While Arsene Wenger's men provided great entertainment, netting 16 goals, the Stamford Bridge side were criticised for playing negative football.

Both Manchester United and Liverpool won through to the 'Group Phase' of the 'UEFA Champions League', though neither team made a great start domestically. On the transfer front, Michael Owen swapped Anfield for the Bernabeu, with Wayne Rooney clinching a switch from Everton to Old Trafford in a deal that could eventually be worth £30m.

Life in the Premiership proved difficult for each of the newcomers. An opening day draw at Norwich earnt Crystal Palace their only point of the month, with the Canaries going just one better. West Brom led the way on three points, though they too were without a victory to their name.

The insecurity of life as a top-flight manager was highlighted as two men lost their jobs. Despite a controversial win against Blackburn in just the second game of the season, Paul Sturrock was relieved of his duties at Southampton. The same fate then befell Sir Bobby Robson at the end of the month, the Newcastle board unhappy with a return of just two points from four games.

While Manchester City made an indifferent start to 2004-05, winger Shaun Wright-Phillips arrived from the bench to mark his England debut with a goal, in a 3-0 trouncing of the Ukraine at St James' Park.

Surprisingly, it was Sam Allardyce's Bolton that topped the Premiership's contingent of Lancashire-based clubs. The Reebok Stadium outfit recorded three wins, most notably against Liverpool, to position themselves third in the table.

August 2004 will long be remembered for the breaking of a notable record. Victory against Blackburn at Highbury saw Arsenal overtake Nottingham Forest's amazing 42-game unbeaten top-flight sequence, set back in 1978.

IN THE NEWS

03RD	Paul Scholes retires from international football after winning 66 caps and scoring 14 goals
08TH	Arsenal win the Community Shield, defeating Manchester United 3-1 in the traditional curtain-raiser to the season
10TH	Charlton splash out over £5m to bring Danny Murphy and Francis Jeffers to the football club, though Paolo Di Canio returns to Italy
18TH	England beat Ukraine 3-0 in a friendly at St James' Park. The goals are scored by David Beckham, Michael Owen and debutant Shaun Wright-Phillips
19TH	Senegalese forward El-Hadji Diouf secures a season-long loan move from Liverpool to Bolton
20TH	England international defender Jonathan Woodgate makes a shock £13.4m move from Newcastle to Real Madrid
25TH	Manchester United join Liverpool in qualifying for the Group Phase of the Champions League
26TH	Chelsea are drawn with Jose Mourinho's former club, FC Porto, in the Group Phase of the Champions League
30TH	West Brom bolster their forward line with the £3m acquisition of Welsh international striker Robert Earnshaw from Cardiff
31ST	Manchester United complete the signing of Wayne Rooney from Everton in a six-year deal reputed to be worth up to £30m

TEAM OF THE MONTH

Petr Cech
Chelsea

Only James Beattie managed to beat the Czech custodian during his first four games in English football. Having excelled at 'Euro 2004' for his country, the keeper provided calm assurance to a team that collected maximum points in the month.

Paulo Ferreira
Chelsea

An ever-present in Chelsea's winning start to the campaign, the Portuguese full-back immediately looked at home in the Premiership. As well as forming part of an almost impregnable defence, the former Porto man looked to get forward at every opportunity.

Noureddine Naybet
Tottenham Hotspur

Brought in to add experience to the Tottenham back-four, the Moroccan international struck up an immediate understanding with Ledley King. Tottenham finished the month unbeaten, laying the foundations for success upon a defence that conceded just two goals in four games.

John Terry
Chelsea

Having been installed as Chelsea captain, the England international led by example. Despite playing with alternating partners at centre-back, Terry's vocal leadership helped inspire his defensive colleagues to three consecutive clean sheets at the start of the campaign.

Franck Queudrue
Middlesbrough

Though the Middlesbrough defence hardly proved watertight in August, Queudrue was always dangerous going forward. The French left-back created three goals during the month, and even chipped in with one of his own at Highbury.

PLAYER OF THE MONTH

Jose Antonio Reyes
Arsenal

The Spaniard began 2004-05 in sparkling form, scoring in each of Arsenal's four games in August. At home either on the left of midfield or in attack, the young starlet proved too hot to handle for Everton, Middlesbrough, Blackburn and Norwich.

"The Gunners have started the new season where they left off, and have done all of this without talismanic captain Patrick Vieira - a very impressive month."

Barclays Awards Panel

MANAGER OF THE MONTH

Arsene Wenger
Arsenal

Maximum points and 16 goals in just four games made Wenger's team the one everybody was talking about in August. Young starlet Cesc Fabregas effortlessly deputised for injured captain Patrick Vieira, as the Gunners blazed a trail at the top of the Premiership.

Premiership Career Statistics
up until end of August 2004
Matches:**300** Wins:**180** Draws:**77** Losses:**43**

"It has been a great start to the season for Arsene Wenger and Jose Antonio Reyes. Arsenal have bagged 16 goals in four games, with Reyes netting four, and they currently sit top of the Barclays Premiership."

Barclays Awards Panel

Leon Osman
Everton

Having spent a successful loan period with Derby last season, Osman was given a chance to shine at Everton this time around. The youngster did not disappoint, starting all four games during the month and netting both goals in the home win against West Brom.

Cesc Fabregas
Arsenal

Big things were expected of this Spanish starlet at Highbury, though few people thought he would be thrust into first-team action so soon. Playing with a confidence that belied his tender years, the midfielder dictated the play for the early-season table-toppers.

Jay-Jay Okocha
Bolton Wanderers

As well as dazzling Premiership crowds with his array of mind-boggling tricks, the Nigerian international captained Bolton to third place. Three goals, including a memorable opening-day free-kick against Charlton, emphasised just how vital Okocha had become to his team.

Dennis Bergkamp
Arsenal

Continuing where he had left off last season, the Dutch master pulled the strings for an inspired Arsenal. Scoring in three of his side's opening four games, Bergkamp also weighed in with two assists as the Gunners fired 16 goals in the month.

Jermain Defoe
Tottenham Hotspur

With his colleagues mainly concentrating on their defensive duties, the former West Ham striker was relied upon heavily for goals. Thankfully for Tottenham, Defoe provided them, scoring in three games as his team finished the month unbeaten.

MONTH IN NUMBERS

39 Games Played

114 Total Goals Scored

2.92 Average Goals Per Game

4 Player With Most Goals (Reyes, Henry)

1 Hat-tricks (Yakubu)

16 Club With Most Goals (Arsenal)

1 Fastest Goal (Beattie)

51.3% Percentage Of Home Wins

20.5% Percentage Of Away Wins

28.2% Percentage Of Draws

4-0 Biggest Win (Manchester City 4 v 0 Charlton Athletic)

86 Total Yellow Cards

3 Total Red Cards

2.2 Average Yellow Cards Per Game

10 Most Disciplinary Points (Naysmith, Dunne, Amoruso)

6 Fastest Booking (Horsfield, Kanoute)

33,336 Average Attendance

Thierry Henry sends a free-kick goalwards

PREMIERSHIP TABLE / TEAM STATISTICS

Pos	(last month)	Team	Played	Won	Drawn	Lost	Goals for	Goals against	Goal diff	Points	Shots on target	Hit woodwork	Shots off target	Failed to score	Clean sheets	Corners	Caught Offside	Players used
1	(-)	Arsenal	4	4	0	0	16	5	+11	12	46	3	18	0	1	29	7	17
2	(-)	Chelsea	4	4	0	0	6	1	+5	12	20	0	29	0	3	19	12	19
3	(-)	Bolton Wanderers	4	3	0	1	7	4	+3	9	29	0	22	1	1	24	10	17
4	(-)	Tottenham Hotspur	4	2	2	0	4	2	+2	8	24	1	23	0	2	13	14	17
5	(-)	Middlesbrough	4	2	1	1	9	8	+1	7	31	0	25	0	1	21	23	18
6	(-)	Aston Villa	4	2	1	1	7	6	+1	7	27	2	22	1	1	37	10	17
7	(-)	Everton	4	2	1	1	6	6	0	7	22	0	22	1	1	15	13	17
8	(-)	Charlton Athletic	4	2	0	2	6	9	-3	6	26	2	12	1	1	18	12	17
9	(-)	Manchester United	4	1	2	1	3	3	0	5	28	2	32	2	1	36	10	20
10	(-)	Manchester City	4	1	1	2	6	4	+2	4	20	0	19	1	1	23	9	16
11	(-)	Portsmouth	3	1	1	1	6	6	0	4	24	0	14	0	0	19	8	17
12	(-)	Liverpool	3	1	1	1	3	3	0	4	20	0	18	1	0	18	6	18
13	(-)	Fulham	4	1	1	2	6	7	-1	4	24	2	21	1	1	21	13	15
14	(-)	Birmingham City	4	1	1	2	2	3	-1	4	17	1	23	2	1	22	9	17
15	(-)	West Brom	4	0	3	1	4	5	-1	3	17	0	18	0	0	27	17	16
16	(-)	Southampton	4	1	0	3	5	8	-3	3	18	0	18	1	0	18	3	17
17	(-)	Newcastle United	4	0	2	2	6	9	-3	2	36	0	24	1	0	36	10	16
18	(-)	Norwich City	4	0	2	2	5	9	-4	2	22	1	17	0	0	21	19	16
19	(-)	Blackburn Rovers	4	0	2	2	4	8	-4	2	14	0	19	1	0	19	17	19
20	(-)	Crystal Palace	4	0	1	3	3	8	-5	1	16	0	21	1	0	20	5	15

TEAM FORM

Pos	Team	Form	Goals For	Goals Against	Pts
1	Arsenal	WWWW	16	5	12
2	Chelsea	WWWW	6	1	12
3	Bolton Wanderers	WLWW	7	4	9
4	Tottenham Hotspur	DWDW	4	2	8
5	Aston Villa	WDLW	7	6	7
6	Middlesbrough	DLWW	9	8	7
7	Everton	LWWD	6	6	7
8	Charlton Athletic	LWWL	6	9	6
9	Manchester United	LWDD	3	3	5
10	Manchester City	DLLW	6	4	4
11	Portsmouth	DLW	6	6	4
12	Liverpool	DWL	3	3	4
13	Fulham	DWLL	6	7	4
14	Birmingham City	DLWL	2	3	4
15	West Brom	DDDL	4	5	3
16	Southampton	LWLL	5	8	3
17	Newcastle United	DLDL	6	9	2
18	Blackburn Rovers	DLLD	4	8	2
19	Norwich City	DLDL	5	9	2
20	Crystal Palace	DLLL	3	8	1

TOP GOALSCORERS

Player	This Month	Total
T.Henry Arsenal	4	**4**
J.Reyes Arsenal	4	**4**
N.Anelka Manchester City	3	**3**
D.Bergkamp Arsenal	3	**3**
A.Cole Fulham	3	**3**
J.Defoe Tottenham Hotspur	3	**3**
J.Hasselbaink Middlesbrough	3	**3**
J.Okocha Bolton Wanderers	3	**3**
H.Pedersen Bolton Wanderers	3	**3**
R.Pires Arsenal	3	**3**
A.Yakubu Portsmouth	3	**3**
J.Beattie Southampton	2	**2**
C.Bellamy Newcastle United	2	**2**
N.Clement West Brom	2	**2**
C.Cole Aston Villa	2	**2**
P.Dickov Blackburn Rovers	2	**2**
T.Gravesen Everton	2	**2**
D.Huckerby Norwich City	2	**2**
F.Jeffers Charlton Athletic	2	**2**
A.Johnson Crystal Palace	2	**2**
O.Mellberg Aston Villa	2	**2**
L.Osman Everton	2	**2**
A.Smith Manchester United	2	**2**

MOST GOAL ASSISTS

Player	This Month	Total
T.Henry Arsenal	6	**6**
F.Ljungberg Arsenal	3	**3**
F.Queudrue Middlesbrough	3	**3**
D.Bergkamp Arsenal	2	**2**
L.Boa Morte Fulham	2	**2**
G.Boateng Middlesbrough	2	**2**
F.Fernandes Southampton	2	**2**
R.Fuller Portsmouth	2	**2**
T.Gravesen Everton	2	**2**
J.Greening West Brom	2	**2**
J.Hasselbaink Middlesbrough	2	**2**
C.Jensen Fulham	2	**2**
F.Kanoute Tottenham Hotspur	2	**2**
R.Kishishev Charlton Athletic	2	**2**
W.Routledge Crystal Palace	2	**2**
N.Solano Aston Villa	2	**2**
S.Wright-Phillips Manchester City	2	**2**

DISCIPLINE

F.A. disciplinary points: Yellow=4 points,
Two Bookable Offences=10 points and Red Card=12 points

Player	Y	SB	R	PTS
L.Amoruso Blackburn Rovers	0	1	0	**10**
R.Dunne Manchester City	0	1	0	**10**
G.Naysmith Everton	0	1	0	**10**
M.Brown Tottenham Hotspur	2	0	0	**8**
J.Defoe Tottenham Hotspur	2	0	0	**8**
R.Delap Southampton	2	0	0	**8**
B.Ferguson Blackburn Rovers	2	0	0	**8**
M.Izzet Birmingham City	2	0	0	**8**
D.Matteo Blackburn Rovers	2	0	0	**8**
L.Osman Everton	2	0	0	**8**
J.Redknapp Tottenham	2	0	0	**8**
J.Samuel Aston Villa	2	0	0	**8**
D.Unsworth Portsmouth	2	0	0	**8**
B.Zenden Middlesbrough	2	0	0	**8**

"I would like to say a special thank you for being given the opportunity to play for the best team in the world."

Michael Owen after joining Real Madrid

"Everybody has been really impressed by what they have seen on the training pitch, with his methods. So if we can work with him for a few years, then we are definitely going to win stuff."

Chelsea captain John Terry praises his new boss

"I didn't think it could be beaten, but, as they say in the business, all records are there to be beaten."

Brian Clough after Arsenal surpassed the 42-match unbeaten top-flight record of his Nottingham Forest team of the late 1970s

"Following discussions over the weekend, Paul Sturrock will be leaving Southampton Football Club, by mutual agreement, with immediate effect."

Southampton club statement

"We are absolutely delighted that Arsene has signed an extension to his contract. Since his arrival in 1996, he has revolutionised the club both on and off the pitch."

Arsenal Chairman Peter Hill-Wood

"After a disappointing start to the Barclays Premiership season, the directors of Newcastle United have informed Sir Bobby Robson that they have decided he is to be replaced as team manager."

Newcastle Utd club statement

"I think he will definitely improve things. That was the main factor in me deciding to stay. He thinks this team are playing to 60 per cent and he thinks he can take the team up a lot more. I agree with him."

Steven Gerrard on new boss Rafael Benitez

"We have, in my opinion, one of the best, if not the best, young managers in the country, a man with huge ambition and drive."

Crystal Palace Chairman Simon Jordan on Iain Dowie

PREMIERSHIP FIXTURE HISTORY

Pl: **13** Draws: **4**	Wins	⚽	Yellow	Red
Aston Villa	4	12	9	0
Chelsea	5	16	11	0

STARTING LINE-UPS

Sorensen

De la Cruz, Delaney, Mellberg (c), Samuel

McCann

Barry, Hitzlsperger

Solano

Angel, Vassell

Drogba, Kezman

J.Cole

Lampard, Tiago

Makelele

Babayaro, Terry (c), Carvalho, Ferreira

Cech

Hendrie, L.Moore, Whittingham, Postma, Davis

Gudjohnsen, Mutu, Smertin, Pidgeley, Gallas

EVENT LINE

HALF TIME 0 - 0

57 **Solano (Off) Hendrie (On)**

61 Cole J (Off) Mutu (On)

61 Kezman (Off) Gudjohnsen (On)

66 Tiago (Off) Smertin (On)

67 **Angel (Off) Moore L (On)**

80 Drogba (Ung.Conduct)

90 **Vassell (Off) Whittingham (On)**

FULL TIME 0 - 0

STATISTICS

Season	Fixture		Fixture	Season
32	5	Shots On Target	10	30
28	6	Shots Off Target	8	37
2	0	Hit Woodwork	1	1
10	0	Caught Offside	2	14
39	2	Corners	9	28
80	9	Fouls	12	62
50%	54%	Possession	46%	55%

LEAGUE STANDINGS

Position (pos before)		W	D	L	F	A	Pts
7 (6)	Aston Villa	2	2	1	7	6	8
2 (2)	Chelsea	4	1	0	6	1	13

Saturday 11th September 2004 | Venue: **Villa Park** | Attendance: **36,691** | Referee: **R.Styles**

ASTON VILLA 0 CHELSEA 0

Eidur Gudjohnsen goes close

"I was delighted with the result, although I thought we got lucky with the penalty incident."
David O'Leary

"We had a lot of chances against Villa, in a game which we controlled for long periods, but couldn't score."
Jose Mourinho

Aston Villa became the first side to prevent Chelsea winning in the Premiership this season, and were good value for a hard-earned point.

David O'Leary sprung a surprise by deploying a midfield diamond, a tactic designed to combat the visitors' identical shape. Gavin McCann anchored the foursome, while Nolberto Solano was given the chance to influence matters from a central position.

With a European adventure under Jose Mourinho set to begin in Paris on Tuesday, the Londoners set their stall out not to be beaten in this fixture. It was no surprise then that both sides cancelled each other out, in a game of few clear-cut chances.

Cheered on by a vociferous home crowd, Villa applied plenty of early pressure. Petr Cech showed just why he had been installed as No.1 at Stamford Bridge, plunging low to his left to keep out a curling Thomas Hitzlsperger free-kick.

Slowly Chelsea clicked into gear, with Mateja Kezman making a nuisance of himself upfront. This was typified in an incident by the corner flag, when the former PSV Eindhoven striker was harshly adjudged to have fouled an out-of-position Thomas Sorensen as he rolled the ball against an upright from the acutest of angles.

That followed a wonderful curling effort from his strike-partner Didier Drogba. The Ivory Coast international seemed to pose little danger when collecting possession 20 yards out, but promptly left Sorensen stranded with an effort that came back off the crossbar.

These chances apart, Mourinho's men were fairly subdued. The threat of Joe Cole was nullified by the presence of McCann to such an extent that the England international made way after 61 minutes.

Villa substitute Luke Moore almost created a late winner for Darius Vassell, but the striker somehow managed to screw his shot wide with the goal at his mercy.

The Londoners were denied a blatant penalty 10 minutes from time when Drogba tumbled under Ulises De la Cruz's untidy challenge. Bizarrely, referee Rob Styles chose to caution the striker for diving, a decision even opposing manager O'Leary couldn't fathom out.

PREMIERSHIP FIXTURE HISTORY

Pl: 6 Draws: 3	Wins	⚽	☐ (yellow)	■ (red)
Bolton Wanderers	0	4	7	1
Manchester United	3	15	7	0

STARTING LINE-UPS

Bolton subs: Diouf, Ferdinand, Hierro, Oakes, Ben Haim

Manchester United subs: Ronaldo, Bellion, Carroll, Spector, Djemba-Djemba

EVENT LINE

39 ☐ **Okocha (Foul)**
44 ⚽ Heinze (Corner)
45 ☐ **Hunt (Foul)**
HALF TIME 0 - 1
46 ⇄ **Pedersen (Off) Diouf (On)**
52 ⚽ **Nolan (Indirect Free Kick)**
64 ⇄ Kleberson (Off) Ronaldo (On)
74 ⇄ van Nistelrooy (Off) Bellion (On)
75 ⇄ **Davies (Off) Ferdinand (On)**
87 ⇄ **Speed (Off) Hierro (On)**
88 ☐ Giggs (Dissent)
90 ⚽ **Ferdinand (Indirect Free Kick)**
90 ⚽ Hunt (Own Goal)
FULL TIME 2 - 2

STATISTICS

Season	Fixture (Bolton)		Fixture (Man Utd)	Season
36	**7**	Shots On Target	**7**	**35**
27	**5**	Shots Off Target	**5**	**37**
0	**0**	Hit Woodwork	**1**	**3**
10	**0**	Caught Offside	**3**	**13**
28	**4**	Corners	**7**	**43**
68	**22**	Fouls	**15**	**57**
48%	**44%**	Possession	**56%**	**53%**

LEAGUE STANDINGS

Position (pos before)		W	D	L	F	A	Pts
3 (3)	**Bolton W**	**3**	**1**	**1**	**9**	**6**	**10**
10 (9)	**Man Utd**	**1**	**3**	**1**	**5**	**5**	**6**

Saturday 11th September 2004 | Venue: **Reebok Stadium** | Attendance: **27,766** | Referee: **M.D.Messias**

BOLTON WANDERERS 2 MANCHESTER UNITED 2

United's slow start to the season continued at the Reebok Stadium, though they were grateful to snatch a point after falling behind in injury time.

Bolton had enjoyed recent success at Old Trafford, and were looking to transfer some of that to home soil against a team that had been underperforming during the current campaign.

The visitors were able to name Ruud van Nistelrooy in their starting line-up for the first time this season, and gave a debut to Olympic gold medallist Gabriel Heinze at left-back.

The opening half proved to be a fairly even contest. Ryan Giggs and Kleberson posed plenty of problems to the home defence down the flanks, while at the other end Kevin Davies was leading the line well.

For United, Alan Smith fired straight at Jussi Jaaskelainen, who also cleared from Mikael Silvestre with his feet. The Trotters went close as Davies failed to connect with a teasing Kevin Nolan cross and Nicky Hunt fired high over the bar, before van Nistelrooy produced a tame header when well-placed.

The first goal of the contest went the way of Sir Alex Ferguson's side in the 44th minute, as new boy Heinze displayed predatory instincts to stab home Silvestre's knockdown from a corner.

Sam Allardyce's men hit back seven minutes into the second half, as Nolan nodded home from eight yards having seen Tim Howard parry his initial deflection of Okocha's low shot.

Wanderers were visibly lifted by the goal, Davies whistling an effort just past the far post and Okocha seeing a goalbound effort deflected to safety by Wes Brown.

Then, Cristiano Ronaldo stepped off the bench to rattle Jaaskelainen's crossbar with an unstoppable 20-yard effort.

Just as the match looked set to end 1-1, Bolton substitute Les Ferdinand capitalised on a defensive mix-up between Silvestre and Howard to slot home what he thought was a 90th-minute winner.

However, for the second away game in succession, United netted a last-gasp equaliser.

Another substitute, David Bellion, was involved, as Smith's back-post header following a right-wing corner struck the Frenchman before spinning slowly into the net off the right leg of defender Hunt.

Les Ferdinand rolls home Bolton's second goal

"We have not defended at two corners, and as a defender once myself, that hurts me."
Sam Allardyce

PREMIERSHIP MILESTONE
Les Ferdinand scored his first Premiership goal for Bolton

PREMIERSHIP MILESTONE
El-Hadji Diouf made his first Premiership appearance in the colours of Bolton

"I've gambled with bringing in Ruud van Nistelrooy, and he's obviously not ready."
Sir Alex Ferguson

PREMIERSHIP MILESTONE
Gabriel Heinze marked his Premiership debut with a goal

PREMIERSHIP FIXTURE HISTORY

Pl: 4 Draws: 0	Wins	Goals	Yellow cards	Red cards
Fulham	0	1	7	0
Arsenal	4	8	11	0

STARTING LINE-UPS

Radzinski, McBride, Crossley, Goma, McKinlay

Reyes, Pennant, Fabregas, Almunia, Clichy

EVENT LINE

22 Vieira (Foul)

HALF TIME 0 - 0

61 Pires (Off) Reyes (On)

62 Ljungberg (Open Play)

64 **van der Sar (Dissent)**

65 Knight (Own Goal)

68 **Legwinski (Foul)**

71 Reyes (Open Play)

73 Ljungberg (Off) Pennant (On)

75 Vieira (Off) Fabregas (On)

76 **Legwinski (Off) Radzinski (On)**

82 Fabregas (Ung.Conduct)

83 **Boa Morte (Off) McBride (On)**

FULL TIME 0 - 3

STATISTICS

Season	Fixture (Fulham)		Fixture (Arsenal)	Season
31	7	Shots On Target	7	53
23	2	Shots Off Target	5	23
2	0	Hit Woodwork	0	3
15	2	Caught Offside	5	12
30	9	Corners	4	33
58	12	Fouls	10	49
50%	40%	Possession	60%	60%

LEAGUE STANDINGS

Position (pos before)	W	D	L	F	A	Pts
15 (13) Fulham	1	1	3	6	10	4
1 (1) Arsenal	5	0	0	19	5	15

Saturday 11th September 2004 | Venue: **Craven Cottage** | Attendance: **21,681** | Referee: **M.R.Halsey**

FULHAM 0 ARSENAL 3

Luis Boa Morte escapes the attentions of Gilberto

PREMIERSHIP MILESTONE

The attendance of 21,681 was a Premiership record at Craven Cottage

"To give the penalty and then not give it is incredible. He said that he changed his mind because of the way the players reacted."

Chris Coleman on referee Mark Halsey

"Fulham decided to surprise us today by going for it in the first half, and that was intelligent by Chris Coleman."

Arsene Wenger

Arsenal's winning start to the season continued, thanks in no small part to some favourable decisions from referee Mark Halsey.

The official initially awarded Fulham a first half penalty, following a challenge by Ashley Cole on namesake Andy, but changed his mind after the reaction of Arsene Wenger's players caused him to consult one of his assistants.

Then, Collins John saw what looked to be a perfectly legal header ruled out for a push, leaving manager Chris Coleman dumbstruck.

The Gunners later took full advantage of their good fortune, as Freddie Ljungberg, a Zat Knight own goal and then Jose Antonio Reyes secured what on paper looked a comfortable victory.

Arsenal began the more brightly of the two sides, with Knight heading clear a dangerous Dennis Bergkamp cross and Ljungberg unsettling Carlos Bocanegra with several tricky runs. The best chances, however, fell to the home team.

Mark Pembridge's corner ended with the ball being cleared off the line and Luis Boa Morte forced a smart stop from Jens Lehmann against his former club, before Halsey played his pivotal role.

With boos still ringing in his ears, Halsey went some way towards appeasing the angry locals by turning down a strong penalty appeal from the visitors. Moritz Volz, another former Gunner, only made contact with Thierry Henry's calf as he tried to win possession in the box, but the referee was unmoved.

After Lehmann had kept out John with his legs at the start of the second period, Wenger introduced Reyes. The ever-improving youngster's impact was immediate, as within a minute he was involved in the move that resulted in a 62nd-minute opener.

Swedish midfielder Ljungberg slotted Henry's unselfish pass low to the right of Edwin van der Sar, before Knight poked the ball beyond his own goalkeeper three minutes later as he attempted a challenge on the Arsenal goalscorer.

Six minutes later Reyes completed the scoring, slamming Bergkamp's measured pass powerfully across van der Sar with his left foot. In doing so, the starlet maintained his amazing record of having netted in every Premiership match thus far.

PREMIERSHIP FIXTURE HISTORY

Pl: 2 Draws: 0	Wins	Goals	Yellow cards	Red cards
Liverpool	2	5	2	0
West Bromwich Albion	0	0	2	1

STARTING LINE-UPS

Liverpool substitutes: Alonso, Baros, Traore, Luzi Bernardi, Diao

West Brom substitutes: Earnshaw, Gera, Kuszczak, Contra, Dobie

EVENT LINE

16 Gerrard (Open Play)

42 Finnan (Open Play)

HALF TIME 2 - 0

53 Horsfield (Off) Earnshaw (On)

60 Garcia (Open Play)

65 Gerrard (Off) Alonso (On)

66 Haas (Off) Gera (On)

68 Kewell (Off) Baros (On)

74 Garcia (Off) Traore (On)

FULL TIME 3 - 0

STATISTICS

Season	Fixture (Liverpool)		Fixture (West Brom)	Season
29	9	Shots On Target	5	22
25	7	Shots Off Target	4	22
0	0	Hit Woodwork	0	0
8	2	Caught Offside	3	20
26	8	Corners	6	33
43	9	Fouls	11	69
56%	51%	Possession	49%	48%

LEAGUE STANDINGS

Position (pos before)	W	D	L	F	A	Pts
8 (12) Liverpool	2	1	1	6	3	7
17 (15) West Brom	0	3	2	4	8	3

Saturday 11th September 2004 | Venue: Anfield | Attendance: 42,947 | Referee: S.W.Dunn

LIVERPOOL 3 WEST BROM 0

Liverpool bounced back from defeat at Bolton with a confident display against Gary Megson's hard-working West Brom side.

Goals from Steven Gerrard, Steve Finnan and the excellent Luis Garcia meant the scoreline was a genuine reflection of the play, as the visitors were overwhelmed in all departments of the pitch.

The Reds were quickly out of the blocks, as Djibril Cisse fired wide when well-placed to end a flowing move in style. The opening goal did not take long to arrive, however, with captain Gerrard the scorer.

The combative midfielder exchanged passes with Garcia in the 16th minute, before beating goalkeeper Russell Hoult with a left-foot shot. The Baggies were on the ropes, and needed Hoult to make a smart save from Sami Hyypia's header in order to keep the deficit at one goal.

Having struggled to get forward during the first half, the last thing West Brom needed was to concede a second before the break. Sure enough, they did just that after 42 minutes.

A long diagonal pass from John Arne Riise picked out Finnan, who danced inside the full-back before pulling his left-foot shot just inside the right-hand upright from 12 yards out.

Little changed after the interval, with Liverpool still in the ascendancy. To their credit, the visitors never gave up, enjoying a sustained spell of corners early on.

A major plus for the home side was the way in which Garcia and Gerrard were linking up.One moment of selfishness from the Spaniard apart, the two seemed to enjoy an almost telepathic understanding. The relationship bore further fruit on the hour mark, as Rafael Benitez's side added a third.

Without even looking up, the Liverpool captain picked out his new teammate in the inside left channel with a crisp first-time pass. Having seen his initial shot from a tight angle saved, the former Barcelona player followed up to squeeze the ball under Hoult from close range.

The final half-hour was short on incident, as the Merseysiders turned their attention towards the upcoming visit of AS Monaco in the Champions League.

"I have no complaints today. How can you find fault after winning 3-0?"
Rafael Benitez

PREMIERSHIP MILESTONE
Steve Finnan and Luis Garcia both netted their first Premiership goals

"The lesson to be learnt from this match is not to give teams too much respect. Sometimes we look as if we're too much in awe of some of the big clubs."
Gary Megson

PREMIERSHIP MILESTONE
Robert Earnshaw made his Premiership debut

Steven Gerrard and Luis Garcia celebrate their success

PREMIERSHIP FIXTURE HISTORY

Pl: 8 Draws: 0	Wins	⚽	□	■
Manchester City	5	20	10	1
Everton	3	10	12	1

STARTING LINE-UPS

Macken, Jihai, Sibierski, Waterreus, Bosvelt

Gravesen, Naysmith, Ferguson, Wright, McFadden

EVENT LINE

45	**Barton (Ung.Conduct)**
45	Carsley (Foul)
	HALF TIME 0 - 0
51	Pistone (Foul)
58	Osman (Off) Gravesen (On)
60	Cahill (Open Play)
61	Cahill (2nd Bookable Offence)
63	**Fowler (Off) Macken (On)**
73	**Sinclair (Off) Sibierski (On)**
73	**Thatcher (Off) Jihai (On)**
73	Bent (Off) Ferguson (On)
73	Kilbane (Off) Naysmith (On)
	FULL TIME 0 - 1

STATISTICS

Season	Fixture		Fixture	Season
24	**4**	Shots On Target	**5**	**27**
28	**9**	Shots Off Target	**1**	**23**
0	**0**	Hit Woodwork	**0**	**0**
12	**3**	Caught Offside	**3**	**16**
32	**9**	Corners	**6**	**21**
70	**14**	Fouls	**9**	**60**
45%	**47%**	Possession	**53%**	**48%**

LEAGUE STANDINGS

Position (pos before)	W	D	L	F	A	Pts
13 (10) Man City	**1**	**1**	**3**	**6**	**5**	**4**
5 (7) Everton	**3**	**1**	**1**	**7**	**6**	**10**

Saturday 11th September 2004 | Venue: **City of Manchester Stadium** | Attendance: **47,006** | Referee: **S.G.Bennett**

MANCHESTER CITY 0 EVERTON 1

Everton continued their encouraging start to the campaign, Tim Cahill's second half header proving decisive in a fixture they had lost 5-1 on the final day of last season.

The victory saw the Toffees climb into the top five, and would have been by a far greater margin had it not been for the heroics of recently dropped England goalkeeper David James. The ex-Liverpool shot-stopper was in sensational form, and was the only home player who didn't deserve to end up on the losing side.

Early chances came and went for Kevin Keegan's side, Sylvain Distin and Trevor Sinclair guilty of missing the target, before James was called upon for the first time on what was to prove a busy afternoon.

City's custodian expertly blocked from Steve Watson as the midfielder burst through on goal, and soon afterwards he was foiling Marcus Bent from point-blank range. Youngster Leon Osman was next to try his luck, though again the Welwyn-born goalkeeper was equal to the task.

Joey Barton, Lee Carsley and Cahill were all booked late in the first period, the latter for an over-zealous challenge in midfield. That caution was to ultimately prove significant, as Everton finally made the breakthrough on the hour mark.

Patient approach play down the right was rewarded when Cahill rose at the back post to nod home Tony Hibbert's right-wing cross from six yards out. Unfortunately for the Australian midfielder, referee Steve Bennett was less than impressed with his celebrations, during which he briefly revealed his torso, and brandished the second yellow card that resulted in his dismissal.

City threw on Jonathan Macken, Sun Jihai and Antoine Sibierski in a bid to make their numerical advantage tell, but seldom looked like penetrating a visiting rearguard expertly marshalled by captain Alan Stubbs.

The half-chances that did drop the home side's way were largely sent high or wide, with Nigel Martyn only being called upon once.

Despite a plethora of off-field sagas, not least the departure of Wayne Rooney, David Moyes has assembled a team that is performing well above expectations. Manchester City, however, are doing quite the opposite.

Shaun Wright-Phillips competes with Marcus Bent

"The game's gone mad. It was probably a rule thought up in Zurich."

Kevin Keegan on Tim Cahill's dismissal

"I honestly didn't know the rules and I will have to get the rulebook out."

Tim Cahill on his sending off

PREMIERSHIP MILESTONE

Tim Cahill's goal was his first in the Premiership

PREMIERSHIP FIXTURE HISTORY

Pl: 3 Draws: 0	Wins	Goals	Yellow cards	Red cards
Middlesbrough	3	8	7	0
Birmingham City	0	4	7	0

STARTING LINE-UPS

Substitutes (Middlesbrough): Riggott, Doriva, Job, Nash, Downing

Substitutes (Birmingham City): Morrison, Bennett, Martin Taylor, Tebily, Clemence

EVENT LINE

27 **Viduka (Open Play)**
42 Heskey (Open Play)
44 **Southgate (Foul)**
HALF TIME 1 - 1
48 **Viduka (Corner)**
55 **Queudrue (Foul)**
60 **Ehiogu (Off) Riggott (On)**
72 **Viduka (Off) Doriva (On)**
75 Johnson (Off) Morrison (On)
77 Izzet (Foul)
79 Yorke (Foul)
81 **Nemeth (Off) Job (On)**
90 Heskey (Dissent)
FULL TIME 2 - 1

STATISTICS

Season	Fixture		Fixture	Season
37	6	Shots On Target	3	20
33	8	Shots Off Target	2	25
0	0	Hit Woodwork	0	1
25	2	Caught Offside	0	9
27	6	Corners	3	25
70	16	Fouls	19	70
52%	49%	Possession	51%	51%

LEAGUE STANDINGS

Position (pos before)		W	D	L	F	A	Pts
4 (5)	Middlesbrough	3	1	1	11	9	10
14 (14)	Birmingham C	1	1	3	3	5	4

Saturday 11th September 2004 | Venue: **Riverside Stadium** | Attendance: **30,252** | Referee: **G.Poll**

MIDDLESBROUGH 2 BIRMINGHAM CITY 1

This fixture failed to live up to the heights of last season, a game Middlesbrough won 5-3, as the home side recorded a third successive Premiership victory.

Both sides had recruited heavily during the summer, and it was new signings Mark Viduka, twice, and Emile Heskey who found the net for their respective clubs. While Steve McClaren's arrivals had gelled sufficiently to see his team occupying fourth after this 2-1 victory, the visitors were left floundering on just four points.

Steve Bruce fielded an attacking line-up, with recent acquisition Dwight Yorke being asked to support the front two from a position on the left of midfield. The decision proved to be a poor one, with the former Aston Villa frontman looking woefully short of match practice.

The game began where it had left off last season, Mikael Forssell and George Boateng both going close in the early exchanges. Gradually Middlesbrough took control, with the aggressive tackling of Ray Parlour key to their dominance in midfield.

Reward arrived in the 27th minute, as Australian Mark Viduka netted his first Riverside goal in the red of his new club. As at Fulham, Jimmy Floyd Hasselbaink was the provider, the Dutchman sending his strike-partner clear with a measured pass that was swept home low to the right of Maik Taylor.

Birmingham responded in spirited fashion, and drew level three minutes before the break. After linking with Forssell, Heskey displayed the power of old, brushing aside Gareth Southgate to dispatch a venomous 15-yard drive across Mark Schwarzer from the inside right channel. It was a strike that the first half performance of the former Leicester City forward fully merited.

Having drawn level, Bruce's side were caught cold three minutes into the second period. A corner was not properly cleared and, after Szilard Nemeth had helped on a cross from the left, Viduka steered home what proved to be a matchwinning header from six yards.

The West Midlands side huffed and puffed, but never looked likely to equalise. They were too often let down by the final ball and clearly missed the tigrish Robbie Savage in the middle of the park.

"Middlesbrough and Birmingham are in contention for a top-six place, so it was important for us to put down a marker."
Steve McClaren

PREMIERSHIP MILESTONE
100 Ugo Ehiogu made his 100th Premiership appearance in a Middlesbrough shirt

"I thought it was an average game to say the least. We need to improve."
Steve Bruce

PREMIERSHIP MILESTONE
Dwight Yorke made his first Premiership appearance for Birmingham

Mark Viduka reels away after scoring

PREMIERSHIP FIXTURE HISTORY

Pl: **10** Draws: **4**

	Wins	Goals	Yellow	Red
Newcastle United	5	17	8	0
Blackburn Rovers	1	8	23	0

STARTING LINE-UPS

Ameobi, Milner, N'Zogbia, Harper, Kluivert

Douglas, Bothroyd, Enckelman, Tugay, Johansson

EVENT LINE

9 **Flitcroft (Own Goal)**

16 **Shearer (Open Play)**

19 Neill (Foul)

24 **Bellamy (Foul)**

HALF TIME 2 - 0

46 Pedersen (Off) Douglas (On)

77 **Bellamy (Off) Ameobi (On)**

78 Emerton (Off) Bothroyd (On)

83 **O'Brien (Indirect Free Kick)**

88 **Dyer (Off) Milner (On)**

89 **Ameobi (Foul)**

90 **Robert (Off) N'Zogbia (On)**

FULL TIME 3 - 0

STATISTICS

Season	Fixture (Newcastle)		Fixture (Blackburn)	Season
40	**4**	Shots On Target	**1**	**15**
27	**3**	Shots Off Target	**4**	**23**
0	**0**	Hit Woodwork	**0**	**0**
13	**3**	Caught Offside	**5**	**22**
44	**8**	Corners	**5**	**24**
61	**10**	Fouls	**19**	**96**
52%	**59%**	Possession	**41%**	**44%**

LEAGUE STANDINGS

Position (pos before)	W	D	L	F	A	Pts
12 (17) Newcastle Utd	**1**	**2**	**2**	**9**	**9**	**5**
19 (19) Blackburn R	**0**	**2**	**3**	**4**	**11**	**2**

Saturday 11th September 2004 | Venue: **St James' Park** | Attendance: **52,015** | Referee: **D.J.Gallagher**

NEWCASTLE UNITED 3 BLACKBURN ROVERS 0

Alan Shearer outmuscles Michael Gray

"I was nervous, but now I've sat in that dugout and we got a great result. It was a great feeling."

Newcastle Caretaker Manager
John Carver

PREMIERSHIP MILESTONE

100 Robbie Elliott made his 100th Premiership appearance

PREMIERSHIP MILESTONE

Charles N'Zogbia made his Premiership debut

"We didn't play very well, and all the players were disappointed with that."

Blackburn Caretaker Manager
Tony Parkes

PREMIERSHIP MILESTONE

Jay Bothroyd made his first Premiership appearance in the colours of Blackburn

Newcastle picked up their first three points of the campaign as a quirk of the fixture list saw them entertain Blackburn Rovers, the team from whom they had just prized manager Graeme Souness.

The Scot had been allowed to leave the Lancashire side on condition that he did not begin work at St James' Park until after this match, meaning that both sides were under the control of caretaker managers. Tony Parkes took the reigns at the visitors for the umptienth time, while former boss Sir Bobby Robson's assistant John Carver was in charge of the Magpies.

The match itself provided clear evidence that Souness had a made a move in the right direction, his new side triumphing 3-0 against his old. A ninth-minute own goal from Garry Flitcroft, a man with whom the former Galatasaray manager had recently fallen out, was followed by strikes from Alan Shearer and defender Andy O'Brien.

Furthermore, referee Dermot Gallagher failed to award the North-East club two penalties, both for clear-cut fouls on Lee Bowyer.

The opening goal arrived inside 10 minutes. An inswinging Laurent Robert corner from the right struck Flitcroft, having come through a crowd of bodies, and flew beyond Brad Friedel. The French winger then drove a fierce 30-yard free-kick inches wide, as Blackburn were penned back in their own half.

The second goal arrived on 16 minutes, and came from a familiar source. The recalled Shearer rose in a fashion all too familiar to the visiting fans, heading Craig Bellamy's centre from the left powerfully past Friedel.

Rovers improved after this, with Brett Emerton firing over from distance and Jon Stead testing Shay Given from a tight angle.

The second period was instantly forgettable, with the exception of a sublime goal from O'Brien. Having gone forward for an 83rd-minute free-kick, the Republic of Ireland international finished in a manner more akin to Thierry Henry, swivelling on Bowyer's pass and then firing home an eight-yard effort from the inside left channel.

Youngster Charles N'Zogbia was handed a fleeting debut, as Newcastle secured the win they needed to kick-start their flagging campaign.

PREMIERSHIP FIXTURE HISTORY

Pl: 1 Draws: 0	Wins	Goals	Yellow	Red
Portsmouth	1	3	0	0
Crystal Palace	0	1	2	0

STARTING LINE-UPS

Taylor, Kamara, Faye, Ashdown, Lua Lua

Ventola, Derry, Hughes, Kiraly, Powell

EVENT LINE

Min	Event
3	**Fuller (Corner)**
12	**De Zeeuw (Off) Taylor (On)**
43	Granville (Corner)
	HALF TIME 1 - 1
47	**Berger (Open Play)**
54	**Fuller (Off) Kamara (On)**
62	**Berkovic (Off) Faye (On)**
70	Kolkka (Off) Ventola (On)
80	Hall (Foul)
85	**Popovic (Own Goal)**
86	Riihilahti (Off) Hughes (On)
86	Routledge (Off) Derry (On)
89	Derry (Foul)
	FULL TIME 3 - 1

STATISTICS

Season	Fixture		Fixture	Season
32	8	Shots On Target	3	19
23	9	Shots Off Target	3	24
0	0	Hit Woodwork	1	1
12	4	Caught Offside	2	7
27	8	Corners	7	27
50	14	Fouls	21	73
51%	60%	Possession	40%	44%

LEAGUE STANDINGS

Position (pos before)	W	D	L	F	A	Pts
9 (11) Portsmouth	2	1	1	9	7	7
20 (20) Crystal Palace	0	1	4	4	11	1

PORTSMOUTH 3 CRYSTAL PALACE 1

An action-packed game ended in disappointment for Crystal Palace, as a penalty miss by Andy Johnson and another Tony Popovic own goal helped Portsmouth to a 3-1 victory.

The result left Iain Dowie's side with just one point from their opening five Premiership fixtures, and few would bet on the South Londoners improving sufficiently enough over the season to survive in the top-flight.

It took Harry Redknapp's side just three minutes to grab the lead. Jamaican Ricardo Fuller stroked home his first goal for the club after Eyal Berkovic had burst into the box following a corner.

Intense home pressure continued for the opening 20 minutes, before Palace came within a whisker of equalising as Danny Granville struck the woodwork with a 25-yard free-kick. The same player did draw his side level two minutes from the break though, meeting Wayne Routledge's right-wing corner with a powerful near-post header.

The visitors again made life difficult for themselves, falling behind just two minutes into the second period. Patrik Berger, a player renowned for his long-range shooting, was afforded all the time and space he could have wished for as he crashed home a 25-yard drive. While the quality of the strike could not be questioned, Julian Speroni should perhaps have done more than help the ball into the net.

A minute later Johnson had a goal ruled out for offside, but the frontman was then handed a perfect opportunity to equalise after 55 minutes when Hungarian Sandor Torghelle was clumsily brought down in the box by Linvoy Primus. Shaka Hislop had other ideas though, comfortably parrying the forward's well-struck spot-kick.

The former Reading goalkeeper then tipped over another Granville free-kick, as Palace threw everything at their South Coast opponents. Hopes were finally extinguished, however, when Popovic produced an even more spectacular own goal than he had managed at Middlesbrough.

With five minutes remaining, the defender met Steve Stone's low cross from the right with the deftest of near-post flicks, sending the ball spiralling beyond Speroni and into the far corner of the net.

"Patrik Berger's goal was a great strike. I told him at half-time that if he connected with the ball properly in this wind he would score."

Harry Redknapp

PREMIERSHIP MILESTONE

Diomansy Kamara and Nicola Ventola both made their Premiership debuts

"We have got to dig deep and be brave, and now we will see what the character in the dressing room is like."

Iain Dowie

PREMIERSHIP MILESTONE

Ricardo Fuller and Danny Granville both netted their first Premiership goals

Aki Riihilahti challenges Diomansy Kamara

PREMIERSHIP FIXTURE HISTORY

Pl: 4 Draws: 1	Wins	Goals	Yellow	Red
Tottenham Hotspur	2	7	4	0
Norwich City	1	4	5	0

STARTING LINE-UPS

Robinson
Naybet, King
Pamarot, Edman
Redknapp (c), Mendes
Brown, Atouba
Kanoute, Defoe
Huckerby, Doherty
Bentley
Holt, Francis
Safri
Drury (c), Edworthy
Charlton, Fleming
Green

Davies, Keane, Jackson, Keller, Gardner

McVeigh, McKenzie, Helveg, Ward, Svensson

EVENT LINE

HALF TIME 0 - 0

50 Charlton (Foul)
65 **Brown (Off) Davies (On)**
69 Safri (Ung.Conduct)
72 **Kanoute (Off) Keane (On)**
75 Safri (Off) McVeigh (On)
83 **Atouba (Off) Jackson (On)**
83 Doherty (Off) McKenzie (On)
84 **Mendes (Foul)**
90 **Redknapp (Foul)**
90 Bentley (Off) Helveg (On)

FULL TIME 0 - 0

STATISTICS

Season	Fixture		Fixture	Season
31	7	Shots On Target	2	24
31	8	Shots Off Target	5	22
2	1	Hit Woodwork	0	1
14	0	Caught Offside	6	25
26	13	Corners	5	26
71	17	Fouls	9	69
46%	42%	Possession	58%	46%

LEAGUE STANDINGS

Position (pos before)		W	D	L	F	A	Pts
6 (6)	Tottenham H	2	3	0	4	2	9
17 (18)	Norwich C	0	3	2	5	9	3

Sunday 12th September 2004 | Venue: **White Hart Lane** | Attendance: **36,095** | Referee: **H.M.Webb**

TOTTENHAM HOTSPUR 0 NORWICH CITY 0

Tottenham spurned the opportunity to go third in the Premiership, denied by the heroics of Norwich keeper Robert Green as they played out a goalless draw at White Hart Lane.

Jacques Santini opted to pair Jermain Defoe with Frederic Kanoute in attack, while Norwich boss Nigel Worthington set his midfield out in a diamond formation. Youssef Safri was handed a first start following his summer move from Coventry, and anchored a foursome that had Arsenal loanee David Bentley at its tip.

A confident Spurs side went at their opponents from the start and were nearly rewarded after 17 minutes. The Canaries had the left-hand upright to thank after Defoe had wriggled free of Damien Francis' challenge and unleashed a low 25-yard drive.

A weak finish from Kanoute failed to crown neat approach play, before Safri was forced to clear off the line from Defoe after captain Adam Drury's weak 24th-minute header.

The returning Gary Doherty tested Paul Robinson with a headed chance in a brief period of respite for the visitors. It was not long until the one-way traffic resumed, however, Jamie Redknapp steering wide from eight yards as Green quickly closed on him.

Norwich were virtual spectators as the North Londoners forced their Chertsey-born goalkeeper into one save after another. A fierce 25-yard effort from Defoe looked certain to break the deadlock in the 58th minute, until the intervention of a strong glove.

Despite their dominance, Tottenham could easily have fallen behind on two occasions. Darren Huckerby weaved his way past several defenders before forcing Robinson to parry, and later looked a certain scorer as he rounded the goalkeeper. Fortunately for Santini's side, Ledley King was alert enough to get back and make a match-saving tackle.

In between times, Green kept out Thimothee Atouba's rising drive. On this evidence it was easy to see why Sven-Goran Eriksson had called the custodian into recent England squads.

Referee Howard Webb's whistle brought to an end what had been a thoroughly entertaining 0-0 draw between two committed teams. The Canaries went home the happier, though Spurs could also take positives from the amount of clear-cut chances they created.

"A lot of my international players were tired after 75 minutes, and it was possible for us to lose the game."
Jacques Santini

PREMIERSHIP MILESTONE
100 Paul Robinson made his 100th Premiership appearance

"Robert Green showed what he can do with some great saves. He has got all the potential to go right to the very top."
Nigel Worthington

Jermain Defoe demonstrates his ability to fly through the air

PREMIERSHIP FIXTURE HISTORY

Pl: 6 Draws: 3	Wins	Goals	Yellow	Red
Charlton Athletic	3	11	7	1
Southampton	0	4	13	1

STARTING LINE-UPS

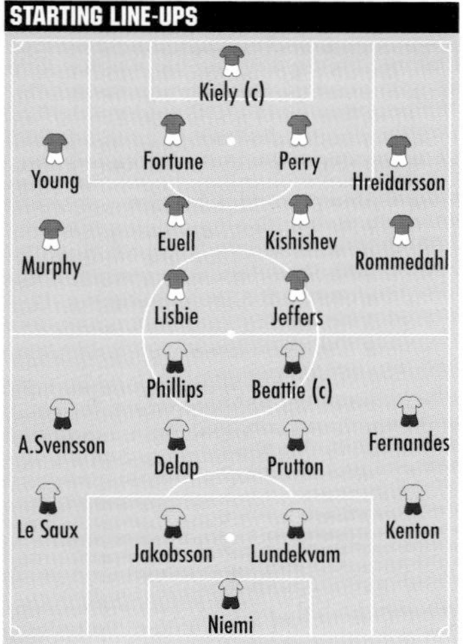

Hughes, Johansson, El Karkouri, Andersen, Konchesky

Nilsson, Crouch, Smith, Best, Higginbotham

EVENT LINE

HALF TIME 0 - 0

58 **Kishishev (Off) Hughes (On)**

67 **Jeffers (Off) Johansson (On)**

73 Kenton (Off) Nilsson (On)

75 **Rommedahl (Off) El Karkouri (On)**

81 Prutton (Foul)

84 Fernandes (Off) Crouch (On)

FULL TIME 0 - 0

STATISTICS

Season	Fixture		Fixture	Season
29	3	Shots On Target	4	22
20	8	Shots Off Target	11	29
2	0	Hit Woodwork	0	0
13	1	Caught Offside	8	11
25	7	Corners	12	30
54	12	Fouls	15	57
45%	42%	Possession	58%	49%

LEAGUE STANDINGS

Position (pos before)	W	D	L	F	A	Pts
10 (11) Charlton Ath	2	1	2	6	9	7
15 (16) Southampton	1	1	3	5	8	4

Monday 13th September 2004 | Venue: **The Valley** | Attendance: **24,263** | Referee: **N.S.Barry**

CHARLTON ATHLETIC 0 SOUTHAMPTON 0

Every so often, even a league as rich in excitement as the Premiership, with its unique brand of free-flowing and action-packed football, produces a game capable of sending all but the most ardent of supporters into a state of slumber - this was such a game.

The contest barely sparked into life throughout the entire 90 minutes, with a pre-match appearance from double Olympic gold medallist Kelly Holmes the only highlight on a miserable evening.

Charlton's lacklustre performance was all the more surprising in light of the fact that they came into this match having won both of their two previous home fixtures. Southampton were clearly wary of the potential threat posed by the Addicks, and set their stall out to try and earn a point.

Swedish international Andreas Jakobsson, a £1m capture from Brondby, was handed a debut alongside fellow Scandinavian Claus Lundekvam at the heart of the visiting defence, as both managers opted for a conventional 4-4-2 formation.

The pace of Dennis Rommedahl threatened several times in a first half low on actual chances, though the winger always seemed to choose the wrong option when well-placed. At the other end, captain Dean Kiely was not called upon to make a save until the 44th minute, when he comfortably kept out a tame effort from James Beattie.

In fact, there was more activity during the half-time break, as Steve Wigley sent his troops out five minutes early to partake in a series of energetic passing exercises. The drills clearly had a positive effect, with Southampton taking charge of proceedings during the second period.

Having just survived their only scare of the evening, when Kevin Lisbie headed straight at Antti Niemi, the Saints enjoyed a dominant spell.

With just over an hour played, Rory Delap's acrobatic effort was brilliantly turned over the bar by his former international teammate Kiely. Moments later, Lundekvam somehow failed to make decent contact with a close-range header from a corner.

The 75th-minute replacement of Rommedahl with the more defensively-minded Talal El Karkouri illustrated that Charlton were on the back foot. The visitors even felt confident enough to introduce a third striker, Peter Crouch, as they unsuccessfully looked to steal a late winner.

Jonathan Fortune gets to grips with Kevin Phillips

"I've criticised our defending, and rightly so over the last couple of away trips, but tonight it probably saved us a point."

Alan Curbishley

PREMIERSHIP MILESTONE

Andreas Jakobsson made his Premiership debut

"The players worked really hard, made more chances and I really think we could have nicked it."

Steve Wigley

PREMIERSHIP FIXTURE HISTORY

Pl: 6 Draws: 2	Wins	Goals	Yellow	Red
Arsenal	4	13	7	0
Bolton Wanderers	0	7	9	2

STARTING LINE-UPS

Arsenal subs: Edu, Bergkamp, Clichy, Almunia, Hoyte

Bolton subs: Pedersen, Ferdinand, Hierro, Oakes, Barness

EVENT LINE

31 Goal **Henry (Open Play)**

43 Yellow card Campo (Foul)

HALF TIME 1 - 0

55 Substitution Davies (Off) Pedersen (On)

55 Substitution Diouf (Off) Ferdinand (On)

63 Goal Jaidi (Corner)

66 Goal **Pires (Indirect Free Kick)**

67 Substitution **Gilberto (Off) Edu (On)**

70 Substitution **Reyes (Off) Bergkamp (On)**

75 Substitution Campo (Off) Hierro (On)

79 Yellow card Ferdinand (Foul)

80 Yellow card Gardner (Foul)

82 Substitution **Pires (Off) Clichy (On)**

84 Yellow card **Lauren (Foul)**

85 Goal Pedersen (Indirect Free Kick)

FULL TIME 2 - 2

STATISTICS

Season	Fixture (Arsenal)		Fixture (Bolton)	Season
59	6	Shots On Target	5	41
28	5	Shots Off Target	3	30
3	0	Hit Woodwork	1	1
14	2	Caught Offside	4	14
36	3	Corners	8	36
62	13	Fouls	17	85
60%	60%	Possession	40%	47%

LEAGUE STANDINGS

Position (pos before)		W	D	L	F	A	Pts
1 (1)	Arsenal	5	1	0	21	7	16
3 (3)	Bolton W	3	2	1	11	8	11

Saturday 18th September 2004 | Venue: **Highbury** | Attendance: **37,010** | Referee: **P.Dowd**

ARSENAL 2 BOLTON WANDERERS 2

Arsenal's perfect start to the season came to an end as gutsy Bolton twice came from behind to earn a share of the spoils at Highbury.

Henrik Pedersen's trickling effort five minutes from the end cancelled out a Robert Pires goal, after Radhi Jaidi's powerful 63rd-minute header had equalised Thierry Henry's first half strike.

Both sides sprung surprises in attack, Arsene Wenger electing to name Dennis Bergkamp as a substitute, while El-Hadji Diouf made his first start for the Trotters on the left.

There was a fairly even opening to the game. Kevin Nolan fired narrowly wide from 30 yards at one end, while Jaidi made last-ditch blocks from both Jose Antonio Reyes and Pires to keep out the Gunners.

As the half wore on, the Londoners increased the tempo. Jussi Jaaskelainen was forced to make a save from point-blank range, before Henry made a 31st-minute breakthrough.

Patrick Vieira was the architect, winning possession in midfield before feeding his teammate in the inside left channel. Seconds later the ball was in the back of the net, a clinical left-foot finish from 15 yards finding the bottom right-hand corner.

Further chances were wasted by the home side, before Sam Allardyce made a double substitution that changed the course of the game. Henrik Pedersen and Les Ferdinand arrived in the 55th minute, bringing with them a greater aerial potency.

Within 10 minutes, Wanderers were level. Tunisian centre-back Jaidi powered home a close-range header from Jay-Jay Okocha's right-wing corner, as the new arrivals deflected some defensive attention in the box.

The effort appeared wasted, however, as Pires restored Arsenal's advantage in the 66th minute. Freddie Ljungberg did all the hard work, beating Ricardo Gardner down the right and laying on a simple chance.

The Swede then had a chance to seal the game himself with a near-post header that flew inches over the crossbar. It was to prove a costly miss, as Pedersen promptly netted an equaliser.

A long free-kick was flicked on by Ferdinand, and the Dane somehow managed to squeeze a left-foot finish through a sea of bodies and into the bottom right-hand corner of the net.

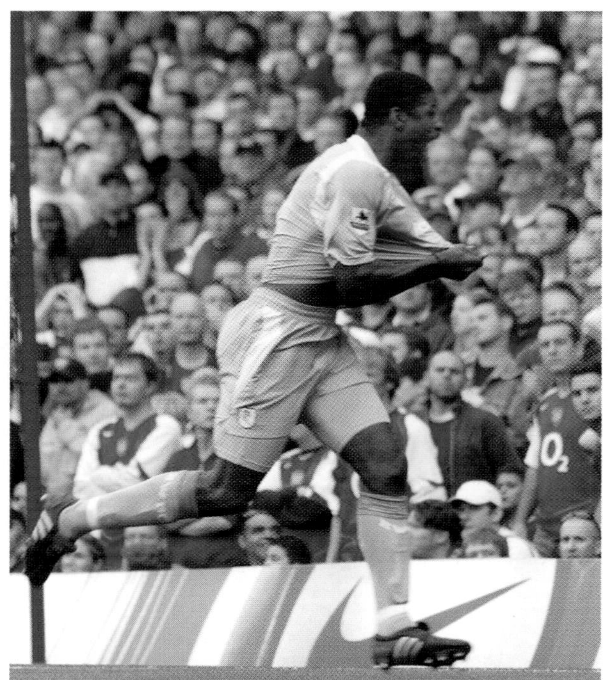

Radhi Jaidi celebrates after equalising with a majestic header

"Sam has done well. Bolton play a direct style and their players all know what they have to do."

Arsene Wenger

"Radhi is becoming a prominent and dominant figure in the centre of defence."

Sam Allardyce

PREMIERSHIP MILESTONE

Radhi Jaidi scored his first Premiership goal

Saturday 18th September 2004	Venue: St Andrew's	Attendance: 27,400	Referee: U.D.Rennie

PREMIERSHIP FIXTURE HISTORY

Pl: 3 Draws: 2	Wins	Goals	Yellow cards	Red cards
Birmingham City	0	3	7	2
Charlton Athletic	1	4	7	0

STARTING LINE-UPS

Dunn, Yorke, Bennett, Martin Taylor, Clemence

Euell, Rommedahl, Andersen, Jeffers, Konchesky

EVENT LINE

HALF TIME 0 - 0

49 Young (Open Play)

57 **Johnson (2nd Bookable Offence)**

61 **Cunningham (Off) Yorke (On)**

61 **Morrison (Off) Dunn (On)**

64 Kishishev (Handball)

68 **Yorke (Corner)**

75 Lisbie (Off) Euell (On)

76 El Karkouri (Off) Rommedahl (On)

84 **Savage (Ung.Conduct)**

85 **Gronkjaer (Ung.Conduct)**

85 Hreidarsson (Ung.Conduct)

FULL TIME 1 - 1

STATISTICS

Season	Fixture		Fixture	Season
22	2	Shots On Target	1	30
27	2	Shots Off Target	1	21
1	0	Hit Woodwork	0	2
13	4	Caught Offside	3	16
37	12	Corners	3	28
82	12	Fouls	16	70
52%	57%	Possession	43%	45%

LEAGUE STANDINGS

Position (pos before)	W	D	L	F	A	Pts
14 (14) Birmingham C	1	2	3	4	6	5
8 (10) Charlton Ath	2	2	2	7	10	8

Danny Murphy beats Robbie Savage to the ball

"For me, Dwight Yorke is going to be a big addition to our ranks, and he proved that today."

Steve Bruce

PREMIERSHIP MILESTONE

Dwight Yorke scored his first Premiership goal for Birmingham

PREMIERSHIP MILESTONE

50 Matthew Upson made his 50th Premiership appearance for Birmingham

PREMIERSHIP MILESTONE

100 Damien Johnson made his 100th Premiership appearance

"I make no apologies for stifling Birmingham after conceding four goals in each of our previous two away games."

Alan Curbishley

BIRMINGHAM CITY 1 CHARLTON ATHLETIC 1

This encounter served to demonstrate that football is indeed 'a funny old game', as 10-man Birmingham battled back from a goal down to earn a point against Charlton.

A tepid first half owed much to the solidity of Alan Curbishley's side. Having shipped eight goals in just two games on their travels, the Londoners understandably fielded a midfield more suited to going backwards than forwards.

Bryan Hughes, a summer arrival from St Andrew's, made his first start for the Addicks on the left of midfield. Having turned down the offer of a new contract in order to make his move, the returning player was not warmly received. This less-than-friendly welcome extended to the pitch, as Damien Johnson was cautioned for catching his former teammate with a high tackle.

While Charlton had reason to stifle the game, Steve Bruce's side rarely looked capable of producing the level of invention needed to make a breakthrough. Instead, they resorted to hitting hopeful long balls in the direction of Emile Heskey, with few chances stemming from this uncultured approach.

Frustration then turned to anxiety for the home side early in the second half. Visiting full-back Luke Young was on hand to capitalise on a rare mistake from Maik Taylor in the 49th minute, tapping home from close range after the goalkeeper had failed to gather Jonatan Johansson's low ball in from the right.

Things then went from bad to worse for Birmingham as they were reduced to ten men in the 57th minute. A swift counter-attack was abruptly ended by a trip from Johnson in the centre-circle, and the midfielder did not hang around to see referee Uriah Rennie show him a second yellow card.

Bizarrely, the dismissal seemed to have a positive effect on the West Midlands side. With 68 minutes on the clock, Dwight Yorke began to repay some of the faith shown in him by his new boss, coming off the bench to head home Muzzy Izzet's right-wing corner.

Although Jason Euell went close for Charlton, it was the home team that finished the stronger. Questions must therefore be asked in the dressing room as to why they only began to perform when faced with adversity.

PREMIERSHIP FIXTURE HISTORY

Pl: 2 Draws: 0	Wins	⚽	Yellow	Red
Blackburn Rovers	1	2	0	0
Portsmouth	1	2	3	0

STARTING LINE-UPS

Blackburn Rovers: Friedel; Neill, Short, Matteo, Gray; Emerton, Ferguson (c), Flitcroft, Pedersen; Stead, Dickov

Portsmouth: Fuller, Yakubu; Berkovic; Berger, Faye, Quashie (c); Unsworth, Stefanovic, Primus, Griffin; Hislop

Subs (Blackburn): Amoruso, Jansen, Bothroyd, Enckelman, Tugay

Subs (Portsmouth): Stone, Kamara, Ashdown, Taylor, Cisse

EVENT LINE

35 Berkovic (Off) Stone (On)

41 **Short (Off) Amoruso (On)**

HALF TIME 0 - 0

55 Griffin (Foul)

58 **Pedersen (Off) Jansen (On)**

64 **Stead (Off) Bothroyd (On)**

75 **Jansen (Open Play)**

76 Berger (Off) Kamara (On)

82 Stefanovic (Foul)

86 Fuller (Ung.Conduct)

FULL TIME 1 - 0

STATISTICS

Season	Fixture		Fixture	Season
18	**3**	Shots On Target	**2**	**34**
33	**10**	Shots Off Target	**4**	**27**
0	**0**	Hit Woodwork	**0**	**0**
23	**1**	Caught Offside	**2**	**14**
37	**13**	Corners	**4**	**31**
109	**13**	Fouls	**15**	**65**
46%	**60%**	Possession	**40%**	**48%**

LEAGUE STANDINGS

Position (pos before)	W	D	L	F	A	Pts
16 (19) Blackburn R	**1**	**2**	**3**	**5**	**11**	**5**
11 (9) Portsmouth	**2**	**1**	**2**	**9**	**8**	**7**

Saturday 18th September 2004 | Venue: **Ewood Park** | Attendance: **20,647** | Referee: **M.Clattenburg**

BLACKBURN ROVERS 1 PORTSMOUTH 0

Having transformed the fortunes of Wales during his five-year tenure, new Blackburn boss Mark Hughes made a dream start to his career in club management.

A tight game was settled by Matt Jansen, a player left out in the cold towards the end of the Graeme Souness regime, who came off the bench to net a 75th-minute winner.

Hughes had started with the same XI that went down 3-0 at Newcastle the previous saturday, adopting a policy that everyone could make a fresh start under his leadership. Portsmouth had enjoyed one of their two away successes last season at Ewood Park, and came into the game on the back of two victories.

The opening 45 minutes were as notable for injuries to Eyal Berkovic and Craig Short as for any of the football that took place. Captain Barry Ferguson went closest for Rovers, while Ricardo Fuller caused moments of panic in the home defence.

Blackburn stepped up a gear after the break, aided by the non-stop endeavour of Paul Dickov and galloping forward forays of Brett Emerton. The diminutive Scottish striker almost broke the deadlock after Shaka Hislop had saved Lorenzo Amoruso's fiercely-struck free-kick, but could not quite convert the rebound.

Andy Griffin was booked for a terrible looking challenge, before Jansen was handed his first appearance of the campaign in the 58th minute. The newcomer was off target shortly after his introduction, as was Aiyegbeni Yakubu when shaking off the attentions of Dominic Matteo soon afterwards.

The Nigerian was made to pay for that miss, as Jansen lit up proceedings 15 minutes from time. Receiving the ball from a marauding Lucas Neill just inside the area, the striker swivelled before dispatching a rapier-like left-foot drive beyond the despairing right hand of Hislop.

Sealing the points was far from a formality after the goal, with referee Mark Clattenburg lending a major helping hand. With four minutes remaining, the official chose to caution Fuller for diving after the striker had been blatantly bundled over in the box by an over-zealous Brad Friedel. Perhaps a change of manager had brought a change of luck?

Patrik Berger and Jonathan Stead go foot-to-foot

"We wanted three points from this game, and it was important to make an immediate impact."
Mark Hughes

"It was a nailed-on penalty. The referee has made a mistake, but we can't do anything to change the result now."
Harry Redknapp on Ricardo Fuller's caution for diving in the box

PREMIERSHIP FIXTURE HISTORY

Pl: 3 Draws: 1	Wins	Goals	Yellow	Red
Crystal Palace	1	3	3	0
Manchester City	1	3	2	0

STARTING LINE-UPS

Kolkka, Ventola, Watson, Kiraly, Powell

Jihai, Waterreus, Bosvelt, Flood, Fowler

EVENT LINE

16 Yellow card Sibierski (Foul)

35 Yellow card **Hall (Foul)**

43 Yellow card Distin (Foul)

HALF TIME 0 - 0

55 Goal Anelka (Corner)

58 Yellow card **Hughes (Foul)**

60 Substitution **Derry (Off) Ventola (On)**

60 Substitution **Torghelle (Off) Kolkka (On)**

64 Goal Anelka (Penalty)

70 Substitution **Riihilahti (Off) Watson (On)**

77 Goal **Johnson (Penalty)**

88 Substitution Macken (Off) Jihai (On)

FULL TIME 1 - 2

STATISTICS

Season	Fixture (Crystal Palace)		Fixture (Manchester City)	Season
21	2	Shots On Target	11	35
26	2	Shots Off Target	4	32
1	0	Hit Woodwork	1	1
12	5	Caught Offside	7	19
29	2	Corners	7	39
89	16	Fouls	16	86
44%	48%	Possession	52%	46%

LEAGUE STANDINGS

Position (pos before)	W	D	L	F	A	Pts
20 (20) Crystal Palace	0	1	5	5	13	1
10 (13) Man City	2	1	3	8	6	7

Saturday 18th September 2004 | Venue: **Selhurst Park** | Attendance: **25,052** | Referee: **M.Atkinson**

CRYSTAL PALACE 1 MANCHESTER CITY 2

A second half double from striker Nicolas Anelka secured a 2-1 victory over Crystal Palace at Selhurst Park and eased the pressure on beleaguered City boss Kevin Keegan.

Pre-match murmurings suggested that the former England boss faced the sack if his side lost this fixture. Yet come the final whistle, the North-West side had moved into the top 10.

The early exchanges were far from encouraging for the visitors. Iain Dowie's side began brightly and should have taken the lead when Hungarian Sandor Torghelle somehow failed to connect with Wayne Routledge's inviting low cross.

If Palace were unlucky on this occasion, they enjoyed an enormous slice of good fortune soon afterwards. When Anelka teed up teammate Antoine Sibierski there appeared to be just one outcome, only for Jonathan Macken to inadvertently block the Frenchman's effort on the goal line.

The tide had turned, with City pouring forward at every opportunity. The only surprise was that the visitors failed to turn their superiority into goals, with Macken particularly wasteful.

However, Keegan's men took just 10 minutes of the second period to find the net. The home side failed to deal with Anelka's corner from the left, enabling the striker to sneak unnoticed into the area before dispatching a crisp 15-yard drive into the far-right bottom corner.

Nine minutes later, the Frenchman extended his team's advantage from the penalty spot. The awarding of the kick was very dubious, Sean Wright-Phillips tumbling under the slightest of contact from Danny Granville, but Anelka brushed aside the protestations to all but secure a much-needed win.

Things were evened out on the penalty front by debutant top-flight referee Martin Atkinson, though on this occasion his decision seemed justified as substitute Nicola Ventola was clumsily upended following a burrowing run. Andy Johnson made light of a miss from 12 yards in his last outing, to fire home what ultimately proved to be a 77th-minute consolation.

Although the margin of victory should have been greater, it was the three points that mattered most to a relieved Manchester City manager.

Richard Dunne and Andy Johnson share a painful collision

"We worked very hard and showed great endeavour. We need to keep our togetherness and try to produce a little more quality."

Crystal Palace Assistant Manager Kit Symons

PREMIERSHIP MILESTONE

Ben Watson made his Premiership debut

"If there were any cracks in our armour, then they would have been exposed here at Selhurst Park today."

Kevin Keegan on rumours of dressing-room unrest

PREMIERSHIP FIXTURE HISTORY

Pl: **4** Draws: **2**

	Wins	Goals	Yellow	Red
Norwich City	1	3	2	0
Aston Villa	1	3	1	0

STARTING LINE-UPS

Norwich City: Green; Edworthy, Fleming, Charlton, Drury (c); Francis, Safri, Holt; Bentley; Doherty, Huckerby

Aston Villa: Vassell, Cole; Barry, Hitzlsperger, McCann, Solano; Samuel, Mellberg (c), Delaney, De la Cruz; Sorensen

Substitutes (Norwich City): McVeigh, McKenzie, Jonson, Ward, Helveg

Substitutes (Aston Villa): Davis, Angel, Postma, L.Moore, Whittingham

EVENT LINE

38 Yellow card **Safri (Foul)**

HALF TIME 0 - 0

57 Substitution Cole (Off) Angel (On)

57 Substitution Solano (Off) Davis (On)

63 Yellow card Delaney (Foul)

77 Substitution **Safri (Off) McVeigh (On)**

78 Substitution Hitzlsperger (Off) Whittingham (On)

80 Substitution **Bentley (Off) McKenzie (On)**

89 Substitution **Doherty (Off) Jonson (On)**

FULL TIME 0 - 0

STATISTICS

Season	Fixture (Norwich)		Fixture (Villa)	Season
27	3	Shots On Target	9	41
33	11	Shots Off Target	9	37
1	0	Hit Woodwork	0	2
28	3	Caught Offside	3	13
27	1	Corners	6	45
77	8	Fouls	12	92
47%	56%	Possession	44%	49%

LEAGUE STANDINGS

Position (pos before)	W	D	L	F	A	Pts
19 (17) Norwich C	0	4	2	5	9	4
7 (7) Aston Villa	2	3	1	7	6	9

Saturday 18th September 2004 | Venue: **Carrow Road** | Attendance: **23,805** | Referee: **B.Knight**

NORWICH CITY 0 ASTON VILLA 0

Norwich remained without a Premiership victory to their name after drawing 0-0 for the second time in a week.

Nigel Worthington kept faith with both the starting XI and midfield diamond formation that had served his team so well at Tottenham, while opposite number David O'Leary reverted back to a traditional 4-4-2 shape.

The game flowed from end to end from the outset. Nolberto Solano saw a shot deflected away for a corner, before Gary Holt fired over from Darren Huckerby's pass. Darius Vassell and Carlton Cole were both wasteful for Villa, while David Bentley almost embarrassed Thomas Sorensen with a clever chip.

Chances continued to come thick and fast, with the best of them falling to Cole. The on-loan Chelsea striker found himself in behind the home defence, only to be denied by a smothering save from the spritely Robert Green. The goalkeeper also did well to beat away a fierce Thomas Hitzlsperger drive in a highly entertaining opening period.

Events continued in the same vain after the break, with Huckerby keeping the Villa defence on their toes. The former Coventry City forward made several meandering runs, the first of which ended with a superbly timed tackle by Mark Delaney.

Though the Canaries were more than matching their opponents in most areas, it was noticeable how the visitors rarely wasted an opportunity to make Green earn his money. This was in stark contrast to the home side, whose efforts were wayward more often than not.

A 74th-minute Gary Doherty shot finally warmed the palms of Sorensen as Worthington's men sensed a chance of victory. Referee Barry Knight waved away a Huckerby penalty appeal, before Norwich were almost punished for becoming too cavalier.

Gavin McCann missed by inches with a header, and then young debutant Steven Davis forced Green into a spectacular reflex stop.

In the end, a draw was probably a fair result. Though Villa registered three times as many shots on target as their East Anglian opponents, the Premiership newcomers enjoyed a greater share of possession.

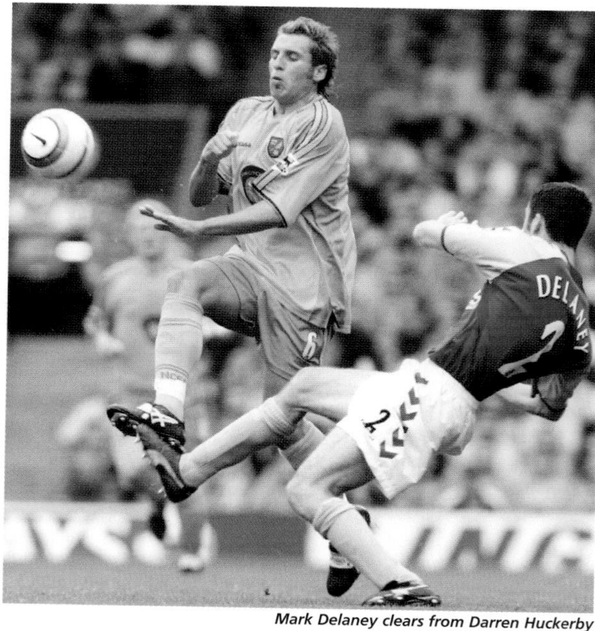

Mark Delaney clears from Darren Huckerby

"We are enjoying what we are doing. If we keep playing how we are playing the results will come."

Nigel Worthington

"I don't think either team deserved to win. It would have been unfair on Norwich if we had won, given what they put into the game."

Aston Villa Assistant Manager Roy Aitken

PREMIERSHIP MILESTONE

150 Gavin McCann made his 150th Premiership appearance

PREMIERSHIP MILESTONE

Steven Davis made his Premiership debut

PREMIERSHIP FIXTURE HISTORY

Pl: 2 Draws: 1	Wins	⚽	Yellow	Red
West Bromwich Albion	1	2	6	1
Fulham	0	1	8	2

STARTING LINE-UPS

West Brom: Kuszczak; Scimeca, Purse (c), Gaardsoe, Robinson; Koumas, Johnson, Clement, Greening; Kanu, Earnshaw

Fulham: Cole, John; Boa Morte, Pembridge, Diop, Legwinski (c); Green, Pearce, Knight, Volz; van der Sar

West Brom subs: Albrechtsen, Dyer, Gera, Murphy, Horsfield

Fulham subs: Radzinski, Crossley, Goma, Malbranque, McBride

EVENT LINE

Min	Event
25	Substitution: **Robinson (Off) Albrechtsen (On)**
27	Yellow: **Purse (Foul)**
29	Yellow: John (Dissent)
30	Yellow: van der Sar (Ung.Conduct)
43	Yellow: Green (Foul)
	HALF TIME 0 - 0
57	Substitution: John (Off) Radzinski (On)
61	Red: Diop (Violent Conduct)
62	Yellow: Knight (Dissent)
63	Yellow: Legwinski (Foul)
66	Substitution: **Johnson (Off) Dyer (On)**
72	Substitution: **Albrechtsen (Off) Gera (On)**
72	Goal: Cole (Open Play)
79	Yellow: **Clement (Ung.Conduct)**
84	Red: **Clement (Foul)**
85	Red: Cole (Violent Conduct)
88	Goal: **Kanu (Corner)**
	FULL TIME 1 - 1

STATISTICS

Season	Fixture (West Brom)		Fixture (Fulham)	Season
27	5	Shots On Target	3	34
26	4	Shots Off Target	6	29
1	1	Hit Woodwork	0	2
24	4	Caught Offside	1	16
44	11	Corners	9	39
78	9	Fouls	10	68
48%	49%	Possession	51%	50%

LEAGUE STANDINGS

Position (pos before)	W	D	L	F	A	Pts
18 (18) West Brom	0	4	2	5	9	4
15 (16) Fulham	1	2	3	7	11	5

Saturday 18th September 2004 | Venue: **The Hawthorns** | Attendance: **24,128** | Referee: **M.L.Dean**

WEST BROM 1 FULHAM 1

Andy Cole celebrates opening the scoring

"That is two points lost as far as I'm concerned."
Gary Megson

PREMIERSHIP MILESTONE
Nwankwo Kanu scored his first Premiership goal in the colours of West Bromwich Albion

PREMIERSHIP MILESTONE
Tomasz Kuszczak made his Premiership debut

Andy Cole and Pape Bouba Diop both reacted badly. But when you have been head-butted and stamped on, how are you expected to react?"
Chris Coleman

PREMIERSHIP MILESTONE
200 Mark Pembridge made his 200th Premiership appearance

Having been involved in the infamous 'Battle of Bramall Lane' in their 2001-02 promotion season, the Baggies played out a similarly bad-tempered affair against Fulham.

All the action came in an explosive last half-hour, in which there were two goals and three straight red cards. Nwankwo Kanu's 88th-minute leveller, his first for the club, cancelled out Andy Cole's 72nd-minute strike, while Cole himself joined Pape Bouba Diop and Neil Clement in being sent for an early bath.

The Cottagers had enjoyed some heated battles with West Brom's near-neighbours Birmingham City in recent seasons, and seemed to have mistaken Gary Megson's side for their West Midlands rivals.

In footballing terms, the opening period was very entertaining. Tomasz Kuszczak, making his debut in the Albion goal, nervously parried a Diop header, while Edwin van der Sar kept out point-blank aerial efforts from both Robert Earnshaw and Kanu.

The best chance of the half fell to the home team, as referee Mike Dean awarded them a 29th-minute penalty. Moritz Volz was adjudged to have handled in the box, but Earnshaw was clearly distracted by van der Sar's delaying tactics and blazed the spot-kick high over the bar. The woodwork then came to the rescue of Chris Coleman's side, Kanu the unlucky man, as the first 45 minutes drew to a close.

The fireworks began after 61 minutes, when Diop was dismissed for violent conduct. The Senegalese midfielder felt that Darren Purse had deliberately stamped on his foot, and reacted by angrily shoving the defender to the ground.

Bizarrely, 10-man Fulham then took a 72nd-minute lead, Cole steering the ball home after Adam Green had got in down the left. The Baggies desperately sought an equaliser, with Neil Clement justifiably cautioned for a blatant dive in the area.

Then, with six minutes remaining, Clement saw red for a professional foul. Heated words were exchanged with a few visiting players, before Cole got himself sent off for throwing a series of punches at the West Brom man.

After peace had been restored, Kanu ensured that the Albion faithful went home relatively happy by heading in Jason Koumas' 88th-minute near-post corner.

Sunday 19th September 2004	Venue: **Stamford Bridge**	Attendance: **42,246**	Referee: **M.A.Riley**

PREMIERSHIP FIXTURE HISTORY

Pl: **13** Draws: **5**	Wins	⚽	☐	■
Chelsea	8	26	15	0
Tottenham Hotspur	0	9	25	2

STARTING LINE-UPS

Chelsea: Cech; Ferreira, Carvalho, Terry (c), Bridge; Makelele; Tiago, Lampard; J.Cole; Gudjohnsen, Drogba

Tottenham Hotspur: Defoe, Keane; Atouba, Mendes, Redknapp (c), Davies; Edman, King, Naybet, Pamarot; Robinson

Chelsea subs: Duff, Kezman, Smertin, Pidgeley, Gallas

Tottenham subs: Brown, Kanoute, Keller, Gardner, Mabizela

EVENT LINE

HALF TIME 0 - 0

50 ☐ King (Foul)

66 **Cole J (Off) Duff (On)**

66 **Tiago (Off) Kezman (On)**

73 ☐ Redknapp (Foul)

74 Atouba (Off) Brown (On)

85 **Bridge (Off) Smertin (On)**

86 Defoe (Off) Kanoute (On)

90 ☐ **Smertin (Foul)**

FULL TIME 0 - 0

STATISTICS

Season	Fixture (Chelsea)		Fixture (Tottenham)	Season
38	8	Shots On Target	3	34
49	12	Shots Off Target	3	34
2	1	Hit Woodwork	0	2
22	8	Caught Offside	2	16
37	9	Corners	6	32
78	16	Fouls	13	84
55%	59%	Possession	41%	45%

LEAGUE STANDINGS

Position (pos before)		W	D	L	F	A	Pts
2 (2)	Chelsea	4	2	0	6	1	14
5 (6)	Tottenham H	2	4	0	4	2	10

CHELSEA 0
TOTTENHAM HOTSPUR 0

Tottenham once more failed to defeat Chelsea in the Premiership, though Jacques Santini's side were more than happy to leave Stamford Bridge with a point on this occasion.

Jose Mourinho's side mounted wave after wave of attacks, threatening to run up a cricket score, but were unable to penetrate a resolute Spurs rearguard. The result ensured that both clubs remained unbeaten, having conceded just three goals between them during the campaign.

The home team were quickly out of the blocks, forcing three corners in the early exchanges. With four minutes gone, Didier Drogba was denied by some alert goalkeeping from Paul Robinson. The visiting custodian rushed from his line to deny the former Marseille striker, before Tiago fired the loose ball high over the vacant goal from 25 yards.

Ledley King denied Eidur Gudjohnsen with a brilliant last-ditch tackle after 19 minutes, following good work from Joe Cole, and the Icelandic international then failed to hit the target with an eight-yard header.

Chelsea continued to stretch the opposition defence throughout the opening period, with Tiago, Gudjohnsen and Drogba all spurning decent chances. It wasn't until the 42nd minute, via a wayward Jamie Redknapp shot from distance, that Tottenham remotely threatened Petr Cech's goal.

The second half was a virtual carbon copy of the first, as Mourinho's men surged at Spurs from every conceivable angle. An audacious overhead effort from Drogba almost brought dividends on 50 minutes, but soon afterwards the visitors almost scored.

In what was to prove the only real threat to the Stamford Bridge side's goal, Robbie Keane somehow saw Cech claw away his point-blank range header. The summer import from Rennes had responded when called upon, and remained virtually untroubled thereafter as the match settled back into a familiar pattern.

Damien Duff and Mateja Kezman were introduced in the search for fresh attacking ideas, but it was midfield stalwart Frank Lampard who forced Robinson into a fantastic reflex save. The woodwork then came to Tottenham's rescue in the final 10 minutes, as Gudjohnsen's 20-yard effort struck a post.

The visitors then survived five minutes of injury time, clinging on desperately to a hard-earned point.

"They brought the bus, and they left the bus in front of the goal."
Jose Mourinho

"When we play against a good team we have to defend. We did have one chance, but Petr Cech made an international class save."
Jacques Santini

Joe Cole welcomes Erik Edman to English football

PREMIERSHIP FIXTURE HISTORY

Pl: 10 Draws: 3	Wins	⚽	☐	■
Everton	5	20	16	0
Middlesbrough	2	10	28	0

STARTING LINE-UPS

Ferguson, McFadden, Wright, Yobo, Naysmith

Doriva, Downing, Job, Nash, Cooper

EVENT LINE

25 ☐ **Kilbane (Foul)**

26 ☐ Boateng (Ung.Conduct)

HALF TIME 0 - 0

46 ⇄ Nemeth (Off) Doriva (On)

47 ⚽ **Bent (Open Play)**

50 ☐ Riggott (Foul)

57 ☐ Doriva (Foul)

59 ⇄ Viduka (Off) Job (On)

59 ⇄ Zenden (Off) Downing (On)

72 ☐ Parlour (Foul)

74 ⇄ **Bent (Off) Ferguson (On)**

81 ⇄ **Watson (Off) McFadden (On)**

FULL TIME 1 - 0

STATISTICS

Season	Fixture		Fixture	Season
36	9	Shots On Target	11	48
25	2	Shots Off Target	5	38
0	0	Hit Woodwork	0	0
20	4	Caught Offside	1	26
27	6	Corners	3	30
73	13	Fouls	12	82
48%	47%	Possession	53%	52%

LEAGUE STANDINGS

Position (pos before)		W	D	L	F	A	Pts
3 (5)	Everton	4	1	1	8	6	13
6 (4)	Middlesbrough	3	1	2	11	10	10

Sunday 19th September 2004 | Venue: **Goodison Park** | Attendance: **34,078** | Referee: **H.M.Webb**

EVERTON 1 MIDDLESBROUGH 0

A single Marcus Bent goal was enough to give Everton victory in this clash between two of the form teams in the Premiership.

Middlesbrough arrived at Goodison Park on the back of three league victories and a midweek win against Banik Ostrava on their debut in European competition. For their part, the Merseysiders had bounced back from an opening-day mauling by Arsenal, to collect 10 points from a possible 12.

Unfortunately, the game proved to be a battle of attrition, with neither side displaying the sort of quality needed to maintain a lofty position in the table.

David Moyes kept faith with the 4-5-1 formation that had served his team so well on recent trips to Manchester, while Steve McClaren fielded a very attacking looking line-up.

Right from the start, the match had an air of lethargy about it. Intricate passing moves were few and far between, though both goalkeepers had plenty of routine saves to make.

Only on one occasion, when Kevin Kilbane headed powerfully goalwards after 12 minutes, was Mark Schwarzer forced into producing a stop of real quality. At the other end, Nigel Martyn was relatively untroubled by a weak effort from Szilard Nemeth.

In fact, the most memorable moment of the opening period came when a strong aerial challenge by Kilbane led to a mass brawl. The visiting players were incensed, believing the Irishman had used his elbow, but referee Howard Webb deemed a yellow card to be sufficient punishment.

Having tested Schwarzer just prior to the interval, Bent broke the deadlock, with the help of a deflection, two minutes into the second half. The pacy frontman latched onto Leon Osman's long ball out of defence, poking a 15-yard effort beyond the onrushing goalkeeper from the inside left channel that may well have gone wide but for the left boot of a sliding Franck Queudrue.

Despite the introduction of both Stewart Downing and Joseph-Desire Job, Middlesbrough never looked likely to mount a fightback. Indeed, it was Everton substitute James McFadden who came closest to scoring, the Scot being superbly denied by Schwarzer.

Thomas Gravesen and George Boateng battle it out

"We've been pleased with the way our season has started. It's probably better than a lot of people expected, maybe even including myself."

David Moyes

PREMIERSHIP MILESTONE

25 Marcus Bent scored his 25th Premiership goal

"Thursday night was not just an extra game for us. It was the first ever European game at the Riverside Stadium, and was an emotional and physical drain on the players."

Steve McClaren

PREMIERSHIP FIXTURE HISTORY

Pl: 12 Draws: 3	Wins	Goals	Yellow	Red
Southampton	8	26	13	1
Newcastle United	1	15	18	0

STARTING LINE-UPS

Southampton: Niemi; Nilsson, Lundekvam, Jakobsson, Le Saux; Fernandes, Prutton, Delap, A.Svensson; Beattie (c), Phillips

Newcastle United: Kluivert, Shearer (c); Jenas, Bowyer, Butt, Bellamy; Bernard, Elliott, O'Brien, Carr; Given

Southampton subs: Crouch, Best, Blayney, Higginbotham, Telfer

Newcastle United subs: Milner, Harper, Hughes, Robert, Ambrose

EVENT LINE

38 Carr (Foul)

45 Prutton (Own Goal)

HALF TIME 0 - 1

48 Bowyer (Foul)

53 **Svensson A (Open Play)**

57 Carr (Indirect Free Kick)

59 Bellamy (Ung.Conduct)

67 **Phillips (Off) Crouch (On)**

67 Kluivert (Off) Milner (On)

76 **Svensson A (Off) Best (On)**

FULL TIME 1 - 2

STATISTICS

Season	Fixture (Southampton)		Fixture (Newcastle)	Season
28	6	Shots On Target	3	43
33	4	Shots Off Target	6	33
0	0	Hit Woodwork	0	0
15	4	Caught Offside	5	18
37	7	Corners	6	50
72	15	Fouls	17	78
49%	50%	Possession	50%	52%

LEAGUE STANDINGS

Position (pos before)	W	D	L	F	A	Pts
17 (17) Southampton	1	1	4	6	10	4
8 (13) Newcastle Utd	2	2	2	11	10	8

Sunday 19th September 2004 | Venue: **Friends Provident St Mary's Stadium** | Attendance: **30,709** | Referee: **C.J.Foy**

SOUTHAMPTON 1 NEWCASTLE UNITED 2

Newcastle celebrated a rare victory at Southampton, as Graeme Souness made a positive start to life in the black and white hot seat.

The Scot had already presided over one victory, against Hapoel Bnei Sakhnin in the UEFA Cup, and sprung a surprise by naming Patrick Kluivert, who scored both goals in that encounter, in his starting line-up. The Dutchman partnered Alan Shearer in attack, forcing Craig Bellamy to revert to a role on the right of midfield.

Graeme Le Saux was the only non-Scandinavian in a home defence that was under pressure from the first whistle. Midfielder David Prutton tracked back to good effect in the eighth minute, blocking a goalbound Lee Bowyer effort, before Alan Shearer somehow missed the target with a free header from a corner.

At the other end, winger Fabrice Fernandes was providing all the sparkle, and he tested Shay Given with a swerving long-range drive. The Frenchman was inspiring his colleagues, James Beattie dancing his way through a sea of legs before a timely block from Andy O'Brien kept him at bay.

The visitors' Irish centre-back then came close to netting his third goal in as many league games, heading narrowly wide from an Olivier Bernard free-kick. However, Newcastle did take the lead on the stroke of half-time.

A pacy break down the left ended when Bellamy's low centre was driven back across goal by Shearer and inadvertently turned into his own net by the recovering Prutton. The Magpies' captain claimed the goal, but his effort would not have gone in without a touch.

Southampton hit back eight minutes after the restart, Anders Svensson finishing smartly after Prutton's blocked shot had fallen to him in the box. Any joy was short-lived, however, as Stephen Carr won the game in the 57th minute.

The full-back was afforded far too much time and space when running onto a quick free-kick from Jermaine Jenas, and duly dispatched a swerving 25-yard effort that flew across goal and beyond the right hand of Antti Niemi.

The Saints huffed and puffed in search of an equaliser, but ultimately got what they deserved from the game - nothing.

Stephen Carr celebrates his goal with Jermaine Jenas

"There is a fine line between success and failure, and Carr's goal separated them today."
Steve Wigley

PREMIERSHIP MILESTONE
Leon Best made his Premiership debut

"I needed to play one or two players out of their preferred positions, but the most important thing was to get the three points."
Graeme Souness

PREMIERSHIP MILESTONE
Stephen Carr netted his first Premiership goal for Newcastle

PREMIERSHIP FIXTURE HISTORY

Pl: 13 Draws: 4	Wins	Goals	Yellow	Red
Manchester United	6	18	18	1
Liverpool	3	10	25	2

STARTING LINE-UPS

Smith, Ricardo, P.Neville, Fletcher, Kleberson

Hamann, Baros, Kirkland, Traore, Diao

EVENT LINE

20 Goal **Silvestre (Indirect Free Kick)**
39 Substitution Gerrard (Off) Hamann (On)
45 Yellow card Josemi (Handball)

HALF TIME 1 - 0

54 Goal O'Shea (Own Goal)
66 Goal **Silvestre (Corner)**
67 Substitution Cisse (Off) Baros (On)
71 Yellow card **Keane (Foul)**
77 Yellow card Alonso (Foul)
85 Substitution **Scholes (Off) Smith (On)**

FULL TIME 2 - 1

STATISTICS

Season	Fixture (Man Utd)		Fixture (Liverpool)	Season
44	9	Shots On Target	3	32
41	4	Shots Off Target	3	28
4	1	Hit Woodwork	0	0
15	2	Caught Offside	5	13
50	7	Corners	2	28
79	22	Fouls	15	58
53%	52%	Possession	48%	55%

LEAGUE STANDINGS

Position (pos before)	W	D	L	F	A	Pts
8 (13) Man Utd	2	3	1	7	6	9
12 (10) Liverpool	2	1	2	7	5	7

Monday 20th September 2004 | Venue: **Old Trafford** | Attendance: **67,857** | Referee: **G.Poll**

MANCHESTER UNITED 2 LIVERPOOL 1

Whilst all the pre-match talk centred on the return to action of Rio Ferdinand after an eight-month suspension, it was the inability of Liverpool's defenders to adjust to Rafael Benitez's newly-introduced 'zonal marking' system that was the major talking point afterwards.

Twice Mikael Silvestre was allowed to head home unchallenged from set-pieces, goals that sandwiched John O'Shea turning the ball into his own net in the 54th minute.

In fairness, United thoroughly deserved their victory. The home side were a class apart from the out-of-sorts Merseysiders, with Ferdinand imperiously dealing with any potential danger in a manner that suggested he had never been away.

Roy Keane was back to his dominant best in midfield, fitting on the day that a legendary former manager of his, Brian Clough, passed away. The Irishman's experience was complemented by the fearlessness of youth, as Portuguese starlet Cristiano Ronaldo delivered a mesmerising display on the right wing.

The former Sporting Lisbon player came closest to turning his team's early pressure into a goal, beating Jerzy Dudek with a powerful drive that came back off a post. Sir Alex Ferguson's side did take the lead, however, after 20 minutes.

Ryan Giggs flighted over an inswinging free-kick from the right, and Silvestre met the ball with a thumping header from six yards out. The Old Trafford outfit wasted further aerial chances to extend their advantage, before both Liverpool and England were dealt a severe injury blow as Steven Gerrard limped away from the action in the 39th minute.

Somehow, Benitez's side drew level early in the second half. Steve Finnan managed to connect with a deep free-kick from the left, turning the ball against the right leg of his international colleague O'Shea and into the back of the net.

Having forced their way back into the match, the visitors succumbed to a 66th-minute corner. Again it was Silvestre who was allowed a free run at Giggs' flag-kick, the Frenchman heading home what proved to be the winner.

Bar a spectacular 40-yard effort from Xabi Alonso, Roy Carroll was rarely tested in the remainder of the game.

Liverpool are made to pay for 'zonal marking'

"It is never easy to pick the game up mentally or physically because eight months out is a long time, but it was nice to get out there again and play."
Rio Ferdinand

PREMIERSHIP MILESTONE

100 Ruud van Nistelrooy and Jerzy Dudek both made their 100th Premiership appearance

PREMIERSHIP MILESTONE

The attendance of 67,857 was a Premiership record

"Xabi Alonso passed me the ball. I was going to turn but my foot stayed in the turf and I heard a crack in it."
Steven Gerrard

Saturday 25th September 2004 | Venue: **Villa Park** | Attendance: **34,843** | Referee: **M.Clattenburg**

ASTON VILLA 1 CRYSTAL PALACE 1

Aston Villa completed a clean sweep of draws against the newly-promoted teams, coming from a goal down to share the points with Crystal Palace.

Former Birmingham City striker Andy Johnson had put the Eagles in front early on, before fellow Englishman Lee Hendrie curled his side level before half-time.

Iain Dowie's side came into the game on the back of five straight league defeats, but had clearly been buoyed by a midweek Carling Cup success against Hartlepool United. It took just six minutes to turn that renewed confidence into something more tangible, as Johnson opened the scoring.

The Villa Park outfit had already survived one scare, Wayne Routledge seeing an effort cleared off the line, when the Londoners' lone striker raced onto a pass from Aki Riihilahti and sent a low left-foot finish back across Thomas Sorensen.

Premiership debutant Gabor Kiraly was barely called into action in the Palace goal during the opening half-hour, as his team produced an assured performance that suggested they would not remain at the bottom of the table for long.

When the equaliser did arrive, after 36 minutes, the visiting players could not be blamed. Collecting possession some 25 yards out, midfielder Hendrie bent an exquisite right-foot shot just inside the goalkeeper's left-hand upright. Referee Mark Clattenburg then booked the home hero for his over-exuberant celebrations.

David O'Leary's men would have been expected to push on from this point, and did finish the opening period strongly as Juan Pablo Angel was denied. However, it was Palace who shaded the game in the second half, with Johnson at the heart of all their good work.

Young midfielder Ben Watson was expertely denied by Sorensen, having been played in by the striker, before the Eagles' Bedford-born frontman headed agonisingly wide from close range. That was as near as either side came to stealing the points.

On this evidence, Aston Villa have much improving to do if they are to repeat the sixth place finish of last season. The West Midlanders appeared toothless in attack and always seemed vulnerable when Dowie's fast-improving outfit ran at them with pace.

Ben Watson challenges Gareth Barry

"A point was all we deserved on our performance. Palace operated their 4-5-1 system extremely well and we could not get to grips with them for long spells."

David O'Leary

"We were tremendous. Some of our football was fantastic and we could easily have won the game."

Iain Dowie

PREMIERSHIP MILESTONE

Gabor Kiraly, Tom Soares and Gonzalo Sorondo all made their Premiership debuts

PREMIERSHIP FIXTURE HISTORY

Pl: 4 Draws: 2	Wins	Goals	Yellow	Red
Aston Villa	2	8	4	0
Crystal Palace	0	3	4	0

STARTING LINE-UPS

Aston Villa: Sorensen; De la Cruz, Delaney, Mellberg (c), Samuel; Solano, Hendrie, McCann, Barry; Vassell, Angel

Crystal Palace: Kiraly; Granville, Popovic (c), Hall, Boyce; Kolkka, Watson, Hughes, Riihilahti, Routledge; Johnson

Aston Villa subs: Hitzlsperger, Cole, Whittingham, Postma, Berson

Crystal Palace subs: Sorondo, Soares, Speroni, Kaviedes, Torghelle

EVENT LINE

6 Goal Johnson (Open Play)
36 Goal **Hendrie (Open Play)**
37 Booking **Hendrie (Ung.Conduct)**
HALF TIME 1 - 1
55 Sub **Hendrie (Off) Hitzlsperger (On)**
61 Sub **Vassell (Off) Cole (On)**
66 Booking Boyce (Foul)
78 Sub Hall (Off) Sorondo (On)
81 Sub **Barry (Off) Whittingham (On)**
81 Sub Kolkka (Off) Soares (On)
88 Booking **Delaney (Foul)**
FULL TIME 1 - 1

STATISTICS

Season	Fixture	Aston Villa / Crystal Palace	Fixture	Season
46	5	Shots On Target	8	29
42	5	Shots Off Target	5	31
2	0	Hit Woodwork	0	1
15	2	Caught Offside	3	15
50	5	Corners	8	37
102	10	Fouls	15	104
49%	47%	Possession	53%	45%

LEAGUE STANDINGS

Position (pos before)		W	D	L	F	A	Pts
8 (7)	Aston Villa	2	4	1	8	7	10
20 (20)	Crystal Palace	0	2	5	6	14	2

PREMIERSHIP FIXTURE HISTORY

Pl: 3 Draws: 1	Wins	Goals	Yellow cards	Red cards
Bolton Wanderers	1	5	5	0
Birmingham City	1	4	5	0

STARTING LINE-UPS

Giannakopoulos, Ferdinand, Poole, Cesar, Hierro

Dunn, Gray, Vaesen, Yorke, Morrison

EVENT LINE

16 **Jaidi (Indirect Free Kick)**

27 Savage (Foul)

HALF TIME 1 - 0

49 Izzet (Indirect Free Kick)

57 **N'Gotty (Ung.Conduct)**

65 **Diouf (Off) Giannakopoulos (On)**

74 **Jaidi (Foul)**

77 Gronkjaer (Off) Dunn (On)

79 **Davies (Off) Ferdinand (On)**

88 Izzet (Off) Gray (On)

FULL TIME 1 - 1

STATISTICS

Season	Fixture (Bolton)		Fixture (Birmingham)	Season
53	12	Shots On Target	2	24
34	4	Shots Off Target	4	31
1	0	Hit Woodwork	0	1
15	1	Caught Offside	3	16
43	7	Corners	2	39
92	7	Fouls	18	100
48%	59%	Possession	41%	50%

LEAGUE STANDINGS

Position (pos before)		W	D	L	F	A	Pts
4 (4)	Bolton W	3	3	1	12	9	12
15 (14)	Birmingham C	1	3	3	5	7	6

Saturday 25th September 2004 | Venue: **Reebok Stadium** | Attendance: **23,692** | Referee: **R.Styles**

BOLTON WANDERERS 1 BIRMINGHAM CITY 1

Muzzy Izzet's first goal for Birmingham was enough to earn a point at the Reebok Stadium, after Tunisian Radhi Jaidi had fired the home side into an early lead.

All the pre-match talk centred around facial injuries to visiting manager Steve Bruce. The former Manchester United defender had been involved in an altercation outside his home in the early hours of the morning, and had the cuts to prove it.

On the pitch, Bruce decided to mirror Bolton's 4-5-1 formation, fielding Emile Heskey as a lone striker. Sam Allardyce was without his inspirational skipper Jay-Jay Okocha and handed the armband to the vastly experienced Gary Speed in his absence.

It was the men in white who began brightly, Henrik Pedersen narrowly failing to reach a dangerous cross and Ivan Campo testing Maik Taylor from distance. The pressure finally told after 16 minutes, as Jaidi followed up his goal at Highbury with an acrobatic right-foot strike following a free-kick.

Referee Rob Styles presented Wanderers with further set-piece opportunities, continually penalising Birmingham for niggly fouls. Robbie Savage was cautioned after 27 minutes, but seemed immune to a second yellow card in spite of some robust challenges.

For all their first half dominance, the home side appeared to lack a cutting edge. Just four minutes after the restart, however, the visitors aptly demonstrated how to find the back of the net.

After Heskey had missed the target from close range, the West Midlanders were awarded a free-kick. The ball was pumped forward and Izzet arrived on cue to drill home off the underside of the crossbar from 15 yards after Jesper Gronkjaer's touch inside.

An offside flag ruled out Pedersen's immediate riposte, while Speed and Stylianos Giannakopoulos both flashed efforts wide.

Birmingham grew in confidence as the game progressed, and should really have snatched an undeserved three points in injury time. Julian Gray somehow contrived to send a shot inches the wrong side of an upright when it seemed easier to score.

As it was, a draw was harsh enough on Bolton. The Trotters had dominated possession, but failed to make the most of their 12 shots on target.

"Their goal really disappointed me, we simply switched off."
Sam Allardyce

"We had more shots on goal in the opening three minutes of the second half than during the entire first period."
Steve Bruce

PREMIERSHIP MILESTONE

Muzzy Izzet scored his first Premiership goal for Birmingham

Kenny Cunningham tries to stop El-Hadji Diouf

PREMIERSHIP FIXTURE HISTORY

Pl: 4 Draws: 1	Wins	Goals	Yellow	Red
Fulham	3	7	1	0
Southampton	0	3	5	0

STARTING LINE-UPS

John, McKinlay, Crossley, Goma, Rehman

McCann, Blayney, Higginbotham, Kenton, Crouch

EVENT LINE

24 **Radzinski (Open Play)**

HALF TIME 1 - 0

61 Svensson A (Off) McCann (On)

72 **Radzinski (Off) John (On)**

85 **Malbranque (Off) McKinlay (On)**

87 McCann (Foul)

FULL TIME 1 - 0

STATISTICS

Season	Fixture		Fixture	Season
40	6	Shots On Target	5	33
34	5	Shots Off Target	10	43
2	0	Hit Woodwork	0	0
21	5	Caught Offside	1	16
44	5	Corners	4	41
79	11	Fouls	22	94
50%	45%	Possession	55%	50%

LEAGUE STANDINGS

Position (pos before)	W	D	L	F	A	Pts
11 (15) Fulham	2	2	3	8	11	8
17 (17) Southampton	1	1	5	6	11	4

Saturday 25th September 2004 | Venue: **Craven Cottage** | Attendance: **19,237** | Referee: **G.Poll**

Steed Malbranque and Graeme Le Saux invent a new dance

"Maybe we didn't deserve to win, and it could have been a different result, but I'm pleased to be sitting here with three points in the bag after what was a mediocre performance."

Chris Coleman

PREMIERSHIP MILESTONE

100 Edwin van der Sar made his 100th Premiership appearance

PREMIERSHIP MILESTONE

Tomasz Radzinski scored his first Premiership goal for Fulham

PREMIERSHIP MILESTONE

Billy McKinlay made his first Premiership appearance for Fulham

"We created enough chances to have won, so we are disappointed not to have got anything."

Steve Wigley

FULHAM 1 SOUTHAMPTON 0

Fulham put the controversy of their last two league games behind them, as they secured an important 1-0 victory against fellow-strugglers Southampton at Craven Cottage.

Canadian Tomasz Radzinski, a summer arrival from Everton, followed up his midweek Carling Cup brace at Boston United with the only goal of the contest after 24 minutes. The striker, deputising for the suspended Andy Cole, met Luis Boa Morte's left-wing centre with a neat near-post header from close range.

It was an inspired moment in what was otherwise a fairly insipid affair. The visitors had the best of the chances, but rarely looked to have the confidence in front of goal to capitalise upon them. Even when they did do everything right, the giant frame of Edwin van der Sar was on hand to keep them at bay.

The South Coast side's first meaningful opening arrived after 12 minutes, James Beattie glancing wide a header from Fabrice Fernandes' cross. A worse miss was to follow from the former England striker just after Radzinski had struck, as he headed over from close range a Graeme Le Saux cross that had goal written all over it.

Fulham emerged after the interval with renewed vigour, and forced Antti Niemi in the Southampton goal to earn his money. However, failure to build on their advantage seemed to have an adverse effect on the Londoners, and they retreated into their shells.

The home team seemed to forget the art of defending, allowing Steve Wigley's charges three presentable opportunities to grab at least a point.

After 75 minutes, van der Sar spectacularly parried away a Beattie volley. The Dutch custodian then held a stinging drive from Kevin Phillips, before brilliantly denying Rory Delap with his legs from point-blank range in the final five minutes.

The final whistle was greeted with sighs of relief amongst the Craven Cottage faithful. Whilst the performance wasn't pretty, the result was all-important.

For Southampton, the situation becomes bleaker by the week. With just one point from five games under Wigley's stewardship, things look set for a winter of discontent.

PREMIERSHIP FIXTURE HISTORY

Pl: 4	Draws: 0	Wins	Goals	Yellow cards	Red cards
Liverpool		3	11	2	0
Norwich City		1	2	6	0

Saturday 25th September 2004 | Venue: **Anfield** | Attendance: **43,152** | Referee: **A.G.Wiley**

LIVERPOOL 3 NORWICH CITY 0

"I was so pleased with the performance, but I would have been happier if we'd scored all our chances in the first half."

Rafael Benitez

PREMIERSHIP MILESTONE

50 Djimi Traore made his 50th Premiership appearance

PREMIERSHIP MILESTONE

150 Dietmar Hamann made his 150th Premiership appearance for Liverpool

"We've got to hand it to Liverpool, they were the better quality side on the day. But I told the lads this loss is part of a learning curve and will do us no harm."

Nigel Worthington

STARTING LINE-UPS

Diao, Traore, Biscan, Kirkland, Josemi

Bentley, McKenzie, Jonson, Ward, Helveg

EVENT LINE

23 **Baros (Open Play)**

26 **Garcia (Open Play)**

HALF TIME 2 - 0

46 Doherty (Off) McKenzie (On)

46 Safri (Off) Bentley (On)

49 **Hamann (Foul)**

64 **Cisse (Indirect Free Kick)**

65 **Alonso (Off) Diao (On)**

71 **Cisse (Off) Traore (On)**

75 McVeigh (Off) Jonson (On)

77 **Warnock (Off) Biscan (On)**

FULL TIME 3 - 0

STATISTICS

Season	Fixture		Fixture	Season
44	12	Shots On Target	1	28
36	8	Shots Off Target	1	34
0	0	Hit Woodwork	0	1
16	3	Caught Offside	1	29
32	4	Corners	2	29
68	10	Fouls	12	89
55%	59%	Possession	41%	46%

LEAGUE STANDINGS

Position (pos before)	W	D	L	F	A	Pts
7 (12) Liverpool	3	1	2	10	5	10
19 (18) Norwich C	0	4	3	5	12	4

Milan Baros opens the scoring

Rafael Benitez's side turned on the style to maintain their 100% winning Premiership record at Anfield.

The three-goal deficit flattered a Norwich team that failed to score for the third consecutive league game, though there was an element of fortune about the first two strikes.

Any fears amongst home supporters that their Spanish manager had so far failed to implement his footballing philosophy were brushed aside in an electrifying first half-hour. The absence of the injured Steven Gerrard was barely noticeable, as Xabi Alonso raised his game with an array of crisp passes rarely seen in recent seasons.

The ball was a friend to Liverpool in the early exchanges, though Djibril Cisse didn't think so when he headed over after a mistake from Robert Green. It was a surprise that a goal didn't arrive until the 23rd minute, when Milan Baros struck.

The young Czech frontman danced across the edge of the box from left to right, before firing home a 25-yard effort that flew in off the back of Simon Charlton. Three minutes later, Luis Garcia got in on the act, capping a fine passing move with a shot from the inside left channel that looped in off the right boot of Craig Fleming.

Suddenly, Nigel Worthington's pre-match plans had been blown apart. The former Northern Ireland defender shuffled his pack at half-time, introducing the attack-minded Leon McKenzie and David Bentley, but it was too late.

Following further home pressure at the start of the second period, the Merseysiders extended their advantage after 64 minutes. A centrally-positioned free-kick was touched off to Cisse some 25 yards out, and the French international unleashed a fearsome low drive beyond the despairing right hand of Green.

The remainder of the game was exhibition stuff, as Liverpool toyed with their East Anglian opponents like a cat with a mouse.

Norwich will have learnt much from this footballing lesson, and should take heart from the fact that they have already played some of their most demanding fixtures. For Benitez's men, the trick will be to transfer Anfield form onto the road.

Saturday 25th September 2004	Venue: **City of Manchester Stadium**	Attendance: **47,015**	Referee: **N.S.Barry**

PREMIERSHIP FIXTURE HISTORY

Pl: **8** Draws: **1**	Wins	⚽	☐	■
Manchester City	0	3	14	0
Arsenal	7	16	10	0

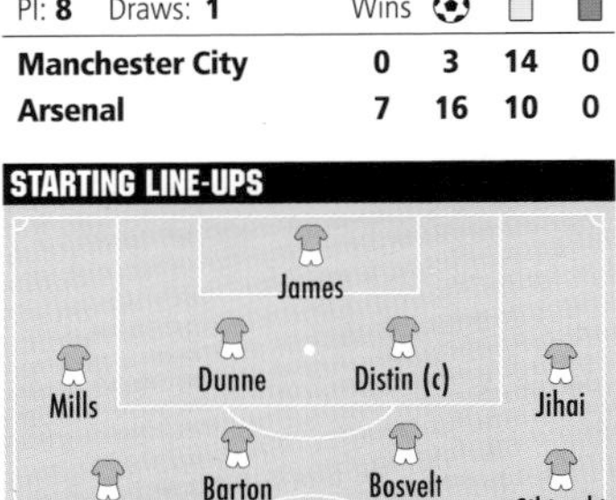

STARTING LINE-UPS

James

Mills, Dunne, Distin (c), Jihai

S.Wright-Phillips, Barton, Bosvelt, Sibierski

Macken, Anelka

Henry, Bergkamp

Reyes, Edu, Vieira (c), Ljungberg

Cole, Campbell, Toure, Lauren

Lehmann

Substitutes: McManaman, Flood, Waterreus, Jordan, B.Wright-Phillips | Clichy, Fabregas, van Persie, Cygan, Almunia

EVENT LINE

14 ⚽ Cole (Open Play)

HALF TIME 0 - 1

47 ☐ **Bosvelt (Foul)**

63 Reyes (Off) Clichy (On)

76 **Bosvelt (Off) McManaman (On)**

76 **Macken (Off) Flood (On)**

88 Bergkamp (Off) van Persie (On)

88 Ljungberg (Off) Fabregas (On)

FULL TIME 0 - 1

STATISTICS

Season	Fixture		Fixture	Season
42	**7**	Shots On Target	**9**	**68**
36	**4**	Shots Off Target	**3**	**31**
1	**0**	Hit Woodwork	**1**	**4**
24	**5**	Caught Offside	**2**	**16**
47	**8**	Corners	**1**	**37**
102	**16**	Fouls	**8**	**70**
46%	**44%**	Possession	**56%**	**59%**

LEAGUE STANDINGS

Position (pos before)	W	D	L	F	A	Pts
14 (11) Man City	2	1	4	8	7	7
1 (1) Arsenal	6	1	0	22	7	19

Ashley Cole threads the ball beyond Shaun Wright-Phillips

PREMIERSHIP MILESTONE
Willo Flood and Robin van Persie both made their Premiership debuts

"It wouldn't surprise me if Arsenal won the Champions League. They are the best side I have ever managed against in the Premier League, and that includes Manchester United."
Kevin Keegan

"Manchester City caught me by surprise and showed me a side of their game I never knew. For 90 minutes they defended tenaciously, and they showed respect for us."
Arsene Wenger

PREMIERSHIP MILESTONE
100 Sol Campbell made his 100th Premiership appearance for Arsenal

PREMIERSHIP MILESTONE
250 Patrick Vieira made his 250th Premiership appearance

MANCHESTER CITY 0 ARSENAL 1

A 14th-minute goal from Ashley Cole proved enough for Arsenal to record an 11th straight victory over Manchester City.

The Londoners had not lost to their opponents since the formation of the Premier League, and were boosted by the return from injury of Sol Campbell. Kevin Keegan's side had put seven goals past Barnsley in a midweek Carling Cup tie, a result that earnt them a home game against Arsene Wenger's side, so came into the match full of confidence.

Both sides had early chances, though only Jonathan Macken forced Jens Lehmann into a save. Nicolas Anelka, Edu and Jose Antonio Reyes all drove wide, before Cole capped a fine passing move with an accomplished left-foot finish from 12 yards out.

Going behind against Arsenal is never a good idea, and only the alertness of David James in rushing from his goal prevented Reyes from adding a quickfire second. Thierry Henry skipped past Richard Dunne and fired inches wide, while Lehmann had to turn over a dipping Antoine Sibierski header as a vibrant half drew to a close.

The second period began with more high-octane stuff. Sun Jihai brilliantly blocked a goalbound Freddie Ljungberg shot, before play switched to the other end as a right-wing centre from Macken saw Anelka denied by a plunging save from the Gunners' German custodian.

City began to exert real pressure on the visiting defence, forcing Wenger to replace Reyes with the more defensively-minded Gael Clichy after 63 minutes. The change afforded Cole greater licence to get forward, and his 70th-minute cross struck the home bar.

Keegan handed a 76th-minute Premiership debut to midfielder Willo Flood as his side continued to press. Fellow substitute Steve McManaman drove straight at Lehmann from distance, while Anelka flashed a free-kick narrowly wide.

Robin van Persie came on for a fleeting Premiership debut, as Arsenal hung on to record their sixth victory in seven league games. The defeat was harsh on a City team that had a real go at the champions, though Cole's goal was deserving of winning any match.

PREMIERSHIP FIXTURE HISTORY

Pl: **10** Draws: **3**

	Wins	Goals	Yellow cards	Red cards
Middlesbrough	3	6	16	1
Chelsea	4	7	23	0

STARTING LINE-UPS

Job, Downing, Morrison, Nash, McMahon

Tiago, Kezman, Huth, Pidgeley, J.Cole

EVENT LINE

36 **Parlour (Off) Job (On)**

HALF TIME 0 - 0

61 Smertin (Foul)

65 Gudjohnsen (Off) Kezman (On)

65 Smertin (Off) Tiago (On)

66 **Job (Off) Downing (On)**

76 **Viduka (Off) Morrison (On)**

81 Drogba (Indirect Free Kick)

88 Duff (Off) Huth (On)

FULL TIME 0 - 1

STATISTICS

Season	Fixture	Middlesbrough / Chelsea	Fixture	Season
52	**4**	Shots On Target	**12**	**50**
42	**4**	Shots Off Target	**5**	**54**
0	**0**	Hit Woodwork	**1**	**3**
29	**3**	Caught Offside	**4**	**26**
33	**3**	Corners	**7**	**44**
92	**10**	Fouls	**14**	**92**
50%	**41%**	Possession	**59%**	**56%**

LEAGUE STANDINGS

Position (pos before)		W	D	L	F	A	Pts
10 (6)	**Middlesbrough**	**3**	**1**	**3**	**11**	**11**	**10**
2 (2)	**Chelsea**	**5**	**2**	**0**	**7**	**1**	**17**

Saturday 25th September 2004 | Venue: **Riverside Stadium** | Attendance: **32,341** | Referee: **M.R.Halsey**

MIDDLESBROUGH 0 CHELSEA 1

Chelsea returned to winning ways at the Riverside Stadium, but left it late to beat a determined Middlesbrough.

Despite dominating proceedings, it appeared that Jose Mourinho's side would have to settle for a third consecutive 0-0 draw. However, with just nine minutes remaining, Didier Drogba fired home the winner from a well-worked free-kick routine.

The Ivory Coast international had already struck the frame of the goal in the first period, his venomous shot leaving keeper Mark Schwarzer powerless as it crashed against the crossbar.

That was one of countless close calls for the home defence, as Chelsea did everything but score. The Londoners overran their opponents in midfield, where Frank Lampard starred again, but appeared to lack the cutting edge needed for victory.

At the other end, Jimmy Floyd Hasselbaink was desperate to prove Mourinho made a mistake in letting him go. Unfortunately for the Dutchman, the only lasting impression he left on this match was an horrific one.

Stooping to head the ball on halfway, the volatile frontman received an accidental kick in the head from former teammate John Terry. Blood gushed from the wound, and Hasselbaink had to leave the pitch for several minutes in order to get it stitched up.

The second period followed a similar pattern to the first, though Middlesbrough did show a greater willingness to commit men forward. That said, Steve McClaren's team conjured up little more than half-chances.

Great work by Damien Duff down the flank led to the visitors' best chance, Drogba wastefully heading over the Irishman's near-post cross from the left. All was forgiven after 81 minutes, however, when the former Marseille striker brilliantly lost his marker to drive home a 15-yard effort from Lampard's low free-kick from the right.

It was a picture-book goal worthy of winning any match, and the least Chelsea deserved in a one-sided contest.

Afterwards, McClaren took heart from the fact that his side had remained on level terms for such a long period of time, despite not playing at their best. In truth, however, that was more a result of the Stamford Bridge outfit's inability to translate dominance into goals, than any stickability on his team's part.

"I think Chelsea are a threat to Arsenal. They have a different style, but at the end of the day it is all about results."

Steve McClaren

"It was a great shot from Didier Drogba which gave us three very important points."

Jose Mourinho

PREMIERSHIP MILESTONE

100 William Gallas made his 100th Premiership appearance

Chelsea celebrate Didier Drogba's winner

PREMIERSHIP FIXTURE HISTORY

Pl: 2 Draws: 0	Wins	Goals	Yellow	Red
Newcastle United	2	5	4	0
West Bromwich Albion	0	2	3	1

STARTING LINE-UPS

Newcastle subs: Robert, Milner, Harper, Hughes, Ambrose

West Brom subs: Horsfield, Gera, Kuszczak, Moore, O'Connor

EVENT LINE

20 Yellow card **Bowyer (Foul)**

22 Yellow card Greening (Foul)

HALF TIME 0 - 0

46 Substitution Earnshaw (Off) Horsfield (On)

51 Yellow card **Elliott (Foul)**

55 Substitution **Bellamy (Off) Robert (On)**

62 Substitution Koumas (Off) Gera (On)

63 Red card Purse (2nd Bookable Offence)

70 Goal **Kluivert (Open Play)**

73 Yellow card **Kluivert (Ung.Conduct)**

77 Substitution **Kluivert (Off) Milner (On)**

78 Goal **Milner (Open Play)**

86 Goal **Shearer (Open Play)**

87 Goal Horsfield (Open Play)

FULL TIME 3 - 1

STATISTICS

Season	Fixture (Newcastle)		Fixture (West Brom)	Season
53	10	Shots On Target	3	30
44	11	Shots Off Target	4	30
2	2	Hit Woodwork	0	1
22	4	Caught Offside	5	29
58	8	Corners	3	47
86	8	Fouls	10	88
53%	64%	Possession	36%	47%

LEAGUE STANDINGS

Position (pos before)		W	D	L	F	A	Pts
6 (9)	Newcastle Utd	3	2	2	14	11	11
18 (19)	West Brom	0	4	3	6	12	4

Saturday 25th September 2004 | Venue: **St James' Park** | Attendance: **52,308** | Referee: **M.A.Riley**

NEWCASTLE UNITED 3 WEST BROM 1

Zoltan Gera pulls back Laurent Robert

"The sending off of their player was the critical moment in the game. We scored three goals and could have scored more."
Graeme Souness

PREMIERSHIP MILESTONE
James Milner scored his first Premiership goal for Newcastle

PREMIERSHIP MILESTONE
250 Alan Shearer made his 250th Premiership appearance for Newcastle

"I thought the first booking was soft and the second even softer."
Gary Megson on the dismissal of Darren Purse

PREMIERSHIP MILESTONE
Geoff Horsfield scored his first Premiership goal for West Brom

Newcastle continued their winning start to life under Graeme Souness, but were made to work hard by a battling West Bromwich Albion side.

The turning point came in the 63rd minute, with the game still goalless, when referee Mike Riley harshly dismissed visiting skipper Darren Purse for a second bookable offence, following a coming together with Patrick Kluivert. If the award of the first yellow card had been soft, for a foul on Craig Bellamy, then the second was positively ludicrous.

From then on the Baggies were unable to contain wave after wave of home attacks. Substitute Geoff Horsfield netted in the 87th minute, but not before Kluivert, James Milner and Alan Shearer had wrapped up the points.

Again, Shearer, Kluivert and Bellamy had all made the Magpies' starting line-up, though on this occasion the Dutchman was at the head of a midfield diamond anchored by summer signing Nicky Butt. For his part, Gary Megson was able to welcome back goalkeeper Russell Hoult from injury.

Newcastle enjoyed the better of the opening period, and were twice denied a penalty. First, an effort from Shearer appeared to strike the hand of Purse, before Lee Bowyer went down under a challenge from Thomas Gaardsoe.

Three presentable openings were sent wide by Bellamy, Kluivert saw two goalbound efforts blocked and Bowyer hit the side-netting, as the Geordies poured forward.

Two minutes after the interval, Neil Clement went close to silencing the home crowd with a 20-yard free-kick. At the other end, Bowyer went even closer, sending a deft chip against Hoult's crossbar.

After Riley had taken centre stage, the goals began to flow. Substitute Laurent Robert fired in a vicious low effort in the 70th minute, and Kluivert was on hand to fire home from 10 yards after the goalkeeper's parry.

Then, after Robert had hit the underside of the bar, another replacement made an immediate impact. Having literally just stepped off the bench, youngster Milner could not miss when presented with a 78th-minute open goal by the industry of Jermaine Jenas.

An 86th-minute Shearer strike was quickly followed by a headed consolation from Horsfield, as Newcastle continued their surge up the table.

PREMIERSHIP FIXTURE HISTORY

Pl: 13 Draws: 2	Wins	Goals	Yellow cards	Red cards
Tottenham Hotspur	3	18	22	0
Manchester United	8	22	20	1

STARTING LINE-UPS

Davies, Jackson, Keller, Gardner, Brown

Miller, Bellion, Ricardo, P.Neville, Kleberson

EVENT LINE

30 **Kanoute (Off) Davies (On)**

42 van Nistelrooy (Penalty)

HALF TIME 0 - 1

61 **Mendes (Foul)**

67 **Mabizela (Off) Jackson (On)**

83 Giggs (Off) Miller (On)

86 van Nistelrooy (Off) Bellion (On)

FULL TIME 0 - 1

STATISTICS

Season	Fixture		Fixture	Season
39	5	Shots On Target	5	49
40	6	Shots Off Target	2	43
2	0	Hit Woodwork	0	4
18	2	Caught Offside	6	21
35	3	Corners	3	53
93	9	Fouls	10	89
45%	47%	Possession	53%	53%

LEAGUE STANDINGS

Position (pos before)		W	D	L	F	A	Pts
9 (5)	Tottenham H	2	4	1	4	3	10
5 (8)	Man Utd	3	3	1	8	6	12

Saturday 25th September 2004 | Venue: **White Hart Lane** | Attendance: **36,103** | Referee: **P.Walton**

TOTTENHAM HOTSPUR 0 MANCHESTER UNITED 1

Ruud van Nistelrooy netted his first Premiership goal of the season, as United became the first team to defeat Jacques Santini's new-look Tottenham.

The Dutchman scored the decisive goal from a 42nd-minute penalty, awarded by referee Peter Walton when Swedish international Erik Edman grabbed hold of John O'Shea's shirt as the Irishman attempted to reach a deep cross from the left.

The victory was just about deserved, though neither side produced the flowing football often seen in this fixture in the past. Rio Ferdinand made a big difference to a visiting defence that had only previously kept one clean sheet in the league, while spirits were visibly lifted by the news that Wayne Rooney was only days away from making his debut.

Having built their solid start around a resolute rearguard, it was somewhat surprising to see the home team line up with three forwards on the pitch. It quickly became clear, however, that Santini had opted for a 4-5-1 formation, with Frederic Kanoute and Robbie Keane operating down the flanks.

The first half offered little by way of creative play, with the best chances coming from opposition mistakes. Cristiano Ronaldo seized on a miscued clearance by Paul Robinson, while Pedro Mendes was gifted possession by Mikael Silvestre, though both men then missed the target.

The bulk of the half-chances fell to Sir Alex Ferguson's side, Ryan Giggs drilling narrowly over from 25 yards and van Nistelrooy seeing a deflected effort pushed away by Robinson, before United's former PSV Eindhoven striker coolly gave his team a half-time lead from the penalty spot.

After Alan Smith had gone close shortly after the restart, Spurs began to take the game to their opponents. The livewire Jermain Defoe embarked on several jinking runs, while Keane continually strived for a killer pass.

A van Nistelrooy effort was controversially ruled out for offside in the 62nd minute, and Silvestre was later denied by an amazing goal-line clearance. At the other end, late attempts from Jamie Redknapp and Keane failed to test Roy Carroll.

While the visitors produced an accomplished display, Tottenham need to show more adventure if they are to make real progress.

Ruud van Nistelrooy celebrates his strike from the penalty spot

"It's a problem for us that we haven't scored many goals, but we played well in the second half."

Jacques Santini

"I think the return of Rio has given a lot of people in the team confidence, in particular Mikael Silvestre."

Sir Alex Ferguson

PREMIERSHIP MILESTONE

50 Rio Ferdinand made his 50th Premiership appearance for Man Utd

PREMIERSHIP FIXTURE HISTORY

Pl: 2 Draws: 0	Wins	⚽	□	■
Portsmouth	0	1	2	0
Everton	2	3	2	0

STARTING LINE-UPS

Lua Lua, Kamara, Ashdown, Taylor, Cisse

Yobo, Ferguson, Wright, McFadden, Campbell

EVENT LINE

HALF TIME 0 - 0

46 **Berkovic (Off) Lua Lua (On)**

46 Stubbs (Off) Yobo (On)

56 Watson (Off) Ferguson (On)

68 **Fuller (Off) Kamara (On)**

76 **Faye (Foul)**

80 Cahill (Indirect Free Kick)

86 Cahill (Foul)

FULL TIME 0 - 1

STATISTICS

Season	Fixture		Fixture	Season
40	6	Shots On Target	2	38
32	5	Shots Off Target	7	32
1	1	Hit Woodwork	0	0
15	1	Caught Offside	0	20
34	3	Corners	6	33
77	12	Fouls	16	89
48%	46%	Possession	54%	49%

LEAGUE STANDINGS

Position (pos before)	W	D	L	F	A	Pts
14 (13) Portsmouth	2	1	3	9	9	7
3 (3) Everton	5	1	1	9	6	16

Sunday 26th September 2004 | Venue: **Fratton Park** | Attendance: **20,125** | Referee: **D.J.Gallagher**

PORTSMOUTH 0 EVERTON 1

Portsmouth suffered their first Premiership defeat at Fratton Park since February, as Tim Cahill headed a resurgent Everton to another three points.

David Unsworth had been part of the Toffees side that enjoyed their only away success of 2003-04 in this fixture, and was made captain for the day by his new employers. The defender's former boss David Moyes kept faith with the 4-5-1 formation that had brought so much success in recent weeks.

It was Harry Redknapp's charges who were quicker out of the blocks. Nigel Martyn was called upon to make a sprawling save in the 12th minute, before Nigel Quashie rattled the crossbar from 25 yards.

As the half wore on, Everton began to take control. Steve Watson was unlucky to see a volley flash the wrong side of the post, while Dejan Stefanovic and Unsworth both had to make desperate last-ditch clearances to deny Marcus Bent and Cahill respectively.

The ineffectual Eyal Berkovic, whose threat had been nullified by Lee Carsley, was replaced by Lomana Tresor Lua Lua at the interval. The visitors also made a change, Joseph Yobo coming on for the injured Alan Stubbs.

The second period continued where the first had left off, with the Merseysiders in the ascendancy. The game runs of Bent were creating space down the middle, and Cahill was only too happy to surge into it at every conceivable opportunity.

With 56 minutes played, Moyes threw on Duncan Ferguson. It was a bold move, clearly demonstrating the manager's belief that his side were more than capable of earning a victory.

The winning goal did not arrive until 10 minutes from time. Lee Carsley swung over a free-kick from the right and Cahill arrived unchallenged to head the ball beyond Shaka Hislop from eight yards out.

Late home pressure failed to result in any clear-cut chances, as Everton recorded their third away win in four league games. The result was richly deserved, and ensured that the Toffees remained hot-on-the-heels of Arsenal and Chelsea at the top of the Premiership.

Everton celebrate their winner in front of a desolate Shaka Hislop

"We are not Arsenal and we are not going to win every week. It's how we respond to defeats that will be important."

Harry Redknapp

"It's basically the same group of players as last season, but we probably did not play as well as we should have last year."

David Moyes

PREMIERSHIP MILESTONE

100 Alan Stubbs made his 100th Premiership appearance in the colours of Everton

PREMIERSHIP FIXTURE HISTORY

Pl: 5 Draws: 1	Wins	Goals	Yellow cards	Red cards
Charlton Athletic	3	7	9	0
Blackburn Rovers	1	5	8	0

STARTING LINE-UPS

Charlton Athletic: Kiely (c); Young, Fortune, Perry, Hreidarsson; Stuart, Murphy, El Karkouri, Hughes; Lisbie, Jeffers

Blackburn Rovers: Friedel; Gray, Matteo, Amoruso, Neill; Jansen, Ferguson (c), Flitcroft, Emerton; Stead, Dickov

Substitutes (Charlton Athletic): Johansson, Kishishev, Euell, Andersen, Rommedahl

Substitutes (Blackburn Rovers): Tugay, Enckelman, Bothroyd, Johansson, Pedersen

EVENT LINE

12 Jeffers (Off) Johansson (On)

HALF TIME 0 - 0

49 El Karkouri (Corner)

70 Flitcroft (Off) Tugay (On)

70 Stead (Off) Bothroyd (On)

76 Hughes (Off) Euell (On)

76 Johansson (Off) Kishishev (On)

83 Stuart (Dissent)

90 Tugay (Foul)

FULL TIME 1 - 0

STATISTICS

Season	Fixture (Charlton)		Fixture (Blackburn)	Season
32	2	Shots On Target	6	24
28	7	Shots Off Target	8	41
2	0	Hit Woodwork	1	1
20	4	Caught Offside	5	28
34	6	Corners	10	47
90	20	Fouls	14	123
44%	36%	Possession	64%	49%

LEAGUE STANDINGS

Position (pos before)	W	D	L	F	A	Pts
7 (12) Charlton Ath	3	2	2	8	10	11
16 (16) Blackburn R	1	2	4	5	12	5

Monday 27th September 2004 | Venue: **The Valley** | Attendance: **26,193** | Referee: **S.W.Dunn**

Talal El Karkouri celebrates his winner

"I saw him play for PSG at right-back, centre-half, left-back and in midfield before I signed him, and his versatility showed through tonight."

Alan Curbishley on matchwinner Talal El Karkouri

PREMIERSHIP MILESTONE

Talal El Karkouri scored his first Premiership goal

"I'm not concerned about our league position at the moment, because if we play as we did tonight we will win more matches than we lose."

Mark Hughes

CHARLTON ATHLETIC 1 BLACKBURN ROVERS 0

Charlton's man from Casablanca, Talal El Karkouri, scored his first goal in English football to give the home side a 1-0 victory over Blackburn Rovers at The Valley.

The Moroccan international, a £1m summer capture from Paris Saint-Germain, met his central midfield partner Danny Murphy's right-wing corner with a powerful near-post header from seven yards out in the 49th minute, thus settling this hard-fought encounter.

The goal ignited a match that had struggled to get going in the first period. The Addicks' best efforts had been deflected to safety, though Garry Flitcroft did hit the post for the visitors with a close-range attempt.

Rovers dominated possession, and new boss Mark Hughes would have been delighted with the way in which his players responded to falling behind. Having forced the game into the Charlton half, the Lancashire side were denied what looked a blatant penalty when Hermann Hreidarsson appeared to handle a cross.

That said, Alan Curbishley's men always looked dangerous on the break, particularly when they were able to utilise the pace of Kevin Lisbie. Brad Friedel was called upon to deny substitute Radostin Kishishev after one such attack, and Lisbie later headed over a golden opportunity.

Matt Jansen, the hero of Hughes' first match in charge, spurned Blackburn's best chance to snatch a point, somehow heading wide when it seemed easier to score. It was an opening that his manager would have gobbled up in his playing days, though the miss was understandable given the former England-U21 international's recent lack of match practice.

The result vindicated the decision to again leave big-name arrival Dennis Rommedahl on the bench, with Graham Stuart and Bryan Hughes providing greater industry in wide areas. Despite woeful away form, the South Londoners climbed to seventh in the table on the back of this win.

By contrast, Rovers remained perilously close to the drop zone after this defeat. Time is needed for Hughes to transmit his ideas to the players, and the signs were encouraging, though it is often hard to move up the table once you have become involved in a relegation dogfight.

Alan Shearer celebrates a goal at Middlesbrough

SEPTEMBER 2004

The month began with a large contingent of Premiership players away on international duty. Manchester City's David James was made the scapegoat for England squandering a two-goal lead in their opening World Cup Qualifier away to Austria, with Tottenham's Paul Robinson taking over in goal for the 2-1 win in Poland a few days later.

Having seen Wales make a stuttering start in their bid to reach Germany in 2006, Mark Hughes moved into Premiership management with Blackburn. The vacancy had arisen when Graeme Souness left Ewood Park to take over at Newcastle. Before agreeing to release Hughes, the Welsh F.A. struck a deal that would see him take charge of their two October internationals.

At the top of the table, both Arsenal and Chelsea remained unbeaten. Three 1-0 victories saw Everton climb into a surprising third place, while a Ruud van Nistelrooy penalty proved enough to condemn Jacques Santini's Tottenham to a first taste of defeat.

Big guns Manchester United, Liverpool and Newcastle all began to move in the right direction. The Magpies enjoyed a particularly profitable September, collecting maximum points to move up 11 places.

League One clubs AFC Bournemouth and Colchester United knocked out top-flight opposition in the 2nd Round of the Carling Cup. The latter defeated struggling West Brom 2-1 at Layer Road, while the men from the South Coast triumphed on penalties after a 3-3 draw at Blackburn.

Even at this early stage of the campaign, the relegation-zone had a predictable look. The three teams that won promotion to the Premiership last season remained without a win between them, though poor form from the likes of Southampton and Birmingham gave them all reason for optimism.

Performance of the month belonged to Wayne Rooney. Having recovered from the foot injury that he picked up playing for England during the summer, the striker marked both his Manchester United and European debut with a stunning hat-trick in a 6-2 demolition of Turkish outfit Fenerbahce.

IN THE NEWS

04TH England squander a two-goal lead as they begin their programme of World Cup Qualifiers with a 2-2 draw in Austria

06TH Graeme Souness agrees to take over the managerial reigns at Newcastle, though not until after they have played his old club Blackburn in their next match

08TH A first international goal from Jermain Defoe helps England to a 2-1 victory in a World Cup Qualifier in Poland

11TH Tim Cahill is controversially shown a second yellow card by referee Steve Bennett after pulling his shirt over his head to celebrate scoring the only goal of the game for Everton at Manchester City

15TH Blackburn appoint Mark Hughes as their new manager, following the departure of Graeme Souness to Newcastle

16TH Middlesbrough defeat Czech side Banik Ostrava 3-0 at the Riverside Stadium in their first ever game in Europe

20TH Rio Ferdinand returns from an eight-month ban for missing a drugs test, performing strongly as Manchester United defeat Liverpool 2-1 at Old Trafford

20TH Steven Gerrard breaks a bone in his foot. The injury will keep the Liverpool and England midfielder out of action for around two months

28TH Wayne Rooney enjoys a sensational Manchester United debut, hitting a hat-trick in a 6-2 demolition of Fenerbahce

TEAM OF THE MONTH

Nigel Martyn
Everton

The veteran keeper was on top form, not conceding a single goal during the month. The likes of Nicolas Anelka, Jimmy Floyd Hasselbaink and Aiyegbeni Yakubu all tried and failed to find a way past Everton's Cornish custodian.

Luke Young
Charlton Athletic

Charlton enjoyed an unbeaten month, keeping two clean sheets in three games. In addition to proving a difficult man to pass at right-back, Young showed himself to be an asset going forward with a goal at Birmingham.

Ricardo Carvalho
Chelsea

Having won the right to partner John Terry at the heart of the Chelsea defence, the Portuguese international played a pivotal role in ensuring that nobody scored a league goal against his side during September.

J'Lloyd Samuel
Aston Villa

Aston Villa responded to what had been a poor month defensively in August with a more solid showing in September. The young full-back was part of a consistent unit that was only breached on one occasion, and surged forward with gusto every time the opportunity arose.

Fredrik Ljungberg
Arsenal

The Swedish midfielder had always been known for his vital goals from midfield, but ably demonstrated his ability to create, as well as score, during the month. A neat finish at Fulham was swiftly followed by an assist, with Robert Pires then benefitting from unselfish work in the home draw with Bolton.

PLAYER OF THE MONTH

Ledley King
Tottenham Hotspur

Though Tottenham failed to score during three matches in the month, two points were still collected as a result of a resolute defence. The back-four were superbly marshalled by an ever-improving King, with Chelsea unable to find a way past and Manchester United reliant on a penalty.

> **"Ledley King's performance against Chelsea at Stamford Bridge was first-class, and he was instrumental in Tottenham's strong defensive record throughout September."**
> Barclays Awards Panel

MANAGER OF THE MONTH

David Moyes
Everton

Three 1-0 wins in September saw Everton climb to the heady heights of third in the table. Astute summer signings Tim Cahill and Marcus Bent fitted neatly into a 4-5-1 formation, with Moyes blending youth and experience into a cohesive unit.

Premiership Career Statistics
up until end of September 2004
Matches:**92** Wins:**35** Draws:**22** Losses:**35**

> **"This award is the result of a real team effort, and I'd never think I could do the job on my own."**
> David Moyes

Jermaine Jenas
Newcastle United

A terrific month for Newcastle saw Jenas cast in the role of principal assistor. The young England international layed on three goals, including two in the win against West Brom at St James' Park.

Tim Cahill
Everton

Two appearances and two winning goals was the Tim Cahill story in September. Headers defeated both Manchester City and Portsmouth on their own grounds, though the midfielder also served a suspension for a harsh dismissal at the City of Manchester Stadium.

Ryan Giggs
Manchester United

Manchester United began to get their season back on track, with the Welsh midfielder recapturing some of his best form. Two wonderful set-piece deliveries created goals against arch-rivals Liverpool, while Giggs found the net himself against Fenerbahce in the 'Champions League'.

Luis Garcia
Liverpool

While not being his natural position, Garcia took to the role of secondary striker like a duck to water. The Spaniard scored one and made one in the victory against West Brom, and added a further goal from his more accustomed role on the right of midfield against Norwich later in the month.

Alan Shearer
Newcastle United

The Newcastle captain led his team to a maximum haul of nine points from the month, scoring against Blackburn and West Brom and forcing an own goal at Southampton. In Europe, Shearer helped himself to a hat-trick in the 5-1 demolition of Israeli outfit Hapoel Bnei Sakhnin.

MONTH IN NUMBERS

30 Games Played

57 Total Goals Scored

1.90 Average Goals Per Game

2 Player With Most Goals (Jaidi, Shearer, Garcia, Cahill, Johnson, Anelka, Viduka, Silvestre)

8 Club With Most Goals (Newcastle United)

3 Fastest Goal (Fuller)

36.7% Percentage Of Home Wins

26.6% Percentage Of Away Wins

36.7% Percentage Of Draws

3-0 Biggest Win (Liverpool 3 v 0 West Brom, Newcastle United 3 v 0 Blackburn Rovers, Liverpool 3 v 0 Norwich City, Fulham 0 v 3 Arsenal)

83 Total Yellow Cards

6 Total Red Cards

2.8 Average Yellow Cards Per Game

16 Most Disciplinary Points (Clement)

16 Fastest Booking (Sibierski)

33,556 Average Attendance

Tim Cahill celebrates moments before his sending-off at Manchester City

PREMIERSHIP TABLE / TEAM STATISTICS

Pos (last month)	Team	Played	Won	Drawn	Lost	Goals for	Goals against	Goal diff	Points	Shots on target	Hit woodwork	Shots off target	Failed to score	Clean sheets	Corners	Caught Offside	Players used
1 - (1)	Arsenal	7	6	1	0	22	7	+15	19	68	4	31	0	3	37	16	20
2 - (2)	Chelsea	7	5	2	0	7	1	+6	17	50	3	54	2	6	44	26	20
3 ▲ (7)	Everton	7	5	1	1	9	6	+3	16	38	0	32	1	4	33	20	17
4 ▼ (3)	Bolton Wanderers	7	3	3	1	12	9	+3	12	53	1	34	1	1	43	15	18
5 ▲ (9)	Manchester United	7	3	3	1	8	6	+2	12	49	4	43	2	2	53	21	25
6 ▲ (17)	Newcastle United	7	3	2	2	14	11	+3	11	53	2	44	1	1	58	22	17
7 ▲ (8)	Charlton Athletic	7	3	2	2	8	10	-2	11	32	2	28	2	3	34	20	19
8 ▲ (12)	Liverpool	6	3	1	2	10	5	+5	10	44	0	36	1	2	32	16	18
9 ▼ (6)	Aston Villa	7	2	4	1	8	7	+1	10	46	2	42	3	3	50	15	18
10 ▼ (4)	Tottenham Hotspur	7	2	4	1	4	3	+1	10	39	2	40	3	4	35	18	19
11 ▼ (5)	Middlesbrough	7	3	1	3	11	11	0	10	52	0	42	2	1	33	29	19
12 ▲ (13)	Fulham	7	2	2	3	8	11	-3	8	40	2	34	2	2	44	21	18
13 ▼ (10)	Manchester City	7	2	1	4	8	7	+1	7	42	1	36	3	1	47	24	17
14 ▼ (11)	Portsmouth	6	2	1	3	9	9	0	7	40	1	32	2	0	34	15	19
15 ▼ (14)	Birmingham City	7	1	3	3	5	7	-2	6	24	1	31	2	1	39	16	20
16 ▲ (19)	Blackburn Rovers	7	1	2	4	5	12	-7	5	24	1	41	3	1	47	28	22
17 ▼ (16)	Southampton	7	1	1	5	6	11	-5	4	33	0	43	3	1	41	16	21
18 ▼ (15)	West Brom	7	0	4	3	6	12	-6	4	30	1	30	1	0	47	29	19
19 ▼ (18)	Norwich City	7	0	4	3	5	12	-7	4	28	1	34	3	2	29	29	16
20 - (20)	Crystal Palace	7	0	2	5	6	14	-8	2	29	1	31	1	0	37	15	20

TEAM FORM

Pos	Team	Form	Goals For	Goals Against	Pts
1	Newcastle United	WWW	8	2	9
2	Everton	WWW	3	0	9
3	Arsenal	WDW	6	2	7
4	Manchester United	DWW	5	3	7
5	Liverpool	WLW	7	2	6
6	Charlton Athletic	DDW	2	1	5
7	Chelsea	DDW	1	0	5
8	Fulham	LDW	2	4	4
9	Portsmouth	WLL	3	3	3
10	Bolton Wanderers	DDD	5	5	3
11	Aston Villa	DDD	1	1	3
12	Middlesbrough	WLL	2	3	3
13	Manchester City	LWL	2	3	3
14	Blackburn Rovers	LWL	1	4	3
15	Tottenham Hotspur	DDL	0	1	2
16	Birmingham City	LDD	3	4	2
17	Norwich City	DDL	0	3	2
18	Southampton	DLL	1	3	1
19	Crystal Palace	LLD	3	6	1
20	West Brom	LDL	2	7	1

TOP GOALSCORERS

Player	This Month	Total
N.Anelka Manchester City	2	**5**
T.Henry Arsenal	1	**5**
J.Reyes Arsenal	1	**5**
A.Johnson Crystal Palace	2	**4**
A.Cole Fulham	1	**4**
H.Pedersen Bolton Wanderers	1	**4**
R.Pires Arsenal	1	**4**
A.Shearer Newcastle United	2	**3**
M.Viduka Middlesbrough	2	**3**
D.Bergkamp Arsenal	0	**3**
J.Defoe Tottenham Hotspur	0	**3**
J.Hasselbaink Middlesbrough	0	**3**
J.Okocha Bolton Wanderers	0	**3**
A.Yakubu Portsmouth	0	**3**

MOST GOAL ASSISTS

Player	This Month	Total
T.Henry Arsenal	1	**7**
F.Ljungberg Arsenal	2	**5**
J.Jenas Newcastle United	3	**3**
R.Giggs Manchester United	2	**3**
J.Okocha Bolton Wanderers	2	**3**
L.Robert Newcastle United	2	**3**
D.Bergkamp Arsenal	1	**3**
L.Boa Morte Fulham	1	**3**
J.Hasselbaink Middlesbrough	1	**3**
W.Routledge Crystal Palace	1	**3**
S.Wright-Phillips Manchester City	1	**3**
F.Queudrue Middlesbrough	0	**3**

DISCIPLINE

F.A. disciplinary points: Yellow=4 points,
Two Bookable Offences=10 points and Red Card=12 points

Player	Y	SB	R	PTS
T.Cahill Everton	2	1	0	**18**
N.Clement West Brom	1	0	1	**16**
A.Cole Fulham	1	0	1	**16**
J.Redknapp Tottenham	4	0	0	**16**
D.Purse West Brom	1	1	0	**14**
P.Diop Fulham	0	0	1	**12**
M.Izzet Birmingham City	3	0	0	**12**
S.Legwinski Fulham	3	0	0	**12**
P.Mendes Tottenham	3	0	0	**12**
Y.Safri Norwich City	3	0	0	**12**
R.Savage Birmingham City	3	0	0	**12**
L.Amoruso Blackburn Rovers	0	1	0	**10**
R.Dunne Manchester City	0	1	0	**10**
D.Johnson Birmingham City	0	1	0	**10**
G.Naysmith Everton	0	1	0	**10**

"I'm interested in football. I intend to do the awards, but I may end up coaching Maidenhead under-nines. You have to start at the bottom, and I intend to do that."

Sir Clive Woodward on his proposed move into football

"If a centre-forward misses ten open goals he can get away with it, but if a goalkeeper makes a mistake he is the worst in the world."

David James shortly after losing his place in the England team

"Arsenal, and maybe Chelsea to a certain degree, seem to have that mentality where they don't look as though they are going to be beaten. Teams playing us think they have got a chance now."

Roy Keane

"I think if you look at the group of players, the top-class performers we've got here, the next step is to win something. I'm sure all the players are aware of that."

Graeme Souness after his appointment as Newcastle manager

"There was an incident on the team bus. I shall be trying to find out what happened. I've given the players the day off on Monday so they can clear their minds and gather their thoughts ahead of this weekend's game against Fulham."

Gary Megson following West Brom's 3-0 defeat at Liverpool

"The day to day job of running the club will be different to what I've experienced, but I'm sure I can handle it. I've been in the game for 25 years."

Mark Hughes after taking over at Blackburn

"It's a great relief to have left Liverpool. The squad was not close-knit, with the French on one side and the English and Czechs on the other."

El-Hadji Diouf after joining Bolton on a season-long loan deal

PREMIERSHIP FIXTURE HISTORY

Pl: 6 Draws: 1	Wins	Goals	Yellow	Red
Arsenal	4	15	8	1
Charlton Athletic	1	8	8	0

STARTING LINE-UPS

Arsenal subs: Pennant, Flamini, van Persie, Almunia, Cygan

Charlton subs: Johansson, Holland, Andersen, Hughes, Rommedahl

EVENT LINE

33 ⚽ **Ljungberg (Open Play)**
36 ▯ **Vieira (Foul)**
38 ▯ Stuart (Foul)
40 ▯ **Ljungberg (Foul)**

HALF TIME 1 - 0

48 ⚽ **Henry (Open Play)**
49 ⇄ **Ljungberg (Off) Pennant (On)**
66 ⇄ Euell (Off) Johansson (On)
66 ⇄ Kishishev (Off) Rommedahl (On)
67 ▯ **Clichy (Foul)**
69 ⚽ **Henry (Open Play)**
70 ⚽ **Reyes (Open Play)**
74 ⇄ Stuart (Off) Holland (On)
82 ⇄ **Fabregas (Off) Flamini (On)**
82 ⇄ **Henry (Off) van Persie (On)**

FULL TIME 4 - 0

STATISTICS

Season	Fixture (Arsenal)		Fixture (Charlton)	Season
77	9	Shots On Target	0	32
37	6	Shots Off Target	4	32
4	0	Hit Woodwork	0	2
18	2	Caught Offside	6	26
43	6	Corners	1	35
83	13	Fouls	15	105
59%	60%	Possession	40%	43%

LEAGUE STANDINGS

Position (pos before)		W	D	L	F	A	Pts
1 (1)	Arsenal	7	1	0	26	7	22
9 (7)	Charlton Ath	3	2	3	8	14	11

Saturday 2nd October 2004 | Venue: **Highbury** | Attendance: **38,103** | Referee: **M.L.Dean**

ARSENAL 4 CHARLTON ATHLETIC 0

Arsenal turned on the style at Highbury as Charlton again conceded four goals away from home.

At least on this occasion the Addicks could point to the fluent football of their on-song opponents as the reason for the hammering. Arsene Wenger's side purred like a well-oiled machine, and could easily have scored more had it not been for Dean Kiely.

That said, the Gunners were slow to get going, possibly feeling the effects of a midweek Champions League trip to Rosenborg. The visitors were unable to make any real inroads, however, and the home side soon slipped into gear.

Firstly, a crisp move ended with a low effort from Dennis Bergkamp that flew narrowly wide of the post. Then, Gael Clichy fired over with the goal gaping, before Jose Antonio Reyes missed the target following a free-kick.

A decent save by Kiely from Bergkamp only served to delay the inevitable. After 33 minutes, Arsenal's Dutch master beat the keeper to a crossfield ball from the left, and promptly kept his composure to lay on a simple finish for the onrushing Freddie Ljungberg.

A woeful 35-yard strike from Talal El Karkouri hardly left the Highbury crowd with a feeling of trepidation going into the interval, and just three minutes after the restart it was 2-0. Having had a fairly quiet afternoon, Thierry Henry dazzled everyone inside the ground with a back-heeled goal that few players would have even attempted.

There followed a sequence of slick interplay, as Arsenal demonstrated why they are worthy Champions. Despite chasing shadows for large periods, Graham Stuart did miss a gilt-edge chance to get his side back in the game. It was to prove costly, as Wenger's men struck twice in quick succession.

A rapier-like Henry drive from the inside left channel made it 3-0 after 69 minutes, and almost immediately Reyes added a fourth. The young Spaniard continued his fine start to the season by latching onto a Bergkamp pass and firing beyond Kiely.

The Irish keeper saved his team from further humiliation with a string of late saves, and on this showing it is difficult to see anyone stopping the North Londoners.

Cesc Fabregas takes a tumble

"I felt the lads were up for it today. They wanted to give a response because there had been reports doubting our team spirit this week."
Arsene Wenger

"It's a very difficult place to come. There are 16 or 17 teams in the league who will really struggle here."
Alan Curbishley

PREMIERSHIP FIXTURE HISTORY

Pl: 11 Draws: 3	Wins	Goals	Yellow	Red
Blackburn Rovers	6	20	11	0
Aston Villa	2	9	16	1

STARTING LINE-UPS

Friedel
Neill, Amoruso, Matteo, Gray
Emerton, Ferguson (c), Tugay, Jansen
Djorkaeff, Dickov

Angel, Cole
Barry, McCann, Hendrie, Solano
Samuel, Mellberg (c), Delaney, De la Cruz
Sorensen

Subs (Blackburn): Flitcroft, Enckelman, Stead, Bothroyd, Johansson

Subs (Aston Villa): Vassell, Postma, Hitzlsperger, Davis, Whittingham

EVENT LINE

25 Angel (Open Play)

30 **Ferguson (Open Play)**

HALF TIME 1 - 1

58 **Jansen (Off) Flitcroft (On)**

60 **Emerton (Dissent)**

60 McCann (Foul)

63 **Emerton (Open Play)**

69 Solano (Foul)

71 **Djorkaeff (Off) Stead (On)**

76 Barry (Off) Hitzlsperger (On)

76 Solano (Off) Vassell (On)

80 Mellberg (Corner)

87 **Neill (Foul)**

FULL TIME 2 - 2

STATISTICS

Season	Fixture (Blackburn)		Fixture (Aston Villa)	Season
31	7	Shots On Target	9	55
47	6	Shots Off Target	6	48
1	0	Hit Woodwork	1	3
32	4	Caught Offside	3	18
53	6	Corners	1	51
137	14	Fouls	17	119
49%	51%	Possession	49%	49%

LEAGUE STANDINGS

Position (pos before)		W	D	L	F	A	Pts
17 (16)	Blackburn R	1	3	4	7	14	6
8 (9)	Aston Villa	2	5	1	10	9	11

Saturday 2nd October 2004 | Venue: Ewood Park | Attendance: 20,502 | Referee: P.Walton

BLACKBURN ROVERS 2 ASTON VILLA 2

Youri Djorkaeff congratulates goalscorer Brett Emerton

"I thought we did enough to win, and to concede from a set-piece was disappointing."
Mark Hughes

PREMIERSHIP MILESTONE

250 Dominic Matteo made his 250th Premiership appearance

PREMIERSHIP MILESTONE

Youri Djorkaeff made his first Premiership appearance for Blackburn

"I thought some of our attacking play was really good and we always looked a threat."
David O'Leary

An Olof Mellberg goal ten minutes from time ensured that the spoils were shared in a highly entertaining battle at Ewood Park.

Aston Villa had taken the lead through Juan Pablo Angel, only to find themselves 2-1 down following strikes from Barry Ferguson and Brett Emerton. In the end a draw was a fair result, though both sides gave everything in search of victory.

Recent acquisition Youri Djorkaeff was handed a starting place by Mark Hughes, and operated just off Paul Dickov in attack. Carlton Cole was preferred to Darius Vassell in the visitors' front line, as David O'Leary's team looked to end a run of three Premiership draws.

Following a high tempo opening, with chances at both ends, the Birmingham outfit made the breakthrough after 25 minutes. It was a goal fashioned in South America as Ecuadorian Ulises De la Cruz burst forward and slipped a pass into the path of Colombian Angel, who hit a low first-time drive beyond Brad Friedel.

The lead was short-lived, however, as Blackburn struck back through their captain Ferguson just five minutes later. Great work by Paul Dickov down the right ended when the Scotland international's near-post cross was expertely turned home from close range by his fellow countryman.

Former Bolton player Djorkaeff was having a positive effect on his new employers' football, and the Frenchman went close to scoring shortly before the break. When the teams re-emerged, Gareth Barry spurned a glorious chance, and Angel saw a headed effort ruled out for offside.

Shortly afterwards, with 63 minutes on the clock, Djorkaeff slipped a clever ball inside the full-back, enabling Brett Emerton to curl a low right-foot effort into the far corner from the inside left channel.

Thomas Sorensen then denied Dickov as Rovers tried to seal the points. At the other end, Friedel had to be at his best to keep out Cole, though he was unable to stop Olof Mellberg from levelling the scores.

The Villa captain confidently steered the ball home from ten yards out, after Mark Delaney had nodded down a corner.

PREMIERSHIP FIXTURE HISTORY

Pl: **13** Draws: **6**	Wins	⚽	□	■
Everton	**2**	**11**	**18**	**0**
Tottenham Hotspur	**5**	**14**	**25**	**3**

STARTING LINE-UPS

Ferguson, Watson, McFadden, Wright, Yobo

Gardner, Ziegler, Keller, Brown, Silva

EVENT LINE

HALF TIME 0 - 0

53 Pamarot (Corner)

58 **Carsley (Off) Ferguson (On)**

60 Redknapp (Foul)

63 **Cahill (Off) Watson (On)**

64 Defoe (Foul)

69 Edman (Off) Gardner (On)

77 **Pistone (Off) McFadden (On)**

80 Defoe (Off) Ziegler (On)

89 **Gravesen (Foul)**

FULL TIME 0 - 1

STATISTICS

Season	Fixture		Fixture	Season
42	**4**	Shots On Target	**2**	**41**
38	**6**	Shots Off Target	**6**	**46**
2	**2**	Hit Woodwork	**0**	**2**
27	**7**	Caught Offside	**8**	**26**
44	**11**	Corners	**2**	**37**
98	**9**	Fouls	**13**	**106**
50%	**60%**	Possession	**40%**	**45%**

LEAGUE STANDINGS

Position (pos before)		W	D	L	F	A	Pts
3 (3)	**Everton**	**5**	**1**	**2**	**9**	**7**	**16**
4 (10)	**Tottenham H**	**3**	**4**	**1**	**5**	**3**	**13**

Saturday 2nd October 2004 | Venue: **Goodison Park** | Attendance: **38,264** | Referee: **G.Poll**

EVERTON 0 TOTTENHAM HOTSPUR 1

Two of English football's former heavyweights slugged it out at Goodison Park, as they both looked to continue their impressive starts to the season.

As it turned out, the game was something of a damp squib, with Noe Pamarot winning the match for Tottenham in the 53rd minute. The defender rose unchallenged to power home a terrific 12-yard header from Robbie Keane's outswinging right-wing corner.

The result was harsh on an Everton side that twice hit the woodwork, through Tim Cahill in the first half and Leon Osman in the second, as Jacques Santini's side registered their fifth clean sheet in eight Premiership outings.

After a nervy opening, it was David Moyes' charges who came closest to breaking the deadlock. Australian Cahill rose majestically to nod Thomas Gravesen's long throw from the right against an upright.

The former Millwall midfielder saw another headed repelled by Paul Robinson, with Marcus Bent firing the loose ball over the bar, before Kevin Kilbane drilled a shot inches wide of the post.

The visitors were under the cosh, but could have taken a lead into the interval had they been awarded a penalty just before the break. Jermain Defoe twisted and turned in the box and enticed a lunging challenge from Alan Stubbs. The striker went down, but referee Graham Poll waved away his protests.

Any lingering feelings of discontent were put to bed, however, when Pamarot converted Spurs' only genuine chance of the match. Moments later, Osman struck the inside of a post, but that was as close as Everton came to an equaliser.

The remainder of the contest was marred by a couple of nasty challenges. Firstly, Cahill hobbled off after an unintentional over-the-ball tackle from Jamie Redknapp. Then, Defoe was lucky to escape with a yellow card following a two-footed lunge on David Weir in front of the dugouts.

Home substitute James McFadden saw a bright run halted by Robinson's agility off his line, and Keane curled a half-chance over from 12 yards, as the game petered out. If both sides are to maintain their lofty positions, they must produce considerably better performances than they served up today.

"I thought we played well enough to win, but football happens like that sometimes."

David Moyes

"I have spent enough time on treatment tables and out injured in my career not to do something like that to a fellow professional."

Jamie Redknapp on his poor challenge on Tim Cahill

PREMIERSHIP MILESTONE

Reto Ziegler made his Premiership debut

PREMIERSHIP MILESTONE

Noe Pamarot netted his first Premiership goal

Noe Pamarot celebrates his goal with Jamie Redknapp

PREMIERSHIP FIXTURE HISTORY

Pl: 1 Draws: 1	Wins	⚽	□	■
Norwich City	0	2	1	0
Portsmouth	0	2	3	0

STARTING LINE-UPS

McVeigh, Svensson, Ward, Helveg, Doherty

Fuller, Lua Lua, Hughes, Ashdown, Mezague

EVENT LINE

37 ⚽ Yakubu (Open Play)
45 □ Griffin (Foul)

HALF TIME 0 - 1

60 ⇄ Kamara (Off) Fuller (On)
62 □ Taylor (Foul)
63 ⚽ **Huckerby (Penalty)**
65 ⚽ Berger (Indirect Free Kick)
67 ⚽ **Charlton (Corner)**
69 □ **Jonson (Foul)**
69 ⇄ Cisse (Off) Lua Lua (On)
72 ⇄ **Jonson (Off) McVeigh (On)**
72 □ Faye (Foul)
78 ⇄ Faye (Off) Hughes (On)
79 ⇄ **McKenzie (Off) Svensson (On)**

FULL TIME 2 - 2

STATISTICS

Season	Fixture (Norwich City)		Fixture (Portsmouth)	Season
37	9	Shots On Target	6	46
42	8	Shots Off Target	7	39
2	1	Hit Woodwork	0	1
30	1	Caught Offside	1	16
37	8	Corners	2	36
102	13	Fouls	7	84
46%	43%	Possession	57%	49%

LEAGUE STANDINGS

Position (pos before)	W	D	L	F	A	Pts
19 (19) Norwich C	0	5	3	7	14	5
13 (14) Portsmouth	2	2	3	11	11	8

Saturday 2nd October 2004 | Venue: **Carrow Road** | Attendance: **23,853** | Referee: **M.D.Messias**

Simon Charlton celebrates levelling the scores

"Apart from the first half at Liverpool last week, I cannot fault my players for the effort that they've put in this season."

Nigel Worthington

PREMIERSHIP MILESTONE

Simon Charlton scored his first Premiership goal for Norwich

"When you get in front twice away from home, you expect to win."

Harry Redknapp

PREMIERSHIP MILESTONE

Aliou Cisse made his first Premiership appearance for Portsmouth

NORWICH CITY 2 PORTSMOUTH 2

Three goals in four minutes midway through the second half enlivened a game that seemed to be drifting towards a narrow away victory after Aiyegbeni Yakubu's first half strike.

No sooner had Darren Huckerby turned home the rebound after his initial penalty had been saved, than Patrik Berger restored Portsmouth's advantage, only for Simon Charlton to then pop up and make it 2-2.

The last two 'Division One' Champions were meeting at Carrow Road in a match that could, even at this early stage of the campaign, be billed as a potential relegation six-pointer. Furthermore, Harry Redknapp was looking to avenge the first defeat he suffered as Pompey boss.

Proceedings opened with a spate of early corners, and David Bentley struck the near post with one such flag-kick. The visitors were looking dangerous on the break, and Diomansy Kamara's mesmeric run deserved a better finish.

After 37 minutes, the Senegalese striker was shown how to find the net by Yakubu. The Nigerian international steered a 10-yard effort into the bottom right-hand corner, after Robert Green had failed to hold a swerving long-range drive from Nigel Quashie.

Shaka Hislop was called upon to keep out a shot from Bentley and then to deny Damien Francis, as the South Coast side went in at half-time with a one-goal advantage.

The second period offered little by way of goalmouth action, before briefly exploding into life. Norwich were awarded a 63rd-minute penalty when Huckerby was bundled over by Matthew Taylor, and the speedy frontman tapped home from close range after Hislop had parried his initial spot-kick.

Just two minutes later, however, all the good work was undone. Patrik Berger scored yet another spectacular goal, driving into the top left-hand corner from 25 yards after David Unsworth had touched a free-kick into his path.

The scoring was not completed though, as Nigel Worthington's team drew level for the second time. A 67th-minute corner found its way to Adam Drury on the left of the area, and the captain sent over a cross that Charlton glanced just inside the far post from seven yards out, to earn his side a valuable point.

PREMIERSHIP FIXTURE HISTORY

Pl: 8 Draws: 3	Wins	Goals	Yellow	Red
Southampton	1	5	8	1
Manchester City	4	9	7	0

STARTING LINE-UPS

Southampton subs: Crouch, Van Damme, McCann, Blayney, Kenton

Manchester City subs: Sommeil, Waterreus, Flood, McManaman, B.Wright-Phillips

EVENT LINE

18 Beattie (Off) Crouch (On)

HALF TIME 0 - 0

46 Le Saux (Off) Van Damme (On)

67 Fernandes (Off) McCann (On)

FULL TIME 0 - 0

STATISTICS

Season	Fixture (Southampton)		Fixture (Man City)	Season
44	11	Shots On Target	11	53
48	5	Shots Off Target	10	46
0	0	Hit Woodwork	0	1
20	4	Caught Offside	5	29
47	6	Corners	14	61
107	13	Fouls	11	113
49%	46%	Possession	54%	47%

LEAGUE STANDINGS

Position (pos before)	W	D	L	F	A	Pts
18 (17) Southampton	1	2	5	6	11	5
12 (13) Man City	2	2	4	8	7	8

Saturday 2nd October 2004 | Venue: Friends Provident St Mary's Stadium | Attendance: 28,605 | Referee: U.D.Rennie

SOUTHAMPTON 0 MANCHESTER CITY 0

Kevin Keegan was left to rue a whole host of missed chances, as his Manchester City side failed to find the goal that would have beaten a woeful Southampton.

The visitors forced 14 corners and managed 21 shots, with Steve Wigley's men only responding in the second period. Yet, despite having three efforts cleared off the line, the North-West side could have gone home empty-handed had Kevin Phillips beaten David James with a last-gasp lob.

Sun Jihai occupied an unaccustomed role on the left of midfield for City, while the Saints kept faith with the team that had lost narrowly at Fulham seven days earlier.

The first half was all one-way traffic. After James Beattie had limped off with a suspected broken toe, the chances began to come thick and fast.

David Prutton was called upon to make goal-line clearances from both Richard Dunne and Sylvain Distin, with Anders Svensson doing so for a third time later on. Then, Ben Thatcher fired a 25-yard free-kick narrowly over, before Jihai somehow pulled a left-foot shot across the face of goal after 35 minutes.

The South Coast side mustered a weak header from Phillips before the interval, and must have been on the sharp end of Wigley's tongue at the break. Whatever was said clearly had a positive effect, as the men in red and white emerged for the second half with renewed vigour.

Rory Delap forced Dunne into the fourth last-ditch clearance of the match, as Southampton began to hit the target with increasing regularity. However, the better openings continued to fall to the visitors, Antti Niemi saving a fierce drive from Jihai and then injuring his face when blocking a Nicolas Anelka effort.

The Finnish keeper recovered to keep out a low strike from Jonathan Macken, while home substitute Peter Crouch saw a header repelled by the visiting custodian. A frantic finish then saw the ball fly across the face of Niemi's goal, before Phillips failed to get enough height on his attempted lob.

Although both teams could have won, Keegan's side had far better chances to do so. On this evidence, neither club looks set for a prosperous campaign.

"I'm prepared to admit that if we play another six times like we did against Manchester City, I don't expect to be here."
Steve Wigley

PREMIERSHIP MILESTONE
200 James Beattie made his 200th Premiership appearance for Southampton

"It's an understatement to say that we should have won easily."
Kevin Keegan

Kevin Phillips beats Ben Thatcher to the ball

PREMIERSHIP FIXTURE HISTORY

Pl: 2 Draws: 1	Wins	⚽	☐	■
West Bromwich Albion	1	3	2	0
Bolton Wanderers	0	2	4	0

STARTING LINE-UPS

Dyer, Kuszczak, Contra, O'Connor, Earnshaw

Diouf, Kaku, Oakes, Barness, Giannakopoulos

EVENT LINE

34 Okocha (Off) Diouf (On)

HALF TIME 0 - 0

57 **Kanu (Open Play)**

58 Pedersen (Off) Giannakopoulos (On)

65 **Gera (Corner)**

65 Campo (Off) Kaku (On)

73 Giannakopoulos (Direct Free Kick)

81 **Albrechtsen (Off) Dyer (On)**

FULL TIME 2 - 1

STATISTICS

Season	Fixture		Fixture	Season
37	7	Shots On Target	7	60
36	6	Shots Off Target	9	43
1	0	Hit Woodwork	2	3
32	3	Caught Offside	1	16
53	6	Corners	5	48
106	18	Fouls	15	107
47%	51%	Possession	49%	48%

LEAGUE STANDINGS

Position (pos before)		W	D	L	F	A	Pts
15 (18)	West Brom	1	4	3	8	13	7
5 (4)	Bolton W	3	3	2	13	11	12

Saturday 2nd October 2004 | Venue: **The Hawthorns** | Attendance: **23,849** | Referee: **M.Clattenburg**

WEST BROM 2 BOLTON WANDERERS 1

West Brom recorded their first victory of the season to climb out of the relegation zone.

Summer signings Nwankwo Kanu and Zoltan Gera netted second half goals for the Baggies, before Greek international Stylianos Giannakopoulos set up a nervous conclusion with a 73rd-minute free-kick.

The home side had begun proceedings at a startling pace, not allowing Bolton to settle on the ball. Having already gone close with a couple of strikes from long range, Gera saw a goalbound shot blocked after Gary Speed had headed Darren Moore's effort off the line.

A poor Jonathan Greening header emphasised West Brom's failings in front of goal, and they were nearly punished in the 25th minute when Kevin Nolan struck a post. The Liverpool-born midfielder narrowly failed to squeeze the ball home from close range after Russell Hoult had kept out Ricardo Gardner's drive.

Hungarian Gera continued to trouble the Trotters' backline, whistling a 20-yarder just the wrong side of an upright on the stroke of half-time. Sam Allardyce's men failed to heed the warning, and they were made to pay after 57 minutes.

Collecting the ball on the right flank, Gera cut inside before firing in a low cross-cum-shot. As the defenders appealed in vain for an offside flag, Kanu poked out a right leg and steered home past the helpless Jussi Jaaskelainen from seven yards.

Eight minutes later, the creator of that goal netted a decisive second. An inswinging Greening corner from the left was glanced home at the near post by Gera, sending the majority of the 23,849-strong crowd into raptures.

Only then did Bolton spark into life, and they pulled a goal back with 17 minutes remaining. A trip on Gardner led to a free-kick in an inside left position some 25 yards out, enabling Giannakopoulos to curl over a ball that evaded a cluster of bodies and crept into the bottom right-hand corner of the net.

Despite late pressure that included a wayward Radhi Jaidi volley from close range, the Baggies hung on to collect a vital three points.

West Brom enjoy their first success of the season

"It's been a long time coming and it's a nice feeling."

Gary Megson on his side's first win of the season

"Overall we were not at our best, and after doing what we have done recently, it is disappointing."

Sam Allardyce

PREMIERSHIP MILESTONE

Blessing Kaku made his Premiership debut

PREMIERSHIP FIXTURE HISTORY

Pl: **3** Draws: **2**

	Wins	Goals	Yellow cards	Red cards
Birmingham City	0	3	7	0
Newcastle United	1	5	6	0

STARTING LINE-UPS

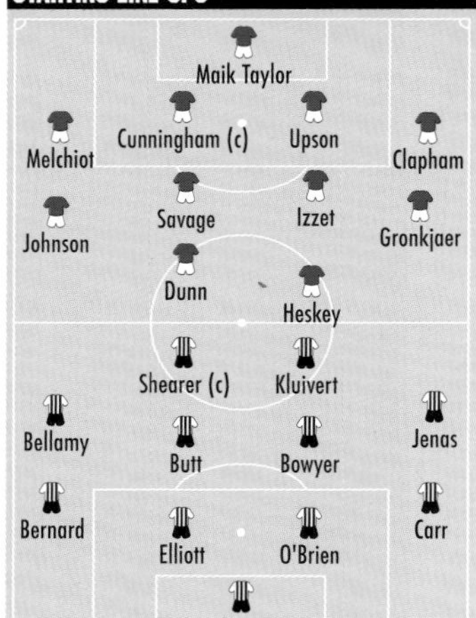

Birmingham City substitutes: Yorke, Clemence, Gray, Bennett, Morrison

Newcastle United substitutes: Milner, Robert, Hughes, Harper, Ambrose

EVENT LINE

Min	Event
3	Goal: Jenas (Open Play)
9	Substitution: **Heskey (Off) Yorke (On)**
23	Goal: **Yorke (Open Play)**
36	Substitution: **Izzet (Off) Clemence (On)**
	HALF TIME 1 - 1
46	Substitution: Kluivert (Off) Milner (On)
48	Booking: Elliott (Foul)
53	Booking: **Dunn (Dissent)**
57	Goal: **Upson (Indirect Free Kick)**
59	Booking: **Clemence (Foul)**
64	Substitution: Bernard (Off) Robert (On)
67	Goal: Butt (Open Play)
73	Booking: Butt (Foul)
81	Substitution: Bowyer (Off) Hughes (On)
83	Substitution: **Dunn (Off) Gray (On)**
90	Booking: **Savage (Foul)**
	FULL TIME 2 - 2

STATISTICS

Season	Fixture (Birmingham)		Fixture (Newcastle)	Season
30	6	Shots On Target	3	56
35	4	Shots Off Target	3	47
1	0	Hit Woodwork	1	3
21	5	Caught Offside	5	27
45	6	Corners	5	63
117	17	Fouls	14	100
50%	50%	Possession	50%	53%

LEAGUE STANDINGS

Position (pos before)		W	D	L	F	A	Pts
15 (16)	Birmingham C	1	4	3	7	9	7
6 (7)	Newcastle Utd	3	3	2	16	13	12

Sunday 3rd October 2004 | Venue: **St Andrew's** | Attendance: **29,021** | Referee: **H.M.Webb**

BIRMINGHAM CITY 2 NEWCASTLE UNITED 2

A terrific encounter ended 2-2 at St Andrew's, leaving both sides to reflect on what might have been.

The visitors drew first blood, taking a third-minute lead through Jermaine Jenas. The England international midfielder expertly slotted across Maik Taylor and into the bottom left-hand corner from 12 yards after Patrick Kluivert's ambitious shot had deflected into his path.

Birmingham were dealt a further blow inside the opening 10 minutes when Emile Heskey had to limp out of the action. The former Liverpool striker was replaced by Dwight Yorke, who made a fairly immediate impact with a well-taken 23rd-minute equaliser.

An astute pass from David Dunn on halfway, making his first start of the season in a role just off the lone frontman, sent Yorke galloping clear in the inside right channel. Having used up all the available time, the Trinidad and Tobago international squeezed a 15-yard shot beyond Shay Given, courtesy of a deflection off the recovering Andy O'Brien.

Driving rain contributed heavily to the exciting fare being served up, and Steve Bruce's team were unlucky not to be awarded a 28th-minute penalty when Stephen Carr appeared to push Yorke as they both jumped for a Damien Johnson cross.

Events continued at a brisk pace after the interval, and the home side took the lead after 57 minutes. An inswinging Robbie Savage free-kick from the left was met by the head of Matthew Upson six yards out, as Birmingham netted more than once for the first time in a 2004-05 Premiership fixture.

The lead lasted just 10 minutes, however, as Nicky Butt opened his Newcastle goalscoring account with a strike that any player would have been proud of. The combative midfielder reacted instantly to a misplaced defensive header, acrobatically sending a swivelling 15-yard volley beyond the outstretched right hand of the goalkeeper.

It needed a fine save from Given to keep out Dunn's close-range effort, while visiting substitute Laurent Robert struck a late free-kick against a post from fully 35 yards, as both teams pushed forward in search of a winner.

Nicky Butt celebrates a rare goal

"If we can keep playing like that, and with a little bit of luck, we should start to enjoy some winning performances."
Steve Bruce

PREMIERSHIP MILESTONE

Matthew Upson scored his first Premiership goal

"Birmingham is a difficult place to visit, and to get a result playing against a struggling team who are desperate for the points was always going to be difficult."
Graeme Souness

PREMIERSHIP MILESTONE

Nicky Butt scored his first Premiership goal for Newcastle

PREMIERSHIP FIXTURE HISTORY

Pl: 13 Draws: 3	Wins	Goals	Yellow cards	Red cards
Chelsea	9	22	12	0
Liverpool	1	6	16	2

STARTING LINE-UPS

J.Cole, Geremi, Tiago, Cudicini, Huth

Baros, Finnan, Hamann, Dudek, Warnock

EVENT LINE

38 **Drogba (Off) Cole J (On)**

HALF TIME 0 - 0

64 **Cole J (Indirect Free Kick)**

71 Josemi (Off) Baros (On)

78 Diao (Off) Hamann (On)

78 Garcia (Off) Finnan (On)

81 **Duff (Off) Geremi (On)**

85 **Smertin (Off) Tiago (On)**

90 Carragher (Foul)

FULL TIME 1 - 0

STATISTICS

Season	Fixture	Chelsea / Liverpool	Fixture	Season
55	5	Shots On Target	3	47
62	8	Shots Off Target	2	38
3	0	Hit Woodwork	0	0
27	1	Caught Offside	2	18
55	11	Corners	2	34
106	14	Fouls	20	88
56%	55%	Possession	45%	54%

LEAGUE STANDINGS

Position (pos before)	W	D	L	F	A	Pts
2 (2) Chelsea	6	2	0	8	1	20
11 (10) Liverpool	3	1	3	10	6	10

Sunday 3rd October 2004 | Venue: **Stamford Bridge** | Attendance: **42,028** | Referee: **P.Dowd**

CHELSEA 1 LIVERPOOL 0

A 64th-minute goal from substitute Joe Cole proved enough to settle this intriguing contest at Stamford Bridge.

The decisive strike was very similar to the Londoners' winner at Middlesbrough, as the young midfielder stole across the front of his marker to divert home Frank Lampard's low free-kick from the right.

In light of the summer managerial changes at both clubs, the match did not resemble a traditional English contest. European football's two most successful managers of 2003-04, Jose Mourinho's Porto won the Champions League while Rafael Benitez's Valencia won the UEFA Cup, locked horns in an intense tactical battle.

The Merseysiders' Spanish boss opted to play a counter-attacking game, with Harry Kewell offering support to lone striker Djibril Cisse, while Chelsea's new man incorporated Damien Duff into a three-pronged strikeforce.

As a consequence, most of the football was played in Liverpool's half. Didier Drogba dragged a fifth-minute effort wide of the target, and Lampard, Duff and Alexei Smertin all failed to test Chris Kirkland, who was making his first start of the season at the expense of Jerzy Dudek, from promising positions.

The Anfield side created nothing more than half-chances during the opening period, Kewell and Cisse both failing to trouble Petr Cech with headers. After Cole had replaced the injured Drogba, a change that saw Eidur Gudjohnsen switched to the central attacking role, Lampard failed to capitalise on a dangerous cross from Duff.

The blank half-time scoreline showed little sign of changing until Cole provided the game with its only genuine moment of inspiration. Mourinho's touchline reaction suggested that the successful free-kick routine had been contrived on the training ground, as the former West Ham midfielder responded positively to his recent exclusion from the starting line-up.

Benitez responded with the 71st-minute introduction of Milan Baros at the expense of Josemi, but Liverpool rarely threatened the home goal in a far-from-exciting conclusion.

Having failed to break down Tottenham under similar circumstances earlier in the campaign, the persistence shown by his players would have delighted the Chelsea manager. The Stamford Bridge outfit are clearly moving in the right direction, but can the same be said of their visitors?

Joe Cole is the Chelsea hero

> **"He has two faces, one is beautiful and one that I don't like. But I can improve him, and he wants to learn."**
>
> Jose Mourinho on Joe Cole

> **"We wanted to keep the ball, but we had to change when they scored."**
>
> Rafael Benitez

PREMIERSHIP FIXTURE HISTORY

Pl: 10 Draws: 2	Wins	Goals	Yellow	Red
Manchester United	5	17	14	1
Middlesbrough	3	12	15	1

STARTING LINE-UPS

Smith, Ricardo, Fortune, Kleberson, Djemba-Djemba

Cooper, Doriva, Graham, Nash, Taylor

EVENT LINE

29 **Keane (Foul)**
33 Downing (Open Play)
35 Parnaby (Off) Cooper (On)
HALF TIME 0 - 1
57 Mendieta (Foul)
69 **O'Shea (Off) Smith (On)**
74 Boateng (Ung.Conduct)
79 Morrison (Off) Doriva (On)
81 **Smith (Open Play)**
87 Downing (Off) Graham (On)
90 Nemeth (Ung.Conduct)
FULL TIME 1 - 1

STATISTICS

Season	Fixture		Fixture	Season
59	10	Shots On Target	9	61
55	12	Shots Off Target	4	46
5	1	Hit Woodwork	0	0
23	2	Caught Offside	2	31
63	10	Corners	2	35
97	8	Fouls	13	105
53%	58%	Possession	42%	49%

LEAGUE STANDINGS

Position (pos before)		W	D	L	F	A	Pts
4 (6)	Man Utd	3	4	1	9	7	13
9 (11)	Middlesbrough	3	2	3	12	12	11

Sunday 3rd October 2004 | Venue: **Old Trafford** | Attendance: **67,988** | Referee: **R.Styles**

MANCHESTER UNITED 1 MIDDLESBROUGH 1

Alan Smith came off the bench to spare United's blushes, heading home Cristiano Ronaldo's 81st-minute cross to earn his side a point against a youthful Middlesbrough.

Despite the visitors' encouraging start to the campaign, few would have expected Steve McClaren's injury-ravaged team to put up such a sterling performance. Names such as Jimmy Floyd Hasselbaink, Mark Viduka and Ray Parlour were absent from a teamsheet that relied heavily on the club's youth academy.

Indeed, it was two products of that system that combined to give the Teesside outfit a 33rd-minute lead. James Morrison, fresh from a midweek UEFA Cup goal in Ostrava, whipped over a dangerous cross from the right, where the highly-rated Stewart Downing arrived to guide the ball into the roof of the net from just inside the six-yard box.

The architects of the goal had lined up on opposite flanks in a 4-5-1 formation. For their part, United had started with a near full-strength side. After his debut hat-trick against Fenerbahce on Tuesday, much was expected of Wayne Rooney on his first Premiership start for the club.

Perhaps the former Everton striker's lack of match practice was catching up with him, as he was largely anonymous in the first half. Sir Alex Ferguson's charges did create openings, however, but Ronaldo, Ryan Giggs and Ruud van Nistelrooy all spurned the chances.

The pattern of play changed little after the interval, with the Old Trafford team largely camped in and around the Middlesbrough box. Yet, it was the visitors who should have extended their lead, as Gaizka Mendieta fired over from 12 yards out with just Roy Carroll to beat.

John O'Shea made way for Smith in the 69th minute, and moments later van Nistelrooy headed against the crossbar. The former PSV Eindhoven forward then blazed over following an astute pass from Rooney, before persistence from Ronaldo down the right saw the Portuguese international pull back a cross that Smith headed beyond Mark Schwarzer.

There followed some hairy moments for McClaren's side, but they hung on to claim a deserved share of the spoils.

Ryan Giggs tries to make something happen

"It was a disappointing result, but it did not reflect the performance in any way."
Sir Alex Ferguson

PREMIERSHIP MILESTONE
Wayne Rooney made his first Premiership appearance for Man Utd

"The result was a real bonus. I don't think anyone who saw the teamsheet before the game gave us any hope."
Steve McClaren

PREMIERSHIP MILESTONE
Anthony McMahon and Danny Graham both made their Premiership debuts

PREMIERSHIP FIXTURE HISTORY

Pl: **1** Draws: **0**

	Wins	Goals	Yellow	Red
Crystal Palace	1	2	1	0
Fulham	0	0	1	1

STARTING LINE-UPS

Crystal Palace: Kiraly; Boyce, Hall, Popovic (c), Granville; Routledge, Riihilahti, Watson, Kolkka; Hughes, Johnson

Fulham: Radzinski, McBride; Malbranque; Pembridge (c), Boa Morte; McKinlay; Green, Pearce, Knight, Volz; van der Sar

Crystal Palace substitutes: Sorondo, Lakis, Kaviedes, Speroni, Torghelle

Fulham substitutes: Goma, Bocanegra, John, Crossley, Rehman

EVENT LINE

6 Pearce (Foul)

9 Radzinski (Off) Goma (On)

33 **Johnson (Foul)**

HALF TIME 0 - 0

46 **Hall (Off) Sorondo (On)**

53 **Johnson (Open Play)**

62 Goma (Off) Bocanegra (On)

62 McBride (Off) John (On)

69 **Riihilahti (Corner)**

72 **Routledge (Off) Lakis (On)**

74 **Riihilahti (Off) Kaviedes (On)**

79 Bocanegra (Foul)

FULL TIME 2 - 0

STATISTICS

Season	Fixture (Crystal Palace)		Fixture (Fulham)	Season
37	**8**	Shots On Target	**5**	**45**
43	**12**	Shots Off Target	**4**	**38**
2	**1**	Hit Woodwork	**0**	**2**
18	**3**	Caught Offside	**0**	**21**
48	**11**	Corners	**2**	**46**
116	**12**	Fouls	**9**	**88**
47%	**58%**	Possession	**42%**	**49%**

LEAGUE STANDINGS

Position (pos before)	W	D	L	F	A	Pts
19 (20) Crystal Palace	**1**	**2**	**5**	**8**	**14**	**5**
14 (14) Fulham	**2**	**2**	**4**	**8**	**13**	**8**

Monday 4th October 2004 | Venue: **Selhurst Park** | Attendance: **21,825** | Referee: **M.A.Riley**

CRYSTAL PALACE 2 FULHAM 0

Aki Riihilahti wheels away after scoring

"It feels great to be off the bottom. It was a long time coming, but now we can be positive and move forward."

Crystal Palace Assistant Manager Kit Symons

"We didn't lose because we had ten men, it was because we were not good enough."

Chris Coleman

PREMIERSHIP MILESTONE

Aki Riihilahti netted his first Premiership goal

PREMIERSHIP MILESTONE

Vassilios Lakis made his Premiership debut

Following in the footsteps of fellow new boys West Brom, goals from Andy Johnson and Aki Riihilahti handed Crystal Palace their first Premiership win of the season.

The South London outfit's cause was aided significantly by the sixth-minute dismissal of Fulham defender Ian Pearce for a professional foul on Johnson, after the livewire striker had picked his pocket.

The incident followed on from an explosive start in which Edwin van der Sar was called upon to make a fine diving stop. The Dutch keeper was also relieved to see Riihilahti head wide of the target from close range.

Strangely, the red card seemed to stifle the home side's attacking play. Chris Coleman's men appeared content to sit back and hit their hosts on the break, while Palace found all routes to goal blocked.

Wayne Routledge failed to capitalise on hesitation by Adam Green as the half drew to a close, while Luis Boa Morte felt aggrieved at not being awarded a penalty when going down under a combined challenge from goalkeeper Gabor Kiraly and Fitz Hall.

Manager Iain Dowie's half-time pearls of wisdom clearly had the desired effect. Eight minutes into the second period, Riihilahti's clever first-time pass enabled Johnson to steer the ball beyond van der Sar from the right side of the six-yard box.

Then, after 69 minutes, Riihilahti turned from creator to goalscorer, rising like a salmon to head home Routledge's outswinging right-wing corner from eight yards.

The remainder of the contest was a completely one-sided affair. The Selhurst Park crowd were buzzing, but had reason to feel disappointed when referee Mike Riley turned down Johnson's appeals for a penalty.

The former Birmingham striker then fired low past the left-hand upright from 15 yards, having been sent clear of the defence. It was a shocking miss, but one that Palace could afford on a comfortable evening.

Substitute Ivan Kaviedes struck a post late on, while Joonas Kolkka saw an effort deflected over, as Dowie's team climbed off the foot of the Premiership in style.

PREMIERSHIP FIXTURE HISTORY

Pl: 13 Draws: 3	Wins	⚽	Yellow	Red
Arsenal	8	21	22	1
Aston Villa	2	10	31	2

STARTING LINE-UPS

Flamini, Pennant, van Persie, Taylor, Cygan

Whittingham, Davis, Angel, Henderson, Solano

EVENT LINE

Min		Event
3	⚽	Hendrie (Open Play)
8	⇄	Barry (Off) Whittingham (On)
17	☐	Cole (Foul)
19	⚽	**Pires (Penalty)**
21	☐	Mellberg (Foul)
33	☐	**Cole (Foul)**
38	☐	**Fabregas (Foul)**
45	⚽	**Henry (Open Play)**
		HALF TIME 2 - 1
46	⇄	Hitzlsperger (Off) Davis (On)
58	⇄	Cole (Off) Angel (On)
63	☐	Samuel (Foul)
66	⇄	**Vieira (Off) Flamini (On)**
72	⚽	**Pires (Open Play)**
73	☐	Hendrie (Foul)
76	⇄	**Reyes (Off) Pennant (On)**
84	⇄	**Pires (Off) van Persie (On)**
		FULL TIME 3 - 1

STATISTICS

Season	Fixture (Arsenal)		Fixture (Aston Villa)	Season
93	16	Shots On Target	2	57
40	3	Shots Off Target	3	51
5	1	Hit Woodwork	0	3
19	1	Caught Offside	1	19
49	6	Corners	3	54
94	11	Fouls	22	141
60%	64%	Possession	36%	47%

LEAGUE STANDINGS

Position (pos before)		W	D	L	F	A	Pts
1 (1)	Arsenal	8	1	0	29	8	25
11 (8)	Aston Villa	2	5	2	11	12	11

Saturday 16th October 2004 | Venue: **Highbury** | Attendance: **38,137** | Referee: **G.Poll**

ARSENAL 3 ASTON VILLA 1

Arsenal produced one of their finest displays under the tutelage of Arsene Wenger, responding from an early setback to brush Villa aside with an exhibition of fluid football.

Stand-in goalkeeper Stefan Postma was called upon to make numerous top-class saves, as the Gunners ran amok at Highbury. The woodwork also came to the rescue of David O'Leary's side, as the North Londoners registered 16 shots on target.

The game began at breakneck pace. Sol Campbell headed Dennis Bergkamp's right-wing free-kick against the bar, before Lee Hendrie fired the visitors into a shock third-minute lead. Receiving the ball on the right edge of the box courtesy of a mishit Carlton Cole effort, the midfielder curled a low 20-yard effort into the bottom left-hand corner of the goal.

Having survived a further scare when substitute Peter Whittingham fired narrowly wide, Arsenal clicked effortlessly into gear. Chances came thick and fast as Bergkamp headed wide, Jose Antonio Reyes missed by inches and Postma saved from both Patrick Vieira and Ashley Cole.

Then, after 19 minutes, the Gunners drew level from the penalty spot. Robert Pires confidently stroked home a deserved equaliser after Thierry Henry had gone down under Mark Delaney's clumsy challenge.

A devastating spell in the lead up to half-time saw Postma foil Reyes, Cesc Fabregas, Bergkamp and Henry, though the Frenchman did score seconds before the break. Having beaten the offside trap to latch onto a pass from Reyes in the inside left channel, Henry advanced to curl a low shot beyond the advancing goalkeeper from 15 yards.

Wenger's men continued to pepper the away goal from all angles after the interval. Amazing stops kept out Pires, Reyes and Henry, though only until the 72nd minute. After Vieira had limped out of the action with a worrying injury, Pires stroked the ball low past the left hand of Postma to make it 3-1 from 15 yards out.

With victory all but assured, Jermaine Pennant and Robin van Persie were given a taste of the action. Opposition substitute Juan Pablo Angel fired wide from distance in a rare visiting attack, as Arsenal maintained their effortless Premiership progress.

"We created chance after chance. Our passing and movement were excellent and it was very enjoyable to watch."
Arsene Wenger

"Arsenal were always a big club, but they've gone on to another level under Arsene, playing a style of football never played when I was there."
David O'Leary

PREMIERSHIP MILESTONE

150 Darius Vassell made his 150th Premiership appearance

Robert Pires takes the applause

PREMIERSHIP FIXTURE HISTORY

Pl: 3	Draws: 1	Wins	⚽	🟨	🟥
Birmingham City		0	1	2	0
Manchester United		2	3	1	0

STARTING LINE-UPS

Anderton, Clapham, Tebily, Bennett, Martin Taylor

Rooney, Scholes, Ricardo, O'Shea, P.Neville

EVENT LINE

HALF TIME 0 - 0

46 **Gronkjaer (Off) Anderton (On)**

51 **Savage (Foul)**

59 Kleberson (Off) Rooney (On)

77 Ronaldo (Off) Scholes (On)

90 **Johnson (Off) Tebily (On)**

90 **Yorke (Off) Clapham (On)**

FULL TIME 0 - 0

STATISTICS

Season	Fixture		Fixture	Season
36	6	Shots On Target	7	66
41	6	Shots Off Target	5	60
1	0	Hit Woodwork	0	5
24	3	Caught Offside	5	28
48	3	Corners	3	66
133	16	Fouls	11	108
50%	50%	Possession	50%	53%

LEAGUE STANDINGS

Position (pos before)		W	D	L	F	A	Pts
14 (15)	Birmingham C	1	5	3	7	9	8
6 (4)	Man Utd	3	5	1	9	7	14

Saturday 16th October 2004 | Venue: **St Andrew's** | Attendance: **29,221** | Referee: **M.R.Halsey**

BIRMINGHAM CITY 0 MANCHESTER UNITED 0

Manchester United's wretched start to the Premiership season continued, as they played out a fifth draw in their opening nine matches.

Despite ending the match with four strikers on the pitch, as well as Paul Scholes, the visitors were unable to add to a woeful tally of just nine league goals. In fact, they had rarely looked like doing so throughout the entire 90 minutes against a resolute Birmingham City.

Sir Alex Ferguson sprang a few surprises with his initial team selection, leaving Wayne Rooney on the bench and fielding Louis Saha on the left of a four-man midfield. Steve Bruce recalled Julian Gray at left-back, perhaps feeling that the winger's pace would be a valuable asset against the trickery of Cristiano Ronaldo.

The opening half-hour served up as dull a contest as you are ever likely to see. Roy Carroll was forced to parry a low drive from Emile Heskey in the only anxious moment experienced by either side.

Things improved dramatically in the 15 minutes before half-time. Maik Taylor made a brilliant reflex save to keep out a close-range effort from Ruud van Nistelrooy, and then did well to repel a blockbuster from Ronaldo.

Despite these scares, Birmingham thoroughly deserved to be on level terms at the break. Just six minutes after the restart, Robbie Savage was cautioned for a strong challenge on Roy Keane, a clear indication that things were hotting up in central midfield.

Again Heskey saw a powerful low drive kept out by Carroll, and Ferguson responded with the introduction of Rooney. The teenager made little impact, causing his manager to throw on Scholes with 13 minutes remaining.

Kenny Cunningham remained unaffected by whoever he came up against, marshalling the defence towards only its second clean sheet of the season. The other shut-out came against United's city neighbours in August.

Alan Smith fired narrowly wide from 20 yards in the final minute, but a visiting goal would have been both cruel and unjust. As it was, Birmingham were more than happy to take a first Premiership point in five attempts from their illustrious opponents.

Robbie Savage and Roy Keane tussle for possession

PREMIERSHIP MILESTONE

300 Darren Anderton made his 300th Premiership appearance and his first in the colours of Birmingham City

"Playing such a quality side as Manchester United is always a good experience, and to keep a clean sheet and earn a point is no mean achievement."

Kenny Cunningham

"You have to give a lot of credit to Birmingham City. They kept coming forward all the time and competed for the entire game."

Sir Alex Ferguson

PREMIERSHIP FIXTURE HISTORY

Pl: **8** Draws: **4**	Wins	⚽	□	■
Blackburn Rovers	2	5	11	1
Middlesbrough	2	8	12	1

STARTING LINE-UPS

Stead, Short, Jansen, Enckelman, Pedersen

Nemeth, Morrison, Nash, Ehiogu, Bates

EVENT LINE

17	□	McMahon (Foul)
30	■	**Tugay (2nd Bookable Offence)**
		HALF TIME 0 - 0
46	⇄	Parnaby (Off) Nemeth (On)
46	⚽	Hasselbaink (Open Play)
50	⚽	Boateng (Open Play)
57	⚽	Hasselbaink (Corner)
60	□	**Matteo (Foul)**
60	⇄	**Dickov (Off) Stead (On)**
63	⇄	**Amoruso (Off) Short (On)**
78	⇄	**Djorkaeff (Off) Jansen (On)**
80	⇄	Mendieta (Off) Morrison (On)
90	⚽	Hasselbaink (Open Play)
		FULL TIME 0 - 4

STATISTICS

Season	Fixture		Fixture	Season
36	**5**	Shots On Target	**10**	**71**
54	**7**	Shots Off Target	**6**	**52**
1	**0**	Hit Woodwork	**0**	**0**
36	**4**	Caught Offside	**1**	**32**
55	**2**	Corners	**10**	**45**
150	**13**	Fouls	**15**	**120**
48%	**44%**	Possession	**56%**	**50%**

LEAGUE STANDINGS

Position (pos before)	W	D	L	F	A	Pts
18 (17) Blackburn R	**1**	**3**	**5**	**7**	**18**	**6**
5 (9) Middlesbrough	**4**	**2**	**3**	**16**	**12**	**14**

Saturday 16th October 2004 | Venue: **Ewood Park** | Attendance: **20,385** | Referee: **M.A.Riley**

BLACKBURN ROVERS 0 MIDDLESBROUGH 4

Middlesbrough, and Jimmy Floyd Hasselbaink in particular, took full advantage of the first half dismissal of Kerimoglu Tugay, to run riot at Ewood Park.

With a tight contest locked at 0-0 after half-an-hour, Rovers' Turkish international midfielder was given his marching orders following a crazy sliding challenge on Gaizka Mendieta. Referee Mike Riley had already cautioned the playmaker for handball, and had little choice but to show him a second yellow card.

Mark Hughes kept faith with the remaining 10 players, opting to drop Frenchman Youri Djorkaeff into a slightly deeper role. The policy seemed to work, as Steve McClaren's visitors struggled to make their numerical advantage tell in the remainder of the half.

However, things began to fall apart for Blackburn shortly after the interval. Within a minute of the restart, Hasselbaink had ran onto Stewart Downing's threaded pass in the inside left channel and fired the ball beyond Brad Friedel from 10 yards out.

Four minutes later, George Boateng popped up with a rare goal to double the lead. The Dutch midfielder steered home past the goalkeeper from seven yards, after latching onto a clever throughball from Mendieta.

Then, after 57 minutes, it was 3-0. Again Downing supplied Hasselbaink, this time with a low cross from the right following a corner, and the former Chelsea striker arrived on cue to turn home an eight-yard near-post effort.

All Rovers could muster in response were a couple of attempts from Djorkaeff, one of which found the net but was ruled out for offside. Paul Dickov, Brett Emerton and Barry Ferguson had all gone close prior to Tugay's red card, but there was clearly no way back into the game now.

Thankfully for Hughes' charges, Middlesbrough took their foot off the accelerator, though there was still time for Hasselbaink to seal a 90th-minute hat-trick. After substitute Szilard Nemeth had won possession, the Dutch forward drilled a low 17-yard effort into the far right-hand corner of the net with his unfavoured left foot.

The finish was every bit as clinical as a scoreline that emphasised the Teesside club's new-found attacking prowess.

Ray Parlour fends off Barry Ferguson

"We need to get on the training ground and address the issues concerning the way we defend."

Mark Hughes

"The sending off obviously had a bearing on the game, because it had been a very close and tight contest up until that point."

Steve McClaren

PREMIERSHIP MILESTONE

George Boateng scored his first Premiership goal for Middlesbrough

PREMIERSHIP FIXTURE HISTORY

Pl: 2 Draws: 0	Wins	Goals	Yellow cards	Red cards
Bolton Wanderers	2	6	3	0
Crystal Palace	0	2	5	1

STARTING LINE-UPS

Pedersen, Fadiga, Barness, Oakes, Ferdinand

Lakis, Freedman, Derry, Speroni, Sorondo

EVENT LINE

16	**Campo (Off) Pedersen (On)**
27	Watson (Foul)
45	**Davies (Indirect Free Kick)**
	HALF TIME 1 - 0
61	Kolkka (Off) Lakis (On)
69	Watson (Off) Freedman (On)
77	**Diouf (Off) Fadiga (On)**
79	Riihilahti (Off) Derry (On)
83	**Davies (Foul)**
90	**Nolan (Off) Barness (On)**
	FULL TIME 1 - 0

STATISTICS

Season	Fixture		Fixture	Season
67	**7**	Shots On Target	**2**	**39**
58	**15**	Shots Off Target	**5**	**48**
3	**0**	Hit Woodwork	**1**	**3**
19	**3**	Caught Offside	**3**	**21**
55	**7**	Corners	**3**	**51**
126	**19**	Fouls	**14**	**130**
49%	**58%**	Possession	**42%**	**46%**

LEAGUE STANDINGS

Position (pos before)		W	D	L	F	A	Pts
4 (7)	**Bolton W**	**4**	**3**	**2**	**14**	**11**	**15**
20 (19)	**Crystal Palace**	**1**	**2**	**6**	**8**	**15**	**5**

Saturday 16th October 2004 | Venue: **Reebok Stadium** | Attendance: **25,501** | Referee: **N.S.Barry**

Khalilou Fadiga takes on Shaun Derry

"Ivan Campo is in hospital and we are hoping it is not a fractured cheekbone or eye socket."
Sam Allardyce

"It's something if you can come to somewhere like Bolton and not get turned over."
Iain Dowie

PREMIERSHIP MILESTONE

Khalilou Fadiga made his Premiership debut

BOLTON WANDERERS 1 CRYSTAL PALACE 0

A late first half goal from Kevin Davies proved enough to give Bolton all three points, in a match marred by an horrific facial injury to midfielder Ivan Campo.

The Spaniard left the field with both a deep gash and suspected broken cheekbone, after a clash of heads with teammate Gary Speed inside the opening 15 minutes. Wanderers' Welsh captain also required stitches following the incident.

Crystal Palace, buoyed by victory over Fulham in their last game, started very brightly. Andy Johnson appeared to be held back in the box, but referee Neale Barry saw nothing wrong with the challenge.

After an understandably lengthy stoppage in play, it was Bolton's turn to be denied a spot-kick. Senegalese international El-Hadji Diouf went tumbling in the area, but again the officials were unmoved.

Hungarian goalkeeper Gabor Kiraly was then called upon to turn a deflected Stylianos Giannakopoulos strike around the post, as Sam Allardyce's team increased the pressure on their spirited opponents.

The Palace custodian was beaten, however, when Davies climbed highest in a crowded penalty box, to nod Bruno N'Gotty's long free-kick into the net with 45 minutes on the clock. The goal was a poor one to concede and would have completely altered Iain Dowie's second half tactics.

The visitors came closest to levelling the scores shortly after the break. Jussi Jaaskelainen spilled a Ben Watson free-kick, and left-back Danny Granville crashed the ball against the bar from close range.

Play soon switched to the other end, with home substitute Henrik Pedersen doing his best to extend Bolton's advantage. The Dane saw a header saved by Kiraly, before having another effort blocked on the line.

Khalilou Fadiga came on for his debut in place of countryman Diouf after 77 minutes, but it was Palace replacement Vassilios Lakis who nearly earned his side a point when narrowly failing to connect with Tony Popovic's downward header.

The final whistle was greeted with a fair amount of relief at the Reebok Stadium, as Wanderers recorded their first Premiership victory in five attempts. Unfortunately for the South Londoners, the defeat saw them return to the bottom of the table.

PREMIERSHIP FIXTURE HISTORY

Pl: 13 Draws: 3	Wins	⚽	▯	■
Everton	9	23	9	0
Southampton	1	7	19	0

STARTING LINE-UPS

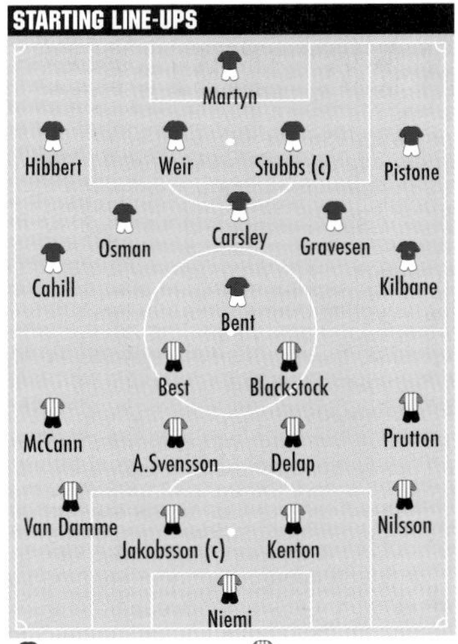

McFadden, Ferguson, Watson, Wright, Yobo

Telfer, Blayney, Fernandes, Griffit, Higginbotham

EVENT LINE

HALF TIME 0 - 0

64 Best (Off) Telfer (On)

77 **Cahill (Off) Ferguson (On)**

77 **Kilbane (Off) McFadden (On)**

88 **Osman (Open Play)**

89 **Bent (Off) Watson (On)**

FULL TIME 1 - 0

STATISTICS

Season	Fixture		Fixture	Season
47	5	Shots On Target	4	48
47	9	Shots Off Target	4	52
2	0	Hit Woodwork	0	0
31	4	Caught Offside	4	24
49	5	Corners	6	53
103	5	Fouls	14	121
50%	47%	Possession	53%	50%

LEAGUE STANDINGS

Position (pos before)		W	D	L	F	A	Pts
3 (3)	**Everton**	6	1	2	10	7	19
19 (18)	**Southampton**	1	2	6	6	12	5

Saturday 16th October 2004 | Venue: **Goodison Park** | Attendance: **35,256** | Referee: **B.Knight**

EVERTON 1 SOUTHAMPTON 0

A goal from Leon Osman two minutes from time ensured that Everton returned to winning ways, while heaping more pressure on under-fire Saints boss Steve Wigley.

The South Coast side remained without a league victory since August, as an afternoon of hard work was undermined by a cruel lapse in concentration. With time running out, substitute Duncan Ferguson flicked on Thomas Gravesen's long throw from the right, and an unchallenged Osman arrived to steer a low 10-yard effort just inside the left-hand upright.

Defeat was particularly harsh on a Southampton side who had competed admirably. Without any recognised strikers available to them, the visitors paired youngsters Dexter Blackstock and Leon Best in an inexperienced attack.

After suffering a loss at home to Tottenham in their previous game, the team sent out by September 'Manager of the Month' David Moyes began brightly. Lone frontman Marcus Bent was extremely lively, linking with Gravesen to almost send Osman clear and then firing in a dangerous cross-cum-shot.

At the other end, Blackstock went close to making it a dream debut when heading a left-wing cross narrowly over the bar. Everton responded as Bent blasted skyward from 12 yards, Kevin Kilbane went close with a free-kick, and Tim Cahill nearly converted following an Osman pass.

A mix-up between Antti Niemi and Jelle Van Damme almost resulted in a goal, but the former Ajax defender recovered to make a desperate last-ditch clearance. The ball was again dramatically kept out from the resulting corner, before Best was nearly released by Neil McCann on a Southampton break.

Paul Telfer was brought on to bolster the visitors' midfield midway through the second half, though Moyes' men continued to carve out some decent chances. A weak shot from Bent proved easy for Niemi, but the keeper could do nothing on 73 minutes as the former Leicester striker's cross evaded both Cahill and Osman in the six-yard box.

With 13 minutes remaining, James McFadden and Ferguson were thrown into the action. Amid scenes of much celebration at Goodison Park, the latter played a significant part in the goal that kept Everton in touch with the Premiership leaders.

Leon Osman is mobbed after scoring the winner

"I think it's a three-horse race now - Everton, Chelsea and Arsenal. That's a tongue in cheek remark, mind you."

David Moyes

"We're not really having much luck at the moment. We worked very hard and competed, and the players are very down."

Steve Wigley

PREMIERSHIP MILESTONE

Dexter Blackstock made his Premiership debut

PREMIERSHIP FIXTURE HISTORY

Pl: 4 Draws: 0	Wins	Goals	Yellow	Red
Fulham	1	6	6	2
Liverpool	3	10	6	1

STARTING LINE-UPS

Fulham subs: John, Crossley, McKinlay, Jensen, Rehman

Liverpool subs: Alonso, Warnock, Biscan, Dudek, Sinama-Pongolle

EVENT LINE

24 **Boa Morte (Open Play)**
30 **Boa Morte (Open Play)**
42 **Green (Foul)**

HALF TIME 2 - 0

46 Diao (Off) Alonso (On)
50 Knight (Own Goal)
61 Garcia (Foul)
64 Traore (Foul)
71 Baros (Open Play)
75 **Radzinski (Off) John (On)**
77 Josemi (2nd Bookable Offence)
79 Alonso (Direct Free Kick)
88 Garcia (Off) Warnock (On)
90 Baros (Off) Biscan (On)
90 Biscan (Open Play)

FULL TIME 2 - 4

STATISTICS

Season	Fixture	Fulham	Fixture	Season
48	3	Shots On Target	3	50
40	2	Shots Off Target	7	45
2	0	Hit Woodwork	0	0
23	2	Caught Offside	9	27
51	5	Corners	6	40
101	13	Fouls	10	98
48%	48%	Possession	52%	53%

LEAGUE STANDINGS

Position (pos before)	W	D	L	F	A	Pts
16 (14) Fulham	2	2	5	10	17	8
7 (11) Liverpool	4	1	3	14	8	13

Saturday 16th October 2004 | Venue: **Craven Cottage** | Attendance: **21,884** | Referee: **S.G.Bennett**

FULHAM 2
LIVERPOOL 4

Luis Boa Morte tries to hold off Salif Diao

PREMIERSHIP MILESTONE

100 Tomasz Radzinski made his 100th Premiership appearance

"I am very disappointed. If you are 2-0 up in a game, you shouldn't lose it."

Chris Coleman

"Xabi Alonso played well when he came on. He plays well with the team as he is a good passer."

Rafael Benitez

PREMIERSHIP MILESTONE

Xabi Alonso and Igor Biscan both netted their first Premiership goals

Liverpool recorded their first away win of the Premiership season in the proverbial 'game of two halves' at Craven Cottage.

Trailing to a Luis Boa Morte brace at the break, Rafael Benitez changed the face of the game through the introduction of substitute Xabi Alonso. An own goal by Zat Knight and a poacher's finish from Milan Baros levelled the scores, before Josemi saw red. In spite of this setback, Alonso himself and Igor Biscan netted to secure a memorable three points.

The opening period offered little by way of encouragement for the visitors. Fulham dominated proceedings from the first whistle, Mark Pembridge going closest to breaking the deadlock with a long-range drive.

After 24 minutes, the West Londoners got the goal their football deserved. American international Brian McBride escaped on the right of the area, and drilled in a low cross that Boa Morte steered home from inside the six-yard box at the back post.

Six minutes later, the Portuguese wide man slotted home a second. A jinking run from the increasingly influential Steed Malbranque ended with a measured pass that was swept under the advancing Chris Kirkland from 12 yards out in the inside left channel.

Chris Coleman would have been a happy manager at the break, but just five minutes after the restart it was 2-1. A hopeful long-range effort from Baros would not have troubled Edwin van der Sar, but the ball struck the head of the unfortunate Knight and looped into the top left-hand corner of the net.

Galvanised by the goal and with Alonso pulling the strings in midfield, Liverpool seized control. After 71 minutes they got their reward, Baros smashing the ball home from close range after Luis Garcia had seen his glancing header miraculously kept out by Fulham's Dutch goalkeeper.

Despite the 77th-minute dismissal of Josemi for a second bookable offence, the result of two fouls, Benitez's side went in front courtesy of a deflected Alonso free-kick with 11 minutes remaining.

Fellow substitute Biscan then secured the points in injury-time, with a cultured right-foot finish from 20 yards.

Saturday 16th October 2004	Venue: **City of Manchester Stadium**	Attendance: **45,047**	Referee: **H.M.Webb**

MANCHESTER CITY 1 CHELSEA 0

Jose Mourinho suffered his first taste of defeat in English football, as a Nicolas Anelka penalty separated the sides at the City of Manchester Stadium.

Chelsea had won the corresponding fixture on the previous five occasions, and squandered plenty of chances to do so again. Eidur Gudjohnsen was particularly guilty, as the Londoners failed to capitalise on having 62% possession of the ball.

The only goal of the game arrived after just 11 minutes. Breaking upfield from one of 10 visiting corners, Anelka chased a long ball over the top into the area. The wet surface definitely contributed to Paulo Ferreira's clumsy challenge, and the striker picked himself up to become only the second player to score past Petr Cech in the Premiership.

Referee Howard Webb could easily have dismissed the Portuguese full-back for a professional foul in the penalty incident, but felt the spot-kick and a yellow card to be punishment enough on a torrid night in the blue half of Manchester.

Mourinho's side did not respond to the early setback in the manner of champions. David James was only called upon to make two real saves, the most impressive coming after a Frank Lampard free-kick had been deflected, as City confidently stroked the ball around.

The second period was a different story, however, as the Stamford Bridge outfit visibly upped the tempo. Midfielder Lampard was the catalyst, forcing his England international colleague to pull off two brilliant diving saves from long-range piledrivers.

Slowly but surely Kevin Keegan's side recovered their composure, hitting the visitors with some spritely counter-attacks. The pacy Shaun Wright-Phillips fired wide on one such breakaway, before teeing up Jonathan Macken for a 73rd-minute effort that hit the side-netting.

With nine minutes remaining, Gudjohnsen missed a glorious chance to level the scores. The Icelandic international was presented with a clear sight of goal inside the area, but somehow side-footed the ball past the right-hand upright.

Chelsea failed to carve out any further noteworthy chances, as Richard Dunne and Sylvain Distin led their defensive colleagues to a hard-earned clean sheet.

Sun Jihai arrives to congratulate goalscorer Nicolas Anelka

"I said to the players before the game that if we are to turn over teams like Chelsea, Arsenal, Manchester United and Newcastle, we need both the work-rate and togetherness."

Kevin Keegan

PREMIERSHIP MILESTONE

50 Robbie Fowler made his 50th Premiership appearance in the colours of Man City

"We have to score more goals. We are defending well, but not scoring. Football is about not conceding and scoring."

Jose Mourinho

PREMIERSHIP FIXTURE HISTORY

Pl: 8 Draws: 1	Wins	Goals	Yellow	Red
Manchester City	1	5	9	0
Chelsea	6	12	14	0

STARTING LINE-UPS

Manchester City: James; Mills, Dunne, Distin (c), Thatcher; S.Wright-Phillips, Jihai, Bosvelt, Sibierski; Macken, Anelka

Chelsea: Gudjohnsen, Kezman; Duff, Lampard, Tiago; Makelele; Gallas, Terry (c), Carvalho, Ferreira; Cech

Substitutes (Manchester City): McManaman, Fowler, Waterreus, Onuoha, Flood

Substitutes (Chelsea): Bridge, J.Cole, Geremi, Cudicini, Parker

EVENT LINE

11 Ferreira (Foul)
11 **Anelka (Penalty)**
43 **Jihai (Off) McManaman (On)**
HALF TIME 1 - 0
46 Gallas (Off) Bridge (On)
54 Lampard (Ung.Conduct)
64 **Mills (Ung.Conduct)**
64 Tiago (Off) Cole J (On)
78 Carvalho (Off) Geremi (On)
88 **Macken (Off) Fowler (On)**
FULL TIME 1 - 0

STATISTICS

Season	Fixture (Man City)		Fixture (Chelsea)	Season
55	2	Shots On Target	3	58
49	3	Shots Off Target	6	68
1	0	Hit Woodwork	0	3
30	1	Caught Offside	3	30
61	0	Corners	10	65
119	6	Fouls	7	113
46%	38%	Possession	62%	56%

LEAGUE STANDINGS

Position (pos before)	W	D	L	F	A	Pts
10 (12) Man City	3	2	4	9	7	11
2 (2) Chelsea	6	2	1	8	2	20

PREMIERSHIP FIXTURE HISTORY

Pl: 1 Draws: 1	Wins	⚽	☐	■
West Bromwich Albion	0	0	2	0
Norwich City	0	0	2	0

STARTING LINE-UPS

Earnshaw, Koumas, Robinson, Kuszczak, Contra

Helveg, McVeigh, Svensson, Ward, Safri

EVENT LINE

42	**Moore (Dissent)**
	HALF TIME 0 - 0
58	**Kanu (Off) Earnshaw (On)**
59	**Johnson (Foul)**
63	McKenzie (Ung.Conduct)
69	**Greening (Off) Koumas (On)**
71	Bentley (Foul)
74	Jonson (Off) Helveg (On)
75	Bentley (Off) McVeigh (On)
80	**Gera (Off) Robinson (On)**
80	McKenzie (Off) Svensson (On)
	FULL TIME 0 - 0

STATISTICS

Season	Fixture		Fixture	Season
39	2	Shots On Target	5	42
43	7	Shots Off Target	7	49
1	0	Hit Woodwork	0	2
33	1	Caught Offside	1	31
56	3	Corners	3	40
121	15	Fouls	23	125
48%	53%	Possession	47%	46%

LEAGUE STANDINGS

Position (pos before)	W	D	L	F	A	Pts
15 (16) West Brom	1	5	3	8	13	8
17 (20) Norwich C	0	6	3	7	14	6

Saturday 16th October 2004 | Venue: **The Hawthorns** | Attendance: **26,257** | Referee: **P.Crossley**

WEST BROM 0 NORWICH CITY 0

The top two 'Division 1' sides of last season were unable to find a goal, in the first ever Premiership meeting between the clubs.

Darren Huckerby was the star performer, terrorising the West Brom defence with a series of mazy runs. The pacy frontman had chosen a move to Norwich in preference to a switch to The Hawthorns during the previous campaign, and demonstrated on countless occasions why Gary Megson had tried to secure his services.

After Zoltan Gera had fizzed a 20-yard effort narrowly wide, the Canaries took control. Former Peterborough striker Leon McKenzie failed to test Russell Hoult from close range, following Huckerby's ball in from the flank.

The home goalkeeper then kept out Huckerby's stinging 24th-minute drive from a mesmeric forward foray, before the former Manchester City player burst through the inside left channel only to slice his effort towards the corner flag.

Swedish international Mattias Jonson was next to be wasteful, firing into the side-netting from close range. At the other end, the Baggies' only genuine attempt on goal came when Robert Green was forced to turn over a miscue from teammate Gary Holt.

The pattern of play changed little after the break, as Norwich continued to look the classier outfit. After 52 minutes, Jonson saw a header from point-blank range repelled by Hoult, while David Bentley was looking lively on the opposite wing.

The introduction of Robert Earnshaw in place of Nwankwo Kanu after 58 minutes breathed new life into West Brom. Almost immediately, Jonathan Greening fired in a 20-yard drive that brought the best out of Green, and the shot-stopper was then alert enough to divert the ball away from the onrushing Geoff Horsfield.

Tired legs and weary bodies meant that the final half-an-hour was not a particularly edifying spectacle. Substitutes Jason Koumas and Paul McVeigh showed glimpses of skill, but there was little by way of any end product.

At the final whistle, Nigel Worthington would certainly have been the happier of the two managers. However, anyone who saw the game would tell you that with better finishing, Norwich could have been celebrating a first Premiership victory.

Paul Robinson tries to stop Darren Huckerby

"The players gave it all they had, but I just felt that a lot of them looked out on their feet."
Gary Megson

"That was a great point for us, and two points dropped for Albion."
Nigel Worthington

PREMIERSHIP FIXTURE HISTORY

Pl: 6 Draws: 4	Wins	Goals	Yellow	Red
Charlton Athletic	1	6	6	0
Newcastle United	1	6	7	2

STARTING LINE-UPS

Charlton subs: Jeffers, Andersen, El Karkouri, Hughes, Euell

Newcastle subs: Robert, Ameobi, Milner, Harper, Hughes

EVENT LINE

39 Bellamy (Open Play)

HALF TIME 0 - 1

51 **Carr (Own Goal)**

66 Ambrose (Off) Robert (On)

66 Bellamy (Off) Ameobi (On)

75 **Stuart (Dissent)**

76 Butt (Off) Milner (On)

79 **Lisbie (Off) Jeffers (On)**

89 Ameobi (Dissent)

FULL TIME 1 - 1

STATISTICS

Season	Fixture (Charlton)		Fixture (Newcastle)	Season
38	6	Shots On Target	8	64
37	5	Shots Off Target	7	54
2	0	Hit Woodwork	0	3
28	2	Caught Offside	2	29
43	8	Corners	9	72
120	15	Fouls	7	107
44%	49%	Possession	51%	53%

LEAGUE STANDINGS

Position (pos before)		W	D	L	F	A	Pts
10 (12)	Charlton Ath	3	3	3	9	15	12
8 (9)	Newcastle Utd	3	4	2	17	14	13

Sunday 17th October 2004 | Venue: **The Valley** | Attendance: **26,553** | Referee: **P.Walton**

CHARLTON ATHLETIC 1 NEWCASTLE UNITED 1

Charlton grab their equaliser

"Expectations are high, but it is very hard to break into the top six and take the club a stage further."

Alan Curbishley

"A draw was a fair result today and either boss would have been upset to lose."

Graeme Souness

PREMIERSHIP MILESTONE

100 Robbie Elliott made his 100th Premiership appearance for Newcastle

The spoils were shared in an entertaining game, as Craig Bellamy turned from hero to villain

Having headed his team into a first half lead that was later cancelled out by a Stephen Carr own goal, Newcastle's Welsh international forward took offence at being replaced midway through the second period. Manager Graeme Souness was on the wrong end of some choice words, and will surely have to discipline his player.

With Patrick Kluivert unavailable, Bellamy had moved to his preferred position alongside Alan Shearer in attack. For the Addicks, Danish international Dennis Rommedahl was recalled to a positive-looking starting XI.

Proceedings began at a high tempo. After Shearer had headed wide and Jermaine Jenas had steered an effort just the wrong side of the post, Graham Stuart saw a well-struck shot expertly turned over the bar by Shay Given.

Further half-chances continued to fall at both ends, before the Magpies grabbed a 39th-minute lead. Full-back Olivier Bernard did brilliantly on the left, battling past defenders before sending over an inviting near-post cross that Bellamy rose to head home from six yards.

The normally lethal Shearer prodded wide just prior to the interval, and the Newcastle captain was made to regret that miss just six minutes after the restart. Pacy forward Kevin Lisbie surged into the area and around Given, with his 15-yard prod finding its way in off the right boot of Carr, despite the best efforts of the covering Andy O'Brien.

Charlton were wearing a special strip to commemorate their centenary, but the air turned blue, not red, when Bellamy was replaced.

After the dust had settled, the match served up a highly entertaining finale. Goal-line clearances seemed to be the order of the day, as Shearer went close at one end and then saved his side at the other.

Both managers urged their men forward, and plenty of frantic scrambles ensued in opposing penalty boxes. However, neither team could conjure up a winner, as Souness remained unbeaten as Newcastle boss.

PREMIERSHIP FIXTURE HISTORY

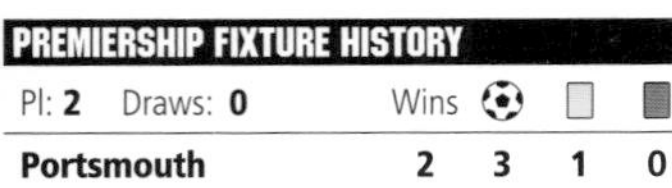

Pl: 2 Draws: 0	Wins	⚽	☐	■
Portsmouth	2	3	1	0
Tottenham Hotspur	0	0	1	0

STARTING LINE-UPS

Portsmouth subs: Fuller, Kamara, Cisse, Ashdown, Taylor

Tottenham subs: Carrick, Kanoute, Jackson, Keller, Ziegler

EVENT LINE

HALF TIME 0 - 0

55 **Berkovic (Off) Fuller (On)**

63 **Yakubu (Open Play)**

72 Brown (Off) Carrick (On)

72 Gardner (Off) Kanoute (On)

75 **Yakubu (Off) Kamara (On)**

80 Atouba (Off) Jackson (On)

85 **Faye (Off) Cisse (On)**

FULL TIME 1 - 0

STATISTICS

Season	Fixture		Fixture	Season
50	4	Shots On Target	5	46
46	7	Shots Off Target	10	56
1	0	Hit Woodwork	1	3
18	2	Caught Offside	0	26
39	3	Corners	5	42
96	12	Fouls	14	120
49%	45%	Possession	55%	46%

LEAGUE STANDINGS

Position (pos before)		W	D	L	F	A	Pts
12 (13)	Portsmouth	3	2	3	12	11	11
9 (9)	Tottenham H	3	4	2	5	4	13

Monday 18th October 2004 | Venue: **Fratton Park** | Attendance: **20,121** | Referee: **U.D.Rennie**

PORTSMOUTH 1 TOTTENHAM HOTSPUR 0

A 63rd-minute Aiyegbeni Yakubu goal was enough to condemn Jacques Santini's Tottenham to a second defeat in three Premiership matches.

The Nigerian international couldn't miss when presented with a free header inside the six-yard box, after his strike partner Lomana Tresor Lua Lua had done the damage down the right.

The home side, and Lua Lua in particular, had begun brightly. The DR Congo international terrorised full-back Noe Pamarot in the early exchanges, and might have done better with a shot from the edge of the area.

A fourth-minute Ledley King header that flew agonisingly over the bar was Spurs' only chance of note amid constant Portsmouth pressure. Goalkeeper Paul Robinson did well to parry a Yakubu effort, but was relieved to see Eyal Berkovic blaze the loose ball skyward.

The former Leeds custodian then did well to keep out Patrik Berger's close-range shot after 24 minutes, and also saved from a Dejan Stefanovic header. The defender atoned for his miss on the stroke of half-time, however, forcing Jermain Defoe to spurn a more-than-presentable chance.

The second period continued in the same vain, with chances at either end. A poor scuffed shot from Berkovic was his last contribution before being replaced by Ricardo Fuller, while Shaka Hislop had to be alert to keep out a long-range Defoe piledriver.

The goalkeeper was helpless moments later though, as stand-in left-back Anthony Gardner headed a free-kick against the post. The livewire Defoe then shot over on the turn from a Robbie Keane cross, and could only watch from a distance as Yakubu netted the decisive goal.

Michael Carrick, the subject of summer interest from Portsmouth prior to his move to White Hart Lane, came on to make a 72nd-minute debut to a cacophony of boos. The midfielder made little impact, perhaps understandable given his recent lack of football.

The best chance of the closing stages fell to Harry Redknapp's side, Senegalese substitute Diomansy Kamara volleying wide when well-placed inside the penalty area eight minutes from time. A second would have added gloss to the scoreline, but the South Coast club were more than happy with a 1-0 victory.

Amdy Faye turns away from Simon Davies

"I was pleased with my entire back four, because we limited Tottenham to only a handful of chances."

Harry Redknapp

"We did not play well. It was a bad evening and a bad game for Tottenham."

Jacques Santini

PREMIERSHIP MILESTONE

Michael Carrick made his first Premiership appearance for Tottenham

PREMIERSHIP FIXTURE HISTORY

Pl: 4 Draws: 0	Wins	Goals	Yellow	Red
Aston Villa	4	10	4	0
Fulham	0	1	4	0

STARTING LINE-UPS

Aston Villa subs: Cole, Davis, Postma, Hitzlsperger, Ridgewell

Fulham subs: Rehman, John, McBride, Crossley, Radzinski

EVENT LINE

10 Pearce (Off) Rehman (On)

16 Volz (Foul)

29 **Solano (Direct Free Kick)**

HALF TIME 1 - 0

62 **Vassell (Off) Cole (On)**

69 Jensen (Off) John (On)

75 **Hendrie (Open Play)**

78 **Whittingham (Off) Davis (On)**

87 **Hendrie (Off) Hitzlsperger (On)**

88 Cole (Off) McBride (On)

FULL TIME 2 - 0

STATISTICS

Season	Fixture (Aston Villa)		Fixture (Fulham)	Season
62	5	Shots On Target	1	49
57	6	Shots Off Target	6	46
3	0	Hit Woodwork	0	2
23	4	Caught Offside	2	25
62	8	Corners	4	55
162	21	Fouls	14	115
48%	54%	Possession	46%	48%

LEAGUE STANDINGS

Position (pos before)	W	D	L	F	A	Pts
8 (13) Aston Villa	3	5	2	13	12	14
17 (16) Fulham	2	2	6	10	19	8

Saturday 23rd October 2004 | Venue: **Villa Park** | Attendance: **34,460** | Referee: **P.Dowd**

ASTON VILLA 2 FULHAM 0

Goals in either half from Nolberto Solano and the in-form Lee Hendrie secured a comfortable victory for Aston Villa.

Not since the end of August had David O'Leary's men tasted Premiership success, but they were rarely troubled by a Fulham side that had also struggled of late. Torrential rain didn't help the quality of the game, as both teams fought against the conditions.

An early injury to Ian Pearce forced Chris Coleman into the introduction of inexperienced youngster Zesh Rehman alongside Zat Knight at the back. The Villans took this as their cue to apply pressure, but were not rewarded until just before the half-hour mark.

After Hendrie had been upended some 25 yards from goal, Peruvian international Solano stepped up to curl a majestic free-kick over the defensive wall and just inside Edwin van der Sar's post.

The visitors failed to respond before the break, Steed Malbranque missing the target with their only semblance of a chance. In fact, the home side would have moved further in front had it not been for several poor misses from the out-of-sorts Darius Vassell.

The England striker limped off to be replaced by Carlton Cole after 62 minutes, following a spell of improved play from Coleman's charges. Although Thomas Sorensen had remained fairly redundant in the Villa goal, the Cottagers were unlucky not to be awarded a penalty when Claus Jensen's free-kick appeared to strike an arm.

Any pressure was short-lived, however, as the team in claret and blue sealed the game with 15 minutes remaining. Substitute Cole was involved, teeing up Hendrie for another long-range cracker that left van der Sar helpless.

Such memorable strikes seemed out of place in an otherwise uninspiring contest. Fulham seemed to give up after the second goal, while O'Leary handed a run-out to Ballymena-born midfielder Steven Davis.

Man of the moment Hendrie was afforded the adulation of the home crowd when he made way for Thomas Hitzlsperger in the final embers of the match. It was fitting reward for an all-action display that did much to secure the points for his team.

Peter Whittingham fires the ball beyond Moritz Volz

"Coming into the game I wanted the three points, and I wasn't concerned how we got them."

David O'Leary

PREMIERSHIP MILESTONE

Nolberto Solano scored his first Premiership goal for Aston Villa

"This is the biggest test of my managerial career. I'm learning more about management than I did in the whole of last season."

Chris Coleman

PREMIERSHIP FIXTURE HISTORY

Pl: **11** Draws: **5**	Wins	⚽	□	■
Chelsea	1	13	14	1
Blackburn Rovers	5	14	19	1

STARTING LINE-UPS

Robben, Tiago, Kezman, Cudicini, Gallas

Pedersen, Johansson, Enckelman, Stead, Bothroyd

EVENT LINE

19 □ Flitcroft (Foul)
37 ⚽ **Gudjohnsen (Open Play)**
38 ⚽ **Gudjohnsen (Open Play)**
41 □ **Parker (Dissent)**

HALF TIME 2 - 0

51 ⚽ **Gudjohnsen (Penalty)**
53 ⇄ Dickov (Off) Bothroyd (On)
53 ⇄ Djorkaeff (Off) Stead (On)
63 ⇄ **Cole J (Off) Robben (On)**
65 ⇄ **Smertin (Off) Tiago (On)**
72 ⇄ **Gudjohnsen (Off) Kezman (On)**
74 ⚽ **Duff (Corner)**
76 □ Neill (Foul)
84 ⇄ Gray (Off) Johansson (On)

FULL TIME 4 - 0

STATISTICS

Season	Fixture 👕		👕 Fixture	Season
72	**14**	Shots On Target	**4**	**40**
72	**4**	Shots Off Target	**3**	**57**
4	**1**	Hit Woodwork	**0**	**1**
33	**3**	Caught Offside	**2**	**38**
77	**12**	Corners	**3**	**58**
124	**11**	Fouls	**11**	**161**
56%	**56%**	Possession	**44%**	**48%**

LEAGUE STANDINGS

Position (pos before)		W	D	L	F	A	Pts
2 (2)	**Chelsea**	**7**	**2**	**1**	**12**	**2**	**23**
19 (18)	**Blackburn R**	**1**	**3**	**6**	**7**	**22**	**6**

Saturday 23rd October 2004 | Venue: **Stamford Bridge** | Attendance: **41,546** | Referee: **G.Poll**

CHELSEA 4 BLACKBURN ROVERS 0

Eidur Gudjohnsen netted a hat-trick as Chelsea finally discovered their scoring touch against Blackburn Rovers at Stamford Bridge.

The Icelandic international netted twice in as many minutes towards the end of the first half, before adding a third from the penalty spot after the break. Winger Damien Duff then completed the rout, against his old club, in the 74th minute.

For Mark Hughes' men, the 4-0 defeat followed hot-on-the-heels of an identical reverse at home to Middlesbrough seven days earlier. On that occasion the result had been influenced by a red card, but this time it was the product of sublime Chelsea football.

Jose Mourinho sprung a couple of surprises, handing starts to the previously overlooked Glen Johnson and Scott Parker. Both players were hungry for the ball, and performed as though they were first-team regulars.

Blackburn came to stifle their more illustrious opponents, and the plan worked perfectly in an opening 35 minutes bereft of clear chances. Things went badly wrong for the Lancashire side, however, when Gudjohnsen punished them twice in quick succession.

Joe Cole was the architect of the opener, chipping over a compact defence for Gudjohnsen to volley home across Brad Friedel from eight yards out in the inside right channel. Then, from the restart, a long ball from Frank Lampard enabled the striker to net his second from an identical position.

The match was 38 minutes old, but effectively dead as a contest. Confidence was rife amongst the men in blue, and they extended their lead in the 51st minute.

Again it was Cole and Gudjohnsen who combined to deadly effect, the Icelander latching onto a neat throughball before being crudely upended. Having picked himself up, the creative forward coolly tucked away the resultant penalty.

Gutsy Blackburn stuck to their task, with Brett Emerton testing Petr Cech from a free-kick. The difference in class between the two sides was further emphasised, however, when Mourinho sent on expensive summer signing Arjen Robben for a belated debut.

The Dutch international lit up Stamford Bridge with some mesmeric dribbling, before fellow winger Duff fired home a low 20-yard drive after working a short-corner routine with Lampard 16 minutes from time.

Eidur Gudjohnsen enjoys a memorable day

"For a striker to get three goals is great for his confidence."

Jose Mourinho on Eidur Gudjohnsen

PREMIERSHIP MILESTONE

Arjen Robben made his Premiership debut

"The moment we lose a goal, the floodgates open. Things need to improve defensively."

Mark Hughes

PREMIERSHIP FIXTURE HISTORY

Pl: 1 Draws: 0	Wins	⚽	Yellow	Red
Crystal Palace	1	3	1	0
West Bromwich Albion	0	0	3	0

STARTING LINE-UPS

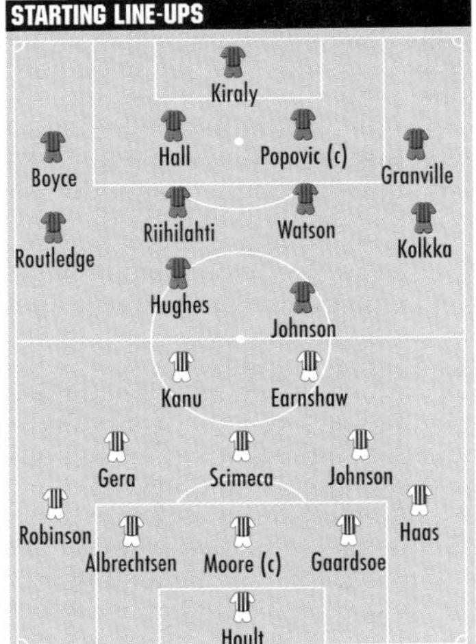

Crystal Palace subs: Lakis, Freedman, Sorondo, Speroni, Torghelle

West Brom subs: Greening, Kuszczak, Inamoto, Horsfield, Hulse

EVENT LINE

5	⚽ **Hall (Corner)**
12	Yellow card: Albrechtsen (Foul)
12	⚽ **Johnson (Penalty)**
24	Sub: Albrechtsen (Off) Greening (On)
39	Yellow card: **Johnson (Ung.Conduct)**
43	Yellow card: Moore (Foul)
	HALF TIME 2 - 0
50	⚽ **Johnson (Open Play)**
62	Yellow card: Robinson (Foul)
69	Sub: **Hughes (Off) Lakis (On)**
80	Sub: **Kolkka (Off) Freedman (On)**
83	Sub: **Watson (Off) Sorondo (On)**
	FULL TIME 3 - 0

STATISTICS

Season	Fixture (Crystal Palace)		Fixture (West Brom)	Season
44	5	Shots On Target	6	45
55	7	Shots Off Target	5	48
3	0	Hit Woodwork	1	2
23	2	Caught Offside	6	39
58	7	Corners	10	66
142	12	Fouls	15	136
46%	46%	Possession	54%	48%

LEAGUE STANDINGS

Position (pos before)	W	D	L	F	A	Pts
15 (20) Crystal Palace	2	2	6	11	15	8
16 (15) West Brom	1	5	4	8	16	8

Saturday 23rd October 2004 | Venue: **Selhurst Park** | Attendance: **22,922** | Referee: **M.D.Messias**

CRYSTAL PALACE 3 WEST BROM 0

West Brom produced a truly abject display as they were ripped apart by a vibrant Crystal Palace at Selhurst Park.

Early goals from Fitz Hall and Andy Johnson left the visitors shell-shocked, before Johnson completed the scoring with a sublime 50th-minute drive. The margin of victory did not flatter Iain Dowie's men, as the Eagles soared above their opponents and out of the relegation zone.

The South Londoners went ahead with just five minutes on the clock. The Baggies failed to properly clear a right-wing corner, allowing Wayne Routledge time and space to send over a deep second ball that was headed home by an unchallenged Hall.

Visiting captain Darren Moore then spurned an immediate chance to reply, sending a downward header into the ground and up over the bar from eight yards out. It was to prove a costly miss, as Palace stretched their lead in the 12th minute.

Referee Matt Messias handed the home side a penalty, when he adjudged that Martin Albrechtsen had illegally prevented Johnson from reaching Joonas Kolkka's low ball across the goalmouth. The Danish defender was cautioned, while Johnson stepped up to tuck away his sixth goal of the season.

Gary Megson's team offered little to encourage their travelling fans before half-time. All 50-50 challenges were won by the men in red and blue, with Danny Granville wasting a decent opportunity to kill the game completely.

To their credit, West Brom began the second period brightly. Robert Earnshaw should have done better when rattling the crossbar from eight yards, before Johnson showed him how to finish.

The former Birmingham striker collected possession on halfway and advanced unchallenged towards goal. Then, as he finally encountered some resistance, the speedy forward drove home a low 20-yard effort that flew in off the foot of the left-hand upright.

The Baggies were a beaten team, though they did carve out some presentable openings. Zoltan Gera fired over and Moore headed wide from a corner, while Earnshaw continued to struggle in front of goal.

Palace substitute Dougie Freedman then took too long when in the clear, but it did not matter as Dowie's men celebrated three crucial points.

Kanu tries to escape the clutches of Wayne Routledge

PREMIERSHIP MILESTONE

Fitz Hall scored his first Premiership goal

"It was pleasing to get another win. We knew it was going to be a hard game and I am delighted with the result."

Iain Dowie

"In terms of performance, this was unacceptable. We started with three centre-backs with the aim of keeping a clean sheet, but it never happened."

Gary Megson

PREMIERSHIP FIXTURE HISTORY

Pl: 6 Draws: 1	Wins	Goals	Yellow cards	Red cards
Liverpool	4	12	4	0
Charlton Athletic	1	5	7	0

STARTING LINE-UPS

Liverpool subs: Kewell, Warnock, Dudek, Diao, Sinama-Pongolle

Charlton subs: Jeffers, El Karkouri, Hughes, Andersen, Euell

EVENT LINE

HALF TIME 0 - 0

52 Goal **Riise (Corner)**

63 Substitution Rommedahl (Off) Jeffers (On)

64 Substitution **Riise (Off) Kewell (On)**

70 Yellow card Jeffers (Foul)

71 Substitution Bartlett (Off) Euell (On)

74 Goal **Garcia (Open Play)**

77 Substitution **Baros (Off) Sinama-Pongolle (On)**

78 Substitution Lisbie (Off) Hughes (On)

86 Substitution **Traore (Off) Warnock (On)**

FULL TIME 2 - 0

STATISTICS

Season	Fixture (Liverpool)		Fixture (Charlton)	Season
57	7	Shots On Target	1	39
55	10	Shots Off Target	2	39
1	1	Hit Woodwork	0	2
30	3	Caught Offside	6	34
52	12	Corners	0	43
107	9	Fouls	11	131
55%	64%	Possession	36%	43%

LEAGUE STANDINGS

Position (pos before)	W	D	L	F	A	Pts
5 (7) Liverpool	5	1	3	16	8	16
11 (10) Charlton Ath	3	3	4	9	17	12

Saturday 23rd October 2004 | Venue: **Anfield** | Attendance: **41,625** | Referee: **A.P.D'Urso**

LIVERPOOL 2 CHARLTON ATHLETIC 0

Liverpool turned back the clock to produce a vintage performance against Charlton Athletic at Anfield.

While the Merseyside club's away form had been poor under the guidance of new boss Rafael Benitez, the side had been playing better and better at home. The Addicks were the latest team to leave empty-handed, and could have no complaints.

Danny Murphy made an emotional return to the venue he had graced for many seasons, and was well-received by his former supporters. The midfielder had little chance to impress, however, as Alan Curbishley's men were subjected to constant early pressure.

Within a minute of the kick-off, Spaniard Luis Garcia fired a skidding drive just wide of the right-hand upright. It was a sign of things to come, as John Arne Riise then wasted a decent opportunity.

Two further gilt-edge chances came and went before half-time as Murphy cleared an effort off the line, before Milan Baros fired over from distance after a surging run from his strike-partner Djibril Cisse.

How Charlton had reached the interval on level terms was a mystery to everyone inside the ground. Poor finishing, rather than stoical defending, was the main culprit, though that changed shortly after the restart.

The Addicks were punished for failing to properly clear a 52nd-minute corner, as Riise was allowed time and space on the edge of the area to run around the ball and fire a left-foot drive beyond the despairing right hand of Dean Kiely.

With the game slipping away from his side, Curbishley introduced ex-Evertonian Francis Jeffers just after the hour mark. The volatile striker was greeted by a cacophony of boos, and soon found himself in referee Andy D'Urso's notebook following a poor challenge.

Steve Finnan then steered an excellent Baros cross straight at Kiely, before Garcia secured the points with a majestic long-range strike.

Collecting a pass from Xabi Alonso some way out from goal, the summer signing from Barcelona advanced unchallenged and unleashed a swerving 25-yard drive that flew high beyond the left hand of the Charlton goalkeeper.

For Liverpool, the acid test will be to repeat this level of performance against the big guns.

"When you have chances and don't score, you'll often pay for it. Fortunately, we managed to score two goals in the second half and secure the win."

Rafael Benitez

"When you're away from home and can't keep hold of the ball for more than three or four passes, then you come under an immense amount of pressure."

Alan Curbishley

PREMIERSHIP MILESTONE

100 Luke Young made his 100th Premiership appearance for Charlton

Luis Garcia savours his magnificent strike

PREMIERSHIP FIXTURE HISTORY

Pl: 4 Draws: 2	Wins	Goals	Yellow cards	Red cards
Norwich City	1	6	2	0
Everton	1	4	7	0

STARTING LINE-UPS

Norwich City substitutes: Svensson, Bentley, Doherty, Ward, Safri

Everton substitutes: Ferguson, Watson, Yobo, Wright, McFadden

EVENT LINE

10 ⚽ Kilbane (Open Play)
37 ▢ Carsley (Foul)
40 ⚽ Bent (Open Play)

HALF TIME 0 - 2

46 ⇄ **Helveg (Off) Svensson (On)**
48 ⚽ **McKenzie (Open Play)**
57 ⚽ **Francis (Corner)**
60 ⇄ Cahill (Off) Ferguson (On)
61 ⇄ Osman (Off) Watson (On)
73 ⚽ Ferguson (Open Play)
76 ▢ Weir (Ung.Conduct)
79 ⇄ Bent (Off) Yobo (On)
83 ⇄ **Jonson (Off) Doherty (On)**
83 ⇄ **McKenzie (Off) Bentley (On)**

FULL TIME 2 - 3

STATISTICS

Season	Fixture (Norwich City)		Fixture (Everton)	Season
52	**10**	Shots On Target	**9**	**56**
61	**12**	Shots Off Target	**4**	**51**
2	**0**	Hit Woodwork	**0**	**2**
34	**3**	Caught Offside	**1**	**32**
51	**11**	Corners	**4**	**53**
134	**9**	Fouls	**16**	**119**
46%	**49%**	Possession	**51%**	**50%**

LEAGUE STANDINGS

Position (pos before)		W	D	L	F	A	Pts
18 (17)	**Norwich C**	0	6	4	9	17	6
3 (3)	**Everton**	7	1	2	13	9	22

Saturday 23rd October 2004 | Venue: **Carrow Road** | Attendance: **23,871** | Referee: **M.Clattenburg**

NORWICH CITY 2 EVERTON 3

If Premiership football was in need of advertising, then this would have been the game to show.

Two fully committed teams served up a feast of football as the Canaries fought back bravely from a two-goal half-time deficit, only to succumb to Everton substitute Duncan Ferguson's back-post header.

The match was played at a frenetic tempo from the outset. Inside the first minute Leon McKenzie headed straight at Nigel Martyn, while Leon Osman soon forced a diving stop from Robert Green.

Then, with 10 minutes played, the visitors took the lead through Kevin Kilbane. A quick break saw Marcus Bent feed Tim Cahill in the inside right channel, and the former Millwall midfielder's low cross was swept home from eight yards out at the back post by the Irish international.

Having initially played their part in the game, the goal rocked Norwich. David Moyes' side enjoyed a sustained spell of pressure, with Thomas Gravesen particularly influential. Home captain Adam Drury did well to prevent a second goal, but the reprieve was short-lived.

Five minutes before the break, former Ipswich forward Bent raced onto a Gravesen pass and tucked a low 15-yard effort past Green and just inside the left-hand upright. With defeat staring them in the face, Nigel Worthington's team hit back shortly after the restart.

Substitute Matthias Svensson played a part in McKenzie's 48th-minute strike, releasing the former Peterborough player on the right. The forward muscled his way towards goal past Alan Stubbs, and duly fired home through the legs of Martyn from six yards out at the near post.

The Canaries continued to force Everton back, and deservedly drew level after 57 minutes. A deep left-wing corner was nodded down by Mattias Jonson, and Damien Francis was on hand to sweep the ball in from close range.

With the match slipping away from his high-flying team, Moyes sent on Ferguson and Steve Watson. The changes proved inspired as, following a surging run from Gravesen, Watson crossed from the right for Ferguson to power home a 73rd-minute close-range headed winner.

Lee Carsley then blocked a goalbound Francis volley, as the visitors hung on for yet another away win.

"We have got to be on the ball for 90 minutes, not 45."
Nigel Worthington

PREMIERSHIP MILESTONE
Leon McKenzie and Damien Francis both scored their first Premiership goals

"Norwich have the pace to cause teams problems, and that is what happened in the second half."
David Moyes

PREMIERSHIP MILESTONE
300 Steve Watson made his 300th Premiership appearance

Leon McKenzie fires his side back into contention

PREMIERSHIP FIXTURE HISTORY

Pl: **6** Draws: **1**	Wins	Goals	Yellow cards	Red cards
Tottenham Hotspur	3	10	6	0
Bolton Wanderers	2	8	10	0

STARTING LINE-UPS

Tottenham substitutes: Defoe, Davis, Ziegler, Keller, Brown

Bolton substitutes: Pedersen, Hierro, Poole, Fadiga, Ferdinand

EVENT LINE

11 Goal: Jaidi (Indirect Free Kick)

41 Goal: **Keane (Open Play)**

HALF TIME 1 - 1

70 Substitution: **Jackson (Off) Defoe (On)**

72 Substitution: Nolan (Off) Pedersen (On)

75 Goal: Pedersen (Corner)

78 Substitution: **Redknapp (Off) Davis (On)**

80 Substitution: **Davies (Off) Ziegler (On)**

81 Substitution: Diouf (Off) Hierro (On)

FULL TIME 1 - 2

STATISTICS

Season	Fixture (Tottenham)		Fixture (Bolton)	Season
51	**5**	Shots On Target	**4**	**71**
59	**3**	Shots Off Target	**2**	**60**
4	**1**	Hit Woodwork	**0**	**3**
29	**3**	Caught Offside	**3**	**22**
44	**2**	Corners	**3**	**58**
134	**14**	Fouls	**17**	**143**
46%	**52%**	Possession	**48%**	**49%**

LEAGUE STANDINGS

Position (pos before)		W	D	L	F	A	Pts
10 (9)	**Tottenham H**	**3**	**4**	**3**	**6**	**6**	**13**
4 (4)	**Bolton W**	**5**	**3**	**2**	**16**	**12**	**18**

Saturday 23rd October 2004 | Venue: **White Hart Lane** | Attendance: **36,025** | Referee: **C.J.Foy**

TOTTENHAM HOTSPUR 1 BOLTON WANDERERS 2

Henrik Pedersen stepped off the bench to settle a hard-fought encounter at White Hart Lane 15 minutes from time.

First half goals from Radhi Jaidi and Robbie Keane had seen the scores locked at 1-1 when the Dane was introduced to deadly effect after 72 minutes. Jacques Santini's men had not previously experienced conceding more than once, and were unable to recover.

The day was a sad one for everyone connected with Tottenham, as the club and its supporters mourned the passing of legendary player and manager Bill Nicholson. In light of this, the result was secondary, though it did serve to highlight how far Spurs had slipped since the halcyon days of his stewardship.

Current boss Santini opted for a strike pairing of Keane and Freddie Kanoute, leaving Jermain Defoe on the bench. The Frenchman's counterpart, Sam Allardyce, was able to welcome back his inspirational captain Jay-Jay Okocha to the starting XI.

Visiting goalkeeper Jussi Jaaskelainen was relieved to see Keane's early effort fly the wrong side of the post, before Tunisian defender Jaidi headed Bolton into an 11th-minute lead. The towering centre-back met Gary Speed's inswinging free-kick from the right with a bullet

close-range header.

After Okocha had drilled an effort wide, the Londoners began to create some decent openings. Young midfielder Johnnie Jackson saw a fierce drive bravely blocked by Jaaskelainen, before the shot-stopper then dived full-length to his left to keep out a 20-yard Kanoute drive.

Then, with the interval fast approaching, a glorious passing move led to an equaliser. Patient build-up play ended when Kanoute cleverly released Keane in the inside right channel, and the Irish forward coolly dispatched a low 12-yard shot across the keeper and inside the far upright.

The Trotters enjoyed the better of the chances after the break, Stylianos Giannakopoulos missing a particularly good one, and grabbed the winner after 75 minutes. Substitute Pedersen had barely touched the ball, when he slotted home from seven yards out after Paul Robinson had made a fine double-save.

Malian international Kanoute immediately headed against a post, but there was no way back for Tottenham.

Bolton players join in with Henrik Pedersen's goal celebration

"I was very disappointed by our performance on the pitch. I always want to win, and wanted to even more so on this day of all days."
Jacques Santini

"I'm delighted with the result. I thought we deserved to take all three points."
Sam Allardyce

PREMIERSHIP FIXTURE HISTORY

Pl: **13** Draws: **4**	Wins	Goals	Yellow cards	Red cards
Manchester United	7	18	19	0
Arsenal	2	5	26	1

STARTING LINE-UPS

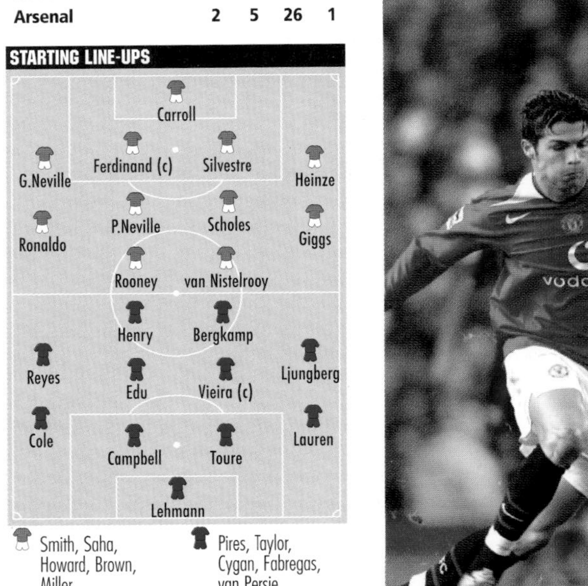

EVENT LINE

35 Cole (Foul)

36 **Neville G (Foul)**

38 **Neville P (Foul)**

HALF TIME 0 - 0

70 Reyes (Off) Pires (On)

73 **van Nistelrooy (Penalty)**

75 Vieira (Foul)

79 Edu (Foul)

85 **Ronaldo (Off) Smith (On)**

90 **van Nistelrooy (Off) Saha (On)**

90 **Rooney (Open Play)**

FULL TIME 2 - 0

STATISTICS

Season	Fixture (Man Utd)		Fixture (Arsenal)	Season
72	6	Shots On Target	6	99
66	6	Shots Off Target	6	46
5	0	Hit Woodwork	0	5
30	2	Caught Offside	1	20
69	3	Corners	3	52
128	20	Fouls	23	117
53%	52%	Possession	48%	58%

LEAGUE STANDINGS

Position (pos before)		W	D	L	F	A	Pts
5 (7)	Man Utd	4	5	1	11	7	17
1 (1)	Arsenal	8	1	1	29	10	25

Sunday 24th October 2004 | Venue: **Old Trafford** | Attendance: **67,862** | Referee: **M.A.Riley**

Cristiano Ronaldo tries to evade Patrick Vieira

"There was a lot of contact out there today, and the referee made decisions that a lot of people were questioning."

Rio Ferdinand

PREMIERSHIP MILESTONE

100 Louis Saha made his 100th Premiership appearance

PREMIERSHIP MILESTONE

Wayne Rooney netted his first Premiership goal for Man Utd

PREMIERSHIP MILESTONE

300 Gary Neville made his 300th Premiership appearance

"We can only master our own performance, and not the referee's performance."

Arsene Wenger

MANCHESTER UNITED 2 ARSENAL 0

Arsenal's magnificent 49-match unbeaten run in the Premiership came to an end, in a bad-tempered clash at Old Trafford.

Ruud van Nistelrooy layed the ghost of his dramatic late penalty miss in the corresponding fixture last season by converting from the spot in the 73rd minute, before Wayne Rooney added a second in injury time.

Arsene Wenger and his team were not happy with the award of the spot-kick, or with the performance of referee Mike Riley. The official failed to punish Rio Ferdinand for what looked to be a professional foul on Freddie Ljungberg, and later took no action when van Nistelrooy ran his studs down the shin of Ashley Cole.

Talking points aside, the game was a poor spectacle. Played in wet conditions, both teams cancelled each other out.

Sir Alex Ferguson's men began the brighter, and nearly found a way to goal in the seventh minute. Kolo Toure did well to block a fiercely struck Rooney drive, before Sol Campbell did likewise after the ball had been worked to Ryan Giggs.

After Riley had enraged the visitors, and gone against the grain, by failing to dismiss a clumsy Ferdinand and aggressive van Nistelrooy, Arsenal carved out their only first-half threat to Roy Carroll's goal.

Edu's long ball found the talismanic Thierry Henry in the inside right channel, but the striker was unable to find a way between the Northern Irish international goalkeeper and his near post from eight yards out.

The game appeared destined to end in stalemate until the referee continued his habit of awarding penalties to Manchester United at Old Trafford. England international Campbell was harshly adjudged to have felled Rooney on the right side of the box, and van Nistelrooy beat Jens Lehmann to make it 1-0.

The Gunners still had time to respond, but were caught on the break as their push for an equaliser became increasingly desperate. Substitutes Louis Saha and Alan Smith led the charge, with the England international squaring a ball from the right that left Rooney with a simple 10-yard finish.

PREMIERSHIP FIXTURE HISTORY

Pl: 2 Draws: 2	Wins	⚽	▢	■
Middlesbrough	0	1	2	0
Portsmouth	0	1	4	1

STARTING LINE-UPS

Nemeth, Cooper, Nash, Ehiogu, Morrison

Taylor, Fuller, Cisse, Ashdown, Berkovic

EVENT LINE

5 ⚽ Kamara (Open Play)

6 ▢ Kamara (Ung.Conduct)

38 **Mendieta (Off) Nemeth (On)**

HALF TIME 0 - 1

46 Unsworth (Off) Taylor (On)

69 Lua Lua (Off) Fuller (On)

74 ⚽ **Downing (Open Play)**

80 Kamara (Off) Cisse (On)

90 **Boateng (Off) Cooper (On)**

90 ▢ Fuller (Ung.Conduct)

FULL TIME 1 - 1

STATISTICS

Season	Fixture		Fixture	Season
82	11	Shots On Target	1	51
67	15	Shots Off Target	2	48
0	0	Hit Woodwork	0	1
35	3	Caught Offside	4	22
54	9	Corners	4	43
129	9	Fouls	5	101
51%	59%	Possession	41%	48%

LEAGUE STANDINGS

Position (pos before)		W	D	L	F	A	Pts
8 (6)	Middlesbrough	4	3	3	17	13	15
11 (13)	Portsmouth	3	3	3	13	12	12

Sunday 24th October 2004 | Venue: **Riverside Stadium** | Attendance: **30,964** | Referee: **M.Atkinson**

MIDDLESBROUGH 1 PORTSMOUTH 1

The points were shared between Middlesbrough and Portsmouth, courtesy of two fine strikes at the Riverside Stadium.

Senegalese forward Diomansy Kamara had drilled the visitors into an early lead after embarking on a mesmeric run, before local lad Stewart Downing danced his way past several defenders to slot home a 74th-minute equaliser.

The goal further strengthened recent claims that Downing could be the long-term answer to England's left-sided problems, though it was the man playing on the left of Harry Redknapp's five-man midfield that did the initial damage.

Collecting possession near the centre-circle, Kamara ran at a startled Middlesbrough defence. As his opponents backtracked, the recent arrival from Modena beat Mark Schwarzer with a left-foot drive from 20 yards that nestled in the bottom right-hand corner of the net.

It was the African's first goal in the Premiership, though referee Martin Atkinson decided to temper his delight by cautioning the player for removing his shirt during the celebrations.

The remainder of the half served up an open and entertaining game, with chances at either end. Shaka Hislop made several fine saves, before young home right-back Anthony McMahon made an excellent last-ditch challenge as Kamara again raced through.

Spaniard Gaizka Mendieta was stretchered off after 38 minutes, but his replacement, Szilard Nemeth, soon forced Aiyegbeni Yakubu into a goal-line clearance.

The second period continued in the same vain, with Hislop certainly the busier of the two custodians. The former Newcastle keeper could do nothing, however, when Downing skipped inside several challenges and placed a 12-yard left-foot shot into the bottom left-hand corner of his goal.

Suddenly Portsmouth were hanging on. The previously anonymous Mark Viduka forced a fine save, as Steve McClaren's team chased a winner. It wasn't to be though, as the Teesside club failed to cash in sufficiently on their 26 goal attempts.

The final whistle was greeted with great satisfaction by fans of the South Coast side. Despite missing out on the three points, the players had shown great resilience and commitment to the cause in the face of some intense pressure.

George Boateng brushes Nigel Quashie aside

"It was a game we should have won. Credit to Portsmouth, after an early goal they put 11 men behind the ball and made it difficult for us."

Steve McClaren

PREMIERSHIP MILESTONE

100 Chris Riggott made his 100th Premiership appearance

"I think he will annoy a few crowds over the next few years, what with him being one of the best players in the country."

Harry Redknapp on Diomansy Kamara

PREMIERSHIP MILESTONE

Diomansy Kamara netted his first Premiership goal

PREMIERSHIP FIXTURE HISTORY

Pl: **7** Draws: **1**

	Wins			
Newcastle United	5	14	4	0
Manchester City	1	5	13	1

STARTING LINE-UPS

Hughes, Milner, Ameobi, Harper, Ambrose

Fowler, Flood, Waterreus, Jordan, Negouai

EVENT LINE

32 **Bernard (Foul)**

HALF TIME 0 - 0

46 Anelka (Off) Fowler (On)

49 **Robert (Direct Free Kick)**

51 Bosvelt (Foul)

58 **Shearer (Penalty)**

58 Macken (Off) Flood (On)

59 **Carr (Off) Hughes (On)**

64 Wright-Phillips S (Open Play)

67 **Butt (Dissent)**

67 Fowler (Penalty)

69 **Elliott (Indirect Free Kick)**

71 **Robert (Off) Milner (On)**

77 Wright-Phillips S (Open Play)

79 McManaman (Ung.Conduct)

89 **Bellamy (Open Play)**

90 **Bellamy (Off) Ameobi (On)**

90 Mills (Ung.Conduct)

FULL TIME 4 - 3

STATISTICS

Season	Fixture		Fixture	Season
76	12	Shots On Target	7	62
59	5	Shots Off Target	5	54
4	1	Hit Woodwork	0	1
30	1	Caught Offside	5	35
79	7	Corners	5	66
120	13	Fouls	14	133
52%	51%	Possession	49%	46%

LEAGUE STANDINGS

Position (pos before)	W	D	L	F	A	Pts
18 (20) Southampton	1	3	6	6	12	6
14 (14) Birmingham C	1	6	3	7	9	9

Sunday 24th October 2004 | Venue: **St James' Park** | Attendance: **52,316** | Referee: **S.W.Dunn**

NEWCASTLE UNITED 4 MANCHESTER CITY 3

A record Premiership crowd at St James' Park of 52,316 watched the proverbial game of two halves.

A dour and uninspiring goalless opening period gave way to an action-packed seven-goal thriller after the interval, as Newcastle edged out their former manager Kevin Keegan's current charges.

The Manchester City boss laid much of the blame for his side's defeat at the door of referee Steve Dunn, though it was difficult to see why in a match that must have transported the home faithful back to the exciting days of the Keegan regime.

A fast and furious first half was short on goalmouth action, and offered little sign of the excitement that was to follow.

Four minutes after the restart, Laurent Robert broke the deadlock from a free-kick. Nicky Butt was adjudged to have been fouled by Paul Bosvelt some 25 yards from goal in a right of central position, and the French winger curled the set-piece over the wall and just inside the right-hand upright.

Then, after 58 minutes, Stephen Carr galloped forward to earn his side a penalty. The Irish international full-back was upended by an advancing David James, and Alan Shearer fired home from the spot.

Having done the hard work, the Magpies then set about squandering their lead. Shaun Wright-Phillips was given the freedom of the city to drill home a 15-yard effort from the inside right channel after 64 minutes, before substitute Robbie Fowler earned and then converted a penalty three minutes later.

However, just as Graeme Souness' men looked set to be overwhelmed, they went back in front through Robbie Elliott. The defender glanced a header from Robert's inswinging free-kick against the left-hand upright, and watched as the ball spun over the line without getting a touch from either Shearer or City centre-back Richard Dunne.

A 77th-minute long throw from the left then fell invitingly for Wright-Phillips to drill home through a crowd of players, yet there was still time for Craig Bellamy to make the right sort of headlines.

With just one minute remaining, the Welsh international sealed the points with a deft 12-yard volleyed effort from the inside left channel.

"Craig Bellamy got all the headlines last week, but he will make them again this week for all of the right reasons."

Graeme Souness

"The referee was not strong enough and made too many mistakes that had a major impact on the game."

Kevin Keegan

Laurent Robert opens the scoring

PREMIERSHIP FIXTURE HISTORY

Pl: 3 Draws: 2	Wins			
Southampton	1	2	3	0
Birmingham City	0	0	4	0

STARTING LINE-UPS

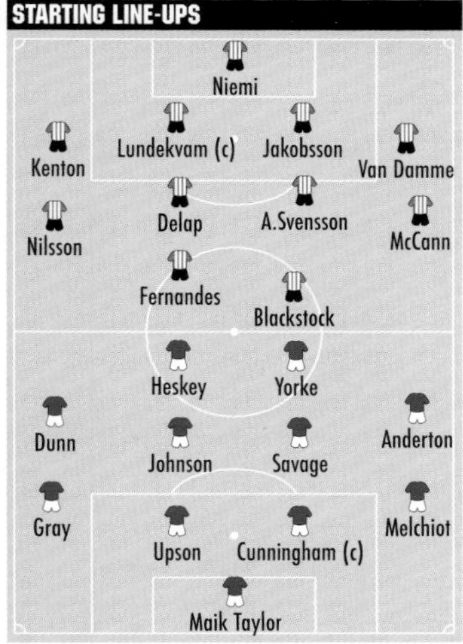

Ormerod, Prutton, Blayney, Best, Higginbotham

Gronkjaer, Clapham, Bennett, Tebily, Martin Taylor

EVENT LINE

	HALF TIME 0 - 0
64	**Nilsson (Off) Ormerod (On)**
64	Yorke (Off) Gronkjaer (On)
71	Anderton (Foul)
81	Dunn (Off) Clapham (On)
89	**Fernandes (Off) Prutton (On)**
	FULL TIME 0 - 0

STATISTICS

Season	Fixture		Fixture	Season
49	1	Shots On Target	2	38
57	5	Shots Off Target	6	47
1	1	Hit Woodwork	0	1
28	4	Caught Offside	6	30
57	4	Corners	4	52
132	11	Fouls	11	144
50%	48%	Possession	52%	50%

LEAGUE STANDINGS

Position (pos before)	W	D	L	F	A	Pts
18 (20) Southampton	1	3	6	6	12	6
14 (14) Birmingham C	1	6	3	7	9	9

Sunday 24th October 2004 | Venue: **Friends Provident St Mary's Stadium** | Attendance: **27,568** | Referee: **M.L.Dean**

SOUTHAMPTON 0 BIRMINGHAM CITY 0

The fact that this game ended scoreless came as little surprise, as both teams continued their disappointing starts to the season.

Neither club had found goals easy to come by prior to this fixture, registering just 13 between them in a combined total of 18 Premiership fixtures. Birmingham also came into the match on the back of four top-flight draws.

A shortage of strikers meant that under-fire Southampton head coach Steve Wigley fielded winger Fabrice Fernandes in support of the youthful Dexter Blackstock. Brett Ormerod, who had played 90 minutes the previous day, was named on the bench after returning from a loan spell at Leeds.

Former Portsmouth man Darren Anderton made his first Premiership start for Steve Bruce's visitors on the right of midfield, while Jesper Gronkjaer was relegated to the bench.

The South Coast club had the better of a dour opening period. Only the woodwork denied Blackstock, when he rose to meet a long throw from the right by Rory Delap. Then, Swede Mikael Nilsson should have done better than hit the side-netting, when rounding goalkeeper Maik Taylor on the right side of the area just before the break.

Antti Niemi was not troubled in the first half, but was called upon to deny David Dunn three minutes after the restart. The Saints' only effort on target of the entire match followed soon afterwards courtesy of Delap, and then Mario Melchiot went close at the other end with a 25-yard drive.

Combative play from Emile Heskey down the right led to a gilt-edge chance for Dunn in the 66th minute, but the midfielder blazed high over the crossbar from around the penalty spot.

Ten minutes later, Anderton was denied what would have been a sweet moment by a fantastic reflex stop from Niemi. The former England international reached a cross from the right and acrobatically dispatched a shot that was arrowing towards the bottom left-hand corner, only for the keeper to somehow fling out a glove and palm the ball away to safety.

The save was breathtaking, and deserved the priceless point that it helped to preserve.

Neil McCann is powerless to stop Mario Melchiot

"I was very pleased with the performance and attitude of my team, and I thought Blackstock did very well playing as a lone striker."

Steve Wigley

"I felt we did enough in the second half to win, but we didn't take our chances."

Steve Bruce

PREMIERSHIP FIXTURE HISTORY

Pl: 13 Draws: 4	Wins	⚽	☐	■
Arsenal	9	32	15	0
Southampton	0	13	37	0

STARTING LINE-UPS

Lehmann
Lauren, Toure, Cygan, Cole
Ljungberg, Vieira (c), Edu, Reyes
Bergkamp, Henry

Ormerod, Blackstock
A.Svensson, Delap, Telfer, Nilsson
Higginbotham, Jakobsson, Lundekvam (c), Kenton
Niemi

Pires, Fabregas, van Persie, Almunia, Senderos

McCann, Prutton, Best, Blayney, Baird

EVENT LINE

18 ☐ Telfer (Foul)

HALF TIME 0 - 0

51 ☐ Kenton (Foul)

61 **Reyes (Off) Pires (On)**

63 ☐ **Vieira (Foul)**

65 **Edu (Off) Fabregas (On)**

67 ⚽ **Henry (Open Play)**

68 ☐ Ormerod (Dissent)

75 Ormerod (Off) McCann (On)

80 ⚽ Delap (Corner)

83 **Ljungberg (Off) van Persie (On)**

85 ⚽ Delap (Indirect Free Kick)

85 Svensson A (Off) Prutton (On)

87 ☐ McCann (Foul)

90 ⚽ **van Persie (Open Play)**

90 Blackstock (Off) Best (On)

FULL TIME 2 - 2

STATISTICS

Season	Fixture (Arsenal)		Fixture (Southampton)	Season
108	9	Shots On Target	4	53
51	5	Shots Off Target	3	60
6	1	Hit Woodwork	1	2
23	3	Caught Offside	5	33
59	7	Corners	7	64
125	8	Fouls	21	153
58%	54%	Possession	46%	49%

LEAGUE STANDINGS

Position (pos before)		W	D	L	F	A	Pts
1 (1)	Arsenal	8	2	1	31	12	26
18 (18)	Southampton	1	4	6	8	14	7

Saturday 30th October 2004 | Venue: **Highbury** | Attendance: **38,141** | Referee: **M.D.Messias**

ARSENAL 2 SOUTHAMPTON 2

Dennis Bergkamp is felled by Darren Kenton

"We had a mental shock when we lost against Manchester United after 49 matches unbeaten, and it was important not to lose the next game."

Arsene Wenger

PREMIERSHIP MILESTONE

Robin van Persie scored his first Premiership goal

"I'd have taken a point before the game, but when we were leading with 15 seconds to go, it was a bitter pill to swallow."

Steve Wigley

PREMIERSHIP MILESTONE

50 David Prutton made his 50th Premiership appearance

Southampton were denied a shock victory at Highbury when Arsenal substitute Robin van Persie fired home a last-gasp equaliser.

A 67th-minute goal from Thierry Henry had looked set to settle the game, before Rory Delap popped up with two headers from set-pieces to put the Saints in front.

Arsene Wenger was forced into one change from the team that had lost their long unbeaten record at Old Trafford, replacing the injured Sol Campbell with Pascal Cygan.

Strangely, the Gunners' last Premiership defeat prior to the Manchester United game, against Leeds in May 2003, was followed by a home match against Southampton - Arsene Wenger's men won 6-1 on that occasion. Many thought a similar result was likely as the champions took to the field against a team that had not won under the leadership of Steve Wigley.

However, after Henry had headed an early chance wide, visiting midfielder Mikael Nilsson struck a post. The Swedish international ghosted in unnoticed to meet a deep cross from the left, and steered an effort back across Jens Lehmann and against an upright.

Then it was the home side's turn to strike the woodwork, as Henry failed to punish Darren Kenton's clumsy 29th-minute challenge from the penalty spot. Further threats to Antti Niemi's goal came from Dennis Bergkamp and Lauren, but the first half ended scoreless.

Unsurprisingly, the second period began with incessant Arsenal pressure. It wasn't until the 67th minute that the deadlock was finally broken though, as Henry expertly brought down a lofted pass from Bergkamp and slotted the ball past Niemi.

The Finnish keeper then denied Freddie Ljungberg, before the game changed completely in a bizarre five minutes. With 10 minutes remaining, substitute Neil McCann's left-wing corner was headed in by Delap. Then, the same two players combined again, as Delap nodded home an inswinging free-kick from the right.

In between the goals, Wenger had introduced van Persie. With time fast running out, the young Dutchman set about making a name for himself at Highbury, checking back onto his left foot in a crowded penalty area and driving a venomous effort into the far top left-hand corner of the net.

Saturday 30th October 2004	Venue: **St Andrew's**	Attendance: **28,916**	Referee: **D.J.Gallagher**

BIRMINGHAM CITY 0 CRYSTAL PALACE 1

Andy Johnson made a perfect return to St Andrew's, scoring the only goal of the game to hand Crystal Palace their first away win in the Premiership.

The result saw former Eagles manager Steve Bruce's expensively assembled side fall below their in-form opponents in the table. For Iain Dowie's men, the victory was a fourth in five matches in all competitions.

Many feared that referee Dermot Gallagher would have his work cut out, as Robbie Savage and Michael Hughes faced each other for the first time since both were sent off during an ugly clash between Wales and Northern Ireland in September.

As it was, the two men were well behaved, and Savage failed to connect with the only decent chance of the opening half-hour. Birmingham continued to press forward, penning the visitors back, but were unable to convert territorial dominance into goals.

The closest Bruce's men came to scoring was when defender Mario Melchiot beat Hungarian goalkeeper Gabor Kiraly, only to see Fitz Hall clear his effort off the line.

While Emile Heskey and Dwight Yorke floundered, Johnson demonstrated what his old club were missing in the 41st minute. The diminutive striker raced onto Wayne Routledge's pass in the inside right channel and scuffed a low shot across Maik Taylor and in off the far post.

Having enjoyed a good rapport with the St Andrew's faithful during his time in the Midlands, Johnson did not celebrate finding the net. In fact, many home fans applauded the player who had just put their team 1-0 down.

With a crucial lead to protect, Dowie's charges offered little going forward in a poor quality second half. The Eagles were content to defend what they had, keeping 10 men behind the ball and working tirelessly for the cause.

Birmingham created several half-chances, though Kiraly seldom had to produce anything other than routine saves. Darren Anderton, Jamie Clapham and Stephen Clemence were all introduced in a desperate attempt to conjure an equaliser, but it wasn't to be.

A dignified Andy Johnson chooses not to celebrate his winner

"We're obviously concerned with what's happening. You can see all the tension and frustration with everyone."
Steve Bruce

"I rate him as an England player, and he certainly wouldn't be out of place in the current international set-up."
Iain Dowie on Andy Johnson

PREMIERSHIP FIXTURE HISTORY

Pl: 1 Draws: 0	Wins	Goals	Yellow	Red
Birmingham City	0	0	1	0
Crystal Palace	1	1	1	0

STARTING LINE-UPS

Birmingham subs: Anderton, Clapham, Clemence, Vaesen, Tebily

Crystal Palace subs: Sorondo, Freedman, Derry, Speroni, Andrews

EVENT LINE

41' Goal: Johnson (Open Play)

HALF TIME 0 - 1

47 Substitution: Popovic (Off) Sorondo (On)

60 Yellow card: **Upson (Foul)**

60 Substitution: **Lazaridis (Off) Anderton (On)**

73 Yellow card: Riihilahti (Foul)

82 Substitution: **Cunningham (Off) Clapham (On)**

85 Substitution: **Johnson (Off) Clemence (On)**

88 Substitution: Kolkka (Off) Freedman (On)

90 Substitution: Hughes (Off) Derry (On)

FULL TIME 0 - 1

STATISTICS

Season	Fixture (Birmingham City)		Fixture (Crystal Palace)	Season
49	11	Shots On Target	1	45
52	5	Shots Off Target	3	58
1	0	Hit Woodwork	0	3
34	4	Caught Offside	4	27
63	11	Corners	3	61
152	8	Fouls	14	156
51%	56%	Possession	44%	46%

LEAGUE STANDINGS

Position (pos before)	W	D	L	F	A	Pts
16 (14) Birmingham C	1	6	4	7	10	9
14 (15) Crystal Palace	3	2	6	12	15	11

PREMIERSHIP FIXTURE HISTORY

Pl: 11 Draws: 4	Wins	Goals	Yellow	Red
Blackburn Rovers	4	22	18	1
Liverpool	3	18	13	0

STARTING LINE-UPS

Blackburn Rovers: Friedel; Short, Johansson, Neill, McEveley; Ferguson (c), Tugay, Reid, Emerton; Bothroyd, Dickov

Liverpool: Baros, Cisse; Riise, Hamann, Alonso, Finnan; Traore, Hyypia (c), Carragher, Josemi; Kirkland

Substitutes – Blackburn Rovers: Stead, Enckelman, Todd, Flitcroft, Djorkaeff

Substitutes – Liverpool: Garcia, Kewell, Diao, Dudek, Warnock

EVENT LINE

7 Riise (Open Play)

16 **Bothroyd (Open Play)**

38 Cisse (Off) Garcia (On)

45 **Emerton (Open Play)**

45 Josemi (Foul)

HALF TIME 2 - 1

54 Baros (Open Play)

55 Finnan (Off) Kewell (On)

61 **Tugay (Foul)**

65 **Bothroyd (Off) Stead (On)**

69 **Stead (Foul)**

81 Hamann (Off) Diao (On)

FULL TIME 2 - 2

STATISTICS

Season	Fixture (Blackburn)		Fixture (Liverpool)	Season
47	7	Shots On Target	9	66
58	1	Shots Off Target	4	59
1	0	Hit Woodwork	0	1
42	4	Caught Offside	3	33
64	6	Corners	6	58
175	14	Fouls	11	118
48%	48%	Possession	52%	54%

LEAGUE STANDINGS

Position (pos before)		W	D	L	F	A	Pts
19 (20)	Blackburn R	1	4	6	9	24	7
6 (6)	Liverpool	5	2	3	18	10	17

Saturday 30th October 2004 | Venue: Ewood Park | Attendance: 26,314 | Referee: R.Styles

BLACKBURN ROVERS 2 LIVERPOOL 2

A terrific 2-2 draw at Ewood Park was marred by an horrific injury to Liverpool striker Djibril Cisse.

The French international was stretchered from the field with a badly broken leg after an innocuous looking challenge with James McEveley near the corner flag. By this point the score was already 1-1.

The visitors had taken a seventh-minute lead when John Arne Riise was afforded time and space in the inside left channel to drill a low 15-yard effort across Brad Friedel from Xabi Alonso's searching pass.

Mark Hughes' team struck back swiftly, however, as Jay Bothroyd guided home his first Premiership goal after Brett Emerton had squared from the left in the 16th minute.

Both sides continued to threaten throughout the remainder of the half. Milan Baros forced a fine save from Friedel after capitalising on a slip by Nils-Eric Johansson, before Emerton sent Rovers into the interval with a 2-1 lead.

The goal was a poor one for Liverpool to concede as they had countless opportunities to clear the danger. Sami Hyypia eventually poked the ball towards the Australian international, who brilliantly dispatched a low curling effort beyond the left hand of Chris Kirkland from just inside the area.

The next goal was always going to be crucial in a match as tightly contested as this, and it went to Liverpool in the 54th minute..

With his mind perhaps elsewhere, given his involvement in the incident that led to Cisse's injury, McEveley presented the ball to Luis Garcia from a free-kick on halfway. The Spaniard quickly picked out Baros, who advanced down the inside right channel and beat Friedel from within his six-yard box.

While that proved to be the end of the scoring, it wasn't through a lack of effort from either team. Promising young goalkeeper Kirkland made a hat-trick of fine saves, tipping over a drive from substitute Jonathan Stead, somehow keeping out a Craig Short header, and then denying Paul Dickov from point-blank range.

At the other end, replacement Harry Kewell stung the palms of the Blackburn custodian, while Riise was also denied a late winner.

Jamie Carragher is hunted by Paul Dickov

"I thought we were excellent from start to finish. We had to make a statement tonight and I think we did that."

Mark Hughes

PREMIERSHIP MILESTONE

100 Paul Dickov and Steve Finnan both made their 100th Premiership appearances

PREMIERSHIP MILESTONE

Jay Bothroyd scored his first Premiership goal

"We played a high tempo game for much of today and controlled the match in parts."

Rafael Benitez

PREMIERSHIP MILESTONE

50 Milan Baros made his 50th Premiership appearance

PREMIERSHIP FIXTURE HISTORY

Pl: 6	Draws: 2	Wins	Goals	Yellow	Red
Charlton Athletic		3	5	10	0
Middlesbrough		1	3	7	0

STARTING LINE-UPS

Charlton subs: Murphy, Lisbie, Konchesky, Andersen, Fortune

Middlesbrough subs: Doriva, Job, Nash, Cooper, Morrison

EVENT LINE

21 El Karkouri (Own Goal)
34 **El Karkouri (Foul)**
HALF TIME 0 - 1
46 **Johansson (Open Play)**
58 Zenden (Open Play)
64 **Perry (Foul)**
66 **Bartlett (Off) Lisbie (On)**
66 **Kishishev (Off) Murphy (On)**
75 Downing (Off) Doriva (On)
79 Viduka (Off) Job (On)
81 **Murphy (Foul)**
82 **Thomas (Off) Konchesky (On)**
FULL TIME 1 - 2

STATISTICS

Season	Fixture (Charlton)		Fixture (Middlesbrough)	Season
46	7	Shots On Target	7	89
40	1	Shots Off Target	4	71
2	0	Hit Woodwork	0	0
37	3	Caught Offside	0	35
46	3	Corners	4	58
145	14	Fouls	8	137
43%	45%	Possession	55%	51%

LEAGUE STANDINGS

Position (pos before)		W	D	L	F	A	Pts
12 (12)	Charlton Ath	3	3	5	10	19	12
4 (8)	Middlesbrough	5	3	3	19	14	18

CHARLTON ATHLETIC 1 MIDDLESBROUGH 2

Charlton suffered their first home defeat of the Premiership campaign, as victory saw Middlesbrough climb into the top four.

The visitors led at half-time thanks to an own goal from Talal El Karkouri, but were pegged back by Jonatan Johansson within 60 seconds of the restart. However, Steve McClaren's side regrouped and conjured up a 58th-minute Boudewijn Zenden winner.

After an even opening in which neither defence had reason to feel unduly concerned, the Teesside club went in front through an extremely fortuitous goal.

Moroccan El Karkouri, occupying a defensive role for the first time since his summer move to The Valley, was a helpless spectator as Jimmy Floyd Hasselbaink's wayward 21st-minute shot struck his right boot and rolled agonisingly into the net.

The Addicks, and El Karkouri in particular, responded via a dangerous set-piece, Mark Schwarzer tipping over a firm header. The goalkeeper was untroubled throughout the remainder of the half, though he was beaten shortly after the restart.

With Alan Curbishley's words of wisdom still fresh in their minds, Jason Euell and Johansson combined for a neat equaliser. The Finnish international latched onto a clever pass from his teammate and cut in from the right past the advancing Schwarzer, before steering the ball home from just inside the area.

Far from being rocked by this early blow, McClaren's charges were galvanised. Dean Kiely saved well from Hasselbaink, but it served only to delay the inevitable.

Just shy of the hour mark, Zenden finished off a move that sliced right through the home defence. After several sharp passes, the final act saw the Dutch midfielder clip the ball in over the advancing Kiely from 10 yards, having been found running into the inside left channel by Mark Viduka.

With over half-an-hour still to play, the visitors may have expected a strong response. This did not materialise, however, as Charlton only managed to muster a couple of weak shots from their goalscorer Johansson.

While Middlesbrough appear set for a strong season, Curbishley's team must find their form quickly if they are to avoid being sucked into a relegation battle.

"I thought the result was a bit harsh, but it's all about results."
Alan Curbishley

"We played an attacking game, and I felt we always looked like getting the points."
Steve McClaren

Boudewijn Zenden steers Middlesbrough in front

PREMIERSHIP FIXTURE HISTORY

Pl: 13 Draws: 4	Wins	Goals	Yellow	Red
Everton	5	13	21	0
Aston Villa	4	13	25	0

STARTING LINE-UPS

Everton: Martyn; Hibbert, Weir, Stubbs (c), Pistone; Watson, Cahill, Osman, Gravesen, Kilbane; Bent

Aston Villa: Cole, Angel; Hitzlsperger, McCann, Hendrie, Solano; Samuel, Mellberg (c), Delaney, De la Cruz; Sorensen

Subs (Everton): Ferguson, McFadden, Wright, Campbell, Fox

Subs (Aston Villa): Ridgewell, Postma, Davis, Whittingham, L.Moore

EVENT LINE

19 Yellow card: Hendrie (Foul)
26 Goal: Hendrie (Open Play)
33 Goal: **Bent (Open Play)**

HALF TIME 1 - 1

49 Yellow card: **Cahill (Foul)**
58 Substitution: Delaney (Off) Ridgewell (On)
60 Substitution: Hitzlsperger (Off) Davis (On)
66 Substitution: **Watson (Off) Ferguson (On)**
77 Substitution: Solano (Off) Whittingham (On)
84 Substitution: **Osman (Off) McFadden (On)**

FULL TIME 1 - 1

STATISTICS

Season	Fixture (Everton)		Fixture (Aston Villa)	Season
64	8	Shots On Target	5	67
63	12	Shots Off Target	4	61
3	1	Hit Woodwork	0	3
33	1	Caught Offside	1	24
61	8	Corners	3	65
127	8	Fouls	17	179
51%	60%	Possession	40%	47%

LEAGUE STANDINGS

Position (pos before)		W	D	L	F	A	Pts
3 (3)	Everton	7	2	2	14	10	23
10 (9)	Aston Villa	3	6	2	14	13	15

Saturday 30th October 2004 | Venue: **Goodison Park** | Attendance: **37,816** | Referee: **S.W.Dunn**

EVERTON 1 ASTON VILLA 1

Tony Hibbert brings down Juan Pablo Angel

"We're trying to keep the players relaxed and not put any pressure on them, but it says a lot when they are disappointed with a draw from this game."
David Moyes

"I can't praise the lads enough after a disappointing result in midweek."
David O'Leary

PREMIERSHIP MILESTONE
25 Lee Hendrie netted his 25th Premiership goal

First half goals from Lee Hendrie and Marcus Bent saw the spoils shared in a highly competitive game at Goodison Park.

The point was reward for some dogged defending by a visiting team that spent much of the match under the cosh. Everton enjoyed the majority of the possession and looked the most likely scorers right from the first whistle.

However, after a series of half-chances had gone begging, it was Aston Villa who took the lead in the 26th minute. Having netted with three wonder strikes in his last four Premiership outings, it should have come as no surprise to see Hendrie curl a 20-yard effort into the top right-hand corner of the net from the inside right channel.

This was a setback for David Moyes' high-flying team, but they responded in positive fashion. Just seven minutes after falling behind, Bent steered a nine-yard effort into the roof of the net from David Weir's slide-rule pass for his third goal in the space of eight days.

It was just reward for the hard-working striker, who harried the visiting defence at every opportunity. Shortly after the restart, the former Ipswich man won possession and centred for Kevin Kilbane, but the Irish midfielder failed to hit the target from close range.

Thomas Sorensen was then relieved to see a looping effort from Bent drift just over, before Duncan Ferguson was introduced in place of Steve Watson. The change saw Everton revert to a 4-4-2 formation as they attempted to find the winning goal that their football deserved.

It didn't materialise, however, and Carlton Cole should really have stolen the points for David O'Leary's charges. The on-loan Chelsea striker found himself unmarked in the box, yet somehow managed to drill a powerful effort high into the crowd.

A Villa goal would have been incredibly harsh on an Everton team that had given everything in the search for victory. The draw kept the Toffees in third place, though the disappointment on the faces of their players at the final whistle reflected how far they had come in such a short space of time.

PREMIERSHIP FIXTURE HISTORY

Pl: 4 Draws: 0	Wins	Goals	Yellow	Red
Fulham	3	7	3	0
Tottenham Hotspur	1	5	5	0

STARTING LINE-UPS

Radzinski, Flitney, Green, Rosenior, McBride

Davies, Kanoute, Carrick, Keller, Taricco

EVENT LINE

24 Bunjevcevic (Foul)

33 **Boa Morte (Open Play)**

41 Brown (Off) Davies (On)

HALF TIME 1 - 0

61 **Cole (Open Play)**

67 Ziegler (Off) Kanoute (On)

70 **John (Off) Radzinski (On)**

83 Davis (Off) Carrick (On)

FULL TIME 2 - 0

STATISTICS

Season	Fixture	Fulham	Tottenham	Fixture	Season
53	4	Shots On Target		1	52
50	4	Shots Off Target		4	63
2	0	Hit Woodwork		0	4
29	4	Caught Offside		11	40
60	5	Corners		4	48
126	11	Fouls		9	143
48%	52%	Possession		48%	46%

LEAGUE STANDINGS

Position (pos before)	W	D	L	F	A	Pts
15 (17) Fulham	3	2	6	12	19	11
11 (10) Tottenham H	3	4	4	6	8	13

Saturday 30th October 2004 | Venue: **Craven Cottage** | Attendance: **21,317** | Referee: **A.G.Wiley**

FULHAM 2 TOTTENHAM HOTSPUR 0

A 2-0 victory saw Fulham end a run of three consecutive Premiership defeats, an unwanted statistic that this result passed on to Tottenham.

Goals in each half from Luis Boa Morte and captain Andy Cole did the damage, as Spurs failed to ignite at any point during the match. Any efforts the visitors did muster were mostly off target, and tended to be the result of lively individual play from Jermain Defoe.

A diabolical first half was punctuated by one moment of real quality after 33 minutes. Home favourite Steed Malbranque collected possession on the left and slipped a perfectly-weighted pass into the path of the onrushing Boa Morte, who coolly slotted low past Paul Robinson from 12 yards out.

It was a picture-book goal, and Zat Knight could have doubled the lead soon afterwards when his header from a free-kick was well saved. A low Defoe drive that fizzed narrowly wide when the game was scoreless was all that Jacques Santini's men could point to by way of chances.

Returning midfielder Sean Davis, who left Fulham under acrimonious circumstances during the summer, saw his every touch booed. Unsurprisingly, this resulted in an under-par performance, and Tottenham lost the midfield battle.

Despite not being at their flowing best, the Cottagers were still more then good enough to win this encounter. A one-goal lead is never secure, however, and it came as a relief to most inside the ground when Cole made it 2-0 after 61 minutes.

This time Boa Morte turned from scorer to provider, battling hard for possession on the left and centring for the striker to nod into the right-hand side of the goal from a central position seven yards out.

A team that had managed just six goals in 10 Premiership games was never likely to recover from such a position, and they seldom threatened to beat Mark Crossley during the remainder of the clash.

The win was an important one for Chris Coleman's charges, moving them back in the right direction, while Santini must be concerned at Spurs' inability to find the net.

"We played better than Tottenham and we deserved the three points. I can't point any fingers when we put in performances like that."

Chris Coleman

"I am not disappointed with the spirit of the players. Today we played with quality, but it wasn't enough to win."

Jacques Santini

PREMIERSHIP MILESTONE

100 Jermain Defoe made his 100th Premiership appearance

Andy Cole heads home Fulham's second goal

Saturday 30th October 2004 | Venue: **Fratton Park** | Attendance: **20,190** | Referee: **N.S.Barry**

PORTSMOUTH 2 MANCHESTER UNITED 0

Manchester United suffered defeat at Fratton Park for the second season in succession, a result that rendered their victory against Arsenal the previous weekend fairly academic.

Much had been made of the importance of following up one good result with another, but a visiting team that lacked Ruud van Nistelrooy didn't possess the cutting edge needed to turn a whole host of presentable openings into goals.

As it was, second half strikes from David Unsworth, via the penalty spot, and Aiyegbeni Yakubu condemned Sir Alex Ferguson's side to a first defeat since the opening weekend of the Premiership season.

Harry Redknapp again managed to accommodate three strikers in a 4-5-1 formation, while Alan Smith replaced the suspended van Nistelrooy in a United team otherwise unchanged from their win against the Gunners.

With confidence understandably high, the North-West outfit began like an express train. Cristiano Ronaldo was at his brilliant best, hitting the side-netting and then forcing two fine saves from Shaka Hislop in a breathless opening.

A curling effort from Smith flew narrowly over, before Portsmouth began to get a foothold in the match. Roy Carroll denied Yakubu after 18 minutes, and then Patrik Berger and Nigel Quashie both went close from distance.

The moments leading up to half-time were even more frantic as Mikael Silvestre cleared off the line from Lomana Tresor Lua Lua, Ronaldo volleyed across goal, and Amdy Faye was denied by a superb one-handed stop.

Eight minutes into the second period the deadlock was finally broken, however, as Unsworth lashed home from the spot after Rio Ferdinand had been adjudged to have brought down Ricardo Fuller.

An immediate response seemed likely when a Ronaldo effort hit the bar and fell invitingly in the direction of Smith. Unfortunately for his team, the striker was unable to contain his forward momentum and diverted the ball high into the crowd.

The miss summed up United's afternoon, and Yakubu sealed the points after 72 minutes. The Nigerian outmuscled two defenders to latch onto Hislop's long kick, and promptly beat the advancing Carroll with a low 15-yard effort that deflected in off Silvestre.

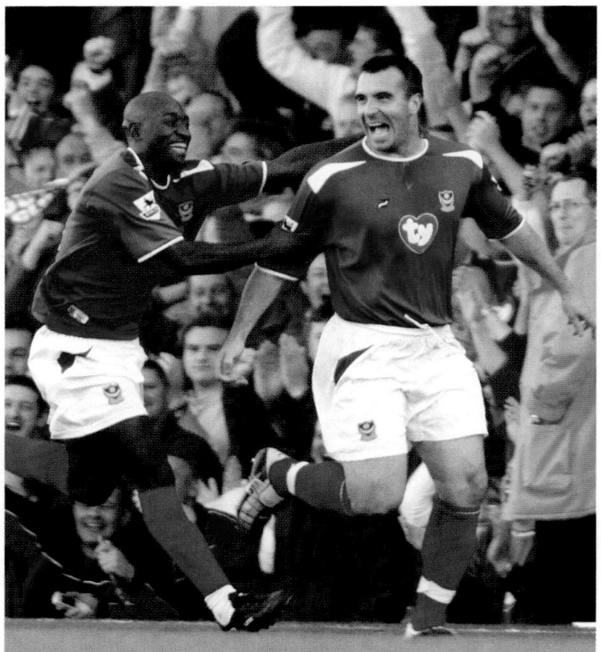

David Unsworth opens the scoring from the penalty spot

PREMIERSHIP FIXTURE HISTORY

Pl: **2** Draws: **0**

	Wins	Goals	Yellow cards	Red cards
Portsmouth	2	3	2	0
Manchester United	0	0	3	0

STARTING LINE-UPS

Portsmouth subs: Fuller, Mezague, Ashdown, Griffin, Cisse

Manchester United subs: Keane, Saha, Brown, Ricardo, Miller

EVENT LINE

32 **Kamara (Off) Fuller (On)**

41 Rooney (Foul)

HALF TIME 0 - 0

46 **Berger (Off) Mezague (On)**

52 Ferdinand (Dissent)

53 **Unsworth (Penalty)**

65 Neville P (Off) Keane (On)

65 Smith (Off) Saha (On)

72 **Yakubu (Open Play)**

80 Neville G (Off) Brown (On)

FULL TIME 2 - 0

STATISTICS

Season	Fixture (Portsmouth)		Fixture (Man Utd)	Season
59	8	Shots On Target	9	81
52	4	Shots Off Target	11	77
1	0	Hit Woodwork	1	6
23	1	Caught Offside	3	33
46	3	Corners	9	78
120	19	Fouls	11	139
47%	42%	Possession	58%	53%

LEAGUE STANDINGS

Position (pos before)		W	D	L	F	A	Pts
9 (11)	Portsmouth	4	3	3	15	12	15
7 (5)	Man Utd	4	5	2	11	9	17

PREMIERSHIP MILESTONE

The attendance of 20,190 was a Premiership record at Fratton Park

"Three years ago we were playing Grimsby or someone. No disrespect to Grimsby, but now we have just beaten Manchester United - It is unreal."

Harry Redknapp

PREMIERSHIP MILESTONE

Valery Mezague made his Premiership debut

"The result against Arsenal last weekend has been totally destroyed. That was a bad, bad performance."

Sir Alex Ferguson

PREMIERSHIP FIXTURE HISTORY

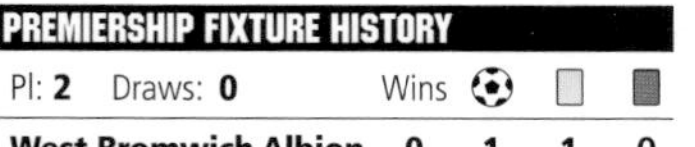

Pl: 2 Draws: 0	Wins	⚽	Yellow	Red
West Bromwich Albion	0	1	1	0
Chelsea	2	6	0	0

STARTING LINE-UPS

Dobie, Koumas, Dyer, Kuszczak, Haos

Carvalho, Robben, Tiago, Cudicini, Kezman

EVENT LINE

45 ⚽ Gallas (Corner)

HALF TIME 0 - 1

46 ⇄ Bridge (Off) Carvalho (On)

46 ⇄ Cole J (Off) Robben (On)

51 ⚽ Gudjohnsen (Open Play)

54 ▯ **Robinson (Foul)**

56 ⇄ **Earnshaw (Off) Dobie (On)**

56 ⚽ **Gera (Open Play)**

59 ⚽ Duff (Open Play)

64 ⇄ **Clement (Off) Koumas (On)**

80 ⇄ **Greening (Off) Dyer (On)**

81 ⚽ Lampard (Open Play)

83 ⇄ Lampard (Off) Tiago (On)

FULL TIME 1 - 4

STATISTICS

Season	Fixture (West Brom)		Fixture (Chelsea)	Season
54	9	Shots On Target	9	81
51	3	Shots Off Target	10	82
2	0	Hit Woodwork	0	4
42	3	Caught Offside	1	34
68	2	Corners	6	83
148	12	Fouls	8	132
48%	46%	Possession	54%	56%

LEAGUE STANDINGS

Position (pos before)		W	D	L	F	A	Pts
17 (16)	West Brom	1	5	5	9	20	8
2 (2)	Chelsea	8	2	1	16	3	26

Saturday 30th October 2004 | Venue: **The Hawthorns** | Attendance: **27,399** | Referee: **B.Knight**

WEST BROM 1 CHELSEA 4

Following the midweek departure of manager Gary Megson, a home match against high-flying Chelsea always threatened to be an uncomfortable afternoon's viewing for caretaker boss Frank Burrows.

The Baggies were well in contention prior to William Gallas' late first half goal, and responded to Eidur Gudjohnsen doubling the lead with a crisp strike from Zoltan Gera, before Damien Duff and Frank Lampard gave the scoreline a one-sided look.

Robert Earnshaw nearly joined the exclusive club of players that had beaten Petr Cech, but saw his third-minute effort well saved. The Welshman's strike-partner, Nwankwo Kanu, then failed to hit the target from close range, and Earnshaw himself fired wide in a bright opening 20 minutes for the home side.

Jose Mourinho's team had not been at their best during the opening period, yet found themselves taking the lead just prior to the interval. Defender William Gallas was the unlikely goalscorer, turning the ball home from within the six-yard box following a corner.

Having waited 45 minutes for a goal, three arrived in an eight-minute spell shortly after the break.

Firstly, Gudjohnsen met Duff's 51st-minute cross from the left with a close-range diving header to make it 2-0. Then, Gera reduced the arrears with a well-struck 20-yard drive into the bottom left-hand corner of the net, before Duff coolly rounded off a smart breakaway by slotting home past Russell Hoult from Lampard's astute pass.

Chances continued to fall at either end as both clubs mustered nine shots on target. Jason Koumas and the pacy Lloyd Dyer were introduced as Burrows went for broke, but it was Chelsea who extended their lead after 81 minutes.

Substitute Arjen Robben battled through a couple of tackles down the left and slipped the ball inside for Lampard to crack home a swerving 25-yard drive. The strike illustrated just how vital the midfielder has become to the Londoners' cause, and ensured a second consecutive four-goal Premiership haul for Mourinho's men.

Coupled with Southampton's draw at Highbury, this result took the Stamford Bridge side level on points with Arsenal at the top of the table.

"If we could have held on for five or ten minutes after we made it 2-1, things might have been different."

Caretaker Manager Frank Burrows

"I'm really happy with the second half display. However, we have to talk about the first half, which I felt was poor."

Jose Mourinho

William Gallas is congratulated on opening the scoring by Wayne Bridge

PREMIERSHIP FIXTURE HISTORY

Pl: 6 Draws: 0	Wins	Goals	Yellow	Red
Bolton Wanderers	4	9	8	1
Newcastle United	2	11	11	0

STARTING LINE-UPS

Bolton subs: Hierro, Pedersen, Barness, Poole, Ferdinand

Newcastle subs: Robert, Ameobi, Bernard, Harper, Bramble

EVENT LINE

HALF TIME 0 - 0

52 **Diouf (Open Play)**

54 **Diouf (Ung.Conduct)**

55 **Jaidi (Off) Hierro (On)**

55 Ambrose (Open Play)

62 **Giannakopoulos (Off) Pedersen (C**

66 Kluivert (Off) Robert (On)

70 **Davies (Indirect Free Kick)**

72 Ambrose (Off) Ameobi (On)

77 Carr (Off) Bernard (On)

84 **Diouf (Off) Barness (On)**

84 Robert (Foul)

FULL TIME 2 - 1

STATISTICS

Season	Fixture (Bolton)		Fixture (Newcastle)	Season
82	11	Shots On Target	4	80
66	6	Shots Off Target	1	60
3	0	Hit Woodwork	0	4
23	1	Caught Offside	6	36
62	4	Corners	5	84
157	14	Fouls	12	132
50%	61%	Possession	39%	51%

LEAGUE STANDINGS

Position (pos before)		W	D	L	F	A	Pts
4 (5)	Bolton W	6	3	2	18	13	21
8 (8)	Newcastle Utd	4	4	3	22	19	16

Sunday 31st October 2004 | Venue: **Reebok Stadium** | Attendance: **27,196** | Referee: **G.Poll**

BOLTON WANDERERS 2 NEWCASTLE UNITED 1

Graeme Souness suffered his first defeat since taking charge of Newcastle, as Bolton overpowered his team at the Reebok Stadium.

On-loan Senegalese forward El-Hadji Diouf bundled home his first goal for the Trotters following a scoreless first half, but this was cancelled out almost immediately by a wonder-strike from Darren Ambrose. Then, with 20 minutes remaining, Kevin Davies pounced to win the game for Sam Allardyce's men.

It was the visitors who began brightly, Craig Bellamy forcing a tidy save from Jussi Jaaskelainen after racing beyond Nicky Hunt. Patrick Kluivert, occupying a slightly deeper role, then almost slipped in Alan Shearer, but Ricardo Gardner made a fine covering challenge.

Wanderers improved as the half progressed, with captain Jay-Jay Okocha's long throws causing no end of problems. A poor kick by Shay Given enabled Diouf to find Davies in space, but the striker pulled his effort wide.

Shortly after the interval, Radhi Jaidi headed a corner straight at the goalkeeper. Newcastle did not heed the warning as the Tunisian bravely rose highest, receiving a punch in the face from Given for his troubles, to nod across goal for Diouf to head home a 52nd-minute opener, following Okocha's right-wing projectile.

Within three minutes of falling behind, the Magpies hit back in spectacular fashion. Battling for the ball in a crowded midfield area, former Ipswich man Ambrose, only playing as a result of Jermaine Jenas' late withdrawal, evaded a couple of challenges and sent a searing 30-yard drive into the top right-hand corner of the net.

The strike was worthy of winning any match, but it turned out not even to be good enough for a point. Having sent on Henrik Pedersen in his quest to find a winner, Allardyce looked on in delight as Davies answered his call.

A free-kick was pumped into the box from deep and found its way towards the Bolton striker, stationed near the right-hand upright, off the head of Stephen Carr. The former Southampton man slid in bravely, not something which could be said of Given, and the ball squirmed into the net from close range.

El-Hadji Diouf remembers how to celebrate scoring a goal

"We thought about taking El-Hadji Diouf off, but then he popped up with a vital goal."
Sam Allardyce

PREMIERSHIP MILESTONE

El-Hadji Diouf scored his first Premiership goal in the colours of Bolton

"I think you know what to expect when you come to the Reebok. There wasn't enough football for me."
Graeme Souness

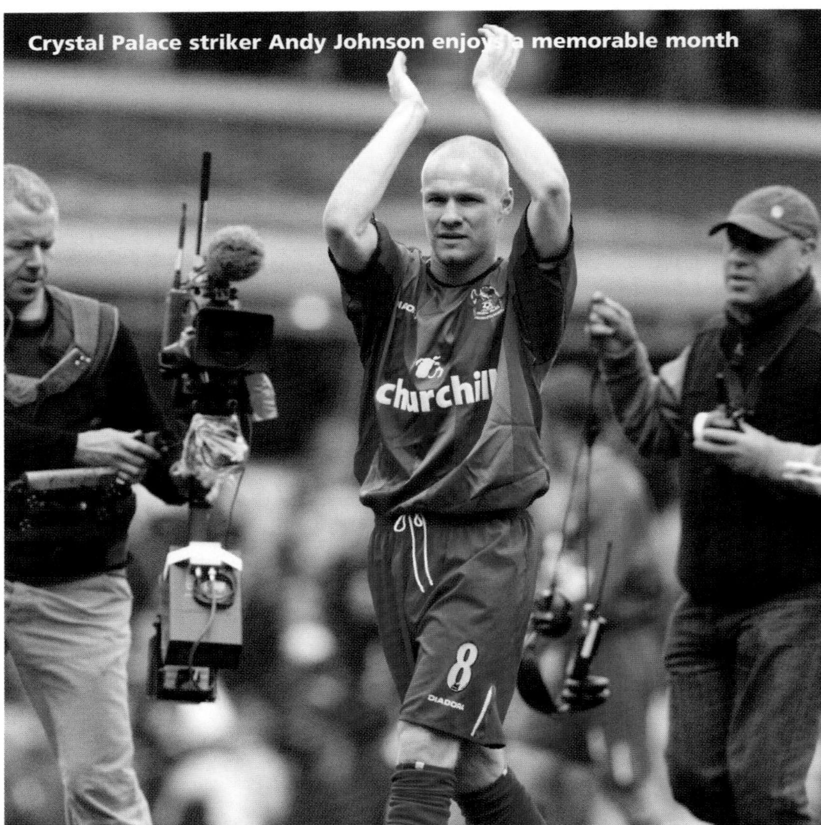

Crystal Palace striker Andy Johnson enjoys a memorable month

OCTOBER 2004

October belonged to Crystal Palace, as the Eagles won three of their four matches to surge out of the bottom three. Fulham, West Brom and Birmingham were all put to the sword, with Andy Johnson firing himself into second place in the scoring charts.

A 3-0 defeat at Selhurst Park proved to be Gary Megson's last game in charge of West Brom. Having stated that he would not be signing a new contract at The Hawthorns when his current deal expired in the summer, the board decided it was best for the two parties to go their separate ways.

The most significant game of the season so far took place at Old Trafford. Manchester United beat Arsenal 2-0 in a bad-tempered affair that ended with allegations of an after-match food fight in the tunnel. The Gunners needed a late Robin van Persie equaliser to avoid defeat at home to Southampton in their next game, while United were beaten at Portsmouth.

Chelsea were the beneficiaries of the heated battle between their two main rivals for the title. A defeat at Manchester City was followed by a couple of convincing wins, as Arjen Robben recovered from injury to breathe new life into an already strong unit.

Bolton, Middlesbrough and Portsmouth all enjoyed strong showings during the month. Sam Allardyce's men recovered from becoming the first team to lose to West Brom by recording three consecutive victories, while neither Steve McClaren or Harry Redknapp experienced defeat.

Six more top-flight sides exited the Carling Cup at the 3rd Round stage, though five of these lost out in all-Premiership encounters. Aston Villa were the exception, producing an abject display in a 3-1 defeat at Championship outfit Burnley.

On the international front, England moved to the top of 'World Cup Qualifying Group Six' with wins against Wales and Azerbaijan. Mark Hughes' men were beaten 2-0 at Old Trafford, in a match best remembered for David Beckham picking up a deliberate booking, before a Michael Owen goal settled matters in Baku.

IN THE NEWS

05TH Arsenal agree a £100m sponsorship deal with 'Emirates Airlines'. As a result, the Gunners' new ground at Ashburton Grove will be known as the 'Emirates Stadium' for its first 15 years of use.

09TH Goals from Frank Lampard and David Beckham ensure that England run out comfortable 2-0 winners against neighbours Wales in a World Cup Qualifier staged at Old Trafford

13TH A Michael Owen goal earns England three points in Azerbaijan, as qualification for the 2006 World Cup begins to look increasingly likely

15TH The Football Association submits a bid for the new Wembley Stadium to hold the 'Champions League' final in 2007.

23RD Legendary Tottenham manager Bill Nicholson, best known for guiding the White Hart Lane club to the league and cup double in 1961, dies at the age of 85 following a long illness

24TH A 2-0 defeat at Old Trafford sees Arsenal's unbeaten Premiership run ended after 49 games

27TH Bolton's Khalilou Fadiga causes concern when he passes out during the warm-up ahead of his side's Carling Cup clash with Tottenham. The Senegalese midfielder previously underwent surgery for an irregular heartbeat.

29TH Chelsea sack striker Adrian Mutu for 'gross misconduct', after the player had failed a random drugs test.

TEAM OF THE MONTH

Gabor Kiraly
Crystal Palace

Having begun the season on the bench, three clean sheets in four games firmly cemented the Hungarian's place as first choice goalkeeper at Selhurst Park. Only Bolton's Kevin Davies found a way past the eccentric custodian, as Palace claimed nine points from a possible 12 in the month.

Tony McMahon
Middlesbrough

With key defenders unavailable through injury, McMahon turned from promising youngster into first-team regular. A debut at Old Trafford did not faze this product of the youth system, as he made the right-back spot his own in an unbeaten October for Steve McClaren's side.

Radhi Jaidi
Bolton Wanderers

The big Tunisian had become a firm favourite at the Reebok Stadium since his summer arrival, and continued to turn in assured performances. Not content with getting the better of Premiership strikers, the defender also chipped in with a goal at Tottenham and an assist against Newcastle.

Matthew Upson
Birmingham City

Since arriving at St Andrew's, Upson had blossomed into an international-class defender. The qualities that brought him to Sven-Goran Eriksson's attention were on display again, as he helped nullify the Manchester United attack. A clean sheet at Southampton followed, while the defender also netted against Newcastle.

David Unsworth
Portsmouth

An unbeaten month for Portsmouth saw David Unsworth on top form. The full-back was part of a defence that kept two clean sheets, and scored from the penalty spot in the memorable 2-0 home win against Manchester United.

PLAYER OF THE MONTH

Andrew Johnson
Crystal Palace

Four goals in four games helped Crystal Palace to three priceless victories that saw them climb clear of the relegation zone. Fulham and West Brom, twice, conceded to the frontman, who also netted the winner on his return to old club Birmingham City.

"Andy Johnson's goals have ensured the Eagles are climbing the table - whether it is England or Poland, international football must surely beckon."

Barclays Awards Panel

MANAGER OF THE MONTH

Harry Redknapp
Portsmouth

Harry Redknapp guided his team into the top half of the table on the back of an unbeaten month. Away draws at Norwich and Middlesbrough provided the platform for progress, as both Tottenham and Manchester United were humbled at Fratton Park.

Premiership Career Statistics
up until en of November 2004
Matches:**317** Wins:**110** Draws:**83** Losses:**124**

"Portsmouth have a habit of beating strong teams at Fratton Park, and thanks to Harry Redknapp's canny acquisitions during the summer they have found a good blend between defence and attack.."

Barclays Awards Panel

Zoltan Gera
West Brom

The Hungarian midfielder was an inspirational figure in his side's first Premiership victory, creating the opener and then scoring a second against Bolton. Though West Brom only managed one further goal during the month, it was a stunning Gera strike against Chelsea.

Lee Hendrie
Aston Villa

Three spectacular efforts from the Birmingham-born midfielder accounted for 50% of Aston Villa's Premiership goals during October. Jens Lehmann, Edwin van der Sar and Nigel Martyn were all beaten by strikes right out of the top drawer.

Frank Lampard
Chelsea

The former West Ham midfielder was exuding confidence as his team battled on three fronts. Four assists and a terrific goal at West Brom helped the cause of his club, while Lampard also struck in England's 2-0 win against Wales in a 'World Cup Qualifier'.

Stewart Downing
Middlesbrough

Another example of the success of Middlesbrough's youth policy, Downing enjoyed a wonderful month on the left wing. A goal at Old Trafford and another at home to Portsmouth earnt his side two draws, while the midfielder set up two at Blackburn and came off the bench to score a winner in Greece in the UEFA Cup.

Thierry Henry
Arsenal

Four goals and two assists from four games domestically was an achievement in itself, but the French striker also netted both on international duty and in the 2-2 'Champions League' draw at Panathinaikos.

MONTH IN NUMBERS

39 Games Played

101 Total Goals Scored

2.59 Average Goals Per Game

4 Player With Most Goals (Johnson, Gudjohnsen, Henry)

2 Hat-tricks (Gudjohnsen, Hasselbaink)

9 Club With Most Goals (Chelsea, Arsenal)

3 Fastest Goal (Hendrie, Jenas)

46.2% Percentage Of Home Wins

20.5% Percentage Of Away Wins

33.3% Percentage Of Draws

4-0 Biggest Win (Arsenal 4 v 0 Charlton Athletic, Chelsea 4 v 0 Blackburn, Blackburn 0 v 4 Middlesbrough)

95 Total Yellow Cards

3 Total Red Cards

2.4 Average Yellow Cards Per Game

14 Most Disciplinary Points (Josemi, Tugay)

6 Fastest Booking (Pearce, Kamara)

32,176 Average Attendance

PREMIERSHIP TABLE / TEAM STATISTICS

Pos (last month)	Team	Played	Won	Drawn	Lost	Goals for	Goals against	Goal diff	Points	Shots on target	Hit woodwork	Shots off target	Failed to score	Clean sheets	Corners	Caught Offside	Players used
1 - (1)	Arsenal	11	8	2	1	31	12	+19	26	108	6	51	1	4	59	23	20
2 - (2)	Chelsea	11	8	2	1	16	3	+13	26	81	4	82	3	8	83	34	22
3 - (3)	Everton	11	7	2	2	14	10	+4	23	64	3	63	2	5	61	33	17
4 - (4)	Bolton Wanderers	11	6	3	2	18	13	+5	21	82	3	66	1	2	62	23	20
5 ▲ (11)	Middlesbrough	11	5	3	3	19	14	+5	18	89	0	71	2	2	58	35	21
6 ▲ (8)	Liverpool	10	5	2	3	18	10	+8	17	66	1	59	2	3	58	33	19
7 ▼ (5)	Manchester United	11	4	5	2	11	9	+2	17	81	6	77	4	4	78	33	26
8 ▼ (6)	Newcastle United	11	4	4	3	22	19	+3	16	80	4	60	1	1	84	36	18
9 ▲ (14)	Portsmouth	10	4	3	3	15	12	+3	15	59	1	52	2	2	46	23	21
10 ▼ (9)	Aston Villa	11	3	6	2	14	13	+1	15	67	3	61	3	4	65	24	19
11 ▼ (10)	Tottenham Hotspur	11	3	4	4	6	8	-2	13	52	4	63	5	5	48	40	22
12 ▼ (7)	Charlton Athletic	11	3	3	5	10	19	-9	12	46	2	40	4	3	46	37	20
13 - (13)	Manchester City	10	3	2	5	12	11	+1	11	62	1	54	4	3	66	35	17
14 ▲ (20)	Crystal Palace	11	3	2	6	12	15	-3	11	45	3	58	2	3	61	27	21
15 ▼ (12)	Fulham	11	3	2	6	12	19	-7	11	53	2	50	4	3	60	29	20
16 ▼ (15)	Birmingham City	11	1	6	4	7	10	-3	9	49	1	52	5	3	63	34	21
17 ▲ (18)	West Brom	11	1	5	5	9	20	-11	8	54	2	51	3	1	68	42	19
18 ▼ (17)	Southampton	11	1	4	6	8	14	-6	7	53	2	60	6	3	64	33	22
19 ▼ (16)	Blackburn Rovers	11	1	4	6	9	24	-15	7	47	1	58	5	1	64	42	25
20 ▼ (19)	Norwich City	10	0	6	4	9	17	-8	6	52	2	61	4	3	51	34	16

Chelsea start to find their form

TEAM FORM

Pos	Team	Form	Goals For	Goals Against	Pts
1	Chelsea	WLWW	9	2	9
2	Crystal Palace	WLWW	6	1	9
3	Bolton Wanderers	LWWW	6	4	9
4	Middlesbrough	DWDW	8	3	8
5	Portsmouth	DWDW	6	3	8
6	Arsenal	WWLD	9	5	7
7	Liverpool	LWWD	8	5	7
8	Everton	LWWD	5	4	7
9	Manchester United	DDWL	3	3	5
10	Newcastle United	DDWL	8	8	5
11	Aston Villa	DLWD	6	6	5
12	Manchester City	DWL	4	4	4
13	West Brom	WDLL	3	8	4
14	Southampton	DLDD	2	3	3
15	Birmingham City	DDDL	2	3	3
16	Tottenham Hotspur	WLLL	2	5	3
17	Fulham	LLLW	4	8	3
18	Norwich City	DDL	4	5	2
19	Blackburn Rovers	DLLD	4	12	2
20	Charlton Athletic	LDLL	2	9	1

TOP GOALSCORERS

Player	This Month	Total
T.Henry Arsenal	4	**9**
A.Johnson Crystal Palace	4	**8**
J.Hasselbaink Middlesbrough	3	**6**
A.Yakubu Portsmouth	3	**6**
R.Pires Arsenal	2	**6**
N.Anelka Manchester City	1	**6**
J.Reyes Arsenal	1	**6**
E.Gudjohnsen Chelsea	4	**5**
A.Cole Fulham	1	**5**
H.Pedersen Bolton Wanderers	1	**5**
L.Boa Morte Fulham	3	**4**
L.Hendrie Aston Villa	3	**4**
M.Baros Liverpool	2	**4**
C.Bellamy Newcastle United	2	**4**
M.Bent Everton	2	**4**
A.Shearer Newcastle United	1	**4**

MOST GOAL ASSISTS

Player	This Month	Total
T.Henry Arsenal	2	**9**
F.Lampard Chelsea	4	**6**
D.Bergkamp Arsenal	3	**6**
W.Routledge Crystal Palace	3	**6**
F.Ljungberg Arsenal	0	**5**
L.Garcia Liverpool	3	**4**
J.Reyes Arsenal	3	**4**
L.Boa Morte Fulham	1	**4**
J.Hasselbaink Middlesbrough	1	**4**
L.Robert Newcastle United	1	**4**
X.Alonso Liverpool	2	**3**
S.Downing Middlesbrough	2	**3**
R.Fuller Portsmouth	1	**3**
T.Gravesen Everton	1	**3**
J.Greening West Brom	1	**3**
F.Kanoute Tottenham Hotspur	1	**3**
R.Giggs Manchester United	0	**3**
J.Jenas Newcastle United	0	**3**
J.Okocha Bolton Wanderers	0	**3**
F.Queudrue Middlesbrough	0	**3**
S.Wright-Phillips Manchester City	0	**3**

DISCIPLINE

F.A. disciplinary points: Yellow=4 points, Two Bookable Offences=10 points and Red Card=12 points

Player	Y	SB	R	PTS
T.Cahill Everton	3	1	0	**22**
K.Tugay Blackburn Rovers	3	1	0	**22**
J.Redknapp Tottenham	5	0	0	**20**
R.Savage Birmingham City	5	0	0	**20**
Josemi Liverpool	2	1	0	**18**
N.Clement West Brom	1	0	1	**16**
A.Cole Fulham	1	0	1	**16**
L.Hendrie Aston Villa	4	0	0	**16**
L.Neill Blackburn Rovers	4	0	0	**16**
P.Vieira Arsenal	4	0	0	**16**
D.Purse West Brom	1	1	0	**14**

"I've had a great seven or eight years here, but I'm under no illusions. If I get it wrong and we are losing games, the most important thing is the club - I can be replaced."

Chris Coleman on the precarious life of a football manager

"We want to make clear that Chelsea has a zero tolerance policy towards drugs. They have no place at our club or in sport."

Chelsea club statement after the sacking of Adrian Mutu

"Gary Megson today informed the board of West Bromwich Albion by letter that he wishes to leave the club at the end of his current contract on 30th June 2005. The club accepts this letter as a resignation and he has been relieved of his duties while contractual matters are resolved."

West Bromwich Albion club statement

"If we're going to win things at this club we need to concentrate on what matters, not this petulance, not people acting like children. It has to stop and it will stop, I guarantee the supporters that."

Graeme Souness on Craig Bellamy's angry reaction to being substituted at Charlton

"We started the season with certain goals, but if those change as the season goes on, it shows how much we have achieved."

David Moyes

"We are looking to gather information from different sources and will see whether we are able to put together a picture of what happened in the tunnel after the game."

An F.A. spokesperson on the alleged events following the Manchester United v Arsenal clash

"If you've got aspirations to be a manager or coach, obviously coaching your country would be a great honour. But you only get one shot at it really, and for me this time I don't think I could give it my full attention."

Gary Speed on speculation linking him with the job of Wales manager

PREMIERSHIP FIXTURE HISTORY

Pl: 4 Draws: 2	Wins	Goals	Yellow cards	Red cards
Manchester City	2	7	4	0
Norwich City	0	3	5	0

STARTING LINE-UPS

Manchester City substitutes: Onuoha, Fowler, Waterreus, McCarthy, B.Wright-Phillips

Norwich City substitutes: Henderson, McVeigh, Ward, Helveg, Mulryne

EVENT LINE

11	Goal: **Flood (Open Play)**
42	Yellow card: **Sibierski (Foul)**
	HALF TIME 1 - 0
46	Goal: Francis (Open Play)
68	Substitution: **Dunne (Off) Onuoha (On)**
81	Substitution: **McManaman (Off) Fowler (On)**
81	Substitution: Jonson (Off) Henderson (On)
87	Substitution: McKenzie (Off) McVeigh (On)
	FULL TIME 1 - 1

STATISTICS

Season	Fixture (Man City)		Fixture (Norwich)	Season
69	7	Shots On Target	3	55
63	9	Shots Off Target	8	69
2	1	Hit Woodwork	0	2
38	3	Caught Offside	12	46
75	9	Corners	4	55
144	11	Fouls	15	149
46%	49%	Possession	51%	47%

LEAGUE STANDINGS

Position (pos before)	W	D	L	F	A	Pts
12 (13) Man City	3	3	5	13	12	12
19 (20) Norwich C	0	7	4	10	18	7

Monday 1st November 2004 | Venue: **City of Manchester Stadium** | Attendance: **42,803** | Referee: **S.G.Bennett**

MANCHESTER CITY 1 NORWICH CITY 1

Norwich recorded their seventh draw in 11 Premiership matches against a Manchester City team still searching for consistency.

The Canaries would gladly have taken a point against a rampant home side if it had been offered to them at half-time, yet they could easily have come away with all three after the second period.

Kevin Keegan's charges began brightly and went in front after just 11 minutes. Irish youngster Willo Flood marked his first Premiership start with a sweetly-struck 20-yard volley from the inside right channel, though Robert Green should really have kept the ball out.

The Norwich custodian was given every opportunity to redeem himself, however, as the men in sky blue launched wave after wave of attacks.

Having prevented their hosts from widening the gap, Nigel Worthington's team began to create some chances of their own. Midfielder Damien Francis twice caused anxiety in the City defence, before netting the equaliser in the first minute of the second half.

Having just kicked off, a ball was launched into the home side's penalty area from the left. Both Danny Mills and Richard Dunne had chances to clear, but things fell kindly for the visitors following Matthias Svensson's challenge and Francis arrived on cue to level the scores from 15 yards.

The Norfolk-based outfit were in the ascendancy and David James had to earn his money on more than one occasion. With victory a distinct possibility, Norwich were perhaps guilty of pushing too many men forward, and were nearly punished.

Goalscorer Flood struck the inside of a post as Shaun Wright-Phillips led a lightning-fast break midway through the half. Then, with time nearly up, Green did brilliantly to deny Nicolas Anelka, with substitute Robbie Fowler's follow-up effort appearing to strike the hand of stand-in captain Craig Fleming.

Somehow the Canaries stood firm, to earn another priceless away point in their battle to beat the drop. A rousing finish could not disguise a poor second half showing by Keegan's men, and they have much work to do if they are to avoid becoming involved in the fight to stay in the Premiership.

Paul Bosvelt practices his Karate skills

"The reason we did not win was because we did not get a second goal."

Kevin Keegan

PREMIERSHIP MILESTONE

Willo Flood scored his first Premiership goal

"It was a very good point, and we showed a lot of character, resolve and team spirit."

Nigel Worthington

PREMIERSHIP MILESTONE

Nedum Onuoha, Jim Brennan and Ian Henderson all made their Premiership debuts

PREMIERSHIP FIXTURE HISTORY

Pl: 2 Draws: 0	Wins	Goals	Yellow cards	Red cards
Aston Villa	2	5	1	0
Portsmouth	0	1	1	0

STARTING LINE-UPS

Aston Villa subs: L.Moore, Davis, Hitzlsperger, Postma, Ridgewell

Portsmouth subs: Griffin, Hughes, Cisse, Ashdown, Taylor

EVENT LINE

15 (Yellow card) **Samuel (Foul)**

18 (Goal) **Whittingham (Open Play)**

25 (Goal) **Angel (Open Play)**

38 (Substitution) Primus (Off) Griffin (On)

40 (Goal) **Solano (Open Play)**

HALF TIME 3 - 0

57 (Yellow card) Unsworth (Foul)

62 (Substitution) Mezague (Off) Hughes (On)

68 (Substitution) **Cole (Off) Moore L (On)**

78 (Substitution) **Hendrie (Off) Davis (On)**

83 (Substitution) Faye (Off) Cisse (On)

85 (Substitution) **Solano (Off) Hitzlsperger (On)**

FULL TIME 3 - 0

STATISTICS

Season	Fixture (Aston Villa)		Fixture (Portsmouth)	Season
76	9	Shots On Target	2	61
62	1	Shots Off Target	5	57
3	0	Hit Woodwork	0	1
27	3	Caught Offside	1	24
71	6	Corners	4	50
187	8	Fouls	13	133
48%	58%	Possession	42%	47%

LEAGUE STANDINGS

Position (pos before)	W	D	L	F	A	Pts
6 (10) Aston Villa	4	6	2	17	13	18
10 (9) Portsmouth	4	3	4	15	15	15

Saturday 6th November 2004 | Venue: Villa Park | Attendance: 32,633 | Referee: M.R.Halsey

ASTON VILLA 3 PORTSMOUTH 0

Aiyegbeni Yakubu fails to find the net for Portsmouth

"Villa were the better team and they deserved their win."
Harry Redknapp

"We started well and the passing and movement was really good"
David O'Leary

PREMIERSHIP MILESTONE

Peter Whittingham scored his first Premiership goal

After victory against Manchester United seven days earlier, Portsmouth were brought back to earth with a bump at Villa Park.

First half goals from Peter Whittingham, Juan Pablo Angel and Nolberto Solano were a just reflection of the home side's dominance, though Harry Redknapp's team did at least salvage some pride in the second period.

Reverting back to a 4-4-2 formation, Pompey were strangely flat right from the off. With 18 minutes played, Whittingham, the only change from the Aston Villa side that drew at Everton last time out, tapped home from close range after persistent play from Carlton Cole down the right.

Any wind was clearly knocked out of the Portsmouth sails by this strike, and seven minutes later it was 2-0. Colombian Angel collected a ball into the box from Ulises De la Cruz and turned away from Dejan Stefanovic, before beating Shaka Hislop from 12 yards out in the inside right channel.

If the first two goals were well constructed, the third was all about the deft skills of Solano. Latching onto an attempted clearance five minutes before the break, the Peruvian expertly lobbed home over the goalkeeper from within the confines of the penalty area.

The in-form Lee Hendrie still had time to draw a scrambling save from Hislop in a half totally dominated by David O'Leary's side.

Having already been forced into one change, and with mainly defensive options on the bench, Redknapp resisted the temptation to tinker with his team during the interval, instead sending out the same group of players to try and make amends.

Though the South Coast club did improve in the second period, Villa were clearly no longer straining every sinew. Aiyegbeni Yakubu missed a decent chance to net a consolation goal, as the game drifted aimlessly towards its inevitable conclusion.

The win ensured that the men in claret and blue maintained their unbeaten home record, while Portsmouth remained without an away victory in the Premiership since an April triumph at Elland Road.

PREMIERSHIP FIXTURE HISTORY

Pl: **13** Draws: **4**

	Wins	Goals	Yellow	Red
Chelsea	8	24	10	0
Everton	1	10	21	1

STARTING LINE-UPS

Chelsea: Cech; Ferreira, Carvalho, Terry (c), Babayaro; Tiago, Makelele, Lampard; Duff, Robben; Gudjohnsen

Everton: Bent; Kilbane, Cahill, Gravesen, Watson, Osman; Pistone, Stubbs (c), Weir, Hibbert; Martyn

Chelsea subs: Kezman, Geremi, Huth, Cudicini, J.Cole

Everton subs: Campbell, McFadden, Chadwick, Turner, Yobo

EVENT LINE

HALF TIME 0 - 0

52 Kilbane (Foul)

58 **Tiago (Off) Kezman (On)**

72 **Robben (Open Play)**

78 **Gudjohnsen (Off) Geremi (On)**

80 Gravesen (Foul)

80 Watson (Off) Campbell (On)

82 **Duff (Off) Huth (On)**

84 Pistone (Off) McFadden (On)

90 **Robben (Ung.Conduct)**

90 Bent (Ung.Conduct)

90 Osman (Off) Chadwick (On)

FULL TIME 1 - 0

STATISTICS

Season	Fixture (Chelsea)		Fixture (Everton)	Season
84	3	Shots On Target	1	65
91	9	Shots Off Target	2	65
5	1	Hit Woodwork	0	3
36	2	Caught Offside	1	34
99	16	Corners	3	64
142	10	Fouls	17	144
56%	60%	Possession	40%	50%

LEAGUE STANDINGS

Position (pos before)		W	D	L	F	A	Pts
1 (2)	Chelsea	9	2	1	17	3	29
3 (3)	Everton	7	2	3	14	11	23

Saturday 6th November 2004 | Venue: **Stamford Bridge** | Attendance: **41,965** | Referee: **M.A.Riley**

CHELSEA 1 EVERTON 0

Dutchman Arjen Robben netted a goal of exquisite quality to see off the challenge of Premiership surprise-package Everton at Stamford Bridge.

Before a ball was kicked in August, few people would have expected this November meeting to be contested between the two clubs positioned second and third in the table. However, David Moyes' hard-working team were up with the leaders on merit and relished the chance to pit themselves against Jose Mourinho's expensively-assembled charges.

The Merseysiders came with a familiar game plan, stringing five men across midfield, but were without pivotal player Lee Carsley. For Chelsea, Robben was handed a first Premiership start on the left of a three-pronged attack.

In a match largely bereft of clear-cut chances, Tim Cahill was denied by a magnificent sprawling save from Petr Cech. With 19 minutes on the clock, Kevin Kilbane burst down the left and delivered a perfect centre that the Australian headed goalwards, only for the giant keeper to repel his effort in miraculous fashion.

That was as close as Everton came as the home side gradually began to click into gear. Just beyond the mid-point of the half, Nigel Martyn had to be at his acrobatic best to tip Robben's stinging drive onto the crossbar.

With that scare behind them, the Toffees continued to defend resolutely. David Weir and Alan Stubbs were like granite boulders, shielding their goal from a bombardment of corners.

Having intoduced Mateja Kezman in a bid to further increase his attacking options, Mourinho saw his team make the vital breakthrough with 18 minutes remaining.

There seemed little danger as Ricardo Carvalho hammered the ball down the right touchline from near his own corner flag. Eidur Gudjohnsen and Robben had other ideas, however, as an astute pass allowed the tricky winger to dash goalwards, before neatly clipping the ball beyond the keeper when challenged by a recovering defender inside the six-yard box.

With Arsenal stuttering to an evening draw at Crystal Palace, the win saw Chelsea climb above their London rivals to the Premiership summit.

Arjen Robben shields the ball

"With Arjen Robben, we are a different team. He is the fastest player we have, is very mature and works for the team."

Jose Mourinho

PREMIERSHIP MILESTONE

Arjen Robben netted his first Premiership goal

"Chelsea have exceptional players, if we had £12m we would have bought Robben."

David Moyes

PREMIERSHIP MILESTONE

150 Kevin Kilbane made his 150th Premiership appearance

PREMIERSHIP FIXTURE HISTORY

Pl: 4 Draws: 2	Wins			
Crystal Palace	0	2	5	0
Arsenal	2	6	9	0

STARTING LINE-UPS

Leigertwood, Lakis, Freedman, Speroni, Torghelle

Bergkamp, Senderos, van Persie, Flamini, Almunia

EVENT LINE

24 **Sorondo (Off) Leigertwood (On)**

HALF TIME 0 - 0

47 Cygan (Foul)

52 **Routledge (Off) Lakis (On)**

63 Henry (Open Play)

65 **Riihilahti (Open Play)**

72 Ljungberg (Off) Bergkamp (On)

72 Pires (Off) van Persie (On)

80 **Kolkka (Off) Freedman (On)**

81 Fabregas (Off) Flamini (On)

FULL TIME 1 - 1

STATISTICS

Season	Fixture		Fixture	Season
46	1	Shots On Target	13	121
60	2	Shots Off Target	6	57
3	0	Hit Woodwork	0	6
33	6	Caught Offside	0	23
62	1	Corners	8	67
166	10	Fouls	8	133
45%	38%	Possession	62%	58%

LEAGUE STANDINGS

Position (pos before)	W	D	L	F	A	Pts
15 (14) Crystal Palace	3	3	6	13	16	12
2 (1) Arsenal	8	3	1	32	13	27

Saturday 6th November 2004 | Venue: **Selhurst Park** | Attendance: **26,193** | Referee: **M.L.Dean**

CRYSTAL PALACE 1 ARSENAL 1

Arsenal surrendered their leadership of the Premiership with a disappointing 1-1 draw against Crystal Palace at Selhurst Park.

The result marked a third league game without a win for Arsene Wenger's side, while Iain Dowie's Eagles made it 10 points from the last 15 available to continue their upward surge.

An intriguing first half saw the Gunners dominate possession without really making the most of it. Hungarian goalkeeper Gabor Kiraly had plenty to do, yet was not called upon to make any truly world-class saves.

Thierry Henry went close early on, firing in a shot that flew just beyond the left-hand upright. Jose Antonio Reyes then drew a comfortable stop from the keeper, before a poor kick from Jens Lehmann nearly gifted Andy Johnson a goal.

Further chances came and went for Kolo Toure and Robert Pires as Arsenal increased the tempo of their football. Then, on the stroke of half-time, Freddie Ljungberg was inches away from connecting with Henry's dangerous ball in from the left.

The second period began in much the same fashion as its predecessor had ended, with Wenger's men pouring forward. A few long-range efforts from Reyes warmed Kiraly's palms and Pires missed the target when well-placed.

Then, with 63 minutes played, Henry made the vital breakthrough. A slick move down the right saw Ljungberg send over an accurate low centre, enabling the French striker to outmuscle his marker and steer the ball home from close range.

A few weeks ago, that would have spelt the end for Palace. As it was, Dowie's team hit back within two minutes courtesy of Aki Riihilahti. Substitute Vassilios Lakis did brilliantly on the right, before sending over an inviting cross that the Finnish international midfielder steered home left-footed ahead of the advancing Lehmann.

Soon afterwards the Eagles could have gone 2-1 up. Having made their equaliser, Lakis somehow contrived to send the ball high over the crossbar from within the six-yard box. It was a poor miss, but didn't prove costly as Palace picked up another valuable point.

"We competed with Arsenal which was pleasing, and now we have some massive games ahead of us."

Iain Dowie

PREMIERSHIP MILESTONE

Mikele Leigertwood made his Premiership debut

"We are going through a difficult period, but the important thing is to stick with it. We will come back."

Arsene Wenger

PREMIERSHIP MILESTONE

50 Jens Lehmann made his 50th Premiership appearance

Lauren is pressured by Joonas Kolkka

PREMIERSHIP FIXTURE HISTORY

Pl: **3** Draws: **1**

	Wins	⚽	Yellow	Red
Liverpool	1	5	5	0
Birmingham City	1	4	3	0

STARTING LINE-UPS

Kirkland

Josemi, Carragher, Hyypia (c), Traore

Garcia, Hamann, Alonso, Riise

Kewell, Sinama-Pongolle

Heskey

Gronkjaer, Izzet, Johnson

Clemence, Savage

Gray, Upson, Cunningham (c), Melchiot

Maik Taylor

Liverpool subs: Finnan, Mellor, Biscan, Dudek, Diao

Birmingham City subs: Lazaridis, Anderton, Clapham, Bennett, Yorke

EVENT LINE

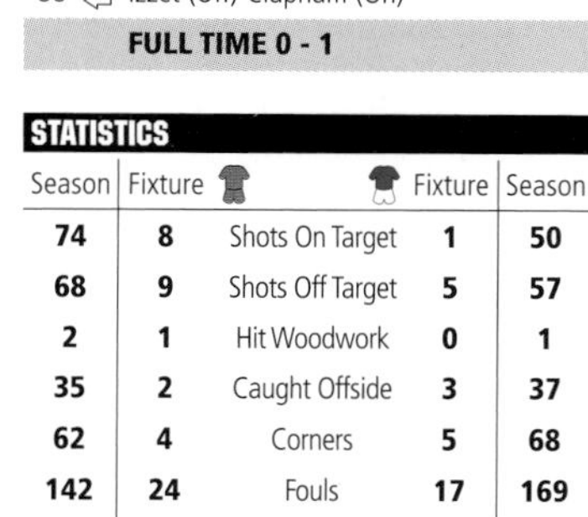

44 Josemi (Foul)

HALF TIME 0 - 0

61 **Garcia (Foul)**

63 Clemence (Off) Anderton (On)

63 Gronkjaer (Off) Lazaridis (On)

65 **Sinama-Pongolle (Off) Finnan (On**

72 **Hamann (Dissent)**

73 **Riise (Off) Mellor (On)**

74 Johnson (Foul)

77 ⚽ Anderton (Corner)

85 **Hamann (Off) Biscan (On)**

88 Izzet (Off) Clapham (On)

FULL TIME 0 - 1

STATISTICS

Season	Fixture (Liverpool)		Fixture (Birmingham)	Season
74	8	Shots On Target	1	50
68	9	Shots Off Target	5	57
2	1	Hit Woodwork	0	1
35	2	Caught Offside	3	37
62	4	Corners	5	68
142	24	Fouls	17	169
54%	54%	Possession	46%	50%

LEAGUE STANDINGS

Position (pos before)	W	D	L	F	A	Pts
7 (6) Liverpool	5	2	4	18	11	17
14 (16) Birmingham C	2	6	4	8	10	12

Saturday 6th November 2004 | Venue: **Anfield** | Attendance: **42,669** | Referee: **U.D.Rennie**

Luis Garcia tries to beat Julian Gray

"It was a frustrating afternoon because we missed lots of clear chances and were punished for one small mistake."

Rafael Benitez

"I'm delighted for Darren Anderton because he's had a really tough time of it through injury."

Steve Bruce

PREMIERSHIP MILESTONE

100 Jesper Gronkjaer made his 100th Premiership appearance

PREMIERSHIP MILESTONE

Darren Anderton netted his first Premiership goal for Birmingham

LIVERPOOL 0 BIRMINGHAM CITY 1

Liverpool's winning start to the Premiership season at Anfield came to an end, as they succumbed to a 77th-minute Darren Anderton goal against Birmingham.

Fresh from an impressive midweek victory away to Deportivo La Coruna in the 'Champions League', and facing a team that had won just one league game all season, few would have expected anything other than three points for Rafael Benitez's side from this encounter.

As it transpired, however, it was Steve Bruce's team that took the spoils. The West Midlands outfit managed a solitary effort on target throughout the entire 90 minutes, yet that moment proved decisive as the ball ended up in the back of Chris Kirkland's net.

The visitors had opted for a five-man midfield in a bid to stifle the Merseysiders' more creative players. With a distinct lack of recognised strikers available to them, the Anfield club lined up with youngster Florent Sinama-Pongolle, supported by Harry Kewell, in attack.

Liverpool began brightly, as Birmingham struggled to clear their lines. Both Kewell and Xabi Alonso forced smart saves fom Maik Taylor, before the returning Emile Heskey attempted to score against the run of play with a flicked header that drifted wide.

The remainder of the half was a scrappy affair, though both sides had opportunities to go in front. A defensive mix-up between Matthew Upson and Julian Gray let in Luis Garcia for what turned out to be a wayward shot, and then Muzzy Izzet failed to beat Kirkland when springing the offside trap.

The home team looked more likely scorers in the second period. Dietmar Hamann fired straight at the keeper from a good position, and the ball later stayed out of the visitors' net three times during a frantic goalmouth scramble.

Then, much to the surprise of most inside the ground, Anderton scored. The midfielder had been on the pitch for just under 15 minutes, when he turned Upson's header back across goal from a left-wing corner into the net from close range.

Despite a few scary moments, Bruce's team held firm to collect a vital three points.

PREMIERSHIP FIXTURE HISTORY

Pl: **4** Draws: **3**

	Wins	⚽	☐	■
Norwich City	1	5	3	1
Blackburn Rovers	0	4	5	1

STARTING LINE-UPS

Henderson, McVeigh, Ward, Helveg, Mulryne

Flitcroft, Enckelman, Thompson, Douglas, Stead

EVENT LINE

37 ☐ **Jonson (Foul)**

44 ■ Bothroyd (Violent Conduct)

HALF TIME 0 - 0

46 **Jonson (Off) Henderson (On)**

56 ⚽ **Svensson (Indirect Free Kick)**

73 Tugay (Off) Flitcroft (On)

79 **McKenzie (Off) McVeigh (On)**

86 ⚽ Dickov (Indirect Free Kick)

90 Dickov (Off) Stead (On)

FULL TIME 1 - 1

STATISTICS

Season	Fixture	Norwich City	Blackburn Rovers	Fixture	Season
60	5	Shots On Target		9	56
76	7	Shots Off Target		6	64
3	1	Hit Woodwork		1	2
47	1	Caught Offside		4	46
62	7	Corners		4	68
170	21	Fouls		15	190
47%	54%	Possession		46%	48%

LEAGUE STANDINGS

Position (pos before)	W	D	L	F	A	Pts
19 (19) Norwich C	0	8	4	11	19	8
20 (20) Blackburn R	1	5	6	10	25	8

Saturday 6th November 2004 | Venue: **Carrow Road** | Attendance: **23,834** | Referee: **S.W.Dunn**

NORWICH CITY 1 BLACKBURN ROVERS 1

Paul Dickov fights to retain possession

"The header that hit the bar was a warning. Now we have got to look forward to the next game and not dwell on this one."

Nigel Worthington

PREMIERSHIP MILESTONE

Matthias Svensson scored his first Premiership goal for Norwich

PREMIERSHIP MILESTONE

100 Marc Edworthy made his 100th Premiership appearance

"The players were superb and created most of the chances in the second half when down to ten men."

Mark Hughes

PREMIERSHIP MILESTONE

25 Paul Dickov netted his 25th Premiership goal

Norwich missed a golden opportunity to record their first win in the Premiership, as they allowed ten-man Blackburn to net a late equaliser.

Mark Hughes' team saw their number reduced just before the interval, when Jay Bothroyd was dismissed for violent conduct. The North-West outfit then went behind to a 56th-minute Matthias Svensson strike, but showed great character to hit back through a Paul Dickov header four minutes from time.

The Canaries had started the game strongly, Svensson heading against the top of the crossbar in the fifth minute. Fellow Swede Mattias Jonson then drilled an effort wide, while Leon McKenzie saw two shots blocked.

Home goalkeeper Robert Green was not an idle spectator during the opening period, twice doing well to beat out piledrivers from Bothroyd. The Blackburn striker made a far less-positive contribution to his team in the 44th minute, however, when he was sent off.

As red cards go, Bothroyd's was undisputable. Contesting possession with Jonson near the corner flag, the former Perugia frontman took exception to the Norwich player's aggressive approach and administered a firm kick to his shins.

After Green had successfully repelled an early second half drive from Kerimoglu Tugay, Nigel Worthington's side made their numerical advantage count. A free-kick eventually made its way to Svensson, stationed just beyond the left-hand upright, and the former Charlton forward drove in his first Premiership goal for the Canaries.

Being both a goal and a man up seemed to cause a crisis of confidence for the men in yellow and green. Rovers began to push forward, and Craig Fleming did well to keep Dickov at bay with an excellent saving challenge.

With nine minutes remaining, Nils-Eric Johansson rattled the crossbar with a header. A goal was coming, and it duly arrived courtesy of Dickov.

Despite being one of the smallest players on the pitch, the Scot was able to meet Lucas Neill's right-wing cross, following a quickly-taken free-kick, with a firm downward header beyond the left hand of Green, to earn his side a well-deserved point.

Saturday 6th November 2004 | Venue: **Friends Provident St Mary's Stadium** | Attendance: **31,057** | Referee: **S.G.Bennett**

PREMIERSHIP FIXTURE HISTORY

Pl: 2 Draws: 1	Wins	Goals	Yellow cards	Red cards
Southampton	1	3	4	0
West Bromwich Albion	0	2	2	0

STARTING LINE-UPS

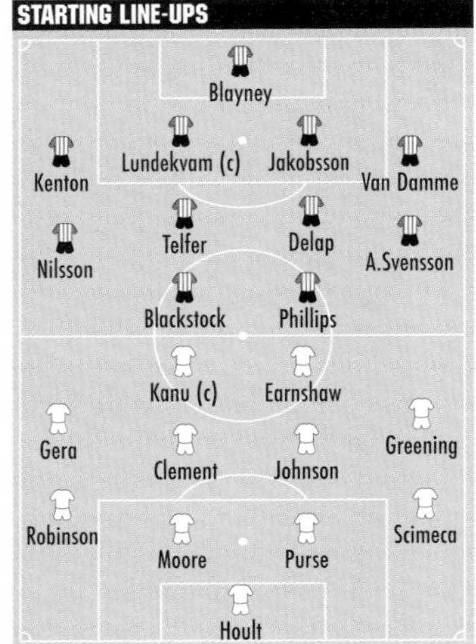

Southampton substitutes: McCann, Ormerod, Prutton, Poke, Higginbotham

West Brom substitutes: Horsfield, Koumas, Kuszczak, Dyer, Albrechtsen

EVENT LINE

28	**Svensson A (Open Play)**
29	Earnshaw (Open Play)
36	**Blackstock (Foul)**
37	Earnshaw (Open Play)
	HALF TIME 1 - 2
60	**Jakobsson (Off) McCann (On)**
63	**Blackstock (Off) Ormerod (On)**
77	Kanu (Off) Horsfield (On)
83	**Kenton (Foul)**
83	Gera (Off) Koumas (On)
84	**Nilsson (Off) Prutton (On)**
87	**Robinson (Own Goal)**
	FULL TIME 2 - 2

STATISTICS

Season	Fixture (Southampton)		Fixture (West Brom)	Season
59	6	Shots On Target	5	59
65	5	Shots Off Target	5	56
2	0	Hit Woodwork	0	2
36	3	Caught Offside	5	47
69	5	Corners	1	69
165	12	Fouls	14	162
50%	59%	Possession	41%	47%

LEAGUE STANDINGS

Position (pos before)	W	D	L	F	A	Pts
18 (18) Southampton	1	5	6	10	16	8
17 (17) West Brom	1	6	5	11	22	9

SOUTHAMPTON 2 WEST BROM 2

With both sides in desperate need of victory, a draw was always the most likely outcome in this encounter.

Each team had won just once in the Premiership coming into the fixture, and it was not hard to see why in an opening 25 minutes that did little to please the football purists. Most of the game was fought out in the middle third of the pitch, with commodities such as skill in short supply.

Then, with 28 minutes played, the match exploded into life. Swedish international Anders Svensson arrived at the back post to head home Paul Telfer's right-wing centre and send a wave of relief around the majority of the stadium.

The home faithful were celebrating too soon, however, as the Baggies struck back within 60 seconds. Welsh striker Robert Earnshaw poached his first top-flight goal, getting the faintest of touches to Jonathan Greening's powerful downward header.

The former Cardiff frontman then repeated the trick eight minutes later. This time he was set up by a poor clearance, driving a 12-yard effort down into the ground and over stand-in goalkeeper Alan Blayney to make it 2-1.

If the Southampton custodian had been partly to blame for West Brom's second goal, he went some way towards redeeming himself with important saves from Greening and Neil Clement shortly after the break.

The managerless Midlanders could also have been celebrating an Earnshaw hat-trick during this period of play, but the diminutive striker somehow hooked a close-range effort just wide of the target.

Despite some bold attacking changes, it looked as though Steve Wigley's team would not be able to break down a resolute away defence. However, with just three minutes remaining, the Saints enjoyed a huge slice of luck.

With the visiting penalty area packed following a corner, Svensson's hopeful low drive from the inside right channel was turned into his own net by left-back Paul Robinson.

The goal was a bitter blow to West Brom, as they paid the price for defending too deeply in the closing stages. For Southampton, a point was better than none, though they still had little reason to celebrate.

"At the moment we are not seen as winners, but I told the players that we need to be competitors."

Steve Wigley

"The lads gave their all, and at least they sent the fans home with something to look forward to."

Caretaker Manager Frank Burrows

PREMIERSHIP MILESTONE

Robert Earnshaw netted his first Premiership goals

Robert Earnshaw stretches for the ball

PREMIERSHIP FIXTURE HISTORY				
Pl: **6** Draws: **3**	Wins	⚽	□	■
Tottenham Hotspur	**0**	**6**	**6**	**1**
Charlton Athletic	**3**	**9**	**6**	**1**

STARTING LINE-UPS

Ziegler, Carrick, Keller, Brown, Silva

Euell, Konchesky, Fortune, Andersen, Jeffers

EVENT LINE

17 ⚽ Bartlett (Open Play)

39 ⚽ Bartlett (Open Play)

HALF TIME 0 - 2

46 ⇄ **Davies (Off) Ziegler (On)**

50 ⚽ Thomas (Open Play)

59 ⇄ **Redknapp (Off) Carrick (On)**

68 ■ Bartlett (Handball)

69 ⚽ **Keane (Penalty)**

77 □ Thomas (Foul)

79 ⚽ **Defoe (Open Play)**

81 ⇄ Johansson (Off) Euell (On)

84 ⇄ Thomas (Off) Konchesky (On)

89 ⇄ Murphy (Off) Fortune (On)

90 □ Young (Dissent)

FULL TIME 2 - 3

STATISTICS

Season	Fixture	(Tottenham)	(Charlton) Fixture	Season
64	**12**	Shots On Target	**3**	**49**
71	**8**	Shots Off Target	**0**	**40**
5	**1**	Hit Woodwork	**0**	**2**
43	**3**	Caught Offside	**3**	**40**
53	**5**	Corners	**1**	**47**
151	**8**	Fouls	**11**	**156**
47%	**53%**	Possession	**47%**	**43%**

LEAGUE STANDINGS

Position (pos before)	W	D	L	F	A	Pts
12 (11) Tottenham H	**3**	**4**	**5**	**8**	**11**	**13**
11 (13) Charlton Ath	**4**	**3**	**5**	**13**	**21**	**15**

Saturday 6th November 2004 | Venue: **White Hart Lane** | Attendance: **35,423** | Referee: **N.S.Barry**

TOTTENHAM HOTSPUR 2 CHARLTON ATHLETIC 3

Robbie Keane tries to get past Talal El Karkouri

"After being 3-0 down we showed our character and almost got a draw. Hopefully we can build on our last 35 minutes of football."

Caretaker Manager Martin Jol

PREMIERSHIP MILESTONE

50 Goran Bunjevcevic made his 50th Premiership appearance

PREMIERSHIP MILESTONE

150 Robbie Keane and Dean Kiely both made their 150th Premiership appearances

"Us going down to ten men changed the complexion of the game. It was a terrific performance up to 3-0, but we were hanging on at the end."

Alan Curbishley

PREMIERSHIP MILESTONE

Jerome Thomas scored his first Premiership goal

In the wake of Jacques Santini's shock resignation on Friday night, caretaker boss Martin Jol presided over an understandable horror show at White Hart Lane.

Charlton capitalised on a disorganised home defence to race into a three-goal lead by the 50th minute, before the dismissal of Shaun Bartlett sparked a spirited fightback that almost earned Tottenham an unlikely point.

It took the Addicks just 17 minutes to get their noses in front. Former Arsenal youngster Jerome Thomas sent over a dangerous near-post ball from the left, and South African Bartlett helped it into the net from seven yards out with his left foot.

Spurs had two chances to draw level after the half-hour mark. Firstly, Ledley King went close with a header from a Robbie Keane cross, and then Frederic Kanoute fired high over the bar from a decent position.

Such profligacy seldom goes unpunished in the Premiership, and, with 39 minutes on the clock, Bartlett added to his and Charlton's tally.

The move that resulted in the goal may have reminded older Tottenham fans of the type of football they had been brought up on. Slick interplay down the right was finished in style, as Luke Young's inviting centre was met with a diving header from inside the six-yard box at the far post.

Things went from bad to worse for Jol's charges five minutes after the break. Having collected a return pass, Thomas' goalbound 17-yard effort from the inside left channel clipped the right boot of King and wrongfooted Paul Robinson to make it 3-0.

The introduction of Michael Carrick, for his home debut, seemed to have a positive impact, and Spurs were given a lifeline after 68 minutes.

Referee Neale Barry had no alternative but to dismiss Bartlett for handball, when the striker illegally kept out Reto Ziegler's goalbound shot. A penalty was duly awarded, and Keane converted from the spot.

Jermain Defoe further reduced the arrears with a fine swivelling effort from Keane's pass after 79 minutes, but, despite intense late pressure, a remarkable comeback remained agonisingly out of reach.

PREMIERSHIP FIXTURE HISTORY

Pl: **8** Draws: **3**

	Wins	⚽	▯	■
Manchester United	5	15	7	2
Manchester City	0	4	19	0

STARTING LINE-UPS

Carroll

G.Neville, Ferdinand, Silvestre, Heinze

Miller, Keane (c), Scholes, Ronaldo

Saha, Smith

Anelka

Sibierski, McManaman, Bosvelt, S.Wright-Phillips, Flood

Jordan, Distin (c), Dunne, Mills

James

Subs (Man Utd): Giggs, Rooney, Howard, Brown, P.Neville

Subs (Man City): Onuoha, Waterreus, McCarthy, Fowler, B.Wright-Phillips

EVENT LINE

22 ▯ **Keane (Foul)**

34 ▯ Jordan (Foul)

HALF TIME 0 - 0

46 **Miller (Off) Giggs (On)**

77 **Scholes (Off) Rooney (On)**

85 ▯ Flood (Foul)

89 ■ **Smith (2nd Bookable Offence)**

FULL TIME 0 - 0

STATISTICS

Season	Fixture		Fixture	Season
91	10	Shots On Target	1	70
82	5	Shots Off Target	2	65
6	0	Hit Woodwork	0	2
39	6	Caught Offside	4	42
94	16	Corners	1	76
149	10	Fouls	10	154
53%	50%	Possession	50%	47%

LEAGUE STANDINGS

Position (pos before)		W	D	L	F	A	Pts
7 (8)	**Man Utd**	4	6	2	11	9	18
13 (13)	**Man City**	3	4	5	13	12	13

Sunday 7th November 2004 | Venue: **Old Trafford** | Attendance: **67,863** | Referee: **G.Poll**

MANCHESTER UNITED 0 MANCHESTER CITY 0

An expensively assembled Manchester United attack failed to find the net for the third time in four Premiership fixtures, as Kevin Keegan's visitors earned a battling draw.

The home side managed five times as many attempts on goal as their opponents during the 90 minutes, but were unable to break the deadlock. To make matters worse, Alan Smith was dismissed near the end following two poor challenges.

Having been deployed as a striker in City's previous game, Shaun Wright-Phillips occupied one of three central midfield roles in a defensively-minded 4-5-1 formation. Fellow youngsters Stephen Jordan and Willo Flood also continued in the starting XI.

With Ruud van Nistelrooy still unavailable, Sir Alex Ferguson opted to partner Smith and Louis Saha in attack. The French striker nearly justified his manager's decision to play him inside the opening five minutes, but Jordan cleared his effort off the line.

Referee Graham Poll then turned down a strong penalty appeal, following Antoine Sibierski's impeding of Saha inside the six-yard box, before Smith saw an acrobatic strike hacked away by Danny Mills.

The visitors were having to weather a serious storm, yet broke dangerously after 10 minutes. A deep left-wing cross from Sibierski picked out lone forward Nicolas Anelka arriving beyond Mikael Silvestre, but the former Arsenal man could only head tamely wide from 12 yards.

That was as close as Keegan's team came in a brave first half showing. The Old Trafford side conjured up several half-chances in the lead up to the break, with David James keeping out one goalbound effort with his legs.

Ryan Giggs was introduced at half-time, and was involved in the 63rd-minute move that ended with Steve McManaman clearing off the line. The Welsh winger then spurned a great chance himself, firing wide when bearing down on goal.

Despite spending the game under the cosh, City could have stolen a late winner through McManaman. Then, with just one minute remaining, Smith was justifiably shown a second yellow card for a lunging tackle on Richard Dunne. The former Leeds man had earlier been booked for a similar challenge on Paul Bosvelt.

Louis Saha directs a late header wide of goal

"In terms of winning the Championship, we're not good enough on that form."
Sir Alex Ferguson

"We had a game plan where we played one up front. We knew it would be a difficult game, but I think we deserved a draw."
Richard Dunne

PREMIERSHIP MILESTONE

150 Richard Dunne made his 150th Premiership appearance

PREMIERSHIP FIXTURE HISTORY

Pl: 5 Draws: 2	Wins	⚽	Yellow	Red
Middlesbrough	2	7	8	0
Bolton Wanderers	1	6	13	1

STARTING LINE-UPS

Middlesbrough: Schwarzer; McMahon, Riggott, Southgate (c), Queudrue; Parlour, Boateng, Zenden, Downing; Hasselbaink, Job

Bolton Wanderers: Davies; Diouf, Giannakopoulos; Speed (c), Hierro, Nolan; Gardner, N'Gotty, Jaidi, Hunt; Jaaskelainen

Middlesbrough substitutes: Viduka, Morrison, Nash, Cooper, Doriva

Bolton Wanderers substitutes: Ben Haim, Pedersen, Poole, Ferdinand, Cesar

EVENT LINE

23 Hunt (Foul)

39 Davies (Foul)

HALF TIME 0 - 0

46 **Job (Off) Viduka (On)**

49 Diouf (Dissent)

53 **Queudrue (Foul)**

54 Hunt (Off) Ben Haim (On)

62 Giannakopoulos (Off) Pedersen (On)

72 Pedersen (Corner)

81 **McMahon (Off) Morrison (On)**

86 Jaaskelainen (Foul)

88 Diouf (Off) Poole (On)

90 **Boateng (Open Play)**

FULL TIME 1 - 1

STATISTICS

Season	Fixture (Middlesbrough)		Fixture (Bolton)	Season
94	5	Shots On Target	4	86
80	9	Shots Off Target	3	69
2	2	Hit Woodwork	0	3
39	4	Caught Offside	2	25
61	3	Corners	3	65
150	13	Fouls	12	169
51%	51%	Possession	49%	50%

LEAGUE STANDINGS

Position (pos before)		W	D	L	F	A	Pts
5 (5)	Middlesbrough	5	4	3	20	15	19
4 (4)	Bolton W	6	4	2	19	14	22

Sunday 7th November 2004 | Venue: **Riverside Stadium** | Attendance: **29,656** | Referee: **P.Walton**

MIDDLESBROUGH 1 BOLTON WANDERERS 1

Gareth Southgate holds off Kevin Nolan

"The players have once again shown fantastic character - they never give up."
Steve McClaren

"If we had kept 11 men on the pitch, we would probably have seen this game out."
Sam Allardyce

In a repeat of last season's Carling Cup final, Middlesbrough salvaged a dramatic late draw against ten-man Bolton.

With time almost up, George Boateng became the Teesside club's unlikely saviour, volleying home from six yards after substitute goalkeeper Kevin Poole had parried Ray Parlour's venomous drive.

The Trotters' veteran shot-stopper had only been on the pitch for a couple of minutes, having come on after regular custodian Jussi Jaaskelainen had been dismissed for a professional foul on Jimmy Floyd Hasselbaink just outside the penalty area.

This late flurry of activity came after Sam Allardyce's side had taken a 72nd-minute lead through Danish super-sub Henrik Pedersen. The forward had been on the field for just 10 minutes, when he diverted Bruno N'Gotty's downward header from a corner past Mark Schwarzer from close range.

Having enjoyed a memorable win against Lazio in the UEFA Cup a few days earlier, Steve McClaren sprang a surprise by naming Joseph-Desire Job as Hasselbaink's partner in attack. This meant Mark Viduka began the game on the bench, as the Middlesbrough boss shuffled his pack.

With their inspirational captain Jay-Jay Okocha missing through injury, Bolton handed a first Premiership start to Real Madrid legend Fernando Hierro in midfield.

The first period was a drab affair. Though the home team could point to their midweek European exertions as a potential reason for tiredness, the visitors had no excuse. It wasn't until the 35th minute that either side produced an effort of note, Parlour firing wide.

Cameroonian frontman Job paid the price for an ineffective 45 minutes, when he was replaced by Viduka at half-time. Shortly after his introduction, the Australian headed Stewart Downing's left-wing cross against an upright.

The match was played at a far greater tempo in the second period, as both clubs looked to build on their encouraging starts to the season. It appeared that Pedersen's 72nd-minute goal would prove decisive, but McClaren's men fought to the bitter end to earn a deserved point.

With at least one Champions League place seemingly up for grabs this season, both teams will fancy their chances of dining at Europe's top table in 2005.

Sunday 7th November 2004 | Venue: **St James' Park** | Attendance: **51,118** | Referee: **H.M.Webb**

NEWCASTLE UNITED 1 FULHAM 4

Fulham triumphed 4-1 at St James' Park, largely thanks to the heroics of goalkeeper Mark Crossley.

The visitors' Welsh shot-stopper had an inspired afternoon, saving everything that was thrown at him. Newcastle hit the target on no less than 20 occasions, but only when they had gone 4-0 down did they find the net.

The opening 25 minutes saw almost constant pressure from the home side. Within the first 100 seconds of play, Lee Bowyer worked a neat one-two with Patrick Kluivert, before forcing a fine parry from Crossley. The ball fell invitingly for Craig Bellamy, but he too was denied.

Further saves followed from Bowyer and Robbie Elliott, as the Magpies became more and more frustrated. Then, with 28 minutes played, frustration turned to despair. Having not featured in the game as an attacking force, a quick Fulham break ended with Collins John beating stand-in custodian Steve Harper from the inside left channel.

Newcastle were angry that they had not been awarded a free-kick in the lead up to the goal, and came agonisingly close to an equaliser before half-time. Dutch international Kluivert did everything right, but could only watch in horror as his potential equaliser struck the unsighted Crossley in the face.

Nine of the North-East team's 19 corners were earned in a positive opening to the second period. Yet, despite growing home pressure, it was Chris Coleman's charges that found the net.

With 65 minutes played, Steed Malbranque lashed home Andy Cole's pass from just outside the area to make it 2-0. Six minutes later, the same player struck again, this time converting from the penalty spot after substitute Tomasz Radzinski had been upended.

Having completely dominated proceedings, Graeme Souness' men now found themselves three goals behind. That margin was briefly extended to four when Luis Boa Morte raced through to clip the ball beyond an advancing Harper after 76 minutes, before Bellamy responded within 60 seconds with a brave header from Bowyer's right-wing cross.

There was still time for one last save from Crossley, as Newcastle were left to reflect on a bizarre defeat.

Steed Malbranque strokes home Fulham's third goal from the penalty spot

"In 35 years of professional football, I've never been involved in a game like that."
Graeme Souness

PREMIERSHIP MILESTONE

25 Craig Bellamy netted his 25th Premiership goal for Newcastle

"The ball bounced for us today, and a few decisions have gone our way. Mark Crossley was fantastic."
Chris Coleman

PREMIERSHIP FIXTURE HISTORY

Pl: 4 Draws: 1	Wins	Goals	Yellow	Red
Newcastle United	2	7	2	0
Fulham	1	6	4	1

STARTING LINE-UPS

Newcastle subs: Robert, Ameobi, Caig, Bramble, Johnsen

Fulham subs: Radzinski, McBride, Rosenior, Legwinski, van der Sar

EVENT LINE

28 ⚽ John (Open Play)
45 ▢ Volz (Foul)
HALF TIME 0 - 1
57 ⇄ **Hughes (Off) Robert (On)**
57 ⇄ John (Off) Radzinski (On)
65 ⚽ Malbranque (Open Play)
68 ⇄ **Bernard (Off) Ameobi (On)**
71 ⚽ Malbranque (Penalty)
76 ⚽ Boa Morte (Open Play)
77 ⚽ **Bellamy (Open Play)**
87 ▢ **O'Brien (Foul)**
FULL TIME 1 - 4

STATISTICS

Season	Fixture	Newcastle / Fulham	Fixture	Season
100	20	Shots On Target	8	61
66	6	Shots Off Target	4	54
4	0	Hit Woodwork	0	2
37	1	Caught Offside	1	30
103	19	Corners	0	60
144	12	Fouls	16	142
51%	54%	Possession	46%	48%

LEAGUE STANDINGS

Position (pos before)		W	D	L	F	A	Pts
9 (9)	Newcastle Utd	4	4	4	23	23	16
12 (16)	Fulham	4	2	6	16	20	14

PREMIERSHIP FIXTURE HISTORY

Pl: 3 Draws: 1	Wins	Goals	Yellow	Red
Birmingham City	1	4	2	1
Everton	1	2	2	1

STARTING LINE-UPS

Birmingham City subs: Lazaridis, Yorke, Anderton, Bennett, Clapham

Everton subs: Ferguson, Watson, Wright, Naysmith, McFadden

EVENT LINE

17 Kilbane (Foul)

HALF TIME 0 - 0

61 **Clemence (Off) Lazaridis (On)**

68 **Izzet (Handball)**

69 Gravesen (Penalty)

73 **Cunningham (Off) Yorke (On)**

81 **Gronkjaer (Off) Anderton (On)**

88 Osman (Off) Ferguson (On)

90 Bent (Off) Watson (On)

FULL TIME 0 - 1

STATISTICS

Season	Fixture	Birmingham City / Everton	Fixture	Season
54	4	Shots On Target	9	74
68	11	Shots Off Target	1	66
1	0	Hit Woodwork	0	3
38	1	Caught Offside	5	39
73	5	Corners	3	67
182	13	Fouls	12	156
50%	50%	Possession	50%	50%

LEAGUE STANDINGS

Position (pos before)		W	D	L	F	A	Pts
15 (15)	Birmingham C	2	6	5	8	11	12
3 (3)	Everton	8	2	3	15	11	26

Saturday 13th November 2004 | Venue: **St Andrews** | Attendance: **28,388** | Referee: **R.Styles**

BIRMINGHAM CITY 0 EVERTON 1

Everton continued their sensational start to the season, with a hard-fought 1-0 win at St Andrew's.

A Thomas Gravesen penalty midway through the second half was enough to secure a fifth away win of the season for David Moyes' well-drilled team. The Merseysiders' cause was also aided by the dismissal of Birmingham midfielder Muzzy Izzet, the former Leicester man seeing red for the deliberate handball that resulted in the award of the decisive spot-kick.

Having recorded a much-needed victory against the red half of Liverpool in their last match, Steve Bruce kept faith with both the personnel and 4-5-1 formation that he had employed at Anfield.

The manager's team selection appeared a good one on the evidence of the early exchanges, as the West Midlands side dominated proceedings. Danish winger Jesper Gronkjaer twice failed to hit the target from good positions, while Izzet tested Nigel Martyn with a 12th-minute header.

With the storm weathered, Everton began to cause problems at the other end. Northern Ireland international goalkeeper Maik Taylor saved from both Leon Osman and Tim Cahill, before he was rescued by Julian Gray after dropping a cross.

Emile Heskey then delighted the visiting fans by firing over the bar on the stroke of half-time. The striker had a chance to redeem himself 20 minutes after the restart, but again he failed to hit the target. The second miss proved extremely costly, with Moyes' men wasting no time in making him pay.

Lee Carsley's 68th-minute drive, following a corner, would have rippled the net had it not been for Izzet's acrobatic intervention. With the Turkish international sent from the field by referee Rob Styles, Gravesen coolly put his side in front from the spot.

Despite having a one-man advantage, the Merseysiders had to endure a couple of scary moments on the road to victory. Tony Hibbert cleared a Heskey header off the line, before substitute Dwight Yorke blazed over in the final minute.

The win kept Everton in third place, while Birmingham slipped ever closer to the relegation zone.

"I shouldn't have done it, but it's the kind of thing you just do."
Muzzy Izzet on his sending off for deliberate handball

"Last season we only won one away from home. It was important that we did something about that and we have."
David Moyes

Thomas Gravesen and Lee Carsley – separated at birth?

Saturday 13th November 2004	Venue: **Reebok Stadium**	Attendance: **25,779**	Referee: **A.P.D'Urso**

PREMIERSHIP FIXTURE HISTORY

Pl: 6 Draws: 1	Wins	⚽	☐	■
Bolton Wanderers	2	7	10	1
Aston Villa	3	9	10	1

STARTING LINE-UPS

Bolton Wanderers: Oakes; Hunt, Jaidi, N'Gotty, Gardner; Nolan, Hierro, Speed (c), Diouf, Pedersen; Davies

Aston Villa: Sorensen; Samuel, Mellberg (c), Delaney, De la Cruz; Whittingham, Hendrie, McCann, Solano; Cole, Angel

Substitutes (Bolton): Campo, Vaz Te, Poole, Ben Haim, Cesar

Substitutes (Aston Villa): L.Moore, Ridgewell, Postma, Hitzlsperger, Davis

EVENT LINE

21 ⚽ **Diouf (Indirect Free Kick)**

24 ☐ **Gardner (Foul)**

41 ⚽ McCann (Open Play)

HALF TIME 1 - 1

63 ⇄ Whittingham (Off) Hitzlsperger (On)

67 ☐ Hendrie (Foul)

75 ⇄ Solano (Off) Moore L (On)

81 ⇄ **Hierro (Off) Campo (On)**

89 ⚽ Hitzlsperger (Open Play)

90 ⇄ **Nolan (Off) Vaz Te (On)**

90 ⇄ Hendrie (Off) Ridgewell (On)

FULL TIME 1 - 2

STATISTICS

Season	Fixture (Bolton)		Fixture (Villa)	Season
93	7	Shots On Target	5	81
77	8	Shots Off Target	5	67
4	1	Hit Woodwork	0	3
25	0	Caught Offside	7	34
74	9	Corners	5	76
179	10	Fouls	17	204
50%	49%	Possession	51%	48%

LEAGUE STANDINGS

Position (pos before)		W	D	L	F	A	Pts
4 (4)	Bolton W	6	4	3	20	16	22
5 (6)	Aston Villa	5	6	2	19	14	21

J'Lloyd Samuel prepares for a header

BOLTON WANDERERS 1 ASTON VILLA 2

"Premiership football is so good that it always punishes you if you don't take your chances."
Sam Allardyce

PREMIERSHIP MILESTONE
Andy Oakes made his first Premiership appearance for Bolton

PREMIERSHIP MILESTONE
50 Kevin Davies made his 50th Premiership appearance for Bolton

"We brought on Thomas Hitzlsperger because he is always likely to do what he did today, and that was score a brilliant goal."
David O'Leary

PREMIERSHIP MILESTONE
Gavin McCann scored his first Premiership goal for Aston Villa

PREMIERSHIP MILESTONE
50 Thomas Sorensen made his 50th Premiership appearance for Aston Villa

PREMIERSHIP MILESTONE
600 Thomas Hitzlsperger netted Aston Villa's 600th Premiership goal

A late thunderbolt from Aston Villa substitute Thomas Hitzlsperger condemned Bolton to their first home defeat of the Premiership campaign.

The German's strike was worthy of winning any match, and came after first half goals from El-Hadji Diouf and Gavin McCann had seen the scores locked at 1-1. As if to add further salt to the Trotters' wounds, the victory was the Midlanders' first on the road this season.

Sam Allardyce would have been pleased with the way in which his team began proceedings. Senegalese international Diouf went close with a header, while Thomas Sorensen had to make a smart save from Kevin Davies.

After Juan Pablo Angel had gone close for the visitors, Bolton took a well-deserved 21st-minute lead. Kevin Nolan was the architect of the goal, firing in a dangerous low ball from the right that Diouf diverted back past the left hand of the keeper.

Jamaican Ricardo Gardner was booked for bringing down Nolberto Solano soon afterwards, and was then lucky to escape a second yellow card from referee Andy D'Urso for a foul on McCann.

Any injustice they might have felt was put to one side by Villa, however, when their former Sunderland midfielder equalised four minutes before the break. Lee Hendrie sent over an inviting cross from the left, and McCann climbed highest to nod the ball beyond Jussi Jaaskelainen from eight yards out.

Again, it was the home side who began more brightly in the second period. Stand-in captain Gary Speed was inches away from connecting with a dangerous cross in the early exchanges, and then fired over the bar when well-placed. The midfielder later teed up Henrik Pedersen, but the Dane could not keep his shot down.

David O'Leary's men grew in confidence as the game progressed. Debutant shot-stopper Andy Oakes saved from Hendrie, while Solano and Angel were both wasteful.

After Nolan and Carlton Cole had both failed to seal the points with headers, Hitzlsperger won the match with a searing 20-yard drive in the 89th minute. A draw would have been a fairer result, but since when has football been fair?

PREMIERSHIP FIXTURE HISTORY

Pl: 1 Draws: 0	Wins	⚽	Yellow	Red
Charlton Athletic	1	4	0	0
Norwich City	0	0	3	0

STARTING LINE-UPS

Konchesky, Euell, Jeffers, Andersen, Fortune

Bentley, Ward, Mulryne, Helveg McVeigh

EVENT LINE

15 ⚽ **Johansson (Indirect Free Kick)**

21 ⚽ **Johansson (Open Play)**

HALF TIME 2 - 0

46 Jonson (Off) Bentley (On)

63 Green (Off) Ward (On)

65 Holt (Off) Mulryne (On)

66 Edworthy (Foul)

74 **Lisbie (Off) Konchesky (On)**

75 ⚽ **Konchesky (Open Play)**

78 **Murphy (Off) Euell (On)**

84 Francis (Foul)

85 **Thomas (Off) Jeffers (On)**

88 ⚽ **Euell (Open Play)**

90 Bentley (Foul)

FULL TIME 4 - 0

STATISTICS

Season	Fixture		Fixture	Season
60	11	Shots On Target	4	64
45	5	Shots Off Target	4	80
2	0	Hit Woodwork	0	3
47	7	Caught Offside	3	50
48	1	Corners	5	67
170	14	Fouls	11	181
44%	48%	Possession	52%	47%

LEAGUE STANDINGS

Position (pos before)	W	D	L	F	A	Pts
9 (11) Charlton Ath	5	3	5	17	21	18
20 (19) Norwich C	0	8	5	11	23	8

Saturday 13th November 2004 | Venue: The Valley | Attendance: 27,057 | Referee: A.Marriner

CHARLTON ATHLETIC 4 NORWICH CITY 0

Norwich were given their harshest beating since returning to the Premiership, as they remained the only winless team in the top-flight.

The Canaries made a poor start to the game, finding themselves two goals down after just 21 minutes, and never fully recovered. One-time transfer target Jonatan Johansson did the early damage, before substitutes Paul Konchesky and Jason Euell added gloss to the scoreline late on.

Despite being at home, Charlton boss Alan Curbishley opted to keep faith with the 4-5-1 formation that had brought success at Tottenham last time out. The policy worked, as Nigel Worthington's team struggled to combat the Addicks' attacking threat from wide areas.

The opening goal came from a free-kick in the 15th minute. Tall former Ipswich defender Hermann Hreidarsson climbed highest to win a header, and Johansson was on hand to nod the ball into the net from close range.

The Finn, operating on the right wing, grabbed his second goal just six minutes later. Robert Green did well to keep out an effort from Danny Murphy, but was unable to prevent Johansson from rifling in the rebound at the back post.

With any game plan blown out of the water, Norwich struggled to get a foothold in the match. Gary Holt and Leon McKenzie spurned half-chances, but Charlton largely kept their visitors at arm's length.

The second period saw plenty of effort from the Carrow Road club. Darren Huckerby and former Addick Matthias Svensson posed plenty of problems for a defence that had struggled to keep clean sheets, though they could not conjure up an all-important goal.

With custodian Green forced off through injury, his replacement, Darren Ward, had little to do except twice pick the ball out of his net.

Firstly, having just arrived from the bench, Konchesky rounded off a smart 75th-minute break down the right by sliding home from close range at the back post. Then, a move down the opposite flank ended when Euell turned home Johansson's low cross after 88 minutes.

At the final whistle, the majority of a Premiership record crowd at The Valley of 27,057 went home very happy with what they had seen.

> **"I'm really pleased for everybody. We have scored seven goals and taken six points from two games, and the confidence seems to be back."**
> Alan Curbishley

> **"The first two goals were down to bad defending, and you get taught harsh lessons in the Premiership if you make mistakes."**
> Nigel Worthington

PREMIERSHIP MILESTONE

Darren Ward made his Premiership debut

PREMIERSHIP MILESTONE

Phil Mulryne made his first Premiership appearance for Norwich

PREMIERSHIP MILESTONE

The attendance of 27,057 was a Premiership record at The Valley

Simon Charlton is harried by Radostin Kishishev

PREMIERSHIP FIXTURE HISTORY

Pl: 4	Draws: 2	Wins	Goals	Yellow	Red
Fulham		0	2	4	0
Chelsea		2	6	8	1

STARTING LINE-UPS

Fulham subs: McBride, van der Sar, Legwinski, Rosenior, Hammond

Chelsea subs: Tiago, Kezman, Huth, Cudicini, Bridge

EVENT LINE

- 23 Yellow card: Makelele (Foul)
- 33 Goal: Lampard (Indirect Free Kick)
- 45 Yellow card: Lampard (Ung.Conduct)

HALF TIME 0 - 1

- 57 Goal: **Diop (Open Play)**
- 59 Goal: Robben (Open Play)
- 63 Substitution: Smertin (Off) Tiago (On)
- 72 Substitution: **Pembridge (Off) McBride (On)**
- 73 Goal: Gallas (Indirect Free Kick)
- 76 Substitution: Duff (Off) Kezman (On)
- 81 Goal: Tiago (Open Play)
- 83 Substitution: Gudjohnsen (Off) Huth (On)

FULL TIME 1 - 4

STATISTICS

Season	Fixture (Fulham)		Fixture (Chelsea)	Season
63	2	Shots On Target	11	95
59	5	Shots Off Target	5	96
2	0	Hit Woodwork	0	5
30	0	Caught Offside	4	40
61	1	Corners	5	104
155	13	Fouls	13	155
48%	43%	Possession	57%	56%

LEAGUE STANDINGS

Position (pos before)	W	D	L	F	A	Pts
13 (12) Fulham	4	2	7	17	24	14
1 (1) Chelsea	10	2	1	21	4	32

Saturday 13th November 2004 | Venue: **Craven Cottage** | Attendance: **21,877** | Referee: **U.D.Rennie**

FULHAM 1 CHELSEA 4

Chelsea continued to set the pace at the top of the Premiership, destroying neighbours Fulham 4-1 at Craven Cottage.

Jose Mourinho's men dominated from start to finish, though they were briefly pegged back at 1-1 by a stunning 57th-minute strike from Pape Bouba Diop. Arjen Robben quickly restored an advantage that had earlier been provided by Frank Lampard, however, and further goals from William Gallas and Tiago sealed the points.

The Stamford Bridge side, and Robben in particular, posed a massive threat in the first period. After Lampard had seen a fine header kept out by Mark Crossley, the Dutch winger took centre stage.

On no less than four occasions in a dazzling 10-minute spell, the former PSV Eindhoven man engineered great chances through his dribbling wizardry. Two high-class saves kept the marauding No.16 at bay, before both Alexei Smertin and Eidur Gudjohnsen failed to profit from their colleague's inspired work.

It seemed only a matter of time until the visitors took the lead, and they did in the 33rd minute. A free-kick was rolled to Lampard some 25 yards out, and the England international midfielder struck a venomous drive that swerved into the right-hand side of the net.

Referee Uriah Rennie turned down two strong penalty appeals from the away side in the lead up to half-time, even booking Lampard for diving, and Fulham took advantage of their good fortune before the hour mark.

Senegalese international Diop capitalised on a poor headed clearance to unleash an unsavable volley from distance, somehow bringing his team level. Home joy was short-lived, however, as within two minutes Robben had netted the goal his performance deserved, following another jinking run.

The Cottagers' resistance was broken, and Chelsea grabbed two more goals. Firstly, Gallas nodded in a right-wing free-kick from close range after 73 minutes. Then, Tiago smartly exchanged passes with Robben, before driving home from the inside left channel nine minutes from time.

In truth, it could have been much worse for Chris Coleman's charges. The home side did not play badly, but were just overrun by opponents at the top of their game.

Arjen Robben and Zat Knight compete for possession

"I think they are even better than Arsenal, and teams like us are well below the two of them. I think Chelsea are favourites for the title."

Chris Coleman

PREMIERSHIP MILESTONE

Pape Bouba Diop scored his first Premiership goal

"In modern football every team is well organised. Chris Coleman is one of the best young managers in England, and his teams have good organisation for the bigger games."

Jose Mourinho

PREMIERSHIP FIXTURE HISTORY

Pl: 4 Draws: 1	Wins	⚽	▢	■
Liverpool	3	10	3	0
Crystal Palace	0	3	8	0

STARTING LINE-UPS

Finnan, Mellor, Dudek, Biscan, Sinama-Pongolle

Lakis, Soares, Speroni, Hudson, Andrews

EVENT LINE

23 ⚽ **Baros (Penalty)**
44 ⚽ Kolkka (Open Play)
45 ▢ Kolkka (Foul)
45 ⚽ **Baros (Indirect Free Kick)**

HALF TIME 2 - 1

52 ⚽ Hughes (Open Play)
62 ⇄ **Riise (Off) Finnan (On)**
65 ⇄ Routledge (Off) Lakis (On)
76 ⇄ Riihilahti (Off) Soares (On)
79 ⇄ **Josemi (Off) Mellor (On)**
79 ▢ Hughes (Dissent)
90 ▢ Kiraly (Ung.Conduct)
90 ⚽ **Baros (Penalty)**
90 ▢ **Baros (Ung.Conduct)**
90 ⇄ **Baros (Off) Sinama-Pongolle (On)**

FULL TIME 3 - 2

STATISTICS

Season	Fixture	Liverpool / Crystal Palace	Fixture	Season
81	7	Shots On Target	4	50
81	13	Shots Off Target	0	60
2	0	Hit Woodwork	0	3
36	1	Caught Offside	2	35
69	7	Corners	1	63
155	13	Fouls	17	183
54%	56%	Possession	44%	45%

LEAGUE STANDINGS

Position (pos before)		W	D	L	F	A	Pts
6 (8)	Liverpool	6	2	4	21	13	20
16 (16)	Crystal Palace	3	3	7	15	19	12

Saturday 13th November 2004 | Venue: **Anfield** | Attendance: **42,862** | Referee: **P.Dowd**

Milan Baros justifies wearing golden boots

"We have a top quality set of strikers here, Milan Baros especially, and hopefully next week another player will take the opportunity to shine as he did today."

Rafael Benitez

"We're absolutely shell-shocked. This result is very difficult to stomach, but we didn't defend very well."

Iain Dowie

PREMIERSHIP MILESTONE

Michael Hughes scored his first Premiership goal in the colours of Crystal Palace

PREMIERSHIP MILESTONE

Joonas Kolkka scored his first Premiership goal

LIVERPOOL 3 CRYSTAL PALACE 2

An inspired showing from Milan Baros gave Liverpool the edge in a five-goal thriller at Anfield.

Iain Dowie's in-form Crystal Palace team twice cancelled out goals from the Czech Republic international, but were eventually undone by a last-gasp penalty that saw the striker claim a richly-deserved hat-trick.

The game was entertaining from the outset. Both Chris Kirkland and Gabor Kiraly were forced to earn their money in the early exchanges, before the men in red went in front midway through the half.

Mikele Leigertwood, making his first start in the Premiership, was adjudged to have brought down Baros, and the nimble forward got up to convert from the spot.

Referee Phil Dowd then turned down appeals for another penalty, as Rafael Benitez's men went in search of a second goal. It was the visitors who equalised just before half-time, however, when Joonas Kolkka hammered a bouncing ball across Kirkland from an acute angle.

That was not the end of the first half scoring though, as Baros steered Liverpool back in front. Harry Kewell did well to fire in a low cross from the right, and the striker managed to poke home from inside the six-yard box.

With the crowd firmly behind them, the Anfield side set about sealing the three points in a spirited start to the second period. Norwegian John Arne Riise forced Kiraly to acrobatically tip an effort over the bar, but it was the Eagles who found the net.

With 52 minutes played, Kolkka turned provider. The Finn did well down the left, and sent over a cross that was nodded powerfully past Kirkland by the onrushing Michael Hughes.

After recovering from the initial shock of conceding another equaliser, it was Benitez's team that pressed for a winner. The Londoners defended valiantly, though were lucky to escape when a Baros header trickled wide of the post.

The Czech was not to be denied, however, earning and converting an injury-time penalty to settle the match. The striker seemed to fall fairly easily when challenged in the box, but was coolness personified as he beat Kiraly from 12 yards.

PREMIERSHIP FIXTURE HISTORY

Pl: 7 Draws: 4	Wins	Goals	Yellow	Red
Manchester City	1	9	12	2
Blackburn Rovers	2	12	13	0

STARTING LINE-UPS

Manchester City: James; Mills, Dunne, Distin (c), Jordan; Flood, Bosvelt, McManaman, Sibierski; Anelka, S.Wright-Phillips

Blackburn Rovers: Stead, Dickov; Emerton, Tugay, Ferguson (c), Reid; McEveley, Johansson, Todd, Neill; Friedel

Substitutes (Manchester City): Reyna, Waterreus, Onuoha, Fowler, B.Wright-Phillips

Substitutes (Blackburn Rovers): Jansen, Thompson, Enckelman, Matteo, Djorkaeff

EVENT LINE

38 Yellow card Todd (Foul)

40 Yellow card **Jordan (Foul)**

45 Goal **Sibierski (Open Play)**

HALF TIME 1 - 0

46 Substitution Stead (Off) Jansen (On)

65 Substitution **Flood (Off) Reyna (On)**

71 Substitution Tugay (Off) Thompson (On)

76 Yellow card McEveley (Foul)

77 Red card **Mills (Foul)**

78 Goal Dickov (Penalty)

79 Yellow card Thompson (Foul)

FULL TIME 1 - 1

STATISTICS

Season	Fixture (Man City)		Fixture (Blackburn)	Season
77	7	Shots On Target	3	59
66	1	Shots Off Target	9	73
2	0	Hit Woodwork	0	2
45	3	Caught Offside	4	50
79	3	Corners	5	73
173	19	Fouls	13	203
47%	49%	Possession	51%	48%

LEAGUE STANDINGS

Position (pos before)	W	D	L	F	A	Pts
12 (13) Man City	3	5	5	14	13	14
19 (20) Blackburn R	1	6	6	11	26	9

Saturday 13th November 2004 | Venue: City of Manchester Stadium | Attendance: 45,504 | Referee: M.Clattenburg

MANCHESTER CITY 1 BLACKBURN ROVERS 1

Shaun Wright-Phillips hurdles Kerimoglu Tugay

"We were a little fortunate to go in 1-0 ahead at half-time, and we didn't look like having another goal in us."

Kevin Keegan

"We showed great determination and if we continue in this vain we will be all right."

Mark Hughes

PREMIERSHIP MILESTONE

50 Brett Emerton made his 50th Premiership appearance

Blackburn climbed off the bottom of the Premiership table thanks to a 78th-minute Paul Dickov equaliser against his former club.

Mark Hughes' men had trailed to a late first half goal from Antoine Sibierski, before Danny Mills was dismissed for a professional foul as Dickov bore down on goal inside the box. The Scottish striker then picked himself up to beat David James from the spot, something he had not managed to do last season when playing for Leicester.

Kevin Keegan kept faith with the same 11 players that had drawn at Old Trafford the previous weekend, though he did revert to a more familiar 4-4-2 formation. Shaun Wright-Phillips was handed the task of partnering Nicolas Anelka in attack, with Sibierski playing wide on the left.

Visiting custodian Brad Friedel had relatively little to do in a dire opening period. Having already repelled a drive from Anelka, the American kept out a well-struck free-kick from the striker.

At the other end, Jonathan Stead, in for the suspended Jay Bothroyd, had Rovers' best opportunities, though he twice failed to beat James. The tall frontman was replaced by Matt Jansen at the interval, but not before City had gone in front.

With 45 minutes played, the tactical switch that had seen Sibierski moved forward midway through the half paid dividends. The Frenchman profited from great work by Wright-Phillips, back patrolling the right flank, as he steered home an inviting low cross.

The overall quality of the match improved little after the break, though Rovers did threaten on a more regular basis. It was the home side, however, who continued to look the more dangerous outfit, with Mills forcing a fine parry from Friedel during their best spell.

Yet, it was Blackburn who grabbed the all-important goal courtesy of Dickov. Allied to the dismissal of Mills, this ensured that it was Hughes' team that came closest to victory.

A deflected Brett Emerton cross was expertly turned over, James parried a fierce David Thompson drive, and then Dickov narrowly missed the target with a late strike.

PREMIERSHIP FIXTURE HISTORY

Pl: 2 Draws: 0	Wins	⚽	Yellow	Red
Southampton	2	5	1	0
Portsmouth	0	1	6	0

STARTING LINE-UPS

Southampton: Keller; Kenton, Lundekvam, Jakobsson, Le Saux; Fernandes, Telfer, Delap, A.Svensson; Beattie (c), Blackstock

Portsmouth: Lua Lua, Yakubu; Berger, Quashie, Faye, O'Neil; Unsworth, Stefanovic, De Zeeuw (c), Primus; Hislop

Southampton subs: Dodd, Phillips, Griffit, Blayney, Crouch

Portsmouth subs: Fuller, Griffin, Taylor, Ashdown, Cisse

EVENT LINE

12 ⚽ Jakobsson (Own Goal)
16 Jakobsson (Off) Dodd (On)
18 ⚽ **Blackstock (Open Play)**
31 **Delap (Foul)**
36 Yakubu (Off) Fuller (On)

HALF TIME 1 - 1

54 Faye (Foul)
68 **Beattie (Off) Phillips (On)**
70 De Zeeuw (Foul)
71 ⚽ **Phillips (Indirect Free Kick)**
79 Berger (Off) Griffin (On)
79 Unsworth (Off) Taylor (On)
80 **Fernandes (Off) Griffit (On)**
86 Quashie (Foul)

FULL TIME 2 - 1

STATISTICS

Season	Fixture	Southampton / Portsmouth	Fixture	Season
64	5	Shots On Target	6	67
71	6	Shots Off Target	7	64
2	0	Hit Woodwork	1	2
36	0	Caught Offside	3	27
73	4	Corners	8	58
178	13	Fouls	12	145
50%	50%	Possession	50%	47%

LEAGUE STANDINGS

Position (pos before)	W	D	L	F	A	Pts
17 (18) Southampton	2	5	6	12	17	11
11 (10) Portsmouth	4	3	5	16	17	15

Saturday 13th November 2004 | Venue: Friends Provident St Mary's Stadium | Attendance: 30,921 | Referee: G.Poll

Dexter Blackstock celebrates levelling the scores

"It's a relief to finally get this first win. It would have been nice if it had come sooner, but I thought we were worth the three points."
Steve Wigley

PREMIERSHIP MILESTONE
Kasey Keller made his first Premiership appearance for Southampton

PREMIERSHIP MILESTONE
Dexter Blackstock netted his first Premiership goal

PREMIERSHIP MILESTONE
75 Kevin Phillips scored his 75th Premiership goal

"It's not been a very good week for me, and what we must do now is pick ourselves up and look to the next match."
Harry Redknapp

PREMIERSHIP MILESTONE
200 Shaka Hislop made his 200th Premiership appearance

SOUTHAMPTON 2 PORTSMOUTH 1

Southampton won their first Premiership match under the leadership of Steve Wigley, coming from behind to seal the points in a vital South-Coast derby.

With speculation about the future of the Saints' boss increasing by the day, his players delivered a perfect tonic. Things did not look good when Andreas Jakobsson headed past his own keeper after 12 minutes, but goals from Dexter Blackstock and substitute Kevin Phillips secured a welcome victory.

With a 5-2 Carling Cup capitulation at Watford still fresh in their minds, the home side got off to the worst possible start. Confusion was the order of the day, as Jakobsson outjumped Lomana Tresor Lua Lua to head a long ball past onrushing loan signing Kasey Keller from just inside the area.

Few fans would have expected a positive response from the men in red and white, but they got one. Just six minutes after falling behind, Blackstock lifted the atmosphere inside St Mary's with a swivelling 12 yard effort, after the ball had broken to him off the arm of James Beattie.

Portsmouth responded with attempts from Lua Lua and Linvoy Primus before the break, but Keller stood firm. The former Leicester keeper then had more than 15 minutes to put his feet up, as Southampton went on the attack after the interval.

Claus Lundekvam somehow failed to head home a long throw from Rory Delap, before Shaka Hislop did well to keep out a near-post strike from midfielder Anders Svensson. Despite this pressure, however, it was Harry Redknapp's visitors that went closest.

With 63 minutes played, Patrik Berger rattled the crossbar with another of his spectacular drives from distance. It was a lucky escape for the Saints, and they took advantage of their reprieve soon afterwards.

Former England international Kevin Phillips had only recently been introduced to the action, when he met fellow substitute Jason Dodd's right-wing free-kick with a firm header past Hislop from seven yards out.

The striker almost added another from distance, before Keller proved his worth with an excellent late save from Jamaican Ricardo Fuller.

Saturday 13th November 2004	Venue: **White Hart Lane**	Attendance: **36,095**	Referee: **S.G.Bennett**

TOTTENHAM HOTSPUR 4 ARSENAL 5

White Hart Lane played host to a pulsating North-London derby, with Arsenal eventually running out 5-4 winners.

Having been confirmed as the successor to Jacques Santini, Martin Jol went through every conceivable emotion in this topsy-turvy encounter. Tottenham led just once during the 90 minutes, though they always remained within striking distance of their near neighbours.

The home side started well, with Jens Lehmann making a sprawling save to deny Pedro Mendes. Jermain Defoe then fired a dangerous ball across the box, before Dennis Bergkamp failed to hit the target with the Gunners' only real opening.

The goal glut began after 37 minutes, when Noureddine Naybet became the first of nine different scorers. An inswinging Michael Carrick free-kick from the left found its way to the Moroccan, and he finished with consumate ease.

Shortly afterwards, Lehmann did well to tip over a looping header from Noe Pamarot. The save proved vital, as on the stroke of half-time Thierry Henry outwitted Ledley King to bring down and then convert Lauren's ball in from the right.

Within 15 minutes of the restart, Arsenal led 3-1. Firstly, Lauren converted a 55th-minute penalty brought about by Pamarot's clumsy challenge on Freddie Ljungberg. Then, Patrick Vieira capitalised on more poor defending to race through and beat Paul Robinson.

The game was not over, however, as Defoe turned and fired an unstoppable 15-yard drive into the far top right-hand corner of the net just 60 seconds later. There followed an exchange of four further goals, Arsene Wenger's team twice stretching the lead, only to see it pegged back.

Great work from Cesc Fabregas enabled Ljungberg to steer home a 69th-minute effort from the inside left channel, though King promptly reduced the deficit by heading home another inswinging Carrick free-kick from the left.

Substitute Robert Pires then appeared to have finally sealed the points by squeezing the ball home from an acute angle, but fellow replacement Frederic Kanoute set up a nervous finale by neatly placing Reto Ziegler's astute throughball past Lehmann two minutes from time.

Patrick Vieira leads by example

"If we can score four against the best team in England, we must be doing something right."
Martin Jol

PREMIERSHIP MILESTONE

Noureddine Naybet scored his first Premiership goal

"I am concerned about the goals we have conceded, but it was a derby."
Arsene Wenger

PREMIERSHIP FIXTURE HISTORY

Pl: **13** Draws: **6**

	Wins	Goals	Yellow	Red
Tottenham Hotspur	4	17	27	0
Arsenal	3	17	27	3

STARTING LINE-UPS

Tottenham Hotspur: Robinson; King (c), Naybet, Pamarot, Edman; Brown, Carrick, Mendes, Ziegler; Defoe, Keane

Arsenal: Henry, Bergkamp; Reyes, Vieira (c), Fabregas, Ljungberg; Cole, Cygan, Toure, Lauren; Lehmann

Tottenham Hotspur substitutes: Davies, Kanoute, Gardner, Fulop, Redknapp
Arsenal substitutes: Pires, van Persie, Almunia, Hoyte, Flamini

EVENT LINE

37 ⚽ **Naybet (Indirect Free Kick)**
38 ▢ **Naybet (Ung.Conduct)**
42 ▢ **Ziegler (Foul)**
45 ⚽ Henry (Open Play)

HALF TIME 1 - 1

55 ⚽ Lauren (Penalty)
59 ▢ **Brown (Foul)**
60 ⚽ Vieira (Open Play)
61 ⚽ **Defoe (Open Play)**
68 ⇄ **Mendes (Off) Davies (On)**
68 ⇄ Reyes (Off) Pires (On)
69 ⚽ Ljungberg (Open Play)
74 ⚽ **King (Indirect Free Kick)**
76 ⇄ **Brown (Off) Kanoute (On)**
81 ⚽ Pires (Open Play)
82 ⇄ Bergkamp (Off) van Persie (On)
88 ⚽ **Kanoute (Open Play)**
90 ⇄ **Keane (Off) Gardner (On)**

FULL TIME 4 - 5

STATISTICS

Season	Fixture		Fixture	Season
71	**7**	Shots On Target	**7**	**128**
74	**3**	Shots Off Target	**3**	**60**
5	**0**	Hit Woodwork	**0**	**6**
48	**5**	Caught Offside	**5**	**28**
56	**3**	Corners	**4**	**71**
171	**20**	Fouls	**9**	**142**
47%	**48%**	Possession	**52%**	**58%**

LEAGUE STANDINGS

Position (pos before)	W	D	L	F	A	Pts
14 (14) Tottenham H	**3**	**4**	**6**	**12**	**16**	**13**
2 (2) Arsenal	**9**	**3**	**1**	**37**	**17**	**30**

PREMIERSHIP FIXTURE HISTORY

Pl: 12 Draws: 3	Wins	Goals	Yellow	Red
Newcastle United	3	20	20	0
Manchester United	6	21	22	2

STARTING LINE-UPS

Newcastle United: Given; Carr, Bramble, Johnsen, Bernard; Bowyer, Butt, Jenas, Bellamy; Shearer (c), Kluivert

Manchester United: Carroll; Heinze, Silvestre, Ferdinand, G.Neville; Keane (c), Scholes, Fletcher; Rooney, Ronaldo; van Nistelrooy

Newcastle subs: O'Brien, Dyer, Robert, Harper, Ameobi

Manchester United subs: Brown, Giggs, Smith, Howard, Saha

EVENT LINE

7 Rooney (Open Play)

18 **Carr (Off) O'Brien (On)**

HALF TIME 0 - 1

54 **Bowyer (Off) Dyer (On)**

57 Silvestre (Off) Brown (On)

62 **Kluivert (Off) Robert (On)**

71 **Shearer (Open Play)**

74 van Nistelrooy (Penalty)

75 **Bramble (Dissent)**

75 **Johnsen (Dissent)**

75 Fletcher (Off) Giggs (On)

83 Ronaldo (Off) Smith (On)

90 Rooney (Open Play)

FULL TIME 1 - 3

STATISTICS

Season	Fixture (Newcastle)		Fixture (Man Utd)	Season
107	7	Shots On Target	8	99
72	6	Shots Off Target	5	87
4	0	Hit Woodwork	0	6
38	1	Caught Offside	5	44
105	2	Corners	7	101
155	11	Fouls	16	165
50%	29%	Possession	71%	54%

LEAGUE STANDINGS

Position (pos before)	W	D	L	F	A	Pts
10 (10) Newcastle Utd	4	4	5	24	26	16
7 (8) Man Utd	5	6	2	14	10	21

Sunday 14th November 2004	Venue: **St James' Park**	Attendance: **52,320**	Referee: **M.L.Dean**

Wayne Rooney celebrates his second goal with Alan Smith

"I was bitterly disappointed with the penalty. I was 50 yards up the pitch and I can see a push on Andy O'Brien, but the referee is ten yards away and he can't see it."

Alan Shearer

PREMIERSHIP MILESTONE

The attendance of 52,320 was a Premiership record at St James' Park

PREMIERSHIP MILESTONE

Ronny Johnsen made his first Premiership appearance for Newcastle

"This win has given us a lot of encouragement. This is not an easy place to come to."

Sir Alex Ferguson

PREMIERSHIP MILESTONE

300 Roy Keane made his 300th Premiership appearance for Man Utd

NEWCASTLE UNITED 1 MANCHESTER UNITED 3

Manchester United finally produced the sort of display their supporters have become accustomed to, defeating Newcastle 3-1 at St James' Park.

Wayne Rooney was on target twice against the side that had competed with the Old Trafford club for his signature, with Ruud van Nistelrooy, from the penalty spot, and Alan Shearer the other men on the scoresheet.

The defeat was the Magpies' third in a row in the Premiership, and left them firmly entrenched in mid-table. Manager Graeme Souness again accommodated Craig Bellamy, Alan Shearer and Patrick Kluivert in his starting XI, though the policy once more failed to bear fruit.

A bright start saw the men in black and white go close on two occasions. Firstly, Roy Carroll saved a Shearer free-kick with his legs, and then Kluivert lashed Bellamy's lay-off inches over the crossbar.

The Dutchman was handed a lesson in how to finish after just seven minutes, however, with Rooney the teacher. Poor positioning from Titus Bramble enabled the young forward to volley Darren Fletcher's ball in from the right across Shay Given, as it dropped over his shoulder in the inside right channel.

Newcastle's Irish goalkeeper then blocked from Cristiano Ronaldo, before Shearer spurned a golden chance to draw the sides level. A rare mistake from Rio Ferdinand sent the striker clear, but he fired narrowly over as Carroll came to meet him.

Sir Alex Ferguson's team were dominating possession, but continued to look vulnerable in defence. A weak backpass from Rooney almost allowed Kluivert to cash in before the break, and Shearer did just that after 71 minutes.

The former England captain robbed substitute Wes Brown and raced into the area, beating Given with a left-footed finish. Just three minutes later, however, United went back in front, van Nistelrooy scoring from the spot after a push on Paul Scholes.

Ronny Johnsen and Bramble were booked for protesting that Andy O'Brien had been pushed in the action proceeding the penalty award, before Rooney, the perceived culprit, lashed home an injury-time third goal after a van Nistelrooy effort had been cleared off the line.

PREMIERSHIP FIXTURE HISTORY

Pl: 2 Draws: 0	Wins	Goals	Yellow	Red
West Bromwich Albion	1	2	0	0
Middlesbrough	1	2	1	0

STARTING LINE-UPS

Horsfield, Hulse, Kuszczak, Gaardsoe, Koumas

Doriva, Nash, Cooper, Morrison, Job

EVENT LINE

32 Purse (Own Goal)

37 **Earnshaw (Open Play)**

HALF TIME 1 - 1

52 Zenden (Open Play)

60 **Earnshaw (Off) Hulse (On)**

60 **Gera (Off) Horsfield (On)**

89 Zenden (Off) Doriva (On)

FULL TIME 1 - 2

STATISTICS

Season	Fixture		Fixture	Season
65	6	Shots On Target	7	101
66	10	Shots Off Target	4	84
2	0	Hit Woodwork	1	3
51	4	Caught Offside	1	40
76	7	Corners	10	71
177	15	Fouls	13	163
48%	53%	Possession	47%	51%

LEAGUE STANDINGS

Position (pos before)	W	D	L	F	A	Pts
18 (18) West Brom	1	6	6	12	24	9
4 (7) Middlesbrough	6	4	3	22	16	22

Sunday 14th November 2004 | Venue: **The Hawthorns** | Attendance: **24,008** | Referee: **S.W.Dunn**

WEST BROM 1 MIDDLESBROUGH 2

In a customary quirk of the fixture list, new boss Bryan Robson began his tenure at The Hawthorns against the club with whom he had started his managerial career.

The former England captain had been a popular player during his time with West Brom, but made a losing start to life in the dugout. A spirited showing from his charges, particularly in the first half, would have been welcome, but Middlesbrough triumphed 2-1.

Romanian Cosmin Contra was handed a belated Premiership debut on the right of midfield, while Neil Clement switched to a more familiar left-back role. For the visitors, Mark Viduka's recall at the expense of Joseph-Desire Job was the only change from their last league match.

The opening period would have pleased the home supporters, as the Baggies responded to an early scare, when Stewart Downing failed to score from close range, by constantly threatening their opponents' goal.

Australian international Mark Schwarzer had to make several important saves, most notably from Nwankwo Kanu and Cosmin Contra, as West Brom piled on the pressure. Failure to capitalise on this impressive spell ultimately cost the Midlanders though, when Darren Purse scored an own goal.

Jimmy Floyd Hasselbaink had already headed against the crossbar, when he was allowed time and space to advance down the left in the 32nd minute. The Dutch striker took full advantage of the situation, firing in a dangerous low ball that Purse diverted past his goalkeeper from within the six-yard box.

A strong response was required, and Robson's men did not disappoint. The away defence was tied in knots by Contra on the right of the area, and failed to deal with the low cross that Robert Earnshaw steered home from 10 yards out.

Unfortunately for their new boss, this was as good as it got for the Baggies. Middlesbrough improved significantly after the break, and netted the decisive goal through Boudewijn Zenden after 52 minutes.

Young starlet Downing created the chance down the left, eventually delivering a ball that his experienced midfield colleague nodded up and over Russell Hoult from 12 yards. A desperate late miss from Kanu then ensured that the points went north.

Boudewijn Zenden celebrates scoring the winning goal

PREMIERSHIP MILESTONE

Cosmin Contra and Rob Hulse both made their Premiership debuts

"It looked far easier to put it into the back of the net than to put it over the bar."

Bryan Robson on Nwankwo Kanu's astonishing miss

"We were disappointed with the first half, which was far too open for us, but we increased the intensity and killed the game in the second period."

Steve McClaren

PREMIERSHIP FIXTURE HISTORY

Pl: 2 Draws: 1	Wins	Goals	Yellow	Red
Arsenal	1	6	3	0
West Bromwich Albion	0	3	3	0

STARTING LINE-UPS

Arsenal: Lehmann; Lauren, Toure, Cygan, Cole; Ljungberg, Fabregas, Vieira (c), Pires; Bergkamp, Henry

West Brom: Hoult; Clement, Moore, Purse, Scimeca; Sakiri, Greening, Johnson, Contra; Gera; Kanu (c)

Arsenal substitutes: Reyes, van Persie, Almunia, Hoyte, Senderos

West Brom substitutes: Earnshaw, Horsfield, Gaardsoe, Kuszczak, Haas

EVENT LINE

HALF TIME 0 - 0

54 **Pires (Open Play)**

75 Contra (Off) Earnshaw (On)

75 Kanu (Off) Horsfield (On)

79 Earnshaw (Open Play)

81 **Fabregas (Off) Reyes (On)**

83 Gera (Foul)

84 Sakiri (Off) Gaardsoe (On)

88 **Bergkamp (Off) van Persie (On)**

FULL TIME 1 - 1

STATISTICS

Season	Fixture	Arsenal / West Brom	Fixture	Season
132	4	Shots On Target	2	67
67	7	Shots Off Target	2	68
6	0	Hit Woodwork	0	2
31	3	Caught Offside	5	56
83	12	Corners	3	79
151	9	Fouls	11	188
58%	65%	Possession	35%	47%

LEAGUE STANDINGS

Position (pos before)	W	D	L	F	A	Pts
2 (2) Arsenal	9	4	1	38	18	31
19 (18) West Brom	1	7	6	13	25	10

Saturday 20th November 2004 | Venue: **Highbury** | Attendance: **38,109** | Referee: **H.M.Webb**

ARSENAL 1 WEST BROM 1

Patrick Vieira challenges Artim Sakiri

"It's frustrating when we can't finish teams off."
Arsene Wenger

"I was very pleased. To go a goal behind at Arsenal and then get a point shows the quality of our performance."
Bryan Robson

PREMIERSHIP MILESTONE

50 Russell Hoult made his 50th Premiership appearance for West Brom

PREMIERSHIP MILESTONE

Artim Sakiri made his Premiership debut

West Brom picked up their first point under the guidance of new manager Bryan Robson, coming from behind to seal a memorable 1-1 draw at Highbury.

After another off-colour performance, it appeared that a 54th-minute Robert Pires goal would be enough to see Arsenal scrape home. Substitute Robert Earnshaw had other ideas, however, netting an equaliser just four minutes after being introduced to the action.

The Baggies were led out by former Gunner Nwankwo Kanu. The Nigerian was played as a lone striker, supported by Zoltan Gera, as the visitors sought to contain Arsene Wenger's side.

The policy proved successful in an opening period that saw the Londoners become increasingly frustrated. Patrick Vieira headed straight at Russell Hoult, Andy Johnson blocked a Thierry Henry drive, and Cesc Fabregas nodded over from a corner.

At the other end, a cross from the left evaded everyone except Gera at the back post. Fortunately for the home team, the Hungarian could only turn the ball into the side-netting.

Having heeded the warning, Arsenal carved out several decent chances either side of the interval. Both Fabregas and Henry forced smart stops from Hoult in the moments before the break, while the Frenchman's burst shortly after the restart should really have resulted in a shot on target.

The Gunners did not have to wait long for a goal though, as Pires' seemingly harmless 20-yard curler slipped through the hands of the goalkeeper and into the net. West Brom were rocked by the mistake, and could have fallen further behind.

Pascal Cygan failed to head home Bergkamp's deep cross, Henry sped past three tackles only to miscue, and Vieira fired wide when well-placed. These misses came back to haunt the Highbury outfit when Earnshaw struck with 11 minutes remaining.

Jonathan Greening did brilliantly to keep in a dropping ball on the right touchline, and delivered an inviting centre that the Welsh striker steered past Lehmann from eight yards out.

The equaliser was just reward for a determined display, but Arsenal really should have won a game in which they spurned so many chances.

PREMIERSHIP FIXTURE HISTORY

Pl: **6** Draws: **1**

	Wins	Goals	Yellow	Red
Chelsea	4	14	10	0
Bolton Wanderers	1	7	10	0

STARTING LINE-UPS

Chelsea subs: Bridge, Cudicini, Johnson, Parker, Kezman

Bolton subs: Giannakopoulos, Campo, Hierro, Poole, Vaz Te

EVENT LINE

1 Goal **Duff (Open Play)**

HALF TIME 1 - 0

48 Goal **Tiago (Corner)**

52 Goal Davies (Indirect Free Kick)

54 Sub Diouf (Off) Giannakopoulos (On)

59 Sub Nolan (Off) Campo (On)

75 Sub Okocha (Off) Hierro (On)

80 Sub **Duff (Off) Kezman (On)**

81 Sub **Gudjohnsen (Off) Johnson (On)**

85 Yellow card **Kezman (Foul)**

87 Goal Jaidi (Indirect Free Kick)

FULL TIME 2 - 2

STATISTICS

Season	Fixture (Chelsea)		Fixture (Bolton)	Season
106	11	Shots On Target	5	98
102	6	Shots Off Target	5	82
6	1	Hit Woodwork	0	4
44	4	Caught Offside	2	27
113	9	Corners	2	76
170	15	Fouls	9	188
56%	56%	Possession	44%	50%

LEAGUE STANDINGS

Position (pos before)		W	D	L	F	A	Pts
1 (1)	Chelsea	10	3	1	23	6	33
6 (5)	Bolton W	6	5	3	22	18	23

Saturday 20th November 2004 | Venue: **Stamford Bridge** | Attendance: **42,203** | Referee: **D.J.Gallagher**

CHELSEA 2 BOLTON WANDERERS 2

Bolton became the first team to breach the Chelsea defence on more than one occasion in the Jose Mourinho era, coming from two goals down to earn a valuable point.

With the kick-off delayed by half-an-hour as a result of a motorway accident that caused traffic chaos, Sam Allardyce's men were caught cold. Frank Lampard released Damien Duff, and the Irish winger strode purposefully forward to round the keeper and score from just inside the left edge of the six-yard box, within the first 60 seconds of play.

Many teams would have gone under at this point, but the Trotters are made of sterner stuff. Though they created few openings of note, the visitors restricted the men in blue to just a couple of half-chances in the remainder of the half.

It was the centre-backs that spurned these opportunities, both John Terry and Ricardo Carvalho heading over Jussi Jaaskelainen's crossbar from Arjen Robben corners.

Having established a foothold in the match, the last thing Bolton needed to do was concede another early goal after the interval. They did just that, however, as Tiago met Robben's near-post corner from the right with a deft finish, under pressure from Nicky Hunt.

The Lancashire side needed an immediate response, and got it courtesy of Kevin Davies in the 52nd minute. The robust forward climbed to meet Gary Speed's inswinging free-kick from the right, though his header appeared to find the net via the back of team-mate Radhi Jaidi.

Eidur Gudjohnsen then had two chances to put the game beyond Allardyce's charges. Firstly, the Icelandic international failed to connect properly with a close-range 58th-minute effort. Then, a marvellous run almost brought reward when his shot rebounded off the woodwork.

Chelsea's inability to net a decisive third goal proved costly, as Jaidi continued his scoring streak in the capital. With important goals at Arsenal and Tottenham already under his belt, the Tunisian rifled home from 15 yards out three minutes from time, after a free-kick from deep had been nodded into his path by Davies.

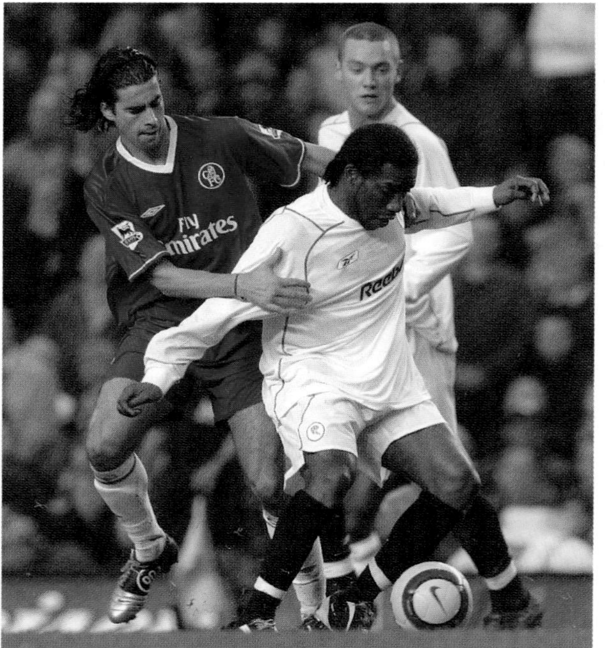

Tiago gets to grips with Jay-Jay Okocha

"I don't like their style of football and I would never play like that, but it's effective."

Jose Mourinho on Bolton

"Our team spirit is fantastic, and ultimately it was that which saw us through."

Sam Allardyce

PREMIERSHIP FIXTURE HISTORY

Pl: 3 Draws: 0	Wins	⚽	▯	■
Crystal Palace	0	1	2	0
Newcastle United	3	5	7	0

STARTING LINE-UPS

Crystal Palace: Kiraly; Boyce, Hall, Popovic (c), Granville; Routledge, Riihilahti, Watson, Kolkka; Hughes; Johnson

Newcastle United: Kluivert, Bellamy; Robert, Jenas (c), Bowyer, Dyer; Bernard, Johnsen, Bramble, Hughes; Given

Crystal Palace subs: Lakis, Freedman, Speroni, Leigertwood, Andrews

Newcastle United subs: Elliott, Milner, Caig, Ambrose, Ameobi

EVENT LINE

6 ▯ Johnsen (Foul)

36 ▯ Bernard (Foul)

HALF TIME 0 - 0

56 ⇄ Johnsen (Off) Elliott (On)

67 ▯ Elliott (Foul)

72 ⇄ Bowyer (Off) Milner (On)

79 ⚽ Kluivert (Open Play)

82 ▯ **Granville (Foul)**

83 ⇄ **Kolkka (Off) Lakis (On)**

84 ⇄ **Riihilahti (Off) Freedman (On)**

88 ⚽ Bellamy (Open Play)

FULL TIME 0 - 2

STATISTICS

Season	Fixture (Crystal Palace)		Fixture (Newcastle United)	Season
55	5	Shots On Target	9	116
62	2	Shots Off Target	8	80
3	0	Hit Woodwork	1	5
38	3	Caught Offside	6	44
66	3	Corners	5	110
196	13	Fouls	10	165
45%	44%	Possession	56%	50%

LEAGUE STANDINGS

Position (pos before)	W	D	L	F	A	Pts
16 (16) Crystal Palace	3	3	8	15	21	12
9 (10) Newcastle Utd	5	4	5	26	26	19

Saturday 20th November 2004 | Venue: Selhurst Park | Attendance: 22,937 | Referee: M.R.Halsey

CRYSTAL PALACE 0 NEWCASTLE UNITED 2

Newcastle made light of Alan Shearer's absence through injury, as the revamped strike-partnership of Patrick Kluivert and Craig Bellamy secured the points at Selhurst Park.

The win ended a run of three consecutive Premiership defeats for the Magpies, though they left it late to net the three points that their performance merited. It wasn't until 11 minutes from time that Kluivert opened the scoring, with Bellamy making the game safe in the 88th minute.

An entertaining opening period yielded plenty of chances. Nobody managed to connect with Laurent Robert's dangerous cross from the left for the visitors, while Joonas Kolkka curled an effort narrowly wide at the other end.

Graeme Souness felt his team could have been awarded two penalties for challenges on Kluivert and Robert, while Lee Bowyer fired over after Bellamy had got the better of Aki Riihilahti.

Having survived that scare, Crystal Palace finished the first half in the ascendancy. Shay Given made magnificent saves from Kolkka and Andy Johnson, before Ben Watson's low drive flew just the wrong side of the upright.

If the opening 45 minutes had produced an even contest, then the second period was certainly a bit more one-sided. Newcastle appeared determined to end their recent downturn in fortunes, and took the game by the scruff of the neck.

A weak finish from Bowyer failed to unduly trouble Gabor Kiraly, but Robert soon tested the keeper with a stinging low drive. Iain Dowie's men continually squandered possession, and were eventually punished in the 79th minute.

A quick break ended when Bellamy and Kluivert combined to deadly effect, the Dutchman nonchalantly converting his team-mate's low ball in from the right with the deftest of near-post flicks.

Any lingering doubts as to the destination of the points were soon dispelled, when Bellamy rammed Robert's measured pass into the roof of the net from 12 yards out after 88 minutes.

With the new-look forward line showing early promise, Alan Shearer may struggle to regain his starting place. Whatever the future holds, the Geordie public will hope that this victory signals the turning point in their season.

"We didn't pass the ball well, and our movement was not there."

Iain Dowie

"I thought Laurent Robert was outstanding, and believe Jermaine Jenas has the potential to be the best midfielder in Europe."

Graeme Souness

PREMIERSHIP MILESTONE

150 Ronny Johnsen made his 150th Premiership appearance

Craig Bellamy celebrates making it 2-0

PREMIERSHIP FIXTURE HISTORY

Pl: 4 Draws: 0	Wins	⚽	▢	■
Everton	4	8	5	1
Fulham	0	2	12	0

STARTING LINE-UPS

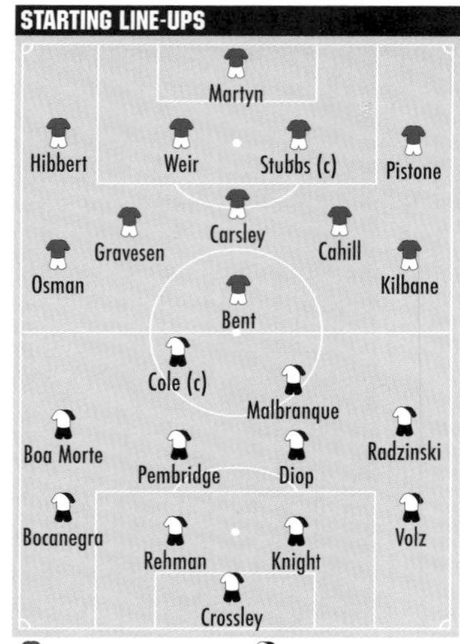

Ferguson, Watson, McFadden, Wright, Yobo

Legwinski, McBride, van der Sar, Pearce, Hammond

EVENT LINE

39 ▢ Diop (Foul)

HALF TIME 0 - 0

54 ⇄ Boa Morte (Off) Legwinski (On)

62 ⇄ **Osman (Off) Ferguson (On)**

67 ⚽ **Ferguson (Corner)**

81 ⇄ Diop (Off) McBride (On)

83 ⇄ **Bent (Off) Watson (On)**

88 ⇄ **Gravesen (Off) McFadden (On)**

FULL TIME 1 - 0

STATISTICS

Season	Fixture	Everton / Fulham	Fixture	Season
81	7	Shots On Target	4	67
72	6	Shots Off Target	2	61
3	0	Hit Woodwork	0	2
41	2	Caught Offside	2	32
79	12	Corners	7	68
165	9	Fouls	22	177
50%	55%	Possession	45%	48%

LEAGUE STANDINGS

Position (pos before)		W	D	L	F	A	Pts
3 (3)	Everton	9	2	3	16	11	29
13 (13)	Fulham	4	2	8	17	25	14

Saturday 20th November 2004 | Venue: **Goodison Park** | Attendance: **34,763** | Referee: **G.Poll**

EVERTON 1 FULHAM 0

A goal from substitute Duncan Ferguson midway through the second half ensured that Everton recorded their sixth 1-0 victory of the season.

The match was not a pretty spectacle, though the majority of the Goodison Park crowd did not let that bother them as they celebrated a win that moved the Toffees closer to both Chelsea and Arsenal in the Premiership table.

David Moyes' men shaded a dire opening period in which industry and commitment were the watchwords. After his acrimonious departure in the summer, Tomasz Radzinski's every touch was greeted with a crescendo of boos.

In truth, this was all either set of fans had to shout about in an insipid opening 20 minutes. Things improved after this, with Tim Cahill heading narrowly over after a fine move down the right involving Leon Osman.

The final five minutes of the half saw a flurry of goalmouth activity. Nigel Martyn did well to keep out a headed flick from Radzinski, while Mark Crossley acrobatically turned over a seven-yard volley from Osman.

While Fulham continued to struggle to find their rhythm after the break, the Merseysiders began to click into gear. Marcus Bent was the catalyst for an improved showing, creating another headed chance for Cahill, and then forcing Crossley into a fine diving save from distance.

The pressure was mounting, with Bent's recently-introduced strike-partner Ferguson making the all-important breakthrough after 67 minutes. A right-wing corner was helped on by Kevin Kilbane, and the tall Scot stooped to nod the ball home from 4 yards out at the back post.

Unsurprisingly, being behind sparked Chris Coleman's team into life. A comedy of defensive errors presented visiting captain Andy Cole with two chances to level the scores, but all the striker succeeded in doing was initiating an ultimately fruitless scramble inside the Everton box.

A last-gasp miss by Radzinski was a further lucky escape for Moyes' men, though the Cottagers did not really deserve anything from a game to which they had contributed very little.

"We're not getting carried away, but I want the fans to enjoy saturdays as much as I am now."
David Moyes

"I thought we competed well with Everton. We worked hard and had some decent chances, but at this level you've got to put those chances away."
Chris Coleman

Moritz Volz tries to fend off Kevin Kilbane

PREMIERSHIP FIXTURE HISTORY

Pl: 6 Draws: 1	Wins	⚽	▢	■
Manchester United	5	14	3	0
Charlton Athletic	0	3	3	0

STARTING LINE-UPS

Manchester United: Carroll; Brown, Ferdinand, Silvestre, Fortune; Fletcher, Scholes, Keane (c), Giggs; Rooney, van Nistelrooy

Charlton Athletic: Bartlett; Thomas, Holland (c), Murphy, Kishishev, Johansson; Hreidarsson, Perry, El Karkouri, Young; Kiely

Subs: Smith, P.Neville, O'Shea, Howard, Ronaldo

Subs: Fortune, Konchesky, Jeffers, Andersen, Euell

EVENT LINE

41 ⚽ **Giggs (Open Play)**

HALF TIME 1 - 0

46 Perry (Off) Fortune (On)

50 ⚽ **Scholes (Open Play)**

57 Thomas (Off) Konchesky (On)

75 Bartlett (Off) Jeffers (On)

76 **van Nistelrooy (Off) Smith (On)**

80 **Keane (Off) Neville P (On)**

84 **Fletcher (Off) O'Shea (On)**

FULL TIME 2 - 0

STATISTICS

Season	Fixture (Man Utd)		Fixture (Charlton)	Season
110	11	Shots On Target	2	62
96	9	Shots Off Target	3	48
6	0	Hit Woodwork	0	2
51	7	Caught Offside	2	49
107	6	Corners	3	51
173	8	Fouls	13	183
54%	55%	Possession	45%	44%

LEAGUE STANDINGS

Position (pos before)		W	D	L	F	A	Pts
5 (7)	Man Utd	6	6	2	16	10	24
10 (9)	Charlton Ath	5	3	6	17	23	18

Saturday 20th November 2004 | Venue: **Old Trafford** | Attendance: **67,704** | Referee: **R.Styles**

MANCHESTER UNITED 2 CHARLTON ATHLETIC 0

Paul Scholes celebrates a return to goalscoring form

"In these sorts of games you have to be patient. We were patient and also played some imaginative football."
Sir Alex Ferguson

PREMIERSHIP MILESTONE

300 Paul Scholes celebrated his 300th Premiership appearance with a goal

"We worked ever so hard to contain and stop United, but had nothing much going the other way."
Alan Curbishley

Goals either side of half-time from Ryan Giggs and Paul Scholes propelled Manchester United towards an important three points in this lunchtime kick-off.

The result was rarely in doubt after Giggs' mazy run ended with a deflected shot past Dean Kiely in the 41st minute, with Scholes then ending a personal goal drought at club level, stretching back to April's F.A.Cup Semi-Final against Arsenal, five minutes after the break.

Charlton contributed very little to the match, with Alan Curbishley's five-man midfield tending to focus more on going backwards than forwards. The opposite was true for the home side, with full-backs Wes Brown and Quinton Fortune surging upfield at every opportunity.

Sir Alex Ferguson's men attacked from the outset. In just the second minute, Kiely repelled a Ruud van Nistelrooy header, following Brown's deep cross from the right. A hat-trick of chances then came and went for Scholes, before United benefitted from a slice of luck.

With four minutes left of the first half, Giggs embarked on a mazy run that took him into the penalty area. With defenders backing off, the Welsh winger hit a 12-yard shot from the inside right channel that found the net via the right boot of Luke Young.

The goal released much of the tension inside Old Trafford, and a second was not long in arriving after the interval. Patient build-up play down the right ended when Scotsman Darren Fletcher centred for Scholes to score with an acrobatic volley.

The Addicks finally conjured up an effort of their own, though Talal El Karkouri's long-range free-kick did not trouble Roy Carroll. Not until the dying embers of the game did the Londoners threaten to any serious extent, with Young and Hermann Hreidarsson both failing to hit the target when well-placed.

In between times, Wayne Rooney had three golden opportunities to extend the lead. The young striker began by blazing over from six yards, then cut in from the left to unleash a drive that was blocked, before finishing with a low shot that was kept out by Kiely.

In the end, 2-0 flattered Charlton more than it did United.

PREMIERSHIP FIXTURE HISTORY

Pl: 10 Draws: 2	Wins	⚽	▯	▮
Middlesbrough	5	13	21	0
Liverpool	3	11	18	0

STARTING LINE-UPS

Schwarzer

McMahon, Riggott, Southgate (c), Queudrue

Parlour, Boateng, Zenden, Downing

Hasselbaink, Viduka

Kewell, Garcia

Riise, Alonso, Hamann, Finnan

Traore, Hyypia (c), Carragher, Josemi

Kirkland

Job, Nemeth, Nash, Cooper, Doriva

Gerrard, Biscan, Dudek, Mellor, Sinama-Pongolle

EVENT LINE

31 ▯ Hyypia (Ung.Conduct)

36 ⚽ **Riggott (Open Play)**

41 ▯ **Zenden (Foul)**

HALF TIME 1 - 0

56 ⇄ Hamann (Off) Gerrard (On)

57 ▯ **Southgate (Foul)**

58 ▯ Josemi (Foul)

62 ⚽ **Zenden (Open Play)**

70 ⇄ Josemi (Off) Sinama-Pongolle (On)

76 ▯ **Boateng (Foul)**

83 ⇄ Alonso (Off) Biscan (On)

86 ⇄ **Hasselbaink (Off) Job (On)**

89 ⇄ **Zenden (Off) Nemeth (On)**

FULL TIME 2 - 0

STATISTICS

Season	Fixture		Fixture	Season
107	6	Shots On Target	10	91
92	8	Shots Off Target	7	88
3	0	Hit Woodwork	0	2
40	0	Caught Offside	1	37
74	3	Corners	5	74
177	14	Fouls	10	165
50%	48%	Possession	52%	54%

LEAGUE STANDINGS

Position (pos before)		W	D	L	F	A	Pts
4 (4)	Middlesbrough	7	4	3	24	16	25
8 (8)	Liverpool	6	2	5	21	15	20

Saturday 20th November 2004 | Venue: **Riverside Stadium** | Attendance: **34,751** | Referee: **S.G.Bennett**

MIDDLESBROUGH 2 LIVERPOOL 0

Middlesbrough made it seven Premiership matches without defeat, as goals in each half from Chris Riggott and Boudewijn Zenden saw off Liverpool at the Riverside Stadium.

With Milan Baros having joined Djibril Cisse on the injury list, Rafael Benitez opted for experience over youth in his attacking partnership, pairing Luis Garcia with Harry Kewell. Despite this lack of strikers, the manager was boosted by the return to the bench of inspirational captain Steven Gerrard.

Little of note took place in the opening half-hour of a tepid contest, though things livened up soon afterwards. Chris Kirkland saved well from Jimmy Floyd Hasselbaink, before Riggott became an unlikely home hero after 36 minutes.

The tall defender remained forward following a set-piece, and was on hand to steer Stewart Downing's left-wing cross into the net from close range with his right foot. The Liverpool keeper could do nothing on this occasion, but soon had to be alert when racing from his line to deny Mark Viduka.

The Merseysiders were then denied an equaliser, when Garcia saw his accomplished finish ruled out for offside. Creditably, visiting heads did not drop, and it was the men from Anfield who looked the likelier scorers after the break.

Mark Schwarzer denied his international team-mate Kewell with a save that is best described as miraculous. The former Bradford custodian appeared beaten, only to divert the ball up and onto the roof of his net with a last-gasp flick of the wrist.

With 56 minutes played, Gerrard ended a two-month injury absence by replacing Dietmar Hamann. Unfortunately for Benitez, his returning leader had little time to adjust to the pace of the game before Middlesbrough went two up.

Dutch midfielder Zenden hit the target for the third time in four Premiership matches, marginally beating the offside trap to collect Hasselbaink's pass and beat Kirkland with a low 12-yard toe-poke.

There was no way back for the visitors after this, with Kewell's failure to capitalise on a gaping goal representing their only real opening. Steve McClaren's team not only won on the day, but may well pip Liverpool to a Champions League place.

Boudewijn Zenden makes it 2-0

"We beat a very good team today. Despite all their injuries, they are still a very good team."

Steve McClaren

PREMIERSHIP MILESTONE

100 Franck Queudrue made his 100th Premiership appearance

"In my opinion, we started well. For 20 minutes, we controlled the game."

Rafael Benitez

Saturday 20th November 2004	Venue: **Carrow Road**	Attendance: **23,706**	Referee: **M.A.Riley**

NORWICH CITY 2 SOUTHAMPTON 1

Damien Francis was the hero, as Norwich came from a goal down to record their first Premiership win of the season.

Southampton arrived at Carrow Road on the back of an important derby victory against Portsmouth, and went in front through a 24th-minute James Beattie strike. The Canaries hit back, however, with a goal in each half from Francis helping to secure the points.

The home side began brightly, with Phil Mulryne forcing an early save from Kasey Keller. Referee Mike Riley then turned down a strong penalty appeal, when Jason Dodd appeared to handle Darren Huckerby's cross.

Paul Telfer and Francis both worked the goalkeepers, before the visitors took an unwarranted lead. There seemed little danger as Beattie prepared to strike an awkwardly bouncing ball from distance, but the former England international managed to find the net with a searing effort that went in off the inside of the left-hand upright.

Far from crumble under the weight of this hammer blow, Norwich drew level just four minutes later. Again a shot went in via a post, but this time it was Francis who steered home from 15 yards after great work by Leon McKenzie.

After a spell of further pressure from the men in yellow, Southampton had two great chances to re-establish an advantage. Dexter Blackstock saw a swivelling shot repelled by Robert Green, with Francis then clearing off the line from Telfer.

Despite opening the second period by forcing a couple of corners of their own, the Saints fell behind from a 52nd-minute flag-kick. Craig Fleming rose well to win the initial header, and Francis nodded the ball past a helpless Keller from inside the six-yard box.

David Bentley continued to trouble the away defence, and delivered an inviting cross from the right that evaded everyone. From then on in all the attacking came from the South Coast team though, as Nigel Worthington's charges defended deeper and deeper.

A nail-biting finish ensued, but Norwich held on to secure a win that drew them level on points with their opponents.

Damien Francis earns Norwich their first Premiership victory

"This was a great result today. We had to do the nasty business first, then go on and win it."
Nigel Worthington

"When you get your nose in front, you expect to go on and win the game."
Steve Wigley

PREMIERSHIP FIXTURE HISTORY

Pl: 4 Draws: 1	Wins	Goals	Yellow	Red
Norwich City	2	9	3	0
Southampton	1	8	6	0

STARTING LINE-UPS

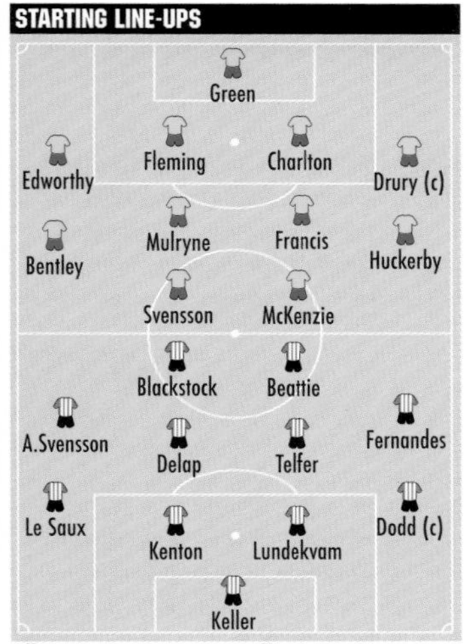

Subs (Norwich): Helveg, Ward, Safri, Jonson, Doherty

Subs (Southampton): Phillips, Nilsson, Crouch, Blayney, Jakobsson

EVENT LINE

24 ⚽ Beattie (Open Play)
28 ⚽ **Francis (Open Play)**
45 ▢ Kenton (Foul)
HALF TIME 1 - 1
52 ⚽ **Francis (Corner)**
60 ⇄ Blackstock (Off) Phillips (On)
67 ▢ **Bentley (Foul)**
72 ⇄ Telfer (Off) Nilsson (On)
83 ⇄ Dodd (Off) Crouch (On)
FULL TIME 2 - 1

STATISTICS

Season	Fixture (Norwich)		Fixture (Southampton)	Season
72	8	Shots On Target	7	71
81	1	Shots Off Target	7	78
3	0	Hit Woodwork	0	2
54	4	Caught Offside	1	37
71	4	Corners	6	79
201	20	Fouls	14	192
47%	43%	Possession	57%	50%

LEAGUE STANDINGS

Position (pos before)	W	D	L	F	A	Pts
18 (20) Norwich C	1	8	5	13	24	11
17 (17) Southampton	2	5	7	13	19	11

PREMIERSHIP FIXTURE HISTORY

Pl: 2 Draws: 0	Wins	⚽	☐	■
Portsmouth	1	5	3	0
Manchester City	1	5	2	0

STARTING LINE-UPS

Portsmouth: Ashdown; De Zeeuw (c), Stefanovic, Primus, Unsworth; Faye, Quashie, O'Neil, Berger; Lua Lua, Fuller

Manchester City: Macken, Anelka; Sibierski, S.Wright-Phillips, Barton, Bosvelt; Jordan, Onuoha, Distin (c), Dunne; James

Substitutes (Portsmouth): Berkovic, Griffin, Wapenaar, Cisse, Taylor

Substitutes (Manchester City): Fowler, Waterreus, Sommeil, Flood, B.Wright-Phillips

EVENT LINE

6 ⚽ Wright-Phillips S (Open Play)

8 ⚽ **O'Neil (Open Play)**

26 **Lua Lua (Off) Berkovic (On)**

27 Anelka (Off) Fowler (On)

38 ☐ **Faye (Foul)**

42 ☐ **Unsworth (Foul)**

45 ☐ **De Zeeuw (Foul)**

HALF TIME 1 - 1

74 **Berger (Off) Taylor (On)**

79 ⚽ Sibierski (Open Play)

85 **Primus (Off) Griffin (On)**

87 ⚽ Bosvelt (Open Play)

FULL TIME 1 - 3

STATISTICS

Season	Fixture		Fixture	Season
74	7	Shots On Target	13	90
66	2	Shots Off Target	5	71
2	0	Hit Woodwork	0	2
30	3	Caught Offside	1	46
66	8	Corners	11	90
153	8	Fouls	15	188
47%	47%	Possession	53%	47%

LEAGUE STANDINGS

Position (pos before)	W	D	L	F	A	Pts
12 (11) Portsmouth	4	3	6	17	20	15
11 (12) Man City	4	5	5	17	14	17

Saturday 20th November 2004 | Venue: **Fratton Park** | Attendance: **20,101** | Referee: **M.D.Messias**

PORTSMOUTH 1 MANCHESTER CITY 3

Joey Barton congratulates Paul Bosvelt on his goal

"With 15 minutes to go, even at half-time, I was looking at my watch and hoping for a draw."

Harry Redknapp

PREMIERSHIP MILESTONE

Jamie Ashdown made his Premiership debut

"I think Shaun Wright-Phillips is the best player in England at the moment in terms of potential."

Kevin Keegan

PREMIERSHIP MILESTONE

Paul Bosvelt scored his first Premiership goal

Shaun Wright-Phillips put the racist taunts he had faced during England's midweek friendly in Madrid behind him, inspiring Manchester City to a 3-1 win at Fratton Park.

The young winger took just six minutes to make an impact, capitalising on some hesitant defending to dispossess Dejan Stefanovic and slot the ball low past Jamie Ashdown from eight yards out.

Portsmouth hit back almost immediately, however, as Gary O'Neil, recently recalled from a loan spell at Cardiff City, volleyed home David Unsworth's left-wing centre from inside the six-yard box.

First half injuries forced both managers into unplanned substitutions. Eyal Berkovic and Robbie Fowler entered the fray at the expense of Lomana Tresor Lua Lua and Nicolas Anelka respectively.

It was Harry Redknapp's charges that finished the opening period with a flourish. Senegalese international Amdy Faye headed over from a free-kick, before City captain Sylvain Distin did well to block a goalbound O'Neil drive.

After the break, it was Kevin Keegan's men that dominated proceedings. Just five minutes in, Wright-Phillips surged past two defenders, only to fire a shot narrowly wide. Stand-in custodian Ashdown then did well to turn away a Paul Bosvelt curler, as the pressure continued to mount.

Former Liverpool striker Fowler was next to test the keeper, and then played a crucial role in the visitors taking a 2-1 lead. With 11 minutes remaining, the substitute got the better of Unsworth, who suspected the ball had gone out, on the right touchline, and sent over a deep cross that Antoine Sibierski drilled into the net from 12 yards.

The scoring was not completed, as Bosvelt added a third in the 87th minute. The Dutchman profited from more great play by Wright-Phillips, tapping into an unguarded goal after Ashdown had denied what would have been a majestic solo effort.

With rumours rife about Redknapp's disappointment at chairman Milan Mandaric's decision to appoint Croatian Velimir Zajec to a role as 'Director of Football' at the club, a 3-1 home reverse was the last thing that Portsmouth's popular boss needed.

PREMIERSHIP FIXTURE HISTORY

Pl: 3 Draws: 3	Wins	⚽	□	■
Blackburn Rovers	0	5	3	1
Birmingham City	0	5	4	0

STARTING LINE-UPS

Blackburn Rovers: Friedel; Todd, Johansson; Neill, McEveley; Ferguson (c), Tugay; Reid, Emerton; Dickov, Jansen

Birmingham City: Morrison, Dunn; Gronkjaer, Anderton, Savage, Johnson; Gray, Upson, Cunningham (c), Melchiot; Maik Taylor

Substitutes (Blackburn): Gallagher, Thompson, Enckelman, Matteo, Pedersen

Substitutes (Birmingham): Clapham, Yorke, Clemence, Vaesen, Martin Taylor

EVENT LINE

4 ⚽ **Jansen (Open Play)**

17 ⚽ Anderton (Open Play)

22 □ Johnson (Foul)

38 ⚽ Savage (Open Play)

45 □ **Ferguson (Foul)**

45 ⚽ Dunn (Open Play)

HALF TIME 1 - 3

46 ⇄ **Jansen (Off) Gallagher (On)**

56 ⇄ **Tugay (Off) Thompson (On)**

57 ⚽ **Reid (Open Play)**

63 ⚽ **Gallagher (Open Play)**

65 ⇄ Morrison (Off) Clapham (On)

74 ⇄ Anderton (Off) Yorke (On)

80 ⇄ Dunn (Off) Clemence (On)

FULL TIME 3 - 3

STATISTICS

Season	Fixture	Blackburn	Birmingham Fixture	Season
69	10	Shots On Target	5	59
78	5	Shots Off Target	3	71
2	0	Hit Woodwork	1	2
53	3	Caught Offside	2	40
79	6	Corners	9	82
215	12	Fouls	9	191
48%	50%	Possession	50%	50%

LEAGUE STANDINGS

Position (pos before)	W	D	L	F	A	Pts
20 (20) Blackburn R	1	7	6	14	29	10
14 (15) Birmingham C	2	7	5	11	14	13

Sunday 21st November 2004 | Venue: **Ewood Park** | Attendance: **20,290** | Referee: **N.S.Barry**

BLACKBURN ROVERS 3 BIRMINGHAM CITY 3

Blackburn and Birmingham served up an unexpectedly thrilling encounter, sharing six goals at Ewood Park.

Having taken an early lead, Rovers found themselves 3-1 down at the interval, but hit back in the second half to rescue a point. Whilst being understandably disappointed with the final outcome, visiting boss Steve Bruce could at least take heart from the fact that his side seemed to have rediscovered their scoring touch.

The opening goal arrived after just four minutes, courtesy of Matt Jansen. The move was right out of the top-drawer, with the former Crystal Palace forward lashing home from just inside the area after Paul Dickov had cleverly dummied Steven Reid's ball inside from the right.

The Midlanders did not have to wait too long to draw level though, Darren Anderton netting for the second away game in succession after 17 minutes. David Dunn inadvertently steered Jesper Gronkjaer's low cross from the left into the path of his team-mate, and the midfielder poked the ball past Brad Friedel with aplomb.

Former Wales manager Mark Hughes then saw his team fall behind to a strike from a vital member of his international outfit. Robbie Savage showed good agility to convert Mario Melchiot's deflected cross, leaving Friedel rooted to the spot.

After Damien Johnson had gone close, another former Rover, Dunn, extended the lead on the stroke of half-time. Again Melchiot was the architect, with the returning hero coolly side-footing home his low right-wing centre from 10 yards.

Few supporters would have expected a Blackburn comeback, but that is exactly what they got. With 57 minutes played, substitute David Thompson released Reid with his first touch, and the former Millwall man fired a deflected drive high into the roof of Maik Taylor's net.

Then, six minutes later, Thompson was involved once more, sending Dickov on a chase behind the Birmingham defence. The tenacious Scot outmuscled Kenny Cunningham to send the ball trickling towards goal, with countryman Paul Gallagher arriving to administer the final touch.

A frantic finish saw Savage clip a post and Taylor thwart Dickov, though a point was probably a fair result.

Barry Ferguson fells Damien Johnson

"We did some very good things today, but there were far too many bad things as well."
Mark Hughes

"Having gone 3-1 up, it was disappointing that we didn't see the game out."
Steve Bruce

PREMIERSHIP MILESTONE

Steven Reid netted his first Premiership goal

Monday 22nd November 2004	Venue: **Villa Park**	Attendance: **35,702**	Referee: **C.J.Foy**

PREMIERSHIP FIXTURE HISTORY

Pl: **13** Draws: **4**	Wins	⚽	▯	▮
Aston Villa	**8**	**18**	**11**	**0**
Tottenham Hotspur	**1**	**8**	**15**	**0**

STARTING LINE-UPS

Barry, L.Moore, Postma, Ridgewell, Whittingham

Ziegler, Keane, Davenport, Fulop, Redknapp

EVENT LINE

HALF TIME 0 - 0

46 Edman (Off) Ziegler (On)

57 **Solano (Corner)**

69 Mendes (Off) Keane (On)

76 **Hitzlsperger (Off) Barry (On)**

83 Defoe (Off) Davenport (On)

86 **Solano (Off) Moore L (On)**

FULL TIME 1 - 0

STATISTICS

Season	Fixture		Fixture	Season
84	**3**	Shots On Target	**5**	**76**
72	**5**	Shots Off Target	**4**	**78**
3	**0**	Hit Woodwork	**0**	**5**
41	**7**	Caught Offside	**3**	**51**
81	**5**	Corners	**5**	**61**
222	**18**	Fouls	**12**	**183**
48%	**47%**	Possession	**53%**	**47%**

LEAGUE STANDINGS

Position (pos before)		W	D	L	F	A	Pts
5 (7)	**Aston Villa**	**6**	**6**	**2**	**20**	**14**	**24**
15 (15)	**Tottenham H**	**3**	**4**	**7**	**12**	**17**	**13**

Olof Mellberg and Frederic Kanoute audition for 'Come Dancing'

"Nolberto Solano is always likely to come up with something special, and it was a great winning goal."

Assistant Manager Roy Aitken

PREMIERSHIP MILESTONE

50 Carlton Cole made his 50th Premiership appearance

"We gave away a sloppy goal, and we didn't expect them to score from a set-piece."

Martin Jol

PREMIERSHIP MILESTONE

Calum Davenport made his first Premiership appearance for Tottenham

ASTON VILLA 1 TOTTENHAM HOTSPUR 0

A moment of individual brilliance from Nolberto Solano was enough to settle this encounter, as Tottenham suffered a sixth consecutive Premiership defeat.

The Peruvian displayed skills more associated with his continental cousins from Brazil, controlling, swivelling and finishing in one fluid movement, after Gavin McCann had helped on Thomas Hitzlsperger's 57th-minute corner from the right.

The goal was a memorable moment in an otherwise forgettable match. Neither side were at their best, with chances restricted to a premium as a result of some assured defending by the likes of Olof Mellberg and Ledley King.

David O'Leary demonstrated his well-known faith in youth by handing Steven Davis a first start in the centre of midfield. For Tottenham, Martin Jol opted to pair Jermain Defoe and Frederic Kanoute in attack, meaning Robbie Keane had to be content with a place on the bench.

Aston Villa shaded a first half that saw some good football played outside the two penalty areas. Juan Pablo Angel was unlucky not to win a penalty, when Erik Edman appeared to prevent him from jumping for an inviting cross.

The Londoners posed a threat on the break, and Michael Brown could have scored after 38 minutes. Fortunately for the home team, Thomas Sorensen was able to comfortably smother the former Sheffield United man's low effort.

The visitors continued to worry their hosts after the interval, as Defoe forced a smart stop from close range and then sent another strike wide of the post. With away hopes raised, it was Solano who then scored what turned out to be the all-important goal.

Having had little chance of denying the former Newcastle midfielder, Paul Robinson bravely prevented him from adding a second. The keeper made full use of his wingspan, as he rushed from his line to produce a vital block.

Tottenham withstood further Villa pressure in the closing stages, with Ulises De la Cruz unlucky not to find the net. Despite the 69th-minute introduction of Keane, the White Hart Lane club lacked the creative spark needed to unlock a resolute defence, thus leaving them empty-handed.

PREMIERSHIP FIXTURE HISTORY

Pl: 1 Draws: 1	Wins	Goals	Yellow cards	Red cards
Birmingham City	0	1	2	0
Norwich City	0	1	1	0

STARTING LINE-UPS

Gronkjaer, Clemence, Yorke, Vaesen, Martin Taylor

McKenzie, Helveg, Ward, Doherty, Jonson

EVENT LINE

9	**Morrison (Open Play)**
33	**Melchiot (Dissent)**
	HALF TIME 1 - 0
46	**Melchiot (Off) Gronkjaer (On)**
54	Brennan (Off) McKenzie (On)
58	Holt (Off) Helveg (On)
64	Huckerby (Open Play)
68	**Dunn (Foul)**
76	**Dunn (Off) Clemence (On)**
79	**Morrison (Off) Yorke (On)**
81	Bentley (Foul)
	FULL TIME 1 - 1

STATISTICS

Season	Fixture		Fixture	Season
69	10	Shots On Target	3	75
77	6	Shots Off Target	4	85
3	1	Hit Woodwork	0	3
40	0	Caught Offside	3	57
88	6	Corners	1	72
205	14	Fouls	12	213
50%	53%	Possession	47%	47%

LEAGUE STANDINGS

Position (pos before)	W	D	L	F	A	Pts
13 (14) Birmingham C	2	8	5	12	15	14
19 (18) Norwich C	1	9	5	14	25	12

Saturday 27th November 2004 | Venue: **St Andrew's** | Attendance: **29,120** | Referee: **G.Poll**

BIRMINGHAM CITY 1 NORWICH CITY 1

In a first meeting since the 2002 'Division One Playoff Final', Birmingham and Norwich were again level after 90 minutes.

An early Clinton Morrison goal looked set to propel Steve Bruce's side towards only their third Premiership victory of the season, but the Canaries hit back through a 64th-minute Darren Huckerby strike.

Things began brilliantly for the West Midlands outfit, as they took the lead inside the opening 10 minutes. Summer signing Emile Heskey headed against the crossbar, with Morrison on hand to nod in the rebound from close range.

The former Crystal Palace forward had chances to complete a first half hat-trick, but was twice thwarted by the impressive Robert Green. Birmingham were completely dominant, and Heskey failed to capitalise on their superiority on two further occasions.

Nigel Worthington's words to his players at the interval would not have been kind ones, and they emerged for the second period as a much stronger force. David Bentley was particularly vibrant, causing many problems with his positive running.

With 64 minutes played, Norwich got the reward their improved performance deserved. Indecisive goalkeeping from Maik Taylor allowed a ball from the right to reach Huckerby at the back post, and the forward slammed home from inside the six-yard box.

From this point on, only one team looked capable of winning the match. The Canaries poured forward in search of a second consecutive Premiership victory, with Matthias Svensson proving a real handful for Kenny Cunningham and Matthew Upson.

Despite their dominance, the Carrow Road club struggled to carve out anything more than half-chances in the latter stages. The best of these fell to goalscorer Huckerby, but he was unable to find a way past Taylor.

There was still time for a scare at the other end, as Robbie Savage headed weakly at Green from close range. The Welsh midfielder was furious with himself, an emotion that summed up how many of the home supporters were feeling.

Boos rang out around St Andrew's at the final whistle, a far cry from the reaction that greeted Birmingham's victorious players on that glorious May bank holiday at the Millennium Stadium.

Darren Huckerby celebrates making it 1-1

"The game should have been over at half-time. We had umpteen chances to have made it 2-0, and at the end frustration crept in."

Steve Bruce

PREMIERSHIP MILESTONE

100 David Dunn made his 100th Premiership appearance

"When it was 1-0, I always thought we could get something from the game."

Nigel Worthington

PREMIERSHIP FIXTURE HISTORY

Pl: **2** Draws: **0**

	Wins	⚽	Yellow	Red
Bolton Wanderers	1	1	1	0
Portsmouth	1	1	2	1

STARTING LINE-UPS

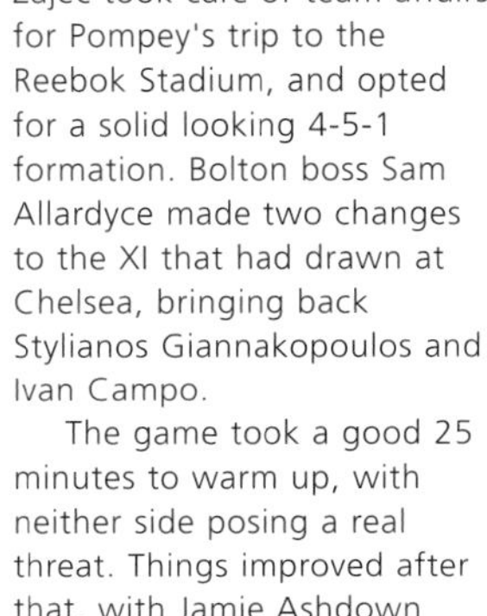

Hierro, Pedersen, Nolan, Oakes, Ben Haim

Faye, Wapenaar, Cisse, Berkovic, Harper

EVENT LINE

45 ⚽ De Zeeuw (Indirect Free Kick)

HALF TIME 0 - 1

57 **Gardner (Off) Hierro (On)**

62 **N'Gotty (Off) Pedersen (On)**

86 Quashie (Foul)

88 **Campo (Off) Nolan (On)**

88 Taylor (Off) Faye (On)

FULL TIME 0 - 1

STATISTICS

Season	Fixture (Bolton)		Fixture (Portsmouth)	Season
108	**10**	Shots On Target	**4**	**78**
91	**9**	Shots Off Target	**4**	**70**
4	**0**	Hit Woodwork	**0**	**2**
28	**1**	Caught Offside	**3**	**33**
83	**7**	Corners	**6**	**72**
201	**13**	Fouls	**14**	**167**
49%	**49%**	Possession	**51%**	**47%**

LEAGUE STANDINGS

Position (pos before)		W	D	L	F	A	Pts
7 (7)	**Bolton W**	**6**	**5**	**4**	**22**	**19**	**23**
11 (12)	**Portsmouth**	**5**	**3**	**6**	**18**	**20**	**18**

Saturday 27th November 2004 | Venue: **Reebok Stadium** | Attendance: **25,008** | Referee: **S.W.Dunn**

BOLTON WANDERERS 0 PORTSMOUTH 1

Portsmouth responded to the departure of manager Harry Redknapp by recording their first Premiership away win of the season.

Captain Arjan De Zeeuw was the hero, heading home the only goal of the game on the stroke of half-time. The same player later showed amazing levels of restraint, failing to react adversely when El-Hadji Diouf spat in his face.

Recently appointed 'Executive Director' Velimir Zajec took care of team affairs for Pompey's trip to the Reebok Stadium, and opted for a solid looking 4-5-1 formation. Bolton boss Sam Allardyce made two changes to the XI that had drawn at Chelsea, bringing back Stylianos Giannakopoulos and Ivan Campo.

The game took a good 25 minutes to warm up, with neither side posing a real threat. Things improved after that, with Jamie Ashdown saving from Diouf and Patrik Berger testing Jussi Jaaskelainen.

With Wanderers beginning to look the more likely scorers, Portsmouth went in front. An inswinging Gary O'Neil free-kick from the left was met by the head of De Zeeuw eight yards out, leaving the keeper with no chance.

The award of the set-piece, following a challenge by Nicky Hunt, seemed a harsh one, though Bolton did not dwell on their misfortune after the break. Within a minute of the restart, both Diouf and Kevin Davies had gone close to an equaliser.

Radhi Jaidi then failed to find the net from six yards, before Gary Speed headed straight at Ashdown. The visitors were not without chances though, Berger ending a run from halfway by shooting narrowly wide and lone striker Ricardo Fuller nearly beating Jaaskelainen at his near post.

As time ebbed away, the Trotters became increasingly desperate. Steve Dunn was unmoved when Diouf tumbled in the box under challenge from Andy Griffin, while Jay-Jay Okocha was a whisker away with a well-struck free-kick.

A goal would not come for the home side, as Zajec demonstrated his tactical acumen to the travelling fans. If there had been one criticism of the Redknapp regime, it was that Portsmouth were too easy to beat on the road - maybe not any more.

Arjan De Zeeuw celebrates with Andy Griffin

"They did to us what we have been doing to other clubs in away games."

Sam Allardyce

"It's been a great end to what has been a tough week for us."

Portsmouth coach Kevin Bond

PREMIERSHIP FIXTURE HISTORY

Pl: 6 Draws: 0	Wins	⚽	□	■
Charlton Athletic	3	10	6	1
Chelsea	3	11	11	0

STARTING LINE-UPS

Kiely

Young, El Karkouri, Fortune, Konchesky

Holland (c), Murphy, Kishishev

Johansson, Thomas

Bartlett

Robben, Gudjohnsen, Duff

Lampard, Makelele, Tiago

Gallas, Terry (c), Carvalho, Ferreira

Cech

Hreidarsson, Euell, Andersen, Jeffers, Rommedahl

Drogba, Geremi, Babayaro, Cudicini, Smertin

EVENT LINE

4 ⚽ Duff (Open Play)

42 □ Terry (Foul)

HALF TIME 0 - 1

47 ⚽ Terry (Corner)

50 ⚽ Terry (Corner)

59 ⚽ Gudjohnsen (Open Play)

61 Gudjohnsen (Off) Drogba (On)

63 **Thomas (Off) Hreidarsson (On)**

64 **Kishishev (Off) Rommedahl (On)**

64 **Murphy (Off) Euell (On)**

71 Duff (Off) Geremi (On)

79 Robben (Off) Babayaro (On)

FULL TIME 0 - 4

STATISTICS

Season	Fixture		Fixture	Season
66	4	Shots On Target	12	118
52	4	Shots Off Target	4	106
2	0	Hit Woodwork	0	6
49	0	Caught Offside	1	45
58	7	Corners	10	123
196	13	Fouls	11	181
43%	36%	Possession	64%	57%

LEAGUE STANDINGS

Position (pos before)	W	D	L	F	A	Pts
12 (10) Charlton Ath	5	3	7	17	27	18
1 (1) Chelsea	11	3	1	27	6	36

Saturday 27th November 2004 | Venue: **The Valley** | Attendance: **26,355** | Referee: **M.Clattenburg**

CHARLTON ATHLETIC 0 CHELSEA 4

Chelsea demonstrated how far they had come under Jose Mourinho, avenging a 4-2 'Boxing Day' defeat with a convincing win at The Valley.

A one-goal half-time lead, courtesy of an early strike from Damien Duff, failed to reflect the visitors' dominance. The game was killed off early in the second period, however, with John Terry netting a brace and Eidur Gudjohnsen completing the scoring just before the hour.

Scott Parker's hopes of facing his former employers were dashed when he didn't even make the 16. The midfielder had been a star performer for the Addicks in this fixture last season, with his absence highlighting fully the depth of the Stamford Bridge side's squad.

It took Chelsea just four minutes to take the lead. A fine pass from Gudjohnsen released Duff, who cut across his defender before squeezing an effort past Dean Kiely from the right edge of the six-yard box.

The remainder of the half was an exhibition of possession football from Mourinho's men. The West Londoners played with a swagger, though only a Ricardo Carvalho header came close to extending their lead.

Charlton were mere spectators for large periods, but did threaten through a couple of Shaun Bartlett headers. Portuguese defender Carvalho also turned the ball against his own post, with Petr Cech left helpless on his line.

Inspirational captain Terry put paid to any home hopes shortly after the restart. Firstly, the England international powerfully headed in Duff's right-wing corner. Then, he converted from close range after another flag-kick had been nodded down by Carvalho.

Icelandic striker Gudjohnsen completed the scoring in the 59th minute, expertly steering Frank Lampard's incisive throughball beyond the onrushing Kiely from 15 yards.

This was Alan Curbishley's cue to ring the changes, though the lack of further Chelsea goals probably had more to do with the withdrawal of Gudjohnsen, Duff and Arjen Robben. Substitutes Hermann Hreidarsson and Jason Euell did at least go close, the latter forcing a decent save from Cech.

With performances like this, it is difficult to see who will take points from Mourinho's men.

"We got a bit of a thumping, so now we go into a run of games where we need to get points."

Alan Curbishley

"The second half was perfect for us. We scored two quick goals, which killed the game."

Jose Mourinho

Paulo Ferreira, Frank Lampard and Damien Duff celebrate

PREMIERSHIP FIXTURE HISTORY				
Pl: **4** Draws: **0**	Wins	Goals	Yellow	Red
Fulham	1	5	4	1
Blackburn Rovers	3	10	6	1

STARTING LINE-UPS

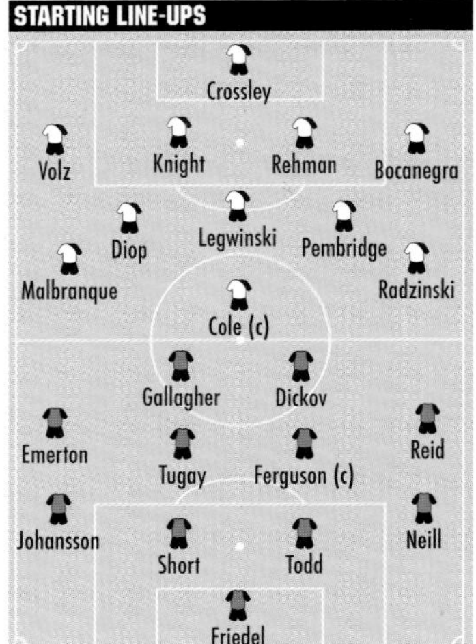

McBride, van der Sar, Pearce, Rosenior, Hammond

Thompson, Matteo, Enckelman, Flitcroft, Pedersen

EVENT LINE

10 Gallagher (Open Play)

23 **Diop (Foul)**

HALF TIME 0 - 1

66 **Legwinski (Off) McBride (On)**

73 **Crossley (Off) van der Sar (On)**

76 **Knight (2nd Bookable Offence)**

77 Dickov (Penalty)

80 Ferguson (Ung.Conduct)

83 Gallagher (Off) Thompson (On)

90 Johansson (Off) Matteo (On)

FULL TIME 0 - 2

STATISTICS

Season	Fixture		Fixture	Season
73	**6**	Shots On Target	**5**	**74**
67	**6**	Shots Off Target	**13**	**91**
2	**0**	Hit Woodwork	**0**	**2**
35	**3**	Caught Offside	**4**	**57**
74	**6**	Corners	**6**	**85**
186	**9**	Fouls	**13**	**228**
48%	**50%**	Possession	**50%**	**48%**

LEAGUE STANDINGS

Position (pos before)	W	D	L	F	A	Pts
14 (13) Fulham	**4**	**2**	**9**	**17**	**27**	**14**
17 (20) Blackburn R	**2**	**7**	**6**	**16**	**29**	**13**

Saturday 27th November 2004 | Venue: **Craven Cottage** | Attendance: **19,103** | Referee: **R.Styles**

FULHAM 0 BLACKBURN ROVERS 2

Paul Dickov converts from the penalty spot

"Blackburn wanted to win the game more than us, and I'm not sure that my players are angry enough about losing."

Chris Coleman

"We haven't been getting the rewards our performances have deserved over the past few weeks, but today we did."

Mark Hughes

PREMIERSHIP MILESTONE

100 Andy Todd made his 100th Premiership appearance

Blackburn ended a sequence of four draws with a well-deserved 2-0 victory at Craven Cottage.

Goals in each half from Scottish strikers Paul Gallagher and Paul Dickov secured the points, with the latter scoring from the spot after Zat Knight had been dismissed for a second bookable offence when conceding the penalty.

Fulham began the match in a lethargic fashion, Brett Emerton coming within inches of connecting with a dangerous low cross from the right. The warning was not heeded, however, as Rovers went in front after just 10 minutes.

Again the ball was delivered from the right, but this time Gallagher nipped in to steer home Steven Reid's near-post centre from close range. Nils-Eric Johansson then nearly headed a second, with the Cottagers' defence all at sea.

Having awoken from their slumber, Chris Coleman's side should have drawn level through Tomasz Radzinski. The former Everton forward found himself bearing down on Brad Friedel, yet could only send an effort the wrong side of an upright.

Further chances came and went at both ends, as the game began to open up. Sylvain Legwinski attempted a spectacular overhead kick, while Reid fired a drive narrowly over the top. Mark Pembridge was the next to go close, with Blackburn maintaining their 1-0 lead going into the break.

Having enjoyed the better of the opening period, Mark Hughes' team had to withstand serious pressure after the restart. Andy Cole fired over, Lucas Neill made a great saving challenge, and Cole then forced a top-class low stop from Friedel with a 65th-minute strike.

With the storm weathered, Rovers went back on the offensive. After Edwin van der Sar had replaced the injured Mark Crossley, events turned very much in the visitors' favour.

With a first half caution for a tackle from behind already to his name, Knight was shown a second yellow card when conceding a 76th-minute penalty. The defender handled the ball when sliding in on Paul Dickov, and the former Leicester man comfortably converted the resultant spot-kick.

A late chance went begging for Brian McBride, as Hughes won the battle of the Welsh managers.

PREMIERSHIP FIXTURE HISTORY

Pl: **8** Draws: **2**	Wins	Goals	Yellow cards	Red cards
Manchester City	**5**	**17**	**12**	**1**
Aston Villa	**1**	**8**	**11**	**1**

STARTING LINE-UPS

Manchester City substitutes: Onuoha, Waterreus, Sommeil, Flood, B.Wright-Phillips

Aston Villa substitutes: Hitzlsperger, Davis, L.Moore, Postma, Ridgewell

EVENT LINE

29 ⚽ **Macken (Open Play)**

38 ⚽ **Wright-Phillips S (Open Play)**

43 Yellow card Delaney (Foul)

HALF TIME 2 - 0

61 Substitution Barry (Off) Hitzlsperger (On)

61 Substitution Cole (Off) Moore L (On)

64 Yellow card **Dunne (Foul)**

72 Substitution **Distin (Off) Onuoha (On)**

90 Red card Hendrie (Violent Conduct)

FULL TIME 2 - 0

STATISTICS

Season	Fixture	Manchester City / Aston Villa	Fixture	Season
97	**7**	Shots On Target	**3**	**87**
76	**5**	Shots Off Target	**4**	**76**
2	**0**	Hit Woodwork	**0**	**3**
47	**1**	Caught Offside	**4**	**45**
98	**8**	Corners	**8**	**89**
202	**14**	Fouls	**19**	**241**
47%	**48%**	Possession	**52%**	**48%**

LEAGUE STANDINGS

Position (pos before)		W	D	L	F	A	Pts
9 (11)	**Man City**	**5**	**5**	**5**	**19**	**14**	**20**
6 (5)	**Aston Villa**	**6**	**6**	**3**	**20**	**16**	**24**

Saturday 27th November 2004 | Venue: **City of Manchester Stadium** | Attendance: **44,530** | Referee: **M.A.Riley**

MANCHESTER CITY 2 ASTON VILLA 0

First half goals from Jonathan Macken and Shaun Wright-Phillips saw Manchester City beat Aston Villa and move into the top ten.

Kevin Keegan's side began proceedings at a high tempo, and never looked back. Four chances went begging prior to Macken's 29th-minute opener, as Thomas Sorensen saved from Antoine Sibierski and Richard Dunne, with another couple of efforts missing the target.

The breakthrough arrived when Danny Mills and Robbie Fowler combined to find Macken in the area. The striker turned smartly, and then found the bottom left-hand corner with a shot that flew between Mark Delaney's legs.

A second goal was not long in coming, courtesy of man-of-the-moment Shaun Wright-Phillips. With 38 minutes on the clock, the England international ran on to a loose ball on the edge of the area, before firing home a rapier-like drive with his unfavoured left foot.

David James was not called into action until the 41st minute, when he brilliantly dived to his right to keep out Lee Hendrie's low effort. Nolberto Solano then provided the midfielder with another great chance, but this time he blazed high into the evening sky.

A third goal would have ended Villa interest, and Sorensen prevented it by tipping over a fiercely-struck Joey Barton drive. There were other openings for Keegan's men, yet they could not manage to wrap things up.

As City began to run out of steam, David O'Leary's team had new hope. Gavin McCann forced a flying save from former Villan James and Hendrie inadvertently blocked a goalbound drive, before Mike Riley awarded the visitors a late penalty.

The decision seemed a harsh one, as Dunne's trip appeared to take place outside the box, but justice was done when James repelled Juan Pablo Angel's penalty. To make matters worse, the Colombian then header the rebound over the crossbar.

There was still time for Riley to produce his customary red card, with Hendrie on the receiving end. The Birmingham-born player feinted to head-butt Danny Mills, and was promptly dismissed for violent conduct.

Shaun Wright-Phillips revels in his wonder-strike

"I cannot think of another player who is better than Shaun Wright-Phillips at what he does."

Kevin Keegan

"Congratulations to Manchester City, who were the better side. We didn't get going today, and the best team won."

David O'Leary

PREMIERSHIP MILESTONE

100 Juan Pablo Angel made his 100th Premiership appearance

PREMIERSHIP FIXTURE HISTORY

Pl: 4 Draws: 1	Wins	Goals	Yellow	Red
Southampton	3	7	6	0
Crystal Palace	0	3	14	0

STARTING LINE-UPS

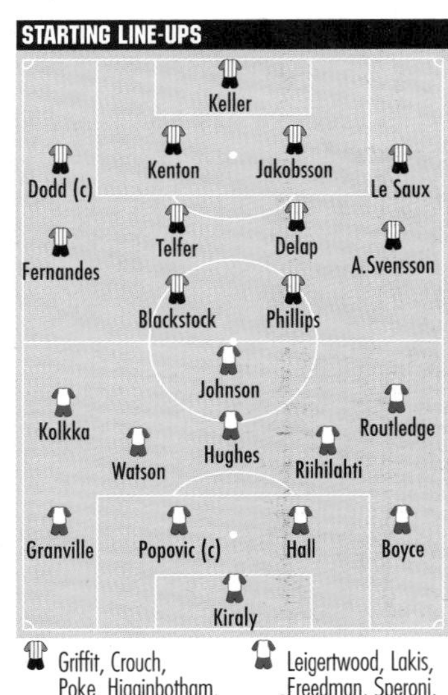

Southampton subs: Griffit, Crouch, Poke, Higginbotham, Ormerod

Crystal Palace subs: Leigertwood, Lakis, Freedman, Speroni, Andrews

EVENT LINE

42 Granville (Foul)

HALF TIME 0 - 0

48 Johnson (Open Play)

50 **Phillips (Open Play)**

54 Jakobsson (Own Goal)

68 **Blackstock (Off) Crouch (On)**

68 **Dodd (Off) Griffit (On)**

76 **Jakobsson (Indirect Free Kick)**

83 Watson (Dissent)

85 Popovic (Dissent)

FULL TIME 2 - 2

STATISTICS

Season	Fixture		Fixture	Season
79	8	Shots On Target	8	63
85	7	Shots Off Target	3	65
2	0	Hit Woodwork	0	3
40	3	Caught Offside	5	43
83	4	Corners	8	74
199	7	Fouls	11	207
50%	44%	Possession	56%	46%

LEAGUE STANDINGS

Position (pos before)	W	D	L	F	A	Pts
18 (17) Southampton	2	6	7	15	21	12
16 (16) Crystal Palace	3	4	8	17	23	13

Saturday 27th November 2004 | Venue: Friends Provident St Mary's Stadium | Attendance: 31,833 | Referee: P.Walton

SOUTHAMPTON 2 CRYSTAL PALACE 2

Peter Crouch gets away from Fitz Hall

"I would like to see how some of the bigger clubs would cope without so many of their best players."
Steve Wigley

"We gave away two soft goals, and there is a sense of disappointment amongst the players at not getting more than a draw."
Iain Dowie

PREMIERSHIP MILESTONE

Andreas Jakobsson netted his first Premiership goal

An exciting 2-2 draw at St Mary's did little to ease the relegation worries of either Southampton or Crystal Palace.

After a scoreless first half, the visitors twice surrendered a lead in the second period. A 48th-minute Andy Johnson header was the first of three goals in a crazy six-minute spell. Kevin Phillips' equaliser was quickly wiped out by an Andreas Jakobsson own goal, before the Swedish international made amends 14 minutes from time.

The opening period will not live long in the memory of those who attended the game. Iain Dowie's men looked more composed, but neither side genuinely threatened to get on the scoresheet.

Everything changed within three minutes of the restart, however, when Johnson broke the deadlock. The striker could already have scored twice in the second half, but had been denied by Kasey Keller on both occasions, when he rose unchallenged to head home Aki Riihilahti's right-wing centre from 10 yards out.

Despite not having threatened prior to conceding, Southampton hit back almost immediately. Fabrice Fernandes' inswinging cross from the right went over the head of Dexter Blackstock, enabling Phillips to ghost in and steer the ball into the roof of the net from close range.

The goal-glut continued, as Palace went back in front. Wayne Routledge cut in from the right touchline and dispatched a left-foot drive, with a major deflection off Jakobsson giving Keller no chance.

Again Steve Wigley's charges responded positively, though Blackstock blazed over from inside the area when the ball fell kindly for him. The striker then made way, much to the annoyance of the home crowd.

His replacement, Peter Crouch, then played a vital role in the 76th-minute equaliser. The former Portsmouth target man nodded a deep free-kick from the left back across goal, where centre-back Jakobsson coolly beat Gabor Kiraly from eight yards out.

Late chances drifted agonisingly wide for the Saints, though defeat would have been incredibly harsh on the men from South London. The draw ensured that Southampton had failed to beat any of the three sides promoted to the Premiership last season, a very worrying black mark against their survival hopes.

PREMIERSHIP FIXTURE HISTORY

Pl: 2 Draws: 0	Wins		
West Bromwich Albion	0	1	0	0
Manchester United	2	6	1	0

STARTING LINE-UPS

West Brom: Hoult; Scimeca, Purse (c), Moore, Clement; Contra, Johnson, Greening, Sakiri; Gera, Earnshaw

Manchester United: van Nistelrooy, Rooney; Giggs, Scholes, Keane (c), Fletcher; Heinze, Silvestre, Ferdinand, Brown; Carroll

Substitutes (West Brom): Gaardsoe, Robinson, Horsfield, Kuszczak, Hulse

Substitutes (Manchester United): Ronaldo, Smith, Howard, O'Shea, Fortune

EVENT LINE

24 **Moore (Off) Gaardsoe (On)**

38 **Contra (Off) Robinson (On)**

HALF TIME 0 - 0

53 Scholes (Open Play)

72 Fletcher (Off) Ronaldo (On)

72 van Nistelrooy (Indirect Free Kick)

75 **Sakiri (Off) Horsfield (On)**

75 van Nistelrooy (Off) Smith (On)

82 Scholes (Corner)

FULL TIME 0 - 3

STATISTICS

Season	Fixture (West Brom)		Fixture (Man Utd)	Season
69	2	Shots On Target	9	119
69	1	Shots Off Target	9	105
2	0	Hit Woodwork	0	6
57	1	Caught Offside	5	56
80	1	Corners	8	115
201	13	Fouls	11	184
46%	34%	Possession	66%	55%

LEAGUE STANDINGS

Position (pos before)	W	D	L	F	A	Pts
20 (19) West Brom	1	7	7	13	28	10
4 (6) Man Utd	7	6	2	19	10	27

Saturday 27th November 2004 | Venue: **The Hawthorns** | Attendance: **27,709** | Referee: **S.G.Bennett**

WEST BROM 0 MANCHESTER UNITED 3

A battling first half display from West Brom made life difficult for Manchester United, before the Old Trafford side stepped up a gear after the break.

Robert Earnshaw replaced Nwankwo Kanu in the only change to the Albion team that had drawn at Highbury last time out. For United, only Gary Neville was unavailable from Sir Alex Ferguson's preferred starting XI, with Cristiano Ronaldo having to settle for a place on the bench.

Though Ryan Giggs missed the target in the seventh minute, the visitors made a sluggish start. An Earnshaw volley flew narrowly wide, before Roy Carroll was forced into a fine save by Hungarian Zoltan Gera.

After Wayne Rooney had gone close from distance, the Baggies lost both Darren Moore and Cosmin Contra to injury. Organisational problems ensued, with Rooney missing a great headed chance from Ruud van Nistelrooy's deep cross.

Fortunately for the former Everton player, he was not made to regret this wasted opportunity. Paul Scholes continued from where he had left off against Charlton, rounding off a smart move with a venomous 25-yard drive in the 53rd minute.

Bryan Robson's men were clearly demoralised by the strike, having given everything in a brave first half display. As United pressed forward in numbers, the only surprise was that it took them until the 72nd minute to add a second goal.

A deep right-wing free-kick was nodded back across goal courtesy of a prodigious leap by Gabriel Heinze, and van Nistelrooy headed in his first Premiership goal of the season that had not come from the penalty spot.

The final nail in the Albion coffin arrived 10 minutes later, and was not dissimilar in style. A corner was never properly cleared, allowing Rooney to set up Scholes for a close range aerial finish.

The victory moved Ferguson's charges up into the final 'Champions League' qualification berth, as the men from Manchester made it nine points from three games. At the other end of the spectrum, West Brom slumped to the bottom of the table.

Paul Scholes unleashes a thunderbolt

PREMIERSHIP MILESTONE

The attendance of 27,709 was a Premiership record at The Hawthorns

"We went to sleep for United's first goal, and once they go in front you know that it is difficult to get the ball back off them."

Bryan Robson

"He is one of the best in the world at appearing at the right time."

Sir Alex Ferguson on Paul Scholes

PREMIERSHIP FIXTURE HISTORY

Pl: 13 Draws: 3	Wins	Goals	Yellow cards	Red cards
Liverpool	7	24	11	0
Arsenal	3	10	25	1

STARTING LINE-UPS

Nunez, Dudek, Biscan, Diao, Warnock

van Persie, Almunia, Hoyte, Senderos, Flamini

EVENT LINE

41 **Alonso (Open Play)**

HALF TIME 1 - 0

57 Vieira (Open Play)

59 Vieira (Foul)

67 Reyes (Off) van Persie (On)

69 **Sinama-Pongolle (Off) Nunez (On)**

84 Henry (Foul)

90 **Mellor (Indirect Free Kick)**

FULL TIME 2 - 1

STATISTICS

Season	Fixture (Liverpool)		Fixture (Arsenal)	Season
98	7	Shots On Target	2	134
92	4	Shots Off Target	1	68
2	0	Hit Woodwork	0	6
39	2	Caught Offside	1	32
80	6	Corners	0	83
171	6	Fouls	16	167
54%	50%	Possession	50%	58%

LEAGUE STANDINGS

Position (pos before)		W	D	L	F	A	Pts
7 (8)	Liverpool	7	2	5	23	16	23
2 (2)	Arsenal	9	4	2	39	20	31

Sunday 28th November 2004 | Venue: **Anfield** | Attendance: **43,730** | Referee: **A.G.Wiley**

LIVERPOOL 2 ARSENAL 1

Neil Mellor fired home a dramatic injury-time goal, sealing a 2-1 win for Liverpool that left Arsenal five points adrift of leaders Chelsea.

The strike was worthy of winning any match, and came when a long free-kick forward was won in the air by a brave Harry Kewell. The bouncing ball sat up perfectly some 25 yards out, providing Mellor with an opportunity to unleash a rocket that flew beyond the despairing right hand of Jens Lehmann.

It was a strike of similar quality that handed Rafael Benitez's team a 41st-minute lead. Spaniard Xabi Alonso side-footed into the top left-hand corner from just outside the area, after running on to captain Steven Gerrard's astute low pass.

A 1-0 advantage was the least Liverpool deserved from a first half showing that made the champions look very ordinary. Both Gerrard and Hamann found their route to goal blocked, while Kewell and Sami Hyypia went close with headers.

The visitors barely registered an attack of note, with one solo run from Thierry Henry representing the sum of their chances. Things had to get better after the break, and they did three minutes before the hour mark.

In a sequence out of keeping with their overall performance, Arsenal carved open the defence with a brand of fluent football not seen in recent weeks. Patrick Vieira started and finished the move, running onto a pass from Robert Pires before clipping over Chris Kirkland from eight yards out.

Having demonstrated the positive side of his game, Vieira was then lucky to escape a red card. A poorly-timed tackle had already brought a yellow, when the away skipper took a dive in midfield. Referee Alan Wiley saw the indiscretion, but decided that a strong word would suffice.

With time running out, Henry was unable to wriggle past a sea of legs in the box. Soon afterwards, the Frenchman let his frustration get the better of him, and was cautioned for a strong challenge.

Then, just as it seemed the match would end level, Mellor came up with a strike that will live long in the memory of those sitting behind it in the 'Kop'.

Jose Antonio Reyes and Dietmar Hamann compete for the ball

"The idea was to control the midfield and not give Arsenal the chance to play."

Rafael Benitez

PREMIERSHIP MILESTONE

Antonio Nunez made his Premiership debut

PREMIERSHIP MILESTONE

Neil Mellor scored his first Premiership goal

"I am not really concerned about Chelsea at this point, I am more focused on sorting out our problems."

Arsene Wenger

PREMIERSHIP MILESTONE

Patrick Vieira netted his 25th Premiership goal

PREMIERSHIP FIXTURE HISTORY

Pl: 12 Draws: 2	Wins	⚽	▯	■
Newcastle United	8	24	12	1
Everton	2	12	32	4

STARTING LINE-UPS

Given
Taylor, Hughes, Bramble, Bernard
Dyer, Bowyer, Jenas (c), Robert
Kluivert, Bellamy

Bent
Kilbane, Cahill, Carsley, Gravesen, Osman
Pistone, Stubbs (c), Weir, Hibbert
Martyn

Ameobi, Harper, Brittain, Ambrose, Milner

Watson, Ferguson, Yobo, Wright, McFadden

EVENT LINE

5 ⚽ **Bellamy (Open Play)**

18 ▯ Cahill (Foul)

45 ▯ Hibbert (Foul)

HALF TIME 1 - 0

49 ▯ **Bramble (Foul)**

56 ⚽ Carsley (Direct Free Kick)

58 ▯ Bent (Dissent)

81 ⇄ **Bowyer (Off) Ameobi (On)**

86 ⇄ Cahill (Off) Watson (On)

88 ⇄ Bent (Off) Ferguson (On)

90 ⇄ Gravesen (Off) Yobo (On)

FULL TIME 1 - 1

STATISTICS

Season	Fixture		Fixture	Season
125	9	Shots On Target	3	84
90	10	Shots Off Target	4	76
7	2	Hit Woodwork	0	3
45	1	Caught Offside	3	44
118	8	Corners	4	83
180	15	Fouls	17	182
51%	58%	Possession	42%	49%

LEAGUE STANDINGS

Position (pos before)	W	D	L	F	A	Pts
10 (10) Newcastle Utd	5	5	5	27	27	20
3 (3) Everton	9	3	3	17	12	30

Sunday 28th November 2004 | Venue: **St James' Park** | Attendance: **51,247** | Referee: **N.S.Barry**

NEWCASTLE UNITED 1 EVERTON 1

A sublime Lee Carsley free-kick cancelled out Craig Bellamy's early strike, as Newcastle and Everton shared the points at St James' Park.

If asked at the start of the season which of these two teams would have been in the top three come the end of November, few followers of football would have suggested Everton. However, this hard-earned point was the Merseysiders' 30th from 15 matches, ensuring that their quest for a European place continued.

After an early scare that saw a Marcus Bent header from a right-wing cross loop just the wrong side of a post, the Magpies took the lead. A clearance from Shay Given reached Bellamy on halfway, and the Welsh international exchanged passes with Patrick Kluivert before racing clear to coolly beat Nigel Martyn from just inside the penalty area.

The goal filled Graeme Souness' charges with self-belief, and they really should have had the points sewn up before half-time. A 14th-minute Laurent Robert free-kick from distance brought the best out of Martyn, before more slick interplay saw Jermaine Jenas foiled.

The young stand-in skipper was later denied by the woodwork, as his acrobatic effort from the inside right channel crashed against the crossbar. Opposing captain Alan Stubbs then cleared off the line from Kluivert, but was soon involved at the other end.

With the interval fast approaching, the former Celtic man forced the first in a series of corners. From the last of these, Tim Cahill somehow scrambled the ball wide from a position just in front of the left-hand upright.

Newcastle created numerous chances at the start of the second period, the best of these seeing Kieron Dyer find the side-netting, before Everton punished their profligacy. A foul on Bent resulted in a free-kick in a fairly central position, and Carsley stepped up to curl a 25-yarder into the top right-hand corner.

Great chances followed at both ends, Bellamy hitting a post, Bent firing wide having rounded the keeper, and finally former Magpie Alessandro Pistone blocking another Bellamy effort in front of an otherwise deserted net.

Patrick Kluivert is the meat in an Everton sandwich

"We played very well, and if we keep playing like that we'll be fine."
Graeme Souness

PREMIERSHIP MILESTONE

250 Lee Bowyer made his 250th Premiership appearance

"This is the best team spirit I have known at any club. It comes from winning and it's getting better."
David Moyes

PREMIERSHIP FIXTURE HISTORY

Pl: 10 Draws: 4	Wins	Goals	Yellow	Red
Tottenham Hotspur	3	10	15	0
Middlesbrough	3	13	15	1

STARTING LINE-UPS

Kanoute, Fulop, Davenport, Redknapp, Brown

Reiziger, Nemeth, Nash, Doriva, Job

EVENT LINE

40 Queudrue (Foul)

41 Boateng (Dissent)

HALF TIME 0 - 0

49 **Defoe (Open Play)**

50 **Defoe (Ung.Conduct)**

68 **Keane (Off) Kanoute (On)**

74 McMahon (Off) Reiziger (On)

76 **Kanoute (Open Play)**

79 Parlour (Dissent)

81 Viduka (Off) Nemeth (On)

FULL TIME 2 - 0

STATISTICS

Season	Fixture (Tottenham)		Fixture (Middlesbrough)	Season
85	9	Shots On Target	3	110
83	5	Shots Off Target	5	97
5	0	Hit Woodwork	0	3
57	6	Caught Offside	3	43
66	5	Corners	7	81
194	11	Fouls	13	190
48%	52%	Possession	48%	50%

LEAGUE STANDINGS

Position (pos before)		W	D	L	F	A	Pts
13 (15)	Tottenham H	4	4	7	14	17	16
5 (5)	Middlesbrough	7	4	4	24	18	25

Sunday 28th November 2004 | Venue: **White Hart Lane** | Attendance: **35,772** | Referee: **P.Dowd**

TOTTENHAM HOTSPUR 2 MIDDLESBROUGH 0

Jermain Defoe celebrates opening the scoring

"It is a terrific feeling to pick up my first Premiership victory."

Martin Jol

"It was a rash challenge from Franck Queudrue, but it did not deserve a red card."

Steve McClaren

Tottenham ended a wretched run of six consecutive Premiership defeats, thanks in no small part to the 40th-minute dismissal of Middlesbrough full-back Franck Queudrue.

The game remained goalless when the Frenchman was given his marching orders by referee Phil Dowd, in a decision that bemused many. The official deemed that the former Lens player had gone in two-footed on an opponent, and wasted no time in producing a straight red card.

Steve McClaren was left fuming by what he deemed to be an overly hasty verdict. Having just returned from a Thursday night UEFA Cup clash in Spain, the last thing the Teesside club needed was to play with a one-man disadvantage for an hour.

Opposing boss Martin Jol had sprung a surprise by naming Rohan Ricketts, recently back from a loan spell at Coventry City, on the right of his midfield quartet. This placed the youngster in direct conflict with man-of-the-moment Stewart Downing.

Indeed, it was Downing that engineered the visitors' clearest opening of the first half after 14 minutes. An inch-perfect cross from the left found the head of Jimmy Floyd Hasselbaink, who nodded down for Ray Parlour to drive narrowly wide of the post.

Thereafter, Tottenham enjoyed the best of the chances. Jermain Defoe struck a free-kick tamely into the wall, but went much closer with his follow-up effort. Mark Schwarzer then turned a strike from Michael Carrick over the bar, before Defoe failed to hit the target when sent through by Reto Ziegler.

Following Queudrue's dismissal and the interval promptings of Jol, Spurs stormed into a 49th-minute lead. Having missed his fair share of chances, Defoe stole a march on his marker to clinically fire home Pedro Mendes' low near-post cross from the right.

Substitute Frederic Kanoute then made sure of the points after 76 minutes, charging down a Schwarzer clearance and watching as the ball rolled into the Middlesbrough net.

The outcome may have been different had McClaren's side not been reduced to ten men, but the supporters at White Hart Lane were just grateful to see their team get back to winning ways.

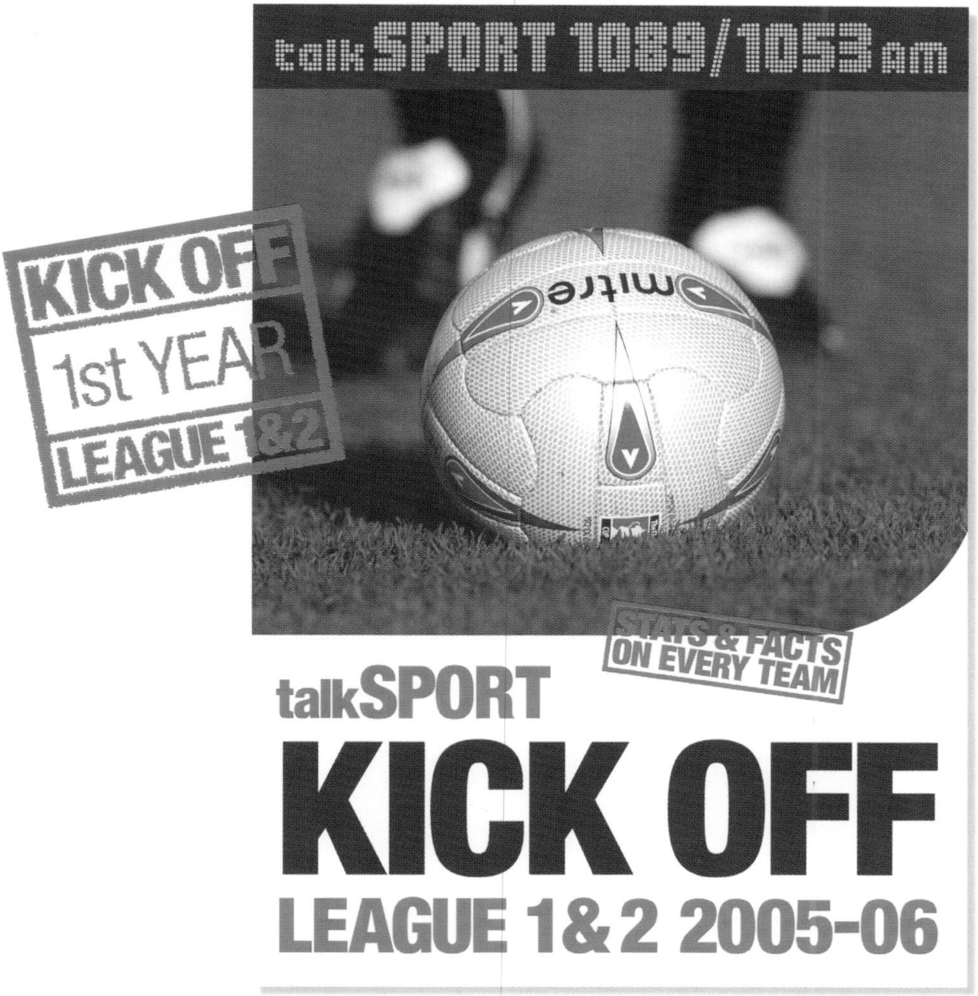

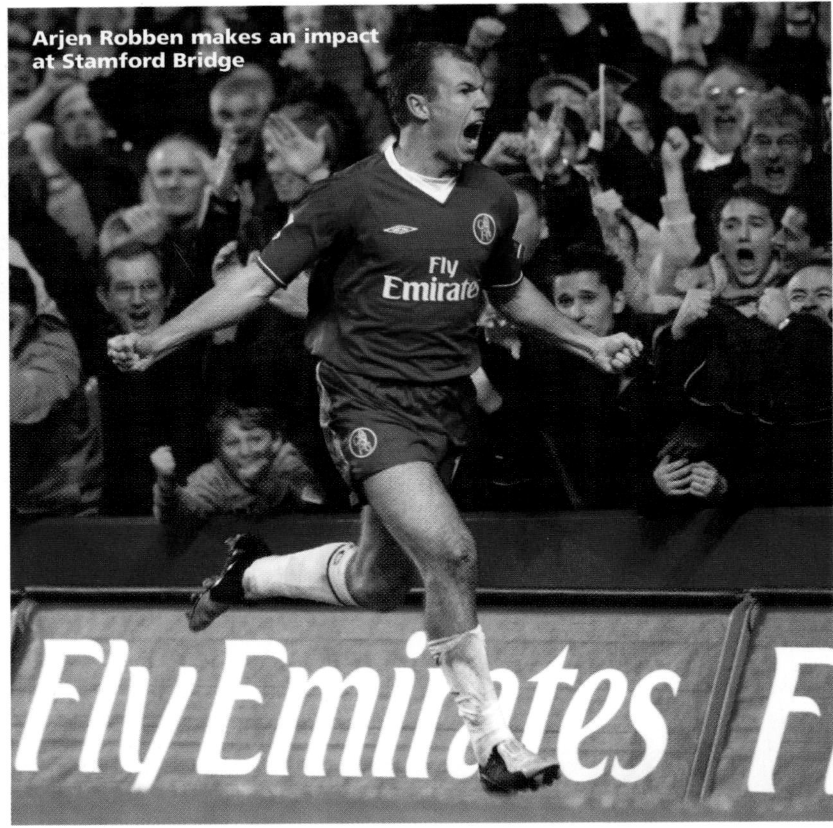

Arjen Robben makes an impact at Stamford Bridge

NOVEMBER 2004

Arsenal continued to wobble in the aftermath of their defeat at Old Trafford, collecting just five points from four matches during November. This poor form opened the door for Chelsea to assume leadership of the Premiership, Jose Mourinho's men picking up 10 points and netting 11 goals during the month.

Worryingly for both of the top two, Manchester United also found their form. A goalless draw in the Manchester derby was followed by three convincing victories, as Sir Alex Ferguson's side moved up into the Champions League places.

Third position still belonged to Everton, however, despite a narrow 1-0 defeat at Stamford Bridge. The Merseysiders' remaining three games yielded seven points, one more than inconsistent neighbours Liverpool were able to collect.

Two managers left their positions during the month, though neither departed as a result of problems on the pitch. Jacques Santini walked out on Tottenham citing personal reasons, with his assistant Martin Jol soon taking over, while Harry Redknapp quit Portsmouth not long after the appointment of Velimir Zajec as 'Executive Director' at Fratton Park.

November was a far happier time for both Kevin Keegan and David O'Leary. Manchester City's former England boss guided his team to an unbeaten month, while three wins on the bounce helped propel Aston Villa into the top six.

A real sense of belief was evident under the new regime at Blackburn. The Ewood Park side were not defeated in their four games, a sequence of results that saw them clamber out of the bottom three.

Championship side Watford proved to be the scourge of the South Coast in the Carling Cup. Southampton and Portsmouth were comprehensively beaten in consecutive rounds, as the Hertfordshire club secured a Semi-Final place.

In Europe, Chelsea and Manchester United qualified for the last 16 of the Champions League before the conclusion of the Group Phase, while Middlesbrough enjoyed a notable UEFA Cup win against Lazio.

IN THE NEWS

02ND	Aston Villa are charged by the Premier League over an alleged illegal approach for Southampton striker James Beattie during the summer
02ND	A 1-0 victory at CSKA Moscow ensures that Chelsea qualify for the Knockout Phase of the Champions League with two matches to spare
04TH	Former Chelsea striker Adrian Mutu is hit with a seven-month suspension and £20,000 fine after admitting to a doping offence at an F.A. disciplinary commission
08TH	Martin Jol is confirmed as the new 'Head Coach' of Tottenham
09TH	Former Liverpool and England captain Emlyn Hughes dies at the age of 57 after battling bravely against a brain tumour for 16 months
09TH	Bryan Robson is named as the new manager of West Brom
12TH	John Toshack is appointed as the new manager of Wales
17TH	Racism mars England's 1-0 friendly defeat in Spain.
24TH	A Blackburn Rovers fan is fined £1,000 and banned from football grounds for five years after admitting racially abusing Birmingham striker Dwight Yorke in a recent game at Ewood Park.
29TH	Bolton's El-Hadji Diouf is charged with 'improper conduct' by the Football Association after spitting in the face of Portsmouth's Arjan De Zeeuw

Roy Carroll
Manchester Utd

The Northern Ireland international had firmly established himself as first choice keeper at Old Trafford, and kept three clean sheets in four Premiership games during the month. A 'Champions League' howler against Lyon could have shaken his confidence, but he returned to action with an assured display at West Brom.

Mario Melchiot
Birmingham City

Having left Chelsea in the summer, Melchiot initially took time to adjust to life at St Andrew's. The full-back was on top form in November, however, helping to secure a 1-0 win at Anfield and marauding forward to set up two goals at Blackburn.

Rio Ferdinand
Manchester Utd

Manchester United put their disappointing October defeat at Portsmouth behind them, as they enjoyed a great month both domestically and in Europe. The success was built on a solid defence, as Ferdinand guided his colleagues to three clean sheets in four Premiership matches.

Alan Stubbs
Everton

Everton continued to prosper, with captain Alan Stubbs in commanding form at the back. The Toffees conceded just twice in four league games, with their former Celtic defender helping to restrict the attacking talents of both Chelsea and Newcastle to just one goal each.

Stephen Jordan
Manchester City

With Ben Thatcher out injured, Jordan was an ever-present in the left-back role for Manchester City. The youngster was outstanding in a rearguard action at Old Trafford, and formed part of a defence that was breached just three times in five games.

PLAYER OF THE MONTH

Arjen Robben
Chelsea

Having recently recovered from an ankle injury, Robben marked his first Premiership start by netting the only goal of the game against Everton. A mesmeric display at Fulham was capped with a fine goal, as the Dutchman helped Chelsea to 10 points in the month.

"Arjen Robben has shown great maturity and strength alongside natural footballing skills, and his performances in November have been all the more impressive when you bear in the mind the severity of his recent ankle injury."

Barclays Awards Panel

MANAGER OF THE MONTH

Jose Mourinho
Chelsea

Chelsea moved to the Premiership summit with victory against Everton, and proceeded to swiftly open up a five-point gap. The return from injury of Arjen Robben was pivotal to this success, but it was Mourinho's 4-3-3 system that provided the Dutchman with the freedom to work his magic.

Premiership Career Statistics
up until end of November 2004
Matches:**15** Wins:**11** Draws:**3** Losses:**1**

"Chelsea have been the dominant force throughout November, with Jose Mourinho exemplifying the spirit that has seen the quest for the title become a reality."

Barclays Awards Panel

Shaun Wright-Phillips
Manchester City

Whatever role he was asked to play during the month, Wright-Phillips shone as his club remained unbeaten. The winger scored against Portsmouth and Aston Villa when playing in his natural position, and weighed in with a couple of assists when occupying a striking berth.

Damien Francis
Norwich City

The former Wimbledon midfielder enjoyed a glorious month, though it ended early through injury. A goal at Manchester City secured a valuable point, before a brace at home to Southampton ensured a first Premiership victory of the season for Norwich.

Boudewijn Zenden
Middlesbrough

A move to central midfield had really benefitted the Dutchman's game, and he scored in wins against both West Brom and Liverpool during the month. On the European stage meanwhile, two goals from the former Barcelona man resulted in a memorable win against Lazio.

Paul Dickov
Blackburn Rovers

Three goals and three assists ensured a happy November for the striker and his club. Blackburn were unbeaten in four games, a run owing much to the Scotsman's late equalisers at Norwich and former employers Manchester City.

Robert Earnshaw
West Brom

Though West Brom only collected two points from a possible 12, their Welsh striker was outstanding. The former Cardiff man netted all four goals scored by his team, including a memorable late leveller in a creditable 1-1 draw at Highbury.

MONTH IN NUMBERS

41 Games Played

118 Total Goals Scored

2.88 Average Goals Per Game

4 Player With Most Goals (Earnshaw)

1 Hat-tricks (Baros)

11 Club With Most Goals (Chelsea)

1 Fastest Goal (Duff)

31.7% Percentage Of Home Wins

36.6% Percentage Of Away Wins

31.7% Percentage Of Draws

4-0 Biggest Win (Charlton Athletic 4 v 0 Norwich City, Charlton Athletic 0 v 4 Chelsea)

91 Total Yellow Cards

9 Total Red Cards

2.2 Average Yellow Cards Per Game

16 Most Disciplinary Points (Hendrie, Queudrue)

6 Fastest Booking (Johnsen)

34,993 Average Attendance

PREMIERSHIP TABLE / TEAM STATISTICS

Pos (last month)	Team	Played	Won	Drawn	Lost	Goals for	Goals against	Goal diff	Points	Shots on target	Hit woodwork	Shots off target	Failed to score	Clean sheets	Corners	Caught Offside	Players used
1 ▲ (2)	Chelsea	15	11	3	1	27	6	+21	36	118	6	106	3	10	123	45	22
2 ▼ (1)	Arsenal	15	9	4	2	39	20	+19	31	134	6	68	1	4	83	32	20
3 - (3)	Everton	15	9	3	3	17	12	+5	30	84	3	76	3	7	83	44	18
4 ▲ (7)	Manchester United	15	7	6	2	19	10	+9	27	119	6	105	5	7	115	56	26
5 - (5)	Middlesbrough	15	7	4	4	24	18	+6	25	110	3	97	3	3	81	43	21
6 ▲ (10)	Aston Villa	15	6	6	3	20	16	+4	24	87	3	76	4	6	89	45	19
7 ▼ (6)	Liverpool	14	7	2	5	23	16	+7	23	98	2	92	4	3	80	39	21
8 ▼ (4)	Bolton Wanderers	15	6	5	4	22	19	+3	23	108	4	91	2	2	83	28	23
9 ▲ (13)	Manchester City	15	5	5	5	19	14	+5	20	97	2	76	5	5	98	47	19
10 ▼ (8)	Newcastle United	15	5	5	5	27	27	0	20	125	7	90	1	2	118	45	22
11 ▼ (9)	Portsmouth	14	5	3	6	18	20	-2	18	78	2	70	3	3	72	33	22
12 - (12)	Charlton Athletic	15	5	3	7	17	27	-10	18	66	2	52	6	4	58	49	20
13 ▼ (11)	Tottenham Hotspur	15	4	4	7	14	17	-3	16	85	5	83	6	6	66	57	24
14 ▲ (16)	Birmingham City	15	2	8	5	12	15	-3	14	69	3	77	6	4	88	40	21
15 - (15)	Fulham	15	4	2	9	17	27	-10	14	73	2	67	6	3	74	35	20
16 ▼ (14)	Crystal Palace	15	3	4	8	17	23	-6	13	63	3	65	3	3	74	43	22
17 ▲ (19)	Blackburn Rovers	15	2	7	6	16	29	-13	13	74	2	91	5	2	85	57	26
18 - (18)	Southampton	15	2	6	7	15	21	-6	12	79	2	85	6	3	83	40	25
19 ▲ (20)	Norwich City	15	1	9	5	14	25	-11	12	75	3	85	5	3	72	57	20
20 ▼ (17)	West Brom	15	1	7	7	13	28	-15	10	69	2	69	4	1	80	57	22

Milan Baros in action against Crystal Palace

TEAM FORM

Pos	Team	Form	Goals For	Goals Against	Pts
1	Chelsea	WWDW	11	3	10
2	Manchester United	DWWW	8	1	10
3	Manchester City	DDDWW	7	3	9
4	Aston Villa	WWWL	6	3	9
5	Middlesbrough	DWWL	5	4	7
6	Everton	LWWD	3	2	7
7	Blackburn Rovers	DDDW	7	5	6
8	Liverpool	LWLW	5	6	6
9	Charlton Athletic	WWLL	7	8	6
10	Norwich City	DDLWD	5	8	6
11	Southampton	DWLD	7	7	5
12	Arsenal	DWDL	8	8	5
13	Birmingham City	WLDD	5	5	5
14	Newcastle United	LLWD	5	8	4
15	Tottenham Hotspur	LLLW	8	9	3
16	Fulham	WLLL	5	8	3
17	Portsmouth	LLLW	3	8	3
18	Bolton Wanderers	DLDL	4	6	2
19	Crystal Palace	DLLD	5	8	2
20	West Brom	DLDL	4	8	2

TOP GOALSCORERS

Player	This Month	Total
T.Henry Arsenal	2	**11**
A.Johnson Crystal Palace	1	**9**
R.Pires Arsenal	2	**8**
M.Baros Liverpool	3	**7**
C.Bellamy Newcastle United	3	**7**
J.Defoe Tottenham Hotspur	3	**6**
E.Gudjohnsen Chelsea	1	**6**
H.Pedersen Bolton Wanderers	1	**6**
N.Anelka Manchester City	0	**6**
J.Hasselbaink Middlesbrough	0	**6**
J.Reyes Arsenal	0	**6**
A.Yakubu Portsmouth	0	**6**
P.Dickov Blackburn Rovers	3	**5**
S.Wright-Phillips Manchester City	2	**5**
L.Boa Morte Fulham	1	**5**
A.Shearer Newcastle United	1	**5**
A.Cole Fulham	0	**5**

MOST GOAL ASSISTS

Player	This Month	Total
T.Henry Arsenal	1	**10**
F.Lampard Chelsea	2	**8**
F.Ljungberg Arsenal	2	**7**
W.Routledge Crystal Palace	1	**7**
S.Wright-Phillips Manchester City	3	**6**
J.Hasselbaink Middlesbrough	2	**6**
D.Bergkamp Arsenal	0	**6**
P.Dickov Blackburn Rovers	3	**5**
E.Gudjohnsen Chelsea	3	**5**
S.Downing Middlesbrough	2	**5**
J.Greening West Brom	2	**5**
L.Boa Morte Fulham	1	**5**
L.Robert Newcastle United	1	**5**

DISCIPLINE

F.A. disciplinary points: Yellow=4 points,
Two Bookable Offences=10 points and Red Card=12 points

Player	Y	SB	R	PTS
L.Hendrie Aston Villa	5	0	1	**32**
T.Cahill Everton	4	1	0	**26**
Josemi Liverpool	4	1	0	**26**
M.Izzet Birmingham City	3	0	1	**24**
D.Mills Manchester City	3	0	1	**24**
K.Tugay Blackburn Rovers	3	1	0	**22**
P.Diop Fulham	2	0	1	**20**
F.Queudrue Middlesbrough	2	0	1	**20**
G.Boateng Middlesbrough	5	0	0	**20**
J.Redknapp Tottenham	5	0	0	**20**
R.Savage Birmingham City	5	0	0	**20**
P.Vieira Arsenal	5	0	0	**20**
D.Johnson Birmingham City	2	1	0	**18**
Z.Knight Fulham	2	1	0	**18**

"My time at Tottenham has been memorable, and it is with deep regret that I take my leave. Private issues in my personal life have arisen which caused my decision."

Jacques Santini on his surprise resignation at Tottenham

"I think that Shaun is potentially the best player in England over the next five years. He has got everything - pace, balance, strength and a big heart."

Kevin Keegan on Shaun Wright-Phillips

"It was my decision and something I have been thinking about for some time. I made it without any pressure from the chairman or the board."

Harry Redknapp on his decision to resign as Portsmouth manager

"I deeply regret my actions and wish to publicly apologise to Arjan De Zeeuw and Portsmouth Football Club. I am a role model to many thousands of fans throughout the world, and my behaviour showed a lack of moral responsibility to the public who support me."

Bolton's El-Hadji Diouf apologises for spitting in the face of Arjan De Zeeuw

"I'm really looking forward to the challenge. You really miss football when you're out of it. What I'd like to achieve is the success I enjoyed as a player here."

Bryan Robson after being appointed West Brom boss

"I don't think anybody back in England or on the England team would have blamed us if we'd walked off the pitch."

Rio Ferdinand on the racist abuse hurled at England's black players during the friendly in Madrid

"If I had to choose between Rooney and Robben, every time I would choose Robben. For me it is a blessing to be able to train him and see him develop."

Dutch coach Marco van Basten

PREMIERSHIP FIXTURE HISTORY

Pl: 3 Draws: 1	Wins	Goals	Yellow	Red
Arsenal	2	5	0	0
Birmingham City	0	0	4	1

STARTING LINE-UPS

Arsenal subs: Clichy, Flamini, Lehmann, Senderos, Owusu-Abeyie

Birmingham subs: Morrison, Yorke, Bennett, Gronkjaer, Martin Taylor

EVENT LINE

33 Goal **Pires (Open Play)**

HALF TIME 1 - 0

57 Substitution Anderton (Off) Gronkjaer (On)

60 Yellow card Upson (Foul)

67 Substitution **Reyes (Off) Clichy (On)**

67 Substitution Dunn (Off) Morrison (On)

72 Substitution **Fabregas (Off) Flamini (On)**

80 Goal **Henry (Open Play)**

81 Substitution Melchiot (Off) Taylor Mar (On)

86 Goal **Henry (Open Play)**

FULL TIME 3 - 0

STATISTICS

Season	Fixture (Arsenal)		Fixture (Birmingham)	Season
138	4	Shots On Target	1	70
71	3	Shots Off Target	1	78
6	0	Hit Woodwork	0	3
33	1	Caught Offside	5	45
87	4	Corners	2	90
174	7	Fouls	15	220
57%	50%	Possession	50%	50%

LEAGUE STANDINGS

Position (pos before)	W	D	L	F	A	Pts
2 (2) Arsenal	10	4	2	42	20	34
15 (14) Birmingham C	2	8	6	12	18	14

Saturday 4th December 2004 | Venue: **Highbury** | Attendance: **38,064** | Referee: **D.J.Gallagher**

Patrick Vieira and Julian Gray fight for possession

"The big target for us was to get back to winning again. The victory was more important than the style."

Arsene Wenger

PREMIERSHIP MILESTONE

50 Robert Pires netted his 50th Premiership goal

PREMIERSHIP MILESTONE

Manuel Almunia made his Premiership debut

PREMIERSHIP MILESTONE

125 Thierry Henry's second goal was his 125th in the Premiership

"People have been asking if Arsenal's bubble has burst. I reckon it's daft the way some people have reacted."

Steve Bruce

PREMIERSHIP MILESTONE

50 Both Maik Taylor and Jamie Clapham made their 50th Premiership appearance in the colours of Birmingham

ARSENAL 3 BIRMINGHAM CITY 0

Arsenal returned to winning ways, though they were not at their best against Birmingham.

A late Thierry Henry brace added to Robert Pires' first half strike, giving Arsene Wenger's men the confidence boost they needed ahead of a crucial 'Champions League' clash with Rosenborg.

Despite the Gunners' indifferent form, Steve Bruce opted to leave out his goalscorer from the previous game, Clinton Morrison. This meant that Emile Heskey had to plough a lone furrow, with David Dunn getting forward to support him whenever possible.

The major team news affected the Highbury side, however, with Jens Lehmann being replaced in goal by Manuel Almunia. With the exception of a first-minute howler, the Spaniard had impressed Wenger during the midweek 'Carling Cup' exit at Old Trafford.

Little happened in an opening half-hour that saw plenty of endeavour. Arguably the biggest cheer of the afternoon occurred during this period though, when Robbie Savage was grounded by a venomous strike from Pires. The impact of the ball on his face bloodied the Welsh international's nose, but he was soon back on his feet.

The home crowd were on edge, and needed something to lift them. With 33 minutes played they got just that, Pires bending a low effort through the legs of former Gunner Matthew Upson and just inside Maik Taylor's right-hand post from 17 yards out.

The Arsenal of earlier in the season would have pushed on from this point, yet that did not happen on this occasion. Birmingham grew in confidence as the game progressed, with Bruce sending on the attack-minded Jesper Gronkjaer and Morrison during the second period.

Within seconds of arriving, the former Crystal Palace striker saw an effort squirm under Almunia, only for the keeper to recover and prevent the ball rolling in. This was a let off for Wenger's men, and Henry then took full advantage.

First, the talismanic forward burst through the inside left channel to score with 10 minutes remaining. This was followed four minutes from time by a simple headed finish from inside the six-yard box, after Freddie Ljungberg's chipped cross from the right.

PREMIERSHIP FIXTURE HISTORY

Pl: 13 Draws: 3	Wins	Goals	Yellow cards	Red cards
Aston Villa	5	15	14	1
Liverpool	5	17	18	1

STARTING LINE-UPS

L.Moore, Berson, Postma, Ridgewell, Whittingham

Josemi, Traore, Dudek, Diao, Sinama-Pongolle

EVENT LINE

16 Kewell (Indirect Free Kick)

35 **Cole (Off) Moore L (On)**

44 **Solano (Direct Free Kick)**

HALF TIME 1 - 1

46 Nunez (Off) Josemi (On)

62 Mellor (Off) Traore (On)

69 **McCann (Off) Berson (On)**

79 **Mellberg (Handball)**

82 Gerrard (Off) Sinama-Pongolle (On)

FULL TIME 1 - 1

STATISTICS

Season	Fixture (Aston Villa)		Fixture (Liverpool)	Season
89	2	Shots On Target	7	105
77	1	Shots Off Target	5	97
3	0	Hit Woodwork	0	2
50	5	Caught Offside	3	42
92	3	Corners	9	89
251	10	Fouls	10	181
49%	53%	Possession	47%	53%

LEAGUE STANDINGS

Position (pos before)		W	D	L	F	A	Pts
6 (6)	Aston Villa	6	7	3	21	17	25
7 (7)	Liverpool	7	3	5	24	17	24

Saturday 4th December 2004 | Venue: **Villa Park** | Attendance: **42,593** | Referee: **M.R.Halsey**

ASTON VILLA 1 LIVERPOOL 1

Despite a vintage first half showing, Liverpool only went away from Villa Park with a point.

Indifferent away form has been the Merseysiders' achilles heel under the guidance of Rafael Benitez, though they played the opening period of this match as if it were at fortress Anfield.

Captain Steven Gerrard was inspirational, revelling in his slightly more advanced role, and played a significant part in Harry Kewell's 16th-minute opener. The England international picked out Jamie Carragher with a deep free-kick from the right, and his header back across goal was nodded in from close range by the Australian.

Many Liverpool fans had been critical of the former Leeds man's lacklustre displays since moving to the club, but Villa boss David O'Leary would have been only too aware of the danger he posed.

The home side tried in vain to get a foothold in the match. While Chris Kirkland was a virtual spectator, his opposite number, Thomas Sorensen, seemed to be constantly involved in the action.

The Danish keeper twice denied Gerrard, and then brilliantly plunged to his left to turn away a swivelling effort from youngster Neil Mellor. It just seemed a matter of time until a goal was scored, though few would have expected it to be netted by the men in claret and blue.

That is what happened, however, as Nolberto Solano curled home a 44th-minute free-kick. Referee Mark Halsey was taken in by Gavin McCann's theatrics some 25 yards out, and Villa's Peruvian international stepped up to hit the target for the fourth home game in succession.

The strike rocked Liverpool, and they were not the same after the break. Midfield colossus Gerrard continued to shine, but those around him seemed to retreat into their shells. For O'Leary's charges, Steven Davis began to look increasingly accomplished.

Chances were suddenly at a premium. Those that were carved out were comfortably saved, with Kirkland's stop from another Solano set-piece representing the closest either side came.

With eight minutes remaining, Benitez withdrew Gerrard. Though one man does not make a team, it was difficult to see how the Merseysiders would achieve anything without him on the pitch.

"We got out of jail on this occasion. I thought we were outplayed in the first half."

David O'Leary

PREMIERSHIP MILESTONE

Mathieu Berson made his Premiership debut

"We need to score more goals and take advantage of the chances we are creating."

Rafael Benitez

Antonio Nunez shields the ball from Gareth Barry

PREMIERSHIP FIXTURE HISTORY

Pl: 11 Draws: 1	Wins	Goals	Yellow cards	Red cards
Blackburn Rovers	5	10	14	1
Tottenham Hotspur	5	13	15	0

STARTING LINE-UPS

Blackburn subs: Bothroyd, Matteo, Enckelman, Flitcroft, Thompson

Tottenham subs: Redknapp, Fulop, Gardner, Kanoute, Pamarot

EVENT LINE

29	Yellow card: **Dickov (Foul)**
	HALF TIME 0 - 0
52	Yellow card: **Tugay (Foul)**
56	Substitution: **Gallagher (Off) Bothroyd (On)**
56	Goal: Keane (Open Play)
65	Substitution: **Tugay (Off) Thompson (On)**
73	Substitution: Ziegler (Off) Redknapp (On)
77	Substitution: Keane (Off) Gardner (On)
82	Yellow card: **Thompson (Handball)**
85	Substitution: **Short (Off) Matteo (On)**
88	Substitution: Defoe (Off) Kanoute (On)
90	Yellow card: Naybet (Foul)
	FULL TIME 0 - 1

STATISTICS

Season	Fixture (Blackburn)		Fixture (Tottenham)	Season
81	7	Shots On Target	8	93
96	5	Shots Off Target	2	85
3	1	Hit Woodwork	0	5
63	6	Caught Offside	6	63
92	7	Corners	5	71
239	11	Fouls	11	205
48%	46%	Possession	54%	48%

LEAGUE STANDINGS

Position (pos before)	W	D	L	F	A	Pts
17 (17) Blackburn R	2	7	7	16	30	13
12 (13) Tottenham H	5	4	7	15	17	19

Saturday 4th December 2004 | Venue: **Ewood Park** | Attendance: **22,182** | Referee: **M.L.Dean**

BLACKBURN ROVERS 0 TOTTENHAM HOTSPUR 1

A 56th-minute goal from Robbie Keane was enough to settle this hard-fought encounter at Ewood Park.

The Republic of Ireland international side-footed home from 15 yards, after Michael Brown had embarked on a determined run from deep inside his own half. The former Sheffield United midfielder surged from a position on the right of defence all the way to the left side of the Blackburn penalty area, before cutting the ball back into Keane's path.

That apart, the game offered very little by way of entertainment. The first half was a particularly lifeless affair, with both teams lacking the imagination required to unlock equally stubborn defences.

Only on one occasion did either manager have genuine cause for concern, Jermain Defoe beating the offside trap before seeing his shot blocked by the legs of Brad Friedel.

Whatever was said at half-time clearly had a positive effect, most notably on Rovers. Paul Gallagher, a scorer on each of his last two appearances, was desperately unlucky to see his snap-shot repelled by Paul Robinson.

Mark Hughes' charges continued to push forward, and were caught on the break by Keane's goal. Things could have gotten worse five minutes later, when Friedel was again on hand to deny Defoe.

That was as close as Tottenham came to extending their lead, as Blackburn gave everything in a bid to extend their five-match unbeaten run.

Substitutes Jay Bothroyd and David Thompson both made an impact. The former Perugia striker was unlucky with a header and might have done better with a shot, while the Birkenhead-born midfielder twice fired narrowly wide from distance.

Then, with the final whistle just moments away, the Ewood Park club won a free-kick on the edge of the box. Fortunately for Spurs, the defensive wall stood firm to block Steven Reid's drive, with Robinson comfortably saving Paul Dickov's follow-up effort.

Defeat was harsh on a Rovers team that could not be faulted in terms of commitment to the cause. With regards Tottenham, Martin Jol seems to be getting his ideas across to the players.

"It was disappointing, but we never really got up a head of steam."

Mark Hughes

"We defended very well, and didn't allow Blackburn to create too much."

Martin Jol

PREMIERSHIP MILESTONE

150 Brad Friedel made his 150th Premiership appearance

Robbie Keane celebrates his winner in customary fashion

PREMIERSHIP FIXTURE HISTORY

Pl: 12 Draws: 4	Wins	⚽	▯	▮
Chelsea	8	23	16	0
Newcastle United	0	5	27	2

STARTING LINE-UPS

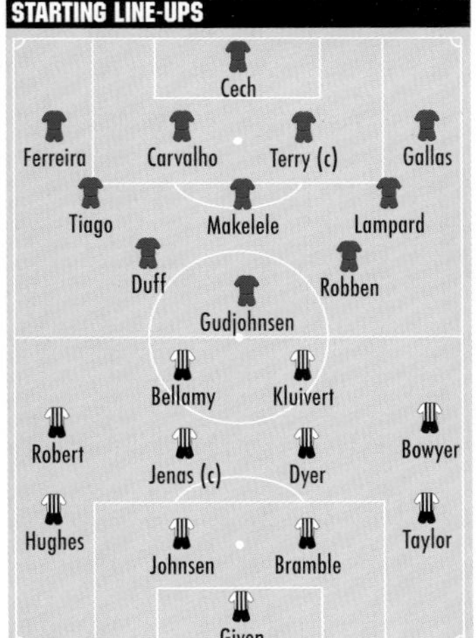

Drogba, Bridge, Kezman, Pidgeley, Parker

Ameobi, Harper, Elliott, Ambrose, Milner

EVENT LINE

16 ▯ **Carvalho (Foul)**

37 ▯ Taylor (Foul)

HALF TIME 0 - 0

46 **Gudjohnsen (Off) Drogba (On)**

61 **Gallas (Off) Bridge (On)**

61 **Tiago (Off) Kezman (On)**

63 ⚽ **Lampard (Open Play)**

65 ▯ Jenas (Foul)

69 ⚽ **Drogba (Open Play)**

77 Robert (Off) Ameobi (On)

89 ⚽ **Robben (Open Play)**

90 ⚽ **Kezman (Penalty)**

FULL TIME 4 - 0

STATISTICS

Season	Fixture (Chelsea)		Fixture (Newcastle)	Season
128	10	Shots On Target	5	130
111	5	Shots Off Target	4	94
7	1	Hit Woodwork	0	7
51	6	Caught Offside	2	47
126	3	Corners	2	120
193	12	Fouls	15	195
56%	51%	Possession	49%	50%

LEAGUE STANDINGS

Position (pos before)	W	D	L	F	A	Pts
1 (1) Chelsea	12	3	1	31	6	39
11 (10) Newcastle Utd	5	5	6	27	31	20

Saturday 4th December 2004 | Venue: **Stamford Bridge** | Attendance: **42,328** | Referee: **R.Styles**

CHELSEA 4 NEWCASTLE UNITED 0

Wayne Bridge beats Patrick Kluivert to the ball

"Newcastle did not deserve to lose 4-0, and I'm sure they will finish in the top six."

Assistant manager Steve Clarke

"Chelsea are the team to catch, but I'm sure that Arsenal and Manchester United are not going to give up."

Graeme Souness

PREMIERSHIP MILESTONE

25 Frank Lampard netted his 25th Premiership goal for Chelsea

PREMIERSHIP MILESTONE

Mateja Kezman scored his first Premiership goal

PREMIERSHIP MILESTONE

100 Shola Ameobi made his 100th Premiership appearance

Chelsea continued their habit of scoring four goals in Premiership matches, though it took them 63 minutes to break the deadlock in this encounter.

Newcastle could take great credit for a strong showing during the first hour of this contest, but boss Graeme Souness would have been concerned by the way in which they fell away when subjected to genuine pressure.

Jose Mourinho's side were not at their best in an opening period lacking in chances. With 17 minutes played, Petr Cech made full use of his giant frame, diving away to his right to turn a fiercely-struck Laurent Robert free-kick around the post.

A similar scene was played out just prior to Chelsea taking the lead. This time Robert went for a curler, bending an effort past the wall towards the bottom left-hand corner, where Cech once more made a plunging stop.

The save took on even greater importance when the home team went in front shortly afterwards. Substitute Didier Drogba was given too much time in the box, and nodded down for Frank Lampard to score with his left foot from 10 yards out.

The roles were reversed just six minutes later, when the former Marseille striker latched onto Lampard's ball over the top and beat Shay Given from just inside the area. The goal represented a first Premiership strike at Stamford Bridge for the Ivorian, and was finished with some aplomb.

Another replacement, Mateja Kezman, then extended his wait for a first goal in the English top-flight, hammering against the right-hand upright. The lead was extended with just a minute remaining, however, when Arjen Robben broke onto Damien Duff's angled pass and slotted into the net.

There was still time for Duff to further ruin his former manager's day, winning a penalty after being upended by fellow Irishman Given. Generosity knew no bounds as Kezman was presented with the chance to open his league account, and the striker confidently chipped home from the spot.

Every Chelsea player went to congratulate the former PSV Eindhoven forward, a clear sign of the amazing team spirit that Mourinho has engendered at the club.

PREMIERSHIP FIXTURE HISTORY

Pl: 6 Draws: 1	Wins	⚽	□	■
Everton	4	13	5	1
Bolton Wanderers	1	7	11	1

STARTING LINE-UPS

Everton: Martyn; Hibbert, Weir, Stubbs (c), Pistone; Bent, Cahill, Carsley, Gravesen, Kilbane; Ferguson

Bolton Wanderers: Davies; Pedersen, Speed, Campo, Okocha (c), Giannakopoulos; N'Gotty, Jaidi, Hierro, Hunt; Jaaskelainen

Everton substitutes: Osman, McFadden, Yobo, Wright, Watson

Bolton substitutes: Nolan, Ferdinand, Poole, Barness, Cesar

EVENT LINE

16 ⚽ Davies (Corner)

37 □ Davies (Foul)

45 ⚽ **Ferguson (Open Play)**

HALF TIME 1 - 1

59 ⚽ Davies (Open Play)

69 ⇄ **Cahill (Off) Osman (On)**

69 ⇄ **Kilbane (Off) McFadden (On)**

74 □ Okocha (Ung.Conduct)

75 ⚽ **Gravesen (Direct Free Kick)**

76 □ Hunt (Dissent)

85 ⚽ **Jaidi (Own Goal)**

86 ⇄ **Ferguson (Off) Yobo (On)**

86 ⇄ Giannakopoulos (Off) Nolan (On)

86 ⇄ Okocha (Off) Ferdinand (On)

FULL TIME 3 - 2

STATISTICS

Season	Fixture	Everton	Bolton Fixture	Season
87	3	Shots On Target	6	114
85	9	Shots Off Target	4	95
3	0	Hit Woodwork	0	4
47	3	Caught Offside	0	28
87	4	Corners	4	87
186	4	Fouls	6	207
49%	49%	Possession	51%	50%

LEAGUE STANDINGS

Position (pos before)		W	D	L	F	A	Pts
3 (3)	Everton	10	3	3	20	14	33
8 (8)	Bolton W	6	5	5	24	22	23

Saturday 4th December 2004 | Venue: **Goodison Park** | Attendance: **35,929** | Referee: **H.M.Webb**

Thomas Gravesen savours his equaliser

"Today was one of our toughest games, and we responded very well."

David Moyes

"We're in the middle of a mini-crisis, and we must learn from what happened today."

Sam Allardyce

PREMIERSHIP MILESTONE

50 Nigel Martyn made his 50th Premiership appearance in the colours of Everton

EVERTON 3 BOLTON WANDERERS 2

A spirited showing saw Everton twice come from behind en route to a thrilling 3-2 victory.

Goals in each half from Kevin Davies were cancelled out by efforts from Goodison Park heroes Duncan Ferguson and Thomas Gravesen, before the match was settled by an unfortunate 85th-minute own goal by Radhi Jaidi.

David Moyes sprang a surprise by drafting Ferguson into his starting line-up. The Scot had impressed as a substitute in recent games, but his inclusion meant that Marcus Bent was moved out to the right-hand side.

For Bolton, an injury to Ricardo Gardner handed a chance to Fernando Hierro, while El-Hadji Diouf was not included in the 16 after his indiscretions of seven days earlier.

The match got off to a scrappy start, with neither team able to assert themselves. Danish international Gravesen came closest to opening the scoring, unleashing a drive that flew narrowly wide of the target.

A goal was not long in coming at the other end, however, as Davies steered a low effort just inside the left-hand post after Nigel Martyn had flapped at a corner. The striker had done well to make space for himself amidst a crowded area.

Tim Cahill missed with an aerial chance as Everton sought an immediate reply, but the Merseysiders had to wait until the 45th minute until they drew level. Alessandro Pistone swung over an inviting centre from the left, and Ferguson scored with a trademark header from six yards.

All the hard work of getting back on level terms was undone just before the hour mark, however, when Davies rose highest to nod a looping effort back over Martyn from Nicky Hunt's right-wing cross.

Controversy followed as Ferguson won a free-kick on the edge of the Bolton box. After the initial strike was blocked, referee Howard Webb penalised Jay-Jay Okocha for encroachment, providing Gravesen with a second chance to drive home hard and low 15 minutes from time

The Trotters never recovered from this blow, and handed victory to the Toffees when Jaidi wildly sliced substitute Leon Osman's drive into his own net.

PREMIERSHIP FIXTURE HISTORY

Pl: 13 Draws: 1	Wins	Goals	Yellow cards	Red cards
Manchester United	12	37	10	0
Southampton	0	12	19	0

STARTING LINE-UPS

Manchester United substitutes: Bellion, Howard, Brown, Fletcher, Miller

Southampton substitutes: Blackstock, Dodd, Fernandes, Blayney, Crouch

EVENT LINE

22 Beattie (Off) Blackstock (On)

HALF TIME 0 - 0

53 **Scholes (Corner)**

58 **Rooney (Open Play)**

61 Lundekvam (Foul)

62 **Smith (Off) Bellion (On)**

86 Delap (Off) Fernandes (On)

87 **Ronaldo (Open Play)**

FULL TIME 3 - 0

STATISTICS

Season	Fixture	Man Utd / Southampton	Fixture	Season
133	14	Shots On Target	0	79
125	20	Shots Off Target	4	89
7	1	Hit Woodwork	0	2
61	5	Caught Offside	0	40
131	16	Corners	2	85
189	5	Fouls	10	209
55%	62%	Possession	38%	49%

LEAGUE STANDINGS

Position (pos before)		W	D	L	F	A	Pts
4 (4)	Man Utd	8	6	2	22	10	30
18 (18)	Southampton	2	6	8	15	24	12

Saturday 4th December 2004 | Venue: **Old Trafford** | Attendance: **67,921** | Referee: **B.Knight**

MANCHESTER UNITED 3 SOUTHAMPTON 0

Manchester United continued their recent upturn in fortunes, with a comfortable 3-0 victory over Southampton at Old Trafford.

It wasn't all plain sailing, however, as it took Sir Alex Ferguson's side 53 minutes to make their superiority count. The Saints were resolute in defence, though they failed to register a single shot on target during the entire 90 minutes.

That was in stark contrast to their hosts, with goals from Paul Scholes, Wayne Rooney and Cristiano Ronaldo representing a poor return from 34 attempts and 16 corners.

As the statistics would suggest, United dominated from start to finish. Only Ruud van Nistelrooy was absent from an otherwise full-strength line-up, with the Dutchman's place going to Alan Smith. For the visitors, Steve Wigley paired James Beattie and Kevin Phillips in attack for the first time in two months.

A wayward 20th-minute drive from Phillips was all the South Coast club could muster in a first half that saw Beattie limp out of the action. Kasey Keller was a busy man, fending off efforts from Gabriel Heinze, Rooney and Ronaldo, while Scholes and Giggs both missed presentable openings.

More of the same followed after the break, before Scholes finally gave the Old Trafford crowd something to cheer. Rio Ferdinand did all the hard work following a corner, chipping into the six-yard box for the flame-haired midfielder to nod home.

A glorious move saw Rooney add a second five minutes later. The young striker sent a 15-yard half-volley flying into the top right-hand corner of the net, after running onto Giggs' perfectly-weighted throughball.

With Southampton at sixes and sevens, it was amazing that Ferguson's men failed to extend their lead for nearly half-an-hour. Both Ronaldo and Scholes were acrobatically denied by Keller, before the woodwork came to the American's rescue.

The Portuguese international did pocket a deserved goal three minutes from the end though, arriving on cue to finish the move he started by volleying home Gary Neville's clipped cross from the right.

Cristiano Ronaldo takes on Graeme Le Saux

"You have to be patient, because teams like Southampton are fighting for every point."
Sir Alex Ferguson

"We did our job in the first half, but we gave away a poor goal early in the second."
Steve Wigley

PREMIERSHIP FIXTURE HISTORY

Pl: **1** Draws: **0**

	Wins	Goals	Yellow	Red
Norwich City	**0**	**0**	**1**	**0**
Fulham	**1**	**1**	**3**	**0**

STARTING LINE-UPS

Green

Edworthy, Fleming, Doherty, Drury (c)

Bentley, Mulryne, Helveg, Huckerby

McKenzie, Svensson

Cole (c), McBride

Malbranque

Pembridge, Legwinski

Diop

Bocanegra, Rehman, Pearce, Volz

van der Sar

Norwich City subs: Safri, Jonson, Ward, Shackell, McVeigh

Fulham subs: Knight, Flitney, Rosenior, Radzinski, Hammond

EVENT LINE

7 Cole (Open Play)

26 Volz (Foul)

HALF TIME 0 - 1

57 **Helveg (Foul)**

62 **Mulryne (Off) Safri (On)**

68 **Svensson (Off) Jonson (On)**

80 Bocanegra (Foul)

84 Cole (Dissent)

FULL TIME 0 - 1

STATISTICS

Season	Fixture	Norwich City / Fulham	Fixture	Season
79	**4**	Shots On Target	**9**	**82**
91	**6**	Shots Off Target	**6**	**73**
3	**0**	Hit Woodwork	**0**	**2**
58	**1**	Caught Offside	**3**	**38**
77	**5**	Corners	**4**	**78**
225	**12**	Fouls	**13**	**199**
47%	**49%**	Possession	**51%**	**48%**

LEAGUE STANDINGS

Position (pos before)	W	D	L	F	A	Pts
19 (19) Norwich C	**1**	**9**	**6**	**14**	**26**	**12**
14 (15) Fulham	**5**	**2**	**9**	**18**	**27**	**17**

Saturday 4th December 2004 | Venue: **Carrow Road** | Attendance: **23,755** | Referee: **A.G.Wiley**

NORWICH CITY 0 FULHAM 1

Andy Cole is congratulated by his team-mates

"Andy Cole was in line with the defenders, there was no daylight between them, and it was a good goal."
Nigel Worthington

"The players really rolled their sleeves up and showed a lot of heart out there."
Chris Coleman

PREMIERSHIP MILESTONE

200 Ian Pearce made his 200th Premiership appearance

A seventh-minute Andy Cole goal proved enough to end Norwich's recent mini-revival, as Fulham got back to winning ways.

The Nottingham-born striker rolled the ball low beyond Robert Green from 12 yards, following fluent approach work involving Steed Malbranque and Brian McBride. The finish was as clinical as the move was swift, leaving the keeper with no chance.

Falling behind seemed to affect Nigel Worthington's men, who offered little for the home crowd to cheer in the opening 45 minutes. The Londoners were dominant in midfield, with Malbranque instigating countless dangerous attacks from his position at the head of a diamond.

Welsh international Mark Pembridge twice tried his luck from long range, forcing a fine save and firing wide, while Pape Bouba Diop also stung Green's hands from distance. The Canaries only really threatened on one occasion, when Edwin van der Sar got down well to keep out a low Matthias Svensson effort.

The second half was more evenly contested, as both sides enjoyed periods of dominance without finding the net. Norwich exerted some early pressure, forcing a mistake that ultimately led to a corner.

At the other end, McBride was inches away from connecting with Cole's dangerous cross from the right. That was as close as Fulham came to extending their advantage, though they did carve out several half-chances during the remainder of the game.

The better opportunities fell to a home side desperately in need of an equaliser. Former Tottenham utility man Gary Doherty headed wide from a Darren Huckerby free-kick, before substitute Mattias Jonson did likewise from a left-wing centre.

David Bentley fired over when he should have tested van der Sar, and then squandered another decent opening in injury time. Again the on-loan Arsenal man drove high into the crowd, though on this occasion there was no time to try and atone for the miss.

Victory would have seen Norwich climb above the visitors in the Premiership table. As it was, defeat ensured that the gap between the two teams widened to five points.

PREMIERSHIP FIXTURE HISTORY

Pl: 1 Draws: 0	Wins	⚽	□	■
Portsmouth	1	3	0	0
West Bromwich Albion	0	2	2	0

STARTING LINE-UPS

Ashdown

Griffin, De Zeeuw (c), Stefanovic, Unsworth

Faye, Berger, Quashie

Stone, Taylor

Fuller

Earnshaw, Kanu (c)

Gera, Haas

Greening, Johnson

Clement, Scimeca

Moore, Purse

Hoult

Primus, Lua Lua, Berkovic, Hislop, Cisse

Gaardsoe, Sakiri, Hulse, Kuszczak, Koumas

EVENT LINE

14 ⚽ Stefanovic (Own Goal)
26 **Unsworth (Off) Primus (On)**
35 ⚽ **Purse (Own Goal)**
43 □ Moore (Foul)
45 ⚽ Earnshaw (Open Play)

HALF TIME 1 - 2

55 **Taylor (Off) Lua Lua (On)**
66 Haas (Off) Gaardsoe (On)
70 Gera (Off) Sakiri (On)
73 □ Hoult (Ung.Conduct)
77 Earnshaw (Off) Hulse (On)
80 **Quashie (Off) Berkovic (On)**
85 ⚽ **De Zeeuw (Indirect Free Kick)**
89 ⚽ **Lua Lua (Open Play)**

FULL TIME 3 - 2

STATISTICS

Season	Fixture		Fixture	Season
88	10	Shots On Target	4	73
74	4	Shots Off Target	6	75
2	0	Hit Woodwork	0	2
36	3	Caught Offside	1	58
80	8	Corners	3	83
181	14	Fouls	12	213
48%	60%	Possession	40%	46%

LEAGUE STANDINGS

Position (pos before)	W	D	L	F	A	Pts
9 (11) Portsmouth	6	3	6	21	22	21
20 (20) West Brom	1	7	8	15	31	10

Saturday 4th December 2004 | Venue: **Fratton Park** | Attendance: **20,110** | Referee: **P.Walton**

PORTSMOUTH 3 WEST BROM 2

Bryan Robson was denied his first victory since taking charge of West Brom, as late goals from Arjan De Zeeuw and Lomana Tresor Lua Lua condemned the Baggies to a 3-2 defeat.

The opening period was a tale of defensive errors. Own goals by Dejan Stefanovic and Darren Purse saw the scores locked at 1-1, before Robert Earnshaw capitalised on a mistake by Matthew Taylor to put the visitors in front for a second time.

Fourteen minutes had elapsed when Stefanovic inadvertently opened the scoring. Neil Clement made a terrific burst down the left, and then drilled in a low ball that the former Sheffield Wednesday defender sliced into his own net from four yards out at the near post.

Not to be outdone, Purse then followed suit at the other end. With the interval 10 minutes away, the centre-back looked set to make a routine clearance from a left-wing cross, yet somehow managed to find a gap between Russell Hoult and the left-hand upright.

West Brom regained their advantage on the stroke of half-time, however, when Riccardo Scimeca dispossessed Taylor and instantly centred for Earnshaw to tap home from a yard out, as the Portsmouth defender tried to prevent a corner.

In truth, the second period failed to produce the same levels of excitement as its predecessor. Former Liverpool midfielder Patrik Berger wasted two good shooting opportunities, as the home side went in search of an equaliser.

A goal looked unlikely prior to the 80th-minute introduction of Eyal Berkovic, but the Israeli proceeded to set up two in the final stages.

Firstly, De Zeeuw powerfully nodded home a curling right-wing free-kick from eight yards out five minutes from time. Then, substitute Lua Lua beat the offside trap to hammer an astute throughball high into the roof of Hoult's net.

The final whistle followed soon afterwards, leaving the visiting players to reflect on what might have been. A Portsmouth victory was tantamount to daylight robbery, though West Brom were guilty of losing concentration when they required it most.

"It was a crazy game of football, but that's what it's like in this country."

First Team Coach Joe Jordan

"We hid away from responsibility, and I have let the players know what I think of the performance."

Bryan Robson

PREMIERSHIP MILESTONE

50 Neil Clement made his 50th Premiership appearance

Nigel Quashie and Andy Johnson battle it out

PREMIERSHIP FIXTURE HISTORY

Pl: 1 Draws: 0	Wins	Goals	Yellow cards	Red cards
Crystal Palace	0	0	2	0
Charlton Athletic	1	1	3	0

STARTING LINE-UPS

Lakis, Freedman, Speroni, Andrews, Leigertwood

Rommedahl, Jeffers, Andersen, Konchesky, Euell

EVENT LINE

19 Johansson (Off) Rommedahl (On)

31 Murphy (Dissent)

44 Kishishev (Dissent)

45 **Watson (Foul)**

HALF TIME 0 - 0

58 El Karkouri (Foul)

76 **Kolkka (Off) Lakis (On)**

76 Bartlett (Off) Jeffers (On)

85 **Riihilahti (Foul)**

86 **Riihilahti (Off) Freedman (On)**

90 Rommedahl (Open Play)

FULL TIME 0 - 1

STATISTICS

Season	Fixture		Fixture	Season
66	3	Shots On Target	8	74
67	2	Shots Off Target	4	56
4	1	Hit Woodwork	0	2
43	0	Caught Offside	2	51
79	5	Corners	3	61
223	16	Fouls	14	210
47%	59%	Possession	41%	43%

LEAGUE STANDINGS

Position (pos before)	W	D	L	F	A	Pts
16 (16) Crystal Palace	3	4	9	17	24	13
10 (13) Charlton Ath	6	3	7	18	27	21

Sunday 5th December 2004 | Venue: **Selhurst Park** | Attendance: **20,705** | Referee: **M.D.Messias**

CRYSTAL PALACE 0 CHARLTON ATHLETIC 1

Gabor Kiraly demonstrates that you can keep goal whilst wearing pyjamas

"The lads are devastated. I felt we dominated the second half, and we defended well for 90 minutes."

Assistant Manager Kit Symons

"It was a great win, and this result will give us a boost."

Alan Curbishley

PREMIERSHIP MILESTONE

100 Francis Jeffers made his 100th Premiership appearance

PREMIERSHIP MILESTONE

Dennis Rommedahl scored his first Premiership goal

Substitute Dennis Rommedahl drilled home an undeserved injury-time winner for Charlton, after Dean Kiely had earlier kept out an Andy Johnson penalty.

The Danish international winger had replaced Jonatan Johansson after just 19 minutes, though rarely threatened prior to his moment of glory. However, the summer signing from PSV Eindhoven became an instant hero with the away supporters, when he cut inside Danny Granville to crisply beat Gabor Kiraly with a low near-post effort.

As is often the case in derby games, the match was not much of a spectacle. Both Aki Riihilahti and Johnson were unable to convert difficult aerial chances for Iain Dowie's men, while Jerome Thomas forced Kiraly into his first meaningful action on the stroke of half-time.

The second period began in similar fashion, before exploding into life just prior to the hour mark. Referee Matt Messias pointed to the spot after the Addicks' Moroccan international defender Talal El Karkouri had clumsily upended the livewire Johnson.

Having seen the Charlton man booked for his challenge, the Eagles' leading scorer then watched in horror as his well-struck penalty was expertly repelled by Kiely.

Though obviously disappointed, the home team kept plugging away. Joonas Kolkka forced another fine save with a shot from distance, as the men in red and blue increased the tempo of their football.

After Kiraly had comfortably dealt with a snap-shot from visiting captain Matt Holland, his opposite number again had to be alert. This time the former Bury custodian raced from his goal to make a brave diving stop at the feet of the ever-persistent Johnson.

Defensive deficiencies then enabled Johnson to latch onto a long clearance, only to find Kiely blocking his path once more, while Wayne Routledge was causing no end of problems on the right wing.

Selhurst Park was gripped by a real sense of frustration, though that turned to desolation as Rommedahl struck. Both Granville and Kiraly were beaten too easily, as the Dane ran on to Danny Murphy's pass and struck a 20-yard dagger through the heart of all Palace fans.

PREMIERSHIP FIXTURE HISTORY

Pl: 6 Draws: 1	Wins	Goals	Yellow	Red
Middlesbrough	5	15	3	1
Manchester City	0	6	11	2

STARTING LINE-UPS

Doriva, Bates, Nash, Davies, Job

Flood, Waterreus, Sommeil, Onuoha, B.Wright-Phillips

EVENT LINE

9 **Viduka (Open Play)**

14 Barton (Ung.Conduct)

32 Mills (Ung.Conduct)

39 Fowler (Open Play)

HALF TIME 1 - 1

46 **Nemeth (Off) Doriva (On)**

54 **Viduka (Open Play)**

65 **Hasselbaink (Direct Free Kick)**

73 Jordan (Foul)

76 Macken (Off) Wright-Phillips B (On)

76 Sibierski (Off) Flood (On)

80 Wright-Phillips B (Indirect Free Kick)

90 **Hasselbaink (Off) Bates (On)**

FULL TIME 3 - 2

STATISTICS

Season	Fixture		Fixture	Season
116	6	Shots On Target	4	101
101	4	Shots Off Target	4	80
3	0	Hit Woodwork	0	2
44	1	Caught Offside	1	48
88	7	Corners	4	102
206	16	Fouls	17	219
50%	48%	Possession	52%	47%

LEAGUE STANDINGS

Position (pos before)		W	D	L	F	A	Pts
5 (5)	Middlesbrough	8	4	4	27	20	28
11 (11)	Man City	5	5	6	21	17	20

Monday 6th December 2004 | Venue: **Riverside Stadium** | Attendance: **29,787** | Referee: **G.Poll**

MIDDLESBROUGH 3 MANCHESTER CITY 2

Mark Viduka and Jimmy Floyd Hasselbaink rediscovered their scoring touch as Middlesbrough narrowly won an entertaining game at the Riverside.

Home boss Steve McClaren was without Chris Riggott, Franck Queudrue and George Boateng from the team that lost at Tottenham last time out, though he was able to welcome back summer signing Michael Reiziger for a first start since returning from injury.

Manchester City came into the game on the back of five Premiership matches without defeat, and manager Kevin Keegan unsurprisingly stuck with the same team that had beaten Aston Villa nine days earlier.

Just under 10 minutes had elapsed when Viduka opened the scoring. The Australian coolly clipped the ball over the advancing David James after latching onto Stewart Downing's clever throughball.

The visitors did not crumble, however, and eventually drew level six minutes before half-time. Strikers Jonathan Macken and Robbie Fowler combined to deadly effect, with the former Liverpool frontman expertly dispatching his partner's knockdown header.

As in the first period, it took Viduka just nine minutes to find the back of the net after the restart. The former Celtic man linked up with Hasselbaink following a throw from the right, before bending a 12-yard effort just inside the far post with the outside of his right boot.

Dutchman Hasselbaink then turned from provider to his more accustomed role of goalscorer in the 65th minute. Having won a free-kick in line with James' right-hand post some five yards outside the area, the powerful forward stepped up to curl home his side's third goal.

At this stage it was hard to see a way back for the men from Manchester, but substitute Bradley Wright-Phillips handed them an 80th-minute lifeline. An inability to properly clear a free-kick cost McClaren's charges, as the young substitute swivelled to steer the ball home from eight yards out just four minutes into his Premiership debut.

Mark Schwarzer then ensured that the home team picked up the three points that their performance just about merited, denying Joey Barton with a magnificent save three minutes from time.

Jimmy Floyd Hasselbaink takes on Joey Barton

"I thought our three goals were magnificent - the quality was tremendous."
Steve McClaren

PREMIERSHIP MILESTONE
Matthew Bates made his Premiership debut

"Tonight, Stewart Downing and Mark Viduka were the key players. If you are looking to solve England's left-sided problem, then Downing looks to be the answer."
Kevin Keegan

PREMIERSHIP MILESTONE
Bradley Wright-Phillips marked his Premiership debut with a goal

PREMIERSHIP FIXTURE HISTORY

Pl: 4 Draws: 2	Wins	⚽	☐	■
Crystal Palace	0	4	4	0
Blackburn Rovers	2	6	4	1

STARTING LINE-UPS

Andrews, Lakis, Torghelle, Speroni, Leigertwood

Stead, Enckelman, Gallagher, Johansson, Thompson

EVENT LINE

41 ☐ Dickov (Dissent)

HALF TIME 0 - 0

53 **Riihilahti (Off) Andrews (On)**

71 Reid (Off) Thompson (On)

73 **Kolkka (Off) Lakis (On)**

80 Bothroyd (Off) Stead (On)

81 ☐ Todd (Foul)

82 **Routledge (Off) Torghelle (On)**

85 ☐ **Hughes (Dissent)**

87 ☐ **Torghelle (Foul)**

88 ■ Thompson (2nd Bookable Offence)

90 ☐ **Andrews (Foul)**

FULL TIME 0 - 0

STATISTICS

Season	Fixture (Palace)		Fixture (Rovers)	Season
67	1	Shots On Target	8	89
74	7	Shots Off Target	8	104
5	1	Hit Woodwork	0	3
45	2	Caught Offside	2	65
81	2	Corners	1	93
242	19	Fouls	22	261
47%	49%	Possession	51%	48%

LEAGUE STANDINGS

Position (pos before)	W	D	L	F	A	Pts
17 (16) Crystal Palace	3	5	9	17	24	14
18 (17) Blackburn R	2	8	7	16	30	14

Saturday 11th December 2004 | Venue: **Selhurst Park** | Attendance: **22,010** | Referee: **A.G.Wiley**

CRYSTAL PALACE 0 BLACKBURN ROVERS 0

Crystal Palace and Blackburn were forced to share the points at Selhurst Park.

Rovers boss Mark Hughes could look back at the chances his side squandered in the first half that would have put this vital six-pointer out of Palace's reach.

To add to Hughes's woes, midfielder David Thompson was ordered off after collecting two yellows with a few minutes to play.

Hungarian Gabor Kiraly produced a five-star performance in the Palace goal, and he was in the thick of the action on 15 minutes, diving full-length to deny Jay Bothroyd's powerful 25-yard free kick – one of 42 awarded on the day.

Paul Dickov had a chance on the half-hour mark, but with only Kiraly to beat, he drove his shot against the keeper and watched as the ball drifted wide.

He had a chance to atone for that miss soon after, driving a shot towards the far corner which Kiraly blocked with his legs.

The loose ball fell for defender Lucas Neill, who also saw his effort blocked by the Eagles keeper.

Rovers skipper Craig Short climbed high above the home defence in the final minute of the half, but his goalbound header was saved by Kiraly on the line.

Palace looked more organised in the second half, but they still managed to give the ball away too cheaply.

Dickov sent a shot over from Brett Emerton's cross before the Australian pounced on a clumsy clearance from Ben Watson, firing a snap-shot which flew wide.

Wayne Andrews' arrival on 53 minutes invigorated Palace, who finally started to threaten the visitors' goal.

Andy Johnson went on a strong solo run midway through the half, working his way through the Rovers defence before seeing his low, right-foot shot touched against the post by Brad Friedel's fingertips.

At the other end, Emerton fired just wide before Kiraly – who wasn't called to work as hard as he had in the opening period – made a fine save to deny Bothroyd.

Substitute Vassilios Lakis missed an easy header from Johnson's cross, but it would have been unfair on Rovers had it gone in.

Jay Bothroyd holds off Emmerson Boyce

"Marvellously entertaining it was not. We were not good enough, and I offer no excuses."

Iain Dowie

PREMIERSHIP MILESTONE

Wayne Andrews made his Premiership debut

"We played very well today and should have won the game. It was a good professional performance."

Mark Hughes

PREMIERSHIP FIXTURE HISTORY

Pl: 13 Draws: 4	Wins	Goals	Yellow	Red
Everton	5	15	26	3
Liverpool	4	14	31	2

STARTING LINE-UPS

Everton: Martyn; Hibbert, Weir, Stubbs (c), Pistone; Osman, Gravesen, Carsley, Cahill, Kilbane; Bent

Liverpool: Mellor; Kewell, Sinama-Pongolle, Hamann, Gerrard (c), Diao; Riise, Hyypia, Carragher, Josemi; Kirkland

Everton subs: Ferguson, Yobo, Watson, Wright, McFadden

Liverpool subs: Nunez, Traore, Alonso, Dudek, Finnan

EVENT LINE

27	Hibbert (Foul)
29	Diao (Foul)
	HALF TIME 0 - 0
58	Riise (Foul)
65	Josemi (Foul)
66	Hamann (Off) Nunez (On)
68	Carsley (Open Play)
75	Sinama-Pongolle (Off) Traore (On)
76	Bent (Off) Ferguson (On)
78	Diao (Off) Alonso (On)
83	Gravesen (Off) Yobo (On)
84	Ferguson (Ung.Conduct)
87	Osman (Off) Watson (On)
	FULL TIME 1 - 0

STATISTICS

Season	Fixture (Everton)		Fixture (Liverpool)	Season
89	2	Shots On Target	5	110
89	4	Shots Off Target	11	108
3	0	Hit Woodwork	0	2
48	1	Caught Offside	5	47
89	2	Corners	7	96
198	12	Fouls	14	195
49%	48%	Possession	52%	53%

LEAGUE STANDINGS

Position (pos before)		W	D	L	F	A	Pts
2 (3)	Everton	11	3	3	21	14	36
7 (7)	Liverpool	7	3	6	24	18	24

Saturday 11th December 2004 | Venue: **Goodison Park** | Attendance: **40,552** | Referee: **S.G.Bennett**

EVERTON 1 LIVERPOOL 0

Lee Carsley curls home the winner

David Moyes's Everton earned a hard-fought victory over their neighbours and bitter rivals, Liverpool.

The Toffees' first derby win in five years lifted them to the lofty position of second in the Premiership, two points clear of champions Arsenal.

Many of the critics who'd predicted they'd fall flat on their faces were now being forced to take them seriously as title contenders.

The 200th Mersey derby got off to a tame start, with both sides carefully feeling each other out.

The Goodison faithful, meanwhile, were waging an energetic chant battle with the Liverpool fans who had made the short walk across Stanley Park.

Liverpool created the game's first real chance, Australia international Harry Kewell picking up the ball just outside the Everton area and making a decisive charge towards goal.

He tricked Alessandro Pistone with a clever turn before unleashing a left-footed shot which was easily handled by Nigel Martyn.

Everton quickly responded with a well-crafted move, Marcus Bent collecting from Thomas Gravesen and running to the byline before flighting a perfect cross into the centre of the box which was headed wide by an unmarked Tim Cahill.

Liverpool nearly took the lead with a series of scrappy shots in the 34th minute.

Champions League goal hero Neil Mellor saw his header cleared off the line by Cahill, the ball travelling only as far as Salif Diao, whose effort was also blocked.

The ball then fell to Steven Gerrard, whose shot was also stopped before being headed over by Mellor.

The Toffees took advantage of Liverpool's dip in confidence as the second half progressed, breaking the deadlock on 68 minutes.

Lee Carsley sent a cross from the left in towards Bent, who quickly switched the ball to Leon Osman.

He in turn found Carsley on the edge of the box, the midfielder curling a brilliant strike past Chris Kirkland for his fourth goal of the season.

Liverpool battled away and had some chances in the last 15 minutes, the best coming from a run into the box by Gerrard, whose shot forced a fine save from Martyn.

"It was an important match for us and the fans. It feels like we've just won the F.A. Cup."

Lee Carsley

PREMIERSHIP MILESTONE

100 Marcus Bent made his 100th Premiership appearance

PREMIERSHIP MILESTONE

The attendance of 40,552 was a Premiership record at Goodison Park

"This was always going to be a difficult game, and we paid the price for a lapse in concentration."

Rafael Benitez

PREMIERSHIP FIXTURE HISTORY

Pl: **8** Draws: **2**	Wins	⚽	Yellow cards	Red cards
Manchester City	**1**	**8**	**11**	**0**
Tottenham Hotspur	**5**	**11**	**12**	**1**

STARTING LINE-UPS

Anelka, Waterreus, Onuoha, Flood, B.Wright-Phillips

Kelly, Gardner, Redknapp, Fulop, Yeates

EVENT LINE

22 Naybet (Foul)

HALF TIME 0 - 0

46 Mendes (Off) Kelly (On)

46 Naybet (Off) Gardner (On)

57 Kanoute (Open Play)

70 **Macken (Off) Wright-Phillips B (O**

71 **Fowler (Off) Anelka (On)**

73 Kelly (Foul)

81 Ricketts (Off) Redknapp (On)

87 **Jordan (Foul)**

FULL TIME 0 - 1

STATISTICS

Season	Fixture		Fixture	Season
104	**3**	Shots On Target	**2**	**95**
85	**5**	Shots Off Target	**3**	**88**
2	**0**	Hit Woodwork	**0**	**5**
55	**7**	Caught Offside	**2**	**65**
108	**6**	Corners	**2**	**73**
227	**8**	Fouls	**9**	**214**
48%	**54%**	Possession	**46%**	**48%**

LEAGUE STANDINGS

Position (pos before)	W	D	L	F	A	Pts
13 (11) Man City	**5**	**5**	**7**	**21**	**18**	**20**
11 (13) Tottenham H	**6**	**4**	**7**	**16**	**17**	**22**

Saturday 11th December 2004 | Venue: **City of Manchester Stadium** | Attendance: **45,805** | Referee: **D.J.Gallagher**

MANCHESTER CITY 0 TOTTENHAM HOTSPUR 1

Tottenham's revival under Martin Jol continued with a narrow victory at Manchester City.

Fredi Kanoute, recently criticised by Jol for giving away the penalty which brought about Spurs' exit from the Carling Cup against Liverpool, went a long way towards finding favour once again with his new boss by scoring the spectacular second-half winner – just his second Premiership goal of the season.

City were shouting for a penalty in the opening minute after Jonathan Macken went down under a challenge from central defender Ledley King, but referee Dermot Gallagher waved play on.

The home side had their first attempt on goal two minutes later, a cheeky chip from Shaun Wright-Phillips which landed on the roof of the net.

Paul Robinson then showed why he was England's number one, flinging himself low to his right to turn a 25-yard drive from Joey Barton around the post.

Spurs' first real opening came on 25 minutes, Rohan Ricketts cutting in from the left and beating Danny Mills before sending his shot just wide.

Robbie Keane had another chance for Spurs on 39 minutes, racing on to Pedro Mendes's long through ball and lofting a shot past the advancing David James which flew a couple of yards wide.

Antoine Sibierski wasted a prime opportunity for City shortly before the break, his diving header from Stephen Jordan's left-wing cross drifting harmlessly wide.

After a turgid start to the second half, Kanoute made the breakthrough on 57 minutes, collecting Michael Brown's terrific crossfield ball and charging in on goal before unleashing an unstoppable shot into the roof of the net from the left side of the penalty area.

Spurs almost doubled their lead soon after, Keane running on to a through ball and rounding James, only for defender Sylvain Distin to make a great goal-line clearance.

Spurs substitute Stephen Kelly was lucky to escape a red card following an extremely aggressive challenge on Wright-Phillips, Mr Gallagher only showing a yellow.

Keane wasted an excellent chance on 78 minutes, blazing over from three yards after being set up by Brown.

Frederic Kanoute celebrates his stunning strike

"As the game went on we passed the ball without any real purpose, and in the end Spurs deserved to beat us."

Kevin Keegan

"It is not about playing terrifically, but about getting a result."

Martin Jol

PREMIERSHIP MILESTONE

Michael Brown made his 50th Premiership appearance

PREMIERSHIP FIXTURE HISTORY

Pl: **2** Draws: **1**

	Wins	⚽	Yellow	Red
Newcastle United	1	4	1	0
Portsmouth	0	1	3	0

STARTING LINE-UPS

Newcastle United: Given; Taylor, Hughes, Bramble, Bernard; Bowyer, Dyer, Jenas (c), Milner; Ameobi, Bellamy

Portsmouth: Fuller; Berger, Faye, Stone, Lua Lua; O'Neil, Stefanovic, De Zeeuw (c), Primus, Griffin; Ashdown

Newcastle United substitutes: Robert, Ambrose, Harper, Elliott, O'Brien

Portsmouth substitutes: Taylor, Cisse, Hislop, Hughes, Berkovic

EVENT LINE

3 ⚽ **Bowyer (Open Play)**

27 ▢ Stone (Foul)

30 ⚽ Stone (Corner)

HALF TIME 1 - 1

57 ⇄ **Milner (Off) Robert (On)**

71 ⇄ **Bowyer (Off) Ambrose (On)**

74 ▢ **Taylor (Foul)**

84 ⇄ Fuller (Off) Taylor (On)

87 ⇄ Lua Lua (Off) Cisse (On)

90 ▢ Griffin (Foul)

FULL TIME 1 - 1

STATISTICS

Season	Fixture (Newcastle)		Fixture (Portsmouth)	Season
132	2	Shots On Target	3	91
107	13	Shots Off Target	3	77
7	0	Hit Woodwork	0	2
47	0	Caught Offside	3	39
126	6	Corners	2	82
207	12	Fouls	15	196
51%	53%	Possession	47%	48%

LEAGUE STANDINGS

Position (pos before)	W	D	L	F	A	Pts
12 (12) Newcastle Utd	5	6	6	28	32	21
10 (9) Portsmouth	6	4	6	22	23	22

Saturday 11th December 2004 | Venue: **St James' Park** | Attendance: **51,480** | Referee: **M.A.Riley**

NEWCASTLE UNITED 1 PORTSMOUTH 1

Steve Stone savours his equaliser

"We allowed ourselves to become a bit nervous in the second half. The crowd became nervous, and so did we."

Graeme Souness

PREMIERSHIP MILESTONE

50 Titus Bramble made his 50th Premiership appearance for Newcastle

"We were spirited and resilient, and we applied ourselves well."

First Team Coach Joe Jordan

Lacklustre Newcastle made it five home games without a win – a run last achieved in the days of Ruud Gullit.

United got off to a dream start with a stunning Lee Bowyer goal inside three minutes, the midfielder's first in the Premiership this season.

Newcastle old boy Lomana LuaLua was looking for a foul on the halfway line after tangling with Bowyer, only for Steven Taylor to seize possession and storm forward.

Bowyer responded immediately, charging ahead before collecting from Taylor and drilling an unstoppable shot beyond Jamie Ashdown and into the top corner.

United almost doubled their lead on the quarter-hour mark, Craig Bellamy robbing Andy Griffin on the halfway line and racing towards goal before unselfishly picking out Kieron Dyer, whose lung-bursting 80-yard run ended with him lifting his left-footed attempt over from eight yards.

Ashdown had a major let-off on 27 minutes after slipping while attempting to clear a Griffin back pass, the ball creeping narrowly past the post for a corner.

Two minutes later, Pompey grabbed a shock equaliser through Gateshead-born Steve Stone.

Bowyer cleared a Ricardo Fuller header off the line, the ball eventually finding its way to former England midfield man Stone, whose 20-yard shot took a deflection off Jermaine Jenas to wrong-foot keeper Shay Given.

James Milner then almost reclaimed the lead for United, his left-foot volley from Taylor's deep cross flying into the side netting.

United sent on Laurent Robert for Milner just before the hour mark and the enigmatic Frenchman immediately brought a save out of Ashdown with what would prove Newcastle's final effort on target.

With Jenas and Bowyer continuing to fire in midfield, the home support were clearly surprised to see the latter lose his place to Darren Ambrose on 71 minutes.

Jenas worked tirelessly in his efforts to restore Newcastle's advantage, helping to pin Pompey back in their own half.

The visitors wasted a gilt-edged chance to take all three points in the 81st minute, Stone collecting from LuaLua on the right and whipping in a pinpoint cross for Gary O'Neil, who planted his header wide of the target from six yards.

PREMIERSHIP FIXTURE HISTORY

Pl: 1 Draws: 0	Wins	Goals	Yellow	Red
Norwich City	1	3	1	0
Bolton Wanderers	0	2	3	0

STARTING LINE-UPS

Norwich City: Green; Edworthy, Fleming (c), Doherty, Charlton; Bentley, Helveg, Safri; Jonson, Huckerby; Svensson

Bolton Wanderers: Davies; Pedersen, Giannakopoulos; Speed, Campo, Okocha (c); N'Gotty, Jaidi, Hierro, Hunt; Jaaskelainen

Norwich City substitutes: McVeigh, Ward, Drury, Shackell, Jarvis

Bolton Wanderers substitutes: Nolan, Ferdinand, Cesar, Oakes, Ben Haim

EVENT LINE

19 Goal Okocha (Penalty)

19 Goal **Svensson (Open Play)**

20 Yellow card **Svensson (Ung.Conduct)**

23 Goal Hierro (Corner)

HALF TIME 1 - 2

60 Yellow card N'Gotty (Foul)

66 Yellow card Campo (Dissent)

69 Goal **Huckerby (Penalty)**

70 Substitution Campo (Off) Nolan (On)

79 Substitution **Jonson (Off) McVeigh (On)**

84 Goal **Svensson (Open Play)**

85 Substitution Okocha (Off) Ferdinand (On)

89 Yellow card Hunt (Foul)

90 Substitution N'Gotty (Off) Cesar (On)

FULL TIME 3 - 2

STATISTICS

Season	Fixture (Norwich)		Fixture (Bolton)	Season
84	5	Shots On Target	4	118
96	5	Shots Off Target	1	96
3	0	Hit Woodwork	0	4
59	1	Caught Offside	3	31
81	4	Corners	4	91
235	10	Fouls	26	233
48%	57%	Possession	43%	49%

LEAGUE STANDINGS

Position (pos before)	W	D	L	F	A	Pts
15 (19) Norwich C	2	9	6	17	28	15
9 (8) Bolton W	6	5	6	26	25	23

Saturday 11th December 2004 | Venue: **Carrow Road** | Attendance: **23,549** | Referee: **B.Knight**

NORWICH CITY 3 BOLTON WANDERERS 2

After slipping up against Fulham in their previous match, Norwich City got their season back on track with a battling win against Bolton.

Norwich threatened in the sixth minute, Darren Huckerby collecting keeper Robert Green's clearance and racing down the left before laying the ball inside to Youssef Safri, whose shot flew wide.

Mattias Jonson fed Huckerby on the left five minutes later, but his low cross was cut out before it reached Mathias Svensson.

Norwich won the first corner of the game on the quarter-hour mark after Radhi Jaidi blocked Jonson's right-wing cross, but nothing came of it.

Referee Barry Knight awarded Bolton a 19th-minute penalty after Gary Doherty handled Gary Speed's long throw.

Jay-Jay Okocha stepped up and confidently slotted into the opposite corner, Green diving to his right.

Norwich equalised within a minute, Svensson heading David Bentley's right-wing cross inside the near post from eight yards.

Fernando Hierro restored Bolton's lead three minutes later, heading Stelios Giannakopoulos's left-wing corner past Green at the near post.

The Norwich keeper kept things close on 37 minutes, making an excellent save to deny Jaidi's header.

Bentley went close three minutes later, his in-swinging free kick from the left eluding everyone in the six yard box before curling inches wide of the far post.

Norwich enjoyed most of the possession in the opening 10 minutes of the second period, though Green had to be alert to tip over a shot from Stelios.

Bruno N'Gotty and Ivan Campo were booked for late tackles on Jonson and Huckerby respectively, as Norwich continued to do most of the attacking.

The Canaries won a penalty of their own on 69 minutes after Bentley was tripped by Speed.

Huckerby took it, sending Jussi Jaaskelainen the wrong way with a right-foot shot inside the keeper's left-hand post for 2-2.

Not surprisingly, the visitors then went on the offensive and Norwich lost some of their momentum.

Paul McVeigh fired a long-range shot over before Norwich grabbed the winner with six minutes to play, Bentley's cross from the right wing finding Svensson, whose powerful header beat the keeper at the far post.

"We deserved the three points. The commitment was there, and the passing was much better than last week."

Nigel Worthington

"Our defending is pathetic at the moment. Defending should be the easy part, but we are getting it wrong."

Sam Allardyce

PREMIERSHIP MILESTONE

Fernando Hierro scored his first Premiership goal

Kevin Davies is challenged by Mark Edworthy

PREMIERSHIP FIXTURE HISTORY

Pl: 10 Draws: 5	Wins	⚽	Yellow	Red
Southampton	3	16	15	1
Middlesbrough	2	13	18	4

STARTING LINE-UPS

Telfer, Smith, Dodd, Griffit, Ormerod

Nemeth, Job, Nash, Davies, Doriva

EVENT LINE

45 ⚽ **Phillips (Open Play)**

HALF TIME 1 - 0

46 **Fernandes (Off) Telfer (On)**

53 **Delap (Foul)**

60 McMahon (Off) Nemeth (On)

64 ⚽ **Crouch (Corner)**

83 Parlour (Off) Job (On)

86 Boateng (Foul)

89 ⚽ Higginbotham (Own Goal)

90 ⚽ Downing (Open Play)

FULL TIME 2 - 2

STATISTICS

Season	Fixture		Fixture	Season
84	5	Shots On Target	7	123
100	11	Shots Off Target	8	109
2	0	Hit Woodwork	1	4
43	3	Caught Offside	1	45
89	4	Corners	6	94
220	11	Fouls	12	218
49%	46%	Possession	54%	50%

LEAGUE STANDINGS

Position (pos before)	W	D	L	F	A	Pts
19 (18) Southampton	2	7	8	17	26	13
5 (5) Middlesbrough	8	5	4	29	22	29

Saturday 11th December 2004 | Venue: **Friends Provident St Mary's Stadium** | Attendance: **29,018** | Referee: **N.S.Barry**

SOUTHAMPTON 2 MIDDLESBROUGH 2

Two Middlesbrough goals in the last two minutes denied Harry Redknapp a win in his first game in charge at Southampton.

Redknapp watched in horror as Saints threw away a precious lead and had to settle for a point when all three were there for the taking.

Southampton opened the scoring just before the break, Kevin Phillips heading home from Graeme Le Saux's centre.

Boro could have been ahead by then, but Jimmy Floyd Hasselbaink shot straight at keeper Antti Niemi, who also made a smart double save from Michael Reiziger and Mark Viduka.

Rory Delap received the game's first booking on 52 minutes, a yellow card for his foul from behind on Stewart Downing.

Hasselbaink took the resulting free kick, firing well over from 22 yards.

Niemi made a superb save to deny Downing an equaliser on the hour, pushing away the midfielder's point-blank shot after he'd ghosted in behind his markers.

Saints looked to have sealed the win with a second goal on 64 minutes, Le Saux's corner from the left headed home by Peter Crouch, who was making his first Premiership start.

Crouch wasted a chance for his second four minutes later, heading Le Saux's floated cross over with the goal at his mercy.

On 72 minutes, Saints midfielder Anders Svensson ran clear from midfield before shooting wide from the edge of the area, but the longer the match went on, the stronger Middlesbrough became.

Viduka and George Boateng both shot wide before the visitors were handed a lifeline in the 89th minute, Danny Higginbotham turning Downing's in-swinging corner from the right over his own line. It was the third time this season an opposing player had netted for Boro.

The visitors then grabbed a shock equaliser a minute into stoppage time, Reiziger playing a ball from the right in towards Downing, who brought it to his left foot before smashing a low drive from 20 yards which gave Niemi no chance.

Redknapp, given a rousing reception by the crowd on his first appearance at St Mary's, scuffed the ground in disgust at the final whistle, having watched his side throw away two precious points.

Stewart Downing celebrates his dramatic late leveller

"The players gave everything, but our nerve cracked a bit."

Harry Redknapp

PREMIERSHIP MILESTONE

300 Paul Telfer made his 300th Premiership appearance

"We got a reprieve with those two late goals, but I am still disappointed with the result."

Steve McClaren

Saturday 11th December 2004	Venue: **The Hawthorns**	Attendance: **24,697**	Referee: **C.J.Foy**

PREMIERSHIP FIXTURE HISTORY

Pl: **2** Draws: **0**	Wins		
West Bromwich Albion	**0**	**0**	**0**	**0**
Charlton Athletic	**2**	**2**	**2**	**0**

STARTING LINE-UPS

Koumas, Horsfield, Kuszczak, Gaardsoe, Hulse

Konchesky, Hughes, Andersen, Euell, Jeffers

EVENT LINE

30 Holland (Indirect Free Kick)

HALF TIME 0 - 1

55 **Contra (Off) Koumas (On)**

65 Rommedahl (Off) Konchesky (On)

85 Thomas (Off) Hughes (On)

88 **Gera (Off) Horsfield (On)**

FULL TIME 0 - 1

STATISTICS

Season	Fixture		Fixture	Season
77	4	Shots On Target	2	76
78	3	Shots Off Target	6	62
2	0	Hit Woodwork	0	2
61	3	Caught Offside	5	56
89	6	Corners	6	67
229	16	Fouls	13	223
46%	56%	Possession	44%	43%

LEAGUE STANDINGS

Position (pos before)	W	D	L	F	A	Pts
20 (20) West Brom	1	7	9	15	32	10
8 (10) Charlton Ath	7	3	7	19	27	24

Matt Holland takes the plaudits at The Hawthorns

"This was a disappointing day, and the boys have got to turn it around now."

Bryan Robson

PREMIERSHIP MILESTONE

50 Neil Clement made his 50th Premiership appearance for West Brom

"Two 1-0 away wins in a week have turned our season around."

Alan Curbishley

PREMIERSHIP MILESTONE

50 Hermann Hreidarsson made his 50th Premiership appearance in the colours of Charlton

WEST BROM 0 CHARLTON ATHLETIC 1

Matt Holland's first goal of the season earned Charlton their second successive win and left struggling West Brom rooted to the bottom of the Premiership.

Holland's 30th-minute strike saw off the challenge of an Albion side who had now taken just one point from a possible 15 under new manager Bryan Robson.

With just one win so far all season, the Baggies were looking increasingly likely candidates for the drop.

West Brom made a bright start, with Jonathan Greening and Andy Johnson testing Dean Kiely from distance.

The former Republic of Ireland international keeper dealt comfortably with both efforts, but he needed the help of Danny Murphy on 26 minutes, the midfielder clearing off the line from Neil Clement's cross.

It proved to be a timely intervention, as Charlton opened the scoring four minutes later with their first shot on target.

The Addicks won a free kick out on the right after Zoltan Gera was rather harshly adjudged to have fouled Dennis Rommedahl.

Murphy took it, whipping in a ball which was cleared by Clement only as far as Holland, who struck a first-time shot through a crowded goalmouth and past the despairing dive of home keeper Russell Hoult.

Albion almost equalised straight afterwards, Gera's header dropping just wide.

Charlton were looking the more dangerous side and really should have doubled their lead on the stroke of half time, Murphy collecting from Rommedahl before dragging his shot narrowly wide.

Murphy missed a chance three minutes into the second period, his close-range shot flying into the side netting after he'd been picked out by a header from Hermann Hreidarsson.

Shaun Bartlett then wasted an excellent opportunity for the visitors, firing wide from Jerome Thomas's cross with only Hoult to beat.

Fortunately for Charlton, Albion were proving equally unsuccessful in front of goal, Kanu's 65th-minute shot deflected over before Gera bundled a cross from Greening just the wrong side of the post six minutes later.

Albion's unhappy fans made their feelings known after the game when they booed their side off the pitch.

PREMIERSHIP FIXTURE HISTORY

Pl: **13** Draws: **4**	Wins	Goals	Yellow cards	Red cards
Arsenal	9	25	18	1
Chelsea	0	14	32	0

STARTING LINE-UPS

Clichy, van Persie, Lehmann, Hoyte, Senderos

Bridge, Drogba, Parker, Cudicini, Kezman

EVENT LINE

2 **Henry (Open Play)**

17 Terry (Corner)

29 **Henry (Direct Free Kick)**

30 Robben (Dissent)

HALF TIME 2 - 1

46 Carvalho (Off) Drogba (On)

46 Tiago (Off) Bridge (On)

46 Gudjohnsen (Indirect Free Kick)

67 Drogba (Foul)

73 Lampard (Foul)

77 Gudjohnsen (Off) Parker (On)

79 **Cole (Foul)**

82 **Bergkamp (Off) van Persie (On)**

82 **Reyes (Off) Clichy (On)**

FULL TIME 2 - 2

STATISTICS

Season	Fixture (Arsenal)		Fixture (Chelsea)	Season
140	2	Shots On Target	4	132
77	6	Shots Off Target	5	116
6	0	Hit Woodwork	0	7
35	2	Caught Offside	6	57
91	4	Corners	6	132
185	11	Fouls	17	210
56%	43%	Possession	57%	56%

LEAGUE STANDINGS

Position (pos before)		W	D	L	F	A	Pts
3 (3)	Arsenal	10	5	2	44	22	35
1 (1)	Chelsea	12	4	1	33	8	40

Sunday 12th December 2004 | Venue: **Highbury** | Attendance: **38,153** | Referee: **G.Poll**

ARSENAL 2 CHELSEA 2

Chelsea twice came from behind to earn a point at Arsenal.

John Terry and Eidur Gudjohnsen cancelled out two strikes from Thierry Henry, as the Blues punished Arsenal's notorious vulnerability in dead ball situations.

Chelsea had still yet to win a league game at Highbury since 1990, but they solidified their position at the top of the Premiership, five points clear of third-placed Arsenal and four ahead of second-placed Everton.

They could have won the game through Frank Lampard and Arjen Robben in the second half, but they almost lost it in the dying minutes when Cesc Fabregas instigated two penetrating moves for the Gunners.

Arsenal manager Arsène Wenger continued with Manuel Almunia in goal, despite criticism of his shaky midweek performance against Rosenborg.

With skipper Patrick Vieira missing through suspension, youngsters Fabregas and Mathieu Flamini filled the central midfield roles.

Chelsea boss José Mourinho stuck with two wingers and Gudjohnsen as a lone striker.

Henry made an explosive start, seizing on Jose Antonio Reyes's header and crashing a left-foot shot past keeper Petr Cech after just 75 seconds.

Chelsea countered with the equaliser on 17 minutes, an unmarked Terry running in to bullet a header across Almunia.

Chelsea lived up to Mourinho's promise to try and win the game, but it was Arsenal who scored next on 29 minutes, Henry's quickly taken free kick on the edge of the box deflecting off Tiago and past the stranded Cech.

Mourinho went with four up front to start the second half, sending on Didier Drogba and Wayne Bridge.

The move paid instant dividends, William Gallas flicking Lampard's free kick on to Gudjohnsen, who nodded past Almunia for a 46th-minute equaliser.

Lampard then wasted a free header from a corner before Robben fired into the side netting.

Arsenal began to fight back, the previously quiet Fabregas at the heart of many of their attacks.

Henry missed a great chance to complete his hat-trick, firing over from Robert Pires's cross after Fabregas had split the defence.

Substitute Robin van Persie almost snatched victory for the Gunners six minutes from time, side-footing inches wide from another slide-rule pass by Fabregas.

"I was a bit frustrated, because we were ahead twice. But we showed great fighting spirit in an intense contest."

Arsene Wenger

PREMIERSHIP MILESTONE

800 Thierry Henry's 2nd goal was Arsenal's 800th in the Premiership

"We're not good enough as a team to gift our opponents two goals."

David O'Leary

Damien Duff and Jose Antonio Reyes collide

PREMIERSHIP FIXTURE HISTORY

Pl: 3 Draws: 1	Wins	⚽	▢	■
Aston Villa	0	3	2	2
Birmingham City	2	6	7	0

STARTING LINE-UPS

Ridgewell, Postma Berson, Whittingham, L.Moore

Gray, Anderton, Clapham, Vaesen, Yorke

EVENT LINE

9 ⚽ Morrison (Open Play)

18 ⚽ Dunn (Open Play)

37 ▢ **Mellberg (Ung.Conduct)**

37 ▢ Johnson (Ung.Conduct)

45 ▢ Dunn (Foul)

HALF TIME 0 - 2

59 ⇄ Dunn (Off) Gray (On)

66 ▢ **Barry (Handball)**

66 ▢ Tebily (Foul)

77 ▢ Carter (Ung.Conduct)

82 ⇄ Morrison (Off) Anderton (On)

90 ⚽ **Barry (Open Play)**

90 ⇄ Lazaridis (Off) Clapham (On)

FULL TIME 1 - 2

STATISTICS

Season	Fixture		Fixture	Season
91	2	Shots On Target	4	74
84	7	Shots Off Target	5	83
3	0	Hit Woodwork	1	4
51	1	Caught Offside	3	48
98	6	Corners	0	90
260	9	Fouls	28	248
50%	68%	Possession	32%	49%

LEAGUE STANDINGS

Position (pos before)		W	D	L	F	A	Pts
6 (6)	Aston Villa	6	7	4	22	19	25
14 (16)	Birmingham C	3	8	6	14	19	17

Sunday 12th December 2004 | Venue: **Villa Park** | Attendance: **41,329** | Referee: **S.W.Dunn**

ASTON VILLA 1 BIRMINGHAM CITY 2

Birmingham celebrate going two goals up

"We're not good enough as a team to gift our opponents two goals."
David O'Leary

"This win is even sweeter after Olof Mellberg's comments. We'd like to dedicate the victory to him."
Robbie Savage

PREMIERSHIP MILESTONE

250 Robbie Savage made his 250th Premiership appearance

An early error by Thomas Sorensen set Birmingham on their way to another derby success against Aston Villa.

The Danish keeper allowed a drive from Clinton Morrison to bounce over him after nine minutes, as the Blues made the perfect start at Villa Park.

Sorensen's defence were guilty of some equally poor play minutes later, letting in David Dunn to score Birmingham's second from eight yards.

Gareth Barry pulled a goal back in second-half stoppage time, but by then the damage had already been done.

Olof Mellberg and defensive partner Mark Delaney presented the visitors with a number of openings early on.

Both backed off when Morrison hit a hopeful effort from 20 yards straight at Sorensen which the keeper contrived to dive beneath, handing Birmingham the lead.

Gavin McCann then fired high and wide with a left-foot drive before City doubled their lead on 18 minutes.

Olivier Tebily played a long ball to Morrison, who beat a man before laying off for Damien Johnson down the right.

Johnson outpaced Jlloyd Samuel and cut inside before crossing low for Dunn to slot home with a first-time shot.

Villa started to come back into the match, with Stephen Davis and McCann bossing the midfield. But they were too reliant on long balls upfield, making it hard for Juan Pablo Angel and Carlton Cole to force an opening.

Emile Heskey almost added a third for Birmingham right before the break, his shot from a tight angle hitting the post.

The second half began in the same vein, with Villa dominating possession and City threatening on the counter.

Barry twice found the back of the net, but both efforts were disallowed – the first for offside, the second for handball.

Birmingham substitute Darren Anderton shot straight at Sorensen when clean through before Barry finally converted for Villa, controlling a long ball before firing past the flailing Maik Taylor.

City held firm for the last couple of minutes to earn the win and remain undefeated in the five Second City derbies they'd played against Villa since their promotion to the Premiership.

PREMIERSHIP FIXTURE HISTORY

Pl: 4 Draws: 3	Wins	Goals	Yellow cards	Red cards
Fulham	0	5	4	0
Manchester United	1	6	9	0

STARTING LINE-UPS

Radzinski, John, Flitney, Knight, Hammond

O'Shea, Howard, Fortune, Fletcher, Bellion

EVENT LINE

33 Smith (Open Play)

HALF TIME 0 - 1

74 **Legwinski (Off) Radzinski (On)**

80 **Diop (Handball)**

83 **Malbranque (Off) John (On)**

87 **Diop (Open Play)**

90 **Radzinski (Foul)**

90 Silvestre (Foul)

FULL TIME 1 - 1

STATISTICS

Season	Fixture		Fixture	Season
85	3	Shots On Target	4	137
80	7	Shots Off Target	12	137
3	1	Hit Woodwork	2	9
39	1	Caught Offside	1	62
84	6	Corners	7	138
215	16	Fouls	14	203
48%	43%	Possession	57%	55%

LEAGUE STANDINGS

Position (pos before)		W	D	L	F	A	Pts
14 (15)	Fulham	5	3	9	19	28	18
4 (4)	Man Utd	8	7	2	23	11	31

Monday 13th December 2004 | Venue: **Craven Cottage** | Attendance: **21,940** | Referee: **P.Dowd**

Mikael Silvestre keeps a tight grip on Andy Cole

"We were delighted to take a point. Some of the football United played was fantastic."
Chris Coleman

PREMIERSHIP MILESTONE

350 Andy Cole made his 350th Premiership appearance

PREMIERSHIP MILESTONE

The attendance of 21,940 was a Premiership record at Craven Cottage

PREMIERSHIP MILESTONE

Liam Rosenior made his Premiership debut

"The thing that makes this result so bad for us is that both our main rivals dropped points yesterday."
Sir Alex Ferguson

PREMIERSHIP MILESTONE

950 Alan Smith scored Man Utd's 950th Premiership goal

FULHAM 1 MANCHESTER UNITED 1

Fulham's Senegal international Papa Bouba Diop scored a stunning equaliser to earn his side a point against Manchester United and put a serious dent in the Red Devils' title challenge.

United were hoping to move two points closer to Premiership leaders Chelsea after the Blues' 2-2 draw at Highbury, and they looked to be on their way following Alan Smith's first-half goal.

But with just three minutes to play, Diop unleashed a ferocious 25-yard shot to steal a point for Fulham.

It was a particularly gratifying result for the Cottagers given the unavailability of first-choice players Luis Boa Morte, Lee Clark, Claus Jensen, Alain Goma, Mark Crossley and Moritz Volz.

United quickly took control of the first half and it seemed only a matter of time before they found the back of the net.

Roy Keane went close on 29 minutes, blasting a 25-yard shot against Edwin van der Sar's left-hand post.

Wayne Rooney then rattled the other upright after collecting a Paul Scholes pass wide on the left and cutting inside.

The opener came on 33 minutes, Smith sliding in to steal Cristiano Ronaldo's low cross from Sylvain Legwinski before getting up and slotting home.

The goal was no doubt greeted with dismay at both Highbury and Stamford Bridge, and United nearly had another five minutes later, Keane's belter well saved by Van der Sar.

Ronaldo took a dive just before the break as he tried to win an undeserved penalty, but referee Phil Dowd wasn't fooled.

The Portuguese striker then had the final chance of the half, dragging his shot narrowly wide from a good position.

Fulham almost equalised a minute into the second half, Diop's header from a corner spectacularly tipped over by Roy Carroll.

Andy Cole went close five minutes later, slamming a right-footed shot against the same post that had earlier denied Keane.

Cole then sent a back header over the bar after Brian McBride had done well to win a high ball on the edge of the box.

Fulham continued to press and were rewarded in the 87th minute, Diop firing home to leave United stunned.

PREMIERSHIP FIXTURE HISTORY

Pl: **2** Draws: **1**

	Wins	⚽	▯	▮
Liverpool	1	4	0	0
Portsmouth	0	1	1	0

STARTING LINE-UPS

Josemi, Harrison, Riise, Mellor, Sinama-Pongolle

Taylor, Berkovic, Hislop, Mezague, Cisse

EVENT LINE

HALF TIME 0 - 0

61 Fuller (Off) Taylor (On)

70 ⚽ **Gerrard (Indirect Free Kick)**

82 **Baros (Off) Sinama-Pongolle (On)**

85 Faye (Off) Berkovic (On)

89 **Nunez (Off) Josemi (On)**

90 ⚽ Lua Lua (Open Play)

FULL TIME 1 - 1

STATISTICS

Season	Fixture		Fixture	Season
117	7	Shots On Target	3	94
111	3	Shots Off Target	4	81
2	0	Hit Woodwork	0	2
47	0	Caught Offside	1	40
99	3	Corners	7	89
199	4	Fouls	6	202
53%	56%	Possession	44%	48%

LEAGUE STANDINGS

Position (pos before)		W	D	L	F	A	Pts
6 (7)	Liverpool	7	4	6	25	19	25
10 (10)	Portsmouth	6	5	6	23	24	23

Tuesday 14th December 2004 | Venue: **Anfield** | Attendance: **35,064** | Referee: **M.Clattenburg**

LIVERPOOL 1 PORTSMOUTH 1

Amdy Faye spins away from Milan Baros

A stoppage-time equaliser from Lomana LuaLua earned Portsmouth a point at Anfield.

Reds boss Rafael Benitez made six changes to his starting line-up following a painful reverse in the Merseyside derby against Everton at the weekend.

Milan Baros returned to freshen up a tired strikeforce, while Xabi Alonso brought some culture and class to midfield. Keeper Jerzy Dudek made his first Premiership start since September, coming in for Saturday's fall guy Chris Kirkland, who was sidelined with a back injury.

Liverpool threatened on eight minutes, a fine ball over the top from Alonso finding Steven Gerrard, whose low cross was intercepted by Jamie Ashdown with Baros lurking.

Dietmar Hamann had a better chance a minute later, but he scuffed his shot wide after Antonio Nunez had flicked on Gerrard's corner.

Portsmouth almost took a surprise lead midway through the half after Steve Finnan was caught out of position, LuaLua curling his effort wide.

A Nunez challenge on 37 minutes gave Harry Kewell a golden opportunity to set the marauding Gerrard free, but the Australian dreadfully over-hit his pass.

Five minutes before the break, a mazy run from LuaLua saw him bypass the entire Liverpool defence, but his tame shot from a tight angle landed comfortably at Dudek's feet.

Gary O'Neil went on an equally impressive run a minute later before curling his shot inches wide.

Gerrard provided a much needed spark of inspiration as the second half got underway, turning beautifully to open space for a shot, only to see his effort creep over the bar.

Benitez's undoubtedly stern half-time words looked to have given the Reds fresh impetus, and the Kop responded by raising the decibel level tenfold.

On 56 minutes, Gerrard nodded a trademark crossfield pass from Alonso into the path of Nunez, who was denied by Ashdown from point-blank range.

Liverpool were looking good for a goal and it finally came from a 70th-minute free kick, Gerrard blasting a 25-yard shot into the top corner from Alonso's lay-off.

But a dreadful error by Dudek in stoppage time undid all of Gerrard's good work, the keeper palming Matthew Taylor's cross out only as far as LuaLua, who nodded home.

"The players are frustrated, as am I, but there's nothing we can do now."

Rafael Benitez

PREMIERSHIP MILESTONE

50 Harry Kewell made his 50th Premiership appearance in the colours of Liverpool

"Liverpool won a lot of trophies by playing right to the end, and I'm absolutely delighted at the way we got the goal."

First Team Coach Joe Jordan

Saturday 18th December 2004	Venue: **St Andrew's**	Attendance: **28,880**	Referee: **M.A.Riley**

PREMIERSHIP FIXTURE HISTORY

Pl: **2** Draws: **0**	Wins	⚽	▢	■
Birmingham City	**2**	**5**	**0**	**0**
West Bromwich Albion	**0**	**0**	**4**	**0**

STARTING LINE-UPS

Anderton, Gray, Clapham, Vaesen, Clemence

Earnshaw, Wallwork, Kuszczak, Dyer, Horsfield

EVENT LINE

4 ⚽ **Savage (Penalty)**

20 ▢ Koumas (Foul)

23 ⚽ **Morrison (Indirect Free Kick)**

30 ⚽ **Heskey (Open Play)**

32 ▢ Haas (Foul)

44 ▢ Greening (Foul)

HALF TIME 3 - 0

46 Gera (Off) Earnshaw (On)

60 ▢ Gaardsoe (Foul)

75 Haas (Off) Wallwork (On)

78 **Johnson (Off) Anderton (On)**

80 ⚽ **Anderton (Direct Free Kick)**

83 **Heskey (Off) Gray (On)**

87 **Savage (Off) Clapham (On)**

FULL TIME 4 - 0

STATISTICS

Season	Fixture		Fixture	Season
79	**5**	Shots On Target	**6**	**83**
86	**3**	Shots Off Target	**3**	**81**
4	**0**	Hit Woodwork	**1**	**3**
52	**4**	Caught Offside	**1**	**62**
92	**2**	Corners	**2**	**91**
262	**14**	Fouls	**20**	**249**
49%	**54%**	Possession	**46%**	**46%**

LEAGUE STANDINGS

Position (pos before)	W	D	L	F	A	Pts
14 (15) Birmingham C	**4**	**8**	**6**	**18**	**19**	**20**
20 (20) West Brom	**1**	**7**	**10**	**15**	**36**	**10**

BIRMINGHAM CITY 4 WEST BROM 0

Birmingham recorded their second derby victory in six days with a comprehensive win over West Brom.

Goals from Robbie Savage, Clinton Morrison, Emile Heskey and Darren Anderton saw the Blues past their local rivals.

With Mario Melchiot still not fit, Birmingham fielded an unchanged starting line-up from the side that had beaten Villa.

Albion defender Darren Purse lined up against Birmingham for the first time since his departure in the summer, while Geoff Horsfield took a seat on the bench.

Birmingham were awarded a penalty in the fourth minute after Purse blatantly held back Morrison in the area.

Savage – the centre of much midweek speculation regarding his future at Birmingham – stepped up and sent Russell Hoult the wrong way, calmly slotting into the bottom-right corner

Zoltan Gera responded for Albion, hitting the post from Kanu's flicked pass.

Jonathan Greening managed to get in a powerful shot from the rebound, but it was well covered by keeper Maik Taylor.

The visitors were then lucky not to concede a second penalty, Purse appearing to handle Damien Johnson's cross after it had been touched on by Heskey.

Birmingham doubled their lead on 23 minutes, Darren Carter receiving David Dunn's quickly taken free kick and drawing the Albion defence before sending a ball into the area for Morrison to drill past Hoult.

It was 3-0 by the half-hour mark, Dunn slipping a good ball through to Heskey, who fired low across Hoult and into the far corner.

West Brom enjoyed a decent spell of pressure before half time, but they never seriously threatened the Blues' goal.

Albion boss Bryan Robson switched things around at the break, replacing Gera with Robert Earnshaw.

The move was greeted by boos and jeers from the travelling fans, who clearly felt that after six matches in charge they were now entitled to get on the manager's back.

Birmingham capped an impressive performance with a fourth goal on 80 minutes, Anderton's low free kick taking a deflection before settling in the back of the net.

Clinton Morrison celebrates with Darren Carter

"They couldn't handle big Emile Heskey, while the return to fitness of Clinton Morrison and David Dunn has been a major boost for us."

Steve Bruce

PREMIERSHIP MILESTONE

100 Clinton Morrison scored Birmingham's 100th Premiership goal

PREMIERSHIP MILESTONE

75 Emile Heskey netted his 75th Premiership goal

"It was shocking defending in the opening half-hour, which allowed Birmingham to take control."

Bryan Robson

PREMIERSHIP FIXTURE HISTORY

Pl: **11** Draws: **2**	Wins	Goals	Yellow	Red
Blackburn Rovers	5	15	19	1
Everton	4	13	18	1

STARTING LINE-UPS

Blackburn subs: Johansson, Gallagher Enckelman, Pedersen, Stead

Everton subs: Ferguson, McFadden, Watson, Wright, Yobo

EVENT LINE

21	**Short (Off) Johansson (On)**
	HALF TIME 0 - 0
57	**Todd (Ung.Conduct)**
62	Hibbert (Foul)
63	Cahill (Off) Ferguson (On)
64	Osman (Off) McFadden (On)
68	Carsley (Foul)
83	**Bothroyd (Off) Gallagher (On)**
87	Bent (Off) Watson (On)
	FULL TIME 0 - 0

STATISTICS

Season	Fixture (Blackburn)		Fixture (Everton)	Season
93	**4**	Shots On Target	**1**	**90**
109	**5**	Shots Off Target	**2**	**91**
4	**1**	Hit Woodwork	**0**	**3**
70	**5**	Caught Offside	**0**	**48**
100	**7**	Corners	**2**	**91**
290	**29**	Fouls	**19**	**217**
48%	**55%**	Possession	**45%**	**49%**

LEAGUE STANDINGS

Position (pos before)		W	D	L	F	A	Pts
16 (18)	**Blackburn R**	**2**	**9**	**7**	**16**	**30**	**15**
2 (2)	**Everton**	**11**	**4**	**3**	**21**	**14**	**37**

Saturday 18th December 2004 | Venue: **Ewood Park** | Attendance: **25,191** | Referee: **M.R.Halsey**

BLACKBURN ROVERS 0 EVERTON 0

Blackburn failed to win at home for the sixth successive time as they played out a goalless draw against second-placed Everton.

On a day when all the other sides in the relegation battle lost heavily, the result represented a wasted opportunity for Blackburn to put some much needed space between themselves and the dropzone.

Everton could also have done with the three points to consolidate their spot in the Champions League qualification places.

Rovers were marginally the better side in a scrappy game of few chances and they took the initiative early on.

Garry Flitcroft set up Paul Dickov in the third minute, but his volley was well blocked by Tony Hibbert.

The resulting corner found Flitcroft unmarked, but he fluffed his shot and Hibbert cleared off the line.

The Rovers midfielder had another chance on eight minutes after Brett Emerton teed him up 20 yards out, but he fired his shot into the crowd.

The first half then descended into a midfield battle, with chances at a premium.

It took until the 29th minute for Blackburn to threaten again, Barry Ferguson sending his effort straight into the arms of Nigel Martyn.

Everton were posing little threat down the other end, their best chance a Kevin Kilbane header on the stroke of half time.

There was little for the crowd to get excited about after the break, as a succession of free kicks interrupted the flow of the game.

The arrival of Duncan Ferguson on 63 minutes livened up Everton's attack, the striker flicking a ball on for Marcus Bent, whose shot on the turn forced a good save from Brad Friedel.

Flitcroft then went close for Rovers, heading Emerton's cross just wide.

Paul Gallagher came on for Jay Bothroyd in the 83rd minute and within two minutes he had the ball in the back of the net, tapping home after Martyn had saved Steven Reid's low shot. But the youngster's goal was ruled out for offside.

If that wasn't enough anguish for the home fans, Emerton then powered a drive from 20 yards which deflected beyond Martyn and flew towards the bottom corner, only to slam back off the foot of the post.

Paul Dickov outpaces Thomas Gravesen

"We are finding it difficult to convert draws into wins, but we are working very hard to get the points we deserve."
Mark Hughes

"We have to be better than that, but at least we managed to secure a point from the game."
Alan Stubbs

PREMIERSHIP FIXTURE HISTORY

Pl: 4 Draws: 1	Wins	⚽	☐	■
Bolton Wanderers	1	4	2	0
Manchester City	2	5	10	1

STARTING LINE-UPS

Vaz Te, Ferdinand, Poole, Hierro, Campo

Onuoha, Waterreus, Flood, Macken, B.Wright-Phillips

EVENT LINE

HALF TIME 0 - 0

52 ⚽ Barton (Open Play)

64 **Okocha (Off) Vaz Te (On)**

75 **Pedersen (Off) Ferdinand (On)**

FULL TIME 0 - 1

STATISTICS

Season	Fixture (Bolton)		Fixture (Man City)	Season
121	3	Shots On Target	1	105
104	8	Shots Off Target	4	89
4	0	Hit Woodwork	0	2
34	3	Caught Offside	1	56
99	8	Corners	1	109
248	15	Fouls	12	239
50%	58%	Possession	42%	47%

LEAGUE STANDINGS

Position (pos before)	W	D	L	F	A	Pts
11 (9) Bolton W	6	5	7	26	26	23
10 (13) Man City	6	5	7	22	18	23

Saturday 18th December 2004 | Venue: **Reebok Stadium** | Attendance: **27,274** | Referee: **U.D.Rennie**

Joey Barton celebrates his winner

""It really was a disappointing defeat for us. We were edgy, and a lot of nervous tension has crept into our game."

Sam Allardyce

PREMIERSHIP MILESTONE

100 Bruno N'Gotty made his 100th Premiership appearance

"I thought everyone played well today. We were committed and showed a lot of resilience."

Kevin Keegan

BOLTON WANDERERS 0 MANCHESTER CITY 1

Bolton Wanderers' poor form continued with a fourth successive Premiership defeat.

The Trotters had now gone seven games without a win, a run which had seen them slip from fourth in the table to the bottom half.

Manager Sam Allardyce made several changes to his starting line-up in an attempt to get his side back on track.

Former Real Madrid players Ivan Campo and Fernando Hierro were dropped to the bench, while Bruno N'Gotty was switched from full back to his more usual central defensive role alongside newcomer Tal Ben Haim.

That left Anthony Barness and Julio Cesar in the full back places, with Kevin Nolan coming in for Campo.

City brought back Nicolas Anelka in place of Jonathan Macken, who was named as one of the substitutes.

Both sides made a cautious start to the game, with Bolton just about having the edge.

Jay-Jay Okocha fired a long-range shot just wide of the target, while Barness probably should have done better with a half-volley from the edge of the area.

But it was City who provided the first real threat, Robbie Fowler forcing a good save from Jussi Jaaskelainen after some neat approach work.

Barness responded for Wanderers, his fierce shot denied by an instinctive save from David James.

After a fairly dull opening period, the game burst into life with City's opener on 52 minutes, Fowler and Anelka both getting clear of their markers before the ball was slipped into the area for Joey Barton to score.

Allardyce responded by replacing captain Okocha with 18-year-old Portuguese striker Ricardo Vaz Te, scorer of 18 goals in the reserves so far this season.

He quickly made his mark in a flowing move that started and finished with Ben Haim, the Israeli mis-hitting his shot in front of goal.

Substitute Les Ferdinand went close with an effort which was saved by James, but generally City looked comfortable as they soaked up everything Wanderers had to offer.

Gary Speed had a chance to snatch a point for Bolton late on, his powerful shot whistling just wide.

PREMIERSHIP FIXTURE HISTORY

Pl: 4 Draws: 0	Wins	Goals	Yellow cards	Red cards
Chelsea	2	9	0	0
Norwich City	2	5	1	0

STARTING LINE-UPS

Drogba, Parker, Kezman, Cudicini Johnson

McKenzie, McVeigh, Ward, Drury, Shackell

EVENT LINE

8 Svensson (Off) McKenzie (On)

10 **Duff (Open Play)**

34 **Lampard (Open Play)**

44 **Robben (Open Play)**

HALF TIME 3 - 0

60 **Gudjohnsen (Off) Drogba (On)**

70 Safri (Off) McVeigh (On)

76 **Tiago (Off) Parker (On)**

78 **Robben (Off) Kezman (On)**

83 **Drogba (Corner)**

FULL TIME 4 - 0

STATISTICS

Season	Fixture (Chelsea)		Fixture (Norwich City)	Season
139	7	Shots On Target	0	84
120	4	Shots Off Target	1	97
7	0	Hit Woodwork	0	3
58	1	Caught Offside	0	59
139	7	Corners	3	84
223	13	Fouls	10	245
56%	58%	Possession	42%	47%

LEAGUE STANDINGS

Position (pos before)	W	D	L	F	A	Pts
1 (1) Chelsea	13	4	1	37	8	43
17 (16) Norwich C	2	9	7	17	32	15

Saturday 18th December 2004 | Venue: **Stamford Bridge** | Attendance: **42,071** | Referee: **M.L.Dean**

CHELSEA 4 NORWICH CITY 0

Chelsea demolished Norwich City 4-0 at Stamford Bridge, the Blues' sixth four-goal rout in their last nine Premiership matches.

The win saw the hosts move six points clear at the top of the table.

Lowly Norwich failed to record a single effort on target, their only attempt an ambitious 26th-minute chip by David Bentley which sailed over Petr Cech's bar.

Chelsea opened the scoring on 10 minutes, Damien Duff intercepting a misplaced Thomas Helveg crossfield ball in centre midfield before racing to the edge of the Norwich area and unleashing a left-foot drive into the bottom-right corner which gave keeper Robert Green no chance.

The Blues doubled their lead on 34 minutes, Arjen Robben collecting a poor Gary Doherty clearance and feeding Frank Lampard, who lashed the ball home with a trademark right-footer into the top-right corner from 25 yards.

Chelsea sealed the win with a third strike just before the break.

This time it was a goal entirely of their own making, with Robben the starter and sublime finisher of a wonderful move.

Quick, precise passing saw the ball move from Robben, to Lampard, to Tiago and finally back to Robben on the edge of the area, the mercurial winger blasting home with his left foot.

Chelsea played much better as a team in the second half, but could only manage one more goal.

Tiago went close four minutes in, his drive from the edge of the area flying inches over.

Lampard was next to threaten for the Blues, his volley from Duff's corner also going over.

Chelsea boss José Mourinho rang the first of his changes on the hour mark, replacing the ineffective Eidur Gudjohnsen with Ivory Coast striker Didier Drogba.

Robben was then denied by Green at the near post before Lampard wasted a chance by firing wide.

Despite still being some way from full fitness, Drogba's play indicated he was starting to round back into form, and he grabbed Chelsea's fourth with nine minutes to play.

Duff set him up with an excellent in-swinging corner, Drogba rising high to head home.

Didier Drogba fends off Craig Fleming

"I told my players at half-time to forget about the 3-0 score. I said they must play collectively and not individually."

Jose Mourinho

"They will be there or thereabouts, but we did alright in the first half in particular."

Nigel Worthington

PREMIERSHIP MILESTONE

150 Damien Duff marked his 150th Premiership appearance with a goal

PREMIERSHIP FIXTURE HISTORY

Pl: 4 Draws: 0	Wins	Goals	Yellow	Red
Manchester United	4	11	0	0
Crystal Palace	0	2	5	0

STARTING LINE-UPS

Carroll
G.Neville, Ferdinand, Silvestre, Fortune
Fletcher, Keane (c), Scholes
Rooney, Smith, Giggs

Johnson
Kolkka, Watson, Hughes (c), Riihilahti, Routledge
Granville, Sorondo, Hall, Boyce
Kiraly

Subs (Manchester United): O'Shea, Howard, P.Neville, Miller, Bellion

Subs (Crystal Palace): Lakis, Soares, Andrews, Speroni, Popovic

EVENT LINE

22 Scholes (Corner)
27 Granville (Corner)
32 Fortune (Off) O'Shea (On)
35 Smith (Corner)

HALF TIME 2 - 1

46 Kolkka (Open Play)
48 Boyce (Own Goal)
49 Scholes (Open Play)
65 Granville (Foul)
69 Hughes (Off) Lakis (On)
69 Riihilahti (Off) Soares (On)
81 Routledge (Off) Andrews (On)
90 O'Shea (Open Play)

FULL TIME 5 - 2

STATISTICS

Season	Fixture (Man Utd)		Fixture (Crystal Palace)	Season
148	11	Shots On Target	3	70
142	5	Shots Off Target	1	75
9	0	Hit Woodwork	0	5
64	2	Caught Offside	1	46
153	15	Corners	3	84
215	12	Fouls	8	250
55%	55%	Possession	45%	47%

LEAGUE STANDINGS

Position (pos before)		W	D	L	F	A	Pts
4 (4)	Man Utd	9	7	2	28	13	34
18 (17)	Crystal Palace	3	5	10	19	29	14

Saturday 18th December 2004 | Venue: Old Trafford | Attendance: 67,814 | Referee: S.W.Dunn

MANCHESTER UNITED 5 CRYSTAL PALACE 2

Two goals from Paul Scholes and a dazzling display by Ryan Giggs proved too much for Crystal Palace at Old Trafford.

Without a goal this season until a month ago, Scholes had now hit six in as many games.

Giggs, meanwhile, played a key part in two United goals and could easily have scored two himself.

Scholes had an early chance, directing a spectacular overhead kick at keeper Gabor Kiraly in the seventh minute.

United were awarded a penalty seconds later after Darren Fletcher went down under a challenge from Danny Granville on the right side of the Palace box.

With United's regular penalty taker, Ruud van Nistelrooy, out with an Achilles injury, Wayne Rooney was entrusted with the kick.

The England youngster stepped up, but his poor right-foot shot towards the bottom-left corner was saved by a diving Kiraly.

United made up for that miss with the opener on 22 minutes, Roy Keane collecting from Giggs on the edge of the Palace area and working the ball inside to Scholes, who sidestepped Ben Watson before curling a sweet right-footer into the top corner from the left edge of the six yard box.

The Eagles equalised five minutes later, Gonzalo Sorondo's header from a Wayne Routledge corner rebounding off Palace striker Andy Johnson and falling for Granville, who converted from 12 yards.

After Kiraly made two brilliant saves to deny Keane and Scholes, Alan Smith reclaimed the lead for United with a 35th-minute header from Scholes's corner.

Palace grabbed their second equaliser a minute into the second half, an unmarked Joonas Kolkka heading home Michael Hughes's cross from 12 yards.

United moved ahead once again two minutes later, Emmerson Boyce turning the ball into his own net from a Scholes header.

It was 4-2 seconds later, Gary Neville's long throw from the right neatly headed on by Smith for Scholes, who scored with a right-foot shot from six yards.

United capped the win with a cheeky goal in stoppage time, Giggs's cross from the left byline finding an unmarked John O'Shea, who fired home from close range.

"You have to give Crystal Palace credit for their attacking play, but our own attacking play was very good."
Sir Alex Ferguson

"I thought we came here and tried to play football, and the scoreline does us no favours."
Iain Dowie

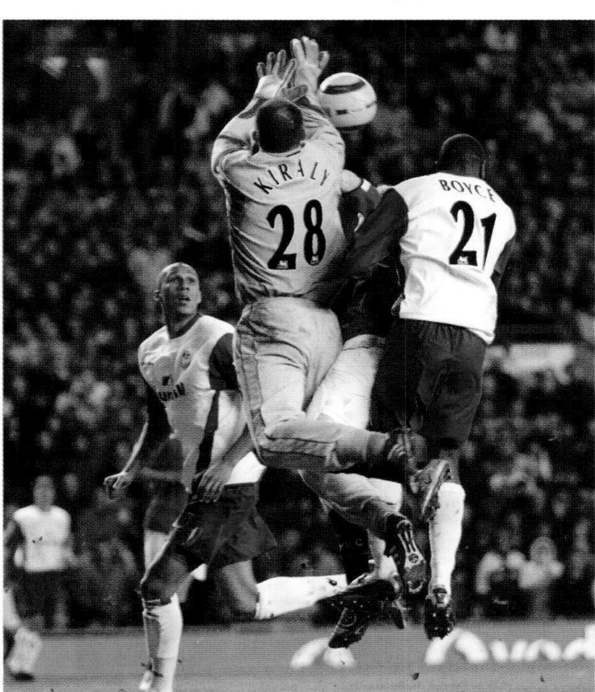

Emmerson Boyce rises to head an unfortunate own goal

PREMIERSHIP FIXTURE HISTORY

Pl: 10 Draws: 2	Wins	Goals	Yellow	Red
Middlesbrough	3	14	14	0
Aston Villa	5	20	8	2

STARTING LINE-UPS

Cooper, Job, Doriva, Nash, Morrison

Berson, Cole, Postma, Ridgewell, L.Moore

EVENT LINE

20 ⚽ **Hasselbaink (Open Play)**
38 **Riggott (Off) Cooper (On)**
45 Whittingham (Foul)
HALF TIME 1 - 0
46 **Viduka (Off) Job (On)**
46 Whittingham (Off) Berson (On)
62 **Nemeth (Off) Doriva (On)**
68 ⚽ **Job (Open Play)**
76 McCann (Off) Cole (On)
88 ⚽ **Reiziger (Open Play)**
FULL TIME 3 - 0

STATISTICS

Season	Fixture		Fixture	Season
130	7	Shots On Target	4	95
110	1	Shots Off Target	7	91
4	0	Hit Woodwork	0	3
48	3	Caught Offside	4	55
102	8	Corners	6	104
225	7	Fouls	18	278
50%	52%	Possession	48%	50%

LEAGUE STANDINGS

Position (pos before)		W	D	L	F	A	Pts
5 (5)	Middlesbrough	9	5	4	32	22	32
8 (7)	Aston Villa	6	7	5	22	22	25

Saturday 18th December 2004 | Venue: **Riverside Stadium** | Attendance: **31,338** | Referee: **A.P.D'Urso**

MIDDLESBROUGH 3 ASTON VILLA 0

Middlesbrough moved up to fourth in the Premiership with a 3-0 win over Aston Villa.

Boro now found themselves seven points clear of Villa and poised for a serious run at a Champions League spot.

The visitors put up a tremendous fight in the second half and often looked the better side, but they were let down by some poor finishing.

Jimmy Floyd Hasselbaink had a chance early on, though his header lacked the pace to seriously trouble keeper Thomas Sorensen.

Gavin McCann countered for Villa, his left-foot drive from Gareth Barry's cross deflected behind for a corner. The resulting ball found its way to Juan Pablo Angel, whose header brushed the crossbar.

Szilard Nemeth could have done better on 13 minutes, firing Olof Mellberg's attempted headed clearance straight at Sorensen from the edge of the box.

Astute defending from Gareth Southgate denied Villa a certain goal six minutes later, as he cleared Barry's effort off the line.

Boro punished the visitors for that miss when they opened the scoring a minute later, Hasselbaink racing down the left wing and cutting inside past Mark Delaney before hammering a shot into the far corner.

It was a stunning goal, easily one of the best seen at the Riverside so far this season.

Stephen Davis wasted an excellent chance for Villa on 27 minutes, sending his shot at the far post over from six yards.

Sorensen kept things close a couple of minutes later with a brilliant save from Southgate's header.

Boro made a substitution on 38 minutes, Colin Cooper coming on for the injured Chris Riggott.

Middlesbrough deserved the lead at the break, but Villa came out for the second half in fighting mood.

Their first chance came five minutes in, Nolberto Solano collecting from Davis and playing a precise ball to Angel, who dragged his shot wide from 14 yards.

Villa continued to stretch the home defence, but Boro held firm and began to push forward, doubling their lead with a Joseph-Desire Job strike on 68 minutes.

Defender Michael Reiziger added a third with two minutes to play, blasting home from 12 yards for his first Premiership goal.

Michael Reiziger surges past Steven Davis

"Our problem last year was that we could not score goals, this season we are scoring from all over the park."

Steve McClaren

PREMIERSHIP MILESTONE

Michael Reiziger netted his first Premiership goal

"I thought we outplayed them at times, but the bottom line is that goals decide games."

David O'Leary

PREMIERSHIP FIXTURE HISTORY

Pl: 13 Draws: 2	Wins	Goals	Yellow	Red
Tottenham Hotspur	9	33	12	1
Southampton	2	13	15	2

STARTING LINE-UPS

Mendes, Keane, Fulop, Davenport, Redknapp

Jakobsson, Folly, Smith, Fernandes, Beattie

EVENT LINE

8 **Defoe (Open Play)**

27 **Defoe (Open Play)**

43 Lundekvam (Foul)

44 **Kanoute (Open Play)**

HALF TIME 3 - 0

46 Nilsson (Off) Jakobsson (On)

47 Crouch (Open Play)

52 Prutton (Foul)

54 Dodd (Off) Folly (On)

61 **Defoe (Open Play)**

66 **Ricketts (Off) Mendes (On)**

83 **Ziegler (Off) Keane (On)**

88 **Keane (Open Play)**

FULL TIME 5 - 1

STATISTICS

Season	Fixture		Fixture	Season
107	12	Shots On Target	4	88
94	6	Shots Off Target	3	103
5	0	Hit Woodwork	0	2
69	4	Caught Offside	2	45
79	6	Corners	3	92
223	9	Fouls	13	233
49%	64%	Possession	36%	48%

LEAGUE STANDINGS

Position (pos before)	W	D	L	F	A	Pts
7 (11) Tottenham H	7	4	7	21	18	25
19 (19) Southampton	2	7	9	18	31	13

Saturday 18th December 2004 | Venue: White Hart Lane | Attendance: 36,054 | Referee: P.Dowd

TOTTENHAM HOTSPUR 5 SOUTHAMPTON 1

Frederic Kanoute celebrates getting on the scoresheet

"I have three top quality strikers at the club in Robbie Keane, Frederic Kanoute and Jermain Defoe, and it is tough for me to leave one out."

Martin Jol

"There is an awful lot of work to do here. I always knew it would be tough, but this is going to be a real struggle."

Harry Redknapp

Jermain Defoe fired a memorable hat-trick to make it four consecutive Premiership wins for new Tottenham manager Martin Jol – the side's best run since 1995.

Defoe picked a good time for his knockout performance, with England boss Sven-Göran Eriksson in attendance.

The Spurs striker was back in the starting line-up following a suspension, with Robbie Keane taking a seat on the bench. Reto Ziegler was also back after time out with an injury.

Spurs opened the scoring on seven minutes, Michael Carrick's superb ball upfield releasing Fredi Kanoute, who raced clear of the Saints defence before cutting back for Defoe to fire past Antti Niemi.

Kevin Phillips had a chance for a Saints equaliser on the quarter-hour mark, his deflected shot going just over.

Anders Svensson went close from the resulting corner, his close-range header flying inches past the post.

Carrick showed some neat footwork on 17 minutes, turning two Southampton defenders before drilling a powerful low drive which was well saved by Niemi.

Defoe should have scored his second on 26 minutes after Michael Brown's pass sent him clear into the area, but he fired straight at the keeper.

Defoe made up for the miss a minute later, springing the Saints offside trap before coolly slotting home.

Kanoute was unlucky not to add a third on 37 minutes, his 25-yard shot superbly pushed away by Niemi diving to his left.

But the Mali international wouldn't have to wait long for a goal, racing on to Carrick's ball in the 44th minute and firing past Niemi.

Peter Crouch wasted a prime opportunity to pull one back just before the break, his close-range shot from David Prutton's pass beaten out by home keeper Paul Robinson.

Just like Defoe, Crouch quickly made up for his error, heading past the stranded Robinson two minutes into the second half after Ledley King had failed to deal with Prutton's ball into the box.

But Defoe stole all the headlines when he completed his hat-trick on the hour mark, converting the rebound after Niemi could only parry Brown's shot.

Keane completed the rout on 87 minutes, slotting past Niemi after Defoe had lobbed the defensive line.

PREMIERSHIP FIXTURE HISTORY

Pl: 12 Draws: 2	Wins	Goals	Yellow	Red
Liverpool	9	29	8	0
Newcastle United	1	15	16	2

STARTING LINE-UPS

Liverpool: Dudek; Finnan, Carragher, Hyypia, Riise; Garcia, Gerrard (c), Alonso, Kewell; Baros, Mellor

Newcastle United: Ameobi, Kluivert; Milner, Jenas (c), Dyer, Bowyer; Bernard, Elliott, Bramble, O'Brien; Given

Liverpool substitutes: Nunez, Traore, Harrison, Hamann, Sinama-Pongolle

Newcastle United substitutes: Robert, N'Zogbia, Ambrose, Harper

EVENT LINE

32 Goal Kluivert (Open Play)
35 Goal **Bramble (Own Goal)**
38 Goal **Mellor (Open Play)**

HALF TIME 2 - 1

57 Yellow card Elliott (Foul)
58 Substitution Kluivert (Off) Robert (On)
61 Goal **Baros (Open Play)**
72 Substitution Milner (Off) N'Zogbia (On)
73 Substitution **Garcia (Off) Nunez (On)**
75 Substitution **Mellor (Off) Sinama-Pongolle (On)**
77 Red card Bowyer (2nd Bookable Offence)
80 Substitution Dyer (Off) Ambrose (On)
83 Yellow card Bernard (Foul)
85 Substitution **Kewell (Off) Traore (On)**

FULL TIME 3 - 1

STATISTICS

Season	Fixture (Liverpool)		Fixture (Newcastle)	Season
122	5	Shots On Target	3	135
122	11	Shots Off Target	4	111
2	0	Hit Woodwork	0	7
50	3	Caught Offside	1	48
104	5	Corners	5	131
210	11	Fouls	13	220
53%	54%	Possession	46%	50%

LEAGUE STANDINGS

Position (pos before)		W	D	L	F	A	Pts
6 (6)	Liverpool	8	4	6	28	20	28
13 (13)	Newcastle Utd	5	6	7	29	35	21

Sunday 19th December 2004 | Venue: **Anfield** | Attendance: **43,856** | Referee: **G.Poll**

LIVERPOOL 3 NEWCASTLE UNITED 1

A Titus Bramble own goal set Liverpool on their way to victory over Newcastle.

Liverpool threatened in the second minute, Milan Baros blazing past a pedestrian Olivier Bernard and cutting the ball back for Luis Garcia, only for the Spaniard to blast a glorious chance wide from seven yards.

After a slow start Newcastle steadily grew in confidence, Bernard rasping a vicious free kick inches wide after Patrick Kluivert had gone down on the edge of Liverpool's box.

United made the breakthrough on 32 minutes, Lee Bowyer running on to a ball from Kieron Dyer and beating the offside trap before squaring for a sliding Kluivert to tap home.

Liverpool equalised from a corner three minutes later, Sami Hyypia rising in front of makeshift right back Bramble and distracting the former Ipswich man enough to force an own goal.

Neil Mellor wasted a chance to put the Reds ahead a minute later, his marauding run ending with a tame shot.

But the new Kop hero made amends on 38 minutes, slotting a side-footed effort into the bottom-left corner from 15 yards following Baros's clever flick.

Garcia had a chance for a third just before the break, bringing Xabi Alonso's long ball down before curling a left-foot shot which was expertly saved by Shay Given.

Liverpool started the second half as they'd ended the first, bombarding the Newcastle box with shots and crosses.

After Baros had an effort ruled out for a foul on Given, Liverpool finally turned their possession into another goal, Harry Kewell sliding a pass through a gaping hole in the Newcastle defence to Baros, who rounded the keeper and tapped home.

Laurent Robert then stung the fingers of Jerzy Dudek in one of Newcastle's few forays into the Liverpool half.

An already difficult task turned desperate on 77 minutes when Bowyer – United's best player on the day – was dismissed for a second bookable offence.

Baros was inches away from a stunning fourth goal five minutes from time, his textbook overhead kick from Antonio Nunez's clipped cross flying just wide.

Milan Baros adds a third goal

"I thought we controlled the game, and it was very good for our future confidence that we managed to come back from 1-0 down."
Rafael Benitez

"It was an entertaining game, but we are very disappointed not to get something out of it."
Graeme Souness

PREMIERSHIP FIXTURE HISTORY

Pl: **2** Draws: **1**	Wins	Goals	Yellow cards	Red cards
Portsmouth	0	1	0	0
Arsenal	1	2	3	0

STARTING LINE-UPS

Portsmouth subs: Yakubu, Berkovic, Hislop, Cisse, Quashie

Arsenal subs: Bergkamp, Lehmann, Hoyte, Senderos, Fabregas

EVENT LINE

HALF TIME 0 - 0

55 (Sub) **Fuller (Off) Yakubu (On)**

68 (Sub) van Persie (Off) Bergkamp (On)

75 (Goal) Campbell (Open Play)

79 (Yellow card) Cole (Foul)

83 (Sub) **Faye (Off) Berkovic (On)**

FULL TIME 0 - 1

STATISTICS

Season	Fixture	Portsmouth / Arsenal	Fixture	Season
98	**4**	Shots On Target	**5**	**145**
87	**6**	Shots Off Target	**7**	**84**
2	**0**	Hit Woodwork	**0**	**6**
45	**5**	Caught Offside	**2**	**37**
94	**5**	Corners	**7**	**98**
217	**15**	Fouls	**10**	**195**
48%	**52%**	Possession	**48%**	**56%**

LEAGUE STANDINGS

Position (pos before)		W	D	L	F	A	Pts
12 (12)	**Portsmouth**	**6**	**5**	**7**	**23**	**25**	**23**
2 (3)	**Arsenal**	**11**	**5**	**2**	**45**	**22**	**38**

Sunday 19th December 2004 | Venue: **Fratton Park** | Attendance: **20,170** | Referee: **H.M.Webb**

PORTSMOUTH 0 ARSENAL 1

Sol Campbell was the unlikely hero as Arsenal moved to within five points of Premiership leaders Chelsea.

Campbell grabbed his first goal in 16 months with a thunderous 25-yard strike on 75 minutes to break the hearts of plucky Portsmouth.

Arsenal were never at their sensational best and Pompey may even have pulled off a shock victory but for a fine display by Gunners keeper Manuel Almunia.

Jamaica international Ricardo Fuller signalled the homes side's intent with an ambitious 35-yard lob in the sixth minute that drifted just over.

Thierry Henry countered for the Gunners five minutes later, but was denied his 16th Premiership goal of the season by a fine save from Jamie Ashdown.

Ashdown was on hand again soon after, pushing a close-range Robert Pires shot around the post after the Frenchman had beaten Pompey's offside trap.

Kolo Toure sent a header over from Henry's corner on 28 minutes before Ashdown saved at Henry's feet three minutes later.

Portsmouth hit back on 33 minutes, Lomana LuaLua's 20-yard curler flying narrowly wide.

Midfielder Gary O'Neil should have put the hosts ahead two minutes later, out-muscling Toure following Steve Stone's hopeful ball upfield, only to fire his shot into the side netting.

Toure then produced a last-ditch block to keep out Fuller's goalbound effort on the stroke of half time after LuaLua had outwitted the Arsenal defence with a cheeky chip.

Fuller wasted a glorious chance three minutes into the second period, slipping over the ball with only Almunia to beat following Patrik Berger's defence-splitting pass.

Portsmouth's caretaker manager Velimir Zajec introduced fit-again top scorer Aiyegbeni Yakubu on 55 minutes.

The move almost paid off 15 minutes later, Berger meeting the Nigerian striker's back-heel with a right-foot shot which was well saved by Almunia.

Campbell then silenced the boisterous home fans with his first goal since scoring against Aston Villa in August, 2003, the England defender collecting from Patrick Vieira and smashing the ball into the bottom-right corner.

Almunia preserved the win with a superb double save 10 minutes from time, palming away Stone's close-range strike before reacting brilliantly to keep out LuaLua's follow-up

"The harsh reality is that we didn't take our chances."

First Team Coach Joe Jordan

PREMIERSHIP MILESTONE

50 Aiyegbeni Yakubu made his 50th Premiership appearance

"He does that in training sometimes, but with defenders the ball either flies in or finishes in the stand."

Arsene Wenger on Sol Campbell's winner

Sol Campbell savours his moment of glory

PREMIERSHIP FIXTURE HISTORY

Pl: 4 Draws: 1	Wins	Goals	Yellow	Red
Charlton Athletic	2	6	6	1
Fulham	1	4	7	0

STARTING LINE-UPS

Charlton Athletic: Kiely; Young, El Karkouri, Fortune, Hreidarsson; Murphy, Kishishev, Holland (c); Rommedahl, Thomas; Bartlett

Fulham: McBride, Cole (c); Malbranque; Pembridge, Legwinski; Diop; Bocanegra, Rehman, Pearce, Rosenior; van der Sar

Charlton substitutes: Jeffers, Konchesky, Euell, Andersen, Hughes

Fulham substitutes: Radzinski, John, Flitney, Volz, Knight

EVENT LINE

18 Diop (Dissent)

27 **Thomas (Indirect Free Kick)**

HALF TIME 1 - 0

63 Malbranque (Off) Radzinski (On)

65 Rosenior (Foul)

66 **El Karkouri (Indirect Free Kick)**

73 Legwinski (Off) John (On)

79 **Bartlett (Off) Jeffers (On)**

81 **Kishishev (Foul)**

82 Radzinski (Corner)

83 **Rommedahl (Off) Konchesky (On)**

87 **Thomas (Off) Euell (On)**

FULL TIME 2 - 1

STATISTICS

Season	Fixture (Charlton)		Fixture (Fulham)	Season
79	3	Shots On Target	4	89
66	4	Shots Off Target	3	83
4	2	Hit Woodwork	0	3
57	1	Caught Offside	7	46
72	5	Corners	3	87
239	16	Fouls	16	231
43%	51%	Possession	49%	48%

LEAGUE STANDINGS

Position (pos before)	W	D	L	F	A	Pts
7 (9) Charlton Ath	8	3	7	21	28	27
15 (15) Fulham	5	3	10	20	30	18

Monday 20th December 2004 | Venue: **The Valley** | Attendance: **26,108** | Referee: **S.G.Bennett**

CHARLTON ATHLETIC 2 FULHAM 1

Radostin Kishishev is the first to congratulate Talal El Karkouri

"I felt that if we had passed the ball better and been more aggressive, then we might have had the game sewn up earlier."

Alan Curbishley

PREMIERSHIP MILESTONE

50 Matt Holland made his 50th Premiership appearance for Charlton

"We got a goal at the end, but we didn't deserve anything from the game."

Chris Coleman

Charlton moved up to seventh in the Premiership after a 2-1 victory over West London neighbours Fulham.

It was the Addicks' third successive win, a fine response to their previously inconsistent form.

A disappointing Fulham pulled a goal back late in the game to cause some mild panic in the home ranks, but Charlton held on for a deserved victory.

Fulham were tormented all night by 21-year-old winger Jerome Thomas.

The youngster had been on a hot steak of late and was one of the main reasons for Charlton's revival.

Fulham striker Andy Cole looked to have opened the scoring on 16 minutes after slotting past Dean Kiely, but the goal was ruled out for offside.

Charlton responded a minute later, Talal El Karkouri rising high to bullet a header from Danny Murphy's corner which Edwin van der Sar did well to keep out.

Thomas moved Charlton ahead on 27 minutes, poking home from seven yards after the Fulham defence had failed to deal with Shaun Bartlett's long-range strike from the right.

Apart from Cole's earlier shot, a Sylvain Legwinski blast from 25 yards was the only effort the Cottagers managed on goal in the first half.

Charlton went close to a second just after the break, El Karkouri hitting the post from the tightest of angles.

Murphy then tried a curling shot which beat Van der Sar, only to come back off the foot of an upright.

It seemed only a matter of time before Charlton scored another goal, and on 66 minutes it duly arrived.

The Addicks were awarded a free kick after Thomas was brought down just outside the area.

Murphy stepped up and curled the ball in towards El Karkouri, whose header just got past Van der Sar.

Fulham pressed hard in the final 20 minutes, sending four men up front.

After Cole fired into the side netting, the Cottagers finally found the back of the net with eight minutes to play, substitute Tomasz Radzinski converting from close range after Charlton had failed to clear a corner.

PREMIERSHIP FIXTURE HISTORY

Pl: 4 Draws: 1	Wins	Goals	Yellow	Red
Arsenal	3	8	5	0
Fulham	0	2	5	0

STARTING LINE-UPS

Almunia
Lauren, Toure, Campbell, Clichy
Ljungberg, Fabregas, Vieira (c), Pires
Bergkamp, Henry

Cole (c)
Radzinski, John
Pembridge, Rehman, Diop
Bocanegra, Knight, Pearce, Volz
van der Sar

Arsenal subs: Flamini, van Persie, Lehmann, Senderos, Pennant

Fulham subs: McBride, Crossley, Fontaine, Legwinski, Malbranque

EVENT LINE

12 Henry (Open Play) – goal

39 Rehman (Foul) – yellow card

43 **Vieira (Foul)** – yellow card

HALF TIME 1 - 0

66 Cole (Off) McBride (On)

71 **Pires (Open Play)** – goal

76 **Ljungberg (Off) Flamini (On)**

78 **Bergkamp (Off) van Persie (On)**

81 Rehman (Off) Malbranque (On)

83 Volz (Foul) – yellow card

FULL TIME 2 - 0

STATISTICS

Season	Fixture (Arsenal)		Fixture (Fulham)	Season
151	6	Shots On Target	1	90
87	3	Shots Off Target	1	84
7	1	Hit Woodwork	0	3
37	0	Caught Offside	2	48
105	7	Corners	6	93
207	12	Fouls	9	240
56%	55%	Possession	45%	47%

LEAGUE STANDINGS

Position (pos before)		W	D	L	F	A	Pts
2 (2)	Arsenal	12	5	2	47	22	41
15 (15)	Fulham	5	3	11	20	32	18

Sunday 26th December 2004 | Venue: **Highbury** | Attendance: **38,047** | Referee: **B.Knight**

ARSENAL 2 FULHAM 0

Robert Pires demonstrates his ball control

"Fulham lacked any creative purpose. They defended deep and strung five men across midfield."
Arsene Wenger

"You don't need to make things easy for a team with players of the quality that Arsenal have, but we managed to do that for both of their goals."
Chris Coleman

PREMIERSHIP MILESTONE

50 Moritz Volz made his 50th Premiership appearance

Arsenal cruised to a comfortable 2-0 win over Fulham at Highbury.

The Gunners were never at their best, but they didn't really need to be against the lacklustre Cottagers.

Fulham had the first real chance on eight minutes, Papa Bouba Diop's header from a left-sided corner cleared off the line by Gael Clichy.

Arsenal responded in the eleventh minute, Robert Pires breaking free just inside the Fulham half before cutting inside and firing straight at Edwin van der Sar.

Arsenal opened the scoring a minute later, Thierry Henry collecting from Pires and racing down the left before twisting past Ian Pearce and firing into the right-hand corner for his 16th goal in 19 Premiership matches.

The Gunners continued to control the game, with Patrick Viera, Pires and Freddie Ljungberg all having opportunities to score.

Henry could have had a second on 53 minutes if 17-year-old Cesc Fabregas had spotted him speeding down the right flank, but the Spaniard sent the ball to Pires, who was quickly closed down.

Kolo Toure wasted a great chance when he met a corner at the far post, only to send his header high over Van der Sar's goal.

Pires went close just before the hour, working his way to the left side of the area before firing a shot from an acute angle which was saved by Van der Sar.

Arsenal keeper Manuel Almunia was on hand to deny Tomasz Radzinski in the 65th minute, coming out quickly to collect an attempted lob.

Arsenal thought they'd scored four minutes later when Henry hit a thunderous half-volley that beat Van der Sar before slamming against the angle.

But it would only take the Gunners another two minutes to find the back of the net.

Fabregas opened up the Fulham defence with a delightful pass, which Dennis Bergkamp stepped over.

Pires collected the ball in space and moved to the left side of the area before firing past the on-rushing keeper.

The rest of the game saw Arsenal playing training ground football as they wound down the clock and collected the points.

PREMIERSHIP FIXTURE HISTORY

Pl: **3** Draws: **0**

	Wins	⚽	▯	■
Birmingham City	3	8	5	0
Middlesbrough	0	1	6	1

STARTING LINE-UPS

Maik Taylor
Tebily, Cunningham (c), Upson, Lazaridis
Johnson, Savage, Carter, Dunn
Heskey, Morrison

Viduka, Hasselbaink
Downing, Zenden, Doriva, Parlour
Queudrue, Southgate (c), Cooper, Reiziger
Schwarzer

Gray, Clapham, Vaesen, Melchiot, Anderton

Job, Nemeth, Nash, McMahon, Morrison

EVENT LINE

10 ⚽ **Morrison (Indirect Free Kick)**
23 Viduka (Off) Job (On)
42 ▯ **Dunn (Ung.Conduct)**
45 ⚽ **Heskey (Corner)**
HALF TIME 2 - 0
50 **Heskey (Off) Gray (On)**
54 **Dunn (Off) Clapham (On)**
61 Doriva (Off) Nemeth (On)
80 **Morrison (Off) Melchiot (On)**
81 Cooper (Off) Morrison (On)
FULL TIME 2 - 0

STATISTICS

Season	Fixture		Fixture	Season
86	**7**	Shots On Target	**3**	**133**
87	**1**	Shots Off Target	**3**	**113**
4	**0**	Hit Woodwork	**0**	**4**
58	**6**	Caught Offside	**6**	**54**
97	**5**	Corners	**3**	**105**
279	**17**	Fouls	**9**	**234**
49%	**49%**	Possession	**51%**	**50%**

LEAGUE STANDINGS

Position (pos before)		W	D	L	F	A	Pts
12 (14)	**Birmingham C**	**5**	**8**	**6**	**20**	**19**	**23**
5 (5)	**Middlesbrough**	**9**	**5**	**5**	**32**	**24**	**32**

Sunday 26th December 2004 | Venue: **St Andrew's** | Attendance: **29,082** | Referee: **S.G.Bennett**

David Dunn tries to make progress

"Despite the injuries we picked up, it was still a very good win against a Middlesbrough side that has been playing so well this season."
Steve Bruce

"If we want to be Champions League challengers we cannot afford these sort of off-days, but we can bounce back."
Steve McClaren

PREMIERSHIP MILESTONE
50 Boudewijn Zenden made his 50th Premiership appearance for Middlesbrough

PREMIERSHIP MILESTONE
150 Colin Cooper made his 150th Premiership appearance in the colours of Middlesbrough

PREMIERSHIP MILESTONE
350 Ray Parlour made his 350th Premiership appearance

BIRMINGHAM CITY 2 MIDDLESBROUGH 0

Birmingham overcame Steve McLaren's Middlesbrough to earn their third successive Premiership victory.

First-half goals from the Blues' in-form strike duo of Clinton Morrison and Emile Heskey settled the encounter, though City would be made to sweat over three injuries picked up by key players, including David Dunn.

Birmingham boss Steve Bruce picked an unchanged side for the second consecutive week, with fit-again Mario Melchiot stuck on the bench and Olivier Tebily continuing at right back.

Middlesbrough had a few injury problems of their own prior to the game, but both Ray Parlour and Mark Viduka passed late fitness tests.

Boro made the stronger start and actually had the ball in the back of the net early on, only for the goal to be ruled out for offside.

But it was Birmingham who opened the scoring on 10 minutes, a long clearance from keeper Maik Taylor flicked on by Heskey for Morrison, who flashed a half-volley past Mark Schwarzer.

Birmingham dominated the rest of the half, with Dunn a constant threat on the left and Morrison and Heskey superb up front.

Boro had a chance five minutes before the break, Jimmy Floyd Hasselbaink firing wide from a Parlour cross.

But again it was City who made it count, grabbing their second goal in first-half stoppage time.

Carter had a low drive deflected wide, setting up a Birmingham corner.

Darren Carter played it short to Robbie Savage, who crossed for Heskey to nod into the far corner.

Morrison threatened early in the second half, but Franck Queudrue was perfectly positioned to intercept and clear.

Heskey and Dunn were then forced off with injuries, Heskey with a knock to the ankle, Dunn with a more serious recurrence of his hamstring problem. Morrison would later join them.

The rest of the match was a bit of a non-event, with Birmingham struggling to adjust to the enforced substitutions and Boro lacking the guile to take advantage.

Savage had City's best chance from a free kick, while Stewart Downing fired wide for Boro late on.

PREMIERSHIP FIXTURE HISTORY

Pl: 10 Draws: 4	Wins	⚽	Yellow	Red
Blackburn Rovers	6	16	11	0
Newcastle United	0	8	15	2

STARTING LINE-UPS

Friedel

Todd, Johansson

Neill, Matteo

Ferguson (c), Flitcroft

Reid, Emerton

Stead, Dickov

Kluivert, Bellamy

Robert, Milner

Jenas (c), Dyer

Elliott, Taylor

Hughes, O'Brien

Given

Thompson, Gallagher, Enckelman, McEveley, Pedersen

Ameobi, Bramble, Bernard, Harper, N'Zogbia

EVENT LINE

6 ⚽ Dyer (Open Play)

26 ⚽ **Dickov (Indirect Free Kick)**

28 ▯ Elliott (Foul)

34 ▯ **Flitcroft (Foul)**

34 ⚽ Robert (Direct Free Kick)

HALF TIME 1 - 2

46 ⇄ **Reid (Off) Thompson (On)**

46 ⇄ Kluivert (Off) Ameobi (On)

54 ⚽ **Todd (Indirect Free Kick)**

60 ⇄ Elliott (Off) Bramble (On)

70 ⇄ Milner (Off) Bernard (On)

78 ▯ Robert (Dissent)

88 ⇄ **Stead (Off) Gallagher (On)**

FULL TIME 2 - 2

STATISTICS

Season	Fixture	Blackburn / Newcastle	Fixture	Season
99	6	Shots On Target	3	138
117	8	Shots Off Target	2	113
4	0	Hit Woodwork	0	7
74	4	Caught Offside	4	52
107	7	Corners	5	136
308	18	Fouls	19	239
48%	46%	Possession	54%	50%

LEAGUE STANDINGS

Position (pos before)	W	D	L	F	A	Pts
16 (16) Blackburn R	2	10	7	18	32	16
14 (13) Newcastle Utd	5	7	7	31	37	22

Sunday 26th December 2004 | Venue: **Ewood Park** | Attendance: **29,271** | Referee: **M.D.Messias**

BLACKBURN ROVERS 2 NEWCASTLE UNITED 2

Graeme Souness's first return to Ewood Park since he left in September ended all-square.

Souness – booed by the home fans every time he went to the touchline – saw his team twice take the lead, only to be pegged back by an enterprising Blackburn.

Rovers went close early on, Steven Reid's powerful header cleared off the line by Laurent Robert.

Newcastle quickly responded with the opener, Robert's ball opening acres of space for Kieron Dyer to drill a shot past Brad Friedel and into the far corner.

Rovers then had a couple of decent chances, Barry Ferguson sending a free kick wide before Garry Flitcroft nodded a looping header inches over Shay Given's crossbar.

Dismal defending had been blamed for Newcastle's recent poor form and that was certainly the case when Blackburn equalised on 26 minutes.

As the Magpies lined up to defend a free kick, Paul Dickov drifted into space 12 yards from goal.

The quick-thinking Ferguson picked out the diminutive striker, who buried a first-time shot into the back of the net.

The home fans were shouting for Robbie Elliott to be given his marching orders after dragging down Jonathan Stead as he headed for goal, but referee Matt Messias opted for yellow instead of red.

Robert, recalled to the starting line-up despite some controversial public comments about his manager during the week, then reclaimed the lead for United with a tremendous 30-yard free kick in the 34th minute.

Both managers shuffled their packs at the break, Mark Hughes sending on David Thompson for Reid, while Souness replaced the ineffective Patrick Kluivert with Shola Ameobi.

Blackburn made a strong start, fashioning three excellent chances in the space of 10 minutes – the last of which brought the equaliser.

Dickov set up Brett Emerton just 17 seconds in, but the Australian winger could only shoot weakly at the advancing Given.

Two minutes later, Thompson found space on the right to cut back to Ferguson, whose drive was well saved by the Newcastle keeper.

Rovers then got the goal their performance deserved, Andy Todd tucking the ball home after Given could only parry a fierce shot from distance.

Aaron Hughes clears the ball, under pressure from Jon Stead

"We find it difficult to go the final yard and convert draws into victories."

Mark Hughes

"We are in a difficult period and we need everyone to stick together and pull in the same direction."

Graeme Souness

PREMIERSHIP FIXTURE HISTORY

Pl: 13 Draws: 2	Wins	Goals	Yellow cards	Red cards
Chelsea	7	13	15	0
Aston Villa	4	10	28	0

STARTING LINE-UPS

Drogba, Smertin, Johnson, Cudicini, Kezman

Solano, L.Moore, Postma, Drobny, S.Moore

EVENT LINE

30 Duff (Open Play)

45 Robben (Foul)

HALF TIME 1 - 0

46 Delaney (Off) Solano (On)

59 Solano (Foul)

60 Ridgewell (Foul)

66 Gudjohnsen (Off) Drogba (On)

69 Tiago (Ung.Conduct)

80 Duff (Off) Smertin (On)

80 Hendrie (Off) Moore L (On)

82 Mellberg (Foul)

86 Terry (Foul)

90 Robben (Off) Johnson (On)

FULL TIME 1 - 0

STATISTICS

Season	Fixture (Chelsea)		Fixture (Aston Villa)	Season
143	4	Shots On Target	4	99
127	7	Shots Off Target	2	93
7	0	Hit Woodwork	0	3
62	4	Caught Offside	0	55
145	6	Corners	6	110
235	12	Fouls	13	291
56%	52%	Possession	48%	49%

LEAGUE STANDINGS

Position (pos before)		W	D	L	F	A	Pts
1 (1)	Chelsea	14	4	1	38	8	46
10 (9)	Aston Villa	6	7	6	22	23	25

Sunday 26th December 2004 | Venue: **Stamford Bridge** | Attendance: **41,950** | Referee: **P.Walton**

CHELSEA 1 ASTON VILLA 0

Chelsea denied Aston Villa any serious chances as they cruised to a comfortable 1-0 win at fortress Stamford Bridge.

The points moved the Blues five clear at the top of the Premiership, while Villa slipped to 10th.

Villa defender Liam Ridgewell made his first start of the season alongside Olof Mellberg. Mark Delaney was shifted to right back, with Ulises de la Cruz moving up the flank into an inexperienced five-man midfield which included 19- and 20-year-olds Stephen Davis and Peter Whittingham. Midfielder Mathieu Berson also made his first start.

José Mourinho, meanwhile, made no changes to the side that had beaten Norwich 4-0 in Chelsea's last game.

Free-roaming wingers Damien Duff and Arjen Robben created most of Chelsea's chances in the opening period, switching from side to side to baffle their markers.

Robben sent in a dangerous cross on four minutes, the ball just failing to reach Eidur Gudjohnsen.

Lee Hendrie countered for Villa with three decent attempts from distance.

Chelsea made the breakthrough on the half-hour mark, Duff storming down the right wing before switching the ball to his right foot and sending a superb shot beyond Thomas Sorensen for his sixth goal in nine games.

Delaney prevented Villa from going two down in the 37th minute, clearing Robben's shot off the line.

Villa then had their best chance of the half, Whittingham's free kick denied by a desperate lunge from Blues keeper Petr Cech.

Chelsea threatened early in the second period, William Gallas sending a diving header wide from Duff's cross on 51 minutes.

Frank Lampard sent a delightful ball in to Gudjohnsen on 64 minutes, but the striker had trouble getting off his shot, which was deflected away by the on-coming Sorensen.

Nolberto Solano responded for Villa six minutes later, his 35-yard drive denied by a good save from Cech.

Robben crossed low across the face of goal on 78 minutes, the ball just eluding striker Didier Drogba.

John Terry was fortunate not to be shown red with four minutes to play following an aggressive challenge on Mellberg.

"I think Villa did a great job. We had to roll our sleeves up and defend at the end."
Jose Mourinho

"Chelsea are up there with the best teams we've played this season. Jose Mourinho's doing an excellent job."
David O'Leary

PREMIERSHIP MILESTONE

200 Gareth Barry made his 200th Premiership appearance

Damien Duff celebrates his winner with Arjen Robben

PREMIERSHIP FIXTURE HISTORY

Pl: 1 Draws: 0	Wins	Goals	Yellow	Red
Crystal Palace	0	0	0	0
Portsmouth	1	1	2	0

STARTING LINE-UPS

Soares, Freedman, Andrews, Speroni, Popovic

Kamara, Fuller, Ashdown, Cisse, Berkovic

EVENT LINE

HALF TIME 0 - 0

56 Mezague (Off) Kamara (On)
56 Yakubu (Off) Fuller (On)
63 **Watson (Off) Soares (On)**
69 Primus (Corner)
70 **Routledge (Off) Freedman (On)**
84 **Riihilahti (Off) Andrews (On)**
84 Fuller (Dissent)
90 Griffin (Foul)

FULL TIME 0 - 1

STATISTICS

Season	Fixture		Fixture	Season
75	5	Shots On Target	4	102
82	7	Shots Off Target	5	92
5	0	Hit Woodwork	1	3
47	1	Caught Offside	3	48
93	9	Corners	7	101
260	10	Fouls	15	232
47%	51%	Possession	49%	48%

LEAGUE STANDINGS

Position (pos before)	W	D	L	F	A	Pts
18 (18) Crystal Palace	3	5	11	19	30	14
9 (12) Portsmouth	7	5	7	24	25	26

Sunday 26th December 2004 | Venue: **Selhurst Park** | Attendance: **25,238** | Referee: **N.S.Barry**

Nigel Quashie fends off Aki Riihilahti

"I am sick and tired of getting nothing out of games we should have got something out of."

Iain Dowie

PREMIERSHIP MILESTONE

Danny Butterfield made his Premiership debut

"There were a few lads throwing themselves about and blocking shots. That is the attitude you want, and that is the attitude that gets you clean sheets."

Joe Jordan

PREMIERSHIP MILESTONE

50 Arjan De Zeeuw made his 50th Premiership appearance in the colours of Portsmouth

PREMIERSHIP MILESTONE

Linvoy Primus scored his first Premiership goal

CRYSTAL PALACE 0 PORTSMOUTH 1

A second-half goal by Linvoy Primus clinched the points for Portsmouth, as Crystal Palace's misery continued at Selhurst Park.

The Pompey central defender was gifted a straightforward header in the 69th minute after Patrik Berger's corner exposed Palace's continuing weakness at set pieces.

The loss meant Iain Dowie's Eagles had managed just three points from their last eight matches.

Portsmouth, meanwhile, were having a much better go of it, with Velimir Zajec taking full-time charge after leading the club to eight points from their last five matches during his caretaker spell.

Nigerian striker Aiyegbeni Yakubu returned to the Pompey starting line-up after a long absence with a knee injury, while Danny Butterfield saw his first action of the season for Palace.

Kick off was delayed by 40 minutes as the groundsmen worked to clear a layer of ice which had formed over the appalling pitch.

Palace had a chance in the opening minute, Butterfield's cross finding Andy Johnson, who was poised to slot home before he was brought down by a Primus challenge. Referee Neale Barry saw nothing illegal and waved play on.

Portsmouth went close on the quarter-hour mark, Yakubu collecting the ball after Michael Hughes made a mess of his clearance and crossing for an unmarked Valery Mezague eight yards out, only for the midfielder to lift his shot over the bar.

Portsmouth keeper Shaka Hislop was tested for the first time on the half-hour, going low to his left to deny Ben Watson's effort.

Steve Stone wasted an excellent chance for the visitors as the second half got underway, firing wide of an open goal from 10 yards.

Arjan De Zeeuw fluffed another chance soon after, hesitating six yards out before seeing his shot easily saved by Gabor Kiraly.

Substitute Ricardo Fuller kept up the pressure with a shot against the Palace post before Portsmouth finally broke the deadlock, Primus charging in to head Berger's corner beyond Kiraly.

Hislop made a brilliant save from Gonzalo Sorondo in the dying seconds to ensure Pompey came away with a deserved three points.

PREMIERSHIP FIXTURE HISTORY

Pl: 8 Draws: 3	Wins	Goals	Yellow	Red
Everton	4	12	8	1
Manchester City	1	8	12	4

STARTING LINE-UPS

Everton: Martyn; Hibbert, Weir, Stubbs (c), Pistone; Gravesen, Carsley, Cahill; Watson, Kilbane; Bent

Manchester City: James; Jordan, Distin (c), Dunne, Mills; Sibierski, Bosvelt, S.Wright-Phillips; Fowler, Macken; Anelka

Everton subs: Ferguson, Yobo, McFadden, Wright, Naysmith

Manchester City subs: Onuoha, Negouai, Waterreus, Barton, Flood

EVENT LINE

22 ⚽ **Cahill (Indirect Free Kick)**

42 ⚽ Fowler (Indirect Free Kick)

43 ▢ Fowler (Ung.Conduct)

HALF TIME 1 - 1

63 ⚽ **Bent (Open Play)**

73 ⇄ **Watson (Off) Ferguson (On)**

73 ▢ Mills (Foul)

74 ▢ **Gravesen (Ung.Conduct)**

80 ⇄ Macken (Off) Negouai (On)

80 ⇄ Mills (Off) Onuoha (On)

81 ⇄ **Gravesen (Off) Yobo (On)**

83 ■ Negouai (Foul)

90 ⇄ **Bent (Off) McFadden (On)**

FULL TIME 2 - 1

STATISTICS

Season	Fixture (Everton)		Fixture (Man City)	Season
95	5	Shots On Target	4	109
94	3	Shots Off Target	4	93
3	0	Hit Woodwork	0	2
51	3	Caught Offside	1	57
95	4	Corners	4	113
231	14	Fouls	21	260
49%	44%	Possession	56%	48%

LEAGUE STANDINGS

Position (pos before)	W	D	L	F	A	Pts
3 (3) Everton	12	4	3	23	15	40
11 (10) Man City	6	5	8	23	20	23

Sunday 26th December 2004 | Venue: **Goodison Park** | Attendance: **40,530** | Referee: **P.Dowd**

EVERTON 2 MANCHESTER CITY 1

Everton extended their unbeaten run to seven games with a hard-fought victory over Manchester City.

Goals from Tim Cahill and Marcus Bent either side of a Robbie Fowler strike consolidated Everton's third place in the table and took their points tally beyond last season's final total.

The visitors ran Everton ragged for the first 20 minutes, as a catalogue of schoolboy errors saw the Toffees continually surrender possession.

But the match took a turn on 22 minutes when Bent was brought down by former Toffee Richard Dunne 20 yards out.

Thomas Gravesen curled the resulting free kick in towards Cahill, who buried a header into the top corner for his third goal of the season.

Steve Watson almost doubled Everton's lead soon after, his shot denied by a fingertip lunge from David James.

City won a free kick on 42 minutes for Cahill's challenge on Antoine Sibierski.

Nicolas Anelka took it, passing the ball to former Liverpool striker Robbie Fowler, who fired into the back of the Gwladys Street net.

Fowler took great delight in scoring against his boyhood heroes, running a full circuit of the pitch and taunting the home fans – and earning himself a yellow card for time-wasting.

City almost moved ahead early in the second half, Danny Mills's strike tipped around the right-hand post.

Everton were shouting for a penalty on the hour mark after Bent looked to have been tripped on the goal line, but referee Phil Dowd waved play on.

The hosts responded by grabbing a second goal three minutes later courtesy of Mills.

The City defender brought down Gary Naysmith to give Everton a free kick 30 yards out.

Again it was Gravesen, this time chipping a perfectly weighted ball in to Bent, who nodded past a diving James.

The match became increasingly ill-tempered, Mills receiving a yellow card for a two-footed tackle on Gravesen before the Everton midfielder was also shown yellow for arguing with Dowd.

Tempers finally boiled over on 83 minutes when City substitute Christian Negouai was sent off for an horrific two-footed tackle less than five minutes after entering the game.

Everton celebrate another home success

"Thomas Gravesen is one of the best players in the Premiership, and he set up both of our goals today."
Assistant Manager Alan Irvine

"Sending off Christian Negouai was the wrong decision, and it really took the wind out of our sails."
Kevin Keegan

PREMIERSHIP MILESTONE

50 Antoine Sibierski made his 50th Premiership appearance

PREMIERSHIP MILESTONE

Christian Negouai marked his Premiership debut with a red card

Sunday 26th December 2004	Venue: **Old Trafford**	Attendance: **67,867**	Referee: **D.J.Gallagher**

PREMIERSHIP FIXTURE HISTORY

Pl: **6** Draws: **1**	Wins	⚽	▢	■
Manchester United	**3**	**11**	**5**	**0**
Bolton Wanderers	**2**	**4**	**10**	**0**

STARTING LINE-UPS

Scholes, Miller, Howard, P.Neville, Bellion

Okocha, Ferdinand, Giannakopoulos, Oakes, N'Gotty

EVENT LINE

10 ⚽ **Giggs (Open Play)**

HALF TIME 1 - 0

51 Diouf (Off) Okocha (On)

63 Davies (Off) Ferdinand (On)

69 **Ronaldo (Off) Scholes (On)**

69 Vaz Te (Off) Giannakopoulos (On)

84 **Rooney (Off) Miller (On)**

89 ⚽ **Scholes (Open Play)**

FULL TIME 2 - 0

STATISTICS

Season	Fixture		Fixture	Season
155	**7**	Shots On Target	**1**	**122**
147	**5**	Shots Off Target	**5**	**109**
9	**0**	Hit Woodwork	**0**	**4**
69	**5**	Caught Offside	**0**	**34**
162	**9**	Corners	**0**	**99**
227	**12**	Fouls	**14**	**262**
55%	**57%**	Possession	**43%**	**49%**

LEAGUE STANDINGS

Position (pos before)		W	D	L	F	A	Pts
4 (4)	**Man Utd**	**10**	**7**	**2**	**30**	**13**	**37**
13 (11)	**Bolton W**	**6**	**5**	**8**	**26**	**28**	**23**

MANCHESTER UNITED 2 BOLTON WANDERERS 0

Ryan Giggs once again let his feet do the talking as he continued his bid to win a contract extension at Old Trafford.

The 31-year-old winger had recently rejected a 12-month contract offer and was seeking an additional two years.

And he looked good value for it after a match-winning performance in the Lancashire derby.

The Welshman scored United's opener and set up their second to prevent Sir Alex Ferguson's men from losing even more ground in the title race.

The win meant United had now gone unbeaten in eight league matches.

Bolton, meanwhile, continued their slide down the table with a fifth successive defeat.

Cristiano Ronaldo and Gabriel Heinze returned to United's starting line-up after mid-season breaks, while John O'Shea came in for flu victim Gary Neville.

Paul Scholes, who was also suffering from flu, stepped down to the bench, while Quinton Fortune was ruled out through injury.

Bolton boss Sam Allardyce made five changes to the side beaten 1-0 by Manchester City, the most notable being the omission of Jay-Jay Okocha.

Bolton's teenage striker Ricardo Vaz Te – making his first league start – threatened early, working his way past Heinze and Darren Fletcher before seeing his shot saved by Roy Carroll.

United settled into their game and opened the scoring on 10 minutes, Heinze's cross from the left getting by a static Bolton defence and running for Giggs, who fired home with a spectacular shot at the far post.

Wanderers keeper Jussi Jaaskelainen then made two brilliant saves to keep things close, denying efforts from Ronaldo and Roy Keane.

Wayne Rooney was lucky not to be sent off shortly before the break when he pushed his hand into the face of Bolton's Israeli defender Tal Ben Haim in a fit of anger. The FA would later hand the United striker a three-match ban for his actions.

Scholes, Rooney and Giggs all forced Jaaskelainen into fine second-half saves as United remained in control.

Scholes sealed the win in the final minute, collecting from Giggs before lashing home a low drive from outside the penalty area.

"It is all about a consistency of performances if we are to keep in the chase with the top two, especially Chelsea."

Sir Alex Ferguson

"My player went down far too easily, but there is no disputing that Rooney put his hand into his face."

Sam Allardyce

PREMIERSHIP MILESTONE

350 Les Ferdinand made his 350th Premiership appearance

Gary Speed keeps a watchful eye on Roy Keane

PREMIERSHIP FIXTURE HISTORY

Pl: 4 Draws: 1	Wins	⚽	☐	■
Norwich City	0	1	2	0
Tottenham Hotspur	3	6	5	0

STARTING LINE-UPS

Green
Edworthy, Fleming (c), Doherty, Charlton
Bentley, Helveg, Safri
Jonson, Huckerby
McKenzie

Keane, Kanoute
Atouba, Carrick, Brown, Mendes
Edman, King (c), Naybet, Pamarot
Robinson

Drury, McVeigh, Mulryne, Lewis, Jarvis

Ziegler, Defoe, Redknapp, Fulop, Gardner

EVENT LINE

8 **Charlton (Off) Drury (On)**
39 **Jonson (Off) McVeigh (On)**
42 **Safri (Foul)**

HALF TIME 0 - 0

46 **Safri (Off) Mulryne (On)**
65 Atouba (Off) Ziegler (On)
71 Kanoute (Off) Defoe (On)
73 Keane (Corner)
77 Brown (Open Play)
87 Brown (Off) Redknapp (On)

FULL TIME 0 - 2

STATISTICS

Season	Fixture		Fixture	Season
89	5	Shots On Target	5	112
104	7	Shots Off Target	8	102
5	2	Hit Woodwork	0	5
65	6	Caught Offside	4	73
94	10	Corners	8	87
256	11	Fouls	9	232
47%	41%	Possession	59%	49%

LEAGUE STANDINGS

Position (pos before)		W	D	L	F	A	Pts
17 (17)	Norwich C	2	9	8	17	34	15
7 (8)	Tottenham H	8	4	7	23	18	28

Sunday 26th December 2004 | Venue: **Carrow Road** | Attendance: **24,508** | Referee: **M.A.Riley**

NORWICH CITY 0 TOTTENHAM HOTSPUR 2

Michael Brown looks to create something for Tottenham

"To come off the pitch with a 2-0 defeat is hard to take. We will play worse this season and win."
Nigel Worthington

PREMIERSHIP MILESTONE

The attendance of 24,508 was a Premiership record at Carrow Road

"It is all about a good mentality and playing football from the back through midfield and up to the front."
Martin Jol

Norwich were punished for not turning their first-half opportunities into goals, as they went down 2-0 to Tottenham at Carrow Road.

The win made it five in a row for a rejuvenated Spurs.

The Canaries were twice denied by the woodwork and saw two other efforts cleared off the line well before Spurs threatened the home goal.

If that weren't bad enough, City also lost three players to injury in the course of the opening period.

Spurs kicked off attacking the Barclay End, Thimothee Atouba sending in a left-wing cross which eluded everyone and went out for a throw.

Norwich were forced into an early substitution after Simon Charlton limped off with a dead leg, to be replaced at left back by Adam Drury.

Darren Huckerby then set up David Bentley, but his shot came back off a post with Paul Robinson well beaten.

The near-miss lifted the home players, Mattias Jonson's fierce drive on 14 minutes just clearing the Spurs bar before Bentley saw his shot beaten away by Robinson.

Fredi Kanoute responded for Spurs, firing over after being put through by Robbie Keane.

Jonson's lay-off opened space for Bentley on 27 minutes, but his snap-shot cleared the bar.

Youssef Safri then sprained his ankle after dispossessing Kanoute inside the City six yard box.

Jonson became the Canaries' third casualty when he left the field with a concussion minutes before the break.

Norwich went close seven minutes into the second period, Huckerby's left-wing corner finding Leon McKenzie, whose header was touched against the bar by Robinson's outstretched fingertips.

Spurs almost scored from the breakaway, Robert Green doing well to gather Keane's pass before it reached Kanoute.

Spurs broke the deadlock on 73 minutes, Pedro Mendes's right-wing corner cleared only as far as Keane, who gave Green no chance with a left-foot blast from 10 yards.

Michael Brown put a broad smile on manager Martin Jol's face four minutes later, collecting a pass from Keane before beating Green high to his left with a shot from 25 yards.

Sunday 26th December 2004	Venue: **Friends Provident St Mary's Stadium**	Attendance: **31,195**	Referee: **S.W.Dunn**

PREMIERSHIP FIXTURE HISTORY

Pl: **6** Draws: **3**	Wins	Goals	Yellow cards	Red cards
Southampton	**3**	**7**	**5**	**0**
Charlton Athletic	**0**	**3**	**5**	**0**

STARTING LINE-UPS

Southampton subs: A.Svensson, Prutton, Ormerod, Smith, Fernandes

Charlton Athletic subs: Konchesky, Andersen, Hughes, Euell, Jeffers

EVENT LINE

HALF TIME 0 - 0

46 **Crouch (Off) Svensson A (On)**

61 **Oakley (Off) Prutton (On)**

74 **Beattie (Off) Ormerod (On)**

87 **Prutton (Foul)**

FULL TIME 0 - 0

STATISTICS

Season	Fixture	Southampton / Charlton	Fixture	Season
91	**3**	Shots On Target	**2**	**81**
109	**6**	Shots Off Target	**7**	**73**
2	**0**	Hit Woodwork	**1**	**5**
49	**4**	Caught Offside	**5**	**62**
97	**5**	Corners	**11**	**83**
240	**7**	Fouls	**12**	**251**
48%	**48%**	Possession	**52%**	**44%**

LEAGUE STANDINGS

Position (pos before)	W	D	L	F	A	Pts
19 (19) Southampton	**2**	**8**	**9**	**18**	**31**	**14**
8 (7) Charlton Ath	**8**	**4**	**7**	**21**	**28**	**28**

Luke Young slides in on Peter Crouch

"We knew the size of the job when we took over, and it looks even bigger now."
Assistant Manager Jim Smith

PREMIERSHIP MILESTONE

200 Rory Delap made his 200th Premiership appearance

PREMIERSHIP MILESTONE

50 Kevin Phillips made his 50th Premiership appearance for Southampton

"People are starting to talk about us getting into Europe, but I would be happy with a top ten finish."
Alan Curbishley

SOUTHAMPTON 0 CHARLTON ATHLETIC 0

Harry Redknapp was still looking for his first win as Southampton manager after Saints were held to a goalless draw by Charlton for the second time this season.

Redknapp had been charged with leading Southampton away from the dropzone following his controversial switch from Portsmouth earlier in the month.

But he was given a stark reminder of the size of the task, as the south coast side extended their winless run to six matches and were lucky to escape with a point.

Redknapp made five changes to his side following the 5-1 hammering at Tottenham, striker James Beattie restored to the starting line-up in a 3-4-3 formation which saw him take a place up front alongside Kevin Phillips and Peter Crouch.

Redknapp also gave midfielder Matthew Oakley his first run out since rupturing knee ligaments in September of last year.

Charlton had the better of the early play and could have been two goals up inside 14 minutes.

Jerome Thomas should have opened the scoring in the 12th minute after Danny Murphy sent him clear, but he fired his shot straight at keeper Antti Niemi.

Shaun Bartlett went closer two minutes later, his header from six yards striking the bar after Southampton had failed to properly clear a Murphy corner.

Hermann Hreidarsson gave the hosts another scare on 20 minutes, his free header from Murphy's free kick flying wide of the left-hand post.

Southampton finally threatened the Charlton goal six minutes later, Danny Higginbotham's close-range effort palmed away by Dean Kiely after Paul Telfer's corner had caused confusion in the Addicks box.

Crouch was denied a fourth goal of the season on 33 minutes, his right-footed drive deflected away by Talal El Karkouri.

The Saints striker wasted an excellent opportunity 10 minutes later, his header from Oakley's pinpoint centre sailing harmlessly wide of Kiely's right-hand post.

Southampton had a late chance to grab all three points, Phillips doing well to hook an 86th-minute Telfer corner across goal, only for substitute Brett Ormerod to head agonisingly into the stand.

PREMIERSHIP FIXTURE HISTORY

Pl: 2	Draws: 0	Wins ⚽	□	■
West Bromwich Albion	0	0	1	1
Liverpool	2	11	1	0

STARTING LINE-UPS

West Brom: Hoult; Scimeca, Purse (c), Gaardsoe, Clement; Contra, Johnson, Greening, Koumas; Horsfield, Earnshaw

Liverpool: Dudek; Traore, Hyypia, Carragher, Finnan; Riise, Hamann, Gerrard (c), Nunez; Baros, Sinama-Pongolle

Substitutes (West Brom): Kuszczak, Robinson, Gera, Hulse, Dyer

Substitutes (Liverpool): Alonso, Garcia, Warnock, Harrison, Diao

EVENT LINE

17 ⚽ Riise (Open Play)

39 ■ **Contra (Handball)**

HALF TIME 0 - 1

46 ⇄ **Johnson (Off) Gera (On)**

51 ⚽ Sinama-Pongolle (Open Play)

55 ⚽ Gerrard (Indirect Free Kick)

62 ⇄ Gerrard (Off) Alonso (On)

66 ⇄ Baros (Off) Garcia (On)

70 ⇄ Finnan (Off) Warnock (On)

72 ⇄ **Earnshaw (Off) Hulse (On)**

82 ⚽ Riise (Open Play)

89 ⚽ Garcia (Open Play)

FULL TIME 0 - 5

STATISTICS

Season	Fixture (West Brom)		Fixture (Liverpool)	Season
84	1	Shots On Target	8	130
82	1	Shots Off Target	8	130
3	0	Hit Woodwork	0	2
72	10	Caught Offside	1	51
95	4	Corners	11	115
261	12	Fouls	13	223
46%	41%	Possession	59%	54%

LEAGUE STANDINGS

Position (pos before)		W	D	L	F	A	Pts
20 (20)	West Brom	1	7	11	15	41	10
6 (6)	Liverpool	9	4	6	33	20	31

Sunday 26th December 2004 | Venue: **The Hawthorns** | Attendance: **27,533** | Referee: **R.Styles**

WEST BROM 0 LIVERPOOL 5

Two-goal John Arne Riise helped to fire Liverpool to a rare away day success against 10-man West Brom at the Hawthorns.

Riise struck once in either half, with Florent Sinama-Pongolle, Steven Gerrard and Luis Garcia also on target in what was just the Merseysiders second road win in the Premiership this season.

In the four Premiership meetings between the sides, Liverpool had now scored 16 and conceded none.

Bryan Robson's men, meanwhile, had now conceded 16 goals in their last five games and failed to score in the previous three, and were in very real danger of being cut adrift.

Gerrard went close with two early long-range drives before Liverpool survived their only major scare of the game.

A misplaced header from Jamie Carragher in the 14th minute fell invitingly for Albion striker Geoff Horsfield.

He advanced on goal and readied a shot, only to be denied by a last-ditch challenge from Sami Hyypia.

Liverpool responded with the opener three minutes later, Gerrard's through ball splitting the West Brom defence and running for Riise, who easily beat Russell Hoult from six yards.

The Reds looked set to double their lead on 38 minutes after Cosmin Contra handled Antonio Nunez's header from a Gerrard corner – an offence which saw Contra red-carded by referee Rob Styles.

Milan Baros stepped up for the penalty, but his weak effort was saved by Hoult diving to his left. The loose ball came back out to Baros, whose shot was cleared off the line by Darren Purse.

Sinama-Pongolle had better luck on 51 minutes, racing into the area to steer home a left-wing cross from Riise for his first league goal of the season.

Liverpool grabbed their third four minutes later, Dietmar Hamann rolling a free kick to Gerrard, who fired a low strike past Hoult for his seventh of the season.

Riise made it 4-0 on 82 minutes, cutting in from the left and blasting home after Albion had failed to clear a cross from Nunez.

And there was still time for a fifth, Riise setting up Garcia for a simple tap-in with a minute to play.

"Once Cosmin Contra was sent off, Liverpool were too good for us."
Bryan Robson

PREMIERSHIP MILESTONE

50 Andy Johnson made his 50th Premiership appearance for West Brom

"It is a very happy Christmas for everyone associated with Liverpool Football Club."
Rafael Benitez

Florent Sinama-Pongolle celebrates his goal

PREMIERSHIP FIXTURE HISTORY

Pl: 13 Draws: 3	Wins	Goals	Yellow cards	Red cards
Aston Villa	2	8	16	0
Manchester United	8	15	22	2

STARTING LINE-UPS

Aston Villa substitutes: L.Moore, S.Moore, Postma, Drobny, Whittingham

Manchester United substitutes: Keane, Ronaldo, Howard, Miller, Bellion

EVENT LINE

36 Yellow card: Ferdinand (Foul)

41 Goal: Giggs (Open Play)

45 Yellow card: O'Shea (Foul)

HALF TIME 0 - 1

54 Substitution: **Cole (Off) Moore L (On)**

60 Substitution: O'Shea (Off) Keane (On)

61 Substitution: Rooney (Off) Ronaldo (On)

67 Substitution: **Hendrie (Off) Whittingham (On)**

75 Yellow card: Heinze (Ung.Conduct)

87 Substitution: **Berson (Off) Moore S (On)**

FULL TIME 0 - 1

STATISTICS

Season	Fixture (Aston Villa)		Fixture (Manchester United)	Season
103	**4**	Shots On Target	**4**	**159**
95	**2**	Shots Off Target	**8**	**155**
3	**0**	Hit Woodwork	**1**	**10**
56	**1**	Caught Offside	**2**	**71**
116	**6**	Corners	**9**	**171**
305	**14**	Fouls	**10**	**237**
49%	**48%**	Possession	**52%**	**55%**

LEAGUE STANDINGS

Position (pos before)	W	D	L	F	A	Pts
11 (10) Aston Villa	**6**	**7**	**7**	**22**	**24**	**25**
3 (4) Man Utd	**11**	**7**	**2**	**31**	**13**	**40**

Tuesday 28th December 2004 | Venue: **Villa Park** | Attendance: **42,593** | Referee: **G.Poll**

ASTON VILLA 0 MANCHESTER UNITED 1

A virtuoso performance from Ryan Giggs saw Manchester United edge a lively encounter at Villa Park.

The win made it 22 points from a possible 24 for United.

United, last beaten at Villa Park in the opening game of the 1995-96 season, were worthy winners, though they took their foot off the pedal in the second half as they sat back and protected their lead.

Giggs was the dominant player in the opening period, mesmerising the hosts with his speed, skill and powerful shooting.

But it was Wayne Rooney who had the visitors' first chance, the £30m striker forcing Thomas Sorensen into a diving save in the first minute.

There was a scare for United on 11 minutes when Rooney appeared to bring down Nolberto Solano in the area, but the referee favoured the England player.

Giggs continued to lead the game with his powerful surges into the heart of Villa's defence, shaking off a challenge from Mathieu Berson, only to see his goalbound shot deflected onto the roof of the net by Ulises de la Cruz.

Villa had a lucky escape soon after, Giggs's shot brilliantly tipped over the bar by Sorensen after the Welshman had caught Gareth Barry napping.

Solano seemed to be relishing the challenge of his confrontation with United's defence, and he set up the hosts' best chance of the match, sending in a cross from the left which Liam Ridgewell headed straight at Roy Carroll.

Villa were finally exposed four minutes before the break, Stephen Davis failing to cut out a John O'Shea pass to Giggs, who fired a low shot past Sorensen as Olof Mellberg closed in to block.

Villa battled bravely in the second half and created an anxious spell for the visitors.

The introduction of Luke Moore for Carlton Cole produced a marked improvement, with United fighting back following the arrival of Roy Keane and Cristiano Ronaldo on the hour.

Ronaldo almost made an immediate impact, his dipping drive flashing inches wide.

Alan Smith wasted a chance for a second United goal in stoppage time, firing against the bar from close range.

Alan Smith gets a shot away

"We have now played two of the top clubs and given them good games."

David O'Leary

PREMIERSHIP MILESTONE

200 Nolberto Solano made his 200th Premiership appearance

"It was a fantastic performance from Ryan Giggs, and he could have scored another couple of goals."

Sir Alex Ferguson

Tuesday 28th December 2004	Venue: Reebok Stadium	Attendance: 27,038	Referee: R.Styles

BOLTON WANDERERS 0 BLACKBURN ROVERS 1

Paul Dickov's early header earned Blackburn their first win in five outings – and their first ever Premiership victory at the Reebok Stadium.

The result saw Bolton continue their dire run of form, slumping to a sixth consecutive defeat.

For Rovers, the three points were a fitting reward for a resolute performance at the back, with central defenders Andy Todd and Nils-Eric Johansson in outstanding form.

Both sides could have had a goal in the opening minute.

Jay Bothroyd went clear after Ricardo Gardner misjudged the bounce of the ball, only to see his shot blocked by home keeper Jussi Jaaskelainen.

At the other end, Kevin Davies was foiled by the outstretched leg of Dominic Matteo as he attempted to tee up El Hadji Diouf inside the area.

Rovers opened the scoring six minutes later, Bothroyd collecting from Johansson and passing to Dickov, who fired into the top corner from just outside the area.

Wanderers stepped up the tempo and went close with a couple of chances, Jay-Jay Okocha's teasing cross into the six yard box beaten out with Stelios Giannakopoulos waiting to pounce, before Davies floated a ball to the far post which Henrik Pedersen volleyed just wide.

Rovers almost capitalised on a lapse in the Bolton defence on 35 minutes, Jon Stead getting clear of his marker, only to head Garry Flitcroft's cross against the bar.

Bolton wasted a great chance in first-half stoppage time, an unmarked Pedersen heading Diouf's cross straight into Brad Friedel's arms.

Wanderers started the second half with a strong penalty claim after Davies went down under the challenges of two defenders, but the referee waved play on.

That led to some spirited play from the home attack, but apart from a wayward volley from Davies, they were finding it difficult to get anywhere near the Rovers goal.

Bolton, who had already brought on Ricardo Vaz Te for Pedersen, then replaced Gary Speed with former Real Madrid captain Fernando Hierro and Stelios with veteran striker Les Ferdinand.

Steven Reid had a chance for a Rovers second in stoppage time, but he sent his shot wide from a good position.

"Every time we lose a game, the next one becomes even tougher."
Sam Allardyce

PREMIERSHIP MILESTONE

100 Ricardo Gardner made his 100th Premiership appearance

"Paul Dickov produced a brilliant goal, and today we got exactly what we deserved."
Mark Hughes

Paul Dickov is mobbed by exuberant team-mates

PREMIERSHIP FIXTURE HISTORY

Pl: 6 Draws: 3	Wins	Goals	Yellow	Red
Bolton Wanderers	2	8	10	0
Blackburn Rovers	1	7	13	3

STARTING LINE-UPS

Bolton Wanderers: Jaaskelainen; Hunt, Jaidi, N'Gotty, Gardner; Giannakopoulos, Speed, Okocha (c); Diouf, Pedersen; Davies

Blackburn Rovers: Bothroyd, Dickov; Emerton, Flitcroft, Ferguson (c), Reid; Matteo, Johansson, Todd, Neill; Friedel

Bolton subs: Vaz Te, Hierro, Ferdinand, Poole, Barness

Blackburn subs: Stead, Enckelman McEveley, Gallagher, Thompson

EVENT LINE

6 Dickov (Open Play)

25 Bothroyd (Off) Stead (On)

28 Ferguson (Foul)

HALF TIME 0 - 1

52 **Pedersen (Off) Vaz Te (On)**

55 **Vaz Te (Ung.Conduct)**

59 Flitcroft (Foul)

72 **Speed (Off) Hierro (On)**

76 **Giannakopoulos (Off) Ferdinand (On)**

87 **Jaidi (Foul)**

FULL TIME 0 - 1

STATISTICS

Season	Fixture (Bolton)		Fixture (Blackburn)	Season
126	4	Shots On Target	3	102
117	8	Shots Off Target	3	120
4	0	Hit Woodwork	1	5
35	1	Caught Offside	6	80
104	5	Corners	1	108
275	13	Fouls	10	318
49%	54%	Possession	46%	48%

LEAGUE STANDINGS

Position (pos before)	W	D	L	F	A	Pts
13 (13) Bolton W	6	5	9	26	29	23
15 (16) Blackburn R	3	10	7	19	32	19

PREMIERSHIP FIXTURE HISTORY

Pl: 6 Draws: 1	Wins	Goals	Yellow	Red
Charlton Athletic	3	9	2	0
Everton	2	7	6	1

STARTING LINE-UPS

Subs (Charlton): Euell, Konchesky, Andersen, Hughes, Johansson

Subs (Everton): Wright, McFadden, Naysmith, Ferguson, Campbell

EVENT LINE

45 Martyn (Off) Wright (On)

HALF TIME 0 - 0

69 **Thomas (Off) Euell (On)**

74 Bent (Off) Ferguson (On)

79 **Rommedahl (Off) Konchesky (On)**

82 **El Karkouri (Corner)**

83 Ferguson (Violent Conduct)

84 Yobo (Off) McFadden (On)

85 **Hreidarsson (Corner)**

FULL TIME 2 - 0

STATISTICS

Season	Fixture		Fixture	Season
93	12	Shots On Target	5	100
77	4	Shots Off Target	5	99
5	0	Hit Woodwork	0	3
64	2	Caught Offside	1	52
91	8	Corners	2	97
264	13	Fouls	11	242
44%	50%	Possession	50%	49%

LEAGUE STANDINGS

Position (pos before)		W	D	L	F	A	Pts
7 (8)	Charlton Ath	9	4	7	23	28	31
4 (3)	Everton	12	4	4	23	17	40

Tuesday 28th December 2004 | Venue: **The Valley** | Attendance: **27,001** | Referee: **M.A.Riley**

CHARLTON ATHLETIC 2 EVERTON 0

Dennis Rommedahl skips away from his countryman Thomas Gravesen

"Whoever scored first was likely to win, and that's what happened."
Alan Curbishley

"It's a good sign that it's a shock to everybody now when Everton lose."
David Moyes

PREMIERSHIP MILESTONE

50 Kevin Kilbane made his 50th Premiership appearance in the colours of Everton

Charlton extended their unbeaten run to five matches with another fine team display at The Valley.

This was a notable scalp for the Addicks, Everton having previously lost just once in nine away matches – and that was against Premiership leaders Chelsea.

The opening period was a real cat and mouse affair with very few opportunities.

Everton's best chance of the half came on the quarter-hour mark, Dean Kiely diving low to his left to push away Marcus Bent's strike.

Charlton's Jonathan Fortune then poked the ball wide from a free kick before Shaun Bartlett headed over.

Tim Cahill had a chance for Everton from Thomas Gravesen's free kick, but he also sent his header over.

Everton lost their keeper Nigel Martyn with a pulled muscle a minute before the break. He was replaced by Richard Wright, who saw his first Premiership action of the season.

The second half was much more open, both sides starting to play the sort of fluid football which had been sorely lacking in the first 45.

Everton went close from Gravesen's corner, Hermann Hreidarsson scrambling the ball off the line.

Wright then made a couple of fine saves to keep things level, denying a blast from Radostin Kishishev before coming off his line to block an effort from Bartlett.

Charlton were starting to dominate play, with Bartlett and Jerome Thomas posing a consistent threat.

The Addicks' pressure was eventually rewarded eight minutes from time, Danny Murphy's corner finding substitute Paul Konchesky, who crossed the ball back into the goalmouth for Morocco international Talal El Karkouri to head home.

There was more bad news for Everton a minute later when Duncan Ferguson, who had only been on the field for eight minutes after coming on as a replacement for Bent, was sent off by referee Mike Riley for elbowing Hreidarsson in the face.

Charlton doubled their lead two minutes later, another Murphy corner causing confusion in the Everton defence, allowing Hreidarsson to volley home at the far post.

Everton might have been having a season to remember, but they met their match at The Valley.

Tuesday 28th December 2004	Venue: **Craven Cottage**	Attendance: **18, 706**	Referee: **M.Clattenburg**

PREMIERSHIP FIXTURE HISTORY

Pl: **3** Draws: **1**	Wins	Goals	Yellow cards	Red cards
Fulham	**0**	**2**	**8**	**0**
Birmingham City	**2**	**4**	**8**	**1**

STARTING LINE-UPS

Fulham subs: Rehman, Malbranque, Hammond, Crossley, Pembridge

Birmingham City subs: Gray, Clemence, Anderton, Vaesen, Martin Taylor

EVENT LINE

25 Goal: Heskey (Open Play)

34 Goal: **Legwinski (Open Play)**

41 Goal: Carter (Open Play)

HALF TIME 1 - 2

46 Substitution: **Pearce (Off) Rehman (On)**

53 Goal: Savage (Open Play)

56 Substitution: **McBride (Off) Malbranque (On)**

57 Substitution: **John (Off) Hammond (On)**

67 Yellow card: **Rehman (Foul)**

75 Substitution: Heskey (Off) Gray (On)

82 Substitution: Morrison (Off) Clemence (On)

86 Substitution: Savage (Off) Anderton (On)

90 Goal: **Radzinski (Corner)**

FULL TIME 2 - 3

STATISTICS

Season	Fixture (Fulham)		Fixture (Birmingham)	Season
95	**5**	Shots On Target	**5**	**91**
87	**3**	Shots Off Target	**1**	**88**
3	**0**	Hit Woodwork	**0**	**4**
53	**5**	Caught Offside	**4**	**62**
98	**5**	Corners	**3**	**100**
249	**9**	Fouls	**13**	**292**
47%	**47%**	Possession	**53%**	**50%**

LEAGUE STANDINGS

Position (pos before)	W	D	L	F	A	Pts
16 (15) Fulham	**5**	**3**	**12**	**22**	**35**	**18**
9 (12) Birmingham C	**6**	**8**	**6**	**23**	**21**	**26**

Robbie Savage is congratulated on a fine strike

"Obviously the players are very disappointed, but we have to get right behind each other and keep on going."

Assistant Manager Steve Kean

PREMIERSHIP MILESTONE

150 Sylvain Legwinski netted Fulham's 150th Premiership goal

"I thought Emile Heskey was excellent today, and he is forming a very good partnership with Clinton Morrison."

Steve Bruce

PREMIERSHIP MILESTONE

150 Stephen Clemence made his 150th Premiership appearance

PREMIERSHIP MILESTONE

Darren Carter scored his first Premiership goal

FULHAM 2 BIRMINGHAM CITY 3

Birmingham's recent revival continued with a good away win at Craven Cottage.

Blues midfielder Robbie Savage, who was being linked with a move to Blackburn Rovers, showed just why the club would hate to lose him.

He was inspirational all afternoon, helping to set up his side's first two goals before rounding things off with a stunning strike of his own.

It was a miserable day for Fulham, who saw Sylvain Legwinski level after Emile Heskey's opener, only for Darren Carter and Savage to reply for Birmingham.

Tomasz Radzinski managed a last-minute consolation, but the home side were still booed off the pitch.

Birmingham took the lead on 25 minutes, Clinton Morrison collecting from Savage and playing in Heskey, who worked his way past a defender before firing into the roof of the net from just inside the area.

Fulham equalised against the run of play eight minutes later.

Papa Bouba Diop fired a shot that looked to be going wide before it was deflected into the path of Radzinski.

The Canadian forward then crossed to Legwinski, who despite falling back while shooting, still managed to find the top corner from 10 yards.

Carter had a chance moments later, but the Blues looked shell-shocked for a time as panic defending set in.

Fulham went close on a couple of occasions before Carter settled the visitors' nerves with a second goal on 41 minutes, coolly slotting past Edwin van der Sar after Heskey had nodded down a cross from Savage.

City could have grabbed another just before the break, Morrison beating the Fulham offside trap to find himself one-on-one with Van der Sar, only for the Dutch keeper to make an easy save.

Under-fire Fulham boss Chris Coleman clearly laid into his side at half time, and they came out flying to start the second period, Andy Cole forcing a save from Maik Taylor.

But on 52 minutes it was all over, as Savage netted Birmingham's third.

Heskey laid the ball off to the Welshman, who flicked it up with his right foot before unleashing a dipping volley with his left that looped over Van der Sar.

PREMIERSHIP FIXTURE HISTORY

Pl: 13 Draws: 4	Wins	Goals	Yellow cards	Red cards
Liverpool	7	28	7	0
Southampton	2	14	19	0

STARTING LINE-UPS

Liverpool subs: Diao, Nunez, Hamann, Harrison, Traore

Southampton subs: A.Svensson, Phillips, Smith, Yahia, Folly

EVENT LINE

- 10 Yellow card Prutton (Foul)
- 26 Yellow card McCann (Foul)
- 28 Yellow card Jakobsson (Foul)
- 29 Substitution **Finnan (Off) Diao (On)**
- 44 Goal **Sinama-Pongolle (Open Play)**

HALF TIME 1 - 0

- 58 Substitution Oakley (Off) Svensson A (On)
- 65 Substitution Blackstock (Off) Phillips (On)
- 68 Substitution **Mellor (Off) Nunez (On)**
- 87 Substitution **Garcia (Off) Hamann (On)**

FULL TIME 1 - 0

STATISTICS

Season	Fixture (Liverpool)		Fixture (Southampton)	Season
138	8	Shots On Target	1	92
137	7	Shots Off Target	1	110
3	1	Hit Woodwork	0	2
52	1	Caught Offside	5	54
122	7	Corners	3	100
229	6	Fouls	12	252
54%	62%	Possession	38%	48%

LEAGUE STANDINGS

Position (pos before)	W	D	L	F	A	Pts
6 (6) Liverpool	10	4	6	34	20	34
19 (19) Southampton	2	8	10	18	32	14

Tuesday 28th December 2004 | Venue: **Anfield** | Attendance: **42,382** | Referee: **M.R.Halsey**

LIVERPOOL 1 SOUTHAMPTON 0

Steven Gerrard and Xabi Alonso provided the few flashes of class in a game where both sides looked like they'd rather be at home eating leftover Christmas turkey.

While he had travelled with the team to Anfield, Saints' star striker James Beattie didn't dress for the game, boss Harry Redknapp explaining that a number of Premiership clubs had expressed interest in the England forward and that Southampton were considering offers so that they could have some cash to spend in the impending transfer window.

Liverpool threatened with the first play of the game, Gerrard's perfectly weighted ball to the left wing finding John Arne Riise, who danced past Paul Telfer before unleashing a cheeky 25-yard effort which produced a fine diving save from Antti Niemi.

Another flurry of creative passes from Gerrard and Alonso moments later put Florent Sinama-Pongolle through on goal, but he fired into the side netting.

Southampton were clearly missing Beattie's presence as they struggled to get the ball out of their own half.

It took them more than 35 minutes to produce a shot at goal, a clumsy effort from David Prutton which drifted six feet wide of the mark.

A trademark side-footed pass from Gerrard then found Sinama-Pongolle with his back to goal.

The Frenchman deftly laid the ball back to his captain, who was unlucky to see his effort saved on the line.

Sinama-Pongolle broke the deadlock on the stroke of half time, running on to a perfect pass from midfield maestro Alonso before rocketing a shot past a helpless Niemi from just inside the area.

Liverpool's play became complacent as the game moved into the second half, especially at the back.

Brett Ormerod found himself with a clear shot on goal, but he was too shocked to produce anything remotely threatening.

Salif Diao left the Anfield faithful wondering what he was doing in the squad – let alone on the pitch – when he gave the ball away three times in the space of two minutes.

It was far from inspiring stuff from the Reds, but they ground out the win to keep themselves in contention for fourth spot.

John Arne Riise does well to keep the ball in

"The most important thing is that we won and have another three points to add to our tally."
Rafael Benitez

"I'm very pleased with the effort we put in. There wasn't much to choose between the two teams."
Harry Redknapp

PREMIERSHIP FIXTURE HISTORY

Pl: 2 Draws: 1	Wins			
Manchester City	0	2	1	0
West Bromwich Albion	1	3	2	2

STARTING LINE-UPS

Onuoha, Waterreus, Flood, Macken, B.Wright-Phillips

Albrechtsen, Hulse, Earnshaw, Kuszczak, Koumas

EVENT LINE

17 Gaardsoe (Foul)

32 **Anelka (Direct Free Kick)**

HALF TIME 1 - 0

46 **Jordan (Off) Onuoha (On)**

64 Scimeca (Off) Albrechtsen (On)

76 Gera (Off) Hulse (On)

82 Greening (Off) Earnshaw (On)

85 Dunne (Own Goal)

FULL TIME 1 - 1

STATISTICS

Season	Fixture		Fixture	Season
113	4	Shots On Target	0	84
100	7	Shots Off Target	0	82
2	0	Hit Woodwork	0	3
61	4	Caught Offside	4	76
124	11	Corners	0	95
267	7	Fouls	10	271
49%	61%	Possession	39%	45%

LEAGUE STANDINGS

Position (pos before)	W	D	L	F	A	Pts
12 (11) Man City	6	6	8	24	21	24
20 (20) West Brom	1	8	11	16	42	11

Tuesday 28th December 2004 | Venue: **City of Manchester Stadium** | Attendance: **47,177** | Referee: **A.P.D'Urso**

MANCHESTER CITY 1 WEST BROM 1

Paul Robinson brushes aside Shaun Wright-Phillips

PREMIERSHIP MILESTONE

100 Shaun Wright-Phillips made his 100th Premiership appearance

"We just couldn't get a second goal, and then we conceded a very poor goal."

Kevin Keegan

"We've not had many breaks since I came here, but hopefully we'll now get some."

Bryan Robson

Ten-man West Brom snatched an unlikely point through a late own goal from Richard Dunne.

The bottom-placed Baggies – forced to play for 73 minutes without dismissed Danish defender Thomas Gaardsoe – went behind to a stunning 32nd-minute strike by Nicolas Anelka.

But City were stunned in the 84th minute when Paul Robinson's long through ball struck Dunne and eluded advancing keeper David James before trickling into an empty net.

The effort, which was West Brom's only attempt on goal, earned Bryan Robson just his second point in eight Premiership matches since succeeding Gary Megson as manager.

Albion, beaten 4-0 and 5-0 in their last two games, set out their stall to frustrate the hosts with a defensive 4-5-1 formation.

City had their penalty appeals waved away on 12 minutes after Darren Purse appeared to handle Robbie Fowler's header in the six yard box.

The visitors lost Gaardsoe five minutes later, the defender shown red for hauling back Fowler as he burst through on goal.

Anelka went close on 23 minutes, his shot from the left edge of the area denied by a superb save from Russell Hoult.

The Frenchman had better luck nine minutes later, drilling a free kick over the wall and into the back of the net after Andy Johnson had handled on the edge of the area.

City almost doubled their lead on 39 minutes, Antoine Sibierski running on to a ball from Anelka before seeing his low shot saved by Hoult. Sylvain Distin headed the resulting corner wide.

City continued to dominate after the break, but were frustrated by some excellent keeping from Hoult, who denied efforts from Shaun Wright-Phillips and Fowler.

The travelling fans turned on Robson when he brought on striker Rob Hulse ahead of top scorer Robert Earnshaw as a replacement for Zoltan Gera, calling for his sacking and singing the praises of former manager Megson.

Then, completely out of the blue, Albion equalised thanks to Dunne's blunder.

Hoult came to West Brom's rescue once again moments later, making a brilliant save to keep out Fowler's volley.

PREMIERSHIP FIXTURE HISTORY

Pl: 2 Draws: 1	Wins	Goals	Yellow cards	Red cards
Middlesbrough	1	5	1	0
Norwich City	0	3	1	0

STARTING LINE-UPS

Middlesbrough subs: Morrison, Nash, McMahon, Davies, Doriva

Norwich City subs: Brennan, Crow, Gallacher, Shackell, McVeigh

EVENT LINE

12 Helveg (Off) Brennan (On)

25 **Zenden (Foul)**

34 Drury (Foul)

HALF TIME 0 - 0

52 **Job (Indirect Free Kick)**

54 **Job (Open Play)**

74 Jarvis (Off) Crow (On)

78 **Nemeth (Off) Morrison (On)**

FULL TIME 2 - 0

STATISTICS

Season	Fixture (Middlesbrough)		Fixture (Norwich City)	Season
143	10	Shots On Target	2	91
119	6	Shots Off Target	7	111
4	0	Hit Woodwork	0	5
55	1	Caught Offside	0	65
113	8	Corners	4	98
247	13	Fouls	10	266
51%	64%	Possession	36%	46%

LEAGUE STANDINGS

Position (pos before)		W	D	L	F	A	Pts
5 (5)	Middlesbrough	10	5	5	34	24	35
18 (17)	Norwich C	2	9	9	17	36	15

Tuesday 28th December 2004 | Venue: **Riverside Stadium** | Attendance: **34,836** | Referee: **H.M.Webb**

MIDDLESBROUGH 2 NORWICH CITY 0

Boro picked up their drive for a top-five Premiership spot with two goals in two minutes from Cameroon international Joseph-Desire Job.

Job, a replacement for injury victim Mark Viduka, took his season goal tally to five as he wrecked City's plans to swamp the Boro attack.

Norwich flooded the midfield and kept Boro at bay in the first half, but Job's quickfire strikes early in the second period sealed the points for the hosts.

Apart from Job, Boro boss Steve McLaren made one other change to his starting line-up, replacing Doriva with Szilard Nemeth.

Norwich boss Nigel Worthington made three changes to his side, inserting Adam Drury, Phil Mulryne and Ryan Jarvis.

City had the first shot on target, David Bentley forcing Mark Schwarzer into a full-length save in the second minute.

Jimmy Floyd Hasselbaink responded for Boro, but his shot from 25 yards lacked the pace to seriously trouble Robert Green.

Norwich lost Thomas Helveg in the 10th minute after he took a sickening blow to the back of the head from his own team-mate, Gary Doherty. He was replaced by Jim Brennan.

Green then made a superb save to deny Job, diving to push away his drive from 20 yards.

There were few real chances for the rest of the half, as both sides struggled to put together any sort of cohesive play.

Job wasted an opening five minutes into the second period, heading Stewart Downing's cross over from close range.

But he made amends two minutes later, guiding Downing's free kick into the back of the net after the Norwich defence had left him unmarked at the far post.

Two minutes later it was game over for the Canaries, Job running on to a pass from Franck Queudrue and beating the offside trap before shooting between Green's legs.

For a time Boro threatened to run riot, but Green held the City backline together with a couple of terrific saves from Downing and Bolo Zenden.

Leon McKenzie had a chance to pull one back on 81 minutes, but Schwarzer came off his line to make the block.

Leon McKenzie is challenged by Michael Reiziger

"Norwich came with a game plan and made us work very hard, but I knew that we would be rewarded if we showed patience."

Steve McClaren

PREMIERSHIP MILESTONE

The attendance of 34,836 was a Premiership record at the Riverside Stadium

"We left Job unmarked to score the first at the far post, and then we tried to play an offside trap which didn't work for the second."

Nigel Worthington

PREMIERSHIP MILESTONE

Ryan Jarvis and Danny Crow both made their Premiership debuts

Tuesday 28th December 2004 | Venue: **Fratton Park** | Attendance: **20,210** | Referee: **A.G.Wiley**

PORTSMOUTH 0 CHELSEA 2

Chelsea's march towards the Premiership title took another decisive step forward with victory over Portsmouth at Fratton Park.

It was the 20th clean sheet in all competitions this season for the Blues, who had now collected a staggering 29 points from a possible 33 since their only defeat in the Premiership against Manchester City in October.

The two-goal margin flattered José Mourinho's table-toppers, but there was no denying they deserved their 15th league win of the season after a solid second-half performance.

They could have won more comfortably if it hadn't been for home keeper Shaka Hislop, who made three outstanding saves.

Hislop kept out a second-minute shot from Didier Drogba before denying the same player on 58 minutes.

After a Glen Johnson header was cleared off the line four minutes later, Hislop was once again Pompey's saviour, denying a close-range effort from substitute Eidur Gudjohnsen on 70 minutes.

In the end, a goal had to come and it did in the 79th minute, Arjen Robben finishing off a five-man move with a deflected left-foot shot past Hislop. The Dutchman celebrated by taking off his shirt and was promptly booked.

Portsmouth offered little resistance for the rest of the game, but Chelsea still had to wait for stoppage time to seal the win, Gudjohnsen setting up a chance for Joe Cole, whose left-foot shot gave Hislop no chance.

Despite producing a plucky first-half performance with plenty of possession, Pompey were unable to create many genuine scoring opportunities.

Their best chance came on 20 minutes, a swerving 25-yard shot from Nigel Quashie which was acrobatically tipped over the bar by giant keeper Petr Cech.

Nigerian striker Aiyegbeni Yakubu had some moments for the home side in the second period, but the Chelsea backline stood firm.

At the final whistle, Mourinho was quickly on to the pitch to greet each member of his side as they walked off in triumph.

Arsenal and the other Championship contenders would have plenty of work to do in the second half of the season if they were to stand any chance of catching them.

"We deserved something from the game, but they had the bit of luck that they needed."
Joe Jordan

PREMIERSHIP MILESTONE

The attendance of 20,210 was a Premiership record at Fratton Park

"Manchester United came here and lost, Arsenal were a bit lucky to win, and we were also a bit lucky."
Jose Mourinho

John Terry puts his head where it hurts

PREMIERSHIP FIXTURE HISTORY

Pl: **2** Draws: **0**	Wins			
Portsmouth	0	0	2	0
Chelsea	2	4	5	0

STARTING LINE-UPS

Fuller, Berkovic, Ashdown, Berger, Cisse

Gudjohnsen, J.Cole, Geremi, Cudicini, Bridge

EVENT LINE

32	**Kamara (Ung.Conduct)**
	HALF TIME 0 - 0
58	Drogba (Off) Gudjohnsen (On)
65	**Kamara (Off) Fuller (On)**
73	Smertin (Off) Cole J (On)
75	Ferreira (Foul)
76	**Stone (Off) Cisse (On)**
79	Robben (Open Play)
80	Robben (Ung.Conduct)
81	Robben (Off) Geremi (On)
83	**Quashie (Off) Berkovic (On)**
84	Lampard (Dissent)
90	Cole J (Open Play)
	FULL TIME 0 - 2

STATISTICS

Season	Fixture		Fixture	Season
104	**2**	Shots On Target	**7**	**150**
94	**2**	Shots Off Target	**3**	**130**
3	**0**	Hit Woodwork	**0**	**7**
51	**3**	Caught Offside	**1**	**63**
106	**5**	Corners	**4**	**149**
244	**12**	Fouls	**15**	**250**
48%	**48%**	Possession	**52%**	**56%**

LEAGUE STANDINGS

Position (pos before)	W	D	L	F	A	Pts
10 (9) Portsmouth	**7**	**5**	**8**	**24**	**27**	**26**
1 (1) Chelsea	**15**	**4**	**1**	**40**	**8**	**49**

207 << **Portsmouth** >> 236 | 220 << **Chelsea** >> 244

PREMIERSHIP FIXTURE HISTORY

Pl: 4	Draws: 3	Wins	Goals	Yellow	Red
Tottenham Hotspur		0	3	5	1
Crystal Palace		1	4	5	1

STARTING LINE-UPS

Tottenham Hotspur: Robinson; Pamarot, King (c), Gardner, Edman; Ricketts, Brown, Carrick, Ziegler; Kanoute, Defoe

Crystal Palace: Johnson; Lakis, Soares, Hughes (c), Riihilahti, Routledge; Granville, Sorondo, Hall, Butterfield; Kiraly

Tottenham Hotspur substitutes: Mendes, Keane, Fulop, Davenport, Redknapp

Crystal Palace substitutes: Torghelle, Speroni, Boyce, Leigertwood, Andrews

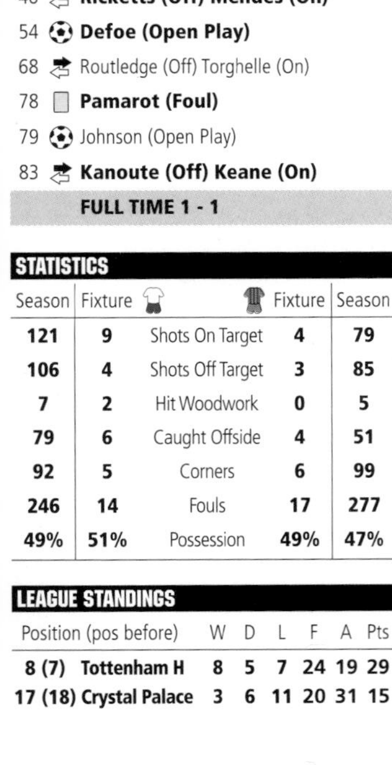

EVENT LINE

HALF TIME 0 - 0

46 **Ricketts (Off) Mendes (On)**

54 **Defoe (Open Play)**

68 Routledge (Off) Torghelle (On)

78 **Pamarot (Foul)**

79 Johnson (Open Play)

83 **Kanoute (Off) Keane (On)**

FULL TIME 1 - 1

STATISTICS

Season	Fixture		Fixture	Season
121	9	Shots On Target	4	79
106	4	Shots Off Target	3	85
7	2	Hit Woodwork	0	5
79	6	Caught Offside	4	51
92	5	Corners	6	99
246	14	Fouls	17	277
49%	51%	Possession	49%	47%

LEAGUE STANDINGS

Position (pos before)	W	D	L	F	A	Pts
8 (7) Tottenham H	8	5	7	24	19	29
17 (18) Crystal Palace	3	6	11	20	31	15

Tuesday 28th December 2004 | Venue: **White Hart Lane** | Attendance: **36,100** | Referee: **U.D.Rennie**

TOTTENHAM HOTSPUR 1 CRYSTAL PALACE 1

Danny Granville tries to evade Michael Carrick

"We were a bit fortunate in the first half and had problems dealing with them."
Martin Jol

"I am very pleased with this performance, and hopefully we can use it as a springboard."
Iain Dowie

Andy Johnson fired a priceless equaliser to keep alive Crystal Palace's hopes of staying in the Premiership and end Tottenham's five-match winning streak.

Despite falling behind to a Jermain Defoe strike, Palace showed they had the fight to beat the drop, even though Paul Robinson shouldn't have been beaten by Johnson's long-range blast.

The Palace striker had the ball in the back of the net on eight minutes after converting the rebound from Vassilios Lakis's initial shot, but the goal was ruled out for offside.

Eagles keeper Gabor Kiraly denied Fredi Kanoute on 27 minutes, pushing his low shot from the edge of the box around the post.

Kanoute went close again just two minutes later, producing a superb turn just outside the area before firing a blistering shot straight into the arms of Kiraly.

Palace then had two golden opportunities to break the deadlock.

The first came on 35 minutes, Tom Soares laying the ball into the path of Lakis, whose close-range shot deflected inches past the post.

The visitors went even closer four minutes later, Johnson's shot from Lakis's ball into the box denied by a fantastic reflex save from Robinson.

Defoe made Palace pay for those misses when he grabbed an early second-half opener.

The England striker's 53rd-minute shot was turned on to the post by Kiraly, but he made no mistake a minute later, racing unchallenged towards the box before firing home off the post.

Kanoute looked to have doubled Spurs' lead soon after, but his effort was ruled out for offside.

Palace then saw their penalty appeals waved away after substitute Sandor Torghelle went down under a challenge from Anthony Gardner.

The visitors continued to battle and were rewarded with the equaliser on 79 minutes, Johnson running on to a ball from Aki Riihilahti before firing a shot from 30 yards which went through the legs of Gardner and somehow managed to trickle its way past Robinson.

Spurs boss Martin Jol replaced Kanoute with Robbie Keane on 83 minutes in the hunt for a late winner.

And Defoe almost found it in the final minute, his effort deflected inches wide.

PREMIERSHIP FIXTURE HISTORY

Pl: 12 Draws: 4	Wins	Goals	Yellow	Red
Newcastle United	4	12	12	1
Arsenal	4	10	22	1

STARTING LINE-UPS

Newcastle United: Given; Taylor, Hughes, Bramble, Bernard; Bowyer, Dyer, Jenas (c); Bellamy, Robert; Ameobi

Arsenal: Henry, van Persie; Pires, Vieira (c), Flamini, Ljungberg; Cole, Campbell, Toure, Lauren; Almunia

Newcastle United substitutes: N'Zogbia, Harper, Ramage, Brittain, Milner

Arsenal substitutes: Clichy, Lehmann, Senderos, Fabregas, Pennant

EVENT LINE

33	**Taylor (Foul)** (booking)
42	Cole (Foul) (booking)
45	Vieira (Open Play) (goal)
	HALF TIME 0 - 1
64	van Persie (Foul) (booking)
72	Lauren (Foul) (booking)
75	Ljungberg (Ung.Conduct) (booking)
76	van Persie (Off) Clichy (On)
87	**Bernard (Off) N'Zogbia (On)**
	FULL TIME 0 - 1

STATISTICS

Season	Fixture	Newcastle United / Arsenal	Fixture	Season
142	4	Shots On Target	4	155
119	6	Shots Off Target	8	95
7	0	Hit Woodwork	0	7
52	0	Caught Offside	1	38
140	4	Corners	8	113
249	10	Fouls	21	228
51%	55%	Possession	45%	55%

LEAGUE STANDINGS

Position (pos before)		W	D	L	F	A	Pts
14 (14)	Newcastle Utd	5	7	8	31	38	22
2 (2)	Arsenal	13	5	2	48	22	44

Wednesday 29th December 2004 | Venue: **St James' Park** | Attendance: **52,320** | Referee: **S.G.Bennett**

Patrick Vieira disappears under a shower of jubilant team-mates

"I'm going home frustrated tonight, because we should have got a point."
Graeme Souness

"In my opinion Newcastle are a very good side. They never gave up and have a very talented midfield."
Arsene Wenger

NEWCASTLE UNITED 0 ARSENAL 1

A stunning strike from skipper Patrick Vieira in first-half stoppage time kept Arsenal in the hunt for back-to-back Premiership titles.

With just one win in their last nine league matches, Newcastle were given a boost when Kieron Dyer declared himself fit for Graeme Souness's injury-ravaged side.

Olivier Bernard returned to the defence with a question mark hanging over his Newcastle career following the speculation that Celestine Babayaro – who had met with chairman Freddie Shepherd the day before – was set to sign for the club during the January transfer window.

United's backline were caught ball-watching in the fourth minute, Robin van Persie ghosting in from the right on the blind side before firing a first-time shot which cannoned behind off the head of keeper Shay Given.

Shola Ameobi came to Newcastle's rescue with a crucial headed clearance off the line on the quarter-hour mark to deny Sol Campbell's header from a corner.

Ameobi then broke free of the Arsenal defence, only to see his pull-back elude the United strikers.

Steven Taylor collected the game's first booking on 33 minutes for a foul on Robert Pires, seconds before Campbell headed a Van Persie corner over the bar.

United were furious not to be awarded a penalty on 39 minutes after Ashley Cole punched a left-wing cross inside the box – right under the nose of referee Steve Bennett.

Ten seconds from the end of the one minute added on for stoppages, Vieira stunned the home side with a goal out of nothing, thumping a cross-shot from 23 yards which took a slight defection off Jermaine Jenas before flying over Given.

Lee Bowyer wasted a chance for United early in the second half, firing well over from just inside the area following good work from Titus Bramble and Craig Bellamy.

Newcastle continued to press, Dyer forcing Manuel Almunia into a full-length save before Laurent Robert's free kick was cleared by the impressive Campbell.

Arsenal's main threat came on the break, Thierry Henry twice trying efforts from just outside the area – the second flying narrowly wide.

O2
14

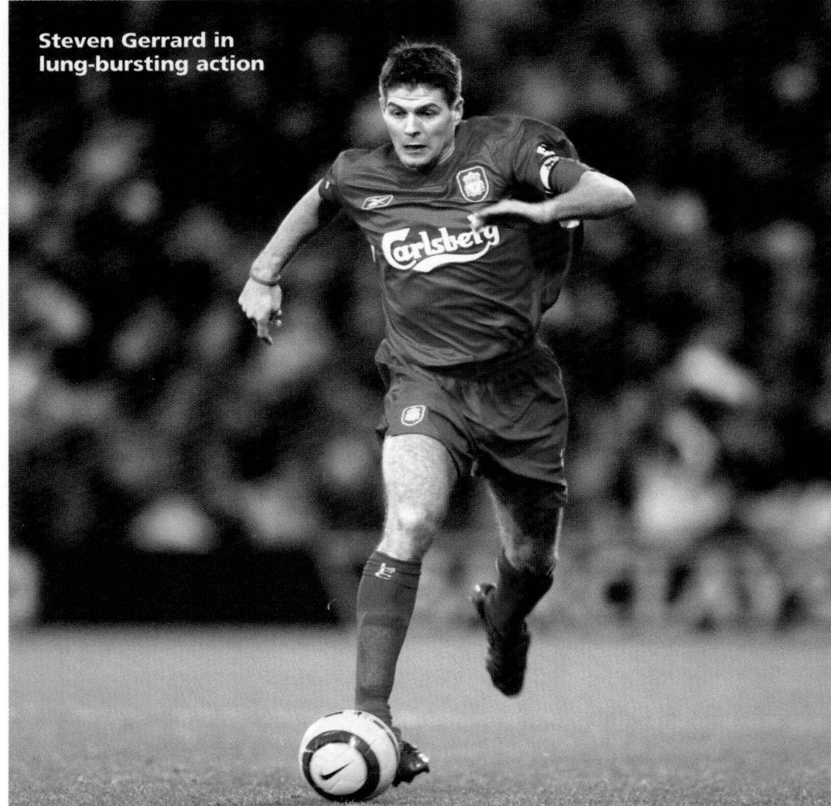

Steven Gerrard in lung-bursting action

DECEMBER 2004

A big month in terms of matches produced big showings from each of the title contenders. The only points dropped by Chelsea and Arsenal came in a 2-2 draw at Highbury, while a late equaliser from Fulham's Pape Bouba Diop was all that stood between Manchester United and five wins.

Tottenham and Charlton were able to match the performances of the top three. Both teams climbed five places as a result of picking up 13 points, with Birmingham doing likewise after a run of four consecutive victories.

At the other end of the spectrum, six clubs failed to win during December. Though Crystal Palace, West Brom and Southampton had been struggling all season, it was a surprise to see such poor form afflicting Aston Villa, Newcastle and Bolton.

If Sam Allardyce's team thought November had been a difficult time, when they earnt just two points from four games, they were in for a shock. The Trotters lost all five of their matches during the month, to plummet down to 13th.

Having left Portsmouth just a couple of weeks earlier, Harry Redknapp emerged as the new boss at neighbours Southampton. It appeared that he would start his reign with an important win, but Middlesbrough scored two very late goals to steal a point at St Mary's.

Arsenal and Liverpool joined Chelsea and Manchester United in ensuring that English football had four representatives in the last 16 of the Champions League for the first time. All the drama came at Anfield, where a late piledriver from Steven Gerrard took his side through at the expense of Olympiakos.

Both Premiership representatives made progress in the UEFA Cup. A 1-1 draw at home to Sporting Lisbon saw Newcastle confirmed as Group D winners, while Middlesbrough defeated Partizan Belgrade 3-0 at the Riverside to secure top spot in Group E.

Domestically, the draw for the Carling Cup Semi-Finals paired Manchester United with Chelsea, leaving Liverpool to take on Watford.

IN THE NEWS

02ND Walter Smith is confirmed as the new manager of Scotland, succeeding German Berti Vogts

03RD 32-year old Birmingham City full-back Martin Grainger is forced to retire as a result of a long-standing knee injury.

05TH All 20 Premiership clubs avoid each other in the F.A.Cup 3rd Round draw. Conference side Exeter are handed a dream trip to Old Trafford, while non-league Yeading take on Newcastle

08TH Harry Redknapp is appointed as the new manager of Southampton, replacing 'Head Coach' Steve Wigley at the helm

10TH Chelsea boss Jose Mourinho is voted 'World Soccer' magazine's 'Coach of the Year' for 2004.

13TH AC Milan's Andriy Shevchenko wins the 'European Footballer of the Year' award. Arsenal's Thierry Henry is placed fourth

16TH Arsene Wenger is fined £15,000 after being found guilty of 'improper conduct' by the F.A. The Arsenal boss was charged after accusing Ruud van Nistelrooy of cheating in the Gunners' 2-0 Premiership defeat at Old Trafford.

20TH Barcelona's Ronaldinho scoops the 'World Footballer of the Year' award. Arsenal's Thierry Henry finishes as runner-up to the Brazilian

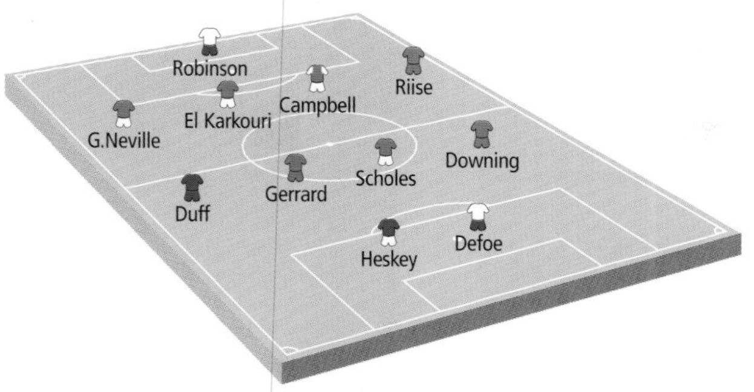

Paul Robinson
Tottenham Hotspur

Tottenham enjoyed a terrific December, with Robinson in fine form. The England international goalkeeper conceded just two goals in the league, and kept clean sheets in each of the three away games that he played in.

Gary Neville
Manchester United

While few would raise questions about the full-back's ability to defend, he has not always been seen in a positive light when going forward. That was not the case in December, however, as Neville created two goals in three appearances.

Talal El Karkouri
Charlton Athletic

Having firmly established himself at the heart of the Charlton defence, El Karkouri helped his team to four victories in five matches. The Moroccan international netted against Fulham and Everton, and was part of a side that kept four clean sheets.

Sol Campbell
Arsenal

Four clean sheets in five matches provided a platform for Arsenal to collect 13 points during December. Sol Campbell organised those around him, and even found time to net a long-range winner at Portsmouth.

John Arne Riise
Liverpool

Whether playing at the back or in midfield, the Norwegian international always gave 100%. A 5-0 win at West Brom owed much to Riise's two goals and two assists, while he was also part of a team that dramatically clinched a place in the last 16 of the Champions League.

PLAYER OF THE MONTH

Steven Gerrard
Liverpool

Inspirational performances from their captain helped Liverpool to make progress both domestically and in Europe. A late wonder-goal against Olympiakos helped book a place in the last 16 of the 'Champions League', while Gerrard also struck from distance against both Portsmouth and West Brom.

"Having him back on top form can only be a good thing for both his club and England, as, on his day, he is one of the best midfielders in the world."

Barclays Awards Panel

MANAGER OF THE MONTH

Martin Jol
Tottenham Hotspur

Having had just one month to transmit his footballing philosophies to his players, Jol guided Tottenham to a return of 13 points from five games. All three away fixtures yielded victories, with Southampton on the end of a 5-1 drubbing at White Hart Lane.

Premiership Career Statistics
up until end of December 2004
Matches:**9** Wins:**5** Draws:**1** Losses:**3**

"Since his appointment in early November, Martin Jol's side has only been beaten twice in the Barclays Premiership. He is often praised for being a progressive coach with immense tactical knowledge and man-management skills, and the performances of his team over the last month are testament to this acclaim."

Barclays Awards Panel

Damien Duff
Chelsea

Two goals and three assists contributed to another fine month for Chelsea, as Duff continued to shine on the right of a three-man attack. Defeat in a meaningless Champions League game at Porto was marked by a goal from the Irish international.

Paul Scholes
Manchester United

Four goals and one assist highlighted the midfielder's return to vintage form. The Old Trafford faithful saw Scholes net in each of United's three home games during the month, with Southampton, Crystal Palace, twice, and Bolton being the victims.

Stewart Downing
Middlesbrough

Growing claims that Downing should be included in the next England squad were strengthened during December. The young left winger created four Middlesbrough goals, and also netted a last-gasp leveller at Southampton.

Emile Heskey
Birmingham City

The much-maligned forward was on fire during the month, scoring in consecutive games against West Brom, Middlesbrough and Fulham. The former Leicester man struck up an understanding with strike-partner Clinton Morrison that helped propel his side to 12 points from five matches.

Jermain Defoe
Tottenham Hotspur

Despite suffering as a result of Martin Jol's policy of rotating his strikers, Defoe still struck four Premiership goals. The England international grabbed a hat-trick against Southampton, and also came off the bench to net in Tottenham's Carling Cup exit at the hands of Liverpool.

MONTH IN NUMBERS

51 Games Played

129 Total Goals Scored

2.53 Average Goals Per Game

5 Player With Most Goals (Henry)

1 Hat-tricks (Defoe)

13 Club With Most Goals (Chelsea)

2 Fastest Goal (Henry)

45.1% Percentage Of Home Wins

31.4% Percentage Of Away Wins

23.5% Percentage Of Draws

0-5 Biggest Win (West Brom 0 v 5 Liverpool)

122 Total Yellow Cards

6 Total Red Cards

2.4 Average Yellow Cards Per Game

16 Most Disciplinary Points (Gaardsoe 1Y1R, Ferguson 1Y1R)

10 Fastest Booking (Prutton)

34,692 Average Attendance

Jermain Defoe gets a shot away

PREMIERSHIP TABLE / TEAM STATISTICS

Pos (last month)	Team	Played	Won	Drawn	Lost	Goals for	Goals against	Goal diff	Points	Shots on target	Hit woodwork	Shots off target	Failed to score	Clean sheets	Corners	Caught Offside	Players used
1 - (1)	Chelsea	20	15	4	1	40	8	+32	49	150	7	130	3	14	149	63	22
2 - (2)	Arsenal	20	13	5	2	48	22	+26	44	155	7	95	1	8	113	38	21
3 ▲ (4)	Manchester United	20	11	7	2	31	13	+18	40	159	10	155	5	10	171	71	26
4 ▼ (3)	Everton	20	12	4	4	23	17	+6	40	100	3	99	5	9	97	52	19
5 - (5)	Middlesbrough	20	10	5	5	34	24	+10	35	143	4	119	4	5	113	55	22
6 ▲ (7)	Liverpool	20	10	4	6	34	20	+14	34	138	3	137	5	5	122	52	21
7 ▲ (12)	Charlton Athletic	20	9	4	7	23	28	-5	31	93	5	77	7	8	91	64	20
8 ▲ (13)	Tottenham Hotspur	20	8	5	7	24	19	+5	29	121	7	106	6	9	92	79	25
9 ▲ (14)	Birmingham City	20	6	8	6	23	21	+2	26	91	4	88	7	6	100	62	22
10 ▲ (11)	Portsmouth	20	7	5	8	24	27	-3	26	104	3	94	5	4	106	51	22
11 ▼ (6)	Aston Villa	20	6	7	7	22	24	-2	25	103	3	95	7	6	116	56	21
12 ▼ (9)	Manchester City	20	6	6	8	24	21	+3	24	113	2	100	6	6	124	61	21
13 ▼ (8)	Bolton Wanderers	20	6	5	9	26	29	-3	23	126	4	117	5	2	104	35	23
14 ▼ (10)	Newcastle United	20	5	7	8	31	38	-7	22	142	7	119	3	2	140	52	22
15 ▲ (17)	Blackburn Rovers	20	3	10	7	19	32	-13	19	102	5	120	8	5	108	80	26
16 ▼ (15)	Fulham	20	5	3	12	22	35	-13	18	95	3	87	7	4	98	53	22
17 ▼ (16)	Crystal Palace	20	3	6	11	20	31	-11	15	79	5	85	6	4	99	51	24
18 ▲ (19)	Norwich City	20	2	9	9	17	36	-19	15	91	5	111	9	3	98	65	22
19 ▼ (18)	Southampton	20	2	8	10	18	32	-14	14	92	2	110	9	4	100	54	27
20 - (20)	West Brom	20	1	8	11	16	42	-26	11	84	3	82	7	1	95	76	23

TEAM FORM

Pos	Team	Form	Goals For	Goals Against	Pts
1	Chelsea	WDWWW	13	2	13
2	Manchester United	WDWWW	12	3	13
3	Tottenham Hotspur	WWWWD	10	2	13
4	Arsenal	WDWWW	9	2	13
5	Charlton Athletic	WWWDW	6	1	13
6	Birmingham City	LWWWW	11	6	12
7	Liverpool	DLDWWW	11	4	11
8	Middlesbrough	WDWLW	10	6	10
9	Everton	WWDWL	6	5	10
10	Portsmouth	WDDLWL	6	7	8
11	Blackburn Rovers	LDDDW	3	3	6
12	Manchester City	LLWLD	5	7	4
13	Fulham	WDLLL	5	8	4
14	Norwich City	LWLLL	3	11	3
15	Crystal Palace	LDLLD	3	8	2
16	Newcastle United	LDLDL	4	11	2
17	Southampton	LDLDL	3	11	2
18	Aston Villa	DLLLL	2	8	1
19	West Brom	LLLLD	3	14	1
20	Bolton Wanderers	LLLLL	4	10	0

TOP GOALSCORERS

Player	This Month	Total
T.Henry Arsenal	5	**16**
J.Defoe Tottenham Hotspur	4	**10**
R.Pires Arsenal	2	**10**
A.Johnson Crystal Palace	1	**10**
J.Hasselbaink Middlesbrough	2	**8**
M.Baros Liverpool	1	**8**
P.Scholes Manchester United	4	**7**
P.Dickov Blackburn Rovers	2	**7**
N.Anelka Manchester City	1	**7**
E.Gudjohnsen Chelsea	1	**7**
C.Bellamy Newcastle United	0	**7**
K.Davies Bolton Wanderers	2	**6**
D.Duff Chelsea	2	**6**
A.Cole Fulham	1	**6**
H.Pedersen Bolton Wanderers	0	**6**
J.Reyes Arsenal	0	**6**
A.Yakubu Portsmouth	0	**6**

MOST GOAL ASSISTS

Player	This Month	Total
F.Ljungberg Arsenal	4	**11**
F.Lampard Chelsea	2	**10**
T.Henry Arsenal	0	**10**
S.Downing Middlesbrough	4	**9**
W.Routledge Crystal Palace	0	**7**
J.Hasselbaink Middlesbrough	2	**8**
D.Duff Chelsea	3	**6**
A.Robben Chelsea	3	**6**
R.Giggs Manchester United	2	**6**
E.Gudjohnsen Chelsea	1	**6**
L.Robert Newcastle United	1	**6**
D.Bergkamp Arsenal	0	**6**
S.Wright-Phillips Manchester City	0	**6**

DISCIPLINE

F.A. disciplinary points: Yellow=4 points,
Two Bookable Offences=10 points and Red Card=12 points

Player	Y	SB	R	PTS
L.Hendrie Aston Villa	5	0	1	**32**
D.Mills Manchester City	5	0	1	**32**
Josemi Liverpool	5	1	0	**30**
P.Diop Fulham	4	0	1	**28**
T.Cahill Everton	4	1	0	**26**
K.Tugay Blackburn Rovers	4	1	0	**26**
M.Izzet Birmingham City	3	0	1	**24**
G.Boateng Middlesbrough	6	0	0	**24**
A.Cole Arsenal	6	0	0	**24**
P.Vieira Arsenal	6	0	0	**24**
D.Johnson Birmingham City	3	1	0	**22**
A.Cole Fulham	2	0	1	**20**
F.Queudrue Middlesbrough	2	0	1	**20**
R.Elliott Newcastle United	5	0	0	**20**
B.Ferguson Blackburn Rovers	5	0	0	**20**
O.Mellberg Aston Villa	5	0	0	**20**
D.Prutton Southampton	5	0	0	**20**
J.Redknapp Tottenham	5	0	0	**20**
R.Savage Birmingham City	5	0	0	**20**
M.Volz Fulham	5	0	0	**20**

"I am happy to announce Velimir Zajec as our manager for the foreseeable future, with Joe Jordan staying on in his coaching role."

Portsmouth Chairman Milan Mandaric

"I was invited to meet Liverpool's representatives on the eve of Porto's Champions League game at Manchester United in March. However, I was preparing for a crucial match and wasn't prepared to leave the hotel to meet another club."

Jose Mourinho

"Chelsea will have a blip, they will lose games. It's then a case of how their players react which will be important. Arsenal and ourselves have got that experience."

Sir Alex Ferguson

"I've got more important things to do than listen to Martin Jol's comments, particularly in light of the comments that I've made, which were not defamatory or personal."

Iain Dowie tries to end his war of words with Tottenham boss Martin Jol

"The manager has no confidence in me and he doesn't talk to me. He says I am lazy in training and tells people I am no good."

A frustrated Laurent Robert

"We'd like to dedicate the win to him. We've delivered every time against Aston Villa and we're delighted to get the three points."

Robbie Savage in the wake of a Birmingham victory at Villa Park inspired by some derogatory Olof Mellberg comments

"I think there is a little bit of an anti-English attitude, but I don't know why. I think it is difficult for people to acknowledge that England has become maybe a super-strong league."

Arsene Wenger on Thierry Henry's failure to win the Ballon D'Or

PREMIERSHIP FIXTURE HISTORY

Pl: 11 Draws: 1	Wins	Goals	Yellow	Red
Aston Villa	5	10	11	0
Blackburn Rovers	5	11	16	0

STARTING LINE-UPS

Aston Villa substitutes: Davis, Postma, Delaney, Berson, S.Moore

Blackburn Rovers substitutes: Gallagher, Thompson, McEveley, Pedersen, Enckelman

EVENT LINE

13 Yellow card **McCann (Foul)**

HALF TIME 0 - 0

59 Substitution Stead (Off) Gallagher (On)

60 Substitution Reid (Off) Thompson (On)

79 Yellow card Dickov (Dissent)

88 Goal **Solano (Corner)**

90 Substitution **Moore L (Off) Davis (On)**

FULL TIME 1 - 0

STATISTICS

Season	Fixture (Aston Villa)		Fixture (Blackburn Rovers)	Season
106	3	Shots On Target	1	103
103	8	Shots Off Target	6	126
3	0	Hit Woodwork	1	6
57	1	Caught Offside	0	80
122	6	Corners	7	115
313	8	Fouls	9	327
49%	49%	Possession	51%	48%

LEAGUE STANDINGS

Position (pos before)		W	D	L	F	A	Pts
9 (11)	Aston Villa	7	7	7	23	24	28
16 (15)	Blackburn R	3	10	8	19	33	19

Saturday 1st January 2005 | Venue: **Villa Park** | Attendance: **34,265** | Referee: **H.M.Webb**

ASTON VILLA 1 BLACKBURN ROVERS 0

A late Nolberto Solano header earned Aston Villa their first win in seven games.

The Peruvian scored with two minutes to play to ease the pressure on the Midlands outfit.

But as Villa's top scorer with just six goals, Solano made it clear that the club needed to acquire a productive striker as soon as possible – preferably Southampton's James Beattie, for whom they'd recently offered £6m.

Villa striker Juan Pablo Angel's poor run of form certainly wasn't helping matters, as he went a ninth game without finding the back of the net.

Blackburn striker Paul Dickov, who had enjoyed something of a revival in recent games, was a handful for Villa's defence, his darting runs creating several openings.

But Rovers' finishing was generally found wanting, with home keeper Thomas Sorensen rarely threatened.

Villa's main concern coming into the match was a goal drought which had seen them score just once in their last four matches, all of which had been losses.

Solano tried desperately hard to provide his strikers with goalscoring service, but Angel still struggled to make any kind of impact.

Jlloyd Samuel created Villa's best chance in a low-key first half, his 60-yard crossfield pass finding Solano, whose first-time shot went just wide.

Solano then sent a useful cross in towards Angel, but the Colombian failed to make contact.

Angel had a chance to redeem himself after Solano cleverly carved out an opening, but he wasted some good approach work by firing into the side netting.

Rovers were looking equally unimpressive in front of goal, their only effort of note in the first half coming from a Brett Emerton right-wing corner which was headed against the outside of the post by Nils-Eric Johansson.

Villa had the first chance of the second period, Luke Moore heading Solano's cross over on 50 minutes.

Solano wasted an opening four minutes later, sending a tame shot straight at Brad Friedel from inside the six yard box.

As the clock wound down, it looked like Blackburn would survive Villa's attacks.

But on 88 minutes, up popped Solano to convert a free header from Gareth Barry's corner and grab a deserved three points.

"We have been struggling to score, and hopefully this will see a change in our fortunes."
David O'Leary

"There were a lot of misplaced passes from both sides, and it was not a pretty spectacle."
Mark Hughes

Juan Pablo Angel tracks Lucas Neill

PREMIERSHIP FIXTURE HISTORY

Pl: 2 Draws: 2	Wins	Goals	Yellow cards	Red cards
Bolton Wanderers	0	2	2	1
West Bromwich Albion	0	2	3	0

STARTING LINE-UPS

Vaz Te, Oakes, Ben Haim, Hierro, Pedersen

Earnshaw, Hulse, Kuszczak, Koumas, Albrechtsen

EVENT LINE

13 Gera (Open Play)

HALF TIME 0 - 1

57 **Davies (Off) Vaz Te (On)**

59 Kanu (Foul)

66 Kanu (Off) Earnshaw (On)

80 Horsfield (Off) Hulse (On)

82 Greening (Off) Albrechtsen (On)

85 **Diouf (Open Play)**

FULL TIME 1 - 1

STATISTICS

Season	Fixture		Fixture	Season
134	8	Shots On Target	4	88
126	9	Shots Off Target	5	87
5	1	Hit Woodwork	1	4
40	5	Caught Offside	3	79
111	7	Corners	3	98
288	13	Fouls	15	286
50%	58%	Possession	42%	45%

LEAGUE STANDINGS

Position (pos before)	W	D	L	F	A	Pts
14 (13) Bolton W	6	6	9	27	30	24
20 (20) West Brom	1	9	11	17	43	12

Saturday 1st January 2005 | Venue: **Reebok Stadium** | Attendance: **25,205** | Referee: **M.L.Dean**

BOLTON WANDERERS 1 WEST BROM 1

Bolton ended a run of six consecutive defeats with a late equaliser against rock-bottom West Brom.

The Baggies opened the scoring on 13 minutes, Zoltan Gera beating Ricardo Gardner on the edge of the area before curling his shot just beyond the reach of veteran keeper Kevin Poole and into the corner of the net.

That made it two goals for the Hungarian against Bolton this season, having also scored in West Brom's 2-1 win at the Hawthorns in October, their only victory of the season so far.

Albion should have doubled their lead a minute later, Geoff Horsfield pulling his shot wide with only the keeper to beat.

Wanderers worked their way back into the game and almost grabbed an equaliser in the 29th minute.

Kevin Davies cut in from the byline and fired a shot which was charged down by keeper Russell Hoult. The loose ball broke for Jay-Jay Okocha, whose shot was cleared off the line.

Albion had a chance just before the break, Neil Clement's free kick flying just wide.

Senegal international El-Hadji Diouf should have done better on 52 minutes, firing his shot straight at Hoult following Kevin Nolan's cut-back.

Andy Johnson responded for Albion, forcing a good save from Poole.

The introduction of Robert Earnshaw for Kanu on 66 minutes livened up the West Brom attack, but it was Bolton who went close on 72 minutes, Okocha slamming a free kick from the edge of the area against Hoult's bar after Ronnie Wallwork had brought down Ricardo Vaz Te.

Nolan then squared a dangerous ball across the six yard box which eluded his team-mates before Diouf volleyed over from a good position.

Wanderers were shouting for a penalty on 83 minutes after Riccardo Scimeca appeared to handle Nolan's shot, but the referee waved play on.

Bolton finally equalised a minute later, Nicky Hunt collecting from Ivan Campo on the right before crossing for Diouf to fire home.

Both sides went in search of a late winner, Hoult diving low to his right to deny Okocha's drive before Earnshaw sent his shot wide.

Ricardo Vaz Te shrugs off Zoltan Gera

"He is the only player I have not rested, so I decided to give him a break."

Sam Allardyce on the exclusion of goalkeeper Jussi Jaaskelainen

PREMIERSHIP MILESTONE

50 Nicky Hunt made his 50th Premiership appearance

"A late lapse by our defence has cost us two points."

Bryan Robson

PREMIERSHIP FIXTURE HISTORY

Pl: 6 Draws: 1	Wins	⚽	Yellow	Red
Charlton Athletic	1	3	10	0
Arsenal	4	11	10	1

STARTING LINE-UPS

Konchesky, Euell, Johansson, Andersen, Hughes

Pires, Senderos, Pennant, Lehmann, Larsson

EVENT LINE

35 ⚽ Ljungberg (Open Play)

45 ⚽ **El Karkouri (Indirect Free Kick)**

HALF TIME 1 - 1

48 ⚽ Ljungberg (Open Play)

56 Cole (Foul)

60 **Thomas (Ung.Conduct)**

64 **Kishishev (Off) Euell (On)**

64 **Thomas (Off) Konchesky (On)**

67 ⚽ van Persie (Open Play)

71 van Persie (Off) Pires (On)

75 **Bartlett (Off) Johansson (On)**

82 Campbell (Off) Senderos (On)

85 Ljungberg (Off) Pennant (On)

FULL TIME 1 - 3

STATISTICS

Season	Fixture (Charlton)		Fixture (Arsenal)	Season
97	4	Shots On Target	5	160
80	3	Shots Off Target	3	98
5	0	Hit Woodwork	0	7
69	5	Caught Offside	4	42
91	0	Corners	2	115
277	13	Fouls	15	243
44%	45%	Possession	55%	55%

LEAGUE STANDINGS

Position (pos before)		W	D	L	F	A	Pts
8 (7)	Charlton Ath	9	4	8	24	31	31
2 (2)	Arsenal	14	5	2	51	23	47

Saturday 1st January 2005 | Venue: The Valley | Attendance: 26,711 | Referee: M.R.Halsey

CHARLTON ATHLETIC 1 ARSENAL 3

Freddie Ljungberg celebrates restoring Arsenal's lead

"The result hurts, although I am delighted by the way in which we went about the game."

Alan Curbishley

"If we remain consistent, we still have a good chance of catching Chelsea."

Arsene Wenger

PREMIERSHIP MILESTONE

Philippe Senderos made his Premiership debut

Arsenal took all three points in a tricky London derby against Charlton.

It was a fourth successive Premiership victory for Arsène Wenger's men, who had now gone unbeaten in their last 31 matches against London's other top-flight clubs, the last defeat coming against Charlton in November, 2001.

With league leaders Chelsea having beaten Liverpool 1-0 earlier in the day, the Gunners knew that only a win would do if they were to maintain their title aspirations.

Wenger recalled Gael Clichy to the starting line-up, moving him into left midfield in place of Robert Pires, while continuing with Robin van Persie up front. He also handed a start to Cesc Fabregas.

Charlton had the best of the early going, Dennis Rommedahl forcing a save from Manuel Almunia in the opening minute before Danny Murphy and Jonathan Fortune both went close.

Arsenal forced their way back into the game and took the lead on 35 minutes with just their second shot on target, Patrick Vieira breaking into the Addicks penalty area and finding Freddie Ljungberg, who turned and rifled the ball past a stranded Dean Kiely.

Charlton countered with a stunning equaliser just before the break, Matt Holland tapping a free kick to Moroccan defender Talal El Karkouri, who fired home from 35 yards.

The goal was El Karkouri's fourth of the season, making him Charlton's top scorer.

Arsenal came out flying at the start of the second half and reclaimed the lead on 48 minutes, Fabregas collecting from Van Persie and slipping a back-heeled pass into the path of Ljungberg, who took the ball on into the area before blasting a shot past Kiely.

Charlton briefly rallied, putting the Gunners under pressure with a series of balls into the box. The only break came from a Thierry Henry free kick which was headed off the line.

Van Persie sealed the points for Arsenal on 67 minutes, bursting into the box after the ball had bounced past two Charlton defenders and firing an unstoppable volley into the bottom corner.

The goal knocked the stuffing out of the Addicks and Arsenal were able to coast home.

PREMIERSHIP FIXTURE HISTORY

Pl: 1 Draws: 0	Wins	⚽	Yellow	Red
Fulham	1	3	1	0
Crystal Palace	0	1	3	0

STARTING LINE-UPS

van der Sar
Volz, Knight, Rehman, Bocanegra
Diop, Malbranque, Pembridge
Radzinski, Boa Morte
Cole (c)

Johnson
Lakis, Routledge
Riihilahti, Hughes, Soares
Granville, Popovic (c), Hall, Butterfield
Kiraly

Rosenior, Clark, John, Crossley, McBride

Torghelle, Andrews, Speroni, Boyce, Leigertwood

EVENT LINE

4 ⚽ **Cole (Open Play)**

35 ⚽ Johnson (Penalty)

HALF TIME 1 - 1

60 ⚽ **Cole (Open Play)**

64 Hughes (Off) Leigertwood (On)

65 Riihilahti (Off) Torghelle (On)

73 ⚽ **Radzinski (Open Play)**

76 **Volz (Off) Rosenior (On)**

79 Lakis (Off) Andrews (On)

79 Soares (Foul)

81 Butterfield (Foul)

82 **Malbranque (Off) Clark (On)**

89 **Boa Morte (Off) John (On)**

90 **Knight (Ung.Conduct)**

90 Popovic (Foul)

FULL TIME 3 - 1

STATISTICS

Season	Fixture	Fulham / Crystal Palace	Fixture	Season
101	6	Shots On Target	3	82
93	6	Shots Off Target	4	89
3	0	Hit Woodwork	0	5
54	1	Caught Offside	2	53
102	4	Corners	2	101
261	12	Fouls	18	295
47%	50%	Possession	50%	47%

LEAGUE STANDINGS

Position (pos before)	W	D	L	F	A	Pts
15 (16) Fulham	6	3	12	25	36	21
18 (17) Crystal Palace	3	6	12	21	34	15

Saturday 1st January 2005 | Venue: **Craven Cottage** | Attendance: **18,680** | Referee: **D.J.Gallagher**

Danny Butterfield fails to prevent a Carlos Bocanegra clearance

FULHAM 3 CRYSTAL PALACE 1

Andy Cole inspired Fulham to a much needed victory with two terrific goals at Craven Cottage.

Palace had an early chance, Tom Soares shooting wide in the second minute after running on to a ball over the top from Fitz Hall.

But it was Fulham who would open the scoring two minutes later.

Tomasz Radzinski turned Andy Johnson and picked out Cole in the box, the striker taking one deft touch before burying a right-footed shot beneath Gabor Kiraly.

Fulham missed a chance for a quick second, Steed Malbranque just failing to get on the end of a pass from Luis Boa Morte.

Wayne Routledge proved a threat all afternoon for the Eagles and on 11 minutes his neat run and cross should have set up the equaliser, Tony Popovic heading the ball back across goal, only for Soares to head over from four yards.

Fulham were next to threaten, Malbranque firing wide after Danny Granville could only half-clear a cross from Cole.

Boa Morte then had a chance from Mark Pembridge's corner, but he sent his header wide.

Palace striker Johnson finally came to life on the half-hour mark, his diving header whistling over the bar.

The Eagles won a penalty three minutes later after Fulham keeper Edwin van der Sar clumsily brought down Johnson inside the area.

Referee Dermot Gallagher wasted no time in pointing to the spot, top scorer Johnson stepping up to crack home his 11th of the season.

Johnson almost moved Palace ahead moments later, his acrobatic overhead kick flying just over.

Aki Riihilahti then tested Van der Sar with a fierce drive before Radzinski curled in a right-footer which was well saved by Kiraly.

Fulham upped the pace in the second half and reclaimed their lead on the hour, Cole taking a pass from Malbranque on the edge of the box before turning and poking past Kiraly.

Routledge wasted a chance for a quick equaliser, his shot flying well over.

Fulham sealed the win with a third goal on 75 minutes, Malbranque charging down the right before cutting the ball back across the six yard box for Radzinski to slide home.

"In the second half we were great and could have had more goals."
Chris Coleman

"We didn't start the second half very well and paid for it."
Iain Dowie

PREMIERSHIP FIXTURE HISTORY

Pl: 13 Draws: 2	Wins	Goals	Yellow	Red
Liverpool	9	25	22	0
Chelsea	2	12	29	4

STARTING LINE-UPS

Nunez, Mellor, Harrison, Diao, Warnock

Drogba, J.Cole, Kezman, Cudicini, Geremi

EVENT LINE

21 Lampard (Foul)

27 **Alonso (Off) Nunez (On)**

HALF TIME 0 - 0

47 **Garcia (Foul)**

61 Gudjohnsen (Off) Drogba (On)

76 Duff (Off) Cole J (On)

80 Cole J (Corner)

83 Robben (Off) Kezman (On)

84 Johnson (Foul)

86 **Riise (Off) Mellor (On)**

90 **Hamann (Foul)**

FULL TIME 0 - 1

STATISTICS

Season	Fixture		Fixture	Season
145	7	Shots On Target	5	155
143	6	Shots Off Target	1	131
3	0	Hit Woodwork	0	7
53	1	Caught Offside	2	65
125	3	Corners	2	151
243	14	Fouls	16	266
54%	54%	Possession	46%	55%

LEAGUE STANDINGS

Position (pos before)		W	D	L	F	A	Pts
6 (6)	Liverpool	10	4	7	34	21	34
1 (1)	Chelsea	16	4	1	41	8	52

Saturday 1st January 2005 | Venue: **Anfield** | Attendance: **43,886** | Referee: **M.A.Riley**

LIVERPOOL 0
CHELSEA 1

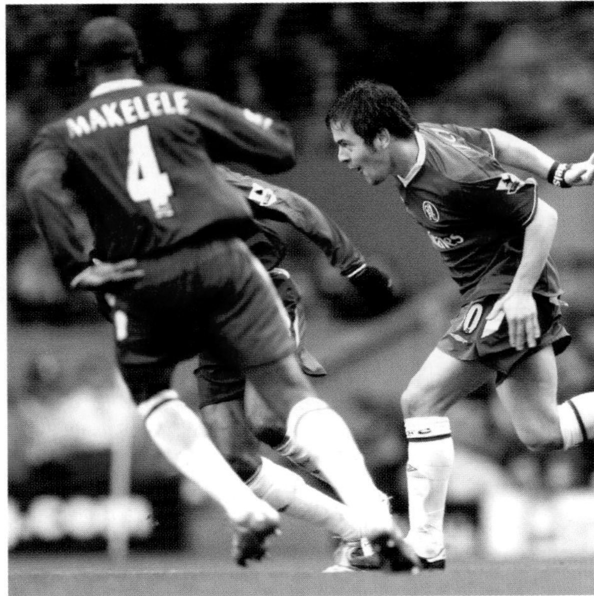

Joe Cole wheels away after netting the winner

"We played an excellent first half and had many opportunities. Chelsea's best player was their goalkeeper."

Rafael Benitez

"If you don't have the right spirit, this is the type of game which you can easily lose."

Jose Mourinho

PREMIERSHIP MILESTONE

50 Claude Makelele made his 50th Premiership appearance

A late strike by substitute Joe Cole earned Chelsea the win at Anfield.

Cole lashed home a deflected shot with 10 minutes to play after it looked as though the visitors would be lucky to escape with a point.

The pre-match build-up inevitably focused on Liverpool skipper Steven Gerrard, who had ultimately resisted the temptation of a summer switch to Stamford Bridge.

In the absence of Milan Baros, who was still struggling with a hamstring injury, Gerrard took responsibility for driving Liverpool forward.

Table-topping Chelsea brought a near full-strength side to Anfield, with only England full back Wayne Bridge missing through injury.

Liverpool made the brighter start, with Florent Sinama-Pongolle giving William Gallas a rough ride early on.

Gerrard then curled a free kick high and wide, the travelling fans responding with chants of: "You'll never play for Chelsea."

Liverpool continued to pen back the visitors as the decibel level on the Kop rose considerably from the early mumblings.

Djimi Traore wasted a glorious chance for the Reds on the quarter-hour mark, sliding his shot directly at keeper Petr Cech after surging on to Sinama-Pongolle's return pass.

Suddenly the visitors sprang into life, Arjen Robben beating the offside trap to run clear on the Liverpool goal, only to see his delayed shot well saved by Jerzy Dudek.

Liverpool responded less than a minute later, John Arne Riise's centre missing Xabi Alonso by inches.

Alonso was forced off on 28 minutes with what proved to be a broken right ankle. He was replaced by former Real Madrid star Antonio Nunez

A slip from Sami Hyypia then let in Tiago, but the Portuguese midfielder's weak shot was easily gathered by Dudek.

Liverpool were furious when their penalty appeals were turned down after Tiago appeared to handle Gerrard's cross.

Chelsea went close to the opener early in the second half, Damien Duff's cross just eluding the sliding Eidur Gudjohnsen.

Gerrard then set up Luis Garcia, but the Spaniard got underneath his shot and blasted over.

With few openings at either end, the game looked to be heading for a goalless draw until Cole converted from 20 yards with 10 minutes to play to maintain the Blues' title charge.

PREMIERSHIP FIXTURE HISTORY

Pl: 8 Draws: 2	Wins	Goals	Yellow cards	Red cards
Manchester City	3	10	10	0
Southampton	3	11	18	1

STARTING LINE-UPS

Manchester City: James; Mills, Dunne, Distin (c), Thatcher; S.Wright-Phillips, Bosvelt, Barton, Sibierski; Anelka, Fowler

Southampton: Phillips (c); McCann, Delap, Oakley, Prutton, Ormerod; Cranie, Higginbotham, Jakobsson, Telfer; Niemi

Substitutes (Manchester City): Macken, Onuoha, McManaman, Flood, Waterreus

Substitutes (Southampton): Fernandes, Crouch, Smith, A.Svensson, Dodd

EVENT LINE

19 Goal: **Bosvelt (Corner)**

40 Goal: **Wright-Phillips S (Open Play)**

HALF TIME 2 - 0

46 Substitution: Oakley (Off) Crouch (On)

46 Substitution: Ormerod (Off) Fernandes (On)

69 Substitution: **Anelka (Off) Macken (On)**

78 Substitution: **Thatcher (Off) Onuoha (On)**

86 Substitution: **Fowler (Off) McManaman (On)**

90 Goal: Phillips (Penalty)

FULL TIME 2 - 1

STATISTICS

Season	Fixture (Manchester City)		Fixture (Southampton)	Season
121	8	Shots On Target	2	94
107	7	Shots Off Target	5	115
2	0	Hit Woodwork	0	2
62	1	Caught Offside	3	57
133	9	Corners	8	108
279	12	Fouls	9	261
49%	49%	Possession	51%	48%

LEAGUE STANDINGS

Position (pos before)	W	D	L	F	A	Pts
10 (12) Man City	7	6	8	26	22	27
19 (19) Southampton	2	8	11	19	34	14

Saturday 1st January 2005 | Venue: City of Manchester Stadium | Attendance: 42,895 | Referee: C.J.Foy

MANCHESTER CITY 2 SOUTHAMPTON 1

Manchester City left their recent indifferent form behind them to register a much needed home victory against struggling Southampton.

With just four points from their last five matches, City were in danger of being dragged back into the dropzone.

A draw against bottom-placed West Brom in their previous fixture had also added to the pressure.

After a nervous start, City dominated the match and should have won by a far wider margin.

In the end, they had to settle for first-half goals from Paul Bosvelt and Shaun Wright-Phillips.

City left back Ben Thatcher returned in place of Stephen Jordan, who had been injured against West Brom.

Southampton restored striker Kevin Phillips to their starting line-up, with Dexter Blackstock dropping out.

City opened the scoring on 19 minutes, Richard Dunne heading Robbie Fowler's corner back across the face of goal for Bosvelt to glance home just his second goal of the season.

Good chances then fell to Nicolas Anelka, Wright-Phillips and Fowler, but none of them could find the back of the net.

Fowler was particularly unlucky, his goalbound header beating keeper Antti Niemi, only to be cleared off the line by Danny Higginbotham.

City eventually doubled their lead on 40 minutes with a brilliant solo goal from Wright-Phillips, the youngster picking up the ball in the centre of the field and beating a couple of opponents on a galloping run before blasting a shot from 30 yards which flew in off an upright.

Southampton boss Harry Redknapp made a double substitution at the break, replacing Brett Ormerod and Matthew Oakley with Peter Crouch and Fabrice Fernandes.

The visitors created more chances in the second period, Phillips seeing a goal ruled out for offside before Crouch was denied by a breathtaking save from City keeper David James.

Saints were handed a lifeline in the final minute when referee Chris Foy ruled that Sylvain Distin had barged Crouch off the ball.

Phillips stepped up for the resulting penalty and smashed the ball home.

City held on for the final few seconds, running out far more comfortable winners than the scoreline suggests.

Martin Cranie is challenged by Antoine Sibierski

"Shaun Wright-Phillips is our most important player. It used to be others, but now it is him."
Kevin Keegan

"If Kevin Phillips' goal had not been ruled out for offside, it would have set up an interesting final half-hour."
Harry Redknapp

PREMIERSHIP MILESTONE

Joey Barton made his 50th Premiership appearance

PREMIERSHIP FIXTURE HISTORY

Pl: **10** Draws: **2**	Wins	Goals	Yellow cards	Red cards
Middlesbrough	1	9	17	0
Manchester United	7	18	20	1

STARTING LINE-UPS

Nemeth, Morrison, Nash, McMahon, Davies

Bellion, Howard G.Neville, Spector, Djemba-Djemba

EVENT LINE

9 Fletcher (Open Play)

HALF TIME 0 - 1

46 **Job (Off) Nemeth (On)**

76 **Parlour (Foul)**

78 **Doriva (Off) Morrison (On)**

78 Ronaldo (Off) Djemba-Djemba (On)

79 Giggs (Open Play)

83 Giggs (Off) Bellion (On)

FULL TIME 0 - 2

STATISTICS

Season	Fixture (Middlesbrough)		Fixture (Manchester United)	Season
145	**2**	Shots On Target	**7**	**166**
123	**4**	Shots Off Target	**6**	**161**
4	**0**	Hit Woodwork	**1**	**11**
55	**0**	Caught Offside	**2**	**73**
120	**7**	Corners	**4**	**175**
260	**13**	Fouls	**9**	**246**
51%	**42%**	Possession	**58%**	**55%**

LEAGUE STANDINGS

Position (pos before)		W	D	L	F	A	Pts
5 (5)	**Middlesbrough**	**10**	**5**	**6**	**34**	**26**	**35**
3 (3)	**Man Utd**	**12**	**7**	**2**	**33**	**13**	**43**

Saturday 1st January 2005 | Venue: **Riverside Stadium** | Attendance: **34,199** | Referee: **A.G.Wiley**

MIDDLESBROUGH 0 MANCHESTER UNITED 2

Manchester United won comfortably at the Riverside Stadium without ever hitting top gear.

The three points made it 26 from a possible 30 for United, who hadn't given up hope of catching leaders Chelsea.

Boro boss Steve McClaren, the former number two at Old Trafford, must have been bitterly disappointed with his side's performance.

They had no answer for United's pace and failed to register a single shot on target.

There was some joy for the hosts, however, as veteran defender Colin Cooper made his 600th league appearance.

Both sides made changes to their starting line-ups, Boro midfielder Doriva taking Szilard Nemeth's spot, while United's Roy Keane and Cristiano Ronaldo came in for John O'Shea and the suspended Wayne Rooney.

Boro made a promising start, Jimmy Floyd Hasselbaink just failing to connect with Stewart Downing's cross to the far post.

Ronaldo countered for United, working his way down the right before firing a shot which bounced back off Mark Schwarzer's right-hand post.

United opened the scoring a minute later, Schwarzer parrying Ryan Giggs's cross-shot only as far as Darren Fletcher, who slotted home from six yards.

United began to up the pressure on the Boro goal, taking advantage of an extremely shaky home defence.

Alan Smith raced through on goal, but his shot from eight yards lacked the power to seriously trouble Schwarzer.

McClaren made a change at the break, replacing Joseph-Desire Job with Slovakia international Nemeth.

Job had had a poor first half, but McClaren could just as easily have withdrawn the disappointing Hasselbaink.

Eric Djemba-Djemba replaced the injured Ronaldo in the 78th minute and he had an instant impact on the match, setting up a low shot from Giggs which rolled over the line.

Middlesbrough managed to force 10 corners in the second half, but they never looked like making any of them count.

The jubilant United fans taunted the home crowd in the final minutes.

"Part-time supporters," they chanted, a comment on the number of Boro fans who were deserting the cause by making their way to the exits before the final whistle.

"You have to be on top form when the leading three clubs come visiting, and we weren't today."

Steve McClaren

"We have a great team spirit. When the sides around us are winning, we are determined to win as well."

Alan Smith

PREMIERSHIP MILESTONE

Darren Fletcher scored his first Premiership goal

PREMIERSHIP MILESTONE

Phil Neville made his 250th Premiership appearance

Darren Fletcher takes on Stewart Downing

PREMIERSHIP FIXTURE HISTORY

Pl: 3 Draws: 0	Wins	Goals	Yellow	Red
Newcastle United	2	3	3	0
Birmingham City	1	2	5	1

STARTING LINE-UPS

Newcastle United: Given; Taylor, Hughes, Bramble, Bernard; Bowyer, Jenas (c), Dyer; Bellamy, Robert; Ameobi

Birmingham City: Morrison, Heskey; Lazaridis, Carter, Savage, Johnson; Tebily, Upson, Cunningham (c), Melchiot; Maik Taylor

Substitutes (Newcastle United): Milner, N'Zogbia, Harper, O'Brien, Ambrose

Substitutes (Birmingham City): Gray, Anderton, Yorke, Vaesen, Clapham

EVENT LINE

6 **Ameobi (Open Play)**
25 Tebily (Off) Gray (On)
35 Savage (Foul)
42 Heskey (Foul)
44 **Bowyer (Open Play)**

HALF TIME 2 - 0

63 **Robert (Off) Milner (On)**
63 Carter (Off) Anderton (On)
64 Heskey (Open Play)
75 **Bellamy (Off) N'Zogbia (On)**
81 **Bernard (Handball)**
84 Cunningham (Off) Yorke (On)

FULL TIME 2 - 1

STATISTICS

Season	Fixture (Newcastle)		Fixture (Birmingham)	Season
146	4	Shots On Target	5	96
123	4	Shots Off Target	2	90
8	1	Hit Woodwork	0	4
54	2	Caught Offside	2	64
146	6	Corners	5	105
257	8	Fouls	11	303
51%	52%	Possession	48%	49%

LEAGUE STANDINGS

Position (pos before)	W	D	L	F	A	Pts
13 (14) Newcastle Utd	6	7	8	33	39	25
12 (9) Birmingham C	6	8	7	24	23	26

Saturday 1st January 2005 | Venue: St James' Park | Attendance: 52,222 | Referee: R.Styles

Kieron Dyer takes a tumble

"I'm pleased for the players. They would have been wondering where the next win was coming from."
Graeme Souness

PREMIERSHIP MILESTONE
100 Olivier Bernard made his 100th Premiership appearance

PREMIERSHIP MILESTONE
700 Lee Bowyer netted Newcastle's 700th Premiership goal

"We were awful in the first half. But all credit to our lads in the second period, we came out and had a right good go."
Steve Bruce

NEWCASTLE UNITED 2 BIRMINGHAM CITY 1

Newcastle United earned their first home Premiership win in two months courtesy of first-half goals from Shola Ameobi and Lee Bowyer.

Birmingham, meanwhile, saw their four-game winning streak come to an end.

The Blues mounted a comeback after the break, with Emile Heskey converting midway through the half, but they couldn't find an equaliser.

United prevailed despite the continued absence of Alan Shearer, whose expected return from a six-week lay-off had been put on hold due to a fresh injury picked up in training the day before.

United boss Graeme Souness kept faith with the team narrowly beaten by Arsenal in midweek, while Steve Bruce made one change to the side that had beaten Fulham, replacing Jamie Clapham with Stan Lazaridis.

United got off to the perfect start, opening the scoring on six minutes.

Craig Bellamy, playing wide on the right for the second game in a row, worked his way past Olivier Tebily and crossed for lone striker Ameobi, who beat Kenny Cunningham to the ball to head past Maik Taylor for his first Premiership goal of the season.

Laurent Robert set Bowyer free down the middle on 21 minutes, but he was denied by a fine save from Taylor.

Tebily was proving no match for Bellamy and was replaced by Julian Gray on 25 minutes. Lazaridis dropped back to left back, with Gray lining up on the wing.

Newcastle continued to press in the pouring rain and added to their lead just before the break, Robert's cross from the left finding Bowyer, who drilled a low shot to the left of a helpless Taylor.

Souness introduced James Milner for Robert on 63 minutes, while Bruce brought on Darren Anderton for Darren Carter a minute later.

Seconds after Anderton's arrival Birmingham had the ball in the back of the net, Heskey running on to a ball from Clinton Morrison before lashing a fierce shot past Shay Given at the near post.

Bruce threw on Dwight Yorke for the final few minutes in place of defender Cunningham, but United resisted the Blues' three-man strikeforce and held on for the win.

PREMIERSHIP FIXTURE HISTORY

Pl: **1** Draws: **1**	Wins	Goals	Yellow cards	Red cards
Portsmouth	0	1	3	0
Norwich City	0	1	0	1

STARTING LINE-UPS

Faye, Fuller, Mezague, Ashdown, Stefanovic

Brennan, Jarvis, Drury, Gallacher, Crow

EVENT LINE

5 Edworthy (Foul)

9 Francis (Open Play)

32 **Griffin (Foul)**

35 **Yakubu (Dissent)**

43 **Taylor (Foul)**

HALF TIME 0 - 1

61 **Yakubu (Penalty)**

61 Mulryne (Off) Brennan (On)

66 **Berger (Off) Faye (On)**

66 **Kamara (Off) Fuller (On)**

67 McKenzie (Off) Jarvis (On)

81 **Taylor (Off) Mezague (On)**

84 Huckerby (Off) Drury (On)

FULL TIME 1 - 1

STATISTICS

Season	Fixture		Fixture	Season
111	**7**	Shots On Target	**4**	**95**
102	**8**	Shots Off Target	**1**	**112**
3	**0**	Hit Woodwork	**0**	**5**
52	**1**	Caught Offside	**0**	**65**
114	**8**	Corners	**5**	**103**
257	**13**	Fouls	**6**	**272**
48%	**60%**	Possession	**40%**	**46%**

LEAGUE STANDINGS

Position (pos before)	W	D	L	F	A	Pts
11 (10) Portsmouth	**7**	**6**	**8**	**25**	**28**	**27**
17 (18) Norwich C	**2**	**10**	**9**	**18**	**37**	**16**

Saturday 1st January 2005 | Venue: **Fratton Park** | Attendance: **20,015** | Referee: **P.Dowd**

PORTSMOUTH 1 NORWICH CITY 1

Robert Green made two outstanding saves to ensure Norwich picked up a point at Fratton Park, despite playing for most of the game with 10 men.

Marc Edworthy was sent off in the fifth minute for bringing down Pompey's Diomansy Kamara as he raced for the ball following a Simon Charlton blunder.

Ten-man City were forced into defensive mode for the rest of the match, with Craig Fleming and Gary Doherty outstanding.

But ultimately it was Green who prevented Portsmouth from snatching a late victory, denying shots from Valery Mezague and full back Andy Griffin.

Mazague was played clear by a shrewd pass from Aiyegbeni Yakubu, only to see his shot blocked by the keeper.

Green then dived to push away a low drive from Griffin at the foot of the post.

Norwich, who entered the game without an away win this season, took a shock lead in the ninth minute with a stunning goal by Damien Francis.

Darren Huckerby's right-wing cross was only half-cleared by Arjan De Zeeuw and Francis picked out the top-left corner with a superb right-footed volley.

Yakubu should have equalised within a minute when Matt Taylor crossed from the left, but the Nigerian striker tucked his header into the side netting.

Charlton then cleared Patrik Berger's shot off the line before Shaka Hislop saved at the feet of Leon McKenzie.

Kamara had the Norwich defence on the ropes again in the 16th minute, twisting his way past two defenders before shooting just wide from the edge of the penalty area.

Kamara had an early chance in the second half, firing narrowly wide with a speculative 25-yard strike. David Bentley responded by going wide for the visitors.

Pompey equalised just past the hour mark thanks to a thrice-taken penalty from Yakubu.

McKenzie was adjudged to have handled inside the box and referee Phil Dowd pointed to the spot.

Yakubu converted, but Dowd spotted Kamara encroaching and ordered a retake.

Yakubu converted again, but again Dowd ruled it out for movement by Kamara.

Once again Yakubu converted, and this time the referee let it stand.

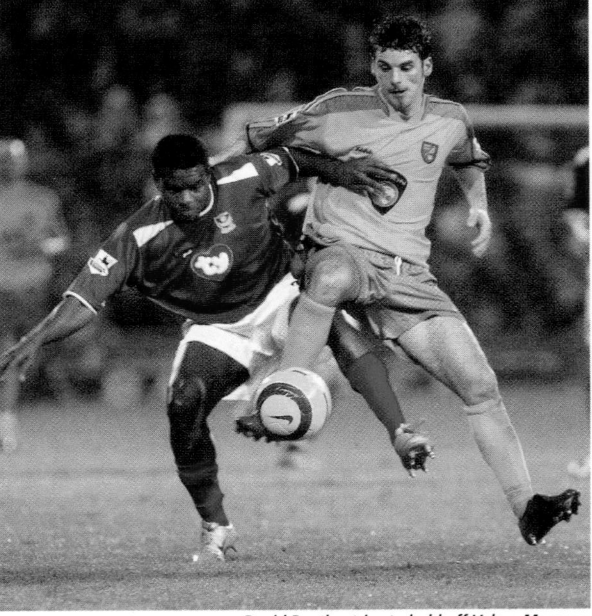

David Bentley tries to hold off Valery Mezague

"It would have been hard on Norwich if they had gone home with nothing."

Joe Jordan

PREMIERSHIP MILESTONE

250 Steve Stone made his 250th Premiership appearance

"Leon McKenzie got a shove in the back, and when that happens your natural reaction is to put your arm out."

Nigel Worthington on the penalty awarded against his side

PREMIERSHIP FIXTURE HISTORY

Pl: **13** Draws: **4**

	Wins	Goals	Yellow	Red
Tottenham Hotspur	**9**	**31**	**15**	**0**
Everton	**0**	**16**	**23**	**0**

STARTING LINE-UPS

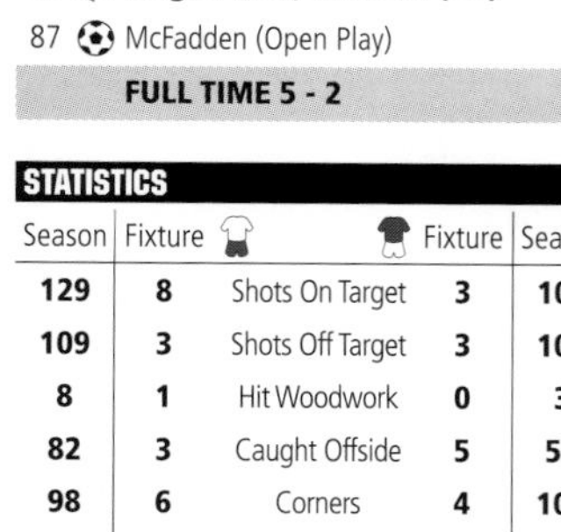

Redknapp, Ricketts, Fulop, Gardner, Davenport

Naysmith, Osman, Campbell, Turner, Chadwick

EVENT LINE

16 **Marney (Open Play)**

27 **Ziegler (Open Play)**

40 Cahill (Open Play)

HALF TIME 2 - 1

59 **Mendes (Open Play)**

68 **Keane (Open Play)**

70 Bent (Off) Osman (On)

70 Pistone (Off) Naysmith (On)

71 Kilbane (Off) Campbell (On)

80 **Marney (Open Play)**

87 **Carrick (Off) Redknapp (On)**

87 **Ziegler (Off) Ricketts (On)**

87 McFadden (Open Play)

FULL TIME 5 - 2

STATISTICS

Season	Fixture		Fixture	Season
129	**8**	Shots On Target	**3**	**103**
109	**3**	Shots Off Target	**3**	**102**
8	**1**	Hit Woodwork	**0**	**3**
82	**3**	Caught Offside	**5**	**57**
98	**6**	Corners	**4**	**101**
254	**8**	Fouls	**13**	**255**
50%	**60%**	Possession	**40%**	**48%**

LEAGUE STANDINGS

Position (pos before)		W	D	L	F	A	Pts
7 (8)	**Tottenham H**	**9**	**5**	**7**	**29**	**21**	**32**
4 (4)	**Everton**	**12**	**4**	**5**	**25**	**22**	**40**

Saturday 1st January 2005 | Venue: **White Hart Lane** | Attendance: **36,102** | Referee: **S.W.Dunn**

TOTTENHAM HOTSPUR 5 EVERTON 2

Dean Marney makes the most of his surprise inclusion

"To score two goals in your first game at home is a terrific achievement. The first goal was a good one, but the second was great."

Martin Jol on Dean Marney

PREMIERSHIP MILESTONE

Dean Marney, Reto Ziegler, Pedro Mendes and James McFadden all opened their Premiership goalscoring accounts

"I would have taken this position at the beginning of the season."

David Moyes

Everton's capital nightmare continued against Spurs at White Hart Lane.

The loss was Everton's second in a row and fifth of the season – all of which had come against London clubs.

Dean Marney netted twice to give the home fans the chance to chant the name of someone other than Jermain Defoe.

Spurs were without their 15-goal top scorer, who was sidelined with the knee injury he'd picked up against Crystal Palace in midweek, but they clearly didn't miss him.

Spurs threatened in the second minute, Fredi Kanoute racing down the right flank and sending in a cross which just eluded Robbie Keane.

James McFadden blew Everton's first chance on 14 minutes, blasting high over the bar after chesting down the rebound from Thomas Gravesen's corner.

Marney, making his full home debut, scored the opener two minutes later, running on to Keane's pass before drilling the ball high into the net.

Keane released Marney again in the 24th minute, only for the midfielder to tangle with Alessandro Pistone in the Everton area. The Spurs players were shouting for a penalty, but the referee waved play on.

The hosts would only have to wait another three minutes for a second goal, Swiss teenager Reto Ziegler perfectly placed to slot Kanoute's flicked header into the bottom corner for his first goal on English soil.

Tim Cahill pulled a goal back for Everton five minutes before the break, his low, powerful shot from Marcus Bent's header into the box beating keeper Paul Robinson.

Portugal international Pedro Mendes made it 3-1 in the 59th minute, firing home from 18 yards.

Marney turned provider on 68 minutes, racing past Pistone before crossing for Keane to calmly tap home his ninth of the season.

Marney all but put his name on the team sheet for the rest of the season in the 80th minute when he scored the goal of the game, a curling 20-yarder into the top-left corner.

McFadden grabbed a late consolation for Everton, but it took nothing away from Marney's brilliant start to 2005.

PREMIERSHIP FIXTURE HISTORY

Pl: 5 Draws: 0	Wins	Goals	Yellow	Red
Blackburn Rovers	4	7	6	0
Charlton Athletic	1	2	7	1

STARTING LINE-UPS

Blackburn Rovers: Friedel; Neill, Todd, Johansson, Matteo; Thompson, Ferguson (c), Flitcroft, Emerton; Stead, Dickov

Charlton Athletic: Kiely; Hreidarsson, Fortune, El Karkouri, Young; Thomas, Holland (c), Murphy, Kishishev, Rommedahl; Johansson

Blackburn subs: Gallagher, Reid, Enckelman, McEveley, Pedersen

Charlton subs: Konchesky, Euell, Hughes, Andersen, Stuart

EVENT LINE

34 Stead (Foul)

41 Emerton (Open Play)

HALF TIME 1 - 0

59 Matteo (Ung.Conduct)

59 Rommedahl (Ung.Conduct)

60 Hreidarsson (Foul)

60 Kishishev (Off) Euell (On)

60 Thomas (Off) Konchesky (On)

71 Hreidarsson (Off) Hughes (On)

80 Stead (Off) Gallagher (On)

88 Thompson (Off) Reid (On)

90 Young (Dissent)

FULL TIME 1 - 0

STATISTICS

Season	Fixture (Blackburn)		Fixture (Charlton)	Season
114	11	Shots On Target	6	103
131	5	Shots Off Target	3	83
6	0	Hit Woodwork	0	5
84	4	Caught Offside	4	73
121	6	Corners	8	99
338	11	Fouls	14	291
48%	53%	Possession	47%	44%

LEAGUE STANDINGS

Position (pos before)	W	D	L	F	A	Pts
15 (16) Blackburn R	4	10	8	20	33	22
8 (8) Charlton Ath	9	4	9	24	32	31

Monday 3rd January 2005 | Venue: **Ewood Park** | Attendance: **19,819** | Referee: **A.G.Wiley**

BLACKBURN ROVERS 1 CHARLTON ATHLETIC 0

A 41st-minute header from Brett Emerton secured Blackburn Rovers' second 1-0 win of the Christmas period.

It was an important result for struggling Blackburn, who bounced back from a late defeat in their previous match against Aston Villa.

The win was just the second of the season at Ewood Park for Rovers, the first coming in Mark Hughes's first game in charge back in September, a 1-0 success against Portsmouth.

Rovers ensured Charlton keeper Dean Kiely was kept warmer than his counterpart Brad Friedel, with Jonathan Stead desperately unlucky not to get his first goal of the season.

Stead couldn't seem to buy a goal, hitting the bar at Bolton last week before being denied here by an inspired Kiely on at least three occasions.

The Irish keeper did well to turn Paul Dickov's low shot around the post midway through the first half.

Dickov's header from the resulting corner was blocked on the line by Danny Murphy, the ball falling nicely for Stead, who was denied by a superb save from Kiely.

Stead went close again from Dickov's right-wing cross before Emerton showed him how it was done four minutes before the break, ghosting in at the far post to head home David Thompson's cross.

Jonatan Johansson then had Charlton's only real chance of the half, his effort denied by a one-handed save from Friedel.

Blackburn quickly countered, Stead muscling Talal El Karkouri off the ball before seeing his fierce drive turned away by Kiely.

Kiely remained the busier of the two keepers as the second half got underway, Stead forcing him into a low save from a tight angle before Thompson tested his reflexes with a free kick.

Rovers had a chance for a second late on, Lucas Neill collecting from Thompson before sending a cross in towards Emerton which the Australian winger headed over.

The Addicks finally applied some pressure to the Rovers goal with a succession of corners and dangerous crosses, but the home defence held firm.

"We really deserved the three points today. It was important psychologically to win."
Mark Hughes

"We never got going today. Perhaps this was one game too many."
Alan Curbishley

Jon Stead and Talal El Karkouri only have eyes for the ball

PREMIERSHIP FIXTURE HISTORY

Pl: 4 Draws: 2	Wins	⚽	▯	▮
Crystal Palace	2	4	5	1
Aston Villa	0	1	10	0

STARTING LINE-UPS

Leigertwood, Boyce, Speroni, Freedman, Shipperley

L.Moore, Postma, Berson, S.Moore, Whittingham

EVENT LINE

33	⚽	**Johnson (Open Play)**
		HALF TIME 1 - 0
50	▯	**Hughes (Foul)**
52	▯	McCann (Dissent)
57	▯	De la Cruz (Foul)
66	⇄	**Watson (Off) Leigertwood (On)**
66	⚽	**Johnson (Penalty)**
66	⇄	Hendrie (Off) Moore L (On)
71	▯	**Granville (Ung.Conduct)**
71	▯	Moore L (Ung.Conduct)
75	⇄	**Butterfield (Off) Boyce (On)**
		FULL TIME 2 - 0

STATISTICS

Season	Fixture		Fixture	Season
92	10	Shots On Target	6	112
94	5	Shots Off Target	6	109
5	0	Hit Woodwork	0	3
55	2	Caught Offside	5	62
108	7	Corners	7	129
302	7	Fouls	14	327
47%	58%	Possession	42%	49%

LEAGUE STANDINGS

Position (pos before)		W	D	L	F	A	Pts
17 (18)	Crystal Palace	4	6	12	23	34	18
9 (9)	Aston Villa	7	7	8	23	26	28

Monday 3rd January 2005 | Venue: **Selhurst Park** | Attendance: **24,140** | Referee: **A.P.D'Urso**

CRYSTAL PALACE 2 ASTON VILLA 0

Gavin McCann gets a piece of Mikele Leigertwood's shirt

"Andy Johnson is fundamental to what we are trying to build at Crystal Palace, and is scoring goals consistently at Premiership level."

Iain Dowie

PREMIERSHIP MILESTONE

Darren Powell made his Premiership debut

"We are a mid-table team at the moment, so we need to push on."

Assistant Manager Roy Aitken

Andy Johnson bagged a brace to earn Crystal Palace their first win since the end of October.

The Palace marksman struck in the 33rd minute before converting his fifth penalty of the season midway through the second period.

The first half was a real cracker, with both sides playing open, attacking football.

Palace had strong claims for a penalty waved away on seven minutes after Wayne Routledge was brought down by Ulises de la Cruz.

Villa's main threat came down the left flank, with Gareth Barry frequently cropping up in good positions.

Barry was put through following smart work from Jlloyd Samuel, but he sent his shot wide of the target.

Johnson countered for the Eagles, his low shot from the edge of the area flying inches wide of Thomas Sorensen's goal.

Palace midfielder Vassilios Lakis went close soon after, working his way down the left before cutting inside and forcing a superb save from Sorensen, tipping the ball over the bar.

Palace opened the scoring on 33 minutes, Sorensen parrying Ben Watson's shot into the path of Johnson, who raced in to convert from 10 yards.

The hosts almost doubled their lead four minutes later, Routledge firing wide from the edge of the area.

Johnson set up a chance for Watson early in the second half, the youngster's right-foot volley dropping wide.

Palace keeper Gabor Kiraly then made a tremendous save to deny Gavin McCann before keeping out a close-range effort from Stephen Davis on the hour mark.

The Eagles were awarded a penalty four minutes later, Villa defender Mark Delaney catching Lakis's ankle following Routledge's cross from the right. Johnson slotted home to take his tally for the season to 13.

Villa worked hard to get themselves back into the match and set up several scoring opportunities, Juan Pablo Angel heading straight into the arms of Kiraly before McCann fired wide.

Nolberto Solano underlined Villa's frustration when his goalbound shot was somehow clawed away by Kiraly, but this was a deserved three points for the Eagles.

PREMIERSHIP FIXTURE HISTORY

Pl: 4 Draws: 1	Wins	Goals	Yellow	Red
Norwich City	1	5	5	1
Liverpool	2	6	9	1

STARTING LINE-UPS

Norwich City: Green; Helveg, Fleming (c), Doherty, Charlton; Francis, Mulryne, Bentley; Jonson, Huckerby; McKenzie

Liverpool: Dudek; Warnock, Hyypia, Carragher, Finnan; Riise, Diao, Gerrard (c), Nunez; Mellor, Garcia

Norwich City substitutes: Brennan, Crow, Jarvis, Gallacher, Drury

Liverpool substitutes: Sinama-Pongolle, Hamann, Traore, Harrison, Raven

EVENT LINE

41	**Francis (Foul)**
	HALF TIME 0 - 0
53	Finnan (Foul)
57	**Bentley (Foul)**
58	Garcia (Open Play)
61	Hyypia (Foul)
61	Mellor (Off) Sinama-Pongolle (On)
64	Riise (Open Play)
67	**McKenzie (Off) Crow (On)**
67	**Mulryne (Off) Brennan (On)**
77	Nunez (Off) Hamann (On)
78	**Francis (Off) Jarvis (On)**
82	Riise (Off) Traore (On)
88	**Jarvis (Open Play)**
90	Warnock (Ung.Conduct)
	FULL TIME 1 - 2

STATISTICS

Season	Fixture (Norwich City)		Fixture (Liverpool)	Season
99	4	Shots On Target	6	151
115	3	Shots Off Target	5	148
5	0	Hit Woodwork	0	3
70	5	Caught Offside	2	55
108	5	Corners	2	127
289	17	Fouls	20	263
46%	49%	Possession	51%	54%

LEAGUE STANDINGS

Position (pos before)		W	D	L	F	A	Pts
18 (17)	Norwich C	2	10	10	19	39	16
5 (6)	Liverpool	11	4	7	36	22	37

Monday 3rd January 2005 | Venue: **Carrow Road** | Attendance: **24,503** | Referee: **H.M.Webb**

NORWICH CITY 1 LIVERPOOL 2

Liverpool had to work hard to complete their double over the Canaries at Carrow Road.

Not for the first time this season, City fell behind when an attacking move broke down. True to recent form, they went on to concede a second shortly afterwards.

But they battled away, Ryan Jarvis pulling one back with two minutes remaining to cause the Reds a brief scare.

Liverpool forced the first corner of the game in the fifth minute after Simon Charlton had given the ball away deep in his own half.

Norwich were reduced to 10 men for a few minutes when Mattias Jonson left the pitch to have a head wound stitched. He returned to the game with his head well bandaged.

Darren Huckerby set up a chance for Jonson, but his half-hit shot failed to trouble Reds keeper Jerzy Dudek.

Steven Gerrard put plenty of power into his rasping drive on 25 minutes, but it flew wide.

John Arne Riise also went wide five minutes later when well positioned inside the Norwich area.

Damien Francis was booked for a challenge on Sami Hyypia four minutes before the break, though referee Howard Webb took a more lenient view when Hyypia was flattened by Leon McKenzie a minute later.

Luis Garcia had the last chance of the half in stoppage time, but he fired high into the Barclay Stand.

Norwich were first to threaten in the second period, a through ball from Phil Mulryne just too long for McKenzie.

Huckerby's left-wing cross was then handled by Jamie Carragher, but Norwich had to settle for a corner.

With City throwing men forward Liverpool scored on the break, Riise's through ball finding Garcia, whose first-time effort from 16 yards cleared the advancing Robert Green and settled in the back of the net.

Liverpool doubled their lead six minutes later, Florent Sinama-Pongolle's initial shot palmed away by Green and falling invitingly for Riise, who smashed home from six yards.

Jarvis came on for Francis in the 78th minute and grabbed a consolation 10 minutes later, controlling Jonson's cross on the edge of the area before beating Dudek high to his right.

Luis Garcia celebrates opening the scoring

"Up to the first goal, there was nothing in it."
Nigel Worthington

PREMIERSHIP MILESTONE

Ryan Jarvis scored his first Premiership goal

"In the first half both teams played well, but after the break we took control of the game."
Rafael Benitez

PREMIERSHIP FIXTURE HISTORY

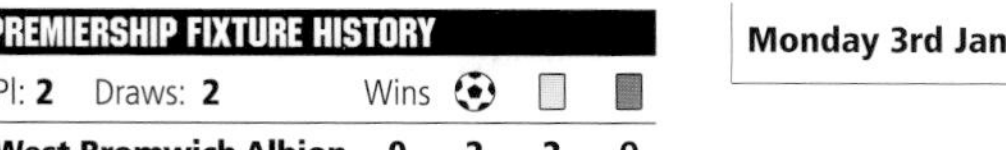

Pl: 2 Draws: 2	Wins	⚽	☐	■
West Bromwich Albion	0	2	2	0
Newcastle United	0	2	0	0

STARTING LINE-UPS

Gera, Kuszczak, Gaardsoe, Contra, Koumas

Milner, Harper, O'Brien, Ambrose, Brittain

EVENT LINE

7 ☐ **Johnson (Dissent)**

25 ☐ **Purse (Dissent)**

HALF TIME 0 - 0

76 N'Zogbia (Off) Milner (On)

83 **Kanu (Off) Gera (On)**

FULL TIME 0 - 0

STATISTICS

Season	Fixture	West Brom	Newcastle Fixture	Season
93	5	Shots On Target	7	153
90	3	Shots Off Target	5	128
4	0	Hit Woodwork	1	9
82	3	Caught Offside	5	59
99	1	Corners	6	152
295	9	Fouls	7	264
45%	46%	Possession	54%	51%

LEAGUE STANDINGS

Position (pos before)	W	D	L	F	A	Pts
20 (20) West Brom	1	10	11	17	43	13
13 (13) Newcastle Utd	6	8	8	33	39	26

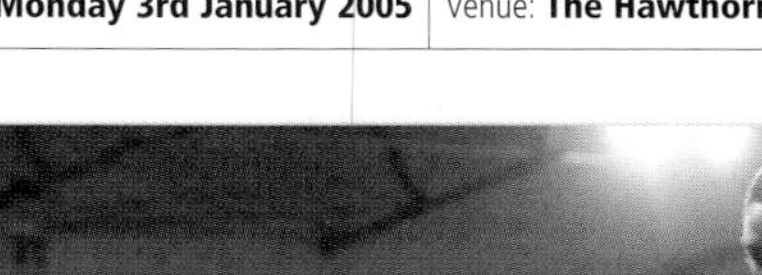

Monday 3rd January 2005 | Venue: **The Hawthorns** | Attendance: **25,259** | Referee: **N.S.Barry**

Russell Hoult bravely denies Shola Ameobi

"We are now unbeaten in the last three games, and that is something we can build on."

Bryan Robson

PREMIERSHIP MILESTONE

50 Geoff Horsfield made his 50th Premiership appearance

"We didn't capitalise when we were dominant early on."

Graeme Souness

PREMIERSHIP MILESTONE

200 Aaron Hughes made his 200th Premiership appearance

WEST BROM 0 NEWCASTLE UNITED 0

West Brom manager Bryan Robson finally collected his first home point at the fifth attempt thanks to a battling display against Newcastle United.

But despite stretching their unbeaten run to three games, Albion still found themselves rooted to the bottom of the Premiership table.

They'd now collected just four points from Robson's 10 games in charge and had yet to win under their new boss.

West Brom had to soak up some intense Newcastle pressure and things could have been very different if United hadn't been missing the injured Alan Shearer, Patrick Kluivert and Craig Bellamy.

That left Shola Ameobi operating as a lone striker, with Lee Bowyer and Kieron Dyer doing the work in midfield.

Newcastle, who had returned to winning ways by beating Birmingham City for their first victory in seven games, had enough chances to win the game comfortably.

But they were frustrated by a combination of poor finishing and some dogged West Brom defending, with Albion skipper Darren Purse in outstanding form.

Russell Hoult denied Titus Bramble in the fifth minute after the central defender had met Laurent Robert's free kick with a powerful close-range header.

Bowyer then volleyed over the bar before Hoult saved from Ameobi on 10 minutes.

West Brom had their only real chance of the first half three minutes later, Kanu heading the loose ball wide after United keeper Shay Given had spilled a long-range drive from Ronnie Wallwork.

The hosts had a double let-off in the 22nd minute, Bowyer's 30-yard drive crashing off the foot of the post before Robert saw his shot from the rebound saved by Hoult.

United's failings in front of goal should really have been punished 10 minutes into the second half.

Albion striker Geoff Horsfield found himself with just the keeper to beat, but his poorly placed shot from 10 yards was easily handled by Given.

The miss sparked West Brom into their best spell of the match, Robert Earnshaw going close with a 67th-minute volley from Paul Robinson's left-wing cross which was well saved by Given.

PREMIERSHIP FIXTURE HISTORY

Pl: 8 Draws: 2	Wins	Goals	Yellow	Red
Arsenal	6	17	9	0
Manchester City	0	4	11	4

STARTING LINE-UPS

Arsenal: Almunia; Hoyte, Toure, Senderos, Cole; Ljungberg, Fabregas, Vieira (c), Pires; van Persie, Henry

Manchester City: Macken, Fowler, S.Wright-Phillips; Sibierski, Bosvelt, Barton; Thatcher, Distin (c), Dunne, Onuoha; James

Arsenal subs: Pennant, Lehmann, Clichy, Larsson, Owusu-Abeyie

Manchester City subs: Flood, McManaman, Waterreus, Sommeil, B.Wright-Phillips

EVENT LINE

31 ⚽ Wright-Phillips S (Open Play)

40 ▢ Thatcher (Foul)

HALF TIME 0 - 1

55 ▢ **Toure (Foul)**

60 ▢ **Fabregas (Foul)**

65 ⇄ **Fabregas (Off) Pennant (On)**

67 ▢ Barton (Foul)

75 ⚽ **Ljungberg (Open Play)**

77 ⇄ Barton (Off) Flood (On)

84 ▢ Bosvelt (Foul)

90 ▢ **Senderos (Foul)**

90 ⇄ Macken (Off) Wright-Phillips B (On)

FULL TIME 1 - 1

STATISTICS

Season	Fixture (Arsenal)		Fixture (Man City)	Season
167	7	Shots On Target	4	125
103	5	Shots Off Target	1	108
8	1	Hit Woodwork	0	2
44	2	Caught Offside	6	68
127	12	Corners	5	138
253	10	Fouls	13	292
55%	59%	Possession	41%	48%

LEAGUE STANDINGS

Position (pos before)		W	D	L	F	A	Pts
2 (2)	Arsenal	14	6	2	52	24	48
9 (10)	Man City	7	7	8	27	23	28

Tuesday 4th January 2005 | Venue: **Highbury** | Attendance: **38,086** | Referee: **R.Styles**

ARSENAL 1 MANCHESTER CITY 1

Shaun Wright-Phillips put the brakes on Arsenal's title challenge with a spectacular 31st-minute strike.

Freddie Ljungberg headed a 75th-minute equaliser to earn the Gunners a point, but the real winners were title favourites Chelsea, who now led Arsenal by seven points after beating Middlesbrough.

The game exposed the lack of depth in Arsenal's injury-hit squad, with Arsène Wenger fielding his youngest Premiership side in more than eight years as Gunners boss.

Nineteen-year-old Swiss centre back Philippe Senderos made his Premiership debut in place of ankle victim Sol Campbell, while 20-year-old right back Justin Hoyte continued to deputise for Lauren.

With Gilberto and Edu still out of action, 17-year-old Cesc Fabregas lined up again alongside Patrick Vieira in central midfield, while Robin van Persie replaced Dennis Bergkamp and Jose Antonio Reyes in partnering Thierry Henry up front.

Robbie Fowler's header forced a good save from Manuel Almunia in the opening minute after the City striker had found space on the right.

Henry responded for the Gunners, whipping in a low centre which flashed across the face of goal.

Arsenal threatened again soon after, Robert Pires missing Henry's 25-yard free kick by inches.

Hoyte surged forward after winning a tackle, but his weak finish failed to trouble City keeper David James.

Ashley Cole was then robbed by a swift challenge following a neat combination with Pires, before Richard Dunne halted Henry with a recovery tackle.

Despite Arsenal's pressure, it was City who opened the scoring on 31 minutes, Wright-Phillips lashing home a trademark 25-yard shot after Vieira had lost the ball on the edge of the Gunners box.

James held Henry's curled free kick two minutes later before Vieira headed wide from a Pires corner with the keeper stranded.

James did well to deny Pires on 70 minutes, tipping his volley against the bar and away to safety.

City finally cracked five minutes later, Ljungberg heading home after Henry's acrobatic overhead kick.

Van Persie almost moved Arsenal ahead on 78 minutes, his free kick slamming against the angle of post and bar.

Henry had a final chance for the Gunners from a Pires cross, but he sent his header over.

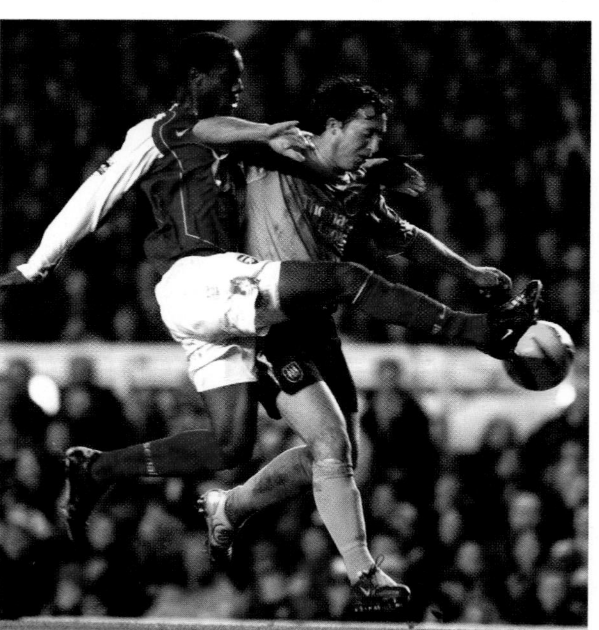

Justin Hoyte makes a vital challenge on Robbie Fowler

"I look upon that result as two points dropped. The second half was all us, and I think we were a bit unlucky not to take all three points in the end."

Arsene Wenger

"We deserved something for our performance, and they deserved something for the way in which they attacked us in the second half."

Kevin Keegan

PREMIERSHIP MILESTONE

100 Richard Dunne made his 100th Premiership appearance for Man City

PREMIERSHIP MILESTONE

350 Shaun Wright-Phillips netted Man City's 350th Premiership goal

PREMIERSHIP FIXTURE HISTORY

Pl: 3 Draws: 0	Wins	Goals	Yellow	Red
Birmingham City	2	6	5	0
Bolton Wanderers	1	3	6	1

STARTING LINE-UPS

Birmingham City: Maik Taylor; Melchiot, Cunningham (c), Upson, Tebily; Johnson, Clemence, Anderton, Lazaridis; Heskey, Morrison

Bolton Wanderers: Jaaskelainen; Gardner, N'Gotty, Jaidi, Hunt; Speed, Campo, Okocha (c); Giannakopoulos, Diouf, Nolan

Substitutes (Birmingham City): Gray, Clapham, Yorke, Vaesen, Martin Taylor

Substitutes (Bolton Wanderers): Pedersen, Hierro, Poole, Ben Haim, Vaz Te

EVENT LINE

17 Goal Diouf (Open Play)

36 Yellow card Diouf (Dissent)

39 Yellow card **Heskey (Dissent)**

40 Yellow card N'Gotty (Dissent)

HALF TIME 0 - 1

57 Substitution Giannakopoulos (Off) Pedersen (On)

64 Substitution **Tebily (Off) Gray (On)**

66 Goal **Upson (Corner)**

73 Substitution **Clemence (Off) Clapham (On)**

76 Substitution Speed (Off) Hierro (On)

77 Substitution **Morrison (Off) Yorke (On)**

83 Yellow card **Upson (Foul)**

90 Goal Nolan (Open Play)

FULL TIME 1 - 2

STATISTICS

Season	Fixture (Birmingham)		Fixture (Bolton)	Season
101	5	Shots On Target	5	139
92	2	Shots Off Target	1	127
5	1	Hit Woodwork	0	5
66	2	Caught Offside	7	47
112	7	Corners	5	116
315	12	Fouls	13	301
50%	56%	Possession	44%	50%

LEAGUE STANDINGS

Position (pos before)	W	D	L	F	A	Pts
13 (12) Birmingham C	6	8	8	25	25	26
11 (14) Bolton W	7	6	9	29	31	27

Tuesday 4th January 2005 | Venue: **St Andrew's** | Attendance: **27,177** | Referee: **U.D.Rennie**

BIRMINGHAM CITY 1 BOLTON WANDERERS 2

A late Kevin Nolan strike secured Bolton's first win in 11 games.

With Darren Carter sidelined with a virus and Robbie Savage dropped after handing in a transfer request, City boss Steve Bruce was forced into two changes in the centre of midfield.

The former Spurs duo of Stephen Clemence and Darren Anderton came in to deputise, while Olivier Tebily kept his place at left back despite his horror show against Craig Bellamy in City's last match against Newcastle.

Jussi Jaaskelainen was back in goal for Wanderers, while Stelios Giannakopoulos took the place of the injured Kevin Davies.

There was a real determination in Bolton's play, the side clearly eager to break out of their prolonged slump.

Wanderers captain Jay-Jay Okocha wasted an early chance when he failed to gain control of a short cross from Nolan.

Maik Taylor then made a good save to deny Nolan, pushing away the midfielder's shot after a clever ball from Okocha had sent him clear.

Livewire Okocha was proving a handful for the City defence and he set up Bolton's opener on 17 minutes, his rocket of a shot parried by Taylor to El-Hadji Diouf, who promptly turned the ball home.

Emile Heskey responded for City, outpacing the Bolton defence before seeing his powerful shot blocked by Jaaskelainen.

The keeper made another good save soon after to deny Tebily's long-range effort.

Referee Uriah Rennie came in for some heated comments from the fans for his long-winded handling of a clash between Heskey and Radhi Jaidi which resulted in both players being booked.

Aussie Stan Lazaridis made some penetrating runs into the heart of the Bolton penalty area, but he was continually denied by Wanderers' solid rearguard.

Birmingham took the offensive initiative in the second period, with Bolton dropping back to defend their slender lead.

Mario Melchiot threatened with a close-range header that dipped just over before City equalised on 66 minutes, Clinton Morrison's overhead kick cannoning off the post and falling for Matthew Upson, who forced the ball home from five yards.

The game looked to be heading for a draw until Okocha inspired Bolton to a late rally, his last-minute shot rebounding off Taylor for Nolan to fire home.

"We didn't deserve to lose, but we were out on our feet in the last five minutes."

Steve Bruce

"I feel that we need to look at this Christmas programme, as I can honestly say I've not seen any entertainment in our last two games."

Sam Allardyce

PREMIERSHIP MILESTONE

100 Matthew Upson made his 100th Premiership appearance

PREMIERSHIP MILESTONE

150 Mario Melchiot made his 150th Premiership appearance

Kevin Nolan is the hero for Bolton

Tuesday 4th January 2005	Venue: Stamford Bridge	Attendance: 40,982	Referee: S.G.Bennett

CHELSEA 2 MIDDLESBROUGH 0

A double from Didier Drogba won the match for Chelsea in what appeared a pivotal night in the Premiership title race.

With Arsenal being held at home by Manchester City and Manchester United also dropping points at home to Spurs, Chelsea moved seven points clear at the top of the table.

Drogba was good value for his man-of-the-match award after scoring two beautiful goals.

They came in a two-minute spell early in the first half, which had started surprisingly well for Middlesbrough.

But after weathering an opening barrage from the visitors, Chelsea soon settled into their customary passing mode and opened the scoring on the quarter-hour mark.

A well-executed counter-attack saw the ball run from Frank Lampard, to Arjen Robben, to Drogba.

The Ivory Coast striker then turned Boro centre back Gareth Southgate inside out, resisting a shirt pull from the former England defender before drilling a low right-footer past keeper Mark Schwarzer from the edge of the penalty area.

Two minutes later, Chelsea won a free kick 20 yards out after Joe Cole had been upended.

Lampard sent a curling ball in towards Drogba, who easily beat defender Colin Cooper to arrow a downwards header into the back of the net.

Questions could be asked about Schwarzer's positioning after he misjudged the flight of Lampard's cross, but the ferocity of Drogba's header was such that the keeper probably wouldn't have made the save even if he'd been ideally placed.

Paulo Ferreira then had a chance for Chelsea's third, collecting from Lampard before seeing his shot clear the Boro bar.

Lampard went close himself shortly before the break, his close-range effort blocked by Schwarzer.

Damien Duff stirred a subdued home crowd into life on 58 minutes, slamming a shot against the bar after Cole had fired wide.

Stewart Downing had Boro's best chance on 66 minutes, his low right-footer well held by Petr Cech.

Lampard responded for the Blues, his low shot from just inside the area denied by Schwarzer.

Former Chelsea man Jimmy Floyd Hasselbaink had a chance for a stoppage-time consolation, but he sent his free kick well over.

Ray Parlour is outmuscled by two-goal striker Didier Drogba

"We set our stall out to get 12 points from these four Christmas games, and that's exactly what we've done."
Assistant Manager Steve Clarke

"I can't fault my players. We could have folded after 17 minutes, but we kept on going."
Steve McClaren

PREMIERSHIP FIXTURE HISTORY

Pl: 10 Draws: 3	Wins			
Chelsea	7	20	18	0
Middlesbrough	0	4	18	0

STARTING LINE-UPS

Tiago, Kezman, Cudicini, Gudjohnsen, Johnson

Job, Morrison, Nash, McMahon, Davies

EVENT LINE

15 **Drogba (Open Play)**
17 **Drogba (Indirect Free Kick)**
25 **Cole J (Foul)**
32 **Robben (Foul)**
HALF TIME 2 - 0
50 **Smertin (Off) Johnson (On)**
60 Nemeth (Off) Job (On)
62 **Cole J (Off) Tiago (On)**
72 Doriva (Off) Morrison (On)
79 **Drogba (Off) Kezman (On)**
82 Parlour (Foul)
FULL TIME 2 - 0

STATISTICS

Season	Fixture		Fixture	Season
164	9	Shots On Target	1	146
136	5	Shots Off Target	1	124
8	1	Hit Woodwork	0	4
66	1	Caught Offside	4	59
155	4	Corners	3	123
281	15	Fouls	9	269
55%	58%	Possession	42%	50%

LEAGUE STANDINGS

Position (pos before)		W	D	L	F	A	Pts
1 (1)	Chelsea	17	4	1	43	8	55
6 (6)	Middlesbrough	10	5	7	34	28	35

PREMIERSHIP FIXTURE HISTORY

Pl: 2 Draws: 0	Wins	⚽	☐	■
Everton	2	3	0	0
Portsmouth	0	1	2	0

STARTING LINE-UPS

Bent, Kilbane, Turner, Weir, Pistone

Cisse, Taylor, Ashdown, Unsworth, Mezague

EVENT LINE

29 ⚽ **Stubbs (Corner)**

31 ⚽ Yakubu (Open Play)

HALF TIME 1 - 1

73 **Campbell (Off) Bent (On)**

73 Faye (Off) Cisse (On)

74 **McFadden (Off) Kilbane (On)**

85 Yakubu (Off) Taylor (On)

90 ⚽ **Osman (Open Play)**

FULL TIME 2 - 1

STATISTICS

Season	Fixture		Fixture	Season
107	4	Shots On Target	5	116
112	10	Shots Off Target	3	105
3	0	Hit Woodwork	0	3
57	0	Caught Offside	1	53
109	8	Corners	1	115
262	7	Fouls	7	264
49%	59%	Possession	41%	48%

LEAGUE STANDINGS

Position (pos before)		W	D	L	F	A	Pts
4 (4)	Everton	13	4	5	27	23	43
12 (11)	Portsmouth	7	6	9	26	30	27

Tuesday 4th January 2005 | Venue: **Goodison Park** | Attendance: **35,480** | Referee: **P.Walton**

EVERTON 2 PORTSMOUTH 1

Shaka Hislop punches away the danger

"I thought we got stronger as the game went on, and we deserved the win because we kept going right until the end."

David Moyes

"I thought we were hard done by. I'm not sure where the ref got all that stoppage time from, but I would like an explanation."

Joe Jordan

Leon Osman grabbed all three points for Everton with a dramatic, last-gasp strike.

The win was an important one for David Moyes's men, re-establishing a safe distance between them and the chasing Champions League pack.

Kevin Campbell had an early chance for the hosts, but his shot was blocked.

Patrik Berger responded for Portsmouth, his shot denied by a diving save from Richard Wright.

Everton were shouting for a penalty on 21 minutes after Arjan De Zeeuw appeared to block James McFadden's shot with his arm, but the referee waved play on.

The Toffees opened the scoring eight minutes later, captain Alan Stubbs rising to head home Thomas Gravesen's corner at the far post.

Aiyegbeni Yakubu levelled two minutes later with a powerful drive into the top corner.

The two sides traded blows, Shaka Hislop saving from Osman before Berger fired a volley over from 25 yards.

Diomansy Kamara almost moved Portsmouth ahead two minutes into the second period, his long-distance shot flying just wide.

Tim Cahill then had a chance for Everton, his diving header going just over.

Berger was next to threaten for Pompey, his shot parried by Wright and falling for Yakubu, whose follow-up was blocked by the keeper.

Cahill responded with a ball over the top for Osman, who pulled his shot wide.

The game turned following the introduction of Marcus Bent, a 73rd-minute replacement for Campbell.

He got a fine reception form the Goodison faithful and his added pace and purpose livened up a previously lacklustre Everton attack.

With seven minutes to play, Gravesen forced Hislop into his first notable save of the second half, working his way past three Pompey players before firing a right-footer which had the keeper at full stretch.

Everton were repeatedly denied by some resilient Portsmouth defending in a frenetic final few minutes.

But with just seconds remaining, Osman turned on a lofted ball into the box and blasted a volley into the top corner.

It was rather harsh on Pompey, but fair reward for Everton's extra endeavour and never-say-die attitude.

PREMIERSHIP FIXTURE HISTORY

Pl: 13 Draws: 2	Wins	⚽	▯	■
Manchester United	11	26	15	0
Tottenham Hotspur	0	4	17	1

STARTING LINE-UPS

Bellion, Miller, Spector, Ricardo, Djemba-Djemba

Gardner, Fulop, Ifil, Bunjevcevic, Yeates

EVENT LINE

37 Giggs (Off) Bellion (On)

HALF TIME 0 - 0

51 Pamarot (Foul)

61 Marney (Foul)

63 Neville P (Foul)

76 Fletcher (Off) Miller (On)

84 Ronaldo (Off) Spector (On)

90 Ricketts (Off) Gardner (On)

FULL TIME 0 - 0

STATISTICS

Season	Fixture		Fixture	Season
182	16	Shots On Target	4	133
168	7	Shots Off Target	3	112
11	0	Hit Woodwork	1	9
82	9	Caught Offside	2	84
183	8	Corners	2	100
257	11	Fouls	13	267
56%	60%	Possession	40%	49%

LEAGUE STANDINGS

Position (pos before)		W	D	L	F	A	Pts
3 (3)	Man Utd	12	8	2	33	13	44
7 (7)	Tottenham H	9	6	7	29	21	33

Tuesday 4th January 2005 | Venue: Old Trafford | Attendance: 67,962 | Referee: M.Clattenburg

MANCHESTER UNITED 0 TOTTENHAM HOTSPUR 0

A controversial decision in the final minutes robbed Tottenham of their first win at Old Trafford since 1989.

With United pressing for a winner, keeper Roy Carroll raced out of his area to clear.

His kick was picked up by Pedro Mendes, who coolly lofted the ball towards the United goal with Carroll now back on his line.

It looked a formality for the Northern Ireland international to take it, but unbelievably he let the ball slip through his hands and was forced to scoop it back from a yard inside his net.

Spurs were ready to celebrate the goal, but instead looked on in disbelief as both the linesman and referee were unmoved.

Spurs had only taken a single point from 12 games at Old Trafford since the inception of the Premiership, but this should surely have been three points for the Londoners.

Until then, United had looked favourites to continue their impressive run, despite the loss of in-form Ryan Giggs to a 37th-minute hamstring injury.

The Red Devils had numerous chances to score, but they found Spurs keeper Paul Robinson in outstanding form.

Robinson twice denied Alan Smith with superb reflex saves from point-blank range in the first half.

Spurs went close just before the break, Mendes collecting from Robbie Keane before curling a shot onto the roof of the net.

Robinson continued his England form in the second period, saving from Cristiano Ronaldo at full stretch before racing off his line to deny Giggs's replacement, David Bellion.

Spurs had a lucky escape in the 59th minute when Noe Pamarot tried to cut out Phil Neville's right-wing cross, only to crash a 10-yard shot against his own post.

Smith had a chance from the rebound, but was denied by a fine block from Ledley King.

Bellion had the next chance for United on 74 minutes, his shot to the near post well saved by Robinson.

The keeper made a superb save to deny United a late winner, acrobatically throwing himself across goal to palm away Gabriel Heinze's vicious free kick from the left edge of the penalty area.

"Technology should play a part in decisions like these. The ball clearly went over the line."

Sir Alex Ferguson on the incorrect decision that saw Tottenham's Pedro Mendes denied a late winner

"You could understand it if it had been a couple of inches over the line, but this was two feet over."

Martin Jol on the goal that never was

Pedro Mendes tries to escape the attentions of Alan Smith

PREMIERSHIP FIXTURE HISTORY

Pl: 4 Draws: 3	Wins	⚽	▢	■
Southampton	1	8	5	0
Fulham	0	6	6	0

STARTING LINE-UPS

McCann, Jakobsson, Smith, Cranie, Ormerod

John, McBride, Fontaine, Crossley, Clark

EVENT LINE

- 20 ⚽ Diop (Indirect Free Kick)
- 21 ⚽ **Phillips (Open Play)**
- 29 ⚽ **Phillips (Open Play)**
- 42 ▢ **Redknapp (Foul)**
- 43 ⚽ Malbranque (Open Play)
- 44 ⇄ **Fernandes (Off) McCann (On)**

HALF TIME 2 - 2

- 50 ⚽ Radzinski (Open Play)
- 61 ⇄ Radzinski (Off) John (On)
- 71 ⚽ **Rosenior (Own Goal)**
- 73 ▢ **Phillips (Ung.Conduct)**
- 73 ▢ Rehman (Foul)
- 84 ⇄ **Davenport (Off) Jakobsson (On)**
- 90 ▢ Cole (Ung.Conduct)
- 90 ⇄ Cole (Off) McBride (On)
- 90 ⇄ Rosenior (Off) Fontaine (On)

FULL TIME 3 - 3

STATISTICS

Season	Fixture		Fixture	Season
99	5	Shots On Target	7	108
118	3	Shots Off Target	5	98
2	0	Hit Woodwork	0	3
61	4	Caught Offside	1	55
110	2	Corners	10	112
277	16	Fouls	17	278
48%	44%	Possession	56%	48%

LEAGUE STANDINGS

Position (pos before)	W	D	L	F	A	Pts
19 (19) Southampton	2	9	11	22	37	15
15 (16) Fulham	6	4	12	28	39	22

Wednesday 5th January 2005 | Venue: **Friends Provident St Mary's Stadium** | Attendance: **27,343** | Referee: **G.Poll**

SOUTHAMPTON 3 FULHAM 3

Steed Malbranque is harried by Rory Delap

Southampton twice came from behind to earn a point against Fulham.

The six-goal thriller left Harry Redknapp still searching for his first win since taking over as Saints manager six games ago.

Southampton were the first to threaten, Danny Higginbotham's deep cross from the left finding Peter Crouch, whose header was saved by Edwin van der Sar.

On 17 minutes, Papa Bouba Diop almost put through his own net when he sliced the ball over the crossbar following Higginbotham's left-wing cross.

Fulham's Senegalese star made up for that near miss three minutes later, out-jumping Claus Lundekvam to head in Mark Pembridge's precise free kick from the right.

Southampton quickly responded, scoring twice in the space of eight minutes to turn the game on its head.

Just seconds after Diop's opener, Kevin Phillips headed home Fabrice Fernandes's centre to level matters.

And on 29 minutes, Phillips exchanged passes with strike partner Crouch before turning defender Zat Knight and curling in his seventh of the season.

But just when it looked like Saints would go in ahead at the break, Steed Malbranque equalised for the visitors, tapping home the rebound from eight yards after Luis Boa Morte's angled shot had been saved by Antti Niemi.

Fulham reclaimed the lead five minutes into the second half, Pembridge's through ball playing in Tomasz Radzinski, who made no mistake from 10 yards.

Andy Cole wasted a chance to move Fulham further ahead three minutes later, shooting well wide from Radzinski's cross.

Cole had a better go on 63 minutes, his right-foot shot turned around the post by Niemi after another good pass from Pembridge.

Pembridge sent the resulting corner in towards substitute Collins John, whose header flew inches over.

Another Pembridge set piece caused havoc on 70 minutes, Niemi somehow keeping out Knight's shot from three yards.

Fulham were made to pay for their missed opportunities a minute later, Anders Svensson finding space down the right before sending in a low cross which was turned into his own net by Liam Rosenior for 3-3.

Referee Graham Poll denied Saints a late penalty, waving away their appeals after Knight appeared to handle in the box.

"We have got to win our home games if we are going to stay up."
Harry Redknapp

PREMIERSHIP MILESTONE
100 Rory Delap made his 100th Premiership appearance for Southampton

PREMIERSHIP MILESTONE
Jamie Redknapp and Calum Davenport both made their first Premiership appearance for Southampton

PREMIERSHIP MILESTONE
50 Peter Crouch made his 50th Premiership appearance

"We controlled the game in the second half, but at the end of the day a point is not a bad result."
Chris Coleman

PREMIERSHIP MILESTONE
100 Luis Boa Morte made his 100th Premiership appearance for Fulham

PREMIERSHIP MILESTONE
Liam Fontaine made his Premiership debut

Saturday 15th January 2005 | Venue: **Villa Park** | Attendance: **38,172** | Referee: **M.A.Riley**

ASTON VILLA 3 NORWICH CITY 0

PREMIERSHIP FIXTURE HISTORY

Pl: 4 Draws: 2	Wins	⚽	▢	■
Aston Villa	1	6	1	0
Norwich City	1	4	2	0

STARTING LINE-UPS

Sorensen

Delaney, Mellberg (c), Ridgewell, Samuel

Solano, Hendrie, Berson, Barry

Angel, Cole

Ashton

Huckerby, Brennan, Mulryne, Francis, Jonson

Drury, Doherty, Fleming (c), Edworthy

Green

Substitutes: L.Moore, Hitzlsperger, Davis, Postma, De la Cruz | McKenzie, Jarvis, Crow, Gallacher, Shackell

EVENT LINE

9 ⚽ **Ashton (Own Goal)**

27 ⚽ **Hendrie (Open Play)**

HALF TIME 2 - 0

46 Mulryne (Off) McKenzie (On)

74 **Cole (Off) Moore L (On)**

76 ⚽ **Solano (Open Play)**

77 **Berson (Off) Hitzlsperger (On)**

82 **Solano (Off) Davis (On)**

85 Ashton (Off) Jarvis (On)

89 Huckerby (Off) Crow (On)

FULL TIME 3 - 0

STATISTICS

Season	Fixture		Fixture	Season
122	10	Shots On Target	1	100
121	12	Shots Off Target	6	121
3	0	Hit Woodwork	0	5
62	0	Caught Offside	2	72
136	7	Corners	6	114
342	15	Fouls	12	301
49%	62%	Possession	38%	46%

LEAGUE STANDINGS

Position (pos before)	W	D	L	F	A	Pts
10 (10) Aston Villa	8	7	8	26	26	31
18 (18) Norwich C	2	10	11	19	42	16

Mark Delaney shields the ball from Darren Huckerby

"I was delighted we scored goals. We have, in general, been playing some good stuff and not getting what we deserve."

David O'Leary

"There is still a lot to play for in the remaining 15 games, and we will keep going to the last whistle of the season."

Nigel Worthington

PREMIERSHIP MILESTONE

Dean Ashton made his Premiership debut

Aston Villa took the points after a comprehensive win over Norwich at Villa Park.

The hosts took full advantage of their struggling opposition for a change to record just their second win in nine outings.

Norwich, meanwhile, were left still searching for their first away win of the season.

The four previous games between the two clubs had ended in draws, but despite some sterling work from Darren Huckerby and Mattias Jonson, the result of this one was never in doubt after Lee Hendrie added to an earlier own goal.

Villa had an early chance, an exciting movement culminating with Juan Pablo Angel setting up Carlton Cole, only for the on-loan striker to blast his low shot wide of the upright.

Dean Ashton, Norwich's recent £3m recruit from Crewe, was showing some neat touches in his first Premiership game, though he wasted an opening when he fired wide from a good position.

Villa moved ahead on nine minutes, Ridgewell meeting Nolberto Solano's free kick with a header that flew in off Ashton.

Angel's failure to score in the last nine games had been cited as the main reason for Villa's indifferent form of late, but there was no arguing with the Colombian's contribution on 27 minutes, setting up Hendrie to convert a low shot past the advancing Robert Green.

Norwich battled away and could have pulled one back four minutes before the break if it weren't for a brilliant reflex save by Thomas Sorensen, the keeper flicking Ashton's shot over the bar after it had taken a deflection off Ridgewell.

Villa had two early chances in the second half, Mathieu Berson's long-distance shot flying inches wide before Green made a superb save to deny Hendrie after the midfielder had linked up with Solano on the edge of the City box.

Former Newcastle United playmaker Solano capped an outstanding performance with Villa's third goal on 76 minutes, heading home a mis-hit shot by Hendrie.

Angel went close to a late fourth for Villa, firing just over with two minutes to play.

PREMIERSHIP FIXTURE HISTORY

Pl: 6 Draws: 2

	Wins	Goals	Yellow cards	Red cards
Bolton Wanderers	2	5	9	1
Arsenal	2	6	9	1

STARTING LINE-UPS

Bolton subs: Pedersen, Hierro, Poole, Fadiga, Vaz Te

Arsenal subs: Reyes, Bergkamp, Lehmann, Senderos, Clichy

EVENT LINE

23 van Persie (Foul)

41 **Giannakopoulos (Open Play)**

HALF TIME 1 - 0

54 **Nolan (Dissent)**

66 Fabregas (Off) Reyes (On)

66 van Persie (Off) Bergkamp (On)

68 **Giannakopoulos (Ung.Conduct)**

79 **Okocha (Off) Pedersen (On)**

87 **Nolan (Off) Hierro (On)**

FULL TIME 1 - 0

STATISTICS

Season	Fixture	Bolton	Arsenal Fixture	Season
142	3	Shots On Target	7	174
133	6	Shots Off Target	4	107
5	0	Hit Woodwork	0	8
56	9	Caught Offside	2	46
124	8	Corners	7	134
311	10	Fouls	9	262
49%	47%	Possession	53%	55%

LEAGUE STANDINGS

Position (pos before)	W	D	L	F	A	Pts
11 (11) Bolton W	8	6	9	30	31	30
2 (2) Arsenal	14	6	3	52	25	48

Saturday 15th January 2005 | Venue: **Reebok Stadium** | Attendance: **27,514** | Referee: **M.Clattenburg**

BOLTON WANDERERS 1 ARSENAL 0

A 41st-minute header by Stelios Giannakopoulos put a serious dent in Arsenal's title hopes.

As usual, the Gunners played a neat and creative game in midfield, but their frontmen failed to cash in on their opportunities.

Bolton keeper Jussi Jaaskelainen was in impressive form, but it was El-Hadji Diouf who stole the show.

He set up the goal for Stelios, went close himself on a number of occasions, and generally created mayhem in the Gunners defence.

While Arsenal were given a tonic with the return from injury of Sol Campbell, Ashley Cole and Freddie Ljungberg, Wanderers suffered a double injury blow that robbed them of two of their most potent players.

Central defender Radhi Jaidi, who had scored against Arsenal in the 2-2 draw earlier in the season, and striker Kevin Davies were both ruled out with hamstring strains.

Arsenal, winners of their last three away games in an unbeaten run of seven Premiership matches, restored Ljungberg alongside Thierry Henry in their attack, while Spanish keeper Manuel Almunia was again preferred to Jens Lehmann.

Almunia was almost caught out in the fifth minute, scrambling the ball away for a corner after Diouf had flashed it across the six yard box.

Patrick Vieira responded for the Gunners, his 25-yard shot flying inches over.

Robin van Persie wasted a good chance on 39 minutes, firing straight at Jaaskelainen.

That miss proved expensive two minutes later, Diouf working his way through the Arsenal defence before crossing to the far post for Stelios to head past a stranded Almunia.

It should have been 2-0 on the stroke of half time when a mix-up between Campbell and his keeper let in Kevin Nolan, but the Bolton midfielder sent his shot over the angle of post and bar.

Jaaskelainen had to be alert to deny Arsenal at the start of the second period, racing out to smother the ball at Ljungberg's feet.

The keeper, who had been linked to a possible move to Highbury, did well a few minutes later, blocking Van Persie's shot before Robert Pires headed the rebound wide.

Wanderers responded with a near miss of their own, Nolan heading wide after good work from Jay-Jay Okocha and Diouf.

Stylianos Giannakopoulos celebrates his winner

"I think we sussed out their formation. They are best going through the middle, but we stopped them."

Sam Allardyce

PREMIERSHIP MILESTONE

50 Stylianos Giannakopoulos made his 50th Premiership appearance

"We allowed Bolton to play the game that suits them."

Arsene Wenger

PREMIERSHIP FIXTURE HISTORY

Pl: 3 Draws: 1	Wins	Goals	Yellow	Red
Charlton Athletic	1	4	3	0
Birmingham City	1	4	3	0

STARTING LINE-UPS

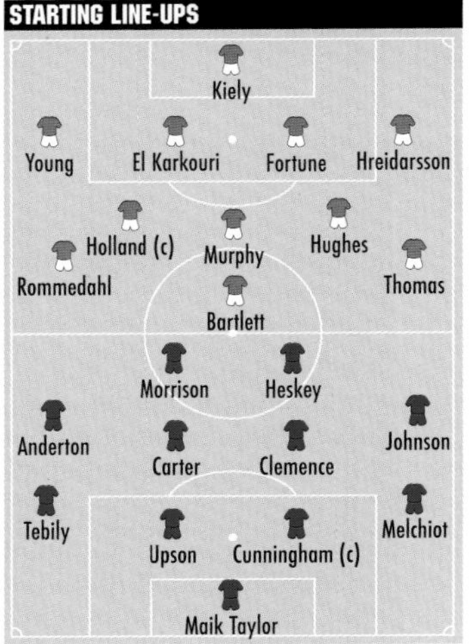

Jeffers, Konchesky, Kishishev, Andersen, Johansson

Gray, Blake, Yorke, Vaesen, Clapham

EVENT LINE

9 **El Karkouri (Direct Free Kick)**
35 Upson (Foul)
HALF TIME 1 - 0
55 Melchiot (Corner)
60 Johnson (Foul)
62 **Rommedahl (Off) Jeffers (On)**
67 **Bartlett (Open Play)**
70 Clemence (Off) Gray (On)
72 **Hughes (Off) Konchesky (On)**
75 **Murphy (Open Play)**
77 Heskey (Off) Blake (On)
80 **Thomas (Off) Kishishev (On)**
82 Anderton (Off) Yorke (On)
FULL TIME 3 - 1

STATISTICS

Season	Fixture		Fixture	Season
109	6	Shots On Target	6	107
86	3	Shots Off Target	4	96
5	0	Hit Woodwork	0	5
76	3	Caught Offside	5	71
103	4	Corners	4	116
302	11	Fouls	10	325
45%	52%	Possession	48%	50%

LEAGUE STANDINGS

Position (pos before)		W	D	L	F	A	Pts
7 (8)	Charlton Ath	10	4	9	27	33	34
14 (13)	Birmingham C	6	8	9	26	28	26

Saturday 15th January 2005 | Venue: **The Valley** | Attendance: **26,111** | Referee: **C.J.Foy**

CHARLTON ATHLETIC 3 BIRMINGHAM CITY 1

An inspired substitution by Charlton manager Alan Curbishley consigned Birmingham to their third successive Premiership defeat.

With the game tied at 1-1 after 62 minutes, Curbishley threw on Francis Jeffers in the hope that the former Everton and Arsenal striker would score the winning goal.

But instead Jeffers turned provider, setting up the two goals which saw Charlton take all three points.

The Addicks should have been more than a goal in front at the break, but their finishing was repeatedly found wanting.

Their failure to kill off the opposition looked like it would cost them when Birmingham equalised early in the second period.

But they focused their attacking intent and were rewarded with goals from Shaun Bartlett and Danny Murphy.

The result was particularly sweet for Charlton, who earned their first Premiership home win over Birmingham.

The Blues, meanwhile, continued to show they were no fans of the London air, having now won just once in their last 16 visits to the capital.

Charlton opened the scoring on nine minutes with one of the most bizarre goals of the season so far, Moroccan defender Talal El Karkouri's 45-yard free kick evading everyone before settling in the back of the Birmingham net.

The goal was El Karkouri's fifth of the season, making him Charlton's top scorer.

He would have had a second from a header soon after if it weren't for a brilliant save by City keeper Maik Taylor.

Birmingham's only first-half effort was a Stephen Clemence shot which was cleared off the line by Bartlett.

Charlton were stunned 10 minutes into the second half when City equalised through Mario Melchiot's firm header from Darren Anderton's corner – the first goal for the defender since his move from Chelsea.

But the Addicks kept their nerve and reclaimed the lead 12 minutes later, Jeffers doing well to cut the ball back for Bartlett, who slid in at the far post for his first goal since November.

Murphy sealed the win in the 75th minute, running on to Jeffers' perfectly weighted through ball before firing past Taylor.

Danny Murphy attempts to evade Darren Anderton

"He found it hard when he first came to us, but we then changed our shape to afford him the luxury of expressing himself."

Alan Curbishley on Danny Murphy

PREMIERSHIP MILESTONE

Danny Murphy scored his first Premiership goal for Charlton

PREMIERSHIP MILESTONE

250 Talal El Karkouri netted Charlton's 250th Premiership goal

"We have a number of key players missing and are light on the ground, but I'm not using that as an excuse."

Steve Bruce

PREMIERSHIP MILESTONE

Mario Melchiot netted his first Premiership goal in the colours of Birmingham

PREMIERSHIP MILESTONE

50 Robbie Blake made his 50th Premiership appearance on his first top-flight outing for Birmingham

PREMIERSHIP FIXTURE HISTORY

Pl: 13 Draws: 2	Wins	⚽	Yellow	Red
Liverpool	4	21	14	1
Manchester United	7	22	24	3

STARTING LINE-UPS

Liverpool: Dudek; Carragher, Hyypia, Pellegrino, Traore; Garcia, Gerrard (c), Hamann, Riise; Baros, Morientes

Manchester United: Saha; Rooney, Scholes, Keane (c), Fletcher, Ronaldo; Heinze, Silvestre, Brown, P.Neville; Carroll

Liverpool subs: Nunez, Biscan, Harrison, Warnock, Sinama-Pongolle

Manchester United subs: O'Shea, Fortune, Bellion, Howard, Miller

EVENT LINE

21 ⚽ Rooney (Open Play)

26 ▢ **Carragher (Foul)**

HALF TIME 0 - 1

65 ■ Brown (2nd Bookable Offence)

67 ⇄ Ronaldo (Off) O'Shea (On)

72 ⇄ **Riise (Off) Sinama-Pongolle (On)**

72 ▢ Rooney (Foul)

75 ⇄ **Morientes (Off) Nunez (On)**

79 ⇄ **Hamann (Off) Biscan (On)**

79 ⇄ Saha (Off) Fortune (On)

82 ▢ Fortune (Foul)

87 ▢ **Nunez (Dissent)**

88 ▢ Keane (Foul)

90 ⇄ Rooney (Off) Bellion (On)

FULL TIME 0 - 1

STATISTICS

Season	Fixture (Liverpool)		Fixture (Man Utd)	Season
156	5	Shots On Target	2	184
156	8	Shots Off Target	3	171
3	0	Hit Woodwork	1	12
57	2	Caught Offside	4	86
136	9	Corners	3	186
272	9	Fouls	22	279
54%	54%	Possession	46%	55%

LEAGUE STANDINGS

Position (pos before)		W	D	L	F	A	Pts
5 (5)	Liverpool	11	4	8	36	23	37
3 (3)	Man Utd	13	8	2	34	13	47

Saturday 15th January 2005 | Venue: **Anfield** | Attendance: **44,183** | Referee: **S.G.Bennett**

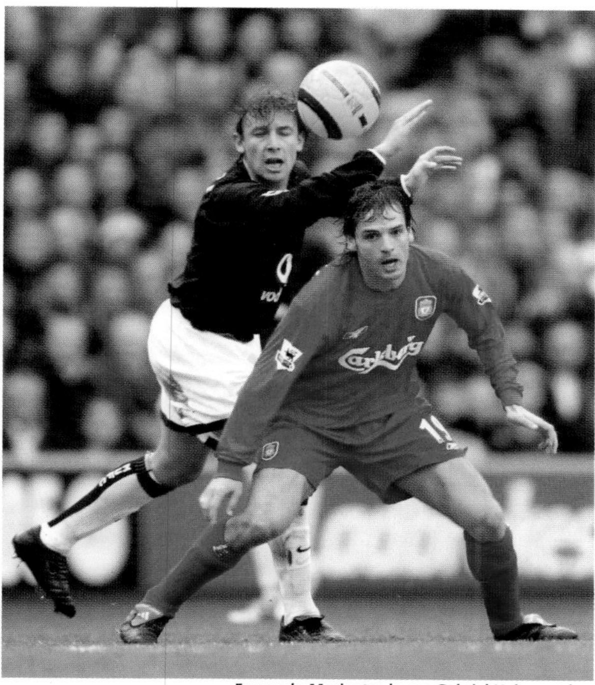

Fernando Morientes keeps Gabriel Heinze at bay

"Jerzy could perhaps have saved the goal, but we still had lots of time to get back in the game."
Rafael Benitez

PREMIERSHIP MILESTONE

Both Fernando Morientes and Mauricio Pellegrino made their Premiership debuts

"It was a great performance. It was a fantastic game, tense and competitive."
Sir Alex Ferguson

LIVERPOOL 0 MANCHESTER UNITED 1

Manchester United striker Wayne Rooney celebrated a trip back to his native city with a stealthy first-half goal.

Much was at stake in this fierce Northwest clash, with both sides trying to play catch-up at the top of the Premiership.

The latest addition to Anfield's Spanish Armada, Fernando Morientes, provided some much needed height up front, but he looked tired on the day and struggled to adapt to the pace of the game.

The Real Madrid export went close early on, his header from Steven Gerrard's pinpoint cross held by United keeper Roy Carroll.

Milan Baros was lively, clearly eager to stay in his boss's good books following the arrival of another star striker.

Rooney looked isolated out on the right and was clearly frustrated by his team-mates' passing ability during the first 20 minutes.

But the precocious teenager should never be underestimated and he scored with virtually his first touch of the game, collecting a quick ball from Cristiano Ronaldo and advancing on goal before converting a low shot to the near post which Jerzy Dudek probably should have saved.

United took advantage of a ragged Liverpool as they went in search of a second, captain Roy Keane trying an ambitious shot from 30 yards which hit the underside of the bar and nearly went in off the back of Dudek.

That effort finally woke Liverpool up, Gerrard putting Morientes clear with a pass round the back of Wes Brown, only for the Spaniard to spoon his shot wide of the mark.

John Arne Riise found Morientes with a clever side-footed pass as the game moved into the second half, but he was blocked inside the area by Gabriel Heinze.

Penalty cries rang out around the stadium, but no foul was called – much to the Kop's disgust.

United were reduced to 10 men on 65 minutes when Brown was shown a second yellow card for a late tackle on Riise – but only after loud protestations from Gerrard and Sami Hyypia.

But even with the man advantage, Liverpool struggled to find a way through as United dropped back to defend their lead.

PREMIERSHIP FIXTURE HISTORY

Pl: 3 Draws: 2	Wins	⚽	☐	■
Manchester City	1	4	2	0
Crystal Palace	0	2	3	0

STARTING LINE-UPS

McManaman, Onuoha, Waterreus, Jordan, B.Wright-Phillips

Andrews, Shipperley, Butterfield, Speroni, Borrowdale

EVENT LINE

12 ⚽ **Wright-Phillips S (Open Play)**

15 ⚽ **Fowler (Open Play)**

32 ⚽ Powell (Indirect Free Kick)

HALF TIME 2 - 1

46 **Sibierski (Off) McManaman (On)**

46 Watson (Off) Andrews (On)

60 Lakis (Off) Borrowdale (On)

67 ☐ **Dunne (Foul)**

72 **Macken (Off) Wright-Phillips B (O**

77 Routledge (Off) Shipperley (On)

81 ☐ Leigertwood (Foul)

90 ☐ **Barton (Foul)**

90 ⚽ **Wright-Phillips S (Open Play)**

90 **Fowler (Off) Onuoha (On)**

FULL TIME 3 - 1

STATISTICS

Season	Fixture		Fixture	Season
134	9	Shots On Target	2	94
115	7	Shots Off Target	5	99
2	0	Hit Woodwork	0	5
72	4	Caught Offside	2	57
145	7	Corners	7	115
302	10	Fouls	11	313
48%	53%	Possession	47%	47%

LEAGUE STANDINGS

Position (pos before)		W	D	L	F	A	Pts
9 (9)	Man City	8	7	8	30	24	31
17 (17)	Crystal Palace	4	6	13	24	37	18

Saturday 15th January 2005 | Venue: **City of Manchester Stadium** | Attendance: **44,010** | Referee: **A.Marriner**

MANCHESTER CITY 3 CRYSTAL PALACE 1

Manchester City put the disappointment of their FA Cup exit at League One Oldham behind them with a hard-earned home victory against Crystal Palace.

The result consolidated City's place in the top half of the Premiership, while leaving Palace mired in the relegation battle.

City manager Kevin Keegan was delighted with the win, but admitted his men made life difficult for themselves.

They could have hit Palace for six goals or more, but at the end were clinging to a slender one-goal advantage until Shaun Wright-Phillips scored City's third – and his second – in the final minute.

Antoine Sibierski and Wright-Phillips both wasted chances in the early stages as City carved open the fragile Palace defence.

But the hosts' pressure was soon rewarded, Wright-Phillips running on to a through ball from Joey Barton in the 12th minute before turning defender Darren Powell and drilling home an angled shot from six yards.

City doubled their lead three minutes later, Robbie Fowler racing on to a Richard Dunne pass and firing home from close range.

City were brimming with confidence and looked like scoring every time they went forward.

They would have moved further ahead if it weren't for some excellent saves from Hungarian keeper Gabor Kiraly to deny Wright-Phillips, Fowler and Jonathan Macken.

It took Palace almost half an hour to muster their first attempt at goal, Andy Johnson bursting clear, only to see his shot deflected behind by Dunne.

The Eagles responded with a goal out of nothing on 32 minutes, Powell popping up at the far post to head home a Wayne Routledge free kick.

Kiraly had to pull off an acrobatic save from Fowler's deflected shot late in the half as City re-imposed their authority.

After an exciting opening period, the second half was a bit of a let-down, with both sides struggling to create chances.

Palace were unlucky not to win a penalty midway through the half after Dunne shoved Powell off the ball in the area.

City sealed the win with a minute to play, Fowler cutting the ball back for Wright-Phillips to slot home.

Shaun Wright-Phillips is challenged by Emmerson Boyce

"All in all 3-1 was probably a fair result, but Palace will probably feel unlucky after their second half showing."

Kevin Keegan

"Overall we didn't have enough quality and guile, though in the second half we pinned City back."

Iain Dowie

PREMIERSHIP MILESTONE

Darren Powell scored his first Premiership goal

PREMIERSHIP MILESTONE

Gary Borrowdale made his Premiership debut

PREMIERSHIP FIXTURE HISTORY

Pl: 12 Draws: 1	Wins	Goals	Yellow	Red
Newcastle United	9	27	12	0
Southampton	2	9	22	1

STARTING LINE-UPS

Newcastle United: Given; Taylor, Boumsong, Bramble, Babayaro; Ameobi, Bowyer, Jenas, Dyer, Bellamy; Shearer (c)

Southampton: Niemi; Higginbotham, Davenport, Lundekvam, Telfer; McCann, Redknapp, Delap, Prutton; Crouch, Phillips (c)

Newcastle United substitutes: Kluivert, Milner, Hughes, Harper, Robert

Southampton substitutes: Smith, A.Svensson, Ormerod, Nilsson, Oakley

EVENT LINE

6 Niemi (Off) Smith (On)

9 **Shearer (Penalty)**

37 Crouch (Foul)

37 Telfer (Foul)

38 **Bramble (Indirect Free Kick)**

42 Crouch (Corner)

HALF TIME 2 - 1

62 **Shearer (Off) Kluivert (On)**

66 McCann (Off) Svensson A (On)

75 **Bellamy (Off) Milner (On)**

86 **Babayaro (Off) Hughes (On)**

87 Phillips (Off) Ormerod (On)

FULL TIME 2 - 1

STATISTICS

Season	Fixture	Newcastle United / Southampton	Fixture	Season
171	18	Shots On Target	6	105
133	5	Shots Off Target	3	121
9	0	Hit Woodwork	0	2
59	0	Caught Offside	0	61
166	14	Corners	4	114
276	12	Fouls	20	297
51%	55%	Possession	45%	47%

LEAGUE STANDINGS

Position (pos before)	W	D	L	F	A	Pts
12 (14) Newcastle Utd	7	8	8	35	40	29
19 (19) Southampton	2	9	12	23	39	15

Saturday 15th January 2005 | Venue: St James' Park | Attendance: 51,266 | Referee: U.D.Rennie

NEWCASTLE UNITED 2 SOUTHAMPTON 1

David Prutton slides in on Patrick Kluivert

PREMIERSHIP MILESTONE

100 Titus Bramble marked his 100th top-flight appearance with his first Premiership goal for Newcastle

"We've got to start scoring more of the chances we create."

Graeme Souness

"Antti Niemi has injured his knee, but we don't know how bad it is. We'll just have to wait and see after a scan."

Harry Redknapp

PREMIERSHIP MILESTONE

Celestine Babayaro made his first Premiership appearance in the colours of Newcastle

PREMIERSHIP MILESTONE

Jean-Alain Boumsong made his Premiership debut

PREMIERSHIP MILESTONE

Paul Smith made his Premiership debut

Graeme Souness repeated the success of his first Premiership game in charge of Newcastle, as the men in black and white defeated Southampton 2-1.

The Magpies welcomed back captain Alan Shearer for his first appearance in two months, and it wasn't long before the local hero made his mark on the game. Just nine minutes had elapsed when the former England international converted a penalty, though he had to wait what seemed an eternity to take it.

Visiting goalkeeper Antti Niemi was stretchered off after colliding with a tumbling Shola Ameobi, the striker having been felled by Calum Davenport, and Paul Smith arrived from the bench to begin his Premiership debut by being beaten from the spot.

The home team then proceeded to spurn plenty of opportunities to extend their advantage. A block denied Ameobi and Lee Bowyer drove over from distance, before Smith kept Craig Bellamy at bay with his legs.

The keeper followed that stop with a more comfortable save from a scuffed effort, and then dived away to his left to keep out a well-struck shot from Jermaine Jenas. Southampton, and Davenport in particular, were fortunate not to concede another penalty, but did fall further behind after 38 minutes.

Titus Bramble was the unlikely scorer, steering the ball home from close range at the near post as Premiership debutant Celestine Babayaro sent over a dipping left-wing free-kick. A two-goal lead was the least Souness' side deserved, but it didn't last long.

Peter Crouch profited from some slack defending from a corner, volleying home from inside the six-yard box after Kevin Phillips had gone close. There was still time for Smith to deny Bellamy again, as the Saints went in at half-time with renewed hope.

The second period was a similar story of Newcastle dominance, though goals weren't forthcoming. Both Ameobi and substitute James Milner forced smart stops from Smith, but it was Harry Redknapp's men that came closest to scoring.

Anders Svensson headed a good chance over the bar, before David Prutton was denied a last-gasp equaliser by a magnificent block.

PREMIERSHIP FIXTURE HISTORY

Pl: 2 Draws: 0	Wins ⚽	⬜	⬛	
Portsmouth	0	1	3	2
Blackburn Rovers	2	3	9	0

STARTING LINE-UPS

Taylor, Fuller, Ashdown, Unsworth, Hughes

Jansen, Reid, Enckelman, Gray, Stead

EVENT LINE

- 14 ⬜ Nelson (Foul)
- 20 **Stone (Off) Taylor (On)**
- 37 ⬜ **O'Neil (Foul)**
- 38 ⬜ Mokoena (Foul)
- 40 ⬜ Johansson (Foul)
- 44 ⬜ Emerton (Foul)

HALF TIME 0 - 0

- 51 ⬛ **Lua Lua (Violent Conduct)**
- 55 ⚽ Pedersen (Open Play)
- 60 ⬜ Tugay (Foul)
- 74 Gallagher (Off) Jansen (On)
- 76 Tugay (Off) Reid (On)
- 86 **Kamara (Off) Fuller (On)**
- 90 ⬛ **Faye (2nd Bookable Offence)**
- 90 ⬜ Dickov (Foul)

FULL TIME 0 - 1

STATISTICS

Season	Fixture		Fixture	Season
117	1	Shots On Target	6	120
115	10	Shots Off Target	8	139
3	0	Hit Woodwork	0	6
53	0	Caught Offside	2	86
120	5	Corners	6	127
280	16	Fouls	21	359
48%	43%	Possession	57%	49%

LEAGUE STANDINGS

Position (pos before)	W	D	L	F	A	Pts
13 (12) Portsmouth	7	6	10	26	31	27
15 (16) Blackburn R	5	10	8	21	33	25

Saturday 15th January 2005 | Venue: **Fratton Park** | Attendance: **19,904** | Referee: **A.P.D'Urso**

Tugay is challenged by Amdy Faye

"I thought the referee was poor, and I'm not just saying that because of the sendings-off."

Joe Jordan

"The match did not warrant the number of yellow cards that were given out."

Mark Hughes

PREMIERSHIP MILESTONE

50 Dejan Stefanovic made his 50th Premiership appearance for Portsmouth

PREMIERSHIP MILESTONE

Aaron Mokoena and Ryan Nelson both made their Premiership debuts

PREMIERSHIP MILESTONE

Morten Gamst Pedersen netted his first Premiership goal

PORTSMOUTH 0 BLACKBURN ROVERS 1

Referee Andy D'Urso took centre-stage at Fratton Park, dismissing two Portsmouth players and cautioning over half the Blackburn team.

Lomana Tresor Lua Lua was the first to see red after 51 minutes, the DR Congo forward inexplicably head-butting visiting captain Andy Todd in an off-the-ball incident near the halfway line.

He was followed down the tunnel in injury time by team-mate Amdy Faye. The midfielder had been lucky to escape with just a yellow card for a shocking challenge shortly before the incident involving Lua Lua, and collected a second caution for an over-zealous lunge at Brad Friedel.

Mark Hughes' team arrived on the South Coast on the back of two wins in their last three Premiership matches, and handed top-flight debuts to recent captures Ryan Nelson and Aaron Mokoena in defence.

In a poor quality opening period, largely disrupted by the referee's whistle, only Lua Lua had a decent scoring opportunity. The former Newcastle man blazed over from close range, an effort that expertly summed up the match as a whole.

Whilst many of the five yellow cards handed out prior to half-time seemed harsh, South African Mokoena was fortunate that his wasn't red for a cynical trip on Diomansy Kamara. Covering defenders and the distance still to travel can have been all that saved the defender from an early bath.

The only goal of the game arrived 10 minutes into the second period. David Thompson picked out Morten Gamst Pedersen in the inside-left channel, and the young Norwegian clipped the ball over Shaka Hislop and into the net.

With the ten men of Portsmouth having to chase the game, Rovers had chances to extend their advantage. Dejan Stefanovic did well to block a goalbound Brett Emerton effort, while Thompson fired over when it seemed easier to hit the target.

Only a fiercely-struck Kamara drive tested Friedel, before Faye was sent off during the six minutes of time added on at the end of the match. The referee had awarded no fewer than 37 free-kicks as a result of what he deemed to be foul challenges, though neither team subscribed to the view that it had been a dirty game.

PREMIERSHIP FIXTURE HISTORY

Pl: 13 Draws: 5	Wins	⚽	▯	▮
Tottenham Hotspur	0	9	15	1
Chelsea	8	24	22	1

STARTING LINE-UPS

Gardner, Marney, Yeates, Fulop, Kelly

Jarosik, Gudjohnsen, J.Cole, Cudicini, Bridge

EVENT LINE

35 ▯ Duff (Dissent)

39 ⚽ Lampard (Penalty)

42 ▯ Johnson (Foul)

HALF TIME 0 - 1

67 **Ziegler (Off) Gardner (On)**

70 Smertin (Off) Jarosik (On)

71 **Pamarot (Off) Marney (On)**

76 Drogba (Off) Gudjohnsen (On)

78 **Mendes (Off) Yeates (On)**

80 Duff (Off) Cole J (On)

85 ▯ Terry (Foul)

86 ▯ **Brown (Ung.Conduct)**

86 ▯ Makelele (Ung.Conduct)

90 ▯ **Yeates (Foul)**

90 ⚽ Lampard (Open Play)

FULL TIME 0 - 2

STATISTICS

Season	Fixture (Tottenham)		Fixture (Chelsea)	Season
137	4	Shots On Target	6	170
120	8	Shots Off Target	7	143
9	0	Hit Woodwork	0	8
86	2	Caught Offside	4	70
104	4	Corners	7	162
279	12	Fouls	14	295
50%	54%	Possession	46%	55%

LEAGUE STANDINGS

Position (pos before)		W	D	L	F	A	Pts
8 (7)	Tottenham H	9	6	8	29	23	33
1 (1)	Chelsea	18	4	1	45	8	58

Saturday 15th January 2005 | Venue: White Hart Lane | Attendance: 36,105 | Referee: G.Poll

TOTTENHAM HOTSPUR 0 CHELSEA 2

Chelsea maintained their remarkable unbeaten Premiership record against Tottenham, as two Frank Lampard goals secured the points.

With Martin Jol's team undefeated in eight top-flight games, many pundits felt that the men from Stamford Bridge could finally come unstuck. Jose Mourinho's charges had other ideas, however, turning in a thoroughly professional display worthy of would-be champions.

The North Londoners began brightly, with full-back Erik Edman firing over in just the second minute. Robbie Keane then headed narrowly wide after a cross from his strike partner, Jermain Defoe, had deflected into his path.

The visitors soon came to life though, Didier Drogba sending a superbly-executed lob over Paul Robinson and just the wrong side of the left-hand upright. The Tottenham custodian was then called into action again, diving full-length to keep out a 12-yard drive from Damien Duff.

Petr Cech parried from Defoe at the other end, before Chelsea earned a debatable 39th-minute penalty. Referee Graham Poll had already turned down an appeal from Arjen Robben, but pointed to the spot as Alexei Smertin tumbled under the challenge of Ledley King. After the protests had subsided, Lampard stepped up to open the scoring.

With just under an hour played, Spurs came within inches of drawing level. An inswinging left-wing corner was horribly sliced by Smertin at the near post, yet somehow managed to escape landing in the back of the net.

That scare apart, Mourinho's men were defending comfortably. In a brave bid to get back into the match, Jol introduced Anthony Gardner and pushed King into attack. The defender offered a more physical threat to John Terry and William Gallas, but neither Defoe or Keane were able to benefit from any knockdowns.

In fact, it was the team from West London that completed the scoring. Inventive play on the left from substitute Eidur Gudjohnsen opened up a shooting chance for Lampard, and the England international hammered home through a forest of legs from just inside the area.

The goal came in injury time, with the on-pitch celebrations after the final whistle showing just how important a victory this was in the chase for the title.

"We played well in midfield, and against any other team we would have created a lot of chances."

Martin Jol

"It was a game we knew was going to be difficult to win, and I think the celebrations at the end tell you how much it meant to us."

Assistant Manager Steve Clarke

PREMIERSHIP MILESTONE

50 Frank Lampard's penalty was his 50th goal in the Premiership

PREMIERSHIP MILESTONE

Jiri Jarosik made his Premiership debut

Frank Lampard celebrates one of his goals

PREMIERSHIP FIXTURE HISTORY

Pl: 2 Draws: 0	Wins	⚽	Yellow cards	Red cards
Fulham	2	4	4	0
West Bromwich Albion	0	0	3	0

STARTING LINE-UPS

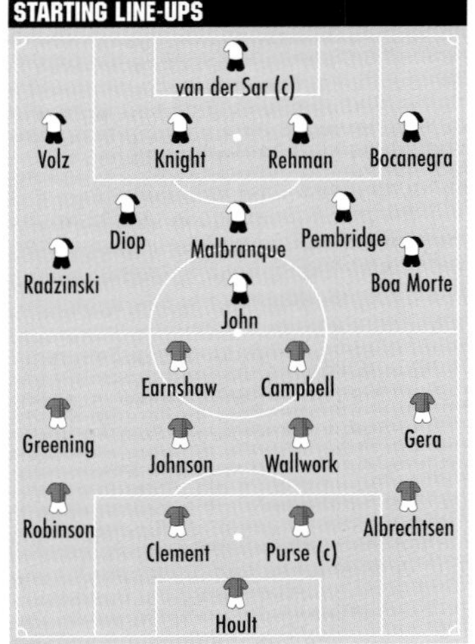

Clark, McBride, Crossley, Rosenior, Legwinski

Scimeca, Kuszczak, Koumas, Kanu, Horsfield

EVENT LINE

22	**Malbranque (Off) Clark (On)**
37	Greening (Foul)
	HALF TIME 0 - 0
67	**Boa Morte (Foul)**
70	Johnson (Off) Scimeca (On)
74	**Bocanegra (Foul)**
79	**John (Off) McBride (On)**
84	**Clark (Foul)**
90	**Diop (Corner)**
	FULL TIME 1 - 0

STATISTICS

Season	Fixture		Fixture	Season
112	4	Shots On Target	7	100
102	4	Shots Off Target	2	92
3	0	Hit Woodwork	0	4
58	3	Caught Offside	3	85
119	7	Corners	5	104
288	10	Fouls	11	306
48%	51%	Possession	49%	45%

LEAGUE STANDINGS

Position (pos before)	W	D	L	F	A	Pts
15 (16) Fulham	7	4	12	29	39	25
20 (20) West Brom	1	10	12	17	44	13

Sunday 16th January 2005 | Venue: **Craven Cottage** | Attendance: **16,180** | Referee: **P.Walton**

FULHAM 1 WEST BROM 0

A last-gasp Pape Bouba Diop header ended West Brom's recent mini-revival, in a game that the visitors should have won.

Debutant Kevin Campbell almost teed up Robert Earnshaw for a first-minute goal, but the Welsh international failed to test Edwin van der Sar with an attempted lob. The former Cardiff striker soon hit the target with a shot on the turn, but the keeper was equal to it.

Luis Boa Morte was his usual lively self on the Fulham left, almost providing for Tomasz Radzinski twice in the early exchanges. The Cottagers were dealt a blow, however, when Steed Malbranque limped off after 22 minutes. The midfielder had been caught on the ankle, and was replaced by club captain Lee Clark.

A woeful mistake by Zat Knight provided Earnshaw with a fantastic sight of goal, but van der Sar was alert enough to make a smothering save. Moments later the Dutch custodian was called into action again, this time repelling a low drive from Ronnie Wallwork.

The Baggies were in the ascendancy, and Campbell twice went close to becoming an instant hero with the travelling fans. The experienced frontman should have done better than fire straight at the keeper when put through, before experiencing the same outcome from a more difficult opening.

At the other end, Russell Hoult made a comfortable save from Boa Morte, and then watched as the former Arsenal man glanced a header narrowly over his crossbar.

The second period differed little from the first, with Bryan Robson's side unable to capitalise on their superiority. Just shy of the hour mark, Earnshaw skipped away from van der Sar but was unable to hit the target from an acute angle.

A 0-0 draw seemed likely as both teams survived late scares. Referee Peter Walton turned down home calls for a penalty as the ball appeared to strike Wallwork's arm, before Campbell deflected a low drive the wrong side of the post.

Fulham still had time for an undeserved winner, however, as an unmarked Diop arrived to head Mark Pembridge's left-wing corner into the net from seven yards out.

Pape Bouba Diop is the hero for Fulham

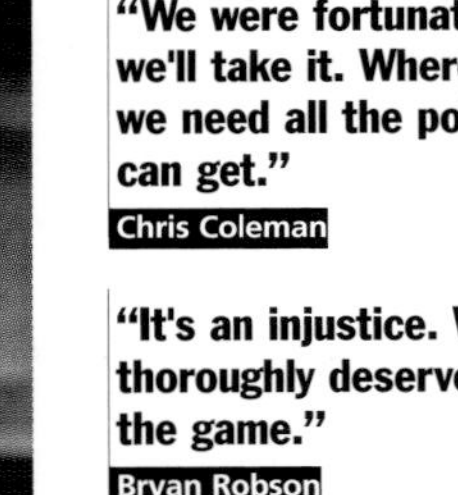

"We were fortunate, but we'll take it. Where we are, we need all the points we can get."

Chris Coleman

"It's an injustice. We thoroughly deserved to win the game."

Bryan Robson

PREMIERSHIP MILESTONE

50 Ronnie Wallwork made his 50th Premiership appearance

PREMIERSHIP MILESTONE

Kevin Campbell made his first Premiership appearance in the colours of West Brom

PREMIERSHIP FIXTURE HISTORY

Pl: 10 Draws: 3	Wins			
Middlesbrough	4	14	13	1
Everton	3	13	17	1

STARTING LINE-UPS

Cooper, Morrison, Nash, McMahon, Graham

Ferguson, Naysmith, McFadden, Turner, Chadwick

EVENT LINE

17 **Ehiogu (Off) Cooper (On)**
26 **Zenden (Open Play)**
43 Hibbert (Foul)
HALF TIME 1 - 0
54 Beattie (Foul)
59 **Nemeth (Off) Morrison (On)**
74 Yobo (Off) Ferguson (On)
76 Cahill (Open Play)
86 Cahill (Off) Naysmith (On)
89 **Zenden (Foul)**
89 Beattie (Off) McFadden (On)
FULL TIME 1 - 1

STATISTICS

Season	Fixture		Fixture	Season
158	12	Shots On Target	5	112
130	6	Shots Off Target	8	120
4	0	Hit Woodwork	2	5
63	4	Caught Offside	3	60
132	9	Corners	6	115
281	12	Fouls	11	273
50%	47%	Possession	53%	49%

LEAGUE STANDINGS

Position (pos before)		W	D	L	F	A	Pts
6 (6)	Middlesbrough	10	6	7	35	29	36
4 (4)	Everton	13	5	5	28	24	44

Sunday 16th January 2005 | Venue: **Riverside Stadium** | Attendance: **31,794** | Referee: **D.J.Gallagher**

James Beattie goes in strongly on Boudewijn Zenden

PREMIERSHIP MILESTONE

100 Szilard Nemeth made his 100th Premiership appearance

"Everton are favourites for the fourth spot in the Champions League race, though we are capable of catching them."

Steve McClaren

"I don't think we were put under any great deal of pressure throughout the game."

David Moyes

PREMIERSHIP MILESTONE

James Beattie made his first Premiership appearance in the colours of Everton

PREMIERSHIP MILESTONE

600 Tim Cahill netted Everton's 600th Premiership goal

MIDDLESBROUGH 1 EVERTON 1

A 76th-minute Tim Cahill goal cancelled out Boudewijn Zenden's first half strike, as the spoils were shared on Teesside.

Middlesbrough welcomed back Ugo Ehiogu to their starting line-up, the defender making his first Premiership appearance in four months. For Everton, James Beattie followed up his F.A.Cup debut at Plymouth with a maiden league outing for the club.

A pacy and competitive opening was temporarily cut short by an injury to the returning Ehiogu. The big defender limped out of the action after just 17 minutes, with veteran Colin Cooper coming on in his place.

Visiting midfielder Lee Carsley then struck the bar following Kevin Kilbane's cross from the left. The former Derby man appeared to be offside, but it didn't matter as the ball rebounded to safety.

Having ridden their luck on that occasion, Steve McClaren's team took a 26th-minute lead. Right-back Tony Hibbert misjudged Jimmy Floyd Hasselbaink's low pass towards the inside-left channel, enabling Zenden to clip a 15-yard effort over the advancing Richard Wright. Alan Stubbs made a brave attempt to clear off the line, but was unable to deny the Dutchman.

The home side were understandably buoyed by the goal, and soon saw a second ruled out for a foul. A venomous Hasselbaink drive then flew just wide, before Marcus Bent was denied by a brilliant save on the stroke of half-time.

The Merseysiders continued in the same vain after the break, Stubbs testing Mark Schwarzer with a header. Middlesbrough were beginning to play on the counter-attack, and Zenden almost netted again with a fiercely-struck near-post shot.

Everton became increasingly dominant as the game progressed, but it looked as though things might go against them when Beattie hit a post. The striker rolled an effort agonisingly against the left-hand upright, after Schwarzer had come unsuccessfully to claim a cross.

The 74th-minute introduction of Duncan Ferguson changed the fortunes of David Moyes' men though. Almost immediately, the big Scot nodded down a right-wing cross for Cahill to sweep home a close-range equaliser.

The giant forward then sparked a 21-man goalmouth brawl, as tempers flared in a highly-competitive encounter.

PREMIERSHIP FIXTURE HISTORY

Pl: 3 Draws: 2	Wins	⚽	Yellow	Red
Birmingham City	0	3	4	1
Fulham	1	4	7	3

STARTING LINE-UPS

Birmingham City: Maik Taylor; Melchiot, Cunningham (c), Martin Taylor, Clapham; Johnson, Diao, Carter, Gray; Heskey, Morrison

Fulham: Cole; Boa Morte, Pembridge, Clark (c), Diop, Radzinski; Bocanegra, Rehman, Knight, Volz; van der Sar

Substitutes (Birmingham City): Blake, Anderton, Yorke, Vaesen, Tebily

Substitutes (Fulham): McBride, Crossley, Rosenior, Legwinski, John

EVENT LINE

HALF TIME 0 - 0

51 ⚽ **Volz (Own Goal)**

53 Yellow card: Boa Morte (Ung.Conduct)

69 Substitution: **Morrison (Off) Blake (On)**

78 ⚽ Cole (Penalty)

82 Yellow card: **Johnson (Foul)**

83 Substitution: **Johnson (Off) Anderton (On)**

83 ⚽ Diop (Indirect Free Kick)

84 Yellow card: Diop (Ung.Conduct)

86 Substitution: **Taylor Martin (Off) Yorke (On)**

89 Substitution: Cole (Off) McBride (On)

90 Yellow card: Bocanegra (Foul)

FULL TIME 1 - 2

STATISTICS

Season	Fixture (Birmingham)		Fixture (Fulham)	Season
112	5	Shots On Target	4	116
99	3	Shots Off Target	3	105
5	0	Hit Woodwork	0	3
72	1	Caught Offside	1	59
121	5	Corners	3	122
339	14	Fouls	10	298
50%	50%	Possession	50%	48%

LEAGUE STANDINGS

Position (pos before)	W	D	L	F	A	Pts
15 (14) Birmingham C	6	8	10	27	30	26
13 (15) Fulham	8	4	12	31	40	28

Saturday 22nd January 2005 | Venue: **St Andrew's** | Attendance: **28,512** | Referee: **P.Dowd**

BIRMINGHAM CITY 1 FULHAM 2

Fulham gained revenge for their recent league defeat at the hands of Birmingham, coming from behind to record a 2-1 victory at St Andrew's.

All the goals came in the second half, following an evenly-contested opening period that lacked any genuine chances at either end. Loan acquisition Salif Diao came up against his international colleague Pape Bouba Diop in a crowded midfield, with the departed Robbie Savage proving a hard act to follow.

It was Steve Bruce's side that took a 51st-minute lead, courtesy of an own goal from German Moritz Volz. Clinton Morrison found his strike partner Emile Heskey, and though Edwin van der Sar kept out his close-range effort, the Dutchman was powerless to prevent the ball from ricocheting back past him via the right knee of his defensive colleague.

Lone frontman Andy Cole then fired narrowly over for the visitors, before referee Phil Dowd chose to caution Luis Boa Morte for diving in an attempt to win a penalty. This was the first in a serious of incidents involving the Portuguese international, and he had better luck 12 minutes from time.

Having committed what appeared to be a clear foul on Diao in midfield, the winger was nudged over by a recovering Damien Johnson a good yard outside the area. The officials had other ideas, however, and provided Cole with the chance to expertly level matters from the penalty spot.

Midfielder Johnson was then cautioned for bringing down Boa Morte on the left wing after 82 minutes. It was to prove a costly foul, as Mark Pembridge sent over a deep free-kick that Diop rose to head powerfully beyond Maik Taylor from six yards out.

It was the third consecutive Premiership game in which the Senegalese international had scored with his head, and the three points moved Chris Coleman's side ever-closer to top-flight survival.

Defeat represented a fourth on the spin in January league action for Birmingham. Much of the good work of December appears to have been undone, and Bruce will no doubt be concerned at the manner in which his team have begun to plummet down the table.

Mark Pembridge is chased by Robbie Blake

"We lost our discipline for the second goal. You cannot allow Diop those sort of chances."

Steve Bruce

"A month ago we lost at home to Birmingham, but now we are looking really good."

Chris Coleman

PREMIERSHIP MILESTONE

Salif Diao made his first Premiership appearance for Birmingham

PREMIERSHIP FIXTURE HISTORY

Pl: 2 Draws: 0	Wins	Goals	Yellow	Red
Chelsea	2	6	0	0
Portsmouth	0	0	0	0

STARTING LINE-UPS

Chelsea: Cech; Ferreira, Gallas, Terry (c), Bridge; J.Cole, Makelele, Lampard; Duff, Robben; Drogba

Portsmouth: Yakubu; Taylor, Berger (c), Hughes, O'Neil, Kamara; Unsworth, Stefanovic, Primus, Cisse; Ashdown

Chelsea subs: Gudjohnsen, Tiago, Kezman, Cudicini, Jarosik

Portsmouth subs: Mezague, Fuller, Hislop, De Zeeuw, Curtis

EVENT LINE

15 **Drogba (Open Play)**

21 **Robben (Open Play)**

39 **Drogba (Direct Free Kick)**

HALF TIME 3 - 0

54 Unsworth (Off) Mezague (On)

65 **Drogba (Off) Gudjohnsen (On)**

65 Yakubu (Off) Fuller (On)

67 **Duff (Off) Tiago (On)**

75 **Robben (Off) Kezman (On)**

FULL TIME 3 - 0

STATISTICS

Season	Fixture	Chelsea / Portsmouth	Fixture	Season
179	9	Shots On Target	5	122
148	5	Shots Off Target	4	119
8	0	Hit Woodwork	0	3
73	3	Caught Offside	1	54
164	2	Corners	3	123
297	2	Fouls	9	289
56%	70%	Possession	30%	47%

LEAGUE STANDINGS

Position (pos before)		W	D	L	F	A	Pts
1 (1)	Chelsea	19	4	1	48	8	61
14 (13)	Portsmouth	7	6	11	26	34	27

Saturday 22nd January 2005 | Venue: **Stamford Bridge** | Attendance: **42,267** | Referee: **M.A.Riley**

CHELSEA 3 PORTSMOUTH 0

Joe Cole tries to fend off Richard Hughes

"It was another three points. There's not much I can add to that."

Assistant Manager Steve Clarke

PREMIERSHIP MILESTONE

750 Didier Drogba's opening goal was Chelsea's 750th in the Premiership

"Unless you get it right, you will be punished by this Chelsea side."

Joe Jordan

After an edgy start, three first half goals proved enough for Chelsea to see off Portsmouth at Stamford Bridge.

As has so often been the case this season, Arjen Robben did most of the damage. The Dutch winger twice played a major part in Didier Drogba strikes, while ending a sweeping move with a finish of his own in between the Ivorian's brace.

The men from the South Coast opted for a five-strong midfield unit, and it seemed to be paying dividends in the early exchanges. The visitors enjoyed their only sustained period of possession during the match, with Jose Mourinho's side looking sluggish.

That soon changed, however, as Drogba fired a warning shot before benefitting from great work by Robben. With 15 minutes played, the former PSV Eindhoven man weaved his way past a string of defenders on the right and squared the ball for his team-mate to tap home.

Six minutes later it was 2-0. Patient build-up play quickly became incisive passing, as Frank Lampard threaded in Robben through the eye of a needle. There was still much to be done, but the brightest star of many on show in West London rounded Jamie Ashdown and squeezed the ball home from the acutest of angles.

Uncharacteristic sloppiness then almost gifted Velimir Zajec's charges a way back into the game. A misplaced Lampard pass was seized upon by a marauding Aiyegbeni Yakubu, who brushed aside John Terry before screwing his low effort wide of goal.

If the Nigerian hadn't realised just how costly a miss that was, then he was soon made to. More mesmerising footwork from Robben saw him win a 39th-minute free-kick in what appeared to be left-foot country. It was Drogba who curled home with his right boot from 20 yards though, ending any realistic hopes of a comeback in the process.

The second half was a poor spectacle, as Chelsea concentrated on ball retention rather than expanding any unnecessary energy. To this end, Mourinho was able to withdraw each member of his attacking trio, a luxury that few other managers can afford.

Saturday 22nd January 2005 | Venue: **Selhurst Park** | Attendance: **23,723** | Referee: **C.J.Foy**

PREMIERSHIP FIXTURE HISTORY

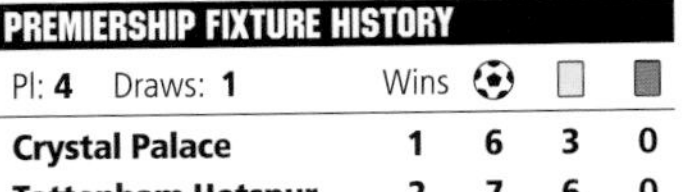

Pl: **4** Draws: **1**	Wins	⚽	☐	■
Crystal Palace	1	6	3	0
Tottenham Hotspur	2	7	6	0

STARTING LINE-UPS

Borrowdale, Andrews, Speroni, Powell, Lakis

Atouba, Yeates, Kelly, Eyre, Gardner

EVENT LINE

20 ☐ Marney (Dissent)

29 ☐ **Hughes (Dissent)**

44 Ziegler (Off) Atouba (On)

HALF TIME 0 - 0

61 ☐ Pamarot (Foul)

66 ⚽ **Leigertwood (Open Play)**

70 ⚽ **Granville (Open Play)**

72 Pamarot (Off) Yeates (On)

77 ⚽ **Johnson (Penalty)**

82 Marney (Off) Kelly (On)

88 **Johnson (Off) Andrews (On)**

88 **Soares (Off) Borrowdale (On)**

FULL TIME 3 - 0

STATISTICS

Season	Fixture		Fixture	Season
102	8	Shots On Target	6	143
101	2	Shots Off Target	6	126
5	0	Hit Woodwork	0	9
61	4	Caught Offside	7	93
120	5	Corners	4	108
322	9	Fouls	14	293
47%	47%	Possession	53%	50%

LEAGUE STANDINGS

Position (pos before)		W	D	L	F	A	Pts
17 (17)	Crystal Palace	5	6	13	27	37	21
8 (8)	Tottenham H	9	6	9	29	26	33

CRYSTAL PALACE 3 TOTTENHAM HOTSPUR 0

A vibrant second half performance from the Eagles saw a previously water-tight Tottenham defence put to the sword.

The visitors had not conceded a goal on their Premiership travels for exactly two months prior to the 11 minute spell that saw them self-destruct at Selhurst Park. Mikele Leigertwood, Danny Granville and Andy Johnson all took advantage of uncharacteristic lapses, as Iain Dowie's men collected an important three points.

The Crystal Palace manager made the bold decision to provide Johnson with a strike partner, in the form of Dougie Freedman. The inclusion of Spurs transfer target Wayne Routledge was also a sign that the home team meant business.

The opening half was as even as they come, with neither side able to establish any level of dominance. Jermain Defoe and Reto Ziegler both went close for the North Londoners, while Granville and Leigertwood weren't far away from scoring at the other end.

Little changed after the break, as both XI's continued to create openings. A decent whipped cross from Routledge narrowly evaded the onrushing Freedman, and a similar scenario then played out in the opposite goalmouth from Thimothee Atouba's dangerous delivery.

The game looked destined to end in a draw, but Leigertwood changed all that after 66 minutes. Youngster Tom Soares delivered an inswinging cross from the left, and the former Wimbledon man guided the ball in via the underside of the bar from six yards out.

Defender Granville added a well-taken second four minutes later, as the floodgates began to open. The left-back exchanged passes with Routledge on the edge of the box, before beating the exposed Paul Robinson with a cool 12-yard finish.

Further gloss was then added to the scoreline from the penalty spot, Johnson converting with consumate ease after he himself had been felled by a clumsy challenge from Pedro Mendes.

Martin Jol's day almost got even worse late on, and the Dutchman must have been at a loss to explain why his team had collapsed so completely in the second half. On the other side of the coin, a three-goal win will have done wonders for a side fighting relegation.

Tom Soares takes on Noe Pamarot

"In the first half we negated each other, but in the second I thought we controlled the match."

Iain Dowie

PREMIERSHIP MILESTONE

Mikele Leigertwood netted his first Premiership goal

PREMIERSHIP MILESTONE

50 Dougie Freedman made his 50th Premiership appearance

"We didn't play particularly well, but I thought we played better than Palace in the first half."

Martin Jol

PREMIERSHIP FIXTURE HISTORY

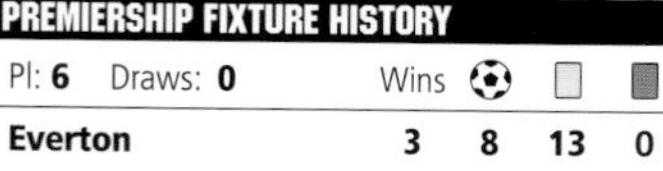

Pl: 6 Draws: 0	Wins	⚽	☐	■
Everton	3	8	13	0
Charlton Athletic	3	6	11	1

STARTING LINE-UPS

Ferguson, McFadden, Turner, Naysmith, Yobo

Johansson, Andersen, Fish, Stuart, Jeffers

EVENT LINE

15 ☐ El Karkouri (Foul)

45 ⚽ Holland (Open Play)

HALF TIME 0 - 1

46 **Bent (Off) Ferguson (On)**

65 **Kilbane (Off) McFadden (On)**

83 ☐ Hughes (Foul)

86 **Pistone (Off) Yobo (On)**

87 Hughes (Off) Johansson (On)

90 ☐ **Stubbs (Ung.Conduct)**

FULL TIME 0 - 1

STATISTICS

Season	Fixture		Fixture	Season
119	7	Shots On Target	3	112
125	5	Shots Off Target	1	87
6	1	Hit Woodwork	0	5
62	2	Caught Offside	2	78
119	4	Corners	5	108
276	3	Fouls	3	305
49%	52%	Possession	48%	45%

LEAGUE STANDINGS

Position (pos before)		W	D	L	F	A	Pts
4 (4)	Everton	13	5	6	28	25	44
7 (7)	Charlton Ath	11	4	9	28	33	37

Saturday 22nd January 2005 | Venue: **Goodison Park** | Attendance: **36,041** | Referee: **H.M.Webb**

EVERTON 0 CHARLTON ATHLETIC 1

Everton suffered a setback in their quest for Champions League football, succumbing to a glorious strike from visiting captain Matt Holland on the stroke of half-time.

There seemed little danger as Hermann Hreidarsson's misplaced cross reared up at the Irish international some 25 yards out. The former Ipswich man had other ideas, however, hitting across the ball in order to make it spin agonisingly away from the left hand of Richard Wright.

James Beattie's home debut almost got off to a dream start when he got on the end of an eighth-minute Leon Osman cross. The centre-forward found himself with just Dean Kiely to beat, but was denied the chance to do so by an offside flag.

Moroccan Talal El Karkouri was cautioned for a bad challenge on the quarter-hour. The tackle was not pretty, though it did inject a bit of passion into an otherwise drab contest.

Wayward efforts from the out-of-position Marcus Bent and skipper Alan Stubbs emphasised the lack of quality on display. The strike from Holland was therefore all the more surprising in light of what had gone before it.

Everton do not sit fourth in the table by accident, and arrived for the second period with renewed vigour. Talismanic figure Duncan Ferguson emerged from the dressing room to spearhead the attack, as David Moyes reverted to a 4-4-2 formation.

The Toffees put in plenty of hard work and commitment, but couldn't find the final pass that was needed to unlock a solid Charlton defence. For their part, the Addicks seemed content to play on the counter-attack, and spent much of the half sitting back and soaking up pressure.

What chances the men in blue did create tended to come from an aerial route. Both Ferguson and Beattie were winning plenty of headers, but for once the ball didn't seem to fall kindly to either Osman or Tim Cahill in the box.

While the defeat came as a great disappointment to Moyes' over-achieving team, few of their rivals were able to cash in. In fact, Charlton were the big winners of the day in the race for European football.

"They scored from 25 yards, and that is about all they created."
David Moyes

"Something has altered, and we're more solid now. We play well much more often."
Alan Curbishley

Alessandro Pistone and Jerome Thomas go to ground

Saturday 22nd January 2005	Venue: **Old Trafford**	Attendance: **67,859**	Referee: **M.R.Halsey**

MANCHESTER UNITED 3 ASTON VILLA 1

A fine individual display from Cristiano Ronaldo inspired Manchester United to a reasonably comfortable 3-1 victory against Aston Villa.

The Portuguese international was both a scorer and a provider in a clash that saw his side's run of five consecutive Premiership clean sheets come to an end.

Sir Alex Ferguson's men dominated the early exchanges, with Louis Saha somehow managing to head over from an inch-perfect Wayne Rooney centre. The miss was soon forgotten, however, as Ronaldo ran on to the striker's pass to drive a 19-yard effort past Thomas Sorensen in just the eighth minute.

The keeper was then relieved to field a weak effort from Rooney, while Roy Carroll was called into comfortable action by both a Nolberto Solano shot and Juan Pablo Angel header at the other end. These were isolated Villa attacks though, and normal service soon resumed.

Mikael Silvestre nodded over the top from a corner and Ronaldo ghosted in to head a cross straight at Sorensen, while Rooney twice went close with decent strikes.

United had forgotten what it was like to concede a goal, one that actually counted anyway, but rediscovered the feeling after eight minutes of the second half. In truth, there was little that the defenders could do to prevent Gareth Barry from ending a flowing move with a venomous 20-yard drive into the far right bottom corner of the net.

After recovering from the initial shock of seeing their lead evaporate, the home side killed off the contest with two goals in a glorious 60 second spell of attacking football.

With 69 minutes on the clock, Saha profited from a surging right-wing burst by Rooney to beat the keeper with a heavily-deflected eight-yard finish. Paul Scholes was then on hand to head into an unguarded net from close range, after Sorensen had parried the fleet-footed Ronaldo's drive from distance.

Captain Roy Keane nearly added a fourth, while visiting substitute Luke Moore fired over when it seemed easier to score. Though the team performance wasn't vintage United, the result was all that mattered.

Nolberto Solano looks to challenge Cristiano Ronaldo

PREMIERSHIP MILESTONE

350 Roy Keane made his 350th Premiership appearance

PREMIERSHIP MILESTONE

50 Cristiano Ronaldo made his 50th Premiership appearance

"That was Cristiano Ronaldo's best game of the season, and he could have had two or three goals."

Sir Alex Ferguson

"We got back into the game after going a goal down, but then had a mad few minutes."

David O'Leary

PREMIERSHIP FIXTURE HISTORY

Pl: **13** Draws: **4**

	Wins	Goals	Yellow	Red
Manchester United	9	22	12	0
Aston Villa	0	5	22	0

STARTING LINE-UPS

Manchester United: Carroll; G.Neville, Ferdinand, Silvestre, Heinze; Fletcher, Keane (c), Scholes; Ronaldo, Rooney; Saha

Aston Villa: Angel; Barry, Solano, Berson, Hendrie, Davis; Samuel, Ridgewell, Mellberg (c), Delaney; Sorensen

Substitutes (Manchester United): Fortune, O'Shea, Giggs, Howard, Brown

Substitutes (Aston Villa): De la Cruz, L.Moore, Postma, Cole, Hitzlsperger

EVENT LINE

8	⚽ **Ronaldo (Open Play)**
11	Delaney (Off) De la Cruz (On)
25	**Keane (Foul)**
27	Berson (Foul)
37	Ridgewell (Ung.Conduct)
38	**Ronaldo (Ung.Conduct)**
45	Hendrie (Foul)
	HALF TIME 1 - 0
46	**Fletcher (Off) Fortune (On)**
46	Berson (Off) Hitzlsperger (On)
51	Samuel (Foul)
53	⚽ Barry (Open Play)
69	⚽ **Saha (Open Play)**
70	⚽ **Scholes (Open Play)**
73	**Rooney (Off) Giggs (On)**
73	**Scholes (Off) O'Shea (On)**
73	Solano (Foul)
74	Solano (Off) Moore L (On)
	FULL TIME 3 - 1

STATISTICS

Season	Fixture		Fixture	Season
195	11	Shots On Target	6	128
178	7	Shots Off Target	4	125
12	0	Hit Woodwork	0	3
92	6	Caught Offside	3	65
190	4	Corners	2	138
290	11	Fouls	21	363
55%	61%	Possession	39%	49%

LEAGUE STANDINGS

Position (pos before)		W	D	L	F	A	Pts
2 (3)	Man Utd	14	8	2	37	14	50
10 (10)	Aston Villa	8	7	9	27	29	31

PREMIERSHIP FIXTURE HISTORY

Pl: 2 Draws: 2	Wins	⚽	☐	■
Norwich City	0	5	0	0
Middlesbrough	0	5	3	0

STARTING LINE-UPS

McKenzie, McVeigh, Holt, Gallacher, Jarvis

Morrison, Graham, Nash, Cooper, Nemeth

EVENT LINE

18 ⚽ **Francis (Open Play)**

22 ☐ Queudrue (Foul)

25 ☐ Parlour (Foul)

34 ⚽ Hasselbaink (Open Play)

HALF TIME 1 - 1

46 ⇄ Doriva (Off) Morrison (On)

49 ⚽ Queudrue (Corner)

53 ☐ McMahon (Dissent)

55 ⚽ Queudrue (Corner)

59 ⇄ **Brennan (Off) McKenzie (On)**

60 ⇄ **Jonson (Off) McVeigh (On)**

64 ⇄ **Mulryne (Off) Holt (On)**

74 ⇄ Job (Off) Graham (On)

78 ⚽ Hasselbaink (Direct Free Kick)

80 ⚽ **Ashton (Indirect Free Kick)**

90 ⚽ **Drury (Corner)**

90 ⚽ **McKenzie (Open Play)**

FULL TIME 4 - 4

STATISTICS

Season	Fixture		Fixture	Season
109	9	Shots On Target	15	173
129	8	Shots Off Target	7	137
5	0	Hit Woodwork	0	4
76	4	Caught Offside	2	65
119	5	Corners	8	140
313	12	Fouls	15	296
46%	45%	Possession	55%	50%

LEAGUE STANDINGS

Position (pos before)	W	D	L	F	A	Pts
19 (18) Norwich C	2	11	11	23	46	17
6 (6) Middlesbrough	10	7	7	39	33	37

Saturday 22nd January 2005 | Venue: **Carrow Road** | Attendance: **24,547** | Referee: **M.D.Messias**

NORWICH CITY 4 MIDDLESBROUGH 4

An incredible game at Carrow Road saw Norwich score three times in the last 10 minutes to salvage an unlikely 4-4 draw against Middlesbrough.

Damien Francis had given the home side an 18th-minute lead, only for braces from both Jimmy Floyd Hasselbaink and Franck Queudrue to make it 4-1 after 78 minutes. Nigel Worthington's men kept going, however, and recovered through goals from Dean Ashton, Leon McKenzie and unlikely hero Adam Drury.

There was little sign of the drama that was to follow in a fairly ordinary opening period. Robert Green denied Stewart Downing and Hasselbaink pulled a left-foot effort wide, while Ashton went close with a volley at the other end.

The deadlock was broken shortly before the mid-point of the half, when Francis tapped in from a yard out following Darren Huckerby's drive across the six-yard box. Steve McClaren's team hit back in fortuitous fashion after 34 minutes though, Hasselbaink diverting Downing's low shot from the left past a stranded keeper.

Within 10 minutes of the restart, Queudrue appeared to have put the game beyond Norwich. The visiting full-back netted twice, heading in a right-wing corner at the near post, and then side-footing home from Gareth Southgate's flick-on following a flag-kick on the opposite flank.

Any lingering hopes of a Canaries comeback appeared to be snuffed out when Hasselbaink bent a 25-yard free-kick over the wall and beyond the right hand of Green 12 minutes from time, but all was not lost.

With 80 minutes played, Ashton, a transfer-window signing from Crewe, beat Mark Schwarzer to an inswinging Huckerby cross from the right to convert from close range.

Then, as the game reached the 90 minute mark, substitute McKenzie was afforded the freedom of the area to divert Huckerby's ball from the left into the bottom right-hand corner with his head.

It seemed that Worthington's charges would be defeated by the clock, but recently-deposed skipper Drury had other ideas. An Ashton free-kick was deflected for a corner on the left, and the full-back arrived unchallenged to nod the resulting delivery into the back of the Middlesbrough net.

"Even though we have only got a point, this was a moral victory."

Nigel Worthington

PREMIERSHIP MILESTONE

Both Dean Ashton and Adam Drury netted their first Premiership goals

PREMIERSHIP MILESTONE

The attendance of 24,547 was a Premiership record at Carrow Road

"This was one of those strange things that happen in football. We seemed in total control at 4-1."

Steve McClaren

Darren Huckerby embarks on another surging run

Saturday 22nd January 2005 | Venue: **Friends Provident St Mary's Stadium** | Attendance: **32,017** | Referee: **A.G.Wiley**

PREMIERSHIP FIXTURE HISTORY

Pl: 13 Draws: 3	Wins	Goals	Yellow	Red
Southampton	5	19	15	1
Liverpool	5	17	13	0

STARTING LINE-UPS

Southampton subs: Jakobsson, Jones, Smith, Oakley, Ormerod

Liverpool subs: Sinama-Pongolle, Raven, Biscan, Carson, Traore

EVENT LINE

5 **Prutton (Open Play)**

22 **Crouch (Open Play)**

38 **Redknapp (Foul)**

HALF TIME 2 - 0

46 Warnock (Off) Sinama-Pongolle (On)

50 Hamann (Foul)

67 Hyypia (Off) Raven (On)

76 **Nilsson (Off) Jakobsson (On)**

78 Hamann (Off) Biscan (On)

89 **Svensson A (Off) Jones (On)**

90 Garcia (Foul)

FULL TIME 2 - 0

STATISTICS

Season	Fixture	Southampton	Liverpool	Fixture	Season
112	7	Shots On Target		2	158
125	4	Shots Off Target		9	165
2	0	Hit Woodwork		0	3
63	2	Caught Offside		2	59
120	6	Corners		3	139
307	10	Fouls		12	284
48%	53%	Possession		47%	53%

LEAGUE STANDINGS

Position (pos before)	W	D	L	F	A	Pts
18 (19) Southampton	3	9	12	25	39	18
5 (5) Liverpool	11	4	9	36	25	37

Key midfielders Jamie Redknapp and Steven Gerrard go head-to-head

PREMIERSHIP MILESTONE

Kenwyne Jones made his Premiership debut

"It was a terrific performance. The lads worked their socks off and played some good stuff."

Harry Redknapp

PREMIERSHIP MILESTONE

50 Danny Higginbotham made his 50th Premiership appearance in the colours of Southampton

"The team worked hard in the second half, but by then it was too late."

Rafael Benitez

PREMIERSHIP MILESTONE

David Raven made his Premiership debut

SOUTHAMPTON 2 LIVERPOOL 0

Early goals from David Prutton and Peter Crouch secured a vital win for Southampton, as Liverpool stuttered to their third defeat in the space of eight days.

Saints manager Harry Redknapp was still awaiting his first Premiership victory since taking charge at the club, and opted to switch to a solid-looking 4-5-1 formation for this vital encounter.

Opposite number Rafael Benitez had been heavily criticised for fielding a weakened side in the midweek F.A.Cup reverse at Burnley, but had all his available big guns back for this lunchtime clash at St Mary's.

Nevertheless, the home team cut a swathe through the away defence after only five minutes. The tall Crouch showed good feet to find Prutton in the inside right channel, and the former Nottingham Forest midfielder beat Jerzy Dudek with a low near-post finish.

The strike didn't waken the Merseysiders from their state of slumber, and they had barely left their own half by the time that Crouch made it 2-0. Sloppiness at the back saw possession squandered in a dangerous area, enabling Prutton to centre from the right for the unmarked ex-Portsmouth man to nod in.

Rory Delap could have made it three as the half ended as it had started. The former Derby player raced towards goal, but was thwarted by an alert Dudek.

Liverpool showed a marked improvement after the interval, though it was not enough to get them back in the match. Milan Baros fired wide after a jinking run, while the previously anonymous Steven Gerrard went close with a shot from distance.

Much of the visitors' best work after the break came about as a result of pacy running from half-time substitute Florent Sinama-Pongolle. The young Frenchman almost netted a deserved consolation with a header that drifted wide, while Baros again went close late on.

The final whistle was greeted with great joy around St Mary's. A few more performances like this would surely be enough to steer the Saints clear of danger, as the fans went home full of optimism for a change.

PREMIERSHIP FIXTURE HISTORY

Pl: 2 Draws: 0	Wins	⚽	Yellow	Red
West Bromwich Albion	1	3	4	0
Manchester City	1	2	2	0

STARTING LINE-UPS

West Brom subs: Horsfield, Gaardsoe, Kuszczak, Contra, Kanu

Man City subs: Waterreus, Sommeil, Onuoha, B.Wright-Phillips, McManaman

EVENT LINE

5 ⚽ **Campbell (Open Play)**

HALF TIME 1 - 0

57 **Earnshaw (Off) Horsfield (On)**

67 Macken (Off) Wright-Phillips B (On)

68 Sibierski (Off) McManaman (On)

81 ⚽ **Wallwork (Open Play)**

83 **Robinson (Ung.Conduct)**

90 **Gera (Ung.Conduct)**

90 **Campbell (Off) Gaardsoe (On)**

FULL TIME 2 - 0

STATISTICS

Season	Fixture (West Brom)		Fixture (Man City)	Season
106	6	Shots On Target	5	139
99	7	Shots Off Target	6	121
4	0	Hit Woodwork	0	2
90	5	Caught Offside	1	73
107	3	Corners	11	156
315	9	Fouls	12	314
45%	46%	Possession	54%	49%

LEAGUE STANDINGS

Position (pos before)	W	D	L	F	A	Pts
20 (20) West Brom	2	10	12	19	44	16
9 (9) Man City	8	7	9	30	26	31

Saturday 22nd January 2005 | Venue: **The Hawthorns** | Attendance: **25,348** | Referee: **G.Poll**

WEST BROM 2 MANCHESTER CITY 0

Goals from Kevin Campbell and Ronnie Wallwork handed West Brom only their second Premiership win of the season, the last coming in early October against Bolton.

Bryan Robson's side had made notable improvements of late, and drew great confidence from taking a fifth-minute lead. Home debutant Kevin Campbell drilled Martin Albrechtsen's low ball from the right into the bottom left-hand corner from 15 yards, though a nick off the right boot of team-mate Robert Earnshaw may have directed the effort goalwards.

The Welsh international then wasted two decent opportunities to extend the lead, though Antoine Sibierski, Shaun Wright-Phillips and Robbie Fowler were also guilty of poor finishing for the visitors.

A late first half flurry saw Wallwork fire over and David James deny Earnshaw. The Baggies were playing well, but 1-0 is a precarious advantage.

Kevin Keegan's team emerged for the second period with the bit between their teeth. Russell Hoult was called upon to deny a near-post Sibierski effort, with captain Darren Purse then making a vital last-ditch clearance.

West Brom gradually regrouped, and nearly went two up just after the hour mark. A Jonathan Greening volley was destined for the top corner until James intervened, the tall custodian flinging out a left hand to divert the ball over the crossbar.

Having nodded a good chance wide just moments earlier, Wallwork secured the victory with his first goal for the club nine minutes from time. Determined play from substitute Geoff Horsfield engineered the opening, enabling the midfielder to arrive on cue to stoop and head into the net from six yards out.

City needed a quick response if they were to salvage anything from a poor evening, and were somewhat unlucky to see a Richard Dunne free-kick ruled out by referee Graham Poll. The official stated that he had not blown his whistle as the Irishman fired a piledriver into the top left-hand corner, though everyone else seemed ready for the set-piece to be taken.

Manager Keegan was fairly philosophical afterwards, choosing to reflect more on the poor performance of his team than on any perceived indiscretions by the man in black.

Antoine Sibierski and Ronnie Wallwork get to grips with each other

"To get that win is a great relief for everyone. We couldn't afford to be any further adrift of the teams above us."

Bryan Robson

PREMIERSHIP MILESTONE

Ronnie Wallwork netted his first Premiership goal

PREMIERSHIP MILESTONE

Kevin Campbell scored his first Premiership goal for West Brom

"It's always disappointing to lose, but I've got no qualms about the result."

Kevin Keegan

PREMIERSHIP FIXTURE HISTORY

Pl: 12 Draws: 1	Wins	⚽	▯	▮
Arsenal	8	23	14	1
Newcastle United	3	11	31	3

STARTING LINE-UPS

Almunia
Lauren, Toure, Campbell, Cole
Pires, Flamini, Vieira (c), Reyes
Bergkamp, Henry

Shearer (c)
Robert, Dyer, Jenas, Bowyer, Ameobi
Bernard, Bramble, Boumsong, Taylor
Given

Arsenal subs: Fabregas, Lehmann, Cygan, Eboue, van Persie

Newcastle subs: Hughes, N'Zogbia, O'Brien, Harper, Kluivert

EVENT LINE

16 ▯ Taylor (Foul)
19 ⚽ **Bergkamp (Open Play)**
44 ▯ Bowyer (Foul)
45 ▯ **Reyes (Foul)**
HALF TIME 1 - 0
46 Taylor (Off) Hughes (On)
56 Robert (Off) N'Zogbia (On)
67 Boumsong (Off) O'Brien (On)
73 ▯ **Vieira (Foul)**
89 **Reyes (Off) Fabregas (On)**
90 ▯ Jenas (Foul)
FULL TIME 1 - 0

STATISTICS

Season	Fixture (Arsenal)		Fixture (Newcastle)	Season
180	6	Shots On Target	1	172
114	7	Shots Off Target	3	136
9	1	Hit Woodwork	0	9
51	5	Caught Offside	2	61
145	11	Corners	1	167
279	17	Fouls	19	295
56%	74%	Possession	26%	50%

LEAGUE STANDINGS

Position (pos before)		W	D	L	F	A	Pts
2 (3)	Arsenal	15	6	3	53	25	51
12 (12)	Newcastle Utd	7	8	9	35	41	29

Sunday 23rd January 2005 | Venue: **Highbury** | Attendance: **38,137** | Referee: **S.W.Dunn**

ARSENAL 1 NEWCASTLE UNITED 0

Thierry Henry leaves Kieron Dyer in his wake

"I was very pleased. We had to win this game to get our momentum back."
Arsene Wenger

"It would have been hard on Arsenal if we'd taken a point."
Graeme Souness

PREMIERSHIP MILESTONE
150 Kieron Dyer made his 150th Premiership appearance

A moment of magic from Dennis Bergkamp settled this one-sided encounter in Arsenal's favour, as Shay Given turned in a performance to remember.

The Dutch master netted possibly the finest goal of his career against the Magpies, and added another gem to his collection in the 19th-minute of this contest. Running onto a neat flick from Mathieu Flamini, the inventive forward brushed past a defender and swept the ball across Given in one fluid movement.

It was Newcastle who provided the interesting team news, with Craig Bellamy not named in their squad of 16 despite being at Highbury. Rumours that the Welsh international had again fallen out with manager Graeme Souness were rife, as the game got underway.

Having produced such an abject display at the Reebok Stadium in their last match, Arsene Wenger's side began in a hurry. Within 30 seconds of the kick-off, a combination of Given and a large slice of luck somehow kept the ball out.

Both Jose Antonio Reyes and Thierry Henry went close prior to Bergkamp's breakthrough, with a fine diving save preventing Arsenal's French striker from increasing their lead shortly afterwards.

Robert Pires and Bergkamp then almost netted from distance, while Lee Bowyer and Shola Ameobi failed to make the most of rare forward forays from the visitors.

An interval scoreline of just 1-0 flattered Souness' men, and it should have been more after the break.

If Given had excelled during the first period, then he was even better in the second half. The Gunners produced some breathtaking football, reminiscent of earlier in the campaign, but were continually thwarted by the Irish international.

Having kept out a well-struck free-kick and smothered the ball at the feet of a marauding Reyes, Given then diverted a low Henry effort against the right-hand upright. An incredible plunging save to his left then denied Pires, as Arsenal continued to be frustrated.

A swivelling Henry drive was soon repelled, before Bowyer shot straight at Manuel Almunia with what was a golden chance to steal a totally undeserved point late on.

PREMIERSHIP FIXTURE HISTORY

Pl: 6 Draws: 2	Wins	Goals	Yellow	Red
Blackburn Rovers	2	10	10	0
Bolton Wanderers	2	8	17	1

STARTING LINE-UPS

Blackburn substitutes: Stead, Enckelman, Johansson, Johnson, Reid

Bolton substitutes: Davies, Pedersen, Fadiga, Poole, Hierro

EVENT LINE

4 Yellow card: Diouf (Foul)
17 Yellow card: **Savage (Foul)**
36 Yellow card: Giannakopoulos (Foul)

HALF TIME 0 - 0

52 Substitution: Okocha (Off) Davies (On)
62 Substitution: **Bothroyd (Off) Johnson (On)**
62 Substitution: **Gallagher (Off) Stead (On)**
66 Yellow card: Nolan (Foul)
67 Substitution: Giannakopoulos (Off) Pedersen (On)
77 Goal: Diouf (Penalty)
78 Substitution: Diouf (Off) Fadiga (On)
90 Yellow card: Davies (Foul)

FULL TIME 0 - 1

STATISTICS

Season	Fixture (Blackburn)		Fixture (Bolton)	Season
124	4	Shots On Target	2	144
143	4	Shots Off Target	5	138
6	0	Hit Woodwork	0	5
88	2	Caught Offside	4	60
134	7	Corners	7	131
377	18	Fouls	18	329
49%	57%	Possession	43%	49%

LEAGUE STANDINGS

Position (pos before)	W	D	L	F	A	Pts
16 (16) Blackburn R	5	10	9	21	34	25
9 (11) Bolton W	9	6	9	31	31	33

Monday 24th January 2005 | Venue: Ewood Park | Attendance: 20,056 | Referee: S.G.Bennett

BLACKBURN ROVERS 0 BOLTON WANDERERS 1

Controversy reigned at Ewood Park, as El-Hadji Diouf won and then scored from a very dubious penalty.

The Senegalese international's 77th-minute goal was enough to settle an otherwise lifeless contest, though he benefitted from a slice of luck to convert from close range after Brad Friedel had saved his initial spot-kick.

Everyone connected with Blackburn was furious with referee Steve Bennett's game-changing decision, claiming that there had been no contact as the on-loan Liverpool man went down under the challenge of Friedel.

The fact that Diouf had been lucky to escape an early red card for an elbow on Rovers captain Andy Todd did not make matters any more palatable.

Mark Hughes gave a debut to new signing Robbie Savage, but was without his main striker Paul Dickov through suspension. A goal from the diminutive Scot had been enough to settle the recent meeting between the two Lancashire sides at the Reebok Stadium.

Unsurprisingly, Sam Allardyce kept faith with the team that had beaten Arsenal last time out. This meant that returning striker Kevin Davies had to make do with a place amongst the substitutes.

Norwegian winger Morten Gamst Pedersen was the first to try his luck, bringing an agile eighth-minute stop from keeper Jussi Jaaskelainen. Next to have a go was full-back Lucas Neill, the former Millwall man again forcing the visiting custodian into a smart parry.

The Trotters offered little going forward, and were somewhat lucky to be on level terms at the interval. David Thompson spurned the best chance of the half, the little midfielder missing by inches with a firm header.

It took 55 minutes before Bolton even remotely threatened the goal of their hosts. Out-of-sorts captain Jay-Jay Okocha had made way for Davies not long beforehand, and the burly striker fired in an effort that narrowly cleared the crossbar.

Chances of any sort were at a premium in the remainder of this insipid contest, though the theatrical skills of Diouf proved enough to break the deadlock.

El-Hadji Diouf celebrates his controversial winner

"The penalty was a diabolical decision, and a disappointing way to lose what was a poor game."

Mark Hughes

PREMIERSHIP MILESTONE

Robbie Savage made his first Premiership appearance in the colours of Blackburn

PREMIERSHIP MILESTONE

Jemal Johnson made his Premiership debut

"It wasn't a particularly good game, scrappy at times, but I thought that we just about shaded it."

Sam Allardyce

John Terry leads his team from strength to strength

JANUARY 2005

Chelsea stretched their lead at the Premiership summit to an enormous 10 points, courtesy of four wins from four games during the month. Petr Cech did not concede a single goal, as Jose Mourinho's men began to establish an air of invincibility.

Defeat at Bolton highlighted how vulnerable Arsenal had become, and a resurgent Manchester United moved to within a point of their great rivals. It wasn't all good news for Sir Alex Ferguson's men, however, as they were beaten over two legs by Chelsea in a hard-fought Carling Cup Semi-Final.

The Londoners' opponents in Cardiff would be Liverpool. Rafael Benitez's men were unconvincing winners over Watford, and failed to cash in on slip-ups from Everton by losing three of their four league games during the month.

Chris Coleman's Fulham took advantage of some matches against struggling sides, to pull clear of relegation danger. The Cottagers collected 10 points from a possible 12, and were the leading scorers during January with nine goals.

Bolton recovered from an appalling two months to get their season firmly back on track. A late El-Hadji Diouf equaliser ended a run of defeats at home to West Brom, before three consecutive victories sent the men from the Reebok Stadium back into the top half of the table.

The F.A.Cup got under way with none of the 20 Premiership teams being drawn against each other. Four sides crashed out away to Championship opposition, most notably an inexperienced Liverpool side in a rearranged tie at Burnley, while Manchester City went down 1-0 at League One neighbours Oldham.

Fielding weakened line-ups almost cost each of the top three. Arsenal and Chelsea had to come from behind to win home games with Stoke and Scunthorpe respectively, and Manchester United needed a replay to see off Conference outfit Exeter after an astonishing 0-0 draw at Old Trafford.

Back in the league, a remarkable game at Carrow Road saw Norwich come from 4-1 down with just 10 minutes remaining to earn a vital point against Middlesbrough.

IN THE NEWS

04TH James Beattie completes a £6m move from Southampton to Everton

10TH Norwich break their transfer record, paying an initial £3m fee to bring in striker Dean Ashton from Crewe

11TH Young winger Wayne Routledge rejects a new contract offer from Crystal Palace. The England under-21 international's current deal expires in the summer

13TH Liverpool complete the signing of Spanish international striker Fernando Morientes for £6.3m from Real Madrid

13TH Italian giants Juventus sign sacked Chelsea striker Adrian Mutu on a five-year contract. The Romanian international's ban ends on May 18

14TH Thomas Gravesen leaves Goodison Park to join Real Madrid for £2.5m

19TH After weeks of speculation, Welsh midfielder Robbie Savage finally moves from Birmingham to Blackburn

25TH Everton goalkeeper Nigel Martyn agrees a one-year contract extension. The deal ties him to the club until the summer of 2006.

31ST Craig Bellamy completes a loan move from Newcastle to Celtic until the end of the season

31ST Nicolas Anelka heads for Turkey, joining Fenerbahce in a £7m move from Manchester City

Petr Cech
Chelsea

The Czech international extended the time since he was last beaten in the Premiership to 691 minutes. In recognition of his achievements, the goalkeeper was presented with a 'special merit' award by the 'Barclays Awards Panel'.

Paulo Ferreira
Chelsea

The Portuguese full-back demonstrated his versatility by operating on both the right and left of the defence during January. Wherever he played the outcome was the same, however, as Chelsea won all four of their Premiership fixtures without conceding a goal.

Andy Todd
Blackburn Rovers

With Barry Ferguson returning to Rangers, Mark Hughes demonstrated his faith in Andy Todd by handing him the captain's armband. The new skipper immediately led his team to a 1-0 victory at Portsmouth, and also guided Blackburn into the F.A.Cup 5th Round.

Gabriel Heinze
Manchester United

In just a few months, the Argentinian full-back had already established himself as a cult hero at Old Trafford. Forming part of a defence that kept three clean sheets in four games, the Olympic gold medallist continued to excite the crowd with many lung-bursting forward runs.

Shaun Wright-Phillips
Manchester City

The young England international weighed in with four goals from the right-hand side of midfield, as City collected seven points during the month. The strike that earnt a point at Highbury was spectacular, as was a low skidding effort that helped secure a win against Southampton.

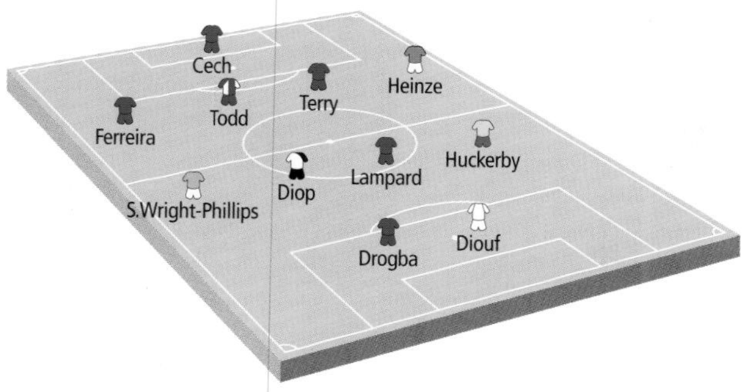

PLAYER OF THE MONTH

John Terry
Chelsea

Chelsea won all four of their league games in January, with the defence stretching their run of Premiership clean sheets to seven. John Terry continued to lead by example, defending as though his life depended on it.

> **"Chelsea have had a blistering start to 2005, aided by Jose Mourinho's tactical sharpness and John Terry's inspirational presence."**
> Barclays Awards Panel

MANAGER OF THE MONTH

Jose Mourinho
Chelsea

Jose Mourinho collected his second managerial award in three months, as Chelsea won all four of their January league games without conceding a goal. The Portuguese maestro also got the better of Sir Alex Ferguson over two legs in the semi-finals of the Carling Cup.

Premiership Career Statistics
up until end of January 2005
Matches:**24** Wins:**19** Draws:**4** Losses:**1**

> **"Jose Mourinho's men now look favourites to scoop the Barclays Premiership - their first domestic league honour for 50 years."**
> Barclays Awards Panel

Pape Bouba Diop
Fulham

Though not renowned for his goalscoring, Diop was on target in three consecutive Premiership matches at the end of the month. Southampton, West Brom and Birmingham all succumbed to powerful headers, as the Senegalese international helped his team to 10 points from four games.

Frank Lampard
Chelsea

Having been outstanding during the previous campaign, Lampard has shone even more brightly under the guidance of Jose Mourinho. The midfielder scored both goals in the win at Tottenham, and also netted in Carling Cup success at Old Trafford.

Darren Huckerby
Norwich City

Operating mainly from wide on the left of a five-man midfield, Huckerby's pace provided Norwich with a real outlet. When he was pushed further forward, as against Middlesbrough, the former Coventry man created each of his side's four goals.

Didier Drogba
Chelsea

The former Marseille striker was on target four times during the month, accounting for half of Chelsea's league goals in January. Braces at home to Middlesbrough and Portsmouth helped secure important wins, as the men from West London extended their Premiership lead.

El-Hadji Diouf
Bolton Wanderers

Having failed to produce his best at Liverpool, the Senegalese forward began to show what he could do at Bolton. A late equaliser against West Brom ended a terrible run of Premiership defeats, while further goals helped secure victories at Birmingham and Blackburn.

MONTH IN NUMBERS

40 Games Played

101 Total Goals Scored

4 Average Goals Per Game

4 Player With Most Goals (S.Wright-Phillips, Drogba, Johnson)

9 Club With Most Goals (Fulham)

4 Fastest Goal (Cole)

52.5% Percentage Of Away Wins

27.5% Percentage Of Home Wins

20% Percentage Of Draws

5-2 Biggest Win (Tottenham 5 v 2 Everton, Aston Villa 3 v 0 Norwich City, Crystal Palace 3 v 0 Tottenham, Chelsea 3 v 0 Portsmouth)

127 Total Yellow Cards

4 Total Red Cards

3.2 Average Yellow Cards Per Game

12 Most Disciplinary Points (Lua Lua, Parlour, Edworthy)

4 Fastest Booking (Diouf)

33,467 Average Attendance

PREMIERSHIP TABLE / TEAM STATISTICS

Pos (last month)	Team	Played	Won	Drawn	Lost	Goals for	Goals against	Goal diff	Points	Shots on target	Hit woodwork	Shots off target	Failed to score	Clean sheets	Corners	Caught Offside	Players used
1 - (1)	Chelsea	24	19	4	1	48	8	+40	61	179	8	148	3	18	164	73	23
2 - (2)	Arsenal	24	15	6	3	53	25	+28	51	180	9	114	2	9	145	51	22
3 - (3)	Manchester United	24	14	8	2	37	14	+23	50	195	12	178	6	13	190	92	26
4 - (4)	Everton	24	13	5	6	28	25	+3	44	119	6	125	6	9	119	62	20
5 ▲ (6)	Liverpool	24	11	4	9	36	25	+11	37	158	3	165	8	5	139	59	24
6 ▼ (5)	Middlesbrough	24	10	7	7	39	33	+6	37	173	4	137	6	5	140	65	22
7 - (7)	Charlton Athletic	24	11	4	9	28	33	-5	37	112	5	87	8	9	108	78	20
8 - (8)	Tottenham Hotspur	24	9	6	9	29	26	+3	33	143	9	126	9	10	108	93	27
9 ▲ (13)	Bolton Wanderers	24	9	6	9	31	31	0	33	144	5	138	5	4	131	60	23
10 ▲ (12)	Manchester City	24	8	7	9	30	26	+4	31	139	2	121	7	6	156	73	21
11 - (11)	Aston Villa	24	8	7	9	27	29	-2	31	128	3	125	8	8	138	65	21
12 ▲ (14)	Newcastle United	24	7	8	9	35	41	-6	29	172	9	136	5	3	167	61	24
13 ▲ (16)	Fulham	24	8	4	12	31	40	-9	28	116	3	105	7	5	122	59	24
14 ▼ (10)	Portsmouth	24	7	6	11	26	34	-8	27	122	3	119	7	4	123	54	22
15 ▼ (9)	Birmingham City	24	6	8	10	27	30	-3	26	112	5	99	7	6	121	72	24
16 ▼ (15)	Blackburn Rovers	24	5	10	9	21	34	-13	25	124	6	143	10	7	134	88	30
17 - (17)	Crystal Palace	24	5	6	13	27	37	-10	21	102	5	101	6	6	120	61	27
18 ▲ (19)	Southampton	24	3	9	12	25	39	-14	18	112	2	125	9	5	120	63	31
19 ▼ (18)	Norwich City	24	2	11	11	23	46	-23	17	109	5	129	10	3	119	76	23
20 - (20)	West Brom	24	2	10	12	19	44	-25	16	106	4	99	9	3	107	90	24

Didier Drogba savours the moment

TEAM FORM

Pos	Team	Form	Goals For	Goals Against	Pts
1	Chelsea	WWWW	8	0	12
2	Manchester United	WDWW	6	1	10
3	Fulham	WDWW	9	5	10
4	Bolton Wanderers	DWWW	5	2	10
5	Arsenal	WDLW	5	3	7
6	Manchester City	WDWL	6	5	7
7	Newcastle United	WDWL	4	3	7
8	Crystal Palace	LWLW	7	6	6
9	Aston Villa	WLWL	5	5	6
10	Charlton Athletic	LLWW	5	5	6
11	Blackburn Rovers	LWWL	2	2	6
12	West Brom	DDLW	3	2	5
13	Southampton	LDLW	7	7	4
14	Tottenham Hotspur	WDLL	5	7	4
15	Everton	LWDL	5	8	4
16	Liverpool	LWLL	2	5	3
17	Middlesbrough	LLDD	5	9	2
18	Norwich City	DLLD	6	10	2
19	Portsmouth	DLLL	2	7	1
20	Birmingham City	LLLL	4	9	0

TOP GOALSCORERS

Player	This Month	Total
T.Henry Arsenal	0	**16**
A.Johnson Crystal Palace	4	**14**
J.Hasselbaink Middlesbrough	2	**10**
J.Defoe Tottenham Hotspur	0	**10**
R.Pires Arsenal	0	**10**
S.Wright-Phillips Manchester City	4	**9**
A.Cole Fulham	3	**9**
D.Drogba Chelsea	4	**8**
A.Yakubu Portsmouth	2	**8**
P.Scholes Manchester United	1	**8**
M.Baros Liverpool	0	**8**
F.Ljungberg Arsenal	3	**7**
K.Phillips Southampton	3	**7**
F.Lampard Chelsea	2	**7**
N.Anelka Manchester City	0	**7**
C.Bellamy Newcastle United	0	**7**
P.Dickov Blackburn Rovers	0	**7**
E.Gudjohnsen Chelsea	0	**7**

MOST GOAL ASSISTS

Player	This Month	Total
F.Lampard Chelsea	3	**13**
S.Downing Middlesbrough	3	**12**
T.Henry Arsenal	1	**11**
F.Ljungberg Arsenal	0	**11**
W.Routledge Crystal Palace	2	**9**
J.Hasselbaink Middlesbrough	1	**9**
A.Robben Chelsea	2	**8**
L.Boa Morte Fulham	2	**7**
R.Giggs Manchester United	1	**7**
E.Gudjohnsen Chelsea	1	**7**
L.Robert Newcastle United	1	**7**
D.Huckerby Norwich City	4	**6**
F.Kanoute Tottenham Hotspur	2	**6**
T.Gravesen Everton	1	**6**
J.Greening West Brom	1	**6**
E.Heskey Birmingham City	1	**6**
D.Bergkamp Arsenal	0	**6**
D.Duff Chelsea	0	**6**
S.Wright-Phillips Manchester City	0	**6**

DISCIPLINE

F.A. disciplinary points: Yellow=4 points, Two Bookable Offences=10 points and Red Card=12 points

Player	Y	SB	R	PTS
L.Hendrie Aston Villa	6	0	1	**36**
P.Diop Fulham	5	0	1	**32**
D.Mills Manchester City	5	0	1	**32**
D.Johnson Birmingham City	5	1	0	**30**
Josemi Liverpool	5	1	0	**30**
K.Tugay Blackburn Rovers	5	1	0	**30**
A.Cole Arsenal	7	0	0	**28**
P.Vieira Arsenal	7	0	0	**28**
T.Cahill Everton	4	1	0	**26**
A.Faye Portsmouth	4	1	0	**26**
A.Cole Fulham	3	0	1	**24**
M.Izzet Birmingham City	3	0	1	**24**
F.Queudrue Middlesbrough	3	0	1	**24**
G.Boateng Middlesbrough	6	0	0	**24**
M.Hughes Crystal Palace	6	0	0	**24**
R.Parlour Middlesbrough	6	0	0	**24**
R.Savage Birmingham City	6	0	0	**24**

"This was a true sporting opportunity. Newcastle really wanted me, and I have the opportunity to play in the Premiership."

Jean-Alain Boumsong after clinching an £8m move to Tyneside

"When I sat on the coach and heard the reports of what the manager was saying, I was in shock. I thought 'not only has he gone behind my back, he's lying."

Craig Bellamy on claims by Graeme Souness that he refused to play for Newcastle at Highbury

"I think you could start off by using it for goal-line decisions. I think that would be an opening into a new area of football."

Sir Alex Ferguson on technology in football

"It's a fantastic job for anybody apart from somebody who has just been the Southampton manager."

Gordon Strachan on the top job at Portsmouth

"We knew it would be a big challenge, but we all thought that we could do it at the start of the season - the players, the staff, the supporters, the people who work within the club - and we will do it."

Nigel Worthington on Norwich's bid to avoid relegation

"My Christmas was pants, the worst I've ever had. I didn't enjoy it and I wasn't very good to be around."

Chris Coleman

"I have a personal opinion about cups. The Premiership team in the cup should always play in the stadium of the lower division team."

Jose Mourinho

"I am convinced that I will play again soon. While watching matches, I cannot see that Manuel Almunia is better than me."

Jens Lehmann on the battle to be No.1 at Arsenal

"When the board decided to sign me, they talked about five years. We need to work with the big picture, to know that it is a long race."

Rafael Benitez

PREMIERSHIP FIXTURE HISTORY

Pl: 13 Draws: 4	Wins	Goals	Yellow cards	Red cards
Arsenal	5	20	20	1
Manchester United	4	17	30	4

STARTING LINE-UPS

Arsenal: Almunia; Lauren, Cygan, Campbell, Cole; Ljungberg, Flamini, Vieira (c), Pires; Bergkamp, Henry

Manchester United: Rooney; Giggs, Scholes, Keane (c), Fletcher, Ronaldo; Heinze, Silvestre, Ferdinand, G.Neville; Carroll

Arsenal subs: Reyes, Hoyte, Fabregas, Lehmann, van Persie

Manchester United subs: O'Shea, Brown, Saha, Howard, P.Neville

EVENT LINE

8 Goal **Vieira (Corner)**
12 Yellow card Heinze (Foul)
15 Yellow card Giggs (Foul)
18 Goal Giggs (Open Play)
29 Yellow card **Pires (Ung.Conduct)**
36 Goal **Bergkamp (Open Play)**
43 Yellow card Rooney (Dissent)

HALF TIME 2 - 1

54 Goal Ronaldo (Indirect Free Kick)
58 Goal Ronaldo (Open Play)
59 Yellow card Ronaldo (Ung.Conduct)
61 Substitution Fletcher (Off) O'Shea (On)
69 Red card Silvestre (Violent Conduct)
70 Substitution **Flamini (Off) Reyes (On)**
70 Substitution Ronaldo (Off) Brown (On)
77 Substitution Giggs (Off) Saha (On)
79 Substitution **Campbell (Off) Hoyte (On)**
83 Substitution **Lauren (Off) Fabregas (On)**
89 Goal O'Shea (Open Play)
90 Yellow card **Reyes (Foul)**

FULL TIME 2 - 4

STATISTICS

Season	Fixture (Arsenal)		Fixture (Man Utd)	Season
190	**10**	Shots On Target	**9**	**204**
115	**1**	Shots Off Target	**1**	**179**
9	**0**	Hit Woodwork	**1**	**13**
54	**3**	Caught Offside	**3**	**95**
151	**6**	Corners	**7**	**197**
299	**20**	Fouls	**16**	**306**
56%	**53%**	Possession	**47%**	**55%**

LEAGUE STANDINGS

Position (pos before)		W	D	L	F	A	Pts
3 (2)	Arsenal	15	6	4	55	29	51
2 (3)	Man Utd	15	8	2	41	16	53

Tuesday 1st February 2005 | Venue: **Highbury** | Attendance: **38,164** | Referee: **G.Poll**

ARSENAL 2 MANCHESTER UNITED 4

Manchester United twice came from behind to win a breathtaking game at Highbury, firmly establishing themselves as the main threat to Chelsea's title hopes in the process.

Having shown signs of rediscovering their early season form in recent weeks, it was Arsenal who began brightly. Roy Carroll had to be alert to deny Freddie Ljungberg, but he could do nothing as Patrick Vieira rose above Gabriel Heinze to glance home the resulting left-wing corner.

The visitors quickly recovered from this eighth-minute setback, and drew level before the mid-point of the half. There was an element of fortune about Ryan Giggs' 19-yard strike, which took a large deflection off Ashley Cole to leave Manuel Almunia stranded, though the neat build-up play between Paul Scholes and Wayne Rooney deserved its reward.

Referee Graham Poll then waved away penalty appeals as Robert Pires fell under challenge from Mikael Silvestre, before Dennis Bergkamp restored the Gunners' advantage. The Dutchman had been in sparkling form all evening, and drove Thierry Henry's measured pass low through the legs of Carroll from an acute angle after 36 minutes.

That proved to be the final goal of a whirlwind opening period, though Rooney spurned a great chance to equalise when firing a low effort against the legs of Almunia.

Whatever Sir Alex Ferguson said at half-time had the desired effect, as before the hour mark United were in front. Cristiano Ronaldo grabbed both goals, ending a sweeping move with a flashing left-foot drive and then tapping home from a yard out after Giggs had taken the ball beyond an errant keeper down the right.

The joint of post and bar was also rattled by a Rooney free-kick in between the Portuguese youngster's brace, as the men from Manchester threatened to overrun their hosts. With 69 minutes played, however, Silvestre's foolish red card for a headbutt on Ljungberg gave Arsenal renewed hope.

Arsene Wenger's men were unable to find a way past the visitors' resolute defence though, and substitute John O'Shea deftly clipped home a fourth goal a minute from time following a spirited surge upfield by Heinze.

John O'Shea celebrates wrapping up the points

"I think we are out of the title race now. Chelsea are playing very well and United have just beaten us at home."
Patrick Vieira

"There are no wimps in my side. We showed a great will to win and played some marvellous attacking football."
Sir Alex Ferguson

PREMIERSHIP FIXTURE HISTORY

Pl: **6** Draws: **2**

	Wins	⚽ (Goals)	□ (Yellow cards)	■ (Red cards)
Bolton Wanderers	**3**	**10**	**4**	**0**
Tottenham Hotspur	**1**	**6**	**12**	**1**

STARTING LINE-UPS

Bolton substitutes: Fadiga, Hierro, Pedersen, Poole, Jaidi

Tottenham substitutes: Defoe, Cerny, Bunjevcevic, Marney, Mido

EVENT LINE

HALF TIME 0 - 0

49 ⚽ **Diouf (Penalty)**

52 □ King (Dissent)

63 ⇄ Edman (Off) Defoe (On)

66 ⚽ Defoe (Open Play)

68 ■ Kanoute (2nd Bookable Offence)

77 ⇄ **Barness (Off) Fadiga (On)**

86 ⚽ **Ben Haim (Corner)**

87 ⚽ **Davies (Open Play)**

88 ⇄ **Giannakopoulos (Off) Hierro (On)**

90 ⇄ **Davies (Off) Pedersen (On)**

FULL TIME 3 - 1

STATISTICS

Season	Fixture (Bolton)		Fixture (Tottenham)	Season
155	**11**	Shots On Target	**5**	**148**
144	**6**	Shots Off Target	**6**	**132**
5	**0**	Hit Woodwork	**0**	**9**
60	**0**	Caught Offside	**3**	**96**
135	**4**	Corners	**6**	**114**
338	**9**	Fouls	**17**	**310**
49%	**49%**	Possession	**51%**	**50%**

LEAGUE STANDINGS

Position (pos before)		W	D	L	F	A	Pts
8 (9)	**Bolton W**	**10**	**6**	**9**	**34**	**32**	**36**
9 (8)	**Tottenham H**	**9**	**6**	**10**	**30**	**29**	**33**

Tuesday 1st February 2005 | Venue: **Reebok Stadium** | Attendance: **24,780** | Referee: **M.L.Dean**

BOLTON WANDERERS 3 TOTTENHAM HOTSPUR 1

Jussi Jaaskelainen enjoys the late show

PREMIERSHIP MILESTONE

100 Henrik Pedersen made his 100th Premiership appearance

PREMIERSHIP MILESTONE

Tal Ben Haim scored his first Premiership goal

"Kevin Davies was our outstanding player. He led the line well and we built from there."
Sam Allardyce

"I don't think I deserved to be sent off, and I still can't quite believe it happened."
Frederic Kanoute

Bolton's recent upturn in fortunes continued, as two late goals helped secure a 3-1 win against Tottenham at the Reebok Stadium.

A goalless opening period was quickly forgotten as El-Hadji Diouf netted a 49th-minute penalty. Visiting substitute Jermain Defoe then arrived from the bench to level matters, before Sam Allardyce's men eventually capitalised on the 68th-minute dismissal of Frederic Kanoute courtesy of Tal Ben Haim and Kevin Davies.

The Londoners had already tasted success at this venue in the Carling Cup and began the match in confident mood. Ivan Campo was caught in possession after just five minutes, but Kanoute flashed his shot narrowly wide.

The French striker then went close with a header, before the home side began to test Paul Robinson. The keeper did well to deal with a swerving Kevin Nolan free-kick, and also repelled an effort from Davies.

The 10 minutes immediately after the break offered as much excitement as the entire first half. Referee Mike Dean's decision to penalise Erik Edman for handball seemed incredibly harsh, but Diouf made no mistake from the spot.

Soon afterwards, the official was at the centre of things again. This time he chose to caution both Kanoute and Ledley King for dissent after the former West Ham forward's free-kick appeared to strike a Bolton arm in the box.

With things going against them, Spurs introduced Defoe into the action. It took just three minutes for the England international to make an impact, collecting Robbie Keane's pass and firing low between the legs of Jussi Jaaskelainen from just outside the area midway through the half.

Much of this good work was undone, however, when Kanoute collected a second yellow card for a rash challenge just moments later. Bolton went for the jugular, bringing on the attack-minded Khalilou Fadiga in place of defender Anthony Barness.

The policy eventually paid dividends as Ben Haim rose to nod home Stylianos Giannakopoulos' 86th-minute right-wing corner, before Davies secured the points by slamming home Diouf's ball in from the right as Tottenham were caught on the break.

Tuesday 1st February 2005	Venue: The Valley	Attendance: 27,102	Referee: N.S.Barry

PREMIERSHIP FIXTURE HISTORY

Pl: 6 Draws: 0	Wins	⚽	▯	▮
Charlton Athletic	3	7	7	0
Liverpool	3	10	8	2

STARTING LINE-UPS

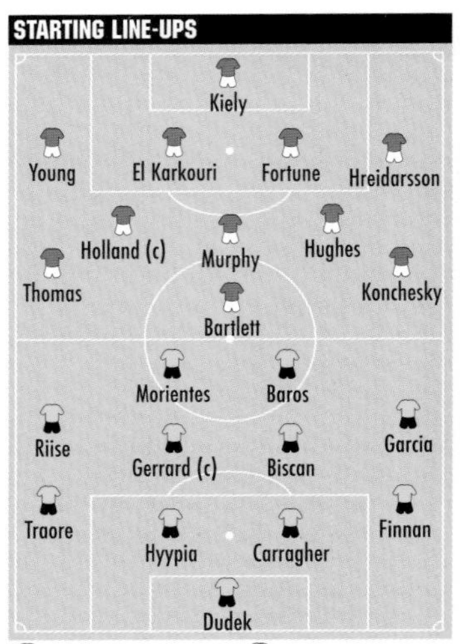

Kishishev, Euell, Jeffers, Andersen, Johansson

Smicer, Warnock, Potter, Carson, Pellegrino

EVENT LINE

20 ⚽ **Bartlett (Corner)**

HALF TIME 1 - 0

59 **Thomas (Off) Kishishev (On)**

61 ⚽ Morientes (Open Play)

66 **Hughes (Off) Euell (On)**

77 **Holland (Off) Jeffers (On)**

79 ⚽ Riise (Open Play)

88 Morientes (Off) Smicer (On)

90 Garcia (Off) Potter (On)

90 Riise (Off) Warnock (On)

FULL TIME 1 - 2

STATISTICS

Season	Fixture		Fixture	Season
115	3	Shots On Target	7	165
88	1	Shots Off Target	12	177
5	0	Hit Woodwork	2	5
86	8	Caught Offside	3	62
111	3	Corners	7	146
316	11	Fouls	15	299
45%	47%	Possession	53%	53%

LEAGUE STANDINGS

Position (pos before)		W	D	L	F	A	Pts
7 (7)	Charlton Ath	11	4	10	29	35	37
5 (5)	Liverpool	12	4	9	38	26	40

Jamie Carragher gets the better of Shaun Bartlett

> **"It was a big game for both sides, and I was disappointed that we didn't perform to our best."**
> Alan Curbishley

PREMIERSHIP MILESTONE

The attendance of 27,102 was a Premiership record at The Valley

> **"Our performance in the second half was at the level and mentality that we need to get us a Champions League spot."**
> Rafael Benitez

PREMIERSHIP MILESTONE

Fernando Morientes scored his first Premiership goal

PREMIERSHIP MILESTONE

Darren Potter made his Premiership debut

CHARLTON ATHLETIC 1 LIVERPOOL 2

Fernando Morientes struck for the first time in English football, as Liverpool recovered from going a goal down to record an important win at The Valley.

Both sides came into the match seven points adrift of fourth-placed Everton in the race for Champions League qualification. While Liverpool are expected to rub shoulders with Europe's elite, few would have predicted that Alan Curbishley's men would be in contention for such a prize at this stage of the season.

A record Premiership crowd at this ground of 27,102 recognised the significance of this fixture. The majority of those in attendance endured a nail-biting opening period, though it was Charlton who went in at half-time with an undeserved lead.

Rafael Benitez's visitors dominated from the first whistle, and should have gone in front early on. Dean Kiely did well to parry a shot from Luis Garcia, with Steven Gerrard then striking his follow-up effort down into the ground and away to safety off the crossbar.

The Liverpool captain was duly punished for his profligacy after 20 minutes, when former team-mate Danny Murphy sent over a right-wing corner that Shaun Bartlett met with a bullet header from six yards out.

Thereafter, the Merseysiders resumed control. Another fine save from Kiely kept Morientes at bay as the half drew to a close.

It was the same story after the break. John Arne Riise rattled the woodwork, before a goal arrived in spectacular fashion. With 61 minutes on the clock, Spaniard Morientes profited from determined work by Milan Baros to unleash a left-foot firecracker that fizzed into the net from just outside the area.

From this point on there was only ever going to be one winner, and the decisive strike arrived 11 minutes from time. Former Barcelona man Garcia benefitted from a lucky ricochet to feed Riise in the inside left channel, and the Norwegian international clinically slid the ball under Kiely from seven yards out.

With Everton not playing until Wednesday night, this Liverpool victory significantly turned up the heat on their city rivals.

PREMIERSHIP FIXTURE HISTORY

Pl: 2 Draws: 0

	Wins	Goals	Yellow	Red
Portsmouth	2	7	1	0
Middlesbrough	0	2	2	0

STARTING LINE-UPS

Skopelitis, Rodic, Ashdown, Curtis, Mezague

McMahon, Job, Graham, Nash, Doriva

EVENT LINE

29 Cooper (Off) McMahon (On)

35 Christie (Indirect Free Kick)

40 **Taylor (Open Play)**

HALF TIME 1 - 1

58 **Yakubu (Open Play)**

60 **Taylor (Foul)**

66 Christie (Off) Job (On)

73 **Fuller (Off) Skopelitis (On)**

80 McMahon (Off) Graham (On)

81 **Berger (Off) Rodic (On)**

90 Parlour (Foul)

90 Zenden (Ung.Conduct)

FULL TIME 2 - 1

STATISTICS

Season	Fixture		Fixture	Season
127	5	Shots On Target	2	175
128	9	Shots Off Target	7	144
3	0	Hit Woodwork	0	4
55	1	Caught Offside	1	66
132	9	Corners	5	145
298	9	Fouls	8	304
47%	54%	Possession	46%	50%

LEAGUE STANDINGS

Position (pos before)		W	D	L	F	A	Pts
12 (14)	Portsmouth	8	6	11	28	35	30
6 (6)	Middlesbrough	10	7	8	40	35	37

Tuesday 1st February 2005 | Venue: **Fratton Park** | Attendance: **19,620** | Referee: **P.Crossley**

PORTSMOUTH 2 MIDDLESBROUGH 1

Portsmouth recorded their first Premiership victory of 2005, to seriously dent Middlesbrough's prospects of Champions League football next season.

The South Coast side recovered from falling behind to a 35th-minute goal from long-term absentee Malcolm Christie, to turn things around through efforts from Matthew Taylor and Aiyegbeni Yakubu.

The inclusion of Christie in attack for the visitors surprised everyone. The striker had not featured in the Premiership for 15 months, but was preferred to Joseph-Desire Job as Jimmy Floyd Hasselbaink's partner.

Velimir Zajec handed a league debut to recent signing Konstantinos Chalkias in goal, and it was from a keeping error that Middlesbrough took the lead. A quick free-kick resulted in a low drive from Ray Parlour that the tall Greek custodian failed to hold, and Christie pounced to steer the ball home from just outside the six-yard box.

The advantage was short-lived, however, as former Luton man Taylor netted for the first time in the top-flight just five minutes later. Mark Schwarzer couldn't hold on to the full-back's initial drive from the left, and was promptly beaten by a right-footed effort as Aliou Cisse returned the ball to his team-mate.

A level scoreline was a fair reflection of the half, but Portsmouth stepped up a gear after the break.

Once Chalkias had raced from his line to deny Christie a second goal, the home side went in front. Just under an hour had elapsed when fancy footwork from Ricardo Fuller on the left of the area resulted in a dangerous low cross that was turned into the net by a combination of Yakubu and defender Franck Queudrue.

The Nigerian had been linked with a move to Teesside during the summer, but was happy to claim what proved to be the winner. To score was particularly sweet in light of the fact that he had seen very strong penalty appeals waved away during the opening period.

Despite strong showings from Parlour and Boudewijn Zenden in the centre of midfield, Steve McClaren's charges were largely restricted to hopeful efforts from distance during the remainder of the game.

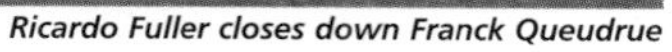

Ricardo Fuller closes down Franck Queudrue

"We're on 30 points with 13 games to go, and this result means that we can control our own destiny."

Joe Jordan

PREMIERSHIP MILESTONE

25 Aiyegbeni Yakubu netted his 25th Premiership goal

PREMIERSHIP MILESTONE

Konstantinos Chalkias, Giannis Skopelitis and Aleksandar Rodic all made their Premiership debuts

PREMIERSHIP MILESTONE

Matthew Taylor marked his 50th top-flight appearance with a first Premiership goal

"We didn't deserve to lose the game, but what we have to do now is remain upbeat."

Steve McClaren

PREMIERSHIP FIXTURE HISTORY

Pl: **1** Draws: **1**

	Wins	⚽	□	■
West Bromwich Albion	0	2	1	0
Crystal Palace	0	2	0	1

STARTING LINE-UPS

Earnshaw, Richardson, Kuszczak, Gaardsoe, Kanu

Powell, Riihilahti, Andrews, Speroni, Lakis

EVENT LINE

12 ■ Sorondo (Foul)

13 ⇄ Freedman (Off) Powell (On)

HALF TIME 0 - 0

47 ⚽ Johnson (Open Play)

55 ⇄ **Horsfield (Off) Earnshaw (On)**

72 ⇄ **Albrechtsen (Off) Richardson (On)**

82 ⚽ **Campbell (Open Play)**

85 □ **Gera (Foul)**

86 ⇄ Powell (Off) Riihilahti (On)

90 ⚽ **Earnshaw (Open Play)**

90 ⇄ Hughes (Off) Andrews (On)

90 ⚽ Riihilahti (Indirect Free Kick)

FULL TIME 2 - 2

STATISTICS

Season	Fixture (West Brom)		Fixture (Crystal Palace)	Season
113	**7**	Shots On Target	**4**	**106**
104	**5**	Shots Off Target	**0**	**101**
6	**2**	Hit Woodwork	**0**	**5**
92	**2**	Caught Offside	**0**	**61**
117	**10**	Corners	**4**	**124**
332	**17**	Fouls	**11**	**333**
46%	**66%**	Possession	**34%**	**47%**

LEAGUE STANDINGS

Position (pos before)	W	D	L	F	A	Pts
20 (20) West Brom	**2**	**11**	**12**	**21**	**46**	**17**
17 (17) Crystal Palace	**5**	**7**	**13**	**29**	**39**	**22**

Tuesday 1st February 2005 | Venue: **The Hawthorns** | Attendance: **25,092** | Referee: **D.J.Gallagher**

Andy Johnson celebrates yet another Premiership goal

"At the moment it feels like two points lost."

Assistant Manager Nigel Pearson

PREMIERSHIP MILESTONE

50 Robert Earnshaw netted West Brom's 50th Premiership goal

PREMIERSHIP MILESTONE

Kieran Richardson made his first Premiership appearance in the colours of West Brom

PREMIERSHIP MILESTONE

50 Darren Purse made his 50th Premiership appearance

"It was an heroic display by the players. They responded excellently to going down to ten men so early in the game."

Iain Dowie

WEST BROM 2 CRYSTAL PALACE 2

An incredible finish saw the spoils shared in this relegation battle at The Hawthorns.

The odds were stacked against Crystal Palace after Uruguayan Gonzalo Sorondo was harshly dismissed for a professional foul just 12 minutes into the contest. Whilst there was no doubt that Geoff Horsfield was upended, few neutrals would support the view that his was a 'clear goalscoring opportunity'.

Frontman Dougie Freedman was sacrificed as Iain Dowie reverted to a battling 4-4-1 formation. Unsurprisingly, West Brom began to dominate possession, though the opening period yielded few clear-cut chances.

That changed almost immediately after the restart, as Andy Johnson stole in to register his 15th Premiership goal of the season. The striker headed a bouncing ball over keeper Russell Hoult from just inside the area, following a terrible misjudgment from his former Birmingham colleague Darren Purse.

Having recovered from the initial shock of falling behind to ten men in such a crucial encounter, the Baggies began to play like a team that was in decent form. It wasn't until the final 10 minutes, however, that they made the breakthrough.

Darren Powell, the defender that had replaced Freedman early on, would have turned Zoltan Gera's dipping right-wing cross into his own net had it not been for the smart reactions of Gabor Kiraly. Unfortunately for the Hungarian, his intervention only delayed the inevitable as Kevin Campbell bundled home the loose ball.

There followed a barrage of home pressure, eventually resulting in what appeared to be a stoppage-time winner. Substitute Robert Earnshaw sprung the offside trap to clip Campbell's astute pass over Kiraly and spark mass celebrations.

Unbelievably, the Eagles somehow found time for an equaliser. Gary Borrowdale's lofted free-kick was nodded back by Emmerson Boyce and turned goalwards by a stretching Aki Riihilahti, with both Gera and Fitz Hall failing to make any sort of contact as the ball looped in.

In a run of the mill fixture this would have been dramatic, on this occasion it may be season changing.

PREMIERSHIP FIXTURE HISTORY

Pl: 3	Draws: 0	Wins	⚽	▢	■
Birmingham City		3	7	0	0
Southampton		0	4	5	1

STARTING LINE-UPS

Maik Taylor

Melchiot, Cunningham (c), Upson, Clapham

Pennant, Johnson, Clemence, Gray

Pandiani, Blake

Crouch

Van Damme, Delap, Redknapp, Prutton, Jones

Bernard, Davenport, Lundekvam (c), Telfer

Niemi

Carter, Tebily, Morrison, Vaesen, Nafti

Camara, A.Svensson, Smith, Jakobsson, Higginbotham

EVENT LINE

12 ⚽ **Pandiani (Open Play)**

41 ⚽ **Blake (Penalty)**

43 ▢ Prutton (Ung.Conduct)

HALF TIME 2 - 0

46 Jones (Off) Camara (On)

48 ▢ Bernard (Foul)

52 ⚽ Camara (Open Play)

69 Van Damme (Off) Svensson A (On)

77 **Pennant (Off) Carter (On)**

80 **Pandiani (Off) Tebily (On)**

90 **Blake (Off) Morrison (On)**

FULL TIME 2 - 1

STATISTICS

Season	Fixture			Fixture	Season
117	5	Shots On Target		3	115
106	7	Shots Off Target		3	128
5	0	Hit Woodwork		0	2
73	1	Caught Offside		4	67
129	8	Corners		1	121
350	11	Fouls		18	325
50%	56%	Possession		44%	47%

LEAGUE STANDINGS

Position (pos before)	W	D	L	F	A	Pts
14 (15) Birmingham C	7	8	10	29	31	29
18 (18) Southampton	3	9	13	26	41	18

Wednesday 2nd February 2005 | Venue: St Andrew's | Attendance: 28,797 | Referee: P.Walton

BIRMINGHAM CITY 2 SOUTHAMPTON 1

Rory Delap keeps Jermaine Pennant at bay

PREMIERSHIP MILESTONE

Jermaine Pennant made his first Premiership appearance for Birmingham

PREMIERSHIP MILESTONE

Walter Pandiani marked his Premiership debut with a goal

PREMIERSHIP MILESTONE

Robbie Blake netted his first Premiership goal in the colours of Birmingham

"The bit of hard work we had to put in to get Walter Pandiani certainly paid off."

Steve Bruce

PREMIERSHIP MILESTONE

Henri Camara marked his first Premiership appearance in the colours of Southampton with a first goal for the club

"We desperately need an away win from somewhere if we are going to get out of the bottom three."

Harry Redknapp

PREMIERSHIP MILESTONE

Olivier Bernard made his first Premiership appearance for Southampton

Southampton's plight worsened as Birmingham ended a run of four consecutive Premiership defeats with a narrow victory.

Several new faces were on show and it was one of them, Walter Pandiani, who opened the scoring after just 12 minutes. Fellow debutant Jermaine Pennant sent over a cross from the right, and the man signed on loan from Deportivo La Coruna powered home a header from six yards out.

Steve Bruce's team were well on top and might have gone further ahead after half-an-hour had it not been for Antti Niemi. The Finn was at full stretch to repel a long-range drive from Jamie Clapham, a save which kept the Saints in contention.

As the pressure increased on the Southampton goal, the manager's son gave away an indisputable penalty. Jamie Redknapp dived in rashly on Mario Melchiot, enabling Robbie Blake to convert his first goal for Birmingham just four minutes before half-time.

Peter Crouch had been an isolated figure in the opening period, but was joined by loan acquisition Henri Camara after the break. It took the Senegalese forward just seven minutes to make an impact, running onto his strike partner's header and unleashing a venomous left-footed half-volley high to the right of Maik Taylor.

Seeing their lead scythed in half clearly rocked the West Midlands side, and David Prutton spurned a great chance to completely shift the momentum of the match.

The introduction of defender Olivier Tebily in place of Pandiani with 10 minutes remaining emphasised Bruce's mindset, though the visitors were unable to conjure up the equaliser that seemed a distant dream at the interval.

Stephen Clemence had a chance to relieve the tension around St Andrew's in the closing stages, but he fired straight at Niemi from six yards. It didn't matter, however, as Birmingham maintained their advantage.

The defeat was a seventh in succession on their Premiership travels for Southampton. With tough home games against the top four still to come, survival amongst English football's elite may well depend on how Harry Redknapp's men fare on the road from here on in.

PREMIERSHIP FIXTURE HISTORY

Pl: 11 Draws: 2	Wins	⚽	▯	■
Blackburn Rovers	5	18	12	1
Chelsea	4	13	19	2

STARTING LINE-UPS

Reid, Enckelman, Amoruso, Tugay, Johnson

J.Cole, Jarosik, Kezman, Cudicini, Johnson

EVENT LINE

5 ⚽ Robben (Open Play)

11 Robben (Off) Cole J (On)

38 ▯ **Matteo (Foul)**

HALF TIME 0 - 1

57 ▯ Terry (Foul)

62 ▯ **Dickov (Foul)**

79 Cole J (Off) Jarosik (On)

81 **Thompson (Off) Reid (On)**

82 Gudjohnsen (Off) Kezman (On)

90 ▯ Kezman (Ung.Conduct)

FULL TIME 0 - 1

STATISTICS

Season	Fixture (Blackburn)		Fixture (Chelsea)	Season
126	2	Shots On Target	4	183
152	9	Shots Off Target	2	150
6	0	Hit Woodwork	0	8
92	4	Caught Offside	3	76
138	4	Corners	4	168
401	24	Fouls	15	312
49%	45%	Possession	55%	56%

LEAGUE STANDINGS

Position (pos before)	W	D	L	F	A	Pts
16 (16) Blackburn R	5	10	10	21	35	25
1 (1) Chelsea	20	4	1	49	8	64

Wednesday 2nd February 2005 | Venue: **Ewood Park** | Attendance: **23,414** | Referee: **U.D.Rennie**

BLACKBURN ROVERS 0 CHELSEA 1

It was a night of mixed fortunes for Chelsea at Ewood Park, with Arjen Robben netting the only goal of the game early on before limping off with a serious looking injury.

The Dutchman struck just five minutes into the contest, driving a low 12-yard effort past Brad Friedel from the inside left channel as the Londoners broke following a Blackburn attack. His night didn't last much longer, however, as a crunching challenge from Aaron Mokoena saw him depart the scene after just 11 minutes.

With a central midfield trio of Mokoena, Robbie Savage and David Thompson, Rovers allowed their visitors little time to settle on the ball. Consequently, Jose Mourinho's men were not at their best, relying more on dogged defending than brilliant attacking to secure the points.

Damien Duff, returning to his old stomping ground, forced Friedel into a smart stop, before Mark Hughes' men went close twice in the space of a minute. Firstly, captain Andy Todd headed wide, and then Savage was not far away from registering a first goal for his new club.

The former Birmingham midfielder then provided team-mate Paul Dickov with a great opportunity to level the scores from 12 yards. The Welsh international tumbled in the box under challenge from Paulo Ferreira, but Petr Cech saved the resultant 34th-minute spot-kick.

Against the West London side's water-tight defence, you are seldom afforded more than one decent chance to score. That proved to be the case in the second half, as Blackburn fought hard without ever really threatening.

Chelsea continued to play on the counter-attack after the break. Joe Cole and Frank Lampard each had a chance to seal the points, before Dickov failed with a glimmer of an opening in the dying embers of the game.

The 1-0 win represented an eighth consecutive Premiership victory for Mourinho's men and was celebrated by the manager ushering his team to throw their shirts into the away section of the crowd. Furthermore, the clean sheet saw Cech set a new Premiership record of 781 minutes without conceding a goal.

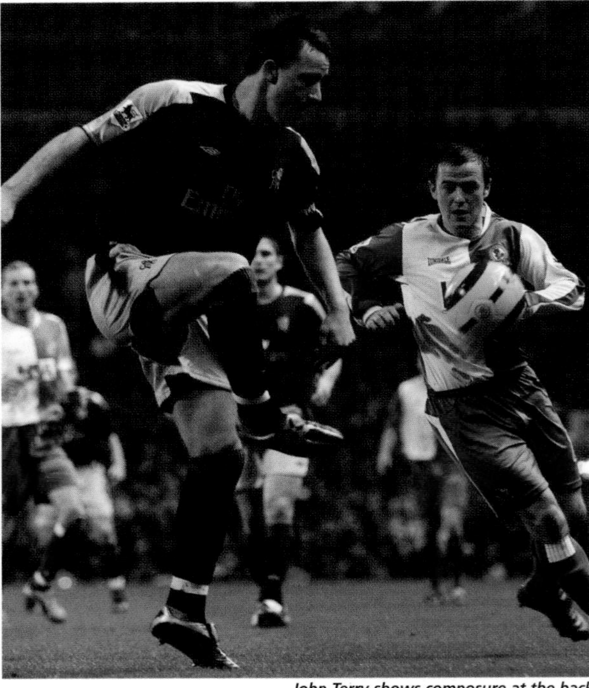
John Terry shows composure at the back

"It's always hard when you let a goal in that early on."
Mark Hughes

"We proved we are ready for a fight if necessary. We will play football, but we are not afraid to battle sometimes."
Jose Mourinho

PREMIERSHIP MILESTONE

Joe Cole made his 50th Premiership appearance for Chelsea

PREMIERSHIP FIXTURE HISTORY

Pl: 4 Draws: 0	Wins	⚽	▯	▮
Everton	2	4	4	0
Norwich City	2	7	3	0

STARTING LINE-UPS

Everton subs: Ferguson, Bent, Naysmith, Wright, Chadwick

Norwich City subs: Stuart, McKenzie, Gallacher, Shackell, McVeigh

EVENT LINE

HALF TIME 0 - 0

46 Drury (Off) Stuart (On)

64 **Weir (Off) Ferguson (On)**

76 **Beattie (Off) Bent (On)**

78 **Doherty (Own Goal)**

81 Jonson (Off) McKenzie (On)

86 **Hibbert (Foul)**

87 **McFadden (Off) Naysmith (On)**

FULL TIME 1 - 0

STATISTICS

Season	Fixture (Everton)		Fixture (Norwich)	Season
123	4	Shots On Target	6	115
139	14	Shots Off Target	5	134
6	0	Hit Woodwork	0	5
63	1	Caught Offside	7	83
122	3	Corners	3	122
288	12	Fouls	16	329
49%	51%	Possession	49%	46%

LEAGUE STANDINGS

Position (pos before)		W	D	L	F	A	Pts
4 (4)	Everton	14	5	6	29	25	47
19 (19)	Norwich C	2	11	12	23	47	17

Wednesday 2nd February 2005 | Venue: **Goodison Park** | Attendance: **37,485** | Referee: **A.G.Wiley**

EVERTON 1 NORWICH CITY 0

A game vital to both ends of the table was settled in Everton's favour by a Gary Doherty own goal 12 minutes from time.

The Merseysiders just about deserved their victory on a pudding of a playing surface at Goodison Park. Dropped points in this fixture would have provided a resurgent Liverpool with renewed hope of stealing up on their city rivals, so the relief around the ground was tangible as the ball found its way into the Norwich net.

David Moyes' men enjoyed the best of the openings during the first 45 minutes. Kevin Kilbane, a scorer at Carrow Road in October, blazed over after James Beattie had dummied a wonderful right-wing cross from James McFadden.

The young Scot was producing some of his best football since arriving at the club from Motherwell, and again delivered a dangerous centre that just evaded both Beattie and Tim Cahill.

At the other end, Darren Huckerby was the main source of danger. The sprightly forward almost beat Nigel Martyn to a weak Alessandro Pistone backpass, and then saw strong penalty appeals turned down after clashing with David Weir.

Little changed after the interval, with Everton in the ascendancy and Norwich looking dangerous on the break.

Transfer-window signing Graham Stuart was afforded a warm reception by all four sides of the ground as he came on for his Canaries debut at the start of the second period. The midfielder played a pivotal role in keeping the Toffees in the top-flight several years earlier, and will always be welcome in the blue half of the city.

Swedish international Mattias Jonson shot weakly at Martyn, whilst Beattie clipped the roof of the net with a 25-yard volley, as a goal began to look increasingly likely. To that end, Duncan Ferguson was introduced in place of David Weir after 64 minutes.

Having ruffled a few feathers, the big Scot was joined in attack by Marcus Bent. Within a couple of minutes the pair had combined to help win the game, Bent forcing Robert Green into a smart parry and Doherty poking the ball into his own net under intense pressure from Ferguson.

"Norwich worked very hard, but I felt we deserved the win."

Assistant Manager Alan Irvine

"We are all very disappointed. It was a tough game, and we were playing on the worst pitch we have seen all season."

Darren Huckerby

PREMIERSHIP MILESTONE

Graham Stuart made his first Premiership appearance for Norwich

Graham Stuart delivers from the left

PREMIERSHIP FIXTURE HISTORY

Pl: 4 Draws: 2	Wins	Goals	Yellow	Red
Fulham	1	4	5	1
Aston Villa	1	4	9	0

STARTING LINE-UPS

Fulham: van der Sar; Volz, Knight, Rehman, Rosenior; Diop, Clark (c), Pembridge, Radzinski, Boa Morte; Cole

Aston Villa: Cole, Angel; Hendrie, Hitzlsperger, Solano; Berson; Barry, Ridgewell, Mellberg (c), De la Cruz; Sorensen

Fulham subs: John, McBride, Crossley, Goma, Legwinski

Aston Villa subs: L.Moore, Davis, Djemba-Djemba, Postma, Laursen

EVENT LINE

32 Yellow card: De la Cruz (Foul)

HALF TIME 0 - 0

46 Substitution: Cole (Off) Moore L (On)

55 Goal: Angel (Corner)

64 Substitution: Hendrie (Off) Davis (On)

68 Substitution: **Radzinski (Off) John (On)**

73 Substitution: **Cole (Off) McBride (On)**

79 Substitution: Solano (Off) Djemba-Djemba (On)

85 Yellow card: **Boa Morte (Foul)**

90 Goal: **Clark (Open Play)**

90 Yellow card: Angel (Ung.Conduct)

90 Yellow card: Davis (Ung.Conduct)

FULL TIME 1 - 1

STATISTICS

Season	Fixture (Fulham)		Fixture (Aston Villa)	Season
121	5	Shots On Target	2	130
112	7	Shots Off Target	10	135
3	0	Hit Woodwork	0	3
61	2	Caught Offside	5	70
126	4	Corners	8	146
310	12	Fouls	17	380
48%	48%	Possession	52%	49%

LEAGUE STANDINGS

Position (pos before)	W	D	L	F	A	Pts
15 (14) Fulham	8	5	12	32	41	29
11 (11) Aston Villa	8	8	9	28	30	32

Wednesday 2nd February 2005 | Venue: **Craven Cottage** | Attendance: **17,624** | Referee: **C.J.Foy**

FULHAM 1 ASTON VILLA 1

Nolberto Solano is too strong for Lee Clark

"We've got a good result on a night when I didn't think it was going to happen for us."

Chris Coleman

"We have to look at this as a positive result, even though we missed two penalties."

Assistant Manager Roy Aitken

PREMIERSHIP MILESTONE

Eric Djemba-Djemba made his first Premiership appearance in the colours of Aston Villa

It was a tale of missed penalties at Craven Cottage, as Fulham and Aston Villa shared a 1-1 draw.

Colombian Juan Pablo Angel could have had a hat-trick, seeing two spot-kicks saved after he had put his team in front in the 55th minute. Former England striker Andy Cole had also missed with a penalty shortly after Angel's opener, but his captain Lee Clark staved off defeat with an injury-time leveller.

The game began at breakneck pace, and Tomasz Radzinski should have tested Thomas Sorensen more severely when presented with a chance inside the opening 30 seconds. Lee Hendrie then fired high and wide for the visitors, as neither side took a grip on proceedings.

A fluent move from the Cottagers deserved a goal, as Luis Boa Morte benefitted from Cole's dummy and exchanged passes with Clark. Unfortunately for the Portuguese international, Sorensen was on hand to repel his right-footed effort.

The remainder of the half offered little by way of noteworthy action. Everything changed soon after the interval, however, as the game exploded back into life.

A startling miss by Hendrie, side-footing Nolberto Solano's inviting cross over the bar, was quickly forgotten as Angel ended a personal goal drought stretching back nearly three months. The striker escaped his marker at the near post to glance Thomas Hitzlsperger's right-wing corner into the net from four yards out.

Shortly afterwards came the first of an incredible three penalty misses. Olof Mellberg was adjudged to have brought down Boa Morte by referee Chris Foy, but Cole dragged his 12-yard effort wide of the post.

As the match reached its final quarter, Angel was presented with an opportunity to seal the points. Moritz Volz was penalised for a challenge on Villa substitute Luke Moore inside the area, though Edwin van der Sar made a terrific save from the spot-kick.

An almost identical scenario played out within the next 10 minutes, Moore winning a penalty, this time after a tackle from Liam Rosenior, and van der Sar denying Angel.

With time almost up, the Colombian was made to feel even worse. A deflected Boa Morte drive reared up in the box, and Clark arrived on cue to drill a 15-yard effort into the bottom right-hand corner of the net.

PREMIERSHIP FIXTURE HISTORY

Pl: 7 Draws: 3	Wins	Goals	Yellow cards	Red cards
Manchester City	3	8	8	0
Newcastle United	1	6	11	0

STARTING LINE-UPS

Manchester City subs: Weaver, Onuoha, Jordan, McManaman, B.Wright-Phillips

Newcastle United subs: Butt, Kluivert, Harper, Hughes, Robert

EVENT LINE

9 Goal Shearer (Open Play)

38 Yellow card Jenas (Foul)

HALF TIME 0 - 1

49 Goal **Fowler (Penalty)**

55 Yellow card Bowyer (Ung.Conduct)

56 Yellow card **Distin (Ung.Conduct)**

63 Substitution Dyer (Off) Butt (On)

65 Substitution Ameobi (Off) Kluivert (On)

71 Yellow card O'Brien (Foul)

83 Yellow card **Bosvelt (Foul)**

84 Substitution **Macken (Off) Wright-Phillips B (On)**

FULL TIME 1 - 1

STATISTICS

Season	Fixture (Man City)		Fixture (Newcastle)	Season
141	2	Shots On Target	1	173
124	3	Shots Off Target	2	138
2	0	Hit Woodwork	0	9
76	3	Caught Offside	5	66
159	3	Corners	1	168
325	11	Fouls	18	313
49%	59%	Possession	41%	50%

LEAGUE STANDINGS

Position (pos before)	W	D	L	F	A	Pts
10 (10) Man City	8	8	9	31	27	32
12 (13) Newcastle Utd	7	9	9	36	42	30

Alan Shearer goes in hard on Ben Thatcher

"But for two serious injuries, Alan Shearer would probably be nearer to 300 Premiership goals."
Kevin Keegan

PREMIERSHIP MILESTONE
Kiki Musampa made his Premiership debut

"I think Alan Shearer is the greatest English centre-forward we've ever seen."
Graeme Souness

PREMIERSHIP MILESTONE
250 Alan Shearer became the first player to net 250 Premiership goals with his ninth-minute strike

PREMIERSHIP MILESTONE
Amdy Faye made his first Premiership appearance for Newcastle

MANCHESTER CITY 1 NEWCASTLE UNITED 1

Alan Shearer became the first man to net 250 Premiership goals, though his ninth-minute strike was not enough to see off Manchester City.

Each side fielded a debutant in their starting XI, Kevin Keegan employing Kiki Musampa on the left of midfield and Graeme Souness parking Amdy Faye in front of his fragile back-four.

After a quiet opening, it was the Magpies that went in front. Much-maligned defender Titus Bramble drilled a glorious pass the length of the field, and Shearer chested the ball beyond Ben Thatcher in the inside right channel before hammering home from 10 yards out.

With Nicolas Anelka sold to Fenerbahce only days earlier, City lacked any real pace through the middle. Shaun Wright-Phillips was the focal point for most of their attacks, but it was in bizarre circumstances that an equaliser nearly arrived.

Recent capture Celestine Babayaro seemed to have coped with a potentially dangerous situation as he played the ball back to Shay Given. The Irish keeper missed his kick, however, and had to make a quick recovery.

It took the men from Manchester just four minutes to draw level after the break. Robbie Fowler stepped up to convert from the spot after Bramble had turned from hero, for his part in Shearer's opener, to villain. The defender made a clumsy challenge on Wright-Phillips, and was very lucky not to be shown a card of either colour by referee Andy D'Urso.

The goals apart, there was only one other shot on target during the entire 90 minutes. This was in stark contrast to the league meeting earlier in the season at St James' Park, when Newcastle triumphed 4-3 in an action-packed second period.

Though the game itself won't live long in the memory, Shearer's landmark strike certainly will. The aging master demonstrated his craft to perfection, and it is hard to see how Souness' side will manage without him next season.

The draw left both teams in mid-table, justifiable positions on the evidence of this encounter.

PREMIERSHIP FIXTURE HISTORY

Pl: **13** Draws: **5**

	Wins	Goals	Yellow cards	Red cards
Aston Villa	3	13	21	1
Arsenal	5	20	24	1

STARTING LINE-UPS

Sorensen

De la Cruz, Mellberg (c), Ridgewell, Samuel

Solano, Davis, Djemba-Djemba, Barry

Angel, L.Moore

Henry, Bergkamp

Reyes, Edu, Vieira (c), Ljungberg

Cole, Cygan, Senderos, Lauren

Lehmann

Substitutes (Aston Villa): Hitzlsperger, Berson, Postma, Laursen, Cole

Substitutes (Arsenal): Flamini, Pires, Fabregas, Almunia, Hoyte

EVENT LINE

10 ⚽ Ljungberg (Open Play)

14 ⚽ Henry (Open Play)

28 ⚽ Cole (Open Play)

HALF TIME 0 - 3

53 ▢ **Samuel (Foul)**

60 ▢ **Djemba-Djemba (Ung.Conduct)**

62 ⇄ **Samuel (Off) Hitzlsperger (On)**

66 ⇄ **Djemba-Djemba (Off) Berson (On)**

74 ⚽ **Angel (Open Play)**

74 ⇄ Bergkamp (Off) Pires (On)

74 ⇄ Edu (Off) Flamini (On)

82 ⇄ Reyes (Off) Fabregas (On)

FULL TIME 1 - 3

STATISTICS

Season	Fixture (Aston Villa)		Fixture (Arsenal)	Season
131	1	Shots On Target	6	196
139	4	Shots Off Target	9	124
3	0	Hit Woodwork	2	11
78	8	Caught Offside	4	58
151	5	Corners	2	153
393	13	Fouls	11	310
49%	46%	Possession	54%	56%

LEAGUE STANDINGS

Position (pos before)		W	D	L	F	A	Pts
11 (11)	Aston Villa	8	8	10	29	33	32
3 (3)	Arsenal	16	6	4	58	30	54

Saturday 5th February 2005 | Venue: **Villa Park** | Attendance: **42,593** | Referee: **S.G.Bennett**

ASTON VILLA 1 ARSENAL 3

Thierry Henry scored for the first time since Boxing Day as Arsenal destroyed Aston Villa in a pulsating opening half-hour.

The Frenchman's goal came in between strikes from Freddie Ljungberg and Ashley Cole, with Juan Pablo Angel restoring some pride via a 74th-minute consolation.

Many observers thought Arsenal might crumble in the wake of their home defeat to Manchester United in midweek, yet they responded to that massive disappointment in the manner of champions.

After Henry had blazed over from Dennis Bergkamp's astute pass, Ljungberg continued his fine recent run of goalscoring form. The Swedish international clipped a 10-yard effort over Thomas Sorensen and into the bottom right-hand corner with his left foot, after latching onto the recalled Edu's neat throughball.

The Gunners' Brazilian midfielder then struck the woodwork, with Henry unable to convert the rebound, as the Highbury side layed siege to the Villa goal. Then, with 14 minutes played, Henry was not so profligate, netting in very similar fashion to Ljungberg after Vieira had won possession and found him in space.

With David O'Leary's side being run ragged, Arsenal added a majestic third. The ball was switched from right to left before Bergkamp supplied Cole with a perfectly-weighted first-time pass, enabling the full-back to hammer home across Sorensen without breaking stride.

The England international was at the centre of rumours suggesting that Chelsea had made an illegal approach for his services, but was clearly unaffected by the controversy.

With half-an-hour gone and the game won, Arsene Wenger's men took their foot off the accelerator. Despite this visible relaxation, it wasn't until 16 minutes from time that makeshift centre-back pairing of Pascal Cygan and Philippe Senderos were exposed.

In their only move of genuine quality throughout the entire game, three South Americans linked up brightly down the right. Peruvian Nolberto Solano fed Ecuadorian Ulises De la Cruz, who in turn supplied Colombian Angel for a crisp near-post finish from seven yards out.

There was still time for the visitors to hit a post, as the game ended with Arsenal stroking the ball effortlessly around Villa Park.

Thierry Henry savours the end of his goal-drought

"The only thing we can take out of the game is our second half performance."

David O'Leary

"I feel the game was a big mental test, and it proved that we are a very good team to come back after the Manchester United defeat."

Arsene Wenger

PREMIERSHIP FIXTURE HISTORY

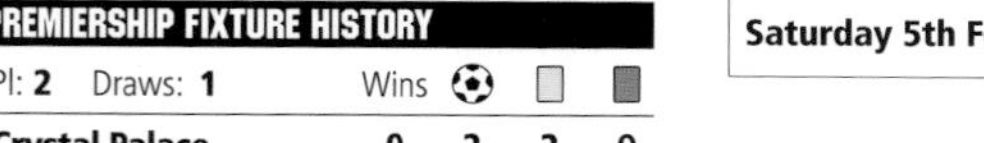

Pl: **2** Draws: **1**	Wins	Goals	Yellow	Red
Crystal Palace	0	2	2	0
Bolton Wanderers	1	3	4	0

STARTING LINE-UPS

Crystal Palace subs: Kolkka, Riihilahti, Andrews, Speroni, Borrowdale

Bolton Wanderers subs: Hierro, Pedersen, Jaidi, Poole, Fadiga

EVENT LINE

31 ⚽ Nolan (Open Play)

45 ▢ Giannakopoulos (Foul)

HALF TIME 0 - 1

59 **Routledge (Off) Kolkka (On)**

64 **Leigertwood (Off) Riihilahti (On)**

64 Campo (Off) Hierro (On)

76 Giannakopoulos (Off) Pedersen (On)

88 **Soares (Off) Andrews (On)**

90 Diouf (Off) Jaidi (On)

FULL TIME 0 - 1

STATISTICS

Season	Fixture (Crystal Palace)		Fixture (Bolton)	Season
113	**7**	Shots On Target	**6**	**161**
111	**10**	Shots Off Target	**3**	**147**
5	**0**	Hit Woodwork	**0**	**5**
64	**3**	Caught Offside	**2**	**62**
130	**6**	Corners	**4**	**139**
349	**16**	Fouls	**10**	**348**
47%	**56%**	Possession	**44%**	**49%**

LEAGUE STANDINGS

Position (pos before)	W	D	L	F	A	Pts
17 (17) Crystal Palace	**5**	**7**	**14**	**29**	**40**	**22**
7 (8) Bolton W	**11**	**6**	**9**	**35**	**32**	**39**

Saturday 5th February 2005	Venue: **Selhurst Park**	Attendance: **23,163**	Referee: **G.Poll**

CRYSTAL PALACE 0 BOLTON WANDERERS 1

Kevin Nolan celebrates his winning goal

"We couldn't create that many chances again and lose."

Iain Dowie

"December was a nightmare, but our good fortune in January and February has seen us go on and on."

Sam Allardyce

Despite a strong showing, Crystal Palace fell to a single-goal defeat at the hands of a resurgent Bolton Wanderers.

Midfielder Kevin Nolan was the match-winner, hooking the ball narrowly over the line from four yards out just after the half-hour mark. Stylianos Giannakopoulos had been denied by Gabor Kiraly, but the Liverpool-born youngster was alert enough to steal in and make it 1-0.

While the home players protested that the whole of the ball had not crossed the line prior to being cleared, television replays showed that the referee's assistant had made the correct decision.

Before falling behind, the Eagles had spurned two great opportunities. Wayne Routledge failed to outwit Jussi Jaaskelainen when running clear in the inside right channel, and Andy Johnson then struck the side-netting when well-placed.

It was the same story after the break, as clear-cut chances came and went for Iain Dowie's men.

Dougie Freedman was at the heart of most of Palace's good work, and conjured up a great chance for his strike partner Johnson. The Scottish forward skipped past a few challenges down the left, before delivering a low near-post cross that was somehow steered wide from inside the six-yard box.

A similar move developed later in the half, but this time Freedman pulled a shot right across the face of goal. Kevin Davies then fired straight at Kiraly on a rare Bolton breakaway, as time began to run out.

Teams fighting relegation need all the luck they can get. Unfortunately for the men in red and blue, they had little of it as this game drew to a close.

A left-wing corner was headed on at the near post, but dropped a yard behind the swinging boot of Freedman. Then, with what proved to be the last chance of the contest, Danny Granville blazed over from close range as the ball fell to his unfavoured right foot in a crowded penalty area.

Defeat was harsh on Dowie's side, though effort and commitment alone will not get them out of trouble.

PREMIERSHIP FIXTURE HISTORY

Pl: 4 Draws: 2	Wins	Goals	Yellow	Red
Liverpool	2	5	2	0
Fulham	0	1	9	0

STARTING LINE-UPS

Liverpool subs: Hamann, Smicer, Warnock, Carson, Pellegrino

Fulham subs: Goma, Crossley, Legwinski, Jensen, McBride

EVENT LINE

9 ⚽ **Morientes (Open Play)**

16 ⚽ Cole (Open Play)

26 ▯ Rehman (Foul)

HALF TIME 1 - 1

52 ▯ Diop (Foul)

63 ⚽ **Hyypia (Indirect Free Kick)**

65 ⇄ **Biscan (Off) Hamann (On)**

69 ▯ Pembridge (Ung.Conduct)

74 ▯ **Garcia (Foul)**

77 ⚽ **Baros (Open Play)**

78 ▯ van der Sar (Dissent)

82 ⇄ **Baros (Off) Smicer (On)**

89 ⇄ **Riise (Off) Warnock (On)**

FULL TIME 3 - 1

STATISTICS

Season	Fixture (Liverpool)		Fixture (Fulham)	Season
172	7	Shots On Target	2	123
180	3	Shots Off Target	4	116
5	0	Hit Woodwork	0	3
63	1	Caught Offside	2	63
150	4	Corners	3	129
311	12	Fouls	13	323
54%	60%	Possession	40%	48%

LEAGUE STANDINGS

Position (pos before)		W	D	L	F	A	Pts
5 (5)	Liverpool	13	4	9	41	27	43
15 (15)	Fulham	8	5	13	33	44	29

Saturday 5th February 2005 | Venue: **Anfield** | Attendance: **43,534** | Referee: **R.Styles**

LIVERPOOL 3 FULHAM 1

Liverpool heaped further pressure on their Merseyside rivals in the chase for Champions League football, defeating a spirited Fulham side 3-1 at Anfield.

A first goal at his new home from Fernando Morientes was soon cancelled out by Andy Cole, before second half efforts from Sami Hyypia and Milan Baros secured the three points for Rafael Benitez's team.

The men in red went in front after just nine minutes, as two Spaniards combined to deadly effect. Luis Garcia sent over an inviting cross from the right, and Morientes lost his marker to angle a perfect header past a static Edwin van der Sar from 10 yards out.

Home joy was short-lived, however, as Chris Coleman's side drew level seven minutes later. Mark Pembridge won possession and fed Luis Boa Morte down the left, with the former Arsenal winger then producing an accurate ball to the back post that a diving Cole headed beyond Jerzy Dudek.

After former Evertonian Tomasz Radzinski had sent a header narrowly wide, great skill from Morientes down the left eventually resulted in a venomous low drive from Igor Biscan that was well kept out by the Cottagers' giant Dutch keeper.

The game continued to be evenly-contested after the interval. John Arne Riise linked up well with Baros on one occasion, while the pace of Boa Morte was a constant threat for the visitors.

Whichever team scored the next goal would have a great chance to win, and it was Liverpool that got it. Steven Gerrard's vicious inswinging free-kick from the left was glanced home by an unmarked Hyypia in the 63rd minute.

Thereafter, the Reds assumed total control. Substitute Dietmar Hamann stung the palms of van der Sar, before Baros slammed the ball home from eight yards after Morientes had released Riise on the left.

The Czech striker was afforded a rapturous reception when he was replaced by his international colleague Vladimir Smicer five minutes later, the home fans fully appreciating the hard work he had put in for the cause.

"We knew that Fernando Morientes would be a good target man for us."
Rafael Benitez

PREMIERSHIP MILESTONE
800 Milan Baros netted Liverpool's 800th Premiership goal.

"You can't afford to nod off and lose your men like we did three times against a good side like Liverpool."
Chris Coleman

PREMIERSHIP MILESTONE
175 Andy Cole scored his 175th Premiership goal

PREMIERSHIP MILESTONE
150 Lee Clark made his 150th Premiership appearance on his 50th top-flight outing for Fulham

Sami Hyypia re-establishes the lead

PREMIERSHIP FIXTURE HISTORY

Pl: 3 Draws: 0	Wins	⚽	Yellow	Red
Manchester United	3	7	2	0
Birmingham City	0	0	6	1

STARTING LINE-UPS

Manchester United substitutes: Fortune, P.Neville, Miller, Howard, Bellion

Birmingham City substitutes: Carter, Morrison, Tebily, Vaesen, Kuqi

EVENT LINE

45 Johnson (Foul)

HALF TIME 0 - 0

55 **Keane (Open Play)**

65 Nafti (Handball)

68 **Saha (Off) Fortune (On)**

72 Blake (Off) Morrison (On)

72 Nafti (Off) Carter (On)

78 **Rooney (Open Play)**

81 Taylor Martin (Off) Tebily (On)

82 **Giggs (Off) Neville P (On)**

82 **Rooney (Off) Miller (On)**

86 **Heinze (Foul)**

90 Pennant (Foul)

FULL TIME 2 - 0

STATISTICS

Season	Fixture (Man Utd)		Fixture (Birmingham)	Season
215	11	Shots On Target	1	118
185	6	Shots Off Target	6	112
13	0	Hit Woodwork	1	6
98	3	Caught Offside	1	74
202	5	Corners	2	131
316	10	Fouls	16	366
55%	56%	Possession	44%	50%

LEAGUE STANDINGS

Position (pos before)		W	D	L	F	A	Pts
2 (2)	Man Utd	16	8	2	43	16	56
14 (14)	Birmingham C	7	8	11	29	33	29

Saturday 5th February 2005 | Venue: **Old Trafford** | Attendance: **67,838** | Referee: **D.J.Gallagher**

Roy Keane leads by example

"In 30 years time, or if this club is still going in 500 years, he will still be one of its greatest ever players."
Sir Alex Ferguson on Roy Keane

"When United needed a piece of inspiration, Roy Keane gave it to them."
Steve Bruce

PREMIERSHIP MILESTONE

Mehdi Nafti made his Premiership debut

PREMIERSHIP MILESTONE

50 Olivier Tebily and Jermaine Pennant both made their 50th Premiership appearance

MANCHESTER UNITED 2 BIRMINGHAM CITY 0

A moment of inspiration from captain Roy Keane set Manchester United on their way to an important 2-0 victory against Birmingham City.

The Red Devils had not been at their best, surviving two major scares, until Keane demonstrated his importance to the side in the 55th minute. Collecting possession courtesy of a Cristiano Ronaldo backheel, the midfielder surged into the box and unleashed a rapier-like drive through the legs of a defender and into the bottom left-hand corner of the net.

From then on the result was in little doubt, and Wayne Rooney sealed the win 12 minutes from time with a deft lob over Maik Taylor after the keeper had initially done well to prevent Ronaldo cashing in on an underhit Kenny Cunningham backpass.

Sir Alex Ferguson's men had enjoyed the better of the first half, without ever really getting anywhere near top gear. An eighth-minute free-kick forced an agile stop from the Birmingham custodian, before Walter Pandiani fired a warning shot from distance for the visitors.

Further chances were spurned by Rooney and Ryan Giggs, and they were inches away from being made to pay for their misses. Uruguayan Pandiani struck a right-footed volley as cleanly as you are ever likely to see, yet the ball struck the underside of the crossbar and somehow stayed out.

If they were unlucky on this occasion, then Steve Bruce's side were wasteful with their other major opening. With the scores locked at 0-0 just after half-time, Julian Gray burst into the box on the left but produced an attempt that seemed somewhere between a cross and a shot.

A deep delivery from Ronaldo almost caught out Taylor in the Birmingham goal, before Keane came up with his vital strike.

The introduction of Quinton Fortune in place of Louis Saha after 68 minutes enabled Rooney to move into the central striking role. The England international almost netted with a ferocious drive from the right side of the area, but was soon able to profit from Cunningham's lapse in concentration.

PREMIERSHIP FIXTURE HISTORY

Pl: 8 Draws: 0	Wins	⚽	Yellow	Red
Middlesbrough	6	12	13	2
Blackburn Rovers	2	8	18	0

STARTING LINE-UPS

Schwarzer
Parnaby, Reiziger, Southgate (c), Queudrue
Morrison, Parlour, Zenden, Downing
Christie, Job
Dickov
Pedersen, Thompson, Mokoena, Savage, Emerton
Matteo, Nelson, Todd (c), Neill
Friedel

Graham, Doriva, Bates, Nash, McMahon

Johnson, Enckelman, Johansson, Flitcroft, Reid

EVENT LINE

13 Mokoena (Foul)

35 **Queudrue (Open Play)**

HALF TIME 1 - 0

49 Matteo (Foul)

60 Mokoena (Off) Johnson (On)

69 **Christie (Off) Graham (On)**

73 **Job (Off) Doriva (On)**

78 Thompson (Off) Reid (On)

89 **Parlour (2nd Bookable Offence)**

90 **Morrison (Off) Bates (On)**

FULL TIME 1 - 0

STATISTICS

Season	Fixture		Fixture	Season
182	7	Shots On Target	3	129
150	6	Shots Off Target	3	155
5	1	Hit Woodwork	0	6
68	2	Caught Offside	7	99
153	8	Corners	10	148
318	14	Fouls	10	411
50%	51%	Possession	49%	49%

LEAGUE STANDINGS

Position (pos before)		W	D	L	F	A	Pts
6 (6)	Middlesbrough	11	7	8	41	35	40
16 (16)	Blackburn R	5	10	11	21	36	25

Saturday 5th February 2005 | Venue: **Riverside Stadium** | Attendance: **30,564** | Referee: **M.A.Riley**

MIDDLESBROUGH 1 BLACKBURN ROVERS 0

An uninspiring game at the Riverside was settled by a 35th-minute goal from full-back Franck Queudrue.

The Frenchman ran on to Stewart Downing's neat pass and cut in from the left, before firing a right-footed effort across Brad Friedel and into the far corner of the net. The former Lens man was developing a taste for scoring, having hit the target twice in the recent 4-4 draw at Norwich.

Steve McClaren was without Jimmy Floyd Hasselbaink, scorer of a hat-trick in his side's 4-0 win at Ewood Park back in October. No fewer than six Academy graduates were named in the Middlesbrough squad, with James Morrison and Stuart Parnaby joining Downing in the starting XI.

Mark Hughes had fewer selection headaches, opting for the same shape and personnel that had competed so well against Chelsea in midweek. That meant Paul Dickov again operating as a lone front runner, in a system that the manager had previously employed so successfully at international level.

After Ray Parlour had collected an early booking for a late challenge on Robbie Savage, the Teesside club began to take control. New-look strikeforce Joseph-Desire Job and Malcolm Christie combined for the former Derby man to head home, only for the effort to be correctly ruled out for offside.

A right-footed Downing effort then hit the side-netting, before Morrison showed a lack of experience when firing straight at Friedel from an acute angle with Christie unmarked in the centre.

Blackburn were woeful in the first half, but improved significantly after the break. Mark Schwarzer was called upon to turn over a Dickov header, before the striker was joined in attack by American youngster Jemal Johnson.

A sturdy challenge by Michael Reiziger could easily have resulted in a Rovers penalty, but referee Mike Riley waved away Dickov's strong appeal.

The official is well known for handing out spot-kicks and red cards like confetti, and there was still time for him to dismiss Ray Parlour. With just a minute remaining, the former Arsenal midfielder received a second yellow card for kicking the ball away in frustration, as a decision went against him.

"With Stewart Downing on the left and James Morrison on the right, we were back to the days of two wingers."
Steve McClaren

PREMIERSHIP MILESTONE
100 Boudewijn Zenden made his 100th Premiership appearance

"We are struggling for goals and it needs someone to step forward and take command of that particular situation."
Mark Hughes

Franck Queudrue enjoys his moment of glory

PREMIERSHIP FIXTURE HISTORY

Pl: 6 Draws: 2	Wins	Goals	Yellow	Red
Newcastle United	3	9	6	0
Charlton Athletic	1	4	11	1

STARTING LINE-UPS

Kluivert, Robert, Harper, Hughes, Butt

Lisbie, Euell, Andersen, Sam, Johansson

EVENT LINE

30 Faye (Foul)

HALF TIME 0 - 0

52 **Dyer (Open Play)**

53 Rommedahl (Open Play)

69 **Ameobi (Off) Kluivert (On)**

70 **Bowyer (Off) Robert (On)**

84 Rommedahl (Off) Lisbie (On)

89 Konchesky (Foul)

90 Murphy (Off) Euell (On)

FULL TIME 1 - 1

STATISTICS

Season	Fixture		Fixture	Season
183	10	Shots On Target	2	117
149	11	Shots Off Target	6	94
10	1	Hit Woodwork	0	5
67	1	Caught Offside	2	88
175	7	Corners	2	113
322	9	Fouls	12	328
50%	59%	Possession	41%	45%

LEAGUE STANDINGS

Position (pos before)	W	D	L	F	A	Pts
12 (12) Newcastle Utd	7	10	9	37	43	31
8 (7) Charlton Ath	11	5	10	30	36	38

Saturday 5th February 2005 | Venue: St James' Park | Attendance: 51,114 | Referee: M.R.Halsey

NEWCASTLE UNITED 1 CHARLTON ATHLETIC 1

Jermaine Jenas tries to stop Shaun Bartlett

"What concerns me is that we cannot win 1-0. If we could, we would be sitting pretty."

Graeme Souness

PREMIERSHIP MILESTONE

100 Shaun Bartlett made his 100th Premiership appearance

"This was a great point for us. We defended fantastically and also had some decent chances."

Alan Curbishley

A crazy 60 seconds of action saw a goal at both ends, as Charlton came from behind to earn a valuable point.

Having endured a frustrating first half, Kieron Dyer's 52nd-minute opener appeared to pave the way for a much-needed Newcastle victory, only for Danish winger Dennis Rommedahl to re-establish parity almost immediately.

The Addicks had often struggled away from home this season, and were put on the back foot right from the start. Dean Kiely smuggled a sixth-minute Alan Shearer shot around the post, before having to touch over a surprise 30-yard drive from centre-back Andy O'Brien.

Further saves were needed to keep out efforts from Shearer and Lee Bowyer, before Danny Murphy fired well wide on a rare foray forward from the visitors.

There was a palpable sense of frustration around St James' Park as the second period got underway. This soon evaporated, however, when Dyer netted from 12 yards. The midfielder arrived on cue to send a deflected effort into the bottom left-hand corner of the net, after Chris Perry had failed to deal with Shearer's header back across goal.

Then, just as Graeme Souness began to think that his side might be on course for a victory, Charlton replied. A loose ball on the left was seized upon by Rommedahl, and within seconds a crisp 20-yard drive was flying into Shay Given's net via the inside of the right-hand upright.

The strike was the Londoners' first on target, though from then on they became a much more prominent attacking force. A tricky run from Rommedahl ended with a low shot that skidded past the left post, before Given then denied the former PSV Eindhoven man with his legs.

Captain Matt Holland and full-back Luke Young both spurned chances to win the game, with Shearer and substitute Patrick Kluivert then unable to cash in on a late goalmouth scramble at the other end.

The final whistle was greeted with derision by a Newcastle public not content with a mid-table position.

Saturday 5th February 2005 | Venue: **Carrow Road** | Attendance: **24,292** | Referee: **C.J.Foy**

PREMIERSHIP FIXTURE HISTORY

Pl: **1** Draws: **0**	Wins	⚽	▢	■
Norwich City	**1**	**3**	**0**	**0**
West Bromwich Albion	**0**	**2**	**3**	**0**

STARTING LINE-UPS

Green
Edworthy, Fleming (c), Doherty, Charlton
Stuart, Francis, Holt
McKenzie, Huckerby
Ashton

Earnshaw, Campbell
Greening, Wallwork, Richardson, Gera
Robinson, Clement, Purse (c), Scimeca
Hoult

Brennan, McVeigh, Gallacher, Safri, Jonson

Horsfield, Kuszczak, Gaardsoe, Chaplow, Kanu

EVENT LINE

41 ⚽ Earnshaw (Open Play)
45 ⚽ **Fleming (Corner)**
45 ▢ Scimeca (Foul)

HALF TIME 1 - 1

46 ⇄ **Charlton (Off) Brennan (On)**
49 ⚽ Richardson (Open Play)
62 ▢ Robinson (Foul)
62 ⚽ **Doherty (Indirect Free Kick)**
68 ⇄ **Stuart (Off) McVeigh (On)**
84 ▢ Greening (Dissent)
85 ⚽ **Francis (Open Play)**
89 ⇄ Greening (Off) Horsfield (On)

FULL TIME 3 - 2

STATISTICS

Season	Fixture		Fixture	Season
122	**7**	Shots On Target	**8**	**121**
140	**6**	Shots Off Target	**7**	**111**
5	**0**	Hit Woodwork	**2**	**8**
84	**1**	Caught Offside	**1**	**93**
125	**3**	Corners	**3**	**120**
346	**17**	Fouls	**14**	**346**
46%	**45%**	Possession	**55%**	**47%**

LEAGUE STANDINGS

Position (pos before)	W	D	L	F	A	Pts
18 (19) Norwich C	**3**	**11**	**12**	**26**	**49**	**20**
20 (20) West Brom	**2**	**11**	**13**	**23**	**49**	**17**

NORWICH CITY 3 WEST BROM 2

Despite twice trailing, it was Norwich who triumphed in this vital battle of the bottom two at Carrow Road.

A recent improvement in form had seen West Brom draw level with their hosts on 17 points prior to kick-off. Conversely, the Canaries had picked up just two points from their last eight matches, and were in desperate need of rediscovering that winning feeling.

Nigel Worthington fielded three forwards in an attack-minded line-up, while Bryan Robson opted to start with Robert Earnshaw in preference to Geoff Horsfield as Kevin Campbell's strike partner.

The Welsh international tested Robert Green after just three minutes, with Dean Ashton then calling Russell Hoult into action at the other end. The home side continued to carve out an array of half-chances, Darren Huckerby and Ashton guilty of several disappointing finishes, but it was the Baggies that went in front.

The normally-reliable Green gifted possession to Jonathan Greening with a poor 41st-minute clearance, and the midfielder played in Earnshaw for a smart left-foot finish through the keeper's legs. The former Cardiff frontman had already rattled the crossbar, while assistor Greening had struck a post.

An interval lead seemed inevitable until captain Craig Fleming levelled matters with a looping header from Graham Stuart's right-wing corner. The effort should have been saved, but Hoult seemed more concerned with claiming a foul than with keeping the ball out.

Seemingly unfazed by the disappointment, West Brom went back in front four minutes after the restart. On-loan midfielder Kieran Richardson needed two attempts to turn Earnshaw's clipped delivery into the net, thus re-establishing a vital lead.

If Fleming's header had been preventable, then Gary Doherty's certainly was. With 62 minutes on the clock, the former Tottenham man rose unchallenged to guide Huckerby's cross from the left into the bottom right-hand corner.

From then on the visitors looked the more likely scorers, with Green called upon to make smart saves from both Greening and Campbell. The Canaries stole the points, however, when Damien Francis rifled a 19-yard drive past the despairing right hand of Hoult from Fleming's cushioned 85th-minute knockdown.

"This was a huge game, hard-fought with some good football."
Nigel Worthington

PREMIERSHIP MILESTONE

Both Craig Fleming and Kieran Richardson netted their first Premiership goal

"We are very disappointed because for long periods we outplayed Norwich."
Bryan Robson

PREMIERSHIP MILESTONE

50 Paul Robinson made his 50th Premiership appearance

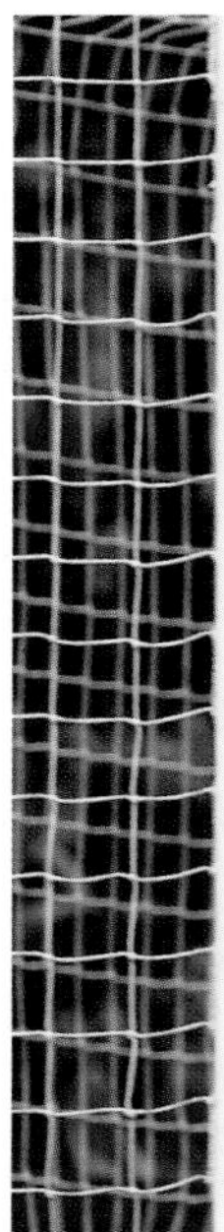

Gary Doherty makes it 2-2

PREMIERSHIP FIXTURE HISTORY

Pl: 2 Draws: 0	Wins	⚽	Yellow cards	Red cards
Tottenham Hotspur	2	7	1	0
Portsmouth	0	4	0	0

STARTING LINE-UPS

Tottenham Hotspur substitutes: Keane, Bunjevcevic, Cerny, Edman, Marney

Portsmouth substitutes: Fuller, Mezague, Skopelitis, Ashdown, Rodic

EVENT LINE

28 ⚽ Kamara (Corner)

34 ⚽ **Mido (Open Play)**

HALF TIME 1 - 1

57 ⚽ **Mido (Open Play)**

62 ⇄ Berger (Off) Fuller (On)

63 ⇄ **Mido (Off) Keane (On)**

63 ⇄ O'Neil (Off) Mezague (On)

83 ⚽ **Keane (Open Play)**

84 ⇄ **Naybet (Off) Bunjevcevic (On)**

89 ⇄ Primus (Off) Skopelitis (On)

FULL TIME 3 - 1

STATISTICS

Season	Fixture (Tottenham)		Fixture (Portsmouth)	Season
158	**10**	Shots On Target	**3**	**130**
140	**8**	Shots Off Target	**3**	**131**
10	**1**	Hit Woodwork	**0**	**3**
99	**3**	Caught Offside	**14**	**69**
123	**9**	Corners	**2**	**134**
319	**9**	Fouls	**8**	**306**
50%	**57%**	Possession	**43%**	**47%**

LEAGUE STANDINGS

Position (pos before)		W	D	L	F	A	Pts
9 (9)	**Tottenham H**	**10**	**6**	**10**	**33**	**30**	**36**
13 (13)	**Portsmouth**	**8**	**6**	**12**	**29**	**38**	**30**

Saturday 5th February 2005 | Venue: **White Hart Lane** | Attendance: **36,105** | Referee: **S.W.Dunn**

Mido tries to hold off Arjan De Zeeuw

"He has got so much experience for someone so young, and we are delighted to have him here."
Martin Jol on Mido

PREMIERSHIP MILESTONE
Andy Reid made his Premiership debut

PREMIERSHIP MILESTONE
Mido marked his Premiership debut with two goals

"I'm disappointed with their first goal, because we should have prevented the cross from Simon Davies."
Joe Jordan

TOTTENHAM HOTSPUR 3 PORTSMOUTH 1

Egyptian striker Mido made a dream start to life in English football, scoring twice as Tottenham came from behind to beat Portsmouth 3-1 at White Hart Lane.

Despite dominating the early exchanges, Spurs fell behind to a 28th-minute Diomansy Kamara header. It did not take long for Mido to restore parity, however, and the loan signing from Roma netted again shortly before the hour mark. Having replaced the two-goal hero, Robbie Keane then made sure of the points late on.

Deadline day signing from Nottingham Forest Andy Reid was another new face in a line-up that began brightly. Just two minutes had elapsed when Mido drove an effort narrowly over the bar, and soon afterwards young full-back Stephen Kelly drew a save from Konstantinos Chalkias.

Captain Ledley King then dragged an effort wide, before a dangerous near-post cross from the left almost produced an own goal. Then, completely against the run of play, Portsmouth went in front.

Czech midfielder Patrik Berger delivered a corner from the right, and Kamara rose highest to flick home a header from six yards out.

Any disappointment was soon forgotten though, as Mido met Simon Davies' centre from the right with a bullet header just over five minutes later.

Martin Jol's men continued to dominate, but it looked like Kamara had caught them out again shortly before half-time. Fortunately for the Londoners, referee Steve Dunn adjudged that the Senegalese forward had handled when evading Paul Robinson and slotting the ball into the back of the net.

The decision proved an important one, as Mido grabbed his second goal after 57 minutes. The tall striker turned home Jermain Defoe's low cross from a yard out, after the visitors had survived a penalty appeal just seconds earlier.

With his work for the day done, Spurs' new hero made way for Keane. The Irish international substitute then sealed the victory seven minutes from time, deftly lobbing Reid's pass over Chalkias after his club and international colleague had struck a post less than 30 seconds beforehand.

PREMIERSHIP FIXTURE HISTORY

Pl: 8 Draws: 3	Wins	Goals	Yellow	Red
Chelsea	4	14	7	0
Manchester City	1	6	8	1

STARTING LINE-UPS

Tiago, J.Cole, Cudicini, Johnson, Smertin

McManaman, Weaver, Onuoha, Jordan, Macken

EVENT LINE

41 Makelele (Foul)

HALF TIME 0 - 0

56 **Jarosik (Off) Tiago (On)**

63 **Kezman (Off) Cole J (On)**

64 **Gudjohnsen (Dissent)**

72 Bosvelt (Foul)

85 Sibierski (Off) McManaman (On)

FULL TIME 0 - 0

STATISTICS

Season	Fixture		Fixture	Season
191	8	Shots On Target	1	142
153	3	Shots Off Target	3	127
8	0	Hit Woodwork	0	2
83	7	Caught Offside	3	79
175	7	Corners	1	160
321	9	Fouls	11	336
56%	54%	Possession	46%	49%

LEAGUE STANDINGS

Position (pos before)	W	D	L	F	A	Pts
1 (1) Chelsea	20	5	1	49	8	65
10 (10) Man City	8	9	9	31	27	33

Sunday 6th February 2005 | Venue: **Stamford Bridge** | Attendance: **42,093** | Referee: **H.M.Webb**

CHELSEA 0 MANCHESTER CITY 0

Manchester City ensured that they would not be beaten by Chelsea this season, earning a hard-earned goalless draw from their trip to Stamford Bridge.

Without Arjen Robben through injury for the first time since a 1-0 defeat in the reverse of this fixture in October, Jose Mourinho's men looked devoid of attacking ideas. That said, they still had chances to win the game, but lacked the finishing touch.

David James may not have been as busy as he might have expected, though he did make several crucial saves. None were more important than the breathtaking injury-time stop from a fiercely struck Frank Lampard volley that will live long in the memory of those who saw it.

With Didier Drogba joining Robben on the injury list, there was a starting place for the misfiring Mateja Kezman. The former PSV Eindhoven striker has struggled to adapt to life in the Premiership, and prodded wide from close range after a low 34th-minute Damien Duff drive had been parried into his path.

This rare moment of excitement sparked both Chelsea and the crowd into life. Soon afterwards, Eidur Gudjohnsen saw a firm header tipped over, and then James denied both Kezman and Lampard in quick succession.

A dramatic goal-line clearance then prevented William Gallas from getting on the scoresheet, and the visitors broke quickly upfield through Shaun Wright-Phillips. The pacy winger eventually delivered a cross from the left, which Robbie Fowler stooped to head wide of a gaping net from close range.

City continued to defend superbly in the second half, restricting their hosts to a handful of chances. Those that were created were quickly snuffed out by James, the keeper touching a dangerous low drive away from the waiting Gudjohnsen and then stopping a low Lampard free-kick with his legs.

The dramatic injury-time stop then ensured that Mourinho's men would be dropping two points, a result which saw their lead at the top of the Premiership cut to single figures. Kevin Keegan's charges have now netted draws away at each of the top three, and have conceded just once in the process.

"With the loss of Drogba and Robben we lacked some creativity, but we did enough today to win the game."

Jose Mourinho

"We deserved the point. We had a plan and looked like a team that wanted to get something from the game."

Kevin Keegan

John Terry climbs above Robbie Fowler

PREMIERSHIP FIXTURE HISTORY

Pl: 13 Draws: 5	Wins	⚽	▢	■
Southampton	6	19	15	1
Everton	2	13	19	1

STARTING LINE-UPS

Jakobsson, Blayney, Telfer, A.Svensson, Ormerod

Bent, Arteta, Ferguson, Wright, Naysmith

EVENT LINE

4 ⚽ Beattie (Open Play)

36 ⚽ **Crouch (Open Play)**

HALF TIME 1 - 1

46 Carsley (Off) Bent (On)

46 ▢ Hibbert (Foul)

55 ⚽ **Camara (Open Play)**

59 Kilbane (Off) Ferguson (On)

59 Stubbs (Off) Arteta (On)

64 ▢ Arteta (Foul)

90 ⚽ Bent (Open Play)

FULL TIME 2 - 2

STATISTICS

Season	Fixture		Fixture	Season
123	8	Shots On Target	3	126
140	12	Shots Off Target	4	143
2	0	Hit Woodwork	0	6
72	5	Caught Offside	4	67
129	8	Corners	3	125
340	15	Fouls	11	299
48%	50%	Possession	50%	49%

LEAGUE STANDINGS

Position (pos before)	W	D	L	F	A	Pts
19 (19) Southampton	3	10	13	28	43	19
4 (4) Everton	14	6	6	31	27	48

Sunday 6th February 2005 | Venue: Friends Provident St Mary's Stadium | Attendance: 31,509 | Referee: A.P.D'Urso

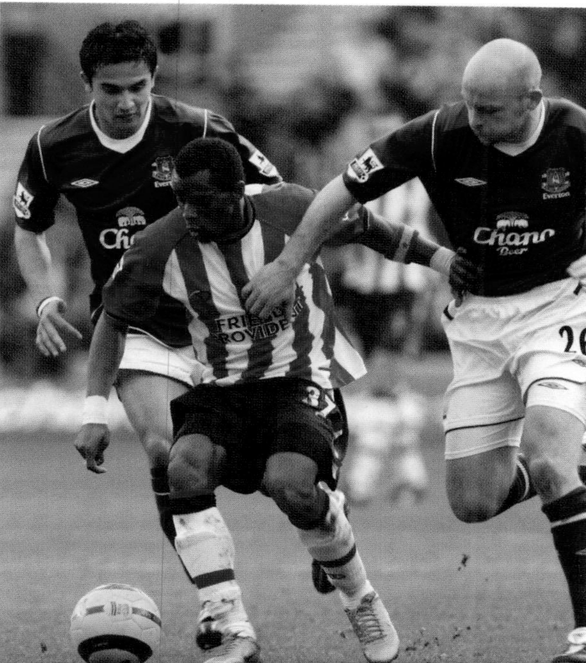

Henri Camara proves a hard man to stop

SOUTHAMPTON 2 EVERTON 2

Substitute Marcus Bent struck a powerful last-gasp equaliser to break Southampton hearts and earn his side a point at St Mary's.

Returning Saint James Beattie had fired his new club into a fourth-minute lead, only for Harry Redknapp's strugglers to turn things in their favour through efforts from Peter Crouch and Henri Camara. It was Bent who had the last laugh, however, netting what may eventually prove to be a vital goal at both ends of the table.

As is so often the case with former players, Beattie came back to haunt his previous employers. The striker drilled an instinctive finish into the roof of Paul Smith's net from the edge of the six-yard box, after the keeper had done well to parry a Tim Cahill header from a long throw on the right.

Ex-Brentford custodian Smith was making his first start for the club, as a result of Antti Niemi undergoing a minor operation a couple of days earlier.

A mistake from visiting captain Alan Stubbs enabled a clearly offside Camara to fire high over the crossbar, before Beattie showed far better technique at the other end with a volley from distance that was touched wide.

Alert goalkeeping then saw Smith make a smothering save from James McFadden, and shortly afterwards Crouch levelled the match. The tall striker made the most of his aerial advantage, climbing above the defenders to head home Rory Delap's 36th-minute long throw from the right.

A second goal nearly followed for the former Portsmouth forward, though Stubbs atoned for his earlier error with an acrobatic goal-line clearance from a well-struck drive.

Southampton remained in the ascendancy after the break, and went in front through Camara. The on-loan Wolves man exchanged passes with David Prutton, skipped past Stubbs, and stroked the ball home at the near post in the 55th minute.

The Saints had further chances to seal the win, but were punished in injury time. Calum Davenport was outpaced by Bent in the inside right channel, and the former Leicester man somehow found the net with a venomous rising drive from an acute angle.

"I've brought in five players during the transfer window, and we look like a proper football team now."
Harry Redknapp

PREMIERSHIP MILESTONE
Nigel Quashie made his first Premiership appearance in the colours of Southampton

"We have got a team spirit that is second to none, and I would not swap it for anything."
David Moyes

PREMIERSHIP MILESTONE
Mikel Arteta made his Premiership debut

PREMIERSHIP MILESTONE
James Beattie marked his return to Southampton with a first Premiership goal in the colours of Everton

PREMIERSHIP MILESTONE
200 Duncan Ferguson made his 200th Premiership appearance for Everton

PREMIERSHIP FIXTURE HISTORY

Pl: 3 Draws: 0	Wins	Goals	Yellow cards	Red cards
Birmingham City	2	4	6	1
Liverpool	1	4	1	0

STARTING LINE-UPS

Birmingham City: Maik Taylor; Melchiot, Cunningham (c), Upson, Clapham; Pennant, Johnson, Clemence, Gray; Heskey, Pandiani

Liverpool: Dudek; Traore, Hyypia, Carragher, Finnan; Riise, Biscan, Hamann, Baros; Morientes, Gerrard (c)

Birmingham City substitutes: Tebily, Nafti, Blake, Bennett, Anderton

Liverpool substitutes: Smicer, Nunez, Pellegrino, Carson, Warnock

EVENT LINE

18 **Melchiot (Off) Tebily (On)**
38 **Pandiani (Penalty)**
45 **Gray (Open Play)**

HALF TIME 2 - 0

46 Biscan (Off) Smicer (On)
50 **Tebily (Foul)**
63 Riise (Off) Nunez (On)
71 **Heskey (Foul)**
79 Finnan (Off) Pellegrino (On)
84 **Pennant (Off) Nafti (On)**
89 **Pandiani (Off) Blake (On)**

FULL TIME 2 - 0

STATISTICS

Season	Fixture	Birmingham City / Liverpool	Fixture	Season
122	4	Shots On Target	2	174
114	2	Shots Off Target	4	184
6	0	Hit Woodwork	0	5
81	7	Caught Offside	2	65
141	10	Corners	4	154
382	16	Fouls	10	321
50%	51%	Possession	49%	53%

LEAGUE STANDINGS

Position (pos before)		W	D	L	F	A	Pts
12 (14)	Birmingham C	8	8	11	31	33	32
5 (5)	Liverpool	13	4	10	41	29	43

Saturday 12th February 2005 | Venue: St Andrew's | Attendance: 29,318 | Referee: H.M.Webb

Emile Heskey fires in a shot

"Considering the opposition and the quality they have, that is as well as we have played in the Premiership for an entire 90 minutes."
Steve Bruce

PREMIERSHIP MILESTONE

Julian Gray scored his first Premiership goal

"We know our problem is that we are not consistent, and we seem to have more difficulties when we play away from home."
Rafael Benitez

BIRMINGHAM CITY 2 LIVERPOOL 0

Liverpool failed to capitalise on Everton's earlier defeat, suffering a thoroughly-deserved 2-0 reverse at the hands of Birmingham at St Andrew's.

Rafael Benitez opted for a solid-looking formation, deploying Milan Baros out of position on the right of midfield. This provided Steven Gerrard with the freedom to roam the pitch in support of lone frontman Fernando Morientes, but the policy clearly didn't work.

The home team were on song right from the first whistle, and Walter Pandiani did well to steer a deep Jermaine Pennant cross anywhere near the target. The roles were then reversed later in the half, as Jerzy Dudek did well to block the winger's route to goal following the Uruguayan's clever pass.

With the Merseysiders posing little threat at the other end, it came as no surprise when Steve Bruce's team took a 38th-minute lead. Sami Hyypia and Emile Heskey embarked upon a wrestling match in the box, and referee Howard Webb decided that the striker had been impeded.

With the scorer of their last spot-kick, Robbie Blake, sat on the bench, Pandiani stepped up to send the keeper the wrong way from the spot.

A fine piece of play from Pennant then helped create a second Birmingham goal on the stroke of half-time. The on-loan Arsenal player tricked his way past two defenders on the right, and then sent over a swerving cross that Julian Gray volleyed in from four yards out at the back post.

A positive interval change saw Vladimir Smicer introduced in place of Igor Biscan, but Liverpool failed to raise their game. A close-range Morientes miss was as near as Benitez's men had come in the first half, and it wasn't until a late Jamie Carragher header was cleared from danger that the men in blue had genuine cause for concern in the second period.

Afterwards Bruce reflected on a terrific display by his players. The usual heart and industry expected from a side managed by such a determined character were supplemented by high levels of skill and creativity. Unfortunately for Liverpool, they displayed none of these qualities.

PREMIERSHIP FIXTURE HISTORY

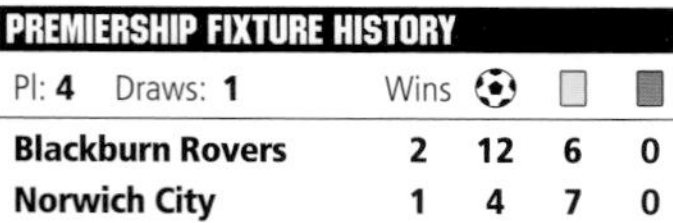

Pl: 4 Draws: 1	Wins	Goals	Yellow cards	Red cards
Blackburn Rovers	2	12	6	0
Norwich City	1	4	7	0

STARTING LINE-UPS

Blackburn subs: Neill, Thompson, Reid, Enckelman, Johnson

Norwich subs: McKenzie, Safri, Gallacher, Shackell, McVeigh

EVENT LINE

17 **Pedersen (Open Play)** (goal)
36 **Tugay (Foul)** (yellow card)
39 **Dickov (Corner)** (goal)

HALF TIME 2 - 0

46 **Mokoena (Off) Neill (On)**
46 Brennan (Off) McKenzie (On)
62 **Dickov (Open Play)** (goal)
66 **Neill (Foul)** (yellow card)
70 **Emerton (Off) Reid (On)**
72 Francis (Ung.Conduct) (yellow card)
76 **Savage (Off) Thompson (On)**
76 Charlton (Off) Safri (On)

FULL TIME 3 - 0

STATISTICS

Season	Fixture (Blackburn)		Fixture (Norwich)	Season
142	**13**	Shots On Target	**6**	**128**
160	**5**	Shots Off Target	**3**	**143**
6	**0**	Hit Woodwork	**0**	**5**
102	**3**	Caught Offside	**3**	**87**
160	**12**	Corners	**3**	**128**
422	**11**	Fouls	**14**	**360**
49%	**63%**	Possession	**37%**	**45%**

LEAGUE STANDINGS

Position (pos before)	W	D	L	F	A	Pts
16 (16) Blackburn R	**6**	**10**	**11**	**24**	**36**	**28**
18 (18) Norwich C	**3**	**11**	**13**	**26**	**52**	**20**

Saturday 12th February 2005 | Venue: **Ewood Park** | Attendance: **20,923** | Referee: **S.W.Dunn**

BLACKBURN ROVERS 3 NORWICH CITY 0

A convincing 3-0 win for Blackburn saw them move eight points clear of both Norwich and the relegation zone.

Home boss Mark Hughes had taken offence to pre-match comments attributed to his opposite number Nigel Worthington that claimed his side employed bully-boy tactics. The Lancashire team did their talking on the pitch, however, with two goals from Paul Dickov and one from Morten Gamst Pedersen securing a comfortable victory.

It was the visitors that began brightly though, Darren Huckerby squandering a great chance when he lashed the ball high over the bar from no more than eight yards out. Brad Friedel then had to be alert to keep out a drive from Damien Francis, before Rovers made the all-important breakthrough.

With 17 minutes played, Pedersen exposed both stand-in right-back Simon Charlton and keeper Robert Green. The Norwegian winger controlled a lofted pass from Kerimoglu Tugay and beat his marker in one movement, before rifling home a 15-yard shot that went straight through the Norwich custodian.

The Canaries had a golden chance to equalise just over five minutes later, when Huckerby unselfishly squared for Jim Brennan. The former Nottingham Forest man seemed shocked by what had occurred though, and proceeded to miss his kick.

It was to prove a costly miss, as Dickov struck six minutes before the break. The diminutive Scot had earned his side a late point at Carrow Road in November, and added another headed goal to his collection by flicking in Pedersen's near-post right-wing corner from the acutest of angles.

Robbie Savage sent a free-kick over the bar as the second half began in atrocious conditions. The hail and driving rain had receded by the time Dickov added a 62nd-minute third, the striker firing in a low 20-yard drive that Green would again have been disappointed not to save.

The keeper did at least prevent a late fourth, producing a marvellous double-save to keep out Steven Reid and then Paul Gallagher. Captain Andy Todd then demonstrated the sense of positivity flowing around Ewood Park, charging forward and crashing a 25-yard shot just past the right-hand upright.

"I thought we made a statement today by the way that we played."
Mark Hughes

"I have no complaints about the defeat, or the way in which Blackburn went about things."
Nigel Worthington

Morten Gamst Pedersen celebrates opening the scoring

PREMIERSHIP FIXTURE HISTORY

Pl: **5** Draws: **2**

	Wins	⚽	Yellow	Red
Bolton Wanderers	3	6	9	0
Middlesbrough	0	2	12	1

STARTING LINE-UPS

Bolton: Jaaskelainen; Barness, Ben Haim, N'Gotty, Gardner; Okocha (c), Campo, Speed; Nolan, Giannakopoulos; Davies

Middlesbrough: Job, Hasselbaink; Downing, Doriva, Morrison; Reiziger, Parnaby; Queudrue, Southgate (c), Riggott; Schwarzer

Bolton subs: Diouf, Vaz Te, Poole, Candela, Hierro

Middlesbrough subs: Nemeth, Nash, McMahon, Bates, Graham

EVENT LINE

HALF TIME 0 - 0

53 **Giannakopoulos (Off) Diouf (On)**

67 Job (Off) Nemeth (On)

81 **Campo (Off) Vaz Te (On)**

90 Morrison (Foul)

FULL TIME 0 - 0

STATISTICS

Season	Fixture (Bolton)		Fixture (Middlesbrough)	Season
169	**8**	Shots On Target	**2**	**184**
152	**5**	Shots Off Target	**3**	**153**
6	**1**	Hit Woodwork	**0**	**5**
66	**4**	Caught Offside	**3**	**71**
142	**3**	Corners	**2**	**155**
359	**11**	Fouls	**15**	**333**
49%	**49%**	Possession	**51%**	**50%**

LEAGUE STANDINGS

Position (pos before)		W	D	L	F	A	Pts
7 (7)	**Bolton W**	**11**	**7**	**9**	**35**	**32**	**40**
6 (6)	**Middlesbrough**	**11**	**8**	**8**	**41**	**35**	**41**

Saturday 12th February 2005 | Venue: **Reebok Stadium** | Attendance: **24,322** | Referee: **A.G.Wiley**

BOLTON WANDERERS 0 MIDDLESBROUGH 0

A repeat of the 2004 Carling Cup final was not a game that will live long in the memory.

Bolton were chasing a record-breaking sixth consecutive top-flight victory, and would have leapfrogged their opponents in the table with a win. Captain Jay-Jay Okocha returned to the team in place of El-Hadji Diouf, in the only change to the side that had won at Crystal Palace last time out.

Visiting manager Steve McClaren surprised everyone by operating a 5-3-2 formation. It was thought that the decision had been forced upon him by injuries, but it later emerged that it had been a purely tactical ploy.

The first chance of the game fell to Middlesbrough. A long kick from Mark Schwarzer dissected the home defence and fell invitingly for Joseph-Desire Job. The Cameroonian international pulled his effort wide of the right-hand upright though, much to the relief of centre-backs Tal Ben Haim and Bruno N'Gotty.

Wanderers responded in positive fashion, and should have taken the lead on the quarter-hour. Kevin Nolan's curling 25-yard effort was brilliantly touched onto the angle of post and bar, yet Kevin Davies was far too careful with a follow-up header that enabled the keeper to make a scrambling recovery save.

A parry from a long-range Anthony Barness drive brought the half to a close, and Bolton continued to pose the greater threat after the break. Twice in quick succession Nolan was inches away from connecting with dangerous balls into the six-yard box.

Jimmy Floyd Hasselbaink fired wide on a rare counter-attack, before both teams came close to snatching victory.

Welsh midfielder Gary Speed did everything right when striking a dropping ball towards the bottom left-hand corner from 15 yards. Unfortunately for the Trotters, his effort flew just the wrong side of the upright, with Schwarzer well-beaten.

If anything, the Middlesbrough opening that followed was even better. Possession broke the way of Hasselbaink in the inside-right channel after a surging run from young James Morrison, but the striker was unable to take the ball around an alert Jussi Jaaskelainen.

"I've told the lads not to be too disappointed, as we tried our best."
Sam Allardyce

"I'm delighted, and I'd have settled for that before the game."
Steve McClaren

Anthony Barness gets a shot away

PREMIERSHIP FIXTURE HISTORY

Pl: 13 Draws: 5	Wins	⚽	▢	■
Everton	3	16	13	3
Chelsea	5	17	34	5

STARTING LINE-UPS

Ferguson, Arteta, Wright, Gerrard, Plessis

Jarosik, Carvalho, Johnson, Cudicini, Smertin

EVENT LINE

8 ■ **Beattie (Violent Conduct)**

33 ▢ **Cahill (Foul)**

HALF TIME 0 - 0

69 ⚽ Gudjohnsen (Open Play)

72 Cole J (Off) Jarosik (On)

73 **Naysmith (Off) Ferguson (On)**

80 ▢ Terry (Ung.Conduct)

85 **Carsley (Off) Arteta (On)**

89 ▢ Jarosik (Ung.Conduct)

90 Duff (Off) Carvalho (On)

90 Tiago (Off) Johnson (On)

FULL TIME 0 - 1

STATISTICS

Season	Fixture		Fixture	Season
128	2	Shots On Target	11	202
145	2	Shots Off Target	14	167
6	0	Hit Woodwork	1	9
67	0	Caught Offside	3	86
128	3	Corners	9	184
309	10	Fouls	15	336
49%	33%	Possession	67%	56%

LEAGUE STANDINGS

Position (pos before)		W	D	L	F	A	Pts
4 (4)	Everton	14	6	7	31	28	48
1 (1)	Chelsea	21	5	1	50	8	68

Saturday 12th February 2005 | Venue: **Goodison Park** | Attendance: **40,270** | Referee: **M.A.Riley**

EVERTON 0 CHELSEA 1

A moment of madness from James Beattie ultimately cost Everton the chance to pit their wits against the Premiership leaders.

Despite his protestations, the striker could have no complaints about his eighth-minute dismissal for violent conduct. Chasing a ball into the corner, the former Southampton man reacted angrily to William Gallas' attempts to block him off, and proceeded to project his head into the back of the Frenchman's in a rhino-like charge.

David Moyes responded to this major setback by moving Marcus Bent forward and switching Joseph Yobo to the right of a four-man midfield. Given that few, if any, sides in English football keep the ball better than Chelsea, the Merseysiders were in for a long afternoon.

The Londoners began to dominate possession, and went close to scoring after 14 minutes. Damien Duff was a whisker away from finding the top left-hand corner with a 20-yard shot, following neat build-up play between Joe Cole and Eidur Gudjohnsen.

Tireless running from Bent made life difficult for the man in possession, but it was at the other end that all the action took place. Portuguese midfielder Tiago fired wastefully over the bar, while the lively Cole twice went close from distance.

The one-way traffic continued after the break. Nigel Martyn made a brilliant close-range stop from Gudjohnsen, and then leapt to his right to turn away a venomous prodded effort from Frank Lampard.

Despite the heroics of their custodian and those in front of him, Everton finally succumbed after 69 minutes. Defender Gallas remained forward following a corner and helped Paulo Ferreira's dipping right-wing cross onto the bar, leaving Gudjohnsen free to tap into an unguarded net from just three yards out.

Creditably, Moyes' men did not lose hope. Lee Carsley brought a save from Petr Cech with a header eight minutes from time, and Gallas was forced into a desperate block that most inside Goodison Park howled had been with his hand.

It wasn't to be, however, as Chelsea held on to register a tenth consecutive top-flight clean sheet. Surely only injuries to key defenders can loosen their ever-tightening grip on the Premiership title now.

Damien Duff gets the better of Alessandro Pistone

"I thought the sending-off ruined the game, but credit to the lads for keeping us in contention."

David Moyes

"We always had the conviction that we would get the three points."

Assistant Manager Steve Clarke

PREMIERSHIP FIXTURE HISTORY

Pl: 2 Draws: 0	Wins	Goals	Yellow	Red
Portsmouth	1	3	4	0
Aston Villa	1	3	3	1

STARTING LINE-UPS

Portsmouth: Chalkias; De Zeeuw (c), Stefanovic; Cisse, Taylor; Hughes, Skopelitis; Stone, Berger; Kamara, Yakubu

Aston Villa: L.Moore, Angel; Barry, Solano; Djemba-Djemba, Hendrie; Samuel, De la Cruz; Ridgewell, Mellberg (c); Sorensen

Portsmouth substitutes: Lua Lua, Fuller, Ashdown, Primus, Mezague

Aston Villa substitutes: Hitzlsperger, Davis, Berson, Postma, Laursen

EVENT LINE

17 De Zeeuw (Own Goal)

21 **Hughes (Foul)**

24 **Yakubu (Penalty)**

HALF TIME 1 - 1

51 **Stefanovic (Foul)**

53 Hendrie (Off) Hitzlsperger (On)

59 Ridgewell (Foul)

66 **Yakubu (Off) Lua Lua (On)**

73 Hitzlsperger (Open Play)

75 Solano (Off) Davis (On)

77 **Skopelitis (Off) Fuller (On)**

90 Moore L (Off) Berson (On)

FULL TIME 1 - 2

STATISTICS

Season	Fixture (Portsmouth)		Fixture (Aston Villa)	Season
134	4	Shots On Target	4	135
137	6	Shots Off Target	2	141
5	2	Hit Woodwork	1	4
71	2	Caught Offside	1	79
140	6	Corners	3	154
320	14	Fouls	22	415
47%	52%	Possession	48%	49%

LEAGUE STANDINGS

Position (pos before)	W	D	L	F	A	Pts
14 (13) Portsmouth	8	6	13	30	40	30
10 (11) Aston Villa	9	8	10	31	34	35

Saturday 12th February 2005 | Venue: **Fratton Park** | Attendance: **20,160** | Referee: **D.J.Gallagher**

PORTSMOUTH 1 ASTON VILLA 2

A stunning strike from substitute Thomas Hitzlsperger won the game for Aston Villa, after Arjan De Zeeuw's own goal had been cancelled out by an Aiyegbeni Yakubu penalty.

The match had echoes of the West Midlands side's only previous Premiership success on their travels this season, at Bolton. On that occasion, Hitzlsperger arrived from the bench to net a spectacular late winner in a 2-1 victory.

Portsmouth handed a first start to Greek midfielder Giannis Skopelitis in the centre of the park, and also welcomed back Steve Stone from injury. With Carlton Cole unavailable, David O'Leary opted to keep faith with Luke Moore in attack.

Diomansy Kamara pulled an effort across the face of goal in a bright opening by the home side, but it was the visitors that went in front after 17 minutes. Moore surged past defenders on the left of the box, before poking over a low near-post cross that the recovering De Zeeuw turned past his stranded keeper from five yards out.

Dejan Stefanovic made a crucial block just 90 seconds later, with Patrik Berger then going close to levelling matters with a fiercely-struck 25-yard drive that rebounded to safety off Thomas Sorensen's right-hand upright.

Referee Dermot Gallagher was then at the centre of two quickfire Portsmouth penalty appeals. He turned down the first when Kamara appeared to be bundled over, but then awarded a dubious second as Stone went down under Gareth Barry's challenge. With 24 minutes played, Yakubu stepped up to confidently equalise from the spot.

The even-nature of the contest did not change after the interval, though Villa created the better openings. Juan Pablo Angel had already forced a save from Konstantinos Chalkias, when he headed against the bar from eight yards out.

The decisive goal was not long in coming though, as a 73rd-minute break ended with Hitzlsperger volleying past a stationary keeper from 20 yards.

The home side tried hard to conjure up their own moment of magic, but saw Kamara blaze wildly into the crowd after Richard Hughes' deflected shot had fallen kindly for him.

"We played well going forward and got ourselves into some good positions, but we didn't get the end product that we were looking for."
Joe Jordan

"We put Thomas Hitzlsperger on because we wanted to win the game and climb the table."
David O'Leary

Thomas Hitzlsperger cannot hide his delight at scoring the winner

PREMIERSHIP FIXTURE HISTORY				
Pl: **8** Draws: **1**	Wins	Goals	Yellow cards	Red cards
Manchester City	2	12	17	0
Manchester United	5	15	14	0

STARTING LINE-UPS

James; Mills, Dunne, Distin (c), Thatcher; Barton, McManaman, S.Wright-Phillips, Musampa; Sibierski, Fowler

Rooney; Fortune, Scholes, Keane (c), O'Shea, Fletcher; Heinze, Brown, Ferdinand, G.Neville; Carroll

Manchester City subs: Macken, Weaver, Onuoha, Flood, B.Wright-Phillips

Manchester United subs: Ronaldo, Giggs, P.Neville, Howard, Bellion

EVENT LINE

33 O'Shea (Off) Ronaldo (On)
38 Rooney (Foul)

HALF TIME 0 - 0

51 Scholes (Foul)
58 Keane (Foul)
64 Fletcher (Off) Giggs (On)
68 **Barton (Off) Macken (On)**
68 Rooney (Open Play)
73 **Fowler (Foul)**
75 Dunne (Own Goal)
77 **Sibierski (Foul)**
83 **Mills (Off) Wright-Phillips B (On)**
84 Scholes (Off) Neville P (On)

FULL TIME 0 - 2

STATISTICS

Season	Fixture (Man City)		Fixture (Man Utd)	Season
145	3	Shots On Target	3	218
133	6	Shots Off Target	7	192
2	0	Hit Woodwork	1	14
79	0	Caught Offside	6	104
164	4	Corners	6	208
345	9	Fouls	14	330
48%	38%	Possession	62%	55%

LEAGUE STANDINGS

Position (pos before)	W	D	L	F	A	Pts
11 (11) Man City	8	9	10	31	29	33
2 (2) Man Utd	17	8	2	45	16	59

Sunday 13th February 2005 | Venue: **City of Manchester Stadium** | Attendance: **47,111** | Referee: **S.G.Bennett**

MANCHESTER CITY 0 MANCHESTER UNITED 2

Wayne Rooney revels in his opening goal

"It was always going to be a tight game, with the first goal proving crucial."
Kevin Keegan

"It was not our best performance of the last two or three months, but all you can do is win."
Sir Alex Ferguson

PREMIERSHIP MILESTONE
250 Rio Ferdinand made his 250th Premiership appearance

PREMIERSHIP MILESTONE
400 Ryan Giggs made his 400th Premiership appearance

Having performed brilliantly all season, Richard Dunne endured a nightmare day at the office in this hard-fought Manchester derby.

The Irish centre-back was unable to prevent Wayne Rooney opening the scoring after 68 minutes, deflecting the young forward's near-post effort beyond David James. Worse then followed seven minutes later, as the burly defender turned a cross from the right into his own net.

Kevin Keegan made one enforced change to the team that had drawn at Chelsea a week earlier, replacing the suspended Paul Bosvelt with Steve McManaman.

The former England manager's counterpart, Sir Alex Ferguson, opted to deploy the hard-working Darren Fletcher and Quinton Fortune in wide areas, leaving both Ryan Giggs and Cristiano Ronaldo on the bench.

It seemed that United's policy was to stifle Shaun Wright-Phillips and Kiki Musampa, though it didn't work early on. Roy Carroll saved a stinging drive from the latter, before City's England international winger fired a dangerous low ball across the box.

The industrious Rooney drilled wide from distance and also forced James into a sprawling save from a curling free-kick, but it was the home side that went closest through McManaman. The former Real Madrid midfielder somehow contrived to steer the ball wide from close range, following a great low near-post delivery from the right.

A first half injury to John O'Shea had seen the introduction of Ronaldo, and he was joined by Giggs after 64 minutes. The visitors stepped up a gear almost immediately, and went in front from a well-worked move.

Gary Neville escaped the attentions of Musampa on the flank, and delivered a low cross that an onrushing Rooney steered home, with the aid of Dunne's deflection, from just outside the six-yard box.

The young starlet then created the second, sending over a 75th-minute cross from the right that Dunne inadvertently steered in via the far left-hand upright.

Late chances came and went for City, Robbie Fowler and Antoine Sibierski both dragging efforts off target, before Giggs struck a post with a powerful drive.

PREMIERSHIP FIXTURE HISTORY

Pl: 4 Draws: 0	Wins	Goals	Yellow	Red
Arsenal	3	10	6	0
Crystal Palace	1	3	8	0

STARTING LINE-UPS

Arsenal: Lehmann; Lauren, Toure, Cygan, Clichy; Pires, Vieira (c), Edu, Reyes; Bergkamp, Henry

Crystal Palace: Johnson; Freedman, Soares, Hughes (c), Riihilahti, Routledge; Granville, Sorondo, Hall, Boyce; Kiraly

Arsenal subs: Flamini, van Persie, Fabregas, Almunia, Senderos

Crystal Palace subs: Leigertwood, Kolkka, Lakis, Speroni, Borrowdale

EVENT LINE

26 Riihilahti (Foul)
31 Riihilahti (Off) Leigertwood (On)
32 **Bergkamp (Open Play)**
35 **Reyes (Open Play)**
39 **Henry (Corner)**
HALF TIME 3 - 0
54 **Vieira (Open Play)**
61 **Edu (Off) Flamini (On)**
63 Johnson (Penalty)
64 **Vieira (Foul)**
64 Freedman (Off) Kolkka (On)
64 Routledge (Off) Lakis (On)
66 Sorondo (Dissent)
77 **Henry (Open Play)**
79 **Bergkamp (Off) van Persie (On)**
80 **Pires (Off) Fabregas (On)**
FULL TIME 5 - 1

STATISTICS

Season	Fixture	Arsenal / Crystal Palace	Fixture	Season
205	9	Shots On Target	4	117
129	5	Shots Off Target	4	115
12	1	Hit Woodwork	0	5
67	9	Caught Offside	3	67
158	5	Corners	1	131
319	9	Fouls	17	366
56%	65%	Possession	35%	47%

LEAGUE STANDINGS

Position (pos before)		W	D	L	F	A	Pts
3 (3)	Arsenal	17	6	4	63	31	57
17 (17)	Crystal Palace	5	7	15	30	45	22

Monday 14th February 2005 | Venue: **Highbury** | Attendance: **38,056** | Referee: **R.Styles**

ARSENAL 5 CRYSTAL PALACE 1

Arsenal overcame a nervous opening to completely overrun Crystal Palace at Highbury.

Three goals in seven minutes towards the end of the first half killed off any hopes of a result that Iain Dowie's side might have harboured. Dennis Bergkamp, Jose Antonio Reyes and Thierry Henry were all on target in a blistering spell of attacking football.

The second period brought little respite for the Eagles, though Andy Johnson did net a penalty in between further efforts from Patrick Vieira and Henry.

It was the men from South London that began brightly. Dougie Freedman, playing on the left of a five-man midfield, forced a smart diving stop from Jens Lehmann, with the German keeper then smothering Johnson's follow-up effort.

A let-off soon followed, as the Gunners' former Borussia Dortmund custodian recovered from failing to connect with a backpass, to dribble the ball safely off his own goal line.

Having slowly warmed to their task, Arsenal took advantage of an enforced substitution to grab the lead. Aki Riihilahti limped out of the action to be replaced by Mikele Leigertwood, and Bergkamp benefitted from defensive uncertainty to guide home Reyes' low cross from seven yards out at the near post.

The Spanish provider then turned goalscorer with a rapier-like drive across Gabor Kiraly from 20 yards, before Henry completed the first half scoring with a 39th-minute thunderbolt following a short-corner on the left.

A potential route back into the match went begging when Freedman steered an effort narrowly wide shortly after the interval. Then, in the 54th minute, Arsene Wenger's men added another, captain Patrick Vieira tapping in from two yards after waltzing round Kiraly.

In between Bergkamp firing inches past the post and Robert Pires striking the right-hand upright, Johnson won and then converted, via the underside of the crossbar, a 63rd-minute penalty.

Arsenal were to have the last laugh, however, as Henry struck a magical fifth. A raking long-distance pass found Bergkamp on the right, and the Dutchman span away from Danny Granville to provide his strike partner with the opportunity to sidestep Gonzalo Sorondo and lash home.

Mathieu Flamini and Mikele Leigertwood tussle in midfield

"Tonight was about us being consistent again. Crystal Palace had a go at us early on, but we responded well after the first ten minutes."
Thierry Henry

PREMIERSHIP MILESTONE
200 Thierry Henry marked his 200th Premiership appearance with two goals

"I did not think it was a 3-0 scoreline at half-time, but that is what they can do to you."
Iain Dowie

PREMIERSHIP FIXTURE HISTORY

Pl: **2** Draws: **1**	Wins	⚽	□	■
West Bromwich Albion	**1**	**1**	**4**	**0**
Southampton	**0**	**0**	**3**	**1**

STARTING LINE-UPS

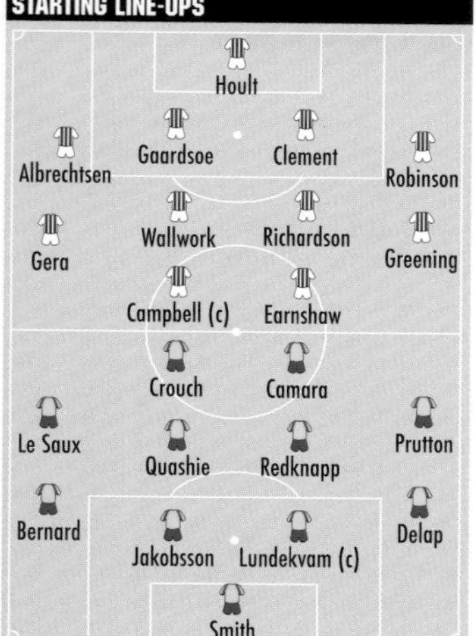

Koumas, Scimeca, Kuszczak, Purse, Horsfield

Higginbotham, Poke, Davenport, Telfer, Phillips

EVENT LINE

25 □ Delap (Foul)

34 □ **Richardson (Foul)**

45 □ **Gera (Foul)**

HALF TIME 0 - 0

47 □ Bernard (Foul)

58 □ Redknapp (Foul)

74 **Richardson (Off) Koumas (On)**

81 **Gera (Off) Scimeca (On)**

FULL TIME 0 - 0

STATISTICS

Season	Fixture		Fixture	Season
124	**3**	Shots On Target	**6**	**129**
117	**6**	Shots Off Target	**6**	**146**
9	**1**	Hit Woodwork	**0**	**2**
95	**2**	Caught Offside	**7**	**79**
127	**7**	Corners	**3**	**132**
361	**15**	Fouls	**15**	**355**
47%	**54%**	Possession	**46%**	**47%**

LEAGUE STANDINGS

Position (pos before)	W	D	L	F	A	Pts
20 (20) West Brom	**2**	**12**	**13**	**23**	**49**	**18**
18 (19) Southampton	**3**	**11**	**13**	**28**	**43**	**20**

Tuesday 22nd February 2005 | Venue: **The Hawthorns** | Attendance: **25,865** | Referee: **M.A.Riley**

WEST BROM 0 SOUTHAMPTON 0

The survival hopes of both West Brom and Southampton suffered a setback, as the two teams played out a spirited 0-0 draw at The Hawthorns.

An evenly-contested opening half, in which Kieran Richardson spanked the crossbar for Bryan Robson's men, was followed by a second period that the visitors shaded, with Henri Camara and David Prutton guilty of some woeful finishing.

The first chance of the match came after seven minutes, Kevin Campbell seeing an effort blocked after Zoltan Gera's shot had been deflected into his path. The Saints hit back soon afterwards though, Peter Crouch's downward header causing a close-range scramble in which Henri Camara was inches away from scoring.

On-loan Manchester United man Richardson then forced Paul Smith into a smart save from a curling free-kick, before play again switched to the other end as Camara lobbed over the advancing Russell Hoult and across the face of goal from wide on the right.

As if to emphasise that there was nothing between them, each side came perilously close to scoring in the final 15 minutes of the half. Firstly, Richardson crashed a 25-yard drive against the angle of post and bar, and then Camara saw a header from point-blank range marvellously turned over by the keeper.

After a bright opening to the second period in which Robert Earnshaw went close from distance, West Brom began to struggle. The visitors upped the tempo of their game, with Jamie Redknapp and Nigel Quashie taking control of the central midfield area.

With 66 minutes played, Camara did everything except score. Collecting possession on the left, the former Celtic man skipped past several challenges and into the box, only to blaze high over the bar from 12 yards out.

A worse miss followed soon afterwards, however, as Prutton volleyed Olivier Bernard's dinked cross from the left over a gaping goal, when it seemed easier to score.

There was still time for a deflected Redknapp free-kick to force a sprawling save from Hoult, but the Baggies held firm to ensure a share of the spoils that would have delighted messrs Worthington and Dowie.

"The positive is that we are now a point closer to Norwich City and Crystal Palace."

Bryan Robson

"It was important that we did not lose, as we did not want to find ourselves on the bottom of the table."

Harry Redknapp

Olivier Bernard slides in on Zoltan Gera.

PREMIERSHIP FIXTURE HISTORY

Pl: 13 Draws: 4	Wins	⚽	Yellow	Red
Aston Villa	8	20	14	0
Everton	1	9	17	2

STARTING LINE-UPS

Hendrie, Vassell, Postma, Laursen, Berson

Ferguson, Naysmith, Wright, Plessis, Vaughan

EVENT LINE

17 ⚽ Osman (Open Play)

34 ▢ **Djemba-Djemba (Foul)**

HALF TIME 0 - 1

46 ⚽ **Solano (Open Play)**

48 ⚽ Cahill (Open Play)

56 ⇄ **Djemba-Djemba (Off) Hendrie (On)**

60 ▢ **Solano (Foul)**

62 ⇄ **Moore L (Off) Vassell (On)**

67 ⚽ Osman (Open Play)

85 ▢ **Hendrie (Foul)**

88 ⇄ Bent (Off) Ferguson (On)

90 ⇄ Cahill (Off) Naysmith (On)

FULL TIME 1 - 3

STATISTICS

Season	Fixture (Aston Villa)		Fixture (Everton)	Season
141	6	Shots On Target	9	137
144	3	Shots Off Target	6	151
5	1	Hit Woodwork	0	6
82	3	Caught Offside	2	69
157	3	Corners	7	135
437	22	Fouls	17	326
49%	48%	Possession	52%	49%

LEAGUE STANDINGS

Position (pos before)	W	D	L	F	A	Pts
10 (10) Aston Villa	9	8	11	32	37	35
4 (4) Everton	15	6	7	34	29	51

Saturday 26th February 2005 | Venue: **Villa Park** | Attendance: **40,248** | Referee: **G.Poll**

Tim Cahill towers above Olof Mellberg.

"Since I've been here, it is probably the worst game we've had."
David O'Leary

"The performance was really good, and there was a real desire to get the points."
David Moyes

ASTON VILLA 1 EVERTON 3

Everton responded to their disappointing F.A.Cup exit at the hands of Manchester United, by recording their first Premiership away win in over three months.

The Merseysiders' last league success on the road also came in the city of Birmingham, with a 1-0 victory at St Andrew's in mid-November. Since then, David Moyes' men had struggled on their travels, but they rediscovered the winning feeling at Villa Park.

Australian Tim Cahill was the driving force for the visitors. The midfielder had been suspended for the previous weekend's cup defeat, and marked his return to the team by creating a well-deserved opening goal.

Finding himself with acres of space on the left wing, the former Millwall man sent over an inviting, inswinging cross that seemed to evade everyone. Leon Osman had other ideas, however, stealing in at the back post to nod the ball home from just a couple of yards out.

Marcus Bent then fired narrowly over from a Mikel Arteta pass, before an inswinging free-kick that clipped the outside of Nigel Martyn's left-hand post provided a rare scare for the Everton defence. Eric Djemba-Djemba shot weakly at the keeper in Villa's only other attack of note.

Whatever David O'Leary said to his troops at half-time clearly did the trick, as the home side drew level straight from the kick-off. Joseph Yobo was robbed by Luke Moore, with Thomas Hitzlsperger taking over to drive in a low effort from the left edge of the six-yard box that Martyn could only push into the path of a grateful Nolberto Solano.

Parity lasted for just two minutes though, as Cahill got the goal his all-action performance deserved. Thomas Sorensen failed to claim Bent's floated cross from the right, enabling the midfielder to rise above Olof Mellberg and head into the net.

From then on, only one team was going to win. Young Osman narrowly missed the top left-hand corner when well-placed, before coolly slotting home after Cahill had danced his way through a static defence in the 67th minute.

With Liverpool not involved in league action over the weekend, the win stretched Everton's lead over their Merseyside rivals to a commanding eight points.

PREMIERSHIP FIXTURE HISTORY

Pl: **1** Draws: **0**

	Wins	⚽	▢	■
Crystal Palace	1	2	3	0
Birmingham City	0	0	3	0

STARTING LINE-UPS

Kiraly

Hall, Sorondo

Boyce, Granville

Leigertwood, Hughes (c)

Soares, Routledge

Freedman, Johnson

Morrison, Pandiani

Gray, Pennant

Clemence, Johnson

Clapham, Tebily

Upson, Cunningham (c)

Maik Taylor

Torghelle, Borrowdale, Lakis, Speroni, Kolkka

Blake, Anderton, Vaesen, Diao, Nafti

EVENT LINE

10 ▢ **Leigertwood (Foul)**
27 ▢ Pennant (Dissent)
32 ▢ Pandiani (Foul)
41 ⚽ **Johnson (Penalty)**

HALF TIME 1 - 0

55 ▢ **Hughes (Foul)**
57 ▢ **Soares (Foul)**
60 ▢ Morrison (Dissent)
63 ⇄ Morrison (Off) Blake (On)
68 ⚽ **Johnson (Penalty)**
73 ⇄ Tebily (Off) Anderton (On)
87 ⇄ **Freedman (Off) Torghelle (On)**
90 ⇄ **Routledge (Off) Lakis (On)**
90 ⇄ **Soares (Off) Borrowdale (On)**

FULL TIME 2 - 0

STATISTICS

Season	Fixture		Fixture	Season
121	4	Shots On Target	5	127
121	6	Shots Off Target	4	118
5	0	Hit Woodwork	0	6
69	2	Caught Offside	2	83
135	4	Corners	7	148
389	23	Fouls	15	397
47%	44%	Possession	56%	50%

LEAGUE STANDINGS

Position (pos before)	W	D	L	F	A	Pts
17 (17) Crystal Palace	6	7	15	32	45	25
12 (12) Birmingham C	8	8	12	31	35	32

Saturday 26th February 2005 | Venue: **Selhurst Park** | Attendance: **23,376** | Referee: **P.Dowd**

CRYSTAL PALACE 2 BIRMINGHAM CITY 0

Andy Johnson ensured that Steve Bruce's return to Selhurst Park was not a happy one, netting twice from the penalty spot to secure a vital win.

The Birmingham boss was given an understandably hostile reception by a home crowd disgusted at the way in which he had deserted them in the search for bigger things. Former Palace players Julian Gray and Clinton Morrison also returned to their old stomping ground for the first time since departing for St Andrew's.

Events were evenly-contested early on. Matthew Upson headed straight at Gabor Kiraly for the visitors, while Johnson tumbled without reward in the box.

Midway through the half, Morrison spurned a great chance to score against his old club. Running onto a throughball from Gray, the striker dragged a low effort just beyond the left-hand upright, much to the delight of the Selhurst Park faithful.

It was to prove a costly miss, as Iain Dowie's men went in front four minutes before the break. Tom Soares' burst into the box was crudely halted by Upson, enabling Johnson to slam home from the spot. Referee Phil Dowd made him retake the kick, however, but the outcome was the same.

Birmingham began the second period brightly, with both Gray and Jermaine Pennant providing a steady supply of crosses from the flanks. Defender Upson met one such delivery with a flying header, but Kiraly was on hand to repel the danger.

It wasn't until the hour mark that the home side responded to an inspirational display from captain Michael Hughes. The midfielder was everywhere, and was involved in the move that saw Dougie Freedman test Maik Taylor from 15 yards out.

Then, with 68 minutes played, Palace grabbed a decisive second goal. Again Upson gave the referee little alternative but to award a penalty, this time upending Johnson, and the Eagles' former Birmingham striker drove the ball straight down the middle of the goal.

The visitors seldom threatened after that, as Dowie's men celebrated establishing a four-point cushion above the relegation zone.

Andy Johnson celebrates beating Maik Taylor from the penalty spot.

"It was a very pleasing performance, and wins are like gold dust for us."
Iain Dowie

PREMIERSHIP MILESTONE
150 Andy Johnson's first goal was the 150th scored by Crystal Palace in the Premiership

"I was not impressed with the referee, and they were soft penalties."
Steve Bruce

PREMIERSHIP MILESTONE
100 Maik Taylor made his 100th Premiership appearance

Saturday 26th February 2005	Venue: **Old Trafford**	Attendance: **67,989**	Referee: **M.R.Halsey**

MANCHESTER UNITED 2 PORTSMOUTH 1

PREMIERSHIP FIXTURE HISTORY

Pl: **2** Draws: **0**	Wins	Goals	Yellow cards	Red cards
Manchester United	2	5	1	0
Portsmouth	0	1	5	0

STARTING LINE-UPS

Howard

G.Neville (c), Brown, Silvestre, Heinze

O'Shea, P.Neville, Scholes

Ronaldo, Rooney

van Nistelrooy

Yakubu

Lua Lua, O'Neil

Skopelitis, Hughes, Stone

Taylor, Stefanovic, De Zeeuw (c), Griffin

Chalkias

Substitutes (Manchester United): Smith, Giggs, Fortune, Ricardo, Saha

Substitutes (Portsmouth): Mezague, Kamara, Hislop, Primus, Fuller

EVENT LINE

8	⚽ **Rooney (Open Play)**
	HALF TIME 1 - 0
46	**Neville G (Off) Smith (On)**
47	⚽ O'Neil (Open Play)
54	Hughes (Off) Mezague (On)
65	**Scholes (Off) Giggs (On)**
79	**Neville P (Ung.Conduct)**
80	Taylor (Ung.Conduct)
81	⚽ **Rooney (Open Play)**
84	O'Neil (Off) Kamara (On)
85	**van Nistelrooy (Off) Fortune (On)**
87	Griffin (Foul)
	FULL TIME 2 - 1

STATISTICS

Season	Fixture (Man Utd)		Fixture (Portsmouth)	Season
224	**6**	Shots On Target	**4**	**138**
199	**7**	Shots Off Target	**4**	**141**
14	**0**	Hit Woodwork	**0**	**5**
105	**1**	Caught Offside	**0**	**71**
212	**4**	Corners	**3**	**143**
345	**15**	Fouls	**15**	**335**
55%	**55%**	Possession	**45%**	**47%**

LEAGUE STANDINGS

Position (pos before)	W	D	L	F	A	Pts
2 (2) Man Utd	**18**	**8**	**2**	**47**	**17**	**62**
14 (14) Portsmouth	**8**	**6**	**14**	**31**	**42**	**30**

Manchester United kept up the pressure on leaders Chelsea, with a 2-1 win against a well-organised Portsmouth side at Old Trafford.

Neither Roy Keane or Rio Ferdinand were named in Sir Alex Ferguson's squad, though Ruud van Nistelrooy followed up his substitute appearance against AC Milan in the Champions League with a starting place.

The Dutchman's return to action meant that Wayne Rooney moved to the left-hand side in a now-familiar 4-5-1 formation. The visitors matched this shape, with lone frontman Aiyegbeni Yakubu drilling wide from distance early on.

It took just eight minutes of the contest for United to make a breakthrough. Stand-in skipper Gary Neville delivered from the right with his left foot, and Rooney ghosted in to sweep the ball low past Konstantinos Chalkias from eight yards out.

The men from the South Coast were visibly rocked by falling behind, and somehow survived a goalmouth scramble that ended with Chalkias blocking from an offside van Nistelrooy. Having recovered their composure, Portsmouth were not genuinely threatened again until Cristiano Ronaldo fired over from point-blank range six minutes before the break.

Having emerged from the dressing room for the second half, the visitors netted a surprise equaliser. Gary O'Neil capitalised on Wes Brown's weak clearance, cutting across the ball from 25 yards out to send it swerving agonisingly beyond the diving left hand of the recalled Tim Howard in goal.

A draw was no good to the Old Trafford side, and they created several half-chances in the quest to go back in front. A 12-yard Rooney volley flew narrowly wide, before substitute Ryan Giggs went close with a curling free-kick.

England international Rooney tried to inspire his colleagues with a run and shot from distance, while van Nistelrooy headed straight at Chalkias 15 minutes from time. The pair were not to be denied, however, combining to deadly effect in the 81st minute.

Controlling a long kick forward with his back to goal, the Dutch striker turned and fizzed a ball into Rooney on the edge of the box. The young star's touch took him away from a defender, and he coolly outmaneuvered the keeper to slot home a vital winner.

"Ruud van Nistelrooy is one of the best strikers in the world, and he played a superb ball for me to score the second goal."
Wayne Rooney

PREMIERSHIP MILESTONE

The attendance of 67,989 was a Premiership record

"We had an awful start, which we could not afford in such a difficult fixture, but we composed ourselves."
Joe Jordan

Wayne Rooney thanks Ruud van Nistelrooy for creating his second goal.

PREMIERSHIP FIXTURE HISTORY

Pl: 13 Draws: 3	Wins	⚽	☐	■
Southampton	4	11	19	2
Arsenal	6	18	21	3

STARTING LINE-UPS

Southampton: Smith; Lundekvam (c), Jakobsson; Delap, Bernard; Redknapp, Quashie; Prutton, Le Saux; Camara, Crouch

Arsenal: Henry, van Persie; Pires, Ljungberg; Vieira (c), Flamini; Cole, Toure; Cygan, Senderos; Lehmann

Telfer, Phillips, Poke, Higginbotham, Davenport

Clichy, Eboue, Taylor, Lauren, Aliadiere

EVENT LINE

45 ■ **Prutton (2nd Bookable Offence)**

45 Pires (Off) Clichy (On)

45 ⚽ Ljungberg (Open Play)

HALF TIME 0 - 1

52 ■ van Persie (2nd Bookable Offence)

67 ⚽ **Crouch (Corner)**

72 **Le Saux (Off) Telfer (On)**

75 Toure (Off) Eboue (On)

85 **Camara (Off) Phillips (On)**

FULL TIME 1 - 1

STATISTICS

Season	Fixture		Fixture	Season
132	3	Shots On Target	12	217
153	7	Shots Off Target	5	134
2	0	Hit Woodwork	0	12
86	7	Caught Offside	3	70
135	3	Corners	5	163
364	9	Fouls	13	332
47%	34%	Possession	66%	56%

LEAGUE STANDINGS

Position (pos before)		W	D	L	F	A	Pts
18 (18)	Southampton	3	12	13	29	44	21
3 (3)	Arsenal	17	7	4	64	32	58

Saturday 26th February 2005 | Venue: **Friends Provident St Mary's Stadium** | Attendance: **31,815** | Referee: **A.G.Wiley**

SOUTHAMPTON 1 ARSENAL 1

Moments of madness from David Prutton and Robin van Persie dominated the headlines from this 1-1 draw at St Mary's.

Both men saw red for second bookable offences, with managers and pundits alike agreeing with the decisions made by referee Alan Wiley.

Southampton's Prutton was the first to go. The midfielder had already been cautioned for a reckless lunge at Mathieu Flamini, when his crunching challenge on Robert Pires saw the Arsenal No.7 stretchered off in first-half injury time.

Though it was impossible to argue with the decision, Harry Redknapp had to run down the touchline and drag away his irate player. The linesman nearest the incident appeared to be the subject of fury, with Prutton also laying hands on Wiley.

The incident sparked into life what had previously been a dull affair, and the visitors immediately took advantage of their extra man. With the half-time whistle just moments away, Thierry Henry single-handedly took on the home defence and turned to tee up Freddie Ljungberg for a simple guided finish from eight yards out.

That should have been that, but van Persie evened up the playing field seven minutes after the break. The Dutchman has won few friends outside of Highbury with his surly attitude, and crazily lunged in on Graeme Le Saux to collect a second yellow card. In truth, many referees would have dismissed him for the strong-arm challenge that resulted in his first caution.

Arsene Wenger was clearly incensed by the actions of his player, expressing his displeasure as van Persie made his exit. Suddenly Southampton had been handed a lifeline, and 15 minutes later they grabbed it with both hands.

A floated left-wing corner from Jamie Redknapp was missed by Jens Lehmann, and Peter Crouch nodded the ball down and up into the roof of the net from seven yards out.

The goal earnt a valuable point, but it was the second half heroics of Paul Smith that proved vital. The keeper parried from Henry on two occasions, as well as making a fine reaction-stop from a header. A superb block from Ashley Cole was also important, while the full-back was denied an injury-time winner by a correct offside flag.

Pascal Cygan challenges Peter Crouch.

"David Prutton knows what he did, and the game is not about the sort of things he was doing."
Harry Redknapp

"Of course I am disappointed not to have won. When you are 1-0 up and the opposition is down to ten men, the immediate target is to keep all 11 of your players on the pitch."
Arsene Wenger

PREMIERSHIP MILESTONE

Emmanuel Eboue made his Premiership debut

PREMIERSHIP FIXTURE HISTORY

Pl: **4** Draws: **1**	Wins	Goals	Yellow cards	Red cards
Tottenham Hotspur	2	7	4	1
Fulham	1	4	7	1

STARTING LINE-UPS

Tottenham subs: Kanoute, Keane, Cerny, Pamarot, Ziegler

Fulham subs: John, McBride, Crossley, Volz, Legwinski

EVENT LINE

HALF TIME 0 - 0

59 Cole (Off) John (On)

73 **Defoe (Off) Kanoute (On)**

77 Clark (Foul)

78 **Kanoute (Direct Free Kick)**

79 **Mido (Off) Keane (On)**

86 Jensen (Off) McBride (On)

90 **Keane (Open Play)**

FULL TIME 2 - 0

STATISTICS

Season	Fixture		Fixture	Season
166	**8**	Shots On Target	**5**	**128**
151	**11**	Shots Off Target	**3**	**119**
10	**0**	Hit Woodwork	**0**	**3**
105	**6**	Caught Offside	**9**	**72**
137	**14**	Corners	**2**	**131**
325	**6**	Fouls	**13**	**336**
50%	**52%**	Possession	**48%**	**48%**

LEAGUE STANDINGS

Position (pos before)		W	D	L	F	A	Pts
8 (9)	**Tottenham H**	**11**	**6**	**10**	**35**	**30**	**39**
15 (15)	**Fulham**	**8**	**5**	**14**	**33**	**46**	**29**

Saturday 26th February 2005 | Venue: **White Hart Lane** | Attendance: **35,885** | Referee: **N.S.Barry**

TOTTENHAM HOTSPUR 2 FULHAM 0

Substitute strikers Frederic Kanoute and Robbie Keane emerged from the bench to settle this London derby in Tottenham's favour.

Spurs came into the game on the back of a terrible recent record in capital clashes. The men from White Hart Lane had won just one of their previous 22 derby matches in the Premiership, and looked set to extend that hopeless record until late on.

Martin Jol opted to revert to the strike pairing of Mido and Jermain Defoe that had served him so well in the last league game against Portsmouth. Andy Reid also returned, having been cup-tied for the F.A.Cup clashes with West Brom and his old club Nottingham Forest.

Opposing boss Chris Coleman welcomed back Danish midfielder Claus Jensen to his top-flight starting XI for the first time since late October. Defender Alain Goma had been absent from Premiership action for slightly longer, and also returned.

It was the home side that began brightly, with Mido a constant threat. The Egyptian dragged a shot wide after just four minutes, and then fired over when picked out inside the box by Welsh midfielder Simon Davies.

The pressure continued apace, as Andy Cole cleared Michael Brown's 22nd-minute effort off the line, before Edwin van der Sar plunged low to his right to turn away a long-range drive from the lively Reid. Captain Ledley King then saw a header deflected narrowly wide, as Tottenham failed to capitalise on their dominance.

Fulham's only attempt worthy of a mention was a powerful shot from distance by Pape Bouba Diop after 43 minutes. Unfortunately for the midfielder, the strike worried the crowd behind the goal more than it did Paul Robinson.

The second period was a carbon copy of the first, except that Jol's team eventually made a breakthrough. Having been on the field just five minutes, Kanoute curled a 25-yard free-kick from the inside-left channel around the wall and into the unguarded bottom right-hand corner of the net.

The Frenchman then teed up Keane for an unbelievable close-range miss, before the Irish international made amends in injury time as he outmuscled Luis Boa Morte and rounded van der Sar to tap home.

Carlos Bocanegra keeps an eye on Simon Davies.

"I don't want to comment on the speculation linking me with the Ajax job."

Martin Jol

PREMIERSHIP MILESTONE

650 Frederic Kanoute netted Tottenham's 650th Premiership goal

"My two central defenders played really well, and you would expect our keeper to deal with the free-kick which Kanoute scored from."

Chris Coleman

PREMIERSHIP FIXTURE HISTORY

Pl: 6 Draws: 5	Wins	Goals	Yellow	Red
Middlesbrough	1	5	4	0
Charlton Athletic	0	3	10	0

STARTING LINE-UPS

Graham, Job, Parnaby, Knight, Cooper

Johansson, Euell, Andersen, Fish, Jeffers

EVENT LINE

14 Holland (Open Play)

HALF TIME 0 - 1

57 Konchesky (Foul)

70 Hreidarsson (Foul)

72 Thomas (Off) Johansson (On)

74 **Riggott (Indirect Free Kick)**

76 Perry (Foul)

78 Murphy (Off) Euell (On)

80 Bartlett (Open Play)

82 **Reiziger (Off) Graham (On)**

86 **Parlour (Off) Job (On)**

86 **Graham (Open Play)**

87 **Nemeth (Off) Parnaby (On)**

FULL TIME 2 - 2

STATISTICS

Season	Fixture		Fixture	Season
202	18	Shots On Target	2	119
156	3	Shots Off Target	3	97
5	0	Hit Woodwork	0	5
72	1	Caught Offside	4	92
165	10	Corners	1	114
345	12	Fouls	15	343
50%	63%	Possession	37%	44%

LEAGUE STANDINGS

Position (pos before)		W	D	L	F	A	Pts
6 (6)	Middlesbrough	11	9	8	43	37	42
9 (9)	Charlton Ath	11	6	10	32	38	39

Sunday 27th February 2005 | Venue: **Riverside Stadium** | Attendance: **29,603** | Referee: **M.A.Riley**

MIDDLESBROUGH 2 CHARLTON ATHLETIC 2

Szilard Nemeth tries to hold off Danny Murphy.

"It's difficult after playing a European game on the Thursday, and there was no great tempo in our first half performance."

Steve McClaren

PREMIERSHIP MILESTONE

50 Stewart Downing made his 50th Premiership appearance

PREMIERSHIP MILESTONE

Danny Graham scored his first Premiership goal

"Dean Kiely made some great saves, and I thought at one stage we could have won the game."

Alan Curbishley

This fixture ended all-square for the fifth consecutive season, as youngster Danny Graham rescued a point for Middlesbrough with his first Premiership goal.

An injury to Mark Schwarzer meant a rare start for Carlo Nash, while Stewart Downing recovered from being stretchered off in the midweek UEFA Cup win against Grazer AK of Austria to take up his position on the left of midfield.

Charlton had not played in the Premiership for three weeks, but came into the game on the back of a demoralising F.A.Cup defeat at the hands of Leicester City. Alan Curbishley's men had been comprehensively outplayed by the Championship side, and were looking to get their season back on track.

The opening period was not a classic, with the visitors establishing a 14th-minute lead. Captain Matt Holland struck a 20-yard drive that deflected past Nash via the left boot of Gareth Southgate, though Shaun Bartlett appeared to control the ball with his arm in the build-up.

Slovakian Szilard Nemeth had a golden chance to equalise before the break, but saw his close-range half-volley sensationally repelled by Dean Kiely after he had exchanged passes with Jimmy Floyd Hasselbaink.

That attack apart, Steve McClaren's side posed little threat in an opening period that the men from South London just about shaded.

Everything changed after the break, however, as Middlesbrough layed siege to the Charlton goal. Former Bury custodian Kiely was in magnificent form, maintaining his team's advantage with a string of miraculous saves.

The keeper denied Chris Riggott with two fine reaction stops, turned over a clever chip from Boudewijn Zenden, and somehow prevented an own goal by Hermann Hreidarsson, before eventually being beaten 16 minutes from time.

The Addicks failed to clear a left-wing free-kick, with Riggott turning home a close-range leveller from a clearly-offside position after Southgate had helped Hasselbaink's shot into his path.

There was still time for both teams to net another goal, Bartlett firing home a bouncing ball following a break down the left in the 80th minute, before substitute Graham bravely nodded home over Kiely from Franck Queudrue's punt forward late on.

PREMIERSHIP FIXTURE HISTORY

Pl: 6 Draws: 1	Wins	Goals	Yellow cards	Red cards
Newcastle United	5	10	4	0
Bolton Wanderers	0	5	8	0

STARTING LINE-UPS

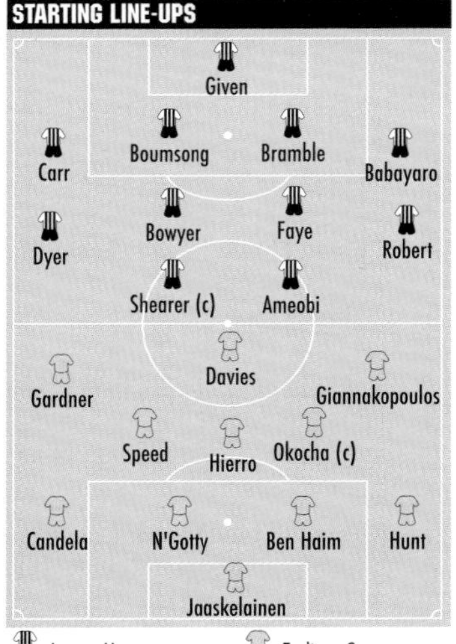

Newcastle subs: Jenas, Harper, Hughes, Butt, Milner

Bolton subs: Fadiga, Campo, Vaz Te, Poole, Jaidi

EVENT LINE

14 Hunt (Off) Fadiga (On)

35 **Bowyer (Open Play)**

41 Giannakopoulos (Open Play)

HALF TIME 1 - 1

47 Ben Haim (Foul)

50 Hierro (Foul)

64 Hierro (Off) Campo (On)

69 **Dyer (Open Play)**

77 **Robert (Off) Jenas (On)**

77 Okocha (Off) Vaz Te (On)

FULL TIME 2 - 1

STATISTICS

Season	Fixture (Newcastle)		Fixture (Bolton)	Season
192	9	Shots On Target	2	171
154	5	Shots Off Target	2	154
10	0	Hit Woodwork	0	6
75	8	Caught Offside	5	71
181	6	Corners	3	145
334	12	Fouls	19	378
50%	49%	Possession	51%	49%

LEAGUE STANDINGS

Position (pos before)		W	D	L	F	A	Pts
11 (13)	Newcastle Utd	8	10	9	39	44	34
7 (7)	Bolton W	11	7	10	36	34	40

Sunday 27th February 2005 | Venue: **St James' Park** | Attendance: **50,430** | Referee: **S.W.Dunn**

NEWCASTLE UNITED 2 BOLTON WANDERERS 1

Having made recent progress in both the F.A.Cup and UEFA Cup, Newcastle made it four consecutive wins in all competitions with a 2-1 victory against Bolton.

rejuvenated Kieron Dyer struck a 69th-minute winner, after first half goals from Lee Bowyer and Stylianos Giannakopoulos had cancelled each other out.

The returning Gary Speed was afforded a warm welcome by the St James' Park crowd, and it was his replacement in the North-East side's engine room, Amdy Faye, who was involved in the incident that saw Nicky Hunt depart the scene injured.

The former Portsmouth midfielder charged down a cross from the full-back, with the ball ricocheting against the defender and seeming to dislocate his shoulder. Khalilou Fadiga emerged from the bench to take his place, with Ricardo Gardner dropping back into a more familiar defensive role.

The Magpies had a great chance to take the lead after 25 minutes. Alan Shearer's low shot was parried out to the right wing by Jussi Jaaskelainen, who then kept out Dyer's close-range header from Titus Bramble's accurate centre.

A Newcastle goal did arrive 10 minutes later, however, with Bowyer starting and finishing the move. The midfielder beat two players and spread the ball out to Stephen Carr on the right, before bursting into the box to head home the Irish international's cross.

The lead lasted just six minutes though, as Giannakopoulos drove an eight-yard effort into the far left-hand corner after a neat build-up involving Jay-Jay Okocha, Kevin Davies and Speed. The Greek international was then denied from a similar position moments later.

Fernando Hierro, preferred to countryman Ivan Campo in the midfield anchor role, was lucky to escape with a 50th-minute yellow card after scything down a marauding Dyer on the edge of the box. The Spaniard was not the last defender, but the foul was cynical in the extreme.

Laurent Robert curled the resulting free-kick over the wall and wide, before Dyer made the breakthrough with a ferocious 12-yard strike after Shearer's effort had been blocked. Further chances were spurned, but Newcastle comfortably maintained their slender advantage.

Kieron Dyer celebrates his winning strike.

"I thought Kieron Dyer was excellent. The more he plays, the more he understands the position in which he is playing."

Graeme Souness

PREMIERSHIP MILESTONE

100 Jermaine Jenas made his 100th Premiership appearance

"I was very disappointed with the final result, and in particular with our second half showing."

Sam Allardyce

PREMIERSHIP MILESTONE

50 Amdy Faye made his 50th Premiership appearance

PREMIERSHIP MILESTONE

Vincent Candela made his Premiership debut

PREMIERSHIP FIXTURE HISTORY

Pl: 4 Draws: 2	Wins	Goals	Yellow cards	Red cards
Norwich City	1	6	6	1
Manchester City	1	6	4	0

STARTING LINE-UPS

Safri, Gallacher, Charlton, McVeigh, Henderson

Sommeil, Weaver, Flood, McManaman, B.Wright-Phillips

EVENT LINE

12 **Ashton (Open Play)**
16 **McKenzie (Open Play)**
17 **Stuart (Foul)**
25 Sibierski (Corner)
37 Fowler (Open Play)

HALF TIME 2 - 2

51 Barton (Foul)
66 **Jonson (2nd Bookable Offence)**
74 **Stuart (Off) Safri (On)**
76 Jordan (Foul)
90 Fowler (Open Play)

FULL TIME 2 - 3

STATISTICS

Season	Fixture		Fixture	Season
131	3	Shots On Target	6	151
145	2	Shots Off Target	9	142
5	0	Hit Woodwork	0	2
89	2	Caught Offside	0	79
131	3	Corners	12	176
373	13	Fouls	8	353
45%	39%	Possession	61%	49%

LEAGUE STANDINGS

Position (pos before)	W	D	L	F	A	Pts
19 (19) Norwich C	3	11	14	28	55	20
10 (12) Man City	9	9	10	34	31	36

Monday 28th February 2005 | Venue: **Carrow Road** | Attendance: **24,302** | Referee: **R.Styles**

Manchester City celebrate their late winner.

"We got two very good goals and we hassled and harried them, but then we stood off."
Nigel Worthington

PREMIERSHIP MILESTONE
Jason Shackell made his Premiership debut

"The one thing we will take out of this game is character. We showed a great spirit to come back from an horrendous start."
Kevin Keegan

PREMIERSHIP MILESTONE
150 Robbie Fowler's first goal was his 150th in the Premiership

PREMIERSHIP MILESTONE
100 Sylvain Distin made his 100th Premiership appearance for Man City

NORWICH CITY 2
MANCHESTER CITY 3

Norwich surrendered a priceless two-goal lead, eventually succumbing to a last-gasp 3-2 defeat at the hands of Manchester City.

Strikers Dean Ashton and Leon McKenzie set the Canaries on the way to what seemed a vital victory, only for Antoine Sibierski and Robbie Fowler, with his 150th Premiership goal, to draw things level prior to the interval. The second half dismissal of Mattias Jonson did not help the home side's cause, and Fowler then popped up with a cruel injury-time winner.

Kiki Musampa fired narrowly wide with the first chance of the match, before Ashton netted an exquisite 12th-minute goal. There seemed little danger as Adam Drury floated the ball forward from deep, but the former Crewe man deftly lobbed over David James and into the far right-hand corner of the net with the outside of his foot.

Four minutes later, Carrow Road erupted again as McKenzie scored. The former Peterborough man raced clear from halfway, eventually scuffing a 15-yard shot through the legs of Sylvain Distin and beyond the committed goalkeeper.

It was all-action at both ends, as Sibierski fired over and Shaun Wright-Phillips forced a save from Robert Green. Then, after 25 minutes, Sibierski was left unchallenged to head home Musampa's inswinging cross from the right.

The tide turned with that goal, and City drew level eight minutes before the break. The ball was worked to Wright-Phillips on the left, and his low centre was expertly steered home by an onrushing Fowler from around the penalty spot.

The pace of the game did not let up after the break, though this time the currency was cards rather than goals. Joey Barton and Jonson were both cautioned for fouls, before the Swede was shown a second yellow for an over-zealous 66th-minute challenge.

Nigel Worthington's men were faced with an uphill task, but seemed to have weathered the storm until Fowler netted. The striker was on hand to scuff the ball home from close range, after Green had parried Wright-Phillips' low drive from the right of the six-yard box.

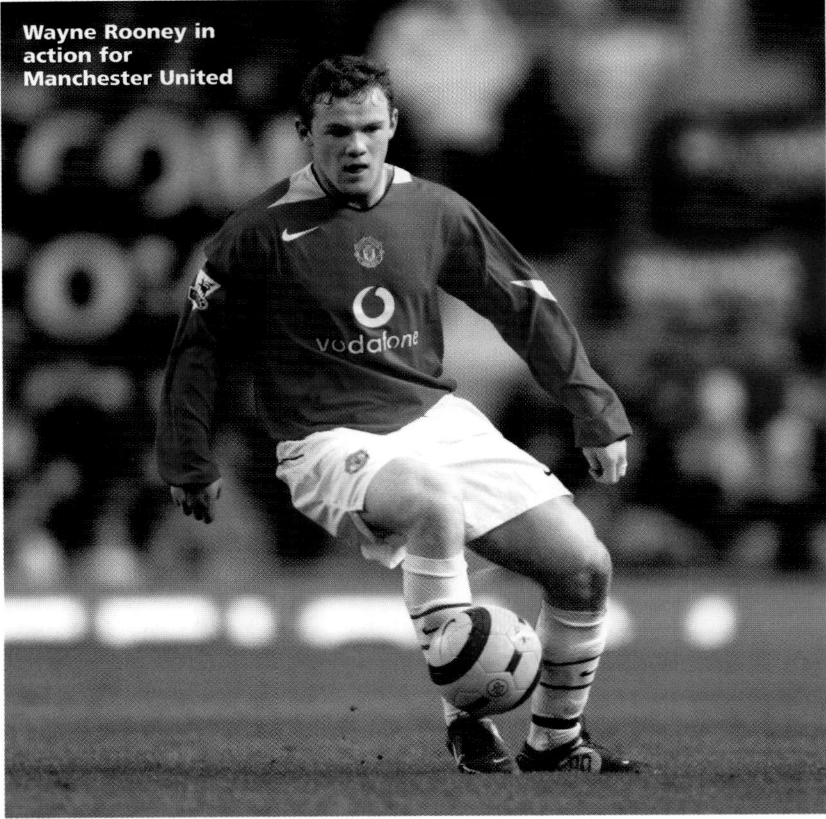

Wayne Rooney in action for Manchester United

FEBRUARY 2005

The first trophy of the season went to Chelsea, as they recovered from conceding a first-minute goal to defeat Liverpool 3-2 after extra-time in the Carling Cup Final. Manchester United took full advantage of the Londoners' absence from league duty, moving to within six points of the leaders after victory at home to Portsmouth.

Sir Alex Ferguson's team had begun February with a 4-2 win against Arsenal at Highbury. The result killed off any lingering title hopes that the Gunners might have had, and Arsene Wenger's men went on to drop two further points at Southampton later in the month.

The 1-1 draw at St Mary's was notable for David Prutton's reaction to being sent off. The former Nottingham Forest midfielder saw red in more ways than one, and had to be restrained by his manager as he attempted to confront the referee's assistant.

Elsewhere in the lower reaches of the table, Crystal Palace established a four-point cushion above the relegation zone. Iain Dowie's Eagles beat Birmingham 2-0, courtesy of a pair of Andy Johnson penalties, to leave the bottom three with much work to do.

By this point, Johnson had already been handed an England debut. Middlesbrough's Stewart Downing also made his international bow in the 0-0 friendly draw with Holland at Villa Park, though neither player was given much of a chance to impress.

It was a time of mixed fortunes for English clubs in Europe. While Newcastle and Middlesbrough both advanced to the last 16 of the UEFA Cup, three of our Champions League representatives suffered first leg defeats.

Liverpool were the good news story, defeating Bayer Leverkusen 3-1 at Anfield, though most of the column inches were devoted to Jose Mourinho. The Chelsea boss kicked up quite a storm with his claims that referee Anders Frisk had spoken with Barcelona chief Frank Rijkaard at half-time during his side's 2-1 defeat at the Nou Camp.

IN THE NEWS

02ND	An Aaron Mokoena challenge results in Arjen Robben breaking two bones in his foot at Blackburn. The winger faces being sidelined for around six weeks as a result of the injury.
02ND	Blackburn captain Andy Todd commits his future to the club by putting pen to paper on a contract that will keep him at Ewood Park until the summer of 2008
04TH	Manchester United announce plans to extend Old Trafford's capacity to 76,000 in time for the start of the 2006-07 season
04TH	Australian international goalkeeper Mark Schwarzer puts an end to speculation about his future by signing a new three-year deal with Middlesbrough
06TH	The F.A. Premier League confirm they are to hold a formal investigation into Chelsea's alleged illegal approach for Arsenal full-back Ashley Cole
09TH	Crystal Palace's Andy Johnson and Middlesbrough's Stewart Downing make their international debuts as second half substitutes in England's 0-0 friendly draw with Holland at Villa Park
10TH	Southampton midfielder Anders Svensson signs a pre-contract agreement to rejoin his former club Elfsborg from July 1
27TH	Chelsea win the Carling Cup, defeating Liverpool 3-2 after extra-time at the Millennium Stadium

TEAM OF THE MONTH

Paul Smith
Southampton

With less than 90 minutes worth of Premiership experience under his belt, Smith was a relative unknown to Southampton supporters. That changed dramatically when injury to Antti Niemi thrust him into the spotlight, as the young keeper turned in a series of heroic performances.

Stephen Carr
Newcastle Utd

The Irish international full-back's performances offered no indication that he had been out injured for the best part of three months. Galloping up and down the touchline as though he had never been away, Carr was part of a team that was not beaten during February.

Tal Ben Haim
Bolton Wanderers

Having struggled to earn a starting place earlier in the season, Ben Haim cemented his position as a first-team regular with a string of fine displays. A late goal helped secure three points against Tottenham, while clean sheets followed in encounters with Crystal Palace and Middlesbrough.

William Gallas
Chelsea

Three Premiership clean sheets during the month ensured that Chelsea had not conceded a top-flight goal since Gallas replaced Ricardo Carvalho at the heart of the defence in mid-December. The French international also found time to set up the winner at Everton.

Ashley Cole
Arsenal

The England international left-back did not let growing transfer speculation affect his performances on the pitch. A goal in Arsenal's 3-1 win at Villa Park highlighted the defender's value at both ends of the field.

PLAYER OF THE MONTH

Wayne Rooney
Manchester United

Whether playing as a lone striker or supporting the frontman from a position wide on the left, Rooney always delivered. Four goals, including one in the 2-0 derby win at Manchester City, were supplemented by two assists.

"Wayne Rooney deserves recognition for his first 'Barclays Player of the Month' award, as his fantastic strike rate has been instrumental in the club's recent run of form."

Barclays Awards Panel

MANAGER OF THE MONTH

Sir Alex Ferguson
Manchester United

Maximum points from their four games during the month propelled Sir Alex Ferguson's side back into the title picture. A stunning 4-2 win at Highbury secured a Premiership 'double' over champions Arsenal, while the Old Trafford side also reached the last eight in the F.A.Cup.

Premiership Career Statistics
up until end of February 2005
Matches:**496** Wins:**310** Draws:**115** Losses:**71**

"Sir Alex's award not only marks a fantastic month for Manchester United, but reinforces his position as one of the most successful managers in club and league history."

Barclays Awards Panel

Cristiano Ronaldo
Manchester United

The winger was in enchanting form during February, netting two vital goals in a win at Arsenal and then turning provider at home to Birmingham. A further strike at Everton in the F.A.Cup 5th Round helped his team make progress.

Claude Makelele
Chelsea

It is no coincidence that Real Madrid have not been the force they were since allowing Claude Makelele to leave. The defensive midfielder is one of the first names on the teamsheet at Stamford Bridge, and helped his side to three Premiership clean sheets during the month.

Roy Keane
Manchester United

The Manchester United captain was back to something resembling his best, and the team responded to their inspirational leader. Never was this more apparent than when Keane lifted his troops at home to Birmingham, driving into the box and rifling home a vital goal.

Morten Gamst Pedersen
Blackburn Rovers

Having initially struggled to establish himself under Mark Hughes, Pedersen had now made the left-wing position his own. Though Blackburn didn't enjoy the best of months, the Norwegian international was the star in a 3-0 victory against Norwich.

Henri Camara
Southampton

The Senegalese international made an explosive start to life at Southampton, scoring within seven minutes of coming on for his debut at Birmingham. A goal against Everton was then followed by an F.A.Cup brace at home to Brentford, as Camara became an instant hit on the South Coast.

MONTH IN NUMBERS

36 Games Played

98 Total Goals Scored

2.72 Average Goals Per Game

4 Player With Most Goals (Johnson, Rooney)

11 Club With Most Goals (Arsenal)

4 Fastest Goal (Beattie)

44.4% Percentage Of Away Wins

27.8% Percentage Of Home Wins

27.8% Percentage Of Draws

5-1 Biggest Win (Arsenal 5 v 1 Crystal Palace)

97 Total Yellow Cards

8 Total Red Cards

2.7 Average Yellow Cards Per Game

16 Most Disciplinary Points (Sorondo)

8 Fastest Booking (Beattie)

34,175 Average Attendance

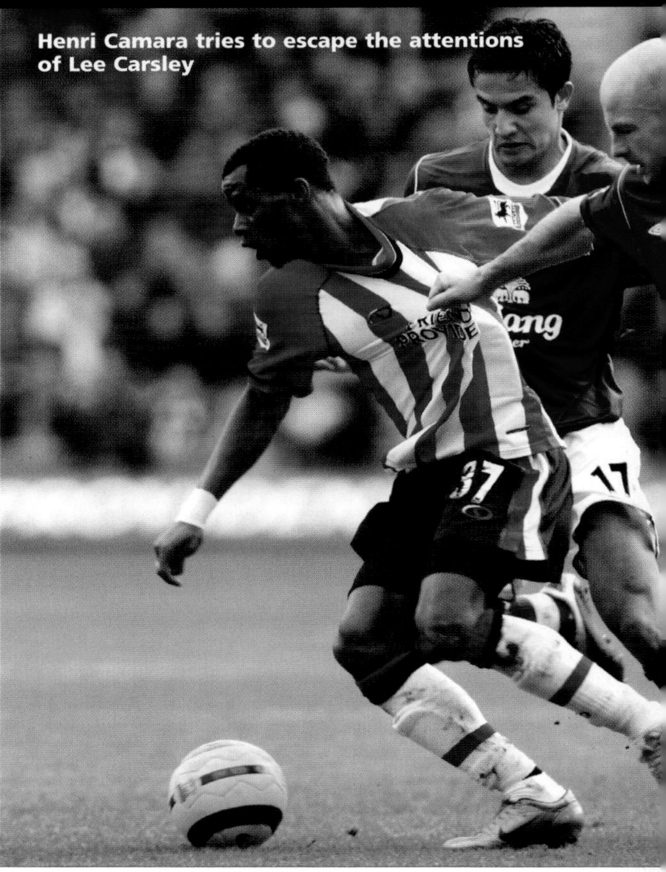
Henri Camara tries to escape the attentions of Lee Carsley

PREMIERSHIP TABLE / TEAM STATISTICS

Pos (last month)	Team	Played	Won	Drawn	Lost	Goals for	Goals against	Goal diff	Points	Shots on target	Hit woodwork	Shots off target	Failed to score	Clean sheets	Corners	Caught Offside	Players used
1 - (1)	Chelsea	27	21	5	1	50	8	+42	68	202	9	167	4	21	184	86	23
2 ▲ (3)	Manchester United	28	18	8	2	47	17	+30	62	224	14	199	6	15	212	105	26
3 ▼ (2)	Arsenal	28	17	7	4	64	32	+32	58	217	12	134	2	9	163	70	23
4 - (4)	Everton	28	15	6	7	34	29	+5	51	137	6	151	7	10	135	69	21
5 - (5)	Liverpool	27	13	4	10	41	29	+12	43	174	5	184	9	5	154	65	26
6 - (6)	Middlesbrough	28	11	9	8	43	37	+6	42	202	5	156	7	7	165	72	24
7 ▲ (9)	Bolton Wanderers	28	11	7	10	36	34	+2	40	171	6	154	6	6	145	71	24
8 - (8)	Tottenham Hotspur	27	11	6	10	35	30	+5	39	166	10	151	9	11	137	105	29
9 ▼ (7)	Charlton Athletic	27	11	6	10	32	38	-6	39	119	5	97	8	9	114	92	20
10 - (10)	Manchester City	28	9	9	10	34	31	+3	36	151	2	142	9	7	176	79	22
11 - (11)	Aston Villa	28	9	8	11	32	37	-5	35	141	5	144	8	8	157	82	22
12 - (12)	Newcastle United	27	8	10	9	39	44	-5	34	192	10	154	5	3	181	75	25
13 ▲ (15)	Birmingham City	28	8	8	12	31	35	-4	32	127	6	118	9	7	148	83	27
14 - (14)	Portsmouth	28	8	6	14	31	42	-11	30	138	5	141	7	4	143	71	25
15 ▼ (13)	Fulham	27	8	5	14	33	46	-13	29	128	3	119	8	5	131	72	24
16 - (16)	Blackburn Rovers	27	6	10	11	24	36	-12	28	142	6	160	12	8	160	102	30
17 - (17)	Crystal Palace	28	6	7	15	32	45	-13	25	121	5	121	7	7	135	69	27
18 - (18)	Southampton	28	3	12	13	29	44	-15	21	132	2	153	10	6	135	86	34
19 - (19)	Norwich City	28	3	11	14	28	55	-27	20	131	5	145	12	3	131	89	25
20 - (20)	West Brom	27	2	12	13	23	49	-26	18	124	9	117	10	4	127	95	25

TEAM FORM

Pos	Team	Form	Goals For	Goals Against	Pts
1	Manchester United	WWWW	10	3	12
2	Arsenal	LWWD	11	7	7
3	Bolton Wanderers	WWDL	5	3	7
4	Everton	WDLW	6	4	7
5	Chelsea	WDW	2	0	7
6	Tottenham Hotspur	LWW	6	4	6
7	Liverpool	WWL	5	4	6
8	Birmingham City	WLWL	4	5	6
9	Newcastle United	DDW	4	3	5
10	Middlesbrough	LWDD	4	4	5
11	Manchester City	DDLW	4	5	5
12	Crystal Palace	DLLW	5	8	4
13	Aston Villa	DLWL	5	8	4
14	Blackburn Rovers	LLW	3	2	3
15	Southampton	LDDD	4	5	3
16	Portsmouth	WLLL	5	8	3
17	Norwich City	LWLL	5	9	3
18	West Brom	DLD	4	5	2
19	Charlton Athletic	LDD	4	5	2
20	Fulham	DLL	2	6	1

TOP GOALSCORERS

Player	This Month	Total
T.Henry Arsenal	3	**19**
A.Johnson Crystal Palace	4	**18**
J.Defoe Tottenham Hotspur	1	**11**
A.Yakubu Portsmouth	2	**10**
A.Cole Fulham	1	**10**
J.Hasselbaink Middlesbrough	0	**10**
R.Pires Arsenal	0	**10**
W.Rooney Manchester United	4	**9**
P.Dickov Blackburn Rovers	2	**9**
F.Ljungberg Arsenal	2	**9**
M.Baros Liverpool	1	**9**
S.Wright-Phillips Manchester City	0	**9**
R.Fowler Manchester City	3	**8**
R.Keane Tottenham Hotspur	2	**8**
E.Gudjohnsen Chelsea	1	**8**
D.Drogba Chelsea	0	**8**
P.Scholes Manchester United	0	**8**

MOST GOAL ASSISTS

Player	This Month	Total
T.Henry Arsenal	4	**15**
S.Downing Middlesbrough	1	**13**
F.Lampard Chelsea	0	**13**
F.Ljungberg Arsenal	0	**11**
S.Wright-Phillips Manchester City	3	**9**
L.Boa Morte Fulham	2	**9**
R.Giggs Manchester United	2	**9**
W.Routledge Crystal Palace	0	**9**
J.Hasselbaink Middlesbrough	0	**9**
D.Bergkamp Arsenal	2	**8**
E.Gudjohnsen Chelsea	1	**8**
A.Robben Chelsea	0	**8**
A.Johnson Crystal Palace	2	**7**
J.Reyes Arsenal	2	**7**
J.Greening West Brom	1	**7**
E.Heskey Birmingham City	1	**7**
D.Huckerby Norwich City	1	**7**
L.Robert Newcastle United	0	**7**

DISCIPLINE

F.A. disciplinary points: Yellow=4 points, Two Bookable Offences=10 points and Red Card=12 points

Player	Y	SB	R	PTS
L.Hendrie Aston Villa	7	0	1	**40**
R.Parlour Middlesbrough	7	1	0	**38**
P.Diop Fulham	6	0	1	**36**
D.Johnson Birmingham City	6	1	0	**34**
D.Prutton Southampton	6	1	0	**34**
K.Tugay Blackburn Rovers	6	1	0	**34**
D.Mills Manchester City	5	0	1	**32**
P.Vieira Arsenal	8	0	0	**32**
T.Cahill Everton	5	1	0	**30**
Josemi Liverpool	5	1	0	**30**
A.Cole Arsenal	7	0	0	**28**
M.Hughes Crystal Palace	7	0	0	**28**
L.Bowyer Newcastle United	4	1	0	**26**
A.Faye Newcastle United	4	1	0	**26**

"I want him around the place, even if it means he doesn't play every week. He is a great example to everyone, and I have not given up hope of him staying."

Graeme Souness on Alan Shearer's impending retirement

"Andy does work that right channel very well, and maybe Sven has seen that, but there is no doubt his strengths are in a central area."

Iain Dowie on Andy Johnson's out-of-position international debut

"Before the game there was all this stuff about anti-racism and anti-bullying. It would be a good idea to start wearing wristbands for anti-diving."

Roy Keane after a 4-2 victory at Arsenal

"I expected much more from my team as the Champions League is very important to us. It's difficult to find a reason as to why we didn't perform. Whether it was down to psychological or physical reasons, I don't know yet."

Arsene Wenger after a 3-1 first leg defeat away to Bayern Munich

"I have a lot of respect for Liverpool fans. What I did, the sign of silence, was not for them, it was for the English press."

Jose Mourinho in the wake of Chelsea's Carling Cup success

"This is a message for possibly the best supporters in the world. We need a 12th man. Where are you? Where are you?"

Delia Smith makes an impassioned half-time plea for greater vocal support after Norwich squander an early two-goal lead at home to Manchester City

"The fact that no English side has won the 'Champions League' since Manchester United in 1999 just goes to show how difficult it is to win."

Steven Gerrard

PREMIERSHIP FIXTURE HISTORY

Pl: 2 Draws: 1	Wins	⚽	▢	▢
Arsenal	1	4	2	0
Portsmouth	0	1	5	0

STARTING LINE-UPS

Arsenal substitutes: Lauren, van Persie, Ljungberg, Almunia, Eboue

Portsmouth substitutes: Primus, Kamara, Hislop, Mezague, Fuller

EVENT LINE

24 ⇄ **Cygan (Off) Lauren (On)**

26 ⇄ Griffin (Off) Primus (On)

39 ⚽ **Henry (Open Play)**

43 ▢ Primus (Foul)

45 ▢ Stefanovic (Foul)

HALF TIME 1 - 0

53 ⚽ **Henry (Open Play)**

70 ⇄ Berger (Off) Kamara (On)

74 ⇄ **Owusu-Abeyie (Off) van Persie (On)**

78 ⇄ **Fabregas (Off) Ljungberg (On)**

85 ⚽ **Henry (Direct Free Kick)**

FULL TIME 3 - 0

STATISTICS

Season	Fixture (Arsenal)		Fixture (Portsmouth)	Season
222	5	Shots On Target	2	140
139	5	Shots Off Target	3	144
12	0	Hit Woodwork	1	6
71	1	Caught Offside	3	74
170	7	Corners	3	146
344	12	Fouls	15	350
56%	56%	Possession	44%	47%

LEAGUE STANDINGS

Position (pos before)		W	D	L	F	A	Pts
3 (3)	Arsenal	18	7	4	67	32	61
15 (14)	Portsmouth	8	6	15	31	45	30

Saturday 5th March 2005 | Venue: **Highbury** | Attendance: **38,079** | Referee: **C.J.Foy**

ARSENAL 3 PORTSMOUTH 0

Ashley Cole is shadowed by Gary O'Neil.

"This was a very solid team performance. It became a comfortable win, but we had to work hard to make it comfortable."

Arsene Wenger

PREMIERSHIP MILESTONE

Quincy Owusu-Abeyie made his Premiership debut

PREMIERSHIP MILESTONE

50 Pascal Cygan made his 50th Premiership appearance

"Today, over the 90 minutes, I can't say that we deserved anything from the game."

Joe Jordan

A hat-trick from Thierry Henry secured the points for a youthful-looking Arsenal side at Highbury.

With Dennis Bergkamp and Jose Antonio Reyes suspended, Quincy Owusu-Abeyie was rewarded for a fine midweek F.A.Cup showing with a place in attack. Elsewhere, Ashley Cole played in advance of Gael Clichy on the left.

Portsmouth arrived at Highbury having collected just four points from the last 27 available. Patrik Berger replaced Richard Hughes in the visitors' five-man midfield, in the only change from the side defeated 2-1 at Old Trafford seven days earlier.

Both teams had openings early on. Lomana Tresor Lua Lua fired straight at Jens Lehmann from distance, before Owusu-Abeyie drilled an effort across the face of goal. Lone striker Aiyegbeni Yakubu then gave the Gunners a massive scare, powerfully heading Matthew Taylor's left-wing centre against the crossbar.

Pompey captain Arjan De Zeeuw headed over from a corner, as Arsenal continued to look vulnerable defensively. Arsene Wenger's men were having no such problems going forward, however, and went in front after 39 minutes.

Lauren, who had replaced the injured Pascal Cygan, overlapped down the right and cut the ball back for Henry. Having received possession some 12 yards out, the French striker found the bottom left-hand corner with a shot that took a slight deflection on its way in.

Patrick Vieira should have made it two before the break, blazing over from close range after Konstantinos Chalkias had inexplicably dropped a corner. The midfielder redeemed himself eight minutes after the interval though, slipping a pass through for Henry to dink over the advancing goalkeeper.

Portsmouth nearly found a way back into the game with 17 minutes remaining, as Yakubu prodded wide from no more than six yards out. Any hope of a comeback seemed to evaporate with that miss, and Henry secured the victory five minutes from time.

Having won a free-kick on the left of the 'D' some 20 yards out, the former Juventus man curled an effort over the defensive wall. A fine save appeared to have kept the score at 2-0, but the ball found the back of the net via the right boot of a falling Chalkias.

ASTON VILLA 2 MIDDLESBROUGH 0

Martin Laursen and Luke Moore scored the goals that swung a dire contest in favour of Aston Villa.

With both managers opting to play a 4-5-1 formation, the midfield proved to be a crowded area. Having not started a top-flight game in over four months, Darius Vassell was surprisingly left to plough a lone furrow in the home attack.

Jimmy Floyd Hasselbaink occupied the same role for the visitors, and came closest to scoring in a half of few chances. The Dutch striker did well to unleash a powerful drive, but the ball was deflected wide via the sliding challenge of J'Lloyd Samuel.

That apart, neither team had genuine cause for concern during the opening 45 minutes. Things picked up after the interval though, as Boudewijn Zenden and Nolberto Solano both caused moments of panic.

Firstly, referee Rob Styles had to be alert to chalk off a Middlesbrough goal, as a tumbling Zenden teed up a simple finish for a team-mate using his hand. Then, Solano was unable to swivel enough when hammering wide of a gaping net from six yards out.

The Peruvian helped atone for his glaring miss by playing a part in Villa's 64th-minute opener. A left-wing corner seemed to be helped on by the arm of Moore, with Laursen arriving to bundle the ball home from close range at the back post.

The Dane had not appeared since picking up a knee injury in late August, and tore down the touchline to celebrate like a man possessed.

The visitors seldom looked like finding a way back into the match, and Moore joined Laursen in netting his first goal for the club. The young forward struck 11 minutes from time, firing into the top right-hand corner from seven yards out after Carlo Nash had parried Solano's dipping near-post free-kick from the left.

David O'Leary's men were worthy winners in the end, showing a greater hunger and desire to earn the three points than their lacklustre opponents. A Stewart Downing drive that flew high over the bar was about as good as it got for the team from Teesside.

"It was a big game for us, and the win was vital."

David O'Leary

PREMIERSHIP MILESTONE

Martin Laursen and Luke Moore both netted their first Premiership goal

"I've just got to write this match off very quickly. There are still nine league games to be played, and we are still in Europe."

Steve McClaren

Stuart Parnaby keeps track of Gareth Barry.

PREMIERSHIP FIXTURE HISTORY

Pl: **10** Draws: **3**	Wins	Goals	Yellow cards	Red cards
Aston Villa	**6**	**14**	**11**	**0**
Middlesbrough	**1**	**5**	**17**	**1**

STARTING LINE-UPS

Aston Villa substitutes: L.Moore, Ridgewell, Hitzlsperger, Postma, Djemba-Djemba

Middlesbrough substitutes: Graham, Job, Knight, Cooper, McMahon

EVENT LINE

HALF TIME 0 - 0

57 Substitution **Vassell (Off) Moore L (On)**

64 Goal **Laursen (Corner)**

65 Substitution Nemeth (Off) Graham (On)

70 Yellow card Doriva (Foul)

73 Yellow card **Davis (Foul)**

78 Yellow card Parlour (Foul)

79 Goal **Moore L (Indirect Free Kick)**

82 Substitution Downing (Off) Job (On)

FULL TIME 2 - 0

STATISTICS

Season	Fixture (Aston Villa)		Fixture (Middlesbrough)	Season
144	**3**	Shots On Target	**1**	**203**
149	**5**	Shots Off Target	**3**	**159**
5	**0**	Hit Woodwork	**0**	**5**
88	**6**	Caught Offside	**2**	**74**
163	**6**	Corners	**5**	**170**
445	**8**	Fouls	**6**	**351**
49%	**56%**	Possession	**44%**	**50%**

LEAGUE STANDINGS

Position (pos before)	W	D	L	F	A	Pts
10 (11) Aston Villa	**10**	**8**	**11**	**34**	**37**	**38**
6 (6) Middlesbrough	**11**	**9**	**9**	**43**	**39**	**42**

PREMIERSHIP FIXTURE HISTORY

Pl: **4** Draws: **2**

	Wins	⚽	Yellow	Red
Crystal Palace	0	1	9	1
Manchester United	2	6	6	1

STARTING LINE-UPS

Crystal Palace: Kiraly; Boyce, Hall, Sorondo, Granville; Hughes (c), Soares, Leigertwood, Routledge, Lakis; Johnson

Manchester United: van Nistelrooy; Giggs, Fortune, Keane (c), P.Neville, Smith; Heinze, Silvestre, Ferdinand, Brown; Howard

Crystal Palace subs: Borrowdale, Speroni, Kolkka, Freedman, Torghelle

Manchester United subs: Scholes, Ronaldo, Rooney, Carroll, O'Shea

EVENT LINE

20 **Hughes (Foul)**

39 **Soares (Foul)**

HALF TIME 0 - 0

49 **Sorondo (Ung.Conduct)**

49 Giggs (Ung.Conduct)

56 Fortune (Off) Scholes (On)

56 Neville P (Off) Ronaldo (On)

64 **Lakis (2nd Bookable Offence)**

65 **Routledge (Off) Borrowdale (On)**

73 Smith (Off) Rooney (On)

79 Rooney (Dissent)

89 Ferdinand (Dissent)

90 **Kiraly (Ung.Conduct)**

90 Heinze (Foul)

FULL TIME 0 - 0

STATISTICS

Season	Fixture (Crystal Palace)		Fixture (Manchester United)	Season
122	**1**	Shots On Target	**9**	**233**
122	**1**	Shots Off Target	**7**	**206**
5	**0**	Hit Woodwork	**0**	**14**
69	**0**	Caught Offside	**7**	**112**
137	**2**	Corners	**7**	**219**
401	**12**	Fouls	**9**	**354**
46%	**45%**	Possession	**55%**	**55%**

LEAGUE STANDINGS

Position (pos before)	W	D	L	F	A	Pts
17 (17) Crystal Palace	**6**	**8**	**15**	**32**	**45**	**26**
2 (2) Man Utd	**18**	**9**	**2**	**47**	**17**	**63**

Saturday 5th March 2005 | Venue: **Selhurst Park** | Attendance: **26,021** | Referee: **M.Clattenburg**

CRYSTAL PALACE 0 MANCHESTER UNITED 0

Manchester United endured a frustrating afternoon at Selhurst Park, a 0-0 draw effectively ending their faint title hopes.

With a difficult Champions League trip to AC Milan on the horizon, Sir Alex Ferguson opted to leave Paul Scholes, Cristiano Ronaldo and Wayne Rooney on a star-studded bench. The manager's opposite number, Iain Dowie, decided to sacrifice striker Dougie Freedman and revert to a more solid 4-5-1 formation.

Crystal Palace began brightly, with Andy Johnson driving a dangerous ball across the six-yard box from the right. The striker then tumbled in the area, but referee Mark Clattenburg thought he had made a meal of a strong challenge.

A routine Tim Howard save from a Mikele Leigertwood drive preceded the visitors' first genuine chance of the contest. Ruud van Nistelrooy rose to head goalwards, but could only watch in amazement as Gabor Kiraly changed direction to scoop the ball away.

Further chances came and went at both ends. A Johnson drive was blocked for the Eagles, while Phil Neville tested the home keeper from distance. Another aerial opening then fell the way of van Nistelrooy, but this time the Dutch striker was off target.

With just over 10 minutes of the second half played, Scholes and Ronaldo joined the action. Soon afterwards, things got even worse for Dowie's side as Vassilios Lakis was sent off.

The Greek midfielder had been cautioned for a foul on Ryan Giggs five minutes prior to his 64th-minute dismissal. The decision seemed harsh, as referee Clattenburg showed him a second yellow card for felling Roy Keane.

There followed wave after wave of United attacks. A Ronaldo volley flew straight at a grateful Kiraly, while Giggs was unlucky to see a free-kick curl the wrong side of the right-hand upright.

With time running out, Ferguson introduced Rooney. The young striker was immediately involved in helping to create the chance of the game for van Nistelrooy, but the Dutchman scuffed his low effort.

Then, with just seconds remaining, Giggs lofted the ball onto the roof of the net after Kiraly had made a smart parry from a well-struck drive.

Alan Smith beats Michael Hughes to the ball.

"It was a big performance against one of the best sides in the league. We did as much as we could today."
Iain Dowie

"It is a bad result for us. When you are going for the Premiership, you need to win these games."
Sir Alex Ferguson

PREMIERSHIP FIXTURE HISTORY

Pl: 4 Draws: 2	Wins			
Fulham	2	3	7	0
Charlton Athletic	0	0	6	0

STARTING LINE-UPS

John, Crossley, Volz, Legwinski, Radzinski

Johansson, Andersen, Fish, Euell, Jeffers

EVENT LINE

12 Boa Morte (Ung.Conduct)

21 Kishishev (Foul)

40 Goma (Foul)

HALF TIME 0 - 0

60 Cole (Ung.Conduct)

60 El Karkouri (Foul)

73 Jensen (Off) John (On)

75 Thomas (Off) Johansson (On)

FULL TIME 0 - 0

STATISTICS

Season	Fixture		Fixture	Season
133	5	Shots On Target	6	125
124	5	Shots Off Target	3	100
3	0	Hit Woodwork	1	6
74	2	Caught Offside	3	95
136	5	Corners	5	119
345	9	Fouls	12	355
48%	47%	Possession	53%	45%

LEAGUE STANDINGS

Position (pos before)		W	D	L	F	A	Pts
14 (15)	Fulham	8	6	14	33	46	30
8 (9)	Charlton Ath	11	7	10	32	38	40

Saturday 5th March 2005 | Venue: Craven Cottage | Attendance: 18,290 | Referee: S.G.Bennett

FULHAM 0 CHARLTON ATHLETIC 0

Fulham moved a point closer to Premiership survival, thanks largely to some poor finishing from Charlton striker Shaun Bartlett.

Despite growing discontent on the terraces, home boss Chris Coleman kept faith with his 4-5-1 formation. Alan Curbishley set out his team in the same fashion, and it was the visitors that began the game brightly.

Paul Konchesky did well on the left of the area and drove dangerously across the six-yard box. It seemed that Bartlett had arrived right on cue for a simple tap-in, but the South African somehow managed to get the ball stuck under his feet, before seeing a swivelling effort blocked.

Fulham defender Zat Knight then came close to opening the scoring twice in quick succession. The tall centre-back rose to head a left-wing corner narrowly wide at the back post, and then forced a plunging save from Dean Kiely as he unleashed a 30-yard drive.

Then came Bartlett's second notable miss, though this time Edwin van der Sar deserved a lot of credit. The Addicks broke down the right, with Matt Holland inadvertently finding his colleague on the left edge of the six-yard box. Again the South African swivelled and fired goalwards, only for the keeper to trap the ball between his right foot and the left-hand upright.

Alain Goma headed wide for the Cottagers, before Danny Murphy tested the keeper's reflexes from distance as the half drew to a close.

Unusually, the second period was less exciting than the first. A sprawling save from Kiely denied Goma, as Fulham's best chances continued to come from set-pieces.

Both Radostin Kishishev and Liam Rosenior resorted to trying their luck from distance, with drives that summed up how poor the game had become. Forwards Collins John and Jonatan Johansson were sent on, as the two managers looked to steal the points.

It was Charlton that came closest to doing just that, as van der Sar acrobatically repelled a Konchesky drive that was destined for the top left-hand corner. A winner for either side would have been unjust, and 0-0 was a fair reflection of the game.

"It has taken Charlton a long time to get to where they are, and it is not going to happen for us overnight."
Chris Coleman

"The players worked their socks off again today, but were just missing that end product."
Alan Curbishley

Luke Young climbs above Luis Boa Morte.

Saturday 5th March 2005	Venue: **St James' Park**	Attendance: **52,323**	Referee: **H.M.Webb**

PREMIERSHIP FIXTURE HISTORY

Pl: **12** Draws: **4**	Wins	⚽	▢	■
Newcastle United	5	16	11	1
Liverpool	3	15	24	1

STARTING LINE-UPS

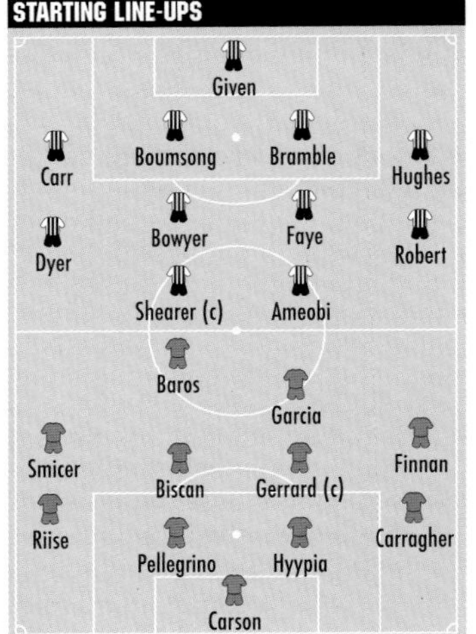

Newcastle subs: Kluivert, Jenas, Butt, Harper, Taylor

Liverpool subs: Nunez, Le Tallec, Warnock, Dudek, Welsh

EVENT LINE

32 ▢ **Faye (Foul)**

34 ▢ **Robert (Foul)**

HALF TIME 0 - 0

58 ▢ Gerrard (Foul)

67 ⇄ **Ameobi (Off) Kluivert (On)**

70 ⚽ **Robert (Direct Free Kick)**

74 ▢ Smicer (Foul)

75 ⇄ Smicer (Off) Nunez (On)

77 ⇄ **Bowyer (Off) Jenas (On)**

82 ⇄ Pellegrino (Off) Le Tallec (On)

88 ⇄ **Dyer (Off) Butt (On)**

88 ⇄ Baros (Off) Warnock (On)

FULL TIME 1 - 0

STATISTICS

Season	Fixture (Newcastle)		Fixture (Liverpool)	Season
196	**4**	Shots On Target	**3**	**177**
163	**9**	Shots Off Target	**3**	**187**
10	**0**	Hit Woodwork	**0**	**5**
80	**5**	Caught Offside	**4**	**69**
186	**5**	Corners	**4**	**158**
345	**11**	Fouls	**16**	**337**
51%	**71%**	Possession	**29%**	**53%**

LEAGUE STANDINGS

Position (pos before)	W	D	L	F	A	Pts
11 (12) Newcastle Utd	**9**	**10**	**9**	**40**	**44**	**37**
5 (5) Liverpool	**13**	**4**	**11**	**41**	**30**	**43**

Laurent Robert celebrates his stunning winner.

PREMIERSHIP MILESTONE

The attendance of 52,323 was a Premiership record at St James' Park

"It was a very special goal that won it. Laurent Robert had an excellent game and contributed in every way."

Graeme Souness

PREMIERSHIP MILESTONE

400 Alan Shearer made his 400th Premiership appearance

"If we don't win our away games, it will be very difficult to reduce the gap on the teams above us."

Rafael Benitez

PREMIERSHIP MILESTONE

Scott Carson made his first Premiership appearance in the colours of Liverpool

NEWCASTLE UNITED 1 LIVERPOOL 0

A wonderfully-struck Laurent Robert free-kick 20 minutes from time handed Graeme Souness his first managerial victory against Liverpool.

The French winger had not always seen eye-to-eye with his manager, but settled the contest with a goal right out of the top-drawer. From a position some 20 yards out on the right of the area, Robert curled a venomous effort into the far top left-hand corner of the net.

The set-piece had been earnt by Newcastle captain Alan Shearer. The former England striker was making his 400th Premiership appearance, and drew a foul from Argentinian defender Mauricio Pellegrino.

Though keeper Jerzy Dudek had turned in one of his better Liverpool performances in the Carling Cup Final, Rafael Benitez decided to replace him with recent signing Scott Carson. The youngster had arrived from Leeds in January, and probably hadn't expected to make his debut so soon into his Anfield career.

Steven Gerrard saw a drive deflected wide as the visitors began brightly, while Lee Bowyer fired high over the crossbar as the home team started to find their feet.

Midway through the half, Titus Bramble was off target following a Robert corner that caused widespread panic in the box. Shola Ameobi was the next to be wasteful, choosing to head Stephen Carr's deep delivery from the right towards goal when others were better placed.

There was still time for Luis Garcia to hook a dipping long-range effort onto the roof of the net before the interval, as the teams went in on level terms.

The second period belonged very much to Robert. The former PSG player flashed a 30-yard free-kick from a central position narrowly wide of Carson's right-hand upright, and then hit an almost identical spot behind the goal with a bobbling left-foot drive from the right wing.

Liverpool did not heed the warnings, though it is difficult to see how anyone could have kept out the winner.

The margin of victory should have been extended late on, as substitute Patrick Kluivert held off Jamie Carragher and dragged a shot wide. A final chance to equalise then fell to Gerrard, but he missed the target.

306 << **Newcastle United** >> 330 | 292 << **Liverpool** >> 324

PREMIERSHIP FIXTURE HISTORY

Pl: 4 Draws: 1	Wins	⚽	Yellow	Red
Norwich City	2	7	2	0
Chelsea	1	5	7	0

STARTING LINE-UPS

Norwich subs: McVeigh, Henderson, Ward, Charlton, Safri

Chelsea subs: Kezman, Jarosik, Cudicini, Huth, Gudjohnsen

EVENT LINE

19 Yellow card **Drury (Foul)**

22 Goal Cole J (Open Play)

39 Yellow card Cole J (Foul)

HALF TIME 0 - 1

58 Yellow card Makelele (Foul)

64 Goal **McKenzie (Open Play)**

67 Substitution Drogba (Off) Gudjohnsen (On)

67 Substitution Tiago (Off) Kezman (On)

71 Goal Kezman (Open Play)

73 Substitution Duff (Off) Jarosik (On)

75 Substitution **Stuart (Off) McVeigh (On)**

79 Goal Carvalho (Corner)

90 Substitution **McKenzie (Off) Henderson (On)**

FULL TIME 1 - 3

STATISTICS

Season	Fixture (Norwich)		Fixture (Chelsea)	Season
136	5	Shots On Target	13	215
148	3	Shots Off Target	10	177
5	0	Hit Woodwork	0	9
91	2	Caught Offside	1	87
138	7	Corners	7	191
387	14	Fouls	15	351
45%	31%	Possession	69%	56%

LEAGUE STANDINGS

Position (pos before)	W	D	L	F	A	Pts
19 (19) Norwich C	3	11	15	29	58	20
1 (1) Chelsea	22	5	1	53	9	71

Saturday 5th March 2005 | Venue: **Carrow Road** | Attendance: **24,506** | Referee: **M.R.Halsey**

NORWICH CITY 1 CHELSEA 3

Chelsea all-but secured a second trophy of the season, winning 3-1 at Carrow Road to extend their Premiership advantage to eight points.

Jose Mourinho's side dominated the first half, and took a lead into the interval courtesy of Joe Cole. Spirited resistance then saw Leon McKenzie head Norwich level after 64 minutes, only for goals from substitute Mateja Kezman and Ricardo Carvalho to wrap up the victory.

Wayward shooting from Damien Duff and Frank Lampard gave the Canaries early hope, before youngster Jason Shackell had to be alert to clear an effort off his own line with a diving header.

Then, after 22 minutes of action, Cole rode a couple of challenges outside the area and fired a 20-yard drive high into the roof of Robert Green's net with his left foot.

Nigel Worthington's men responded with a couple of shots from striker Dean Ashton, while Green had to be alert to prevent Cole from reaching Lampard's diagonal pass.

The second period continued to produce plenty of goalmouth incident. Didier Drogba was off target with a header from a free-kick, and then drove straight at the keeper after running onto a neat pass.

A left-wing corner was glanced wide by Ashton, before McKenzie became the first player in 1,025 minutes of Premiership football to beat Petr Cech. The former Peterborough man fed the ball out to Darren Huckerby on the left, and then met his team-mate's inswinging cross with a firm header from seven yards out.

Chelsea responded by introducing Kezman and Eidur Gudjohnsen, and were rewarded almost immediately. The Icelandic international was involved in the move that saw his fellow substitute tap his side in front from close range after Lampard had lifted the ball over a stranded keeper.

Eight minutes later the points were secured, Carvalho rising unchallenged to head home a left-wing corner from five yards out.

The home side could take plenty of positives from their brave second half showing, but defeat left Worthington's men with a mountain to climb if they were to stave off the threat of relegation.

Mateja Kezman is congratulated after making it 2-1.

"First of all my players did well to get back into the game, but to see Kezman and Gudjohnsen warming up must have worried them a bit."

Nigel Worthington

"I think in the first half we were very comfortable, but in the second half they gave us a good game and deserved their goal."

Jose Mourinho

PREMIERSHIP MILESTONE

Ricardo Carvalho scored his first Premiership goal

Saturday 5th March 2005	Venue: **Friends Provident St Mary's Stadium**	Attendance: **31,903**	Referee: **P.Walton**

SOUTHAMPTON 1 TOTTENHAM HOTSPUR 0

PREMIERSHIP FIXTURE HISTORY

Pl: **13** Draws: **3**	Wins	⚽	▯	▮
Southampton	8	15	19	1
Tottenham Hotspur	2	8	25	0

STARTING LINE-UPS

Southampton subs: Nilsson, A.Svensson, Blayney, Cranie, Phillips

Tottenham subs: Keane, Kanoute, Ziegler, Cerny, Pamarot

EVENT LINE

HALF TIME 0 - 0

- 50 **Delap (Off) Nilsson (On)**
- 51 ⚽ **Quashie (Open Play)**
- 57 Mido (Off) Kanoute (On)
- 68 Kelly (Off) Ziegler (On)
- 72 ▯ Edman (Foul)
- 75 Reid (Off) Keane (On)
- 87 ▯ **Quashie (Ung.Conduct)**
- 88 **Le Saux (Off) Svensson A (On)**
- 90 ▯ Brown (Dissent)

FULL TIME 1 - 0

STATISTICS

Season	Fixture (Southampton)		Fixture (Tottenham)	Season
136	**4**	Shots On Target	**8**	**174**
158	**5**	Shots Off Target	**5**	**156**
2	**0**	Hit Woodwork	**0**	**10**
93	**7**	Caught Offside	**5**	**110**
139	**4**	Corners	**10**	**147**
371	**7**	Fouls	**11**	**336**
47%	**47%**	Possession	**53%**	**50%**

LEAGUE STANDINGS

Position (pos before)	W	D	L	F	A	Pts
18 (18) Southampton	**4**	**12**	**13**	**30**	**44**	**24**
9 (8) Tottenham H	**11**	**6**	**11**	**35**	**31**	**39**

Nigel Quashie reels away in celebration of his winner.

"We're playing well at the moment, and over the last five or six weeks we've really started to lift off."

Harry Redknapp

PREMIERSHIP MILESTONE

Nigel Quashie scored his first Premiership goal for Southampton

"We should have got at least a draw, but it was just one of those days."

Martin Jol

PREMIERSHIP MILESTONE

50 Frederic Kanoute made his 50th Premiership appearance in the colours of Tottenham

Nigel Quashie took the plaudits at St Mary's, heading home a priceless 51st-minute goal to secure three points against Tottenham.

With David Prutton beginning a draconian 10-match ban for his reaction to being sent off against Arsenal, Paul Telfer came in on the right of midfield. Elsewhere, Danny Higginbotham partnered Claus Lundekvam at the heart of the Southampton defence.

Buoyed by their F.A.Cup triumph in midweek, Spurs began brightly. Egyptian striker Mido found himself one-on-one with Paul Smith, but was denied by the legs of the in-form goalkeeper.

Senegalese forward Henri Camara almost profited from defensive uncertainty at the other end, blazing over under pressure after Anthony Gardner had gifted him possession.

Harry Redknapp's team then had a major escape, as Jermain Defoe found himself in the clear. Again Smith was the hero, staying on his feet for as long as possible and deflecting the England international's drive over the bar.

Opposing custodian Paul Robinson then kept out Camara's weak attempt at a lob, before breathing a huge sigh of relief in the moments leading up to the interval. The keeper could do nothing as Peter Crouch guided Camara's low cross towards the bottom right-hand corner of his net, but was grateful to see the ball drift wide.

The second period was just six minutes old when Quashie struck. The former Portsmouth midfielder nodded powerfully home from just outside the six-yard box, after Swedish international Mikael Nilsson had literally stepped off the bench to deliver a pinpoint centre from the right wing.

The points could have been secured when Robinson kept out Crouch's downward header a couple of minutes later, before Tottenham regained their composure.

Twice Smith kept out goalbound efforts from Defoe, as the Saints were pushed further and further back in defence of their lead. Then, with just three minutes remaining, the young keeper solidified his hero status by denying substitute Frederic Kanoute in another one-on-one situation

Having given away possession cheaply in the move that led to Everton's late equaliser at St Mary's a month earlier, Crouch helped make sure of the points by running down the clock in the corner.

PREMIERSHIP FIXTURE HISTORY

Pl: **11** Draws: **1**	Wins	⚽	Yellow	Red
Everton	**4**	**8**	**16**	**0**
Blackburn Rovers	**6**	**13**	**22**	**3**

STARTING LINE-UPS

Ferguson, McFadden, Wright, Stubbs, Plessis

Stead, Enckelman, Short, Tugay, Gallagher

EVENT LINE

14 Dickov (Off) Stead (On)

24 **Arteta (Off) Ferguson (On)**

36 **Weir (Foul)**

HALF TIME 0 - 0

64 Mokoena (Dissent)

65 **Carsley (Foul)**

71 Stead (Open Play)

75 Stead (Foul)

76 **Pistone (Off) McFadden (On)**

80 **Cahill (Foul)**

FULL TIME 0 - 1

STATISTICS

Season	Fixture		Fixture	Season
141	**4**	Shots On Target	**5**	**147**
159	**8**	Shots Off Target	**6**	**166**
6	**0**	Hit Woodwork	**0**	**6**
69	**0**	Caught Offside	**4**	**106**
141	**6**	Corners	**3**	**163**
341	**15**	Fouls	**20**	**442**
49%	**53%**	Possession	**47%**	**49%**

LEAGUE STANDINGS

Position (pos before)		W	D	L	F	A	Pts
4 (4)	**Everton**	**15**	**6**	**8**	**34**	**30**	**51**
14 (16)	**Blackburn R**	**7**	**10**	**11**	**25**	**36**	**31**

Sunday 6th March 2005 | Venue: **Goodison Park** | Attendance: **32,406** | Referee: **P.Dowd**

EVERTON 0 BLACKBURN ROVERS 1

Jonathan Stead was the unlikely hero, as Blackburn secured an important 1-0 victory at Goodison Park.

Having not found the net in 19 Premiership appearances this season, few would have put money on the former Huddersfield striker netting the winner in this game. Funnily enough, Stead's last goal away from Ewood Park was the winner in this fixture during the last campaign.

David Moyes kept faith with the Everton team that had won so convincingly at Aston Villa last time out, while opposite number Mark Hughes had to do without the services of midfielders Robbie Savage and Brett Emerton.

Visiting striker Paul Dickov was injured in a collision with Nigel Martyn, and had to give way to Stead after only 14 minutes. Then, just 10 minutes later, Mikel Arteta limped out of the action to be replaced by Duncan Ferguson, with the Toffees switching to a 4-4-2 formation.

Marcus Bent seemed to benefit from the presence of a strike partner. The former Leicester man outmuscled Aaron Mokoena to find himself bearing down on goal, but Brad Friedel stood up tall to block his effort.

Next to go close was Lee Carsley. The bald-headed former Derby player curled a delightful free-kick up and over the defensive wall, only to see the ball drop the wrong side of the right-hand upright.

Thereafter, Rovers were largely untroubled by their hosts. Solid defending ensured that Ferguson was unable to keep down a header from a right-wing cross, while chances started to fall at the other end.

Ex-Liverpool midfielder David Thompson should have done better than volley tamely wide from the inside-right channel, before Stead struck what proved to be the only goal of the game from a similar position.

A poor ball out of defence gifted possession to Blackburn, and within an instant Stead was running onto Steven Reid's accurate pass and dispatching a 15-yard drive across Martyn and into the bottom left-hand corner of the net.

The 71st-minute strike knocked the stuffing out of Everton, as they squandered a great chance to put one foot in next season's Champions League.

Marcus Bent and Ryan Nelson go head-to-head.

"I'm disappointed we couldn't build on a terrific performance at Aston Villa."
David Moyes

"When you come to Everton you know it's going to be a physical challenge, and every one of my players stood up to it."
Mark Hughes

PREMIERSHIP FIXTURE HISTORY

Pl: 2 Draws: 1	Wins	Goals	Yellow cards	Red cards
West Bromwich Albion	1	3	4	0
Birmingham City	0	1	2	1

STARTING LINE-UPS

West Brom subs: Kanu, Scimeca, Moore, Chaplow, Earnshaw

Birmingham subs: Lazaridis, Anderton, Blake, Vaesen, Morrison

EVENT LINE

28 Diao (Foul) (yellow card)

37 Tebily (Off) Lazaridis (On)

HALF TIME 0 - 0

53 **Clement (Corner)** (goal)

64 **Campbell (Open Play)** (goal)

68 Diao (Off) Anderton (On)

68 Gray (Off) Blake (On)

73 **Wallwork (Foul)** (yellow card)

86 **Horsfield (Off) Kanu (On)**

90 **Richardson (Off) Scimeca (On)**

FULL TIME 2 - 0

STATISTICS

Season	Fixture (West Brom)		Fixture (Birmingham)	Season
129	5	Shots On Target	0	127
122	5	Shots Off Target	7	125
10	1	Hit Woodwork	1	7
100	5	Caught Offside	3	86
140	13	Corners	3	151
377	16	Fouls	18	415
47%	53%	Possession	47%	50%

LEAGUE STANDINGS

Position (pos before)	W	D	L	F	A	Pts
19 (20) West Brom	3	12	13	25	49	21
13 (13) Birmingham C	8	8	13	31	37	32

Sunday 6th March 2005 | Venue: **The Hawthorns** | Attendance: **25,749** | Referee: **S.W.Dunn**

WEST BROM 2 BIRMINGHAM CITY 0

Second half goals from Neil Clement and Kevin Campbell settled an important West Midlands derby in favour of the Baggies.

Bryan Robson locked horns with former Manchester United team-mate Steve Bruce, keen to avenge a 4-0 drubbing in the December meeting between the two sides at St Andrew's.

Former Birmingham striker Geoff Horsfield was given a start alongside Campbell in the home team's attack, while Salif Diao made only his second appearance since joining the visitors on loan from Liverpool in January.

West Brom dominated the opening period, with Kieran Richardson and Jonathan Greening at the heart of most of their good work. The latter beat two players down the left to carve out a half-chance in the early exchanges, while his less-experienced colleague grazed a post with a shot from distance.

In between times, Campbell was unlucky to see a follow-up effort hooked off the line, after Maik Taylor had got down well to parry a fiercely-struck drive from the edge of the box.

Emile Heskey failed to make contact with Walter Pandiani's cross from the left, in a rare foray forward from Bruce's men. In fact, the visitors didn't manage a single shot on target during the first 45 minutes.

The Baggies finally got the goal their performance deserved eight minutes after the restart. Defender Neil Clement had not scored since August, but rose unchallenged to head home Richardson's right-wing corner from seven yards out.

West Brom would not have had that set-piece but for the hard work of Zoltan Gera. The Hungarian somehow prevented a goal kick, clambered back to his feet, and played the ball against the legs of an opponent.

Stung by falling behind, Birmingham almost hit back immediately. The base of the right-hand post felt the full force of a Heskey header.

Then, with 64 minutes played, Campbell added a decisive second. The former Arsenal man guided the ball home from close range at the back post, after Horsfield and Greening had combined down the left.

There was still time for the January signing from Everton to head narrowly past the left-hand upright from a clipped Horsfield centre, though the miss didn't do too much harm.

"Results like this breed confidence, as does the fact that we are now off the bottom of the table."

Bryan Robson

"I have got no excuses. West Brom wanted it more from the first minute to the last, and that is something I will not accept."

Steve Bruce

Kieran Richardson holds off Salif Diao.

PREMIERSHIP FIXTURE HISTORY

Pl: 4 Draws: 0	Wins	⚽	Yellow	Red
Manchester City	3	9	3	1
Bolton Wanderers	1	3	8	0

STARTING LINE-UPS

Manchester City: James; Mills, Dunne, Distin (c), Sommeil; Flood, Reyna, Bosvelt, Musampa; Sibierski, Fowler

Bolton Wanderers: Davies; Diouf, Giannakopoulos; Okocha (c), Hierro, Nolan; Gardner, N'Gotty, Ben Haim, Candela; Jaaskelainen

Manchester City subs: McManaman, Croft, Weaver, Bischoff, B.Wright-Phillips,

Bolton Wanderers subs: Speed, Campo, Jaidi, Poole, Pedersen

EVENT LINE

45 ⚽ Diouf (Indirect Free Kick)

45 Okocha (Off) Speed (On)

HALF TIME 0 - 1

46 **Flood (Off) McManaman (On)**

56 Candela (Foul)

65 **Dunne (Foul)**

68 **Bosvelt (Off) Wright-Phillips B (On**

83 **Sibierski (Off) Croft (On)**

86 Hierro (Off) Campo (On)

89 Candela (Off) Jaidi (On)

90 Ben Haim (Foul)

FULL TIME 0 - 1

STATISTICS

Season	Fixture (Man City)		Fixture (Bolton)	Season
151	0	Shots On Target	4	175
149	7	Shots Off Target	5	159
2	0	Hit Woodwork	0	6
80	1	Caught Offside	8	79
181	5	Corners	5	150
366	13	Fouls	20	398
49%	54%	Possession	46%	49%

LEAGUE STANDINGS

Position (pos before)	W	D	L	F	A	Pts
12 (12) Man City	9	9	11	34	32	36
6 (7) Bolton W	12	7	10	37	34	43

Monday 7th March 2005 | Venue: City of Manchester Stadium | Attendance: 43,050 | Referee: A.G.Wiley

Willo Flood attempts to halt Ricardo Gardner.

"The game kept going dead. We never got any tempo, and it suited them better than us."

Kevin Keegan

PREMIERSHIP MILESTONE

Lee Croft made his Premiership debut

PREMIERSHIP MILESTONE

50 Paul Bosvelt made his 50th Premiership appearance

"After we lost at Newcastle people suggested we might slip into a bad run, but now we have shown we are a great team."

Sam Allardyce

PREMIERSHIP MILESTONE

250 El-Hadji Diouf netted Bolton's 250th Premiership goal

MANCHESTER CITY 0 BOLTON WANDERERS 1

Bolton greatly enhanced their prospects of qualifying for European football next season, with a 1-0 win against a depleted Manchester City side.

Chelsea's victory in the Carling Cup Final ensured that, barring a miraculous sequence of results, a sixth place finish would bring with it a UEFA Cup place in season 2005-06. That is exactly the position that this victory took Sam Allardyce's men into.

Without Shaun Wright-Phillips, Joey Barton and a recognised left-back, Kevin Keegan handed places in his starting line-up to Willo Flood, Claudio Reyna and David Sommeil. The French defender was making his first appearance in the Premiership since January 2004, while Reyna had seen his campaign decimated by injury.

The game was far from being a classic, and the winning goal epitomised that. A free-kick was not properly cleared, enabling Stylianos Giannakopoulos to drive low across the six-yard box for El-Hadji Diouf to tap home from a yard out on the stroke of half-time.

Moments earlier Bolton had lost inspirational captain Jay-Jay Okocha through injury. Thankfully for the Trotters, they were able to send on the most experienced player in the Premiership, Gary Speed, as his replacement.

Though the home team never really clicked into gear, they should already have been in front. Robbie Fowler was guilty of being too deft with his finish, as he sent the ball up and over both Jussi Jaaskelainen and the crossbar.

Steve McManaman was brought on at the interval in a bid to bring fresh attacking impetus, but it was the visitors that continued to look the more likely scorers after the break.

Senegalese international Diouf danced his way across the City back-line from right to left, though his wayward final shot failed to match the sparkling approach work. Lone striker Kevin Davies then forced a smart save from David James, before heading another chance wide from a good position.

Despite their dominance, Allardyce's men almost squandered two points right at the death. Kiki Musampa ghosted in unmarked to meet a right-wing centre with his head, yet somehow directed the ball narrowly wide of the top right-hand corner of the net.

PREMIERSHIP FIXTURE HISTORY

Pl: 2 Draws: 0	Wins	Goals	Yellow	Red
Chelsea	2	3	0	0
West Bromwich Albion	0	0	2	0

STARTING LINE-UPS

Cech

Ferreira, Huth, Terry (c), Gallas

Gudjohnsen, Makelele, Lampard

J.Cole, Duff

Drogba

Kanu

Horsfield, Campbell (c)

Wallwork, Gera, Richardson

Robinson, Clement, Gaardsoe, Albrechtsen

Hoult

Chelsea substitutes: Jarosik, Kezman, Smertin, Cudicini, Carvalho

West Brom substitutes: Earnshaw, Greening, Kuszczak, Moore Scimeca

EVENT LINE

16 Clement (Foul)

26 **Drogba (Open Play)**

HALF TIME 1 - 0

74 **Gudjohnsen (Off) Jarosik (On)**

83 Horsfield (Off) Earnshaw (On)

86 **Cole J (Off) Kezman (On)**

86 Richardson (Off) Greening (On)

90 **Duff (Off) Smertin (On)**

FULL TIME 1 - 0

STATISTICS

Season	Fixture (Chelsea)		Fixture (West Brom)	Season
220	5	Shots On Target	4	133
194	17	Shots Off Target	3	125
9	0	Hit Woodwork	0	10
88	1	Caught Offside	4	104
199	8	Corners	3	143
364	13	Fouls	10	387
56%	53%	Possession	47%	47%

LEAGUE STANDINGS

Position (pos before)	W	D	L	F	A	Pts
1 (1) Chelsea	23	5	1	54	9	74
19 (19) West Brom	3	12	14	25	50	21

Tuesday 15th March 2005 | Venue: **Stamford Bridge** | Attendance: **41,713** | Referee: **N.S.Barry**

CHELSEA 1 WEST BROM 0

A 26th-minute goal from Didier Drogba proved enough to secure a victory that took Chelsea 11 points clear at the top of the Premiership.

The former Marseille striker was on hand to guide Damien Duff's low cross from the left past an exposed Russell Hoult in the West Brom goal from around nine yards out, after Frank Lampard had threaded a neat ball inside visiting right-back Martin Albrechtsen.

Both managers made interesting team selections. Bryan Robson boldly opted to deploy three strikers, believing they would be able to maintain possession high up the pitch, while Jose Mourinho fielded Eidur Gudjohnsen in a midfield role.

Unsurprisingly, it was the home side that dominated the early proceedings. A corner from the right was headed goalwards by John Terry, only for Gudjohnsen to help it wide from inside the six-yard box.

A clumsy challenge by Ronnie Wallwork could easily have resulted in a penalty, before Geoff Horsfield had a goal correctly ruled out for offside at the other end. The same fate befell the striker soon afterwards, while Drogba twice failed to make a decent connection when well-placed.

Having opened the scoring, Chelsea's Ivory Coast international should have quickly doubled their lead. Racing onto a pass from Joe Cole and skipping around Hoult, the forward was muscled away from danger by the covering Albrechtsen.

West Brom had proved determined foes in the opening period, though they were lucky to be just one behind. Events followed a similar pattern after the break, but the home side were unable to add to their advantage.

Once again the major misses came from Drogba. A low left-foot effort found the side-netting, a free header from seven yards out sailed wide, and another presentable opening was blazed high over the bar.

German defender Robert Huth bravely nodded Nwankwo Kanu's fiercely-struck volley away from danger, in what proved to be the Baggies' most promising attack of the match. Despite their undoubted commitment, an equaliser would have been unjust on the balance of play.

"The manager is not bothered by criticism - the only thing that bothers him is winning trophies."

Assistant Manager Steve Clarke

PREMIERSHIP MILESTONE

150 Eidur Gudjohnsen made his 150th Premiership appearance

"We played three up front in order to give them a game. Too many teams have played five in midfield here and not got out of their own half."

Bryan Robson

Didier Drogba wheels away after scoring the only goal of the game.

PREMIERSHIP FIXTURE HISTORY

Pl: 6 Draws: 0	Wins	Goals	Yellow	Red
Charlton Athletic	3	9	8	0
Tottenham Hotspur	3	10	7	0

STARTING LINE-UPS

Kiely
Young, El Karkouri, Perry, Hreidarsson
Holland (c), Murphy, Konchesky
Rommedahl, Thomas
Bartlett

Kanoute, Keane
Ziegler, Reid
Carrick, Brown
Edman, Pamarot
Gardner, King (c)
Robinson

Substitutes (Charlton): Johansson, Euell, Fish, Andersen, Jeffers

Substitutes (Tottenham): Defoe, Davis, Kelly, Cerny, Atouba

EVENT LINE

4 **Thomas (Open Play)**

HALF TIME 1 - 0

53 **Rommedahl (Off) Johansson (On)**
55 Pamarot (Foul)
60 Edman (Ung.Conduct)
60 Ziegler (Off) Defoe (On)
62 Brown (Foul)
70 Carrick (Off) Davis (On)
70 Reid (Ung.Conduct)
71 **Bartlett (Off) Euell (On)**
76 **Thomas (Off) Fish (On)**
79 **Euell (Ung.Conduct)**
85 **Murphy (Direct Free Kick)**
86 Pamarot (Off) Kelly (On)

FULL TIME 2 - 0

STATISTICS

Season	Fixture		Fixture	Season
127	2	Shots On Target	4	178
103	3	Shots Off Target	3	159
6	0	Hit Woodwork	0	10
100	5	Caught Offside	5	115
124	5	Corners	2	149
371	16	Fouls	17	353
45%	44%	Possession	56%	50%

LEAGUE STANDINGS

Position (pos before)		W	D	L	F	A	Pts
7 (8)	Charlton Ath	12	7	10	34	38	43
9 (9)	Tottenham H	11	6	12	35	33	39

Wednesday 16th March 2005 | Venue: The Valley | Attendance: 26,870 | Referee: C.J.Foy

CHARLTON ATHLETIC 2 TOTTENHAM HOTSPUR 0

Danny Murphy celebrates making it 2-0.

"We got off to a great start, but they played really well in the first 45 minutes."
Alan Curbishley

"Since I came to the club I think our football has improved, and if you keep playing good football the results will come."
Martin Jol

PREMIERSHIP MILESTONE
100 Mark Fish made his 100th Premiership appearance in the colours of Charlton

Stunning strikes from Jerome Thomas and Danny Murphy handed Charlton a 2-0 victory against Tottenham in the race for European football.

The game took just four minutes to spring into life, as Thomas opened the scoring in spectacular fashion. The former Arsenal youngster received possession some 25 yards out in the inside-left channel, and proceeded to unleash a right-footed rocket that flew in via the far upright.

From that point on, the visitors dominated the half. Shortly after falling behind, Robbie Keane headed an inswinging Andy Reid cross wide of the post, and then fellow striker Frederic Kanoute failed to connect with a similar delivery.

The same trio were involved in Spurs' best chance of the opening 45 minutes. A clever flick from Keane saw Dean Kiely rush from his goal to foil Kanoute, with Reid hastily hammering the rebound over the bar.

Despite being largely outplayed, Charlton always looked dangerous on the counter-attack. Danny Murphy led one such charge, but saw his attempted chip deflected narrowly past the post by Ledley King.

A very optimistic Tottenham penalty shout was dismissed by referee Chris Foy in the early stages of the second period. There was a coming together in the box between Kanoute and Hermann Hreidarsson, though the former West Ham forward was the only man inside the ground who believed he had been fouled.

The Addicks raised their game as Martin Jol's side pressed for an equaliser. After Kiely had comfortably saved a low drive from Keane, Murphy struck a swerving effort over the top of Paul Robinson's crossbar.

With chances proving much harder to carve out after the break, the result centred around two free-kicks. A goalbound set-piece from Reid was headed off the line by Shaun Bartlett, before Murphy secured the points five minutes from time.

The former Liverpool man was presented with a dead-ball opportunity after Hreidarsson had been tripped by Noe Pamarot some 20 yards out in the inside-left channel. The wall proved to be no obstacle, as Murphy found the net via Robinson's right-hand upright.

PREMIERSHIP FIXTURE HISTORY

Pl: 11 Draws: 4	Wins	Goals	Yellow	Red
Liverpool	6	18	7	0
Blackburn Rovers	1	7	16	0

STARTING LINE-UPS

Liverpool: Dudek; Finnan, Carragher, Pellegrino, Warnock; Garcia, Hamann, Gerrard (c), Smicer; Baros, Morientes

Blackburn Rovers: Stead; Pedersen, Flitcroft, Mokoena, Reid, Emerton; Johansson, Nelson, Todd (c), Neill; Friedel

Liverpool subs: Riise, Nunez, Biscan, Carson, Hyypia

Blackburn Rovers subs: Matteo, Gallagher, Enckelman, Tugay, Johnson

EVENT LINE

20 **Hasselbaink (Open Play)**

38 **Riggott (Off) Cooper (On)**

45 Whittingham (Foul)

HALF TIME 1 - 0

46 **Viduka (Off) Job (On)**

46 Whittingham (Off) Berson (On)

62 **Nemeth (Off) Doriva (On)**

68 **Job (Open Play)**

76 McCann (Off) Cole (On)

88 **Reiziger (Open Play)**

FULL TIME 3 - 0

STATISTICS

Season	Fixture		Fixture	Season
178	1	Shots On Target	0	147
192	5	Shots Off Target	4	170
5	0	Hit Woodwork	0	6
73	4	Caught Offside	7	113
169	11	Corners	3	166
351	14	Fouls	15	457
53%	59%	Possession	41%	49%

LEAGUE STANDINGS

Position (pos before)	W	D	L	F	A	Pts
5 (5) Liverpool	13	5	11	41	30	44
14 (14) Blackburn R	7	11	11	25	36	32

Wednesday 16th March 2005 | Venue: **Anfield** | Attendance: **37,763** | Referee: **B.Knight**

LIVERPOOL 0 BLACKBURN ROVERS 0

Liverpool failed to make the most of their game-in-hand on fourth-placed Everton, being held 0-0 at Anfield by a determined Blackburn Rovers side.

The Merseysiders came into the match full of confidence, having progressed to the last eight of the Champions League in fine style seven days earlier. Sami Hyypia and John Arne Riise found themselves on the bench, as Rafael Benitez decided to shuffle his pack.

The visitors made two changes to the team that had scraped past Leicester to reach the Semi-Finals of the F.A.Cup. Both David Thompson and Paul Dickov were missing, their places going to weekend substitutes Brett Emerton and Jonathan Stead respectively.

Little happened in an opening period that served to highlight just how organised Mark Hughes' charges had become. Liverpool enjoyed plenty of possession in the right half of the field, though they never looked like making a breakthrough.

It took around 40 minutes of the contest before either goalkeeper was forced into any sort of meaningful action. Brad Friedel was easily able to gather in a low drive from Mauricio Pellegrino, before the Argentinian centre-back volleyed another effort over the bar from close range.

Vladimir Smicer made way for John Arne Riise at the interval, and it took the Norwegian international just three minutes to make an impact. After bursting into the area on the left the substitute picked out Baros with an accurate cut-back, only for the striker to wildly miss the target with a side-foot finish.

A wayward shot from Stead was all that Blackburn could offer in response, and Ryan Nelson was then fortunate not to concede a penalty. The New Zealander had already tugged at the shirt of Jamie Carragher from a 62nd-minute corner, when he prevented him from rising to meet the delivery with a push in the back.

Frustration amongst the Anfield crowd almost turned to dejection, as Steven Reid came within inches of stealing the points for the visitors. There were just 12 minutes to play when the former Millwall man sent a low free-kick narrowly past the post.

"Blackburn were excellent in defence today, and we found it hard to cross the ball and create chances."
Rafael Benitez

"Tonight we've built on the great results we've had of late."
Mark Hughes

Fernando Morientes stretches to retain possession.

PREMIERSHIP FIXTURE HISTORY

Pl: 11 Draws: 2	Wins	Goals	Yellow	Red
Blackburn Rovers	3	12	17	2
Arsenal	6	17	17	1

STARTING LINE-UPS

Blackburn Rovers: Friedel; Neill, Todd (c), Nelson, Matteo; Thompson, Reid, Mokoena, Flitcroft, Pedersen; Dickov

Arsenal: Reyes, van Persie; Cole, Vieira (c), Flamini, Fabregas; Clichy, Senderos, Toure, Lauren; Lehmann

Blackburn Rovers substitutes: Johansson, Tugay, Emerton, Enckelman, Stead

Arsenal substitutes: Cygan, Taylor, Eboue, Ljungberg, Owusu-Abeyie

EVENT LINE

42 Matteo (Off) Johansson (On)

43 van Persie (Open Play)

HALF TIME 0 - 1

46 Todd (Off) Tugay (On)

60 Flitcroft (Off) Emerton (On)

61 Clichy (Foul)

72 Dickov (Dissent)

90 Neill (Foul)

90 Reid (Foul)

FULL TIME 0 - 1

STATISTICS

Season	Fixture (Blackburn)		Fixture (Arsenal)	Season
149	2	Shots On Target	8	230
177	7	Shots Off Target	2	141
6	0	Hit Woodwork	1	13
119	6	Caught Offside	2	73
170	4	Corners	6	176
479	22	Fouls	8	352
49%	46%	Possession	54%	56%

LEAGUE STANDINGS

Position (pos before)	W	D	L	F	A	Pts
14 (14) Blackburn R	7	11	12	25	37	32
3 (3) Arsenal	19	7	4	68	32	64

Saturday 19th March 2005 | Venue: Ewood Park | Attendance: 22,992 | Referee: G.Poll

BLACKBURN ROVERS 0 ARSENAL 1

A 43rd-minute goal from Robin van Persie proved enough to secure three points for Arsenal in a poor game at Ewood Park.

The Dutchman's effort was a rare moment of quality in a bleak spectacle, as he turned past a defender on the edge of the box and waltzed around Brad Friedel to slot into an empty net from no more than three yards out.

Blackburn had based their improvement under Mark Hughes on a solid defence, and it was no surprise that the Gunners struck just moments after an injury to Dominic Matteo had forced the home side into a change.

Having been paired together in the draw for the F.A.Cup Semi-Finals, a cagey contest was always likely. Neither team was at their best, though the Lancashire outfit did create a few early half-chances.

David Thompson was the first to try his luck, cutting in from the right and dragging a low shot tamely past the near post. Then, Norwegian Morten Gamst Pedersen headed straight at Jens Lehmann when he should have done better.

With the exception of a couple of long-range efforts, Arsene Wenger's men rarely threatened to score during the first half. When the goal did arrive, therefore, it was a particularly bitter pill for Rovers to swallow.

With home captain Andy Todd forced off at the interval due to injury, Arsenal set about extending their lead at the start of the second period. It took a fine save to keep out van Persie, before Jose Antonio Reyes again called Friedel into action.

The two strikers then combined to dissect the home defence, as Reyes found his team-mate with a cut-back from the right. Taking all the time available to him, van Persie curled a left-footed effort past the keeper but against the crossbar from around eight yards out.

Substitute Brett Emerton gave Blackburn a lift, and flashed a dangerous drive across the face of goal from the right. Irish international Steven Reid then had a late chance to earn his side a share of the spoils, but struck a bouncing ball harmlessly wide from just outside the area.

Lucas Neill gets physical with Robin van Persie.

"We've had a very difficult spell, and there were signs of tiredness."
Mark Hughes

PREMIERSHIP MILESTONE

50 Both Andy Todd and David Thompson made their 50th Premiership appearance in the colours of Blackburn

"Our league form has been very good, and I suppose you could say that the victory here gives us an advantage in terms of the F.A.Cup semi-final next month."
Arsene Wenger

PREMIERSHIP FIXTURE HISTORY

Pl: 1 Draws: 0	Wins	⚽	▯	▮
Bolton Wanderers	1	1	3	0
Norwich City	0	0	1	0

STARTING LINE-UPS

Bolton Wanderers: Jaaskelainen; Hunt, Ben Haim, N'Gotty, Candela; Nolan, Hierro, Speed (c), Giannakopoulos, Gardner; Davies

Norwich City: Green; Drury, Shackell, Fleming (c), Edworthy; Huckerby, Holt, Francis, Stuart; McKenzie, Ashton

Bolton subs: Jaidi, Poole, Campo, Okocha, Pedersen

Norwich subs: Jonson, Doherty, Ward, Charlton, Safri

EVENT LINE

42 ⚽ **Giannakopoulos (Corner)**

HALF TIME 1 - 0

56 ▯ **Hunt (Foul)**

60 ⇄ Stuart (Off) Jonson (On)

73 ▯ **N'Gotty (Ung.Conduct)**

73 ▯ McKenzie (Ung.Conduct)

88 ⇄ Edworthy (Off) Doherty (On)

90 ▯ **Giannakopoulos (Ung.Conduct)**

90 ⇄ **Candela (Off) Jaidi (On)**

FULL TIME 1 - 0

STATISTICS

Season	Fixture (Bolton)		Fixture (Norwich)	Season
185	10	Shots On Target	2	138
165	6	Shots Off Target	4	152
7	1	Hit Woodwork	0	5
80	1	Caught Offside	1	92
157	7	Corners	6	144
418	20	Fouls	16	403
49%	57%	Possession	43%	45%

LEAGUE STANDINGS

Position (pos before)		W	D	L	F	A	Pts
5 (6)	Bolton W	13	7	10	38	34	46
20 (20)	Norwich C	3	11	16	29	59	20

Saturday 19th March 2005 | Venue: Reebok Stadium | Attendance: 25,081 | Referee: P.Walton

BOLTON WANDERERS 1 NORWICH CITY 0

A moment of magic from Stylianos Giannakopoulos was enough to beat a spirited Norwich side and lift Bolton up to fifth in the table.

European football beckons for a team that have won seven of their last nine Premiership fixtures, while Nigel Worthington's men now look certainties to be plying their trade in the Championship next season.

With El-Hadji Diouf suspended, Sam Allardyce opted to push Ricardo Gardner back into the more advanced role he had begun in at Newcastle. The Canaries kept faith with the XI that had battled so bravely against Chelsea last time out.

Though Bolton shaded the first half, it was the visitors that created the two best openings. Both chances fell to Damien Francis, the midfielder beating Jussi Jaaskelainen with a drive that flew inches wide, before seeing Tal Ben Haim block another dangerous effort.

Home midfielders Gary Speed and Fernando Hierro both tried their luck from distance, while Kevin Davies felt he had been pushed over in the box. Then, three minutes before half-time, the Trotters went in front.

Having seen his corner from the left only half-cleared, Giannakopoulos was on hand to look up and bend a 20-yard effort high to the left of Robert Green in the Norwich goal. Moments later, Vincent Candela struck the crossbar, as the game threatened to run away from the visitors.

Openings were less clear-cut after the break, with neither keeper being unduly troubled for much of the half. The opportunities that did arise came late on, and all seemed to fall the way of Hierro.

Having gone close with a deflected drive seconds earlier, the Spaniard forced Green into a smart diving save to his left with another strike from distance.

With West Brom winning at Charlton earlier in the day, Worthington's men could ill afford this fourth successive defeat. At the other end of the table, Bolton moved to within just five points of Everton, sparking thoughts of Champions League football at the Reebok Stadium next season.

"Norwich were very resilient, and it took a little bit of individual brilliance to beat them."
Sam Allardyce

"If my lads continue to play football like that, we won't go far wrong."
Nigel Worthington

Kevin Davies shields the ball from Craig Fleming.

Saturday 19th March 2005 | Venue: **The Valley** | Attendance: **27,104** | Referee: **M.R.Halsey**

PREMIERSHIP FIXTURE HISTORY

Pl: **2** Draws: **0**	Wins	⚽	▯	▮
Charlton Athletic	**1**	**2**	**2**	**1**
West Bromwich Albion	**1**	**4**	**3**	**0**

STARTING LINE-UPS

Robert Earnshaw savours a memorable afternoon at The Valley.

Euell, Rommedahl, Hughes, Andersen, Perry

Moore, Earnshaw, Chaplow, Kuszczak, Kanu

EVENT LINE

9 ⚽ Horsfield (Open Play)
22 ⇄ Gaardsoe (Off) Moore (On)
24 ⚽ Johansson (Open Play)
29 ▮ El Karkouri (Foul)
HALF TIME 1 - 1
64 ⇄ Richardson (Off) Earnshaw (On)
70 ⇄ Johansson (Off) Euell (On)
73 ⚽ Earnshaw (Open Play)
77 ⇄ Murphy (Off) Rommedahl (On)
82 ⇄ Bartlett (Off) Hughes (On)
84 ⚽ Earnshaw (Open Play)
86 ⇄ Gera (Off) Chaplow (On)
90 ⚽ Earnshaw (Penalty)
FULL TIME 1 - 4

STATISTICS

Season	Fixture	(Charlton)	(West Brom) Fixture	Season
132	**5**	Shots On Target	**10**	**143**
106	**3**	Shots Off Target	**5**	**130**
6	**0**	Hit Woodwork	**0**	**10**
102	**2**	Caught Offside	**1**	**105**
127	**3**	Corners	**9**	**152**
382	**11**	Fouls	**8**	**395**
44%	**32%**	Possession	**68%**	**48%**

LEAGUE STANDINGS

Position (pos before)	W	D	L	F	A	Pts
7 (7) Charlton Ath	**12**	**7**	**11**	**35**	**42**	**43**
19 (19) West Brom	**4**	**12**	**14**	**29**	**51**	**24**

"It was always going to be tough playing for an hour with ten men, so we just have to take it on the chin."
Alan Curbishley

PREMIERSHIP MILESTONE
The attendance of 27,104 was a Premiership record at The Valley

PREMIERSHIP MILESTONE
Richard Chaplow made his Premiership debut

"This result has been coming for a long while. We've been playing well away from home, but haven't had the breaks."
Bryan Robson

CHARLTON ATHLETIC 1 WEST BROM 4

Substitute Robert Earnshaw arrived from the bench to stun 10-man Charlton with a 17-minute hat-trick, helping to secure a first Premiership away win of the season for West Brom.

Earlier, a Geoff Horsfield header had been cancelled out by an effort from Jonatan Johansson, before Talal El Karkouri saw red for an over-zealous challenge on Hungarian Zoltan Gera in the 29th minute.

Bryan Robson decided to revert to a 4-4-2 formation for this trip to The Valley. That meant Nwankwo Kanu dropping to the bench, with Jonathan Greening coming in on the left of midfield.

The tactics worked perfectly, as the recalled midfielder's ball in was eventually turned back across goal by Gera and headed home by Horsfield. Just nine minutes had elapsed, and the lead would already have been greater but for some smart saves from Dean Kiely.

With the Midlands club having laid on free coach travel to its supporters, there were no empty seats in the away section behind Russell Hoult's goal. The keeper had nowhere to hide, therefore, when Johansson rode his challenge to equalise with a simple 15-yard finish.

The momentum was now with Charlton, but that changed five minutes later. Defender El Karkouri lunged at Gera with both feet off the ground, leaving referee Mark Halsey with little alternative but to show the Moroccan a straight red card.

The Baggies initially struggled to make their one-man advantage count, and Hermann Hreidarsson was unlucky to see a header cleared off the line. Things changed after the 64th-minute introduction of Earnshaw, however, as the striker fired his team to three vital points.

With Wales securing the 'RBS Six Nations' grand slam and Craig Bellamy hitting a hat-trick to send Celtic back to the top in Scotland, it was fitting that it was another Welshman that was the hero in this encounter.

A close-range header from Horsfield's knockdown was followed by a calm finish when sent clear by Gera, before the hat-trick was completed from the penalty spot after Bryan Hughes had upended debutant Richard Chaplow.

PREMIERSHIP FIXTURE HISTORY

Pl: **4** Draws: **1**	Wins	Goals	Yellow	Red
Chelsea	**3**	**13**	**3**	**0**
Crystal Palace	**0**	**4**	**5**	**1**

STARTING LINE-UPS

Chelsea: Cech; Johnson, Carvalho, Terry (c), Ferreira; Gudjohnsen, Makelele, Lampard; J.Cole, Duff; Drogba

Crystal Palace: Kiraly; Granville, Sorondo, Hall, Boyce; Soares, Hughes (c), Leigertwood, Riihilahti, Routledge; Johnson

Chelsea substitutes: Tiago, Robben, Kezman, Cudicini, Huth

Crystal Palace substitutes: Torghelle, Freedman, Watson, Speroni, Borrowdale

EVENT LINE

29 **Lampard (Open Play)**

42 Riihilahti (Corner)

HALF TIME 1 - 1

54 **Cole J (Open Play)**

63 **Drogba (Off) Tiago (On)**

73 Routledge (Off) Torghelle (On)

74 **Duff (Off) Robben (On)**

74 Sorondo (Off) Freedman (On)

77 **Gudjohnsen (Off) Kezman (On)**

78 **Kezman (Open Play)**

80 **Terry (Dissent)**

88 Riihilahti (Off) Watson (On)

90 **Kezman (Corner)**

FULL TIME 4 - 1

STATISTICS

Season	Fixture (Chelsea)		Fixture (Crystal Palace)	Season
233	**13**	Shots On Target	**3**	**125**
201	**7**	Shots Off Target	**3**	**125**
9	**0**	Hit Woodwork	**0**	**5**
93	**5**	Caught Offside	**2**	**71**
209	**10**	Corners	**4**	**141**
377	**13**	Fouls	**16**	**417**
56%	**56%**	Possession	**44%**	**46%**

LEAGUE STANDINGS

Position (pos before)		W	D	L	F	A	Pts
1 (1)	**Chelsea**	**24**	**5**	**1**	**58**	**10**	**77**
17 (17)	**Crystal Palace**	**6**	**8**	**16**	**33**	**49**	**26**

Saturday 19th March 2005 | Venue: **Stamford Bridge** | Attendance: **41,667** | Referee: **P.Dowd**

CHELSEA 4 CRYSTAL PALACE 1

Chelsea had to work hard to secure victory against a determined Crystal Palace side at Stamford Bridge.

It took nearly half-an-hour for Jose Mourinho's men to make a breakthrough, and even then it needed a spectacular effort. Collecting Joe Cole's pass infield from the left some 25 yards out, Frank Lampard arrowed a venomous drive beyond the left hand of a diving Gabor Kiraly.

Normally one goal is enough for the West London side, particularly at home, but on this occasion the visitors drew level. Just three minutes of the first half remained when Lampard failed to clear Wayne Routledge's low corner from the left, enabling Aki Riihilahti to steal in and poke a deflected four-yard effort past Petr Cech.

Amazingly, the Eagles should have been in front at the break. The ball found its way to Andy Johnson in a crowded penalty area, and the usually composed striker hurried a low shot across the face of goal.

That proved to be the last genuine opening for Iain Dowie's side, as Chelsea raised their game after the interval. Within 10 minutes of the restart, the in-form Joe Cole latched onto Eidur Gudjohnsen's weighted pass in the inside-right channel and fired home through the legs of a defender.

There was little Kiraly could do about that effort, but he was entirely responsible for the third goal. Substitute Mateja Kezman had been on the pitch for around 60 seconds when the Hungarian keeper allowed his hopeful curler from the left-wing to go right through him.

The mistake was very similar to that made by Italian Massimo Taibi for Manchester United against Southampton several years earlier, though Kiraly soon set about making amends by tipping over Tiago's rising drive.

Gloss was added to the scoreline in injury-time, as Kezman netted a second. A corner was not properly cleared, with the former PSV Eindhoven forward swivelling to turn the ball home from five yards out after Lampard's low shot had been bravely blocked.

With games running out, Chelsea seem set to end their 50-year wait for the league title.

"It was a tricky game at first, but it opened up after we scored our second goal."
Joe Cole

"Chelsea have good players, and they will win the title because they are versatile in their play."
Iain Dowie

Mateja Kezman celebrates one of his two goals.

PREMIERSHIP FIXTURE HISTORY

Pl: 4 Draws: 0	Wins	Goals	Yellow cards	Red cards
Manchester United	3	8	6	0
Fulham	1	5	5	0

STARTING LINE-UPS

Smith, O'Shea, P.Neville, Carroll, G.Neville

Legwinski, Radzinski, Crossley, Volz, John

EVENT LINE

21 **Ronaldo (Open Play)**

HALF TIME 1 - 0

51 Diop (Foul)

64 Diop (Off) Legwinski (On)

77 **van Nistelrooy (Off) Smith (On)**

83 **Rooney (Off) O'Shea (On)**

89 Jensen (Off) Radzinski (On)

90 **Scholes (Off) Neville P (On)**

FULL TIME 1 - 0

STATISTICS

Season	Fixture		Fixture	Season
245	**12**	Shots On Target	**6**	**139**
213	**7**	Shots Off Target	**4**	**128**
14	**0**	Hit Woodwork	**1**	**4**
114	**2**	Caught Offside	**2**	**76**
237	**18**	Corners	**3**	**139**
361	**7**	Fouls	**11**	**356**
55%	**59%**	Possession	**41%**	**47%**

LEAGUE STANDINGS

Position (pos before)		W	D	L	F	A	Pts
2 (2)	**Man Utd**	**19**	**9**	**2**	**48**	**17**	**66**
16 (15)	**Fulham**	**8**	**6**	**15**	**33**	**47**	**30**

Saturday 19th March 2005 | Venue: **Old Trafford** | Attendance: **67,959** | Referee: **A.P.D'Urso**

MANCHESTER UNITED 1 FULHAM 0

Cristiano Ronaldo fires home the winner.

"We've scored two goals in our games with Fulham this season, but we should have comfortably won both of them."

Sir Alex Ferguson

"We were cautious in the first half, but went out in the second with more belief and had chances to equalise."

Chris Coleman

Manchester United made hard work of beating Fulham, and were nearly made to pay for their profligate finishing late on.

Sir Alex Ferguson's side dominated the opening period, as the visitors barely crossed the halfway line. Cristiano Ronaldo was at the heart of all his team's good work, and netted the only goal of the game after 21 minutes.

Receiving possession from Roy Keane on the left, the Portuguese winger cut inside Liam Rosenior and hammered a 20-yard effort into the top right-hand corner. The former Sporting Lisbon youngster had already headed narrowly wide, and was proving a constant menace to Chris Coleman's defence.

Prior to the goal, United had carved out a plethora of chances. Wayne Rooney missed the target with a flicked effort, Paul Scholes tried his luck with a header, and both Roy Keane and Gabriel Heinze went close from distance.

Having opened the scoring, Ronaldo then spurned a great opportunity to add a second when he failed to make proper contact with a 12-yard volley. A deflected Heinze strike then flew wide, as the home side went in at the interval with just a 1-0 lead.

The second 45 minutes began in a similar vain. Edwin van der Sar made two smart saves to keep out long-range Rooney attempts, while Ronaldo twice failed to hit the target. Two further stops from stinging Heinze drives kept the Cottagers in contention.

Having completely run the show for 80 minutes, the Old Trafford side appeared to run out of steam. A Beckham-esque clipped effort from halfway by Alan Smith was all that Ferguson's men could muster, as Fulham came perilously close to an equaliser on three occasions.

Firstly, visiting captain Lee Clark saw his strike deflected against a post, with Carlos Bocanegra's follow-up somehow staying out. Then, Tim Howard deflected away the returning Andy Cole's low drive, before late substitute Tomasz Radzinski failed to make decent contact with an inviting ball in from the right.

Victory left United in second place, though they will struggle to hold onto it if they continue to be so wasteful in front of goal.

PREMIERSHIP FIXTURE HISTORY

Pl: 2 Draws: 2	Wins	Goals	Yellow	Red
Portsmouth	0	2	7	0
Newcastle United	0	2	6	0

STARTING LINE-UPS

Hughes, Fuller, O'Neil, Chalkias, Kamara

Jenas, Milner, Kluivert, Harper, Taylor

EVENT LINE

8 **Skopelitis (Foul)**
29 **De Zeeuw (Foul)**
39 **Primus (Foul)**
41 **Yakubu (Ung.Conduct)**
42 Carr (Dissent)
43 Dyer (Indirect Free Kick)
45 **Stone (Open Play)**

HALF TIME 1 - 1

48 **Lua Lua (Foul)**
54 Bowyer (Foul)
68 Faye (Off) Jenas (On)
72 O'Brien (Foul)
76 Robert (Off) Milner (On)
81 **Berger (Off) Hughes (On)**
82 Butt (Ung.Conduct)
85 **Yakubu (Off) Fuller (On)**
86 **Stone (Off) O'Neil (On)**
87 Butt (Off) Kluivert (On)

FULL TIME 1 - 1

STATISTICS

Season	Fixture		Fixture	Season
146	6	Shots On Target	6	202
151	7	Shots Off Target	5	168
6	0	Hit Woodwork	1	11
79	5	Caught Offside	0	80
150	4	Corners	3	189
365	15	Fouls	19	364
47%	42%	Possession	58%	51%

LEAGUE STANDINGS

Position (pos before)	W	D	L	F	A	Pts
15 (16) Portsmouth	8	7	15	32	46	31
11 (11) Newcastle Utd	9	11	9	41	45	38

Saturday 19th March 2005 | Venue: **Fratton Park** | Attendance: **20,165** | Referee: **M.D.Messias**

PORTSMOUTH 1 NEWCASTLE UNITED 1

Gateshead-born Steve Stone scored the equaliser against Newcastle in a 1-1 draw for the second time this season.

The result brought an end to the Magpies' eight-match winning sequence in all competitions, though it stretched their unbeaten record to 12 games.

Having successfully deployed Kieron Dyer as a second striker in the resounding 4-0 win against Olympiakos in the UEFA Cup in midweek, Graeme Souness kept faith with the policy on the South Coast.

Given the confidence levels of the two teams, it was somewhat surprising to see Portsmouth in charge early on. Captain Arjan De Zeeuw headed powerfully over the top, while Aiyegbeni Yakubu, a possible transfer target for Newcastle, dragged a left-footed effort across goal.

The visitors began to threaten as the half wore on, and Laurent Robert was unlucky to see a header strike the underside of the crossbar. In the ensuing melee, Nicky Butt almost found the net in bizarre fashion as he charged down a clearance.

Shay Given made an acrobatic save from a Patrik Berger screamer, before Souness' charges grabbed a 43rd-minute lead. Lee Bowyer received possession from a short free-kick on the right, and his deflected cross struck Linvoy Primus before being nodded in by an alert Dyer.

The advantage was short-lived, however, as former Magpie Lomana Tresor Lua Lua twisted and turned on the left, making space for a low centre that Stone diverted home from just inside the six-yard box.

The second period was a scrappy affair, not helped by referee Matt Messias. The official added four yellow cards to the five he had handed out during the opening 45 minutes, though there was not a bad tackle in the game.

Newcastle came closest to pinching the points, when Jamie Ashdown kept out a crisp strike from Bowyer 11 minutes from time. The keeper had been preferred to eccentric recent acquisition Konstantinos Chalkias in goal, much to the delight of the Fratton Park faithful.

In the end, a draw was a fair result. While cup competitions have become the away side's priority, Portsmouth are in danger of being dragged into a relegation battle.

Matthew Taylor keeps Stephen Carr at bay.

"It was nice for Steve Stone to score because he's a Geordie lad, and he seems to save all his goals up for Newcastle."

Joe Jordan

PREMIERSHIP MILESTONE

50 Steve Stone marked his 50th Premiership appearance for Portsmouth with a goal

"Portsmouth are battling for every point at the moment, and it was always going to be hard to come down here and get something."

Graeme Souness

PREMIERSHIP MILESTONE

50 Lee Bowyer made his 50th Premiership appearance in the colours of Newcastle

PREMIERSHIP FIXTURE HISTORY

Pl: 8 Draws: 2	Wins	⚽	▢	■
Tottenham Hotspur	5	10	8	0
Manchester City	1	6	15	0

STARTING LINE-UPS

Robinson

Kelly, Naybet, King (c), Atouba

Davies, Carrick, Brown, Reid

Defoe, Mido

Fowler

Musampa, Sibierski, Bosvelt, Barton, Reyna

Jordan, Distin (c), Dunne, Onuoha

James

Kanoute, Gardner, Keane, Cerny, Davis

Flood, Mills, Macken, Weaver, Sommeil

EVENT LINE

16 ⚽ **Defoe (Open Play)**

44 ⚽ Reyna (Open Play)

HALF TIME 1 - 1

65 ⇄ **Mido (Off) Kanoute (On)**

76 ⇄ **Naybet (Off) Gardner (On)**

76 ⇄ Sibierski (Off) Flood (On)

80 ⇄ **Reid (Off) Keane (On)**

83 ⇄ Onuoha (Off) Mills (On)

84 ⚽ **Keane (Open Play)**

88 ▢ **Atouba (Ung.Conduct)**

89 ⇄ Bosvelt (Off) Macken (On)

89 ▢ Dunne (Ung.Conduct)

89 ▢ Fowler (Ung.Conduct)

90 ▢ **Defoe (Dissent)**

90 ▢ Barton (Foul)

FULL TIME 2 - 1

STATISTICS

Season	Fixture		Fixture	Season
187	9	Shots On Target	7	158
162	3	Shots Off Target	4	153
10	0	Hit Woodwork	0	2
122	7	Caught Offside	7	87
155	6	Corners	4	185
366	13	Fouls	13	379
50%	56%	Possession	44%	49%

LEAGUE STANDINGS

Position (pos before)	W	D	L	F	A	Pts
9 (9) Tottenham H	12	6	12	37	34	42
12 (12) Man City	9	9	12	35	34	36

Saturday 19th March 2005 | Venue: **White Hart Lane** | Attendance: **35,681** | Referee: **B.Knight**

Claudio Reyna closes down Andy Reid.

"Sometimes you play well and don't get the points, but today we did the reverse."
Martin Jol

"Joey Barton has a cut on his eye and feels that Thimothee Atouba elbowed him or something like that. But as I said to him, these things happen in the game."
Stuart Pearce

TOTTENHAM HOTSPUR 2 MANCHESTER CITY 1

Stuart Pearce began his nine-match reign as Manchester City boss with an undeserved 2-1 defeat against Tottenham at White Hart Lane.

The former England left-back had been given until the end of the season to prove that he was the man to take over permanently at the City of Manchester Stadium, and would have seen his case helped by the performance of his team.

Paul Robinson and Thimothee Atouba did their best to hand the visitors the initiative early on, as Claudio Reyna almost profited from a bizarre piece of play. The American international saw a goalbound effort cleared to safety by Ledley King, after the Spurs keeper had been unable to deal with a strong throw from his Cameroonian team-mate.

Soon afterwards, a mistake at the other end was punished in clinical fashion. Nedum Onuoha, preferred to Danny Mills at right-back, was dispossessed by Andy Reid, who centred for Simon Davies to mishit a shot that Jermain Defoe nodded home from close range.

The England international had already tested David James with a low drive, and strike-partner Mido came close to doubling the lead following a corner.

The men from Manchester recovered from their 16th-minute setback, and began to create some chances of their own. Antoine Sibierski produced a tame header, before Joey Barton was denied by the legs of Robinson after dancing into the box.

An equaliser did arrive, however, as half-time approached. Robbie Fowler's deft flick from the edge of the area was meant for Barton, but Reyna ghosted in to find the net via the inside of the right-hand post with a left-footed half-volley.

Kiki Musampa ran out of room and fired into the crowd, as he attempted to hand the visitors the lead just after the hour mark. Play quickly switched to the other end, with Reid forcing James to acrobatically tip over his stinging drive.

Tottenham's 84th-minute winner had an air of controversy about it. Substitute Robbie Keane guided Davies' deflected drive into an unguarded net from just a couple of yards out, but Barton needed several stitches above his eye following an off-the-ball clash with Atouba in the build up.

PREMIERSHIP FIXTURE HISTORY				
Pl: **3** Draws: **1**	Wins	⚽	□	■
Birmingham City	**2**	**5**	**8**	**0**
Aston Villa	**0**	**0**	**7**	**0**

STARTING LINE-UPS

Nafti, Gray, Morrison, Vaesen, Blake

Vassell, Cole, Hitzlsperger, Postma, Ridgewell

EVENT LINE

- 30 □ **Melchiot (Foul)**
- 40 □ **Upson (Foul)**
- 41 □ **Johnson (Ung.Conduct)**
- **HALF TIME 0 - 0**
- 52 ⚽ **Heskey (Open Play)**
- 54 □ Berson (Foul)
- 57 □ Laursen (Foul)
- 60 Berson (Off) Vassell (On)
- 60 Moore L (Off) Cole (On)
- 71 Solano (Off) Hitzlsperger (On)
- 76 **Clemence (Off) Nafti (On)**
- 80 **Lazaridis (Off) Gray (On)**
- 88 **Pandiani (Off) Morrison (On)**
- 89 ⚽ **Gray (Open Play)**
- 90 □ Hendrie (Foul)
- **FULL TIME 2 - 0**

STATISTICS

Season	Fixture		Fixture	Season
131	**4**	Shots On Target	**3**	**147**
133	**8**	Shots Off Target	**2**	**151**
7	**0**	Hit Woodwork	**1**	**6**
87	**1**	Caught Offside	**1**	**89**
153	**2**	Corners	**3**	**166**
427	**12**	Fouls	**20**	**465**
50%	**52%**	Possession	**48%**	**49%**

LEAGUE STANDINGS

Position (pos before)	W	D	L	F	A	Pts
13 (13) Birmingham C	**9**	**8**	**13**	**33**	**37**	**35**
11 (10) Aston Villa	**10**	**8**	**12**	**34**	**39**	**38**

Sunday 20th March 2005 | Venue: **St Andrew's** | Attendance: **29,382** | Referee: **M.A.Riley**

BIRMINGHAM CITY 2 ASTON VILLA 0

Birmingham extended their unbeaten Premiership record against Aston Villa to six matches, winning 2-0 against their bitter rivals at St Andrew's.

As is often the case in derbies, the game was not much of a spectacle. Steve Bruce's side deserved to win more than their opponents, though once again they benefitted from a goalkeeping howler.

Thomas Sorensen had been culpable for Clinton Morrison's opener in the reverse fixture at Villa Park, and should have saved Emile Heskey's low drive towards the very goal in which Peter Enckelman made his infamous error.

David O'Leary signalled his intentions by sending his team out in a 4-5-1 formation. Inexperienced striker Luke Moore was given the task of leading the line, with both Darius Vassell and Carlton Cole left on the bench.

Kenny Cunningham and Matthew Upson had little trouble in outmuscling the visitors' isolated forward, and the ball kept coming back at Villa as a result. By contrast, Heskey and Walter Pandiani gave their markers a real physical examination right from the outset.

Home-grown midfielder Darren Carter twice came close to putting his team in front, drilling a low effort just past the right-hand upright and then firing straight at Sorensen from a Stan Lazaridis pass.

Then, after encroachment from Damien Johnson had seen a free-kick marched forward 10 yards, Maik Taylor had to fling himself to his right to turn Nolberto Solano's set-piece strike against a post.

This was a warning that Birmingham heeded, as they went in front seven minutes after the break. A hopeful punt forward was seized upon by Heskey, who struck a low angled shot that crept under Sorensen at his near post.

The keeper then went some way to redeeming himself with a smart save from a Pandiani header, before substitute Cole fired over for O'Leary's men.

Home replacement Julian Gray then sealed the points with a minute remaining, capitalising on a defensive mix-up to slide the ball into the bottom left-hand corner from 12 yards out. It could have been 2-1 moments later when Cole was denied from point-blank range, but it just wasn't Villa's day.

"We were back to our best today, and Emile Heskey was outstanding."
Steve Bruce

PREMIERSHIP MILESTONE
300 Emile Heskey marked his 300th Premiership appearance with a goal

"Birmingham must love playing against us, because we keep gifting them points."
David O'Leary

Emile Heskey is congratulated after opening the scoring.

PREMIERSHIP FIXTURE HISTORY

Pl: 13 Draws: 6	Wins	Goals	Yellow cards	Red cards
Liverpool	5	15	12	3
Everton	2	11	29	2

STARTING LINE-UPS

Liverpool: Dudek; Finnan, Carragher, Pellegrino, Warnock; Garcia, Gerrard (c), Hamann, Riise; Morientes, Baros

Everton: Bent; Kilbane, Yobo, Cahill, Carsley, Osman; Pistone, Stubbs (c), Weir, Hibbert; Martyn

Substitutes (Liverpool): Nunez, Biscan, Smicer, Carson, Hyypia

Substitutes (Everton): Beattie, Ferguson, Watson, Wright, Naysmith

EVENT LINE

21 **Warnock (Off) Nunez (On)**

27 **Gerrard (Indirect Free Kick)**

32 **Garcia (Open Play)**

39 Weir (Foul)

40 **Hamann (Off) Biscan (On)**

41 Yobo (Foul)

43 **Morientes (Off) Smicer (On)**

45 Osman (Foul)

HALF TIME 2 - 0

46 Yobo (Off) Beattie (On)

55 Bent (Off) Ferguson (On)

77 **Baros (Foul)**

82 Cahill (Indirect Free Kick)

84 **Finnan (Ung.Conduct)**

84 Pistone (Off) Watson (On)

86 Hibbert (Foul)

FULL TIME 2 - 1

STATISTICS

Season	Fixture	Liverpool / Everton	Fixture	Season
186	8	Shots On Target	2	143
199	7	Shots Off Target	2	161
6	1	Hit Woodwork	0	6
75	2	Caught Offside	3	72
174	5	Corners	1	142
364	13	Fouls	15	356
53%	45%	Possession	55%	49%

LEAGUE STANDINGS

Position (pos before)		W	D	L	F	A	Pts
5 (6)	Liverpool	14	5	11	43	31	47
4 (4)	Everton	15	6	9	35	32	51

Sunday 20th March 2005 | Venue: **Anfield** | Attendance: **44,224** | Referee: **R.Styles**

LIVERPOOL 2 EVERTON 1

Luis Garcia celebrates doubling his side's lead.

"This is our best performance in the league since I joined the club. I think we can close the gap on Everton now."

Rafael Benitez

PREMIERSHIP MILESTONE

25 Steven Gerrard netted his 25th Premiership goal

"I thought Liverpool were magnificent today. They did things they have not done all season."

David Moyes

The battle for Champions League football took a new twist, as Liverpool beat Everton 2-1 to move to within four points of their great rivals.

Rafael Benitez's men responded to an electric atmosphere inside Anfield by going for the jugular right from the off. Marcus Bent cut a lonely figure in attack for the Toffees, with almost all of the action taking place in the other half of the field.

Despite their territorial dominance, it took the home side 27 minutes to make a breakthrough. Luis Garcia was felled right on the edge of the box, and Steven Gerrard threaded Dietmar Hamann's lay-off from the set-piece through a sea of legs.

Five minutes later, it was 2-0. Nigel Martyn could only touch a dipping Fernando Morientes shot up onto his crossbar, and was unable to recover in time to keep out Garcia's close-range follow-up header.

Though things were going well for Liverpool, they were not helped by a succession of injuries. Stephen Warnock had already been forced off with ankle trouble, when Hamann and Morientes joined him on the treatment table before half-time.

David Moyes brought on James Beattie in place of Joseph Yobo at the start of the second period, and he was soon joined in attack by Duncan Ferguson. With Garcia clearly struggling with a knock he picked up just before the break, Everton were effectively playing against 10 men.

Despite this disadvantage, the home team continued to create the better chances. A slip from Alan Stubbs saw Milan Baros race clear, but the striker's hesitation enabled Tony Hibbert to get back and make a challenge.

The Czech international was then denied by the left leg of Martyn in another one-on-one situation, before things went from bad to worse as he was shown a straight red card for a high challenge on Stubbs.

With eight minutes remaining, Tim Cahill handed his side a lifeline with a sweet 15-yard half-volley from Ferguson's knockdown that beat Jerzy Dudek at his near post. That was as good as it got for Everton though.

Sunday 20th March 2005 | Venue: **Riverside Stadium** | Attendance: **30,082** | Referee: **U.D.Rennie**

PREMIERSHIP FIXTURE HISTORY

Pl: **10** Draws: **2**	Wins	Goals	Yellow	Red
Middlesbrough	4	15	10	2
Southampton	4	14	14	2

STARTING LINE-UPS

Middlesbrough: Schwarzer; Parnaby, Riggott, Southgate (c), Queudrue; Nemeth, Doriva, Zenden, Downing; Hasselbaink, Job

Southampton: Camara, Crouch; Le Saux, Quashie, Redknapp, Telfer; Bernard, Jakobsson, Lundekvam (c), Delap; Niemi

Substitutes (Middlesbrough): Reiziger, Graham, Jones, Cooper, Wheater

Substitutes (Southampton): Phillips, A.Svensson, Smith, Davenport, Higginbotham

EVENT LINE

14 Jakobsson (Indirect Free Kick)

41 **Hasselbaink (Open Play)**

HALF TIME 1 - 1

60 Crouch (Open Play)

67 Crouch (Corner)

68 **Nemeth (Off) Graham (On)**

68 **Parnaby (Off) Reiziger (On)**

69 Camara (Off) Phillips (On)

80 Le Saux (Off) Svensson A (On)

FULL TIME 1 - 3

STATISTICS

Season	Fixture		Fixture	Season
211	8	Shots On Target	7	143
165	6	Shots Off Target	5	163
5	0	Hit Woodwork	0	2
78	4	Caught Offside	2	95
173	3	Corners	6	145
371	20	Fouls	17	388
50%	49%	Possession	51%	47%

LEAGUE STANDINGS

Position (pos before)		W	D	L	F	A	Pts
9 (8)	Middlesbrough	11	9	10	44	42	42
17 (18)	Southampton	5	12	13	33	45	27

MIDDLESBROUGH 1 SOUTHAMPTON 3

Southampton moved out of the relegation zone courtesy of an impressive 3-1 win at Middlesbrough.

Harry Redknapp's side were full value for the three points, as they won on their Premiership travels for the first time this season. A second half brace from Peter Crouch did the damage, after Andreas Jakobsson's early goal had been cancelled out by Jimmy Floyd Hasselbaink.

With the home team having been knocked out of the UEFA Cup in Lisbon on Thursday, the Saints set about taking the game to their potentially tired opponents. They were rewarded for doing so after just 14 minutes, as Jakobsson turned home Henri Camara's low cross from the left following a free-kick.

Joseph-Desire Job fired over as Steve McClaren's men sought an immediate response, while Camara tried to end a bright run with a finish from an impossible angle at the other end.

A rare mistake from the recalled Antti Niemi then gifted Middlesbrough an equaliser four minutes before half-time. The Finn was unable to hold Boudewijn Zenden's drive from distance, enabling Job to nip in and steer the rebound into the path of a grateful Hasselbaink.

The keeper made amends moments later, however, foiling Szilard Nemeth from point-blank range. The save was to prove crucial, as Southampton used the interval to regain their composure.

With an hour played, Peter Crouch made the most of his height to head the visitors back in front. The striker rose above Gareth Southgate to meet Olivier Bernard's deep cross from the left with a powerful eight yard header that left Mark Schwarzer with no chance.

Seven minutes later, the former Aston Villa forward was on target again from a similar position. Graeme Le Saux did well to retrieve a corner and clip the ball into the area, where Crouch was well-placed to guide home a precise volley from around 12 yards out.

Middlesbrough seldom threatened to find a way back into the match, and the final whistle was greeted with boos from the Riverside faithful. The South Coast supporters were delirious with joy, however, celebrating as though survival had already been ensured.

Peter Crouch helps Southampton towards an important away victory.

"There are eight games to go, and we need our injured players back. It is important we stick together."
Steve McClaren

"We knew we would not stay up if we did not get an away win."
Assistant Manager Jim Smith

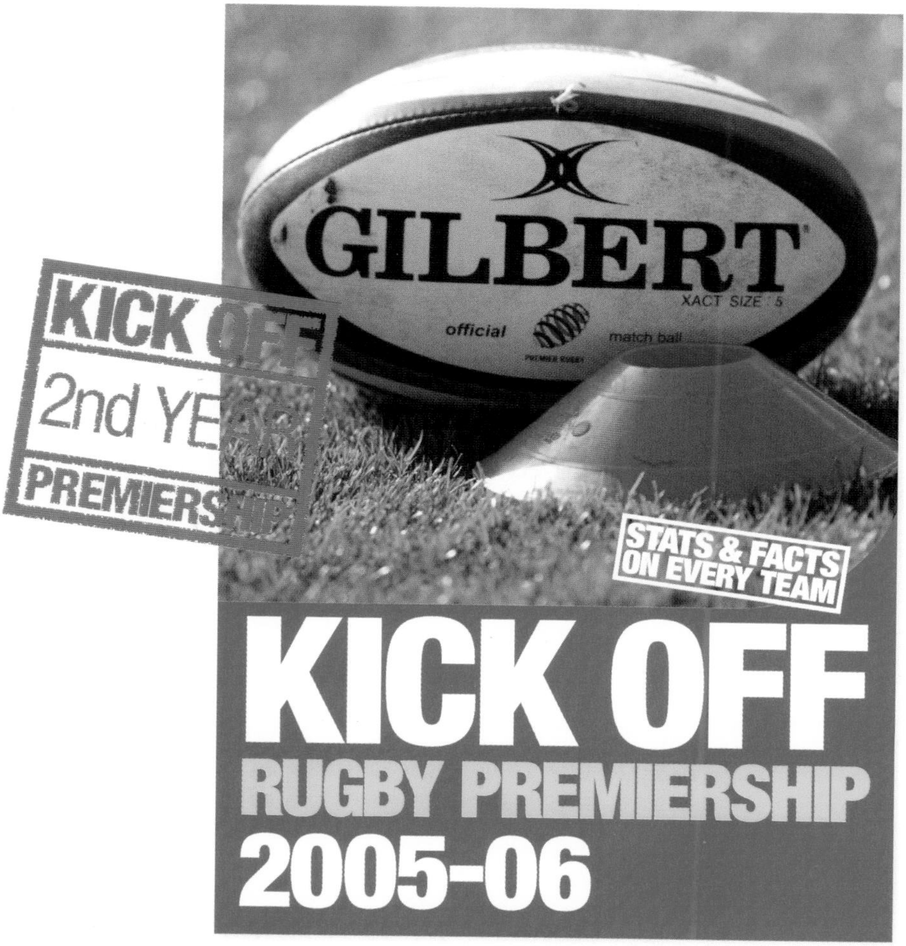

Mateja Kezman finds his shooting boots

MARCH 2005

In a month of just 23 Premiership matches, a surprising amount of action took place at both ends of the table.

Liverpool beat neighbours Everton to close to within four points of their rivals in the race for Champions League football, while Bolton also threw their hat into the ring by picking up all six of the points available to them.

At the bottom, West Brom and Southampton were the teams in form. A first Premiership away win of the season, 3-1 at Middlesbrough, took the Saints out of the relegation zone, while Bryan Robson's men won two of their three matches to increase hopes of survival.

Chelsea took advantage of fixtures against the three sides promoted to the top-flight last season, collecting maximum points and scoring eight goals. These wins stretched the Londoners' lead to 11 points, with Arsenal clawing back some ground on Manchester United in the race for second place.

The battle for UEFA Cup football continued to rage, though only Newcastle made any genuine progress. North-East neighbours Middlesbrough went in the other direction, failing to collect a single point as they fell to ninth.

In the F.A.Cup, Arsenal, Manchester United, Blackburn and Newcastle won through to the last four. Only Sir Alex Ferguson's side triumphed by more than a one-goal margin, setting up a semi-final clash with Alan Shearer and friends.

The men from Old Trafford saw their Champions League adventure end in Milan, with Bayern Munich doing just enough to prevent Arsenal from progressing. Jose Mourinho's Chelsea overturned a first-leg deficit against Barcelona to set up a tie with the Germans, while Liverpool lined up a poignant clash with Juventus.

Qualification for the World Cup was back on the agenda, as England won home matches with Northern Ireland and Azerbaijan 4-0 and 2-0 respectively. Poland and Austria also collected maximum points, however, keeping things interesting at the top of Group Six.

IN THE NEWS

02ND	Lee Bowyer and Kieron Dyer are sent off for fighting each other during Newcastle's 3-0 home reverse at the hands of Aston Villa. Defender Steven Taylor is also dismissed for deliberate handball, though is unlucky not to win an oscar for his attempts to convince referee Barry Knight that the ball struck him in the stomach.
07TH	Former Marseille boss Alain Perrin is appointed as Portsmouth's new manager. The Frenchman will be able to call upon the experience of David Pleat until the end of the current campaign.
08TH	Referee Mike Dean is formally suspended until 31 May following an investigation into his involvement with a betting website.
10TH	England international Michael Owen is on target in Real Madrid's 4-2 win against arch-rivals Barcelona in Spain's 'La Liga'.
13TH	Liverpool secure a 0-0 draw with Juventus in Turin, a result that sets up an intriguing 'Champions League' semi-final against Chelsea.
24TH	London's 'Grosvenor House' hotel plays host to a prestigious awards ceremony that sees Chelsea captain John Terry named 'PFA Player of the Year'.
30TH	A 2-0 win at Bolton sees Chelsea confirmed as Premiership champions. Frank Lampard nets both the goals, as Jose Mourinho guides the club to a first league title in 50 years.

TEAM OF THE MONTH

Shay Given
Newcastle Utd

Newcastle carried their fine form from February into March, winning four of their five games in all competitions. Only two goals were conceded during the month, with Given turning in a particularly inspirational display in the 1-0 F.A.Cup Quarter-Final victory against Tottenham.

Wes Brown
Manchester Utd

Though not playing in his favoured position, Brown looked more than at home in the role of right-back. Only AC Milan's Hernan Crespo managed to breach the United defence, and Gary Neville had to be content with a place on the bench when returning from injury.

Jamie Carragher
Liverpool

A series of consistent performances helped Liverpool reach the last eight of the Champions League and defeat Everton 2-1 in a crucial Merseyside derby. The defender also drew praise from fellow England centre-back John Terry during the month.

Philippe Senderos
Arsenal

The Swiss youngster established himself at the heart of an Arsenal defence that did not concede a single goal during March. A starring performance against Bayern Munich highlighted how much Senderos had developed in such a short space of time.

Olivier Bernard
Southampton

Six points from two games took the Saints out of the relegation zone, with Bernard playing an important role at both ends of the pitch. Resolute defending helped keep Tottenham at bay at St Mary's, while the Frenchman created a crucial goal in the win at Middlesbrough.

PLAYER OF THE MONTH

Joe Cole
Chelsea

A run of games on the right at last saw Cole begin to develop some of his potential. The former West Ham man scored against both Norwich and Crystal Palace, as well as turning in a mesmeric display against Barcelona. Furthermore, the midfielder forced his way into Sven-Goran Eriksson's England team.

"Joe Cole has become a very important player for Chelsea. His left-footed strike against Norwich showed just how good a player he is."
Barclays Awards Panel

MANAGER OF THE MONTH

Harry Redknapp
Southampton

Beginning the month four points adrift of safety, Redknapp led his team out of the relegation zone with wins against Tottenham and Middlesbrough. The 1-0 home success against Spurs was a performance of real character, with the 3-1 victory at the Riverside Stadium representing a first Premiership away win of the season.

Premiership Career Statistics
up until end of March 2005
Matches:**334** Wins:**113** Draws:**89** Losses:**132**

"Harry Redknapp's Southampton are enjoying a great run of form, which has seen the Saints move out of the relegation zone."
Barclays Awards Panel

Mathieu Flamini
Arsenal

With Gilberto and Edu ruled out through injury, Flamini saw off the challenge of Cesc Fabregas to firmly establish himself as Patrick Vieira's regular partner in central midfield. Tigerish tackling and an ability to cover every blade of grass have made the Frenchman a vital part of the team.

Kieran Richardson
West Brom

While thought of more as a winger at Old Trafford, Richardson has performed admirably in central midfield during his loan spell at The Hawthorns. Never afraid to try his luck from distance, the youngster has arguably been the catalyst for West Brom's improved results.

Laurent Robert
Newcastle Utd

The former PSG player benefitted from an extended run in the first XI, turning in a string of impressive performances. Stunning free-kicks brought goals against Liverpool and Olympiakos, with Newcastle looking a stronger side with Robert on the pitch.

Mateja Kezman
Chelsea

Having disappointed in his first season in England, Kezman hit the goal trail in March. Despite not starting a Premiership game during the month, the striker emerged from the bench to net three goals, two of which came in predatory fashion.

Peter Crouch
Southampton

Four goals in four games in all competitions highlighted the value of a confident striker. The former Aston Villa man began the month by scoring twice in a 3-1 away win, at Brentford in the F.A.Cup, and finished it in the same manner at Middlesbrough in the league.

MONTH IN NUMBERS

23 Games Played

45 Total Goals Scored

1.96 Average Goals Per Game

3 Player With Most Goals (Earnshaw, Henry, Kezman)

2 Hat-tricks (Earnshaw, Henry)

8 Club With Most Goals (Chelsea)

4 Fastest Goal (Thomas)

56.5% Percentage Of Home Wins

26.1% Percentage Of Away Wins

17.4% Percentage Of Draws

4-1 Biggest Win (Chelsea 4 v 1 Crystal Palace, Charlton Athletic 1 v 4 West Brom, Arsenal 3 v 0 Portsmouth)

81 Total Yellow Cards

3 Total Red Cards

3.5 Average Yellow Cards Per Game

16 Most Disciplinary Points (El Karkouri)

8 Fastest Booking (Skopelitis)

33,792 Average Attendance

PREMIERSHIP TABLE

Pos (last month)	Team	Played	Won	Drawn	Lost	Goals for	Goals against	Goal diff	Points
1 - (1)	Chelsea	30	24	5	1	58	10	+48	77
2 - (2)	Manchester United	30	19	9	2	48	17	+31	66
3 - (3)	Arsenal	30	19	7	4	68	32	+36	64
4 - (4)	Everton	30	15	6	9	35	32	+3	51
5 - (5)	Liverpool	30	14	5	11	43	31	+12	47
6 ▲ (7)	Bolton Wanderers	30	13	7	10	38	34	+4	46
7 ▲ (9)	Charlton Athletic	30	12	7	11	35	42	-7	43
8 - (8)	Tottenham Hotspur	30	12	6	12	37	34	+3	42
9 ▼ (6)	Middlesbrough	30	11	9	10	44	42	+2	42
10 ▲ (12)	Newcastle United	29	9	11	9	41	45	-4	38
11 - (11)	Aston Villa	30	10	8	12	34	39	-5	38
12 ▼ (10)	Manchester City	30	9	9	12	35	34	+1	36
13 - (13)	Birmingham City	30	9	8	13	33	37	-4	35
14 ▲ (16)	Blackburn Rovers	30	7	11	12	25	37	-12	32
15 ▼ (14)	Portsmouth	30	8	7	15	32	46	-14	31
16 ▼ (15)	Fulham	29	8	6	15	33	47	-14	30
17 ▲ (18)	Southampton	30	5	12	13	33	45	-12	27
18 ▼ (17)	Crystal Palace	30	6	8	16	33	49	-16	26
19 ▲ (20)	West Brom	30	4	12	14	29	51	-22	24
20 ▼ (19)	Norwich City	30	3	11	16	29	59	-30	20

TEAM STATISTICS

Shots on target	Hit woodwork	Shots off target	Failed to score	Clean sheets	Corners	Caught Offside	Players used
233	9	201	4	22	209	93	23
245	14	213	7	17	237	114	26
230	13	141	2	11	176	73	24
143	6	161	8	10	142	72	21
186	6	199	11	6	174	75	28
185	7	165	6	8	157	80	24
132	6	106	9	11	127	102	20
187	10	162	11	11	155	122	29
211	5	165	8	7	173	78	24
202	11	168	5	4	189	80	25
147	6	151	9	9	166	89	22
158	2	153	10	7	185	87	24
131	7	133	10	8	153	87	27
149	6	177	14	10	170	119	30
146	6	151	8	4	150	79	25
139	4	128	10	6	139	76	24
143	2	163	10	7	145	95	34
125	5	125	8	8	141	71	27
143	10	130	11	5	152	105	26
138	5	152	13	3	144	92	25

Robert Earnshaw fires West Brom towards Premiership safety

TEAM FORM

Pos	Team	Form	Goals For	Goals Against	Pts
1	Chelsea	WWW	8	2	9
2	Arsenal	WW	4	0	6
3	West Brom	WLW	6	2	6
4	Southampton	WW	4	1	6
5	Bolton Wanderers	WW	2	0	6
6	Newcastle United	WD	2	1	4
7	Manchester United	DW	1	0	4
8	Liverpool	LDW	2	2	4
9	Blackburn Rovers	WDL	1	1	4
10	Charlton Athletic	DWL	3	4	4
11	Aston Villa	WL	2	2	3
12	Birmingham City	LW	2	2	3
13	Tottenham Hotspur	LLW	2	4	3
14	Fulham	DL	0	1	1
15	Portsmouth	LD	1	4	1
16	Crystal Palace	DL	1	4	1
17	Everton	LL	1	3	0
18	Manchester City	LL	1	3	0
19	Norwich City	LL	1	4	0
20	Middlesbrough	LL	1	5	0

TOP GOALSCORERS

Player	This Month	Total
T.Henry Arsenal	3	**22**
A.Johnson Crystal Palace	0	**18**
J.Defoe Tottenham Hotspur	1	**12**
J.Hasselbaink Middlesbrough	1	**11**
R.Earnshaw West Brom	3	**10**
A.Cole Fulham	0	**10**
R.Pires Arsenal	0	**10**
A.Yakubu Portsmouth	0	**10**
P.Crouch Southampton	2	**9**
D.Drogba Chelsea	1	**9**
R.Keane Tottenham Hotspur	1	**9**
M.Baros Liverpool	0	**9**
P.Dickov Blackburn Rovers	0	**9**
F.Ljungberg Arsenal	0	**9**
W.Rooney Manchester United	0	**9**
S.Wright-Phillips Manchester City	0	**9**

MOST GOAL ASSISTS

Player	This Month	Total
F.Lampard Chelsea	3	**16**
T.Henry Arsenal	1	**16**
S.Downing Middlesbrough	0	**13**
F.Ljungberg Arsenal	0	**11**
W.Routledge Crystal Palace	1	**10**
E.Gudjohnsen Chelsea	1	**9**
A.Robben Chelsea	1	**9**
L.Boa Morte Fulham	0	**9**
R.Giggs Manchester United	0	**9**
J.Hasselbaink Middlesbrough	0	**9**
S.Wright-Phillips Manchester City	0	**9**
J.Greening West Brom	1	**8**
D.Huckerby Norwich City	1	**8**
D.Bergkamp Arsenal	0	**8**

DISCIPLINE

F.A. disciplinary points: Yellow=4 points, Two Bookable Offences=10 points and Red Card=12 points

Player	Y	SB	R	PTS
L.Hendrie Aston Villa	8	0	1	**44**
R.Parlour Middlesbrough	8	1	0	**42**
P.Diop Fulham	7	0	1	**40**
D.Johnson Birmingham City	7	1	0	**38**
T.Cahill Everton	6	1	0	**34**
D.Prutton Southampton	6	1	0	**34**
K.Tugay Blackburn Rovers	6	1	0	**34**
D.Mills Manchester City	5	0	1	**32**
M.Hughes Crystal Palace	8	0	0	**32**
P.Vieira Arsenal	8	0	0	**32**
L.Bowyer Newcastle United	5	1	0	**30**
Josemi Liverpool	5	1	0	**30**
A.Cole Fulham	4	0	1	**28**
T.El Karkouri Charlton Athletic	4	0	1	**28**
A.Cole Arsenal	7	0	0	**28**
P.Dickov Blackburn Rovers	7	0	0	**28**
T.Hibbert Everton	7	0	0	**28**

"If he does join permanently, we'll do all we can to try and help him. Education is the big thing. Jermaine needs a bit of guidance."

Steve Bruce after on-loan winger Jermaine Pennant is handed a three-month jail sentence for motoring offences

"Manchester City Football Club announces that by mutual agreement our manager Kevin Keegan will leave the club with immediate effect. We all believe that this is in the best interest of the club."

Manchester City club statement

"There is £34m available and, subject to where we lie at the end of the season, there could be more."

Aston Villa Chairman Doug Ellis on David O'Leary's summer transfer budget

"I am happy to play for West Bromwich Albion. This is the ideal club for me and I feel extremely good here."

Zoltan Gera

"My biggest regret is not being able to play for Wales again while John Toshack is in charge. It's completely outrageous what he's done, it goes beyond football matters."

Robbie Savage on his exclusion from the Wales squad picked to face Austria in two 'World Cup' qualifiers

"When I say life, I mean it. I want to stay here. I've never even thought about leaving."

Jamie Carragher on his plans for the future

"He is a good player, there is no doubt about that. But I think when you call your manager a 'liar' on television, that speaks for itself. I think it would be very difficult for him to return."

Newcastle Chairman Freddy Shepherd on the future of loaned-out forward Craig Bellamy

"I have played with a lot of players and it's difficult for me to say this, but Dennis Bergkamp is the best player that I have ever played with as a partner."

Thierry Henry

Saturday 2nd April 2005	Venue: **Highbury**	Attendance: **38,066**	Referee: **A.G.Wiley**

ARSENAL 4 NORWICH CITY 1

PREMIERSHIP FIXTURE HISTORY

Pl: 4 Draws: 1	Wins	Goals	Yellow	Red
Arsenal	2	11	3	0
Norwich City	1	6	3	0

STARTING LINE-UPS

Arsenal: Lehmann; Lauren, Toure, Cygan, Cole; Ljungberg, Gilberto, Flamini, Pires; Reyes, Henry (c)

Norwich City: Ashton, McKenzie; Huckerby, Holt, Francis, Stuart; Drury, Shackell, Fleming (c), Edworthy; Green

Arsenal subs: Fabregas, van Persie, Clichy, Almunia, Eboue

Norwich City subs: Safri, Svensson, Helveg, Ward, Doherty

EVENT LINE

19 **Henry (Open Play)**
22 **Henry (Open Play)**
30 Huckerby (Corner)
36 **Flamini (Off) Fabregas (On)**
HALF TIME 2 - 1
50 **Ljungberg (Open Play)**
59 Holt (Off) Safri (On)
66 **Henry (Open Play)**
70 **Reyes (Off) van Persie (On)**
71 McKenzie (Off) Svensson (On)
73 Edworthy (Off) Helveg (On)
77 **Pires (Off) Clichy (On)**
89 **Cygan (Foul)**
FULL TIME 4 - 1

STATISTICS

Season	Fixture	Arsenal	Fixture	Season
245	15	Shots On Target	1	139
147	6	Shots Off Target	2	154
13	0	Hit Woodwork	0	5
74	1	Caught Offside	4	96
186	10	Corners	3	147
360	8	Fouls	11	414
56%	56%	Possession	44%	45%

LEAGUE STANDINGS

Position (pos before)		W	D	L	F	A	Pts
2 (3)	Arsenal	20	7	4	72	33	67
20 (20)	Norwich C	3	11	17	30	63	20

Premiership top scorer Thierry Henry tore struggling Norwich apart with a hat-trick as Arsenal climbed above Manchester United in the race for England's second automatic Champions League spot.

The Gunners moved ahead on goal difference after United were held 0-0 at home by Blackburn.

Henry took his Premiership total to 25 goals with two trademark curling shots and an opportunist goal. Freddie Ljungberg added Arsenal's fourth, as the best attack in the league overwhelmed the weakest defence.

Things were looking increasingly desperate for the bottom-placed Canaries in their battle against relegation.

They now stood seven points behind the 17th-placed team with just seven games to go.

Arsenal welcomed back Brazilian midfielder Gilberto after a seven-month absence with a fractured vertebra. He replaced skipper Patrick Vieira, who was feeling the effects of France's World Cup qualifiers.

The movement of Henry and José Antonio Reyes was soon causing the Norwich defence all sorts of problems

Centre back Craig Fleming blocked a second-minute volley from Reyes, before Henry blasted a 30-yarder on the turn that was well held by keeper Robert Green on six minutes.

Green came to Norwich's rescue again soon after, diving to palm away Reyes's shot after Henry had slipped the Spaniard through inside the box.

Henry made the breakthrough in the 19th minute, collecting a neat pass from Robert Pires before sidestepping two defenders and burying a low curler past Green.

The Arsenal striker added his second three minutes later, cutting into the box and beating two defenders again before bending another shot beyond Green.

Norwich responded with a goal out of nothing on the half-hour mark, Darren Huckerby cutting in from the left and sweeping a shot past Jens Lehmann after Pascal Cygan and Kolo Toure had failed to clear Green's long kick.

It was the first goal Arsenal had conceded since Peter Crouch's equaliser at Southampton on February 26.

The Gunners re-established their two-goal advantage in the 50th minute, Lauren breaking to the byline and chipping for Ljungberg to score with a close-range header.

Henry made it 4-1 on 66 minutes, reacting fastest to knock home the loose ball after Reyes had been tackled in the box.

Jose Antonio Reyes holds off Craig Fleming.

"It's been an interesting day for us. The good thing is that our 'Champions League' situation is back in our own hands."

Arsene Wenger

PREMIERSHIP MILESTONE

150 Robert Pires made his 150th Premiership appearance

"We stuck at it, but Arsenal's quality simply came through."

Nigel Worthington

PREMIERSHIP FIXTURE HISTORY

Pl: 3 Draws: 2	Wins	Goals	Yellow	Red
Birmingham City	1	3	4	0
Tottenham Hotspur	0	2	6	0

STARTING LINE-UPS

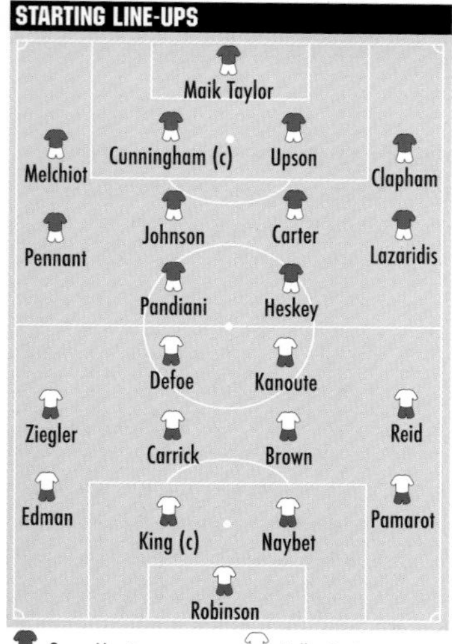

Subs (Birmingham): Gray, Morrison, Nafti, Vaesen, Blake

Subs (Tottenham): Kelly, Davis, Mido, Cerny, Keane

EVENT LINE

13 Pamarot (Off) Kelly (On)

38 Ziegler (Off) Davis (On)

HALF TIME 0 - 0

56 **Pennant (Off) Gray (On)**

59 Kelly (Open Play)

64 Brown (Ung.Conduct)

66 **Carter (Open Play)**

67 **Pandiani (Off) Morrison (On)**

71 **Lazaridis (Off) Nafti (On)**

71 Naybet (Off) Mido (On)

FULL TIME 1 - 1

STATISTICS

Season	Fixture (Birmingham)		Fixture (Tottenham)	Season
138	7	Shots On Target	5	192
140	7	Shots Off Target	4	166
7	0	Hit Woodwork	0	10
92	5	Caught Offside	5	127
156	3	Corners	3	158
433	6	Fouls	10	376
50%	54%	Possession	46%	50%

LEAGUE STANDINGS

Position (pos before)		W	D	L	F	A	Pts
13 (13)	Birmingham C	9	9	13	34	38	36
9 (8)	Tottenham H	12	7	12	38	35	43

Saturday 2nd April 2005 | Venue: **St Andrew's** | Attendance: **29,304** | Referee: **H.M.Webb**

BIRMINGHAM CITY 1 TOTTENHAM HOTSPUR 1

Clinton Morrison wasted a glorious opportunity to break open a 1-1 tie in stoppage time and steal all three points for Birmingham.

The Republic of Ireland striker, who had taken over from out-of-form Walter Pandiani, went wide with a close-range shot against a Spurs outfit looking for their first away win since Boxing Day.

Youngster Jermaine Pennant started for City, but lacked his usual sparkle after spending the last month in jail for motoring offences.

He was eventually replaced by Julian Gray in the 55th minute, leaving the pitch to a standing ovation from the home support.

Spurs broke the deadlock three minutes later, substitute Stephen Kelly converting a low cross-shot following a defence-splitting pass from Michael Carrick.

Birmingham responded on 65 minutes, Darren Carter playing a neat one-two with Pandiani on the edge of the Spurs box before jinking his way towards goal and poking the ball past Spurs keeper Paul Robinson.

Spurs generally looked the sharper side, but they lacked a cutting edge, repeatedly failing to take advantage of some skilful approach work by Andy Reid.

The former Nottingham Forest man was a constant threat, going just wide with a couple of fine efforts.

There was an anxious first-half moment for City when Fredi Kanoute's cross was mis-hit by Jermain Defoe and Jamie Clapham got himself in a tangle clearing the ball off the line.

Birmingham, meanwhile, rarely threatened in the opening 45, with Pandiani looking completely out of touch.

Emile Heskey battled bravely and was involved in several tussles with Ledley King in which the Spurs skipper usually came out on top.

Birmingham keeper Maik Taylor made two excellent reflex saves to keep his side in the game late on, denying a Mido header on 76 minutes before parrying Kanoute's half-volley from a corner.

Defoe had a chance with two minutes to play, bursting into the box before being denied by an excellent last-ditch tackle from Matthew Upson.

Then came Morrison's agonising miss, the striker failing to find the target after Gray had headed Damien Johnson's cross back across goal.

England strikers Jermain Defoe and Emile Heskey do battle.

"He wanted to get his first appearance out of the way, and now he just wants to get on with rebuilding his career and life."

Steve Bruce on Jermaine Pennant

"We badly needed a win, but I can live with a draw as we had problems with our substitutes."

Martin Jol

PREMIERSHIP MILESTONE

Stephen Kelly scored his first Premiership goal

PREMIERSHIP FIXTURE HISTORY

Pl: 4 Draws: 2	Wins	Goals	Yellow	Red
Charlton Athletic	1	8	6	1
Manchester City	1	7	4	0

STARTING LINE-UPS

Charlton Athletic: Kiely; Young, Perry, Fish, Hreidarsson; Holland (c), Murphy, Konchesky; Johansson, Thomas; Bartlett

Manchester City: Fowler, Macken; Musampa, Barton, Sibierski, Reyna; Jordan, Distin (c), Dunne, Onuoha; James

Charlton subs: Fortune, Jeffers, Lisbie, Andersen, Hughes

Manchester City subs: Mills, Weaver, Sommeil, Croft, B.Wright-Phillips

EVENT LINE

4 Hreidarsson (Own Goal)
10 **Bartlett (Open Play)**
38 Fowler (Corner)
HALF TIME 1 - 2
46 **Fish (Off) Fortune (On)**
46 **Johansson (Off) Jeffers (On)**
64 **Young (Foul)**
76 **Hreidarsson (Off) Lisbie (On)**
90 **Perry (Open Play)**
FULL TIME 2 - 2

STATISTICS

Season	Fixture	Charlton	Man City Fixture	Season
135	3	Shots On Target	8	166
112	6	Shots Off Target	8	161
7	1	Hit Woodwork	0	2
105	3	Caught Offside	2	89
133	6	Corners	7	192
388	6	Fouls	8	387
44%	44%	Possession	56%	49%

LEAGUE STANDINGS

Position (pos before)		W	D	L	F	A	Pts
8 (7)	Charlton Ath	12	8	11	37	44	44
12 (12)	Man City	9	10	12	37	36	37

Saturday 2nd April 2005 | Venue: **The Valley** | Attendance: **26,436** | Referee: **R.Styles**

CHARLTON ATHLETIC 2 MANCHESTER CITY 2

Charlton manager Alan Curbishley lambasted his team's performance after they scrambled to a 2-2 draw against Manchester City at The Valley.

The Addicks grabbed a stoppage-time equaliser that just about kept alive their hopes of playing European football for the first time.

New City boss Stuart Pearce was understandably frustrated by his side's failure to take all three points, particularly after dominating the game for long periods.

City opened the scoring in the fourth minute, Richard Dunne's header from a Robbie Fowler corner deflecting into the net off Charlton defender Hermann Hreidarsson.

Jonathan Macken, scorer of just one goal in 23 games for City, squandered two gilt-edged opportunities before Charlton levelled through Shaun Bartlett on 10 minutes, the striker bundling the ball over the line after keeper David James had failed to hold on to a cross from Jerome Thomas.

City worked hard to restore their advantage, Fowler getting off a shot which was well saved by Dean Kiely before the Addicks keeper twice blocked efforts from Macken with his legs.

City laid siege to the Charlton goal, launching a number of well-worked attacks as the Addicks resorted to the long ball.

Antoine Sibierski tried a shot from distance before Claudio Reyna went just wide under pressure from Hreidarsson.

The visitors' efforts were eventually rewarded six minutes before the break, the lively Fowler netting a poacher's goal from Joey Barton's corner.

Curbishley responded by replacing Mark Fish and Jonatan Johansson with Jonathan Fortune and Francis Jeffers, and reverting to a 4-4-2 system.

His side showed a marked improvement as the second half progressed and were unfortunate not to equalise when skipper Matt Holland, who was making his 500th career appearance, rattled the crossbar with a header.

Kiki Musampa then went close for City, his powerful strike beaten away by Kiely.

City looked to be heading for the win before Chris Perry scored his first goal of the season in stoppage time, converting a close-range effort at the far post after Luke Young's cross had been headed across the face of goal by Jeffers.

Jonathan Macken shields the ball from Mark Fish.

"Our performance in the first half was abysmal and really shocked me. We made Manchester City look like Brazil."
Alan Curbishley

PREMIERSHIP MILESTONE

200 Danny Murphy made his 200th Premiership appearance

"I thought we were exceptional at times today, and had enough chances to win comfortably."
Stuart Pearce

PREMIERSHIP FIXTURE HISTORY

Pl: 2 Draws: 0	Wins	⚽	□	■
Crystal Palace	1	4	0	0
Middlesbrough	1	2	5	0

STARTING LINE-UPS

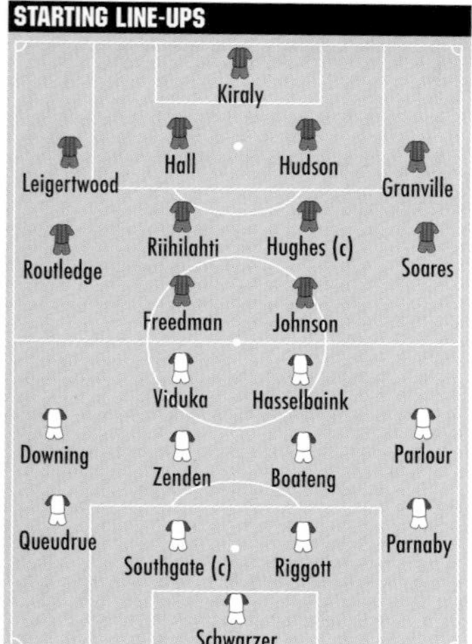

Borrowdale, Lakis, Andrews, Speroni, Watson

Nemeth, Doriva, Graham, Jones, Cooper

EVENT LINE

12 Viduka (Off) Nemeth (On)
35 ⚽ Queudrue (Corner)
42 □ Riggott (Foul)

HALF TIME 0 - 1

53 Zenden (Off) Doriva (On)
54 **Granville (Off) Borrowdale (On)**
58 □ Queudrue (Foul)
71 **Soares (Off) Lakis (On)**
76 □ Boateng (Foul)
79 **Riihilahti (Off) Andrews (On)**
80 Nemeth (Off) Graham (On)
90 □ Hasselbaink (Foul)

FULL TIME 0 - 1

STATISTICS

Season	Fixture (Palace)		Fixture (Boro)	Season
138	13	Shots On Target	5	216
135	10	Shots Off Target	2	167
6	1	Hit Woodwork	0	5
73	2	Caught Offside	2	80
149	8	Corners	3	176
423	6	Fouls	19	390
47%	51%	Possession	49%	50%

LEAGUE STANDINGS

Position (pos before)		W	D	L	F	A	Pts
18 (18)	Crystal Palace	6	8	17	33	50	26
7 (9)	Middlesbrough	12	9	10	45	42	45

Saturday 2nd April 2005 | Venue: **Selhurst Park** | Attendance: **24,274** | Referee: **S.W.Dunn**

CRYSTAL PALACE 0 MIDDLESBROUGH 1

Franck Queudrue's goal 10 minutes before the break was enough to sustain Middlesbrough's hopes of a top-six finish, as they won away in the league for the first time since November.

Iain Dowie's Eagles, meanwhile, remained mired in the bottom three and would need to make a serious improvement over the last few games if they were to stave off relegation.

Palace dominated the early going and should have moved ahead in the fifth minute, Andy Johnson blazing wide from 10 yards after being set up by a clever ball from Dougie Freedman.

Jimmy Floyd Hasselbaink responded for the visitors, latching on to Mark Schwarzer's long punt upfield and rounding keeper Gabor Kiraly, only to see his effort roll narrowly wide.

Johnson then went even closer with a 25-yarder which slammed against the post.

Freedman was next to threaten for Palace, his right-foot shot through a crowd flying wide.

Queudrue's opener arrived on 35 minutes, the French defender rising above a motionless Palace defence to firmly head Stewart Downing's corner into the roof of the net.

Kiraly denied Ray Parlour a second goal for Boro just before the break, blocking the ball after the former Gunner had collected from Hasselbaink on the right side of the penalty area.

Palace enjoyed most of the possession in the second half, but all too often were guilty of giving the ball away cheaply.

Ex-Eagle Gareth Southgate was having an outstanding game for Boro at the heart of defence as the visitors sat back and tidied up with comfort, with Schwarzer forced into just one second-half save, a routine stop from Mark Hudson.

Palace continued to press, but despite the non-stop running of Johnson, they lacked the creativity to break down the Boro rearguard.

Still, there were two late chances for the Eagles to snatch a point.

First, Freedman tried a curler from 15 yards which drifted inches wide with Schwarzer stranded.

Then, in stoppage time, Johnson saw his header deflected off the line by Boro's best player on the day – Southgate.

Boudewijn Zenden leads the celebrations after Franck Queudrue's goal.

"We are very disappointed with the result, but not with the performance."

Assistant Manager Kit Symons

"It was never going to be an easy game, and we showed great character to hold on to our goal."

Steve McClaren

PREMIERSHIP MILESTONE

450 Franck Queudrue netted Middlesbrough's 450th Premiership goal

PREMIERSHIP FIXTURE HISTORY

Pl: **6** Draws: **1**	Wins	Goals	Yellow cards	Red cards
Liverpool	**5**	**14**	**4**	**0**
Bolton Wanderers	**0**	**5**	**14**	**0**

STARTING LINE-UPS

Liverpool substitutes: Le Tallec, Smicer, Morientes, Dudek, Hyypia

Bolton substitutes: Okocha, Pedersen, Campo, Poole, Jaidi

EVENT LINE

32 Hierro (Foul)

HALF TIME 0 - 0

50 Hunt (Off) Okocha (On)

60 **Riise (Off) Le Tallec (On)**

64 Giannakopoulos (Off) Pedersen (On)

73 **Welsh (Off) Smicer (On)**

73 Ben Haim (Foul)

74 **Pellegrino (Foul)**

79 **Nunez (Off) Morientes (On)**

82 Candela (Handball)

83 Hierro (Off) Campo (On)

86 **Biscan (Corner)**

FULL TIME 1 - 0

STATISTICS

Season	Fixture (Liverpool)		Fixture (Bolton)	Season
193	**7**	Shots On Target	**5**	**190**
202	**3**	Shots Off Target	**8**	**173**
6	**0**	Hit Woodwork	**0**	**7**
76	**1**	Caught Offside	**1**	**81**
178	**4**	Corners	**12**	**169**
370	**6**	Fouls	**13**	**431**
52%	**49%**	Possession	**51%**	**49%**

LEAGUE STANDINGS

Position (pos before)		W	D	L	F	A	Pts
5 (5)	**Liverpool**	**15**	**5**	**11**	**44**	**31**	**50**
6 (6)	**Bolton W**	**13**	**7**	**11**	**38**	**35**	**46**

LIVERPOOL 1 BOLTON WANDERERS 0

A late Igor Biscan header moved Liverpool to within a point of neighbours Everton in the race for the Champions League.

The much-maligned Croatian stooped at the far post to meet Djimi Traore's 85th-minute cross to salvage a poor Liverpool display.

Sam Allardyce's high-flying team of over-achievers came to Anfield in the hope of leapfrogging Liverpool in the table as they looked to secure Champions League football for the first time in club history.

Controversial on-loan Liverpool star El-Hadji Diouf was denied the chance to play against his current employers due both to suspension and a clause in the loan deal, but otherwise the visitors were at full strength.

Reds boss Rafael Benitez rewarded tough-tackling youngster John Welsh with his first Premiership start following a series of impressive performances at England Under-21 level.

Bolton, willed on by a buoyant army of travelling Lancastrians, went close to a fourth-minute opener, keeper Scott Carson beaten to a well-struck corner by Ricardo Gardner.

It took a magnificent save from Carson to deny Stelios Giannakopoulos's sweetly struck half-volley soon after as Wanderers laid siege to the youngster's goal.

The Kop were shouting for a penalty on 20 minutes after John Arne Riise appeared to be dragged down in the area by Nicky Hunt, but referee Steve Bennett didn't spot the incident.

Confusion in the Liverpool defence saw Jamie Carragher nod past the on-rushing Carson, with Stelios just failing to reach the loose ball.

Steven Gerrard went close on 26 minutes, his beautifully struck 25-yard free kick denied by an equally impressive save from visiting keeper Jussi Jaaskelainen.

Vincent Candela kept things level on 34 minutes, his dramatic goal-line clearance preventing a certain tap-in for Luis Garcia.

Liverpool upped the tempo after the break and almost took the lead through Antonio Nunez's far-post volley, Jaaskelainen struggling to gather.

Riise then diverted a great cross from Steve Finnan goalwards, only to be denied by smart work on the line from Tal Ben Haim.

The home faithful grew increasingly restless as the clock wound down, but they reckoned without the mighty Biscan, who stole the points with a fine header.

Jussi Jaaskelainen gets the better of Anthony Le Tallec in this aerial duel.

"In the end we thought one goal would be enough to win the game, and that proved to be the case."
Rafael Benitez

"I'm absolutely gutted, but the fact is we should have had the game wrapped up in the first ten minutes with the amount of chances we had."
Sam Allardyce

PREMIERSHIP FIXTURE HISTORY

Pl: **11** Draws: **3**

	Wins	Goals	Yellow cards	Red cards
Manchester United	8	22	13	0
Blackburn Rovers	0	9	20	2

STARTING LINE-UPS

Manchester United substitutes: Keane, Smith, Carroll, Brown, P.Neville

Blackburn Rovers substitutes: Emerton, Gallagher, Enckelman, Amoruso, Tugay

EVENT LINE

6 **Giggs (Off) Keane (On)**

35 **Neville G (Foul)**

HALF TIME 0 - 0

63 **van Nistelrooy (Off) Smith (On)**

68 Mokoena (Off) Emerton (On)

71 Stead (Foul)

76 **Keane (Foul)**

78 Pedersen (Off) Gallagher (On)

82 **Smith (Foul)**

89 Nelson (Foul)

FULL TIME 0 - 0

STATISTICS

Season	Fixture (Man Utd)		Fixture (Blackburn)	Season
254	9	Shots On Target	3	152
227	14	Shots Off Target	6	183
16	2	Hit Woodwork	0	6
116	2	Caught Offside	3	122
246	9	Corners	3	173
382	21	Fouls	18	497
55%	60%	Possession	40%	49%

LEAGUE STANDINGS

Position (pos before)	W	D	L	F	A	Pts
3 (2) Man Utd	19	10	2	48	17	67
14 (14) Blackburn R	7	12	12	25	37	33

Saturday 2nd April 2005 | Venue: **Old Trafford** | Attendance: **67,939** | Referee: **M.A.Riley**

MANCHESTER UNITED 0 BLACKBURN ROVERS 0

Manchester United missed out on two precious points at Old Trafford as they failed to break through Blackburn's massed defensive ranks.

Arsenal's 4-1 home win over Norwich saw the Gunners leapfrog United into second place on goal difference, increasing the likelihood of a tricky Champions League qualifier for the Red Devils before the start of next season.

Rovers striker Jonathan Stead had the first chance after just 50 seconds, firing straight at keeper Tim Howard from 12 yards after Rio Ferdinand had failed to cut out a long ball into the United penalty area.

The hosts responded 20 seconds later, Wayne Rooney's cross from the left side of the Rovers box coming back to the England youngster, whose 10-yard header was pushed away by a diving Brad Friedel.

Rovers missed their best chance of the match on 13 minutes.

Steven Reid's blistering 25-yard drive took a wicked deflection off Quinton Fortune, forcing Howard to hurl himself across goal to make a fine save.

The loose ball ran to Andy Todd six yards out, but with Howard still grounded the Blackburn skipper ballooned his shot over the bar.

United went close six minutes later, Mikael Silvestre's downward header from Paul Scholes's free kick to the far post brilliantly saved by Friedel.

A piece of Rooney magic almost broke the deadlock on 25 minutes, his screaming 30-yarder crashing against the post with Friedel beaten.

The woodwork came to Blackburn's rescue again on 38 minutes, Roy Keane racing on to Cristiano Ronaldo's ball from the right before hitting a low shot against the post from the edge of the area.

United threatened again two minutes later, Scholes sending a fine cross from the right in towards Silvestre, whose powerful header at the far post was cleared off the line by Morten Gamst Pedersen.

There was a chance for Rovers on the hour mark, Stead clipping his 12-yard shot narrowly wide.

Alan Smith replaced the ineffective Ruud van Nistelrooy three minutes later, United's first-half momentum having dropped off dramatically.

United's only serious chance of the second period came with five minutes to play, Gary Neville's mis-hit shot forcing a diving save from Friedel.

"Brad Friedel made some fantastic saves, like he did against us at Ewood Park earlier in the season, but we should have scored five in the first half."
Sir Alex Ferguson

"We know we have limitations, but our work ethic and the way we apply ourselves cannot be beaten."
Mark Hughes

Morten Gamst Pedersen makes a dramatic goal-line clearance.

PREMIERSHIP FIXTURE HISTORY

Pl: 12 Draws: 2	Wins	⚽	Yellow	Red
Newcastle United	8	24	13	6
Aston Villa	2	12	22	3

STARTING LINE-UPS

Given
Carr, Boumsong, O'Brien, Hughes
Jenas, Bowyer, Butt, Robert
Dyer, Shearer (c)
Angel, Vassell
Barry, Hitzlsperger, Davis, Hendrie
Samuel, Mellberg (c), Laursen, Delaney
Sorensen

Newcastle subs: Taylor, Ameobi, Faye, Harper, Milner
Aston Villa subs: Ridgewell, Solano, Cole, Postma, Berson

EVENT LINE

5 ⚽ Angel (Open Play)
32 Yellow Hitzlsperger (Foul)
41 Yellow Mellberg (Foul)

HALF TIME 0 - 1

46 Sub Mellberg (Off) Ridgewell (On)
52 Sub O'Brien (Off) Taylor (On)
63 Sub Jenas (Off) Ameobi (On)
73 Red Taylor (Handball)
73 ⚽ Barry (Penalty)
79 Yellow Carr (Foul)
80 ⚽ Barry (Penalty)
82 Red Bowyer (Violent Conduct)
82 Red Dyer (Violent Conduct)
84 Sub Robert (Off) Faye (On)
84 Sub Hendrie (Off) Solano (On)
88 Sub Angel (Off) Cole (On)

FULL TIME 0 - 3

STATISTICS

Season	Fixture	Newcastle / Aston Villa	Fixture	Season
214	12	Shots On Target	7	154
176	8	Shots Off Target	3	154
11	0	Hit Woodwork	1	7
82	2	Caught Offside	7	96
197	8	Corners	6	172
378	14	Fouls	24	489
51%	56%	Possession	44%	49%

LEAGUE STANDINGS

Position (pos before)	W	D	L	F	A	Pts
11 (10) Newcastle Utd	9	11	10	41	48	38
10 (11) Aston Villa	11	8	12	37	39	41

Saturday 2nd April 2005 | Venue: **St James' Park** | Attendance: **52,306** | Referee: **B.Knight**

NEWCASTLE UNITED 0 ASTON VILLA 3

Shamed Newcastle had three players sent off as Aston Villa won for only the second time in the Premiership at St James' Park.

Referee Barry Knight, who hadn't shown red all season, dismissed substitute Steven Taylor for handling the ball on the goal line in the 72nd minute.

Then, nine minutes from time, United team-mates and fellow England internationals Lee Bowyer and Kieron Dyer were given their marching orders following an off-the-ball brawl with each other.

United were stunned when Villa raced into a fourth-minute lead, Jermaine Jenas's attempted clearance of a Steve Davis right-wing cross going straight to Juan Pablo Angel, who fired past keeper Shay Given.

England midfielder Jenas then wasted two opportunities to redeem himself within the space of 90 seconds, volleying over from six yards before scuffing the ball wide from a good position.

Dyer went close on 18 minutes, volleying Stephen Carr's right-wing cross narrowly over.

Gareth Barry almost doubled Villa's lead on the half-hour mark, cutting in from the left and beating Given, only to see his shot strike the foot of the post.

Jenas wasted another good chance in first-half stoppage time, finishing weakly after being teed up by Dyer.

United were furious not to be awarded a penalty two minutes after the restart, Alan Shearer's header from Laurent Robert's telling cross deflecting off the hand of Jlloyd Samuel before being saved by Thomas Sorensen.

Dyer threatened on 64 minutes, but was denied by a well-timed challenge from Samuel on the edge of the area as he readied his shot.

United were reduced to 10 men on 72 minutes after Taylor, a 53rd-minute replacement for Andy O'Brien, deliberately handled the ball on the line to prevent a certain Darius Vassell goal.

Barry stepped up for the penalty and hammered the ball home for 2-0.

Villa were awarded a second penalty on 78 minutes for Carr's block on Vassell, Barry converting with a carbon copy of his first goal.

United were down to eight men three minutes later after Dyer and Bowyer squared up to each other, Bowyer landing a right hook to Dyer's head as Barry and Carr rushed in to separate them.

Gareth Barry celebrates netting one of his two penalties.

"I have been told by Kieron Dyer that he did not throw any punches. As for Lee Bowyer, his actions are indefensible."
Graeme Souness

"I don't care that we might not get the credit we deserve. All I care about is the three points."
David O'Leary

PREMIERSHIP FIXTURE HISTORY

Pl: 13 Draws: 2	Wins	Goals	Yellow	Red
Southampton	4	13	16	0
Chelsea	7	18	23	0

STARTING LINE-UPS

Southampton: Niemi; Delap, Lundekvam (c), Jakobsson, Bernard; Telfer, Redknapp, Quashie, Le Saux; Camara, Crouch

Chelsea: Kezman; Duff, J.Cole; Lampard, Makelele, Gudjohnsen; Gallas, Terry (c), Huth, Johnson; Cech

Southampton subs: A.Svensson, Phillips, Smith, Higginbotham, Davenport

Chelsea subs: Tiago, Drogba, Jarosik, Cudicini, Carvalho

EVENT LINE

22 Goal: Lampard (Direct Free Kick)

39 Goal: Gudjohnsen (Open Play)

HALF TIME 0 - 2

46 Sub: Cole J (Off) Tiago (On)

62 Yellow: Kezman (Foul)

63 Sub: Camara (Off) Phillips (On)

63 Sub: Le Saux (Off) Svensson A (On)

65 Sub: Kezman (Off) Drogba (On)

69 Goal: Phillips (Corner)

80 Sub: Duff (Off) Jarosik (On)

83 Goal: Gudjohnsen (Open Play)

89 Yellow: Tiago (Foul)

FULL TIME 1 - 3

STATISTICS

Season	Fixture	Southampton		Chelsea Fixture	Season
146	3	Shots On Target		8	241
164	1	Shots Off Target		4	205
2	0	Hit Woodwork		0	9
97	2	Caught Offside		3	96
149	4	Corners		3	212
399	11	Fouls		10	387
47%	45%	Possession		55%	56%

LEAGUE STANDINGS

Position (pos before)	W	D	L	F	A	Pts
17 (17) Southampton	5	12	14	34	48	27
1 (1) Chelsea	25	5	1	61	11	80

Saturday 2nd April 2005 | Venue: Friends Provident St Mary's Stadium | Attendance: 31,949 | Referee: M.R.Halsey

SOUTHAMPTON 1 CHELSEA 3

Eidur Gudjohnsen struck twice at St Mary's to move Chelsea a step closer to the Premiership crown.

José Mourinho's Blues now stood 13 points clear of their nearest challengers Arsenal and Manchester United, and could wrap up their first title since 1955 with three wins in their remaining seven matches.

Mourinho recalled Glen Johnson in place of Paulo Ferreira, who was sidelined with a foot injury. He also inserted giant German defender Robert Huth into the starting line-up in an attempt to counter in-form Saints striker Peter Crouch.

Chelsea took control of proceedings early on and opened the scoring in the 22nd minute following Andreas Jakobsson's foul on Mateja Kezman, Frank Lampard's fearsome 35-yard free kick taking a deflection off the wall to give Saints keeper Antti Niemi no chance.

Harry Redknapp's Saints, unbeaten at home in the league since September, should have equalised in the 32nd minute through defender Claus Lundekvam.

Rory Delap's long throw from the right found the Norwegian unmarked just six yards out, but he sent his header wide – much to the relief of keeper Petr Cech.

Niemi then pulled off two wonder-saves to prevent his side going further behind, deflecting a back pass from Lundekvam for a corner at full stretch before getting down smartly to his left to block a well-struck effort from Huth.

But the Finn was powerless to deny Gudjohnsen his 13th goal of the season on 39 minutes, the striker applying a clinical finish inside the left upright after being set up by Johnson.

Resolute Southampton battled away and were rewarded with a goal on 69 minutes, Kevin Phillips side-footing home after Paul Telfer had picked him out with a pinpoint cross from the byline.

Saints surged forward in the hope of an unlikely equaliser before Gudjohnsen killed off the match with his second goal seven minutes from time.

The Icelandic star exchanged a neat one-two with Didier Drogba on the right side of the area before steering a shot across the face of goal and inside the left upright.

Eidur Gudjohnsen celebrates his first goal with Mateja Kezman.

"I thought there was very little in the game. We came in 2-0 down at half-time, but I thought that was a bit unjust."

Harry Redknapp

"We are very happy with the result. It wasn't the best performance that we've produced this season, but we were up against a good team."

Robert Huth

PREMIERSHIP MILESTONE

50 Eidur Gudjohnsen's 2nd goal was his 50th in the Premiership

PREMIERSHIP MILESTONE

50 Damien Duff made his 50th Premiership appearance in the colours of Chelsea

PREMIERSHIP FIXTURE HISTORY				
Pl: 2 Draws: 0	Wins	Goals	Yellow	Red
Fulham	2	5	3	0
Portsmouth	0	1	6	1

STARTING LINE-UPS

Fulham subs: McBride, Radzinski, Bocanegra, Crossley, John
Portsmouth subs: O'Neil, Kamara, Fuller, Chalkias, Hughes

EVENT LINE

5 Stefanovic (Foul)
32 Lua Lua (Open Play)

HALF TIME 0 - 1

57 **Rosenior (Handball)**
57 **Jensen (Off) McBride (On)**
63 **Cole (Open Play)**
64 **Legwinski (Off) Radzinski (On)**
77 Stone (Off) O'Neil (On)
79 **Goma (Foul)**
80 Skopelitis (Foul)
81 **McBride (Open Play)**
82 **Boa Morte (Ung.Conduct)**
82 Berger (Off) Kamara (On)
83 O'Neil (Foul)
84 **Clark (Off) Bocanegra (On)**
88 Yakubu (Off) Fuller (On)
90 **Boa Morte (Open Play)**

FULL TIME 3 - 1

STATISTICS

Season	Fixture (Fulham)		Fixture (Portsmouth)	Season
146	7	Shots On Target	5	151
133	5	Shots Off Target	4	155
4	0	Hit Woodwork	0	6
78	2	Caught Offside	5	84
144	5	Corners	5	155
370	14	Fouls	10	375
48%	61%	Possession	39%	47%

LEAGUE STANDINGS

Position (pos before)	W	D	L	F	A	Pts
14 (16) Fulham	9	6	15	36	48	33
16 (15) Portsmouth	8	7	16	33	49	31

Sunday 3rd April 2005 | Venue: **Craven Cottage** | Attendance: **20,502** | Referee: **M.Clattenburg**

FULHAM 3 PORTSMOUTH 1

Fulham produced a superb second-half performance to ease their relegation worries and drop Portsmouth back into the scrap at the bottom of the table.

The first chance fell to the visitors, Lomana LuaLua working his way down the left flank before drilling a dangerous ball across the face of goal for Steve Stone, who was just beaten to it by keeper Edwin van der Sar.

There was an opening for Patrik Berger soon after following some neat set-up play from LuaLua, but the Czech international's first touch let him down.

It took a stunning save from Van der Sar to deny Portsmouth on 22 minutes, the Dutchman reacting brilliantly to turn LuaLua's point-blank header from Stone's cross over the bar.

Sylvain Legwinski then had a rare chance for Fulham, steering his header wide from a good position.

It seemed only a matter of time before Portsmouth scored the goal their dominating play deserved and on 32 minutes it duly arrived, LuaLua cutting back on the left side of the area and taking the ball past Zat Knight and Moritz Volz before curling a shot into the bottom corner from 18 yards.

The Cottagers wasted a prime opportunity to level matters on the stroke of half time after Dejan Stefanovic handled Andy Cole's cross into the Saints area, Steed Malbranque's penalty saved by Jamie Ashdown diving to his left.

Fulham came out for the second period looking far more determined and were rewarded with a 63rd-minute equaliser, Luis Boa Morte working his way down the left before pulling the ball back for Cole to side-foot into the top corner.

Cole almost grabbed a second with 15 minutes to play, his sliding effort striking the inside of the post and rebounding back into play.

Aiyegbeni Yakubu then fired narrowly wide for Portsmouth before substitute Brian McBride moved Fulham ahead on 81 minutes, intercepting Arjan De Zeeuw's attempted header back to the keeper and sending a looping shot over Ashdown.

LuaLua responded with a dangerous ball into the box, but Van der Sar made the grab.

Boa Morte sealed the win in the dying stages, robbing Linvoy Primus and rounding Ashdown before slotting home.

Andy Cole and Brian McBride celebrate a Fulham goal.

"Our second half performance was magnificent. That's the sort of character you need when you're in the position we are."
Chris Coleman

"We weren't as clinical as we should have been. We could have done with the points, so we're a bit frustrated."
Joe Jordan

PREMIERSHIP MILESTONE

Linvoy Primus made his 50th Premiership appearance

PREMIERSHIP FIXTURE HISTORY

Pl: 2 Draws: 0	Wins	Goals	Yellow cards	Red cards
West Bromwich Albion	1	2	3	0
Everton	1	2	4	0

STARTING LINE-UPS

West Brom substitutes: Moore, Scimeca, Chaplow, Kanu, Earnshaw

Everton substitutes: Yobo, Ferguson, Watson, Wright, Plessis

EVENT LINE

27 Yellow card: Cahill (Foul)

28 Yellow card: **Richardson (Foul)**

45 Yellow card: Arteta (Ung.Conduct)

45 Substitution: Pistone (Off) Yobo (On)

HALF TIME 0 - 0

63 Goal: **Gera (Open Play)**

75 Substitution: Carsley (Off) Ferguson (On)

85 Substitution: Stubbs (Off) Watson (On)

86 Substitution: **Richardson (Off) Moore (On)**

89 Substitution: **Albrechtsen (Off) Scimeca (On)**

FULL TIME 1 - 0

STATISTICS

Season	Fixture (West Brom)		Fixture (Everton)	Season
147	4	Shots On Target	2	145
134	4	Shots Off Target	6	167
11	1	Hit Woodwork	0	6
108	3	Caught Offside	3	75
159	7	Corners	7	149
410	15	Fouls	20	376
47%	43%	Possession	57%	49%

LEAGUE STANDINGS

Position (pos before)	W	D	L	F	A	Pts
18 (19) West Brom	5	12	14	30	51	27
4 (4) Everton	15	6	10	35	33	51

Sunday 3rd April 2005 | Venue: **The Hawthorns** | Attendance: **26,805** | Referee: **G.Poll**

WEST BROM 1 EVERTON 0

Champions League-chasing Everton crashed to their third successive defeat against lowly West Bromwich Albion.

The win was West Brom's third in four games, moving them level on points with fourth-from-bottom Southampton.

Everton, meanwhile, had now collected just four points from the last 18, and apart from a late rally, never really looked like ending their poor run.

West Brom went close on 10 minutes, Thomas Gaardsoe rising above the Everton defence, only to see his header crash against the bar with keeper Nigel Martyn beaten.

Everton, who started with Marcus Bent as a lone striker, struggled to break down Albion's rearguard.

On the one occasion in the first half when they did create an opening after a neat through ball from Tony Hibbert, Bent fluffed the chance by shooting weakly at Russell Hoult.

West Brom took a hold of the game in the latter stages of the opening period, Tim Cahill needing to be well placed to clear a goalbound header from Neil Clement.

Everton looked much more threatening as the second half got underway, with Leon Osman and Cahill providing strong midfield support for some penetrating runs by Bent into the home defence.

But the finished product continued to prove elusive, Bent wasting an excellent chance in the 61st minute by firing high over the bar from the edge of the area after being set up by Mikel Arteta.

It proved to be a costly miss, as the hosts broke the deadlock just two minutes later.

West Brom left back Paul Robinson collected Ronnie Wallwork's free kick on the left wing before feeding a short pass to Jonathan Greening.

The former Manchester United midfielder whipped a perfect cross in towards Hungary international Zoltan Gera, who beat Martyn at the far post with a precise header for his fifth of the season.

West Brom were denied by the woodwork once again on 71 minutes, Martin Albrechtsen rattling the post with a low drive.

Gera had a chance for his second with two minutes to play, but his shot from a Geoff Horsfield cross was blocked by Martyn.

Kieran Richardson gets the better of Mikel Arteta.

"This win is all down to team spirit. You could see everyone fighting for each other out there."

Kevin Campbell

"We've never really been thinking about the 'Champions League'. We've only been thinking about having the best season we possibly can."

David Moyes

PREMIERSHIP FIXTURE HISTORY

Pl: 11 Draws: 2	Wins	Goals	Yellow	Red
Blackburn Rovers	8	17	10	0
Southampton	1	7	16	1

STARTING LINE-UPS

Emerton, Tugay, Stead, Enckelman, Amoruso

Phillips, A.Svensson, Poke, Davenport, Higginbotham

EVENT LINE

11 **Pedersen (Open Play)**

30 Camara (Handball)

HALF TIME 1 - 0

46 **Thompson (Off) Emerton (On)**

46 Le Saux (Off) Phillips (On)

48 **Jakobsson (Own Goal)**

49 **Flitcroft (Off) Tugay (On)**

50 **Emerton (Foul)**

55 **Reid (Corner)**

74 **Reid (Foul)**

74 **Reid (Off) Stead (On)**

75 Camara (Off) Svensson A (On)

83 Bernard (Off) Higginbotham (On)

FULL TIME 3 - 0

STATISTICS

Season	Fixture (Blackburn)		Fixture (Southampton)	Season
160	8	Shots On Target	3	149
190	7	Shots Off Target	6	170
6	0	Hit Woodwork	0	2
129	7	Caught Offside	1	98
177	4	Corners	2	151
516	19	Fouls	14	413
49%	54%	Possession	46%	47%

LEAGUE STANDINGS

Position (pos before)	W	D	L	F	A	Pts
14 (15) Blackburn R	8	12	12	28	37	36
17 (17) Southampton	5	12	15	34	51	27

Saturday 9th April 2005 | Venue: **Ewood Park** | Attendance: **20,726** | Referee: **N.S.Barry**

BLACKBURN ROVERS 3 SOUTHAMPTON 0

Two goals in the space of seven minutes at the start of the second half saw Blackburn Rovers to a comfortable win over strugglers Southampton.

After an evenly matched opening spell, Morten Gamst Pedersen opened the scoring for Rovers in the 11th minute.

Brad Friedel rolled the ball out to Aaron Mokoena, who sent a 50-yard pass over the head of Rory Delap and into the path of the on-rushing Pedersen.

The Norwegian's first touch was as sublime as the finish, delicately cushioning the ball down before lashing it through the legs of a helpless Paul Smith from an acute angle for his seventh of the season.

Rovers were quickly back on the offensive, Mokoena splitting the Saints defence with a precision ball, only for David Thompson to be flagged for offside.

Southampton's best chance of the half came on 20 minutes, Nigel Quashie's corner finding an unmarked Henri Camara, whose right-foot effort curled agonisingly wide.

Paul Dickov then went close for Rovers, his near-post header from Pedersen's vicious corner well saved by Smith.

Peter Crouch had a chance down the other end, his volley from 20 yards held by Friedel.

The second half kicked off in blistering fashion, with Rovers grabbing two scrappy goals in quick succession to effectively kill off the game.

The first came on 48 minutes, Saints defender Andreas Jakobsson turning the ball into his own net following Steven Reid's drilled ball across the face of goal.

Seven minutes later and it was 3-0, left back Dominic Matteo collecting Pedersen's corner on the edge of the area before picking out Reid to calmly slot home from 12 yards.

Substitute Brett Emerton went within inches of making it four midway through the half, firing just wide from 20 yards after Dickov's first touch from Lucas Neill's ball over the top had dropped kindly into his path.

Jonathan Stead, a 74th-minute replacement for Reid, then had a couple of decent chances, but was denied by Smith on both occasions.

Saints continued to battle and almost grabbed a late consolation, Kevin Phillips firing narrowly over from inside the Rovers area.

Morten Gamst Pedersen celebrates his opening goal.

"I thought the players were magnificent. Each and every one of them put in a committed performance today."
Mark Hughes

"Blackburn look a strong outfit, and I think they can give Arsenal a good game next week in the F.A.Cup."
Harry Redknapp

PREMIERSHIP FIXTURE HISTORY

Pl: 4 Draws: 2	Wins	Goals	Yellow cards	Red cards
Bolton Wanderers	1	3	3	0
Fulham	1	3	6	1

STARTING LINE-UPS

Bolton subs: Gardner, Fadiga, Poole, Jaidi, Pedersen

Fulham subs: Radzinski, John, Crossley, Bocanegra, Pembridge

EVENT LINE

12 Red card Jensen (Handball)

13 Yellow card Rosenior (Dissent)

13 **Okocha (Penalty)**

33 **Nolan (Open Play)**

HALF TIME 2 - 0

47 Boa Morte (Open Play)

54 **Giannakopoulos (Open Play)**

61 Yellow card Boa Morte (Foul)

80 Malbranque (Off) Radzinski (On)

82 Cole (Off) John (On)

84 **Candela (Off) Gardner (On)**

84 **Hierro (Off) Fadiga (On)**

FULL TIME 3 - 1

STATISTICS

Season	Fixture (Bolton)		Fixture (Fulham)	Season
201	**11**	Shots On Target	**4**	**150**
178	**5**	Shots Off Target	**3**	**136**
7	**0**	Hit Woodwork	**0**	**4**
88	**7**	Caught Offside	**4**	**82**
173	**4**	Corners	**6**	**150**
437	**6**	Fouls	**14**	**384**
49%	**54%**	Possession	**46%**	**48%**

LEAGUE STANDINGS

Position (pos before)	W	D	L	F	A	Pts
6 (6) Bolton W	**14**	**7**	**11**	**41**	**36**	**49**
16 (14) Fulham	**9**	**6**	**16**	**37**	**51**	**33**

Saturday 9th April 2005 | Venue: **Reebok Stadium** | Attendance: **25,493** | Referee: **D.J.Gallagher**

BOLTON WANDERERS 3 FULHAM 1

Bolton Wanderers stayed on track for a possible European place with a convincing victory over 10-man Fulham.

Wanderers boss Sam Allardyce made one change to the side beaten at Liverpool the previous week, recalling captain Jay-Jay Okocha following the Nigerian's recovery from a knee injury.

Fulham boss Chris Coleman also made a change, opting to start Brian McBride up front alongside Andy Cole.

The visitors were reduced to 10 men on 12 minutes after former Wanderer Claus Jensen used his arm to block a Bruno N'Gotty header which was destined for the back of the net. Okocha fired home the resulting penalty.

Wanderers pressed for a second goal, Kevin Nolan and Gary Speed both wasting chances from good positions before Nolan beat Edwin van der Sar from close range on 33 minutes for his fourth of the season.

Fulham pulled one back on 47 minutes, Cole doing well to hold play up on the edge of the area before knocking a ball to the far post for Luis Boa Morte to slide home.

Fulham's joy was short-lived, however, as seven minutes later Stelios Giannakopoulos converted his sixth of the season to restore Bolton's two-goal advantage.

The hard-working Fulham midfield began to tire as the half progressed, opening extra space for Okocha and Stelios to attack Van der Sar's goal.

Despite Wanderers' dominance, Fulham still managed to create a few good chances, McBride just missing out on Moritz Volz's ball from the right across the face of goal.

Coleman brought on Tomasz Radzinski and Collins John for Steed Malbranque and Cole for the final 10 minutes in the hope that fresh legs might catch out Wanderers.

Allardyce responded with two substitutions of his own, introducing Ricardo Gardner and Khalilou Fadiga for Vincent Candela and Fernando Hierro.

Okocha then wasted a chance for a Wanderers fourth, firing a free kick from a dangerous position straight into the defensive wall.

John looked to have grabbed a late goal for Fulham when he knocked the ball towards an empty net, only for Gardner to race back and clear off the line with an overhead kick.

Stylianos Giannakopoulos wheels away after scoring.

"After the bit of luck with the penalty, we won with two quality goals."

Sam Allardyce

"After the sending off it was always going to be an uphill struggle, but the boys never stopped working."

Assistant Manager Steve Kean

PREMIERSHIP FIXTURE HISTORY

Pl: 3 Draws: 2	Wins	Goals	Yellow cards	Red cards
Chelsea	1	4	5	0
Birmingham City	0	1	5	0

STARTING LINE-UPS

Gudjohnsen, Drogba, Jarosik, Cudicini, Carvalho

Lazaridis, Gray, Morrison, Vaesen, Blake

EVENT LINE

21	Cunningham (Foul)
	HALF TIME 0 - 0
46	**Kezman (Off) Drogba (On)**
46	**Smertin (Off) Gudjohnsen (On)**
50	Nafti (Foul)
60	Carter (Off) Lazaridis (On)
65	**Cole J (Foul)**
65	Pandiani (Indirect Free Kick)
66	**Tiago (Foul)**
69	**Johnson (Off) Jarosik (On)**
80	Pennant (Off) Gray (On)
82	**Drogba (Open Play)**
87	Pandiani (Off) Morrison (On)
	FULL TIME 1 - 1

STATISTICS

Season	Fixture (Chelsea)		Fixture (Birmingham)	Season
253	**12**	Shots On Target	**1**	**139**
212	**7**	Shots Off Target	**1**	**141**
10	**1**	Hit Woodwork	**0**	**7**
98	**2**	Caught Offside	**0**	**92**
220	**8**	Corners	**5**	**161**
404	**17**	Fouls	**12**	**445**
56%	**59%**	Possession	**41%**	**50%**

LEAGUE STANDINGS

Position (pos before)		W	D	L	F	A	Pts
1 (1)	**Chelsea**	**25**	**6**	**1**	**62**	**12**	**81**
13 (13)	**Birmingham C**	**9**	**10**	**13**	**35**	**39**	**37**

Saturday 9th April 2005 | Venue: **Stamford Bridge** | Attendance: **42,031** | Referee: **C.J.Foy**

CHELSEA 1 BIRMINGHAM CITY 1

Didier Drogba spared Chelsea blushes with a late equaliser against Birmingham City.

The visitors took a 65th-minute lead before Drogba, a second-half substitute, scored his 10th league goal of the season with eight minutes to play.

Chelsea threatened on 22 minutes, Frank Lampard arrowing a trademark free kick from 20 yards through the Birmingham wall, only for Maik Taylor to make a comfortable save.

Joe Cole went off on a jinking run in the 33rd minute, slicing through three defenders and nutmegging Kenny Cunningham before driving a daisy-cutter from just outside the six yard box which beat Taylor before skimming the upright and running out of play.

Tiago set up Chelsea's next chance three minutes later, dispossessing a sleepy Mario Melchiot on the byline before sending a left-footer across the face of goal which just eluded the on-rushing Lampard.

Chelsea boss José Mourinho made two substitutions at the break, replacing Alexei Smertin and Mateja Kezman with Drogba and Eidur Gudjohnsen.

Birmingham almost grabbed the opener on 49 minutes, Darren Carter's left-foot volley denied by a brilliant reflex save from Petr Cech. The loose ball fell for Walter Pandiani, but John Terry snuffed out his shot.

A Drogba header and a Lampard shot then both went wide before Birmingham broke the deadlock on 65 minutes, Matthew Upson heading Jermaine Pennant's lofted free kick back into the area towards Pandiani, whose right-foot blast deflected off Terry and the underside of the bar before settling in the back of the net.

With time ticking away and Chelsea's unbeaten home record this season looking doomed, they launched another in a series of attacks on the Birmingham rearguard.

Lampard collected the ball close to the six yard box and in one quick movement managed to squeeze it into the path of Drogba, who curled a low right-footer past the diving Taylor.

Chelsea threw everyone forward in the final minutes in the hunt for a winner, Terry heading just wide before Jiri Jarosik's volley flew into the side netting with practically the last kick of the game.

Matthew Upson thwarts Didier Drogba.

"It was a bad performance in the first half. It looked like a friendly that was played in the heat of August."

Jose Mourinho

"We deserved to get something from this game. It would have been special to win, but I'm happy with the point."

Steve Bruce

347 << **Chelsea** >> 370 | 341 << **Birmingham City** >> 360

PREMIERSHIP FIXTURE HISTORY

Pl: 8 Draws: 5	Wins	⚽	Yellow	Red
Manchester City	2	10	7	0
Liverpool	1	11	6	0

STARTING LINE-UPS

Mills, Weaver, Negouai, Croft, B.Wright-Phillips

Smicer, Welsh, Traore, Dudek, Hyypia

EVENT LINE

33 Carragher (Foul)

45 **Barton (Ung.Conduct)**

HALF TIME 0 - 0

67 **Onuoha (Off) Mills (On)**

68 Garcia (Off) Smicer (On)

73 **Bosvelt (Off) Croft (On)**

78 Morientes (Off) Welsh (On)

82 Riise (Off) Traore (On)

83 **Sibierski (Off) Wright-Phillips B (On)**

90 **Musampa (Open Play)**

FULL TIME 1 - 0

STATISTICS

Season	Fixture		Fixture	Season
174	8	Shots On Target	1	194
165	4	Shots Off Target	5	207
3	1	Hit Woodwork	0	6
94	5	Caught Offside	6	82
197	5	Corners	2	180
395	8	Fouls	11	381
49%	53%	Possession	47%	52%

LEAGUE STANDINGS

Position (pos before)	W	D	L	F	A	Pts
11 (12) Man City	10	10	12	38	36	40
5 (5) Liverpool	15	5	12	44	32	50

Saturday 9th April 2005 | Venue: **City of Manchester Stadium** | Attendance: **47,203** | Referee: **M.A.Riley**

MANCHESTER CITY 1 LIVERPOOL 0

Lacklustre Liverpool wasted a glorious opportunity to move ahead of rivals Everton into the fourth Champions League spot.

Only seconds of normal time remained when Kiki Musampa struck the goal which earned a first win for new City manager Stuart Pearce in his third game in charge.

Until then the game had looked to be heading for a gloomy goalless draw, a result which would still have been sufficient for Liverpool to move ahead of Everton on goal difference.

But as had happened so often this season, Liverpool once again failed to deliver after a European fixture.

In the 10 matches which had immediately followed Champions League games, Liverpool had managed just two victories.

And once again the Reds disappointed, this time four days after their impressive win against Italian giants Juventus.

City had the first chance on 11 minutes, captain Sylvain Distin's downward header from Stephen Jordan's free kick well saved by teenage keeper Scott Carson diving low to his right.

Igor Biscan forced David James into his first save of the match in the 33rd minute, the City keeper diving smartly to his left to keep out a long-range shot from the Croatian midfielder before kicking away the loose ball as Anthony Le Tallec went in for the rebound.

City almost grabbed the lead on the stroke of half time, Carson racing out of his goal to block at the feet of Antoine Sibierski.

The hosts had a penalty appeal waved away on 62 minutes after Robbie Fowler went down under a challenge from Mauricio Pellegrino. Television replays confirmed that the City striker had taken a dive.

Musampa went within inches of putting City ahead midway through the half, his volley striking the upright with Carson beaten.

Steven Gerrard wasted a great chance for Liverpool with eight minutes to play, firing into the side netting after being released on the right side of the penalty area by Vladimir Smicer's crossfield pass.

But it was City who would steal the points with Musampa's 90th-minute strike, a terrific shot on the run from 12 yards flying low to the left of Carson.

Paul Bosvelt challenges Fernando Morientes.

"It was probably poetic justice to score the winner in the last minute after what happened at Charlton last week."

Stuart Pearce

PREMIERSHIP MILESTONE

Kiki Musampa scored his first Premiership goal

"What was upsetting was that the goal came from our throw-in."

Rafael Benitez

PREMIERSHIP FIXTURE HISTORY

Pl: 10 Draws: 0	Wins	Goals	Yellow	Red
Middlesbrough	2	6	11	3
Arsenal	8	24	10	1

STARTING LINE-UPS

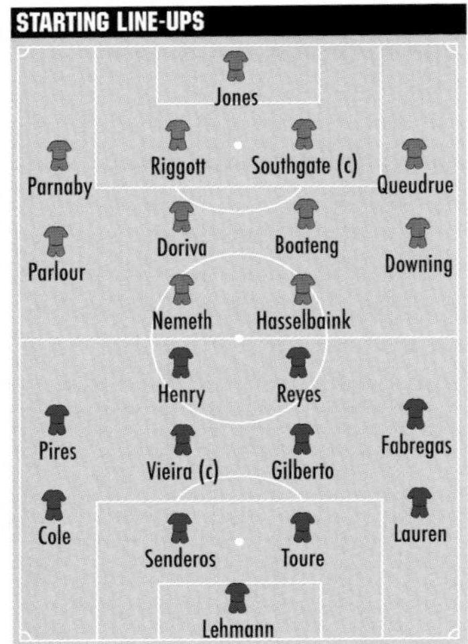

Graham, Ehiogu, Cooper, Johnson, Kennedy

Bergkamp, Almunia, Cygan, Eboue, van Persie

EVENT LINE

2 Lauren (Foul)

43 **Queudrue (Foul)**

HALF TIME 0 - 0

46 Reyes (Off) Bergkamp (On)

73 Pires (Open Play)

86 **Doriva (Off) Graham (On)**

90 **Parlour (Off) Ehiogu (On)**

FULL TIME 0 - 1

STATISTICS

Season	Fixture		Fixture	Season
222	6	Shots On Target	1	246
170	3	Shots Off Target	6	153
6	1	Hit Woodwork	0	13
85	5	Caught Offside	1	75
181	5	Corners	3	189
402	12	Fouls	9	369
50%	36%	Possession	64%	56%

LEAGUE STANDINGS

Position (pos before)		W	D	L	F	A	Pts
7 (7)	Middlesbrough	12	9	11	45	43	45
2 (2)	Arsenal	21	7	4	73	33	70

Saturday 9th April 2005 | Venue: **Riverside Stadium** | Attendance: **33,874** | Referee: **P.Dowd**

MIDDLESBROUGH 0 ARSENAL 1

Arsenal's victory at the Riverside Stadium followed by Manchester United's defeat at Carrow Road saw the Gunners solidify their hold on second spot in the Premiership table.

The points were valuable in Arsenal's quest for a Champions League place, but manager Arsène Wenger couldn't have been happy with the Gunners' overall display, his men lacking the hunger they'd shown in recent performances.

Middlesbrough had been cruelly hit by injuries this season and there was another blow shortly before kick off, keeper Mark Schwarzer suffering a back injury in the warm-up which saw fellow Australian Brad Jones hastily called up for a rare first-team opportunity.

Boro boss Steve McClaren just had time to call up the teenage midfield player Adam Johnson for a place among the substitutes.

Boro came into the game hoping to boost their challenge for a UEFA Cup spot next season, while Arsenal were looking to record their fourth league win on the trot.

Boro were the first to threaten, Jimmy Floyd Hasselbaink pulling the ball back for Brazilian midfielder Doriva, whose powerful shot grazed the outside of the post.

Arsenal played at a slow tempo and surprisingly failed to trouble the inexperienced Jones before the break.

Dennis Bergkamp came on for the injured José Antonio Reyes to start the second half.

As the game progressed, Arsenal continued to lack the urgency one would expect from a side chasing the number two spot in the Premiership.

They never looked in danger of losing, but there was a real lack of penetration from their attack.

Credit should be given to some strong Boro defending, with George Boateng a powerhouse in midfield.

Arsenal finally made the breakthrough on 73 minutes, Franck Queudrue's attempted clearance striking Doriva and falling for Robert Pires, who beat Jones with a left-foot shot from seven yards.

Hasselbaink had a great chance for an equaliser shortly after, breaking through to face Jens Lehmann one-on-one, only for the keeper to make an excellent save to deny the former Leeds United striker his 15th of the season.

Robert Pires celebrates with Ashley Cole.

"I thought the lads were heroic, and I just cannot believe we have lost the game."

Steve McClaren

PREMIERSHIP MILESTONE

50 Stuart Parnaby made his 50th Premiership appearance

"We enjoy playing football and giving entertainment to people. Defensively we have become more stable in the past month, and that has been very good for us."

Arsene Wenger

PREMIERSHIP FIXTURE HISTORY

Pl: 4 Draws: 0	Wins	⚽	Yellow	Red
Norwich City	1	3	4	0
Manchester United	3	7	4	0

STARTING LINE-UPS

Bentley, Svensson, Jonson, Ward, Doherty

Ronaldo, Rooney, Carroll, O'Shea, van Nistelrooy

EVENT LINE

22 Saha (Off) Ronaldo (On)

HALF TIME 0 - 0

46 **Stuart (Off) Bentley (On)**

46 Fortune (Off) Rooney (On)

54 Rooney (Foul)

55 **Ashton (Indirect Free Kick)**

63 Kleberson (Off) van Nistelrooy (On)

66 **McKenzie (Open Play)**

67 **McKenzie (Ung.Conduct)**

68 Scholes (Foul)

83 **Bentley (Ung.Conduct)**

84 **Ashton (Off) Svensson (On)**

86 **Huckerby (Off) Jonson (On)**

FULL TIME 2 - 0

STATISTICS

Season	Fixture		Fixture	Season
144	5	Shots On Target	8	262
156	2	Shots Off Target	8	235
5	0	Hit Woodwork	0	16
97	1	Caught Offside	1	117
150	3	Corners	4	250
433	19	Fouls	18	400
45%	43%	Possession	57%	55%

LEAGUE STANDINGS

Position (pos before)	W	D	L	F	A	Pts
20 (20) Norwich C	4	11	17	32	63	23
3 (3) Man Utd	19	10	3	48	19	67

Saturday 9th April 2005 | Venue: **Carrow Road** | Attendance: **25,522** | Referee: **H.M.Webb**

NORWICH CITY 2 MANCHESTER UNITED 0

Goals from Dean Ashton and Leon McKenzie saw lowly Norwich to victory over Premiership giants Manchester United at Carrow Road.

The loss was United's first in the league in 21 games.

Home keeper Robert Green was called into action early on, easily gathering a scuffed shot from Kleberson after good work on the right by Gary Neville.

McKenzie countered for Norwich, whipping in a dangerous cross from the left wing which was intercepted before it could reach the well-placed Damien Francis.

Cristiano Ronaldo, a 22nd-minute replacement for the injured Louis Saha, sent over a good cross from the right wing, but neither Alan Smith nor Kleberson were ready for it.

Another Ronaldo cross on the half-hour mark produced the first corner of the game, but the energetic McKenzie was on hand to head away to safety.

Norwich then forced three corners of their own, but couldn't make any of them count.

Ronaldo threatened shortly before the break, cutting in from the right before seeing his shot fly wide.

Both sides made a change at the break, Norwich striker David Bentley making a first appearance after a long lay-off through injury to replace Graham Stuart, while Wayne Rooney came on for Quinton Fortune.

Bentley was quickly into the action, sending a cross from the right in towards Ashton, who was unable to test Tim Howard with his header.

Good work by Darren Huckerby and Adam Drury released McKenzie, but his angled shot was saved by Howard.

Norwich wouldn't have to wait much longer for the opener, Ashton outjumping the visiting defence to head Bentley's free kick inside the far post on 55 minutes.

Ronaldo then fired wide from the edge of the area before McKenzie doubled Norwich's advantage, blasting home a left-foot volley from 12 yards after a perfect pass from Ashton.

United created a couple of decent chances, Ruud van Nistelrooy seeing a header blocked by Craig Fleming before Green saved from Rooney.

Francis responded for Norwich, his volley blocked after Huckerby had picked him out on the edge of the United penalty area.

Rooney went close with a late chance, his ambitious shot from 35 yards tipped over by Green.

Leon McKenzie volleys home Norwich's second goal.

"At half-time the boss told us to keep believing, keep playing and keep getting in their faces."
Craig Fleming

PREMIERSHIP MILESTONE
The attendance of 25,522 was a Premiership record at Carrow Road

"That wasn't good enough from start to finish."
Gary Neville

PREMIERSHIP FIXTURE HISTORY

Pl: 2 Draws: 0	Wins	⚽	Yellow	Red
Portsmouth	1	5	4	0
Charlton Athletic	1	4	5	0

STARTING LINE-UPS

Kamara, Rodic, Primus, Chalkias, O'Neil

Thomas, Lisbie, Johansson, Andersen, Hughes

EVENT LINE

3 ⚽ **Yakubu (Open Play)**
14 Murphy (Dissent)
19 Kishishev (Off) Thomas (On)
20 ⚽ **Stone (Indirect Free Kick)**
22 ⚽ Fortune (Indirect Free Kick)
43 Hreidarsson (Foul)
45 ⚽ Murphy (Direct Free Kick)

HALF TIME 2 - 2

55 Perry (Foul)
60 **Skopelitis (Off) Kamara (On)**
61 Bartlett (Off) Lisbie (On)
72 **Berger (Off) Rodic (On)**
80 **Taylor (Off) Primus (On)**
83 ⚽ **Kamara (Open Play)**
88 Perry (Off) Johansson (On)
90 ⚽ **Lua Lua (Open Play)**
90 **Lua Lua (Ung.Conduct)**

FULL TIME 4 - 2

STATISTICS

Season	Fixture		Fixture	Season
160	9	Shots On Target	4	139
159	4	Shots Off Target	4	116
7	1	Hit Woodwork	0	7
90	6	Caught Offside	1	106
160	5	Corners	4	137
386	11	Fouls	14	402
47%	59%	Possession	41%	44%

LEAGUE STANDINGS

Position (pos before)	W	D	L	F	A	Pts
15 (16) Portsmouth	9	7	16	37	51	34
8 (8) Charlton Ath	12	8	12	39	48	44

Saturday 9th April 2005 | Venue: **Fratton Park** | Attendance: **20,108** | Referee: **G.Poll**

PORTSMOUTH 4 CHARLTON ATHLETIC 2

Portsmouth overcame a spirited Charlton revival to snatch two late goals and relieve the pressure on new manager Alain Perrin.

Pacing the technical area two days after arriving in England to begin a new career as Pompey's latest manager, the Frenchman couldn't have hoped for a better start, Aiyegbeni Yakubu converting a free header from Steve Stone's centre in the third minute for his 15th goal of the season.

Charlton, still eyeing a UEFA Cup place, had Danny Murphy booked on 14 minutes before losing Radostin Kishishev with a facial injury in the 19th minute, to be replaced by Jerome Thomas.

Thomas's first contribution was to give away a free kick, Patrik Berger floating in a delightful ball which was glanced home by Stone for 2-0.

The visitors were thrown a lifeline two minutes later when they were awarded a free kick on the left, Murphy sending a quick ball in towards big defender Jonathan Fortune, who headed home.

Hermann Hreidarsson was booked for a foul on Stone just before the break and then in first-half injury time the Addicks pulled level, Murphy stepping up to bend a free kick beyond the defensive wall and past a static Jamie Ashdown after Thomas had been brought down on the edge of the area.

Portsmouth had the better chances as the second half got underway, Yakubu blazing over from 12 yards before Giannis Skopelitis saw his shot blocked on the line by Shaun Bartlett.

Yakubu hit the post in the 65th minute, while Ashdown made up for his part in Charlton's second with a fine save to deny another quickly taken free kick by Murphy.

The match appeared to be heading for a draw before Portsmouth shocked the visitors with two late goals.

The first came with eight minutes to play, Lomana LuaLua sending a right-wing corner in towards substitute Diomansy Kamara, who stole in ahead of the keeper to score with a stunning header.

Then, in stoppage time, Yakubu played a perfect pass to LuaLua, who worked his way past an advancing Charlton defender before beating Dean Kiely with a low shot into the far corner.

Yakubu nets an early goal.

"I think the benefit of my arrival was mainly psychological. The players responded to a new manager."

Alain Perrin

PREMIERSHIP MILESTONE

25 Steve Stone netted his 25th Premiership goal

PREMIERSHIP MILESTONE

50 Aliou Cisse made his 50th Premiership appearance

"For some reason we have got a big problem at the back, and Portsmouth got in two or three headers which they should never have been allowed."

Alan Curbishley

PREMIERSHIP FIXTURE HISTORY

Pl: 2 Draws: 1	Wins	⚽	▢	■
Aston Villa	1	3	3	2
West Bromwich Albion	0	2	3	1

STARTING LINE-UPS

De la Cruz, Cole, Postma, Hitzlsperger, Berson

Kanu, Earnshaw, Scimeca, Kuszczak, Moore

EVENT LINE

27 ⚽ **Vassell (Corner)**

HALF TIME 1 - 0

51 ▢ Robinson (Foul)

52 ▢ **Laursen (Foul)**

61 ■ **Ridgewell (Violent Conduct)**

61 ■ Greening (Violent Conduct)

64 **Solano (Off) De la Cruz (On)**

71 Campbell (Off) Kanu (On)

71 Horsfield (Off) Earnshaw (On)

80 **Angel (Off) Cole (On)**

80 Albrechtsen (Off) Scimeca (On)

85 ▢ Kanu (Foul)

90 ⚽ Robinson (Open Play)

FULL TIME 1 - 1

STATISTICS

Season	Fixture		Fixture	Season
161	7	Shots On Target	5	152
161	7	Shots Off Target	2	136
8	1	Hit Woodwork	0	11
97	1	Caught Offside	4	112
177	5	Corners	5	164
495	6	Fouls	10	420
49%	54%	Possession	46%	47%

LEAGUE STANDINGS

Position (pos before)	W	D	L	F	A	Pts
10 (10) Aston Villa	11	9	12	38	40	42
17 (18) West Brom	5	13	14	31	52	28

Sunday 10th April 2005 | Venue: **Villa Park** | Attendance: **39,402** | Referee: **R.Styles**

ASTON VILLA 1 WEST BROM 1

A dramatic last-minute equaliser by Paul Robinson moved West Bromwich Albion out of the bottom three for the first time since last November.

Robinson, who had just signed a new two-year contract, headed home substitute Riccardo Scimeca's cross at the far post to notch his first ever goal for Albion.

The match was marred by dismissal's for either side, Villa's Liam Ridgewell and the Baggies' Jonathan Greening both sent off in the 61st minute for head-butting.

Darius Vassell, who had struggled for Villa following a spate of injuries, was proving a real nuisance for the West Brom defence, his pacey runs on goal opening some good scoring opportunities.

West Brom, meanwhile, were doing little to suggest they might earn their first win at Villa Park since 1979.

They did well to survive some early Villa pressure, but were unable to push forward themselves with any real conviction.

Fortunately for the visitors, keeper Russell Hoult was in good form, bravely blocking an effort from Vassell before saving a long-range blast from Lee Hendrie.

He made another brilliant save to flick over a cross from Jlloyd Samuel, but from Nolberto Solano's corner Villa took the lead, Hoult parrying Ridgewell's powerful header only as far as Vassell, who headed home from close range for his first Premiership score since the opening match of the season.

It wasn't until the last few minutes of the half that West Brom finally managed to test Thomas Sorensen with a shot from Zoltan Gera and a Kevin Campbell header which the Villa keeper held at the second attempt.

The visitors threatened again five minutes into the second period, Martin Laursen clearing off the line as Geoff Horsfield closed in to apply the finishing touch.

The game became rather frantic following the dismissals of Ridgewell and Greening, with chances opening up at either end.

Vassell then went close for Villa, his effort denied by a great save from Hoult.

Sorensen made an equally fine save to deny Robinson after he'd been put clear by Campbell.

The points looked to be Villa's until former Watford defender Robinson popped up to grab the late equaliser.

Neil Clement holds off Darius Vassell.

"In the first half we outplayed them totally and should have been well ahead, but then we were a shadow of ourselves in the second period."

David O'Leary

"I think Paul Robinson is an underrated player. His goal illustrates the mood in the camp at the moment."

Bryan Robson

PREMIERSHIP MILESTONE

Paul Robinson scored his first Premiership goal

PREMIERSHIP FIXTURE HISTORY

Pl: 4 Draws: 0	Wins	Goals	Yellow cards	Red cards
Everton	2	8	3	0
Crystal Palace	2	5	10	0

STARTING LINE-UPS

Everton subs: Watson, Carsley, Vaughan, Wright, McFadden

Crystal Palace subs: Watson, Torghelle, Speroni, Hudson, Borrowdale

EVENT LINE

Min	Event
7	Kiraly (Handball) (booked)
7	**Arteta (Direct Free Kick)** (goal)
26	**Stubbs (Off) Watson (On)**
	HALF TIME 1 - 0
47	**Cahill (Open Play)** (goal)
54	**Cahill (Open Play)** (goal)
57	Lakis (Off) Torghelle (On)
57	Riihilahti (Off) Watson (On)
60	**Hibbert (Foul)** (booked)
67	**Bent (Off) Carsley (On)**
74	**Naysmith (Off) Vaughan (On)**
87	**Vaughan (Open Play)** (goal)
	FULL TIME 4 - 0

STATISTICS

Season	Fixture (Everton)		Fixture (Crystal Palace)	Season
153	8	Shots On Target	3	141
172	5	Shots Off Target	8	143
6	0	Hit Woodwork	1	7
80	5	Caught Offside	1	74
153	4	Corners	9	158
386	10	Fouls	14	437
49%	53%	Possession	47%	47%

LEAGUE STANDINGS

Position (pos before)	W	D	L	F	A	Pts
4 (4) Everton	16	6	10	39	33	54
19 (19) Crystal Palace	6	8	18	33	54	26

Sunday 10th April 2005 | Venue: **Goodison Park** | Attendance: **36,519** | Referee: **U.D.Rennie**

EVERTON 4 CRYSTAL PALACE 0

Everton regained the momentum in the big city battle to reach the Champions League with a 4-0 thumping of Crystal Palace at Goodison Park.

A Tim Cahill double, a fine effort from Mikel Arteta and a debut goal from 16-year-old James Vaughan increased the Toffees' advantage over Merseyside neighbours Liverpool in the race for fourth place.

Everton boss David Moyes restored Duncan Ferguson to the starting line-up in an attempt to halt a run of three straight defeats.

Kevin Kilbane had the first chance for Everton in the second minute, his 25-yard volley landing on the roof of Gabor Kiraly's net.

A mistake from Kiraly led to Everton's opener five minutes later, the keeper carrying the ball out of the box and setting up a free kick which Spanish journeyman Arteta curled beautifully into the top corner.

The ever-mobile Andy Johnson twisted and turned his way into a shooting position on 24 minutes before Everton skipper Alan Stubbs was forced off with a shoulder injury.

Tom Soares went close with a 40th-minute header from Danny Granville's cross before Kiraly made up for his error with one of the saves of the season to deny Ferguson's free header a minute later.

Leon Osman wasted a prime opportunity to double Everton's lead just before the break, heading over an open goal from 12 yards.

But the hosts didn't have to wait long for their second goal, Cahill charging on to Marcus Bent's flicked cross in the 47th minute and blasting an unstoppable drive into the roof of the net.

The Australian struck again seven minutes later, nodding home an easy goal after Kilbane had been granted a free run through the heart of the Eagles defence.

Palace made a brief show of resistance, Sandor Torghelle hitting the post before Wayne Routledge fired wide from 10 yards.

With four minutes to go, substitute Vaughan, who at 16 years and 271 days had just become the youngest first-team player in Everton history, knocked home Kilbane's clipped cross to become Everton's youngest ever first-team goalscorer, breaking the record held by one Wayne Rooney.

James Vaughan becomes the youngest scorer in Premiership history.

"Our passing was much better today, and we had the penetration which was so lacking against West Brom."

Assistant Manager Alan Irvine

PREMIERSHIP MILESTONE

James Vaughan marked his Premiership debut with a goal

PREMIERSHIP MILESTONE

Mikel Arteta scored his first Premiership goal

"My players owe the supporters some performances after that showing in the second half."

Iain Dowie

PREMIERSHIP FIXTURE HISTORY

Pl: 12 Draws: 1	Wins	Goals	Yellow cards	Red cards
Tottenham Hotspur	7	21	8	2
Newcastle United	4	14	18	2

STARTING LINE-UPS

Davis, Keane, Ziegler, Cerny, Bunjevcevic

Milner, N'Zogbia, Ambrose, Caig, Hughes

EVENT LINE

14 **Brown (Foul)**
19 Faye (Foul)
42 **Defoe (Open Play)**
HALF TIME 1 - 0
46 Shearer (Off) Milner (On)
51 Ameobi (Foul)
55 **Brown (Off) Davis (On)**
62 Butt (Off) Ambrose (On)
62 Robert (Off) N'Zogbia (On)
78 **Defoe (Off) Keane (On)**
84 **Davies (Off) Ziegler (On)**
86 **Davis (Foul)**
FULL TIME 1 - 0

STATISTICS

Season	Fixture		Fixture	Season
198	6	Shots On Target	3	217
179	13	Shots Off Target	3	179
10	0	Hit Woodwork	0	11
134	7	Caught Offside	2	84
162	4	Corners	7	204
385	9	Fouls	15	393
50%	45%	Possession	55%	51%

LEAGUE STANDINGS

Position (pos before)		W	D	L	F	A	Pts
7 (9)	Tottenham H	13	7	12	39	35	46
12 (12)	Newcastle Utd	9	11	11	41	49	38

Sunday 10th April 2005 | Venue: **White Hart Lane** | Attendance: **35,885** | Referee: **S.G.Bennett**

TOTTENHAM HOTSPUR 1 NEWCASTLE UNITED 0

A first-half goal from Jermain Defoe kept Spurs on track for European football.

The England striker slotted home his 22nd of the season after a dreadful error by stand-in Newcastle keeper Steve Harper.

It was sweet revenge for Spurs, who had been knocked out of the FA Cup by the same scoreline at Newcastle last month.

Graeme Souness's men would now turn their attention to big matches against Sporting Lisbon and Manchester United in the UEFA Cup and FA Cup respectively.

Spurs boss Martin Jol made three changes to his starting line-up, introducing Stephen Kelly, Anthony Gardner and Simon Davies for Noe Pamarot, Noureddine Naybet and Reto Ziegler.

United were without the banned Lee Bowyer and Kieron Dyer. They were also missing the suspended Stephen Taylor and injured trio Patrick Kluivert, Titus Bramble and keeper Shay Given.

The best early chance fell to the visitors, Jermaine Jenas's inch-perfect cross to the far post finding an unmarked Shola Ameobi, whose downward header bounced up and over the bar.

Spurs were looking the livelier side and their efforts were rewarded with the 42nd-minute opener, Harper's attempted clearance from Celestine Babayaro's back pass cannoning off Davies and falling for Defoe, who made no mistake.

Spurs continued to dominate as the game moved into the second half, but they were finding it difficult to convert their possession into goalscoring opportunities.

The biggest cheers of the day – other than for Defoe's goal – came when Davies roasted former Spurs captain Stephen Carr down the left flank, much to the delight of the Tottenham fans.

United wasted an excellent chance to move level on 57 minutes, miscommunication between Spurs keeper Paul Robinson and England team-mate Ledley King opening space for James Milner, who chipped woefully wide with Robinson out of position.

Fredi Kanoute could have sealed the points with 15 minutes to play after being put through on goal by strike partner Defoe, but he ballooned his shot over.

United threatened late on with a flurry of set pieces, but stout defending from Spurs kept all three points at home.

Jermain Defoe celebrates his winning goal.

"If we can pick up a few more wins we have a chance of getting into Europe."
Martin Jol

"These things happen when you are playing reserve team football every week."
Graeme Souness on Steve Harper's costly error

PREMIERSHIP FIXTURE HISTORY

Pl: 2 Draws: 1	Wins	Goals	Yellow	Red
Birmingham City	1	2	2	0
Portsmouth	0	0	5	0

STARTING LINE-UPS

Birmingham City: Maik Taylor; Melchiot, Cunningham (c), Upson, Clapham; Pennant, Johnson, Nafti, Lazaridis; Heskey, Pandiani

Portsmouth: Lua Lua, Kamara; O'Neil, Hughes, Skopelitis, Stone; Griffin, De Zeeuw (c), Primus, Cisse; Ashdown

Substitutes (Birmingham City): Gray, Morrison, Carter, Vaesen, Blake

Substitutes (Portsmouth): Berger, Fuller, Mezague, Hislop, Rodic

EVENT LINE

HALF TIME 0 - 0

- 48 Cisse (Foul)
- 59 **Lazaridis (Off) Gray (On)**
- 59 **Pandiani (Off) Morrison (On)**
- 64 Stone (Off) Berger (On)
- 69 Kamara (Foul)
- 70 **Nafti (Foul)**
- 71 Kamara (Off) Fuller (On)
- 76 **Nafti (Off) Carter (On)**
- 83 Skopelitis (Off) Mezague (On)

FULL TIME 0 - 0

STATISTICS

Season	Fixture (Birmingham)		Fixture (Portsmouth)	Season
143	4	Shots On Target	4	164
146	5	Shots Off Target	1	160
7	0	Hit Woodwork	0	7
92	0	Caught Offside	4	94
168	7	Corners	5	165
461	16	Fouls	12	398
50%	51%	Possession	49%	47%

LEAGUE STANDINGS

Position (pos before)	W	D	L	F	A	Pts
12 (13) Birmingham C	9	11	13	35	39	38
15 (15) Portsmouth	9	8	16	37	51	35

Saturday 16th April 2005 | Venue: St Andrew's | Attendance: 28,883 | Referee: P.Walton

BIRMINGHAM CITY 0 PORTSMOUTH 0

Portsmouth edged closer to Premiership survival, picking up a point at St Andrew's in Alain Perrin's first away game in charge.

Having beaten Charlton 4-2 in a thrilling first match under new management, the South Coast outfit showed a different side to their game in this clash. Not since a Boxing Day victory at Crystal Palace had Pompey kept a clean sheet on the road, but that was about to change.

While the visitors were looking to dispel any lingering relegation fears, Birmingham had little to play for. Positioned somewhere between the battles for European football and to avoid the drop, Steve Bruce's men were ideal opponents to be facing at this stage of the season.

Former Newcastle striker Lomana Tresor Lua Lua almost handed his team a dream start, heading a Gary O'Neil cross just wide. That was as close as either side came in an opening period that was devoid of any creative ideas.

Australian international Stan Lazaridis was the only player in a blue shirt that offered any positive contribution during the first 45 minutes. The tricky left winger twice tried his luck from distance, though neither effort forced Jamie Ashdown into action.

Buoyed by the ease with which they had kept Birmingham at bay, Portsmouth were a little more adventurous after the break. The talented O'Neil embarked upon a jinking run into the box, only to see his goalbound strike turned away by Maik Taylor.

The action quickly switched to the other end, as Linvoy Primus cleared an Emile Heskey header off the line. Soon afterwards the former Leicester striker had a new partner, Clinton Morrison taking the place of Uruguayan Walter Pandiani.

Julian Gray was introduced at the same juncture, though neither of the ex-Crystal Palace men made a real impact on the final half-hour. In fact, it was visiting substitute Patrik Berger that came closest, forcing a smart save from Taylor with a low drive from distance.

Full-back Mario Melchiot nearly engineered a late home winner with a dangerous low cross from the right, but Portsmouth stood firm to collect a valuable point.

Emile Heskey battles with Arjan De Zeeuw

"What was disappointing for me was the fact that we again struggled to take points off a team below us in the Premiership."
Steve Bruce

PREMIERSHIP MILESTONE

50 — Patrik Berger made his 50th Premiership appearance for Portsmouth

"We came here to get a point, but after 50 minutes we were looking for more."
Alain Perrin

PREMIERSHIP FIXTURE HISTORY

Pl: 4	Draws: 1	Wins	⚽	Yellow cards	Red cards
Charlton Athletic		0	4	1	0
Bolton Wanderers		3	7	3	0

STARTING LINE-UPS

Charlton substitutes: Johansson, Euell, Kishishev, Andersen, Fuller

Bolton substitutes: Diouf, Gardner, Campo, Poole, Fadiga

EVENT LINE

7 ⚽ Okocha (Penalty)

29 ⚽ **Jeffers (Indirect Free Kick)**

HALF TIME 1 - 1

55 Davies (Off) Diouf (On)

58 ⚽ Diouf (Open Play)

59 Ben Haim (Foul)

66 **Thomas (Off) Johansson (On)**

74 Candela (Off) Gardner (On)

78 **Hughes (Off) Euell (On)**

79 **Konchesky (Off) Kishishev (On)**

89 Okocha (Off) Campo (On)

FULL TIME 1 - 2

STATISTICS

Season	Fixture	Charlton	Bolton Fixture	Season
149	10	Shots On Target	6	207
124	8	Shots Off Target	6	184
7	0	Hit Woodwork	0	7
110	4	Caught Offside	2	90
145	8	Corners	2	175
412	10	Fouls	14	451
44%	49%	Possession	51%	49%

LEAGUE STANDINGS

Position (pos before)		W	D	L	F	A	Pts
10 (9)	Charlton Ath	12	8	13	40	50	44
5 (6)	Bolton W	15	7	11	43	37	52

Saturday 16th April 2005 | Venue: **The Valley** | Attendance: **26,708** | Referee: **A.G.Wiley**

CHARLTON ATHLETIC 1 BOLTON WANDERERS 2

Bolton turned up the heat on fourth-placed Everton, winning 2-1 at Charlton to move to within just two points of a 'Champions League' place.

Substitute El-Hadji Diouf netted what proved to be the winner with virtually his first touch, after an early Jay-Jay Okocha penalty had been cancelled out by a deflected effort from Francis Jeffers.

The men from the Reebok Stadium started in confident mood, and were quite literally handed the chance to take the lead after seven minutes. Referee Alan Wiley did well to spot the ball striking the arm of Hermann Hreidarsson in the box, and Okocha stepped up to send Dean Kiely the wrong way from the penalty spot.

It was illegal use of the hand at the other end that led to Charlton drawing level just before the half-hour mark. Goalkeeper Jussi Jaaskelainen was penalised for inadvertently carrying the ball outside his area, and Jeffers swept home Danny Murphy's square pass from the resultant free-kick with the aid of two deflections.

The equaliser had been coming, with Murphy sending a dipping effort narrowly over and then forcing a save with a low drive from an acute angle. The Addicks were somewhat lucky to reach half-time at 1-1, however, as a sprawling Jonathan Fortune seemed to block Kevin Davies' 15-yard strike with his arm.

Bolton did regain their lead after 58 minutes though. Senegalese forward Diouf arrived right on cue to cushion a nine-yard header over Kiely, after Gary Speed had nodded a right-wing centre from Stylianos Giannakopoulos back across goal.

The on-loan Liverpool man then caused further problems, battling away to create an opening for Kevin Nolan. The midfielder's strike was parried, with Fernando Hierro fizzing a long-range drive just past the left-hand upright less than 30 seconds later.

Alan Curbishley's charges tried to find a way back into the game as time began to run out. Left-back Hreidarsson drew a comfortable catch from Jaaskelainen, before one Finn denied another as the keeper was perfectly positioned to comfortably keep out Jonatan Johansson's close-range stretching volley.

Jerome Thomas is watched closely by Nicky Hunt

"I feel we have to score twice to get anything out of a game, because we're defending so badly and letting in so many silly goals."

Alan Curbishley

PREMIERSHIP MILESTONE

25 Francis Jeffers netted his 25th Premiership goal

"Maybe it's time we started looking up and not down for a change, worrying about who we've got to pass rather than who might pass us."

Sam Allardyce

PREMIERSHIP FIXTURE HISTORY

Pl: **3** Draws: **1**

	Wins	Goals	Yellow	Red
Crystal Palace	0	4	2	0
Norwich City	2	6	5	0

STARTING LINE-UPS

Crystal Palace subs: Soares, Torghelle, Popovic, Speroni, Riihilahti

Norwich City subs: Holt, Svensson, Jonson, Ward, Doherty

EVENT LINE

5 **Kolkka (Indirect Free Kick)**

12 Helveg (Ung.Conduct)

22 Ashton (Open Play)

36 **Granville (Foul)**

HALF TIME 1 - 1

46 Ashton (Open Play)

53 McKenzie (Corner)

59 Shackell (Foul)

65 **Leigertwood (Off) Soares (On)**

66 **Hughes (Foul)**

72 **Butterfield (Off) Torghelle (On)**

73 **Hughes (Open Play)**

83 **Johnson (Penalty)**

84 **Kolkka (Off) Popovic (On)**

88 Francis (Off) Holt (On)

88 McKenzie (Off) Svensson (On)

90 Huckerby (Off) Jonson (On)

FULL TIME 3 - 3

STATISTICS

Season	Fixture	Crystal Palace / Norwich City	Fixture	Season
152	11	Shots On Target	8	152
145	2	Shots Off Target	4	160
7	0	Hit Woodwork	0	5
77	3	Caught Offside	6	103
165	7	Corners	3	153
454	17	Fouls	21	454
47%	51%	Possession	49%	45%

LEAGUE STANDINGS

Position (pos before)	W	D	L	F	A	Pts
19 (19) Crystal Palace	6	9	18	36	57	27
20 (20) Norwich C	4	12	17	35	66	24

Saturday 16th April 2005 | Venue: **Selhurst Park** | Attendance: **25,754** | Referee: **R.Styles**

Dougie Freedman gets away from Youssef Safri

"At 3-1 down we were dead and buried, but we came back and were worthy of the point."

Assistant Manager Kit Symons

"The penalty was harsh, but I thought we were lucky not to give away two earlier on."

Nigel Worthington

CRYSTAL PALACE 3 NORWICH CITY 3

Two teams facing the threat of an immediate return to the second tier of English football served up a six-goal thriller at Selhurst Park.

Despite propping up the table, victory at home to Manchester United in their last game meant that Norwich arrived in South London full of confidence. This was in stark contrast to Iain Dowie's side, the Eagles having lost 4-0 at Everton last time out.

The form book went out of the window after just five minutes, however, as Crystal Palace took the lead. Woeful marking enabled winger Joonas Kolkka to lash home Michael Hughes' floated left-wing free-kick from just wide of the six-yard box at the back post.

Ten minutes later Robert Green showed why he has been a regular member of recent England squads, diving full-length to his left to repel a 12-yard Dougie Freedman header. It was to prove a crucial stop, as the Canaries drew level midway through the half.

Midfielder Damien Francis did the hard work, bursting into the box on the left and squaring for Dean Ashton to guide the ball into an unguarded net from no more than four yards out.

Referee Rob Styles then became the focus of attention, denying the home side what appeared to be two certain penalties before half-time. Firstly Andy Johnson appeared to be bundled over by the inexperienced Jason Shackell, before Youssef Safri seemed to be guilty of handball.

Nigel Worthington's men took full advantage of these escapes, taking the lead straight from the kick-off in the second period. Fitz Hall misjudged a clip forward from the back, giving Ashton the chance to run at Gonzalo Sorondo and drive a low 15-yard effort in off the far left-hand upright.

Seven minutes later the points seemed secure, as Leon McKenzie turned home Darren Huckerby's low cross from the left from inside the six-yard box. The Eagles had other ideas though, Michael Hughes meeting Johnson's ball in from the right with a stunning header on the run after 73 minutes.

Then, 10 minutes later, Johnson salvaged a point from the penalty spot after Shackell was adjudged to have upended him.

PREMIERSHIP FIXTURE HISTORY

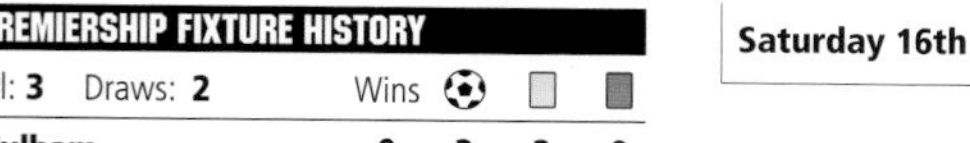

Pl: **3** Draws: **2**

	Wins			
Fulham	**0**	**3**	**2**	**0**
Manchester City	**1**	**4**	**7**	**0**

STARTING LINE-UPS

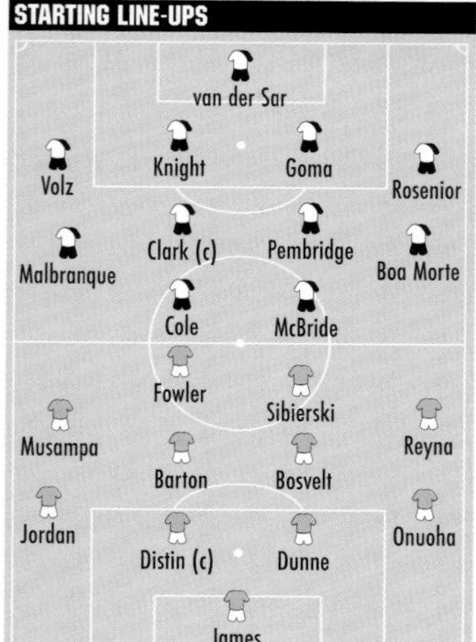

Radzinski, John
Crossley, Bocanegra
Rehman

S.Wright-Phillips
B.Wright-Phillips
Weaver, Thatcher
Mills

EVENT LINE

20 Reyna (Open Play)

HALF TIME 0 - 1

62 Fowler (Off) Wright-Phillips S (On)

66 **Malbranque (Off) Radzinski (On)**

69 **Cole (Off) John (On)**

76 **Boa Morte (Open Play)**

81 Dunne (Foul)

86 Musampa (Off) Wright-Phillips B (On)

FULL TIME 1 - 1

STATISTICS

Season	Fixture		Fixture	Season
153	**3**	Shots On Target	**3**	**177**
141	**5**	Shots Off Target	**4**	**169**
5	**1**	Hit Woodwork	**0**	**3**
84	**2**	Caught Offside	**11**	**105**
156	**6**	Corners	**8**	**205**
393	**9**	Fouls	**19**	**414**
48%	**45%**	Possession	**55%**	**49%**

LEAGUE STANDINGS

Position (pos before)	W	D	L	F	A	Pts
16 (16) Fulham	**9**	**7**	**16**	**38**	**52**	**34**
11 (11) Man City	**10**	**11**	**12**	**39**	**37**	**41**

Saturday 16th April 2005 | Venue: **Craven Cottage** | Attendance: **21,796** | Referee: **N.S.Barry**

FULHAM 1 MANCHESTER CITY 1

Sylvain Distin beats Andy Cole to the ball

"Results elsewhere went our way, so a point is not the end of the world."

Chris Coleman

"It was a good fighting performance, and the players have again responded to what I have asked them to do."

Stuart Pearce

PREMIERSHIP MILESTONE

50 David James made his 50th Premiership appearance in the colours of Man City

It was a return to the days of good old-fashioned centre-forward play at Craven Cottage, as Luis Boa Morte profited from a strong Brian McBride challenge to earn his side a point.

A suspiciously offside-looking Claudio Reyna, a one-time Fulham transfer target, had turned the visitors into a 20th-minute lead, before parity was restored 14 minutes from time.

Edwin van der Sar had already been forced to turn over a curling Antoine Sibierski effort, when he was called upon to deny the Frenchman for a second time. The Dutch custodian could only parry a diving header, enabling Reyna to steer home the loose ball from close range.

An angled Boa Morte drive was touched onto the base of the far right-hand upright by David James, as the Cottagers sought to find a way back into the match as half-time approached.

Home hopes should have been extinguished in the early stages of the second period. Sloppy play from several men in white shirts handed Robbie Fowler a decent sight of goal, but the former Liverpool striker drove the ball wide of the near post with his unfavoured right foot.

Stuart Pearce acted swiftly to replace his misfiring frontman with Shaun Wright-Phillips. The England international was making a welcome return from injury, and was soon followed onto the pitch by Tomasz Radzinski and Collins John.

It was John that almost made an immediate impact, firing in a deflected 20-yard effort that looped just the wrong side of the right-hand upright. A Fulham goal was not long in coming, however, as Boa Morte struck in the 76th minute.

Lee Clark hoisted over a deep cross from the right that McBride challenged for with the keeper. The ball broke loose as the two players collided, with the American international having the presence of mind to tee up Boa Morte for a crisp 13-yard finish through a sea of bodies.

The visiting players felt that James had been fouled, but referee Neale Barry waved away their protests. There was still time for both teams to go close, through Kiki Musampa and Radzinski, but a draw was probably a fair result.

PREMIERSHIP FIXTURE HISTORY

Pl: 13 Draws: 4	Wins	Goals	Yellow	Red
Liverpool	8	27	12	0
Tottenham Hotspur	1	12	22	1

STARTING LINE-UPS

Liverpool substitutes: Riise, Cisse, Biscan, Carson, Traore

Tottenham substitutes: Ziegler, Defoe, Cerny, Bunjevcevic, Marney

EVENT LINE

12 Edman (Corner)

35 **Warnock (Off) Riise (On)**

44 **Garcia (Open Play)**

HALF TIME 1 - 1

55 Keane (Indirect Free Kick)

63 **Hyypia (Corner)**

72 Reid (Off) Ziegler (On)

77 **Nunez (Off) Cisse (On)**

84 **Alonso (Off) Biscan (On)**

88 Keane (Off) Defoe (On)

FULL TIME 2 - 2

STATISTICS

Season	Fixture (Liverpool)		Fixture (Tottenham)	Season
201	7	Shots On Target	6	204
219	12	Shots Off Target	3	182
7	1	Hit Woodwork	0	10
88	6	Caught Offside	4	138
192	12	Corners	3	165
386	5	Fouls	7	392
53%	71%	Possession	29%	49%

LEAGUE STANDINGS

Position (pos before)		W	D	L	F	A	Pts
6 (5)	Liverpool	15	6	12	46	34	51
7 (7)	Tottenham H	13	8	12	41	37	47

Saturday 16th April 2005 | Venue: **Anfield** | Attendance: **44,029** | Referee: **M.R.Halsey**

LIVERPOOL 2 TOTTENHAM HOTSPUR 2

After their 'Champions League' heroics in midweek, Liverpool continued to stutter on the domestic scene.

Rafael Benitez's men twice came from behind to earn a point against Tottenham, a result that further jeopardised their chances of participating in next season's premier European competition.

The Spaniard's team selection proved very interesting, as he opted to employ three centre-backs. Further forward, Antonio Nunez and Luis Garcia were asked to support striker Fernando Morientes from wide areas.

After 12 minutes of getting used to their new system, Liverpool fell behind. Swedish international Erik Edman struck a contender for goal of the season, drilling the ball into the top right-hand corner of the net from at least 35 yards out.

Despite enjoying plenty of possession, the home side were unable to carve out any decent chances. The only brief moment of worry for a Tottenham defence containing debutant Michael Dawson came when Nunez fired tamely across the face of goal.

Then, just as the two managers had finished preparing their half-time words of wisdom, Garcia struck a stunning leveller. The former Barcelona player turned his man on the edge of the box and curled a left-footed effort beyond the right hand of Paul Robinson.

Shortly afterwards, the keeper did well to maintain parity, repelling a firm Morientes header. It was to prove a vital save, as Spurs went back in front 10 minutes after the restart.

Frederic Kanoute whipped over a pinpoint cross from the right, and Jerzy Dudek was left helpless as Robbie Keane's eight-yard header took a massive deflection off Jamie Carragher.

Captain Steven Gerrard earned an immediate chance to draw his side level, winning a penalty as Michael Carrick halted his surge into the box. The skipper was unable to complete the job, however, blazing his spot-kick wide of the right-hand post.

The miss was soon forgotten though, as Sami Hyypia added to his recent stunning volley against Juventus with another picture-book strike. A corner was cleared to the edge of the area, where the tall Finn sent it back with interest to make it 2-2.

Steve Finnan drove wide, Gerrard struck a post and Morientes fired over, but Tottenham clung on for a point.

Luis Garcia celebrates his equaliser

"I don't believe fourth position is out of our reach yet, we have plenty more opportunities to win games."
Rafael Benitez

"When you come to Liverpool it's always hard. We had a good start, but they were on a high from the 'Champions League'."
Martin Jol

PREMIERSHIP MILESTONE

50 Steve Finnan made his 50th Premiership appearance for Liverpool

PREMIERSHIP MILESTONE

Michael Dawson made his Premiership debut

PREMIERSHIP MILESTONE

Erik Edman scored his first Premiership goal

Saturday 16th April 2005 | Venue: **Friends Provident St Mary's Stadium** | Attendance: **31,926** | Referee: **A.P.D'Urso**

PREMIERSHIP FIXTURE HISTORY

Pl: **13** Draws: **2**	Wins	⚽	▯	▮
Southampton	5	20	12	1
Aston Villa	6	19	17	2

STARTING LINE-UPS

Davenport, Le Saux, Camara, Smith, Higginbotham

Cole, Solano, L.Moore, Postma, Berson

EVENT LINE

4 ⚽ **Phillips (Open Play)**

13 ⚽ **Crouch (Open Play)**

27 ▯ **Redknapp (Foul)**

32 ▯ Hendrie (Dissent)

36 ⇄ Vassell (Off) Cole (On)

HALF TIME 2 - 0

46 ⇄ **Jakobsson (Off) Davenport (On)**

46 ⇄ Laursen (Off) Solano (On)

55 ⚽ Cole (Open Play)

63 ⇄ **Svensson A (Off) Le Saux (On)**

65 ▯ Barry (Handball)

70 ⚽ Solano (Corner)

72 ⚽ Davis (Open Play)

74 ⇄ **Telfer (Off) Camara (On)**

77 ⇄ Angel (Off) Moore L (On)

FULL TIME 2 - 3

STATISTICS

Season	Fixture (Southampton)		Fixture (Aston Villa)	Season
157	8	Shots On Target	7	168
178	8	Shots Off Target	4	165
3	1	Hit Woodwork	0	8
99	1	Caught Offside	0	97
156	5	Corners	8	185
423	10	Fouls	17	512
47%	47%	Possession	53%	49%

LEAGUE STANDINGS

Position (pos before)	W	D	L	F	A	Pts
18 (18) Southampton	5	12	16	36	54	27
9 (10) Aston Villa	12	9	12	41	42	45

Former Villan Peter Crouch gets a shot away

"We needed the three points today, that's for sure, and it's going to be very hard to get out of trouble."
Harry Redknapp

"Even at two goals down I felt we could get back into the game if we scored quickly after the break, and that's what happened."
David O'Leary

PREMIERSHIP MILESTONE

Steven Davis netted his first Premiership goal

SOUTHAMPTON 2 ASTON VILLA 3

Southampton took a giant step towards relegation from the Premiership, going down 3-2 at home to Aston Villa having established a two-goal interval lead.

The Saints were two up inside 13 minutes, strikers Kevin Phillips and Peter Crouch doing the damage. However, the half-time introduction of Nolberto Solano sparked the visitors into life, the Peruvian netting in between goals from Carlton Cole and Steven Davis.

Harry Redknapp's team got off to a dream start, as Phillips poked them into a fourth-minute lead. J'Lloyd Samuel was dispossessed near the corner flag by Crouch, and the tall forward pulled the ball back for his strike partner to evade a defender and net from seven yards out.

Nine minutes later, Crouch grabbed a goal of his own. An astute pass from Jamie Redknapp found the former Villa man in the inside-left channel, and he dispatched a low drive across Thomas Sorensen and into the far corner.

Visiting captain Gareth Barry missed the target with a free header from around the penalty spot, before Sorensen was relieved to see Crouch fail to make proper contact after he had parried a Phillips effort.

Then, with 55 minutes played, Cole, a first half replacement for the injured Darius Vassell, stroked Solano's cushioned touch into the bottom left-hand corner. The goal drained the Southampton players of belief, and only a sprawling parry from Niemi denied Cole a second from close range.

The reprieve was only temporary, however, as David O'Leary's charges grabbed two goals in as many minutes. A guided seven-yard finish by Solano from a right-wing corner drew the teams level, before Davis rounded off a flowing move by diverting home Ulises De la Cruz's 72nd-minute drive.

A poor miss by Cole gave the Saints renewed hope, but substitute Henri Camara was even more wayward in his finishing at the other end. The Senegalese international did the hard work, only to fire against the advertising hoardings.

PREMIERSHIP FIXTURE HISTORY

Pl: 6 Draws: 4	Wins	⚽	□	■
Bolton Wanderers	0	2	10	0
Southampton	2	4	7	2

STARTING LINE-UPS

Jaaskelainen
Hunt, Ben Haim, N'Gotty, Candela
Okocha (c), Hierro, Speed
Giannakopoulos, Diouf, Nolan

Crouch, Phillips
A.Svensson
Quashie, Telfer
Le Saux, Delap
Higginbotham, Jakobsson, Lundekvam (c)
Niemi

Davies, Gardner, Jaidi, Poole, Campo

Oakley, Nilsson, Smith, Davenport, Camara

EVENT LINE

25 ⚽ **Giannakopoulos (Open Play)**

HALF TIME 1 - 0

46 Le Saux (Off) Oakley (On)

61 □ **Ben Haim (Foul)**

65 **Nolan (Off) Davies (On)**

69 ⚽ Phillips (Open Play)

73 □ **Giannakopoulos (Dissent)**

80 Svensson A (Off) Nilsson (On)

87 **Candela (Off) Gardner (On)**

90 **Giannakopoulos (Off) Jaidi (On)**

FULL TIME 1 - 1

STATISTICS

Season	Fixture		Fixture	Season
223	16	Shots On Target	4	161
195	11	Shots Off Target	5	183
8	1	Hit Woodwork	0	3
96	6	Caught Offside	4	103
181	6	Corners	2	158
460	9	Fouls	10	433
50%	58%	Possession	42%	47%

LEAGUE STANDINGS

Position (pos before)		W	D	L	F	A	Pts
5 (5)	Bolton W	15	8	11	44	38	53
17 (18)	Southampton	5	13	16	37	55	28

Tuesday 19th April 2005 | Venue: **Reebok Stadium** | Attendance: **25,125** | Referee: **M.Clattenburg**

BOLTON WANDERERS 1 SOUTHAMPTON 1

The spoils were shared in a hard-fought contest that had implications at both ends of the Premiership table.

With Everton not in action, Bolton knew that a victory would see them climb into fourth place. The home fans had reason to feel confident when Stylianos Giannakopoulos headed the Trotters into a 25th-minute lead, but Kevin Phillips netted a 69th-minute equaliser that saw his side move out of the relegation zone.

El-Hadji Diouf was rewarded for his winning goal at Charlton by taking the place of Kevin Davies in attack. Harry Redknapp rang the changes for the South Coast club, switching to a 5-3-2 formation that saw Anders Svensson operating behind the strikers.

It was the team with Europe on their minds that began brightly. A right-wing corner caused havoc inside the penalty area, with Nigel Quashie having to be alert to keep out both Kevin Nolan and Giannakopoulos in a goalmouth scramble.

Bolton's Greek international wasn't to be denied, however, stealing a march on Claus Lundekvam to dive and head home Diouf's ball across the six-yard box from the right, after the Senegalese international had tricked his way past Graeme Le Saux.

With confidence understandably low, Southampton were rocking. Antti Niemi was forced to parry a near-post Diouf drive, before surviving a potentially embarrassing moment as Jay-Jay Okocha's speculative strike bounced awkwardly in front of him.

The second half began in similar fashion, Diouf blazing over when it seemed easier to score after Niemi had brilliantly kept out Gary Speed's downward header.

The heroics of their goalkeeper, allied to an interval reshuffle, seemed to have a positive effect on the visiting players. Jussi Jaaskelainen made a remarkable double-save to keep out Peter Crouch and substitute Matthew Oakley, but was unable to deny Phillips.

There were just over 20 minutes remaining when the former Sunderland man netted a priceless equaliser. Rory Delap's long ball forward found the striker unmarked in the inside-right channel, and his quickly-taken shot found its way in via the keeper's right leg.

Bolton substitute Davies then struck a post, before Niemi pulled off a string of vital saves.

Nigel Quashie makes his point to Kevin Nolan

"We played some wonderful football at times and created some fantastic chances, but we just couldn't get that second goal."
Sam Allardyce

"Every point is vital for us, and it was nice to get away from the bottom three."
Harry Redknapp

PREMIERSHIP FIXTURE HISTORY

Pl: 4 Draws: 2	Wins	Goals	Yellow cards	Red cards
Middlesbrough	2	7	7	0
Fulham	0	5	6	0

STARTING LINE-UPS

Middlesbrough subs: Kennedy, Knight, Davies, Wheater, Doriva

Fulham subs: Malbranque, Crossley, Bocanegra, Rehman, Jensen

EVENT LINE

22 Yellow card **Southgate (Foul)**

HALF TIME 0 - 0

82 Substitution John (Off) Malbranque (On)

82 Goal McBride (Open Play)

86 Substitution **Cooper (Off) Kennedy (On)**

90 Goal **Zenden (Penalty)**

FULL TIME 1 - 1

STATISTICS

Season	Fixture (Middlesbrough)		Fixture (Fulham)	Season
227	5	Shots On Target	2	155
173	3	Shots Off Target	5	146
6	0	Hit Woodwork	1	6
90	5	Caught Offside	3	87
183	2	Corners	6	162
413	11	Fouls	12	405
50%	52%	Possession	48%	48%

LEAGUE STANDINGS

Position (pos before)		W	D	L	F	A	Pts
8 (8)	Middlesbrough	12	10	11	46	44	46
15 (16)	Fulham	9	8	16	39	53	35

Tuesday 19th April 2005 | Venue: **Riverside Stadium** | Attendance: **30,650** | Referee: **R.Styles**

Franck Queudrue is chased by Tomasz Radzinski

"We salvaged a point, and that could be valuable at the end of the season."

Steve McClaren

"It was disappointing to say the least. We should be going home with three points."

Chris Coleman on Middlesbrough's dubious late penalty

PREMIERSHIP MILESTONE

Jason Kennedy made his Premiership debut

PREMIERSHIP MILESTONE

150 Luis Boa Morte made his 150th Premiership appearance.

PREMIERSHIP MILESTONE

50 Brian McBride made his 50th Premiership appearance

MIDDLESBROUGH 1 FULHAM 1

A poor game sprang into life in the final 10 minutes, with Brian McBride's goal being cancelled out by a highly controversial last-gasp penalty.

With more points required to ensure their Premiership survival, Fulham looked hungrier than their UEFA Cup chasing opponents. An early free-kick nearly led to a goal, as McBride directed a six-yard header just the wrong side of the left-hand upright.

Edwin van der Sar was a virtual spectator during the opening period, and looked on as Jimmy Floyd Hasselbaink tumbled in the box. Referee Rob Styles justifiably waved away his appeals, though the striker was not happy.

Despite being clearly offside, a McBride header that flew over would have counted. That effort followed a wayward finish from Collins John, the young striker blazing over from a central position inside the area.

The Cottagers remained on top after the interval, and were desperately unlucky not to take the lead from a Luis Boa Morte free-kick. Stand-in goalkeeper Brad Jones was left rooted to the spot, as the Portuguese international's curling effort struck the top of his crossbar.

Just 13 minutes remained when Middlesbrough carved out their first genuine chance of the contest. Boudewijn Zenden whipped in a near-post delivery from the left, and Hasselbaink got across his marker to glance a header dangerously across the face of goal.

Five minutes later, Fulham went in front. Tomasz Radzinski was allowed to make progress down the right, with McBride on hand to sweep his low cross back from the direction it came and just inside the far upright from 15 yards out.

Given the way in which their team had performed, the Riverside Stadium faithful had little reason to expect a reply. They got one, however, as the referee handed them a late lifeline.

Custodian van der Sar charged from his goal in an attempt to clear the ball from danger, but succeeded only in upending Hasselbaink. Despite the foul taking place a good yard outside the area, Styles awarded a penalty that Zenden was comfortably able to convert.

PREMIERSHIP FIXTURE HISTORY

Pl: **6** Draws: **1**	Wins	⚽	▢	■
Aston Villa	4	10	6	1
Charlton Athletic	1	6	7	1

STARTING LINE-UPS

Vassell, L.Moore
Postma, Berson
Djemba-Djemba

Euell, Perry
Andersen, Fuller
Thomas

EVENT LINE

18 ▢ Jeffers (Dissent)

HALF TIME 0 - 0

72 **Hendrie (Off) Vassell (On)**

76 Rommedahl (Off) Euell (On)

84 **Cole (Off) Moore L (On)**

87 Hreidarsson (Off) Perry (On)

FULL TIME 0 - 0

STATISTICS

Season	Fixture		Fixture	Season
173	**5**	Shots On Target	**3**	**152**
173	**8**	Shots Off Target	**9**	**133**
8	**0**	Hit Woodwork	**0**	**7**
97	**0**	Caught Offside	**5**	**115**
191	**6**	Corners	**5**	**150**
526	**14**	Fouls	**9**	**421**
49%	**49%**	Possession	**51%**	**44%**

LEAGUE STANDINGS

Position (pos before)	W	D	L	F	A	Pts
9 (9) Aston Villa	**12**	**10**	**12**	**41**	**42**	**46**
10 (10) Charlton Ath	**12**	**9**	**13**	**40**	**50**	**45**

Wednesday 20th April 2005 | Venue: **Villa Park** | Attendance: **31,312** | Referee: **B.Knight**

Carlton Cole focuses on the ball

"Charlton are the team delighted with the outcome as they came not to be beaten."
David O'Leary

"The clean sheet was more important to us than the point in view of what has happened in recent weeks."
Alan Curbishley

ASTON VILLA 0 CHARLTON ATHLETIC 0

Two teams very much in the hunt for a UEFA Cup place did little to improve their prospects in a drab encounter at Villa Park.

Europe must seem a long way off to a Charlton side that has managed just one win since the start of February. The Addicks have become renowned for their poor form during the final weeks of the season in recent years, and have started their slide even earlier this time round.

With poor defending costing them points of late, Alan Curbishley sent out his team with a cautious mentality. This came as a relief to David O'Leary, who had to field a makeshift central defensive pairing of Mark Delaney and J'Lloyd Samuel due to injuries.

What chances there were during a poor first half fell to Aston Villa. Midfielder Thomas Hitzlsperger, who had just agreed a summer move to VfB Stuttgart in his native Germany, unleashed a 25-yard thunderbolt that Dean Kiely did well to get in the way of.

Then, Carlton Cole burst into the box on the left and delivered an inviting low ball across the face of goal. Strike partner Juan Pablo Angel was inches away from making contact, but Charlton survived.

The deadlock was almost broken just past the hour mark, when Nolberto Solano curled an effort towards the far post following a short corner. Though the keeper was beaten, Danny Murphy was able to repel the danger with his head.

Play quickly switched to the other end, as Hermann Hreidarsson nodded a right-wing set-piece just past the left-hand upright. This was as close as the visitors had come, and the Icelandic international knew he had missed a golden opportunity to steal the points.

Though the Addicks didn't contribute a great deal coming forward, defeat would have been harsh on a team that worked so hard. Such a fate nearly befell them, however, as Hitzlsperger flashed a low shot beyond Kiely's right-hand post in the dying embers of the game.

On this evidence, neither side is ready for Europe.

PREMIERSHIP FIXTURE HISTORY

Pl: 4 Draws: 1	Wins	⚽	□	■
Blackburn Rovers	2	6	5	0
Crystal Palace	1	5	6	0

STARTING LINE-UPS

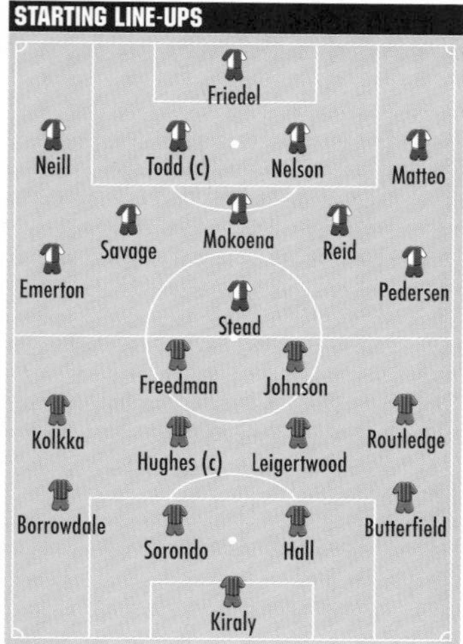

Tugay, Thompson Enckelman, Flitcroft Gallagher

Soares, Torghelle Popovic, Speroni Shipperley

EVENT LINE

29 □ **Savage (Foul)**
31 □ Sorondo (Foul)
45 ⚽ **Pedersen (Indirect Free Kick)**
HALF TIME 1 - 0
46 ⇄ **Savage (Off) Tugay (On)**
46 ⇄ Kolkka (Off) Soares (On)
57 □ Butterfield (Foul)
60 ⇄ Freedman (Off) Torghelle (On)
75 ⇄ **Pedersen (Off) Thompson (On)**
76 □ **Reid (Foul)**
76 ⇄ Butterfield (Off) Popovic (On)
78 □ **Mokoena (Foul)**
FULL TIME 1 - 0

STATISTICS

Season	Fixture		Fixture	Season
167	7	Shots On Target	3	155
201	11	Shots Off Target	1	146
6	0	Hit Woodwork	0	7
137	8	Caught Offside	1	78
188	11	Corners	6	171
527	11	Fouls	19	473
49%	55%	Possession	45%	47%

LEAGUE STANDINGS

Position (pos before)	W	D	L	F	A	Pts
12 (14) Blackburn R	9	12	12	29	37	39
19 (19) Crystal Palace	6	9	19	36	58	27

Wednesday 20th April 2005 | Venue: **Ewood Park** | Attendance: **18,006** | Referee: **P.Walton**

Tom Soares is chased by Aaron Mokoena

"We feel that we are definitely safe now and everyone is delighted."
Mark Hughes

"One thing I won't do is roll over. I've not thrown the towel in yet."
Iain Dowie

BLACKBURN ROVERS 1 CRYSTAL PALACE 0

A late first half goal from Morten Gamst Pedersen virtually secured Blackburn's Premiership survival, while dealing a further blow to Crystal Palace's hopes of beating the drop.

With Paul Dickov unavailable through injury, Jonathan Stead was handed the role of lone striker. The former Huddersfield man almost justified his inclusion with a firm downward header from an early right-wing corner, but could only watch as Gabor Kiraly made an excellent one-handed save.

The next significant chance also fell to Rovers, New Zealander Ryan Nelson crashing a drive against the outside of the right-hand upright after the visitors had failed to execute an offside trap.

Brett Emerton tested Kiraly after a jinking run infield from the right, before Robbie Savage was cautioned for a mistimed challenge on Mikele Leigertwood. The Welsh international then escaped a second booking after hacking down Wayne Routledge on the edge of the box.

Having seen the ugly side of Savage's game, the locals were given a taste of what he could do with a football. With half-time fast approaching, the former Leicester midfielder delivered an inviting left-wing free-kick that Pedersen steered in off the underside of the crossbar from five yards out.

The experienced Kerimoglu Tugay replaced Savage at the break, with rumours abounding about an altercation in the tunnel during the interval.

Blackburn could have doubled their lead midway through the second period. Dominic Matteo stole across the front of a defender to meet Pedersen's low delivery from the left, but could only divert the ball into the side-netting.

The onslaught continued as Steven Reid inexplicably missed with a free header from seven yards out, with Stead then arriving to poke an effort narrowly beyond Kiraly's right-hand post.

The Eagles had been a million miles from their best, with Brad Friedel only briefly called into action when comfortably saving twice from Andy Johnson in the moments after half-time.

In fact, the margin of defeat would have been greater had either Reid or Stead been able to find a way past Kiraly in late one-on-one situations.

PREMIERSHIP FIXTURE HISTORY

Pl: 13 Draws: 5	Wins	Goals	Yellow	Red
Chelsea	3	13	24	4
Arsenal	5	18	27	2

STARTING LINE-UPS

Tiago, Kezman
Jarosik, Cudicini
Huth

van Persie, Aliadiere
Almunia, Campbell
Edu

EVENT LINE

HALF TIME 0 - 0

52 **Cole J (Dissent)**
74 Vieira (Foul)
78 Bergkamp (Off) van Persie (On)
79 **Cole J (Off) Tiago (On)**
81 Fabregas (Off) Aliadiere (On)
85 **Duff (Off) Kezman (On)**
90 **Gudjohnsen (Off) Jarosik (On)**
90 Pires (Foul)
90 Reyes (Ung.Conduct)

FULL TIME 0 - 0

STATISTICS

Season	Fixture (Chelsea)		Fixture (Arsenal)	Season
256	3	Shots On Target	4	250
218	6	Shots Off Target	2	155
10	0	Hit Woodwork	1	14
103	5	Caught Offside	3	78
222	2	Corners	2	191
414	10	Fouls	16	385
56%	49%	Possession	51%	56%

LEAGUE STANDINGS

Position (pos before)		W	D	L	F	A	Pts
1 (1)	Chelsea	25	7	1	62	12	82
2 (2)	Arsenal	21	8	4	73	33	71

Wednesday 20th April 2005 | Venue: **Stamford Bridge** | Attendance: **41,621** | Referee: **S.G.Bennett**

CHELSEA 0 ARSENAL 0

William Gallas puts Cesc Fabregas under pressure

"It will be difficult for anyone apart from us to win the title now. We wanted to stop giving silly goals away, and that is what we did."
Assistant Manager Steve Clarke

"I take big satisfaction from the quality of our performance and display, especially as we had so many young players out there."
Arsene Wenger

Chelsea moved a step closer to the Premiership title, surviving an early Arsenal onslaught to draw 0-0 with their nearest challengers at Stamford Bridge.

The visitors began in lightning-quick fashion, Robert Pires crashing a 15-yard volley against Petr Cech's crossbar after Jose Antonio Reyes had climbed above Glen Johnson at the back post.

Play switched to the other end as Frank Lampard forced Jens Lehmann into a comfortable low save, before Pires missed what turned out to be the best chance of the match. A ricochet in the box saw the ball fall perfectly for the Frenchman eight yards from goal, but he dragged his effort the wrong side of the far left-hand upright.

Having weathered the Gunners' early storm, Jose Mourinho's men started to show some of the form that had taken them to the top of the league. Didier Drogba should have done better than fire against the legs of Lehmann, while Eidur Gudjohnsen drew an important clearance from the omnipresent Pires.

Both sides continued to create chances as the half progressed. William Gallas did well to block a fiercely-struck Gilberto drive when covering from left-back, while the in-form Joe Cole blazed over from a tight angle at the other end.

The second period was less exciting than the first, though Chelsea did go close to snatching victory on a couple of occasions.

After Reyes had curled a weak shot into the arms of Cech, Drogba came within inches of opening the scoring. The former Marseille striker received the ball with his back to goal near the penalty spot, before spinning and bending an effort just the wrong side of the right-hand post.

Inspirational midfielder Lampard then failed to hit the target with a measured 15-yard strike, following fine approach play involving Gallas and Drogba.

A goal rarely seemed likely at the other end, though Arsene Wenger could point to a decent penalty claim earlier in the half. Dennis Bergkamp outmuscled Johnson on the left edge of the six-yard box, with Reyes seemingly upended by Claude Makelele as he attempted to reach the Dutchman's cutback.

All in all, a draw was a fair result. With Everton beating Manchester United at Goodison Park, the point also enhanced Arsenal's prospects of securing second place.

PREMIERSHIP FIXTURE HISTORY

Pl: 13 Draws: 1	Wins	Goals	Yellow	Red
Everton	2	11	26	1
Manchester United	10	26	17	2

STARTING LINE-UPS

Everton subs: Osman, Beattie, McFadden, Wright, Vaughan

Manchester United subs: Silvestre, O'Shea, Carroll, Fortune, Smith

EVENT LINE

27 Arteta (Handball) — yellow card

HALF TIME 0 - 0

52 Ferguson (Foul) — yellow card

55 Ferguson (Indirect Free Kick) — goal

58 Hibbert (Foul) — yellow card

72 Brown (Off) Silvestre (On)

72 Neville G (Violent Conduct) — red card

76 Bent (Off) Osman (On)

76 Fletcher (Off) O'Shea (On)

80 Ferguson (Off) Beattie (On)

86 Cahill (Off) McFadden (On)

89 Ronaldo (Ung.Conduct) — yellow card

90 Scholes (2nd Bookable Offence) — red card

FULL TIME 1 - 0

STATISTICS

Season	Fixture (Everton)		Fixture (Man Utd)	Season
155	2	Shots On Target	6	268
174	2	Shots Off Target	5	240
6	0	Hit Woodwork	0	16
81	1	Caught Offside	1	118
156	3	Corners	2	252
400	14	Fouls	13	413
49%	42%	Possession	58%	56%

LEAGUE STANDINGS

Position (pos before)		W	D	L	F	A	Pts
4 (4)	Everton	17	6	10	40	33	57
3 (3)	Man Utd	19	10	4	48	20	67

Wednesday 20th April 2005 | Venue: **Goodison Park** | Attendance: **37,160** | Referee: **P.Dowd**

EVERTON 1 MANCHESTER UNITED 0

Gabriel Heinze clears the danger

"The crowd were awesome tonight. If you've seen a better atmosphere than that recently, I'll be surprised."
David Moyes

"I think Everton knew we had a weak referee, and they exploited that to the full from the very start."
Sir Alex Ferguson

Everton strengthened their grip on fourth place, as they defeated Manchester United for the first time since the 1995 F.A.Cup final.

In fact, the Merseysiders' last Premiership win against the men from Old Trafford came three months prior to that memorable day in the Wembley sunshine. On that occasion, a Duncan Ferguson goal was enough to secure a 1-0 victory at Goodison Park, and history repeated itself here.

Wayne Rooney, returning to his former stomping ground for the second time, forced Nigel Martyn into the first meaningful save of the contest, the Cornish goalkeeper plunging to his right to repel a well-struck drive from distance.

A clumsy 33rd-minute challenge on Mikel Arteta brought about a caution for Paul Scholes. From the resulting free-kick, Wes Brown was called upon to kick an acrobatic Tim Cahill effort off the line.

Shortly after the interval, Scholes came close to giving the visitors the lead. Picked out by an astute pass from Rooney, the flame-haired midfielder was brilliantly denied by a sprawling Martyn.

It was to prove a crucial stop, as Everton scored from their next attack. An inswinging Arteta free-kick from the left was met by a trademark Ferguson header, the Scot losing his marker to beat Tim Howard from eight yards out.

Sir Alex Ferguson's men responded like a wounded animal, with Scholes fizzing a drive narrowly over the top from just outside the box. Gary Neville took things too far, however, kicking the ball deliberately into the crowd to earn a 72nd-minute red card.

The increasingly unpopular Rooney nearly made light of his side's numerical disadvantage, skipping past several challenges before pulling a left-footed effort just past the right-hand upright.

A Rio Ferdinand header was kicked away to safety as the late pressure increased, with frustration then getting the better of Scholes in injury time. The former England international made a wild lunge at Kevin Kilbane to collect his second booking of the contest, an incident that sparked a war of words between the two managers.

PREMIERSHIP FIXTURE HISTORY

Pl: 3 Draws: 1	Wins	Goals	Yellow	Red
Manchester City	2	4	1	1
Birmingham City	0	0	3	0

STARTING LINE-UPS

Manchester City substitutes: B.Wright-Phillips, Croft, Weaver, Mills, McManaman

Birmingham City substitutes: Lazaridis, Blake, Pandiani, Bennett, Martin Taylor

EVENT LINE

41 Clapham (Off) Lazaridis (On)

HALF TIME 0 - 0

55 **Taylor Maik (Own Goal)**

66 Clemence (Off) Blake (On)

76 Anderton (Off) Pandiani (On)

80 **Dunne (Indirect Free Kick)**

81 **Fowler (Off) Wright-Phillips B (On)**

85 Morrison (Dissent)

86 **Sibierski (Penalty)**

90 **Wright-Phillips S (Off) Croft (On)**

FULL TIME 3 - 0

STATISTICS

Season	Fixture (Man City)		Fixture (Birmingham)	Season
182	5	Shots On Target	1	144
173	4	Shots Off Target	4	150
3	0	Hit Woodwork	1	8
108	3	Caught Offside	2	94
213	8	Corners	3	171
425	11	Fouls	9	470
49%	51%	Possession	49%	50%

LEAGUE STANDINGS

Position (pos before)	W	D	L	F	A	Pts
11 (11) Man City	11	11	12	42	37	44
13 (12) Birmingham C	9	11	14	35	42	38

Wednesday 20th April 2005 | Venue: City of Manchester Stadium | Attendance: 42,453 | Referee: M.Atkinson

MANCHESTER CITY 3 BIRMINGHAM CITY 0

Three second half goals strengthened Stuart Pearce's case for becoming the permanent boss at Manchester City.

A fit-again Shaun Wright-Phillips made a first start since late February on the right of the home midfield, but it was down the left that the first chance arrived.

Robbie Fowler got on the end of Kiki Musampa's low cross to angle an effort beyond Maik Taylor and against the far right-hand upright within the first 60 seconds of play, only for an evidently-rusty Wright-Phillips to blaze the rebound over the bar from close range.

Birmingham then conjured up a decent opening of their own, as a clever flick from the marauding Mario Melchiot set up Emile Heskey for a venomous drive that was marginally too high.

That was as good as it got in an opening period woefully short of incident, but the game burst into life after the break.

Republic of Ireland international Clinton Morrison saw a well-taken goal from Jermaine Pennant's right-wing centre correctly ruled out for offside, with the home team responding to that scare by swiftly going in front.

A decent Musampa delivery from the left was met by the head of Fowler some 12 yards out, with the ball finding its way into the net via the body of keeper Taylor after it had initially struck the right-hand post.

A Pennant free-kick that clipped the woodwork was as close as Steve Bruce's team came to an equaliser, with the men in sky blue effectively sealing the points through a Richard Dunne effort 10 minutes from time.

Again there was an element of fortune about the goal, the centre-back's header from a left-wing Fowler free-kick deflecting in off the head of Heskey.

A late penalty added further gloss to the scoreline, Antoine Sibierski just beating Taylor from the spot after handball had been awarded against either Darren Carter or Morrison.

Though Birmingham have played better this season, a 3-0 result was not a fair reflection of the game. Luck was certainly on Pearce's side in this encounter, and they say it is better to be a lucky manager than a good manager.

Matthew Upson tussles with Antoine Sibierski

"We have four games left and we will be trying to win them all and see where that takes us."

Stuart Pearce

PREMIERSHIP MILESTONE

Richard Dunne scored his first Premiership goal

"People will look at 3-0, but that scoreline was cruel and flatters Manchester City."

Steve Bruce

PREMIERSHIP MILESTONE

300 Kenny Cunningham made his 300th Premiership appearance.

PREMIERSHIP FIXTURE HISTORY

Pl: 3 Draws: 0	Wins	⚽	▢	■
Norwich City	2	5	0	0
Newcastle United	1	4	0	0

STARTING LINE-UPS

Norwich City: Green; Helveg, Fleming (c), Shackell, Drury; Bentley, Francis, Safri, Huckerby; Ashton, McKenzie

Newcastle United: Shearer (c), Ameobi; Robert, N'Zogbia, Butt, Milner; Elliott, O'Brien, Boumsong, Carr; Given

Norwich City substitutes: Jonson, Svensson, Holt, Ward, Edworthy

Newcastle United substitutes: Ambrose, Kluivert, Harper, Ramage

EVENT LINE

HALF TIME 0 - 0

46 **Huckerby (Off) Jonson (On)**

63 Milner (Off) Ambrose (On)

68 ⚽ **Safri (Open Play)**

76 Ameobi (Off) Kluivert (On)

82 **McKenzie (Off) Svensson (On)**

89 **Bentley (Off) Holt (On)**

90 ⚽ Kluivert (Open Play)

90 ⚽ **Ashton (Open Play)**

FULL TIME 2 - 1

STATISTICS

Season	Fixture (Norwich)		Fixture (Newcastle)	Season
160	8	Shots On Target	10	227
167	7	Shots Off Target	14	193
5	0	Hit Woodwork	0	11
111	8	Caught Offside	1	85
159	6	Corners	6	210
466	12	Fouls	11	404
45%	46%	Possession	54%	51%

LEAGUE STANDINGS

Position (pos before)	W	D	L	F	A	Pts
20 (20) Norwich C	5	12	17	37	67	27
14 (13) Newcastle Utd	9	11	12	42	51	38

Wednesday 20th April 2005 | Venue: **Carrow Road** | Attendance: **25,503** | Referee: **A.Marriner**

Thomas Helveg and Shola Ameobi go head-to-head

"We have got to stick to it and keep our good run going. We are still thinking we can beat the drop."
Dean Ashton

"It was hard on us. We did not deserve to lose, but all credit to Norwich who kept going right to the end."
Graeme Souness

PREMIERSHIP MILESTONE
200 Dean Ashton netted Norwich's 200th Premiership goal.

PREMIERSHIP MILESTONE
Youssef Safri scored his first Premiership goal

NORWICH CITY 2 NEWCASTLE UNITED 1

Norwich continued their recent revival with a dramatic last-gasp win against a Newcastle side struggling for any kind of form.

Substitute Patrick Kluivert looked to have earnt his side a point with a 90th-minute goal that cancelled out Youssef Safri's stunning effort, only for Dean Ashton to send Carrow Road into a state of delirium with a majestic headed winner.

The visitors were first to go close, captain Alan Shearer ghosting in to drive the ball just the wrong side of the far left-hand upright. Then, at the other end, striker Leon McKenzie was unable to make contact with Darren Huckerby's dangerous delivery from the left.

A dipping Laurent Robert free-kick was then spilled by Robert Green, with Shearer inexplicably failing to capitalise on the situation as he missed the target from no more than four yards out.

Controversial French winger Robert blazed over the bar after his initial volley had been saved, before play switched to the other end with Shay Given producing a world-class save to keep out a close-range header from Damien Francis.

Shola Ameobi drilled narrowly over the top as the game continued at a frantic pace, and there was to be no let up after the break.

Nigel Worthington's team came out with all guns blazing at the start of the second period. A goalmouth scramble saw a wayward finish from Francis, before Safri perfectly demonstrated how to strike a ball in the 68th minute.

Few Newcastle players would have been worried as the Moroccan international lined up a shot from fully 35 yards out, but his swerving strike crashed in off the woodwork to give the Canaries a priceless lead.

An Ashton goal was then ruled out for offside, with Kluivert taking full advantage to find the bottom corner of the net as the ball broke to him near the penalty spot.

A point was of little use to Norwich, and they amazingly won all three deep into injury time. Former Crewe striker Ashton beat Given with a towering header from Thomas Helveg's right-wing centre, sparking scenes of great joy inside the stadium.

Wednesday 20th April 2005	Venue: **Fratton Park**	Attendance: **20,205**	Referee: **H.M.Webb**

PORTSMOUTH 1 LIVERPOOL 2

Liverpool maintained their challenge for 'Champions League' football next season, winning 2-1 at Portsmouth despite captain Steven Gerrard starting on the bench.

Rafael Benitez decided that his skipper was in need of a rest, and also chose to keep faith with the three centre-backs system he had employed against Tottenham last time out.

The first five minutes of the contest contained as much goalmouth action as you often see in entire games. Lomana Tresor Lua Lua harshly saw an effort ruled out for offside, before Milan Baros was foiled by the legs of Jamie Ashdown in the home goal.

The visitors did go in front less than 60 seconds later, however, as Fernando Morientes turned the ball in at the second attempt, following good work from John Arne Riise down the right.

Liverpool's former Real Madrid striker missed a presentable headed chance midway through the half, while Jerzy Dudek did well to recover his ground and keep out a Lua Lua lob at the other end.

Portsmouth did draw level after 34 minutes though. Arjan De Zeeuw saw his attempt from a right-wing corner cleared off the line, with Diomansy Kamara on hand to bundle the ball home from close range via Dudek and Steve Finnan.

After two scrappy goals, the Merseysiders re-established their lead in classic fashion on the stroke of half-time. Norwegian Riise delivered from the left, and Luis Garcia stole across the front of his marker to plant a 12-yard header firmly into the bottom left-hand corner of the net.

The former Barcelona man did not re-emerge after the interval, but Liverpool remained on top. Again Ashdown made a vital save with his legs, this time from Riise, while the keeper also had to turn over a cultured Xabi Alonso strike.

In between times, Steve Stone was unable to turn home Matthew Taylor's driven cross.

The closing stages saw long-range drives from Patrik Berger and Alonso at opposite ends of the pitch, though both keepers were equal to them.

PREMIERSHIP FIXTURE HISTORY

Pl: **2** Draws: **0**	Wins	Goals	Yellow cards	Red cards
Portsmouth	1	2	3	0
Liverpool	1	2	2	0

STARTING LINE-UPS

Portsmouth subs: Primus, Berger, Fuller, Hislop, Rodic

Liverpool subs: Smicer, Gerrard, Cisse, Carson, Pellegrino

EVENT LINE

4 Morientes (Open Play)

34 **Kamara (Corner)**

45 Garcia (Open Play)

HALF TIME 1 - 2

46 **De Zeeuw (Off) Primus (On)**

46 Garcia (Off) Smicer (On)

51 **Hughes (Foul)**

66 **Stone (Off) Berger (On)**

67 Biscan (Off) Gerrard (On)

76 **Lua Lua (Off) Fuller (On)**

79 Baros (Off) Cisse (On)

FULL TIME 1 - 2

STATISTICS

Season	Fixture	Portsmouth	Liverpool	Fixture	Season
170	6	Shots On Target		12	213
162	2	Shots Off Target		7	226
7	0	Hit Woodwork		0	7
98	4	Caught Offside		3	91
170	5	Corners		4	196
408	10	Fouls		8	394
47%	47%	Possession		53%	53%

LEAGUE STANDINGS

Position (pos before)	W	D	L	F	A	Pts
16 (16) Portsmouth	9	8	17	38	53	35
5 (6) Liverpool	16	6	12	48	35	54

Milan Baros tries to find a way past Arjan De Zeeuw

"The game was as tough as I expected because Liverpool are a strong team."
Alain Perrin

"We know that we cannot change results on other pitches, and the result at Everton means that picking up league points is important for us."
Rafael Benitez

Wednesday 20th April 2005 | Venue: **White Hart Lane** | Attendance: **35,885** | Referee: **C.J.Foy**

PREMIERSHIP FIXTURE HISTORY

Pl: 2 Draws: 1	Wins	Goals	Yellow cards	Red cards
Tottenham Hotspur	1	4	4	0
West Bromwich Albion	0	2	1	0

STARTING LINE-UPS

Tottenham Hotspur: Robinson; Kelly, Dawson, King (c), Edman; Davies, Davis, Carrick, Reid; Defoe, Keane

West Brom: Campbell (c), Kanu; Richardson, Chaplow, Wallwork, Gera; Robinson, Clement, Gaardsoe, Scimeca; Hoult

Tottenham Hotspur substitutes: Atouba, Mido, Ziegler, Cerny, Marney

West Brom substitutes: Inamoto, Moore, Earnshaw, Kuszczak, Albrechtsen

EVENT LINE

8 (yellow card) **Dawson (Foul)**

23 (substitution) Richardson (Off) Inamoto (On)

24 (goal) Gera (Corner)

HALF TIME 0 - 1

46 (substitution) **Davis (Off) Mido (On)**

46 (substitution) **Edman (Off) Atouba (On)**

52 (goal) **Keane (Open Play)**

60 (substitution) Campbell (Off) Moore (On)

75 (substitution) **Defoe (Off) Ziegler (On)**

83 (substitution) Kanu (Off) Earnshaw (On)

90 (yellow card) **Reid (Foul)**

FULL TIME 1 - 1

STATISTICS

Season	Fixture (Tottenham)		Fixture (West Brom)	Season
209	**5**	Shots On Target	**4**	**156**
192	**10**	Shots Off Target	**6**	**142**
10	**0**	Hit Woodwork	**1**	**12**
142	**4**	Caught Offside	**6**	**118**
172	**7**	Corners	**3**	**167**
404	**12**	Fouls	**12**	**432**
50%	**56%**	Possession	**44%**	**47%**

LEAGUE STANDINGS

Position (pos before)		W	D	L	F	A	Pts
7 (7)	**Tottenham H**	**13**	**9**	**12**	**42**	**38**	**48**
17 (18)	**West Brom**	**5**	**14**	**14**	**32**	**53**	**29**

Robbie Keane celebrates his goal

"It is important for Tottenham to get into Europe because of the confidence and prestige it will give to the players."

Martin Jol

"It gives the players confidence that we are out of the bottom three, but there are still five tough games to come."

Bryan Robson

PREMIERSHIP MILESTONE

Junichi Inamoto made his first Premiership appearance in the colours of West Brom

TOTTENHAM HOTSPUR 1 WEST BROM 1

The Baggies continued their recent upturn in form, moving back out of the relegation zone courtesy of a 1-1 draw at White Hart Lane.

The visitors nearly made a dream start, Zoltan Gera sliding the ball agonisingly past the right-hand upright after Nwankwo Kanu had been denied by a last-gasp challenge inside the box.

Bryan Robson's men continued to dominate, centre-back Neil Clement striking the outside of a post with a free-kick from 25 yards out after Kieran Richardson had been brought down in full flight.

Russell Hoult needed to be alert to prevent a Thomas Gaardsoe own goal, before West Brom grabbed a 24th-minute lead. Hungarian Gera found acres of space inside the penalty area following a left-wing corner, and wasted no time in lashing home a 15-yard drive.

Former Burnley midfielder Richard Chaplow was then denied by Paul Robinson as he arrived to meet Kanu's low ball across the box. A second goal at this point might have been decisive, and the save kept Spurs in touch going into the break.

Martin Jol was clearly not happy with what he had seen during the first 45 minutes, forcing him into a double substitution at half-time. Thimothee Atouba replaced Erik Edman in a like-for-like switch, while striker Mido came on for Sean Davis as Tottenham opted for a three-man attack.

The introduction of Mido almost paid immediate dividends. The Egyptian forward danced through a forest of legs when cutting inside from the left, only to fire into the side-netting when a shooting chance presented itself.

Disappointment was short-lived, however, as Robbie Keane profited from the presence of a more physical forward to net a 52nd-minute leveller. The Republic of Ireland international guided a bouncing ball just inside the left-hand upright from 17 yards out, following a bit of 'route one' football.

From then on, the game could have swung either way. Junichi Inamoto and Gera both went close for West Brom, while Andy Reid and Mido were not far away for Tottenham.

PREMIERSHIP FIXTURE HISTORY

Pl: 6	Draws: 2	Wins	⚽	Yellow	Red
Aston Villa		3	9	7	0
Bolton Wanderers		1	7	13	0

STARTING LINE-UPS

Aston Villa subs: Cole, Postma, Hendrie, L.Moore, Djemba-Djemba

Bolton subs: Campo, Jaidi, Nolan, Poole, Pedersen

EVENT LINE

26 ⚽ **Hierro (Own Goal)**

HALF TIME 1 - 0

46 Hierro (Off) Campo (On)

49 Hunt (Off) Jaidi (On)

54 ⚽ Speed (Open Play)

56 Campo (Foul)

70 Okocha (Off) Nolan (On)

75 Nolan (Foul)

79 **Solano (Off) Cole (On)**

FULL TIME 1 - 1

STATISTICS

Season	Fixture (Aston Villa)		Fixture (Bolton)	Season
183	10	Shots On Target	6	229
176	3	Shots Off Target	6	201
8	0	Hit Woodwork	0	8
101	4	Caught Offside	1	97
198	7	Corners	5	186
543	17	Fouls	13	473
49%	49%	Possession	51%	50%

LEAGUE STANDINGS

Position (pos before)		W	D	L	F	A	Pts
9 (9)	Aston Villa	12	11	12	42	43	47
6 (6)	Bolton W	15	9	11	45	39	54

Saturday 23rd April 2005 | Venue: **Villa Park** | Attendance: **36,053** | Referee: **U.D.Rennie**

Bruno N'Gotty and Juan Pablo Angel prepare for the arrival of the ball

"I would say Sam Allardyce is jumping for joy at taking a point."

David O'Leary

"It was a point won rather than two lost, as Jussi Jaaskelainen had to make some really good saves."

Sam Allardyce

PREMIERSHIP MILESTONE

Gary Speed scored his first Premiership goal for Bolton

ASTON VILLA 1 BOLTON WANDERERS 1

Bolton failed to capitalise on both Merseyside clubs dropping points, as they stuttered to a 1-1 draw at Villa Park.

Sam Allardyce's men were not at their best, and fell behind in the 26th minute. Nolberto Solano sent over an inswinging corner from the left, with former Real Madrid captain Fernando Hierro rising to meet the ball with a firm downward header into his own net.

By this point, the visitors could easily have been in front. Greek international Stylianos Giannakopoulos somehow contrived to head Jay-Jay Okocha's pinpoint cross from the right past the left-hand upright from no more than five yards out.

Jussi Jaaskelainen then had to be at his best to turn away an effort from Juan Pablo Angel. The Colombian striker climbed highest to meet Ulises De la Cruz's centre, thus forcing the keeper into an agile plunging save.

Though Bolton's Finnish custodian could do little to prevent Hierro's own goal, he soon ensured that David O'Leary's team would not be increasing their lead before the break. Darius Vassell robbed Tal Ben Haim and surged forward, but Jaaskelainen stood up tall to foil the pacy frontman.

Parries from J'Lloyd Samuel and Steven Davis either side of the interval kept the Trotters in the game, with Gary Speed arriving right on cue to head home a 54th-minute equaliser from El-Hadji Diouf's right-wing cross.

Aston Villa responded positively to the setback, carving out two great opportunities to regain the lead. Firstly, a powerful Angel header was pushed away by a strong right hand from Jaaskelainen, before a flowing move ended when Davis was unable to find a way past the shot-stopper.

The visitors then had two decent chances of their own. Substitute Kevin Nolan steered the ball just over the bar after a free-kick from deep had caused havoc in the box, with Diouf soon frustrating his team-mates as he selfishly fired wide when others were better placed.

A late appeal for a penalty fell on deaf ears when Bruno N'Gotty proved too strong for Angel, though if any side deserved to win this encounter, it was Villa.

PREMIERSHIP FIXTURE HISTORY

Pl: 7 Draws: 1	Wins	⚽	▢	■
Blackburn Rovers	4	10	6	0
Manchester City	2	6	6	0

STARTING LINE-UPS

Thompson, Gallagher Enckelman, Tugay Flitcroft

B.Wright-Phillips, Croft, Weaver, Mills Thatcher

EVENT LINE

HALF TIME 0 - 0

69 **Savage (Off) Thompson (On)**

76 **Pedersen (Off) Gallagher (On)**

77 Musampa (Off) Croft (On)

86 Fowler (Off) Wright-Phillips B (On)

FULL TIME 0 - 0

STATISTICS

Season	Fixture		Fixture	Season
172	5	Shots On Target	1	183
207	6	Shots Off Target	6	179
6	0	Hit Woodwork	0	3
137	0	Caught Offside	1	109
194	6	Corners	2	215
547	20	Fouls	17	442
49%	56%	Possession	44%	49%

LEAGUE STANDINGS

Position (pos before)	W	D	L	F	A	Pts
12 (12) Blackburn R	9	13	12	29	37	40
10 (11) Man City	11	12	12	42	37	45

Saturday 23rd April 2005 | Venue: **Ewood Park** | Attendance: **24,646** | Referee: **C.J.Foy**

BLACKBURN ROVERS 0 MANCHESTER CITY 0

Manchester City stretched their unbeaten run to five games, with a hard-fought goalless draw at Ewood Park.

The match got off to a cagey start, with long-range drives the order of the day. Joey Barton was not a million miles away with his 25-yard effort, before Jonathan Stead curled the ball just the wrong side of David James' right-hand upright from the edge of the box.

A moment of real controversy followed as the game headed towards the half-hour mark. Shaun Wright-Phillips was clearly upended by Dominic Matteo as he surged into the area from his position on the wing, but referee Chris Foy was unmoved.

That was as exciting as things got in a fairly dull opening 45 minutes. Possession was often squandered cheaply in a crowded midfield area, while decent chances were at a premium.

Unfortunately for the 24,646-strong crowd, there was little improvement after the interval. On a positive note, however, James was at least called into meaningful action in the City goal.

Full-back Matteo seemed an unlikely scorer, but he came very close following a throw on the left. The former Leeds man returned a clearance with interest, only to see James keep out his deflected volley with a sprawling save.

Set-pieces presented Blackburn with several half-chances either side of Matteo's effort. Brett Emerton tested the keeper when meeting a Morten Gamst Pedersen corner, while Andy Todd, Ryan Nelson and Steven Reid were all off target with their aerial attempts.

Stuart Pearce then saw another penalty appeal from his side waved away. Antoine Sibierski tangled with Nelson inside the six-yard box, though the Frenchman's dramatic fall did little to help his cause.

Mark Hughes' team nearly stole the points as the match drifted towards its conclusion. Striker Stead almost profited from a break of the ball on the edge of the area, turning to fire in a shot that temporarily got away from James.

Though this clash will not live long in the memory, credit must be given to two managers for whom organisation is a vital part of success.

Antoine Sibierski looks to control the ball

"They had a couple of penalty claims, one of which may have been a decent call, but apart from that we created more and could have nicked it."

Mark Hughes

"I was delighted with the players, and I told them that this was more pleasing than the one or two victories we have had at home."

Stuart Pearce

Saturday 23rd April 2005 | Venue: **Stamford Bridge** | Attendance: **42,081** | Referee: **A.G.Wiley**

CHELSEA 3 FULHAM 1

Chelsea moved to within touching distance of their first league title in 50 years, defeating neighbours Fulham 3-1 at Stamford Bridge.

PREMIERSHIP FIXTURE HISTORY

Pl: 4	Draws: 1	Wins	Goals	Yellow	Red
Chelsea		3	9	6	0
Fulham		0	5	5	0

STARTING LINE-UPS

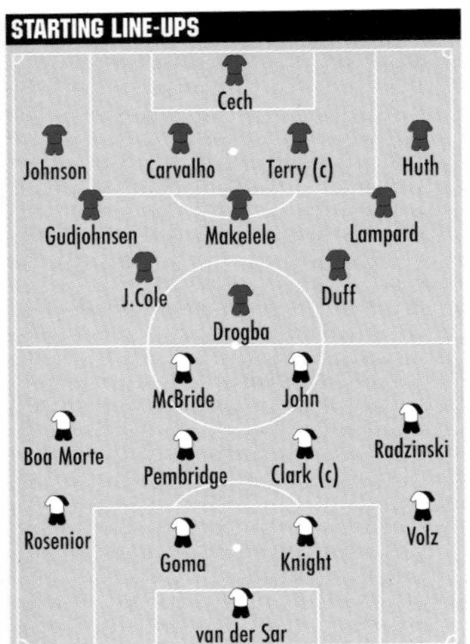

Chelsea subs: Jarosik, Robben, Tiago, Cudicini, Kezman

Fulham subs: Malbranque, Crossley, Bocanegra, Rehman, Jensen

EVENT LINE

17 ⚽ **Cole J (Open Play)**
41 ⚽ John (Open Play)
43 ▯ **Terry (Foul)**
HALF TIME 1 - 1
46 ⇄ **Cole J (Off) Robben (On)**
46 ⇄ **Huth (Off) Jarosik (On)**
53 ▯ John (Handball)
64 ⚽ **Lampard (Open Play)**
74 ⇄ **Drogba (Off) Tiago (On)**
84 ⇄ Pembridge (Off) Malbranque (On)
87 ⚽ **Gudjohnsen (Open Play)**
FULL TIME 3 - 1

STATISTICS

Season	Fixture (Chelsea)		Fixture (Fulham)	Season
263	7	Shots On Target	4	159
223	5	Shots Off Target	6	152
10	0	Hit Woodwork	0	6
114	11	Caught Offside	1	88
226	4	Corners	6	168
421	7	Fouls	11	416
56%	52%	Possession	48%	48%

LEAGUE STANDINGS

Position (pos before)		W	D	L	F	A	Pts
1 (1)	Chelsea	26	7	1	65	13	85
16 (15)	Fulham	9	8	17	40	56	35

Joe Cole's 17th-minute opener was cancelled out by Collins John four minutes before the break, with second half strikes from Frank Lampard and Eidur Gudjohnsen ensuring that the Premiership trophy would be heading to West London if nearest challengers Arsenal failed to beat Tottenham two days later.

With a 'Champions League' semi-final meeting with Liverpool on the horizon, Jose Mourinho would have been hoping for a comfortable afternoon. That looked a possibility when Cole was allowed to turn on the edge of the box and curl an effort just inside the right-hand post.

Thereafter, Chelsea enjoyed a decent spell. Didier Drogba, who had earlier headed narrowly over from a Damien Duff cross, came close to making it two when he spun and quickly sent an effort just past the left-hand upright.

The Cottagers weathered the storm, however, and began to create chances of their own as the half progressed. Brian McBride fired over after good work from Liam Rosenior down the left, before John made it 1-1.

The powerful young forward seemed second favourite to reach Luis Boa Morte's ball behind the defence, but he got the better of Ricardo Carvalho to slot past Petr Cech from just inside the six-yard box.

Arjen Robben was introduced at the start of the second half, as he returned from a month on the sidelines. The Dutchman set about making an immediate impact, setting up Gudjohnsen for a disallowed goal and then teeing up Lampard for a strike that did count.

The England international arrived in customary fashion in the 64th minute, placing a 15-yard effort low to the right of a wrongfooted Edwin van der Sar.

Tomasz Radzinski showed that Fulham were still a threat with a shot from distance that called Cech into action, but Gudjohnsen sealed the points with three minutes remaining as he raced onto Tiago's pass and slotted the ball under the keeper.

Collins John tries to find a way through a wall of blue

"I do not want to win the league on Monday. I am hoping Arsenal can beat Tottenham, and I want to transmit this mentality to my players."
Jose Mourinho

"I thought our guys played very well. I think we pushed them from the first to the last minute."
Chris Coleman

PREMIERSHIP FIXTURE HISTORY

Pl: 4 Draws: 1	Wins	Goals	Yellow cards	Red cards
Crystal Palace	1	3	7	0
Liverpool	2	10	8	0

STARTING LINE-UPS

Crystal Palace: Kiraly; Sorondo, Hall, Popovic, Granville; Leigertwood, Riihilahti, Hughes (c); Routledge, Soares; Johnson

Liverpool: Morientes, Baros; Gerrard (c), Le Tallec, Welsh; Traore, Finnan; Pellegrino, Hyypia, Carragher; Dudek

Crystal Palace substitutes: Watson, Speroni, Lakis, Torghelle, Ventola

Liverpool substitutes: Potter, Riise, Cisse, Carson, Biscan

EVENT LINE

34 Goal Johnson (Open Play)
35 Booking Carragher (Foul)
37 Substitution Baros (Off) Potter (On)
45 Booking **Routledge (Ung.Conduct)**
45 Booking Morientes (Foul)

HALF TIME 1 - 0

54 Substitution Pellegrino (Off) Riise (On)
55 Booking **Granville (Foul)**
60 Booking Gerrard (Foul)
69 Substitution Traore (Off) Cisse (On)
77 Booking Finnan (Foul)
88 Booking Riise (Foul)
90 Substitution **Soares (Off) Watson (On)**

FULL TIME 1 - 0

STATISTICS

Season	Fixture (Crystal Palace)		Fixture (Liverpool)	Season
158	3	Shots On Target	7	220
149	3	Shots Off Target	2	228
7	0	Hit Woodwork	0	7
80	2	Caught Offside	7	98
175	4	Corners	1	197
492	19	Fouls	14	408
46%	38%	Possession	62%	53%

LEAGUE STANDINGS

Position (pos before)		W	D	L	F	A	Pts
17 (19)	Crystal Palace	7	9	19	37	58	30
5 (5)	Liverpool	16	6	13	48	36	54

Saturday 23rd April 2005 | Venue: **Selhurst Park** | Attendance: **26,043** | Referee: **D.J.Gallagher**

Fernando Morientes tries to shield the ball from Tony Popovic

"There will be some really hostile atmospheres to face between now and the end of the season, but I'm convinced we can churn out the results."

Assistant Manager Kit Symons

"I thought we controlled the game in the first half, but when we conceded the goal it was difficult."

Rafael Benitez

CRYSTAL PALACE 1 LIVERPOOL 0

A 34th-minute Andy Johnson header proved enough to beat Liverpool and move Crystal Palace out of the bottom three.

Australian international defender Tony Popovic was lucky to avoid a booking for a poor challenge on Milan Baros, before rising to meet a Michael Hughes free-kick with a header that forced Jerzy Dudek into an acrobatic stop.

Iain Dowie's men were first to every ball, with Johnson running the Merseysiders' three centre-backs ragged. The Eagles' positive approach was eventually rewarded, Johnson angling a 12-yard header beyond the right hand of Dudek from Wayne Routledge's wayward volley.

After Baros had been forced to limp out of the action, the livewire Johnson nearly made it two. Outmuscling Mauricio Pellegrino and Jamie Carragher on the edge of the box, the striker was harshly penalised by the referee as he drilled an effort narrowly wide.

Though the visiting fans may have expected a response from their team after the break, it was the men in red and blue that continued to threaten. Tom Soares had a great chance to put the match out of Liverpool's reach, but saw Pellegrino clear his scuffed close-range attempt.

Still Rafael Benitez's charges continued to struggle, with Palace captain Hughes almost finding the bottom right-hand corner of the net with a dipping 25-yard strike.

The introduction of Djibril Cisse lifted the Anfield side in the closing 20 minutes. Fernando Morientes leapt prodigiously to meet Steven Gerrard's flicked pass with a powerful header, though the attempt didn't unduly trouble Gabor Kiraly.

A last-gasp Popovic tackle then prevented the Spaniard from getting a clear sight of goal, while home-grown youngster Darren Potter tried to conjure up an equaliser with a well-struck low drive.

After Johnson had nearly latched onto a clipped ball through from Routledge, Kiraly made a crucial save from Gerrard. The Liverpool skipper set his aim for the bottom right-hand corner, but the Hungarian made an agile parry.

Despite enduring some more nervous moments, the Eagles held on for an uplifting victory.

PREMIERSHIP FIXTURE HISTORY

Pl: 3 Draws: 2	Wins	⚽	▯	▮
Everton	1	3	2	1
Birmingham City	0	2	6	0

STARTING LINE-UPS

Everton subs: Watson, Ferguson, Bent, Wright, McFadden

Birmingham City subs: Blake, Clemence, Martin Taylor, Bennett, Morrison

EVENT LINE

5 ⚽ Heskey (Open Play)
24 ▯ **Carsley (Dissent)**
32 ▯ Melchiot (Foul)

HALF TIME 0 - 1

46 **Carsley (Off) Ferguson (On)**
46 **Pistone (Off) Watson (On)**
61 **Beattie (Off) Bent (On)**
68 Pandiani (Off) Blake (On)
69 ▯ Cunningham (Foul)
79 Anderton (Off) Clemence (On)
81 ▯ Clemence (Ung.Conduct)
86 ⚽ **Ferguson (Corner)**
89 Pennant (Off) Taylor Martin (On)
90 ▯ **Watson (Foul)**

FULL TIME 1 - 1

STATISTICS

Season	Fixture		Fixture	Season
161	6	Shots On Target	4	148
179	5	Shots Off Target	5	155
6	0	Hit Woodwork	0	8
82	1	Caught Offside	0	94
165	9	Corners	5	176
418	18	Fouls	18	488
49%	50%	Possession	50%	50%

LEAGUE STANDINGS

Position (pos before)		W	D	L	F	A	Pts
4 (4)	Everton	17	7	10	41	34	58
13 (13)	Birmingham C	9	12	14	36	43	39

Saturday 23rd April 2005 | Venue: **Goodison Park** | Attendance: **36,828** | Referee: **A.P.D'Urso**

EVERTON 1 BIRMINGHAM CITY 1

Duncan Ferguson came off the bench to net what may yet prove to be a crucial equaliser against Birmingham at Goodison Park.

Though the home faithful would have expected three points on the back of victory against Manchester United, favourable results later in the day meant that this was a point gained rather than two lost.

Things began disastrously for David Moyes' men, as former Liverpool striker Emile Heskey grabbed an early goal. Just five minutes had elapsed when the powerful frontman controlled Jermaine Pennant's ball forward with his first touch, before firing a 20-yard effort into the bottom left-hand corner of the net with his second.

After his heroic exploits in midweek, Ferguson found himself back amongst the substitutes for this encounter. That meant a start for £6m transfer-window signing James Beattie, and the former Southampton man was guilty of a poor headed miss from Leon Osman's excellent cross from the right flank.

The normally-deadly Tim Cahill was next to miss an aerial chance, failing to hit the target from eight yards out after Osman had again done well. The Australian midfielder seemed to mistime his jump, though the opening was nowhere near as clear as Beattie's.

Joseph Yobo was unable to find a way past Maik Taylor as he rose to meet a corner, while Heskey almost increased the size of the task facing Everton when he ghosted between Nigel Martyn and the Nigerian defender to loop an effort agonisingly wide of the left-hand upright.

Though Ferguson was introduced at the start of the second half, it wasn't until he was joined by Marcus Bent just after the hour that things began to happen. A break involving the two strikers caused havoc in the Birmingham defence, but Kevin Kilbane was unable to capitalise.

By this point, Tunisian Mehdi Nafti should have headed the visitors in front, while Heskey was inches away from connecting with another dangerous Pennant centre.

The failure to extend their lead ultimately cost Steve Bruce's team, as Ferguson swept home an 86th-minute leveller after both Cahill and Bent had been denied.

Tim Cahill keeps an eye on Damien Johnson

"We know we are close to making European football, and it would be nice if that happens."
David Moyes

"It feels like a defeat to come so close and then concede an equaliser right at the end."
Steve Bruce

PREMIERSHIP MILESTONE

350 Nigel Martyn made his 350th Premiership appearance.

PREMIERSHIP MILESTONE

100 Kenny Cunningham made his 100th Premiership appearance in the colours of Birmingham

PREMIERSHIP FIXTURE HISTORY

Pl: 2 Draws: 0	Wins	⚽	▢	■
Middlesbrough	2	7	1	0
West Bromwich Albion	0	0	2	0

STARTING LINE-UPS

Davies, Parlour Graham, Knight Wheater

Inamoto, Kanu Horsfield, Kuszczak Moore

EVENT LINE

22 ▢ Gaardsoe (Foul)

27 ⚽ **Nemeth (Open Play)**

33 ⚽ **Hasselbaink (Open Play)**

37 ⇄ **Cooper (Off) Davies (On)**

37 ⚽ **Nemeth (Open Play)**

HALF TIME 3 - 0

46 ⇄ Albrechtsen (Off) Inamoto (On)

46 ⇄ Campbell (Off) Kanu (On)

55 ▢ **Downing (Foul)**

65 ⇄ **Zenden (Off) Parlour (On)**

79 ⇄ Gera (Off) Horsfield (On)

87 ⇄ **Nemeth (Off) Graham (On)**

90 ⚽ **Downing (Direct Free Kick)**

FULL TIME 4 - 0

STATISTICS

Season	Fixture (Middlesbrough)		Fixture (West Brom)	Season
235	8	Shots On Target	9	165
177	4	Shots Off Target	6	148
6	0	Hit Woodwork	0	12
93	3	Caught Offside	2	120
184	1	Corners	4	171
425	12	Fouls	12	444
49%	42%	Possession	58%	48%

LEAGUE STANDINGS

Position (pos before)		W	D	L	F	A	Pts
7 (8)	Middlesbrough	13	10	11	50	44	49
19 (17)	West Brom	5	14	15	32	57	29

Saturday 23rd April 2005 | Venue: **Riverside Stadium** | Attendance: **32,951** | Referee: **H.M.Webb**

MIDDLESBROUGH 4 WEST BROM 0

Bryan Robson's return to Middlesbrough was not a happy one, as his West Brom side suffered a damaging four-goal defeat.

Having received a standing ovation from the home faithful for the job he had done when in charge at the club, Robson watched as his new team made a confident start to proceedings.

Captain Kevin Campbell saw a low drive touched just past the far right-hand upright by goalkeeper Brad Jones, while the Australian custodian then raced from his line to deny Robert Earnshaw in a one-on-one situation.

In between times, Jimmy Floyd Hasselbaink went close with a downward header, though this was an isolated attack.

Midway through the half, a left-wing free-kick caused further problems in the home defence. A stooping near-post header from Campbell tested the reflexes of the keeper, with Thomas Gaardsoe just unable to get to the rebound.

Having dominated the match, West Brom were stunned by three Middlesbrough goals in the space of 10 minutes.

Slovakian international Szilard Nemeth got the ball rolling in the 27th minute, steering a low 12-yard drive just inside the far right-hand post after Hasselbaink had been denied by Hoult.

Steve McClaren's strikers then linked up again, as Hasselbaink hammered home from a yard out after Hoult had inadvertently palmed Nemeth's cross from the left edge of the six-yard box back towards his own net.

Four minutes later, it was three. The visiting custodian was partially at fault once more, parrying Hasselbaink's venomous drive straight onto the head of a grateful Nemeth.

Despite being all at sea defensively, the Baggies continued to pose a threat going forward. Twice Earnshaw could have reduced the arrears, but he missed the target with both a free header and an improvised hooked finish.

The second half proved to be nowhere near as exciting as its predecessor. Nwankwo Kanu was denied from point-blank range, while fellow substitute Geoff Horsfield was also unable to find a way past the inspired Jones.

To make matters worse for the West Midlands side, Stewart Downing stepped up to curl a 90th-minute free-kick into the top right-hand corner of their net.

Ronnie Wallwork maintains possession

"There was a lot of pressure on our team today, and it was a great result for us."

Steve McClaren

"Football is all about taking your chances. We had three or four really good chances today, but we missed them all."

Bryan Robson

Saturday 23rd April 2005	Venue: **Carrow Road**	Attendance: **25,459**	Referee: **M.Atkinson**

NORWICH CITY 1 CHARLTON ATHLETIC 0

PREMIERSHIP FIXTURE HISTORY

Pl: **1** Draws: **0**	Wins		
Norwich City	1	1	1	0
Charlton Athletic	0	0	1	0

STARTING LINE-UPS

Huckerby, Svensson
Holt, Ward
Brennan

Euell, Thomas
Andersen, Perry
Lisbie

EVENT LINE

20 **Helveg (Foul)**

23 El Karkouri (Foul)

HALF TIME 0 - 0

62 Hughes (Off) Euell (On)

63 **Jonson (Off) Huckerby (On)**

80 **Bentley (Off) Svensson (On)**

82 Johansson (Off) Thomas (On)

88 **Svensson (Open Play)**

90 **McKenzie (Off) Holt (On)**

FULL TIME 1 - 0

STATISTICS

Season	Fixture		Fixture	Season
166	6	Shots On Target	6	158
174	7	Shots Off Target	5	138
5	0	Hit Woodwork	1	8
114	3	Caught Offside	0	115
166	7	Corners	8	158
474	8	Fouls	9	430
45%	56%	Possession	44%	44%

LEAGUE STANDINGS

Position (pos before)	W	D	L	F	A	Pts
18 (20) Norwich C	6	12	17	38	67	30
11 (10) Charlton Ath	12	9	14	40	51	45

Brave defending keeps Charlton at bay

"Winning breeds confidence, but we're still in the bottom three and can't take our feet off the pedal."

Nigel Worthington

"It's been a disappointing period, but you've got to look at the overall picture."

Alan Curbishley

PREMIERSHIP MILESTONE

100 Jonathan Fortune made his 100th Premiership appearance

Norwich's remarkable bid for Premiership survival continued apace, as Matthias Svensson netted a late winner against his former club Charlton.

Just two weeks ago the Canaries looked doomed to Championship football next season, but 10 points from the last four games has given the Carrow Road outfit a genuine chance of survival.

Despite some promising build-up play, chances were few and far between in the early exchanges. Jonatan Johansson nearly found himself one-on-one with Robert Green, while a right-wing corner sailed just too high for an unmarked Dean Ashton at the other end.

As the minutes ticked by, opportunities became more prevalent. Danny Murphy should have done better than blaze high into the crowd after Johansson's cutback from the right, with David Bentley driving just over the Charlton crossbar from 25 yards out.

Nigel Worthington's side have benefitted from the excellent link-up play between strikers Ashton and Leon McKenzie in recent weeks. The pair combined brilliantly again on the stroke of half-time, but Ashton dragged his effort wide of the left-hand post following his partner's flick-on.

The Addicks began the second period in the ascendancy, and created several decent openings. Talal El Karkouri forced Green into a diving stop with a drive from the edge of the box, Johansson almost got on the end of a dangerous Francis Jeffers cross, and a jinking Dennis Rommedahl run ended with a weak attempt.

Norwich responded with a long-range Damien Francis drive that was comfortably saved by Dean Kiely, before McKenzie missed a gilt-edged chance. The former Peterborough striker did well to get his head to Bentley's mishit volley, though he could only nod the ball wide.

With 10 minutes remaining, Svensson entered the fray. From then on, all the action seemed to revolve around the Swede, culminating in his crucial 88th-minute winner.

Having been foiled by an alert Kiely seconds after coming onto the pitch, the striker made a last-ditch challenge at the other end after Murphy had struck a post with a free-kick. Not content with this contribution, the former Charlton man promptly won the match with an acrobatic 10-yard finish.

PREMIERSHIP FIXTURE HISTORY

Pl: 12 Draws: 5	Wins	Goals	Yellow cards	Red cards
Manchester United	7	23	16	1
Newcastle United	0	8	17	1

STARTING LINE-UPS

Manchester United subs: Ronaldo, Kleberson, Silvestre, Carroll, O'Shea

Newcastle United subs: Kluivert, Robert, Harper, Brittain, McClen

EVENT LINE

27 ⚽ Ambrose (Open Play)

37 ⇄ **Heinze (Off) Ronaldo (On)**

40 ▢ Carr (Foul)

HALF TIME 0 - 1

50 ▢ **Rooney (Foul)**

57 ⚽ **Rooney (Open Play)**

61 ⇄ **Fletcher (Off) Kleberson (On)**

66 ⇄ Shearer (Off) Kluivert (On)

75 ⚽ **Brown (Corner)**

76 ⇄ **Keane (Off) Silvestre (On)**

82 ⇄ Ramage (Off) Robert (On)

FULL TIME 2 - 1

STATISTICS

Season	Fixture	Man Utd / Newcastle	Fixture	Season
278	10	Shots On Target	5	232
248	8	Shots Off Target	6	199
16	0	Hit Woodwork	0	11
123	5	Caught Offside	0	85
261	9	Corners	4	214
421	8	Fouls	21	425
56%	59%	Possession	41%	51%

LEAGUE STANDINGS

Position (pos before)		W	D	L	F	A	Pts
3 (3)	Man Utd	20	10	4	50	21	70
14 (14)	Newcastle Utd	9	11	13	43	53	38

Sunday 24th April 2005 | Venue: **Old Trafford** | Attendance: **67,845** | Referee: **N.S.Barry**

MANCHESTER UNITED 2 NEWCASTLE UNITED 1

Newcastle failed to gain revenge for their F.A.Cup semi-final defeat, surrendering a half-time advantage as they went down 2-1 at Old Trafford.

Visiting manager Graeme Souness set his team out in a defensively-minded 4-5-1 formation. Irish international Stephen Carr took up a position just in front of the back four, a move seemingly designed to counter the attacking threat of Wayne Rooney.

It took 10 minutes for Sir Alex Ferguson's men to click into gear. Ryan Giggs was the first player to test Shay Given, darting in from the right to curl a left-footed effort straight down the keeper's throat.

The Magpies responded with an attempt of their own. Darren Ambrose met Gabriel Heinze's headed clearance with a well-struck 20-yard volley, but the ball flew just past Tim Howard's left-hand post.

Then, after Rooney had forced a near-post save from Given and Alan Shearer had been denied by the alertness of Rio Ferdinand, Newcastle were gifted a 27th-minute lead.

A routine clearance was made a hash of by Howard, enabling Ambrose to exchange passes with Shola Ameobi and skip through to slot past the keeper.

To make matters worse for the home side, full-back Heinze had to be stretchered off before half-time following an innocuous looking collision with Ameobi.

There seemed no great urgency from the Old Trafford side as the second period got underway. Graeme Souness' men were defending comfortably, and seemed to have done so again as a hopeful ball forward was headed clear in the 57th minute.

They hadn't counted on a magnificent 25-yard volley from Rooney though. The England international didn't break stride as he found the top left-hand corner of a helpless Given's net.

From then on there was only likely to be one winner, and Wes Brown scored the goal that sealed the points 15 minutes from time. The Manchester-born centre-back rose to meet Giggs' outswinging corner from the left with a header that crept just inside the right-hand post.

There was no way back for the visitors, with Robbie Elliott somewhat fortunate to avoid netting a bizarre late own goal.

"It took a fantastic goal from Wayne Rooney to change the game. It was a phenomenal strike."

Sir Alex Ferguson

"We were unlucky to lose today, and I feel we got it right with the formation."

Graeme Souness

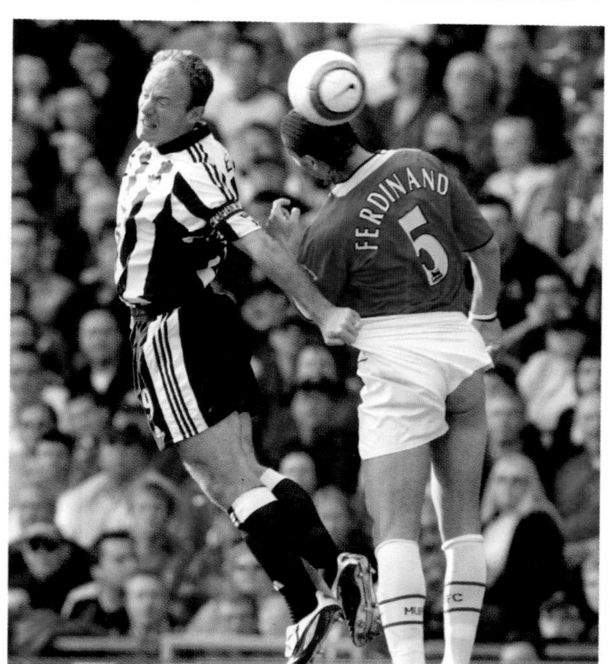

Alan Shearer climbs with Rio Ferdinand

PREMIERSHIP MILESTONE

25 Wayne Rooney netted his 25th Premiership goal

PREMIERSHIP MILESTONE

Wes Brown scored his first Premiership goal

PREMIERSHIP MILESTONE

200 Alan Smith made his 200th Premiership appearance.

PREMIERSHIP MILESTONE

250 Shay Given made his 250th Premiership appearance

PREMIERSHIP MILESTONE

Peter Ramage made his Premiership debut

PREMIERSHIP FIXTURE HISTORY

Pl: 2 Draws: 0	Wins	⚽	☐	■
Portsmouth	2	5	2	0
Southampton	0	1	4	0

STARTING LINE-UPS

Portsmouth: Ashdown; Griffin, De Zeeuw (c), Stefanovic, Taylor; Stone, Hughes, Berger, O'Neil; Lua Lua, Yakubu

Southampton: Phillips, Camara; Telfer, Quashie, Redknapp, Oakley; Higginbotham, Jakobsson, Lundekvam (c), Delap; Niemi

Portsmouth subs: Kamara, Cisse, Skopelitis, Hislop, Fuller

Southampton subs: Bernard, Smith, Davenport, Nilsson, A.Svensson

EVENT LINE

- 4 ⚽ **Yakubu (Penalty)**
- 17 ⚽ **De Zeeuw (Indirect Free Kick)**
- 20 ⚽ Camara (Open Play)
- 22 ⚽ **Lua Lua (Open Play)**
- 27 ⚽ **Lua Lua (Open Play)**
- 28 ⇄ **Lua Lua (Off) Kamara (On)**
- 32 ☐ **Hughes (Foul)**
- 40 ☐ Lundekvam (Foul)

HALF TIME 4 - 1

- 46 ⇄ Oakley (Off) Bernard (On)
- 57 ⇄ **Berger (Off) Cisse (On)**
- 63 ☐ Redknapp (Foul)
- 78 ⇄ **Yakubu (Off) Skopelitis (On)**
- 85 ☐ **Griffin (Foul)**

FULL TIME 4 - 1

STATISTICS

Season	Fixture (Portsmouth)		Fixture (Southampton)	Season
179	9	Shots On Target	8	169
172	10	Shots Off Target	3	186
7	0	Hit Woodwork	0	3
103	5	Caught Offside	1	104
174	4	Corners	7	165
423	15	Fouls	12	445
47%	54%	Possession	46%	47%

LEAGUE STANDINGS

Position (pos before)	W	D	L	F	A	Pts
15 (15) Portsmouth	10	8	17	42	54	38
20 (20) Southampton	5	13	17	38	59	28

Sunday 24th April 2005 | Venue: **Fratton Park** | Attendance: **20,210** | Referee: **S.W.Dunn**

Olivier Bernard is pressured by Andy Griffin

"It's very good for people to see a win like that. We were relaxed after the early goals."
Alain Perrin

"I have got to lift the players and keep believing in them, and hopefully we can turn things around."
Harry Redknapp

PREMIERSHIP MILESTONE

200 Patrik Berger and Kevin Phillips both made their 200th Premiership appearance.

PORTSMOUTH 4 SOUTHAMPTON 1

Harry Redknapp endured a miserable return to Fratton Park, as his struggling Southampton side were torn apart inside the opening half-hour.

Lomana Tresor Lua Lua was very much the star of the show, winning an early penalty that was converted by Aiyegbeni Yakubu. Arjan De Zeeuw and Henri Camara then exchanged goals, before a spectacular Lua Lua brace completed the scoring after just 27 minutes of high octane football.

The day began badly for the visitors, with striker Peter Crouch having to pull out at the last moment due to injury. It was at the other end that the men from St Mary's seemed to be disorganised, however, and they quickly fell behind.

A rush of blood saw Antti Niemi charge from his line to upend Lua Lua, with Yakubu finding the roof of the net from the penalty spot. Dejan Stefanovic then went close with a near-post flick, as Portsmouth dominated the early exchanges.

After 17 minutes, it was 2-0. Captain De Zeeuw rose majestically to power home Patrik Berger's deep free-kick from the right, though Camara quickly handed his team a lifeline with a venomous drive across Jamie Ashdown that flew into the bottom left-hand corner.

The match was being played at breakneck speed, with the next goal arriving just two minutes later. Again Niemi was at fault, losing out to Lua Lua as he rushed from his area. The former Newcastle forward still had much to do, but superbly clipped the ball beyond a covering defender from 20 yards out.

Things looked bleak for Redknapp's men, and they quickly got worse. A counter-attack appeared to have lost its momentum when Danny Higginbotham challenged Steve Stone on the edge of the box, but Lua Lua somehow curled an effort in off the right-hand upright.

Injury meant a premature end to the Democratic Republic of Congo international's afternoon, and the game suffered for his departure. Diomansy Kamara and Berger ensured that Niemi remained the far busier keeper, with only Nigel Quashie really testing Ashdown.

On this evidence, time is running out on Southampton's stay in the top-flight.

PREMIERSHIP FIXTURE HISTORY

Pl: 13 Draws: 5	Wins	Goals	Yellow cards	Red cards
Arsenal	7	18	17	1
Tottenham Hotspur	1	9	30	2

STARTING LINE-UPS

Arsenal substitutes: Bergkamp, Edu, Aliadiere, Almunia, Campbell

Tottenham Hotspur substitutes: Mido, Keane, Ziegler, Cerny, Naybet

EVENT LINE

17	Davis (Foul)
22	**Reyes (Open Play)**
	HALF TIME 1 - 0
54	Edman (Foul)
68	Kanoute (Dissent)
69	**van Persie (Off) Bergkamp (On)**
70	**Fabregas (Off) Edu (On)**
70	Kanoute (Off) Mido (On)
72	Dawson (Foul)
78	Defoe (Off) Keane (On)
79	Davis (Off) Ziegler (On)
88	**Reyes (Off) Aliadiere (On)**
	FULL TIME 1 - 0

STATISTICS

Season	Fixture (Arsenal)		Fixture (Tottenham)	Season
251	1	Shots On Target	1	210
167	12	Shots Off Target	7	199
15	1	Hit Woodwork	0	10
82	4	Caught Offside	5	147
195	4	Corners	7	179
403	18	Fouls	14	418
56%	46%	Possession	54%	50%

LEAGUE STANDINGS

Position (pos before)		W	D	L	F	A	Pts
2 (2)	Arsenal	22	8	4	74	33	74
8 (8)	Tottenham H	13	9	13	42	39	48

Monday 25th April 2005 | Venue: **Highbury** | Attendance: **38,147** | Referee: **M.A.Riley**

ARSENAL 1 TOTTENHAM HOTSPUR 0

A solitary Jose Antonio Reyes strike midway through the first half was enough to settle this North London derby.

Anything other than an Arsenal victory would have seen Chelsea confirmed as Premiership champions, but the current title-holders ensured that Jose Mourinho's men would have to wait a little longer to get their hands on the glittering prize.

Tottenham were second best in the opening 45 minutes, and should have fallen behind inside 60 seconds. Incisive passing found Reyes in the inside-right channel, but he could only hit the side-netting having taken the ball around England international Paul Robinson.

Jens Lehmann made a smart save from Jermain Defoe on the one occasion that Martin Jol's men posed a genuine threat to his goal, before Reyes broke the deadlock.

The Spaniard atoned for his earlier miss with a crisp drive into the far bottom right-hand corner of the net, after Michael Dawson had played him onside from Cesc Fabregas' defence-splitting pass.

The points could have been secured before half-time, as Patrick Vieira, Robin van Persie and Fabregas all spurned chances to score. The efforts were all off target though, giving Spurs renewed hope as the second period got underway.

Having not featured much as an attacking force earlier in the game, Tottenham started to gain the upper hand. Philippe Senderos and Kolo Toure stood firm at the heart of the Arsenal defence, however, restricting their opponents to no more than hopeful attempts.

The introduction of Dennis Bergkamp and Edu saw Arsene Wenger's men rediscover their rhythm and carve out a plethora of chances. The Brazilian midfielder nonchalantly clipped an effort against the base of the left-hand upright soon after coming on.

After Reyes and Bergkamp had both gone close to capping sweeping moves, the Gunners were given a real scare. Substitute Robbie Keane ghosted between two defenders to meet a cross from the left, but could only direct his header wide of goal.

A late Spurs penalty appeal, when Ashley Cole appeared to handle the ball, then fell on deaf ears, as Arsenal secured an important win in the race for second place.

"I feel Tottenham fought in a fair way. They tried to play football as well."
Arsene Wenger

"To lose 1-0 I can live with, but on the other hand it would have been nice to have got a point."
Martin Jol

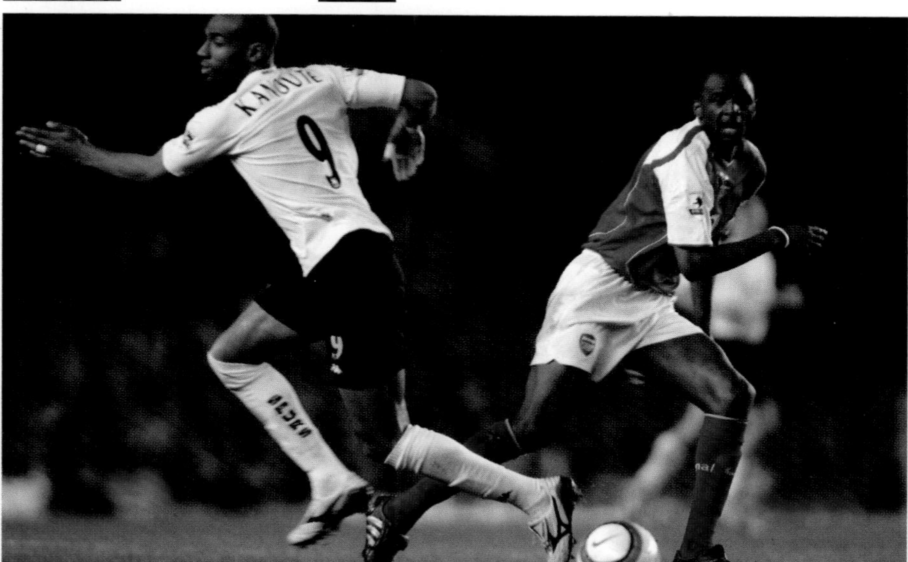

Frederic Kanoute spins away from Patrick Vieira

PREMIERSHIP FIXTURE HISTORY

Pl: 2 Draws: 1	Wins	⚽	Yellow	Red
West Bromwich Albion	0	1	4	0
Blackburn Rovers	1	3	5	0

STARTING LINE-UPS

West Brom: Hoult; Albrechtsen, Gaardsoe, Clement, Robinson; Gera, Wallwork, Richardson, Chaplow; Horsfield, Campbell (c)

Blackburn Rovers: Stead; Pedersen, Savage, Mokoena, Reid, Emerton; Matteo, Nelson, Todd (c), Neill; Friedel

Substitutes (West Brom): Scimeca, Kanu, Earnshaw, Kuszczak, Moore

Substitutes (Blackburn): Tugay, Thompson, Gallagher, Flitcroft, Enckelman

EVENT LINE

3 Yellow **Horsfield (Ung.Conduct)**
32 ⚽ **Richardson (Direct Free Kick)**
34 Yellow Matteo (Dissent)
44 Yellow **Robinson (Foul)**

HALF TIME 1 - 0

56 Sub Mokoena (Off) Tugay (On)
59 Yellow Neill (Dissent)
60 Yellow Pedersen (Foul)
61 Yellow Todd (Foul)
63 Sub **Campbell (Off) Scimeca (On)**
63 Sub **Chaplow (Off) Kanu (On)**
64 ⚽ Emerton (Open Play)
79 Sub **Horsfield (Off) Earnshaw (On)**
83 Sub Pedersen (Off) Thompson (On)
87 Sub Savage (Off) Gallagher (On)
90 Yellow **Scimeca (Foul)**

FULL TIME 1 - 1

STATISTICS

Season	Fixture	West Brom / Blackburn	Fixture	Season
168	3	Shots On Target	7	179
154	6	Shots Off Target	8	215
12	0	Hit Woodwork	1	7
124	4	Caught Offside	4	141
177	6	Corners	4	198
458	14	Fouls	16	563
48%	51%	Possession	49%	49%

LEAGUE STANDINGS

Position (pos before)	W	D	L	F	A	Pts
18 (19) West Brom	5	15	15	33	58	30
12 (12) Blackburn R	9	14	12	30	38	41

Tuesday 26th April 2005 | Venue: **The Hawthorns** | Attendance: **25,154** | Referee: **S.G.Bennett**

WEST BROM 1 BLACKBURN ROVERS 1

With games against Arsenal and Manchester United to follow, West Brom could ill afford to only draw 1-1 in this encounter.

The Baggies led at half-time thanks to a stunning Kieran Richardson free-kick, but were pegged back after the break by a well-taken goal from Australian international winger Brett Emerton.

Bryan Robson's men began the match on the front foot. Geoff Horsfield received an early booking for diving in the box, while Zoltan Gera flashed a low drive narrowly wide of Brad Friedel's right-hand post from all of 25 yards out.

Blackburn responded with a Dominic Matteo header from a left-wing throw that was just too high, before Kevin Campbell was denied a penalty when he appeared to be wrestled to the ground by visiting captain Andy Todd when trying to get on the end of an inswinging free-kick.

Having missed this obvious foul, referee Steve Bennett then harshly penalised Ryan Nelson as he challenged Horsfield on the edge of the box. The home side took full advantage of the referee's generosity, Richardson stepping up to clip the ball over the wall and into the top right-hand corner of the net after 32 minutes.

Jonathan Stead had found goals hard to come by this season, but did everything right as he came close to an equaliser. The striker pounced on a clearing header to beat Russell Hoult from 15 yards, only to see his effort rebound to safety off the inside of the keeper's left-hand post.

With that scare behind them, West Brom began the second half brightly. Neil Clement had two chances to score, heading wide from an unmarked position four yards out as the rain poured down, before testing Friedel with a stinging drive.

Then, with 64 minutes on the clock, Rovers drew level. Morten Gamst Pedersen did the hard work down the right and delivered a low cross that was missed by Stead, enabling Emerton to pass the ball into the roof of the net from 10 yards out.

Late chances then went begging at both ends, notably for Pedersen and Clement, as the game ended all square.

Zoltan Gera gets to grips with Morten Gamst Pedersen

"What we really needed was a second goal to ease our nerves, and I think that would have been decisive."
Bryan Robson

"I was very pleased with how we played in the second half, and felt that we probably deserved to win."
Mark Hughes

PREMIERSHIP FIXTURE HISTORY

Pl: **9** Draws: **2**	Wins	⚽	Yellow	Red
Newcastle United	6	15	8	0
Middlesbrough	1	6	19	2

STARTING LINE-UPS

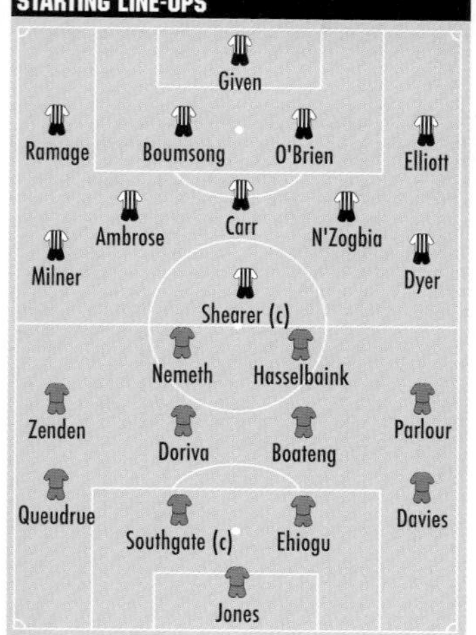

Ameobi, Harper Brittain, Robert Kluivert

Downing, Graham Knight, Reiziger Wheater

EVENT LINE

35 **Dyer (Off) Ameobi (On)**

HALF TIME 0 - 0

63 **Ambrose (Foul)**

65 Zenden (Off) Downing (On)

83 Nemeth (Off) Graham (On)

88 Hasselbaink (Foul)

90 Doriva (Foul)

FULL TIME 0 - 0

STATISTICS

Season	Fixture (Newcastle)		Fixture (Middlesbrough)	Season
237	5	Shots On Target	3	238
205	6	Shots Off Target	2	179
11	0	Hit Woodwork	0	6
85	0	Caught Offside	2	95
223	9	Corners	1	185
433	8	Fouls	7	432
51%	47%	Possession	53%	50%

LEAGUE STANDINGS

Position (pos before)		W	D	L	F	A	Pts
14 (14)	Newcastle Utd	9	12	13	43	53	39
7 (7)	Middlesbrough	13	11	11	50	44	50

Andrew Davies challenges Kieron Dyer

> **"My players gave everything, and I can't ask for any more than that."**
> Graeme Souness

> **"We gave a great disciplined performance. At the end of the season, this could be a valuable point."**
> Steve McClaren

NEWCASTLE UNITED 0 MIDDLESBROUGH 0

Newcastle and Middlesbrough drew for the second time this season, though this match was nowhere near as exciting as their clash on the opening day.

Despite being at home, Graeme Souness kept faith with the 4-5-1 formation that had troubled Manchester United for nigh on an hour at Old Trafford. Kieron Dyer came into the starting XI in place of Shola Ameobi, and lined up on the left of midfield.

Little happened in a tedious opening. Stand-in right-back Andrew Davies made a vital tackle on Dyer as he surged into the box, while Jimmy Floyd Hasselbaink failed to trouble Shay Given after being picked out by Szilard Nemeth at the other end.

A weakly-struck James Milner volley handed goalkeeper Brad Jones a rare feeling of the ball, before Dyer was eventually forced off after appearing to pull his hamstring. The former Ipswich man's replacement, Ameobi, then missed the target with a downward header from a right-wing corner.

The second 45 minutes offered more by way of clear-cut chances. Slovakian Nemeth drilled inches the wrong side of the left-hand upright from the edge of the box, after running onto Ray Parlour's dangerous low cross from the right flank.

Then, after Ameobi had again failed to test Jones from a decent position, Hasselbaink spurned a great chance to open the scoring. The former Leeds striker momentarily got in behind the defence, but could only clip a tame effort straight into the arms of a grateful Given.

Newcastle responded with two attempts of their own. Charles N'Zogbia found the side-netting with a shot from a left-wing corner, before Jones made a fantastic reaction stop to keep out Milner's sweetly-struck 15-yard half-volley.

A clash of heads between Shearer and Gareth Southgate resulted in the Middlesbrough man having to be bandaged up, and he was powerless to prevent what should have been a last-gasp winner.

The Magpies' No.9 burst down the right and delivered a low near-post cross, with N'Zogbia somehow managing to blaze the ball over the bar from no more than four yards out.

Saturday 30th April 2005	Venue: St Andrew's	Attendance: 28,621	Referee: B.Knight

PREMIERSHIP FIXTURE HISTORY

Pl: 3 Draws: 0	Wins	⚽	Yellow	Red
Birmingham City	1	2	3	1
Blackburn Rovers	2	6	4	0

STARTING LINE-UPS

Birmingham City: Maik Taylor; Melchiot, Cunningham (c), Upson, Lazaridis; Pennant, Johnson, Nafti, Anderton; Heskey, Pandiani

Blackburn Rovers: Stead; Pedersen, Reid, Mokoena, Flitcroft, Emerton; Johansson, Nelson, Todd (c), Neill; Friedel

Subs: Clemence, Blake, Morrison, Vaesen, Martin Taylor

Subs: Thompson, Tugay, Gallagher, Short, Enckelman

EVENT LINE

13 ⚽ Stead (Open Play)

22 **Anderton (Off) Clemence (On)**

44 Mokoena (Foul)

HALF TIME 0 - 1

59 **Nafti (Off) Blake (On)**

59 Pedersen (Off) Thompson (On)

61 ⚽ **Blake (Open Play)**

67 Johansson (Off) Tugay (On)

76 **Heskey (Dissent)**

76 Emerton (Off) Gallagher (On)

80 ⚽ **Heskey (Open Play)**

84 **Pandiani (Off) Morrison (On)**

90 **Morrison (Ung.Conduct)**

FULL TIME 2 - 1

STATISTICS

Season	Fixture		Fixture	Season
154	6	Shots On Target	1	180
159	4	Shots Off Target	4	219
9	1	Hit Woodwork	0	7
95	1	Caught Offside	2	143
182	6	Corners	1	199
503	15	Fouls	16	579
50%	57%	Possession	43%	49%

LEAGUE STANDINGS

Position (pos before)	W	D	L	F	A	Pts
12 (13) Birmingham C	10	12	14	38	44	42
13 (12) Blackburn R	9	14	13	31	40	41

Mehdi Nafti battles with Steven Reid

"Emile Heskey has had his critics, but he has done fantastically well for us."
Steve Bruce

"Once Birmingham equalised, it was difficult for us to get back into the game."
Mark Hughes

PREMIERSHIP MILESTONE

100 Damien Johnson made his 100th Premiership appearance in the colours of Birmingham.

BIRMINGHAM CITY 2 BLACKBURN ROVERS 1

Former Burnley man Robbie Blake came off the bench to help turn a one-goal deficit into a 2-1 Birmingham victory against Blackburn at St Andrew's.

The visitors had taken a 13th-minute lead, courtesy of Jonathan Stead's second goal of the season, but were pegged back by Blake just past the hour mark. Then, with 10 minutes remaining, Emile Heskey drove home the winning goal.

Team news centred around the non-inclusion of Robbie Savage in the Rovers side. An agreement between the clubs meant that the Welsh midfielder was precluded from taking part in the game, much to the displeasure of Mark Hughes.

Roared on by the home faithful, it was Steve Bruce's men that were in the ascendancy early on. Uruguayan striker Walter Pandiani hit a post and went close with a header, before Blackburn stole in front.

Former Huddersfield forward Stead started and finished the move, finding Brett Emerton on the right wing and continuing his run into the box. Having beaten his international colleague Stan Lazaridis, Emerton sent over an inviting cross that was nodded home from eight yards out.

Another opportunity for Pandiani apart, the West Midlands side rarely threatened Brad Friedel's goal during the remainder of the first half. Things continued in a similar vain after the break, prompting the Birmingham boss into action.

Just under an hour of the contest had elapsed when Bruce took the positive step of bringing on the attack-minded Blake in place of Tunisian midfielder Mehdi Nafti. The change brought an almost instant reward, as the substitute pounced on a loose ball to slot home past the keeper.

Blackburn were unable to respond to the equaliser, and fell behind 10 minutes from time.

A scrappy passage of midfield play ended with the ball landing at the feet of Heskey, with the striker demonstrating why he had recently won a recall to the England squad by firing low past Friedel from 20 yards out with his unfavoured left foot.

At the final whistle, both sets of fans were left to ponder how things might have been different if Savage had been allowed to play.

PREMIERSHIP FIXTURE HISTORY

Pl: 6 Draws: 2	Wins	Goals	Yellow	Red
Bolton Wanderers	2	6	10	0
Chelsea	2	8	8	1

STARTING LINE-UPS

Bolton Wanderers: Jaaskelainen; Candela, Ben Haim, N'Gotty, Gardner; Okocha (c), Hierro, Speed; Giannakopoulos, Davies, Diouf

Chelsea: Cech; Gallas, Terry (c), Carvalho, Geremi; Makelele; Jarosik, Lampard, Tiago; Gudjohnsen, Drogba

Bolton Wanderers subs: Nolan, Pedersen, Jaidi, Poole, Fadiga

Chelsea subs: Huth, J.Cole, Smertin, Cudicini, Kezman

EVENT LINE

Min	Event
5	Makelele (Ung.Conduct)
	HALF TIME 0 - 0
51	**Candela (Foul)**
58	**Diouf (Foul)**
60	Lampard (Open Play)
60	**Jaaskelainen (Dissent)**
63	**Giannakopoulos (Off) Pedersen (On)**
63	**Okocha (Off) Nolan (On)**
65	Drogba (Off) Huth (On)
76	Lampard (Open Play)
77	**Candela (Off) Jaidi (On)**
85	Gudjohnsen (Off) Cole J (On)
89	**Nolan (Ung.Conduct)**
90	Makelele (Off) Smertin (On)
	FULL TIME 0 - 2

STATISTICS

Season	Fixture (Bolton)		Fixture (Chelsea)	Season
234	**5**	Shots On Target	**5**	**268**
209	**8**	Shots Off Target	**3**	**226**
8	**0**	Hit Woodwork	**0**	**10**
100	**3**	Caught Offside	**3**	**117**
193	**7**	Corners	**2**	**228**
490	**17**	Fouls	**14**	**435**
50%	**55%**	Possession	**45%**	**56%**

LEAGUE STANDINGS

Position (pos before)		W	D	L	F	A	Pts
6 (6)	**Bolton W**	**15**	**9**	**12**	**45**	**41**	**54**
1 (1)	**Chelsea**	**27**	**7**	**1**	**67**	**13**	**88**

Saturday 30th April 2005 | Venue: **Reebok Stadium** | Attendance: **27,653** | Referee: **S.W.Dunn**

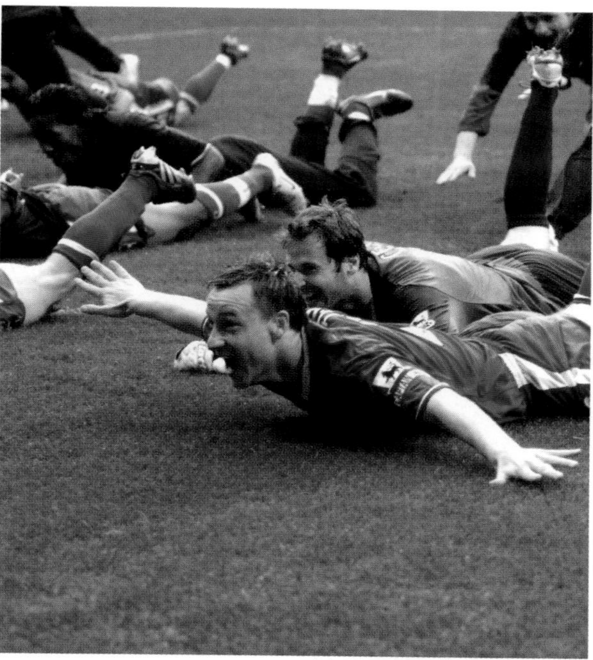

John Terry leads the title celebrations

"Two things cost us victory today, our finishing in the first half and the referee."

Sam Allardyce

"Nobody speaking with fairness and sense can say we don't deserve this title. I'm very happy for the fans, but the players deserve this more than anybody."

Jose Mourinho

PREMIERSHIP MILESTONE

450 Gary Speed made his 450th Premiership appearance.

BOLTON WANDERERS 0 CHELSEA 2

Two Frank Lampard goals secured victory at Bolton and ensured that Chelsea finally ended their 50-year wait for the league title.

Jose Mourinho's men had looked certain to finish the season on top for many months, with this 2-0 win at the Reebok Stadium officially confirming the Londoners as Premiership champions.

Cameroonian international Geremi was a surprise inclusion at right-back for the team from Stamford Bridge, while Joe Cole had to be content with a place on the bench as he was given a rest ahead of the crucial 'Champions League' clash with Liverpool in midweek.

With the prospect of European football in Bolton next season growing increasingly likely, Sam Allardyce's charges made a positive start. Stylianos Giannakopoulos could only direct an effort straight at Petr Cech following a long throw, with Gary Speed then testing the keeper with a firm header.

Burly striker Kevin Davies should have done better with a free header from seven yards out midway through the opening period, as Chelsea looked anything but potential title-winners.

Speculative long-range strikes had been the order of the day for Mourinho's men during the opening 45 minutes, but the manager's half-time words of wisdom seemed to have the desired affect.

With an hour played, talismanic midfielder Frank Lampard drilled his team into the lead. The former West Ham man had much to do when running onto Didier Drogba's flick, but outmuscled Vincent Candela to cut in from the left and beat Jussi Jaaskelainen from 12 yards out.

Custodian Cech then demonstrated why he has won rave reviews this season, leaping to his right to somehow keep out Geremi's misplaced near-post header from a long throw by Speed.

The save proved vital, as Lampard soon netted the goal that confirmed a first league title since 1955. Claude Makelele picked out his team-mate on halfway as Chelsea broke forward from a Bolton corner, with the midfielder surging upfield to take the ball around the keeper before slotting home.

The final whistle brought jubilant scenes both on the pitch and in the stands, with Roman Abramovich joining the players in their celebrations.

PREMIERSHIP FIXTURE HISTORY

Pl: 4 Draws: 0	Wins	Goals	Yellow cards	Red cards
Fulham	4	8	4	2
Everton	0	1	7	1

STARTING LINE-UPS

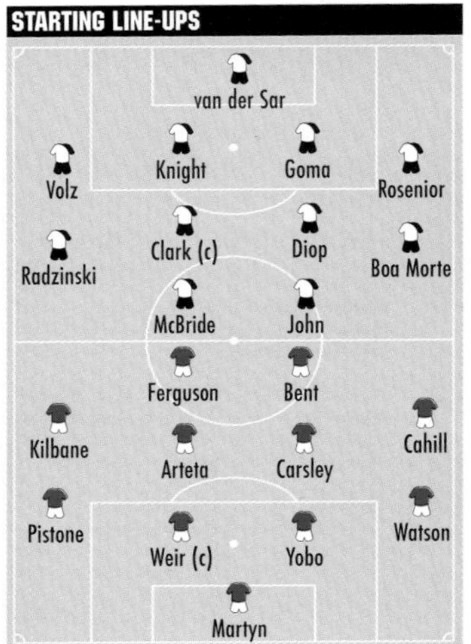

Fulham substitutes: Cole, Jensen, Crossley, Bocanegra, Pembridge

Everton substitutes: Osman, McFadden, Beattie, Wright, Plessis

EVENT LINE

11 Yellow card: Pistone (Ung.Conduct)

13 Substitution: Cahill (Off) Osman (On)

15 Goal: **John (Open Play)**

39 Goal: **McBride (Open Play)**

HALF TIME 2 - 0

61 Substitution: **John (Off) Cole (On)**

63 Substitution: **Radzinski (Off) Jensen (On)**

64 Yellow card: Arteta (Foul)

64 Substitution: Arteta (Off) McFadden (On)

64 Substitution: Bent (Off) Beattie (On)

76 Red card: **Diop (2nd Bookable Offence)**

79 Yellow card: McFadden (Dissent)

FULL TIME 2 - 0

STATISTICS

Season	Fixture (Fulham)		Fixture (Everton)	Season
165	6	Shots On Target	4	165
157	5	Shots Off Target	7	186
6	0	Hit Woodwork	0	6
90	2	Caught Offside	9	91
171	3	Corners	7	172
434	18	Fouls	16	434
48%	52%	Possession	48%	49%

LEAGUE STANDINGS

Position (pos before)	W	D	L	F	A	Pts
15 (16) Fulham	10	8	17	42	56	38
4 (4) Everton	17	7	11	41	36	58

Saturday 30th April 2005 | Venue: **Craven Cottage** | Attendance: **21,881** | Referee: **S.G.Bennett**

FULHAM 2 EVERTON 0

Tim Cahill produces an uncompromising challenge

"This season we have been too inconsistent, and today we showed exactly what we are capable of."

Chris Coleman

PREMIERSHIP MILESTONE

100 Alessandro Pistone made his 100th Premiership appearance for Everton.

"We have put in a lot of good performances, but we didn't play well today."

David Moyes

First half goals from Collins John and Brian McBride saw off the challenge of Everton, and confirmed that Fulham would be playing Premiership football again next season.

David Moyes' men almost got off to a dream start, when Kevin Kilbane thought he had opened the scoring. The Republic of Ireland international was correctly ruled offside, however, as he touched home David Weir's header from a free-kick.

Star midfielder Tim Cahill then limped off after 13 minutes, with the Cottagers taking the lead shortly afterwards. Former Toffee Tomasz Radzinski saw his shot charged down, but John reacted quickly to lash the ball home from near the penalty spot.

The game was very open, with both sides continuing to create chances. Goalscorer John dragged a low effort past the left-hand upright, before Marcus Bent whipped in a dangerous angled drive from the right side of the area at the other end.

The next goal was going to prove vital, and it went to Chris Coleman's team. Luis Boa Morte seemed to take an eternity before delivering from the left, but his patience was rewarded as McBride rose to plant a towering 14-yard header beyond the reach of Nigel Martyn after 39 minutes.

There was still time for Edwin van der Sar to foil a clearly-offside Bent with his legs before half-time, with Lee Carsley then shanking wide a 12-yard volley from an unmarked position during the early stages of the second period.

Pape Bouba Diop was booked for a lunging challenge on Leon Osman after 68 minutes, and was then harshly shown a second yellow card by referee Steve Bennett for minimal contact with Everton substitute James McFadden.

Another replacement, James Beattie, went close with a free-kick in the final minute, but 10-man Fulham held on to record an important victory.

With other results going their way, the Merseysiders remained on course for 'Champions League' football next season. The Goodison Park side have struggled during the latter half of the campaign, but will be difficult to catch at this late stage.

PREMIERSHIP FIXTURE HISTORY

Pl: 10 Draws: 4	Wins	Goals	Yellow	Red
Liverpool	6	19	7	1
Middlesbrough	0	5	16	0

STARTING LINE-UPS

Liverpool: Dudek; Finnan, Carragher, Pellegrino, Warnock; Nunez, Gerrard (c), Alonso, Riise; Kewell, Morientes

Middlesbrough: Jones; Queudrue, Southgate (c), Ehiogu, Davies; Zenden, Doriva, Boateng, Parlour; Hasselbaink, Nemeth

Liverpool subs: Garcia, Cisse, Hamann, Carson, Hyypia

Middlesbrough subs: Downing, Parnaby, Knight, Reiziger, Morrison

EVENT LINE

4 Goal: Nemeth (Open Play)
28 Yellow card: **Nunez (Ung.Conduct)**
HALF TIME 0 - 1
46 Substitution: **Pellegrino (Off) Garcia (On)**
52 Goal: **Gerrard (Open Play)**
58 Yellow card: Doriva (Foul)
62 Substitution: Nemeth (Off) Downing (On)
72 Yellow card: Parlour (Foul)
73 Substitution: **Nunez (Off) Cisse (On)**
74 Yellow card: **Garcia (Foul)**
78 Substitution: Parlour (Off) Parnaby (On)
82 Yellow card: Zenden (Foul)
84 Substitution: **Warnock (Off) Hamann (On)**
FULL TIME 1 - 1

STATISTICS

Season	Fixture	Liverpool / Middlesbrough	Fixture	Season
226	6	Shots On Target	3	241
234	6	Shots Off Target	3	182
7	0	Hit Woodwork	0	6
100	2	Caught Offside	3	98
204	7	Corners	4	189
418	10	Fouls	20	452
53%	58%	Possession	42%	49%

LEAGUE STANDINGS

Position (pos before)		W	D	L	F	A	Pts
5 (5)	Liverpool	16	7	13	49	37	55
7 (7)	Middlesbrough	13	12	11	51	45	51

Saturday 30th April 2005 | Venue: **Anfield** | Attendance: **43,250** | Referee: **P.Dowd**

LIVERPOOL 1 MIDDLESBROUGH 1

A wonder-goal from captain Steven Gerrard was only good enough to earn his side a point, as Liverpool prepared for their 'Champions League' semi-final in disappointing fashion.

Middlesbrough made a brilliant start to the match, with Slovakian international Szilard Nemeth opening the scoring after just four minutes. The striker latched onto Jimmy Floyd Hasselbaink's chested pass, and beat Jerzy Dudek with a composed left-footed finish from just outside the area.

John Arne Riise then set about a single-handed quest to level the scores. The Norwegian international glanced over an Antonio Nunez cross, before testing Brad Jones with a longe-range volley and then sending a similar effort just wide.

A deflected drive from Doriva flew over the Liverpool crossbar, with Mauricio Pellegrino somewhat lucky to avoid turning the ball into his own net from the resulting corner. The former Valencia defender made way for Luis Garcia at the interval, in what was a bold statement of intent by Rafael Benitez.

The switch almost paid off immediately, as the diminutive Spaniard climbed highest to meet Steve Finnan's right-wing cross with a firm header. Unfortunately for the Anfield faithful, Jones was able to make a fine reaction save.

Moments later, however, 'The Kop' was in full voice. A clipped pass found Gerrard in space on the right, and he wasted little time in unleashing a 30-yard thunderbolt that flew into the top left-hand corner of the net.

Harry Kewell, starting a match for the first time since the Carling Cup final, then got the better of Andrew Davies and tested the keeper with a near-post drive, as the pressure increased on the visitors.

Steve McClaren's men stood firm though, with the bandaged-up Gareth Southgate leading by example at the heart of their defence. Both Fernando Morientes and Garcia spurned half-chances, as hopes of a home victory ebbed away.

The final whistle saw an unusually angry reaction from Benitez. The Liverpool boss was clearly unhappy about the lack of time added on at the end of the game, and forcibly made his point to referee Phil Dowd.

John Arne Riise attempts to shrug off Andrew Davies

"There are lots of things which were not good. We have one more point, but one less game."
Rafael Benitez

"I thought we were fantastic in the first half, and it was our best display since we've been coming to Anfield."
Steve McClaren

PREMIERSHIP MILESTONE
250 Jamie Carragher made his 250th Premiership appearance.

PREMIERSHIP MILESTONE
400 Gareth Southgate made his 400th Premiership appearance

PREMIERSHIP MILESTONE
50 Doriva made his 50th Premiership appearance

Saturday 30th April 2005	Venue: City of Manchester Stadium	Attendance: 46,454	Referee: A.Marriner

MANCHESTER CITY 2 PORTSMOUTH 0

Manchester City kept alive their slim hopes of qualifying for the UEFA Cup, beating Portsmouth 2-0 thanks to a couple of early goals.

Captain Sylvain Distin got the ball rolling with a fourth-minute header, with Robbie Fowler sealing the victory by curling home a free-kick shortly after the quarter-hour mark.

The win stretched the home side's unbeaten run to six matches, further strengthening Stuart Pearce's bid to be handed the managerial reigns on a permanent basis. The former Nottingham Forest defender is clearly getting the best out of his players, and could count himself very unlucky if he did not land the job.

The opening goal was a fairly scrappy affair, as Distin looped a six-yard header over Matthew Taylor on the line. Jamie Ashdown had failed to reach Fowler's right-wing corner ahead of Richard Dunne, providing City's French skipper with the chance to make a rare appearance on the scoresheet.

It was 2-0 after 16 minutes, as Fowler found the bottom left-hand corner of the net with a 25-yard free-kick from the inside-right channel. Portsmouth had every reason to feel aggrieved about the award of the set-piece though, with Richard Hughes being harshly penalised for a fair tackle on Shaun Wright-Phillips.

Surprise inclusion Aleksandar Rodic was thwarted by a combination of Dunne and David James in the visitors' most dangerous attack of the opening period, and came even closer early in the second half when denied by Ben Thatcher at point-blank range.

A well-struck Gary O'Neil free-kick tested the Manchester City keeper as Alain Perrin's men bravely attempted to establish a foothold in the match, while Antoine Sibierski could have made it three with a late header that he directed straight at Ashdown.

Despite enjoying a fairly comfortable victory, Pearce's afternoon wasn't entirely without incident. Both Perrin and his first team coach Joe Jordan were angered when the former England international prevented Taylor from taking a throw from what he felt was the wrong position.

An interval apology was accepted by the Portsmouth staff, as Pearce learnt that management is not all about what happens on the pitch.

Shaun Wright-Phillips tries to outwit Matthew Taylor

"Why not put pressure on ourselves by striving to qualify for Europe?"
Stuart Pearce

"We didn't show enough concentration at the start of the game. I was disappointed to concede two goals from set-pieces."
Alain Perrin

PREMIERSHIP FIXTURE HISTORY

Pl: 2 Draws: 1	Wins	⚽	☐	■
Manchester City	1	3	2	0
Portsmouth	0	1	4	0

STARTING LINE-UPS

Thatcher, Croft, Mills, Weaver, B.Wright-Phillips

Fuller, Mezague, Hislop, Stone, Skopelitis

EVENT LINE

4 ⚽ **Distin (Corner)**
11 ☐ O'Neil (Foul)
16 ⚽ **Fowler (Direct Free Kick)**
HALF TIME 2 - 0
46 **Jordan (Off) Thatcher (On)**
66 Rodic (Off) Fuller (On)
68 **Fowler (Off) Croft (On)**
85 Cisse (Off) Mezague (On)
87 **Musampa (Off) Mills (On)**
FULL TIME 2 - 0

STATISTICS

Season	Fixture		Fixture	Season
190	7	Shots On Target	3	182
185	6	Shots Off Target	4	176
3	0	Hit Woodwork	0	7
111	2	Caught Offside	5	108
222	7	Corners	5	179
457	15	Fouls	6	429
49%	56%	Possession	44%	47%

LEAGUE STANDINGS

Position (pos before)	W	D	L	F	A	Pts
8 (10) Man City	12	12	12	44	37	48
16 (15) Portsmouth	10	8	18	42	56	38

PREMIERSHIP FIXTURE HISTORY

Pl: 3 Draws: 1	Wins	⚽	▢	■
Newcastle United	1	4	6	0
Crystal Palace	1	4	7	0

STARTING LINE-UPS

Ramage, Robert
Kluivert, Harper
O'Brien

Torghelle, Speroni
Watson, Lakis
Ventola

EVENT LINE

9 ▢ Popovic (Foul)

HALF TIME 0 - 0

46 **Elliott (Off) Ramage (On)**

69 **Ambrose (Off) Kluivert (On)**

69 **Ameobi (Off) Robert (On)**

83 ▢ **N'Zogbia (Foul)**

90 ▢ Leigertwood (Foul)

90 Routledge (Off) Torghelle (On)

FULL TIME 0 - 0

STATISTICS

Season	Fixture		Fixture	Season
246	**9**	Shots On Target	**4**	**162**
212	**7**	Shots Off Target	**4**	**153**
11	**0**	Hit Woodwork	**0**	**7**
90	**5**	Caught Offside	**2**	**82**
228	**5**	Corners	**2**	**177**
450	**17**	Fouls	**16**	**508**
51%	**55%**	Possession	**45%**	**46%**

LEAGUE STANDINGS

Position (pos before)	W	D	L	F	A	Pts
14 (14) Newcastle Utd	**9**	**13**	**13**	**43**	**53**	**40**
18 (17) Crystal Palace	**7**	**10**	**19**	**37**	**58**	**31**

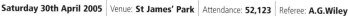

Saturday 30th April 2005 | Venue: **St James' Park** | Attendance: **52,123** | Referee: **A.G.Wiley**

Michael Hughes chases Charles N'Zogbia

"We're disappointed with the result. We had a lot of chances, but not the quality in the final third."

Assistant Manager Alan Murray

"We did not get our passing game going, but we gave a gritty display."

Iain Dowie

PREMIERSHIP MILESTONE

250 Shay Given made his 250th Premiership appearance for Newcastle.

NEWCASTLE UNITED 0 CRYSTAL PALACE 0

Newcastle extended their winless Premiership run to seven matches, as Crystal Palace picked up a valuable point at St James' Park.

The Eagles nearly had their wings clipped after just three minutes, as Gabor Kiraly had to be at his best to deny Alan Shearer. The home favourite got across the front of his marker to meet Stephen Carr's cross with a low six-yard shot, but the keeper kept the ball out with his legs.

Graeme Souness' side continued to look threatening. Again Shearer tested Kiraly, this time from James Milner's left-wing cross, before Charles N'Zogbia completely lost his composure when blazing a half-volley wide from a decent position.

Iain Dowie's men survived a half-hearted penalty appeal as Gonzalo Sorondo got the better of Milner, with play quickly switching to the other end as a marginally-offside Tom Soares missed his kick from Michael Hughes' clipped left-wing cross.

Newcastle began the second period as they had the first. A deep corner from the left was dropped by Kiraly, and Darren Ambrose rifled a volley wide of the right-hand upright in the ensuing scramble.

Still the chances continued to fall. Jean-Alain Boumsong was just wide with a downward header, while Milner saw an aerial effort of his own hooked to safety by a combination of Sorondo and Tony Popovic on the line.

The deadlock appeared to have been broken when Steven Taylor ghosted in at the back post to turn home substitute Laurent Robert's inviting free-kick from the left. Unfortunately for the Magpies, referee Alan Wiley was not ready for the set-piece to be taken.

Another replacement, Patrick Kluivert, then saw a goal harshly ruled out for offside, as events seemed to conspire against the men in black and white.

Having somehow kept their hosts at bay, Crystal Palace almost snatched all three points. Andy Johnson showed why he had been nominated for the PFA 'Player of the Year' award, embarking on a solo run from halfway that almost ended in a brilliant goal.

PREMIERSHIP FIXTURE HISTORY

Pl: 4 Draws: 1	Wins	Goals	Yellow cards	Red cards
Southampton	2	8	5	1
Norwich City	1	5	9	0

STARTING LINE-UPS

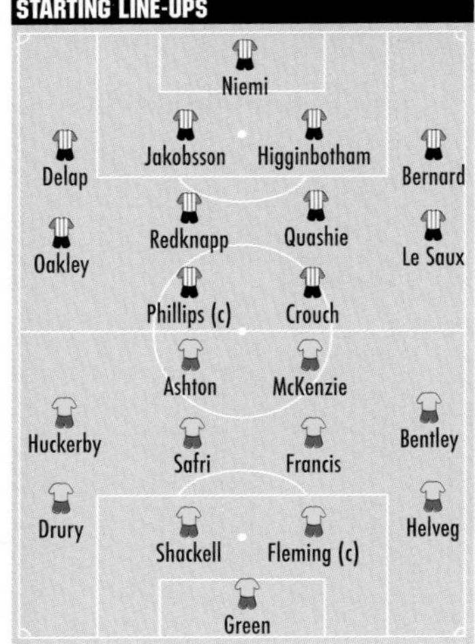

Southampton subs: Lundekvam, Telfer, Camara, Smith, Ormerod
Norwich City subs: Charlton, Svensson, Ward, Holt, Jonson

EVENT LINE

3 ⚽ Bentley (Open Play)
7 ⚽ **Oakley (Open Play)**
20 ⚽ **Crouch (Open Play)**
25 ▢ Fleming (Foul)
31 ⚽ Higginbotham (Own Goal)
39 ⚽ **Le Saux (Indirect Free Kick)**
45 ⚽ McKenzie (Open Play)

HALF TIME 3 - 3

46 ⇄ **Delap (Off) Telfer (On)**
46 ⇄ **Jakobsson (Off) Lundekvam (On)**
54 ▢ Helveg (Foul)
69 ⇄ Huckerby (Off) Charlton (On)
72 ▢ **Le Saux (Foul)**
73 ⇄ **Le Saux (Off) Camara (On)**
76 ▢ **Bernard (Foul)**
82 ⇄ Ashton (Off) Svensson (On)
88 ⚽ **Camara (Open Play)**
88 ▢ **Camara (Ung.Conduct)**

FULL TIME 4 - 3

STATISTICS

Season	Fixture (Southampton)		Fixture (Norwich City)	Season
178	9	Shots On Target	7	173
193	7	Shots Off Target	7	181
3	0	Hit Woodwork	1	6
105	1	Caught Offside	5	119
171	6	Corners	8	174
463	18	Fouls	14	488
47%	55%	Possession	45%	45%

LEAGUE STANDINGS

Position (pos before)	W	D	L	F	A	Pts
17 (20) Southampton	6	13	17	42	62	31
20 (19) Norwich C	6	12	18	41	71	30

Saturday 30th April 2005 | Venue: **Friends Provident St Mary's Stadium** | Attendance: **31,944** | Referee: **G.Poll**

SOUTHAMPTON 4 NORWICH CITY 3

An incredible game at St Mary's saw Southampton edge out Norwich in a seven-goal thriller that could have a massive bearing on who remains in the top-flight.

Leon McKenzie had already caused two scares when he teed up David Bentley for the visitors' third-minute opener. The striker shrugged off his marker and put in a deep looping cross, with Bentley arriving at the back post to steer home a volley.

If the majority of those inside the stadium feared the worst, they were wrong. Just four minutes later, Matthew Oakley ran onto Nigel Quashie's perfectly-weighted pass and drove a low effort across Robert Green and just inside the left-hand post.

Dean Ashton struck an upright and Jamie Redknapp went close with a free-kick, before Harry Redknapp's men went in front midway through the half. Rory Delap delivered an inviting centre from the right, and Peter Crouch stole in to stroke home a volley from 10 yards out.

Still there was no let up to the action. After Green had parried from goalscorer Crouch, Danny Higginbotham stuck out a right leg to turn Darren Huckerby's low cross agonisingly beyond his helpless keeper.

Antti Niemi was able to keep out good efforts from both Huckerby and Bentley, with Graeme Le Saux taking advantage of these reprieves in the 39th minute. A free-kick from deep was nodded down by Crouch and touched back by Quashie, enabling the left-sided player to volley into the bottom right-hand corner of the net from just inside the area.

That was not the end of the first half scoring, however, as McKenzie grabbed a deserved goal. The striker had just been penalised for a foul when hitting the woodwork, and got on the end of Ashton's flick to steer the ball past an onrushing custodian.

The second period was no less exciting, though it lacked the drama of six goals. Norwich had the better chances, with Niemi making world-class saves to keep out Simon Charlton and McKenzie.

The stops were to prove vital, as Henri Camara emerged from the bench to crack home a low 25-yard winner in the 88th minute.

Adam Drury beats Peter Crouch to the ball

"I thought we played some really good football for our goals, but we had a problem every time they came forward."

Harry Redknapp

"I thought it was going to finish 10-10 judging by the first half, but I can't fault my players."

Nigel Worthington

PREMIERSHIP MILESTONE

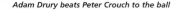

Graeme Le Saux scored his first Premiership goal for Southampton

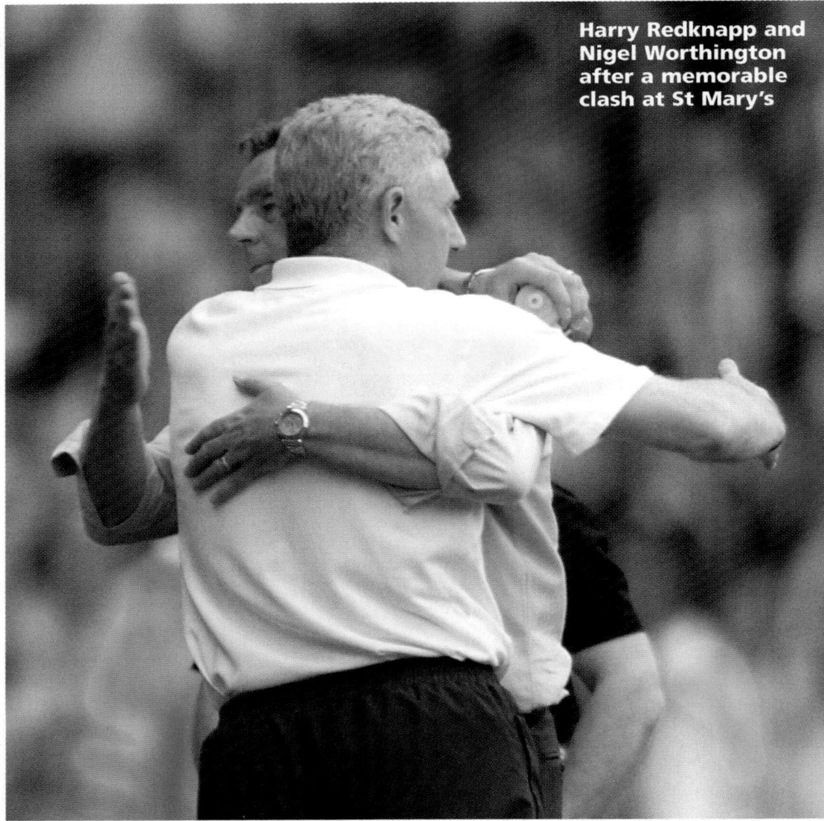

Harry Redknapp and Nigel Worthington after a memorable clash at St Mary's

APRIL 2005

Chelsea secured their first title of the Premiership era, winning 2-0 at Bolton on the final day of the month to end a 50-year wait for league success. Talismanic midfielder Frank Lampard netted both goals, as Jose Mourinho's men registered a 24th top-flight clean sheet.

The men from West London also made progress on the European stage, edging out Bayern Munich 6-5 on aggregate in a thrilling tie. The victory set up a showdown with Liverpool, as Rafael Benitez's men deservedly saw off the challenge of Juventus. After a goalless first leg at Stamford Bridge, the outcome of this all-English affair remains in the balance.

In the F.A.Cup, Arsenal and Manchester United set up a dream final. Both sides ran out comfortable winners in their semi-final encounters, the Gunners beating Blackburn 3-0 and Sir Alex Ferguson's charges defeating Newcastle 4-1.

That defeat capped a miserable week for the Magpies, who crashed out of the UEFA Cup at the hands of Middlesbrough's conquerors, Sporting Lisbon. With Lee Bowyer and Kieron Dyer having been dismissed for fighting each other against Aston Villa earlier in the month, it was not a great time to be Graeme Souness.

A major story during April was the form of Norwich City. Seven points adrift of safety at the end of March, the Canaries moved to within touching distance of salvation thanks to a return of 10 points from six games.

Frenchman Alain Perrin was handed the task of taking Portsmouth forward, and the former Troyes boss made an encouraging start. An alarming slump in form had forced chairman Milan Mandaric into making an appointment earlier than he had planned.

With the campaign drawing to a close, Charlton once again seemed to press the self-destruct button. Two points from five games did little for the Addicks' league position, as they endured yet another end-of-season blip.

IN THE NEWS

02ND Lee Bowyer and Kieron Dyer are sent off for fighting each other during Newcastle's 3-0 home reverse at the hands of Aston Villa. Defender Steven Taylor is also dismissed for deliberate handball, though is unlucky not to win an oscar for his attempts to convince referee Barry Knight that the ball struck him in the stomach.

07TH Former Marseille boss Alain Perrin is appointed as Portsmouth's new manager. The Frenchman will be able to call upon the experience of David Pleat until the end of the current campaign.

08TH Referee Mike Dean is formally suspended until 31 May following an investigation into his involvement with a betting website.

10TH England international Michael Owen is on target in Real Madrid's 4-2 win against arch-rivals Barcelona in Spain's 'La Liga'.

13TH Liverpool secure a 0-0 draw with Juventus in Turin, a result that sets up an intriguing 'Champions League' semi-final against Chelsea.

24TH London's 'Grosvenor House' hotel plays host to a prestigious awards ceremony that sees Chelsea captain John Terry named 'PFA Player of the Year'.

30TH A 2-0 win at Bolton sees Chelsea confirmed as Premiership champions. Frank Lampard nets both the goals, as Jose Mourinho guides the club to a first league title in 50 years.

TEAM OF THE MONTH

Brad Jones
Middlesbrough

Having made just one Premiership appearance in his fledgling career, Jones found himself thrust into action as a result of an injury to regular custodian Mark Schwarzer. The youngster excelled himself, producing countless memorable saves as he was beaten just three times in five games.

Nedum Onuoha
Manchester City

Given his chance at the expense of Danny Mills, the young defender took to the role of right-back like a duck to water. Part of a Manchester City side that kept four clean sheets during the month, Onuoha won plenty of admirers.

Richard Dunne
Manchester City

As well as helping his team to four clean sheets and an unbeaten month, the Irish international also found time to net one goal and set up two more. Having been in fine form all season, the defender was rewarded with a new two-year contract.

Gareth Southgate
Middlesbrough

Whether partnering Chris Riggott or the returning Ugo Ehiogu, Southgate was always in control of Middlesbrough's defensive unit. The captain led his team to three clean sheets in six games, and demonstrated his commitment to the cause by playing on with a bandaged head at Newcastle.

Dominic Matteo
Blackburn Rovers

Though not the most eye-catching of players, Matteo has been a consistent performer throughout his career. This was highlighted during April, as Blackburn conceded just once during the five league matches in which he played.

PLAYER OF THE MONTH

Frank Lampard
Chelsea

In addition to the high standard of his performances, Lampard scored some more vital goals for his club. Four Premiership strikes, including the two that clinched the title at Bolton, were added to by three more in the 'Champions League' success against Bayern Munich.

"Frank is fast becoming one of the world's top midfielders. He has become Chelsea's top scorer, no mean feat for a midfielder in the Barclays Premiership."

Barclays Awards Panel

MANAGER OF THE MONTH

Stuart Pearce
Manchester City

Under pressure to prove his management credentials, Pearce led Manchester City to an unbeaten month. Three home victories were consolidated upon by three away draws, as a team with renewed confidence climbed four places up the table and into contention for a UEFA Cup place.

Premiership Career Statistics
up until end of April 2005
Matches:**27** Wins:**8** Draws:**12** Losses:**7**

"Stuart Pearce's passion for the game is there for all to see, and with 12 points from six games, it looks like his positive approach has had an immediate effect on the City players."

Barclays Awards Panel

Eidur Gudjohnsen
Chelsea

Operating in a deeper midfield role as the season reached a crucial stage, Gudjohnsen excelled both domestically and in Europe. The Icelandic international found more freedom in which to express himself, and still managed to find the net on three occasions.

Gilberto
Arsenal

Arsenal are not the same team without Gilberto, and he showed exactly why during April. Returning from a lengthy absence through injury, the Brazilian midfielder helped his team keep three clean sheets in four league games, as well as playing an important role in the Gunners' F.A.Cup semi-final success.

Luis Boa Morte
Fulham

A frustrating player at times, Boa Morte showed just what he is capable of when he plays to his potential. Three goals and three assists were testament to the positive impact that the Portuguese winger had on Fulham's fixtures during the month.

Lomana Tresor Lua Lua
Portsmouth

A match-winning performance against bitter rivals Southampton elevated Lua Lua to cult status at Fratton Park, but that was just one of several fine displays. Over the course of the month, the former Newcastle forward netted four times and registered two assists.

Dean Ashton
Norwich City

Striking up an almost telepathic understanding with fellow forward Leon McKenzie, Ashton scored four goals and collected two assists during the month. The former Crewe man grabbed a late winner against Newcastle, and helped re-ignite his team's survival hopes.

MONTH IN NUMBERS

55 Games Played

131 Total Goals Scored

2.38 Average Goals Per Game

4 Player With Most Goals (Ashton, Lua Lua, Lampard)

1 Hat-tricks (Henry)

12 Club With Most Goals (Norwich City)

3 Fastest Goal (Yakubu, Bentley)

47.3% Percentage Of Home Wins

14.5% Percentage Of Away Wins

38.2% Percentage Of Draws

4-0 Biggest Win (Middlesbrough 4 v 0 West Bromwich Albion, Everton 4 v 0 Crystal Palace)

158 Total Yellow Cards

9 Total Red Cards

2.9 Average Yellow Cards Per Game

16 Most Disciplinary Points (Neville G 1Y1R)

2 Fastest Booking (Lauren)

33,718 Average Attendance

PREMIERSHIP TABLE / TEAM STATISTICS

Pos	(last month)	Team	Played	Won	Drawn	Lost	Goals for	Goals against	Goal diff	Points	Shots on target	Hit woodwork	Shots off target	Failed to score	Clean sheets	Corners	Caught Offside	Players used
1	- (1)	Chelsea	35	27	7	1	67	13	+54	88	268	10	226	5	24	228	117	23
2	▲ (3)	Arsenal	34	22	8	4	74	33	+41	74	251	15	167	3	14	195	82	25
3	▼ (2)	Manchester United	34	20	10	4	50	21	+29	70	278	16	248	10	18	261	123	26
4	- (4)	Everton	35	17	7	11	41	36	+5	58	165	6	186	10	12	172	91	22
5	- (5)	Liverpool	36	16	7	13	49	37	+12	55	226	7	234	13	7	204	100	29
6	- (6)	Bolton Wanderers	36	15	9	12	45	41	+4	54	234	8	209	8	8	193	100	24
7	▲ (9)	Middlesbrough	36	13	12	11	51	45	+6	51	241	6	182	10	10	189	98	27
8	▲ (12)	Manchester City	36	12	12	12	44	37	+7	48	190	3	185	11	11	222	111	24
9	▼ (8)	Tottenham Hotspur	35	13	9	13	42	39	+3	48	210	10	199	12	12	179	147	30
10	▲ (11)	Aston Villa	35	12	11	12	42	43	-1	47	183	8	176	10	11	198	101	22
11	▼ (7)	Charlton Athletic	35	12	9	14	40	51	-11	45	158	8	138	11	12	158	115	20
12	▲ (13)	Birmingham City	36	10	12	14	38	44	-6	42	154	9	159	12	9	182	95	27
13	▲ (14)	Blackburn Rovers	36	9	14	13	31	40	-9	41	180	7	219	16	14	199	143	30
14	▼ (10)	Newcastle United	35	9	13	13	43	53	-10	40	246	11	212	9	6	228	90	26
15	▲ (16)	Fulham	35	10	8	17	42	56	-14	38	165	6	157	10	7	171	90	24
16	▼ (15)	Portsmouth	36	10	8	18	42	56	-14	38	182	7	176	10	5	179	108	25
17	- (17)	Southampton	36	6	13	17	42	62	-20	31	178	3	193	11	7	171	105	34
18	- (18)	Crystal Palace	36	7	10	19	37	58	-21	31	162	7	153	12	10	177	82	27
19	- (19)	West Bromwich Albion	35	5	15	15	33	58	-25	30	168	12	154	12	6	177	124	27
20	- (20)	Norwich City	36	6	12	18	41	71	-30	30	173	6	181	13	5	174	119	25

Chelsea celebrate winning the league

TEAM FORM

Pos	Team	Form	Goals For	Goals Against	Pts
1	Manchester City	DWDWDW	9	3	12
2	Chelsea	WDDWW	9	3	11
3	Arsenal	WWDW	6	1	10
4	Norwich City	LWDWWL	12	12	10
5	Middlesbrough	WLDWDD	7	3	9
6	Aston Villa	WDWDD	8	4	9
7	Blackburn Rovers	DWWDDL	6	3	9
8	Fulham	WLDDLW	9	9	8
9	Liverpool	WLDWLD	6	6	8
10	Bolton Wanderers	LWWDDL	7	7	8
11	Everton	LWWDL	6	4	7
12	Portsmouth	LWDLWL	10	10	7
13	Birmingham City	DDDLDW	5	7	7
14	Tottenham Hotspur	DWDDL	5	5	6
15	West Bromwich	WDDLD	4	7	6
16	Crystal Palace	LLDLWD	4	9	5
17	Manchester United	DLLW	2	4	4
18	Southampton	LLLDLW	9	17	4
19	Charlton Athletic	DLLDL	5	9	2
20	Newcastle United	LLLLDD	2	8	2

TOP GOALSCORERS

Player	This Month	Total
T.Henry Arsenal	3	**25**
A.Johnson Crystal Palace	2	**20**
J.Defoe Tottenham Hotspur	1	**13**
F.Lampard Chelsea	4	**12**
A.Yakubu Portsmouth	2	**12**
J.Hasselbaink Middlesbrough	1	**12**
E.Gudjohnsen Chelsea	3	**11**
P.Crouch Southampton	2	**11**
R.Keane Tottenham Hotspur	2	**11**
A.Cole Fulham	1	**11**
R.Pires Arsenal	1	**11**
K.Phillips Southampton	3	**10**
R.Fowler Manchester City	2	**10**
D.Drogba Chelsea	1	**10**
F.Ljungberg Arsenal	1	**10**

MOST GOAL ASSISTS

Player	This Month	Total
F.Lampard Chelsea	1	**17**
T.Henry Arsenal	0	**16**
J.Hasselbaink Middlesbrough	5	**14**
S.Downing Middlesbrough	1	**14**
L.Boa Morte Fulham	3	**12**
W.Routledge Crystal Palace	1	**11**
F.Ljungberg Arsenal	0	**11**
D.Huckerby Norwich City	2	**10**
R.Giggs Manchester United	1	**10**
A.Robben Chelsea	1	**10**
S.Wright-Phillips Manchester City	1	**10**
A.Johnson Crystal Palace	2	**9**
J.Greening West Bromwich Albion	1	**9**
E.Gudjohnsen Chelsea	0	**9**

DISCIPLINE

F.A. disciplinary points: Yellow=4 points, Two Bookable Offences=10 points and Red Card=12 points

Player	Y	SB	R	PTS
P.Diop Fulham	7	1	1	**50**
L.Hendrie Aston Villa	9	0	1	**48**
R.Parlour Middlesbrough	9	1	0	**46**
L.Bowyer Newcastle United	5	1	1	**42**
T.Cahill Everton	7	1	0	**38**
D.Johnson Birmingham City	7	1	0	**38**
T.Hibbert Everton	9	0	0	**36**
M.Hughes Crystal Palace	9	0	0	**36**
P.Vieira Arsenal	9	0	0	**36**
D.Prutton Southampton	6	1	0	**34**
K.Tugay Blackburn Rovers	6	1	0	**34**
T.El Karkouri Charlton Athletic	5	0	1	**32**
D.Mills Manchester City	5	0	1	**32**

"I would like to apologise to the fans, chairman, manager, staff, all the players and everyone connected to Newcastle who witnessed what happened on the football field. I am sincerely sorry."

Lee Bowyer apologises for fighting with Kieron Dyer

"If we have a disagreement, we shouldn't be fighting on the football field in front of 50,000 fans. I'm deeply sorry about what happened, and at such a crucial stage of the season."

Kieron Dyer apologises for his part in the fight with Lee Bowyer

"Anyone you bring in would be a gamble, but Alain is a solid football man and a good coach. He will mould the team, and he was candidate number one."

Portsmouth Chairman Milan Mandaric on the appointment of Alain Perrin

"I want Robbie Keane to stay, but you never know. We will have to wait and see what happens at the end of the season. The most important thing is to achieve with Spurs, on an individual level it is not important.

Martin Jol

"If Michael Owen was available, he would be first on our list. We already have two former Real Madrid players here in Fernando Hierro and Ivan Campo, so you could never actually write off the fact that we might get a third."

Sam Allardyce on his ambitious transfer plans

"We have four of the best centre-halves in the world in John Terry, Ricardo Carvalho, William Gallas and Robert Huth. We don't need a central defender."

Chelsea Assistant Manager Steve Clarke on speculation linking the club with Rio Ferdinand

"Everyone at this club needs to look at themselves and ask whether they are giving 100%. I am not sure all the players can say they are, and that is a crime in itself."

Roy Keane

Sunday 1st May 2005 | Venue: **The Valley** | Attendance: **26,789** | Referee: **D.J.Gallagher**

PREMIERSHIP FIXTURE HISTORY

Pl: 6 Draws: 1	Wins	Goals	Yellow cards	Red cards
Charlton Athletic	0	4	4	2
Manchester United	5	15	9	0

STARTING LINE-UPS

Lisbie, Perry
Euell, Kiely
Hughes

P.Neville, Kleberson
Fortune, Howard
Ronaldo

EVENT LINE

34 Scholes (Corner)
36 Scholes (Foul)
44 Fletcher (Open Play)

HALF TIME 0 - 2

49 Keane (Foul)
56 **Jeffers (Off) Lisbie (On)**
62 Smith (Open Play)
64 Scholes (Off) Neville P (On)
65 Keane (Off) Kleberson (On)
67 Rooney (Open Play)
68 **Kishishev (Off) Perry (On)**
68 **Rommedahl (Off) Euell (On)**
69 Rooney (Off) Fortune (On)
85 **Perry (Foul)**

FULL TIME 0 - 4

STATISTICS

Season	Fixture	Charlton		Man Utd Fixture	Season
162	4	Shots On Target		12	290
140	2	Shots Off Target		6	254
8	0	Hit Woodwork		1	17
117	2	Caught Offside		3	126
159	1	Corners		7	268
436	6	Fouls		15	436
44%	38%	Possession		62%	56%

LEAGUE STANDINGS

Position (pos before)	W	D	L	F	A	Pts
11 (11) Charlton Ath	12	9	15	40	55	45
3 (3) Man Utd	21	10	4	54	21	73

Alan Smith goes to ground

"When you play the top sides, you need for it all to go your way - that didn't happen."

Alan Curbishley

"There's great character in this side, we've shown that before, and we won't give up second place without a fight."

Sir Alex Ferguson

PREMIERSHIP MILESTONE

Stephan Andersen made his Premiership debut

CHARLTON ATHLETIC 0 MANCHESTER UNITED 4

Charlton's end-of-season slump continued, as they suffered a humiliating 4-0 reverse at the hands of Manchester United.

Defeat extended the Addicks' winless sequence to seven games, but it was the manner of the loss that manager Alan Curbishley found hard to swallow. The home team were second best from the first whistle, and were quite fortunate to only lose by four goals.

The visitors almost took the lead inside the opening 30 seconds, Wayne Rooney skipping around debutant keeper Stephan Andersen and clipping over a cross that Darren Fletcher could only glance wide.

In a rare foray forward, Francis Jeffers drew a smart parry from Roy Carroll, while Rooney then went close at the other end with a low drive from distance.

As Sir Alex Ferguson's side turned up the heat on their hosts, Andersen began to make a name for himself. The Danish custodian somehow reacted quickly enough to keep out a point-blank range Alan Smith effort, before denying Paul Scholes in a one-on-one situation.

Having made two such fine saves, the keeper was then at fault as United grabbed a 34th-minute lead. A low Rooney drive following a right-wing corner took a slight deflection, but should not have been spilt into the path of a grateful Scholes.

The goalscorer then escaped with a booking as he lunged in on Dennis Rommedahl, and was soon involved in the move which led to Fletcher making it 2-0. The Scottish international produced an accomplished 19-yard finish, after he had been spotted by Scholes.

The home team didn't appear to have the necessary fight to stage a comeback, and nearly fell three behind early in the second half. A ball over the top of a static defence released Rooney, though the England international struck his effort against the base of the far left-hand upright.

Two more goals were forthcoming, however, as Smith raced through to slot past Andersen from just outside the area, before Rooney capped a fine sequence of passing with a nonchalent touch beyond the keeper.

An appalling afternoon for Charlton then got worse, as substitute Chris Perry saw red for an 85th-minute professional foul on Wes Brown.

PREMIERSHIP FIXTURE HISTORY

Pl: 13 Draws: 4	Wins	Goals	Yellow cards	Red cards
Tottenham Hotspur	6	19	19	0
Aston Villa	3	14	18	0

STARTING LINE-UPS

Tottenham subs: Cerny, Defoe, Mido, Bunjevcevic, Ziegler

Aston Villa subs: Hendrie, L.Moore, Sorensen, Cole, De la Cruz

EVENT LINE

- 6 ⚽ **Kanoute (Open Play)**
- 6 ▢ Postma (Ung.Conduct)
- 17 ▢ **Davis (Foul)**
- 19 ⚽ **King (Corner)**
- 27 ⚽ **Kanoute (Corner)**
- 45 ⚽ Barry (Penalty)

HALF TIME 3 - 1

- 59 ⇄ Angel (Off) Moore L (On)
- 59 ⇄ Hitzlsperger (Off) Hendrie (On)
- 64 ⇄ **Robinson (Off) Cerny (On)**
- 67 ⚽ **Reid (Open Play)**
- 78 ⇄ **Kanoute (Off) Mido (On)**
- 78 ⇄ **Keane (Off) Defoe (On)**
- 90 ⚽ **Kelly (Open Play)**
- 90 ▢ Solano (Foul)

FULL TIME 5 - 1

STATISTICS

Season	Fixture	Tottenham / Aston Villa	Fixture	Season
224	14	Shots On Target	4	187
205	6	Shots Off Target	1	177
11	1	Hit Woodwork	0	8
150	3	Caught Offside	7	108
188	9	Corners	3	201
431	13	Fouls	16	559
50%	57%	Possession	43%	49%

LEAGUE STANDINGS

Position (pos before)	W	D	L	F	A	Pts
7 (9) Tottenham H	14	9	13	47	40	51
10 (10) Aston Villa	12	11	13	43	48	47

Sunday 1st May 2005 | Venue: **White Hart Lane** | Attendance: **36,078** | Referee: **M.Clattenburg**

TOTTENHAM HOTSPUR 5 ASTON VILLA 1

Aston Villa were torn apart by a rampant Tottenham, as the men from White Hart Lane climbed above Middlesbrough and into the final UEFA Cup qualification spot.

It was David O'Leary's men that began brightly. Young midfielder Steven Davis saw his low drive expertly kept out by Paul Robinson, before the keeper played an important part in the opening goal.

A marauding Mark Delaney appeared to be felled in the box by Erik Edman, but referee Mark Clattenburg waved play on. Within seconds the ball was at the other end, Frederic Kanoute latching onto Robinson's punt forward and finding the bottom left-hand corner of the net via the body of stand-in custodian Stefan Postma.

Spurs then made it two from a 19th-minute corner. Captain Ledley King had seen a header saved in the early stages of the match, but finished clinically from eight yards out after a low Andy Reid drive had struck the base of the right-hand post.

The goal rush continued, with Kanoute grabbing his second before 30 minutes had been played. Again the visitors failed to deal with a corner, brought about by a fine save from a Sean Davis header, allowing the Malian international to sweep home from inside the six-yard box.

There seemed to be no way back for Villa, but they were handed, quite literally, a lifeline in first half stoppage time. Michael Dawson blocked Juan Pablo Angel's strike with his arms, enabling Gareth Barry to convert from the penalty spot.

The opening 20 minutes of the second period were nervy for Tottenham. Twice Darius Vassell was denied by Robinson, with the keeper being forced off through injury after colliding with his international team-mate.

Any anxiety amongst the White Hart Lane faithful soon disappeared though, as Reid burst forward to hammer home a memorable goal. The midfielder ran unchallenged from halfway, before finding the net with a 25-yard blockbuster.

Substitute Jermain Defoe was then unlucky not to score, with Stephen Kelly adding a fifth in injury time. The full-back ran onto Davis' majestic flick and outmuscled J'Lloyd Samuel to beat Postma from close range.

Robbie Keane demonstrates his ball skills

"Aston Villa are a very good side, but that was one of our best performances of the season."
Martin Jol

"We conceded too many soft goals, and we let ourselves down today."
David O'Leary

PREMIERSHIP MILESTONE

Andy Reid scored his first Premiership goal

PREMIERSHIP MILESTONE

Radek Cerny made his Premiership debut

PREMIERSHIP FIXTURE HISTORY

Pl: 2	Draws: 0	Wins	Yellow	Red
West Bromwich Albion	0	1	1	0
Arsenal	2	4	0	0

STARTING LINE-UPS

Kanu, Horsfield Earnshaw, Kuszczak Scimeca

Edu, Bergkamp Almunia, Campbell Aliadiere

EVENT LINE

HALF TIME 0 - 0

66 van Persie (Open Play)

74 Fabregas (Off) Bergkamp (On)

74 van Persie (Off) Edu (On)

80 **Albrechtsen (Off) Earnshaw (On)**

80 **Campbell (Off) Horsfield (On)**

80 **Gera (Off) Kanu (On)**

90 Edu (Open Play)

FULL TIME 0 - 2

STATISTICS

Season	Fixture (West Brom)		Fixture (Arsenal)	Season
169	1	Shots On Target	4	255
161	7	Shots Off Target	5	172
12	0	Hit Woodwork	0	15
129	5	Caught Offside	1	83
186	9	Corners	0	195
470	12	Fouls	12	415
48%	50%	Possession	50%	56%

LEAGUE STANDINGS

Position (pos before)		W	D	L	F	A	Pts
19 (19)	West Brom	5	15	16	33	60	30
2 (2)	Arsenal	23	8	4	76	33	77

Monday 2nd May 2005 | Venue: **The Hawthorns** | Attendance: **27,351** | Referee: **N.S.Barry**

WEST BROM 0 ARSENAL 2

West Brom remained deep in the relegation mire, as second half goals from Robin van Persie and Edu condemned them to a 2-0 defeat.

Bryan Robson opted for a defensively-minded 5-4-1 formation, leaving former Gunner Kevin Campbell isolated in attack. The home game plan was to deny Arsenal space in which to operate, and things worked well during the first hour of the contest.

Arsene Wenger's men were unable to generate any fluency in their play, and it was the Baggies that enjoyed the better opening. Zoltan Gera, Ronnie Wallwork and Kieran Richardson all had half-chances during this spell, though Jens Lehmann was largely untroubled.

More than half-an-hour had elapsed before the visitors began to pose a genuine threat. Captain Patrick Vieira curled a 20-yard effort just over the crossbar, while Russell Hoult had to rush from his line to intercept a dangerous throughball.

The keeper was then called upon to make a vital save, standing up tall to block from van Persie after Lauren had released the Dutchman in the inside-right channel. This was a warning, and Wallwork soon delivered one of his own with a shot that flew just over.

Both Lauren and Gilberto made important blocks as the second period got underway, before van Persie netted a vital 66th-minute goal. Jose Antonio Reyes found his strike partner with a crisp pass, and the young forward stepped across a defender to curl home from 15 yards out with his favoured left foot.

Five minutes later, the points should have been sealed. Neil Clement showed his value to the Albion cause, making a potentially-crucial last-gasp clearance as Reyes skipped beyond Hoult to slot the ball goalwards.

The home team had to find a way back into the game, and Robson went for broke by sending on three strikers. It was the Arsenal substitutes that did the damage though, as Dennis Bergkamp's measured pass enabled Edu to clip an injury-time second over the advancing Hoult.

While West Brom still harbour hopes of beating the drop, a trip to Old Trafford next time out does not look a very inviting fixture.

Robin van Persie fires home the opening goal

"We matched them all over the pitch, and until they scored I can't remember a chance they created."
Bryan Robson

"It is a big disappointment to have lost the title, but Chelsea deserve congratulations."
Arsene Wenger

PREMIERSHIP FIXTURE HISTORY

Pl: 4 Draws: 0	Wins	Goals	Yellow	Red
Fulham	2	8	4	0
Newcastle United	2	8	9	1

STARTING LINE-UPS

Fulham: van der Sar; Volz, Knight, Goma, Rosenior; Pembridge; Radzinski, Boa Morte; Clark (c); Cole, McBride

Newcastle United: Kluivert; Ameobi, Milner; N'Zogbia, Faye, Ambrose; Taylor, Boumsong (c), Bramble, Carr; Given

Fulham subs: Jensen, Crossley, Bocanegra, Pearce, Rehman

Newcastle United subs: O'Brien, Harper, Ramage, Brittain, Robert

EVENT LINE

18 Ambrose (Open Play)

HALF TIME 0 - 1

62 Kluivert (Corner)

62 **van der Sar (Dissent)**

66 **Cole (Off) Jensen (On)**

67 Taylor (Foul)

75 Ameobi (Corner)

86 **Radzinski (Open Play)**

FULL TIME 1 - 3

STATISTICS

Season	Fixture (Fulham)		Fixture (Newcastle)	Season
168	3	Shots On Target	3	249
160	3	Shots Off Target	1	213
6	0	Hit Woodwork	0	11
97	7	Caught Offside	6	96
172	1	Corners	2	230
445	11	Fouls	13	463
48%	62%	Possession	38%	50%

LEAGUE STANDINGS

Position (pos before)	W	D	L	F	A	Pts
16 (15) Fulham	**10**	**8**	**18**	**43**	**59**	**38**
12 (14) Newcastle Utd	**10**	**13**	**13**	**46**	**54**	**43**

Wednesday 4th May 2005 | Venue: **Craven Cottage** | Attendance: **19,003** | Referee: **G.Poll**

FULHAM 1
NEWCASTLE UNITED 3

Newcastle rediscovered that winning feeling, picking up three points for the first time since early March.

Darren Ambrose, Patrick Kluivert and Shola Ameobi were on target for the Magpies, with former Everton man Tomasz Radzinski netting what proved to be nothing more than a late consolation for the home side.

The major team news centred around the non-appearance of Alan Shearer. The striker had not registered a Premiership goal in three months, and asked manager Graeme Souness if he could be rested for this trip to West London.

The absence of their captain did not seem to affect Newcastle, as they made the better start. A right-wing cross was turned into the side-netting by Kluivert, while a neat move ended with the sting being taken out of an Ambrose drive.

The former Ipswich midfielder did not have long to wait for a goal, however, steering the ball home from nine yards out after James Milner's deflected back-post header had fallen into his path.

All Fulham chances during the opening 45 minutes fell to former Magpies. Centre-back Alain Goma missed with an early header, before Lee Clark nodded just over following Shay Given's challenge on Andy Cole.

Dutchman Kluivert had been guilty of a poor aerial miss in the first half, but made amends just past the hour mark. Charles N'Zogbia delivered a vicious inswinging corner from the right, and the former Barcelona man arrived to power home a near-post header.

One-time Newcastle transfer target Luis Boa Morte fizzed a 15-yard effort narrowly wide of the left-hand upright, as the Cottagers tried to respond.

Any hopes of a home comeback were put to bed after 75 minutes, however, as Ameobi made it three. This time Chris Coleman's men failed to defend a corner from the opposite flank, with the striker rising virtually unopposed at the back post to convert Milner's delivery.

The Craven Cottage faithful were at least given an 86th-minute goal to cheer. Liam Rosenior won possession and fed Radzinski, with the Canadian international neatly tucking the ball under Given and into the far right-hand corner of the net.

Moritz Volz tries to stop Shola Ameobi

"I'm very disappointed tonight, particularly after the way we played on saturday."

Chris Coleman

"Alan Shearer did not play because he has been drained psychologically and physically since our UEFA Cup defeat."

Graeme Souness

PREMIERSHIP MILESTONE

Stephen Carr made his 250th Premiership appearance

PREMIERSHIP FIXTURE HISTORY

Pl: 8 Draws: 4	Wins	⚽	☐	■
Aston Villa	2	9	11	1
Manchester City	2	8	10	0

STARTING LINE-UPS

Djemba-Djemba
Solano, L.Moore
Postma, Ridgewell

B.Wright-Phillips
Croft, Weaver
Jordan, Sommeil

EVENT LINE

5 ⚽ Wright-Phillips S (Open Play)

12 ⚽ Musampa (Open Play)

HALF TIME 0 - 2

46 **Hitzlsperger (Off) Solano (On)**

46 **Samuel (Off) Djemba-Djemba (On)**

61 ⚽ **Angel (Open Play)**

71 Sibierski (Off) Wright-Phillips B (On)

75 ☐ **Solano (Foul)**

78 **Hendrie (Off) Moore L (On)**

79 Macken (Off) Croft (On)

85 ☐ Barton (Foul)

FULL TIME 1 - 2

STATISTICS

Season	Fixture (Aston Villa)		Fixture (Man City)	Season
195	8	Shots On Target	4	194
184	7	Shots Off Target	6	191
8	0	Hit Woodwork	1	4
114	6	Caught Offside	3	114
207	6	Corners	2	224
567	8	Fouls	18	475
49%	61%	Possession	39%	49%

LEAGUE STANDINGS

Position (pos before)	W	D	L	F	A	Pts
10 (10) Aston Villa	12	11	14	44	50	47
8 (9) Man City	13	12	12	46	38	51

Saturday 7th May 2005 | Venue: **Villa Park** | Attendance: **39,645** | Referee: **R.J.Beeby**

ASTON VILLA 1 MANCHESTER CITY 2

Having just been named 'Manager of the Month' for April, Stuart Pearce led his team to a potentially vital 2-1 victory at Villa Park.

Early goals from wingers Shaun Wright-Phillips and Kiki Musampa knocked the stuffing out of the home side, though Juan Pablo Angel did at least set up a nervous final half-hour for the visitors with a strike of his own.

Just five minutes had been played when Wright-Phillips opened the scoring. The England international only seems to find the net in spectacular fashion, and did so again as he waltzed through a static defence to drill a low 12-yard effort across Thomas Sorensen.

A second goal was not long in arriving. Antoine Sibierski's cross from the right was touched on by Jonathan Macken, with Musampa taking full advantage of the acres of space he was afforded in the box to crash the ball into the top right-hand corner of the net.

Steven Davis was presented with two very good opportunities to give his team a foothold in the game before half-time. The young midfielder found the side-netting from Lee Hendrie's pass, and was then denied by former Villan David James as he capitalised on some overly-casual defending by Ben Thatcher.

The interval saw the introduction of Eric Djemba-Djemba and Nolberto Solano, and the changes had the desired effect. The Peruvian met Angel's astute header with an angled drive, but his shot was blocked.

Both substitutes were soon involved in the early part of a move that ended with Angel reducing the deficit. Eventually, Ulises De la Cruz's low pass was dummied by Hendrie, with the Colombian striker holding off Danny Mills to fire under James from nine yards out in the inside-right channel.

The closing stages offered plenty of excitement, though most of it came at the Villa end. Both Wright-Phillips and Musampa came within inches of sealing the points, with the latter poking a low effort against Sorensen's left-hand upright.

A Gareth Barry header drifted just beyond the far post, but City held on to set up a showdown with Middlesbrough next Sunday in the battle for a UEFA Cup place.

Steven Davis fends off Joey Barton

"We gave them two gift-wrapped goals, but afterwards we should have scored quite a few. It has been that type of season."

David O'Leary

"We should have beaten Aston Villa more convincingly. We came out of the blocks and played really well."

Stuart Pearce

Saturday 7th May 2005	Venue: **Ewood Park**	Attendance: **18,991**	Referee: **P.Dowd**

PREMIERSHIP FIXTURE HISTORY

Pl: 4 Draws: 0	Wins	Goals	Yellow	Red
Blackburn Rovers	2	6	8	1
Fulham	2	6	8	1

STARTING LINE-UPS

Blackburn Rovers: Friedel; Neill, Short (c), Nelson, Johansson; Reid, Mokoena, Savage; Emerton, Pedersen; Stead

Fulham: McBride, Malbranque; Boa Morte, Pembridge, Clark (c), Radzinski; Rosenior, Goma, Knight, Volz; van der Sar

Substitutes (Blackburn): Thompson, Tugay, Derbyshire, Taylor, Enckelman

Substitutes (Fulham): Bocanegra, Crossley, Pearce, Rehman, Timlin

EVENT LINE

6 **Neill (Open Play)**
20 Malbranque (Open Play)
32 **Reid (Off) Thompson (On)**
37 **Neill (Foul)**
HALF TIME 1 - 1
53 McBride (Corner)
67 **Mokoena (Off) Tugay (On)**
69 **Short (Violent Conduct)**
69 Boa Morte (Foul)
70 Rosenior (Violent Conduct)
75 **Stead (Foul)**
77 Malbranque (Open Play)
82 **Pedersen (Off) Derbyshire (On)**
90 Pembridge (Ung.Conduct)
FULL TIME 1 - 3

STATISTICS

Season	Fixture	Blackburn / Fulham	Fixture	Season
185	5	Shots On Target	7	175
227	8	Shots Off Target	1	161
8	1	Hit Woodwork	0	6
151	8	Caught Offside	0	97
207	8	Corners	5	177
591	12	Fouls	23	468
49%	54%	Possession	46%	48%

LEAGUE STANDINGS

Position (pos before)	W	D	L	F	A	Pts
14 (14) Blackburn R	9	14	14	32	43	41
15 (16) Fulham	11	8	18	46	60	41

Robbie Savage closes down Mark Pembridge

"We found we had no gas left in our tank, and it was a poor performance by recent standards."
Mark Hughes

"I was pleased with the effort of the team. We showed great character and a lot of composure on the ball."
Chris Coleman

PREMIERSHIP MILESTONE
Matt Derbyshire made his Premiership debut

PREMIERSHIP MILESTONE
100 Alain Goma made his 100th Premiership appearance in the colours of Fulham.

PREMIERSHIP MILESTONE
25 Steed Malbranque's second goal was his 25th in the Premiership

BLACKBURN ROVERS 1 FULHAM 3

Fulham produced a vintage display at Ewood Park, becoming the first team to net three goals against Blackburn in a Premiership match since late November.

Mark Hughes' team got off to a dream start, as Lucas Neill opened the scoring after just six minutes. The goal had an Australian flavour to it, as the full-back surged onto Brett Emerton's pass and beat Edwin van der Sar from 12 yards out.

That was as good as it got for Rovers, however, with the Cottagers drawing level midway through the half. Captain Lee Clark ran onto a Moritz Volz chip and intelligently pulled the ball back from the right, where Steed Malbranque was waiting to slot home.

Things might have been different had Jonathan Stead's left-footed curler not drifted just the wrong side of van der Sar's right-hand upright, but Fulham capitalised on their reprieve.

Zat Knight saw an early second half header ruled out for climbing on a defender at a corner, before Brian McBride netted after 53 minutes. A flag-kick from the right was flicked on by Clark, with the American international controlling and then sweeping the ball home from seven yards out at the back post.

An unmarked Emerton should have done better than strike the outside of a post, while Robbie Savage saw a penalty saved after Luis Boa Morte had hauled down Morten Gamst Pedersen at a free-kick.

It was after this that the fireworks really began. A crude Boa Morte challenge on Ryan Nelson provoked an angry reaction from Craig Short, with the stand-in Blackburn skipper receiving a red card for raising his hands.

Then, just a minute later, a rush of blood to the head saw Liam Rosenior shove Savage to the ground. The defender clearly didn't like the former Leicester midfielder's strong challenge on his Portuguese team-mate, but left referee Phil Dowd with little option but to dismiss him.

With both teams down to 10 men, Fulham took advantage of the space on offer. An away victory was duly confirmed, as Malbranque rounded off a sweeping move by beating Brad Friedel with the outside of his right boot.

PREMIERSHIP FIXTURE HISTORY

Pl: 6 Draws: 0	Wins	Goals	Yellow	Red
Chelsea	4	8	15	0
Charlton Athletic	2	4	7	0

STARTING LINE-UPS

Jarosik, Forssell
Pidgeley, Huth
Kezman

Fish, Kiely
Fuller, Rommedahl
Euell

EVENT LINE

	HALF TIME 0 - 0
67	**Johnson (Off) Jarosik (On)**
67	**Tiago (Off) Forssell (On)**
82	**Cudicini (Off) Pidgeley (On)**
90	**Makelele (Penalty)**
	FULL TIME 1 - 0

STATISTICS

Season	Fixture (Chelsea)		Fixture (Charlton)	Season
274	6	Shots On Target	4	166
235	9	Shots Off Target	3	143
12	2	Hit Woodwork	0	8
126	9	Caught Offside	1	118
230	2	Corners	5	164
442	7	Fouls	14	450
56%	57%	Possession	43%	44%

LEAGUE STANDINGS

Position (pos before)	W	D	L	F	A	Pts
1 (1) Chelsea	28	7	1	68	13	91
11 (11) Charlton Ath	12	9	16	40	56	45

Saturday 7th May 2005 | Venue: **Stamford Bridge** | Attendance: **42,065** | Referee: **M.A.Riley**

Claude Makelele enjoys his moment in the limelight

"Every title has the same taste, but to win it in England is different in that it is more difficult to do."

Jose Mourinho

"I am fed up of going on holiday with a bad taste in my mouth. We have worked hard all season, but people just remember the last couple of months."

Alan Curbishley

PREMIERSHIP MILESTONE

Claude Makelele scored his first Premiership goal

PREMIERSHIP MILESTONE

Lenny Pidgeley made his Premiership debut

CHELSEA 1 CHARLTON ATHLETIC 0

On the day that Chelsea were presented with the Premiership trophy, they left it very late to secure a 1-0 win against Charlton at Stamford Bridge.

The game appeared to be drifting towards a tame goalless draw, when inspirational midfielder Frank Lampard was upended by Jonathan Fortune as he surged into the box. The visiting players argued that the offence had taken place outside the area, but referee Mike Riley pointed to the spot.

With little resting on the result, Claude Makelele was given the chance to net his first goal for Chelsea. The French midfielder saw his weak penalty saved, but reacted quickly to scuff home the rebound.

With a midweek 'Champions League' semi-final defeat at the hands of Liverpool still fresh in their minds, Chelsea made a sluggish start to proceedings. Stand-in goalkeeper Carlo Cudicini reminded everyone of his quality though, racing from his line to deny Bryan Hughes.

As the half progressed, Jose Mourinho's men began to warm to their task. Former West Ham player Lampard was guilty of a poor headed miss from William Gallas' cross, while Joe Cole's long-range drive was touched onto the bar by Stephan Andersen.

The second period began in a similar vain, captain John Terry meeting Glen Johnson's right-wing cross with a looping six-yard header that rebounded to safety off the angle of post and bar.

The Addicks hit back, however, with Matt Holland forcing a world-class save from Cudicini. The Italian custodian somehow managed to get his right hand down to a low drive, turning the ball just past the left-hand upright in the process.

Another keeper, Lenny Pidgeley, was introduced, as Cudicini left the field to rapturous applause. The former Watford loanee did well to keep out Hughes in a goalmouth scramble, before Chelsea made their 90th-minute breakthrough.

The final whistle enabled the party to begin at Stamford Bridge, with the 1955 title-winners joining their modern day counterparts in the celebrations. A sea of blue and white streamers flew into the sky, highlighting the emergence of a new force in English football.

PREMIERSHIP FIXTURE HISTORY

Pl: 4 Draws: 3	Wins	⚽	☐	■
Crystal Palace	0	4	7	1
Southampton	1	5	11	1

STARTING LINE-UPS

Kiraly

Sorondo, Hall, Popovic, Granville

Leigertwood, Hughes (c), Riihilahti

Routledge, Soares

Johnson

Camara, Crouch

Le Saux, Quashie (c), Redknapp, Oakley

Bernard, Higginbotham, Lundekvam, Telfer

Niemi

Watson, Ventola, Speroni, Lakis, Freedman

Phillips, Delap, McCann, Smith, Davenport

EVENT LINE

22 ☐ **Johnson (Foul)**

34 ⚽ **Hall (Indirect Free Kick)**

37 ⚽ Crouch (Penalty)

HALF TIME 1 - 1

58 ■ Crouch (Violent Conduct)

59 ■ **Sorondo (Violent Conduct)**

62 ☐ **Hall (Ung.Conduct)**

63 Le Saux (Off) Phillips (On)

64 **Popovic (Off) Ventola (On)**

64 **Riihilahti (Off) Watson (On)**

72 ⚽ **Ventola (Open Play)**

74 ☐ **Ventola (Foul)**

76 Oakley (Off) Delap (On)

79 Redknapp (Off) McCann (On)

86 ☐ Phillips (Foul)

90 ⚽ Higginbotham (Open Play)

FULL TIME 2 - 2

STATISTICS

Season	Fixture		Fixture	Season
168	6	Shots On Target	4	182
161	8	Shots Off Target	4	197
7	0	Hit Woodwork	0	3
86	4	Caught Offside	4	109
182	5	Corners	2	173
525	17	Fouls	18	481
46%	53%	Possession	47%	47%

LEAGUE STANDINGS

Position (pos before)	W	D	L	F	A	Pts
19 (18) Crystal Palace	7	11	19	39	60	32
18 (17) Southampton	6	14	17	44	64	32

Saturday 7th May 2005 | Venue: **Selhurst Park** | Attendance: **26,066** | Referee: **H.M.Webb**

CRYSTAL PALACE 2 SOUTHAMPTON 2

A 2-2 draw did little to boost either side's chances of Premiership survival, though Danny Higginbotham's late equaliser could yet prove vital come the final day.

The game was deep into stoppage time when the former Manchester United defender arrived at the back post to guide home Kevin Phillips' low cross from the left. His run to the opposite end to celebrate in front of the Southampton supporters highlighted just how much the goal meant.

Earlier, Fitz Hall had opened the scoring with a spectacular strike, only for Peter Crouch to level things up almost immediately from the penalty spot. The tall striker and Uruguayan Gonzalo Sorondo were then dismissed, before substitute Nicola Ventola netted what appeared to be a Crystal Palace winner.

There was an understandable amount of tension on display in the opening half-hour. Tom Soares, Wayne Routledge and Jamie Redknapp all forced comfortable saves, while Matthew Oakley was unable to make contact with Olivier Bernard's driven cross.

The breakthrough arrived after 34 minutes, with Hall drilling a dagger into the heart of his former employers. The centre-back was forward for a free-kick, and capitalised on confusion to send a swivelling 17-yard effort just inside Antti Niemi's left-hand upright.

Harry Redknapp's charges responded in a positive fashion, however, with Henri Camara winning a penalty by flicking the ball against the arm of defender Tony Popovic. Despite the pressure of the situation, Crouch kept his head to beat Gabor Kiraly from 12 yards.

Visiting custodian Niemi made a brilliant one-handed save from Michael Hughes as the half drew to a close, while Soares fired inches wide with a 20-yard drive just after the restart.

An explosive incident then saw both teams reduced to 10 men just before the hour mark. Striker Crouch was dismissed for swinging a leg and then an arm at Sorondo, while the home defender was given his marching orders for cuffing Graeme Le Saux in the melee that followed.

A well-taken goal from Ventola, his first for the Eagles, looked to have secured a vital win for Iain Dowie's side after 72 minutes, but Higginbotham had other ideas.

Nicola Ventola celebrates making it 2-1

"If you give a goal away that late, it is disappointing. It just proves that the show is never over."
Iain Dowie

"It's a rarity for Danny Higginbotham to score, but we had no choice but to put everyone forward at the end."
Harry Redknapp

PREMIERSHIP MILESTONE

Nicola Ventola netted his first Premiership goal

PREMIERSHIP MILESTONE

Danny Higginbotham scored his first Premiership goal for Southampton

PREMIERSHIP FIXTURE HISTORY

Pl: 12 Draws: 3	Wins	Goals	Yellow	Red
Everton	5	14	21	1
Newcastle United	4	14	24	3

STARTING LINE-UPS

Everton: Martyn; Hibbert, Yobo, Weir (c), Watson; Carsley, Cahill, Arteta, Kilbane; Bent, Ferguson

Newcastle United: Kluivert; Ameobi, N'Zogbia, Jenas, Ambrose, Milner; Babayaro, Boumsong (c), Bramble, Carr; Given

Everton subs: Beattie, McFadden, Stubbs, Wright, Pistone

Newcastle United subs: Ramage, Shearer, Harper, O'Brien, Robert

EVENT LINE

34 Carsley (Foul)
43 Weir (Indirect Free Kick)

HALF TIME 1 - 0

46 Carr (Off) Ramage (On)
56 Ameobi (Violent Conduct)
57 Cahill (Foul)
59 Cahill (Open Play)
63 Ferguson (Off) Beattie (On)
74 Bent (Off) McFadden (On)
82 Arteta (Ung.Conduct)
82 Kluivert (Ung.Conduct)
82 Milner (Off) Shearer (On)
89 Cahill (Off) Stubbs (On)

FULL TIME 2 - 0

STATISTICS

Season	Fixture	Everton	Newcastle Fixture	Season
171	6	Shots On Target	4	253
188	2	Shots Off Target	5	218
6	0	Hit Woodwork	0	11
92	1	Caught Offside	1	97
175	3	Corners	2	232
456	22	Fouls	11	474
49%	42%	Possession	58%	51%

LEAGUE STANDINGS

Position (pos before)		W	D	L	F	A	Pts
4 (4)	Everton	18	7	11	43	36	61
12 (12)	Newcastle Utd	10	13	14	46	56	43

Saturday 7th May 2005 | Venue: **Goodison Park** | Attendance: **40,438** | Referee: **B.Knight**

EVERTON 2 NEWCASTLE UNITED 0

Everton all-but-secured a spot in next season's 'Champions League', beating Newcastle 2-0 at Goodison Park to move six points clear of Liverpool in fourth place.

With Bolton being held to a draw at Portsmouth, only their Merseyside rivals can now overhaul David Moyes' men in the table.

An early Mikel Arteta free-kick drew a fine diving save from Shay Given, before the visitors began to take charge of proceedings. Buoyed by a midweek win at Fulham, Graeme Souness' men started to carve out a plethora of decent chances.

Darren Ambrose overran the ball when bearing down on Nigel Martyn after 18 minutes, while Patrick Kluivert twice went close. The former Barcelona man dragged a low effort just past the right-hand upright, and then missed with a downward header from inside the six-yard box.

James Milner stung the palms of the goalkeeper as the half drew to a conclusion, though there was still time for captain David Weir to head Everton in front. A clumsy Jean-Alain Boumsong challenge resulted in a deep Arteta free-kick from the left, with the Scottish international defender nodding home unchallenged from four yards out.

The marking was non-existent, and Newcastle's predicament worsened 11 minutes into the second period. Shola Ameobi was dismissed for violent conduct, after reacting to a bit of shirt pulling by pushing Tim Cahill in the face.

The Merseysiders' Australian international midfielder went on to find the net just three minutes later, passing the ball into the top left-hand corner from eight yards out after Arteta's mishit shot had found him in space.

There was no way back for the Magpies, despite the 82nd-minute introduction of Alan Shearer. The former England captain had returned from his rest to find himself warming the bench, though he had little chance to make a late impact given his side's numerical disadvantage.

The final whistle was greeted with scenes of great joy around Goodison Park. With Liverpool facing a daunting trip to Highbury the following day, most Evertonians were confident that they would be watching European football's elite next season.

Joseph Yobo jumps with James Milner

"I keep telling David Weir that he doesn't get enough goals, but that one today was a very important one."

David Moyes

"You'd have wondered who the home side was before Everton scored, but suddenly we found ourselves a goal down thanks to a poor decision."

Graeme Souness

PREMIERSHIP FIXTURE HISTORY

Pl: 2 Draws: 1	Wins	⚽	▯	▮
Manchester United	1	2	2	0
West Bromwich Albion	0	1	1	1

STARTING LINE-UPS

Subs (Man Utd): Scholes, Rooney, Saha, Howard, Miller

Subs (West Brom): Kuszczak, Kanu, Inamoto, Moore, Scimeca

EVENT LINE

21	⚽	**Giggs (Direct Free Kick)**
22	⇄	Hoult (Off) Kuszczak (On)
		HALF TIME 1 - 0
47	▯	**Smith (Foul)**
63	⚽	Earnshaw (Penalty)
66	⇄	Horsfield (Off) Kanu (On)
67	⇄	**Kleberson (Off) Rooney (On)**
67	⇄	**Neville P (Off) Scholes (On)**
67	⇄	**Smith (Off) Saha (On)**
83	⇄	Gera (Off) Inamoto (On)
		FULL TIME 1 - 1

STATISTICS

Season	Fixture (Man Utd)		Fixture (West Brom)	Season
304	14	Shots On Target	1	170
267	13	Shots Off Target	2	163
18	1	Hit Woodwork	0	12
128	2	Caught Offside	3	132
280	12	Corners	0	186
446	10	Fouls	13	483
56%	59%	Possession	41%	48%

LEAGUE STANDINGS

Position (pos before)		W	D	L	F	A	Pts
3 (3)	Man Utd	21	11	4	55	22	74
20 (19)	West Brom	5	16	16	34	61	31

Saturday 7th May 2005	Venue: Old Trafford	Attendance: 67,827	Referee: M.R.Halsey

MANCHESTER UNITED 1 WEST BROM 1

A virtuoso performance from substitute goalkeeper Tomasz Kuszczak earnt West Brom an unlikely point at Old Trafford.

The Baggies were second best from the first whistle, as Manchester United set about putting them to the sword. Quinton Fortune drew a smart save from Russell Hoult, with the custodian then appearing to injure his groin as he scrambled across his six-yard box.

A willingness to play on through the pain ultimately cost his side, however, as Ryan Giggs curled a 20-yard free-kick over the wall and into the net. The keeper was still organising his defenders as the ball was struck, and pulled up sharply as he tried to get across his goal to make a save.

The remainder of the half was one-way traffic, with Kuszczak turning in an inspired performance. After Giggs had gone perilously close to a second from an acute angle, the Polish shot-stopper began to make save after save.

A point-blank range header from Fortune was parried to safety, while Cristiano Ronaldo twice forced sprawling stops. Alan Smith then nodded a dangerous cross from the left straight into the grateful arms of the custodian, as West Brom went in at half-time with just a one-goal deficit.

John O'Shea's header almost let in visiting captain Kevin Campbell as the second period got underway, but Sir Alex Ferguson's men were soon back on the offensive.

Portuguese starlet Ronaldo was unlucky to see the ball trickle just the wrong side of the left-hand upright as he stole in behind the defence, while Kleberson was guilty of a wayward finish following great work from Fortune down the left.

No team can afford to miss as many chances as United did, and they were made to pay just after the hour mark.

Geoff Horsfield grappled with O'Shea as he tried to reach Campbell's lofted pass, with referee Mark Halsey surprisingly choosing to award a penalty. Welsh international Robert Earnshaw kept his cool, sending Roy Carroll the wrong way from the spot.

In a dramatic finale, Scholes struck a post from distance and substitute Wayne Rooney was denied by the impressive Kuszczak.

Roy Keane drives his team forward

"It was a terrible result considering the amount of chances we had."

Sir Alex Ferguson

"It was a good result for us. After a poor first half, we came back out in the second and started to pass the ball well."

Bryan Robson

Saturday 7th May 2005 | Venue: **Riverside Stadium** | Attendance: **34,766** | Referee: **D.J.Gallagher**

PREMIERSHIP FIXTURE HISTORY

Pl: **10** Draws: **3**	Wins	⚽	□	■
Middlesbrough	5	14	12	0
Tottenham Hotspur	2	8	25	2

STARTING LINE-UPS

Doriva, Knight Reiziger, Cooper Morrison

Keane, Mido Ziegler, Fulop Bunjevcevic

EVENT LINE

6 □ Davis (Ung.Conduct)
11 ⚽ **Boateng (Open Play)**
18 □ Carrick (Ung.Conduct)
39 □ **Southgate (Foul)**
HALF TIME 1 - 0
58 ⇄ Defoe (Off) Keane (On)
69 ⇄ Reid (Off) Mido (On)
70 □ Mido (Foul)
78 ⇄ **Zenden (Off) Doriva (On)**
83 ⇄ Kanoute (Off) Ziegler (On)
FULL TIME 1 - 0

STATISTICS

Season	Fixture		Fixture	Season
249	8	Shots On Target	2	226
190	8	Shots Off Target	3	208
7	1	Hit Woodwork	0	11
102	4	Caught Offside	3	153
193	4	Corners	3	191
466	14	Fouls	10	441
49%	49%	Possession	51%	50%

LEAGUE STANDINGS

Position (pos before)		W	D	L	F	A	Pts
7 (8)	Middlesbrough	14	12	11	52	45	54
9 (7)	Tottenham H	14	9	14	47	41	51

Franck Queudrue is chased by Simon Davies

"I think experience won the game today. Spurs are an up and coming side, but we had the big game experience."
Steve McClaren

"We were not on top of our game, to say the least."
Martin Jol

MIDDLESBROUGH 1 TOTTENHAM HOTSPUR 0

Middlesbrough seized pole position in the race for UEFA Cup football, beating closest rivals Tottenham 1-0 at the Riverside Stadium.

The home side started in fine style, with Slovakian international Szilard Nemeth curling a 25-yard effort against stand-in goalkeeper Radek Cerny's crossbar.

Play then switched to the other end, as Frederic Kanoute clipped over a dangerous ball from the right that had to be headed behind by Stuart Parnaby.

With such a high-octane opening, it came as little surprise when a goal arrived after just 11 minutes. George Boateng was the scorer, firing in a deflected 20-yarder after Nemeth had retrieved an overhit centre.

Things settled down from this point onwards, and the crowd had to wait until just before the interval to get genuinely excited again. Stewart Downing burst into the Tottenham box on the left, but saw his low drive miss the far post by centimetres.

Having replaced the ineffective Jermain Defoe just prior to the hour mark, Robbie Keane was unlucky not to score with a volley very reminiscent of David Platt's for England against Belgium in the 1990 World Cup.

Visiting captain Ledley King, off of whom the ball had deflected for Boateng's goal, should then have done better with a near-post header from an inswinging Andy Reid free-kick.

Middlesbrough responded to Spurs' greater threat by pushing forward. Jimmy Floyd Hasselbaink tested Cerny from 20 yards with his left foot, but then blazed over in horrible fashion having been picked out in the box by Downing.

The lively Nemeth was not far away with a curling effort as the game drew to a close, skipping inside Michael Dawson and bending the ball just beyond the far right-hand upright. Martin Jol's men had long since ceased to pose a real threat, with the Teessiders earning a deserved victory.

With Manchester City also collecting three points, Steve McClaren's men travel to the City of Manchester Stadium in search of the final day draw that would book a second consecutive season in the UEFA Cup.

PREMIERSHIP FIXTURE HISTORY

Pl: 1 Draws: 0	Wins	Goals	Yellow	Red
Norwich City	1	1	1	0
Birmingham City	0	0	5	1

STARTING LINE-UPS

Holt, Charlton Svensson, Lewis Jonson

Clemence, Morrison Blake, Vaesen Martin Taylor

EVENT LINE

16 Nafti (Foul)
19 Lazaridis (Off) Clemence (On)
31 Johnson (Violent Conduct)
45 Cunningham (Foul)
45 **Ashton (Penalty)**

HALF TIME 1 - 0

46 Pandiani (Off) Morrison (On)
48 Morrison (Handball)
58 Pennant (Foul)
63 **Safri (Off) Holt (On)**
67 **McKenzie (Foul)**
71 Clemence (Foul)
72 **Drury (Off) Charlton (On)**
78 Cunningham (Off) Blake (On)
86 **McKenzie (Off) Svensson (On)**

FULL TIME 1 - 0

STATISTICS

Season	Fixture		Fixture	Season
178	5	Shots On Target	9	163
185	4	Shots Off Target	13	172
6	0	Hit Woodwork	3	12
122	3	Caught Offside	2	97
175	1	Corners	7	189
508	20	Fouls	10	513
45%	42%	Possession	58%	50%

LEAGUE STANDINGS

Position (pos before)	W	D	L	F	A	Pts
17 (20) Norwich C	**7**	**12**	**18**	**42**	**71**	**33**
13 (13) Birmingham C	**10**	**12**	**15**	**38**	**45**	**42**

Saturday 7th May 2005 | Venue: **Carrow Road** | Attendance: **25,477** | Referee: **S.G.Bennett**

NORWICH CITY 1 BIRMINGHAM CITY 0

Despite not being at their best, Norwich rode their luck to record a victory that saw them leap out of the relegation zone with just one game remaining.

Nigel Worthington's men were rescued by the woodwork on no fewer than three occasions, as a Dean Ashton penalty just before half-time proved enough to see off a spirited challenge from 10-man Birmingham.

The Canaries made a nervous start to proceedings, and were somewhat lucky to avoid conceding a penalty. Former Ipswich man Jamie Clapham's shot appeared to be blocked by the arm of captain Craig Fleming, with Walter Pandiani unable to get enough power behind his follow-up strike.

The Uruguayan striker then hit the bar with his standing foot, after taking a wild swing at Mario Melchiot's low delivery from the right.

With just a solitary Ashton run to show for their efforts, Norwich were handed a 31st-minute boost. Damien Johnson inexplicably punched Danish international Thomas Helveg in the stomach, resulting in an instantaneous red card from referee Steve Bennett.

Steve Bruce's team remained comfortable until the dying embers of the half, when Darren Huckerby burst into the box and was upended by Kenny Cunningham. Former Crewe man Ashton took responsibility, sending Maik Taylor the wrong way from the spot.

Clinton Morrison was booked for a stupid handball that denied team-mate Emile Heskey a clear headed chance as the second period got underway, while Ashton was soon drawing a save from Taylor from an acute angle.

Leon McKenzie was denied from point-blank range as the game became more stretched, before Morrison struck the woodwork twice in quick succession.

The former Crystal Palace striker swivelled to loop a deflected 15-yard effort against the bar, and then met Jermaine Pennant's right-wing centre with a glancing header that hit almost the exact same spot.

Somehow Norwich held on to their one-goal lead, recording a victory that leaves them very much in charge of their own destiny. If the Canaries pick up a first away win of the season at Fulham, they will avoid relegation to the Championship.

Leon McKenzie battles with Matthew Upson

"At this stage of the season, the result is more important than the performance."
Nigel Worthington

"It was a travesty. We slaughtered them, but the luck has gone their way today."
Steve Bruce

PREMIERSHIP MILESTONE

200 Darren Huckerby made his 200th Premiership appearance

PREMIERSHIP FIXTURE HISTORY

Pl: **2** Draws: **1**

	Wins	⚽	Yellow	Red
Portsmouth	1	5	2	0
Bolton Wanderers	0	1	6	0

STARTING LINE-UPS

Keene, Fuller Cisse, Hislop Rodic

Nolan, Jaidi Pedersen, Poole Fadiga

EVENT LINE

11 ⚽ Diouf (Open Play)

45 Gardner (Foul)

HALF TIME 0 - 1

55 Giannakopoulos (Off) Nolan (On)

60 **Kamara (Off) Keene (On)**

60 **Skopelitis (Off) Fuller (On)**

72 ⚽ **Yakubu (Indirect Free Kick)**

76 Candela (Off) Jaidi (On)

77 **Mezague (Off) Cisse (On)**

82 Diouf (Foul)

84 Diouf (Off) Pedersen (On)

FULL TIME 1 - 1

STATISTICS

Season	Fixture		Fixture	Season
186	4	Shots On Target	4	238
181	5	Shots Off Target	8	217
7	0	Hit Woodwork	1	9
112	4	Caught Offside	0	100
181	2	Corners	9	202
441	12	Fouls	23	513
47%	53%	Possession	47%	50%

LEAGUE STANDINGS

Position (pos before)	W	D	L	F	A	Pts
16 (15) Portsmouth	10	9	18	43	57	39
6 (6) Bolton W	15	10	12	46	42	55

Saturday 7th May 2005 | Venue: **Fratton Park** | Attendance: **20,188** | Referee: **M.D.Messias**

PORTSMOUTH 1 BOLTON WANDERERS 1

A 1-1 draw at Portsmouth clinched a place in Europe for the first time in Bolton Wanderers' history.

Though El-Hadji Diouf's first half goal was cancelled out by a fortuitous Aiyegbeni Yakubu effort, the point guaranteed Sam Allardyce's men a top seven finish and the UEFA Cup spot that goes with it.

Tal Ben Haim fired an early warning shot for the visitors, before Diouf handed them an 11th-minute lead. The Senegalese international withstood an understandable torrent of boos, as he capitalised on a defensive mix-up to round Dejan Stefanovic and fire home under Jamie Ashdown.

Neither Arjan De Zeeuw, who refused to shake his hand prior to the kick-off, or the Pompey faithful had forgotten the notorious spitting incident in the reverse fixture earlier in the season, but the enigmatic forward let his feet do the talking on this occasion.

A more popular African, Jay-Jay Okocha, then fizzed a 20-yard effort just the wrong side of the right-hand upright, with Bolton very much in the ascendancy against a Portsmouth team that had little to play for.

Alain Perrin can't have been happy with the first half showing, and would have been buoyed by an improved start to the second period. A long range drive forced a scrambling save from Jussi Jaaskelainen, with both Yakubu and Gary O'Neil trying their luck from the rebound.

Visiting substitute Kevin Nolan then crashed the ball against the outside of a post following a floated free-kick from deep, before play switched to the other end.

After Richard Hughes had taken a tumble, fellow midfielder O'Neil delivered an inswinging set-piece from the left. A sea of bodies competed for the cross, with a ricochet off the chest of Yakubu resulting in an equaliser.

The remaining 18 minutes saw Bolton back on the offensive. Chances were at a premium, however, with Okocha scuffing the best of them well wide from distance.

On a normal day, the Trotters would have been disappointed with just a point. This was not a normal day though, and Allardyce's men can now start to dream of their European adventure.

James Keene gets the better of Vincent Candela

"Once again we started slowly and conceded in the first 15 minutes, but we improved in the second half and deserved a draw."

Alain Perrin

"Leading us into Europe is the crowning glory for Sam, his finest hour."

Assistant manager Phil Brown

PREMIERSHIP MILESTONE

James Keene made his Premiership debut

PREMIERSHIP MILESTONE

200 Kevin Davies made his 200th Premiership appearance

PREMIERSHIP FIXTURE HISTORY

Pl: 13 Draws: 4	Wins	Goals	Yellow cards	Red cards
Arsenal	4	13	16	2
Liverpool	5	11	23	2

STARTING LINE-UPS

Arsenal substitutes: Edu, Bergkamp, Aliadiere, Almunia, Campbell

Liverpool substitutes: Kewell, Cisse, Smicer, Carson, Biscan

EVENT LINE

15 Baros (Handball)
23 Hamann (Foul)
25 **Pires (Direct Free Kick)**
29 **Reyes (Open Play)**

HALF TIME 2 - 0

46 Baros (Off) Cisse (On)
46 Riise (Off) Kewell (On)
51 Gerrard (Indirect Free Kick)
68 **Pires (Off) Edu (On)**
68 **van Persie (Off) Bergkamp (On)**
68 Hamann (Off) Smicer (On)
86 **Reyes (Off) Aliadiere (On)**
90 **Fabregas (Open Play)**

FULL TIME 3 - 1

STATISTICS

Season	Fixture	Arsenal / Liverpool	Fixture	Season
263	**8**	Shots On Target	**6**	**232**
175	**3**	Shots Off Target	**5**	**239**
15	**0**	Hit Woodwork	**0**	**7**
90	**7**	Caught Offside	**4**	**104**
196	**1**	Corners	**4**	**208**
428	**13**	Fouls	**10**	**428**
55%	**46%**	Possession	**54%**	**53%**

LEAGUE STANDINGS

Position (pos before)		W	D	L	F	A	Pts
2 (2)	**Arsenal**	**24**	**8**	**4**	**79**	**34**	**80**
5 (5)	**Liverpool**	**16**	**7**	**14**	**50**	**40**	**55**

Sunday 8th May 2005 | Venue: **Highbury** | Attendance: **38,119** | Referee: **G.Poll**

Xabi Alonso tracks countryman Jose Antonio Reyes

"We made a nervy start today, but then we got into our stride and played some top-class football."
Arsene Wenger

"We must do better in the league. We've lost far too many away games."
Rafael Benitez

ARSENAL 3 LIVERPOOL 1

Despite a brave second half showing, Liverpool were unable to recover from the damage done to them by Arsenal before the break.

The Gunners were in imperious form during the opening 45 minutes, establishing a two-goal lead thanks to strikes from Robert Pires and Jose Antonio Reyes. Steven Gerrard then reduced the arrears shortly after the restart, before Cesc Fabregas sealed the points in injury time.

Spaniard Reyes almost gave his team a dream start, turning the ball home from close range after Jerzy Dudek had fumbled Robin van Persie's low strike. Unfortunately for Arsene Wenger's men, an offside flag was correctly raised.

John Arne Riise was foiled by Jens Lehmann and Fabregas fired narrowly wide from distance, before Milan Baros saw a goal disallowed. The Czech striker finished calmly from 13 yards out, but earnt a booking for using his hand in the build-up.

Full-back Lauren somehow failed to open the scoring from six-yards out, with Robert Pires passing the ball just beyond the far right-hand upright moments later. It proved to be just a sighter for the Frenchman, as he curled a free-kick over the wall and into the net after 25 minutes.

An unfortunate slip by Jamie Carragher quickly let in Reyes for a second, the forward surging into the box and drilling home through the legs of the keeper.

Rafael Benitez took affirmative action at the break, sending on Harry Kewell and Djibril Cisse in place of Riise and Baros. Though not directly involved in the 51st-minute goal, their arrival lifted Liverpool.

Unsurprisingly, Gerrard was the man that gave his side hope. Dietmar Hamann touched a free-kick into the path of his captain, and the England international unleashed a shot that took a wicked deflection on its way in.

The Merseysiders desperately hunted an equaliser, with Luis Garcia coming closest, but it wasn't to be. Then, in injury time, Fabregas latched onto a magnificent Dennis Bergkamp touch to poke home a decisive third.

Perhaps the happiest team at the final whistle were Everton. An Arsenal victory meant that David Moyes' men had qualified for the 'Champions League'.

PREMIERSHIP FIXTURE HISTORY

Pl: **13** Draws: **6**

	Wins	⚽	▯	▮
Manchester United	**3**	**18**	**22**	**0**
Chelsea	**4**	**20**	**31**	**1**

STARTING LINE-UPS

Saha, Howard O'Shea, Fortune Smith

Jarosik, Morais Grant, Cech Forssell

EVENT LINE

- 7 ⚽ **van Nistelrooy (Corner)**
- 17 ⚽ Tiago (Open Play)
- 31 ▯ **Keane (Foul)**
- **HALF TIME 1 - 1**
- 51 ▯ Makelele (Dissent)
- 61 ⚽ Gudjohnsen (Open Play)
- 63 ▯ **van Nistelrooy (Dissent)**
- 64 ▯ Lampard (Foul)
- 72 ⇄ **Fletcher (Off) Saha (On)**
- 72 ⇄ Johnson (Off) Jarosik (On)
- 73 ▯ Gallas (Dissent)
- 82 ⚽ Cole J (Open Play)
- 86 ⇄ Gudjohnsen (Off) Morais (On)
- 90 ⇄ Cole J (Off) Grant (On)
- **FULL TIME 1 - 3**

STATISTICS

Season	Fixture		Fixture	Season
306	**2**	Shots On Target	**4**	**278**
275	**8**	Shots Off Target	**1**	**236**
19	**1**	Hit Woodwork	**0**	**12**
132	**4**	Caught Offside	**0**	**126**
287	**7**	Corners	**0**	**230**
457	**11**	Fouls	**15**	**457**
56%	**52%**	Possession	**48%**	**55%**

LEAGUE STANDINGS

Position (pos before)		W	D	L	F	A	Pts
3 (3)	**Man Utd**	**21**	**11**	**5**	**56**	**25**	**74**
1 (1)	**Chelsea**	**29**	**7**	**1**	**71**	**14**	**94**

Tuesday 10th May 2005 | Venue: **Old Trafford** | Attendance: **67,832** | Referee: **G.Poll**

MANCHESTER UNITED 1 CHELSEA 3

Chelsea emphasised the gulf in class between themselves and Manchester United, winning 3-1 at Old Trafford to extend the gap between the sides to a massive 20 points.

When you consider that the starting XI fielded by Jose Mourinho was missing players such as John Terry, Petr Cech, Damien Duff, Arjen Robben and Didier Drogba, it becomes apparent just how demoralising a defeat this was for Sir Alex Ferguson's men.

Most pundits were expecting the home side to turn on the style in a bid to show that they will be a force next season. This was exactly what happened in the early stages, with Ruud van Nistelrooy notching a poacher's goal after just seven minutes.

A Wayne Rooney corner from the left eventually found its way back to the England international, with his low cross-cum-shot being steered into the back of the net from inside the six-yard box by United's Dutch striker.

Chelsea's depleted side responded in the manner of champions, with Tiago drawing them level within 10 minutes. The Portuguese midfielder let fly with a speculative 30-yard drive, with Roy Carroll left rooted to the spot as the ball flew in.

If the remainder of the first half was evenly contested, then the second period belonged to the Londoners. A Darren Fletcher drive that spanked the crossbar apart, the Old Trafford team barely threatened.

Chelsea could already have scored three times after the break, when Eidur Gudjohnsen made it 2-1. The Icelandic international beat the offside trap to latch onto Tiago's pass, nonchalantly clipping home over the advancing Carroll in the 61st minute.

Joe Cole then ensured that his team would break the record for most points collected in a Premiership season, turning in Frank Lampard's low cross from within the confines of the six-yard box eight minutes from time.

The 'Theatre of Dreams' had emptied on a scale not seen for many years by the time referee Graham Poll blew his final whistle. Much work will have to be done over the summer if Ferguson's men are to mount a serious title challenge next season.

Geremi challenges Mikael Silvestre

"The passing from both teams was excellent, but when we lost the second goal I thought they took control."

Sir Alex Ferguson

"We did not panic when we went a goal down, and kept on playing well."

Jose Mourinho

PREMIERSHIP MILESTONE

150 Frank Lampard made his 150th Premiership appearance in the colours of Chelsea

PREMIERSHIP MILESTONE

50 Glen Johnson made his 50th Premiership appearance

PREMIERSHIP MILESTONE

Both Nuno Morais and Anthony Grant were handed a Premiership debut

PREMIERSHIP FIXTURE HISTORY

Pl: 13 Draws: 1	Wins	Goals	Yellow	Red
Arsenal	11	37	12	1
Everton	1	11	23	3

STARTING LINE-UPS

Arsenal: Lehmann; Lauren, Senderos, Campbell, Cole; Pires, Vieira (c), Edu, Reyes; van Persie, Bergkamp

Everton: Wright; Pistone, Weir (c), Yobo, Hibbert; Kilbane, Arteta, Carsley, Watson, McFadden; Beattie

Arsenal subs: Flamini, Henry, Fabregas, Almunia, Toure

Everton subs: Bent, Ferguson, Turner, Stubbs, Plessis

EVENT LINE

8 **van Persie (Open Play)**
12 **Pires (Open Play)**
37 **Vieira (Open Play)**

HALF TIME 3 - 0

46 **van Persie (Off) Henry (On)**
46 **Vieira (Off) Flamini (On)**
46 Beattie (Off) Bent (On)
50 **Pires (Open Play)**
56 **Flamini (Foul)**
64 **Pires (Off) Fabregas (On)**
70 **Edu (Penalty)**
75 Arteta (Off) Ferguson (On)
77 **Bergkamp (Open Play)**
79 **Campbell (Foul)**
85 **Flamini (Open Play)**

FULL TIME 7 - 0

STATISTICS

Season	Fixture (Arsenal)		Fixture (Everton)	Season
276	13	Shots On Target	3	174
182	7	Shots Off Target	5	193
15	0	Hit Woodwork	0	6
93	3	Caught Offside	3	95
200	4	Corners	2	177
437	9	Fouls	14	470
56%	65%	Possession	35%	48%

LEAGUE STANDINGS

Position (pos before)		W	D	L	F	A	Pts
2 (2)	Arsenal	25	8	4	86	34	83
4 (4)	Everton	18	7	12	43	43	61

Wednesday 11th May 2005 | Venue: **Highbury** | Attendance: **38,073** | Referee: **A.G.Wiley**

ARSENAL 7 EVERTON 0

Dennis Bergkamp rolled back the years, aptly demonstrating why he is arguably the finest player ever to have graced the Premiership arena.

The Dutch master was at his mesmeric best, and Everton simply had no answer to his promptings. With their No.10 pulling the strings, Arsenal ripped through the visiting defence at will.

The first of seven unanswered goals arrived after just eight minutes. The strike was made in Holland, as Robin van Persie swept Bergkamp's measured ball into the net from around the penalty spot.

Robert Pires made it two at the second attempt, looping home a 12-yard header after former Gunner Richard Wright had parried his initial drive from Jose Antonio Reyes' left-wing cutback.

With just 12 minutes played, the match already seemed beyond David Moyes' men. Patrick Vieira then confirmed as much eight minutes before half-time, cleverly lofting an effort over the advancing keeper from another precise Bergkamp pass.

There was no respite after the interval, with Thierry Henry emerging from the bench. The Frenchman was involved in a 50th-minute fourth, Pires slotting past Wright following a challenge on his countryman.

Edu, reportedly playing his last game at Highbury before a summer exit, signed off in style by converting a penalty 20 minutes from time. Lee Carsley was penalised for handling a chip by Henry, and the Brazilian just found the net from 12 yards.

All that was missing was a Bergkamp goal, and the fans did not have long to wait. Having pulled a ball out of the sky, the Arsenal legend threaded a neat finish just inside the left-hand upright.

The rout was completed five minutes from time, as Mathieu Flamini bobbled home an eight-yard effort. The donkey work was done by Henry and Reyes, with the midfielder arriving right on cue.

Coupled with Manchester United's poor showing against Chelsea 24 hours earlier, Arsene Wenger's men are fast emerging as favourites for their upcoming F.A.Cup Final clash. On this evidence, Bergkamp has to be given a starting place in Cardiff.

Thierry Henry embraces Arsenal legend Dennis Bergkamp

"You have to be special to play at that level at the age of 36, and you saw how Dennis created the first three goals. You don't meet a Dennis Bergkamp on every street corner."
Arsene Wenger

"I can't blame my players, but this evening as a manager, I was embarrassed."
David Moyes

PREMIERSHIP MILESTONE
Mathieu Flamini scored his first Premiership goal

PREMIERSHIP FIXTURE HISTORY

Pl: 3 Draws: 0	Wins	Goals	Yellow	Red
Birmingham City	1	2	4	0
Arsenal	2	8	4	0

STARTING LINE-UPS

Morrison, Tebily
Martin Taylor, Vaesen
Blake

Edu, Aliadiere
Flamini, Almunia
Eboue

EVENT LINE

HALF TIME 0 - 0

62 **Carter (Off) Morrison (On)**
68 Ljungberg (Off) Edu (On)
68 van Persie (Off) Aliadiere (On)
75 Fabregas (Off) Flamini (On)
78 **Melchiot (Off) Tebily (On)**
80 **Pandiani (Corner)**
81 **Pandiani (Ung.Conduct)**
88 Bergkamp (Open Play)
90 **Heskey (Open Play)**
90 **Pandiani (Off) Taylor Martin (On)**

FULL TIME 2 - 1

STATISTICS

Season	Fixture		Fixture	Season
167	4	Shots On Target	5	281
177	5	Shots Off Target	6	188
12	0	Hit Woodwork	1	16
103	6	Caught Offside	3	96
192	3	Corners	2	202
523	10	Fouls	8	445
50%	48%	Possession	52%	56%

LEAGUE STANDINGS

Position (pos before)	W	D	L	F	A	Pts
12 (13) Birmingham C	11	12	15	40	46	45
2 (2) Arsenal	25	8	5	87	36	83

Sunday 15th May 2005 | Venue: **St Andrew's** | Attendance: **29,302** | Referee: **D.J.Gallagher**

BIRMINGHAM CITY 2 ARSENAL 1

Birmingham ended an indifferent season on a high, beating in-form Arsenal 2-1 at St Andrew's.

All the goals came in a dramatic final 10 minutes. Uruguayan Walter Pandiani got things started, before late strikes from Dennis Bergkamp and Emile Heskey caused disappointment and then joy amongst the home faithful.

It was Steve Bruce's team that carved out the best chance of the opening period. Midfielder Stephen Clemence should have at least hit the target, but blazed his effort high over the bar after Pandiani had dispossessed Philippe Senderos.

The Gunners' only real opportunity of the first 45 minutes fell to Robin van Persie. In truth, the young Dutchman did well to divert Kolo Toure's deflected cross goalwards, but Maik Taylor was able to make a comfortable save.

The second half began in worrying fashion for Birmingham, as Arsenal scythed through their defence at lightning speed. A van Persie pass picked out Bergkamp in the inside-left channel, but his lofted finish flew right across the face of goal.

Home substitute Clinton Morrison was denied by an alert Jens Lehmann, while Toure drove against the outside of a post at the other end. Then, just as the game seemed destined to end 0-0, the deadlock was broken.

A deep corner from the right was played back into the danger area by Clemence, where, following a series of ricochets, Pandiani was on hand to stab the ball into the net from marginally outside the six-yard box.

Eight minutes later, Bergkamp looked to have atoned for his earlier miss by salvaging a point. The Highbury legend peeled away from his marker to control a dipping Patrick Vieira pass, and then squeezed a shot under the body of Taylor.

That was not the end of the scoring though, as Heskey rifled in a 90th-minute winner. Swiss centre-back Senderos was caught napping, as the former Leicester striker suddenly darted across his path to beat Lehmann with a venomous drive.

The defeat was of little consequence to Arsene Wenger's men, but will provide the West Midlands side with real confidence going into next season.

Cesc Fabregas surveys the scene

"We deserved the win, although I didn't think we would get it when Bergkamp equalised."
Steve Bruce

"It appeared to me that we had an eye on the F.A.Cup final, and we lost too many 50-50 tackles."
Arsene Wenger

PREMIERSHIP FIXTURE HISTORY				
Pl: 6 Draws: 3	Wins	⚽	Yellow	Red
Bolton Wanderers	2	9	10	2
Everton	1	7	7	1

STARTING LINE-UPS

Candela, Nolan O'Brien, Poole, Vaz Te — Osman, Stubbs Vaughan, Martyn, Pistone

EVENT LINE

9 ⚽ Cahill (Open Play)
17 ▢ **Diouf (Dissent)**
28 ▢ **Davies (Foul)**
45 ■ **N'Gotty (Violent Conduct)**
45 ▢ Cahill (Ung.Conduct)

HALF TIME 0 - 1

53 ⚽ **Jaidi (Indirect Free Kick)**
59 ⇄ Cahill (Off) Osman (On)
61 ⚽ **Davies (Open Play)**
63 ⚽ Carsley (Corner)
66 ⚽ **Giannakopoulos (Corner)**
67 ⇄ **Hierro (Off) Candela (On)**
68 ⇄ **Giannakopoulos (Off) Nolan (On)**
71 ⇄ Arteta (Off) Stubbs (On)
80 ⇄ Hibbert (Off) Vaughan (On)
82 ⇄ **Diouf (Off) O'Brien (On)**

FULL TIME 3 - 2

STATISTICS

Season	Fixture	(Bolton) / (Everton)	Fixture	Season
247	9	Shots On Target	5	179
225	8	Shots Off Target	5	198
9	0	Hit Woodwork	0	6
103	3	Caught Offside	1	96
207	5	Corners	6	183
525	12	Fouls	19	489
50%	56%	Possession	44%	48%

LEAGUE STANDINGS

Position (pos before)		W	D	L	F	A	Pts
6 (6)	Bolton W	16	10	12	49	44	58
4 (4)	Everton	18	7	13	45	46	61

Sunday 15th May 2005 | Venue: **Reebok Stadium** | Attendance: **27,701** | Referee: **N.S.Barry**

Radhi Jaidi competes with Duncan Ferguson

"The players have finished the season on a magnificent high, the only disappointment being the sending-off of Bruno N'Gotty."
Sam Allardyce

"We could and should have won the match, but it was a good end of season game."
David Moyes

PREMIERSHIP MILESTONE
Joey O'Brien made his Premiership debut

BOLTON WANDERERS 3 EVERTON 2

Two over-achieving sides served up a thrilling game of football on the final day, with 10-man Bolton eventually running out 3-2 winners.

With both clubs having already secured a European place, there was little riding on the 90 minutes. This was far from obvious, however, as the match proved to be hard-fought from the first whistle.

It took just nine minutes for Tim Cahill to do what he does best. The former Millwall midfielder profited from confusion at the back post, finding the net with a perfectly-executed overhead kick from within the six-yard box.

After El-Hadji Diouf, Gary Speed and Stylianos Giannakopoulos had all failed to level the scores, the task facing Sam Allardyce's men became even harder when they were reduced to 10 men.

Moments before half-time, Bruno N'Gotty became involved in an off-the-ball altercation with Cahill. The Everton man appeared to swing an arm at the centre-back, who earnt a red card by slapping his opponent on the back of the head.

Far from having a negative impact on their play, the dismissal seemed to galvanize the home troops. Radhi Jaidi rose majestically to head in Fernando Hierro's 53rd-minute free-kick from the left, before Kevin Davies completed the turnaround.

Just over an hour had been played when Diouf picked out Giannakopoulos in the box, with the Greek international teeing up Davies for a deflected 15-yard effort that left Richard Wright with no chance.

The lead lasted just two minutes, however, as Lee Carsley drew the Merseysiders level from a corner. Quick feet from substitute Leon Osman provided Duncan Ferguson with a chance, and his mishit effort fell invitingly for his bald-headed team-mate.

Still the goals kept coming, with Giannakopoulos netting what proved to be the winner after 66 minutes. Again a set-piece caused problems, with the Bolton No.7 prodding the ball home from close range after Davies' header had been parried.

Almost immediately, legend of the game Hierro was withdrawn to a standing ovation. The Spaniard had announced that this would be his last game before retirement, and went out on a real high.

PREMIERSHIP FIXTURE HISTORY

Pl: 1 Draws: 1	Wins	⚽	Yellow	Red
Charlton Athletic	0	2	2	0
Crystal Palace	0	2	2	0

STARTING LINE-UPS

Thomas, Sam
Rommedahl, Perry
Andersen

Freedman, Powell
Riihilahti, Speroni
Ventola

EVENT LINE

30 ⚽ **Hughes (Open Play)**
39 Soares (Foul)
HALF TIME 1 - 0
47 **Konchesky (Foul)**
56 Butterfield (Off) Freedman (On)
58 ⚽ Freedman (Open Play)
67 **Holland (Off) Thomas (On)**
69 **Fortune (Handball)**
71 ⚽ Johnson (Penalty)
71 Johnson (Ung.Conduct)
76 **Murphy (Off) Sam (On)**
79 **Bartlett (Off) Rommedahl (On)**
82 ⚽ **Fortune (Indirect Free Kick)**
86 Soares (Off) Powell (On)
89 Watson (Off) Riihilahti (On)
FULL TIME 2 - 2

STATISTICS

Season	Fixture		Fixture	Season
171	5	Shots On Target	7	175
146	3	Shots Off Target	2	163
8	0	Hit Woodwork	0	7
123	5	Caught Offside	5	91
167	3	Corners	8	190
464	14	Fouls	14	539
44%	54%	Possession	46%	46%

LEAGUE STANDINGS

Position (pos before)	W	D	L	F	A	Pts
11 (11) Charlton Ath	12	10	16	42	58	46
18 (19) Crystal Palace	7	12	19	41	62	33

Sunday 15th May 2005 | Venue: The Valley | Attendance: 26,870 | Referee: M.Clattenburg

CHARLTON ATHLETIC 2 CRYSTAL PALACE 2

Having been just eight minutes away from survival, a Jonathan Fortune header ensured that Crystal Palace became the first team to be relegated from the Premiership on four occasions.

The Eagles dominated the early exchanges, showing little sign of nerves. Defender Fitz Hall nearly opened the scoring with a scrappy effort, while Ben Watson tested Dean Kiely with a curling free-kick from distance.

The Charlton keeper then made a far more impressive save, diving away to his left to turn a venomous Wayne Routledge drive around the post. It was to prove a crucial stop, as the Addicks scored against the run of play soon afterwards.

Former Birmingham man Bryan Hughes did the damage, timing his run infield from the left to perfection. The midfielder was spotted by team-mate Radostin Kishishev, and found the net via the inside of the right-hand upright.

Jonatan Johansson then had a chance to condemn the visitors to Championship football next season, but volleyed inches wide from a right-wing Danny Murphy free-kick.

Simply playing well would not keep Crystal Palace in the division, so Iain Dowie went in search of goals. Dougie Freedman entered the arena after 56 minutes, and lobbed his team level from just inside the area with his first touch.

With the results at Craven Cottage and St Mary's going their way, the Eagles knew that a victory would keep them up. With just under 20 minutes remaining, they were handed a great chance to achieve one.

Defender Fortune used his arm to prevent Freedman's cross from reaching Andy Johnson, resulting in the award of a penalty. Custodian Kiely had saved a Johnson spot-kick in the reverse fixture, but was sent the wrong way on this occasion.

For the first time during an afternoon of twists and turns, the Selhurst Park side moved out of the relegation zone. Within 11 minutes they fell back into trouble, however, as Fortune met a left-wing Jerome Thomas free-kick with a powerful close-range header.

There was to be no late winner for Dowie's men, with news of West Brom's success bringing with it confirmation of relegation.

A desolate Andy Johnson faces up to relegation

"I'm not happy that we finished outside the top ten, because I thought we were a bit better than that."
Alan Curbishley

"We can feel sorry for ourselves and slide away into nothingness, or get out of the traps like a bunch of greyhounds next season - I know which response I'm after."
Iain Dowie

PREMIERSHIP MILESTONE
150 Paul Konchesky made his 150th Premiership appearance

PREMIERSHIP MILESTONE
Lloyd Sam made his Premiership debut

PREMIERSHIP MILESTONE
Bryan Hughes netted his first Premiership goal in the colours of Charlton

PREMIERSHIP MILESTONE
Dougie Freedman scored his first Premiership goal for Crystal Palace

PREMIERSHIP FIXTURE HISTORY

Pl: 1 Draws: 0	Wins	⚽	▯	▮
Fulham	1	6	0	0
Norwich City	0	0	1	0

STARTING LINE-UPS

Cole, Crossley Pearce, Rehman Pembridge

Holt, Jonson Svensson, Ward Charlton

EVENT LINE

10 ⚽ **McBride (Open Play)**
18 ▯ Helveg (Foul)
33 ⇄ Safri (Off) Holt (On)
35 ⚽ **Diop (Direct Free Kick)**
HALF TIME 2 - 0
46 ⇄ Helveg (Off) Jonson (On)
54 ⚽ **Knight (Corner)**
59 ⇄ Bentley (Off) Svensson (On)
72 ⚽ **Malbranque (Open Play)**
86 ⚽ **McBride (Open Play)**
87 ⇄ **Boa Morte (Off) Cole (On)**
90 ⚽ **Cole (Open Play)**
FULL TIME 6 - 0

STATISTICS

Season	Fixture		Fixture	Season
184	9	Shots On Target	0	178
165	4	Shots Off Target	2	187
7	1	Hit Woodwork	0	6
98	1	Caught Offside	5	127
181	4	Corners	13	188
479	11	Fouls	12	520
48%	56%	Possession	44%	45%

LEAGUE STANDINGS

Position (pos before)	W	D	L	F	A	Pts
13 (15) Fulham	12	8	18	52	60	44
19 (17) Norwich C	7	12	19	42	77	33

Sunday 15th May 2005 | Venue: **Craven Cottage** | Attendance: **21,927** | Referee: **S.W.Dunn**

FULHAM 6 NORWICH CITY 0

Having battled hard to gain control of their Premiership destiny in recent weeks, Norwich exited the top-flight with something of a whimper.

The Canaries came into the game knowing that a first away win of the season would ensure survival, but suffered a humiliating six-goal drubbing that saw them return to the Championship at the first time of asking.

Nigel Worthington's men actually made an impressive start. Darren Huckerby's low drive was deflected wide, while Fulham players had to make several last-ditch challenges.

The visitors were dealt a hammer blow after just 10 minutes, however, as Brian McBride opened the scoring. Tomasz Radzinski created the chance, slipping a ball into the inside-right channel that his team-mate poked under Robert Green.

Dean Ashton was then harshly penalised for a foul as he rifled in what he thought was an equaliser, before Pape Bouba Diop stunned the travelling fans by netting an exquisite 25-yard free-kick in the 35th minute.

A stretching McBride hit the bar as half-time approached, and a third goal did arrive within 10 minutes of the restart. Defender Zat Knight was the unlikely scorer, lashing a 15-yard drive through a crowd of bodies at a corner.

The Canaries were now completely reliant on other results going their way, and went 4-0 down with 18 minutes remaining. Luis Boa Morte was given time and space in the box, eventually picking out Steed Malbranque for a cool 12-yard finish.

As Delia Smith watched on with her fellow supporters, McBride made it five. The American was released in the inside-left channel by Malbranque, and drove the ball comfortably past Green and into the far corner.

Andy Cole, who scored the winner in the reverse fixture, then emerged from the bench to add a cheeky sixth. The former England international deftly flicked home McBride's low cross, capping a miserable day for Norwich.

With only the result at St Mary's going in their favour, Worthington's team ended the day in 19th place. This defeat highlighted the two main reasons for their relegation - poor away form and a leaky defence.

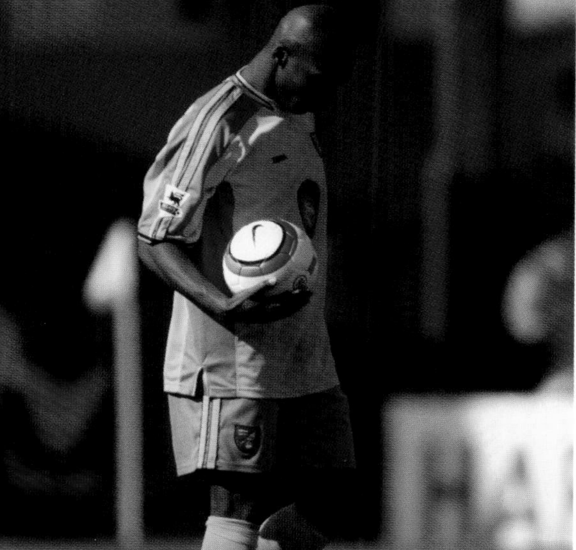
A disappointed Damien Francis trudges off

"It was great to go out with a result like that, but of course I feel sorry for Nigel Worthington."
Chris Coleman

"The occasion got to one or two of my players, but credit must go to Fulham for a very professional performance."
Nigel Worthington

PREMIERSHIP MILESTONE
Zat Knight scored his first Premiership goal

PREMIERSHIP FIXTURE HISTORY

Pl: 13 Draws: 2	Wins	⚽	▯	▮
Liverpool	8	23	12	1
Aston Villa	3	12	16	0

STARTING LINE-UPS

Baros, Hamann Finnan, Dudek Hyypia

L.Moore, Samuel Cole, Henderson McCann

EVENT LINE

20 ⚽ **Cisse (Penalty)**

27 ⚽ **Cisse (Open Play)**

HALF TIME 2 - 0

46 Vassell (Off) Moore L (On)

48 Hendrie (Off) Samuel (On)

60 **Kewell (Off) Baros (On)**

64 Angel (Off) Cole (On)

67 ⚽ Barry (Open Play)

70 **Biscan (Off) Hamann (On)**

79 **Nunez (Off) Finnan (On)**

FULL TIME 2 - 1

STATISTICS

Season	Fixture (Liverpool)		Fixture (Aston Villa)	Season
240	8	Shots On Target	4	199
247	8	Shots Off Target	9	193
8	1	Hit Woodwork	1	9
106	2	Caught Offside	3	117
217	9	Corners	5	212
438	10	Fouls	16	583
53%	46%	Possession	54%	49%

LEAGUE STANDINGS

Position (pos before)		W	D	L	F	A	Pts
5 (5)	Liverpool	17	7	14	52	41	58
10 (10)	Aston Villa	12	11	15	45	52	47

Sunday 15th May 2005 | Venue: **Anfield** | Attendance: **43,406** | Referee: **B.Knight**

LIVERPOOL 2 ASTON VILLA 1

A brace from Djibril Cisse helped Liverpool to a 2-1 win against Aston Villa, thus securing a fifth-placed finish.

With a 'Champions League' final on the horizon, Rafael Benitez decided to rest several important players. Steven Gerrard and Luis Garcia were not amongst the 16, while the bench was packed with first-team regulars.

Lee Hendrie tested Scott Carson with an early effort for the visitors, before stand-in skipper Jamie Carragher embarked on a run from his own half that ended with a shot into the side-netting.

The defender's forward surge clearly inspired his colleagues, with Cisse winning a penalty moments later. Harry Kewell's low drive from distance was smartly parried, and Mark Delaney then crazily upended Liverpool's former Auxerre striker as the ball ran away from goal.

The French international took the spot-kick himself, calmly finding the bottom left-hand corner of the net from 12 yards.

That was after 20 minutes, and the Anfield crowd did not have to wait too long for a second. Again Cisse was the scorer, slotting the returning Josemi's cutback from the right past a bewildered Thomas Sorensen.

Aston Villa's Danish custodian did well to deny Antonio Nunez at the start of the second period, while visiting substitute Luke Moore drew a decent save from Carson.

Midway through the half, David O'Leary's men found a way back into the game. Captain Gareth Barry lashed the ball high into the net from seven yards out, after Nolberto Solano had nodded Steven Davis' clipped pass into the danger area.

The woodwork then came to the rescue of both teams. John Arne Riise clipped the top of the bar with a stinging drive, before Moore rose majestically to head against the frame of the goal at the other end.

There was little incident of note in the remainder of the game, as Liverpool completed their Anfield campaign with a win. Striker Cisse was the main beneficiary of this 90 minutes, making a strong case for inclusion in Benitez's starting line-up in Istanbul.

Young guns Stephen Warnock and Steven Davis fight for possession

"Djibril scored two good goals, and we now have two options in attack for the 'Champions League' final."

Rafael Benitez

"I think we deserved something from the game for our second half performance."

David O'Leary

PREMIERSHIP MILESTONE

Thomas Sorensen made his 200th Premiership appearance

PREMIERSHIP FIXTURE HISTORY

Pl: 6 Draws: 3	Wins	Goals	Yellow	Red
Manchester City	0	2	9	0
Middlesbrough	3	5	18	0

STARTING LINE-UPS

Manchester City: James; Mills, Onuoha, Distin (c), Thatcher; S.Wright-Phillips, Reyna, Barton, Musampa; Sibierski, Fowler

Middlesbrough: Nemeth, Hasselbaink; Zenden, Doriva, Boateng, Parlour; Queudrue, Southgate (c), Ehiogu, Parnaby; Schwarzer

Substitutes (Manchester City): B.Wright-Phillips, Croft, Weaver, Jordan, Macken

Substitutes (Middlesbrough): Downing, Morrison, Reiziger, Knight, Cooper

EVENT LINE

23 Hasselbaink (Direct Free Kick)
33 **Barton (Foul)**
35 Queudrue (Foul)
42 **Distin (Foul)**
45 Zenden (Foul)

HALF TIME 0 - 1

46 **Musampa (Open Play)**
50 Boateng (Foul)
54 **Sibierski (Off) Wright-Phillips B (On)**
54 Nemeth (Off) Downing (On)
62 Parlour (Foul)
69 Parlour (Off) Morrison (On)
84 **Mills (Off) Croft (On)**
84 Morrison (Off) Reiziger (On)
88 **Reyna (Off) Weaver (On)**

FULL TIME 1 - 1

STATISTICS

Season	Fixture (Man City)		Fixture (Middlesbrough)	Season
199	5	Shots On Target	4	253
196	5	Shots Off Target	1	191
4	0	Hit Woodwork	0	7
114	0	Caught Offside	6	108
234	10	Corners	3	196
487	12	Fouls	15	481
49%	60%	Possession	40%	49%

LEAGUE STANDINGS

Position (pos before)		W	D	L	F	A	Pts
8 (8)	Man City	13	13	12	47	39	52
7 (7)	Middlesbrough	14	13	11	53	46	55

Sunday 15th May 2005 | Venue: **City of Manchester Stadium** | Attendance: **47,221** | Referee: **R.Styles**

MANCHESTER CITY 1 MIDDLESBROUGH 1

Mark Schwarzer was the hero for Middlesbrough, saving an injury-time Robbie Fowler penalty to secure a UEFA Cup place for his side.

The visitors knew that a point would be enough to clinch a place in Europe, and took a 23rd-minute lead courtesy of a venomous Jimmy Floyd Hasselbaink free-kick. Kiki Musampa then levelled matters at the start of the second half, as Manchester City hunted the win that would have brought them European football.

It is often difficult to be at your best in a match in which you just need to avoid defeat, and Steve McClaren's team struggled early on. After Musampa had flashed a dangerous ball across the six-yard box, Antoine Sibierski did likewise from the other side.

Shaun Wright-Phillips was the next man to go close, running at defenders and exchanging passes with Fowler. The England international found himself clean through, but dinked an effort just the wrong side of the right-hand upright.

Somehow Middlesbrough had remained on level terms, and they soon took a shock lead. Striker Hasselbaink was upended some 35 yards from goal, providing him with the chance to unleash a ferocious drive that flew in off the underside of the crossbar.

Stuart Pearce's men took a while to recover from the setback, but Wright-Phillips fired narrowly over as the interval approached. Then, within 60 seconds of the restart, City equalised.

Joey Barton found Musampa on the edge of the box, with the winger spinning away from his marker to create a shooting chance. Having advanced to within eight yards of goal, a crisp finish through the legs of the keeper brought an eruption of noise.

Ben Thatcher's header from a corner nearly found a way in, before Pearce made a surprising substitution. Nicky Weaver replaced Claudio Reyna, enabling David James to change into a specially-prepared outfield shirt and move into attack.

The keeper made a nuisance of himself, and might have scored but for a Franck Queudrue handball. Referee Rob Styles spotted the offence and pointed to the spot, but Schwarzer dived to his left to deny Fowler.

Mark Schwarzer is the hero for Middlesbrough

"I don't think we could have done much more than what we did. The rest was in the lap of the gods."
Stuart Pearce

"There is a fine line between success and failure, and I am pleased to be on the right side."
Steve McClaren

PREMIERSHIP MILESTONE

400 David James marked his 400th Premiership appearance by playing as a striker for the final few minutes

PREMIERSHIP FIXTURE HISTORY

Pl: 12 Draws: 3	Wins	Goals	Yellow	Red
Newcastle United	6	18	11	0
Chelsea	3	11	28	1

STARTING LINE-UPS

Newcastle United: Given; Carr, Bramble, Boumsong, Babayaro; Jenas, Ambrose, N'Zogbia, Milner, Kluivert; Shearer (c)

Chelsea: Gudjohnsen; J.Cole, Jarosik; Lampard (c), Makelele, Tiago; Johnson, Carvalho, Huth, Geremi; Cudicini

Newcastle United subs: Taylor, Chopra, Harper, O'Brien, Robert

Chelsea subs: Oliveira, Morais, Watt, Cech, Grant

EVENT LINE

33 Geremi (Own Goal)
34 Babayaro (Foul)
35 Lampard (Penalty)
37 N'Zogbia (Foul)
41 Cole J (Dissent)

HALF TIME 1 - 1

46 Carr (Off) Taylor (On)
54 Kluivert (Dissent)
59 Carvalho (Foul)
59 Tiago (Ung.Conduct)
60 Jenas (Foul)
76 Kluivert (Off) Chopra (On)
78 Geremi (Foul)
84 Gudjohnsen (Off) Oliveira (On)
89 Cole J (Off) Morais (On)
90 Jarosik (Off) Watt (On)

FULL TIME 1 - 1

STATISTICS

Season	Fixture	Newcastle United / Chelsea	Fixture	Season
256	3	Shots On Target	8	286
222	4	Shots Off Target	5	241
11	0	Hit Woodwork	0	12
100	3	Caught Offside	8	134
238	6	Corners	4	234
485	11	Fouls	17	474
50%	44%	Possession	56%	55%

LEAGUE STANDINGS

Position (pos before)	W	D	L	F	A	Pts
14 (12) Newcastle Utd	10	14	14	47	57	44
1 (1) Chelsea	29	8	1	72	15	95

Sunday 15th May 2005 | Venue: St James' Park | Attendance: 52,326 | Referee: H.M.Webb

NEWCASTLE UNITED 1 CHELSEA 1

A 1-1 draw at St James' Park ensured that Chelsea finished the season with just one Premiership defeat to their name.

Jose Mourinho was without a large number of first-team members for this trip to the North East, and named a bench with limited top-flight experience. Graeme Souness recalled captain Alan Shearer to the starting line-up, and his skipper was involved in the opening goal.

A Jiri Jarosik shot apart, neither keeper had been unduly tested in a disappointing opening half-hour. The game then sprang into life, as Charles N'Zogbia's right-wing corner was flicked on by Shearer and turned into his own net by Geremi.

The former Middlesbrough player had been under pressure from Titus Bramble at the back post, and could do nothing as the ball struck his right boot and flew in.

The champions responded immediately, with Eidur Gudjohnsen tumbling under the challenge of former team-mate Celestine Babayaro in the box. Referee Howard Webb had no hesitation in pointing to the spot, from where Frank Lampard made it 1-1.

Carlo Cudicini would surely be a first-team regular at any other Premiership club, and demonstrated why after 71 minutes. The Chelsea custodian had not been called into action too often, but plunged to his right to keep out a goalbound Patrick Kluivert header.

Shay Given then demonstrated his credentials, producing a marvellous reaction save to keep out a deflected Jarosik drive. The keeper was unsighted, but thrust out a right hand to earn his side a confidence-boosting result.

The draw left Mourinho's men with 95 points, an incredible return from just 38 games. For their part, Newcastle finished the season 51 points adrift in 14th place. The supporters will not accept another season of abject failure, with Souness under pressure to turn things around.

One player unlikely to be at St James' Park next season is Laurent Robert. The French winger was an unused substitute on the day, and signed off by stripping to his pants and throwing his kit into the crowd.

Glen Johnson is faced with James Milner

"It promises to be an interesting summer for us. It's fair to say we are looking for big improvements next season."
Graeme Souness

"Next season I think will be harder. Everyone knows the team we have and what we can do."
Jose Mourinho

PREMIERSHIP MILESTONE
The attendance of 52,326 was a Premiership record at St James' Park

PREMIERSHIP MILESTONE
Steven Watt made his Premiership debut

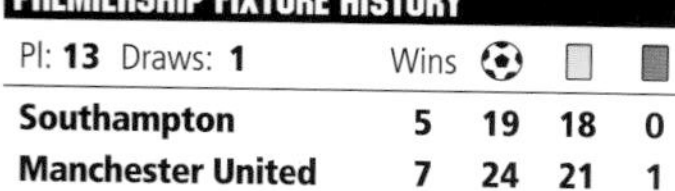

PREMIERSHIP FIXTURE HISTORY

Pl: 13 Draws: 1	Wins	⚽	▢	■
Southampton	5	19	18	0
Manchester United	7	24	21	1

STARTING LINE-UPS

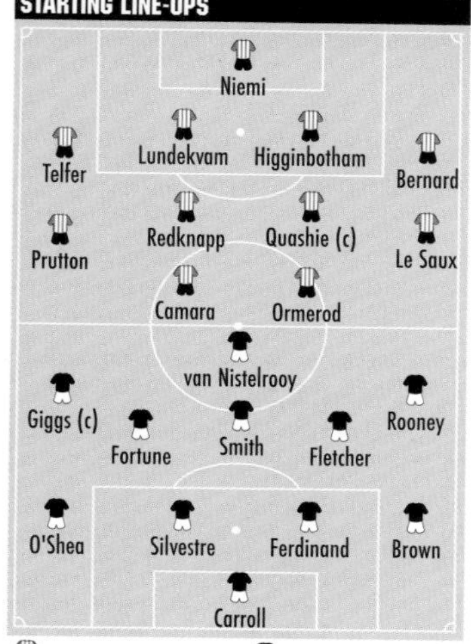

Delap, Phillips Davenport, Smith Oakley

Saha, P.Neville Ricardo, Keane Kleberson

EVENT LINE

10 ⚽ **O'Shea (Own Goal)**
17 ▢ Brown (Foul)
19 ⚽ Fletcher (Open Play)
28 ▢ Silvestre (Foul)
31 ▢ **Lundekvam (Foul)**

HALF TIME 1 - 1

63 ⚽ van Nistelrooy (Open Play)
71 ⇄ **Le Saux (Off) Delap (On)**
71 ⇄ **Prutton (Off) Phillips (On)**
74 ⇄ Rooney (Off) Saha (On)
78 ⇄ **Bernard (Off) Davenport (On)**
87 ⇄ van Nistelrooy (Off) Neville P (On)

FULL TIME 1 - 2

STATISTICS

Season	Fixture	Southampton / Man Utd	Fixture	Season
184	2	Shots On Target	8	314
206	9	Shots Off Target	8	283
4	1	Hit Woodwork	0	19
114	5	Caught Offside	2	134
179	6	Corners	3	290
495	14	Fouls	13	470
47%	38%	Possession	62%	56%

LEAGUE STANDINGS

Position (pos before)	W	D	L	F	A	Pts
20 (18) Southampton	6	14	18	45	66	32
3 (3) Man Utd	22	11	5	58	26	77

Sunday 15th May 2005 | Venue: **Friends Provident St Mary's Stadium** | Attendance: **32,066** | Referee: **S.G.Bennett**

SOUTHAMPTON 1 MANCHESTER UNITED 2

Southampton's 27-year stay in the top-flight of English football came to an end, as Manchester United left St Mary's with a 2-1 victory.

A 10th-minute John O'Shea own goal lifted the Saints out of the relegation zone, only for Darren Fletcher's 19th-minute equaliser to leave them on a knife-edge. At half-time, Harry Redknapp's team remained in a position of safety, but a Ruud van Nistelrooy header saw them end the day at the bottom of the table.

After a nervous opening, the home side struck first. Graeme Le Saux's inswinging corner from the right was inadvertently touched on by Mikael Silvestre, and flew into the net via the right thigh of O'Shea.

Captain Nigel Quashie had put the defender under enormous pressure, and it would soon have been 2-0 but for the agility of Wes Brown.

Midfielder David Prutton, returning from a 10-game ban, raced onto a Jamie Redknapp pass and took the ball around Roy Carroll. The former Nottingham Forest man then centred from the right, with Brown somehow managing a last-ditch volleyed clearance under intense pressure from Brett Ormerod.

Play quickly switched to the other end, as O'Shea atoned for his earlier indiscretion by setting up Fletcher. The Irish full-back delivered an inswinging cross from the left, which his Scottish team-mate headed home on the run from around 12 yards out.

Chances continued to fall at both ends of the pitch. Antti Niemi turned over a van Nistelrooy drive and Le Saux cleared off the line from O'Shea, while in between times Carroll foiled Henri Camara and Ormerod nodded over from a corner.

With Norwich and Crystal Palace trailing, Southampton knew that a second half winner would probably keep them up. Then, as news of unfavourable goals at both The Valley and The Hawthorns filtered through, United went 2-1 in front.

Alan Smith burst into the box on the right and floated the ball to the back post. With Niemi unable to make up the ground quickly enough, van Nistelrooy was able to use his head to break Southampton hearts.

Southampton's players face up to relegation

"It was always going to be a tough day, but we have been relegated over the course of the season."

Harry Redknapp

"Harry and Jim Smith have just come here too late. If they had overseen a full season with their own players, I think they would be in a far safer position."

Sir Alex Ferguson

PREMIERSHIP FIXTURE HISTORY				
Pl: **11** Draws: **2**	Wins	Goals	Yellow	Red
Tottenham Hotspur	5	12	11	1
Blackburn Rovers	4	14	20	1

STARTING LINE-UPS

Defoe, Marney, Fulop, Bunjevcevic, Ziegler

Johnson, Enckelman, Johansson, Tugay, Douglas

EVENT LINE

		HALF TIME 0 - 0
52	Yellow	Savage (Foul)
61	Sub	**Reid (Off) Defoe (On)**
61	Sub	Stead (Off) Johnson (On)
71	Sub	**Davis (Off) Marney (On)**
76	Yellow	**Naybet (Foul)**
83	Yellow	Neill (Ung.Conduct)
88	Yellow	**Marney (Foul)**
		FULL TIME 0 - 0

STATISTICS

Season	Fixture		Fixture	Season
233	7	Shots On Target	8	193
214	6	Shots Off Target	4	231
11	0	Hit Woodwork	0	8
155	2	Caught Offside	8	159
196	5	Corners	7	214
451	10	Fouls	14	605
50%	50%	Possession	50%	49%

LEAGUE STANDINGS

Position (pos before)		W	D	L	F	A	Pts
9 (9)	Tottenham H	14	10	14	47	41	52
15 (14)	Blackburn R	9	15	14	32	43	42

Sunday 15th May 2005 | Venue: **White Hart Lane** | Attendance: **35,797** | Referee: **A.G.Wiley**

TOTTENHAM HOTSPUR 0 BLACKBURN ROVERS 0

Needing a convincing win to maintain their slim hopes of qualifying for the UEFA Cup, Tottenham were held to a goalless draw by Blackburn.

The North London side made a decent start, Robbie Keane forcing a save of sorts from Brad Friedel with a dipping 20-yard snapshot on the run.

Mark Hughes' men responded with a great chance of their own. Captain Andy Todd found himself unmarked at the back post following a left-wing corner, but saw Radek Cerny turn over the six-yard volley that he drove into the ground.

Simon Davies then forced a sprawling save from Friedel as a sea of white shirts descended on the visiting goal, before Erik Edman made a great last-ditch block to deny Brett Emerton when play switched to the other end.

From the resulting corner, David Thompson somehow nodded Morten Gamst Pedersen's deep delivery the wrong side of the left-hand upright from no more than two yards out.

The rest of the half was dominated by Tottenham. Having forced Friedel into an easy stop, Frederic Kanoute then drew an excellent low save from the American, who also parried a venomous Sean Davis drive to safety.

The second period was no less frenetic than the first, with chances at both ends. Rovers midfielder Thompson hit a long-range drive that Cerny was equal to, while a stretching Noureddine Naybet was just unable to turn home Andy Reid's inswinging free-kick.

With an hour played, Keane came as close as anyone to breaking the deadlock. Collecting the ball with his back to goal in the inside-right channel, the Irish international turned and bent a left-footed effort just past the far post.

In a desperate attempt to win the game, Martin Jol sent on Jermain Defoe and changed to a three-man attack. The tactical switch did not work, with the trio of forwards being largely deprived of possession in dangerous areas of the pitch.

Though Spurs missed out on a UEFA Cup place, the draw between Manchester City and Middlesbrough meant that even a win in this fixture would not have been enough to secure European football.

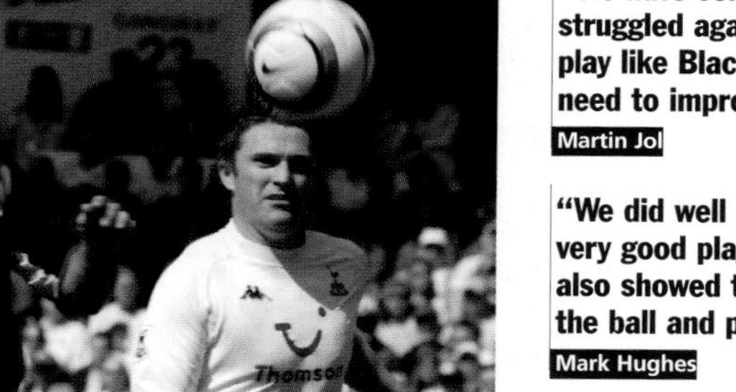

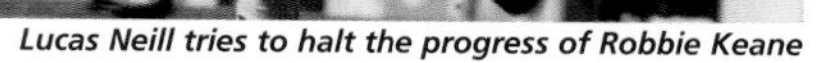

Lucas Neill tries to halt the progress of Robbie Keane

"We have sometimes struggled against teams who play like Blackburn, and we need to improve on that."

Martin Jol

"We did well against some very good players, and we also showed that we can get the ball and play a bit."

Mark Hughes

PREMIERSHIP MILESTONE

50 Jermain Defoe made his 50th Premiership appearance for Tottenham

Sunday 15th May 2005 | Venue: **The Hawthorns** | Attendance: **27,751** | Referee: **M.A.Riley**

WEST BROM 2 PORTSMOUTH 0

West Brom pulled off the 'great escape', beating Portsmouth 2-0 to become the first team bottom of the Premiership table at Christmas to avoid the drop.

The Baggies began the day at the foot of the table, needing all three relegation rivals to fail to win if they were to have any chance of survival. Even if this trio of results went their way, Bryan Robson's side would also need to pick up three points of their own.

Just five minutes had elapsed when Robert Earnshaw spurned a great chance to fire Albion in front. The Welsh international burst onto Kieran Richardson's pass, but could only direct the ball wide of the right-hand upright from near the penalty spot.

With the atmosphere inside the ground constantly changing as goals flew in elsewhere, the nervous tension seemed to transmit itself to the home players. Ricardo Fuller nearly benefitted from the uncertainty on display, but missed the target thanks to pressure from Martin Albrechtsen.

Young James Keene forced a diving save from Tomasz Kuszczak for Alain Perrin's charges, before Kevin Campbell stung the palms of Jamie Ashdown with a near-post drive at the other end of the pitch.

With his team giving everything in their search for a goal, Robson sent on Geoff Horsfield and switched to a 4-3-3 formation. Within 60 seconds of his introduction, the striker had found the net with a nine-yard volley that would potentially keep the West Midlands side up.

With just under 20 minutes remaining, news filtered through that Crystal Palace had taken the lead at Charlton. Soon afterwards, Kieran Richardson scored to muted applause, collecting a backheel from Horsfield and drilling low past Ashdown from 13 yards out.

The Baggies needed a Charlton equaliser if they were to stay up, and it duly arrived eight minutes from time. The final whistle brought a nervous wait for confirmation of other results, followed by unconfined joy and a mass celebratory pitch invasion.

On a day when all four relegation-threatened clubs spent some time above the drop zone, it was West Brom that finished there.

Kevin Campbell and Kieran Richardson celebrate the 'great escape'

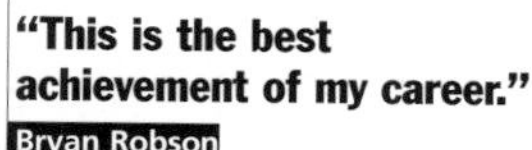

"This is the best achievement of my career."
Bryan Robson

"You have to give credit to West Brom, as they wanted it more than us."
Alain Perrin

PREMIERSHIP MILESTONE

The attendance of 27,751 was a Premiership record at The Hawthorns

PREMIERSHIP FIXTURE HISTORY

Pl: 1 Draws: 0	Wins	Goals	Yellow	Red
West Bromwich Albion	1	2	0	0
Portsmouth	0	0	1	0

STARTING LINE-UPS

Subs (West Brom): Horsfield, Kanu, Murphy, Moore, Inamoto
Subs (Portsmouth): Skopelitis, Rodic, Mezague, Chalkias, Duffy

EVENT LINE

33 Fuller (Foul)

HALF TIME 0 - 0

50 Hughes (Off) Skopelitis (On)
58 Greening (Off) Horsfield (On)
58 Horsfield (Open Play)
65 Kamara (Off) Rodic (On)
75 Richardson (Open Play)
81 Keene (Off) Mezague (On)
84 Earnshaw (Off) Kanu (On)

FULL TIME 2 - 0

STATISTICS

Season	Fixture (West Brom)		Fixture (Portsmouth)	Season
175	5	Shots On Target	2	188
167	4	Shots Off Target	6	187
12	0	Hit Woodwork	0	7
134	2	Caught Offside	3	115
193	7	Corners	1	182
495	12	Fouls	14	455
48%	52%	Possession	48%	47%

LEAGUE STANDINGS

Position (pos before)	W	D	L	F	A	Pts
17 (20) West Brom	6	16	16	36	61	34
16 (16) Portsmouth	10	9	19	43	59	39

MAY 2005

The Premiership season reached a dramatic conclusion, with unresolved issues going right to the wire. Three teams were battling for a UEFA Cup place, while three of four clubs would end up filling the relegation spots.

On a final day that saw Norwich, Southampton, West Brom and Crystal Palace all fighting to stay up, it was the Baggies that achieved their goal. All four teams spent some time above the safety line during the afternoon, but a 2-0 win against Portsmouth helped Bryan Robson's side climb from bottom to 17th.

With Tottenham failing to register the convincing win against Blackburn that they needed to maintain any hopes of qualifying for the UEFA Cup, attention switched to the City of Manchester Stadium. Mark Schwarzer's injury-time penalty save from Robbie Fowler ensured that it was Middlesbrough, and not their opponents, who secured the place in Europe.

The Teesside club would be joined in the competition by Liverpool and Bolton. Sam Allardyce had guided the Trotters to a first season of continental football, while Rafael Benitez hoped that victory in the 'Champions League' final would see his team allowed to

Chelsea end a 50-year wait for the league title

defend their trophy.

As things stood, England's four representatives in the premier European club competition would be champions Chelsea, Arsenal, Manchester United and Everton. David Moyes' men had been expected to battle against relegation, but secured fourth place with two games to spare.

Jose Mourinho's team were worthy title-winners, finishing the season with a record Premiership haul of 95 points. Second-placed Arsenal were 12 points further back, as the Stamford Bridge outfit suffered just one league defeat.

With several key players unavailable, Sven-Goran Eriksson included a few new faces in his England squad for the trip to America. Peter Crouch, Scott Carson, Zat Knight and Kieran Richardson were all given the chance to impress the Swede.

IN THE NEWS

03RD	**On a memorable night at Anfield, Luis Garcia's disputed goal proves enough for Liverpool to upset Chelsea and reach the final of the 'Champions League'.**
05TH	**In the wake of speculation suggesting that Liverpool would be awarded England's fourth 'Champions League' place in the event of winning the trophy and finishing fifth in the league, the F.A. announce that this is not the case.**
06TH	**Frank Lampard wins the 'Football Writers' Player of the Year' award.**
07TH	**A 1-1 draw at Portsmouth is enough to see Bolton Wanderers book a place in Europe for the first time in their history.**
08TH	**Liverpool's 3-1 defeat at Highbury guarantees Everton a place in the 2005-06 'Champions League', an incredible achievement by a team tipped for relegation at the start of the campaign.**
12TH	**Peter Crouch and Scott Carson are the new names in Sven-Goran Eriksson's squad for a two-game tour of America. Kieran Richardson and Zat Knight are later added to a party that will take on the U.S.A. and then Colombia.**
15TH	**West Brom become the first team bottom of the table at Christmas to survive in the Premiership. Furthermore, the Baggies begin the last day at the bottom, climbing to 17th position and safety by the final whistle.**

MONTH IN NUMBERS

26	Games Played
81	Total Goals Scored
3.12	Average Goals Per Game
3	Player With Most Goals (Malbranque, Pires, McBride)
0	Hat-tricks ()
13	Club With Most Goals (Arsenal)
5	Fastest Goal (Wright-Phillips S)
46.2%	Percentage Of Home Wins
26.9%	Percentage Of Away Wins
26.9%	Percentage Of Draws
7-0	Biggest Win (Arsenal 7 v 0 Everton)
74	Total Yellow Cards
8	Total Red Cards
2.8	Average Yellow Cards Per Game
12	Most Disciplinary Points (Rosenior 1R, Sorondo 1R, N'Gotty 1R, Johnson 1R, Crouch 1R, Perry 1R, Short 1R, Ameobi 1R)
6	Fastest Booking (Davis, Postma)
35,118	Average Attendance

Bryan Robson guides West Brom to Premiership survival

PREMIERSHIP TABLE / TEAM STATISTICS

Pos (last month)	Team	Played	Won	Drawn	Lost	Goals for	Goals against	Goal diff	Points	Shots on target	Hit woodwork	Shots off target	Failed to score	Clean sheets	Corners	Caught Offside	Players used
1 - (1)	Chelsea	38	29	8	1	72	15	+57	95	286	12	241	5	25	234	134	30
2 - (2)	Arsenal	38	25	8	5	87	36	+51	83	281	16	188	3	16	202	96	25
3 - (3)	Manchester United	38	22	11	5	58	26	+32	77	314	19	283	10	19	290	134	26
4 - (4)	Everton	38	18	7	13	45	46	-1	61	179	6	198	11	13	183	96	22
5 - (5)	Liverpool	38	17	7	14	52	41	+11	58	240	8	247	13	7	217	106	29
6 - (6)	Bolton Wanderers	38	16	10	12	49	44	+5	58	247	9	225	8	8	207	103	25
7 - (7)	Middlesbrough	38	14	13	11	53	46	+7	55	253	7	191	10	11	196	108	27
8 - (8)	Manchester City	38	13	13	12	47	39	+8	52	199	4	196	11	11	234	114	25
9 - (9)	Tottenham Hotspur	38	14	10	14	47	41	+6	52	233	11	214	14	13	196	155	31
10 - (10)	Aston Villa	38	12	11	15	45	52	-7	47	199	9	193	10	11	212	117	22
11 - (11)	Charlton Athletic	38	12	10	16	42	58	-16	46	171	8	146	13	12	167	123	22
12 - (12)	Birmingham City	38	11	12	15	40	46	-6	45	167	12	177	13	9	192	103	27
13 ▲ (15)	Fulham	38	12	8	18	52	60	-8	44	184	7	165	10	8	181	98	24
14 - (14)	Newcastle United	38	10	14	14	47	57	-10	44	256	11	222	10	6	238	100	27
15 ▼ (13)	Blackburn Rovers	38	9	15	14	32	43	-11	42	193	8	231	17	15	214	159	31
16 - (16)	Portsmouth	38	10	9	19	43	59	-16	39	188	7	187	11	5	182	115	26
17 ▲ (19)	West Bromwich Albion	38	6	16	16	36	61	-25	34	175	12	167	13	7	193	134	27
18 - (18)	Crystal Palace	38	7	12	19	41	62	-21	33	175	7	163	12	10	190	91	27
19 ▲ (20)	Norwich City	38	7	12	19	42	77	-35	33	178	6	187	14	6	188	127	25
20 ▼ (17)	Southampton	38	6	14	18	45	66	-21	32	184	4	206	11	7	179	114	34

TEAM FORM

Pos	Team	Form	Goals For	Goals Against	Pts
1	Arsenal	WWWL	13	3	9
2	Chelsea	WWD	5	2	7
3	Manchester United	WDLW	8	5	7
4	Fulham	LWW	10	4	6
5	Tottenham Hotspur	WLD	5	2	4
6	Bolton Wanderers	DW	4	3	4
7	Middlesbrough	WD	2	1	4
8	Manchester City	WD	3	2	4
9	West Brom	LDW	3	3	4
10	Newcastle United	WLD	4	4	4
11	Birmingham City	LW	2	2	3
12	Liverpool	LW	3	4	3
13	Norwich City	WL	1	6	3
14	Everton	WLL	4	10	3
15	Crystal Palace	DD	4	4	2
16	Southampton	DL	3	4	1
17	Portsmouth	DL	1	3	1
18	Blackburn Rovers	LD	1	3	1
19	Charlton Athletic	LLD	2	7	1
20	Aston Villa	LLL	3	9	0

TOP GOALSCORERS

Player	This Month	Total
T.Henry Arsenal	0	**25**
A.Johnson Crystal Palace	1	**21**
R.Pires Arsenal	3	**14**
J.Hasselbaink Middlesbrough	1	**13**
F.Lampard Chelsea	1	**13**
A.Yakubu Portsmouth	1	**13**
J.Defoe Tottenham Hotspur	0	**13**
A.Cole Fulham	1	**12**
P.Crouch Southampton	1	**12**
E.Gudjohnsen Chelsea	1	**12**
T.Cahill Everton	2	**11**
R.Earnshaw West Bromwich Albion	1	**11**
W.Rooney Manchester United	1	**11**
R.Keane Tottenham Hotspur	0	**11**
E.Heskey Birmingham City	1	**10**
S.Wright-Phillips Manchester City	1	**10**

MOST GOAL ASSISTS

Player	This Month	Total
F.Lampard Chelsea	2	**19**
T.Henry Arsenal	1	**17**
J.Hasselbaink Middlesbrough	1	**15**
L.Boa Morte Fulham	2	**14**
S.Downing Middlesbrough	0	**14**
D.Bergkamp Arsenal	4	**12**
J.Reyes Arsenal	3	**11**
D.Huckerby Norwich City	1	**11**
F.Ljungberg Arsenal	0	**11**
W.Routledge Crystal Palace	0	**11**
E.Gudjohnsen Chelsea	1	**10**
R.Giggs Manchester United	0	**10**
A.Robben Chelsea	0	**10**
S.Wright-Phillips Manchester City	0	**10**
J.Greening West Bromwich Albion	0	**9**

DISCIPLINE

F.A. disciplinary points: Yellow=4 points, Two Bookable Offences=10 points and Red Card=12 points

Player	Y	SB	R	PTS
P.Diop Fulham	7	1	1	**50**
D.Johnson Birmingham City	7	1	1	**50**
R.Parlour Middlesbrough	10	1	0	**50**
L.Hendrie Aston Villa	9	0	1	**48**
T.Cahill Everton	9	1	0	**46**
L.Bowyer Newcastle United	5	1	1	**42**
G.Sorondo Crystal Palace	3	0	2	**36**
F.Queudrue Middlesbrough	6	0	1	**36**
J.Barton Manchester City	9	0	0	**36**
T.Hibbert Everton	9	0	0	**36**
M.Hughes Crystal Palace	9	0	0	**36**
R.Keane Manchester United	9	0	0	**36**
L.Neill Blackburn Rovers	9	0	0	**36**
P.Vieira Arsenal	9	0	0	**36**

"I said yesterday that with the supporters on our side and the solidarity of the players, we could win. We played with a strong mentality and it showed on the pitch in our performance."

Rafael Benitez after 'Champions League' success against Chelsea

"With Wayne Rooney it is a question of education. He should receive a clip around the ear from the management."

Fifa President Sepp Blatter

"I hope Liverpool will go on to win the 'Champions League', but there's no denying Everton are the best team in the city this season."

David Moyes

"He has been amazing throughout all the years that he has been here and, if it was down to me, I would give him another year."

Thierry Henry on Dennis Bergkamp

"The players have been terrific, as they have had to cope with all this stuff saying if they were bottom of the table at Christmas they could not survive."

Bryan Robson on West Brom's final day survival

"I sat at home and thought that if we were drawing and looking to launch it route one, David James may upset them."

Stuart Pearce on his decision to play his goalkeeper in attack for the final few minutes against Middlesbrough

"He is a Premiership-quality player, but he has signed for us for four or five years. He's certainly an outstanding player, but he has signed a contract."

Iain Dowie on the future of Andy Johnson

"He has trouble with a lot of the players. I want to leave Newcastle because getting on with Graeme Souness is not possible."

Laurent Robert

"Marseille is in my heart. I said it when I left, and I haven't changed my mind in a few months. Now I'm English champion and, one day, I want to be French champion."

Didier Drogba

TEAM OF THE SEASON

MANAGER OF THE SEASON

Jose Mourinho

Chelsea

The best signing Chelsea made last summer was undoubtedly their manager. Arriving at Stamford Bridge just days after winning the 'Champions League' with unfancied Porto, Mourinho brought with him a real sense of belief. Narrow early season victories gave way to convincing wins, as the West London club made light work of securing the Premiership crown. Success in the Carling Cup meant two trophies in the cabinet, and they are likely to be the first of many with the self-proclaimed 'special one' in charge.

Premiership Career Statistics
until end of May 2005
Matches:**38** Wins:**29** Draws:**8**
Losses:**1**

Petr Cech

Chelsea

Appearances: **35** Clean sheets: **24**

A deserving winner of the 'Barclays Golden Glove' award, the Czech custodian kept a staggering 24 clean sheets in the league. During an amazing spell between December and February, Cech went a Premiership record 1,025 minutes without conceding a goal. The former Rennes shot-stopper was beaten just 13 times during his 35 top-flight appearances, with only Bolton and Arsenal managing to score twice past him in a game.

Gabriel Heinze

Manchester United

Appearances: **26** Goals: **1** Assists: **1**

Having missed the start of the campaign as he won Olympic gold with Argentina, Heinze marked his Manchester United debut with a goal at Bolton. Though he didn't add to that strike, the full-back endeared himself to the Old Trafford faithful with a string of all-action displays. Uncompromising in the tackle and with a seemingly endless supply of energy, the former PSG defender has become a vital member of Sir Alex Ferguson's rearguard.

John Terry

Chelsea

Appearances: **36** Goals: **3** Assists: **1**

The '2005 Professional Footballers' Association Player of the Year' led his team to both Premiership and Carling Cup success. An inspirational figure on the pitch, the England international was handed the captaincy in a pre-season vote amongst his team-mates. As well as marshalling a record-breaking defensive unit, Terry also netted some vital goals. A header that knocked Barcelona out of Europe typified his steely determination and never-say-die approach.

Jamie Carragher

Liverpool

Appearances: **38** Assists: **2**

Given the chance to play in his preferred position of centre-back by new boss Rafael Benitez, the Bootle-born defender attracted widespread praise. An ever-present in the Premiership, Carragher captained the side to victory on the final day against Aston Villa. Liverpool's progress in Europe owed much to the heroics of their England international, who turned in world-class performances against both Juventus and Chelsea.

Luke Young

Charlton Athletic

Appearances: **36** Goals: **2** Assists: **2**

Voted 'Player of the Year' by the Charlton supporters, the full-back was Mr.Consistent at The Valley. Early season goals against Aston Villa and Birmingham showed that the defender had added a new string to his bow, while he also registered a couple of assists. With Hermann Hreidarsson and Paul Konchesky unavailable for the trip to Norwich, Young showed his versatility by successfully operating at left-back.

Stewart Downing
Middlesbrough

Appearances: **35** Goals: **5** Assists: **14**

Even Steve McClaren must have been surprised at the startling progress of his young winger. Beginning the season on the bench, Downing soon ensured that he was one of the first names on the teamsheet with a series of top-class displays. Whether at home or in Europe, the former Sunderland loanee terrorised defences, earning himself an England cap in the February friendly with Holland.

Tim Cahill
Everton

Appearances: **33** Goals: **11** Assists: **6**

Widely regarded as the signing of the season, Cahill finished up as the leading scorer at Goodison Park with 11 Premiership goals. Few players can have made such an impact when stepping up a level from the Championship, as the former Millwall man played a pivotal role in improving Everton's fortunes. Generally operating as the link between midfield and attack, the Australian international quickly established himself as a firm favourite with supporters.

PLAYER OF THE SEASON

Frank Lampard
Chelsea

Appearances: **38**
Goals: **13** Assists: **19**

Named both 'Football Writers' Player of the Year' and 'Barclays Premiership Player of the Year', Lampard was the heartbeat of Chelsea's season. The midfielder finished as top scorer at the West London club, netting 13 goals in the league and a further six in cup competitions. No player created more Premiership goals either, as the former West Ham man topped the table for assists with 19.

Shaun Wright-Phillips
Manchester City

Appearances: **34** Goals: **10** Assists: **10**

This was the season that saw Shaun Wright-Phillips emerge from the shadow of his step-father to fully demonstrate his own credentials. A goalscoring international debut against the Ukraine seemed to lift the winger to a new level, and he got better with every game for his club. No defender looked forward to facing such a uniquely gifted player, with pace and direct running resulting in a return of 10 Premiership goals and a further 10 assists.

Thierry Henry
Arsenal

Appearances: **32** Goals: **25** Assists: **17**

The Highbury faithful were treated to another season of Henry magic, as the Frenchman netted more goals than anyone else in the top-flight. An improvised backheel past Dean Kiely highlighted the striker's undoubted quality, while only Frank Lampard managed more assists. Though Arsenal didn't do themselves justice in Europe, their talismanic forward still managed to score five times in eight matches.

TEAM OF THE SEASON STATISTICS

91	Total Goals Scored
81	Total Assists
41	Total Yellow Cards
1	Total Red Cards
35	Average Number of Appearances
27	Oldest Player **Thierry Henry**
20	Youngest Player **Stewart Downing**

Andy Johnson
Crystal Palace

Appearances: **37** Goals: **21** Assists: **9**

Without Johnson's goals, Crystal Palace would have been relegated long before the final day of a brave campaign. The diminutive striker found the net on no fewer than 21 occasions, accounting for over half of his club's Premiership tally. An England cap was fully merited, and the former Birmingham man was named in Sven-Goran Eriksson's squad for the end-of-season trip to America.

FINAL WHISTLE MATCH FINDER

Use the grid below to look up the page number for the game you're looking for.

HOME TEAM / AWAY TEAM	Arsenal	Aston Villa	Birmingham City	Blackburn Rovers	Bolton Wanderers	Charlton Athletic	Chelsea	Crystal Palace	Everton	Fulham	Liverpool	Manchester City	Manchester United	Middlesbrough	Newcastle United	Norwich City	Portsmouth	Southampton	Tottenham Hotspur	West Brom
Arsenal		92	172	26	58	82	189	218	415	203	413	242	272	22	266	340	312	112	385	147
Aston Villa	282		190	228	376	368	48	68	300	102	173	404	213	313	32	248	127	4	156	357
Birmingham City	416	332		388	243	59	14	113	137	258	292	24	93	204	88	157	360	277	341	193
Blackburn Rovers	325	83	155		267	238	278	369	194	405	114	377	33	94	205	293	60	350	174	5
Bolton Wanderers	249	138	69	214		6	389	95	417	351	40	195	49	294	120	326	158	366	273	229
Charlton Athletic	230	27	250	77	361		159	418	215	202	274	342	400	115	100	139	15	57	323	327
Chelsea	370	206	352	103	148	406		328	128	378	89	290	12	244	175	196	259	34	64	322
Crystal Palace	129	239	301	182	283	180	25		16	91	379	61	314	343	149	362	207	407	260	104
Everton	13	116	380	319	176	261	295	358		150	183	208	371	65	408	279	245	96	84	35
Fulham	50	280	216	160	17	315	140	231	390		97	363	191	28	403	419	348	70	117	256
Liverpool	164	420	130	324	344	105	232	141	333	284		18	251	391	200	71	192	217	364	51
Manchester City	72	161	372	142	321	36	98	252	52	7	353		297	421	281	126	392	233	184	218
Manchester United	108	262	285	345	209	151	414	197	41	329	67	134		90	383	19	302	177	246	409
Middlesbrough	354	198	53	286	135	305	73	37	257	367	152	181	234		8	219	109	334	410	381
Newcastle United	222	346	235	54	306	287	422	393	165	136	316	110	145	387		29	185	253	20	74
Norwich City	38	62	411	131	186	382	317	9	106	178	240	307	355	263	373		85	153	210	288
Portsmouth	201	296	10	254	412	356	220	55	76	42	374	154	118	275	330	236		384	101	179
Southampton	303	365	111	21	30	211	347	162	291	247	264	86	423	187	66	394	143		318	132
Tottenham Hotspur	144	401	39	424	107	133	255	221	237	304	11	331	75	166	359	56	289	199		375
West Brom	402	23	320	386	87	188	119	276	349	63	212	265	163	146	241	99	425	299	31	